Twentieth-Century Literary Criticism

Guide to Gale Literary Criticism Series

When you need to review criticism of literary works, these are the Gale series to use:

If the author's death date is: **You should turn to:**

After Dec. 31, 1959
(or author is still living)

CONTEMPORARY LITERARY CRITICISM

for example: Jorge Luis Borges, Anthony Burgess,
William Faulkner, Mary Gordon,
Ernest Hemingway, Iris Murdoch

1900 through 1959

TWENTIETH-CENTURY LITERARY CRITICISM

for example: Willa Cather, F. Scott Fitzgerald,
Henry James, Mark Twain, Virginia Woolf

1800 through 1899

NINETEENTH-CENTURY LITERATURE CRITICISM

for example: Fyodor Dostoevsky, Nathaniel Hawthorne,
George Sand, William Wordsworth

1400 through 1799

LITERATURE CRITICISM FROM 1400 TO 1800
(excluding Shakespeare)

for example: Anne Bradstreet, Daniel Defoe,
Alexander Pope, François Rabelais,
Jonathan Swift, Phillis Wheatley

SHAKESPEAREAN CRITICISM

Shakespeare's plays and poetry

Antiquity through 1399

CLASSICAL AND MEDIEVAL LITERATURE CRITICISM

for example: Dante, Homer, Plato, Sophocles, Vergil,
the Beowulf Poet

Gale also publishes related criticism series:

CHILDREN'S LITERATURE REVIEW

This series covers authors of all eras who have written for the preschool through high school audience.

SHORT STORY CRITICISM

This series covers the major short fiction writers of all nationalities and periods of literary history.

POETRY CRITICISM

This series covers poets of all nationalities and periods of literary history.

DRAMA CRITICISM

This series covers dramatists of all nationalities and periods of literary history.

ISSN 0276-8178

_R_

Volume 43

Twentieth-Century Literary Criticism

**Excerpts from Criticism of the
Works of Novelists, Poets, Playwrights,
Short Story Writers, and Other Creative Writers
Who Died between 1900 and 1960,
from the First Published Critical Appraisals
to Current Evaluations**

**Laurie DiMauro
Editor**

**David Kmenta
Marie Lazzari
Thomas Ligotti
Bridget Travers
Thomas Votteler
Associate Editors**

 Gale Research Inc. • _DETROIT_ • _LONDON_

STAFF

Laurie DiMauro, *Editor*

David Kmenta, Marie Lazzari, Thomas Ligotti, Bridget Travers, Thomas Votteler, *Associate Editors*

Ian A. Goodhall, Elizabeth P. Henry, James Poniewozik, Johannah Rodgers, *Assistant Editors*

Jeanne A. Gough, *Permissions & Production Manager*

Linda M. Pugliese, *Production Supervisor*

Paul Lewon, Lorna Mabunda, Maureen Puhl, Camille Robinson, Jennifer VanSickle, *Editorial Associates*

Donna Craft, Brandy C. Johnson, Sheila Walencewicz, *Editorial Assistants*

Maureen Richards, *Research Supervisor*

Mary Beth McElmeel, *Editorial Associate*

Kathleen Jozwiak, Amy Kaechele, Julie Karmazin, Tamara C. Nott, Julie Synkonis, *Editorial Assistants*

Sandra C. Davis, *Permissions Supervisor (Text)*

Maria L. Franklin, Josephine M. Keene, Denise M. Singleton, Kimberly F. Smilay, *Permissions Associates*

Rebecca A. Hartford, Michele Lonoconus, Shelly Rakoczy (co-op), Shalice Shah, Nancy K. Sheridan, *Permissions Assistants*

Margaret A. Chamberlain, *Permissions Supervisor (Pictures)*

Pamela A. Hayes, *Permissions Associate*

Nancy Rattenbury, Karla Kulkis, Keith Reed, *Permissions Assistants*

Mary Beth Trimper, *Production Manager*

Mary Winterhalter, *Production Assistant*

Arthur Chartow, *Art Director*

C. J. Jonik, *Keyliner*

This volume is dedicated to our friend and colleague
David Kmenta, 1965-1991.

Contents

Preface   ix

Acknowledgments   xiii

Preface

Since its inception more than ten years ago, *Twentieth-Century Literary Criticism* has been purchased and used by nearly 10,000 school, public, and college or university libraries. *TCLC* has covered more than 500 authors, representing 58 nationalities, and over 25,000 titles. No other reference source has surveyed the critical response to twentieth-century authors and literature as thoroughly as *TCLC*. In the words of one reviewer, "there is nothing comparable available." *TCLC* "is a gold mine of information—dates, pseudonyms, biographical information, and criticism from books and periodicals—which many libraries would have difficulty assembling on their own."

Scope of the Series

TCLC is designed to serve as an introduction to authors who died between 1900 and 1960 and to the most significant interpretations of these authors' works. The great poets, novelists, short story writers, playwrights, and philosophers of this period are frequently studied in high school and college literature courses. In organizing and excerpting the vast amount of critical material written on these authors, *TCLC* helps students develop valuable insight into literary history, promotes a better understanding of the texts, and sparks ideas for papers and assignments. Each entry in *TCLC* presents a comprehensive survey of an author's career or an individual work of literature and provides the user with a multiplicity of interpretations and assessments. Such variety allows students to pursue their own interests; furthermore, it fosters an awareness that literature is dynamic and responsive to many different opinions.

Every fourth volume of *TCLC* is devoted to literary topics that cannot be covered under the author approach used in the rest of the series. Such topics include literary movements, prominent themes in twentieth-century literature, literary reaction to political and historical events, significant eras in literary history, prominent literary anniversaries, and the literatures of cultures that are often overlooked by English-speaking readers.

TCLC is designed as a companion series to Gale's *Contemporary Literary Criticism,* which reprints commentary on authors now living or who have died since 1960. Because of the different periods under consideration, there is no duplication of material between *CLC* and *TCLC*. For additional information about *CLC* and Gale's other criticism titles, users should consult the Guide to Gale Literary Criticism Series preceding the title page in this volume.

Coverage

Each volume of *TCLC* is carefully compiled to present:

- criticism of authors, or literary topics, representing a variety of genres and nationalities

- both major and lesser-known writers and literary works of the period

- 11-15 authors or 4-6 topics per volume

- individual entries that survey critical response to each author's work or each topic in literary history, including early criticism to reflect initial reactions; later criticism to represent any rise or decline in reputation; and current retrospective analyses.

Organization of This Book

An author entry consists of the following elements: author heading, biographical and critical introduction, list of principal works, excerpts of criticism (each preceded by an annotation and followed by a bibliographic citation), and a bibliography of further reading.

- The **author heading** consists of the name under which the author most commonly wrote, followed by birth and death dates. If an author wrote consistently under a pseudonym, the pseudonym will be listed in the author heading and the real name given in parentheses on the first line of the biographical and critical introduction. Also located at the beginning of the introduction to the author entry are any name variations under which an author wrote, including transliterated forms for authors whose languages use nonroman alphabets.

- The **biographical and critical introduction** outlines the author's life and career, as well as the critical issues surrounding his or her work. References are provided to past volumes of *TCLC* and to other biographical and critical reference series published by Gale, including *Short Story Criticism, Children's Literature Review, Contemporary Authors, Dictionary of Literary Biography,* and *Something about the Author.*

- Most *TCLC* entries include **portraits** of the author. Many entries also contain reproductions of materials pertinent to an author's career, including manuscript pages, title pages, dust jackets, letters, and drawings, as well as photographs of important people, places, and events in an author's life.

- The **list of principal works** is chronological by date of first book publication and identifies the genre of each work. In the case of foreign authors with both foreign-language publications and English translations, the title and date of the first English-language edition are given in brackets. Unless otherwise indicated, dramas are dated by first performance, not first publication.

- **Criticism** is arranged chronologically in each author entry to provide a perspective on changes in critical evaluation over the years. All titles of works by the author featured in the entry are printed in boldface type to enable the user to easily locate discussion of particular works. Also for purposes of easier identification, the critic's name and the publication date of the essay are given at the beginning of each piece of criticism. Unsigned criticism is preceded by the title of the journal in which it appeared. Some of the excerpts in *TCLC* also contain translated material. Unless otherwise noted, translations in brackets are by the editors; translations in parentheses or continuous with the text are by the critic. Publication information (such as publisher names and book prices) and parenthetical numerical references (such as footnotes or page and line references to specific editions of works) have been deleted at the editors' discretion to provide smoother reading of the text.

- Critical excerpts are prefaced by **annotations** providing the reader with information about both the critic and the criticism that follows. Included are the critic's reputation, individual approach to literary criticism, and particular expertise in an author's works. Also noted are the relative importance of a work of criticism, the scope of the excerpt, and the growth of critical controversy or changes in critical trends regarding an author. In some cases, these annotations cross-reference excerpts by critics who discuss each other's commentary.

- A complete **bibliographic citation** designed to facilitate location of the original essay or book follows each piece of criticism.

- An annotated list of **further reading** appearing at the end of each author entry suggests secondary sources on the author. In some cases it includes essays for which the editors could not obtain reprint rights.

Cumulative Indexes

- Each volume of *TCLC* contains a cumulative **author index** listing all authors who have appeared in Gale's Literary Criticism Series, along with cross-references to such biographical series as *Contemporary Authors* and *Dictionary of Literary Biography.* For readers' convenience, a complete list of Gale titles included appears on the first page of the author index. Useful for locating authors within the various series, this index is particularly valuable for those authors who are identified by a certain period but who, because of their death dates, are placed in another, or for those authors whose careers span two periods. For example, F. Scott Fitzgerald is found in *TCLC*, yet a writer often associated with him, Ernest Hemingway, is found in *CLC*.

- Each *TCLC* volume includes a cumulative **nationality index** which lists all authors who have appeared in *TCLC* volumes, arranged alphabetically under their respective nationalities, as well as Topics volume entries devoted to particular national literatures.

- Each new volume in Gale's Literary Criticism Series includes a cumulative **topic index,** which lists all literary topics treated in *NCLC, TCLC, LC 1400-1800,* and the *CLC* Yearbook.

- Each new volume of *TCLC*, with the exception of the Topics volumes, contains a **title index** listing the titles of all literary works discussed in the volume. In response to numerous suggestions from librarians, Gale has also produced a **special paperbound edition** of the *TCLC* title index. This annual cumulation lists all titles discussed in the series since its inception and is issued with the first volume of *TCLC* published each year. Additional copies of the index are available on request. Librarians and patrons will welcome this separate index: it saves shelf space, is easy to use, and is disposable upon receipt of the following year's cumulation. Titles discussed in the Topics volume entries are not included in the *TCLC* cumulative index.

A Note to the Reader

When writing papers, students who quote directly from any volume in Gale's Literary Criticism Series may use the following general forms to footnote reprinted criticism. The first example pertains to material drawn from periodicals, the second to material reprinted from books.

[1] T. S. Eliot, "John Donne," *The Nation and the Athenaeum,* 33 (9 June 1923), 321-32; excerpted and reprinted in *Literature Criticism from 1400 to 1800,* Vol. 10, ed. James E. Person, Jr. (Detroit: Gale Research, 1989), pp. 28-9.

[2] Clara G. Stillman, *Samuel Butler: A Mid-Victorian Modern* (Viking Press, 1932); excerpted and reprinted in *Twentieth-Century Literary Criticism,* Vol. 33, ed. Paula Kepos (Detroit: Gale Research, 1989), pp. 43-5.

Suggestions Are Welcome

In response to suggestions, several features have been added to *TCLC* since the series began, including annotations to excerpted criticism, a cumulative index to authors in all Gale literary criticism series, entries devoted to criticism on a single work by a major author, more extensive illustrations, and a title index listing all literary works discussed in the series since its inception.

Readers who wish to suggest authors or topics to appear in future volumes, or who have other suggestions, are cordially invited to write the editors.

Acknowledgments

The editors wish to thank the copyright holders of the excerpted criticism included in this volume, the permissions managers of many book and magazine publishing companies for assisting us in securing reprint rights, and Anthony Bogucki for assistance with copyright research. We are also grateful to the staffs of the Detroit Public Library, Wayne State University Purdy/Kresge Library Complex, and the University of Michigan Libraries for making their resources available to us. Following is a list of the copyright holders who have granted us permission to reprint material in this volume of *TCLC*. Every effort has been made to trace copyright, but if omissions have been made, please let us know.

COPYRIGHTED EXCERPTS IN *TCLC*, VOLUME 43, WERE REPRINTED FROM THE FOLLOWING PERIODICALS:

Annals of Scholarship: Metastudies of the Humanities and Social Sciences, v. 3, 1984. Reprinted by permission of the publisher.—*Browning Institute Studies,* v. 13, 1985. Copyright © 1985 by the Browning Institute, Inc. Reprinted by permission of the publisher.—*Chasqui,* v. 14, November, 1984. Reprinted by permission of the publisher.—*Chicago Review,* v. 16, Winter-Spring, 1963. Copyright © 1963 by *Chicago Review.* Reprinted by permission of the publisher.—*CLA Journal,* v. XXX, March, 1987. Copyright, 1987 by The College Language Association. Used by permission of The College Language Association.—*CLIO,* v. 8, Spring, 1979 for "Literary Criticism as History: The Example of Auerbach's Mimesis" by Thomas M. DePietro; v. 10, Winter, 1981 for "Auerbach's 'Mimesis': Aesthetics as Historical Understanding" by W. Wolfgang Holdheim. © 1979, 1981 by Robert H. Canary and Henry Kozicki. Both reprinted by permission of the respective authors.—*Commentary,* v. 11, May, 1951. Copyright 1951, renewed 1979 by the American Jewish Committee. All rights reserved. Reprinted by permission of the publisher.—*Conradiana,* v. VII, 1975. Reprinted by permission of the publisher.—*Critical Inquiry,* v. 1, December, 1974 for "Virginia Woolf's Criticism: A Polemical Preface" by Barbara Currier Bell and Carol Ohmann. Copyright © 1974 by The University of Chicago. Reprinted by permission of the publisher and Barbara Currier Bell.—*Critical Quarterly,* v. 8, Autumn, 1966 for "Lord Jim: The Romance of Irony" by G. S. Fraser. Reprinted by permission of the Literary Estate of G. S. Fraser.—*Dalhousie Review,* v. 49, Winter, 1969-70 for "Sartre and Conrad: Lord Jim as Existential Hero" by Ira Sadoff. Reprinted by permission of the publisher and the author.—*Freedomways,* v. 3, Summer, 1963; v. 14, first quarter, 1974. Copyright © 1963, 1974 by Freedomways Associates, Inc. Both reprinted by permission of *Freedomways.*—*The Hudson Review,* v. VII, Spring, 1954. Copyright 1954 by The Hudson Review, Inc. Reprinted by permission of the publisher.—*Journal of the History of Ideas,* v. XXII, January-March, 1961 for "Philosophy or Philology: Auerbach and Aesthetic Historicism" by Charles Breslin. Copyright 1961, Journal of the History of Ideas, Inc. Reprinted by permission of the publisher and the author.—*Luso-Brazilian Review,* v. 21, Summer, 1984. Copyright © 1984 by the Board of Regents of the University of Wisconsin System. Reprinted by permission of The University of Wisconsin Press.—*The Midwest Quarterly,* v. XXV, Winter, 1984. Copyright, 1984, by *The Midwest Quarterly,* Pittsburg State University. Reprinted by permission of the publisher.—*MLN,* v. 81, December, 1966. © copyright 1966 by The Johns Hopkins University Press. All rights reserved. Reprinted by permission of the publisher.—*Mosaic: A Journal for the Interdisciplinary Study of Literature,* v. XX, Winter, 1987 for "Mimesis: The Representation of Reality in the Post-War British Novel" by Margaret Drabble. © *Mosaic* 1987. Acknowledgment of previous publication is herewith made. Reprinted by permission of the publisher and the author.—*Nineteenth-Century Fiction,* v. 32, March, 1978 for "The Country House Ideals in Meredith's 'The Egoist' " by Maaja A. Stewart. © 1978 by The Regents of the University of California. Reprinted by permission of the publisher and the author.—*PHYLON: The Atlanta University Review of Race and Culture,* v. XL, December, 1979. Copyright, 1979, by Atlanta University. Reprinted by permission of *PHYLON.*—*The Phylon Quarterly,* v. XVIII, Second Quarter, 1957. Copyright, 1957, renewed 1985 by Atlanta University. All rights reserved. Reprinted by permission of *PHYLON.*—*Studies in the Novel,* v. III, Spring, 1971. Copyright 1971 by North Texas State University. Reprinted by permission of the publisher.—*Textual Practice,* v. 4, Summer, 1990. © Routledge 1991. All rights reserved. Reprinted by permission of the publisher.—*The Times Literary Supplement,* n. 3326, November 25, 1965. © The Times Supplements Limited 1965. Reproduced from *The Times Literary Supplement* by permission.—*Victorian Poetry,* v. 15, Spring, 1977. Reprinted by permission of the publisher.—*Western Humanities Review,* v. XIX, Summer, 1965. Copyright, 1965, University of Utah. Reprinted by permission of the publisher.—*The Yale Review,* v. XXXII, Winter, 1943. Copyright 1942, renewed 1970 by Yale University. Reprinted by permission of the editors.

thor.—Slochower, Harry. From *Three Ways of Modern Man.* International Publishers, 1937. Copyright, 1937, renewed 1965 International Publishers Co., Inc. Reprinted by permission of the publisher.—Stone, Donald David. From *Novelists in a Changing World: Meredith, James, and the Transformation of English Fiction in the 1880's.* Cambridge, Mass.: Harvard University Press, 1972. Copyright © 1972 by the President and Fellows of Harvard College. All rights reserved. Excerpted by permission of the publishers and the author.—Swanson, Donald R. From *Three Conquerors: Character and Method in the Mature Works of George Meredith.* Mouton, 1969. © copyright 1969 Mouton & Co., Publishers. Reprinted by permission of Mouton de Gruyter, a Division of Walter de Gruyter & Co.—Tomlins, Jack E. From an introduction to *Hallucinated City: Paulicea desvairada.* By Mário de Andrade, translated by Jack E. Tomlins. Vanderbilt University Press, 1968. Copyright © 1968 Vanderbilt University Press. Reprinted by permission of the publisher.—Trilling, Diana. From *Claremont Essays.* Harcourt Brace Jovanovich, 1964. Copyright 1948, © 1964 by Diana Trilling. Reprinted by permission of the author.—Van Ghent, Dorothy. From *The English Novel: Form and Function.* Holt, Rinehart and Winston, 1953. Copyright 1953, renewed 1981, by Dorothy Van Ghent. Reprinted by permission of the Literary Estate of Dorothy Van Ghent.—Wellek, René. From *A History of Modern Criticism: 1750-1950, Vol. 5.* Yale University Press, 1986. Copyright © 1986 by Yale University. All rights reserved. Reprinted by permission of the publisher.—Wellek, René. From "Auerbach and Vico," in *Vico: Past and Present.* Edited by Giorgio Tagliacozzo. Humanities Press, 1981. Copyright © 1981 by Humanities Press, Inc. All rights reserved. Reprinted by permission of the editor.—Weygandt, Cornelius. From *The Time of Yeats: English Poetry of To-Day against an American Background.* D. Appleton-Century, 1937. Copyright, 1937 by D. Appleton-Century Company, Inc. Renewed 1964 by Cornelius N. Weygandt. Reprinted by permission of the Literary Estate of Cornelius Weygandt.

PHOTOGRAPHS AND ILLUSTRATIONS APPEARING IN *TCLC,* VOLUME 43, WERE RECEIVED FROM THE FOLLOWING SOURCES:

Joao Cândido Portnari: **p. 1;** The Granger Collection, New York: **p. 184;** Schomberg Center for Research in Black Culture, the New York Public Library, Astor, Lenox and Tilden Foundations: **p. 220;** Frontispiece and title page of *The New Negro: An Interpretation,* edited by Alain Locke. Albert and Charles Boni, 1925. Reprinted by permission of W. W. Norton & Company, Inc.: **p. 233;** Courtesy of the Danish Information Office, N.Y.: **p. 307;** Copyright 1936 by Twentieth Century-Fox Film Corp.: **p. 372;** Lenare: **p. 378;** Photograph by Gisele Freund: **pp. 396, 412;** Courtesy of Alex Reid & Lefevre Ltd., London: **p. 404;** Courtesy of Mrs. Angelica Garnett: **p. 422.**

Mário de Andrade

1893-1945

INTRODUCTION

(Full name Mário Raul de Morais Andrade; also wrote under the pseudonym Mário Sobral) Brazilian novelist, poet, critic, essayist, and short story writer.

A central figure in the development of the Modernist movement in Brazilian literature during the early part of the twentieth century, Andrade is best known as the author of the poetry volume *Paulicea desvairada (Hallucinated City)*, one of the first important Modernist works in South America, and *Macunaíma,* an experimental novel that incorporates Brazilian folklore and regional dialects. In these and other works Andrade sought to produce a distinctly Brazilian form of literary expression, and toward this end synthesized a wide variety of literary influences and trends, including native South American legends and the orthography and grammar of Brazilian Portuguese.

Born into an upper-middle-class family in São Paulo, Andrade was the son of an accountant. After graduating from high school, he attended the Dramatic and Musical Conservatory of São Paulo. In 1917, using the pseudonym Mário Sobral, Andrade published *Há uma gôta de sangue em cada poema,* a volume of poetry influenced by the work of the French Parnassian poets, who rejected the emotionalism of Romantic poetry and advocated the use of highly structured, traditional verse forms. Andrade wrote most of the poems in *Hallucinated City* during one week in December 1920 and revised them throughout the following year. Andrade's reading of several of these works created a sensation at the Semana de Arte Moderna in São Paulo, a festival held in February 1922 featuring Brazilian artists, musicians, and writers. Published later the same year, *Hallucinated City* established Andrade's reputation as an important figure in Brazilian literary circles. In 1927 Andrade published his first novel, *Amar, verbo intransitivo (Fräulein),* which concerns a German woman hired by a wealthy Brazilian to provide his teenage son with his first sexual experience. His next major work, *Macunaíma* was the result of several years of research in linguistics, ethnography, and Brazilian folklore. During the mid-1930s Andrade served as the director of the Department of Culture of São Paulo, organizing research of Brazilian folklore and music; he was later appointed director of the Institute of Arts of the University of the Federal District in Rio de Janeiro. In 1940 Andrade returned to São Paulo, where he continued to write and later published several volumes of critical essays. Shortly before his death in 1945, Andrade completed "A meditação sôbre o Tietê," a long free-verse poem containing numerous references to his earlier poetry.

Inspired by the Belgian poet Émile Verhaeren's *Les villes tentaculaires* (1895), *Hallucinated City* is a collection of

twenty-two free-verse poems dedicated to the city of São Paulo. At the request of his publisher and several friends who felt that these poems might be misunderstood, Andrade wrote what he termed a "Prefácio interessantíssimo" ("Extremely Interesting Preface") in which he explained his poetic theories and objectives. Rejecting the formal rigidity of the Parnassians as well as the artistic strictures that resulted from the influence of Italian Futurism on Brazilian literature, Andrade emphasized subjectivity and lyricism in his poetry, arguing that the poet should employ the harmonic and polyphonic structures of music. He also defended his usage of Brazilian grammar, rather than follow the linguistic models of literary Portuguese. Although Andrade declared that the preface, "with all the nonsensical theories which it contains, is not worth a damn," critics recognize this work, which served as a manifesto for the Modernists, and his essay *A escrava que não é Isaura* as important statements of Modernist poetic theory. While the poems in *Hallucinated City* have been faulted for lack of philosophical depth, and many of Andrade's contemporaries dismissed them as nonsense, this volume has been credited with shaping the development of the Modernist movement in Brazil after 1922.

1

Most recent commentary on Andrade's work has been devoted to *Macunaíma*. This novel is largely based on a native South American folktale concerning Makunaíma, a mischievous trickster with magical powers. The opening chapters of Andrade's novel reveal Macunaíma's origins and development in the forests of the Amazon region, focusing primarily on his playful antics with the women of his village and with his brothers Jiguê and Maanape. Together they conquer Ci, the Mother of the Forest, and Macunaíma becomes the new Emperor of the Virgin Forest and Ci's lover. During the course of his adventures Macunaíma loses the *muiraquitã*, an amulet given to him by Ci, and must travel to São Paulo to recover it from the Peruvian trader Venceslau Pietro Pietra, who is also identified as the giant Piaimã, Eater of Men—Macunaíma's traditional foe in native legend. In São Paulo Macunaíma has numerous adventures and writes a letter to his subjects concerning life in the city and his attempts to recover the amulet. After wounding Piaimã during an African magic ceremony, Macunaíma finally kills the giant by tricking him into falling into a cauldron of macaroni. Having recovered the amulet, Macunaíma returns to the forest, where his brothers die, and he loses the *muiraquitã* a second time. Weary of life in this world, Macunaíma recounts his adventures to a parrot and then ascends into the sky to become the Great Bear constellation.

Although Andrade's aim in *Macunaíma* was to create a distinctly Brazilian form of literary expression, many early commentators found his mixture of regional dialects, slang, and native South American and Afro-Brazilian words unintelligible. Some of his contemporaries also considered the work pornographic; the original edition contained a passage relating Macunaíma's rape of Ci, which Andrade significantly shortened for later editions of the novel. Macunaíma's letter to his subjects is noted for its skillful mockery of the accounts of early Portuguese explorers and the pedantic formality of classical Portuguese literary language, while the novel as a whole has been discussed as a parody of Luís de Camões's epic poem *Os Lusíadas* (1572; *The Lusiads*). Critics further note that the narrative serves both etiological and elegiacal functions, providing mythical explanations for various aspects of modern Brazilian life, such as the origins of soccer and numerous idiomatic expressions and gestures, and evoking a lament for the rapid disappearance and assimilation of native cultures. While Andrade's reputation in English-speaking countries has been limited by a scarcity of translations and critical discussion, he is nevertheless recognized for his contributions to Brazilian literature. Thomas R. Hart commented that "the Modernist movement gave to Brazilian literature much that is of lasting value and surely the writings of Mário de Andrade are not the least of its gifts."

PRINCIPAL WORKS

Há uma gôta de sangue em cada poema [as Mário Sobral] (poetry)   1917
Paulicea desvairada (poetry)   1922
   [*Hallucinated City,* 1968]
A escrava que não é Isaura (essay)   1925

Losango cáqui (poetry)   1926
Primeiro andar (short stories and plays)   1926; revised and enlarged edition, 1943
Amar, verbo intransitivo (novel)   1927
   [*Fräulein,* 1933]
Clã do jabuti (poetry)   1927
Macunaíma (novel)   1928; also published as *Macunaíma: O herói sem nenhum caráter* [revised edition], 1944
   [*Macunaíma,* 1984]
Remate de males (poetry)   1930
Belazarte (short stories)   1934; also published as *Histórias de Belazarte* [enlarged edition], 1944
O movimento modernista (essay)   1942
Aspectos da literatura brasileira (essays)   1943
O empalhador de passarinho (essays)   1944
Lira Paulistana (poetry)   1946
Contos novos (short stories)   1947
Cartas de Mário de Andrade a Manuel Bandeira (letters)   1958
Setenta e uma cartas de Mário de Andrade (letters)   1963
Mário de Andrade escreve a Alceu, Meyer e outros (letters)   1968
O turista aprendiz (journal)   1977
Poesias Completas (poetry)   1987

Mário de Andrade   (essay date 1922)

[*In the following excerpt from his "Extremely Interesting Preface" to* Hallucinated City, *Andrade discusses his literary theories.*]

Reader:

Hallucinism has been launched.

This preface—although interesting—useless.

A few facts. Not all of them. No conclusions. For those who accept me, both facts and conclusions are useless. The curious will have the pleasure of discovering my conclusions, by comparing the work with the facts. As for those who reject me, it is wasted effort to explain to them what they have rejected even before they have read it.

When I feel the lyric impulse upon me, I write without thinking all that my unconscious shouts out to me. I think afterward: not only to correct but also to justify what I have written. Hence the reason for this **"Extremely Interesting Preface."**

Furthermore, in this kind of chit-chat it is very difficult to know where the *blague* leaves off and the serious begins. I do not even know myself.

And forgive me for being so behind the times regarding present-day artistic movements. I am old-fashioned, I confess. No one can liberate himself once and for all from the grandaddy-theories he has imbibed, and the author of this book would be a hypocrite if he pretended to represent a modern orientation which as yet he himself does not totally comprehend.

A book obviously impressionistic. Now, according to the moderns, a grave error, Impressionism. The architects flee from the Gothic style as well as from the new art, allying themselves—beyond historical time—with elemental shapes: cube, sphere, etc. The painters scorn Delacroix as well as Whistler and take refuge in the constructive serenity of Raphael, Ingres, el Greco. In sculpture Rodin is horrendous; imaginary Africans are good. The musicians despise Debussy: genuflections before the cathedral polyphony of Palestrina and Johann Sebastian Bach. Poetry . . . "tends to despoil man of all his contingent and ephemeral aspects in order to grasp the humanity in him." I am old-fashioned, I confess.

"This Koran is nothing more than a jumble of confused and incoherent dreams. It is not inspiration drawn from God, but created by the author. Muhammed is not a prophet; he is a man who writes verses. Let him represent himself as some revealing sign of his destiny, like the ancient prophets." Perhaps they will say of me what they said of the creator of Allah. A notable difference between the two of us: Muhammed represented himself as a prophet; I have deemed it more proper to represent myself as a madman.

Have you read St. John the Evangelist? Walt Whitman? Mallarmé? Verhaeren?

For almost ten years I metrified and rhymed. Example?

"Artist"

> I fain would paint—like Leonardo be,
> Whose art in pious scenes refined became;
> The vast corolla unto worldly fame
> I'd ope of this exalted dream in me . . .
>
> I yearn upon life's backdrop dun to see
> Venetian tints the murkiness inflame,
> To give in rose and gold, as alms, the same
> Fair tones where'er the stone and thistle be.
>
> When I shall find that tinted fountainhead
> And brush sublime, oh Veronese, borne
> By you upon the upraised frieze o'erhead,
>
> I'll in the land where Sorrows dwell sojourn;
> And I shall live by painting smiles of red
> Upon the lips of those who curse or mourn.

Senhores Laurindo de Brito, Martins Fontes, and Paulo Setúbal published their verses, although they obviously do not have the scope of Vicente de Carvalho or Francisca Julia. And they do very well. I could, like them, publish my metrical poetry.

I am not a Futurist (after Marinetti). I have said so before and I repeat it. I have points of contact with Futurism. When Oswald de Andrade called me a Futurist, he was wrong. The fault was mine. I knew of the existence of his article, and I allowed it to be published. The scandal was so great that I wished the whole world dead.

I was vain. I was trying to break free of obscurity. Today I am proud. I would not mind returning to obscurity. I thought my aims would be discussed. Even now I do not

remain silent. They would mock my silence as much as they mock this uproar. I shall go through life with my arms outstretched, like the "L'indifférent" of Watteau.

"When some readers read these phrases (the poetry quoted), they did not understand immediately. I even think that it is impossible, without a bit of practice, to understand entirely, on a first reading, thoughts schematized in this way. But it is not for that reason that a poet can complain about his readers. Where these readers are contemptible is in their not thinking that a writer who signs his work does not write asininities for the sheer joy of testing his ink; and that beneath that apparent extravagance there was perhaps some extremely interesting significance, that there was something to understand." Jean Epstein.

There is in this world a gentleman named Zdislas Milner. And he wrote the following: "The fact that a work departs from already learned precepts and rules does not give the measure of its value." Excuse me for granting some value to my book. No father will abandon his hunchback child, who is drowning, to save the beautiful heir of his neighbor, for the simple reason that he *is* a father. The wet nurse who did that in the story was a completely unnatural ham.

Every writer believes in the worth of what he writes. If he shows it, it is out of vanity. If he does not show it, it is also out of vanity.

I do not flee from the ridiculous. I have illustrious companions.

The ridiculous is often subjective. It does not depend on the greater or lesser goal of the one who suffers it. We create it in order to garb in it the person who wounds our pride, ignorance, or sterility.

A little theory?

I believe that lyricism, born in the subconscious, purified into a clear or confused thought, creates phrases which are entire verses, without the necessity of counting so many syllables with predetermined accentuation. Run-on lines are a welcome respite to those poets who are trapped in the Alexandrine prison. There are only rare examples of that in this book. As the twig is bent. . . .

Inspiration is short-lived, violent. Any obstacle whatever upsets it and even silences it. When Art is added to Lyricism to create Poetry, this process does not consist of halting the mad dash of the lyric state in order to warn it of the stones and barbed-wire fences along the road. Let it stumble, fall, and wound itself. Art is a subsequent weeding out of all irksome repetitions, romantic sentimentalities, and useless or unexpressive details.

Let Art, therefore, not consist of ridding verses of colorful exaggerations. Exaggeration: ever-new symbol of life as well as of the dream. Through exaggeration, life and dreams are linked. And, employed consciously, it is not a defect, rather a legitimate means of expression.

"The wind sits in the shoulder of your sail!" Shakespeare. Homer had long ago written that the earth groaned beneath the feet of men and horses. But you must know that there are millions of exaggerations in the works of the masters.

Taine said that the artist's ideal consists of "presenting not the objects themselves, but rather of presenting clearly and completely any essential and outstanding characteristic of them, by means of the systematic alteration of the natural relationship between their parts, so as to make that characteristic more visible and dominant." However, I recognize that Senhor Luis Carlos has the right to quote the same thing in defense of his "Columns."

Have you ever thought about so-called "hideous beauty"? That is too bad. Hideous beauty is a subterfuge created according to the size of the ears of certain philosophers to justify the attraction which the hideous exercises, at all times, over the artist. Do not come to me and say that the artist, reproducing the ugly, the hideous, is creating a beautiful work. To call beautiful that which is ugly and hideous, only because it is expressed with intensity, agitation, or art, is either to devalue or to ignore the concept of beauty. But "ugly" equals "sin." It is attractive. Anita Malfatti was talking to me the other day about the ever-new charm of the ugly. Anita Malfatti has undoubtedly not yet read Emile Bayard: "The logical purpose of a canvas is to be pleasing to the eye. However, artists take delight in expressing the singular charm of ugliness. The artist makes everything sublime."

Beauty in art: arbitrary, conventional, transitory: a matter of fashion. Beauty in nature: immutable, objective, natural. It possesses whatever eternity nature may possess. Art does not succeed in imitating nature, nor is this its object. All the great artists, whether consciously (the Raphael of the Madonnas, the Rodin of the Balzac, the Beethoven of the Pastoral, the Machado de Assis of the Braz Cubas) or unconsciously (the greater part of them) were deformers of nature. From which I infer that artistic beauty will be more artistic, more subjective, the more it withdraws from natural beauty. Let others infer what they will. I could not care less.

Our senses are fragile. Our perception of external things is dim, obstructed by a thousand veils which derive from our physical and moral defects: illness, prejudice, indisposition, antipathy, ignorance, heredity, circumstances of time and place, etc. . . . Only ideally can we conceive of objects as acts in their beautiful or in their ugly integrity. Even when art derives its themes from the objective world, it is developed through comparisons which are remote, exaggerated, without apparent exactitude; or it indicates objects, as universals, without any qualifying delimitation whatever. It has the power of leading us to that free, musical idealization. This free and subjective idealization permits one to create a whole atmosphere of ideal realities where sentiments, beings and things, beauties and defects, are presented in their heroic plenitude, which surpasses the defective perception of the senses. I do not know what kind of Futurism can exist in one who practically embraces the esthetic concepts of Fichte. Let us flee from nature! Only in this way will art not be offended by the ridiculous weakness of photography . . . colored.

I am no longer amused at all by the fact that people submit their emotions to the couch of Procrustes in order to obtain a conventional number of syllables in conventional rhythm. In my first book, I indifferently used several me-

ters, without feeling any obligation to employ only regular meter. Now I free myself also from that preconception. I acquire others. Should I be scorned because of that?

I do not shun the dancer's trained balance found in *redondilhas* and decasyllables. It happens sometimes that emotions fit into those molds. Sometimes they go, then, into the rhythmic cabaret of my verses! In this question of meter, I am not an ally; I am like Argentina: I grow rich.

Concerning order? As a matter of fact, I am disgusted by what Musset called: "L'art de servir à point un dénouement bien cuit."

There is the order of children leaving school, two by two, holding hands. There is the order of students in the upper grades going downstairs, four at a time, prettily jostling one another. There is the even higher order of the unleashed fury of the elements.

He who lectures on Brazilian history will follow an order which surely does not consist in studying the Paraguayan War before the illustrious discovery of Pedro Alvares. He who sings his subconscious will follow the unforeseen order of his emotions, of the association of images, of external contacts. It happens that the theme sometimes gets off the track.

The lyric impulse cries out inside us like the madding crowd. It would be highly amusing if we said to the crowd: "Slow down there! Let each cry out when it is his turn; and let the one who has the strongest argument keep it for the end!" The crowd is apparent confusion. He who knows how to withdraw ideally from the confusion will see the imposing development of that collective soul speaking the exact rhetoric of vindication.

My vindication? Freedom. I use it; I do not abuse it. I know how to bridle it for my philosophical and religious truths, because philosophical and religious truths are not conventional like art: they are true. I do not abuse to that degree. I do not pretend to make anyone follow me. I am accustomed to going it alone.

Virgil and Homer did not use rhyme. Virgil and Homer have admirable assonances.

The Brazilian language is one of the richest and most sonorous. And it possesses that really splendid sound *ão*.

Marinetti was wonderful when he rediscovered the suggestive, associative, symbolic, universal, and musical power of the liberated word. Beyond that: it is as old as Adam. Marinetti was wrong: he made a system out of the liberated word. It is merely an extremely powerful auxiliary. I employ liberated words. I feel that my cup is too large for me, and yet I drink from the cups of others.

I am capable of constructing ingenious theories. Do you want to see one? Poetics is far more backward than music. Maybe even before the eighth century, music abandoned the regimen of melody, which at most dared to use octaves, in order to enrich itself with the infinite resources of harmony. Poetics, with rare exception down to the middle of the nineteenth century in France, was essentially melodic. I consider melodic verse the same as musical melody: a horizontal arabesque of consecutive tones (sounds) which contain intelligible thought. Now, if instead of using only verses which are horizontally melodic, such as:

> Mnesarete, the divine, the pale Phryne
> Appears before the austere and stern assembly
> of the supreme Areopagus . . .

we have words follow each other without any immediate connection among themselves, these words, for the very reason that they do not follow intellectually and grammatically, overlie one another for the gratification of our senses, and no longer form melodies but rather harmonies. I shall explain more fully. Harmony: combination of sounds. Example:

> Ravishments . . . Struggles . . . Arrows . . .
> Songs . . . Populate!

These words have no connection. They do not form a series. Each one is a phrase, an elliptical period, reduced to the telegraphic minimum. If I pronounce "Ravishments," since it does not belong to a phrase (melody), the word calls our attention to its detachment and it continues to vibrate, waiting for a phrase which will give it meaning, a phrase which DOES NOT FOLLOW. "Struggles" gives no conclusion whatever to "Ravishments"; and, under the same conditions, as we are not made to forget the first word, it continues to vibrate along with the other word. The other voices do the same. Thus: instead of melody (grammatical phrase) we have an arpeggiated chord, harmony—the harmonic verse. But, if instead of using only disconnected words, I use disconnected phrases, I get the same sensation of overlay, not now of words (notes) alone but of phrases (melodies). Hence: poetic polyphony. Thus in **Hallucinated City** are employed melodic verse:

> São Paulo is a stage for Russian ballets;

harmonic verse:

> Pack of dogs . . . Stock Market . . .
> Gambling . . . ;

poetic polyphony (one and sometimes two and even more consecutive verses):

> The gears palsy . . . The mist snows . . .

And so? Do not forget, however, that another will come along to destroy everything that I have constructed here.

Add this to theory:

1

The poetic geniuses of the past succeeded in giving greater importance to melodic verse by making it more beautiful, more varied, more moving, more surprising. Some even succeeded in formulating harmonies, at times extremely rich. Harmonies, nonetheless, unconscious, sporadic. I can prove the unconscious part: Victor Hugo, very often harmonic, exclaimed after he had heard the Quartet from *Rigoletto:* "Just let them make it possible for me to combine several phrases simultaneously and they'll see what I'm capable of." I find the anecdote in Galli, Esthetics of Music. Se non é vero. . . .

2

There are certain figures of speech in which we can see the embryo of oral harmony, just as we find the germ of musical harmony in the reading of the symphonies of Pythagoras. Antithesis: genuine dissonance. And if it is so greatly appreciated, that is proper because poets, like musicians, have always felt the great charm of dissonance, of which G. Migot speaks.

3

Commentary on the words of Hugo. Oral harmony is not effected, like musical harmony, in the senses, because words are not fused like notes; rather they are shuffled together, and they become incomprehensible. The creation of poetic harmony is effected in the intellect. The comprehension of the arts expressive of the succession of time is never immediate, rather it is intermediate. In the diachronic arts we co-ordinate consecutive acts of the memory which we assimilate in a final whole. This whole, the result of successive states of mind, renders the final and complete comprehension of music, poetry, and finished dance. Victor Hugo was wrong when he wished to effect objectively that which is effected subjectively within ourselves.

4

Psychologists will not accept the theory. Merely answer them with the "Só-quem-ama" by Bilac. Or with Heine's verses from which Bilac derived the "Só-quem-ama." If, perhaps, some shocking and unforeseen thing has happened to you (it has, naturally), recall the disordered tumult of the many ideas which at that moment coursed through your brain. Those ideas, reduced to the telegraphic minimum of the word, did not persevere because they did not belong to any sentence; they had no reply, solution, or continuity. They quivered, echoed, massed, heaped. Without juncture, with no apparent agreement—although they were born of the same occurrence—they formed, in rapid succession, true simultaneity, true harmonies accompanying the energetic and grand melody of the occurrence.

5

The Bilac of *Tarde* often represents an attempt at poetic harmony. Hence, in part at least, the new style of the book. He discovered for the Brazilian language that particular poetic harmony rarely employed before him. (Gonçalves Dias brilliantly in the fight scene, Y-Juca-Pirama). Bilac's defect lay in the fact that he did not methodize his finding, did not extract all the consequences of it. His defect can be explained historically: *Tarde* is an apogee. Decadence does not follow apogee. Apogee is already decadence, because, since it is stagnation, it cannot in itself contain progress, an ascending evolution. Bilac represents a destructive phase in poetry, because all perfection in art signifies destruction. I can imagine your alarm, reader, as you read this. I do not have time to explain: study it, if you will. Our primitivism represents a new constructive phase. It falls to us to schematize and methodize the lessons of the past. I will return to the poet. He behaved like the creators of the medieval Organum: he accepted the harmonies of fourths and fifths while he scorned thirds, sixths, and all the other intervals. The number of his harmonies is extremely restricted. Thus " . . . the air and the earth, the flora and fauna, the grass and the bird, the stone and the trunk, the nests and the ivy, the water and the reptile, the leaf and the insect, the flower and the beast" gives the impression of a long and monotonous series of medieval fifths: boring, excessive, useless, incapable of stimulating the hearer and giving him the feeling of dusk in the forest.

Lyricism: a sublime affective state—the next thing to sublime madness. Preoccupation with metrics and rhyme hinders the free naturalness of objectified lyricism. Therefore sincere poets confess that they have never written their best verses. Rostand, for instance; and, among us, more or less, Senhor Amadeu Amaral. I have the good fortune of writing my best verses. Better than that I cannot do.

Ribot said somewhere that inspiration is a telegram in code sent by unconscious activity to conscious activity which decodes it. Both the poet and the reader may share that conscious activity. In this way the poet does not denude or thoroughly analyze the lyric moment, and he magnanimously concedes to the reader the glory of collaborating in the poems.

"Language permits the ambiguous form which marble does not permit." Renan.

"Between the plastic artist and the musician stands the poet who approaches the plastic artist with his conscious production, while he achieves the possibilities of the musician in the dark depths of the unconscious." Wagner.

You are beginning to see how accustomed I am to going it alone. . . .

Sir Lyricism, when he disembarked from the El Dorado of the Unconscious at the pier of the Land of the Conscious, is inspected by the ship's doctor, Intelligence, who cleanses him of quirks and of all sickness whatever that might spread confusion and obscurity in this progressive little land. Sir Lyricism undergoes one more visit from the customs officials, a visit discovered by Freud who called it Censure. I am a smuggler! I am against the vaccination laws.

It appears that I am all instinct. That is not true. There is in my book—and it does not displease me—a pronounced intellectualist tendency. What do you expect? I smuggle my silk in without paying the duties. But it is psychologically impossible for me to liberate myself from vaccinations and tonics.

Grammar appeared after languages were organized. It so happens that my unconscious knows nothing of the existence of grammars or of organized languages. And my unconscious, like Sir Lyricism, is a smuggler. . . .

You will easily note that if grammar is sometimes scorned in my poetry, it does not suffer serious insults in this extremely interesting preface. Preface: skyrocket of my higher self. The poems: landscape of my deeper self.

Pronouns? I write Brazilian. If I use Portuguese orthography, it is because it furnishes me an orthography without altering the result.

In my opinion, to write modern art never means to represent modern life through its externals: automobiles, movies, asphalt. If these words frequent my book, it is not because I think that I write "modern" with them; but since my book is modern, these things have their reason for being in it.

Besides, I know that there may be a modern artist who seeks inspiration in the Greece of Orpheus or in the Lusitania of Nun' Alvares. I recognize furthermore the existence of eternal themes, open to adoption because of their modernity: universe, homeland, love and the presence-of-the-absent, ex-bitter-pleasure-of-wretches.

Neither did I seek to attempt insincere and cross-eyed primitivism. We are actually the primitives of a new epoch. Esthetically: I sought an expression more human and freer from art among the hypotheses of psychologists, naturalists, and critics of the primitives of past ages.

The past is a lesson to be meditated, not to be imitated.

> E tu che sé costí, anima viva,
> Pártiti da cotesti che son morti.

For many years I sought myself. I have found myself. Do not tell me now that I seek originality because I have already discovered where it was: it belongs to me, it is mine.

When one of the poems in this book was published, many people told me: "I did not understand it." There were some, however, who confessed: "I understood it, but I did not feel it." As for my dear friends . . . I saw more than once that they felt it, but they did not understand it. Evidently my book is good.

A famous writer said about me and my friends that we were either geniuses or jackasses. I think that he is right. We feel, I as well as my friends, the desire to be showoffs. If we were sheep to the point of forming a collective school, this would surely be "Showoffism." Our desire: to illuminate. The extreme left in which we have stationed ourselves will not permit half-way solutions. If we are geniuses: we will point the road to follow; if we are jackasses: shipwrecks to avoid.

I sing in my own way. What do I care if no one understands me? You say that I do not have enough strength to universalize myself? What do I care! Singing to the accompaniment of the complex lute that I have constructed, I strike out through the wild jungle of the city. Like primitive man, at first I shall sing alone. But song is an engaging fellow: it gives rebirth in the soul of another man—predisposed or merely sincerely curious and free—to the same lyric state provoked in us by joys, sufferings, ideals. I shall always find some man or some woman who will be rocked in the hammock of the libertarian cadence of my verses. At that moment: a new, dark and bespectacled Amphion, I shall make the very stones rise up like a wall at the magic of my song. And within those walls we shall sequester our tribe.

My hand has written about this book that: "I neither had nor do I now have the slightest intention of publishing it." *Jornal do Comércio,* June 6. Read the words of Gourmont concerning contradiction: first volume of the *Promenades littéraires.* Rui Barbosa has a lovely page on contradiction, I do not remember where. There are a few words also in Jean Cocteau, *La noce massacrée.*

But this whole preface, with all the nonsensical theories which it contains, is not worth a damn. When I wrote *Hallucinated City* I did not think about any of this. I guarantee, however, that I wept, sang, laughed, and bellowed . . . I am alive!

Besides, verses are not written to be read by mute eyes. Verses are meant to be sung, bellowed, wept. If you cannot sing, do not read **"Landscape I."** If you cannot bellow, do not read **"Ode to the Bourgeois Gentleman."** If you cannot pray, do not read **"Religion."** Scorn: **"The Escalade."** Suffer: **"Colloque sentimental."** Forgive: the lullaby, one of the solos of My Madness from **"The Moral Fibrature."** I will not go on. It disgusts me to hand over the key to my book. If you are like me, you already have the key.

So the poetic school of "Hallucinism" is finished.

In the next book I will found another school.

And I do not want disciples. In art: School equals the imbecility of the many for the vanity of a single man.

I could have quoted Gorch Fock. I would have been spared this **"Extremely Interesting Preface."** "Every song of freedom is born in prison." (pp. 5-18)

> *Mário de Andrade, "Extremely Interesting Preface," in his* Hallucinated City: Paulicea desvairada, *translated by Jack E. Tomlins, Vanderbilt University Press, 1968, pp. 5-18.*

Jack E. Tomlins   (essay date 1967)

[*Tomlins is an American educator and translator who specializes in Spanish and Portuguese literature and who translated Andrade's* Paulicea desvairada. *In the following excerpt from his introduction to that work, Tomlins discusses the composition of the poems in* Hallucinated City *and the importance of the "Extremely Interesting Preface" in the Modernist movement in Brazilian literature.*]

Since his untimely death in 1945 the Brazilian writer Mário Raul de Morais Andrade has become the object of ever-increasing interest to his own countrymen as well as to students of Brazilian culture in the English-speaking world. Literary historians and critics in both Americas study the role that he played in the early twenties as instigator and artificer of Brazil's most significant literary event of this century: the Modernist Movement. Of this Movement he has been variously named prophet, pope, and lawgiver. It has been repeatedly said of Mário de Andrade that it was he who most profoundly understood the spirit and the mission of Modernism and that it was he who, in his creative life, most effectively embodied the Modernism that he had helped to create. Still, the totality of the man—poet, novelist, critic, folklorist, musicologist—remains largely a mystery. Even the wisest historian of Brazilian Modernism admits that it is perhaps best to speak ultimately of Mário de Andrade as a presence, a

man whose creative and critical personality genially hovered over the literary scene from 1922 to 1945.

The young poet was something more human than presence or myth, however, when he participated in the Week of Modern Art in his native São Paulo in February of 1922. Among the artists who took part in this series of three festivals devoted to modern Brazilian culture were sculptors, painters, writers, and musicians. Three separate sessions convened between February 13 and 17 in the Municipal Theatre. There *paulistas* stared bemused or aghast at the paintings of Anita Malfatti, the sculpture of Brecheret; they heard readings of modern Brazilian poetry and the music of Villa-Lobos. What today seems a quaint preview of things to come struck the Brazilian public of 1922 as wildly extravagant, insanely paranoiac.

In the years just before and after World War I, the young Brazilians, like the young North American writers, had gone to Europe. A tropical lost generation, they had come in contact with such liberated spirits as Jean Cocteau, Filippo Marinetti, Blaise Cendrars, Jean Epstein; they subsequently wanted a Brazilian art that was truly modern in the European esthetic tradition they had recently discovered. They wanted at the same time an art that was authentically and thematically Brazilian. Such was the complex revolution of the Week of Modern Art and such the juncture at which Mário de Andrade purposefully entered the literary scene.

By 1922, Mário and his fellow poets had surveyed the literary landscape of their country, and they saw a horizon littered with volumes of played-out Symbolism and Parnassianism. Mário himself, in 1917, had paid his own debt to the old schools in his volume of youthful, imitative verse, *There is a Drop of Blood in Every Poem (Há uma gota de sangue em cada poema).* He continued to read the French poets—Verhaeren, Rimbaud. He learned from the former that the modern world, constantly animated by the press of violent human and social change, might admirably furnish the material of a new poetry. Both influenced and dazzled by Verhaeren, the Brazilian poet later conceived his own *paulista Villes Tentaculaires:* a volume of "modern" poems composed in free verse and devoted to his beloved São Paulo. During most of the year 1921 he was busy with the polishing of this volume, the *Hallucinated City (Paulicea desvairada).* When he discovered that individual poems from the collection had an irritating effect on the overwhelming middle-class sensibilities of São Paulo, he knew it was time to bring his book before the general public and his fellow poets. This he did in the following July of 1922, the year of Modern Art.

Hallucinated City is a slender volume of twenty-two poems preceded by a short dedication from the poet to the poet and an **"Extremely Interesting Preface,"** [see excerpt dated 1922] as Mário immodestly qualified his foreword. This preface, often called the bible of Brazilian Modernism, in reality constitutes the first formal poetics of the Movement. As such, it is largely responsible for the direction which the Brazilian lyric took after 1922. Rather than bible, the **"Extremely Interesting Preface"** might more justly be termed missal: text of the proper thing to write, rubric directing the creator as to how he shall write it.

The poet himself, however, would have objected to the term "missal." It smacks of school, and he hated the rigidity of the literary school. He remarked at the conclusion of his preface that in art, schools served the vanity of the founder-poet and merely emphasized the imbecility of the followers of the founder. Sheep after the shepherd. There is undoubtedly here the poet's constantly reiterated desire to divorce himself from the appellation of "Futurist," after the manner of Marinetti, a title which he had shortly before received from his fellow poet, Oswald de Andrade. With customary tongue-in-cheek, Mário states that in order to prove his divorcement from Futurism he will found his own school: Hallucinism. Next week he will found another.

This, in itself, is not to be taken seriously. What the Brazilian admired in Marinetti was the liberated word: "the suggestive, associative, symbolic, universal, and musical power of the liberated word." He did not, however, appreciate the petrification of the liberated word in a modern poetic system. This is the gulf that separates Mário from the Italian Futurist. This freedom from the stricture of school points always, in Mário, away from Futurism and toward Modernism. Unlike the Futurists, Mário writes of modern things only because they are part of his world; they are neither to be systematized nor to be deified. They are to be used as an extremely powerful auxiliary in the composition of modern poetry. So it is that in the *Hallucinated City* Brazil's first revolutionary Modernist writes of the Cadillac (belonging to Oswald), streetcars, factories, trains, airplanes: the complex ordure of modern civilization.

Although the poet shuns the rigidity of the school, he takes especial delight in his own literary theories:

a. Poetry is equated with lyricism. The two terms are synonymous. Lyricism is the same as the poet's inspiration: whatever his unconscious cries out to him, he writes down on paper. Art later enters the process to weed out all dull repetition, romantic sentimentality, or useless detail.

b. Colorful exaggeration is perfectly suited to the lyric. Neither Homer nor Shakespeare hesitated to employ the daring image, the extravagant figure of speech.

c. The true lyric poet should never be restrained by such useless bonds as metrics, rhyme, or grammar. Free verse is the ideal; however, the modern poet will not eschew the standard and traditional meters if it happens that he can, at the moment of creation, cast the tumultuous passions of his life in those old-fashioned molds. After all, modern poetry can well be made with old-fashioned subjects. The modern poet is not bound to write solely of gasoline and asphalt.

d. The modern lyric should follow the historical development of music in the progression: melody, harmony, polyphony.

Melodic verse is the old-fashioned, nineteenth-century declarative statement, containing a complete thought:

São Paulo is a stage for Russian ballets.

Harmonic verse is the combination of distinct words which bear no immediate relationship to one another and, therefore, do not form a logical series:

Pack of dogs . . . Stock Market . . . Gambling. . . .

Polyphonic verse is the combination not of words, as above, but rather of distinct phrases to achieve the same effect as harmonic verse:

The gears palsy . . . The mist snows. . . .

Thus is expressed Mário's version of literary simultaneism put to the service of the lyrical impulse.

e. Lyric poetry should never be read by "mute eyes." The modern lyric poet writes his verses down so that subsequently they may be "sung, bellowed, wept" as they were at the moment of creation.

f. Finally, Mário admits that he did none of this theorizing at the moment of inspiration. Probably his theories are "not worth a damn." He only recalls that he "wept, sang, laughed, and bellowed." He was most alive when he set his inner turmoil down on paper in the form of lyric poetry. That was quite enough for him. He condemns schools and theories for what they are worth.

In a lecture delivered twenty years after the publication of the *Hallucinated City,* the poet recalled the events that immediately led to the composition of the poems in that volume. In 1920 he and his fellow poets had recently discovered the sculptor Victor Brecheret, who at that time had returned from his studies in Italy just as Anita Malfatti had returned before the War from her expressionist and cubist experiences in Germany. At great expense to his pocketbook, Mário was able to purchase a "Bust of Christ" from the sculptor, who was then all the rage among the young artists of São Paulo. Mário recalls proudly unwrapping his acquisition in the bosom of the family:

There was the devil to pay. They yelled and screamed. That monstrosity was a mortal sin, screeched my old auntie the matriarch of the family. Who ever heard of a Christ with braids! Hideous! Frightful! Maria Luisa, your son is totally depraved.

I was delirious, I swear. I honestly wanted to whack someone. I ate alone in an unbelievable state of distress. Later, at dusk, I went up to my room with the intention of pulling myself together, going out, relaxing a bit, setting off a bomb at the middle of the world. I recall that I went to the balcony, looked down at the square below without actually seeing it. Noises, lights, the ingenuous bantering of the taxi drivers: they all floated up to me. I was apparently calm and was thinking about nothing in particular. I don't know what suddenly happened to me. I went to my desk, opened a notebook, and wrote down a title that had never before crossed my mind: *Hallucinated City.* After almost a year of soul-searching anguish, the explosion had come at last. In the midst of disappointments, pressing labors, debts, arguments, in a little more than a week I had scrawled on paper a barbaric canticle maybe twice as long as it was to be after I had cleared out all extraneous material.

Thus it was that the first authentically revolutionary and significant volume of Modernist verse was born. Owing to the nature of its genesis, it is not surprising that, like all the representative lyrical works of the first decade of Brazilian Modernism, the *Hallucinated City* is, to a certain extent, a flawed book. It represents perhaps too much the impassioned outcry of the moment, notwithstanding Mário's definition of Art. This verse frequently lacks philosophical depth; it often reveals a want of simple meditation. On the other hand, it is legitimately the portrait of a young poet with all the baggage of his sincerity weighing lightly on his back. Later, in 1931, Mário was to write that, in his opinion, youths under twenty-five should be prohibited by law from publishing books of poetry! His final word on that point.

Nonetheless, if the poems which figure in the *Hallucinated City* had been deeply meditated and meditative, the work would have lacked the agitated revolutionary spirit so essential to the renovation of Brazil's fading Parnassianism. It is not foolhardy, then, to declare that this small volume of poetry was effectively instrumental in changing the direction of Brazilian letters for all time. After the *Hallucinated City* and the Modernist revolution followed the more durable and mature Modernist spirit. Brazilian Portuguese became once and for all a fitting tool for the composition of the lyric and the novel. The sociological prose fiction of the Northeast, largely a product of the thirties, would not have been possible without the literary housecleaning of the poets of the twenties. Because Mário de Andrade sang a vehement hymn of love to his São Paulo—and by extension to his Brazil—the path was opened to all Brazilian writers to compose such hymns, each in his way, with varying degrees of profundity. And so they did.

The poems in the *Hallucinated City* have weathered the years since 1922 with admirable vigor and freshness because they are essentially good and honest verses. From the outset, in the first poem of the collection, Mário states his **"Inspiration"**:

> São Paulo! tumult of my life . . .
> Gallicism crying in the wilderness of America!

He had clarified this point in his Preface: São Paulo is his love and his agitation, and he sings of this passion with a Gallic voice untainted by Italian Futurism.

His vision of São Paulo is, of course, hallucinated as it is flashed through a surrealistic prism. It must be noted, however, that the simultaneous images of Mário's private surrealism are always orderly and structural within the framework, or formality, of the individual poem. Lêdo Ivo speaks of the poet as a "glosser of lucid and workaday moments" and describes the *Hallucinated City* as a "collection of the most lucid, rational and well-planned poems in all of Modernism."

One scene rapidly follows another, like a nude descending a staircase, like delirious motion picture images. The overall blurred impression on the retina, however, proceeds from an ingenious series of daring images:

> . . . the gray of the goose-fleshed streets
> chats a lament with the wind . . .

> . . . a sorcerer sun is shattered
> in a Persian triumph of emeralds, topazes, and
>   rubies . . .

> Nude bronze statues eternally coursing,
> in a fixed disdain for velocities . . .

> . . . the trolleys pass by like a skyrocket,
> clicking their heels on the tracks . . .

> The sky is all a conventional battle of white con-
>   fetti;
> and the gray wildcats of the mountains in the
>   distance . . .

> The little pigeons [girls] from the Normal School
> flutter between the fingers of the mist . . .

> And the grand golden chorus of sacks of coffee!

Out of this paradoxical combination of the bleary and the brilliant, Mário de Andrade fashioned his little book. In it he jeered the drudgery of middle-class existence, governmental hypocrisy, and the destructive self-satisfaction of the masses. He gloried in his racy Brazilian language and gave it dignity. He danced a lyrical harlequinade and, like the sprite in diamond tights, he rejoiced in his freedom. Toward the end of his life, when the clowning and prancing were over, he glanced back. In the midst of a vigorous literary career, he spoke of himself and his companions with the balance and consummate good sense that had always characterized his creative efforts:

> I think that we Modernists of the Week of Modern Art should serve as an example to no one. However, we may well serve as a lesson. . . . Human life is something other than arts and sciences and professions. It is in that other life that freedom has some meaning. Freedom is not a prize; it is a sanction. Yet to come.

> (pp. xi-xviii)

Jack E. Tomlins, in an introduction to Hallucinated City: Paulicea desvairada by *Mário de Andrade, translated by Jack E. Tomlins, Vanderbilt University Press, 1968, pp. xi-xviii.*

Thomas R. Hart   (essay date 1968)

[*In the following excerpt, Hart examines Andrade's critical theories, focusing primarily on the ideas presented in* A escrava que não é Isaura *and the preface to* Hallucinated City *(excerpted above).*]

The most important current in Brazilian literature in the first half of the twentieth century was the Modernist movement of the twenties, which first attracted widespread attention as a result of the *Semana de Arte Moderna* held in São Paulo in February 1922. Just who conceived the idea of the *Semana* is not clear; it seems to have arisen spontaneously out of the conversations of a group of young poets and painters. Mário de Andrade [in *Aspectos da literatura brasileira*] denied the idea was his, yet it is surely fair to say that no one played a more significant role than he in the early history of Modernism. The most important literary work of the movement's first phase is his book of poems, ***Paulicéia desvairada;*** its most comprehensive theoretical statement is his long essay, ***A escrava que não é Isaura.***

Written in December 1920, the poems of ***Paulicéia desvairada*** were widely known in São Paulo literary circles even before Mário read some of them at the second evening program of the *Semana de Arte Moderna,* a reading repeatedly interrupted by whistles and catcalls from the audience. They were not published until July 1922, a half-year after the *Semana,* and were preceded by a **"Prefácio interessantíssimo,"** written, according to Mário, at the insistence of some friends and one enemy ("por insistência de amigos e dum inimigo"). The "enemy" was the publisher and short-story writer, Monteiro Lobato, who insisted, as a condition for publishing the book, that Mário write a preface explaining his aims; Monteiro Lobato, however, finally decided not to publish it. Many points touched on in the preface to ***Paulicéia*** are more fully developed in ***A escrava que não é Isaura.*** Written in April and May 1922, shortly after the *Semana de Arte Moderna,* the little book was not published until January 1925. In a note at the end dated November 1924, Mário speaks of the "lamentable position" of "those who write books in Brazil and lack money to have them published immediately, at least a certain kind of books which try to break new ground and a certain kind of writers who are quite unconcerned with posterity and with vanity." Some of his own views, he declares, have been considerably modified since he wrote the book, an assertion which has led the Brazilian critic Jamil Almansur Haddad, in a perceptive study of Mário's poetics, to disregard ***Escrava*** on the ground that it represents a stage of Mário's thought which he had abandoned even before the work was published. Mário himself compares the book to a photograph taken in April 1922 and insists that "the main lines have remained intact" [***Escrava***]. Indeed, it is possible to argue that "the main lines" will be retained throughout the rest of his career, a period of only twenty years, cut short by his death at the age of fifty-one in February 1945.

The ideas presented in the preface to ***Paulicéia*** and in ***Escrava*** are fundamentally the same—not surprisingly, since the two essays were written at almost the same time—and it will be convenient to consider them together. The tone, too, is more or less the same, sometimes frankly intended to shock the bourgeois reader or even to insult him openly, sometimes pleading for understanding—a note Mário may have borrowed from Apollinaire's poem "La jolie rousse," a brief quotation from which comes at the very end of the twenty pages of appendixes printed at the end of ***Escrava.*** Both essays make lavish use of capital letters, italics, and occasional very short paragraphs composed of a single phrase or even a single word. The language, while often violent, is not slangy or even colloquial, nor is it self-consciously Brazilian. In ***Paulicéia,*** Mário repeatedly calls into question the seriousness of his own writing: "Besides, it's very hard to tell in this stuff where I leave off joking and begin to talk seriously. Even I can't tell." Near the end of the preface he insists that "this whole preface, with all the wild theories there are in it, isn't worth a damn. When I wrote ***Paulicéia desvairada,*** I didn't think about any of

this stuff." And, a moment later, "And that's the end of the 'Hallucination' school of poetry. In my next book I'll found another." In ***Escrava,*** his tone is more serious, though still far from solemn. There are other, perhaps more important, differences. The preface to ***Paulicéia*** is an introduction to Mário's own poetry, at once a manifesto and an apology. ***Escrava,*** on the other hand, is concerned with Mário's creative work only secondarily and by implication. It is a manifesto combined with an annotated anthology of works by French, Italian, and Brazilian poets, two of the latter, incidentally, represented by poems in French; significantly, none of Mário's own poems is included. It is, in short, exactly what its subtitle proclaims it to be, a lecture on some tendencies of modernist poetry, "discurso sobre algumas tendências da poesia modernista." [The critic adds in a footnote: "It will be noted that Mário does not use the term 'Modernist' to refer to the group of Brazilian poets we now call by this name; he uses it rather to refer to contemporary poets in general, or at any rate to those who share a particular aesthetic orientation. In the preface to ***Paulicéia,*** he had used '*futurista*' in the same way, as a label for an international movement in poetry, rather than limiting it to Marinetti and his followers."]

Few of the ideas in either essay could have seemed shocking, or even very new, to anyone familiar with the debates over the new poetry which had been going on in France and Italy for more than a decade. That the Modernists could arouse so much incomprehension and hostility in São Paulo has much less to do with their ideas than with the prevailing climate of opinion in the city, and especially with the fact that the new ideas were introduced all at once rather than emerging gradually in the course of a prolonged public debate. Both the incomprehension and the hostility were nevertheless very real. The *Semana de Arte Moderna,* which marked the first public appearance of the Modernists as a group, was a *succès de scandale* in the most literal sense: in some São Paulo families, the *Semana* was considered a flagrant breach of morality, not to be mentioned in the presence of children or women. Mário himself recalled, years later [in ***Aspectos da literatura brasileira***], the difficult position in which he had found himself among the members of his own family and even before the *Semana* itself. It is perhaps partly for this reason that he takes such pains in both essays to insist that his revolutionary ideas are confined to the realm of aesthetics and do not touch on morality or religion: "My demands? Liberty. I use it; I don't abuse it. I know how to keep it under control in my philosophical and religious truths; because philosophical and religious truths aren't conventional like Art, they're truths. I don't go that far!" [***Paulicéia***] Even within the realm of aesthetics, Mário insists that he is not presenting Truth itself but only his own version of Truth: "Christ said: 'I am the truth.' And he was right. I always say: 'I am my Truth.' And I'm right, too. The Truth of Christ is immutable and divine. Mine is human, aesthetic, and transitory" [***Escrava***].

I should not want, however, to suggest that Mário is here only making a concession to spare the feelings of his family and friends. On the one hand, there is abundant evidence that he was a practicing Catholic who took his religion very seriously; on the other, a distinction between nature and art is at the very center of his aesthetic theories. The distinction is precisely that art, unlike nature, is not concerned with eternal values but with ever-changing conventions. The essential quality of art at any moment is its newness, its difference from everything that has preceded it. Artistic beauty is thus quite different from natural beauty:

> The beautiful in art is arbitrary, conventional, transitory—a question of fashion. The beautiful in nature is unchanging, objective, natural—it has whatever permanence nature has. Art doesn't succeed in reproducing nature, nor is this its aim. All the great artists . . . have distorted nature. From which I infer that the beautiful in art will be artistic and subjective in proportion to its distance from natural beauty [*Paulicéia*].

The artist must not take nature for his model: "Let us flee nature! Only thus can art escape the ridiculous weakness of color photography" [*Paulicéia*]. And again, still more succinctly, in *Escrava*: "The poet doesn't photograph: he creates."

Poetry resides, not in the poet's subject matter, which may be ugly or merely commonplace, but in his treatment of it. The poet, moreover, does not choose his subject matter. He simply takes whatever his subconscious offers him:

> The lyrical impulse is free; it doesn't depend on us, nor on our intelligence. It can spring from a bunch of onions as easily as from a lost love. . . . Inspiration may be called forth by a sunset and by a Matarazzi factory chimney, by the divine body of a Nize and by the divine body of a Cadillac. All subjects are *alive*. There is no such thing as a subject poetic in itself [*Escrava*].

Since the subconscious takes its materials from the external world, the poet, if he is true to himself, must also deal with that world. It is for this reason that true poets have always been Modernists:

> The Modernists haven't forced themselves to take sports, machinery, eloquence, and exaggeration as the [underlying] principle of all lyricism. Not at all. Like true poets in all periods, like Homer, like Virgil, like Dante, they sing the epoch in which they live. And it's just because they follow the old poets that the Modernists are so new [*Escrava*].

But the poet's job is not done when he has transcribed the message sent him by his subconscious: "It is inspiration which is subconscious, not creation. In all creation there is an effort of will. . . . *Lyricism* isn't the same thing as *poetry*." In the preface to *Paulicéia,* Mário gives this account of his own method of composition: "When I feel the lyrical impulse I write down, without thinking, everything my unconscious shouts to me. I think later: not only to correct, but also to justify, what I've written. That's the reason for this **'Very Interesting Preface'**." Later in the preface he restates the same proposition as a definition of poetry in general, in a formula borrowed from the French poet Paul Dermée, "Lyricism + Art = Poetry":

Art, which, added to lyricism, gives poetry, doesn't consist of holding back the mad race of the lyrical moment in order to warn it about the stones and barbed-wire fences along the road. Let it stumble, fall, hurt itself! Art is a matter of weeding out, later on, annoying repetitions, bits of romantic sentimentality, unnecessary or inexpressive details [*Paulicéia*].

The same idea is developed at much greater length in *Escrava* and with still more stress on the poet's conscious control of his material in the interest of making his work intelligible to his readers. For Dermée's formula, Mário now substitutes his own revision, intended to stress the importance for the artist's work of the medium he had chosen: "Pure lyricism + [self-] criticism + language = poetry," though he adds, somewhat inconsistently, that "some men are poets who have written only prose—or never written anything at all. D'Annunzio's finest poem is the Fiume adventure." But this seems to be a momentary slip; in the rest of the essay, Mário returns again and again to his view of the poet as a conscious craftsman (though one whose materials are given him by his subconscious). He defines the work of art as "a machine for producing emotions" and refers in a footnote to Poe's essay "The Philosophy of Composition"; a few pages later he defines a poet as "one who has achieved what he set out to do."

The poet has an obligation to make his meaning clear, though Mário recognizes that what is clear for one reader may not be clear for another: "Hermeticism must be resisted without quarter. But I don't mean by that that poems have to be so plain that a yokel from Xiririca can understand them as well as a cultivated man who is familiar with psychology, aesthetics, and the historical development of poetry." The poet, then, has obligations to the reader, but the reader has some obligations of his own:

> [Georges] Ribot has said somewhere that inspiration is a telegram in code sent by the unconscious to be translated by the consciousness. That conscious activity may be divided between the poet and the reader. Thus the poet doesn't coldly strip the lyrical moment and break it into little pieces: he generously grants the reader the glory of collaborating in his poems [*Paulicéia*].

Mário returns to the same analogy in *Escrava:* "It is the reader who must raise himself to the level of the poet's sensibility, not the poet who must stoop to the level of the reader's sensibility. It's up to him [the reader] to translate the telegram!"

The reader's collaboration becomes particularly crucial in the case of much modern poetry because of its use of juxtaposition: the poem offers a disconcerting series of apparently unrelated elements unconnected by logical transitions which would guide him in establishing a meaningful relationship among them. In the preface to *Paulicéia* Mário calls this type of verse "harmonic": "If . . . we place words one after another without joining them together in any way, then these words, by the very fact that they don't follow each other intellectually or grammatically, will be superposed one upon another, so that we shall have the sensation of hearing, not melodies, but harmonies." As an example of harmonic verse, Mário cites a line which might be an extraordinarily condensed and evocative account of the settlement of his native state of São Paulo:

> "Ecstasies . . . Struggles . . . Arrows . . . Songs . . . To Settle [a new land]! . . ." These words aren't joined together. . . . Each one is a separate phrase, an elliptical sentence, reduced to a telegraphic minimum. If I say the word "ecstasies," since it doesn't form part of a phrase (a melody), it calls attention to its isolation and keeps on vibrating, waiting for a phrase that will give it a meaning and that DOES NOT COME. "Struggles" doesn't make any sort of conclusion for "ecstasies"; and, by the same token, without making us forget the first word, it keeps on vibrating together with it. The other words do the same thing.

In a footnote, Mário declares that he had discovered the theory for himself and discussed it with his friends six or eight months before learning that the same phenomenon had been discussed by the French critic Jean Epstein in the review *Esprit nouveau* under the name *"simultanisme."* In *Escrava,* he presents the same theory at much greater length and gives it a new name, "polyphonism." This time his claim to originality is limited to the name itself and, by implication, to the presentation of the phenomenon in terms of an analogy with music, though he is careful to repeat and to amplify his assertion in *Paulicéia* that the analogy is to be understood only in a figurative sense. Now he is anxious to invoke the authority of European poets and critics: "I give the name 'polyphonism' to the Simultaneity of the French, with Epstein as their spokesman, the Simultanism of Fernand Divoire, the Synchronism of Marcello-Fabri" [*Escrava*]. Polyphonism, however, is not to be equated with simultaneity in the ordinary sense of two or more things which happen at the same time. It demands a deliberate effort of analysis, a "vontade de análise," and the intention, on the artist's part, of creating a unified total effect.

Mário does not present polyphonism as a program for future poets: "I have no pretensions to creating anything at all. 'Polyphonism' is the theoretical formulation of certain techniques employed every day by certain modernist poets." It is not even something entirely new, or rather its effect is not wholly different from that of older, more traditional poetry: "In all the arts of time, there could not be understanding without the sum of successive acts of memory, each relating to a single isolated sensation. Even in an old-fashioned sonnet, it is the complex total, final sensation produced by this sum, which determines the emotional effect of the work." The difference is that in traditional poetry ideas are presented one at a time and the logical connections between them spelled out by the poet, while in Modernist poetry the elements are simply juxtaposed, with the relations between them left to be filled in by the reader. Yet "left" is not quite the right word; the connections may remain implicit, but the poet must take care to see that they are present. Here, as always, Mario holds fast to his premise that *the poet doesn't photograph the subconscious";* every poem must be subjected to revision to ensure its ability to stand alone, independent of the more or less accidental circumstances of its composition.

The value of *Escrava* does not lie in the originality of its insights into the distinctive qualities of twentieth-century poetry. Mário's basic thesis that poetry consists of inspiration plus craftsmanship underlies most twentieth-century thought on the subject, uniting poets as far apart as Paul Valéry and André Breton. The former is quite willing to admit the existence of inspiration, though he tends to minimize its importance; the latter confesses that no Surrealist poem is wholly a product of the subconscious. The real importance of *Escrava* is its revelation of the mind of the young poet-critic at a crucial point in his development and its role as a transmitter of the new European theories of poetry, and of the poetry itself, to the younger Brazilian writers of the twenties; the latter reason alone would be more than enough to give Mário an honored place among those intermediaries whose activities have traditionally attracted the attention of students of comparative literature.

Mário's essay on Brazilian Modernization holds a special place among his writings. Originally a lecture celebrating the twentieth anniversary of the *Semana de Arte Moderna,* it was first published separately as a book and then incorporated in the second edition of his collection of essays, *Aspectos da literatura brasileira.* It is both a fascinating autobiographical document and an important source for the history of Modernism written by one of its central figures, but it has relatively little to say about the aesthetic theories with which we are primarily concerned. It is not that Mário repudiates the ideas presented in his earlier essays; what he rejects is the refusal of the Modernists, and especially his own refusal, to play an active role in attempting to solve the social and political problems of the day. The end of the essay, in particular, is a frank confession of guilt, in which Mário invites his former comrades to join. He recognizes that the aims of the movement were not, in practice, identical with those he had proclaimed in the preface to *Paulicéia* and in *Escrava.* He now sees Modernism as essentially destructive, an accusation he had taken great pains to refute in his earlier essays. Although he had insisted there that the artist's matter has no bearing on the value of his work, he now introduces an important distinction: subject matter is irrelevant to the "aesthetic intelligence" itself, but this intelligence is manifested in art, which is concerned with the needs of society, and, as such, has "a pragmatic human function which is of greater importance than the hedonistic creating of beauty." He is now convinced that the Modernists' preoccupation with aesthetic problems was by no means as disinterested and idealistic as it had appeared to them at the time: "With a few unconvincing exceptions, we were victims of our pleasure in life and of the merrymaking with which we destroyed our virility. If we transformed everything about ourselves, there is one thing we forgot to transform: our attitude of self-seeking toward contemporary life. And this was the most important thing!" The Modernists, he concludes, "should not serve as an example to anyone. But we can serve as a lesson. Man is passing through a wholly political phase. . . . Refusals to take part and eternal values can wait till later."

The whole essay offers an excellent example of the tone of moral seriousness and personal involvement characteristic of Mário's later essays and in striking contrast to the flippancy, though not the intensity, of the preface to *Paulicéia* and of *Escrava.* In its concern with the social value of art and the writer's duty to take part in the social and political struggles of his time, it is typical of Mário's mature critical writing.

Both the preface to *Paulicéia* and *Escrava* represent attempts to make European culture, specifically contemporary European poetry, more widely known and accepted in Brazil. Indeed, one is tempted to say that it is precisely this preoccupation with Europe—which Mário never visited—that links his work with that of a great many other writers in both Spanish and Portuguese America. In *Escrava,* Mário boasts of his familiarity with European culture, his firm belief that he is a citizen of the world. At the same time he insists that this does not make him any less Brazilian, offering as proof his willingness to stay in Brazil and do what he can to help his country enter into the life of the contemporary world—though one must not fail to note his ironical tone when he says that he accepts his wretched position in Brazil so that his country "may one day come to understand that the telegraph, the steamship, the telephone, and the Fox Movietone News exist, and that SIMULTANEITY EXISTS."

The later essays, on the other hand, deal exclusively with Brazilian topics. They have been collected in two volumes of Mário's *Obras completas, Aspectos da literatura brasileira,* which contains a dozen essays written between 1931 and 1943, and in *O empalhador de passarinho,* a collection of shorter occasional pieces (mostly reviews of recent books), first published between 1939 and 1944. Not all the essays are primarily concerned with literature. That on Tristão de Ataíde, in *Aspectos,* aside from a few brief remarks on the latter's literary criticism, is given over to a refutation, based on Mário's extensive knowledge of Brazilian folklore and popular traditions, of Tristão's assertion that Brazilian culture is essentially Catholic; the essay **"Elegia de abril"** in the same volume is a series of reflections on the role of the intellectual in Brazilian society. I shall limit my discussion to two essays on nineteenth-century novelists, both included in *Aspectos da literatura brasileira*—that on Manuel Antônio de Almeida and that on Machado de Assis.

The essay on Almeida, first published in 1940 as the introduction to an edition of his novel *Memórias de um sargento de milícias,* is a good example of Mário's mature criticism. It is obvious that he finds Almeida an attractive subject, partly, no doubt, because of the latter's interest in folklore. At the same time, Mário is careful to point out that Almeida did not see the beauty of the folk traditions he describes with such precision, adding that "from his material difficulties, the poverty he knew as a child, the artist retained no pity for the poor, no charitable understanding of lowly suffering and of humble people" [*Aspectos*]. This is, of course, fundamentally moral criticism, as is Mário's charge that Almeida was too much an aristocrat to interest himself in the problems of the poor, even too much a coward to take an active part in trying to bet-

ter their situation. The harshness of Mário's judgment on this point, as so often in the later essays, is surely not unrelated to the fact that the flaws he points out in the authors he studies are those which troubled him in his ceaseless examination of his own actions and of his motives for them. Here, for example, one senses a connection between Mário's appraisal of Almeida and his increasing sensitivity, in the last years of his life, to the charge that he, like some of the other Modernists, had refused to play an active part in the struggle to create more equitable social and political conditions in Brazil. It is hardly an exaggeration to say that Mário accuses Almeida of the same error he saw in his own conduct, his failure to love his fellowmen, his sense that he had been a victim of his own individualism, "vítima do meu individualismo": "I've come, in my declining years, to the conviction that I've lacked humanity. My sense of my own superiority has hurt me."

Mário praises the naturalness and precision of Almeida's style; his language, like his treatment of folk traditions, offers material of great value to historians of Brazilian society. Mário notes Almeida's ironic play with the sentimental exaggerations of the romantics but denies that the book should be considered either realistic or naturalistic. Almeida takes neither himself nor his subject so seriously; he has no interest in social reform. His book belongs to the tradition of the picaresque novel or, more inclusively, to that of the comic adventure novel which begins with Apuleius and Petronius. Despite its wealth of accurate historical information, it is not a portrait from life, but a caricature; Mário remains firmly convinced that "the artist doesn't photograph: he creates."

Mário begins his essay on Machado de Assis with a question to the reader: "Do you love Machado?" [*Aspectos*] The implication is clearly that he fears the answer will be "No," and this is indeed Mário's own answer. One can admire an author without loving him, and this is the case with Machado; Mário finds him unattractive as a man, though he can derive great aesthetic pleasure from his work. The work, moreover, has a moral value, that morality of technique, "a moralidade da técnica," to which Mário refers so often, with an insistence that surely comes in part from his feeling that the Modernists, with their stress on freedom from formal constraints, had encouraged slovenliness and amateurishness in a generation of Brazilian writers. But the perfection of Machado's style, though it is a triumph of dedication, of conscious effort, is also a kind of double betrayal, both a refusal on Machado's part to reveal himself as he really was and a denial of the essential nature of art by equating it with conscious calculation. One recalls Mário's definition of poetry in the preface to *Paulicéia* and in *Escrava;* Machado, he is saying in effect, is so preoccupied with technique that he leaves no room for lyricism. His victory, moreover, is incomplete: "He was unable to conquer his own unhappiness." Unable to escape the limitations of a world-view shaped by his own misfortunes, Machado saw them as the universal lot of mankind.

Although Mário praises Machado for his probity both as a public official and as a private citizen, he suggests that the security Machado fought so hard to achieve was bought at the price of estrangement from the real problems of his time. Machado refused to concern himself with social and political questions; as a result the world of his novels is quite different from the real world in which he lived, and still more different from our own modern world. Here one may feel that Mário's attack on Machado springs in part from his dissatisfaction with the lack of social involvement in the work of the Modernists; the essay was written in 1939 when he was coming increasingly to feel the absence of social commitment in his own earlier work as a grave moral error. In the same way, it is possible to see Mário's rejection of Machado's pessimism as a counterpart to his harsh judgment of his own earlier writings on the ground that they represent the views of a man devoted solely to pleasure and to the cultivation of his own mind, unaware that for most men, certainly for most Brazilians, the struggle for mere existence makes such a pursuit of pleasure inconceivable.

In the preface to *Aspectos da literatura brasileira,* Mário expresses his hope that his readers will recognize in the essays collected there "not the aim of meting out justice, which I consider petty in the art of criticism, but a passionate effort to love and understand." Such a view must not, however, be taken to mean that value judgments have no place in criticism. To speak of justice implies adherence to an impersonal standard, whereas criticism, for Mário, means the examination of one's own disciplined responses. It is the product not merely of understanding and love, but of the will to understand and love something which at first may seem meaningless or repugnant to us. Criticism, in short, is a record of the critic's search for a vantage point from which the writers he studies can be shown to have a positive value *for him.* Mário would surely have endorsed Baudelaire's view that "[the use of] *I,* rightly considered impertinent in many cases, implies nevertheless a great modesty; it confines the writer within the strictest limits of sincerity. By reducing his task, it makes it easier." Criticism is thus always essentially moral criticism: it involves both an attempt to understand and judge the writer as he is revealed by his work and a constant reappraisal by the critic of his own tastes and values; it is perfectly understandable that Mário's criticism of other writers should reflect so often his uneasiness about the social usefulness of his own work and, ultimately, the moral value of his life.

Mário's role in the creation of Modernism was by no means limited to his critical writing; his own fiction and poetry were of far more importance. Nor was his role limited to his published works; he was a tireless correspondent whose letters to a great number of other writers or would-be writers, many of them not personally known to him, did much to further the spread of Modernist ideas throughout Brazil. His letters to the Brazilian poet Manuel Bandeira [collected in *Cartas de Mário de Andrade a Manuel Bandeira*] are of particular importance, for they are our best source for studying the development of Mário's thought on the problems of creating a distinctively Brazilian literary language.

Any poet might claim that his goal is to "donner un sens plus pur aux mots de la tribu," but for the writer who undertakes to create a new literary language, and not just his own personal style, this means a concern with problems of grammar which need not worry the writer in the more established literary traditions; it may mean, for instance, in the case of Brazilian Portuguese, something as simple as deciding whether to place object pronouns before or after the verb. When the writer must use a dialect of a language which already has an established literary tradition in another country—when, in other words, he is an ex-colonial, as any Latin-American writer must be—his problems, both practical and psychological, become still more complex.

Mário was proud of his knowledge of Portuguese. In a letter of 1925 to Manuel Bandeira, he declares that "I've studied Portuguese and I'm aware of my mistakes. At least of the great majority of them." In another, written ten years later, he says: "It's funny, but I have a secret desire to speak Portuguese well and to write it correctly." In a newspaper article reprinted in *O empalhador de passarinho,* he insists that the writer must be thoroughly familiar with the literary language in its traditional form, even though he may choose to depart from its prescriptions: "only someone who knows the rules has a right to break them. Only then does a mistake cease to be a mistake and become a matter of going beyond the established conventions, which have been made useless by the new demands of a new form of expression." This is one more instance of Mário's insistence that art necessarily contains a large measure of craftsmanship, a note he had stressed from his earliest writings on poetry and one he came increasingly to feel had not been sufficiently understood by his contemporaries; in his lecture on the Modernist movement [in *Aspectos*] he remarks sadly that "today, with respect to the general level of the literary language, our position is worse than it was a hundred years ago." Already in 1929, in a letter to Bandeira, he reveals misgivings about his own role in creating a new Brazilian language: "I even recognize that a dash of cold water on the Brazilianizing mania won't do any harm. I'm very much to blame for all that has happened and if I'd dreamed the fashion would catch on in such a big way I would certainly have been more moderate."

Though Mário insists that the writer must know the literary language, he realizes that this very knowledge makes his task more difficult: "At every moment I find myself using needless Lusitanisms [forms or idioms characteristic of European Portuguese]. It's only natural. Remember that I've been writing Portuguese for 32 years. . . . Rome wasn't built in a day. They're my new barbarisms." To write Brazilian is very different from speaking it: it demands a conscious effort, which Mário aptly calls one of translation. In a letter of 1925 to Bandeira he speaks of the early book of poems *Losango Cáqui,* "which I translated completely into Brazilian." In another, he says: "Here's that poem I wrote a year ago. I've spent a year, off and on, in correcting it. . . . Finally I've Brazilianized the whole thing."

Mário was perfectly aware that the writer's problem could not be solved simply by urging him to write as he speaks. In his long letter of 1925 to Manuel Bandeira, he offers a remarkable perspective of the problems of the writer who must make use of what Mário calls "a language which is not yet a language," *língua que ainda não é língua.* He rejects Bandeira's accusation that he is writing, not Brazilian, but the dialect of São Paulo: "A grave injustice. I'm not writing *paulista.* On the contrary. Rather, in the Brazilian language I'm writing now, I combine terms from both North and South." And, a little further on: "It's a question of a learned systematization and not a photograph of popular speech. . . . And that systematization must inevitably be a personal one. . . . I don't want to think my Brazilian—*the style I've adopted*—will be the Brazilian language of tomorrow. I don't have that pretension, I swear it. Besides, if I didn't systematize in that way, I would be a folksy writer and I want to be a cultivated and literary one." Fifteen years later, in an essay, he says much the same thing:

> The standard language, especially when it is used for literary purposes, is a living language, too. Indeed, it's the only living language which reconciles within itself all the partial forms [i.e. the regional, social, and professional dialects] of a language. And of other languages. . . . If, in São Paulo, talking with my sister who's a *paulista,* I should ask her to go into the *camarinha* [bedroom] and get my slippers, I would be as much an anarchist and a pedant as if I spoke to her in the style of Camões. But as an artist, I insist on my right to use *"camarinha"* in my short story or in my poem, whether for the sake of regionalism, or that of picturesqueness and comedy, or simply that of sonority and rhythm. And the use of the word may nevertheless be a simple and very useful fact of personal psychology. I've traveled through the Northeast, there I've slept in lots of *camarinhas,* there I've used the word to make myself more readily understood, there I've dreamed, there I've had illusions, there I've suffered. So the word may spring up within me, a flower of my own garden. And I, as an artist, have the right to express myself by means of it [*O empalhador de passarinho*].

This notion of the literary language as the sum of the possibilities offered by its various specialized forms recalls that offered by Dante in *De vulgari eloquentia,* and indeed Dante's name often appears in Mário's remarks on language and style. Mário, however, is careful to insist that his own role is not that of Dante but the humbler one of those poets of the *dolce stil novo* who prepared the way for him: "Dante didn't just spring up all by himself. Before him, a lot of poets had begun to write in the vernacular and they *prepared the way* for Dante" [*Cartas*]. But the fate of writers who prepare the way for those who will come after them is to be superseded. In the letters to Bandeira, Mário returns again and again to the theme that his linguistic experiments will be no more than a passing phase, though a necessary one. They demand a deliberate sacrifice, which Mário willingly accepts. In a letter of November 8, 1924, he declares that "I am ready to sacrifice myself. It's necessary to give courage to those poor fellows who still don't have the courage to write Brazilian." Again, in 1925, he speaks of "the Messianic element in my struggle, sacrificing my works, writing them in a language which is not yet a language."

This sacrifice is twofold. In the first place, it means giving up the place one might have had in posterity, a consideration Mário repeatedly declares is of no concern to him: "I don't attach the slightest importance to fame or to posterity. I've none of that kind of vanity." And again: "It isn't my destiny to survive. . . . What do I care about being praised in 1985?" He insists that it is not really a question of sacrifice, but simply of accepting his own limitations: "I said I'm sacrificing myself. But that isn't quite true. I've only given up, sensibly, a pretension I mustn't have: to be famous and have a place in the histories [of literature] as an important writer. . . . I'm convinced my destiny is to be transitory. That neither saddens me nor makes me proud. It's just a fact." On this point, Mário is perhaps speaking with something less than perfect candor; one recalls the remark of his good friend Bandeira that "certain aspects of his powerful personality are even difficult to classify; are we to call them virtues or defects? For example, his pride, which was immense, but frequently expressed itself in forms of apparent humility, forms which intrigued Mário himself."

But there is another, though not unrelated, sense in which the sacrifice must have been very real: Mário's realization that for what we may call polemical reasons his writings could not take the form he himself would have preferred to give them. In a letter of 1929 to Bandeira, he declares that his style is now less self-consciously Brazilian "simply because there's no longer any reason to exaggerate," *simplesmente porque já não há mais razão pra forçar a nota.* "You know I either told you or wrote you that I was experimenting and that I had no intention of continuing to exaggerate in that way." Such a conception of the task at hand implies rejecting those means of expression which are not themselves arms in the war to create a Brazilian language: "You understand, Manuel, I've impoverished my means of expression. I've got no doubts about that. I've impoverished them deliberately. There is a phrase of Machado [de Assis] which constantly throbs in my memory: 'Something must be sacrificed.' " But this, in turn, goes counter to one of Mário's most deeply held convictions about the nature of literary creation, that it is a spontaneous revelation of the unconscious. The polemical aim of his attempt to create a distinctively Brazilian style, coupled with the many decisions on minute points of grammar inherent in the attempt itself, meant that he could not give free rein to his creative powers: "My naturalness now is affectation because the problem preoccupies me at every moment and therefore distorts my natural style. I am in a period of transition. I am creating a new natural style. For the time being, it looks like a great affectation." Four years later, in 1929, he insists that this phase has already passed: "As for what you call willful and premeditated [in my style], I've examined my conscience and I know it's not that at all. It's just a new habit I've picked up. . . . My pronouns and Brazilianisms . . . pour forth now like water from a spring with no special effort on my part."

Yet the danger was real, and the damage done to Mário's work remains, as even very sympathetic critics have conceded. It is the judgment which Mário himself extended to the other Modernists [*in Aspectos da literatura brasileiro*]: "The Modernist movement was essentially destructive. Even destructive of ourselves, because the pragmatism of our experiments always weakened our freedom to create." To weaken, however, is not the same as to destroy. The Modernist movement gave to Brazilian literature much that is of lasting value and surely the writings of Mário de Andrade are not the least of its gifts. (pp. 265-88)

> *Thomas R. Hart, "The Literary Criticism of Mário de Andrade," in* The Disciplines of Criticism: Essays in Literary Theory, Interpretation, and History, *Peter Demetz, Thomas Greene, and Lowry Nelson, Jr., eds., Yale University Press, 1968, pp. 265-88.*

David T. Haberly   (essay date 1983)

[*In the following excerpt, Haberly examines Andrade's views on Brazilian racial diversity and national identity as expressed in* Hallucinated City *and* Macunaíma *and presents a deconstructive reading of the latter work.*]

Mário de Andrade was widely regarded in his own time as the "Pope" of Modernism. He vehemently rejected this title, but his position at the epicenter of the Modernist tumult has nonetheless remained a critical constant in the years since his death. There is general agreement today that Mário—through his learning, his personality, and his many activities—served as the intellectual focus of the Modernist generation and, in a very real sense, as its conscience. (pp. 135-36)

The general emphasis upon Mário's importance as a cultural presence, however, has tended to obscure his literary contributions. His writings, long praised but too often either misread or unread, have only recently begun to receive the attention they deserve. A number of Brazilian scholars have produced analyses of Mário's readings, his language and allusions, his poetics, and the evolution of his ideas about Brazil. As a result, we know what most of the words mean, we know what Mário had read, and we have a fairly good idea of the poetic and fictive devices he utilized. Nonetheless, the reasoning behind Mário's language and techniques, the ultimate meaning of the works themselves, remains elusive.

Mário, then, is still presented as an important and highly talented intellectual whose tragically flawed works are too chaotic and too intensely personal to be deciphered and understood. (p. 136)

My intention here is to suggest another context, a new way of looking at Mário's works that can help us to understand the poems of **Hallucinated City (Paulicéia desvairada)**, published in 1922, and Mário's "rhapsody," **Macunaíma** (1928). This new interpretation begins with a simple statement of fact, but one that will distress and even anger his family and friends: Mário de Andrade must be read as a nonwhite writer. It is true that he came from an upper-middle-class family in São Paulo; his maternal grandfather had been a provincial governor, and his father was a successful accountant. But Mário was, in fact, as much the genetic and somatic embodiment of the traditional racial trinity as Gonçalves Dias. Mário's skin color was the legacy of Indian ancestors; the contours of his nose and lips, so evident in photographs, portraits, and caricatures, were clearly African. Mário occasionally referred to his triple ancestry, and at least some of his friends and colleagues, aware of these nonwhite somatic traits, perceived his "mulatto character, expressed in his ostentatious toothiness," as an important element in Mário's position as a permanent "show"—the term is Oswald's [the Brazilian writer Oswald de Andrade (no relation to Mário de Andrade)]—at the center of the Modernist festivities.

We know very little about Mário's life, and even less about his private feelings regarding his ancestry and appearance. As I have suggested, there are a few overt and extremely important references in his works to his nonwhiteness, to his "soul spotted with races." Nonetheless, a close reading of **Hallucinated City** and **Macunaíma** provides convincing evidence that Mário had thought seriously and originally about the problem of his own racial identity and about the parallel question of national identity, and that he endeavored to express his conclusions in his writings.

Perhaps the most fundamental theme in Mário's works is his own multiplicity, which derives from the absence of any single, unified personal identity. "I am three hundred, three hundred and fifty," he wrote, and though he hoped that "one day, at last, I'll bump into myself," that single self does not appear in his works. Mário rejected the commonplace idea that the three races were intermingled and fused, in Brazil or in his own being; he saw himself, rather, as multiple: simultaneously black, red, and white.

One can hypothesize several reasons for Mário's innovative elaboration of the idea of racial juxtaposition rather than fusion. First, fusion meant miscegenation, widely believed to lead to degeneracy. Mário appears to have been particularly sensitive to the term *mulato*, denoting miscegenation, which he sometimes employed in a pejorative sense to imply phoniness and dissimulation. The concept of racial fusion also seems to have disquieted him because it suggested to him the domination and potential destruction or absorption of one race by another. If no single identity could exist for Mário, it was vital for the separate and parallel racial selves to survive intact, balanced in an uneasy truce. He described the "sickness of America"—and, by extension, his own psychic malaise—as the result of the forcible domination of the African and Indian identities by a white self that had been strengthened and emboldened by external cultural and political influences as well as by European immigration.

The concept of parallel and multiple racial identities, existing simultaneously at a number of separate points on the continuum, also made it possible for Mário to believe that other, nongenetic identities could be added by education or taste. Thus he claimed that he was not only red and black and white, but French, as a result of his schooling; Italian, because of his love for music; North American, because he admired the United States; and so on. The simultaneous coexistence of these inherited and assumed identities was a comforting idea, one that could work to preserve him from the fear and self-doubt that marked other non-white Brazilian writers, but two critical problems remained: How could these separate and often contradictory identities be united, and how could they be utilized to produce literature?

Mário's solution was to try to submerge and unify his own multiplicity through identification with and description of far larger but equally multiple and contradictory collective entities: the city of São Paulo, in *Hallucinated City;* Brazil itself—and, by extension, all of South America—in *Macunaíma.* He described the composition of the first of these works as the direct result of an intense *comoção,* a word best translated not as "commotion," but as "shock," the shock of recognition and identification. (pp. 137-39)

The twenty-two poems of *Hallucinated City,* begun in the heat of a family argument, appear to have been written down rapidly, during a single week in December of 1920. Mário then drastically edited the manuscript, cutting it to half its original length. He finally read portions of it to a few astonished friends, but it is not clear that he intended to publish the work. Oswald de Andrade forced the issue, however, by quoting one poem in a 1921 article on Mário. (p. 139)

Reactions to the disjointed and fragmentary blank verse of the poem Oswald cited were so intense and so negative that Mário's friends persuaded him to write some sort of explanation to prove his sanity. When the full text of *Hallucinated City* was finally published, in July of 1922, it included a long introduction to which Mário gave the ironic, Machadian title **"Extremely Interesting Preface."** Although this carefully evasive explanation served as a basic text of Modernist poetics and introduced Brazilian readers to a number of contemporary European aesthetic theories, it was written well after the fact and refers to authors Mário probably had not yet read at the time he wrote the poems themselves. "I did not think about any of this" then, he declares, and he urges us not to take the preface too seriously; it is "not worth a damn," since he is not sure himself "where the *blague* leaves off and the serious begins."

Most critics have tended to start post facto, studying the ideas and techniques set forth in the **"Extremely Interesting Preface"** and then tracing their presence in the poems. It seems more useful, however, to reverse this process—to begin with the poetic text. The central image of that text is the harlequin, for Mário the primary "catalyst of associations." [The critic adds in a footnote: "The figure of the harlequin—and, more generally, of the clown—was part of what Mário described as the universal 'waters of modernity' in which he moved. Mário, however, took a symbol that was commonly used in European and Brazilian literature and art of the period and made it his own, as a representation of racial diversity."] The figure of the harlequin, with his suit of many colors, symbolizes both the contradictory diversity of São Paulo and the parallel multiplicity of the poet; it is, therefore, the basis for Mário's identification with the city.

The image of the harlequin, in the first edition of *Hallucinated City,* began with the volume's cover: a pattern of diamond-shaped lozenges of contrasting colors. In his later **"Improvisation on the Sickness of America" ("Improviso do mal da América"),** written in 1928, Mário made it clear that these colored lozenges referred to his own multiple racial identities, the red and white and black that "weave my harlequinate costume." The harlequin also implies a pose—the madcap, apparently nonrational hilarity and essential marginality of the clown. But the evasive mask of carefree indifference Mário's harlequin wears hides the same sorrow and bitterness felt by Cruz e Sousa's "Acrobat of Pain": "And they say that clowns are happy!" Mário exclaims; "I never rattle the little bells in my harlequinate interior! . . . "

The link between poet and city is the adjective *desvairada,* which appears in the volume's title. The word refers to the hallucinatory lunacy of the clown, induced by the city's multiplicity, and defines the superficially incoherent character of the text; it also means "disoriented" or "lost." The chaotic poems of *Paulicéia desvairada* describe the poet's frenetic wanderings—his odyssey or *odisséia*—through the city of São Paulo, maddened by the juxtaposed contradictions of his own multiplicity; he describes himself, in fact, as "a Tupi Indian strumming a lute." His goal is the discovery, within the city he loves, of a single, satisfying identity that will compensate for his own disunity. No such unity exists, however, for the city is itself lost, contradictory, harlequinate. The end of the search, therefore, is not identity, but identification in disunity.

If the poet is a racial harlequin, the harlequinate character of São Paulo is based upon Mário's perception of several orders of juxtaposed contradictions in its nature. The first order is climactic. The book's initial poem is preceded by a quotation from a classical Portuguese stylist, Friar Luís de Sousa: "Where even at the height of summer there were storms of wind and cold like unto the harshest winter." The city's weather changes constantly, and the poems refer again and again to the sudden and violent shifts from light to mist, from heat to cold. These shifts are replicated within the poet, the city's troubador:

> The vernal seasons of sarcasm
> intermittently in my harlequinate heart . . .
> Intermittently . . .
> Other times it is a sick man, a chill
> in my sick soul like a long round sound . . .

Additional contradictions can be found within the city, a crazy quilt of twentieth-century asphalt and primeval dust and mud, of conflicting architectural styles, of races and ethnic groups, of samba dancers and the Ballets Russes. At the heart of the city's disunity is its history. A few reminders of a more glorious past survive amid what Mário sees as the tawdry present of prostitutes, immigrants, politicians, and the cheap semiprecious stones of progress—a contrast that fills him with bitterness and a profound sense of loss. The Tietê River, once the route to the west of heroic pioneers, now trickles through a world of Italian social clubs and alien languages. The poet, reduced by time to the impotent jocularity of the harlequin, sits on a trolley and observes the city:

> But . . . behold, oh my eyes longing after yester-
>   days,

that enchanted spectacle of the Avenue!
Revive, oh ancestrally *paulista* gauchos!
and oh horses of blood-red rage!

Oranges, oranges, oranges!
Avocados, cambucás and tangerines!
Guardate! At the applause of the whizzing
    clown,
heroic heir of that lordly race of pioneers,
an immigrant's son elegantly passes by,
blondly taming a motor car!

The two basic colors of São Paulo's harlequin costume are gold and gray—symbols, at one level, of climactic diversity: sunshine and mist, summer and winter. The same two colors are also used, however, to suggest a number of additional contradictions. The gold of the pioneer past has become the ash and smoke of the present, but the quest for gold remains a constant in the city's life, transformed into the capitalistic greed of the hated bourgeoisie and the "grand golden chorus of sacks of coffee!. . . ." The most damaging consequence of the new lust for gold is industrialization, the gray smoke of factories and the ashen faces of their tubercular workers. The land has been cheapened and changed beyond recognition: Cotton fields have become dance halls, rice paddies are now red-light districts, and the forests of banana trees have been replaced by joyless public parks dominated by the statuary of foreign cultures.

Stylistically, the poems of *Hallucinated City* were revolutionary; they appeared formlessly chaotic and utterly meaningless to many Brazilian readers in the twenties. Traditional meter and rhyme are absent, and the vocabulary includes created words and elements drawn from the nonpoetic lexicon of the machine. In a few instances, Mário was carried away by his emotions to shout and preach; it is also true that some of his references were so personal, so topical, that they can no longer be fully understood.

On the whole, however, the book has to be regarded as an enormous and innovative success. In the best poems, form and content merge, like the poet and his city. The lozenges of contradictory ideas and images are suddenly and outrageously juxtaposed, like the colors of the harlequin's costume; they are frequently stitched together by internal rhyme. Poetic and consciously antipoetic words and phrases collide like past and present, sun and rain; the languages of the city, as varied as its races and ethnic groups, are forced into coexistence. Thus São Paulo, the vast and contradictory "Gallicism crying in the wilderness of America," is portrayed through a text that is just as chaotic, just as alien, just as harlequinate—a strident shout in the cultural wasteland of pre-Modernist Brazil.

The **"Extremely Interesting Preface"** is something of a let-down after the poems of *Hallucinated City.* Its value is largely external, as a good-humored, reasonably clear, and very useful exposition of contemporary ideas about poetics and aesthetics, topics Mário later covered in greater detail in his 1925 *The Slave-Girl Who Is Not Isaura (A escrava que não é Isaura).* Much of the preface deals with questions that now seem either obvious or excessively topical—Mário's defense of free verse, for example. The pref-

ace, however, is also a brilliant demonstration of Mário's ability to avoid revelation as he hides behind a mask of verbiage and theory. There are no specific references to the book's central image of harlequinate diversity and conflict, an image drawn from the poet's own racial multiplicity. Moreover, because the most obvious stylistic technique in the poems—the juxtaposition of contradictory and discordant elements—might lead readers to perceive the personal implications of the text, Mário cleverly uses allusion and misdirection to create the complicated theory (which he openly admits is nonsensical) of melodic, harmonic, and polyphonic verse.

During the three years following the publication of *Hallucinated City,* Mário came to realize that "São Paulo is not the only harlequinate city" in Brazil. The best poem of this period, the 1923 **"Carnival in Rio" ("Carnaval Carioca"),** provided a new tool, metamorphosis, which could be used to express that diversity. In *Hallucinated City,* the various parallel identities of poet and city coexisted in concrete, immutable form—the multicolored lozenges of the harlequin's suit. In **"Carnival,"** each participant in the festivities can move from one potential identity to another, from one lozenge to another, simply by changing costume. Thus the dancers—even the most extreme case and the focus of Mário's poem, the male cashier who transforms himself into a sexy Bahian girl—do not become what they are not, but what they also, simultaneously, are.

By 1925 Mário had become convinced that it was his responsibility to try to create a single literary work that would sum up Brazil's diversity. He prepared for this task by reading everything he could find, endeavoring to transform himself intellectually, to move from the dominant identity of urban whiteness implicit in his education to another potential identity, based upon his nonwhiteness, that would be more truly Brazilian. In the second volume of *Vom Roroima zum Orinoco,* by the German anthropologist Theodor Koch-Grünberg, Mário discovered a series of native folktales dealing with the exploits of Macunaíma, the culture hero and trickster of one Amazonian tribe.

Mário immediately felt the intense *comoção* of self-recognition, and decided to use the character of Macunaíma, the "hero without character," as the central figure in a long prose text. The hero's lack of character functions at two levels, ethical and national: He is inconsistent and amoral in his actions; and his harlequinate lack of any fixed racial or cultural identity is that of Brazil as a whole, still formless and without "either a civilization of its own or a traditional sense of self," in Mário's words. Macunaíma, moreover, is more South American than Brazilian; he is born where Guyana and Venezuela meet Brazil, and his travels take him from the Amazon to the Andes to the pampas of Argentina.

Mário claimed to have written the first draft of *Macunaíma* during a single week in December of 1926, but that draft was based upon several years of intensive ethnographic and linguistic research, and was drastically revised before publication in 1928. He produced several different prefaces to the text, but decided not to publish any of them; he also referred to *Macunaíma* in his correspondence and in articles. All of these explanations and justifications, however, are as contradictory and evasive as the **"Extremely Interesting Preface."** Mário sometimes claimed, for example, that there were no symbols in the text, but his 1943 analysis of the role of Vei—his only detailed explication of any portion of the book—reveals a tightly structured allegorical symbolism.

What are we to make of these contradictions? I believe, first, that *Macunaíma* was far more personal than Mário was ever publicly willing to admit, and that this is one reason for the evasiveness of his accounts of its composition and meaning. Secondly, although the text is a highly conscious creation, the product of hundreds of hours of research and rewriting, we must also accept Mário's assertion that the final utilization of the materials he had collected was in large measure determined by his subconscious, which created symbolic relationships and meanings he had not planned.

Mário was enormously excited when he finished the final draft of *Macunaíma* in 1927, astonished at what his learning and his unconscious mind had combined to create. He was therefore shocked and embittered by the almost universally negative reactions of his contemporaries. The book was harshly criticized, by other Modernists as well as by older writers whose opinions Mário respected; to make matters worse, the text was published shortly after the "Anthropophagist Manifesto," and some readers appear to have been convinced that Mário had simply put Oswald's theory into practice. Mário frequently complained that no one had ever understood the text that he regarded as his masterpiece, and finally concluded that it had been a failure.

It is easy to feel sympathy for Mário's distress, but the reactions of his readers are understandable. *Macunaíma* is written in an artificial and extremely difficult language, Mário's own invention, which combines popular syntax with a lexicon drawn from a number of native and foreign languages as well as from every regional dialect within Brazilian Portuguese. The structure of *Macunaíma,* moreover, appears as chaotic as its language—a formless series of utterly illogical events. The book is also obscene; many of Mário's contemporaries were shocked by what they viewed as pure pornography, but even the book's Rabelaisian bawdiness appears pointless. In addition, large sections of *Macunaíma* are found texts, sometimes copied almost word for word from Koch-Grünberg and other collectors of Brazilian Indian folktales, which have been tossed together without any obvious logic. When Mário was accused, rather gently, of plagiarism, he admitted, "I copied everybody," but also insisted, "I made things up whenever I felt like it and, above all, whenever I needed to make sure that my creation would remain art and not the dry documentation of scholarship."

I believe, however, that this biography of the "hero without character," if read as I am convinced Mário consciously and unconsciously intended it to be, is not a failed text but one of the two or three greatest works of Brazilian literature—the high point in a long national tradition but also a work far ahead of its time, the independent precursor of what is now generally described as the "magic realism" of the Spanish-American novel of the fifties and six-

ties. And, finally, despite its riotously funny and often scatological humor, Mário's text is perhaps the most profoundly tragic work in Brazilian literature, a native *Don Quijote.*

The complexity of this utterly untranslatable book begins with its genre. It has often been classified as a novel—sometimes, most erroneously, as a picaresque novel—although Mário never referred to it as such. The book was first advertised as a *história,* a term that combines the historical context of the text and its folkloric origins as a story. When it was published, the title page defined it as a *rapsódia,* another term with a double meaning. In music, a rhapsody is a light diversion, a variation using popular national themes; in literature, it is the creation of the rhapsodist, the personification, in Mário's definition, of a tradition that flowed directly from the ancient bards of pre-Homeric Greece to the oral literature of northeastern Brazil in the twentieth century. The function of the rhapsodist, Mário declared, remained the transformation of contemporary and historical events into authentic literary expressions of the popular mind.

Mário's rhapsodic text—the story of Macunaíma's origins in the Amazonian forests, his trip to São Paulo, and his return to the jungles before he ascends into the heavens to become the Big Dipper—is far less chaotic than several generations of critics have claimed. Though it does not have a standard novelistic framework, the rhapsody is quite rigidly organized around a series of complex internal structures that are symbolic or allegorical in content. These structures, perhaps most usefully described as codes, are both the source of *Macunaíma's* multiplicity and apparent incoherence and the key to its meaning. It is worthwhile, therefore, to deconstruct the text in order to look closely at several of the codes that coexist within it.

The chronological and cosmogonic codes—In *Macunaíma,* what we call time, the fixed chronology of civilization, exists only within the calendars and clocks of São Paulo. Time outside the city is multiple and simultaneous, like the harlequinate juxtapositions of past and present in *Hallucinated City.* Thus the chronology of the real world of São Paulo in the twenties coexists with all of Brazilian history and with a primitive vision of multiple and parallel chronologies, of worlds being created and destroyed.

The multiplicity of time is a function, in fact, of the multiple character of the universe, which exists simultaneously at various stages of development and in which there are few fixed forms: Humans become plants, mountains, and waterfalls; animals and insects were once human; machines were once animals, and people can become machines; the Moon and stars are still being created, formed of birds and snakes and human beings.

This cosmogonic multiplicity and simultaneity is the basis for the magic metamorphoses that take place within the text. The hero, in part because he has no fixed character of his own, realizes that every identity carries within it a series of other potential identities: those which once existed and those which may yet come to be—a more elaborate form of Mário's vision of **"Carnival in Rio."** Magic simply involves moving oneself or others from one identity to another. Thus, to give but one example, the hero is magically and instantly transformed from infant to adult, a metamorphosis possible because the hero's adult identity is already implicit within the child, the father of the man. Only Macunaíma's head remains baby-sized; it is also rhomboid—the diamond shape of the lozenges in the harlequin's suit.

The petrological code—The opposite of metamorphosis is petrification—the irreversible foreclosure of potential options for existence as the multiple identities become forever fixed in a single, often ironic form. Macunaíma uses this implicit petrous identity as the basis for some of his magic: He turns a visiting Englishman into the stone structure of the London Bank; when Macunaíma leaves São Paulo to return to the forest, he looks back, like Lot's wife, and changes the whole bustling metropolis into an enormous stone sloth.

Stones retain some trace of their original identities, however, and this is the basis for the power of the *muiraquitã*, the magic talisman that Ci, the Empress of the Forests and the Queen of the Amazon Women, gives to Macunaíma before she ascends into the heavens. The hero quickly loses the stone, and his journey to São Paulo to recover it from the villain, Venceslau Pietro Pietra, forms the major portion of the plot. Macunaíma finally kills Pietra and regains the *muiraquitã*, but he loses it a second time at the end of the book and gives up on the world. Pietra is a foreigner, a Peruvian-Italian trader, and is used on one level to satirize São Paulo's immigrants and their pretensions. The conflict between the hero and Pietra is not, however, a simple allegory for the native-foreigner dialectic; the trader is also, simultaneously, the evil giant Piamã—Macunaíma's traditional foe in native folklore. Pietra-Piamã, therefore, is a universal symbol of evil, combining the sins of greed and of sacrilege in his mania for collecting stones—the petrified remains of animals, of human beings, even of entire civilizations. This obsession is implicit in the giant's Italian name.

Macunaíma is too free a spirit to contain a petrous identity within his multiplicity. At the end of the book, the Tupi Indians have all been petrified; a gigantic stone turtle, their traditional totemic animal, is all that remains of their race. The hero writes his own epitaph upon its surface—"I DID NOT COME INTO THIS WORLD TO BE A STONE!"—and departs to become the Big Dipper.

The celestial code—Superior, nonpetrous spirits can rise, like Macunaíma, to become stars—an idea Mário took from Indian mythology. Their ascent is proof of their basic goodness, but the stellar option also represents frustration, sorrow, and evasion; it is, in fact, as much a final, irreversible fixation of identity as is petrification. Thus Iriqui, one of the wives of Macunaíma's brother Jiguê, becomes a star in the Pleiades when she can no longer attract the hero. When their infant son dies, Macunaíma's wife Ci transforms herself into Beta Centauri.

The heavens contain other symbols. Macunaíma endeavors, during his stay in São Paulo, to teach the city's inhabitants the true nature of the universe, the real and multiple identity of all things. Perhaps his greatest single good deed, within the context of the text, is that he saves the *paulistas* from the false and banal cosmography of the state. The hero ridicules the national stellar symbol, the Southern Cross, and shows his audience that the constellation is really the final transformation of Pauí-Pódole, the Father of the Curassows, the first and greatest of that species of birds. This revelation so moves the sophisticated and cosmopolitan *paulistas* that they become as little children, and go back to their homes afraid that they will wet their beds during the night.

Another aspect of the celestial code, which Mário himself explained in 1943, is the relationship between the hero and Vei, the feminine Sun. Vei intends that Macunaíma, as Brazil, should marry one of her daughters; the nation would thereby attain its potential identity as a great tropical civilization, like ancient Egypt and Mexico. The hero, however, wanders off to fornicate with a Portuguese girl, causing Vei to change her mind. Vei gets her revenge at the very end of the text, when she warms the hero's body to rekindle his dormant lust. As a result, Macunaíma dives into a lake to copulate with a seductive water-spirit, the Uiara; a swarm of piranhas devour most of his body, he loses the *muiraquitã* again, and he decides to abandon the Earth for life among the stars.

The entomologic code—Mário uses insects to establish and describe the ideal relationship between primitive man and his environment. Man is master of the insect world, and primitive society is built around a series of vital insect-centered rituals of human interaction: shooing away mosquitoes, searching for ticks, picking lice. This ancient relationship breaks down in São Paulo. Suzi, the city girl who is Jiguê's third wife, utterly deforms ritual by picking her own lice, an act symbolizing the shift from primitive communality to urban individualism, from public virtue to private vice. She even takes off her head of hair in order to find the insects more efficiently, thereby deforming nature as well. Macunaíma also realizes that ants are literally taking over São Paulo and Brazil. The image of the vast urban ant hill was a Modernist commonplace and appears in *Hallucinated City,* but the hero's preoccupation is now concrete rather than metaphoric: The insect world is escaping from civilized man's control. Macunaíma cannot save modern Brazil from its ants, nor can he restore the traditional model of symbiosis and respect. He can only warn Brazilians, through his famous dictum, "TOO MANY ANTS AND TOO LITTLE HEALTH: / SUCH IS THE SICKNESS OF BRAZIL."

The epidemiological code—There is, it appears, no disease in the forests where the hero is born. São Paulo's grayness, in *Hallucinated City,* is related to its diseases, laryngitis and tuberculosis. The São Paulo Macunaíma enters is filled with a far greater assortment of diseases, and he catches almost all of them: erysipelas, scarlet fever, thrush, measles, and so on. Precisely because he has never really grown up, he is particularly susceptible to the illnesses of civilized children. The hero, moreover, perceives that disease is an integral part of the city's life; the monstrous animal-machines that sweep the streets, for example, are designed to stir up bacteria and thereby kill enough people to stabilize the population.

Macunaíma is no more healthy when he leaves São Paulo to return to the forest. His diseases simply become more tropical, providing etiologies for such ailments as malaria and leprosy. He finally becomes not merely the victim of disease but its active agent, as he consciously infects Jiguê with the leprosy that will destroy his entire family. Only Macunaíma escapes this disease, but its effects are symbolically repeated in his final maiming by the piranhas.

The ornithological code—Birds have two vital functions within the text. First, they provide continuity for the plot, reflecting the transformations of the hero. Macunaíma's nobility—as Ci's husband, he becomes Emperor of the forests and ruler of the single-breasted Amazons—and his original integration into the natural world are symbolically represented by the bright canopy of parrots that always flies above his head. When he enters São Paulo—a world in which the riches of the forest are almost worthless, quickly dissipated on lobsters, champagne, and prostitutes—the parrot canopy flies away.

The birds return only when the hero goes back to the forest, protecting him from the heat of vengeful Vei, but he has changed and they slowly begin to drift away. He barely notices, for he now cares only about the two chickens he has brought back from São Paulo—helpless, flightless birds without function in the forest. Macunaíma is no longer attracted to Iriqui, one of Jiguê's Indian wives, and part of his imperial canopy goes with her to form the Pleiades. The rest depart when he betrays and infects his brothers with leprosy. Only one parrot remains to converse with Macunaíma, to witness his ascension into the sky, and to teach the hero's language and deeds to a stranger and, thereby, to us. The parrot then flies away, like Machado's Tristão and Fidélia, to find a new life in Portugal.

The ornithological code is also the primary source of one of the most important concepts in the book, the archetypal model—the Pódole—of every living species. The Pauí-Pódole, the Father of the Curassows, has left his descendents behind on earth, and is now what Brazilians incorrectly call the Southern Cross. As a result of Macunaíma's mindless treachery, toward the end of the text, Jiguê is devoured by leprosy and becomes the ghost leper that infects and digests the oldest brother, Maanape, and the beautiful princess who is their companion. The multiple, all-consuming ghost then attacks the Father of the Vultures, the archetypal king vulture, and receives a new identity as the bird's second head. [The critic adds in a footnote: "The reference is to the very prominent crop of this species. From a distance, the king vulture appears to have two heads, one above the other."] The Father of the Vultures does not join the Father of the Curassows in the heavens, however; the world of the forest is dying, and scavengers must remain to feed upon it and thereby purify it.

The code of the machine—When Macunaíma first encounters the city of São Paulo, he is astonished by its machines, artifacts he can comprehend only in terms of the natural world he knows. He adapts quickly to this new environ-

ment, however, because he perceives that the multiplicity and potentiality of his cosmogonic vision still apply to modern man and his machines. After pondering the question, he concludes that "the men were in fact machines and the machines were in fact men." Once this multiple and simultaneous identity is established, Macunaíma can extend the magic of metamorphosis to this new order, turning his brother Jiguê into a telephone whenever he needs to make a call.

The hero, in another of his rare good deeds, transmits his perception of technology as merely one of the potential identities of nature to a chauffeur—a social type described, in one of Mário's most important nonfolkloric sources, as the prototype of the new man of the twentieth century, the "technicalized savage" who is the master of the machine. In a replication of the Southern Cross incident, Macunaíma tells a chauffeur and his girlfriend the story of the jaguar who became the first automobile and of her vast, sexually differentiated litter of male Fords and female Chevrolets. The authenticity of this etiology provides the chauffeur with a tradition rooted in the real Brazil, leaving him and the girl speechless and in tears.

The hero, however, is also tempted by the machine—a word he extends to include all manufactured articles. Vei gives him the *vatá,* the magic fire stone, but this most precious of objects in the forest is of no interest in a world of matches and lighters, and Macunaíma trades it away to get his picture in the papers. When he leaves São Paulo, he takes with him two of its artifacts: a Smith-Wesson revolver and a Pathek watch. These objects are as useless in the forest as his chickens, but Macunaíma clings to these artificial talismans during his last days on Earth, managing to recover them from the piranhas and take them with him up to the heavens. The *muiraquitã,* the real talisman, is lost forever.

The racial code—Macunaíma, like Mário's harlequin, is at once black and red and white: He is born a black-skinned Indian, but becomes white, blond, and blue-eyed when he bathes in the water that fills a footprint left by Saint Thomas. In a standard folk etiology of racial diversity, the hero so muddies the water that Jiguê, who bathes second, becomes a red-skinned Indian; even less water is left for Maanape, who can only lighten his palms and the soles of his feet. In this symbolic baptism, Jiguê and Maanape, previously no more than foils for the hero's childish pranks, acquire definition as independent personalities; but their new forms, as the Indian and the African, are simply personifications of two somatic and cultural identities already implicit in Macunaíma the harlequin.

Maanape is the sorcerer, a symbol of the survival of African religion and magic in Brazil; it is he who cures the hero's many urban diseases. Once the three brothers leave São Paulo to return to the Indian forests, Maanape becomes a lost and alien figure without function; he cannot even cure his own leprosy. Jiguê the Indian is braver than Macunaíma, but he is not very intelligent, particularly where women are concerned. He comes into his own, however, when the brothers reenter the forest. As the hero's sexual appeal and potency fade, the pattern of seduction is reversed; it is Jiguê who beds the beautiful princess who would seem to be Macunaíma's natural mate. Jiguê also retains the ancestral Indian magic of hunting and fishing, which Macunaíma literally throws away in mindless fits of jealous impotence. The alienated envy of the tragically whitened and weakened hero leads him to infect Jiguê with leprosy, thereby destroying his companions and his own future on earth.

The sexual code—Macunaíma is born lustful and moves magically from infantile sexuality to adult potency. He seduces all three of Jiguê's wives, and has three other important sexual relationships—with Ci, with the anonymous princess, and with the Uiara. He also tries to bed every female he meets, and generally succeeds, at least until the final chapters of the text.

The sexuality that pervades *Macunaíma* has several important and related functions. First, it provides a metaphor for the primitive-urban dialectic: Sex is freely given and taken among the Indians, but Macunaíma usually has to pay for it in São Paulo, a fact that astonishes and puzzles him. Fascinated by the city's prostitutes—most of whom are foreign and all of whom claim to be French—and by their use of such machine-made aids to seduction as rouge and lipstick, the hero transforms himself into a French whore, with banana stalks for breasts, and tries to seduce Pietra in order to regain the *muiraquitã*. The attempt fails when Pietra gets too physical, but the episode is the first hint that Macunaíma, in the city, is slowly losing his masculinity; by the time he returns to the forest, he is so asexual that the monster Mapinguari, who likes only girls, pursues him by mistake.

Sex in *Macunaíma* is often extremely violent. The hero's sexual encounters with Jiguê's first two wives, Sofará and Iriqui, involve mutual flagellation and mutilation, elements replicated in his final copulation with the Uiara. Macunaíma rapes Ci violently, while his brothers hold her down, and their sexual relationship after marriage is frequently and graphically sadomasochistic. [The critic adds in a footnote: "This section was considerably longer and more explicit in the first two editions, but Mário cut it for the third."] All of this sexual aggression is meaningful, within the context of the text, because it emphasizes that sex is power, and that Macunaíma's gradual impotence is merely a metaphor for the dissipation of his primitive powers that results from his contact with the white, urban world of São Paulo.

The link between sex and power is most explicit in the episode of the *macumba* ("voodoo") ritual in Rio, a tangle of inverted sexual identities and the most brutal and terrifying section of the text. The ceremony calls up Exu, the male African deity of evil, who takes over the body of a fat Polish whore. As Macunaíma copulates with the whore possessed by Exu, it becomes clear that the hero is really Exu's son, and is therefore fornicating with his own father. As a reward for Macunaíma's sexual prowess, Exu works sympathetic magic: The hero beats and tortures the whore's body in a fit of almost incomprehensible sadism, but all her wounds are transferred to the body of Pietra in São Paulo—Macunaíma's first victory over his great adversary.

This sexual sadomasochism also symbolizes Macunaíma's destiny as a destructive rather than a creative force. A web of allusions and symbols make it clear that the hero's exaggerated natural sexuality reflects one supreme potential identity within his multiplicity—as the procreator of a race, as a Pódole. Thus Macunaíma's first liaison, with Sofará, refers to the cosmogony implicit in the ending of Alencar's *The Guarani Indian:* Sofará, in Indian legend, was the wife of the only man to survive the Deluge, and is therefore the mother of mankind. Jiguê sends Sofará home to her father, short-circuiting the generative potential of her identity. The same possibility exists in Macunaíma's relationship with Iriqui, who is described in terms that suggest Alencar's Iracema, but she rises to the Pleiades without bearing children. The episode of the hero's marriage to Ci, the Mother of the Forest and another Iracema figure, is more promising, for a child is born, a new Moacir. The Edenic potential is destroyed when the infant dies and Ci also departs for the heavens.

Macunaíma, weakened and contaminated by the modernity of São Paulo, is still obsessed with sex, but his generative potential is forever eliminated during his stay there. He has lost so much of his native cunning that a monkey easily tricks him into smashing his own testicles with a rock. The shock kills Macunaíma, but Maanape brings him back to life and gives him a pair of coconuts as substitutes. The hero's ability to serve as a Pódole, however, is lost. He becomes a voyeur, observing the lovemaking of the chauffeur and his girl. Once back in the forest, the hero gradually loses all interest in sex, even with the beautiful princess; his encounter with the Uiara is the last, artificially induced spasm of lust, and the piranhas devour his coconuts.

The linguistic code—Mário sought to use the artificial language in which *Macunaíma* is written to "deregionalize" the nation, to unify Brazilian Portuguese by juxtaposing words taken from every regional dialect. The language is also intended to suggest that the text itself refers to the nation as a whole rather than to any single area. In addition, loan words from European languages coexist with Africanisms and borrowings from a number of native Indian tongues to form the harlequinate lexicon of the text. Enumeration, one key technique in Mário's effort to unify Brazil linguistically through *Macunaíma,* has greatly puzzled and irritated readers. These long intercalated lists of synonyms drawn from a number of dialects—words for "fish" or "parrot," for example—nonetheless serve two functions: to make the book, and its author, more truly and completely Brazilian; and to present nonmeaningful tone poems, brief melodic interludes of sounds and rhythms that reproduce the rhapsodist's accompaniment on the lyre, gusla, or guitar.

Macunaíma begins to talk rather late in his brief childhood, but he is as fascinated by language as Mário. When he goes to São Paulo, he tries—like a new Adam in a concrete Eden—to give names to what he sees, juxtaposing the natural and the mechanical: The marmoset-elevator climbs up the palm-tree-building, for example. He also uses, or at least pretends to use, the city's alien languages: English, French, and Italian. He is most intrigued, however, by a more curious linguistic phenomenon, the almost total discontinuity between what Brazilians say and what they write; between the spoken language and formal, pretentious written Portuguese.

Macunaíma masters this alien second tongue and writes the long "Letter to the Amazons" in it, asking for more funds and showing off what he has learned. The letter is a delightful linguistic *tour de force,* combining meaningless quotations from the classics, grammatical overcorrection, bureaucratic discourse, and pompous allusions that are often not quite exact. This brilliant satire on the traditional reactions of foreign travelers to Brazil, from Pêro Vaz de Caminha on, is also an attack on the ignorance implicit in the high-flown, verborrheic style every educated and semieducated Brazilian, in Mário's view, dreamed of mastering.

The hero's ability to use this style, however, is also evidence of his transformation and contamination by the urban civilization of policemen, whores, and politicians he praises in this letter. As he adopts this obsolete and dysfunctional language, he begins to lose his own tongue and his own identity. Thus, for example, it is thanks to Macunaíma's influence that the *paulistas* learn to replace an imported gallicism, *boutonnière,* with an authentic native term, *puíto,* an Indianism for "anus." This is one of the hero's minor accomplishments in a series of conscious or unconscious efforts to give the city's inhabitants their Brazilian roots, but Macunaíma is later startled when a German girl offers to put a flower in his *puíto,* and at first does not understand her.

Macunaíma is also increasingly fixated upon obscenity, upon just plain talking dirty. This fixation is symbolic of his gradual loss of sexual potency, the substitution of language for action. And, like Mário himself, the hero becomes a collector of words. When he sees Pietra's collection of stones—concrete and potentially powerful artifacts, past beings and civilizations in petrified form—Macunaíma is tempted to start one of his own. He decides, however, that it sounds like too much work, and makes up his mind to gather words rather than things; he amasses a vast repertoire of dirty words from every language and every country. Macunaíma attempts to use the words against Pietra, but the giant is intrigued rather than frightened or insulted; a few drops of rain have a far greater effect upon the enemy than all of the hero's obscenities, which are as ultimately useless as Mário's careful collection of regional synonyms. And, in the final destruction of Macunaíma's tribe and world, language itself is lost. The mute hero rises to the silence of the heavens; his language and that of his tribe, no longer used by humans, is preserved only in the rote memory of a parrot.

. . . . .

If we now reconstruct the text, reintegrating these separate codes, it becomes clear that Mário managed to combine within it the two traditional functions of Indianism: etiology, explaining the present; and elegy, mourning the loss of the past while finding lessons in it for the present. Macunaíma is a genuine culture hero, both in his folkloric origins and in his role within Mário's text. It is through

him that an incredibly diverse series of natural and social phenomena are explained: why the Moon and stars exist, why the Sun is yellow, where automobiles come from, why Brazil has soccer, soft drinks, and obscene gestures. The hero and his brothers also explain Brazil's racial diversity: It is a nation that was once primarily Indian and African, that has been whitened by Christianity but remains, simultaneously and harlequinately, white and red and black.

The etiological function of *Macunaíma,* however, includes the explanation of negative national characteristics, a departure from the optimism of Alencar. Brazilians had long perceived their nation and its culture as not yet fully formed, not yet adult. Macunaíma is indeed both infant and man, for he never grows up; the magic of the agouti rodent gives him the body of an adult, but his head—the seat of intelligence and sensibility—remains small and deformed, with the "nauseating baby face of a child." This transformation, like all of the hero's other metamorphoses, also reflects Brazil's lack of a fixed and true identity.

Although Macunaíma fulfills his etiological function, he utterly fails to live up to his creative potential as an authentic culture hero, one who not only explains the present but also, as a Pódole, preserves the past and engenders the future. That failure, the central theme of the text, moves *Macunaíma* beyond the tradition of Alencar. The book is not only an etiological myth of national creation, but an explanation of the annihilation of the future, a myth of national destruction. Macunaíma is the Brazil that might have been: the creative, balanced coexistence of the three races within a culture rooted in the traditions of the past, conscious of the potential of its multiplicity, and destined to flourish as a great tropical civilization. When the mutilated and impotent hero departs for the heavens, still clutching his chickens, his watch, and his revolver, he leaves no descendants; his tribe—and Brazil's future—vanishes. All that remains is the world of ants and machines and disease, the city of stone and its petrous inhabitants.

The text, therefore is elegiac, mourning the lost future as well as the lost past. Mário may well have hoped that there was still time to unify Brazilians through the language and allegory of his text, to warn them of the perils of sterility, disease, and dependency. These goals help explain Mário's bitter despair when his warning was criticized and misunderstood. But *Macunaíma* is also, I believe, a very personal document, as much a journal of life on the continuum as the works of Gonçalves Dias, Machado, or Cruz e Sousa. Through the hero, Mário seeks to identify himself with the real Brazil—and, in fact, with the whole of Latin America. His own identity, like that of the nation and the continent, is harlequinate and multiple, and must remain so. Mário's **"Improvisation on the Sickness of America,"** written a few months before *Macunaíma* was published, describes the greatest of all the ailments afflicting him and the nation, and one that Macunaíma shared: the disease of whiteness that is slowly destroying the other racial identities that color both his harlequin's suit and his soul, foreclosing his multiple options for existence on the racial continuum.

Even as he wrote his rhapsodic text, Mário de Andrade appears to have feared that his warning might go unheeded. All he had to offer Brazilians were his words, words that, as Macunaíma discovers, are less powerful than a few drops of rain. Moreover, those who might have understood and heeded his message—those Brazilians not yet contaminated by cultural dependency, those who still retained tradition and racial and cultural diversity—could not read. Despite all of Mário's efforts to nationalize the vocabulary and syntax of his text, it is as pointless as the ridiculous letter Macunaíma writes to the illiterate Amazons—a text to which there can be no reply. Those who attempt the impossible task of saving Brazil from modernity and whiteness by endeavoring to show the nation its roots and by celebrating its harlequinate racial diversity may, like Macunaíma, escape petrification as "mute statues in the corners of public gardens a hundred years from now," as Mário wrote of himself in 1936. The fate that awaits them, however, is the same evasive fixation of identity the frustrated and despairing hero chooses in the end: "the useless brilliance of the stars"—a destiny Mário de Andrade assigned to José de Alencar, and a destiny he also predicted for himself. (pp. 139-60)

> David T. Haberly, "The Harlequin: Mário de Andrade," in his Three Sad Races: Racial Identity and National Consciousness in Brazilian Literature, *Cambridge University Press,* 1983, pp. 135-60.

Renata R. Mautner Wasserman   (essay date 1984)

[*In the following excerpt, Wasserman focuses on Andrade's synthesis of European and native cultural influences in* Macunaíma.]

Sometimes literature is said to discover the individual to himself; sometimes it is said to discover the Other to the self. But literature can also discover a community to itself and provide readers with a language in which to speak of themselves as a generalized public whose reaction to a work is part of its meaning. Widely read and accepted works draw their meanings from, and spill them back into an extraliterary reality; they articulate and modify, affirm, juggle, and contest ideologies. This (Jaussian) modification of reader-response criticism, which considers response as a social and historical, rather than simply individual, process, yields unexpected dividends when applied to the literatures of communities that are not at the center of political and economic power, for it throws ideologies into sudden relief as the vocabularies associated with them are put to new uses and subjected to new scrutiny. One finds in these literatures that literary vocabularies drawn from more powerful communities bring urgency to questions of national identity (or group identity) that they are also called upon to settle. In the process of articulating a language to express identity, these literatures enter into a complicated relationship with those of the centers of power; they strive to differentiate themselves from the ideologies that assert power over them, but also need to use the terms of those ideologies in order to make themselves understood, even to themselves.

Around the time of their independence from assorted European nations, countries of the New World produced literatures in which one central preoccupation was to affirm and define themselves. Each new nation proudly showed that it had its own independent intellectual and artistic life, that it could think and speak about itself in its own language. But, of course, it did not: one does not, if one wants to be understood, invent one's own language *ex nihilo.* Thus the new nations were caught in the paradox of having to assert difference and independence in terms that of necessity preexisted them and limited the scope of that same affirmed difference. Fenimore Cooper's work, for instance, asserts difference in its defense of republican ideas and its use of authochtonous subject matter, but it also depends on the stereotypes of European romantic fiction for the terms in which it speaks of the novelty it offers. And while the problem of affirming difference and defining nationality has become less critical for the United States as the nation became more powerful and richer (the preoccupation lingers in the works of Southern writers, for example, and in criticism of these works), it is still important in the literatures of most other nations of the hemisphere. These literatures express the need to define nationality and to come to terms with the powerful Other to whom the definition is, in part, addressed and against whom it is formulated. At the same time, as they become known, these literatures play a role in the ideological economy of the dominant cultures: Vargas Llosa and García Márquez are vital and elemental and fresh; their realism is magical, in contrast with the humdrum variety grown domestically in Europe or the United States, and the violence they write of is almost redemptive in the primitive context where it takes place. They can offer, instantly and automatically, the "estrangement" of which Russian formalists spoke, for they use the language of power idiosyncratically to free themselves from it.

In *Macunaíma* (1928), by the Brazilian Mário de Andrade, the problematic relation between national identity and foreign influence appears clearly. Though the work places itself in a tradition of attempts to define nationality, it speaks the language of a French literary movement useful insofar as it is iconoclastic at its origin. The Other against whom the self-definition becomes necessary is diverse: an enviable and unavoidable political and economic power resides in England and the United States, while France and Italy, as intellectual and artistic models, provide the impulse for the creation of a language in which the confrontation can take place, and a German ethnologist provides the science, the raw data upon which Andrade's tale is built.

Six years before the publication of *Macunaíma,* Mário de Andrade had taken part in the "Week of Modern Art," held in the Municipal Theater of São Paulo. In that most conventional of forums, hired for the occasion by an editor of the *Jornal do Comércio,* a respectable daily of wide circulation, there was a week's bedlam. A full house chanted the refrains of poetry by Manuel Bandeira, whistled and stomped at music by Villa Lobos, gasped at paintings by Leger's student Anita Malfatti, listened to Graça Aranha and Oswald de Andrade demolish established poets and literary figures. For the Modern Art people, the "Week" had been a culmination of years of experimentation and of contacts with European movements like Dada, Futurism, Surrealism, and with the works of Apollinaire, Verlaine, Mallarmé, Marinetti, Verhaeren and others. In these few days the São Paulo rebels became the established avant-garde. Their works were published not only in little magazines brought out by themselves, but in the literary pages of large newspapers like the *Correio da Manhã*, whose editors were sympathetic to their efforts at transforming and renewing artistic expression in Brazil, and who saw these efforts as part of a larger program to propel the country out of its provincial corner into the larger world, where its ability to speak the language of power might allow its participation. The Brazilian Modernists were to transform expression, along models arising in France and Italy, to express transformations along models arising in England and in the United States. In their work an authentic spirit of Brazilian nationality was to find a language characteristic of the nation and "legible" within the syntactic and semantic rules of the models, if close to the limits of that legibility. But the task became possible only because the models themselves were then open to that particular kind of renewal and willing to encourage it: French artists looked to African and other primitive art for inspiration, and the economically dominant nations were investing in "primitive" markets, whose rapid urbanization was, paradoxically and inevitably, a desired sign of progress.

Macunaíma participates in this process of change. It is written as the coffee-rich state of São starts to become urban and industrialized, and the author's native city of São Paulo begins its tremendous growth, attracting floods of immigrants from all over Brazil and the world, and challenging older centers of national political power. The process is seen, on the whole, as desirable, and the book, which tries to find the continuity between modernization and primitive substratum, is well received despite its difficulties. There is no lack of friendly and understanding reviewers able and qualified to read it. Even those who do not like it, praise it for being "talented nonsense." Lately the book has become part of a popular culture: in 1974 Portela, one of the main "samba schools" in Rio de Janeiro, made it into the theme of its presentation in the great Carnival parade; a movie, based on the tale, was successful domestically and shown in Paris and New York; *Macunaíma* became a play in 1977. In short, the book does not mark one of those moments in literature when a select group talks to itself about itself: from the beginning it has been seen as integrated in the fabric of a national life, and its present reworking into other media and other levels of discourse shows that it has not become simply the symbol of a historical moment.

Nationalistic in its reference, modernistic in its referent, *Macunaíma* answers the newly urgent need to create a language in which to express a national reality, and to define a national self. Both imply opposition: to the old language, and to the Other, both holders of power. As Cavalcanti Proença shows [in his *Roteiro de Macunaíma*], it is not the first time in the history of Brazilian letters that the process has taken place. He notes that *Macunaíma* like, for instance, the texts of the romantic author José de Alencar,

whom Andrade respected as a forerunner, accomplishes a revaluation of "national subject matter"; these texts form a tradition of opposition to outdated literary canons, and to a certain kind of external domination. Romantics, writing within half a century of their country's independence, set themselves the conscious task of formulating the difference between the new American nation and the colonial power which till then had determined its political, economic, and cultural life. In the case of the modernists, the source of the domination is more diffused, but the need remains to define what is national, and to stress its opposition to outside determination of its nature and its value. Romantics and modernists also have in common the use of external sources to legitimize their valuation of what they had decided to show as valuable in the difference between their nation and others: Alencar's best-known creations are his Indian heroes, the man Peri and the woman Iracema; and the works in which they appear owe much to the greatly successful romances of Chateaubriand, Scott, and Fenimore Cooper. These affinities with literary works from other literatures and cultures could simply attest to cultural contacts. But the question is not whether there was a direct influence of these foreign authors on Alencar—what is important for this discussion is the congruence between the valuation of the Indian for internal, Brazilian use, and his valuation outside Brazil. Chateaubriand and others who wrote about romanticized noble savages did so in order to present an example to their European readers, to revitalize their moral lives, or to entertain them with tales from strange lands and peoples. Alencar, however, took that Europeanized Indian, the model for which had originally come from descriptions of widely-read travel accounts like de Léry's, and in bringing him back, so to speak, to his native land, encased him in a different, non-European context, and made him, the Other, into one of the components in the image of an authentic Brazilian self. On both sides of the Atlantic the value of that Indian figure lay in its difference: in Europe he was the foil of the tired and decadent European criticized by romantic writers and thinkers; in Brazil he stood for the distinctive trait separating the new Brazilian nation from Portugal, its former colonizer. But for Brazilians there was another, paradoxical value in the figure of the Indian, and that was the very value that the Europeans placed upon him.

Similarly, when Mário de Andrade takes Macunaíma for his hero, a process of valuation of the primitive had been going on in Paris for about a decade. African carvings and bronzes were admired in Parisian museums, and prominent Frenchmen were travelling to the tropics to be conduits for the culture of the French and the nature of the newer lands. Raul Bopp [in his *Movimentos modernistas no Brasil, 1922-1928*] tells that in 1917 Paul Claudel comes to Rio, on a diplomatic mission, bringing Darius Milhaud with him. They are delighted with the country, fill the embassy with tropical plants and parrots given them by their astonished Brazilian friends, and Milhaud makes "O Boi no Telhado," a popular song, into "Le Boeuf sur le Toit." Soon, on both sides of the Atlantic, one "narrated an imaginary Brazil, with colorful landscapes, like a land of utopia." And "the Brazilians who went to Paris on their vacations began to like that cordial 'Brazil' in all its primitive freshness." When these travellers came back to Brazil, they brought with them a new valuation of certain aspects of the nation that had been neglected for a while. At the Week of Modern Art much of the art presented and of the theoretical work behind it was concerned not only with the renewal of artistic forms that was part of modernism, but also with a rethinking of the meaning of nationality and a reevaluation of its distinctive characteristics.

The specifically literary movement the young modernists fought against and replaced, "Parnassianism," had stressed the elements of regularity in form and universality in subject that would allow products of Brazilian artists to merge into production from elsewhere. But the moderns had other aims. Oswald de Andrade expressed them as well as anyone else, even to the outrageousness of some of his propositions, in the "Manifesto of Anthropophagy," published in the same year as **Macunaíma.** "Anthropophagy," an all-encompassing artistic and intellectual movement, was to be "a descent to the genuine, still pure, origins of the nation, which would capture the germs of renewal, repossess the subjacent Brazil . . . and strive to reach a specific cultural synthesis, with greater emphasis on a national consciousness." Oswald de Andrade demythifies grandiose concepts of nationalism and culture with monumental jokes (he proposes as a patron saint the—historical—Bishop Sardinha, eaten by coastal cannibals when his ship sank off the shore of Pernambuco), and rejects European influence (the greatest national holiday was to be October 11, the last day of freedom for the Americas). But in his earlier call for the production of "a literature for export" he accepts the concept of literature as a consumer product: nationalism, and even the eventual return to the cannibals, should give rise to something desired by the rejected European culture, and has to take into consideration the tastes of a targeted market.

Mário de Andrade was not one of the Anthropophagists, but critics and reading public quickly established a connection between the literary manifesto that took cannibals as models for intellectual endeavors, claiming them as ancestors of present-day Brazilians and source of their desired difference from other cultures, and the modernistic novel whose anti-hero, a representative of the authentic Brazilian, was an Indian. Thus, despite disclaimers, and the growing disaffection between the two writers, Mário de Andrade often found himself working in the same vein as Oswald de Andrade, since he was embarked, like his namesake, in the production of a recognizably Brazilian literature which defined a recognizably Brazilian character. Oswald de Andrade thought about placing a national literature on the international market, while Mário de Andrade turned toward the internal audience for his works and, like Macunaíma (who refused to ask the government for a grant to study art in Paris), made it a point never to leave Brazil. But even if he was not so concerned about the insertion of Brazilian literature in the class of phenomena called world literature (which does not necessarily include all the literature of the world, but only those works "legible" outside the boundaries of countries where they are produced), he was in contact with other literatures, and the international literary movements of his time provided him with a language in which to frame the definition of

nationality he was seeking to formulate. Despite differences in methods and personalities, Mário and Oswald de Andrade's choice of the figure of an American Indian to signify Brazilianness is, in the end, a traditional gesture among national authors. Once again, also, they are not only defining an internal phenomenon, but also purveying exotic fare, for which an outside interest has opened the internal markets. Those Brazilian friends of Claudel's who provided him with tropical plants and parrots, and those travelling Brazilians who, in Paris, became enamored of their own primitive, unspoiled, redemptive, and hopeful country, were participating in a recurring process of exchange of cultural goods for values between the less and the more powerful.

Mário de Andrade is aware that primitivism is not a representation of reality, but a language. In a letter to the critic Tristão de Athayde [collected in **Cartas de Mário de Andrade**], he explains that he uses the "primitive" not because he wants to recreate a state he cannot authentically claim, since he is a cultivated man, but because he is at the beginning of a process: that of defining a Brazilian culture distinct even from that of countries like Russia, in which an exportable literature is relatively new: "I am primitive because I belong to a beginning phase." He also claims that his technical innovations are attempts at systematizing what has already been formed in Brazil, that they do not create but reflect a reality (linguistic and other) of which writers and other intellectuals have not yet become entirely aware because they have been too preoccupied with whether Brazilian productions measure up to, or are sufficiently distinctive from, European ones. In other words, he claims for his work an independence from current literary trends which parallels the independence he wishes for his country, but which his very intellectual development, his library, his friends' trips to Paris for inspiration and verification, must deny. With his primitive heroes, his revolutionary language, and his claims of isolation and independence he creates a useful fiction from within which he can recount certain developments in his land; it is a little like the useful fictions of isolation that allow scientists to study certain phenomena in their laboratories. Rather than turning his eyes upon the world and trying to adapt its offerings to a Brazilian reality defined as insufficient and incomplete, he looks upon what Brazil has to offer in isolation. He claims that this entity Brazil, which he tries to capture, has already produced a typical idiom to express a typical reality, and that he is just tapping a flourishing and till then neglected popular culture, not out of a desire to abandon his intellectual formation, but in order to give a more accurate account of the level at which the differentiating elements of nationality are to be found. The wording of his explanations shows that in his presentation the linguistic element is privileged, and that it is programmatically subjected to a reevaluation: "When I started to write wrong Portuguese, didn't I immediately announce that I was making a Brazilian grammar, with which announcement I simply intended to show that I was not improvising, but doing something thought out and systematic . . . ?" In his use of it, the opposition right/wrong appears with its values reversed, and comes to stand for the political dichotomy between national and alien, for the logical one between false and true, and for the epistemological one between random and systematic: the positive value of rationality is attributed, not to traditional criteria for judging literature and language, but to their reevaluation. His reversals of customary evaluation do not affect all dichotomies in the same way—system and rationality are positive, as is "wrong" grammar—and this may be one reason why Mário de Andrade had to spend so much effort dissociating himself from the more anarchic antics of Oswald de Andrade and his group, whose efforts arise from a much more naive concept of primitivism, of its authentic presence in Brazil, and of its representativeness of Brazilian culture. In the end, Mário de Andrade's work on language and on the integration of popular culture in learned discourse had the same abrasiveness and destructiveness as that of the Anthropophagists, and has proved more lasting; at the time, however, it too could be mistaken for a fall into chaos rather than an attempt at a new, subversive order.

However, both authors are linked in that they appropriate the European rebellion against received forms and turn it into a sign of nationalistic affirmation. As a rebellion, it promises a language free from compromise with established internal or external power structures in which to redefine national reality. But by the same token it depends upon those same structures to establish the scope and orientation of its opposition. In *Macunaíma,* Mário de Andrade attempts to evade the dilemma: he uses Indians and the language of exoticism to characterize Brazilianness but his work redefines the enterprise in the way in which it modifies, in use, the old signifiers of nationality. He tries to codify the relation between an authentic national expression and the language of exoticism, and to confront the problematic relation between a national character defined as unique and the ethical or esthetic paradigms which, not being unique, yet, because they are current and established, guarantee the intelligibility and legitimacy of such a definition.

The enterprise is problematic because exoticism is a category in the discourse of power. It is the way in which the more powerful speak of the less powerful, and also the way in which the less powerful speak of themselves in order to be heard by those whose attention is necessary to the process of self-assertion and self-definition. Exoticism allows the holders of the language to set terms in which others will talk about themselves, and thus to hold their differences at bay, to control and domesticate that which might, in the discourse of others, represent a challenge to the ethical justification, or to the actuality of their own power. The past provides an illustration of the demands of exoticism in the contrast between the reception of Fenimore Cooper's *Notions of the Americans,* which attempts to speak of America in terms Europeans were used to applying to themselves, and of the Leatherstocking tales, which speak of America in terms of exoticism: the former was execrated at its publication and is now forgotten, but the latter made their author into an international best-seller and the creator of a national American literature. Thus the exoticism of certain literatures is inevitable, since the discourse of power defines the terms in which they can be spoken. They face the problem of how to articulate differ-

ence or identity, even for internal consumption, within an externally established set of meanings and values.

Macunaíma chooses to turn exoticism on its head. By following very closely the collection of tales about the original Taulipang trickster Macunaíma, published by [Theodor] Koch-Grünberg in *Vom Roroima zum Orinoco,* Mário de Andrade models his discourse on the discipline of ethnology, which could claim to be value-neutral. Thus his Indian protagonist is offered, not as a representative of primitive virtue who will redeem a tired and corrupt civilization (as were Alencar's heroic Indians), but as a malicious innocence redefined into enlightened provocation that will make a tired and corrupt civilization more aware of itself. Macunaíma is free from the European-imposed, and formerly Brazilian-accepted load of virtue and villainy that burdened previous literary Indians; he is the prototype for a recognizable national character that defines itself not as either in conformity, or in opposition to, some European model, but as characteristically undefinable. A "hero without any character at all," as he is identified in the subtitle, Macunaíma is subversive of moral, psychological, and literary orders, and at the same time indicative of an alternative structuration. The refusal to define a modern man by recourse to a psychology of easily identifiable characteristics, the introduction of immotivation into the vocabulary available for the presentation of literary characters, are themselves traits that distinguish modernist texts from those they set themselves against. If one wants to invoke the *Zeitgeist,* one can mention that Musil's *Mann ohne Eigenschaften* was being written at the same time as *Macunaíma.* But Mário de Andrade used this redefinition of literary character, whether he too invented it, or whether he picked up the idea from some of

Grande Otelo as Macunaíma in the 1969 film adaptation of Andrade's novel.

his extensive reading, for a purpose traditional in Brazilian literature: the definition of nationality.

In part this conjunction of the new and the traditional in the work was as important in determining the ready acceptability of the book as was the author's personal position in a group of artists who, well placed in the local social hierarchy, were exercising the recognized and accepted role of revolutionizers and revitalizers of the intellectual landscape. These artists prepared the way for the intellectual acceptance of the change from an agrarian to an industrial economy, the growth of the cities and shift of populations, the influx of immigrants. All of these reopened the possibility, probably not as visible since Independence, for the insertion of Brazil in a more prominent position in the international concert of nations. This integrative function takes place whether Mário de Andrade is for or against the changes taking place: the fact that **Macunaíma** incorporates the phenomena of change and raises the problems they cause is what makes the narrative pivotal not only in the development of Brazilian literature, but more generally, in the development of a language in which the country can speak of itself in its new garb.

The thread from which Macunaíma's adventures loosely hang is his voyage from the small Indian village where he is born to São Paulo and back, in a loop whose squiggles and curlicues cover almost the entire Brazilian territory. At first he is simply fleeing from hunger; later he is on a quest for the magic stone given him by the woman he married and lost. The flight, which has Macunaíma and his brothers abandoning their home of famine and discord, eventually becomes subsumed in the quest, and that allows Mário de Andrade to transport his hero from North to South without making him a refugee: what he seeks is valuable, but what he abandons is not value-less. Throughout, Mário de Andrade refuses to establish hierarchies: Macunaíma lives in a world of levelled values which embraces not only all the regions of the country, their people and stories, but also all events and decisions.

Macunaíma marries a spirit of the forest. After giving him much pleasure and a child who dies, she is sucked dry by a snake and climbs into heaven. The magic stone she had given him ends up in the hands of a capitalist and adventurer with the vaguely Italo-American name of Venceslau Pietro Pietra, who lives in São Paulo and is also the giant Piaimã of Amazonian Indian mythology. In his quest for the stone, Macunaíma is like a traditional hero of epics and folktales. He does not, however, have the usual heroic qualifications: at the inception or climax of any given action, bellicose or romantic, he is as likely as not to yawn, "I feel sooo lazy," and go to sleep. He pursues his enemy only fitfully, and does what he can to avoid meeting him "man to man," by dressing up as a French prostitute or by sending in a surrogate. When he meets a monster, he flees, like a sensible person, but certainly not like a hero. He eats too much and is cheerfully incapable of resisting any temptation of the flesh. When forced to fight, he resorts to ruses, but even so he is one of the more vincible figures in literature. He is a trickster of flickering cleverness and innocent malice, charming, guileful, unpredictable, irresponsible, stubborn, lewd: one could not derive

from him anything like a traditional literary character, or from his motives and actions anything like a code of preferred behavior. On the contrary, he negates the steadiness, reliability, and goal-orientedness necessary to achieve the kind of success that depends on hard work and delay of gratification, and with that his laziness becomes a challenge to power. Macunaíma is of many minds, and follows them all, challenging also traditional notions of character, plot, causality, and verisimilitude. Thus he throws into question the qualities needed for success as defined in the world that calls him primitive. At the same time, however, his subversion of literary and conceptual categories falls into a known category: he is an anti-hero, transposed into the primitive mode; the primitive, however, is another known category thought to capture the essence of the New World.

In this double characterization Macunaíma is shown not as model, but as instance: he refers to the myth of the primitive and demythifies it. He dribbles past the demands that Western literary and ideological traditions place upon the primitive, because he cannot be considered either a noble or a redemptive creation: he is not Adam before the fall, but the unsayable id. But he also dribbles past the more recent association attached to the anti-hero because he is not in opposition to any well-known literary figure, but an alternative to it; he is not the hope of a tired and disillusioned civilization that can find renewal, because it can still find itself, in denial, but the denial of that very need. His antics do not foreground the problems of good or evil, of conformity to tradition or of freedom acquired by experimentation on the borders of the acceptable or imaginable; they evade those problems. Macunaíma does not do what is good or evil, what will make him progress or remain backward; he does what will get him into or out of trouble, what will bring him pleasure, cause him pain, or throw him into danger.

He is born as aware of his surroundings as Oskar in *The Tin Drum;* with just as little child-like innocence, he seduces his sister-in-law by turning himself from an insufferable brat at home into a gorgeous young man in the forest (she gladly suffers beatings from her husband to protect her pleasure with little Macunaíma). Later, when he is wandering in the forest with his brothers, he kills, more or less by chance, a monster who is threatening a young maiden. When the monster's head pursues him to offer its everlasting magical services, he flees ignominiously and never lets it get close enough to make the offer. Macunaíma is not noble and courageous; he is not a defender of helpless women; he does not uphold the values of the family; he is not even alert enough to profit from magic help when it is offered him. He is Other. The antidote he would offer to a tired Western civilization is not that of its own neglected virtues; what he brings to the growing metropolis of São Paulo is not the higher morality of a simpler life.

The episode with Vei, the sun (Chapter 8), contextualizes Macunaíma's otherness in literary and ideological terms. He finds himself in one of the classic fairy-tale trial situations: he is promised wealth and one of the sun's daughters for a wife, if he stays on a little island off Rio and keeps away from women for one whole day while the sun goes on her round. He complies for a while, then becomes restless, goes out to explore the city and falls in, and into bed, with a Portuguese fishwife, recently immigrated. As he is caught, he loses his chance of making something of himself, and from there on the sun punishes him, and at several other points in the tale mercilessly burns his back. The passage can be read allegorically: incapable of delaying gratification; innocent in the pursuit of sensual pleasure; ready to yield to the appeal of the best, but also the most undemanding, that the former colonial power can offer him, Macunaíma shows some of the most charming and also some of the most destructive traits generally attributed to the Brazilian character. Because of that he forfeits the opportunity to become as successful as the heroes of the former colony to the North, that was already raising questions about the values of alternative cultures. Macunaíma loses his chance to make the tropical sun work for his advancement and justifies the association of the tropics with irresponsible backwardness. In this reading, the conjunction of the Iberic heritage and the merciless sun condemns him to a hand-to-mouth existence, narrated in his eventual return from the developed city of São Paulo (whose development is thus also thrown into question), to the Amazonian forest, where he dies. However, the allegorical reading disregards the surface texture of the tale. The writing and the details of the episode are full of wit; the description of a Macunaíma covered with bird-droppings washed and put to dry by Vei on the island off Rio; the zest with which the hero explores the city and "plays" with the fishwife, and the implication that the condition imposed by the sun is unreasonable, counterbalance the regret at the lost opportunity and confirm the value of Macunaíma's refusal to play the game of "order and progress." That positivistic motto, which graces the Brazilian flag, the chapter seems to say, expresses neither the reality nor the authentic aspirations of the nation.

Macunaíma subverts the usual order of things not only by shuffling hierarchies and values, but also by blurring the boundaries that help organize thought and identity. In line with the traditional view Brazil has of itself as a place of exemplary race relations, where differences in color are absorbed into a multi-hued national culture, *Macunaíma* blurs the distinctions between the races. Its hero is born black, "son of the fear of the night." A bath in a magic pool makes him white, and turns his brother Jiguê's skin copper-colored, while his second brother, Maanape, remains black because the other two used up all the magic water. The races that make up the population are thus shown to have the same family origin; their differences are accidental. Later, Macunaíma enlists the help of the African spirit Exu, who had descended upon a young Polish woman, to win his first victory over the giant Piaimã and Mário de Andrade, who includes himself and several of his friends in the scene, is able at the same time, to complete the cycle of representation of his hero as encompassing all races, to include in one scene the cultural contributions of several population groups, to refer to characteristically Brazilian religious synchretism, and to make fun of Macunaíma's usual incompetence. When Macunaíma leaves the ceremony at which the "possession" took place, in the company of the author's friends, Mário de Andrade also blurs the boundaries between fantasy and extra-literary reality. Macunaíma's transformation and the ritual scene refer to the casual treatment of race, believed, both internally and abroad, to be one of the most striking characteristics distinguishing Brazil from other nations, and reaffirm one of the most emphatically stressed Brazilian characteristics and values. One notes, however, that when he bathes in the magic pool, Macunaíma becomes not just white, but precisely tall and blond, as is the woman receiving the African spirit: Mário de Andrade's text registers the common Brazilian self-characterization as a nation where all races are equal and equally respected, while the details he chooses for his representation contradict the central, privileged message. In its illustration of the ideology of racial harmony, Macunaíma accords with part of the reality of the composition of Brazilian national consciousness; in the choice of terms expressing this accord, however, Mário de Andrade incorporates a set of observable data contradicting the ideological representation. The clash between the two is as much as part of what is characteristically national as are the clashing elements. This layering of contradictory references also serves to strip the African ceremony of its exoticism by removing it from a system of simple oppositions between primitive and European cultures.

In the works of Mário de Andrade's predecessor Alencar, the violence attendant upon the contact between different peoples in the Americas appears as a sort of background volume, like the noise of the kettledrums in a romantic symphony, while virtuous and heroic Indians are foregrounded. But when Macunaíma goes to Exu, he does not show or acquire virtue—just effectiveness; the chapter foregrounds violence and then, by making it serve satire, turns it from a condition of extra-literary reality into a tool of literary expression. When Exu, the African trickster god, possesses the young woman of Polish origin, Macunaíma feels a great urge to take part in the rite. He "plays" with the woman while she is in a trance, and thus becomes the "son" of Exu. Then he joins the line of petitioners asking favors of the god in the woman: a butcher wanting people to buy his tainted meat (granted), a lover asking that his girl be given a teaching job so they can get married (granted), a farmer wishing his farm freed of ants and malaria (not granted), a doctor asking for the ability to write elegant Portuguese (not granted); the witty formulation of these matters just barely keeps under control of satire the cruelty of rape and dishonesty. The levelling of values, the demythification of the hero, and the deromanticizing of the exotic all coalesce when Macunaíma asks Exu to make Venceslau Pietro Pietra/Piaimã suffer. Macunaíma then wins his first victory over the giant, who is transported into the medium's body, thrashed and tortured till Exu himself cries out and the woman lies half-dead on the ground. At intervals, the narrator repeats: "It was horrible." At the end, a modified, vaguely sacrilegious recital of the Lord's Prayer restores Exu and the woman to health, while the giant lies on the floor of his palace, howling, gored and beaten, burnt and cut, bleeding and foaming at the mouth. Exu leaves. Among the others who leave is a group known to have once accompanied Mário de Andrade to such a ceremony; the author's name has been replaced with that of Macunaíma.

With this blurring of boundaries—between races, religions, literary and extra-literary reality, author and creature—Mário de Andrade characterizes otherness, and questions the definitions of the world as known and accepted; he also avoids exoticism, not only because by dismantling the comfortable and accustomed order of things he dismantles the thisness against which otherness measures itself, but also because the explicit violence of the process makes it difficult to accept the otherness as redemptive of the discomforts of the familiar. The specific ingredients of the anarchic stew he concocts are a recognizable part of everyday Brazilian life, and the satire that spices it serves to link it to a reality with which readers are familiar and of which they can be expected to disapprove. But the violence of the incidents described and their satirical intention also work against the movement toward internal exoticism that Bopp mentions, and make the typical into a source of discomfort as much as a reason for pride in uniqueness. *Macunaíma* throws all values into question, including the one which might be expected to underlie its own creation: the affirmation of national identity.

A similar form of estranging integration is the result of the "degeographication" of which Mário de Andrade speaks in his Prefaces to *Macunaíma.* The hero's origins and adventures make geographical boundaries irrelevant to the definition of a national character. Macunaíma is born somewhere in the Guianas, while his opponent, Piaimã is from somewhere else: in the Taulipang myth his name means "stranger." The spirits who help and annoy the hero are from anywhere in South America or Africa. His heritage, as promised by Vei (but not delivered) is, as in the Brazilian saying, Europe, France and Bahia ("Oropa França e Bahia . . . ") The language in which his tale is told consists of a large number of words of Amerindian origin, of Africanisms, gallicisms, anglicisms, and regional expressions from everywhere in the country, in such a linguistic riot that a reader, while recognizing all as Brazilian, and delighted at finding childhood words lost in the homogenization of schools and standard written language, will also find it difficult to read the specialized vocabulary of his fellow-countrymen's childhood words. The three great spheres of Macunaíma's activities—the forest, the countryside, the city—are independent of national boundaries: in the book they co-exist, as in the domain of the giant Piaimã, whose house is an urban palace in the middle of a rural sylvan grotto, developed by an English company in the city of São Paulo. Thus, on one hand, degeographication is an expansive force, and allows Macunaíma to chase and be chased over the entire Brazilian territory, from forest to town to field in one paragraph, madly galloping through the folk tales, customs and idioms of the entire country. On the other hand, degeographication is centripetal, showing the possibility—at a time when the first great push for industrialization was concentrating in São Paulo a mad jumble of peoples from the entire world and from all levels of technological development—of an integration of disparate elements, creating a modern version of the traditional view of Brazil as a place where integration is possible.

But, as practiced by Mário de Andrade, this sort of unification is also corrosive, since it implies that the notion of nationality will not be based on the easy patriotism that derives pride and identity from more or less arbitrary national borders. At the only clearly official, patriotic gathering Macunaíma attends, he displaces the designated orator, and by telling an Indian tale immediately accepted by the public, subverts the occasion and deflects feeling away from univocal, official symbols like the flag to "natural" multivalent signs like the constellation of the Southern Cross. Though from the official point of view the abolition of geographic boundaries and the subversion of patriotic occasions introduce disorder into the body politic, within *Macunaíma* the dissolution of these expected distinctions begins to establish a more appropriate basis for a feeling of national affiliation. The play with political boundaries also calls into question the position of the nation in the world: relations, including (or especially) relations between nations, depend on boundaries, and unstable boundaries, like Macunaíma's laziness, disconcert power.

More tellingly, however, Mário de Andrade blurs the accustomed boundaries between nature and culture, the latter represented not so much by all possible products of human activity, as in accordance with the more common classification which assigns to the developed, Western nations the realm of culture, and to those of the New World that of nature. There too, Mário de Andrade deromanticizes the primitive, even while referring to it. When the nations of the New World are placed in the realm of the primitive, they are cast in the role of redeemers of the discontents of the civilized world, and at the same time, and apparently justly, denied the voice and power that are the birthright of civilization. The primitive Macunaíma guards against the excesses of government power, or the evils of a nationalism that turns more or less accidental geopolitical boundaries into matters of pride and criteria for definition; he reinforces the ideals of racial equality on which his nation had always prided itself and through which it had claimed a higher moral status than nations which based their sense of superiority on, and legitimated their economic domination by, a parallel insistence upon preserving the races distinct; he integrates the national territory as no other literary creation had done, and offers a way out of the fragmentation of national literature into a series of competing regionalisms, each with its own claim to representativeness. In the end, however, when confronted with the superior technological sophistication of those who provide the new nations with guns, internal combustion engines, and telephones, he is helpless, and his powers become inadequate, leaving him and what he represents dependent on the providers of these necessities of civilized life.

He might have remained pure by refusing the products of civilization. But this solution is generally chosen by refugees from civilization, and not by those they take refuge with. In São Paulo Macunaíma comes into contact with the technological progress at the center of economic power, and sees the roots of the economic development that Brazil will have to take into consideration both in its claims to parity with, and in its affirmation of difference from the rest of a world that would define it. Unwilling to deny the reality of Brazil's desire for parity, and unable to force the truth by denying the desirability of the products of technology, Mário de Andrade undermines their importance by making the magic of their production accessible to Macunaíma within an entirely different system. When Macunaíma finds out about taxis and telephones and the need for money other than the load of *cacy* he had brought with him from the Amazon, he immediately takes possession of this new world by turning his brother Jiguê into whatever gadget he happens to need at the moment: "He turned Jiguê into the machine telephone, called up the giant Piaimã and called his mother names." He turns his brother into the "machine taxi" when he needs transportation, or, conversely, looks up to the "machine moon" in the sky. And when the need arises, he goes to the Englishmen who own the whiskey, gun, and ammunition orchards and asks them to give their trees a shake for him. Through magic and nerve Macunaíma obtains the products of civilization, and by causing primitive magic to produce telephones and trees to produce guns, Mário de Andrade invalidates distinctions between nature and culture.

But this is the rub: despite his magic and his ability to make the Englishmen shake guns off their trees whenever he wants them to, those trees are still not his, and in the end the episodes freeze him in the same role that his (and presumably the Brazilians') ancestors had filled: he is as incapable as they were of resisting the lure of weapons and firewater that the Europeans had offered them. Thus he remains outside of a historical process in which he could, at least to some extent, dictate the language in which he is spoken. All that remains open to him is the power of use over those artifacts. By subjecting machines to Indian magic and referring to the "machine moon" he eliminates the distinction that had defined his position within the realm of the powerless, and demands a reevaluation of the world. But since he cannot do that in fact from the position of powerlessness which he occupies, Macunaíma becomes, not a figure of actualities, but a fantasy of possibility, an imaginative way of rearranging the world. The anarchy that is his medium cannot realistically be raised to a principle of government and interpretation, an ordering of political and epistemological meanings, but it can at least remind its readers that the arrangements they take for granted are not facts of nature, and that differences are imaginable. Macunaíma represents a subversion by imagination; he has the nerve to posit a different arrangement from that which obtains in a world where he would otherwise be perpetually exotic.

At the end of the book Macunaíma finally beats the giant in a Rabelaisian scene which ends with him swinging madly from a liana in the giant's entrance hall and the giant falling into his own spaghetti sauce pot where he melts together with a multitude of other ingredients into a unified soup. Macunaíma wins back his stone and returns to the place of his birth. But his victory is not apotheotic. When he goes back his friends are gone, he is hungry, the sun beats on his back. His brothers and his women die. He knocks on the doors of various forest spirits for shelter and company, and one of them finally takes pity on him and turns him into a constellation, an arbitrary design imposed upon amorphous eternity.

There is left a story-telling parrot, who wanders off into the distance, on the shoulder of a man to whom it spins the tale of Macunaíma, so it can be told to us. The legacy of the parrot is the innovative, revolutionary language Mário de Andrade invents for his work, incorporating the vocabularies of the many nations that form Brazil, respecting a popular, native syntax and, cultivated man that he never denied being, transforming it into a new, flexible, expressive, recognizably Brazilian literary language. It asserts a cultural independence from the former colonial power, which till then had dominated the former colony's mode of expression, if not its economy, and it opens the way for the possibility of expressing a critical view of the world that is subversive of the customary perception of national reality. That language represents the final and lasting affirmation of Mário de Andrade's work: in it man and parrot, culture and nature, join in the creation of the anarchic Macunaíma who, if he does not solve the problems of exoticism, of domination, of economic and cultural dependency, finally becomes part of what is understood as Brazilianness by creating a different articulation of all these problems, and enters a national mythology through the book that has become one of the basic texts of Brazilian literature. (pp. 99-114)

Renata R. Mautner Wasserman, "Pregüiça and Power: Mário de Andrade's 'Macunaíma'," in Luso-Brazilian Review, *Vol. 21, No. 1, Summer, 1984, pp. 99-116.*

David George   (essay date 1984)

[*In the following excerpt, George discusses* Macunaíma *as a parody of the Portuguese poet Luís de Camões's epic poem* Os Lusíadas *(1572;* The Lusiads).]

Significant studies have been published regarding the structural configuration of **Macunaíma.** It has been compared variously to the mosaic, the fairy tale, the model of composition of Brazilian popular music, and the author himself defined his narrative as a rhapsody. The very structural complexity of Mário de Andrade's work requires a variety of approaches, and it is not my intention to deny the contributions of previous scholars. There is, however, one essential narrative dimension of **Macunaíma** which has not been examined in depth; I refer to the text's epic structure.

It is not unusual to compare novels and other lengthy narratives to the epic. Using loose definitions of the genre such as "the various adventures of a closely watched hero," critics have included a wide variety of prose works within the category of epic and mock epic: *Gone With the Wind, Uncle Tom's Cabin, Tom Jones, Don Quijote.* Studies on the relationship of epic and prose narrative are instructive, but they do not provide a clear analysis of what it meant by epic and therefore fail to illuminate the connections between genres. It is my contention that by defining the epic in terms of a general set of thematic and structural principles one finds embedded in **Macunaíma** echoes of the genre in its variegated forms and stages: tribal chronicle, lays, oral epic, and literary epic, especially *The Lusiads.* Bringing into focus the relationship between Camões' epic and the Brazilian work will demonstrate that *Macunaíma* constitutes in effect a mock epic, a parody. My intention, therefore, is to juxtapose the two works in the light of the epic features outlined below, to show how—and why——the parody functions. First, however, I want to discuss *Macunaíma* in terms of some general notions of epic, to demonstrate that different stages of the genre are indeed embedded in the Modernist rhapsody.

Paul Merchant [in *The Epic*] examines the relationship of history and myth in the epic. In its beginnings the epic is a tribal chronicle. On this most primitive level, *Macunaíma* is the epic chronicle of the Tapanhumas tribe's last member, Macunaíma himself. According to Merchant, history in later stages of the epic often becomes nostalgia for glories past. The Brazilian work satirizes this notion by presenting a decrepit colonial past and its continued existence in the form of neo-colonial exploitation, a topic that I will explore later in this article. Merchant goes on to say that epic history and myths "look back to a period of extraordinary significance in an attempt to define in some way the nature of man and his relationship to the world." In *Macunaíma* Mário de Andrade weaves an elaborate tapestry of myth and history. Utilizing etiological tales and other forms of oral history, the author pushes the boundaries of Brazilian history beyond the colonial beginnings to the period of Amerindian myth. Indeed, he breaks down the barriers between myth and history so that distinctions become a matter of degree. In doing so he attempts to Brazilianize history in the Modernist sense. That is, he creates a kind of oral epic that emphasizes the extra-European origins of Brazilian reality. In the manner of the *Manifesto Antropófago*, *Macunaíma* represents an attempt to shatter Brazil's colonial veneer, and its use of epic forms adds force to that effort. If one considers Mário de Andrade's narrative on some levels a parody of *The Lusiads*, epic structure is clearly a useful means to decolonize national conceptions of art, ontology, and history.

A comparison of the two titles—*Os Lusíadas*/*Macunaíma*—is the first thing that suggests parody, for they possess striking morphological similarities. Although the titles are in some ways alike phonetically, the similarity in phonemic structure is especially convincing. "Lusíadas" is built on "luso" and is thus the epic chronicle of the Portuguese people. If one surmises that "macunaíma," a legendary Indian name, is based on the tribal designation "macuna," then the Modernist work becomes a chronicle not only of an Indian hero but of a tribe and by extension of Amerindian civilization itself. The parallels with *The Lusiads* become even clearer upon examination of epic structure.

Several major categories that pertain to the epic in general but particularly to the literary epic *The Lusiads*:

The epic is dominated by a hero with a purpose or quest who embodies the ideals of a people or nation and who must surmount great obstacles to fulfill his quest and to achieve heroic stature.

The hero of the oral epic has superhuman stature; he fights and is ready to die for individual glory and honor. The hero of the literary epic represents a highly organized society with no room for individualism; his heroic sacrifice and glory consist in his service to the state or empire. The hero of the oral epic (e.g., Roland) is [according to C. M. Bowra in his *From Virgil to Milton*] a "noble barbarian," representing the heroic ideal of "societies that have burst through the stiff forms of primitive societies." Vasco da Gama, hero of the literary epic *The Lusiads*, achieves heroic stature by fulfilling his duties to a complex and highly organized civilization, a budding empire ruled by the monarch Sebastian, and built by conquering worlds inhabited by barbarians.

Mário de Andrade manipulates the notion of epic hero in an ironic fashion, for he has created a *herói sem nenhum caráter* (hero with no character). Both oral and literary epic heroes represent highly moral qualities: rectitude, honor, and courage. Macunaíma is an amoral character: one may say that his actions and concerns lie outside the scope of Western conceptions of morality. He is akin to the oral epic hero in his individualism, but he is decidedly unheroic. His relation to Vasco da Gama is ironic, for in *The Lusiads* Macunaíma would be an ignoble barbarian, an infidel dog, fit only for conquest or destruction at the hands of the Portuguese hero. If the barbarian is not exactly now in charge, he at least has a fighting chance to survive. Craft and cunning—*experteza, astúcia*—are required for survival. Macunaíma is also lazy. The seemingly negative quality, however, corresponds to what Telê Ancona Lopes calls his *pensée sauvage*, which is creative laziness and fantasy: "perplexed at Cartesian puzzles of unexpected solution, this is the dialectical reason of an undefined personality." Macunaíma's lack of character, his imagination, replace the courage of the epic hero; they help him overcome obstacles and therefore to survive. Survival through imagination should thus be seen as an ideal of the Brazilian people.

The epic hero is inextricably tied to a quest. In Mário de Andrade's rhapsody that notion functions on two levels. Macunaíma's most obvious goal is to rescue the *muiraquitã*, the lost talisman, while the goal of Vasco da Gama in *The Lusiads* is to reach India. In both cases the objective is tangible. There is a further symbolic correspondence in the case of the Brazilian work. The talisman represents the lost Indian roots sought by the hero, as well as the national patrimony appropriated by outside forces, which are symbolized by the foreigner/man-eating monster Venceslau Pietro Pietra/Piaimã. An even more fundamental objective is that Macunaíma, and with him the Brazilian people, must overcome a myriad of obstacles in order to survive. There are plagues, *a sol traiçoeira* (the treacherous sun woman), the beasts and fantastic beings of the forest, and of course the foreign exploiter. The epic hero always fulfills his quest, as does Macunaíma with the rescue of the *muiraquitã*. The question of survival is more ambiguous. And although the hero dies physically, he achieves mythic survival in the form of the constellation Ursa Major.

Macunaíma, then, parodies the concept of epic hero in order to reveal the necessary response of the Brazilian people to their own reality. They do not give their loyalty to the ideal of empire, colony, Western civilization. Those have all meant exploitation.

A fundamental narrative element of the epic is the voyage.

All epic literature contains a narrative core made up of a voyage or voyages. Great epic journeys may be by land or sea. *The Lusiads* tells the story of the great maritime voyages of the Portuguese explorers, and the principal narrative trajectory is Vasco da Gama's opening of the passage to India. The subsequent journey to the Isle of Love is the symbolic reward, administered by Venus and her nymphs, for achievement of the Portuguese quest. Mário de Andrade parodies the Portuguese epic by sending Macunaíma on journeys along the rivers of Brazil, but instead of traveling on a great ship he floats along on a raft.

The Lusiads contains several secondary threads, particularly the voyages to the East that precede and follow those of Vasco da Gama. Mário de Andrade's rhapsody contains many voyages in addition to the attempt to recover the *muiraquitã*. There are constant searches for buried treasure. If one casts a skeptical and reductionist look at the Portuguese explorations they are no more than that; a search for treasure, spices, gold, and slaves. The irony of the parallel deepens if one considers that the buried treasure in *Macunaíma* dates back to the colonial period. Moreover, the treasure hunts of Macunaíma and his brothers constitute a modern reference to financial speculation, the search for a quick profit that characterizes much of economic behavior in dependent countries like Brazil, behavior that continues the economic patterns begun in the age when Brazil was a Portuguese colony.

The supernatural element, the marvellous, is a fundamental aspect of most epics.

The oral epic accepts the marvellous as part of the real world. In the literary epic supernatural elements belong to the realm of fancy, although fancy serves the higher purpose of indirect presentation of the truth.

There are very close parallels between *The Lusiads* and *Macunaíma* in their utilization of the marvellous. Both works refer back to a pagan antiquity in relation to a dominant Catholic ideology. Camões pays a debt to classical antiquity by recreating the mythology of the Olympian gods and giving them a major role in his epic. Catholic ideology, however, forces him to disclaim their reality. They are symbols of cultural, spiritual, and natural forces. Venus becomes the spirit of the West, light and providence, and Bacchus the spirit of the East, darkness and deceit. One aids Vasco da Gama's quest and the other hinders it.

Mário de Andrade also harks back to antiquity, to the mythology of the Amerindian and the Afro-Brazilian. He does so not only in the face of a monolithic Catholic ideology, but against a colonial history of submission to many imported ideologies, both religious and philosophical, from the Catholicism of the Portuguese empire to the Positivism of 19th-century Europe. The important thing is that those ideologies deny the validity of Brazil's pagan antiquity which still lives in the present. Mário de Andrade brings that barbaric antiquity in the very heart of the Brazilian symbol of Western civilization: São Paulo. Whereas Camões attempts to place pagan mythology at the service of Catholic truth, Mário de Andrade allows

Amerindian mythology to possess its own truth and indeed to form the basis of a Brazilian ontology.

There are two supernatural levels in *Macunaíma*: Indian animism and cosmogony and Afro-Brazilian magic. The Brazilian forest is inhabited by fantastic beings and forces, Vei the sun woman, rocks with souls, monsters of all sorts. With supernatural aid the hero becomes a man, turns white, dies, and is resuscitated. Macunaíma and other characters are aggrandized when they become stars or constellations, which creates a Brazilian sky and therefore cosmos. Indian cosmogony is also applied to the great metropolis of São Paulo. The essential element in this cosmogony is the machine (*máquina*), which in an inversion of values becomes a mythical archetype or paradigm. For example, Macunaíma magically turns his brother Jiguê into the *máquina-telefone*. Moreover, the prefix *máquina-* is used for all objects and institutions of the city: *máquina-roupa* (clothing), *máquina-negócios* (business), *máquina-amor* (love), and so forth. That is, Macunaíma reinterprets civilization on the basis of a primitive cosmogonic vision. *Máquina* is transformed into a cosmogonic paradigm: all machines are repetitions or recreations of the archetypal machine. Mário de Andrade thus suggests an ontological definition of Brazil through Indian archetypes, which constitute the deepest roots of national culture.

African magic plays an important role as well. It is through Macumba (Afro-Brazilian magic system) that Macunaíma manages to administer a beating to the man-eating giant Piaimã. The hero is consecrated as a son of Exu and in that way he is aggrandized. [The critic adds in a footnote: "Exu, often associated with the Devil, is known variously in Brazilian Macumba as the messenger of the gods, the Trickster, and the Man of the Crossroads."] The narrator makes it clear, moreover, that Macumba pervades all social classes, for he places within the temple of the *mãe-de-santo* (priestess) Tia Cinta members of all social levels, including such Modernist writers as Raul Bopp and Manuel Bandeira.

A number of supernatural beings that play an important role in *Macunaíma* can be compared to those of Camões' epic. Venus and Vei possess a phonetic relationship, and their characteristics and narrative functions are similar. Both figures are related to a celestial body—the morning star and the sun, respectively—that serves to guide the hero on his journey. Both represent light on many levels: the light of a heavenly body and the light of Western civilization and Vei the dazzling light of tropical civilization. Both are accompanied by lesser female entities who have an erotic dimension, Venus and her nymphs and Vei and her daughters of light. While the former reward the Portuguese on the Isle of Love, Vei and her daughters provide warmth and comfort for the hero on a deserted isle in Guanabara Bay. The isle had formerly been inhabited by a nymph, which makes the parallel even more striking. Vasco da Gama is Venus' chosen one. Macunaíma is Vei's; she wishes to make him her son-in-law. Camões makes it clear that Vasco da Gama deserves Venus' aid because of his heroic qualities. If Mário de Andrade's protagonist is a parody of the epic hero, it follows that his lack of heroic qualities will influence his relationship with Vei. That is precisely what happens. Macunaíma's infidelity brings down upon him the wrath and vengeance of the sun woman, which leads in the end to his destruction. And the Indian hero's demise symbolizes that of Amerindian civilization.

In a manner similar to the parallels between Venus and Vei, there is a parodic relationship between Bacchus and Exu. Both represent malevolent forces of darkness. Bacchus symbolizes the evils of the East, particularly infidel Africa, that which is non-Christian and non-European. He represents forces which either hinder the Portuguese colonial venture or are swallowed up by it. Exu is identified with the devil, and his origin is African. His continuance in Brazil subverts the colonial order, and Mário de Andrade clearly utilizes him to that end. In the Macumba ceremony, Exu is Macunaíma's vehicle for vengeance against Piaimã/Venceslau, the symbol of neo-colonialist exploitation. By placing the Bacchus-like Exu on the side of Macunaíma, Mário de Andrade parodies one of *The Lusiads'* fundamental narrative devices and overturns the ideology of Christian imperialism.

Camões is forced by the pressures of Catholic ideology to claim that his supernatural creatures are the stuff of allegory. Although the fantastic beings that inhabit Mário de Andrade's rhapsody have many symbolic references, they are assigned a place in the world of here-and-now. Quite consciously and aggressively, the Modernist work strikes a blow against Catholic ideology and other forms of imposed culture.

The language of the literary epic is sublime.

Bowra makes several distinctions between oral and literary epics on the basis of technique. Mário de Andrade uses oral and literary epic techniques. **Macunaíma** includes features of the oral epic such as stock phrases, repetitions, formulas, epithets, and recurring themes that are the machinery of improvisational story-telling. The work also displays the variation and dense texture of literary epics.

Colin Smith states [in his 1972 edition of the *Poema de mío Cid*] that epic style is sublime, its tone is elevated. That is certainly the case with *The Lusiads*. In fact, *língua de Camões* (language of Camões) was a standard for much of Brazilian letters until early in the 20th century. That standard had fossilized by Mário de Andrade's time into a taste for Latinized syntax and other forms of linguistic pedantry. The Modernists' search for Brazilian language was in large part a reaction to *língua de Camões,* which they parodied. Mário de Andrade not only mocks the latter-day imitators of Camões, he goes to the very source *The Lusiads,* for his parody, and it is in the chapter entitled "Carta pràs Icamiabas" ("Letter to the Icamiabas," the women of Macunaíma's tribe), where he exposes the fossilization of the Latinized linguistic system.

The "carta" itself has many parallels with *The Lusiads*. For example, there is a long section in the Portuguese epic (cantos III-IV) which Vasco da Gama narrates. The Brazilian hero is the narrator of the "carta". Camões' entire epic is a sort of report to the king on the strange customs and beliefs in the new lands. The point of view is that of the emissary from civilization observing the barbarians.

The "carta" is a report of the new land of São Paulo from the Emperor of the Virgin Forest to his subjects. The point of view is that of the barbarian observing civilization.

A less obvious dimension of the parody is the use of folkloric modes with a strong Indian and African influence in vocabulary and syntax, which the surveyors of *língua de Camões* denigrated. Those modes are in general a component of the Modernist conception of an autochthonous Brazilian literary language.

Other linguistic processes of the epic are parodied in **Macunaíma.** One of the salient characteristics of *The Lusiads* is the so-called catalogue or enumeration. There are catalogues of Portuguese heroes, great feats, historical events, and royal lineage. Mário de Andrade's text incorporates catalogues of parrots, ants, monkeys, plagues and *artes de brincar* (arts of love-making), elements of Brazilian reality that have little to do with sublimity. The author, however, confers upon his catalogues a kind of national sublimity by placing them within a musical structure. That is, they constitute variations on Brazilian themes; they are another piece in the mosaic, a passage in the rhapsody.

The epic world is always masculine: military code, leadership, courage.

Mário de Andrade parodies the epic vision of masculinity and military code at every turn. When danger appears, his hero usually flees. In the battle against Venceslau to recover the lost talisman the hero avoids open combat. Although he goes into the countryside to seek strength (*campear força*) like a traditional epic hero, to achieve victory he utilizes the weapons of the barbarian, the primitive: cunning and magic.

Camões, according to Bowra, follows the chivalrous epic: jousts, tournaments, damsels in distress, and gallant knights. Mário de Andrade parodies all this. The "damsel" Ci actually beats up the hero. Instead of defending her honor he rapes her, with the help of his brothers of course.

There is no doubt that Mário de Andrade's rhapsody portrays an essentially masculine universe, since the main characters are Macunaíma and his two brothers, Maanape and Jiguê. But women appear at every turn, from the hero's mother and the women of the forest to the prostitutes of São Paulo. The only truly military figure is Ci, Mother of the Forest, an effort to undo the identification of the epic masculine principle. To clarify Mário de Andrade's purpose, the *Manifesto Antropófago* bears further mention at this point.

Subversion of the masculine code is closely related to the concept of utopian matriarchy elucidated in the *Manifesto Antropófago*. By that Oswald de Andrade means a future world of child-like happiness in which instinctual liberation and Eros would reign. In the utopian matriarchy the feminine principle would hold sway over the masculine. The guiding force, in Jungian terms, would be anima: imagination, intuition, unconscious, and in general the irrational and nonlinear mentality of the primitive. To achieve that state it would be necessary to overcome the legacy of colonialism and catechism, embodied in the masculine principle of animus: reason, instinctual repression, and linear mentality. [The critic adds in a footnote: "By catechism Oswald de Andrade means imposed dogma, repressive moral codes, and Metropolitan linguistic codes."]

There is treachery, but good triumphs in the end.

Vasco da Gama and the *lusos* who accompany him in the search for a maritime route to India must contend with the treachery of Bacchus and his African allies. The Portuguese triumph in the end with the aid of Venus. Macunaíma must confront three types of treachery: that of men, the foreigner Venceslau; that of nature, plague; that of supernatural forces. The hero without a character has three weapons at his command to combat treachery: magic, cunning, and flight. According to the norms of the epic, triumph would be fulfillment of the quest, recovery of the *muiraquitã,* as well as survival. The notion of epic triumph is subverted because though the hero regains the talisman, he loses it in the end. He dies a final physical death due to the treachery of Vei and the phantom Ujara, but also because of his own lust. Everything in **Macunaíma** is parodied and mitigated. Since there is no hero properly speaking, there is no absolute treachery. The lack of physical survival and of triumph over treachery brings to mind one of the work's essential paradoxes. In a book filled with phantasmagoria, magic, creation myths, and surrealism what stands out is the skeptical, demystifying, and cruelly realistic vision of Brazil. That is, Mário de Andrade portrays a land without heroics, where disease and hunger take their toll, there is cruelty toward fellow men, and foreign domination holds sway. One can conclude from the text that triumph over treachery would mean an end to injustice, survival of the native Brazilian ethos, and the nation's effective independence from foreign domination, both economic and cultural. That triumph is still in the balance.

The hero is temporarily removed from society, from civilization; he achieves greatness in isolation, in the wilderness; he is acclaimed upon his return.

Vasco da Gama separates himself voluntarily from Portuguese society; he achieves greatness in isolation (he reaches India); but he is not acclaimed so much upon his return as on the Isle of Love, a fantastic place. The Brazilian hero is separated temporarily from society (the Virgin Forest) because of treachery (Venceslau's usurpation of the talisman). In isolation he achieves a kind of greatness: he is consecrated a *filho de exu* (son of Exu), a chosen one, he recovers the talisman, and he slays the giant. Upon his return to the Virgin Forest, however, there is no acclamation. Macunaíma finds the village deserted, and only a single parrot remains to recount the hero's feats. As in the case of *The Lusiads* acclamation comes from outside the world, but in the form of astral metamorphosis.

Mário de Andrade parodies the epic principle in this case by reversing the relative positions of civilization and wilderness, or "barbarism", which Sarmiento denominated *civilización y barbarie.* Civilization is to be found in the forest, which early in the book coincides in many ways with the Tupi Golden Age imagined by Oswald de Andrade in the *Manifesto Antropófago.* [The critic adds in a

footnote: "The pre-colonial Golden Age envisioned by Oswald de Andrade was characterized by equal sharing of goods, instinctual liberation, and the unhindered pursuit of pleasure."] Macunaíma's abandonment of his society symbolizes the Amerindian's loss of his edenic universe as a result of Portuguese incursions. My contention here is that Venceslau represents the colonizer, formerly associated with "civilization". The city of São Paulo itself becomes for the hero wilderness (*barbarie*), a dehumanized place where, "os homens é que eram máquinas e as máquinas é que eram homens" (men were machines and machines were men). The city is the focus of the colonial legacy against which Oswald de Andrade rails in the *Manifesto Antropófago:* pedantry, dogma, and authoritarianism. The deserted village that the hero discovers on his return symbolizes the destruction under colonialism of the aboriginal civilization. That civilization and its ontology persist in legend, disseminated by the parrot at the end of the book. I have discussed above the continuing significance of primitive ontology in Mário de Andrade's vision of Brazil. In the author's inversion of the epic formula, then Macunaíma's civilization corresponds to the barbarous lands in *The Lusiads* that are the object of colonization.

Epics are usually poems of hope.

The principle deals with the fundamental question of the future. In the case of oral epics like *El Cid Campeador* there is no doubt: the poem suggests a vision of great hope in a glorious Castilian future; the reconquest is in full swing; the process of national consolidation has begun under the aegis of the Castilian banner. The case of *The Lusiads* is less clear. There is hope, because the work narrates the beginning of the colonial adventure. At the same time, there is pessimism because Camões composed his epic during the early stages of Portuguese decline. The case of **Macunaíma** is perhaps more ambiguous. There is certainly optimism and hope in the attempt to formulate a conception of the national character and to establish a Brazilian literary language. But there is pessimism, almost a note of despair: plague—*os males do Brasil*—, foreign economic domination, the disappearance of the aboriginal culture. The ending is in itself equivocal. The return to the primordial expresses a tone of sadness, *saudades,* desolation. However, that may also represent a *tabula rasa:* a new Brazil may now be created. Furthermore, the creations of this new Brazil can be exported. [The critic adds in a footnote: "The reader will recall that at the end of the book Macunaíma's story is carried to Portugal by a parrot."] One of the fundamental intentions of Modernism was to export Brazilian art, which would reverse the pattern of imposition and imitation in Brazil of foreign cultural models. To this date, that intention has been only partially fulfilled.

I conclude from the evidence I have presented that **Macunaíma** deserves an expanded structural definition, based on epic principles, as well as a new generic description, that of mock-epic. Merchant places within the genre such works as *Don Quijote, Tom Jones, Tristam Shandy,* as well as the picaresque tradition. One could add to that list a Spanish American work: Lizardi's *El Periquillo Sar-*

niento. Mario de Andrade's rhapsody therefore heirs to a very distinguished tradition.

I have attempted in this article to shed further light on the structural complexities of what many consider to be the outstanding work of Brazilian Modernism. By overturning epic principles and the ideology of *The Lusiads,* *Macunaíma* ridicules the national penchant for imitation of and reverence for imported literary forms. Mario de Andrade's work points the way toward the establishment of an autochthonous literature founded on both the primitive roots of Brazilian ontology and the diversity of national culture. (pp. 41-50)

> David George, " 'Macunaima', a Parody of 'The Lusiads'?" in Chasqui, Vol. 14, No. 1, November, 1984, pp. 41-52.

Nancy Gray Díaz   (essay date 1988)

[*In the following excerpt, Díaz examines the theme of metamorphosis in* Macunaíma.]

In [Alejo Carpentier's] *El reino de este mundo* and [Miguel Angel Asturias's] *Hombres de maíz,* the novel as genre engages myth as paradigm and myth-making as historical process. Reverence for myth enters Carpentier's novella as motive for political change and founds Asturias' novel as precious primordial element vital to the survival of culture. Mário de Andrade's novel *Macunaíma,* on the other hand, although it too grows out of mythical and legendary material, belongs to a different narrative tradition subsumed by the novel, that of satire. Less interested in the social and historical conditions in which Brazilian Indians live than in their legends, music, and dance, Andrade recasts selected folkloric material—especially legends of the Taulipang and Arekuná peoples of Northwest Brazil and Venezuela, collected by Theodor Koch-Grünberg in *Vom Roroima zum Orinoco*—in such a way as to create a pan-Brazilian hero/anti-hero and to signal, to lament, and to deride certain aspects of Brazilian national life and character. Haroldo de Campos, one of several outstanding interpreters of *Macunaíma,* has analyzed the novel in the light of Vladimir Propp's *Morphology of the Folktale.* According to Campos [in his *Morfologia do Macunaíma*], at the same time that Propp was studying the Russian folktale in order to construct his morphology of the basic elements common to all folktales, Andrade was studying the Brazilian folktale in order to create his meta-tale.

> De fato, operando com sinal inverso em relação a Propp, Mário tratou, por assim dizer, de recombinar as "variantes" de uma fábula virtual, de base, numa polimorfa metafábula. A "polimorfia", salientada por Propp no estudo do seu material, convertia-se, para Mário de Andrade, não numa dificuldade a superar, para fins de clarificação metodológica, mas, precisamente, no horizonte fascinante aberto aos seus desígnios de invenção textual, de "texto-síntese".

> (In fact, operating inversely with relation to Propp, Mário tried, one could say, to recombine the basic "variants" of a potential folktale into a polymorphous metafable. The "polymor-

phousness," emphasized by Propp in the study of his material, became for Mário de Andrade, not a difficulty to overcome, for the purposes of methodological clarification, but rather, precisely, a fascinating horizon open to his designs for textual invention, for a "text-synthesis.")

In his study Campos convincingly demonstrates that Andrade, having grasped the same fundamental structures that Propp systematically delineates, incorporates those structures into *Macunaíma* in such a way as to form an intricately and authentically ordered myth/legend/satire/novel. (pp. 51-2)

Mário de Andrade has referred to *Macunaíma* both as satire and as rhapsody. Although ambivalent about the symbolic nature of his hero, the author admits that by subtitling the work "O herói sem nenhum caráter," he identifies the mode of the novel as satire [in his 1928 preface to *Macunaíma*].

> E resta a circunstância da falta de caráter do herói. Falta de caráter no duplo sentido de indivíduo sem caráter moral e sem caraterístico. Está certo. Sem esse pessimismo eu não seria amigo sincero dos meus patrícios. E a sátira dura do livro. Heroísmo de arroubo é fácil de ter. Porêm o galho mais alto dum pau gigante que eu saiba não é lugar propício prá gente dormir sossegado.

> (And there remains the circumstance of the lack of character of the hero. Lack of character in the double sense of individual without moral character and without characteristic. Yes. Without that pessimism I would not be a sincere friend to my compatriots. This is the tough satire of the book. A rapturous heroism is easy to have. But the highest branch of a gigantic tree which I might know of is not a propitious place for people to sleep peacefully.)

But *Macunaíma* is satire in the original sense of the Latin word *satura* ("mixture") as well. The novel is a mélange, a fusion of extremely disparate levels and regions of discourse. In order to create a sense of pan-Brazilianism, Andrade incorporates words from various Brazilian Indian and African languages as well as street language, formal literary language, technological words, magical and mythical words, baby talk, folk songs, comic words, coined words, and obscenities. Both the thrust of the satire and the daring linguistic mix are meant to shock and unsettle, and they belong rightfully to the literary revolution that characterizes Brazilian Modernism. When Andrade uses the words *rapsodismo* and *rapsódicas* in the first preface to *Macunaíma,* he both explains the style and excuses the sexual explicitness (he calls it pornography) of the book as typical of religious books and popular rhapsodism.

> Quanto a estilo, empreguei essa fala simples tão sonorizada música mesmo por causa das repetições, que é costume nos livros religiosos e dos cantos estagnados no rapsodismo popular. Foi pra fastarem de minha estrada essas gentes que compram livros pornográficos por causa da pornografia. Ora se é certo que meu livro possui além de sensualidade cheirando alguma pornografia e mesmo coprolalia não haverá quem con-

teste no valor calmante do brometo dum estilo assim.

(As for the style, I used such simple, sonorous, musical language exactly because of the repetitions, which are the custom in religious books and of the songs stagnated in popular rhapsodism. It was to drive away those people who buy pornographic books for the sake of the pornography. Now if it is true that my book goes beyond sensuality, smelling of some pornography and indeed of obscenity, there will not be any one who can contest the calming value of the bromide of a style such as this.)

Rhapsody thus refers to the oral, popular, folkloric sources to which *Macunaíma* is heir and also draws on the musical connotations of the term as a composition irregular in form, seemingly an improvisation. The first edition of *Macunaíma* (1928) is specifically called "historia" ("tale"), but Andrade changed the designation of the second edition (1937) to "rapsódia." In the third (1944) and subsequent editions the title page has simply read *Macunaíma: O herói sem nenhum caráter.*

In order for us to clarify the ways in which modern satire interweaves with indigenous legend in the rhapsody, it will be helpful to examine a key episode in some detail. Chapter 8, "Vei a Sol," is based on a Taulipang legend collected by Koch-Grünberg. According to the legend, in ancient times there existed a very high tree. Walo'ma, the frog, climbed to the highest point in the tree. A man named Akalapijeíma waited every afternoon at the foot of the tree to catch the frog. Walo'ma said that if Akal were to catch him, he would throw him into the sea. The man caught him, and Walo'ma dragged the man through the water to an island, leaving him there. The *urubus* (Brazilian black vultures) defecated on him until he was smeared and stinking. Being very cold, Akal appealed to the morning star to take him to the sky, but she refused because he had always offered mandioca cakes to the sun but never to her. Then he asked her for fire and again was told to ask the sun. He asked the moon either to return him to his own land or to give him fire, but the moon also directed him to the sun. Then Wei the sun came and took Akal into his canoe, ordering his daughters to wash him and to cut his hair. Wei wanted him for a son-in-law. Akal asked Wei to warm him, and Wei crowned himself with a headdress of parrot feathers, carrying Akal higher and higher in the sky. When Akal became too hot, Wei gave him clothes to cool him. Wei warned Akal not to involve himself with other women so that he could marry one of the daughters of the sun, but when Akal returned to earth, he fell in love with the daughters of the *urubus.* Wei became very angry and told Akal that if he had followed Wei's advice, he would have stayed young and handsome. Now he would grow old and die. "[Akal] foi nosso ancestral, o pai de todos os índios. Por isso ainda hoje vivemos assim. Ficamos jovens e bonitos por tempo muito curto, tornandonos então feios e velhos" ([Akal] was our ancestor, the father of all of the Indians. That is why we live as we do. We stay young and handsome for a very short time, then become ugly and old).

Andrade closely follows the basic outline of this myth of the loss of immortality, giving the name "Volomã" to the tree itself and making it the antagonist. That is, the vegetation itself is fruitful, yet unyielding. Nevertheless, Macunaíma, cast here in the role of Adam assaulting a reluctant Tree of Life, utters the incantation, "Boiôiô, boiôiô! quizama quizu," which, according to M. Cavalcanti Proença [in his *Roteiro de Macunaíma*], is the Indian name of the tree, and he thereby forces the angry tree to give up its fruits. The tree, in turn, hurls Macunaíma beyond the bay of Guanabara to a deserted island formerly inhabited by Alamoa, an evil nymph who came to Brazil with the Dutch. Macunaíma falls asleep in midair. Like Akal, he is lambasted in his sleep by the *urubus* and wakes up cold. Thus, for violating the first interdiction Macunaíma is punished by being hurled into cold isolation and attacked by the excrement of birds of death. Furthermore, he is asleep and it is night. Alamoa, being associated both with the Dutch colonialists and with greed, is the first sign of foreign intervention in Brazil in the chapter, and Macunaíma has no hesitation in seeking her treasure. Instead of the treasure, however, he finds only a species of ants. He asks the morning star to take him to heaven, but the star answers, "Vá tomar banho" (Go take a bath), thus inventing a common expression used by Brazilians to address certain European immigrants (also an expression of disbelief or discontentment). The moon also refuses to help and directs him to the sun. In the novel Vei is feminine, and she is good to Macunaíma because she remembers that he always offered mandioca cakes to her. The sun and her daughters clean and comfort him, and desiring him for a son-in-law, the sun offers him "Oropa, França e Bahia" as a dowry if he will renounce other women. Soon after their arrival in Rio de Janeiro, however, Macunaíma, left alone, takes up with a Portuguese woman. In defiance he declares, "Pois que fogo devore tudo! . . . Não sou frouxo agora pra mulher me fazer mal" (To hell with everything!. . . . I'm not so flabby that a woman can hurt me). Then he utters what will be his definitive and repeated denunciation of the evils by which his country is beset. "POUCA SAUDE E MUITO SAUVA, OS MALES DO BRASIL SAO" (Too little vigor and too many ants are the troubles of Brazil). Just as in the legend, when Vei discovers his betrayal, she tells him he has lost his chance for immortality. He protests that he was lonely and "if he had only known." Vei then gives him the Vató stone, but he trades it for a picture in the paper.

Thus, in the novel the sun grants several benefits to Macunaíma and holds out the promise of more. She cleans and purifies him, symbolically restoring him to life. She offers him love, leisure, contentment, and, implicitly, immortality. She also brings him to the city. There he finds his own companionship and has no need for her stone/fire. . . . Macunaíma trades tropical fulfillment for intercourse with a Portuguese woman, a contravention so powerful that he pays for it not just by aging and by being beset by a monster but also by being mutilated at the end of the novel in Vei's final ambush.

Macunaíma's lack of character thus originates in the legends themselves, but it is carefully and consistently adapted to the modern character of his country. He exploits nature by force, consorts with colonial interests, goes back on his word, trades the durable for the ephemeral, and sets individual desire as the prime motive for action. Andrade, then, not only preserves the beauty and the richness of the Indian legends but also stretches them in such a way as to explore their potential for expressing contemporary psychological, ethical, and political concerns. As in the works of Carpentier and Asturias, a return to indigenous culture in *Macunaíma* opens a new route toward an understanding of modern heterogeneous and colonized culture.

Mutability especially expresses itself in *Macunaíma* by (1) the collapsing of space and time, (2) the operations of manipulative and mythical magic, and (3) the recurrent motif of a lost Golden Age, which, as in Ovid's *Metamorphoses,* gives the sense of entities having formerly been other and of culture in transition.

We do not know the date of Macunaíma's birth. It is lost in the darkness of the primeval forest. Chronology in the first four chapters and in the last three is measured by Macunaíma's personal growth—which is affected several times by magic and metamorphosis so as to obfuscate any perception of natural human development—and by his decline at the end of the story. His constant recourse to popular wisdom and his teachings of Indian belief, indeed his use of magic itself, show Macunaíma to be an original source of ageless knowledge, and we are told at the end that he is the descendant of the *jaboti,* the first of all the races. [The critic adds in a footnote: "The *jaboti* or *jabuti* is a Brazilian fruit-eating land turtle. In 1927 Andrade published a collection of poetry, *Clã do jaboti,* in which he represents the *jaboti* as the totem animal of Brazil."] Furthermore, except for the deepening sadness over the loss of Ci and the changes resulting from the alteration in skin color, Macunaíma's personality experiences very little growth from the beginning of the book to the end. On the other hand, the chapters during which Macunaíma inhabits the city (chapters 5-14) belong to a specific historical period (the mid-1920s), clearly designated by the naming of machines and gadgets of the era. Thus, city time and jungle time are carefully distinguished, the former being characterized as a microcosmic moment in history, the latter as a macrocosmic, mythical process slowly moving toward eventual decline.

In both spheres realistic perceptions of time are constantly subverted, coinciding with subversions of spatial relationships. Here M. M. Bakhtin's concept of chronotope [from his essay "Forms of Time and of the Chronotope in the Novel"] is a useful tool for analysis.

> We will give the name chronotope (literally, "time space") to the intrinsic connectedness of temporal and spatial relationships that are artistically expressed in literature. . . . In the literary artistic chronotope, spatial and temporal indicators are fused into one carefully thought-out, concrete whole. Time, as it were, thickens, takes on flesh, becomes artistically visible; likewise, space becomes charged and responsive to the movements of time, plot and history. This intersection of axes and fusion of indicators characterizes the artistic chronotope.

Macunaíma may be seen to have the following five major chronotopes: (1) the virgin forest, whose passage of time has been described above; (2) the city street, which has also been characterized; (3) the pension that Macunaíma occupies in São Paulo and other enclosed dwellings (the sun's boat, the *malocas* in which Macunaíma lived with his family and with Ci), whose time is defined by Macunaíma's labored interaction with others, his expressions of melancholy, his illnesses; (4) the points of encounter with the Piaimã and other characters who at the same time belong to legend and to the realm of social satire—the cannibals, i.e., the currupira, Ceiuci, Oibê (The most important of these is the house of the giant in São Paulo, to which Macunaíma returns five times. The places are usually situated with a geographical exactness, for example, "Venceslau Pietro Pietra morava num tejupar maravilhoso rodeado de mato no fim da rua Maranhão olhando pra noruega do Pacaembu" [Venceslau Pietro Pietra lived in a marvelous hut surrounded by woods at the end of Maranhão street facing the valley of Pacaembu]. Time in these latter episodes is filled in by frantic action, intrigue and deception, rapid metamorphoses, and the chase); and (5) the sky, about which more will be said later in this chapter.

The fourth chronotope most especially illustrates the collapsing of space and time in *Macunaíma,* and we find one of the important manifestations of this chronotope in chapter 11, "A Velha Ceiuci." Toward the end of this chapter Macunaíma goes fishing in the Tieté and is caught by Ceiuci, the Piaimã's wife. Rescued by her younger daughter, who then becomes a comet, Macunaíma sets out to flee the old woman, who is the *caapora* (an evil forest goblin).

This chase returns us to . . . the opposition set forth by Carpentier between authentic American magic and the so-called contrived magic of Surrealism. Macunaíma starts out from the giant's house in São Paulo on horseback.

> Caminhou caminhou caminhou e já perto de Manaus ia correndo quando o cavalo deu uma topada que arrancou chão. No fundo do buraco Macunaíma enxergou uma coisa relumeando. Cavou depressa e descobriu o resto do deus Marte, escultura grega achada naquelas paragens inda na Monarquia e primeiro-de-abril passado no Araripe de Alencar pelo jornal chamado Comércio do Amazonas. Estava comtemplando aquele torso macanudo quando escutou "Baúa! Baúa!". Era a velha Ceiuci chegando. Macunaíma esporeou o cardão-pedrês e depois de perto de Mendoza na Argentina quasi dar um esbarrão num galé que também vinha fugindo da Guiana Francesa, chegou num lugar onde uns padres estavam melando.

> (He galloped and galloped and galloped and near Manaus he was moving rapidly when the horse stumbled and pulled up some ground. At the bottom of the hole Macunaíma caught sight of something shining. He quickly dug it up and discovered the remains of the god Mars, a Greek sculpture found in those parts back in the time of the Monarchy and last April Fool's Day in Araripe of Alencar by the journal named Comércio do Amazonas. He was contemplating that

wonderful torso when he heard, "Baúa! Baúa!"
It was the old woman Ceiuci coming up behind
him. Macunaíma spurred on the spotted horse
and after almost running into a galley which was
fleeing from French Guiana near Mendoza, Argentina, he came to a place where some priests
were making honey.) (*Macunaíma*)

During the chase, Macunaíma crisscrosses Brazil several
times, touching most, perhaps all, of the states of the country at least once, entering Argentina and Peru and nearing
the borders of Bolivia, Uruguay, and Paraguay. He finds
the statue (an actual find had been reported in the newspapers and then dismissed as an April Fool's joke), meets a
galley (presumably of slaves), is hidden by Argentinian
priests, deciphers or does not decipher Indian rock inscriptions in various parts of the country, is hidden by the
surucucu (the largest of Brazil's poisonous snakes)—
whom he rewards with a ring turned into four hundred
contos worth of carts of millet, some manure, and a secondhand Ford—meets a woman hiding from the Dutch
(since the time of the wars with the Dutch, 1640-1654),
and finally is brought home by the *tuiuiu* (wood ibis) who
metamorphoses into an airplane. We do not know how
long the journey lasts, but he meets the *surucucu* on the
fourth day.

The flight of Macunaíma recalls the flight of Lautréamont's Maldoror as the latter outsmarts and outlasts the
police by being today in Madrid, tomorrow in St. Petersburg, yesterday in Peking. . . . Carpentier attacked
Lautréamont and the Surrealists for the absence of popular faith, myth, and history in their versions of the fantastic. The flight of Macunaíma, and indeed the entire tale
of his adventures, provide, perhaps, a necessary intermediary between the revolutionary myth of Mackandal,
grounded in recent history, and the purely imaginary Maldoror (who nevertheless rebels against authentic currents
of European intellectual history). Macunaíma is a genuine
folk hero, borrowed by Andrade from tribal legend and
adapted to a new series of modern adventures perfectly in
keeping with the hero's more ancient deeds and his traditional personality. Andrade simply contemporizes the legend and thereby gives it renewed meaning.

The chase chronotope telescopes extensive geographical
space into a conceivable, graspable whole, a unity that can
be reduced to the sum of its parts. Overwhelmed, as one
must be, by Brazil's magnitude and diversity, Andrade
nevertheless conceptualizes Brazil and its culture as a totality, one set within the larger totality of Latin America.
[The critic adds in a footnote: "Andrade makes the point,
in his second preface, that Macunaíma is not even Brazilian (he is from an area in Venezuela)."] The statue of Mars
in the passage quoted above refers to a magazine article
about the discovery of fragments of a marble statue near
Manaus, perhaps a representation of Mars, and the inscriptions to contemporary theories that such inscriptions
were left in Brazil by the Phoenicians. The aid tendered
by animals situates Macunaíma in the legendary plane,
whereas the references to priests, galleys, the Monarchy,
and the Dutch place him in history. Thus time in the chase
chronotope, as well as space, is disjoined and telescoped,
and in addition, at least three types of discourse used to

record and interpret human activities—journalism, legend, and history—are evoked and fused.

The old woman Ceiuci is the wife of Venceslau Pietro
Pietra, thus a capitalist. She is also a cannibal, a theme to
which we will return in the discussion of the Golden Age.
Telê Lopez, in her excellent study of Andrade's intellectual life [*Mário de Andrade: Ramais e caminho*], outlines the
theme of the old woman as one of major interest to Andrade in his collections of popular stories, ballads, and
songs. These materials treat the old woman as faded beauty and lost fertility. For Andrade the old woman is a rem-
nant of ancient matriarchal systems, now brought low,
feared and ridiculed. This chase sequence thus embodies
two manifestations of mutability that operate in *Macunaíma* at once. The old woman's threat is cannibalization, a
particularly fearful form of mutability and one that functions both at the primitive, carnal level and at the modern,
economic level. But furthermore, this chronotope creates
both a geography corresponding in its detail to actual
places, displaced and rearranged into an imaginative cohesion, and a history fused to legend and reordered into a
digestible, comic, otherworldly chronology.

The second of the major principles of mutability operating
in *Macunaíma* is magic, and although many entities and
characters employ magic in the novel, the principal magic
users are Macunaíma and his brother Maanape, the sorcerer. Macunaíma's magical manipulations are often connected to the breaking of taboos, and the view of taboos
in the novel is almost certainly derived from Freud's
Totem and Taboo, which Andrade probably read in 1925.
Macunaíma turns himself into a prince, for example, in
order to have sex with his sister-in-law (incest); he moves
the family hut to higher ground in order to be alone with
his mother (and it was really with her, instead of Sofará,
that he wanted to frolic in the jungle). Several times he
turns Jiguê into a telephone, which violates a taboo against
consorting with machines, a transgression against the ethical code of the novel. In the Macumba episode he uses
magic against the Piaimã, who can be interpreted as a father figure to the fatherless Macunaíma. In the legends
collected by Koch-Grünberg, the giant is the father of
magic and the master magician who teaches young apprentices his arts (see legend 21, for example). He is a cannibal and the personification of darkness, and his conflicts
with Makunaíma represent solar and lunar eclipses. Thus
his large size, his status as constant older antagonist, the
fact that Macunaíma sleeps with his daughter, make of the
Piaimã a dominant, patriarchal, father image. Macunaíma's use of magic against him and his eventual killing of
him thus represent the breaking of another most powerful
taboo.

Many of the breakers of taboos in *Macunaíma*—for example, Ci, who as an Amazon is required to remain a virgin;
the Piaimã's daughter, who betrays her parents and
Macunaíma himself—metamorphose into heavenly bodies
at points of crisis. In addition, we learn that Carlos
Gomes, who had been a famous composer, is now a little
star in the sky. This latter remark serves to link the breaking of taboos with artistic creativity. The legendary
Makunaíma [as described in Theodor Koch-Grünberg's

"Mitos e lendas dos Indios Taulipang e Arekuná"] was the great creator and transformer.

> Makunaíma é, como todos os heróis tribais, o grande transformador. Transforma pessoas e animais, algumas vêzes por castigo, na maior parte, porém, pelo prazer da maldade, em pedras. . . . Também é criador. Ele fêz, como já foi dito, todos os animais de caça, bem como os peixes. Após o incêndio universal, que liquida todos os homens, cria novos homens. Nesta tarefa, inicialmente, apresenta falta de habilidade. Modela-os em cêra, de forma que, expostos ao sol, se derretem. Depois os modela em barro para em seguida transformá-los em homens.

> (Makunaíma is, like all tribal heroes, the great transformer. He transforms people and animals, sometimes as punishment, mostly, however, for the pleasure of the mischief, into stones. . . . He is also creator. He made, as we have already said, all the animals of prey, as well as the fish. After the universal fire, which destroys all men, he creates new men. In this task, initially, he shows a lack of skill. He models them in wax, so that, exposed to the sun, they melt. Later he models them in mud in order subsequently to transform them into men.)

Thus, it is in the fundamental nature of Andrade's hero to work magic, to transform, to create. However, it is the satiric aspect of this modern Macunaíma that begins to predominate in many of the episodes in which he uses his magic, for we begin to have a foreboding that the light-hearted contraventions of modern "tribal" and "natural" laws may have catastrophic consequences. Although Macunaíma is the great hero, he is human enough to suffer. Since Macunaíma's implementation of magic is connected to the breaking of prohibitions, its results for him are either minimal (the black magic of the Macumba wounds but does not kill the Piaimã) or it brings short-term pleasure and long-term punishment (he enjoys sex with Sofará but is triply punished by Jiguê by being beaten, deprived of food, and separated from Sofará).

Maanape, on the other hand, is the tribal healer. His beneficent magic resurrects Macunaíma three times after, in each case, Maanape had warned him against doing the things that would cause him to be killed. Maanape cures Macunaíma's wounds and restores him from illness. Maanape is, as well, the mediator between Macunaíma and Jiguê and is the wise possessor of secret knowledge. Unlike his brothers, he knows no women, enters into no conflict. He is the sage, the healer, the peacemaker. In social terms, magic as practiced by Macunaíma and Maanape has opposite effects. Macunaíma's magic is usually at the service of individualistic goals and it is often mischievous as well. It separates him from the community and makes him an isolated figure. Maanape's magic, however, derives from the ancient practices of his tribe and is a support and a comfort for others. It unites and gives continuity to the community. Magic, then, as mutability principle, has to do with creation and transformation and has far-reaching social and ethical implications as well.

The concept of a golden age and of culture in transition in *Macunaíma* relates both to Oswald de Andrade's "Manifesto antropófago," published in the first number of the *Revista de Antropofagia,* along with an advertisement for the forthcoming *Macunaíma* (May 1928), and to the ideas about cultural epochs expressed by Count Hermann Keyserling in *The World in the Making.* In his prose-poem manifesto Oswald (no relation to Mário) sets up a dialectic between, on the one hand, prehistoric primitivism, which for him was matriarchal and cannibalistic, sensual, leisurely, and ruled by the collective, and, on the other hand, the historical period, which is patriarchal and slave owning, logical, imperialist, and dominated by the father figures: conqueror, priest, and capitalist. The manifesto calls for revolution and return. . . . According to Telê Lopez [in *Macunaíma: A margem e o texto*],Mário de Andrade did not consider himself part of the *Antropofagia* group, but he could associate himself with their celebration of the primitive and of Brazilian-ness. And we shall see . . . that Mário had in mind a similar kind of matriarchal/patriarchal dialectic in the composition of *Macunaíma.*

Count Keyserling's book describes the contemporary period as the age of the chauffeur, an age of mechanistic, as opposed to spiritual, consciousness. Nevertheless, he believes the latter kind of age may and will come. The age of the chauffeur believes in progress, "the range of whose vision is so much narrower and shallower [than the Romantic Age of Hegel]. Briefly explained, it stands for nothing more than this: that the material, moral and mental circumstances of our life shall completely satisfy life's meaning," a crude and barbarous belief to Keyserling's way of thinking. At another point he calls the chauffeur the "technicalized savage."

In *Macunaíma* we find constant reference to past ages. In chapter 10, for example, Macunaíma, outraged by a patriotic speech on the nature of the Southern Cross, takes over the speaker's platform. He explains that the constellation known as the Southern Cross is really the *Pai do Mutum* (father or original ancestor of the *mutum,* a Brazilian species of pheasant), and he tells the Indian legend of the origin of the constellation. In the course of the speech, he makes reference to two separate past ages, one in which animals were people, "like us," and the age in which the legend itself took place. According to Koch-Grünberg, the primitive concept of animals does not differentiate man and animal, although the primitive imagination settles on the special characteristics of each animal. He indicates that the "primitive era" was an earlier epoch, the time of Makunaíma and the other legendary beings and occurrences. Our Macunaíma, the hero of Andrade's novel, inhabits three ages (that is, he moves imperceptibly from one to another almost simultaneously): the primary age in which animals are undifferentiated from humans (he, after all, speaks often with animals and communicates their messages to others), the following age in which he recognizes that animals were once people but are now a separate order of beings, and the third age which is contemporary and corresponds to Keyserling's mechanized age.

One of the most consistent motifs of the novel is Macunaíma's interaction with machines. When he first arrives in São Paulo, he perceives machines as an order of beings new to him and as the centers of power. Therefore, he sets out to have sex with them in order to conquer them, as he had done with Ci. In the end he is symbolically conquered by the pernicious charms of mechanization, for as he leaves São Paulo for the last time he takes with him to his native region a Smith & Wesson revolver and a Pathek watch. Of these two he makes his ear-pendants and from his lower lip he suspends the *muira-quitã* (the talisman given to him by Ci).

Thus in *Macunaíma,* time and distance contract into themselves so that Brazilian history and geography may be conceptualized as a unity that transcends the seeming separation of regions, cultures, language groups, and historical periods. Magic pervades action, functioning both as individualistic evil and as collective benefit. And culture is seen in helter-skelter transition from primitive cultural purity to mechanized and colonized corruption. Mutability as structural principle provides the novel with a sense that chaos, diversity, and magnitude can be overcome, at least intellectually; and mutability as satire warns against social tendencies and transformations that are perhaps more problematic for Brazil than the "muito saúva e pouca saúde" of which Macunaíma so often complains.

The individual metamorphoses of Macunaíma and other characters participate in the various modalities of mutability in the narrative world described above and bear their own existential meanings as well. The many metamorphoses of Macunaíma form a pattern that finds parallels in the metamorphoses of other entities and culminates in the most significant and crucial transformation, that is, the last one.

As has already been noted, Macunaíma, the hero of the Taulipang and Arekuná legends, is the great transformer. In addition, when missionaries translated the Bible into these languages, they named Christ "Makunaíma." [The critic adds in a footnote: "Andrade was a Christian and a Catholic at least through the twenties, so that it is improbable that religious irony is intended in the characterization of Macunaíma."] Thus, the hero of the novel, in his status as originator, inheritor, and transmitter of legendary culture, is rightfully endowed with powers of metamorphosis. He personally undergoes eleven metamorphoses before the final one, and often they occur in groups of three. (He also experiences death and resurrection three times.) He becomes a prince three times in order to frolic with Sofará; he changes into an insect, a plant, and then a man in order to frolic with Iriquí; he becomes an ant (*caxipara,* male *saúva*) in order to harass Venceslau Pietro Pietra; he turns into a fish three times to try to steal the Englishman's fishhook; and then he becomes the *piranha,* which enables him finally to lay hold of the hook. These minor metamorphoses allow him to satisfy instinctual desires in artful and comic ways, for Macunaíma is never satisfied with the mundane. They are spicy and frivolous. The last metamorphosis, however, is entirely other; it makes Macunaíma's story and life, if not tragic, surely profoundly poignant. In addition, to the extent to which Macunaíma embodies Brazil, his final metamorphosis is a painful and despairing vision of the destiny of that nation.

Although Macunaíma is in some ways a super-human character and although he is objectified and satirized, he may be said to embody a self in [two ways]. . . . He embodies a distinct spatio-temporal history, which he remembers and carries with him, and he is a unity that comprehends contradictions. Remembering Johnstone's definition of the self as one who can know what he or she is to do and not do it, we note in Macunaíma the propensity for lying, which he cannot explain, and his excuse to Vei: "If I had only known." With regard to the third characteristic of selfhood—the ability to reflect on one's own self and being—Macunaíma, although capable of introspection, refuses to engage in it, both out of pride and because he is a man of action. On the other hand, in his second preface to *Macunaíma,* Andrade asserts that Macunaíma represents the *Sein* ("Being") of Keyserling.

> Me repugnaria bem que se enxergasse em Macunaíma a intenção minha dele ser o herói nacional. E o herói desta brincadeira, isso sim, e os valores nacionais que o animam são apenas o jeito dele possuir o "Sein" de Keiserling, a significação imprescindível a meu ver, que desperta empatia. Uma significação precisa de ser total pra ser profunda. E é por meio de "Sein" (ver o prefácio do tradutor em *Le monde qui naît*) que a arte pode ser aceita dentro da vida. Ele é que fez da arte e da vida um sistema de vasos comunicantes, equilibrando o líquido que agora não turtuveio em chamar de lágrima.
>
> (It would repel me if in Macunaíma were to be seen any intention of mine to make of him a national hero. He is the hero of this plaything [the novel], yes, and the national values that animate him are only his tendency to possess the "Sein" of Keyserling, an indispensable meaning to my way of thinking, which arouses empathy. A meaning does not need to be total in order to be profound. It is by way of "Sein" (see the translator's preface to *Le monde qui naît*) that art can be integrated into life. It is what makes of art and life a system of communicating vessels, balancing the liquid that I now do not hesitate to call tears.)

This *Sein* stands in opposition to "action" in Keyserling's terms because action is associated with a lack of sensibility, consciousness, conscience, and spirituality. In Andrade's novelistic adaptation of Keyserling's ideas, we can see that Macunaíma is emphatically a man of feeling, that he leaves his conscience on an island before entering the city (and when he returns for it, he takes that of a Spanish American instead), and that his spirituality consists in his sense of and respect for ancient tradition and in his intimate relations with the creatures of nature and the cosmos.

In the analysis of changes of body, perception, will, and time, Macunaíma must be considered at three levels of representation: as human, as hero, and as symbol. To take the form of a constellation is to give up motility and all forms of relating physically to the world. He will no longer eat, sleep, be sick, fight, flee, hunt, fish, or frolic. His sole physical manifestation will be purely to shine, to give off light (at night, which is associated with hunger, cold, loneliness and death, as we have seen in the analysis of chapter

8). "Ia ser o brilho bonito mas inútil porém de mais uma constelação" (He was going to be the brilliance, pretty but useless, of one more constellation). He says he did not come into the world to be a stone. By removing himself from earth, he deliberately cuts himself off from contact with vegetable, animal, and especially human forms. As a collection of points of light with an animal name, he rejects any further involvement in human-ness. In Heideggerian terms, he gives up "care," which is the function of Being-in-the-World. As hero, Macunaíma remains in full view of all, tricking some into thinking he is the Saci because of his one leg. [The critic adds in a footnote: "According to Proença . . . , the *saci* is an entity from Indian mythology, sometimes evil, sometimes funny and jeering, represented by a small black man with one leg, a red stocking cap, and pipe; he makes himself known by a mysterious hissing, difficult to locate at night, and he amuses himself by frightening travelers and dispersing cattle herds from the ranches and horses from their pastures."] He has recovered his other parts (after being dismembered in the pool by the *piranhas*), and they will be visible along with his ear-pendants, the revolver, and the clock. Symbolically, his corporal transformation suggests inertia and stasis. However, the inertia is not the *lazer* related to artistic creativity. It is sterility, spiritless emanation.

We have seen that Macunaíma's sensory perceptions are acute and highly developed, but they reach satiation and then begin to torture him. At the end of the book he cannot bear the heat of the sun, the cold of the water, his nagging sexual desires. At the next level of perception, his emotional life is in ruins. He is lonely and heartsick, and he can find no more resources within himself to change his condition. Unlike Carpentier's Ti Noel, he has no final flash of insight, no introspective leap. His transformation signals his despair. Yet he displays no sign of guilt or remorse because he does not reflect on his past actions any more than he does on his current condition. His consciousness remains at the affective level, unable to attain the realm of judgment. And it is this lack of judgment, of self-criticism—manifested by his lack of foresight and insight, as well as by his breaking of taboos—that leads to his disastrous final disillusionment. Without judgment, one cannot have "character," for character, in the ethical sense, presupposes the ability to weigh alternative possibilities and to choose according to a system of values. For Andrade, this aspect of Macunaíma's character is indigenous to the Brazilian national character. According to Telê Lopez [in *Mario de Andrade: Ramais e caminho*], Andrade believes, as a result of his studies of popular forms of social criticism, that the Brazilian's ability to analyze and to criticize stops at well-meaning irony and sarcasm. (pp. 52-65)

At the human level, we see Macunaíma all too disposed to act out of impulse, instinct, desire. Yet paradoxically, as we have noted, he is meant to personify not action, but being, in Keyserling's sense of the word. Macunaíma is moved to action by discomfort, but his ultimate goal is always inaction, or at least play (especially sexual) or profit. His complaints against ants and ill health are ironic and result from his feeble powers of analysis, for the true impediments to his goal of leisurely contentment are the fa-

ther figure/cannibal/capitalist Venceslau, and the matriarchal tropical sun Vei, whose friendship he throws away precisely through his lack of character. Pathetically, the inaction of the useless star will comprehend neither play, nor music, nor sex. It will be being in its purest form, empty presence.

In its temporal dimension, Macunaíma's final metamorphosis represents a contrast both to Ti Noel's final choice and to Nicho Aquino's. Ti Noel elects a human death and assumption into the natural cycle of decay and reification. Nicho Aquino's metamorphosis allows transcendence and eternal participation in the fullness of natural and divine mysteries. On the other hand, Macunaíma, as human, simply stops, and his extinction is the extinction of his people. In his role as tribal hero, as we have seen, he embodies the comprehensive past of his people and is spokesperson as well. In this capacity he survives, for the memory of his existence continues in literature, and his presence will eternally manifest itself in the evening sky. As symbol of Brazil, Macunaíma represents the continuity of ancient Indian traits in the contemporary, multi-racial society. According to this formulation, it is a society that lives for its present, unable to plan systematically for the future, indeed negating the value of such planning. For the Brazilian the present moment achieves richness and meaning in being, not action, in contemplation and feeling, rather than in successive accomplishments. The temporal paradox reveals itself in the nothingness and vacuity of any future unforeseen and unprepared for. Macunaíma's final metamorphosis turns out to symbolize the nihilistic destruction of destiny by a people accused of being without character.

Having established the personal, existential meaning of Macunaíma's metamorphosis, we need now to analyze the transformational crisis in the full context of the values of the narrative world. The two keys to this perspective are the metamorphosis of Macunaíma's brothers and the parable of Taína-Cã, which Macunaíma relates to the parrot directly before his final confrontation with Vei and his metamorphosis. In these episodes we return to the dominant themes of the novel: leisure/work, creativity/sterility, life/death, earth/heaven, indigenous Brazilian culture/colonial culture. These dualities in some ways closely resemble those that come into play in the metamorphosis and death of Ti Noel and the conclusion of *El reino de este mundo*.

Macunaíma leaves the city for the last time with his foreign, manufactured acquisitions (not just the revolver and the clock but two Leghorns, a foreign hybrid, as well), thinking like an engineer: "Pois então Macunaíma adestro na proa tomava nota das pontes que carecia construir ou consertar pra facilitar a vida do povo goiano" (Then Macunaíma, resting in the prow, took note of the bridges which needed to be built or repaired to make life easier for the people of Goiás). As a city dweller, he has become enormously creative, not the least of his creations being new words, as we shall see. However, on his return to his native region, he falls ill with malaria. Indeed, he no longer lives in harmony with these surroundings. Whereas before he had had enormous energy and extraordinary magical powers for sexual activities, hunting and fishing, now he does not have the strength, the talent, or the will. He foils his brothers' efforts to provide for the group as well and schemes to poison Jiguê. Once Jiguê has become the shadow, he swallows both Maanape and the princess (who is a metamorphosed tree). As the shadow/Jiguê pursues Macunaíma, the latter comes upon an ox (*boi*), which he kicks, causing a stampede of oxen. In the confusion Jiguê attaches him/herself (shadow [*sombra*] is feminine) to the ox and proceeds to eat all of its food. The ox finally dies, and there is great rejoicing among all the species of vultures and buzzards. They dance and sing around the rotting corpse, and then they feast on it. Jiguê becomes the second head of the Father of the Vultures.

The *boi* is a sacrificial animal in many regions of Brazil, especially in the northeastern states, and Andrade took a particular interest in the sacrificial ceremonies, making an extensive collection of folk songs about the *boi*. In his marginalia to the tenth chapter of Frazer's *The Golden Bough,* "Relics of Tree Worship in Modern Europe" (which Andrade read in French), Andrade signals what he considers to be a parallel between European vegetation/fertility rites and Brazilian rituals among cattle-herding communities. He concludes that since Brazil has its economic focal point in cattle rather than in the earth, the value of the ox is raised to mythical status. "O Boi mal comparando, parece assumir uma posição de Dionisio, símbolo de refloresci-mento e do tempo fecundo" (The ox, comparing loosely, seems to assume the position of Dionysus, symbol of reflorescence and fertile season). And again: "O Boi é realmente o rei do criação" (The ox is truly the king of creation). Indeed, he goes even further and declares: "O boi é realmente o principal elemento unificador do Brasil" (The ox is truly the principal unifying element of Brazil). The death of the Boi in Brazilian festivals produces rejoicing, popular singing, and dramatic dances which are at the same time communal and primordial to native tradition. Furthermore, each part of the ox's body is committed to a practical use benefiting the collectivity. In **Macunaíma** Andrade rewrites the ceremonies to make the collectivity a community of vultures. By so doing he represents, as Carpentier was to do later, the natural cycle of animals consuming others, death giving life. As we have seen in the chapter on Vei, the defecation of vultures leads the human being to seek light, warmth, and cleansing, and these comforts, in turn, drive him back to union with the birds of death. And so the cycle perpetuates itself. In effect, then, Jiguê and Maanape are consigned to the cycle of nature and belong eternally to the earth.

In contrast, Macunaíma makes the choice that was available to Ti Noel, which the latter rejected, that is, transformation into an unearthly, eternal form, breaking with the natural cycle. In Macunaíma's parable of Taína-Cã, he spells out some of the implications of that choice. Taína-Cã is the evening star, and Imaerô, the older daughter of a Carajá chief, fell in love with him because of his beauty and brilliance and wanted to marry him. One evening he presented himself to her in human form, and they became engaged. Her younger sister Denaquê was very jealous. The next day, however, Taína-Cã appeared old and wrinkled, and Imaerô refused to marry him. De-

naquê, on the other hand, accepted him, and they were married. Taína-Cã, in spite of his aged looks, was very energetic sexually, and he made Denaquê idyllically happy. Every day Taína-Cã would leave their hut and would tell Denaquê not to follow him. He was clearing land and planting, which was something new and unheard of by the Carajá. He would go back and forth from earth to heaven bringing back everything that the Carajá lacked. But Denaquê began to follow him, and she fell in love with other, little, stars. Saddened and embittered by her infidelity, Taína-Cã returned to heaven and stayed there. "Si a Papaceia [Taína-Cã] continuasse trazendo as coisas do outra lado de lá, céu era aqui, nosso todinho. Agora é só do nosso desejo" (If the evening star had continued bringing things from the other side, the sky would be here, all ours. Now it is only our desire).

According to the myth, the separation of earth and heaven came about through betrayal; paradoxically, Macunaíma partakes of all three participants in this drama. He is Imaerô, who cannot recognize true value, for he was seduced by the glitter of technology. He is Denaquê, the unfaithful, for he has betrayed the values of primitivism, the collectivity, his mother, his brothers, the tropical sun. He is also Taína-Cã, for he has been both provider—intermediary between humans and natural forces—and potent sexual force. His story illustrates also the futility of work, agriculture being the destruction of the hunter-gatherer culture to which Macunaíma truly belongs. Thus, the beginning of agriculture, indeed of progress, results in material and spiritual loss and leads eventually to the advent of the technicalized savage.

As Telê Lopez points out, according to Andrade's understanding of Indian culture, the Indians' indolence is linked to creativity, specifically to verbal creativity. . . . One day, while he is living in São Paulo, a flower vendor gives Macunaíma a flower for his buttonhole, but since Macunaíma does not know the word for button-hole, he falls into confusion and irritation, finally blurting out the word *puíto* (an Indian word for anus). The flower vendor repeats the word, and soon Macunaíma discovers that all of São Paulo is calling buttonholes "puítos." He also studies languages and writes the hilariously inventive letter to the Amazon women. Thus, Macunaíma's *preguiça* (his laziness) is of value; it is something that is especially harmonious with his nature, since he is the great transformer and verbal artist. However, since he misuses his magical powers, as we have seen, his leisure becomes progressively sterile and uncreative as it becomes more and more isolated. In addition, for all of his frolicking, he engenders only one child, who is the fruit of transgression and must die. Andrade was emphatic in his belief that art must be involved in social concerns.

> O ideal seria então o artista só publicar aquilo que sua consciência social reputa bom e sua consciência pessoal reputa belo? E um engano, R. F., porque ambas estas duas consciências são contraditórias. Quem tem a segunda é um egoísta, que se indiferentiza no individualismo e não pode obter a primeira. E esta primeira despreza a segunda e a repudia. *A lealdade pra com a consciência social é a única que nobilita o artista, e o*

*justifica satisfatòriamente em sua humanidade.
E por ela que o artista faz a arte evoluir, pois êle
está consciente que transformando a arte, cor-
responde a uma precisão pública.*

(The ideal would be, then, for the artist only to
publish that which his social conscience reckons
good and his personal conscience reckons beautiful? This is a fraud, R. F., because these two
consciences are contradictory. Whoever has the
second one is an egoist who becomes indifferent
in individualism and cannot achieve the first.
And this first despises the second and repudiates
it. *The loyalty to the social conscience is the only
thing that ennobles the artist and satisfactorily
justifies him in his humanity. It is because of it
that the artist makes art evolve, for he is conscious
that by transforming art, he is responding to a
public need.*)

Leisure, life, and art come together as a vitally dynamic
union in the young Macunaíma. In the progression of
Macunaíma's career, Andrade dramatizes the decline of
the individualistic artist.

As we have seen, *preguiça* is one of the gifts of the tropical
sun. Before his initial encounter with Vei, Macunaíma was
her special favorite, and we have seen as well that the legendary Makunaíma was even a sun-figure himself. Haroldo de Campos, because of his concern with Proppian
structures in **Macunaíma,** points to Venceslau Pietro
Pietra as Macunaíma's principal antagonist. However, the
tropical sun, not the *muiraquitã,* is the key to happiness
and fulfillment for Macunaíma and the Brazilian, according to Andrade's ethic. The defeat of the father is relatively insignificant as compared to the magnitude of the conflict with the mother. Here, for a second time, we find the
theme of metamorphosis closely tied to the conflict between male and female dominance. In *Hombres de maíz,*
the metamorphosis of Nicho Aquino signals the decline of
the matriarchal age. In **Macunaíma,** the metamorphosis
of the hero occurs directly as a result of the matriarchy's
reassertion of her power. In [Carlos Fuentes's] *Zona sagrada* we will find yet another, this time pathological, linkage between metamorphosis and matriarchy.

Angel Rama [in "Mario de Andrade: Fundador de la
nueva narrativa"] has described Mário de Andrade as the
founder of the new Latin American narrative.

El orden narrativo que pone en juego, siendo
verosímil, nunca es meramente realista. Se gobi-
erna con leyes que fijan un distanciamento, se or-
ganiza al parecer caprichosamente, pero siguien-
do rígidas leyes que animan el juego.

Hay en este manejo de la literatura (que estaba
siendo el modo en que Kafka venía tratando los
"particulares" narrativos desde *La metamorfo-
sis*) una secreta, no confesa supeditación al subje-
tivismo. Este ensambla el conjunto y lo unifica
por una mirada del autor: ella es candorosa y hu-
morística a la par. La levedad de este material,
su apariencia inconsútil, juguetona y hasta in-
genua, la limpieza y pulcritud de la composición,
la constante humildad del asunto y de su trata-
miento, no disimulan la sabiduría de un estilo

con el que se pone en movimiento la narrativa
nueva del continente.

(The narrative order which he puts into play,
being probable, is never merely realistic. It is
governed by laws that fix an objectivity, orga-
nizes itself as though capriciously, but following
rigid laws that put the game into motion.

There is in this handling of literature [which was
the way in which Kafka was treating the "peculiar" narratives from *The Metamorphosis* on] a
secret, unconfessed subduing of subjectivism.
This joins the whole and unifies it through one
look by the author: it is candid and humorous
at the same time. The lightness of this material,
its seamless appearance, playful and ingenuous,
the cleanness and beauty of the composition, the
constant humility of the subject and its treatment, do not hide the wisdom of the style with
which he sets in motion the new narrative of the
continent.)

Being satire, **Macunaíma** is both comical and didactic.
Throughout this [discussion] we have been concerned
with the ethical code because satire by its very nature demands attention to ethics. Nevertheless, **Macunaíma**
serves as an appropriate transition between works in
which metamorphosis is involved in myth and magic (*El
reino* and *Hombres*) and works in which it is involved in
play and the game ([Julio Cortázar's] "Axolotl" and *Zona
sagrada*). **Macunaíma** may be considered a legitimate forerunner of Magic Realism in Latin American literature,
and it prefigures the Boom as well. (pp. 65-71)

> *Nancy Gray Díaz, "Metamorphosis as Cosmic
> Refuge: 'Macunaíma',"* in her The Radical
> Self: Metamorphosis to Animal Form in
> Modern Latin American Narrative, *Universi-
> ty of Missouri Press, 1988, pp. 51-71.*

FURTHER READING

Albuquerque, Severino João. "Construction and Destruction
in *Macunaíma.*" *Hispania* 70, No. 1 (March 1987): 67-72.
  Linguistic and thematic analysis of the Portuguese text
  of *Macunaíma.*

Béhague, Gerard. *Music in Latin America: An Introduction,*
pp. 115ff. Prentice-Hall History of Music Series, edited by H.
Wiley Hitchcock. Englewood Cliffs, N.J.: Prentice-Hall,
1979.
  Briefly mentions Andrade's contributions to Brazilian
  musicology.

Chambers, Leland H. Review of *Hallucinated City (Paulicea
desvairada),* by Mário de Andrade. *The Denver Quarterly* 3,
No. 4 (Winter 1969): 127-28.
  Notes the importance of Andrade's poetry while criticizing Jack E. Tomlins's 1968 translation.

Foster, David William. "Some Formal Types in the Poetry

of Mário de Andrade." *Luso-Brazilian Review* 2, No. 2 (December 1965): 75-95.

Identifies five main structural forms in Andrade's poetry.

George, David. "The Staging of *Macunaíma* and the Search for National Theatre." *Latin American Theatre Review* 17, No. 1 (Fall 1983): 47-58.

Discusses the Grupo Pau-Brasil's 1979 adaptation and performance of *Macunaíma* as a drama.

Haberly, David T. "The Depths of the River: Mário de Andrade's 'Meditação sôbre o Tietê'." *Hispania* 72, No. 2 (May 1989): 277-82.

Close reading of Andrade's last poem, "A meditação sôbre o Tietê."

Johnson, Randal. "Macunaíma as Brazilian Hero: Filmic Adaptation as Ideological Radicalization." *Latin American Literary Review* 7, No. 13 (Fall-Winter 1978): 38-44.

Focuses on differences between Joaquim Pedro de Andrade's 1969 film adaptation of *Macunaíma* and Andrade's original text. Johnson comments: "The adaptation of *Macunaíma* . . . is not merely an attempt at expressing the ideas of the 1928 work in a different medium, but rather a reinterpretation and an ideological radicalization of Mário de Andrade's original text cast in terms of the social, economic, and political realities of the late 1960s."

———. "Joaquim Pedro de Andrade: The Poet of Satire." In his *Cinema Novo X 5: Masters of Contemporary Brazilian Film*, pp. 13-51. Latin American Monographs (Institute of Latin American Studies), no. 60. Austin: University of Texas Press, 1984.

Includes further discussion of the 1969 film adaptation of *Macunaíma*.

Martins, Wilson. *The Modernist Idea: A Critical Survey of Brazilian Writing in the Twentieth Century*. Translated by Jack E. Tomlins. New York: New York University Press, 1970, 345 p.

Critical study of the historical background, representative works, and important authors associated with Brazilian Modernism. Martins includes a section on Andrade and discussion of *Pauliceia desvairada, A escrava que não é Isaura,* and *Macunaíma.*

Nist, John. "Mário de Andrade." In his *The Modernist Movement in Brazil*, pp. 59-70. Austin: University of Texas Press, 1967.

Appraises Andrade's contribution to the Modernist movement.

Schelling, Vivian. "Mário de Andrade and Paulo Freire: Two 'Primitive' Intellectuals." *Portuguese Studies* 3 (1987): 106-25.

Examines similarities between the intellectual aims of Andrade and the Brazilian educator Paulo Freire. Schelling proposes: "Without discussing their work as a whole, I would however like to argue that, firstly, their discourses are linked in a significant manner by their common attempt to create a cultural project for the emancipation from dependence and underdevelopment, and secondly, that their identity as 'primitive intellectuals' arises out of this common, although differently manifested, endeavour."

———. "Mário de Andrade: A Primitive Intellectual." *Bulletin of Hispanic Studies* 65, No. 1 (January 1988): 73-86.

Examines Andrade's efforts to synthesize diverse elements in Brazilian culture, language, and art.

Zilberman, Regina. "Myth and Brazilian Literature." In *Literary Anthropology: A New Interdisciplinary Approach to People, Signs, and Literature,* edited by Fernando Poyatos, pp. 141-59. Amsterdam: John Benjamins Publishing Co., 1988.

Analyzes the use of myth as a novelistic narrative form in *Macunaíma* and José de Alencar's *Iracema.*

Erich Auerbach

1892-1957

INTRODUCTION

German critic, philologist, historian, and educator.

Regarded as a seminal figure in twentieth-century literary criticism, Auerbach demonstrated that the study of literature is integral to any complete understanding of history, sociology, and philosophy. In his highly acclaimed work *Mimesis: Dargestellte Wirklichkeit in der abendländischen Literatur* (*Mimesis: The Representation of Reality in Western Literature*), Auerbach surveyed Western literature from Homer to Virginia Woolf and investigated the cultural and societal implications of variations in the definition of realism throughout the history of literary expression. As a Jewish intellectual writing during and after the rise of the Nazi regime, Auerbach felt a particular responsibility attendant upon him as a commentator on Western cultural traditions in a world that, in his view, was "pregnant with disaster" because it had misinterpreted its own history and heritage.

Born to an upper middle-class family in Berlin, Auerbach was educated at the highly reputed Französisches Gymnasium, which was known at the time for its emphasis on classical studies and French literature. He later attended universities in Berlin, Freiburg, and Munich and completed his doctorate of jurisprudence at the University of Heidelberg in 1913. After serving in the German army during World War I, Auerbach abandoned his law career and attained a doctorate in Romance philology at the University of Greifswald. In 1923 he became a staff member at the Prussian State Library. Although not as prestigious as a teaching position, the post at the library offered Auerbach the time and resources to continue his studies. The following year, Auerbach published his translation of the Italian philosopher Giambattista Vico's *Principi di una Scienza Nuova* (1725; *New Science*), a work that greatly influenced many of Auerbach's later writings. In 1929 Auerbach was appointed chair of Romance philology at the University of Marburg, where he completed his first major work on Dante, *Dante als Dichter der irdischen Welt* (*Dante, Poet of the Secular World*), along with several other essays. In 1935, after two years of increasing discrimination against Jewish faculty at the university, the Nazi government dismissed Auerbach from his academic post and forced him to leave Germany. Auerbach settled in Turkey, where many German Jews sought refuge during the war, and he began teaching at the State University of Istanbul. During his tenure in Turkey he published his textbook on Romance philology *Introduction aux études de philologie romane* (*Introduction to Romance Languages and Literature*) and, from 1942 to 1945, wrote *Mimesis*. *Mimesis* and Auerbach's continuing research on Dante established the paradigms for his later works, which were completed in the United States after leaving Turkey with his wife and son in 1947. Auerbach briefly taught at Pennsylvania State University and was later affiliated with the Institute for Advanced Study at Princeton University until being appointed professor of Romance philology at Yale University in 1950. The atmosphere of internationalism and the intellectual climate at Yale led Auerbach to write to Harry Levin that the situation was "almost ideal." Auerbach was named Sterling Professor at Yale and was planning a major work on medieval literature when he died in 1957.

Auerbach's literary criticism is generally valued for its innovative formulations of the relationship between literature and history. In *Dante, Poet of the Secular World*, Auerbach studied the influence of classical literature and philosophy on Dante's *Divina commedia* (1321; *The Divine Comedy*) by examining Dante's familiarity with Attic and Roman literary theories, which proposed that authors select an appropriate style—high, middle, or low—to reflect the import and aim of the subject treated. In addition to his interest in the separation of styles as a recurring construct in the history of literature, Auerbach also examined "figural interpretation," a method used in medieval hermeneutic studies concerned with the origins of symbols in the Bible. Auerbach's 1938 essay "Figura" analyzes the differences between the typological view of history, in which history is both figurative and literal, and the chronological, which defines history as a succession of factual events. According to a typological historiography, the sacrifice of Isaac acts as a "figura," or a prefiguration of the sacrifice of Christ; the two events are related neither causally nor temporally but symbolically. Auerbach utilized his investigation of a figural understanding of history as a means of discerning the way in which the understanding of history in the Middle Ages effected a change in methods of representation and resulted in the increasing influence of sacred texts on secular literary works. Auerbach's interest in biblical hermeneutics coincided with his active opposition to National Socialism in Germany. His interpretations of the Bible were guided by his desire to disprove the validity of the claim made by anti-Semitic Christians in Germany that a fundamental opposition between the Old Testament and the New Testament licensed discrimination against the Jews. During and after the war years, Auerbach continued to develop a critical methodology relevant to the times: "At an early date, and from then on with increasing urgency, I ceased to look upon the European possibilities of Romance philology as mere possibilities and came to regard them as a task specific to our time—a task which could not have been envisaged yesterday and will no longer be conceivable tomorrow." Thereafter, Auerbach applied his critical efforts to historical and historiographical studies of literature. Auerbach's historical and linguistic study "Passio als Leidenschaft," written in 1941, was strongly influenced by the works of Vico, who is credited as the first thinker to assert that historical phenomena were solely the consequence of human actions and thus possessed an order that could be analyzed. In addition, Vico emphasized the relevance of philology in historical investigations and introduced a radical historiography that questioned the adequacy of language to convey historical information. Vico's humanism and his emphasis on the relationship between language and history structure Auerbach's investigations of literary realism in *Mimesis.*

Composed of general reflections on language, literature and cultural history, *Mimesis* does not contain the detailed philological analyses that are characteristic of Auerbach's other scholarly works. Writing *Mimesis* during his exile in Turkey, Auerbach did not have the resources on Western literature that would have otherwise been available to him in Germany. Auerbach adapted his study to this restriction by limiting his commentary to brief passages considered in isolation from larger literary or critical contexts and by extending the scope of his work to include a broad range of examples from world literature. *Mimesis* begins with a comparison of the styles of representation found in the *Odyssey* and the New Testament and proceeds to a consideration of texts from various periods of literary history, ranging from the Middle Ages to the Modern period. A combination of close textual analyses and broad historiographical enquiries facilitate Auerbach's discussion of continuity and variation in the history of mimetic representation, which is defined as the approach taken by an author to achieve verisimilitude in the description of human experience. For instance, Auerbach cites the fact that both Gustave Flaubert's novel *Madame Bovary* and Homer's *Odyssey* attend to descriptions of the everyday lives of their characters. Flaubert rendered the minute details of middle-class life and Homer repeatedly described the rituals and appearance of Odysseus's household. Auerbach noted, however, that the boredom that plagues the characters in *Madame Bovary* and the limited narrative perspective Flaubert used are in contrast to the dynamic events of the *Odyssey* and the narrator's omniscient viewpoint in the depiction of those episodes. According to Auerbach, the differences and similarities between these and other literary works that are from widely varying historical periods suggest that the mode of representation presented in each work comments not only on the historical period in which it was written, but also, as a result of the text's relationship to the literary tradition out of which it arises, reflects the history of literature and culture in general. The presentation in *Mimesis* of the way in which literature aids the interpretation of history and historiography, as well as Auerbach's proposal that literary history is a continuum rather than a succession of isolated periods, have both had a lasting impact on literary criticism.

Auerbach's later work investigates concerns that are outlined in *Mimesis.* The essays that make up *Literatursprache und Publikum in der lateinischen Spätantike und im Mittelalter* (*Literary Language and Its Public in Late Latin Antiquity and in the Middle Ages*), a philological work that was intended as a supplement to *Mimesis,* and *Scenes from the Drama of European Literature* include considerations of the separation of styles, the secularization of sacred texts, and literary history. Although literary critics have contested the coherence of Auerbach's theo-

ries and the usefulness of his critical methodology, they have nevertheless acknowledged the acumen and profundity that Auerbach brought to the study of literature, history, and culture.

(See also *Contemporary Authors,* Vol. 118.)

PRINCIPAL WORKS

Dante als Dichter der irdischen Welt   (criticism)   1929
   [*Dante, Poet of the Secular World,* 1961]
Uber die ernste Nachahmung des Alltäglichen   (criticism)
   1937
Neue Dantestudien   (criticism)   1944
*Mimesis: Dargestellte Wirklichkeit in der abendländischen
   Literatur*   (criticism)   1946
   [*Mimesis: The Representation of Reality in Western Literature,* 1953]
Introduction aux études de philologie romane   (criticism)
   1949
   [*Introduction to Romance Languages and Literature,*
   1961]
*Vier Untersuchungen zur Geschichte der französischen
   Bildung*   (criticism)   1951
Typologische Motive in der mittelalterlichen Literatur
   (criticism)   1953
Literatursprache und Publikum in der lateinischen Spätantike und im Mittelalter   (criticism)   1958
   [*Literary Language and Its Public in Late Latin Antiquity and in the Middle Ages,* 1965]
Scenes from the Drama of European Literature   (criticism)   1959
Gesammelte Aufsätze zur romanische Philologie   (criticism)   1967

*This work includes translated portions of *Neue Dantestudien* and *Vier Untersuchungen zur Geschichte der französischen Bildung.*

Francis Fergusson   (essay date 1954)

[*Fergusson is one of the most influential American drama critics of the twentieth century. In his seminal study,* The Idea of a Theater *(1949), he claims that the fundamental truths present in all drama are defined exclusively by myth and ritual, and that the purpose of dramatic representation is, in essence, to confirm the "ritual expectancy" of the society in which the artist works. Fergusson's method has been described as a combination of the principles of Aristotle's* Poetics *and the principles of modern myth criticism. In the following excerpt, he outlines Auerbach's conceptions of literary representation presented in* Mimesis.]

Professor Auerbach, now at Yale, has been in this country since the end of the War. . . . He has published an important work on Dante in German, *Dante als Dichter der irdischen Welt,* many articles on Romance languages and literatures, and **"Figura,"** a study of the development of Dante's allegory. *Mimesis,* written in Istanbul during the War, is his most extensive work, and the best one in which to study his original and illuminating methods of literary analysis.

Professor Auerbach studies the representation of reality in twenty chapters, each based on one or more short passages from works of literature, beginning with the *Odyssey* and ending with *To the Lighthouse*. On the way he considers Petronius, two late Latin narratives, three Medieval texts, the Farinata-Cavalcante episode from the *Inferno,* bits of Rabelais, Shakespeare and Cervantes; samples of French neoclassic literature, and of Stendhal, Balzac, Flaubert, the Goncourts, and Zola. This slight indication of the contents of the book will show how vast its scope is, and how impossible it would be, even for one with the requisite erudition, to estimate its success in detail. Professor Auerbach's methods make things easy for the reader who lacks much knowledge of Latin style in the dark ages, for example: each passage analyzed is short, and the elucidations are very effective. Every chapter is good reading, both because of the light shed on the particular text, and because of the fascination of Professor Auerbach's methods, ostensibly philological *explication de texte,* actually the analysis, in the small example, of the author's basic attitudes to "reality", and of his strategies for representing it. But I will not attempt to discuss it in detail, but rather to enquire what Professor Auerbach means by the theme of the book as a whole, which is suggested in the title.

Five of the chapters seem to me especially important for understanding Professor Auerbach's theme. The reader inevitably wants to know how "reality" and "representation" are understood. Professor Auerbach does not define either term, for his method is to concentrate upon the analyses of particular texts, and to rely upon the reader to derive his understanding of the general ideas from common sense and from the material itself. Thus his concept "reality" is based upon Dante's Aristotelian-Christian realism, and also modern realism as exemplified in the French novel of the Nineteenth Century. His notion of representation rests upon the distinction between the classic notion of three separate styles, the elevated, middle, and low, and realistic styles (both Medieval and modern) in which the sublime, the everyday, and the low, or grotesque, or comic, or disgusting, are mixed. The five chapters in which these ideas are clearest, are 1, "Odysseus' Scar"; 8, "Farinata and Cavalcante"; 15, "The Faux Dévol"; 18, "In the Hotel de la Mole", and 19, "Germinie Lacerteux."

The first chapter begins with an analysis of the episode in the *Odyssey* in which Odysseus' old nurse, Eurycleia, giving him a bath, recognizes him by a scar on his thigh. What Professor Auerbach has to say about the way reality is represented in this episode: its bright, uniform illumination; its rigidly-held present tense—for the interpolation which recounts Odysseus' wounding by the boar, years ago, is as present as the bath—the sensuous immediacy of everything; the serenity of the narrative movement—is very just and illuminating. But the point of the chapter is clear only when the Homeric episode is compared with the Abraham-Isaac story in the Old Testament. In reading Homer, "It does not matter whether we know that all this is only legend, 'make-believe'. The oft-repeated reproach

that Homer is a liar takes nothing from his effectiveness, he does not need to base his story on historical reality." The Old Testament narrative, on the contrary, is rooted in time and history; in Abraham's past, and in the past of his tribe. It is far darker and more mysterious than Homer; all is directed toward the partly-hidden will of God; but it offers itself as literally true. Because of this basic attitude to its reality, the tiniest episode, however humble or grotesque, may be as "problematic" (one of the author's favorite words), as significant and intense, as the sublimest tragedy. Because it is true, mysterious, and related at every point to the will of God, it requires, and has of course received, endless interpretation. Homer, on the other hand, being immediately clear, completely expressed, neither requires nor admits interpretation. The Old Testament story represents reality much more than Homer does; Homer, though he wrote before the classic doctrine of the separation of styles, stands for that classic conception of art which Professor Auerbach uses throughout to contrast with the various kinds of realism.

The full scope of Professor Auerbach's conception of the Hebraic-Christian realism does not emerge until he comes to Dante. Chapter 8, on the Farinata-Cavalcante episode in the *Inferno,* is offered as an example of Dante's realism, or, as it may be described, his *mixture* of styles. The point is that Dante can compass both common speech and the humblest subjects, classically associated with comedy, and at the same time the most "sublime" emotions and rhetorical effects, classically associated with tragedy and epic. Dante's realism, like that of the Old Testament, is religious: it is the eye of God upon every detail of human life which guarantees its timeless value and meaning, yet at the same time firmly anchors it in time and place. Religious realism in this tradition deals with human individual fates of all kinds. The classic notion of three styles, on the other hand, tends to be general, typical, moralistic, or "esthetic". It is usually associated with a rigid class structure, and the low style for servants, the high style for princes, is supposed to reflect some natural and permanent stratification in human society. The *Divine Comedy* and the Old Testament narratives, on the other hand, envisage a "reality" much more fundamental than any social order, any abstract moral system, or any absolute conception of style.

Professor Auerbach's conception of this religious realism, starting in the Old Testament and culminating in Dante, contains, I think, his most original and illuminating insights. It would not be possible to do justice to it in a review; I'm not even sure that **Mimesis** makes it sufficiently clear. The early book on Dante, the monograph, **"Figura,"** in which the development of Dante's realism from its ancient sources is traced, and a number of shorter studies of Dante's methods which have appeared in various journals, would perhaps be required for full understanding of Professor Auerbach's views. I hope that this material will soon be collected and made available in English, for I think it is of first importance in our present literary studies.

I have more reservations about the application of these concepts to more modern literature in the remainder of the book. Chapter 15, "The Faux Dévot" (one of La Bruyère's *Caractères*) is in effect a brief study of French neo-classicism in relation to Professor Auerbach's theme. In general, he sees the age of Louis XIV as governed by the classic "separation of styles" with all that goes with it—the sense of reality, as one might put it, strained through social, moral, and esthetic conventions. It is this chapter, therefore, where one may best study the classic or neoclassic conception of literary representation which Professor Auerbach opposes to realism. The reservations I have are due less to the author's native understanding of this literature than to the focus of the book as a whole, which is not well designed to bring out what Racine and Molière, for example, do offer. Professor Auerbach, following his line of enquiry, does not seek to expound what *they* achieved, so much as to estimate their "realism". Even from this point of view one might have questions: is there no "reality" in Molière's rational norms, conventional though they are, or in Racine's moral paradoxes, abstract though *they* are?—It depends, of course, upon what one means by reality.

In chapters 18 and 19 Professor Auerbach discusses Stendhal, Balzac, Flaubert, the Goncourts and Zola; and these chapters, taken together, show what is meant by modern realism. Modern realism is quite different from Dante's, yet Professor Auerbach accepts it as "real" also, and perhaps even more real. He defines it as follows: "The serious treatment of everyday reality, the rise of more extensive and socially inferior human groups to the position of subject matter for problematic-existential representation, on the one hand; on the other, the embedding of random persons and events in the general course of contemporary history, the fluid historical background—these, we believe, are the foundations of modern realism". I do not quarrel with this definition, nor with the fine analyses of passages from particular works. If these chapters do not quite satisfy me, that is perhaps because we have so much modern realism which fulfills the definition, yet strikes me as insignificant and not very "real". Are the differentia of this school or style as significant as Professor Auerbach seems to maintain? Do we not usually, and rightly, think that the best modern realists are those who reveal most about human nature and destiny *beyond* the temporal facts, and who construct the most rich and satisfying poetic forms?

Such questions as these are perhaps inappropriate, because of the focus and method of the whole of *Mimesis.* But raising them may help us to understand the point of view which gives the book its great scope, its kind of objectivity, and its deep, if hidden consistency. There is, for example, the view of history and its importance which is implied in Professor Auerbach's definition of modern realism. In Dante's realism history has its crucial place, but so do moral truth and God, the ultimate object of faith and hope; both of them are outside the temporal sequence itself, though in perpetual relation to it. If God is not in the picture at all, and the "truths" of the moral life vary with the shifts of time and place and circumstance, then "history" is the ultimate reality. The modern realists' concern with "the general course of contemporary history, the fluid historical background", would make their realism realer than Dante's—for his view of the shifting scenes of history is formed by his belief in the timeless realities of God and moral truth. For the purposes of *Mimesis* as a whole, Professor Auerbach has accepted, I think, the view that history is the realest or final reality. This does not prevent him from appreciating Dante to the full—on the contrary; but it makes it unnecessary, and even irrelevant, to compare Dante's realism with Flaubert's: the relation is historic. There is, as I suggested, a *kind* of objectivity in this view; Professor Auerbach speaks at one point of the "incomparable historical vantage point which [this age] affords". But questions of permanent value, whether moral, artistic, or religious, are ruled out.

Questions of artistic value are ruled out too. I must hasten to say that this does not mean that Professor Auerbach fails to see artistic values; his poetic sensibility is evident again and again, it is one of the things that give *Mimesis* its great value. But he is investigating the representation of reality and not poetry as such. For that reason he never raises the questions which chiefly concern modern American criticism: the unity and coherence of the poem or play as a whole, the integrity and inner order of the art-work. That is one reason why his method of analyzing short passages from longer works is so effective for his purposes: he wants to know, not what the author made, but how he represents a reality outside the poem altogether. It is amazing how much this method reveals incidentally about poetry and poems. But from time to time it leads Professor Auerbach to judgments which I question, for example, that Dante's characters are so real that the coherence of the Canto or Cántica is lost: I should prefer to say that the larger units of the composition are there to be seen, if one is looking for them. His treatment of Shakespeare, based on the analysis of a short scene between Prince Hal and Poins, though it illustrates his theme well and most interestingly, is hardly adequate for Shakespeare. His unit is the play; I do not think one can assess his success in representing reality on the basis of a shorter selection.

The great value of *Mimesis* for us lies in its unfashionable focus: it is time we raised once more the ancient question of art's truth to reality. On the basis of a common sense and historistic conception of reality, Professor Auerbach has written a work of extraordinary learning, perceptiveness, and rigor. I think its methods, its ideas, and its particular insights should keep us busy for a long time. (pp. 123-27)

Francis Fergusson, "Two Perspectives on European Literature," in The Hudson Review, *Vol. VII, No. 1, Spring, 1954, pp. 119-27.*

H. Marshall McLuhan   (essay date 1956)

[*McLuhan was a Canadian critic, educator, and media analyst. In his discussions of the media and advertising, McLuhan stresses the importance of considering mass communications in any sociology of the modern world. His pioneering efforts in the study of popular culture and its effect on the individual and society have had a substantial influence in the fields of sociology, history, and cultural studies. In the following review, he discusses what Auerbach calls the "stylistic" approach to the analysis of literature in* Mimesis.]

Erich Auerbach belongs with that group of scholars whose approach to literature and culture has been described as "stylistic." Many Americans are already familiar with this approach; they have met it in the work of Curtius, Leo Spitzer, Helmut Hatzfeld, and Ulrich Leo. It is an approach which is not unrelated to the methods worked out for art and culture by Burckhart and his student, Wölfflin. As for myself, I met it first in Siegfried Giedion's *Space, Time, and Architecture.* Giedion is a disciple of Wölfflin much greater than his master.

As for the approach itself, it may be said to accept any work of art or any portion of human expression (a road, a town, a building, a poem, a painting, an ash-tray, or a motor-car) as a preferential ordering of materials. Since all art expresses some preference, any portion of anything made by man can be spelled out. Every art object and every art situation represents a preferential response to reality, so that the precise techniques chosen for the manipulation and presentation of reality are a key to the mental states and assumptions of the makers. Thus, the art object or situation (a city or a factory) may be a non-verbal affair, but its "meaning" can easily be verbalized to the person skilled in the language of vision or stylistics.

This is an approach to literature and art which, superficially, dispenses with history. In practice it provides a technique, both massive and minute, of historical documentation and awareness. What we have in the past four centuries come to accept as historical explanation has typically been linear. Linear perspective comes into painting and writing (via format of the printed page) at the same time. And it consists in the discovery that a single, fixed point of view is possible to the spectator both in time and space. This extremely artificial and arty discovery was very exciting and useful at first. It seemed to be a great improvement on medieval non-lineality in time and space.

But lineal perspective was supplanted in the visual arts by the techniques of *lo spettatore nel centro del quadro* or the spectator in the center of the picture, which, in poetry, gives the novelty of Wordsworth's "Solitary Reaper." The very fact of poetry appearing almost entirely in the printed form, however, long disguised this shift from lineality, and helps, for example, to explain Hopkins' insistence on his poetry being heard.

The purpose of these remarks is to reveal that Auerbach's **Mimesis** is very much in line with those developments in English poetry and criticism which we link with the names of Pound, Eliot, Richards, Empson, Leavis, and Brooks: "A work of art has the power of imposing its own assumptions." The business of the reader or spectator is to discover the stylistic assumptions of a work of art, not to extract meanings and ideas from it. For some people biographical and historical data, as well as meanings and ideas, appear to help in the art experience. For most they tend to be a substitute for such experience. But for all types of reader the stylistic analyses in **Mimesis** will come as a series of new insights and sympathies with many authors from Homer to Virginia Woolf (From Beowulf to Virgina Woolf, as it were).

Auerbach is able to get startling results from such unex-pected works as Gregory of Tours' *History of the Franks,* in which the sentences and points of view have shifted from the autocratic position of earlier imperial writers to an interest in "everything that can impress the people."

It is impossible to illustrate Auerbach's procedure in a review. But it should be said that it is a way of seeing and doing that he offers and not a set of conclusions or ideas. Even agreement or disagreement with his particular perceptions and discussions is unimportant, because it is the enterprise of making the whole of world literature available *on its own terms* that is here valuable. Moreover, this method not only promotes exact attention to the modalities of experience incorporated in particular works and makes those modalities luminously available, but it incidentally reveals the mode of existence of any type of art and its natural function within a culture.

Today, with 30,000 new titles a year in English alone, it is nothing less than a necessity to make of the book a tool of perception. The book has a new role in our new technological culture—just the role that Auerbach and his associates have discovered. The book having lost its monopoly as a channel of information or as an avenue of recreation, now assumes a higher role as tool and trainer of perception in all the arts. And it is just because the Auerbachs have perfected the techniques of literary stylistics that these techniques can be extended to music, painting, architecture, and town planning. (pp. 99-100)

> *H. Marshall McLuhan, in a review of "Mimesis: The Representation of Reality in Western Literature," in* Renascence, *Vol. IX, No. 2, Winter, 1956, pp. 99-100.*

Charles Breslin   (essay date 1961)

[*In the following excerpt, Breslin considers Auerbach's achievements as a historian, philologist, and literary critic.*]

The cultural phenomenon known as historicism has made a somewhat belated appearance in American intellectual life. This concept is still an innovation for us and that accounts, perhaps, for its very imperfect assimilation into our pragmatic thought patterns. Fanatic espousal and total excoriation both betray a shallow understanding of historicism, which in reality is not a single idea but an historical complex of ideas. The field of literary studies reflects the inadequacy of our assimilation to quite a pronounced degree. "After the year 1858 came the year 1859, that is historicism." Such are the words of an eminent American critic and man of letters. Most of our avowed historicists and, conversely, their critics, are far more concerned with what they believe to be the essential philosophical implications of historicism, viz. relativism, scepticism, moral and aesthetic indifferentism, etc., than with historicism as a hermeneutic principle and general intellectual orientation through which a literary work of art, in all its richness and plenitude, can be made to reveal itself meaningfully to the human spirit.

This is not to say that the logical nature of the category of historicism is free from conceptual confusion. In a recent study the Crocean Carlo Antoni has viewed historicism as a multifaceted concept formed by the liberal historicism of XVIIIth-century Europe, Vico's humanistic historicism, the romantic historicism of Herder, Savigny, and Jakob Grimm, the dialectical historicism of Hegel, Marx's materialistic historicism, and the absolute historicism of Benedetto Croce. Those with a philosophical turn of mind might legitimately inquire whether historicism denotes a determinate mode of thought, a heuristic or scientific method, an historical theory of knowledge, an interpretation of history, or a completed *Weltanschauung* or philosophy. What rôle, for instance, would the concept play in the construction of a formal logic of history or of a material philosophy of history? These epistemological complexities need not be elucidated here; they are mentioned only to give some intimation of the kind of problems that surround the idea of historicism. It certainly confronts us with issues that are among the deepest, the most basic, and the most mysterious of those which perpetually engage the powers of the human understanding. As a help toward perspective, however, we can do no better than to consider the words of Friedrich Meinecke and Ernst Troeltsch, two of the most sensitive and learned investigators of this movement. For Meinecke "the essence of historicism consists in the substitution of an individualizing view toward historical-human forces for a generalizing one, . . . one of the greatest revolutions that human thought has undergone." For Troeltsch the phenomenon signified "the radical historicizing of our entire knowledge and perception of the spiritual world"; he regarded historicism and naturalism as the "two great scientific creations of the modern world."

In order to define the relation of literary study to historicism we must first of all turn to the work of Erich Auerbach, a scholar who has brilliantly realized the full depth and range of potentialities encompassed by aesthetic historicism. His understanding of this concept is stated with clarity and eloquence in a passage from his well-known book *Mimesis: The Representation of Reality in Western Literature:*

> When people realize that epochs and societies are not to be judged in terms of a pattern concept of what is desirable absolutely speaking but rather in every case in terms of their own premises; when people reckon among such premises not only the natural factors like climate and soil but also the intellectual and historical factors; when, in other words, they come to develop a sense of historical dynamics, of the incomparability of historical phenomena and of their constant inner mobility; when they come to appreciate the vital unity of individual epochs, so that each epoch appears as a whole whose character is reflected in each of its manifestations; when, finally, they accept the conviction that the meaning of events cannot be grasped in abstract and general forms of cognition and that the material needed to understand it must not be sought exclusively in the upper strata of society and in major political events but also in art, economy, material and intellectual culture, in the depths of the workaday world and its men and women, because it is only there that one can grasp what is unique, what is

animated by inner forces and in a constant state of development; in other words, as a piece of history whose everyday depths and total inner structure lay claim to our interest both in their origins and in the direction taken in their development. Now we know that the insights which I have just enumerated and which taken all together represent the intellectual trend known as Historismus were fully developed during the second half of the eighteenth century in Germany.

The above is obviously a most comprehensive statement of the historistic view of life and one that also illuminates its convergence with the tradition of *Geistesgeschichte.* This way of looking at things has ever been latent in the secularization and intense historical dynamism of the West; it has progressively disclosed new dimensions in the historical being of the human race. Auerbach's conception is akin to the aesthetic historicism which pertains to the inner freedom and individual creativity of the historian. This type of historicism is exemplified in the writings of Carlyle, Michelet, and Burckhardt; it arose in the XIXth century as a reaction against the monistic strictures of naturalistic and metaphysical historicism, the one seeking to subsume historical phenomena within the categories of exact or positive science, the other seeking to formulate a metaphysical principle that would unify the realms of nature and history. Its rise was also a consequence of the prodigous accumulation and pillaging of cultural-historical materials, a process which alienated the study of human history from its vital context and obscured all possibility of genuinely fruitful creativity. The doctrine of *L'histoire pour l'histoire* provoked Nietzsche's famous *Zweite Unzeitgemässe,* which deplored the submergence of human life beneath a monstrous antiquarianism. Another aspect of this condition was the historian's proclivity to lapse into a kind of aesthetic, sceptical, or ironic contemplation in the face of a multitude of individualities, endless transformations, and vast interplay of forces. The fact that resignation, pessimism, and enervating relativism could result from this aesthetic historicism was a contingency Auerbach himself recognized when he spoke of general and aesthetic historicism as "a precious (and also very dangerous) acquisition of the human mind." His own conception is derived from the breadth and diversity of the contemporary aesthetic horizon and is grounded in the belief that historical relativism or perspectivism has a two-fold aspect: "it concerns the understanding historian as well as the phenomenon he understood." The historical antecedents for these views are, of course, to be found in the XIXth and in the latter part of the XVIIIth century. Aesthetic historicism for Auerbach was a product of German romanticism, and it rests on the conviction that "every civilization and every period has its own possibilities of aesthetic perfection; that the works of art of different peoples and periods, as well as their general forms of life, must be understood as products of variable individual conditions, and have to be judged each by its own development, not by absolute rules of beauty and ugliness."

The real import and validity of Auerbach's historistic approach to literature will become apparent if we recall that he was imbued with all that was most fertile in the XIXth-century German tradition of philology, a tradition for which we have no exact counterpart in this country. Indeed, for many of us the word philology itself, a term which has a very wide signification in German, tends to evoke thoughts suggesting the most concentrated and arid sort of pedantry. Yet Theophil Spoerri, a critic reminiscent of René Wellek in his preoccupation with literature and value theory, has described the philologist as one who is concerned with "the reflections of life, with shining appearances, which are the products of a creative process, of a transformation, and a transfiguration." If we are to believe the mature *Philolog* (Auerbach, E. R. Curtius, Leo Spitzer, Karl Vossler, Helmut Hatzfeld, are probably the best known in America), the discipline of philology must be regarded as an indispensable prolegomenon to genuine literary criticism; in fact, it is the source and foundation of any sound literary judgment which has as its object a work of art whose medium is language. Philology is more than an auxiliary, or instrumental science; actually it forms an integral and necessary part of what we call literary criticism.

For Auerbach the highly developed critical faculty consists of a special sense for significant facts and for a synoptic comprehension of the "breadth of the general culture, which rests on the passionate inclination to absorb everything that could be useful for the interest under pursuit." The literary critic must ultimately possess an imagination of considerable innate vitality and revelatory power if he ever hopes to penetrate language, which itself is not only the substance of the literary art work but also the most fundamental of symbolic forms. Through the manifold expressions of linguistic activity the historical dimension of human existence makes itself known to men, in the words of Giambattista Vico, a thinker highly esteemed by Auerbach, *il mondo delle nazione.* The critical acumen requisite for their comprehension is not transmissible pedagogically, it cannot be reduced to questions of method, but is rather the function and telos of all method. Methodology, however extensive or finely wrought, will remain sterile if it fails to culminate in the critical qualities that Auerbach mentions. One might think that literary criticism as it is currently practised often exhibits these very qualities and in most cases without benefit of that laborious background in grammar, lexicography, source and textual criticism, bibliography, techniques of collecting, etc., which Auerbach considers so essential. But he also states that if the critical virtues cannot be taught they can and must be formed and sharpened. It is philology that will enable us to re-evoke, to re-know the past structures of the human spirit and to repossess them internally whether this be done through a literary or any other kind of linguistic document. This process is not equivalent to an identification of literature with history, using literature as a kind of external 'source' for historical knowledge. But literature is the embodiment of an image or vision of human life, and this image is inevitably reflected only through the prism of its own historical matrix. What we try to define as the aesthetic qualities of a literary work are indissolubly welded to its particular vision of reality, its representation of human life. (pp. 369-73)

According to Auerbach, then, it is philology that engenders and cultivates a "state of mind capable of revealing in itself all varieties of human experience, of rediscovering them in its own 'modifications.' " Our modern world picture is a realization of certain potentialities inherent within the total structure of human existence, but the present is nevertheless only one particular stage in the collective consciousness of humanity. Auerbach speaks of our being here and now historically "with all the richness and limitedness that this contains." The sheer preponderance and singularity, the pervasive immediacy and ubiquity of the modern world-view act as a hindrance in the effort to re-experience the life of a literature which is itself the emanation of a remote or alien mental formation or cultural complex. Following Vico, Auerbach sees philology as both the inchoate science of spirit in the great breadth of its positive moments and as the hermeneutic or method for the intrinsic rediscovery of these moments through the medium of their documents, that is, through their historical 'words,' their *umana Voci.*

Auerbach's interest in the method of *explication de texte* will become clear if it is seen within this philological context. *Explication* compels the literary scholar to read "with a fresh, spontaneous, and sustained attention" and abstain scrupulously from premature judgments. In other words it will assist him to attain "the greatest possible freedom from world-view or other dogmatic preconceptions." In the age of Malraux's imaginary museum when works of art have become isolated from their cultural function and from the center of their epoch it is no doubt correct to refer to these works—cf. T. S. Eliot and René Wellek—as monuments rather than documents. Yet works of literature are not inert monuments in the same sense as are works of plastic art or of architecture or even of music. The verbal medium, unlike the stones or the colors of the architect and painter, is essentially living, dynamic, progressing, and is constantly transforming itself. Also the thoroughly rationalistic and positivistic trends of the XXth century must first apprehend the art of a Pindar or Dante or Cervantes as a literary document and then, through manifold explication, attempt to relive the vital experience it contains and symbolizes, to perceive its singular nature. Such a process, which takes place within the modifications of the reader's own mind and within the depths of his own consciousness, is antecedent to the development and application of formal aesthetic categories. A work of literature does not have to be 'reconstructed' as do the events of an historical narrative, but its complete physical availability to us does not obviate the necessity of explication, which is subtle and difficult enough. Without such a heuristic the literary document can quite easily become subject to what Herbert Read has aptly called the fallacy of retrospective interpretation. Through the pervasiveness and ossification of established modes of thought, a work's real character and its importance as *Anthropologie,* as commentary on the essential nature of man, could be forever lost to us. In Auerbach's words "it is a difficult and infinite task to understand the particular character of historical forms and their interrelations, a task requiring, apart from learning and intelligence, a passionate devotion, much patience, and something which may well be called magnanimity." This magnanimity is connected ideologically with the *Verstehen* of Dilthey and Schleiermacher, with Winckelmann's interpretation of art works, and Herder's empathy. C. S. Lewis in our own time voices similar thoughts when he states that in order to enjoy our full potentialities we ought, so far as possible, "to contain within us, and on occasion to actualize all the modes of thinking and feeling through which man has passed."

The analyses in *Mimesis* show that *explication de texte*—whether its vantage point originates from a special semantic, syntactic, aesthetic, or sociological problem—can effectively illuminate the aesthetic value of a text, the psychology of its author, or even the spirit of a literary epoch. Nor does the method disengage a work of literature from its living milieu; both pedagogically and scientifically this is a most sane and fertile approach to literature. Among the many currents of modern thought which have contributed to its scientific development is Croce's conception of the identity of linguistics and aesthetics wherein the latter is seen as the science of expression and general linguistic. Of equal importance is the phenomenology of Edmund Husserl which strives, in its search for *Wesensschau,* to intuit and elucidate the essence of phenomena. The importance of this philosophy for literary theory has been amply demonstrated through the intensive studies of Roman Ingarden. Heinrich Woelfflin's theory of art history has also been a notable contribution. The method of explication has received considerable enrichment from philologists like Leo Spitzer who seeks the 'inner life-center' of a literary work and Karl Vossler for whom aesthetic criticism can be the quintessence of philology. A radical historicism is, of course, an undeniable presupposition of the *explication* procedure. (pp. 374-76)

Auerbach considers one of Vico's axioms of particular importance for the understanding of historicism and the modern conception of cultural or period style: "The nature of (human or historical) things is nothing but their coming into being at certain times and in certain fashions. Whenever the time and fashion is thus and so, such and not otherwise are the things that come into being." The burden of this *degnita* is that man has no other nature than his history, that human nature is a function of history. Ingarden is saying much the same thing when he writes: "It is an acknowledged fact that each epoch in the development of human culture possesses its special types of understanding, of aesthetic and extra-aesthetic values, its determinate presuppositions in regard to exactly such and not other ways of comprehension of the world generally, but also of works of art." This condition governs artistic creation as well as aesthetic interpretation. The vicissitudes of history subject a literary work of art to unpredictable transmutations, retrogressions, renascences. Analogically a work can even 'die' a natural death if it should become totally alien or incomprehensible to the readers of a given period. Hence the immediate task of literary criticism is necessarily an historical one, involving certain predispositions imparted by the historicist attitude; the scholar must labor to restore the original significance of the text, to uncover its proper form, to disclose its individual essence. Nicolai Hartmann, speaking in the language of ontology, observed that such a labor will be crowned by experiencing "the resurrection or rebirth of an historically dead spirit" which has been infused with life once again after a prolonged interval of silence.

Auerbach's early book on Dante contains some thoughts that will illustrate Ingarden's analysis. Dante's work is not so remote from us in time that more than a minimum of historical empathy is required to gain entrance into its poetic world, but neither a powerful sense of such empathy nor the most searching scholarship will be of any avail if the 'will' or mind remain unmoved and is recalcitrant toward Dante's poetry. Auerbach concedes that historical concretions can exhibit new dimensions within the being of the human spirit's great creations without mutilating or destroying their identity or actuality. Yet in the Divine Comedy "there is a limit of its power to transmute itself." He believes this limit was reached when readers of the *Commedia* tried to dissociate its poetic beauties from the doctrine and the object or substance of the poem and to evaluate them as purely sensuous phenomena. The *Commedia* cannot be read as "pure poetry" because "the object and doctrine of the poem are not an incidental work, but the roots of its poetic beauty . . . they are the moving forces, the form of this matter, they animate and kindle the high imagination; they first lend to the visionary appearance along with its true form the power to seize and enchant." The linguistic character of the Divine Comedy is determined by the fusion of several elements: one involves the hard, realistic, and authentic reporting of actual events, the other didactic or dogmatic promulgation of rational doctrine concerning the world's order. In the poem itself these two elements are nowhere completely separable and their coalescence is so perfect that the characteristic element of the poetic, the imagination, has forfeited its autonomy. Simply stated, chimerical criticism can be avoided only if we judge a work "in the same spirit that its author wrote," and aesthetic historicism cultivates a temper of mind through which the original spirit of a work or an age can manifest itself, and can become knowable within its own "historical space." (pp. 377-78)

Historicism in literary study, however, does not envisage an ultimately philosophical goal, one whose aim would be the ideal restoration of the human spirit's total presence. This Platonic idea, or *verum* (to use Vico's technical term), partially realizes itself in the vision of life and sense of order present in every historical age. It represents all of man's diverse efforts toward self-understanding which have received and will receive symbolic expression throughout history. The initial concern of Auerbach as literary scholar is to read literary documents in terms of the historical conditions that they immediately reflect and express, to read them, that is, in the light of their positive moments or stages. This orientation enables him to cope with what students of language often consider the most difficult problem of meaning, viz. the influence of context or situation. Such extreme historicism eventuates in relativism which, in Auerbach's estimation, is the "prerequisite for all serious and comprehensive historical work." It is Vico, once again, who furnishes him with an antidote against what is pernicious in philosophical relativism. The historically diverse forms of human thought can be rediscovered, or recreated within the structure, the potentialities, the *modificazioni* of the human mind. Consequently, the literature of former ages is not in any sense radically or irrevocably alien to man's spirit at its present juncture, but its re-assimilation by us can be effected only if this literature is addressed and explored in such a way that it reveals itself in both its uniqueness and historical dimension. This is what Auerbach means when he says that "it is from the material itself that he [the critic] will learn to extract the categories or concepts which he needs for describing and distinguishing the different phenomena," and that any valid methodological approach or point of departure "must be pregnantly and precisely, not only analogically, applicable to the historical object."

Since historicism is an ineradicable component of our modern world-view, its dialectical development has confronted us with another momentous task, one which transcends and absorbs the study of particular historical manifestations. The modern investigator must now concern himself with continuity, interrelations, and synthesis. According to Auerbach historicism as a spiritual movement has compelled us to proceed from historical individualities to an 'historical Typology,' and finally to the conception of a "synthetic-historical philosophy." The stupendous growth in our knowledge or concrete experience of the forms of historical life and the refinement of our methodological techniques has rendered the need for comparison and synthesis inevitable, but supremely difficult. *Geistesgeschichte,* the inner goal of Auerbach's investigations, has become a real possibility and we now need to develop what Fritz Saxl once called "the aesthetic historical sensibility." The present object of philology is to seek a whole formed in such a way that "it works as a dialectical unity, like a drama, or as Vico once said, like a serious poem." But the *serioso Poema,* which is European civilization, is approaching an end; its unity as a spiritual configuration is destined for amalgamation within the greater unity of world history.

At the turn of the XIXth century Friedrich Schlegel prophesied that the study of literature in the modern world would demand a scholar, a free and educated man, who had the power "to attune himself at will to philosophy or philology, to criticism or poetry, to history or rhetoric, to the ancient or the modern." Surely Erich Auerbach possessed this very power. (pp. 380-81)

> Charles Breslin, "Philosophy or Philology: Auerbach and Aesthetic Historicism," in Journal of the History of Ideas, *Vol. XXII, No. 1, January-March, 1961, pp. 369-81.*

The Times Literary Supplement   (essay date 1965)

[*In the following review, the critic commends the scholarship and critical insight of Auerbach's* Literary Language and Its Public in Late Latin Antiquity and in the Middle Ages.]

When enthusiasts have had ten years or more to get their teeth into a really great critical book, the last papers of the scholar who wrote it can sometimes be meanly treated by ambitious younger scholars, or envious older ones. But a new book by Erich Auerbach, even if it were much thinner textured than these four excellent and elaborate papers, [in *Literary Language and Its Public in Late Latin Antiquity and in the Middle Ages*], would always command the gratitude and excitement of everyone who learnt from *Mi-*

mesis; his method is empirical, and every new essay is a re-creation of the powerful electric charge that book administered. Before *Mimesis* appeared, there were whole areas of the relations between language and life we had sensed, but not realized could be coherently understood. The sharp scholarship and strong sensibility of which those early studies are the monument did not die out in exhaustion or restlessness: the formula of their combination remained the same, and they continued to break into new material until Auerbach's death in 1957.

The relation between the literary language of certain periods with its public, and the way in which the language used by writers predetermines and limits them, the bombshell effects on literary possibilities of the intellectual and social crises of late antiquity, will not be unfamiliar themes to Auerbach's admirers. But the precise ground he covers and many of the suggestions he throws out are in fact new, and this book, like its predecessor, is necessary reading. His first study deals with the Christian crisis of *sermo humilis,* the necessity that Augustine felt to speak simply and the very interesting and specifically Christian mixed style which was the result. In spite of his vast output, Auerbach was not a comprehensive but a triumphantly selective scholar, who worked by isolating key problems and by paying attention to the questions they raised prior even to his lively appreciation of actual texts. He was one of a generation of European scholars who grew supple by wrestling with the spirit of Vico. His strength in this typical, and typically suggestive, study of *sermo humilis* is the combination of unremitting intellectual limelight with a deep, concrete grasp of what Augustine's, Bernard's, anyone's Latin is actually like.

If one could wish anything different about his work, it might be the inclusion of new areas, or languages (more Greek for instance), which could have modified his sense of literary history. There are many questions one might have asked him about the humbler genres of non-Christian Latin, about the non-correspondence of Greek to Latin literary history, and about the Carolingian restoration of official Latin language, which he could surely have answered if he chose. In everything Auerbach wrote, there is matter for disagreement, modification and discussion; mistakes are rare. He is, as a matter of fact, wrong once in this volume about a formula used by Gregory of Tours to future copyists, warning them not to add to or subtract from his writings. The formula goes back through the Bible (the end of the book of Revelations) to the blessings and curses attached to ancient epitaphs and the earliest inscribed laws. Auerbach does from time to time show uncertainty in dealing with literary formulas of this kind, but there are few tricks he misses, and there have not been many scholars to equal him even for sheer breadth of exact information.

The second and third of these last four studies are again a kind of appendix and enlargement to *Mimesis.* His paper on Latin prose in the early Middle Ages is at once a literary and a social history of the Latin language in that period. Its grasp of the shifts and differences of Latin, and of what changes underlay them, is much sharper than would have seemed possible before it was written. His paper on the sublime in the Middle Ages is the shortest but the pithiest and most wholly convincing in the book. It would be unfair to repeat his detailed, empirical argument in a bare résumé, but it may be said to end with an analysis of the early and late Dante which ranks among Auerbach's finest achievements, a few pages in which all his sympathetic, historical and critical powers are in majestic play.

One is often forced to ask oneself for what public Auerbach is writing. What readers are there good enough to know Dante properly, to have a real grasp of medieval Latin, to understand Homer, the *Chanson de Roland,* the sermons of the fathers, and to have some feeling for the early origins of the Romance languages? (Even when direct quotations are all translated.) The poet Apollinaire would have liked this book: W. H. Auden has been recommending *Mimesis* for many years. It is not so much a sourcebook for academic men, which of course it is and will be for a long time, as a piece of direct speech to those who understand what literature is, or who want to understand it: the limitations and the possibilities. There is a sense in which the final study which has given its name to this volume is mirrored in Auerbach's own position. His penetration of the western public and its language is both subtle and powerful, not to be overthrown. The existence and the delights of his book and of the lifework it completed are an enormous beacon burning against despair.

> *"Language without Limits," in* The Times Literary Supplement, *No. 3326, November 25, 1965, p. 1072.*

Wolfgang Bernard Fleischmann   (essay date 1966)

[*Fleischmann is an Austrian-born American educator and critic. In the following essay, he analyzes Auerbach's application of linguistic and historical criticism to the study of literature.*]

In the course of his introduction to his last, and perhaps greatest book, *Literary Language and Its Public in Late Latin Antiquity and in the Middle Ages,* Erich Auerbach refers to Vico's conception of the total phenomenon of history as an eternal Platonic state in spite of constant change displayed by the historic process. If one were to seek a phrase to describe the contours and perspectives of Auerbach's accomplishments as a philologist and critic, Vico's metaphor yields a clue. Early and late, Auerbach's work is permeated by a genial, though limited, set of ideas on literary process which serve to illuminate and explain a kaleidoscopic variety of literary phenomena. His republic of letters is a Platonic state, in which the multiplicity of appearances, the flux of languages, styles, and texts is, through Auerbach's skill, continually made relevant to structures of ideas which, by dint of serving in many instances to show order in diversity, help define the nature of historic process.

Any attempt to seize upon and describe Auerbach's set of structures, as they illuminate his work with literature, would send one to the "Epilogue" of *Mimesis.* For it is here that we find a kind of genetic development for three of these: From an apposition of Plato's ranking *mimesis* as third after truth, in Book 10 of *The Republic* with

"Dante's assertion that in the *Commedia* he presented true reality," and from a keeping in mind of this apposition as he proceeded to a wide study of the interpretation of human events in European literature, Auerbach states having crystallized out "three closely related ideas" which in turn form the methodological base for *Mimesis.* These are, first and second, the two "breaks with the doctrine of stylistic levels", in the literary history of the West—the breakthrough to realism in the early nineteenth century with its representation of random individuals in the context of "serious, problematical, and even tragic" situations being paralled earlier in the tradition by a "first break with the classical theory . . . (through) . . . the story of Christ, with its ruthless mixture of everyday reality and the highest and most sublime tragedy." Unlike the Romantic breakthrough, however, the Christ story did not foreshadow realistic representation in literature. Much rather, New Testament theology gave rise to what Auerbach terms figural interpretation, the seeing of one occurrence in terms of the new, "the connection between occurrences . . . (being) . . . not regarded as primarily a chronological or causal development but as a oneness within the divine plan, of which all occurrences are parts and reflections." The "figural . . . conception of reality in late antiquity and the Christian Middle Ages" is Auerbach's third key idea for the intellectual dimensions of *Mimesis.*

A fourth guiding concept in Auerbach's work is his notion of deriving insight into the nature of a literary audience through the exploration of key phrases having to do, within a given stage of linguistic and literary developments, with author-reader relationships, with social status in relation to readership, or with the description of readers, as such. Here, Auerbach's early study on the phrase "La Cour et la Ville" as revelatory of the nature of reading publics in late seventeenth-century France is paradigmatic, as to method, for the interconnecting series of essays on late classical and medieval reading publics which constitute *Literary Language.*

It will be noticed that all four of Auerbach's key concepts for approaching literary phenomena are firmly grounded in a historic process. Three of these—the notions of breaks in traditional stylistic conventions through the literary portrayal of commonplace persons in the *New Testament* and in the Romantic novel, as well as the concept of assessing a literary public through a study of its habituated language—are deeply concerned with the relationship between literature and society. Auerbach's thoughts on "figural interpretation" are, by contrast, less historical and societal in conception, than they are historical and theological. While the methodological part of his essay **"Figura"** purports to be the analysis of an idea strongly represented in medieval modes of literary interpretation and useful for a modern interpretation of medieval literature, the terms of its applicability are visualized along theological lines. Having demonstrated the often complex ways in which the "prophetic" writings of the Church fathers had interpreted the Old Law as foreshadowing the New by means of endowing *figurae* in the former with eschatological significance for the latter and by way of anticipating his own "figural" approach to the *Divine Comedy,* Auerbach admits: "There is something scholarly, indirect, even abstruse about . . . [figural interpretation] . . . , except on the rare occasions when a gifted mystic breathes force into it."

Is the Auerbach of *Mimesis* a "gifted mystic" on this order? In part, my answer would be "yes"; in part, "no." My positive answer would be strongest for a case like Auerbach's interpretation of Virginia Woolf's *To the Lighthouse,* in the chapter of *Mimesis* entitled "The Brown Stocking," where a misreading of the novel as fragmented and disorganized is presented with such force of conviction that even a reader objectively certain that Auerbach is wrong is carried along by his argument. There is, secondly, an almost uncanny quality about Auerbach's choice of texts for inclusion in *Mimesis:* Why do seemingly random passages from texts often of doubtfully representative quality for the period of literary history envisaged work so well in bringing not only the work from which they are taken but also the whole period of their origin to life? Finally, a reading of *Mimesis,* especially when it is done at one sitting, will give one the illusion of having recapitulated, in that series of essays acknowledged by their author to have been presented on eclectic and fragmentary principles, the whole of the Western tradition in literature. There is no doubt that *Mimesis* is infused with a kind of providential spirit, seeming effortlessly to make the chaos whole, which is hard to find in twentieth-century literary criticism and which is, besides, explicitly prefigured in the author's methodological assumptions.

Yet in other, equally important contexts, *Mimesis* is by no means a theological work and Auerbach, the sum total of his writings considered, no theologian. For one, Auerbach's commitments to eminently secular notions of history and society (discussed below) would qualify any purely theological, let alone mystical stand. For another, Auerbach suffers too strongly from the "philological conscience" of his academic generation to be less than skeptical of metaphysical commitment. He feels compelled to justify his genial ideas on "figurative interpretation" by prefatory excursions on a strictly etymological order. An attempt is made to anchor every chapter of *Mimesis* in the grounds of accepted literary history, by means of a comparative epilogue. When Auerbach writes either for students or for the public presumed to be beyond his field, he takes distance from ideas to which he confesses elsewhere being very close, and assumes a stance of scholarly "objectivity." No student using Auerbach's textbook *Introduction aux études de philologie romane* could feel that the discussion of Leo Spitzer's philological methods, to which Auerbach admits on many occasions having been signally indebted, was written by any but the most dispassionate knowledgeable observer. Readers of the *Journal of Aesthetics and Art History,* seeing Auerbach's cool and uncommitted discussion of **"Vico and Aesthetic Historicism"** could get no sense of the author's strong intellectual attachment to Vico, which amounts to a discipleship.

Auerbach seems thus, in communicating to a student or general public, to be able to stand outside his own commitments, to act as a distant, dispassionate commentator upon ideas very close to his scholarly life and work. For

a critic as interested as is Auerbach in levels of literary understanding as these related to the place of authors and readers in their social and educational structure, such a pronouncement of exoteric doctrine, with one's own working essentials viewed from an objective distance, is not very surprising. "Philosophy," says Vico in enunciating the sixth element of his *New Science,* "considers man as he should be and so can be of service to but very few, who wish to live in the Republic of Plato, not to fall back into the dregs of Romulus."

Wish to live in the Republic of Plato, where the essentials of his quest are concerned, Auerbach does. What he has in mind is a *Geistesgeschichte* which understands, through a seizing upon of all phenomena possibly relevant to it, the totality of its spiritual, intellectual, aesthetic, political, and social essence. Studying the portrayal of reality in a given era, on the one hand, and the relationship between literary language and its reading public, on the other, defines the character of the era. Breaks in stylistic levels signify demarkation points between eras. Ways of interpreting events from one era through significations derived from another, the Old Law in terms of the New, create a dynamic in the inter-relationship of historic process which, all at once, prevents one from a static view of literary "periods" anchored in the past and also permits the flow of history to emerge into the present and thence into the future. All phenomena are studied in relation to phenomena of their own era as well as to those of eras in their past. At the same time they stand ready, as it were, to be reinterpreted by future eras and in terms of these.

While the critic reasons, the present shifts; the future becomes the past. The task of what Auerbach calls, in *Literary Language,* his "radical relativism" is thus unending— "a task of infinite dimensions which everyone must attempt for himself, from his own point of observation." In the process of the critic's study, all "extrahistorical and absolute categories" vanish; legitimate categories of cognition are derived from the historical process itself, but they are, by reason of the nature of this process, necessarily "elastic" and temporary." Nothing is final or absolute *except,* when it comes to the flow of history and to its beholder, the relativity of the process itself.

Plato, in replacing *mimesis* third from truth assumed truth, in the context of the tenth book of *The Republic* to be absolute. The maker of the painted bed in question here, i.e. the carpenter, is second from truth. The true maker of the archetypal bed is God. Divine Providence was, for Vico, the moving force behind the historic process. Historical relativity was a function of divine decree. To quote Auerbach, "Divine Providence makes human nature change from period to period; the distinction between human nature and human history disappears; as Vico puts it, human history is a permanent Platonic state." Auerbach's Platonic state finds what permanency lies behind it in the dialogue of the historic process itself. "The general image," he says, "which seems to me capable of representation, is the view of a historic process; something like a drama which contains no theory but a paradigmatic exposition of human fate. Its subject, in the broadest sense, is Europe; I try to seize upon this in a number of individual critical attempts." Yet Auerbach hints, elsewhere, that the end of the process he is concerned with is in view. Civilizations will either be destroyed, in short order, or become as one. In the latter case, consciousness of the diversity of historic process will disappear. By an implication not stated by Auerbach, the disappearance of historical consciousness would mean the end of a continuation of historic process, as he understands this. Past history could be looked at from a static point of observation; what had been discovered about it would assume permanence. The drama of European literature would cease to be part of a shifting dialectic, subject to modification by future participants; its different acts would assume the nature of perennial human paradigms.

In the time immediately preceding Auerbach's early death, we know that he engaged in the study of minute and technical problems in Dante. By way of personal reading, he was intensively preoccupied with the *Essais* of Montaigne. It seems almost as if he wished to convince himself, and perhaps posterity, of the absence either of theological concern or commitment on his part. I cannot but believe, however, that the strength and momentum needed by Auerbach in attempting over and again to seize the variety of Occidental literary phenomena in structures were based upon an intimation either of a cessation of historic process which would give these structures permanence or of a hope, on a theological order, that these were part of a meaningful plan. At the same time, the nature of Auerbach's work makes it abundantly clear that the difficulties of maintaining a radical relativism, uninformed by a certain belief in the eventual relevance of the historic patterns discovered upon a plane of absolute truth, took their toll in denying the work eventual coherence. What unifies the work is its method. Once this is understood, the hard covers placed about either **Mimesis** or **Literary Language** could melt, revealing a series of brilliant individual essays, of fragments yielding luminous insights into the varied eras of literary history their topics connote.

We can learn much from the work of Erich Auerbach, but not the sort of literary historiography which will allow students and teachers a working knowledge about any given era. If the synthetic survey of Romance literatures in Auerbach's **Introduction aux éudes de philologie romane** fails to relate the author's scholarly ways to the student, this lack of contact may be due not only to Auerbach's consciousness for the need of simplified generalizations in a manual of this sort but also to an inability to relate, on a broad canvas, the highly specific insights his discoveries convey. If **Mimesis,** for all its semblance of unity, presents no "coverage" in the sense of historic continuity, this is due less to the great intrinsic difficulty of coping with the Occidental tradition from Homer to Virginia Woolf within the scope of one volume than to the fundamental lack of belief, on Auerbach's part, in either the possibility or relevance of such an attempt.

Again, it would be folly to use Auerbach's method as a dogma. By his own admission, some of the essentials required of a philologist cannot be taught. Breadth of cultural horizon, wealth of personal experience, power to re-experience imaginatively the work of art, ability to seize

upon what is important—these are, for Auerbach, necessary but personal accomplishments, on this order. Whether or not a teacher can do anything to further these factors is a matter for debate but the fact that Auerbach considers them unteachable points to a view of his own work, which I share, as a highly personal, creative achievement. To send graduate students to **Mimesis,** as is occasionally done, with a view of having them hunt for Auerbach's specific structures in texts not treated by him seems a dubious undertaking. "**Mimesis,**" as its author says, "is quite consciously a book written by a certain kind of man, in a certain kind of situation at the beginning of the 1940's." What students and critics can learn from Auerbach's method, however, is a lesson in the possibility of combining essentially structural criticism with the most detailed philological study, of keeping form in mind without needing to forget the ever present multiplicity of detail.

On the practical level this means that a critic learning from Auerbach can make stylistic studies without wedding himself beforehand to a system of categories. Much rather, the categories his critical exposition necessarily must contain can evolve, as it were, from the text, the probability of their truth being assured by a vigilant exercise of those scholarly virtues Auerbach considers teachable—"grammar and lexicography, the use of sources and textual criticism, bibliography . . . (and) . . . careful reading." What will emerge will have the advantages of creative originality and of relevance to the text, without for a moment sacrificing that accuracy and exactitude only the application of linguistic and historical insight can achieve—in short, the advantage of Auerbach's own work, at its very best. (pp. 535-41)

Wolfgang Bernard Fleischmann, "Erich Auerbach's Critical Theory and Practice: An Assessment," in MLN, *Vol. 81, No. 5, December, 1966, pp. 535-41.*

Harry Levin   (essay date 1969)

[*Levin is an American educator and critic whose works reveal his wide range of interests and expertise, from Renaissance culture to the contemporary novel. He has long been an influential advocate of comparative literature studies, and he has written seminal works on the literature of several nations, including* The Power of Blackness: Hawthorne, Poe, Melville *(1958),* The Gates of Horn: A Study of Five French Realists *(1962), and* James Joyce: A Critical Introduction *(1941; rev. ed. 1960). The latter work was in part inspired by Joyce's comment that Levin had written the best review of* Finnegans Wake *(1939). Levin has noted that his "focal points have been the connection between literature and society" and that his "ultimate hope is for a kind of criticism which, while analyzing the formal and aesthetic qualities of a work of art, will fit them into the cultural and social pattern to which it belongs." In the following excerpt, he recounts his friendship with Auerbach and comments on Auerbach's writings.*]

The literary event to which I owe my acquaintance with Erich Auerbach happens to have been the birth of Cervantes. In the fall of 1947, four hundred years afterward, it was being commemorated at Harvard University by a series of lectures and conferences. Américo Castro, whom I likewise had the privilege of meeting on that occasion, was naturally among the presiding spirits. One of the private receptions took place at the home of Amado Alonso, who himself had twice become an emigré. As a young Spaniard, trained at the Centro de Estudios Históricos in Madrid, he had emigrated to Buenos Aires, where he had been placed in charge of the Instituto de Filología. As a leader in the academic opposition to Perón, he had lately been compelled to leave Argentina a year before. His decision to settle in the United States signalized a revival of Hispanic studies at Harvard—though his leadership of it would, alas, be cut short by his premature death in 1952. From the hospitable Don Amado I gathered that Auerbach, of whose work I then had barely heard, was present by a happy accident. He had just come for the first time to America, where he would be spending the rest of his career, and was here in Cambridge to visit a son who was studying chemistry at the Harvard Graduate School.

The man I met was slight and dark, gentle to the point of diffidence, yet lively and engaging in conversation, speaking mostly French at that time, and looking not unlike one of those kindly ferrets in the illustrations of children's books. Though he had recently published **Mimesis,** and would shortly have his Swiss publisher send me a copy, he was not sanguine about its impact on either side of the Atlantic. Though he was on leave of absence from his chair of Romance philology at the Turkish State University in Istanbul, he spoke with candor and modesty about his possible willingness to accept an American professorship. Finding that we had much to talk about, both on a theoretical and on a practical plane, we agreed to lunch together a few days later. Our lunching place deserves at least a footnote in the annals of cultural migration. The Window Shop was started during the nineteen-thirties, by a group of Harvard faculty wives, as a means of finding employment for German and Austrian refugees. Having flourished, it had moved along into a well-known habitat on Brattle Street, which had formerly been a New England tearoom and originally the smithy of Longfellow's Village Blacksmith. Where the spreading chestnut tree had stood, *Sacher Torte* was now the specialty of a Viennese menu.

Regularly favored by the patronage of the stately Hellenist, Werner Jaeger, and of other scholarly expatriates, this was our local Cantabrigian symbol of the great American melting pot. Auerbach seemed pleased to be taken there, and our dialogue opened with a polite exchange about the tenor of life in Cambridge, Massachusetts. Prompted by his questions, I found myself repeating an old byword about the Galata Bridge at Istanbul: that, if you sat there long enough, all the world would pass by. Auerbach, whose penetrant eyes had been inspecting the situation, did not immediately respond. Instead he rose, excused himself, and walked to a neighboring table. Its occupant, who warmly greeted him, was—as Auerbach explained on his return—an American with whom he had been acquainted in Istanbul. Coincidence had reinforced my groping parallel. In the ensuing discussion he made it clear why he no longer wished to sit and wait at his Turk-

ish bridge. Whether, by crossing the seas, he had come to another Byzantium, worthier of Yeats's ideals for a holy city of the arts, might well have been in doubt. But America, at any rate, had niches ready to be filled by wandering sages. Belatedly yet wholeheartedly, Auerbach joined that throng of European intellectuals who passed by the transatlantic bridge, to the vast enrichment of our culture. (pp. 463-64)

One of his anecdotes casts a comic light upon the sense of disconnection from which he must have suffered [at his teaching position in Istanbul, Turkey]. On taking up his official duties at Istanbul, he was introduced to various Turks with whom, it was presumed, he would have much in common. One of them, understandably, was the Turkish translator of Dante, whose rendering of the *Commedia* had been accomplished in less than two years; indeed it would have been completed sooner, he boasted, had he not also been translating potboilers during the same interim. When Auerbach congratulated him on his presumable grasp of the language, this colleague blandly confessed that he knew no Italian at all. His brother did; but that was scarcely a help, since the brother had been away at the time. To Auerbach's obvious question, his informant replied that he had worked from a French translation. Auerbach, doing his best to keep his eyebrows from twitching, asked which one. "I don't recall the name," said the Turk, "but it was a large brown book." What could be expected, under these circumstances, from so highly qualified a *Gelehrter* as Auerbach? He would be working, as he liked to put it, *"dans un grenier."* After he had used up his backlog of notes, he would have to suspend his medieval researches. In the absence of learned journals, compilations, and commentaries, how could one continue to be a scholar?

To be sure, there was a fair collection of the major authors of the West. And it is true that, in countries where seminars were grinding out professors and bibliographical tools were being multiplied, critics had begun to wonder whether all the philological apparatus was not obscuring the literary artistry. A certain correlation was suspected between the short-sightedness of footnote-scholarship, *Anmerkungswissenschaft,* and the acquiescence of the German universities to the Hitler régime. Auerbach, at all events, could never be deprived of his own learning and training. His artistic perceptions, innately keen, had been broadened by historical perspectives acquired from Vico and from Vico's modern apostle, Benedetto Croce. He found himself perforce in the position of writing a more original kind of book than he might otherwise have attempted, if he had remained within easy access to the stock professional facilities. There is not a single footnote in the English edition of **Mimesis,** and the only ones in the German edition are simply Auerbach's translations of the texts already cited in foreign languages. Each of these is the theme of a chapter devoted to its stylistic interpretation. But the sequence of twenty chapters also comprises an anthology—or, better, an imaginary museum—of European civilization extending, across three millennia and eight languages, from Homer to Virginia Woolf.

Ever since Aristotle expostulated with Plato over the imitation of nature, *mímesis* has been the central and most problematic concept of esthetics and criticism. Auerbach's subtitle pins it down to the representation of reality by means of words, so that textual explication becomes the key to a concrete understanding of the occidental past. Realism in the explicit sense, as practised by the French novelists, is telescoped into two dense chapters toward the end of the book. Equally real, for Auerbach, are a mob scene under the Roman Empire and the stream of Mrs. Ramsay's consciousness in *To the Lighthouse*. The selection of passages to be chronologically analyzed is always interesting and often surprising. The recognition of Odysseus by Euryclea, Eve and the serpent in a mystery play, Manon Lescaut and her lover at supper, Pantagruel's mouth viewed as a microcosm—these are privileged moments if not epiphanies. We are plunged into particularity without any introduction. Auerbach shies away from generalization, though a brief epilogue draws together the guiding threads of his approach. His starting point is the canonical assumption of traditional rhetoric, the separation it maintained between grand and humble styles, plus the subsequent conditions of their intermixture, so deliberate in the Bible and elsewhere, with an effect of elevating the commonplace which has social as well as esthetic implications.

His other key idea, which more peculiarly bears the stamp of his thinking and derives from his work as a medievalist, is the exegetical device of *figura*. That rhetorical term of the ancients had been utilized by the early Christians, when they saw the personages and events of the Gospels prefigured in the narratives of the Old Testament. In the Middle Ages it was invoked to show how a particular manifestation could express a transcendental reality. Thus it illuminates the vivid concreteness of Dante's otherworldly allegory. Auerbach had traced and formulated this conception through an article first published in Italy at the outset of the Second World War. (A decade afterward I sat next to him at a meeting of the Modern Language Association, watching his weary smile and hearing his wry comment, as an American colleague made effective but unacknowledged use of his method.) Since *mímesis* is realistic by definition, and *figura* is a symbolic mode, one of the contributions of Auerbach's book is to demonstrate precisely how they conjoin and enmesh. He wrote to me that his European reviewers, though they were friendly, looked upon *Mimesis* as no more than "an amusing series of analyses [in?] of style." Having hoped that his integrating ideas would be noticed and discussed, he transferred his hopes to the English edition, which was laboriously being prepared under the sponsorship of the Bollingen Foundation.

Meanwhile he had received his first American appointment from Pennsylvania State College, where—in addition to his teaching in Romance languages—he taught a course in Goethe for the German Department. After a mutually satisfactory year he would have been given tenure, but for a technicality which arose when the prerequisite medical examination revealed a heart condition. He was enabled to spend a congenial interlude at the Institute for Advanced Study in Princeton, where he also gave one of the Christian Gauss Seminars. In 1950 he was called to Yale, and he passed his last years on that distinguished

faculty which includes such cosmopolitan figures as Henri Peyre and René Wellek. His position there he described as "almost ideal." He had occupied the transitional years in "filling up the enormous lacunae in bibliography, and western life in general, caused by the eleven years in Turkey—adaptation to academic and literary life in USA . . . " He was delighted to have generous hours for reading and writing, along with a few courses wholly devoted to medieval subjects. His essay applying the stylistic theories of *Mimesis* to Baudelaire and modern poetry, he declared, would be his farewell to modernity. My feelings of loss were all the more poignant, when he died in the fall of 1957, because he had accepted an invitation to teach the course in Dante at Harvard that year. "Had we but world enough and time . . . "

Marvell's line is quoted on the title page of *Mimesis,* whose dates of composition are given on the verso: "*Mai 1942 bis April 1945.*" Partly to fill in temporal gaps from the resources of American libraries, Auerbach's later investigations were again specialized and concentrated on more distant periods. They are vivified by a percipient reader's concern with the nature of the reading public, manifested earlier through a study of the role the audience had played in French classicism. His illumination of the dark ages before the invention of printing should counterbalance the postliterate sociology of Marshall McLuhan. The introduction to Auerbach's final volume harks back to his earliest mentor, Vico, and reaffirms the commitment to historicism they shared. In contrast to the medievalism of Ernst Robert Curtius, Auerbach stresses changes rather than continuities. History, as he conceives it, is recorded consciousness, to be interpreted by continual scrutiny of the surviving records. For the questionable absolutes of *Geistesgeschichte,* he would substitute a relativistic perspective, which seeks realities in those different places where our differing predecessors have found it. What confers a unity on this outlook is a vision of Europe intensified by successive expatriations to the east and west. A posthumous collection is entitled *Scenes from the Drama of European Literature.* Now and then an elegiac tone hints to us that the drama is a tragedy which has entered its last act. (pp. 465-69)

Harry Levin, "Two 'Romanisten' in America: Spitzer and Auerbach," in The Intellectual Migration: Europe and America, 1930-1960, *edited by Donald Fleming and Bernard Bailyn, Cambridge, Mass.: The Belknap Press of Harvard University Press, 1969, pp. 463-84.*

René Wellek (essay date 1978)

[*In the following essay originally presented at the 1978 Vico/Venezia conference, Wellek discusses Giambattista Vico's influence on Auerbach's understanding of literary history and aesthetics.*]

Erich Auerbach, the Romance philologist and Dante scholar who is best known for his book *Mimesis: The Representation of Reality in Western Literature* (1946), was a life-long student of Vico. His first paper on Vico dates from 1922; his last posthumous book, *Literary Language and Its Public in Late Latin Antiquity and in the Middle Ages,* in a statement of "Purpose and Method" contains a grateful acknowledgement of Vico's profound influence on his thinking. In the thirty-five years between these pronouncements, Auerbach produced an abbreviated translation of *The New Science* into German in 1924, a translation of Croce's book on Vico (1927), and a series of essays, comments and reviews on Vico. The thirteen items expressly devoted to Vico do not exhaust Auerbach's absorbing interest in Vico. Vico's conception of Dante is discussed in other contexts, allusions to Vico are frequent in many papers, and the name of Vico is invoked as a star witness in a few declarations of faith.

The introduction to the German translation of *The New Science* (1924) is Auerbach's most elaborate and comprehensive account of Vico's thought. Unfortunately it is little known: it is not reprinted in the **Gesammelte Aufsätze zur romanischen Philologie** (1967), and even copies of the translation seem to be rare today. The introduction starts with an informative sketch of Vico's life and some remarks on his reputation and influence. Vico's isolation in his own time is then emphasized extravagantly. "We must not think of Hobbes, Descartes, Grotius, and Montesquieu but of Bach and Johann Balthasar Neumann [1687-1753, the architect of the church at Vierzehnheiligen.] We must not look for the contemporaries among whom he belongs, among the philosophers and men of letters, but among composers and architects." Something like a baroque time-spirit is assumed. Vico is resolutely taken out of the history of thought. But I trust that this passage should be understood mainly as an expression of Auerbach's admiration for Vico's grand imaginative architectonics and originality. Actually, Auerbach expounds then Vico's opposition to Descartes and the epistemological foundation of Vico's thought: the identity of *verum* and *factum,* of knowledge and creation. In the sketch of Vico's reputation, Auerbach had recognized Croce's merit for the rediscovery of Vico, and he was to translate Croce's monograph, but in expounding Vico's theory of knowledge and the position he assigned to mathematics, Auerbach doubts that Croce could be right in detecting irony in Vico's view of mathematics. Vico, Auerbach states, thought in terms of medieval Realism or, as he says himself, Platonically. The frontiers between logical abstraction and metaphysical reality are often blurred in him. Rather, Auerbach sees in Vico's concept of mathematics an anticipation of Kant's phenomenalism. When Vico calls mathematics an "operative science," he comes close to Kant's view. But Auerbach knows that Vico did not have a concept of the "necessary form of intuition" and rather helped himself with "an arbitrary act," "a mystical abstraction." Vico did not recognize this. He was deluded by the pleasure of uniting Platonic, Christian and empirical ideas. I cannot pretend to any competence in the history of the concept of mathematics, but Auerbach's trust in Kant's solution has not, I believe, been borne out, if one thinks of such recent theories as Gödel's; Vico is closer to present-day views. Auerbach's attempt to make him a precursor of Kant on this issue seems ill-advised. But, in any case, Auerbach dismisses the early writings of Vico: *De nostri temporis studiorum ratione* and *De Antiquissima sapientia,* as not really original. Even the principle of the coincidence of creating

and knowing was formulated before by Francisco Sanchez, but the discussion and rejection of Cartesian rationalism was a necessary preparation for the writing of the *New Science.*

Auerbach then hails Vico's proclamation of the primacy of historical science, quoting paragraphs 331 and 349, voicing Vico's rapture at his discovery. Vico has created the possibility of a philosophy of history and is not disturbed by the open conflict between this foundation and his system. Auerbach sees the conflict in Vico's retreat from the view announced in these sentences in which greater certainty for history than for mathematics is claimed. Vico's three stages, the *corsi* and *ricorsi,* deny man the knowledge of history which God has of nature. The subject of knowledge has disappeared: free will is in mystical harmony with nature along with Providence. Man collaborates with history: we know history from inside intuitively better than we know nature. But saying that man creates and knows history is, in its radical version, misleading. The universally human, in myth, law and language, the common sense of mankind, is not knowledge in the same sense in which God knows perfectly. Vico thought of himself as a man at a point of history when the mystery of Providence reveals itself to the fully developed man of reason. But Vico does not see that this man would be like a Cartesian man of reason. There remains, Auerbach concludes, an insoluble contradiction.

Auerbach then quotes Croce paraphrasing Vico that "man creates the human world, creates it by transforming himself into the facts [*cose*] of society; by thinking it he recreates his own creations . . . and thus knows them with full and true knowledge. Here is really a world, and man is really the God of this world." Auerbach, however, doubts that this is Vico's opinion. For Vico, Providence and not man is the God of history. *The New Science* is called in its second paragraph "una teologia civile ragionata della Providenza divina." Logically one can, like Croce, draw the consequence from the maxim of the identity of *verum* and *factum* that man is the God of the historical world, but Vico's concept of history is a theology, an attempt to probe the ways of God. Croce thus disapproves of the climax of Vico's system. In Vico, the mysterious interplay of Providence and society seems a mystical synthesis of contraries: of empirical history and God's foreknowledge (*ewiger Ratschluss*), of transcendence and immanence, of God and the world. The stages of history are, in their totality, the common sense of man. They are, at each stage, simultaneously the expression of the empirical state of the time and the eternal divine reason, so that the postulate of a union of philosophy and philology can only be felt but not known rationally.

Auerbach then explains that philology as used by Vico includes all moral sciences and that he demands that they be united with philosophy, i.e., that every empirical fact be understood in terms of the general law and every general law in terms of the individual state of affairs. But the eternal law is not only immanent, not even pre-formed harmony, but a transcendent God is at the same time immanent. How this can be remains obscure.

Croce discovered these contradictions because he is hostile

to any transcendence and tries to separate what Vico put together. He rejects Vico's view that empirical history is also "typical" history or even "ideal eternal history." He rejects the "universale fantastico": a universal based on sensibility rather than on reason. This might have satisfied Croce's philosophical conscience but not Vico's. Vico wanted to abolish the Here and There and put the One in its place. He wanted to unify Reason and Sense in the history of Divine Providence. Croce speaks of Vico's limited horizon, but Auerbach protests that he towers over all his successors. Compared to Vico, Herder's humanity, the "conservatism of feeling" embraced by the Romantics, and even the Absolute Spirit of Hegel, bear the stamp of a homely orderliness in which the *I* either believes or demands or dreams of a cosy point of repose. Vico's Catholic God is, Auerbach grants,

> a dogma: but it is not simply postulated or dreamt up but a living myth, an ineffable mystery, totally un-human, while the corresponding schemes of later times, with their lukewarm temperature, have no sensual power and do not rise to the high dignity of the metaphysical idea; for they were constructed on the analogy of man around the *I* that has become so important that an attempt is made to assimilate the world to the *I,* to make it feel at home in it. An atmosphere of a close room is created where many sit together in order to discuss things, while Vico, hotter than all the others, stands alone in the icy air of a glacier, and above him stretches the immense baroque horizon of the vault of heaven.

This unusually florid passage, which I have translated literally with all its shifting metaphors, is used to support the argument that Vico, while opposed to Descartes and the whole of the eighteenth century, should not be put together with Romantic and post-Romantic philosophers of history. Pantheism and conservatism of feeling was quite alien to him. The fact that the Germans at that time ignored him only proves the point.

Auerbach then expounds familiar matters: Vico's objections to the contract theory and his concept of poetry and language. For Auerbach, Vico is "undoubtedly, if only in underground manner, as it were, the founder of modern aesthetics and anthropology." Croce's aesthetics is a modern paraphrase of his thought. Vico's concept of poetry as myth and metaphor is more radical than anybody's in German literature since, with the possible exceptions of Hölderlin's and Nietzsche's. For Vico, the poetic age is only poetic and mythological; even its ethics, politics and sciences are poetic. Croce objects to this view strenuously: there never could be or have been poetic ethics, politics or sciences. Auerbach rejects however Croce's saying that this is "one of the corners that remain in shadow" in Vico's thought. Rather, it shows the abyss that divides Vico's thinking from that of the nineteenth or twentieth centuries. We understand him better today because we have learned to take heed of the irrational and poetic elements of the human mind. Still, we remain rationalists. It is the insoluble paradox of Vico's being that he was the first to attempt to design a "godless" system of history. He should have been a poet; a new *Divine Comedy* would have

come about—but he knew that this could not be in a rational age.

Vico's concept of the evolution of law confirms Auerbach's view that Vico had no contact with the Enlightenment. He treated it with a show of respect but actually with secret contempt and quickly saddled it with the "barbarism of reflection" and with decadence. Vico did not pave the way for the Romantic concept of law. He had no interest in *Volksgeist.* He contemplated man and society in general and called it the history of divine providence or sometimes "storia dell' autorità," the history of traditional norms. He looked at men and circumstances not out of interest in their peculiarity but as expressions of God; he contemplated God and not men; in the *New Science* the icy and sometimes passionate breath of the unconditioned blows; it is the air of Spinoza and Leibniz, not the air of Romanticism or of the science of the nineteenth century. Nothing dynamic, organic, or whatever you call it can change this.

Providence implants the religious conception into the hearts of men; without it order could not come about and would not last for a moment. History is the path of Providence, it leads society from anarchy to order according to God's decree. But where does history lead? Where is its fulfillment, its last aim? Here, Auerbach thinks, is an astonishing gap. Vico began with the fall of man; he should have ended with the Last Judgment, but there is not a word about it. He does discuss the history of the Jews separately, but the appearance of Christ is no milestone for him. History after Christ seems not essentially different from ancient history and, above all, the Last Judgment is missing. At the end of the *corso* comes the *ricorso:* everything begins anew. Seeing that Vico depicts the modern absolute monarchy rather perfunctorily as the highest point or human development, it would seem that he did not envisage a better state of the world than the enlightened and rational state. We would think that Vico would merely refrain from considering its further development as achieving a state of absolute felicity and that he would rather see the germs of decadence and of a new beginning in it. But this would be an error. Vico cannot be considered a partisan of the enlightened state. Every state was good for him in its specific time. He has not described the happy City of God. He wanted to and could describe only secular history. One cannot, on the other hand, present Vico as the discoverer and believer in an immanent Providence and regret that his deplorable Catholicism prevented him from finding the modern concept of progress. His Providence acts in the empirical stages of history, but it is the experience of a believer who looks at it as transcendent reality. It was Vico's intention to present religion as the basic condition of modern society, to equate God and order, and to tie the proud man of reason of his time to God and the earth.

I have paraphrased and at times translated this introduction not only for its intrinsic interest as Auerbach's fullest statement on Vico but also because it differs sharply from his later pronouncements in its emphasis on Vico's belief in Providence and its rejection of Croce's interpretations. The Introduction was preceded by an article buried in *Der neue Merkur* which anticipates it, sometimes literally. The emphasis is the same; Vico was the last to succeed in interpreting history as the eternal way of Providence, as the expression of God. The picture of the Enlightenment mind is drawn even more harshly, in contrast to the "unexpressed, with the architects and musicians, on altars and wooden saints" for which man and history were nothing. The sketch of the course of history according to Vico is more highly compressed and the rejection of Croce's interpretations as secular and wrong is even more emphatic. The article concludes with the passage repeated in the Introduction to Vico "standing in the icy air of a glacier" and on his aim to bind the "proud man of reason of his time to God and the earth."

All discussions after these two early pieces focus on specific aspects, are comments or developments on what is said in the Introduction and, in some later papers, single out ideas which Auerbach felt inspired and justified his own concept of scholarship.

The review of Richard Peters, *Der Aufbau der Weltgeschichte bei Vico* (1929) reasserts Auerbach's emphasis on the metaphysical basis of a Catholic nature behind Vico's scheme. It gives it its vivifying power, which lends an admirable unity to the system. Peters, while diligent and careful in his exposition, goes even further than Croce in seeing Vico's religion as a "a sort of mimicry which hides his real ideas." The emphasis on the rationalistic Enlightenment elements in Vico is misleading.

An article on **"Die Entdeckung Dantes in der Romantik"** (1929), Auerbach's inaugural lecture at the University of Marburg, expounds Vico's view of Dante as a Tuscan Homer as an important anticipation of Romantic notions but disapproves of Vico's view that Dante would have been a greater poet had he known nothing of Scholasticism and Latin. In Auerbach's contemporary book, ***Dante als Dichter der irdischen Welt*** (1929), Vico's view of Dante is again expounded but rejected. Dante's work, "umana ragione tutta spiegata," Dante the supposed barbarian, was superior to Vico in "subtlety of reason," in the exactitude and purity of thinking. But Vico was an important precursor of the Romantic conception.

Still, in the next paper, **"Vico und Herder"** (1931), a lecture at Cologne, while expounding Vico's anticipations of Herder's ideas, Auerbach emphasized rather their fundamental differences. Herder in speaking of early poetry thought of folksongs in which the poetic mind of primitive times played about, while early poetry was for Vico a "harder, more concrete substance in which law and poetry, sociology and theology were interlocked." There is no *Volksgeist* in Vico, no interest in the particular conditions of nations, no patriotism, no egotism, no romantic folklore, no domestic feeling of closeness, no idyllic joy in the beautiful and noble in man. "The little schoolmaster Vico stood in admiration and awe before the giant figures that had sprung from his head." In conclusion, Auerbach contrasted Vico's Providence as transcendent and unchangeable with Herder's belief in immanence.

Both the papers on the discovery of Dante in Romanticism and the Vico and Herder piece were originally public

lectures which kept an urbane tone of exposition and persuasion. Auerbach's last paper before his emigration to Istanbul, **"Giambattista Vico und die Idee der Philologie"** (1936), is a heavily documented and footnoted survey of the meanings Vico gave to the terms "Scienza nuova" and "natura." Auerbach argues that the concept of nature is completely historicized in Vico. It means the state of development, a view buttressed in a special paper, **"Sprachliche Beiträge zur Erklärung der Scienza nuova von G. B. Vico"** (1937). There Auerbach distinguishes between Vico's various uses of the term, singling out passages in which, he argues, human-social nature is identified with history. Human nature is neither a remote original state nor enlightened reason. Vico's historicism is absolutely natural, but his concept of nature is also specifically historical. In the paper **"G. Vico und die Idee der Philologie,"** Auerbach expounds Vico's idea of the mentality of primitive man, emphasizing that "poetic" does not have the modern meaning of lyrical or enthusiastic. The imagination of primitive man is rather severe, formulaic, pictorial, cruel and epic-historical. In a term which Auerbach must have borrowed from Ernst Cassirer, he speaks of Vico's analysis of the "symbolic forms" of human expression. Vico transfers hermeneutics from writers to myths and laws and finds the master-key in the study of the structure of primitive language. The common sense of mankind, a predisposition, not a truth but rather a certitude, allows him and us to understand primitive man. The *certum* is the subject of hermeneutic philology, the new art of criticism. Its main tool is the interpretation of documents: whether of Homer or of the Twelve Tables. Philology is thus the study of the Principles of Humanity. Philologists include poets, historians, orators, grammarians and jurists. Thus the *New Science* is the first work of "verstehende Philologie," a science of man insofar as he is a historical being. It presupposes a common world of man, not in the cultured, enlightened and progressive sense but in the whole great and terrible reality of history. Behind this sober exposition one feels that Auerbach now knows: *tua res agitur*. In expounding Vico, he expounds his own concept of philology as understanding, as interpretation and as history "in its terrible reality."

The war brought an interruption in Auerbach's concern with Vico. It allowed him to write *Mimesis* in Istanbul. Vico is there discussed only briefly as a parallel figure to the Duke of Saint-Simon; both, "in opposition to the rationalist-antihistorical attitude of their time, regard man as deeply imbedded in the historical data of his existence." When, after the war, Auerbach emigrated to the United States, he soon had occasion to review the English translation of the *New Science* by Thomas G. Bergin and Max Fisch as "the most complete and accurate translation in any language" and to restate, this time in English, Vico's conception of historical evolution and his anticipation of almost all the basic principles of modern ethnology. In the same year, Auerbach gave a lecture at the convention of the American Society for Aesthetics in Cambridge, Massachusetts, on **"Vico and Aesthetic Historicism"** in which he clearly formulated his own creed. Today we admire, he argues, Giotto, Michelangelo, Rembrandt, Picasso and Persian miniatures; Racine and Shakespeare, Chaucer and Alexander Pope, Chinese lyrics and T. S. Eliot. The breadth of our aesthetic horizon is a consequence of our historical perspective. It is based on "historism" (Auerbach uses the German form learned from Troeltsch and Meinecke), i.e., "the conviction that every civilization and every period has its own possibilities of aesthetic perfection." Auerbach then appeals to Vico and expounds the relevant views closely following his earlier paper, **"Vico und die Idee der Philologie."** New is Auerbach's mention of Robert T. Clark's discovery of a tenuous link between Vico and Herder through Cesarotti's notes to Ossian, and new is a mention of Joyce as influenced by Vico. In summary, Auerbach praises again Vico's discovery of the magic formalism of primitive man and Vico's theory of knowledge. Vico created the principle of historical understanding entirely unknown to his contemporaries, and Vico created and passionately maintained the concept of the historical nature of man. "He identified human history and human nature; he conceived human nature as a function of history."

Auerbach came to Yale in 1959 and understandably had other things to do. He was planning the book *Literatursprache und Publikum in der lateinischen Spätantike und im Mittelalter.* Still, Vico remained very much in the back of his mind. The new intellectual atmosphere at Yale, where Auerbach encountered many who did not believe in his secular religion of historicism—New Critics or simply old positivists or religious believers—induced him to restate his creed with an appeal to the authority of Vico. A paper entitled **"Philologie der Weltliteratur"** (1952), shows Auerbach's concern for the decay of historical perspectivism and concern for the incursions into philology of the problems and categories of contemporary literary criticism, which seem to him disruptive of an empathic surrender to concrete problems of the past. Vico is referred to only quite incidentally.

Auerbach's review of my *History of Modern Criticism* (or rather of its first two volumes [1955]) must be seen in the context of a defense of his own position, also in reaction against my review of the English translation of *Mimesis* [see Further Reading]. Auerbach says many laudatory things about my books but protests against my reservations about historical perspectivism, which, in my view, led later to eclecticism, mere antiquarianism and finally to extreme relativism and critical paralysis. Auerbach argues that we need not fear even radical relativism. Quoting Vico that all forms of the human can be found again "dentro le modificazioni della medesima nostra mente umana," he states that the historian "does not become incapable of judging; he learns what judging means. Indeed he will soon cease to judge by abstract and unhistorical categories; he even will cease to search for such categories of judgment." Not surprisingly, in comments on individual sections of my book, Auerbach complains of my brief treatment of Vico (only a retrospective one, for he precedes the starting point of the book, the middle of the eighteenth century) as inadequate. I should have followed Croce and seen that Vico's poetics was "the very first modern poetics" and that he was the founder of historism. Admittedly I was then impressed by Franco Amerio's *Introduzione allo studio di G. B. Vico* (1947) and cannot even today share Croce's concept of poetry and history. I mention Auerbach's review not for any personal reasons (though our discussions became important for, I hope, both of us in these years of close association) but because the very same passage, somewhat changed in detail, was then used in English translation in an article published posthumously as **"Vico's Contribution to Literary Criticism"** and then again in the Preface on "Purpose and Method" of *Literatursprache und Publikum in der lateinischen Spätantike und im Mittelalter* (1958). In these two almost identical pronouncements we have the fullest statement of Auerbach's creed with the strongest appeal to the precedence of Vico. In **"Vico's Contribution to Literary Criticism"** he again expounds Vico's "first methodical theory of understanding of history," which he interprets as an advocacy of empathy by our own inner experience. He praises Vico's insight into the unity of the various kinds of human activity. "Vico has expressed with unequalled grandeur and consistency, the modern idea of 'style.'" Finally, Vico is considered the father of historicism when Auerbach quotes: "Natura di cose non è che nascimento di esse in certi tempi e con certe guise." "Thus together with the concept of style, historicism was created; it is, I believe, the 'Copernican' discovery in the field of historical studies. Our historistic way of feeling and judging is so deeply rooted that we have ceased to be aware of it. The variety of periods and civilizations no longer frightens us." Auerbach then alludes to me and others when he says that "the tendency to ignore historical perspectivism is wide-spread and is, especially among literary critics, connected with the prevailing antipathy to philology of the nineteenth-century type. Thus many believe that historicism leads to antiquarian pedantry, to the overevaluation of biographical detail, to complete indifference to the values of the work of art; therefore to a complete lack of categories with which to judge, and finally to arbitrary eclecticism." But to Auerbach these consequences, rehearsed very much in the terms of my arguments, are only signs of the ineptitude of particular scholars. Historicism is not eclecticism. Auerbach then repeats the passage from the review of my *History of Modern Criticism* almost verbatim and goes on to assert that Vico also succeeded in defining the essence of poetry, the *universale fantastico,* which is at the same time general and concrete. Vico confined poetry, wrongly in Auerbach's view, to the early stages of man's history, but even this primitivism produced some of the most important ideas of modern criticism: the folk genius, the poetic symbol, and the distinction between poetic expression and the ordinary language of communication. In Vico, philology comprehends all the historical humanities: it becomes almost identical with the German term *Geistegeschichte.* Auerbach concludes: "This is Vico's idea of philology, which I learned from him."

The introduction to *Literatursprache und Publikum* differs from the article by expressing an apprehension for the decay of Europe and a sense of the end of a period. It then formulates most strongly Auerbach's sense of obligation to Vico. "Early in my studies I became acquainted with Vico's conception of philology and the 'world of nations'; in a very specific way this conception has complemented and molded the ideas deriving from German historicism." Then Auerbach again reproduced word for word what he

had said in **"Vico's Contribution to Literary Criticism."**
Vico, he continues, is the inspiration for a synthetic philology, which he sees as an urgent task now that the sense
of history is diminishing. He grants that Vico's own enterprise did not succeed completely: much of his erudition is
erroneous and even absurd. The difficulties of mastering
the task have since multiplied. A general synthesis has become impossible but, Auerbach argues, we can reach it by
selecting characteristic particulars and following up their
implications. We must isolate key problems. Auerbach
recommends the interpretation of textual passages as a
starting point: the method he himself had practiced with
supreme success in *Mimesis.* If we assume with Vico that
every age has its characteristic unity, then every text will
provide a partial view on the basis of which a synthesis is
possible. But Auerbach sets his method off from stylistics
in the manner of Leo Spitzer. His purpose is always to
write history. Vico is called upon for the last time when
Auerbach doubts that there are general laws in history.
Even dialetical materialism seems to him of only limited
validity. He himself can only convey a historical process,
a kind of drama which advances no theory but only a pattern of human destiny.

Auerbach said once that he wanted to write a book "without any general expressions." He did not admit that his
mind was saturated with a knowledge of historical grammar and syntax, intellectual and general social and political history, Hegelian and Marxist generalizations. Vico allowed him to retreat into concreteness, empathy, intuition, "understanding," as the justification of a praxis
which combined stylistics, *Geistesgeschichte* and Hegelian-
ism (mainly in the guise of Lukács' *Theory of the Novel*),
with a stupendous grasp of theology, literary history and
many older forms of thinking. But trying to characterize,
analyze and possibly criticize Auerbach's work would lead
us far beyond the confines of this paper. (pp. 85-96)

> René Wellek, "Auerbach and Vico," in Vico:
> Past and Present, edited by Giorgio Tagliacoz-
> zo, Humanities Press, 1981, pp. 85-96.

Thomas M. DePietro   (essay date 1979)

[*In the following essay, DePietro examines what he considers the limitations of Auerbach's methodology in* Mimesis, *specifically the conflation of history and legend
and imposition of modern critical assumptions on ancient and medieval texts.*]

"My purpose," Auerbach states, "is always to write history." In **Mimesis: The Representation of Reality in Western Literature,** his immediate and explicit historical concern is to capture and record the whole of European civilization through an examination of select literary fragments. He discusses excerpts of prose works, plays, poems,
and letters, asking of these fragments what he believes to
be the appropriate questions. But Auerbach's idea of history, as it unfolds throughout *Mimesis,* lacks the theoretical underpinning that we have come to expect of modern
historians. He believes that the laws and categories of de-
terministic methods for understanding the past (as for example dialectical materialism or psychoanalysis) can only

explain a small segment of the past. The "levelling of western culture" and the engulfment of Europe into a larger,
more complex civilization demand the writing of a "lucid
and coherent picture of this civilization"—a sketch of the
"pattern of human destiny." The socio-political conditions of Europe before and after World War II, the apparently steady dissolution of moral and political order, and
the rise of the barbaric "new order" justify the sense of urgency and fear that surfaces throughout *Mimesis.* But to
view the book as a mere response to its immediate historical surroundings obviously minimizes its theoretical assumptions and their consequences for the practical study
of literary history.

The underlying premises of *Mimesis* are that literary style
and language (for example, syntax, grammar, organization of detail) portray the view of reality in a given text;
that the chronological organization of these views explains
the "movement" or change of literary styles in European
literature; and finally, that through an understanding of
an individual's style and of "stylistic movement" (the synchronic and the diachronic) we can understand the view
of reality, or, more broadly, the general milieu of a given
historical period. True, Auerbach's system does not easily
conform to such a neat reduction, because he often goes
beyond the limitations of stylistic concerns and considers
other forms of evidence (most notably, the biographical
data concerning Stendhal). Yet Auerbach does impose a
sense of unity on the apparently eclectic accumulation of
non-stylistic evidence in *Mimesis.* Specifically, it is his
own presence—the subjective "I" of personal experience—which carefully selects from the enormous amount
of potential non-textual evidence the data relevant to a
given text or to the movement of historical periods.

The synchronic view of the text in *Mimesis* does not separate the text as an individual piece of language from its period. Instead, Auerbach, like his teacher Vico, believes
that the "largeness of our aesthetic horizon is a consequence of our historical perspective; it is based on
historism. . . ." He elaborates this principle in succinct,
self-evident terms: ". . . every civilization and every period has its own possibilities of aesthetic perfection. . . .
the works of art of the different peoples and periods, as
well as their general forms of life, must be understood as
products of variable individual conditions, and have to be
judged each by its own development. . . ." In the epilogue to *Mimesis,* Auerbach explains that his concern
with the ancient conception of the three levels of style refined itself into the basic question: what does an author
take to be sublime or significant? But Auerbach's historicism prevents him from asking the same questions of
Homer and Virginia Woolf. Instead, the question becomes
a series of more specific questions or, as he calls them,
"points of departure." Again, his technique relies on a Vi-
conian principle. Briefly, Vico posits a holistic view of history and believes that insight into one aspect of a cultural
period such as law, logic, or poetry provides a key to all
the other aspects of a period. Auerbach extends this idea
into a theory of literary method which uses the interpretation of a literary passage as the initial key to understanding the whole work. He does not apply the "loose analogies" or terms of departure used by such critics as A. O.

Lovejoy (for example, "classic," "romantic," or "baroque"). Instead, his questions arise from important words *within* the texts, as for example, "*figura*" in Dante or "*la cour et la ville*" in Moliere and Racine. Once the meaning of these terms is established, they are, at least in theory, applicable to any text of the period.

For Auerbach, the synchronic elements of the text are then intrinsically bound to the diachronic elements so that the questions for a text can only be answered in terms of language and style. He therefore demonstrates how the two principal styles (the Homeric and the Biblical) mingle, dissolve, and are distorted. This concern, along with his belief in the continuity of western culture, explains the seemingly injudicious comparison of Homer and Petronius, writers as far apart in history as the Beowulf poet and Robert Lowell. Consequently, a comparative principle is at the middle of all of Auerbach's statements about writers. Without a discussion of Rabelais' style, how could he discuss Montaigne's style, since the language for discussion would then have to have an *a priori*, ideal existence outside of history (in which Auerbach rightly does not believe)? By closely examining the application of these ideas in chapter one of **Mimesis,** I hope to clarify the premises and to draw out some of the problematic theoretical consequences of this method.

Although Auerbach acknowledges that his study must begin *in medias res*, his choice of the Old Testament and the *Odyssey* as starting points is neither arbitrary nor unjustified. By beginning with these two works, he emphasizes the enormous and distinct influences that they exert on later representations of reality in western literature. A study of Homer's digressions provides Auerbach with the best means for understanding the style of the *Odyssey*. The clarity of detail and the orderly "syntactical connection between part and part" (i.e., the use of hypotaxis or causal connectives between dependent clauses) that characterize Homer's style reflect the orderly thoughts and feelings of his characters. The digressions in the *Odyssey* (Auerbach chooses the recognition of the scar as his example) neither produce suspense nor create perspective; rather they serve to illuminate the narrative proper, leaving nothing in darkness. Instead of mentioning the scar and leaving its origins unknown for a moment, Homer uses its first mention as an opportunity to describe its background: all is "externalized." Because Homer "knows only foreground" or the objective present, there is no tension between the past and the present. Homer narrates all the past details only as they are related to the present, creating the effect of transposing the material of the digressions (the past) to the immediate present. Auerbach supports these claims with stylistic evidence. For example, the digressions are introduced by syntactical constructions ("once long ago") which indicate that the material to follow happened in the past. When he resumes the narrative he continues in the present tense. Other linguistic devices (such as conjunctions, adverbs, or participles) help to place everything in the *Odyssey* into fixed "spatial and temporal relations." Consequently, the descriptions of people are precise, the relationships between the characters are clear, and we know where everyone is, at what time, and why they are there.

In contrast, the narrative of the Old Testament, exemplified by Genesis 22:1, is obscure and defined only by the unity imposed by a formless God. We do not know who is narrating and God enters from an unknown place. There are wide gaps in the narrative of the story of Abraham and Isaac—gaps which are left for the reader to fill. Along with vague language and obscure characterization—Isaac could be anyone—the Biblical author uses certain linguistic devices which support Auerbach's view. The sentence structure is often paratactical: there is no causal relationship indicated by conjunctions or connectives in the sentence, "Behold, here I am." In the *Odyssey,* Homer represents "absolute objects" in order to "prevent the reader from concentrating exclusively on a present crisis," whereas in the Old Testament incidents are obscurely narrated in order to achieve complete suspense. The motives, the emotions, and the thoughts of the characters are "unexternalized." The author of Genesis "knows only background": the reader can understand Abraham's actions only if he remembers God's promises. The Biblical characters are explained by history alone. And they carry their history, as individual members of the chosen people, wherever the action leaves them in time and space. Although, in most cases, it is neither clear where they are nor what time it is.

Because Auerbach's purpose is to determine how an author represents reality, and not merely to point out stylistic devices, he must define or at least suggest the nature of the relationship between reality, truth, and fiction. According to Auerbach, the "real" in the *Odyssey* is the orderly world constructed by Homer and not a reality based on historical fact or truth. Homer does not ignore "the basic facts of human existence," but he neither examines their complexity nor responds to them in an evaluative manner. In other words, Homer neither rebels against nor embraces the various facts of contemporary life such as the gods or the heirarchical class structure. The Biblical author, on the other hand, avoids stimulating our senses with detailed descriptions. His sole concern is to translate "moral, religious, and psychological phenomena" into concrete matter. The Old Testament therefore demands to be received as absolute truth because its author believed in the truth of the story whether or not it was, in fact, true. According to Auerbach we must subject ourselves to the "truth" (the author's belief that it was true) of the Old Testament because its end is only the portrayal of truth and any other forms of realism are mere by-products. This universal claim to truth of the Bible accounts for its lack of narrative unity: the vision of God and the hope of Salvation alone bind its stories together.

Auerbach acknowledges that we cannot easily determine if the world within the Bible is in fact "true" or "synthetic." But by the stylistic evidence outlined above we can distinguish between the legendary and the historical. The *Odyssey* contains only legend and no history: "Legend arranges its material in a simple and straightforward way; it detaches it from its contemporary historical context, so that the latter will not confuse it; it knows only clearly outlined men who act from few and simple motives and the continuity of whose feelings and actions remains uninterrupted." The confusion of the Bible is thus created by the narrator's being "true" to the historical nature of what must be narrated. The narrative and its subject matter are confused because they lack a present purpose and make sense only in terms of an other-worldly universal history. In Homer, the sublime ("what an author takes to be significant") is the elevated and orderly representation of the ruling class. Only unproblematic idyllic realism enters into the narrative. In the Old Testament, "the sublime, tragic, and problematic take shape precisely in the domestic and commonplace."

The reason for my descriptive, non-critical discussion of chapter one is to unravel the complexity of Auerbach's method of stylistic analysis and to suggest the unfortunate consequences of an analysis based primarily on the synchronic. One limitation of his method is that he avoids examining the religious attitudes held by Homer's audience. Surely, were he to examine other cultural evidence of ancient Greece (since theoretically what he says of Homer should be true of the period) he would discover, especially in Greek tragedy, a completely different view of the gods. For example, the *Bacchae* (which is later than Homer but part of the same period) is characterized by its use of "everyday reality" and presents an ambiguous, often sarcastic view of the gods. This evidence would then call into question the idea of Homer's lack of ambiguity. But this criticism does not take into consideration the premises of the chapter because in the first chapter and the majority of those following, Auerbach is neither interested in how style arises for a specific society within a larger period nor in the attitudes held by the authors in regard to given institutions.

A far more important criticism of Auerbach's synchronic analysis results from his mistaken distinction between history and legend. This distinction, which underlies the differences between Homer and the Bible, also accounts for the differences between Petronius and Tacitus as historiographers. It explains as well why Gregory of Tours' work is not a history but a memoir and why the Song of Roland is a fable. In general, the difference between history and legend underlies the major distinctions between reality and fiction throughout *Mimesis.*

Given Auerbach's statements about the portrayal of truth in the Old Testament, an atheist cannot grasp the Bible because he is not able to subject himself to the Biblical claim for absolute truth. Auerbach gives five basic points concerning the difference between history and legend:

> 1) "It is a difficult matter . . . to distinguish the true from the synthetic."
> 2) " . . . it is easy to separate the historical from the legendary in general."
> 3) "Their structure is different."
> 4) [Legend] "detaches it [its material] from its contemporary historical context."
> 5) "To write history is so difficult that most historians are forced to make concessions to the technique of legend."

My first impulse is to wonder whether Auerbach sufficiently establishes the distinction between the first and second points or does he merely say that history has more truth in it and that legend has more falsehood? It seems that he does not adequately distinguish the historical from the truthful on the one hand, and the legendary from the synthetic on the other. If I am correct on the first point, then the problem is clear. How can any historical narrative claim absolute validity? In order to do so, its author would have to exist outside of time. Otherwise he could not see the beginning and the end (the totality of history) which would be necessary for any full (true) account. But this is not an entirely fair representation of Auerbach's view, since he does assert in the third point that the historical narrative is different *in structure* from the narrative of legend. Historical narration is confused because it must be "true" to the complexity of historical events. Legendary narrative presents an orderly view because it removes itself from history (point four). It has no obligation to the truth of events. To restate this in other terms, Auerbach asserts that the language of a synthetic reality (Homer) is different from the language of religious belief and historical "reality" (the Bible). This points to two problematic consequences. We realize that Auerbach's question to the texts at hand is a singularly modern concern. The Biblical narrative and its language lead him to believe that its author's intention is to be realistic. However, we must realize that this is realism as he (a twentieth-century reader-critic) defines it. The result of his distinction is that we cannot read the Bible, or Gregory of Tours, as an artificial, or, more precisely, "constructed" reality. In defense of Auerbach's question to the text, I think he would not deny its modernity (a point to which I will return).

The consequence of his later assertion is more severe and pertinent at this point. By asserting a difference between history and legend, Auerbach supposes that there are fundamental differences between the languages of historical and legendary narratives, or, to restate, that there are fundamental differences between a language that portrays events as they have been witnessed by or told to the author and a language that relies on the author's imagination. But, to return to the first point, we can never be absolutely sure what is true or false in the events described, because our means for ascertaining their validity is subject to revision. And, corollary to this point, if the subject matter of legend removes itself from an historical context (point four), then so must its language, because, as Auerbach himself believes, language is inextricably bound to its subject matter. Also, Auerbach certainly would not want to be reduced to saying that either subject matter or language can exist outside its own period. Finally, and this is the most important counter-argument, all discourse, written or spoken, relies on artifice. Among the many modern examples of proseworks that rely most clearly on both history and fiction are *War and Peace,* Neale's *Queen Elizabeth I,* and Norman Mailer's recent article on Jimmy Carter in *The New York Times Magazine.* Auerbach, who often anticipates our objections, seems almost to state this himself in point five. But all of these objections result from his reliance on a purely synchronic view of the text. These objections do not apply to the entire book, because in later chapters more attention is given to the diachronic aspects of the text.

When considering the diachronic, Auerbach accepts the traditional definitions of periods in history. Only one work, Augustine's *Confessions,* defies the given categories. Augustine, unlike his contemporaries, "ever more passionately pursued and investigated the phenomenon of conflicting and united inner forces, the alternation of antithesis and synthesis in their relations and effects." These concerns, reflected in Augustine's style, set his work outside of his period. Therefore, since Auerbach's historicism acknowledges that it is the critic who defines an epoch, he adopts the obvious solution: he redefines the epoch in order to allow Augustine a separate place in literary history. I raise this point by way of demonstrating Auerbach's uneasiness with non-stylistic evidence. And instead of sorting out the particulars of Auerbach's discussion of periodization, I think that a consideration of his analyses of form and genre (especially in chapter seven) will suggest the major consequences of movement or change as represented in *Mimesis.*

The emergence of Christian Scripture in the later Middle Ages prevented the separation of styles. According to Auerbach, it was necessary for late medieval authors to mix styles since Christianity "cuts vertically" through the heirarchy of class structure. Thus, in the play, *Mystère d'Adam,* we find the representation of both the sublime (the idyllic reality of a superior class) and the humble (the tragic everyday reality of the common people). Auerbach elaborates this idea as follows:

> In antique theory, the sublime and elevated style was called *sermo gravis* or *sublimis;* the low style was *sermo remissus* or *humilus;* the two had to be kept strictly separated. In the world of Christianity, on the other hand, the two are merged, especially in Christ's Incarnation and Passion, which realize and combine *sublimitas* and *humilitas* in overwhelming measure.

The mixture of styles accounts for the form of the Adam and Eve play, which opens with a liturgical reading of Scripture and then presents, in dramatic form, the events of the Fall. Interspersed between the Fall and the announcement of the coming of Christ are scenes which portray "everyday contemporary life." All of these scenes are then given larger meaning by being placed into a "Biblical and world-historical frame." That is to say, "every occurrence . . . is simultaneously a part in a world-historical context through which each part is related to every other, and thus is likewise to be regarded as being of all times or above all time." Thus, if in a medieval play a character falls from a high position, he reenacts the fall of Adam and suggests the coming of Christ, the Redeemer of man fallen in sin.

Auerbach's view of medieval drama anticipates the more recent method of the Robertsonian school of medieval interpretation. But it is not necessary to repeat here the well-known arguments of R. S. Crane, who rigorously counters the Augustinian approach to medieval literature. Instead, I will draw out the implications of Auerbach's assertions as they relate to the study of genres and thereby suggest the limitations of this view.

According to Auerbach, the medieval drama (like all drama) can be classified in terms of form and style within its period. But as styles change, historical movement (that is, new periods of style) requires that we alter the way in which we view a dramatic work written in a distinct period of the past. Consequently, throughout *Mimesis,* Auerbach concerns himself only with what is different (mostly in terms of style) between the drama (or any other genre) of two distinct periods. Since a genre or form is so bound by style to its cultural period, it would be of no importance, for Auerbach, to seek out formal similarities between the use of a genre in different historical periods. He would consider it unimportant to discover similarities between the English Drama of the Middle Ages and of the Renaissance. He would not be interested in accounting for the survival of medieval vice figures in the plays of Shakespeare and Marlowe in which one-dimensional characters are used in the medieval emblematic manner. To return to the actual scope of the book, he suggests why Rousseau chose to write *Confessions* but never considers why Augustine, more than a thousand years before, also chose to call his book *Confessions.*

Writers, regardless of period, choose to write a drama or a poem (or a mixture of both) for reasons which pertain to the intrinsic qualities of the form and the subject matter. Among the many reasons Chaucer chose to write the *Canterbury Tales* with a narrative prologue and links was to allow for a diversity of forms (romance, homily, prose, and so on) each with its distinct purpose within his larger structure. The exigencies of time and finance prompted Johnson's *Rasselas,* his only attempt at prose fiction—a genre for which he had normally little patience and less understanding. Authors, then, are not merely the recipients of received forms. An alteration of form often results from the author's conscious intention to suit his subject matter to an appropriate medium. If an author's reasons for choosing a specific form are unimportant, as Auerbach seems to suggest, then there is no explanation for Johnson, primarily an editor and essayist, choosing to write *Rasselas* or *Irene,* his only dramatic tragedy.

Auerbach's discussion of authorial intention in relation to *Le rouge et le noir,* although inadequate as a discussion of why Stendhal as an individual chose the style he did, indicates that Auerbach would probably entertain the above objections. This does not mean that Auerbach's decision to include non-stylistic evidence (for example, a discussion of audience in relation to Montaigne or sociological theory in relation to Racine) reflects an unsystematic eclecticism. Instead, his selection from potential external evidence suggests a methodological concept that informs the entire book. That concept, as I have suggested earlier, is Auerbach's awareness of his own position in history. He acknowledges that this basic question (what does the author take to be significant?) is somewhat circular, since it is a twentieth-century question. And the answers to this question can only be derived from the mind of the twentieth-century critic. He acknowledges his own limitations as an individual reader and the limitations of his critical edifice. He believes with Vico "that the world of civil society has certainly been made by men, and that its principles are therefore to be found within the modifications of our own human mind." *Mimesis* is his attempt to understand texts as part of the world around him in order to understand himself as an individual in society. Together with his brilliant stylistic analyses of individual texts, this principle accounts for Auerbach's importance as a critic. In **Mimesis,** he has given us his careful scholarly opinions and asks us to accept or reject them (in a like rigorous manner) as we, individual readers, begin to understand and revise our own position in society and history. (pp. 377-86)

Thomas M. DePietro, "Literary Criticism as History: The Example of Auerbach's 'Mimesis'," in CLIO, *Vol. 8, No. 3, Spring, 1979, pp. 377-87.*

W. Wolfgang Holdheim   (essay date 1981)

[*Holdheim is a German-born American educator and critic. In the following essay, he focuses on what he calls the "symphonic structure" of Auerbach's writings on literary history.*]

[In his *Linguistics and Literary History*] Leo Spitzer bitterly complained about the sociological bias he detected in Erich Auerbach's criticism. It would be better, actually, to speak of a historiographical bias which often takes on a sociological emphasis. Now Spitzer's approach as well is strongly historical, but for him, history remains a tool for the aesthetic elucidation of a work and for the spiritual communion with its writer. The historical lines of force that traverse an author and his creation should be recognized, but their identification is merely the precondition for understanding the *individuum ineffabile:* "the particular form of language, the particular work or the particular poet" [Auerbach, **Literatursprache und Publikum in der lateinischen Spätantike und Mittelalter**]. Auerbach's purpose, by his own admission, is more general. The questions he asks the individual texts are squarely historical in nature: "again and again I have the purpose of writing history." The aesthetic dimension *per se* seems to play a secondary role in his critical preoccupations. He uses the very term rarely and usually in a limited context; unlike history, the aesthetic component seems self-evident and scarcely in need of explanation; after all, we are all imbued with the spirit of our time and need no professor to understand Rilke, Yeats, or Gide. This appears to be Auerbach's express opinion. In practice, however, he brilliantly elucidates aesthetic aspects and procedures, such as the transitions in Dante's Farinata episode. But there is more: his very way of writing history (in **Mimesis,** for example) is strikingly aesthetic. There is a seeming contradiction here. Can it be dismissed as a fortuitous case of individual ability, a mere indication that Auerbach just happened to be good at writing and at organizing his material? I do not think so. Auerbach's adeptness at exposition has a deeper significance—one which he himself (less a theorist than a practician) has not clearly formulated. But he did want to illustrate how literary history *should* be written, and his aesthetic practice tells us something about the nature of historical knowledge itself.

Let us look at **Mimesis,** his best-known and in certain ways most ambitious enterprise along these lines, and let us concentrate on the first eight chapters (up to and including Dante), which are probably the best and make up something of a whole in their own right. There are certain recurrent themes that should engage our attention. The two principal cultural strands of our Western tradition (the Greek and the Judeo-Christian) are first identified and contrasted (perhaps too neatly), then are artfully interwoven with a third strand exemplified by medieval romance. This is done, however, by reference to certain particular trends or notions that can give some focus to the process. I shall start by concentrating on that notion (that "question") which, by his own testimony, was Auerbach's primary point of departure: the problem of the levels of style.

Already the elevated style of the Homeric poems largely excludes the lower classes, reflecting the static hierarchy of a feudal society. On the other hand, the sublime and the tragic readily merge with the domestic amongst the movable nomadic peoples of the Old Testament. This Jewish *mélange des genres* is sharply intensified in the New Testament, as witness the story of Peter's three denials of the Savior. Christ's Incarnation and Passion gives a powerful impetus to the sublimity of everyday life; and neither the extreme pendulum swing between triumph and misery in the creature's soul (already a characteristic of the Old Testament), nor the vivid sense of collectively active historical forces would be compatible with a separation of stylistic spheres, such as it persists in Petronius' comical depiction of low life. While this division is not overcome even in the Latin decadence of the Fourth Century, the integrative power of the Incarnation is dramatically expounded in Auerbach's chapter on that period, and is related to Augustine's theorizing on the *sermo humilis.* The theme can be touched upon only in passing in the midst of the stylistic breakdown of the era of Gregory of Tours—and just as briefly in the discussion of eleventh-century epic: although social elevation occupies the foreground, the *chanson de geste* is popular in nature, no doubt because the classes were intellectually homogeneous. As for the romances of chivalry, they are held in a pleasant intermediate mode: the later trend towards separation (note the anticipation!) will be due to the revived influence of Antiquity. The theme culminates in chapter VII: the Christian convergence of humility and sublimity expands from the ethico-theological to the aesthetico-stylistic domain, finding its intellectual form in St. Bernard (who draws upon an extensive patristic tradition—note the flashback!), finding its literary expression in the mystery plays, and finally finding its existential embodiment in St. Francis. In the *Divina Commedia* at last, the union of opposites prevails in practice against Dante's own rhetorical preconceptions, but the tension between the poles is so extreme that it comes close to exploding all style. What is the pattern that emerges? The interplay of motifs resembles that in a symphony. The static motif is the separation of styles, and its staticity is artistically contrasted with the dynamism of stylistic intermingling, which seems to expand from chapter to chapter as it presents and represents itself from ever new perspectives, in an ever broader scope and intenser form. Then for some time the entire polarity goes underground, surfacing just enough so that it may not be forgotten—only to burst forth (in its dynamic pole) in full splendor and with hitherto unattained expansion, moving towards a high point of intensity from whence it advances towards self-transcendence.

At the moment of its apotheosis, the mixture of styles merges with the representational power of the figural conception of reality (among others). It is important to trace how the notion of the *figura,* one of Auerbach's foremost contributions to literary scholarship and intellectual history, progresses through the early parts of his book. It is essentially Christian, so that the initial pages on the Old Testament introduce it but unobtrusively and prefiguratively—much like a theme in a symphonic overture. Thereafter, it appears with reference to the Pauline mission among the Gentiles, which was forced to interpret the events of the Old Testament as "figural" anticipations of the New. Superficially, this passage looks like a brief final digression in chapter II; actually it prepares us for the initial effects of the figural conception, which will be non-realistic: the sensory impact of the occurrences will tend to get lost in the theoretical meanderings of theological interpretation. This perspective is renewed and expanded about twenty-five pages further down, when the concept is for the first time defined and treated at some length: in the figural view of reality, two events or persons distant in time are related in such a way that the first signifies the second, while the latter fulfills the former, yet each retains autonomous temporal and historical existence; it is here that the fruitful term "omnitemporality" is introduced. Yet it is in vain that Augustine tries to accord the figures' meaning as determined by exegesis, their vertical relation to a transcendent order, with their horizontal interconnection and their concrete vitality: the time is not ripe for a union of the two worlds; the exegetic verticality of the figures will triumph for many years to come. Helped along by the rigidification of life in late Antiquity and the early Middle Ages, this leads to the unproblematical schematization of characters which we find in such works as the *Song of Roland* and the *Song of Alexis.* The dramatic possibilities of a figural realism finally develop in the period of the mystery plays, of St. Bernard and of the triumphant *sermo humilis.* The vital historical concreteness of events now asserts itself against all dilution into typological signification, and the living example of St. Francis shifts the center of gravity to the country in which Dante will appear. The *Commedia* brings the completion and apotheosis of this view of reality—and at the same time its end, because the intensity of the realism literally bursts the frame which made it possible. Here again we seem to have followed the progressive expansion and the multifarious variation of a musical motif. With a difference, though: the progression is less linear than in the case of the mixture of styles, the variety is more important. What looms largest is the capacity of the figural trend to take various and even opposite forms (realistic plenitude as against bloodless schematization, for example) in different contexts and at various times.

We have a complex structure of contrast and expansion, the perspectivist variation and progression of a theme. Is this exclusively an "aesthetic" procedure, perhaps a series of rhetorical tricks to persuade by arousing our pleasure and interest? Quite the contrary: I want to argue that it is genuinely cognitive, reflecting the nature of the historical phenomenon in its multi-layered complexity. The difference between history and legend (Auerbach once writes) can be easily determined at first sight, because in legend things go far too smoothly. History is not linear;

its events are not merely stages in a demonstrative progression; chronology is a mere bloodless skeleton of time. In fact, historical events are not "facts" in the preferred sense of the natural sciences, methodically abstracted from reality—neutral "data" that can be grasped and manipulated by a pre-established ideal of cognition. They are not dogmatic but speculative—not staunchly self-identical entities, invariably and reliably "this" or "that," but inherently variable complexes contextually related to the whole of historical reality, subject to infinite modifications, radiating and opalizing in manifold ways. Auerbach's procedures bring out how we can make sense of history—the sense, *nota bene,* which it projects (or adumbrates) by itself. The treatment of the *figura* admirably reflects the principle of contextuality, showing how a general trend will have contrary manifestations at different periods.

A *general* trend: the *figura* (just like the notion of stylistic levels) is of course a universalizing concept. Auerbach once wrote that he would ideally have liked to avoid all generalities, and to restrict himself to a suggestive account of particulars. The remark, of course, can be interpreted as merely directed to the strategy of exposition, expressing Auerbach's congenital and justified suspicion of clichés—of rigid concepts (such as "romanticism" or "classicism") that are all too easily foisted upon the material in self-sufficient and inconsequential splendor. Yet I believe that there is more to it: we here catch a glimpse of Auerbach's occasional over-reliance on the more extreme turn-of-the-century forms of historicism, a limitation in his theoretical self-understanding that sometimes occurs but is nearly always overcome by his critical practice. Thus in this case he does use general notions, and how indeed could he do otherwise? Sheer particularity is itself an abstraction, and generality is an integral part of both historical life and historical understanding. In history, *universalia sunt realia,* there are active and supra-individual "historical forces," as Auerbach himself elsewhere declares. But these universals only remain real if in conceptualizing them we do not transform them into reified unchangeable entities. Historical concepts are not Platonic Ideas. Auerbach, I submit, uses his universals exactly in the right way. The *figura* concept, for example, emerges as a genuine historical tendency, maintaining and asserting its identity not above and despite, but precisely *in and through* all differences. Nor does such a trend need to be explicitly formulated or even institutionalized in its own time. What he has written is a history of literary reality, not of literary doctrines (so Auerbach argued against Curtius' criticisms), and the notion of stylistic levels as he uses it was formulated about 1940 by a German professor living in Istanbul. Of course institutionalization does occur, but it is far from being a necessary concomitant of historical trends and forces. Where it exists, in fact, it makes for reification, in literature as in other walks of life. Aspects of the concept of stylistic levels, as also of the *figura* syndrome, have been unequally codified in varying degrees at different times, and surely the periods of their institutional influence and theoretical self-consciousness have not always been those of their greatest vitality.

This is quite obviously so in the case of another prime

motif in the early parts of **Mimesis:** that of stylistic parataxis. It is shown to be most effective in the story of Isaac's sacrifice, but in such an unselfconscious manner that the *terminus technicus,* revealingly, is not mentioned. In St. Augustine, a deliberately Biblical parataxis merges with (and tries to control) a consciously classical hypotaxis, in an attempted unification of the two worlds that is never quite successful. In the barbarized age of Gregory, parataxis (again appropriately unnamed) prevails simply because the organizational power of language has declined. In the Eleventh Century, juxtaposition becomes the creative principle of the elevated style of the *Song of Roland.* In chapter VII, it appears briefly as a Biblically inspired incursion of eloquent directness in the letters of St. Francis. But then in the ensuing analysis of Dante, the concept recurs with an insistence that is surprising, for what is really being established is that the *Commedia* is not paratactic at all. That work is, on the contrary, a masterpiece of hypotactic sophistication, whose various episodes are contrasted with each other in a consummately artistic way. But it is precisely this procedure that is still distantly reminiscent of parataxis. More precisely, hypotaxis has been carefully blended with a technique of transitional juxtaposition, creating a synthesis in which parataxis has in effect been changed into counterpoint. The Hegelian flavor of this *Aufhebung* is too evident to need belaboring. But also the other two concepts I have examined reach their end point in the Dante chapter: *figura,* style mixture, and parataxis, in a state of extreme maturity, are intertwined with superior *raffinement.* Is the historian here overdoing things for purposes of aesthetic symmetry that are no longer cognitive? Generally, Auerbach's art of balancing and interconnecting strands and subjects is remarkable. Thus chapter VII, gravitating toward the central theme of the *mélange des genres,* advances persuasively from the French *Mystère d'Adam* via Bernard de Clairvaux, St. Augustine, and the Church Fathers to St. Francis and finally a dramatic Passion poem by Jacopone da Todi that is set off against the initial play. Once more: is this merely a compositional *tour de force*? I think that it is also a masterpiece of pertinent historical exposition. Consider the tremendous range (generic, theological, existential) covered by this picture of the period with its roots and prefigurations, and the ease with which the cultural focus shifts from France to Italy. As for the Dante section, note that the three guiding concepts converge not only at their point of culmination but at their moment of self-transcendence. Parataxis becomes contrapunctuality; the fulfillment of figural realism explodes the figural frame; and the mingling of styles moves towards a violation of all style. Historical trends truly are born, develop, overlap, manifest themselves variously in many contexts, and finally change their nature as if driven by their own inherent dynamics. The forces whose meanderings we have followed after all do come to a head and shed their skins in Dante, who convincingly emerges as the end and the beginning of an era.

But how do we know that in the story of Abraham parataxis creates a mysterious intermediate space in which unsaid complexities and hidden depths can be divined, whereas in the *Song of Roland* (for example) the same technique stops up all interstices and leaves an impression of rough-hewn simplicity and airless immutability? How can we be sure that these manifestations have just those meanings and yield precisely those results? Of course we cannot merely read them off, with absolute certainty, from "objectively given" texts or events, the way we can note computations from a calculator. Historical understanding is an active, hermeneutic appropriation by an interpretive mind. The putative discovery of objective laws or patterns that deserve universal application is itself merely a type of interpretation—a concealed and distorted one that does not recognize itself as such. In this respect as well, aesthetic prehension coincides with historical understanding.

We are here touching upon an eternal controversy: can historical knowledge be truly scientific, or is Clio really a muse? In recent times, however, some of us have begun to question the aestheticist view which would reduce the domain of the muses to a self-enclosed sphere of non-cognitive ideality. Art and literature are also forms of knowledge: in view of this insight, the terms of the old controversy have tended to shift. The line now no longer runs between knowledge and (for example) enjoyment, but rather between two different conceptions of knowledge. Is history to strive for an analytic, a "scientific" ideal of cognition, seeking universally valid "covering laws" or perhaps abstract patterns to which the wealth of its phenomena can be reduced? Or is it to be a form of hermeneutic understanding, with features that are related to aesthetic understanding—with *narrative* features, to be more precise? In the latter view, reading a story is an act of cognition that is also a model for historical prehension. What is crucial is that we are always dealing with an act of following, a process unfolding in time. The possibility of repeated rereading does not abolish this processuality at all. At each subsequent reading we grasp new aspects, see new and richer filiations; the pattern is refined but never exhausted; the point where we could collapse everything into a formula or (heaven help us!) into a diagram is never reached. The aspiration for a divine *nunc stans* vision is an exercise in reductive futility. And this is by no means a deficiency, as if a timeless and total comprehension were still the ideal to be approximated, unattainable only because of the regrettable finiteness of our minds. Rather, this finiteness—which makes knowledge ever a process, never a stance of attainment—is the creative mainspring of its infinite expandibility. The very nature and value of historical cognition lies in its ever-repeated and ever-varied sequentiality, that supreme principle of constant accretion and growth.

The basis of this conception of historicity is given in the theological tradition of the Old Testament, which cannot be grasped by ideal systematic constructs but only through narrative re-creation and reinterpretation. The exemplary significance of **Mimesis** is largely due to Auerbach's acute awareness of this fact. I have emphasized the symphonic aspects of his procédés to bring out their aesthetic characteristics; now, to stress their cognitive impact, I must add that they are also (and ultimately) narrative. **Mimesis** shows that the writing of literary history, and of the history of ideas, is a narrative enterprise. I am not speaking on the superficial level of interesting plots. No, there is a pervasive pattern of parallels and contrasts, flashbacks and anticipations, fruitful associations and digressions, that is "narrative" in a much more essential sense.

The most striking and conclusive point to that effect, actually, still remains to be made. Speech is coextensive with human life, and not just because we often communicate verbally. Rather, such communication is itself only a particular expression of a more basic discursivity of existence that is not exhausted by the act of speaking. Language is merely "the outspokenness of discourse" [Martin Heidegger, *Sein und Zeit*]. And narration is the particular mode of that outspokenness which is most essentially mimetic, which most completely represents and reproduces our experience as beings evolving in time. All our narrative techniques reflect and sharpen the way we really deal with our temporality. No rhetoric of narration, if it wants to be more than an exercise in superficial taxonomizing, can afford to forget that its object of study (in Barbara Hardy's words) "merely heightens, isolates, and analyzes the narrative motions of human consciousness" ["Towards a Poetics of Fiction," *Novel* (1968)]. It is this privileged grounding in existence that accounts for the cognitive primacy of narrativity. Historical understanding is intimately related to the understanding of stories, and we tell and grasp stories as we live our lives.

Nowhere has this transition between life and literature, life and knowledge been better described than in André Jolles's book on *Einfache Formen.* It deals with the "simple forms" which, arising from experience and shaping themselves as it were out of language itself, underlie and found the full-fledged literary modes and genres. The foundation of historical writing is the memorabile, which already on a pre-literary level exhibits a proto-aesthetic structure of *Hervorhebung* (of "heightening" or "bringing into relief "). As an existential reality, not a mere methodical superimposition, the process is essentially temporal. It is perfectly described by the Latin verb *concresco, concrescere,* which means "to harden," "to congeal," and, more originally, "to grow together." In the newspaper account of a millionaire's suicide, and in an historical account of the assassination of William of Orange, Jolles shows how the dispersed strands of temporal unfolding converge, congeal into a *concrete* event that stands out in the flux of time. It is not a timeless configuration but a slowdown of time itself, placing its essence in relief, distilling its concentrated meaning into an intensified and intensely suggestive picture of the period.

What we have here is a veritable phenomenology of concreteness, that quality which Auerbach's historical representation always seeks. Concreteness is what he demands from his famous *Ansatz,* the point of departure or initiation from which such representation is to start out. The *Ansatz* should be well circumscribed, profiled and precise ("prägnant und genau"). Above all it should not be an abstract category, applied from the outside, but an "intrahistorical" phenomenon which, "brought out and unfolded" ("hervorgehoben und entfaltet"), has grown out of the historical object itself and clarifies it in its particularity and in its relation to other objects. This *Hervorhebung* and *Entfaltung* (note that "unfolding" is also the term Gerhard von Rad uses to designate historical development in

the Old Testament) is, therefore, a clarification of what is given. History is not an additive collection of facts, it is radiation; the *Ansatz* "must radiate, so that world history can be carried on à propos of it." Auerbach here describes with great precision what he actually does in *Mimesis* and elsewhere. Historiography becomes an (in itself almost mimetic) interplay of concepts and forces in which literary understanding coincides with historical understanding, in which the text radiates in all directions and on many levels, so that the distinction between the "intrinsic" and the "extrinsic" becomes almost impossible to maintain. Note the striking (and, I think, conclusive) parallel with the memorabile. In the concrete texts that serve as Auerbach's points of initiation, and whose lines of radiation overlap to form an ever-deepening picture of a period, we have those events, those concrescences that Jolles has identified as the very stuff of historical knowledge. Narrativity is the principle of such knowledge on the most essential level there can be.

Occasionally it sounds as though Auerbach saw his approach as something of a *pis aller,* in an era where the inflation of facts and specializations renders synthesis increasingly difficult. Once we have found a fruitful *Ansatz* (so he writes), we can proceed on the strength of "a modest overall knowledge, supported by some advice." In the face of this modesty, this Auerbachian "bescheidene übersichtwissen," we cannot repress a wistful smile. Though he was well aware of the growing nostalgia for antihistorical barbarization, and in fact wrote **"Philologie der Weltliteratur"** to warn against it, even Auerbach could hardly foresee just how *bescheiden* we could get. But his approach is definitely not a mere compromise under the pressure of increasing odds. When he argues that the very discovery of the *Ansatz* is a matter of intuition, and that the broad horizon we need must ultimately be acquired without deliberation and guided by the instinct of personal curiosity, he is not throwing up his hands in resignation but is formulating positive principles of hermeneutic understanding: knowledge is not detached and "objective," the adherence to a methodologically pre-established pattern; rather, it is *Wirkungsgeschichte,* radiation, living appropriation, dependent upon an *esprit de finesse* that cannot be predetermined or codified. If he proceeds as he does, it is not because he cannot do any better but because this is the way history should be apprehended if it is to remain history. And this is why his work is a model even now—especially now—no matter how this or that specialist may evaluate this or that particular literary analysis. It is a model in a time that is desperately in need of such examples. "Everywhere there are lurking ready-made concepts that seldom fit exactly, sometimes seductive by virtue of their sound and of the dictates of fashion, ready to pop up the very moment a writer is forsaken by the energy of the substantive and the concrete." Who wrote those words? Erich Auerbach. When? During the 1950s. What he meant to offer was a diagnosis. No doubt he also meant it as a prognosis. And alas! Here I cannot even console myself by hoping that he mercifully may not have realized just how prophetic he really was. (pp. 143-52)

W. Wolfgang Holdheim, "Auerbach's 'Mimesis': Aesthetics as Historical Understanding," in CLIO, *Vol. 10, No. 2, Winter, 1981, pp. 143-54.*

Edward W. Amend   (essay date 1984)

[*In the following essay, Amend challenges the adequacy of Auerbach's analysis of literary representation and realism in* Mimesis.]

The story is familiar of how Erich Auerbach came to write his panoramic survey of European literature, ***Mimesis: The Representation of Reality in Western Literature.*** As a refugee in Turkey from the Nazi persecution, Auerbach was separated from the major libraries of Europe, and he had access to only a few of the secondary materials regarding the literary texts in which he was interested. Therefore, he found the boldness necessary to deal with the texts largely by themselves. And, consequently, through the careful analysis of small portions of those texts Auerbach traced the history of certain major motifs throughout the tradition of European literature "from Homer to Virginia Woolf," as is often stated.

Probably because of personal preference as well as that isolation, Auerbach avoided the philosophical discussion of what he was doing and of the theories of literature which most interested him. He regarded himself as an "historicist" in the traditions of Herder, Vico, Meinecke, and Croce. He obviously had benefitted greatly from the philosophical legacy of Hegel; indeed, Auerbach's study of Dante, including his *Habilitationsschrift,* ***Dante: Poet of the Secular World,*** he himself regarded as almost a footnote to Hegel's own comments in the *Aesthetik.* Beyond those and parallel influences, Auerbach mentions also in the Epilogue of ***Mimesis*** an argument that he is conducting with Plato regarding the ranking of *mimesis* in Book X of the *Republic.* Auerbach believed that literature was more representative of reality than to be regarded as at a "third remove." This philosophical starting point led him next to Dante and then virtually to the entire corpus of major European narrative literature.

This emphasis on Plato, however, conceals another argument that Auerbach was engaged in, which he himself only mentions passingly, but which is more profound and more relevant to the modern philosophical understanding of literature. That argument was with Plato's great disciple. For, in contrast to Aristotle, Auerbach constantly seeks and persistently stresses the historical content of literary works. Rather, therefore, than considering *poesis* as more philosophical and serious than *historia,* as Aristotle does in Chapter IX of *The Poetics,* Auerbach wishes to call attention to poetic possibilities beyond this abstraction and generalization of the literary work. For Auerbach believes that the literary work "grasps" truth as it becomes full of history and of the concreteness that history provides. So literary symbolism does not emphasize only imaginative possibilities, as Aristotle contends; works also become profoundly symbolic through the very density of the historical details which they carry and convey. Auerbach was thus attempting to develop a contrasting account of literary reality to that of Aristotle's. The power of poetry, at least in the Christian-influenced West, derives from the representation of concrete detail as much as from the outline of universal symbols.

Erich Auerbach never identified his approach to literature in relation to the various schools of twentieth-century criticism. Auerbach's critical methods displayed elements of a number of modern literary theories. Literature represented reality, and to that extent his concept involved imitation. *Nachahmung* was an important word in an early embryonic essay. Literary art, however, did not refer simply to the world of nature but also to the complex processes of social and historical existence. Under the concept of representation, Auerbach also noted the pragmatic influence of literature upon its audience, and especially in its shaping of a reading public as in the title of his last work, ***Literary Language and Its Public in Late Latin Antiquity and in the Middle Ages.*** A work's relation to a particular public provided a unifying symbol of the group's life. Literature, therefore, was also expressive, though not simply of one person's feelings but of the aspirations of an entire society.

All such aspects of representation Auerbach found within the dynamics of the work itself, thus in a sense making his approach also an objective one. By means of the work's language, form, and "grasp" of the world, Auerbach was led to meanings outside the work. The isolated work was for him neither an end nor a world in itself. For he conceived literary art to be, most fundamentally, an index (*Ansatz*) of human destiny. He was steadfast in his conviction that the larger significances of literature are to be discovered only when it is studied in relation to its total historical matrix.

The essays in ***Mimesis*** focus on single passages of individual works. While Auerbach seldom detailed his interpretation of the whole structure of any given work, he obviously felt quite secure with each text in its totality. But that structure was far more a presumed background for the analysis of style than an explicit pattern of meaning. Small details of language and technique caught his attention, and, for the sake of those, he set aside questions of aesthetic structure. His search was always for the significant detail. Auerbach's approach joins the art object closely to the cultural development of which it is a part. In his vision, literature somehow always assumes an heuristic role.

Auerbach made it plain that a work's external relationships have an effect upon its internal dynamics. Montaigne's *Essays* "manifests the excitement which sprang from the sudden and tremendous enrichment of the world picture and from the presentiment of the yet untapped possibilities." Because of the historical confidence gained from Christianity, the Mystery Plays of the Middle Ages did not require a unifying plot but could, nonetheless, encompass a wide variety of events. "Since, for the believing Christian, all history was concentrated on a single conflict—the Fall of Man through original sin, redeemed by the sacrifice of Christ—he had no need of external unity in order to relate all events to this one central point." In twentieth-century literary developments the Aristotelian concepts of poetic causality and resolution no longer apply so well as they once did: works attempt less and less to give an imitation of one single event but rather give a great number of events, parts of events, and images which have only a loose relation to one another, not transpiring after each other and almost never guided toward an "end" in the earlier meaning of this term. . . . This notion of the unity of action is generally in decline; the method of the pure resolution of an event out of the collected life of the world appears in the twentieth century to undermine the authenticity of that which is real.

Thus literary art changes with the reality it represents, as a new relationship emerges between the symbol and its historical setting.

In the great variety of artistic developments that Auerbach described, a kind of process emerges to which Harry Levin has also pointed: "Generally speaking, art seems to oscillate between two poles, the symbolistic and the realistic—or, we might say, the typical and the individual." In the essays of *Mimesis,* a balance somehow is maintained similarly between the givens of life (social developments, personal experiences, psychological processes) and their aesthetic assimilation and registration (as style, subject matter, form, order, or aim). Auerbach's "dialectical" history of literary representation discerns periods of extension, when new aspects and dimensions of human life were registered, and periods of aesthetic intensification, when new forms and wholes developed out of a raw kind of realism. The change he observed especially from the literature of the early Middle Ages to that of the Renaissance could be characterized as realism followed by symbolism. At times literary works move toward inclusiveness and accuracy, while at other times they draw symbolistically toward integration and unity.

Hence realism and symbolism are the poles of an ongoing heuristic role that literature assumes in Western history. For *Mimesis* is in many ways a history of "firsts"; here Auerbach traced new aspects of human life as they were first identified by great literary works. Dante's *Divine Comedy* "was the first to lay open the panorama of the common and multiplex world of human reality." Through another medieval text Auerbach discovered "that the practical vicissitudes of a human being in his everyday existence have been here given a literary existence which did not exist earlier." Much later, in the work of Stendhal "contemporary political and social conditions are woven into the action in a manner more detailed and more real than had been exhibited in any earlier novel." Indeed, Stendhal introduced no less than the "modern consciousness of reality."

Other writers and literary movements could be more broadly described as "capturing" or "awakening" or "emancipating" the human imagination and self-consciousness. But, above all, in whatever form it took, a new discovery arose through literary art. "The inner history of the last millenia," according to Auerbach, "is constituted by the documents of an intense and venturesome advance of human beings toward the awareness of their circumstances and the realization of their potentialities."

Generally, in Auerbach's critical account, the features of class level, random daily experience, sensory vividness,

and social movement provide the outlines of a serious "outer reality" that literature over the centuries was developing. Yet Auerbach found that this exterior environment was complemented by an "inner world" manifesting the depths of human consciousness. As for biblical figures, according to Auerbach, each had an enormous inwardness. Emotional dilemmas created within Abraham and Peter great movements of "pendulation." Dante portrayed, in a similar fashion, inner layers of consciousness through the gestures of the various individuals in his *Inferno.* "More accurately than antique literature was ever able to present it, we are given to see, in the realm of timeless being, the history of man's inner life and unfolding."

This conception of literature as penetrating outer and inner worlds illustrates further Auerbach's primarily heuristic approach. From the time of Homer, storytelling moved in both directions. In this broadened range of representation, literature granted tragic sympathy to groups of people and situations before regarded as unworthy of consideration. New attention was also given to the inner life of ordinary individuals, whether their activities were routine or violent, whether they took place in boredom or in squalor.

Auerbach's idea of literature has thus in it the strong note of a necessary openness to random, ordinary experience. Literary representation must provide an open perspective, a love of being, which includes the masses of humanity as well as the moments of existence.

It is precisely here that Auerbach disagreed most with the Aristotelian concept of *poesis.* Aristotle too greatly imposed his ideal of order upon the aims of art; he did not leave room for the "encompassing" action of literary works. "Aristotle did not try to fathom the part of actuality which resists rational formulation, but dropped it as having neither law nor purpose."

Consequently, Auerbach found that the historical inclusiveness of Western literature served important ethical purposes. New perceptions of outer and inner reality became, in an expression adopted from Vico, "modifications" of the human self. Greater appreciation of historical existence made possible a new clarity of understanding in the present. "A change in our manner of viewing history will of necessity soon be transferred to our manner of viewing current conditions." As a result, literature serves as a unifying force upon the life of mankind:

> The more numerous, varied, and simple the people are who appear as subjects of such random moments, the more effectively must what they have in common shine forth. . . . The strata of societies and their different ways of life have become inextricably mingled.

The seriousness of modern literature is characterized by this expanded awareness of historical existence. History weighs with significance the problems faced by ordinary people in their daily lives. Lowly individuals live in a world where human ideals are constantly subject to change. In this ongoing process of transformation, the universe is described as open and elastic. In Auerbach's own words, "modern movements, which were no longer called forth by Christian concerns, have preserved in their aims and propaganda an element of Christian eschatological unrest." The vertical relationship with God that formerly had intensified Christian realism is in the modern world transferred into an expanding horizon of history.

The daily activities of ordinary individuals become significant as the focus of great events that shape human destiny. In nineteenth-century works the problems of the century come to a head in everyday conflicts and in the resulting personal confusion and despair. Characters such as Julien Sorel, Emma Bovary, and the working class of Zola's *Germinal* face the dilemmas of an unsettled world. No fixed solution can be applied to the predicaments encountered by such persons. Each individual must instead learn his or her own methods of self-orientation, and his or her fate is intensified by this necessity. Historical existence has its grounding in the "workaday" world wherein men and women come to grips with the great issues that surround and seem ready to engulf them.

Even, or perhaps especially, "random" portions of this everyday life convey the general movements of an entire age. A twentieth-century work such as James Joyce's *Ulysses* has demonstrated how a single day can epitomize the turmoils of a civilization. "Multiple and multivalent reflections of consciousness" fill so short a span of time with the awareness of "a Europe unsure of itself, overflowing with unsettled ideologies and ways of life, and pregnant with disaster." But the result is not simply so negative or gloomy a picture, for out of such random experience new "forms of order and interpretations" emerge that are intrinsic to the age itself. This process of interpretation the theologian Friedrich Gogarten in an essay on Auerbach calls the "density" of history. The individual life gains a "qualitative" character in its "historicity," when "the entirety of 'destiny' is sought not in the whole chronological course of life but rather in the 'totality of fate' as it appears in 'small events that are externally unimportant as turning points of destiny.' "

Certain events, in particular, speed up this process of transformation through the upheavals and new crises they bring about. In Auerbach's opinion the French Revolution was one such event. World War I can be readily regarded as another. A new tempo results from such world-shaking developments or, in Auerbach's own term, *Erschütterungen,* that is, "convulsions." Modern literature registers both the consequences of such events and also their premonition. Stendhal's *The Red and the Black* portrays the shifts in society coming about after the French Revolution; Zola's *Germinal* forewarns of the coming tidal wave of labor agitation and reform. Such great events break through the process of gradual change by drastically reshaping the conceptions of life and destiny.

As ordinary people in the modern world experience rapid changes, the human sensibility is extended by new forms of self-consciousness and social relationship. When the French Realists were writing at the peak of their abilities, each penetrated one step further in the exploration of historical existence: Stendhal identified the "rootlessness" of post-revolutionary man; Flaubert brought forth the "un-

concrete despair" that underlay the drabness of bourgeois relationships; and Zola articulated the powerful threat about to spring out of the inequities of industrial society. Historical existence, as presented in modern works, provides an openness to the unexpected developments yet to come for mankind. Western literature in recent centuries has shown "the powerful and adventurous thrust of men toward the consciousness of their situation and toward the realization of the possibilities given to them." Literary traditions and conventions lay the basis upon which new techniques are attempted and new patterns formulated. Modern works test out common assumptions through a constant process of questioning.

The seriousness of modern literature that Auerbach describes has, therefore, the character of what Jürgen Moltmann calls a "moving historic horizon." This movement is not "history" simply because it accepts the human conditions of the past and present. It is also history inasmuch as it forces attention to the transformations of existence that are yet to be experienced. Modern literary realism, according to Auerbach, has so defined man's historical existence that ordinary life has an eschatological character evident before only in the Christian figuralism of Dante. In this changing horizon human beings encounter new self-understanding and the appreciation of how rich a destiny they have in this historically complex world. Though such a horizon may not yet be equated with the medieval reverence for God, still it is more than a simple humanism. The vertical perspective, though replaced by history, has not been entirely lost in the transformation. Human beings still live in the presence of a world they can only intimate, a world inviting them to possibilities and perceptions not yet imagined.

Erich Auerbach's criticism is basically a survey of literary works that contain a fullness, a richness of historical detail. Of most interest to him were the developments of that realism in the Middle Ages and in the nineteenth century. He analyzed both the figuralism of medieval literature and the historical existence stressed in modern works, providing a comprehensive study of these general patterns of Western literary symbolism.

Auerbach's concept of representation is limited by his treatment of literature as a form of human knowledge. Literary works are often used by him as sources of information about human life in general. Like other proponents of *Geistesgeschichte,* his own analysis of art stresses the view or attitude that depends on a union of the writer's creative act with the reader's perceptions. But literary symbolism also involves sensibility, motivation, and the integration of human life; its effects cannot be so narrowly limited to epistemology. Auerbach's research deals with the growing understanding that results from literature, but it generally neglects the reintegration of human existence that occurs through the impact of especially powerful symbolic works. While Auerbach shows how a new image of mankind resulted from the art of Dante and Stendhal, he overlooks the equal or even greater effects of the works of Homer, Shakespeare, and Cervantes.

While many of Auerbach's conclusions suggest intriguing philosophical possibilities, he is reluctant to analyze the contrast between Christian-Medieval and modern-historical forms of literary seriousness. He thus avoids a philosophical interpretation of the varied relationships between literary symbolism and human reality. Even though his essays provide a wealth of insight into the "grasp of reality" in literature, his criticism is confined often to the more narrow features of literary language and, more specifically, to the historical references of imagery.

Auerbach's observations about the connections between literature and history are more significant to philosophical study than is his concept of representation. He wanted to show how literary works are grounded in the historical events of their time and in the categories of their contemporary life; that is, he wanted to deal with their "historicity," although he himself rarely used the word. Literary language and imagery reflect current happenings in the historical world. The details of personal, domestic, political, and "workaday" existence all thereby become part of the symbolism of literature.

This historicity is of special importance for the major literary traditions reviewed in *Mimesis.* The works of both Christianity and modern fiction are closely connected to the events of their time. Early Christian documents echo the emotional struggles caused by a faith that sets men apart from the society around them. The images of French Realism during the decades after the Revolution display the enormous power social and political changes have over people. In each case, contemporary events press new categories of existence into the imaginative world of literary art.

The forms of historicity differ, however, in the figuralism and the historicism of the literature discussed by Auerbach. Dante's epic, for example, gives primary attention to the precise definition of each individual, of the concreteness of human character. Modern realist works, on the other hand, show their historicity more in the terms of social movements and historical forces. Their description of an individual is complicated and enriched by his or her participation in the upheavals of political and social order.

Thus, although the medieval and modern forms of historicity differ, a common principle still unites them. In both, the vitality of literary art derives from its presentation of recent happenings and newly discovered aspects of mankind's being. In effect, the highly specific images of contemporary life become literary symbols.

Even in the historicity of literature there is a more complex process of representation involved than that which Auerbach describes. For the realistic features of literature have both an original significance and a continued symbolic meaning. Neither realism nor historicity is merely the accurate portrayal of contemporary life. The forms of earlier existence are still meaningful to modern man.

And in this sense Auerbach demonstrates his own movement toward Existentialist philosophy. In his study of Augustine's *Confessions,* for example, Auerbach is not interested in the attractions of the various Roman philosophies, presumably of intense interest during Augustine's time. Instead, Auerbach stresses the ethical dilemma of Alypius, an experience much like that a young man might

endure today. Likewise, the use of apocalyptic imagery in the Gospel of St. Mark could illustrate the major concern shared by the author with his intended audience. Yet Auerbach focuses attention on the shifting attitudes of a disciple whose loyalty is being tested; and this test is far closer to the modern imagination than pictures of the returning Son of Man.

Auerbach sees literary representation as more than merely the depiction of everyday life. In his study of literature he draws from each text those aspects of its setting that can still be appreciated and that still retain symbolic power: historicity includes both relevant details from contemporary life and the continued viability of those images in later culture. For Auerbach writers best represent reality when they select from life those details most symbolic of man's enduring existence on earth.

This resonance of historical imagery is a specific form of the overall symbolism in literature. Auerbach did not examine at length works from classical or neoclassical periods, yet there, too, one finds a realism, of a more abstract kind. Those works are historical and contain historicity also, but in quite a different way from the Christian writings and the modern novels studied by Auerbach. His research emphasizes the historical particularity inherent in his models; he neglected the historical generality of classical and neoclassical works.

The tragic action, for example, is a paradigm of the age old human engagement with death and destruction. The power of the literary symbol in that case is derived from a concept of destiny meaningful to far more than one era. The elimination and concentration of detail, and not the inclusion of detail, is necessary for such symbolism to be most effective. Unlike the historicity stressed by Auerbach, the realism of the more abstract literary works must not be so circumscribed by any one time that the work cannot "represent" human fate at other times. As the categories of concrete human life transcend a specific culture in the realism described by Auerbach, so the more abstract realism of classical works aims at transcending immediate time by presenting human reality for all time.

Even if realistic style is conceived as a form of historicity, still Auerbach's account of literary representation is not sufficient for a complete understanding of the literary symbol's relation to the ongoing historical world. Auerbach's approach to literature often shows the historian's bias of wanting to discover mainly how it was in the past. The "position" of a work is therefore a matter of past reality. Yet such a definition in terms of a past milieu does not account adequately for the enduring symbolism of literature. Auerbach did not make clear how a category of the present can be used by the literary artist as a model for the future. For literature is not only an affirmation of its age through what it registers and highlights but also an expectation beyond its age through the thrust of its symbolism toward some new pattern for mankind. The imaginative worlds of artists are partly a turning away from their times, as they project images beyond what they see and know and feel.

Even those texts of modern literature dealt with by Auerbach show how writers such as Zola were influenced by their visions of the future of man. Moreover, realism is by no means an adequate name for the more recent trends in twentieth-century fiction. Such writings not only present many areas of life; they are also revolutionary in the complexity of the images they expose from this life. Writers like Joyce, Kafka, Faulkner, and others have helped shape modern intellectual life through the drastic changes they have made on literary form and style. Their works not only reflect the modern world; they also transform it into patterns that shock human beings into new self-understanding.

This distinction between a work's relation to the present and to the future makes possible a somewhat clearer comparison between the main forms of realism that Auerbach identifies. Works of both medieval and modern realism affirm the categories of everyday life. The personal experiences of ordinary men are placed in contexts of great significance. This common principle connects ancient Christianity and modern art. Realist literature of the last two centuries preserves a form of human dignity that was granted through the example of Christ's Incarnation. The "seriousness of everyday life" has become an accepted affirmation in the literature of the West.

Beyond this concern with ordinary existence, however, modern works display far different expectations of human life than do the documents of Christianity. Daily life was meaningful for Christians of the Middle Ages, because there a person's ethical decisions either fulfilled or resisted God's eternal purpose. But, in modern realist fiction, the common person's lot is serious because of the political and social consequences it represents. Importance is no longer granted through the assurance of life everlasting but rather through some reordering of present existence. Resurrection, final judgment, and immortality are no longer the means whereby human beings gain significance. Modern writers have substituted complex patterns of human society and consciousness for these Christian ideas of eternal life.

Erich Auerbach tried ever so diligently and comprehensively to give an account of the reality of Western literature. Yet he was only partly successful in this endeavor. Simply the quasi-objective and semi-mystical terms he used—"style," "view," and "reality"—show how his research resists organization into a systematic theory of representation. Auerbach's account of historicity in literature is evidence, however, of the way concrete experience in one period becomes a part of the symbolism of later culture and of humanity in general. Literature transforms raw existence into images of life's durability, conferring hope and excitement on human prospects in a world yet to come. Concerning that process Erich Auerbach's critical scholarship gives bountiful and inspired testimony. (pp. 15-26)

> *Edward W. Amend, "Mimesis as History: Erich Auerbach's Theory of Literary Representation," in* Annals of Scholarship: Meta-studies of the Humanities and Social Sciences, *Vol. 3, No. 1, 1984, pp. 15-27.*

Timothy Bahti   (essay date 1985)

[*In the following excerpt, Bahti analyzes the relationship between fiction and reality in Auerbach's understanding of history and history writing.*]

Auerbach's **Mimesis** continues to do service as an immensely useful—indeed, uncontested—pedagogic tool in [the] popular dissemination of literary high culture. (p. 127)

[The] work's exemplary status rests primarily on a recognition of its particular disciplinary or institutional achievements as a literary-historical argument. **Mimesis** established a term and concept—that of the "levels of style" and their mimetic power—as an indispensible element, at once thematic and methodological, in our literary-critical vocabulary. Considered thematically, the notion of "levels of style" is a key cog—apparently (and by his own word) *the* key cog—in Auerbach's machine of historical continuity. He traces the now well-known path from the classical doctrine of strictly distinguishable levels of style to that doctrine's initial disruption by the *sermo humilis* of the New Testament and its story of Christ's incarnation and passion. His narrative then moves on to the theoretical development of *sermo humilis* under Jerome, Augustine, and the exegetical method of figural interpretation; to the combination of mixed styles and figural representation in Dante; to the further levelling and inmixing of stylistic differences in such figures as Rabelais and Montaigne, Shakespeare and Schiller; until the final destruction of distinct levels of style is achieved, along with the fullest representation of contemporary social reality, by nineteenth-century French realism.

But this enormous accomplishment—the historical argument about the mixing and levelling of levels of style for which **Mimesis** is probably best known—is, as I hinted, only one side of the book's critical achievement, the thematic side, that is. The other side is the *methodological* employment of style in Auerbach's work: not the historical theme of style as an object of study, then, but the critical practice of *stylistics* as a surprisingly elastic method. One recalls how almost every chapter begins with a stylistic analysis of a brief passage, and how Auerbach can then move from the passage to the work in question, from the work to the author, from the author to the period, and from the period to the history of all periods. This method—one might call it a synecdoche turned into metonymy's revenge—offers as powerful and influential a critical tool *qua* method as does Auerbach's argument regarding levels of style and representations of reality *qua* historical themes; and one may remark that in this metonymic elasticity of stylistics, his method represents philology at its most ambitious, implying a methodological continuum that extends from the smallest etymon or morphological unit to the largest dimensions of the histories of languages and literatures.

I do not wish to contest Auerbach's demonstrable achievements; they are what give **Mimesis** its critical value and make it worthy of critical scrutiny in its own right. Rather, in what follows I wish to expose and consider the structure whereby Auerbach comes to tell his historical story and arrive at these effects. But first let me situate Auerbach's work in its German intellectual milieu. Germany is exemplary of the problem of history and theory because the so-called "crisis" or "loss of faith" in historiography, and in literary history in particular, played itself out earlier and more decisively there than elsewhere in the West. Our own non-Germanic perspective may prevent our recognition of the stakes involved. French historians today are perhaps more positivistic, and more self-assured in their positivism, than ever; in America, we have many models—psychohistory, cliometrics, demographics, etc.—that professional historians employ with confidence. But since the war years, there have been virtually no outstanding German literary historians or "true believers" in the efficacy of literary historiography: instead there have been "work-immanent" interpreters, theoretical or Hegelian "Frankfurt School" analysts, or religious brooders on the one hand, and more or less vulgar historical materialists on the other. In fact, one can say that the most ambitious literary-historical projects by Germans were undertaken in states of exile: Benjamin's unfinished studies of Baudelaire and Paris in the nineteenth century, written in Paris; Curtius's *European Literature and the Latin Middle Ages,* written in what he called an "inner exile" within Hitler's Germany; Auerbach's *Mimesis,* written in Istanbul, followed by other historical studies written in this country. Indeed, it is my contention that even as Germany was the country that believed most profoundly and productively in the centrality of historical thinking in the nineteenth century, this heritage—largely the work of Hegel, Ranke, and Dilthey—runs aground or decays from within the German intellectual context at about the same time that it is being most powerfully absorbed into the larger Western context. As literary history flourished in France, England, Italy, and America from the 1860s to the early twentieth century, Germany witnessed the general and devastating critique of historicism delivered by Nietzsche and then Heidegger, and such specific and interestingly failed attempts at literary *history* as Nietzsche's *Birth of Tragedy,* Lukács's *Theory of the Novel,* and Benjamin's late studies.

Auerbach was aware of this "crisis" in German historical thinking after Hegel and the nineteenth century. On the one hand, he remained devoted to the tradition and saw his discipline of Romance philology as its heir; on the other hand, he sought alternative models for rejuvenated historical studies. As I have written elsewhere, Auerbach found such an alternative model in an amalgam of Vicö's *New Science* with biblical and medieval figural interpretation ["Vico, Auerbach and Literary History," *Philological Quarterly* (1981)]. These two concerns—both as objects of historical study and as models for historiography—were in turn associated by Auerbach with the Hegelian problem of the "sublation" (*Aufhebung*) of historical change. The sublation of historical temporality involves the recuperation of change, loss, negation, and sheer difference through their systematic elevation from contingency to proper—that is, philosophic—meaning. Historical change is sublated within the philosophic process into the form and concept of *its meaning;* most succinctly, the truth of time—time's true meaning—manifests itself as the presence of truth, or absolute knowledge. I will have to summarize several points from this earlier essay before we turn

to Auerbach's **Mimesis** to examine the construction of its history and the figural structure of its narrative. My first point is that Vico's apparent understanding of human nature—its languages, its institutions, its history (what he called its *cose*)—postulated at one and the same time the immanent unfolding of historical change *and* the providential *storia ideale eterna.* This synthesis is crucial to Auerbach's understanding of his project as a philologist and a literary historian. A second point is that Auerbach's understanding of Vico, while avowedly an attempt to distinguish him from German idealism and historicism, was nonetheless a highly Hegelian understanding, a fact explainable by the assimilation of Vico into post-Hegelian idealism before Auerbach, as well as by Auerbach's own Hegelian leanings. And a third point is that if Auerbach did not explicitly understand Vico's *New Science* as a treatise on the rhetorical *method* of historical construction and interpretation—as a work of rhetorical *historiography* in the sense of the figurative construction and operation of history in its narration and interpretation—this is because he did not need to: having already in hand his understanding of *figura* as a rhetorical structure at work within historiography.

Now what are the main points of Auerbach's understanding of *figura?* Briefly they are as follows. First, and essential to bear in mind, is his historical and philological thesis about *figura. Figura* could not have developed its exegetical and representational meaning and power without having first unfolded from its service as a philosophic term for the translation of the Greek *schēma* and *typos.* From this, *figura* becomes a rhetorical term for the verbal distinctions between the real and the apparent or seeming, the straightforward and the stylized, the model and the copy, the true and the concealing—most basically, the distinction between the literal and the figurative. In other words, one cannot raise the objection that Auerbach's historical understanding of *figural* interpretation might have little to do with the theory of *figurative* language; on the contrary, "figural" in Auerbach's historical sense is grounded upon "figurative" in our conventional sense. A second crucial point may be made by juxtaposing several of Auerbach's definitional remarks on *figura* in the sense of figural biblical interpretation as it was developed by Tertullian, Jerome, Augustine, and other early church fathers. On the one hand, the relational understanding of the *figura* as an event (in the Old Testament, and in history more broadly) that is prefigural or prophetic of a spiritual event and meaning (in the New Testament, and in Christian or salvation history more broadly) that would fulfill the figure—this relation between the figure and its fulfillment must be, Auerbach insists, between two equally real, concrete, historical events. "Real historical figures are to be interpreted spiritually, but the interpretation points to a carnal, hence historical fulfillment—for the truth has become history or flesh."

> Figural interpretation establishes a connection between two events or persons, the first of which signifies not only itself but also the second, while the second encompasses or fulfills the first. . . . Both, being real events or figures, are within time, within the stream of historical life. Only the understanding of the two persons or events

is a spiritual act, but this spiritual act deals with concrete events whether past, present, or future . . . since promise and fulfillment are real historical events, which either have happened . . . or will happen.

And in a third quotation, this time from the epilogue to *Mimesis,* we read that "an occurrence on earth signifies not only itself but at the same time another, which it predicts or confirms, without prejudice to the power of its concrete reality here and now." Auerbach's main point regarding figural interpretation is precisely that the "figural schema permits both its poles—the figura and its fulfillment—to retain the characteristics of concrete historical reality . . . so that figure and fulfillment—although the one 'signifies' the other—have a significance which is not incompatible with their being real." But if this is his main point, Auerbach must also recognize that the second pole, event, or sign is necessarily privileged over the first. He writes: "The fulfillment is often designated as *veritas* . . . and the figure correspondingly as *umbra* or imago"; but against the obvious disjunction and difference thus established between one event or sign as truthful, the other as merely shadow or image (or, in another patristic formulation, as merely *imitatio veritatis,* "the imitation of truth"), Auerbach then immediately adds: "But both shadow and truth are abstract only in reference to the meaning first concealed, then revealed; they are concrete in reference to the things or persons which appear as vehicles of the meaning." Truth and its shadow or foreshadowing are each concretely situated in the real, historical events which are the "vehicles of their meaning," and this despite the implied tension in the concept of *figura* as a relation between two signs, both of which are to remain real and historical, but the latter of which is to be the truth of the former's mere prefiguration.

The character of this tension may be further indicated by reference to two more aspects of Auerbach's essay **"Figura."** For one thing, Auerbach makes explicit the rhetorical or, more precisely, the *figurative* structure which underwrites this interpretive ambivalence between figural truth and its mere prefiguration:

> Beside the opposition between *figura* and fulfillment or truth there appears another, between *figura* and *historia; historia* or *littera* is the literal sense or the event related; *figura* is the same literal meaning or event in reference to the fulfillment cloaked in it, and this fulfillment is *veritas,* so that *figura* becomes a middle term between *littera-historia* and *veritas.*

In other words, the tension between prefiguration and fulfillment—wherein the latter, as truth, would make the former be less than true, thereby endangering its value as concrete, historical reality—this tension is reduplicated in, or, more accurately, is already implied in the *rhetorical* structure of figural interpretation: one event, the *figura,* is historically literal but interpretively figural; the second, fulfilling event, also a historical event, is figuratively the truth (*veritas*) of the *figura.* Thus, there is already a first opposition between literal and figural in the *figura* or prefiguration itself; this then reappears as an opposition between the *figura* as historical sign, and the later figural

truth (*veritas*) which "fulfills" it, or which reveals the "true" figurative meaning of that first figure.

The last aspect to which I would call attention in Auerbach's **"Figura"** essay regards this same point, and helps move our discussion back toward **Mimesis** and the question of its historiography. Auerbach must repeatedly attempt to explain how the fulfillment of a previous figure can avoid annihilating the value of the former's historical reality; he once writes that the latter term "fulfills and annuls" (*erfüllt und aufhebt*) the former; twenty pages later, he writes that the *veritas* will "unveil and preserve" (*enthüllend und bewahrend*) the *figura.* Cancel and preserve—this implies all the difficulty of sublation or *Aufhebung* in its speculative, Hegelian meaning. The initial *figura* has the double structure of *littera-historia and* spiritual meaning, although that meaning is not fulfilled until the advent of the *veritas* (say, Moses as a historical figure and as the sign of the Christ to come). Within the *figura,* then, the operation of cancelling-and-preserving the literal-historical event in the production of a spiritual sign seems to obey the economy of sublation. In the same manner, the *veritas* or fulfillment of this historical *figura* follows the pattern of the Hegelian "idealization" of phenomenal and historical experience, and so the *veritas* cancels-and-preserves the historical reality of the previous *figura* in fashioning truth through this elevation-and-negation. Yet that initial *figura,* as we have seen, itself displays the double structure of the figurative sign, that is, it is both literal and figurative. What would it mean for the *veritas* to cancel-and-preserve this sublation of the literal into the figurative which occurs *within* the very *figura* which the *veritas* fulfills? What is sublated, what is cancelled-and-yet-preserved, is precisely this first rhetorical sublation of the historical, the very double structure already at play within the beginning *figura.* Whatever the prior historical event might be, when it is taken to prefigure some later meaning, it becomes doubled (literal and figural), but the later "fulfillment" of the former's prefigural meaning must at once preserve the former's figural character—as the latter's sign, after all, as its prefiguration—*and* cancel it, render it nothing but a mere *littera,* annihilate it into a non-thing, a dead letter or a corpse. This is, I will now argue, the structure and operation of **Mimesis:** history, as historical reality and as the history of its realistic literary representation, is the *historia et littera* which, rendered figurative in the hands of Auerbach's figural interpretation, must at one and the same time perpetuate or preserve its figural character in a later fulfillment, and—*as this very fulfillment*—cancel itself to the extent that it is then merely the dead letter of some other figural meaning of "history."

I take as the operative instances of **Mimesis's** literary history the chapters on Dante and Flaubert: they are privileged by Auerbach in his epilogue as the two decisive moments, medieval and modern, in realism's overcoming of the doctrine of the levels of style; but as I shall show, Dante and Flaubert are also, in the exact language and texture of Auerbach's chapters, related to one another as prefiguration and fulfillment. When Dante is said by Auerbach to fulfill the structure of figural *representation* implied in the Christian and medieval concept of *figura,* and thereby to overcome the very concept which prizes the fulfillment over the literal figure, the spiritual truth over the literal historical event or life, he is also seen to carry over the structure of *figura* toward Flaubert, so that Dante prefigures the "real" fulfillment of Western realism in nineteenth-century French realism: Dante becomes the figure for Flaubert's truth. But if the fulfillment of figural interpretation by Dante is supposed to preserve and value the real *historia et littera* of the fulfilled figure, then when Flaubert fulfills the *figura* of Dante, there occurs necessarily the cancellation of Dante's apparent "truth" (now mere prefiguration of *figura*) and the revelation of a different *veritas* behind that "first" truth of Dante's fulfillment. This new *veritas* would be the realization of a lived *historia et littera*. There are, in other words, three figural moments in this story of Auerbach's about Dante and Flaubert: Dante's realism as figural fulfillment, Flaubert's realism as such, and the figural relation between the two.

Readers of the Dante chapter will recall the exquisite stylistic analysis which is so patiently sustained in the initial treatment of the encounter between the Dante-pilgrim and Farinata and Cavalcante in canto ten of *Inferno* (it is perhaps the best such example of applied stylistics in **Mimesis,** and certainly among the best studies of Dante's style that we have in Dante criticism). After Auerbach recounts the nearly "incomprehensible miracle" and "unimaginable" achievement of Dante's mixing of styles in this passage, and after his discussion accounts more largely for the mixture of the sublime and the trivial or comic which the *Commedia* represents, his discourse turns thematic:

> The *Commedia* . . . [is] a literary work which imitates reality and in which all imaginable spheres of reality appear: past and present, sublime grandeur and vile vulgarity, history and legend, tragic and comic occurrences, man and nature. . . . Yet, in respect to an attempt at the elevated style, all these things are not so new and problematic as in Dante's undisguised incursion into the realm of a real life neither selected nor preordained by aesthetic criteria. And indeed, it is this contact with real life which is responsible for all the verbal forms.

Auerbach now begins to argue that the *Commedia,* with its subject of the *status animarum post mortem,* represents "God's design in active fulfillment," and yet these dead souls, represented as judged for eternity by God, "produce the impression not that they are dead—though that is what they are—but alive." "Here," Auerbach continues,

> we face the astounding paradox of what is called Dante's realism. Imitation of reality is imitation of the sensory experience of life on earth—among the most essential characteristics of which would seem to be its possessing a history, its changing and developing. Whatever degree of freedom the imitating artist may be granted in his work, he cannot be allowed to deprive reality of this characteristic, which is its very essence. But Dante's inhabitants of the three realms lead a "changeless existence." [Auerbach borrows here a phrase from Hegel's *Aesthetik, wechselloses Dasein,* and continues with Hegel as he adds:] Yet into this changeless existence Dante

> "plunges the living world of human action and endurance and more especially of individual deeds and destinies."

As Auerbach characterizes it, the existence of the personae is "final and eternal, but they are not devoid of history. . . . We have left the earthly sphere behind, . . . and yet we encounter concrete appearance and concrete occurrence." Though not yet named here, the basis of Auerbach's Dante interpretation is obviously his understanding of figural interpretation—already foreshadowed in his much earlier book on Dante, and introduced in the last section of his **"Figura"** essay. The characters are more themselves, more fulfilled in "reveal[ing] the nature proper to each" here in their state of eternal judgment than they were in their real, historical lives: "We behold an intensified image of the essence of their being, . . . behold it in a purity and distinctness which could never for one moment have been possible during their lives upon earth." Auerbach first explains these claims within the context of the poem's theological thematics: God has judged Farinata and Cavalcante, and "not until He has pronounced that judgment has He fully perfected it and wholly revealed it to sight." But when Auerbach then writes of Cavalcante that "it is not likely that in the course of his earthly existence he ever felt his faith in the spirit of man, his love for the sweetness of light and for his sons so profoundly, or expressed it so arrestingly, as now, when it is all in vain"—this statement is saved from absurdity (a "man" more real in literature than in life?) by two particular facts: that Cavalcante, like Farinata, was indeed a real, historical persona; and that the theological thematics of Dante's poem do indeed confirm Auerbach's judgment that the characters' lives are more fulfilled in God's eternal world than they could have been in their real, earthly, historical lives.

Here, with the examples of human beings represented as more real and more fully themselves after death than in life, thereby retaining "earthly historicity in [the] beyond" as "the basis of God's judgment [and] the absolute realization of a particular earthly personality in the place definitively assigned to it," Auerbach finally and explicitly announces the figural "conception of history" as "the foundation for Dante's realism, this realism projected into changeless eternity": "It is precisely [the] 'full notion of their proper individuality' which the souls attain in Dante's beyond by virtue of God's judgment; and specifically, they attain it as an actual reality, which is in keeping with the figural view. . . . [The dead in Dante represent] the relation of figure fulfilled . . . in reference to their own past life on earth." Auerbach then refers to that feature of the figural conception which I mentioned above, the privileging of the fulfillment as truth over the figure as mere prefiguration: "Both figure and fulfillment possess . . . the character of actual historical events and phenomena. The fulfillment possesses it in greater and more intense measure, for it is, compared with the figure, *forma perfectior*. This explains," Auerbach concludes, "the overwhelming realism of Dante's beyond."

But with the phrase *"overwhelming* realism of Dante's beyond," something is set in motion. For the remaining pages now stand this thematic and theologically orthodox understanding on its head as Auerbach goes on to preserve the literal and historical reality *beyond* the realism of its spiritual fulfillment in Dante's depiction of the afterlife. Auerbach asserts that, in personae such as Farinata and Cavalcante, "never before has this realism been carried so far; never before . . . has so much art and so much expressive power been employed to produce an almost painfully immediate expression of the earthly reality of human beings." Beyond the thematic and theological justification, then, Auerbach refocuses on Dante's style and its "expressive power."

> Figure surpasses fulfillment, or more properly: the fulfillment serves to bring out the figure in still more impressive relief. . . . What actually moves us is not that God has damned them, but that the one [Farinata] is unbroken and the other [Cavalcante] mourns so heartrendingly for his son and the sweetness of the light.

In other words, as fulfillment overcomes or surpasses its *figura*'s literal, historical, *real* life, it also preserves and even elevates that *figura* to the point where it surpasses its fulfillment. Auerbach seizes upon this counter-surpassing of the fulfillment (the thematic, theological representation of divine judgment) by the *figura* (the stylistic realism of Dante's representation of the characters' lives in the afterlife) to conclude with these three crucial points. First, this "impression" of the realism of life beyond its thematic fulfillment ("the listener is all too occupied by the figure in the fulfillment," he writes)—this impression "is so rich and so strong that its manifestations force their way into the listener's soul *independently of any interpretation.*" Second,

> the principle, rooted in the divine order, of the indestructibility of the whole historical and individual man turns *against* that order, makes it subservient to its own purposes, and obscures it. The image of man eclipses the image of God. Dante's work made man's Christian-figural being a reality, and destroyed it in the very process of realizing it.

Third—as if the previous point were not Hegelian enough—Auerbach closes the chapter by saying: "In [the] fulfillment, the figure becomes independent. . . . We are given to see, in the realm of timeless being, the history of man's inner life and unfolding [*wir erfahren . . . im zeitlosen Sein das innergeschichtliche Werden*]."

These three closing points of Auerbach's thus expound two kinds of "independence" enacted by a quasi-dialectical *Aufhebung* on the far side of figural representation: the lived, historical realism of that figural representation of an ahistorical, eternal afterlife becomes so powerful as to be "independent of any interpretation"; the *figura* as such consequently becomes "independent" of its spiritual meaning in fulfillment. Both of these effects are brought about by the "dialectic" of figural representation itself: an "obscuring," "eclipsing" or *concealing* of revelation *in* revelation; a "destruction" of fulfilled truth *in* its "realization"; the figure free of fulfillment *in* the fulfillment itself; or the literal and historical—the real—returning *in* its having been turned into the figural and ahistorical or eternal. Auerbach's figural understanding of Dante can there-

fore be summarized as follows: the historical reality (the past lives of real, historical characters) is made to serve as the *figura* for its fulfillment in divine judgment, but the representation of this fulfillment by its *figura* is so realistic—more real than life, history, reality itself—that the fulfillment becomes in turn a figure whose fulfillment is the realism of—but now *independent of*—the figural representation; the fulfillment of that historical reality itself in its realism. *Figura* in its Christian, spiritual interpretation thus becomes lived reality "independent of any interpretation."

It should already be clear how this conclusion to Auerbach's chapter on Dante foreshadows his treatment of French realism as the fulfillment of Western literature's development toward the objective representation of contemporary social reality. Briefly, the real, historical world whose representation is promised by Dante's achievement (the realism promised by reality set free) no longer receives its literary representation *within* the domain of figural fulfillment—the spiritual setting of the afterlife in Dante's *Commedia*—but rather is now fulfilled by the realism of the French novelist, a realism not of an afterlife larger and more real than life as *lived,* but of the real social-historical lived world itself. No longer would there be a *décalage* between figure and fulfillment; rather, the real, historical world of nineteenth-century France will be both *littera* and *figura* for the novels, the realism of which—like Dante's realism—will now be that literal figure's fulfillment within the very letters of literal figures. Such realistic representation of historical reality is also, then, *Mimesis*'s fulfillment of the *figura* of Dante in Flaubert. Most generally, this unfolding of the "independence" of the *figura* from its fulfillment and from its spiritualist interpretation is, in Auerbach's literary history, the enactment of Western history according to a double-edged structure of secularization. That is, the argument for the historical secularization of literary realism is coextensive with a writing of literary history according to the model of figural representation, of *figura* (Dante as medieval figural realism) and fulfillment (Flaubert as modern social-historical realism). Thus, a history of literary secularization is a figural writing of history, a *literary* history with the accent on the adjective—an *allegory* of history as its own literalization.

But the matter is not this simple. The tensions between *figura* and fulfillment are between the literal *figura* (Dante's liberated realism of life) and the figural meaning of literal representation (the letters of French realism made figurative of a higher meaning in Auerbach's interpretive construction of Flaubert's place in history). We need to investigate these tensions more closely now by turning to the chapter on French realism. In striking antithesis to the beginning of the Dante chapter, it begins without a word of stylistic commentary, offering instead several pages of historical information on 1830 and its preceding years as background material necessary for an understanding of a passage extracted from Stendhal's *Le rouge et le noir.* But this antithesis is not at all surprising; it is rather the first sign of the chapter's figural relation to the Dante chapter. If there one began and ended with literary *style* as the locus of realism, prior to and finally beyond the poem's thematics of fulfilled judgment, then here one begins with real social-historical detail as the beginning *and* end, *figura* and fulfillment, of the novel's realism. But a second contrast to the Dante chapter is perhaps more genuinely surprising, and it foreshadows things to come. While the Dante chapter began and ended by extolling the passionate and vital expression of the characters' fullest possible lives—"We cannot but admire Farinata and weep with Cavalcante," Auerbach wrote—here Auerbach begins with a discussion of boredom:

> No ordinary boredom . . . [no] fortuitous personal dullness, [but] a phenomenon politically and ideologically characteristic of the Restoration period . . . an atmosphere of pure convention, of limitation, of constraint and lack of freedom . . . mendaci[ty] . . . [people] no longer themselves believ[ing] in the thing they present . . . talk[ing] of nothing but the weather . . . unashamed baseness . . . fear . . . pervading boredom.

This is all in the first paragraph. What has happened here, where the history of realistic Western literature is to reach its triumphant fulfillment? When the chapter, after sections on Stendhal and Balzac, finally arrives at its treatment of Flaubert, the discussion focuses immediately, for the third time and again in the first paragraph, on Emma Bovary's situation of "mediocrity . . . boredom . . . unrest and despair . . . cheerlessness, unvaryingness, grayness, staleness, airlessness, and inescapability." What has happened to Auerbach's argument? Here his analysis must be followed in precise detail.

In remarking upon the selected passage—Emma and her husband at dinner in Tostes ("toute l'amertume de l'existence lui semblait servie sur son assiette")—Auerbach first comments that the reader "sees [directly] only Emma's inner state; he sees what goes on at the meal indirectly, from within her state, in the light of her perception." But if the reader sees through Emma, Auerbach then notes that Emma sees through Charles:

> When Emma looks at him and sees him sitting there eating, he becomes the actual cause of the *elle n'en pouvait plus,* because everything else that arouses her desperation—the gloomy room, the commonplace food, the lack of a tablecloth, the hopelessness of it all—appears to her, and through her to the reader also, as something that is connected with him, that emanates from him, and that would be entirely different if he were different from what he is.

With this reference to Charles as the "actual cause" of what Emma sees, and of what the reader therefore also sees, one must ask whether it is Auerbach's own voice or his imitation of Flaubert's *style indirect libre*—that is, of Emma's consciousness—that says all "would be entirely different if he were different from what he is." Is it Emma, in the plot of the novel, wishing Charles were different so that her life might be different as well? Or is it Auerbach imagining that if Charles were different, Emma would be, too, and the reader—Auerbach—would see a different world? The question is especially germane since the suggestion of a possibly different life that could be available

for representation recalls that larger, fuller, more vital life represented in Farinata and Cavalcante by Dante.

The next paragraph answers our question, and does so with a sentence I find the most bizarre in all of *Mimesis.* Auerbach begins by recapitulating: "We are first given Emma and then the situation through her," but not in "a simple representation of the content of Emma's consciousness, of *what* she feels *as* she feels it"; rather, "the light which illuminates the picture proceeds from her, [but] she is yet herself part of the picture. . . . Here it is not Emma who speaks, but the writer." Indeed, if the reader gets the scene through Emma, and Emma gets it through Charles, the reader actually gets both through Flaubert. Well enough; but then—in contrast to Flaubert's felicitously phrased expressions, says Auerbach—Emma

> would not be able to sum it all up in this way. . . if she wanted to express it, it would not come out like that; she has neither the intelligence nor the cold candor of self-accounting necessary for such a formulation. To be sure, there is nothing of Flaubert's life in these words, but only Emma's; Flaubert does nothing but bestow the power of mature expression upon the material which she affords, in its complete subjectivity.

Auerbach's remarks about Emma's lack of self-expression, "intelligence," and "candor" still conform to the critic's conventional thematic commentary on the representation of a character; but then he speaks of her "life" and her "subjective material." And now the bizarre sentence: "If Emma could do this herself, she would no longer be what she is, she would have outgrown herself and thereby saved herself."

"She would no longer be what she is." She would no longer be Emma, the unhappy and doomed heroine of Flaubert's novel. Perhaps—surely in part—Auerbach means she would be a different character, less unhappy, less doomed. But who is "she"? "She" is not, as Farinata or Cavalcante was, a once real and historical person. "She" is the "real" Emma Bovary who is not. A realistic representation of a fictional character is taken by Auerbach as a person—a "complete subjectivity"—who might have been otherwise than she is, that unhappy fiction. And to be real—"she would no longer be what she is"—would be to develop ("outgrow herself") and to be fulfilled ("save herself").

I can now move rapidly to my conclusion. In Dante, realistic representation translates historical lives into the apotheosis of their actuality, until this fullness of representation saves them from their thematic depiction as dead souls in the afterlife of hell; to recall Auerbach's formulation, they "produce the impression not that they are dead—though that is what they are—but alive." The *figurae* of their thematic fulfillment surpassed and cancelled their own spiritual fulfillment, and were *refigured* as literal, living, historical figures. Now, with Flaubert, the opposite occurs. The power of the realistic representation of a fictional life set in real, social-historical circumstances appears to Auerbach as the unfulfilled promise of a more spiritually real life that might have been—really, historically, literally. That absent fulfillment would "save" Emma, who is otherwise an inauthentic, unfulfilled, fictional yet realistic *figura.* To adapt Auerbach, she produces the impression not that she is fiction—though that is what she is—but real. Her *figura,* as the letters on the pages of *Madame Bovary* producing (signifying, representing) the figure of a real person, would be fulfilled (surpassed, overcome, cancelled) in her becoming more (but also less) than she is—in her becoming *disfigured* as a figure (a representation of a reality), and being made literal, historical, real. The move, in other words, from Dante to Flaubert is from real historical life transformed into a literature which is more than a reality, to a realistic fictional life transformed into a reality which would be more, should be more, but *is* not: *plus de réalité*—more, and no more, reality.

Thus, when Auerbach moves, on the next page, to speak of Flaubert's artistic practice, he speaks of "selecting events and translating them into language" as if they were already there, like real, historical lives or a real history, a real past; and he adds: "This is done in the conviction that every event, if one is able to express it purely and completely, interprets itself far better and more completely than any opinion appended to it could do." This exact echo of the claim made for Dante—realism "independent of any interpretation"—is made here in the absence of an authorial judgment: the self-sufficient truth of verbal representation, or what Auerbach calls "a profound faith in the truth of language." But the truth of language here, its *veritas,* is the fulfillment or unveiling of Flaubert's *figure*—Emma—as *letters;* not as a literal, historical being ("a complete subjectivity"), but as *litterae* or letters. The truth of literary realism becomes the revelation of the falseness, the fictionality, of its rhetorical or figural representation in and through literal letters.

The truth of modern realism is the "no more reality" that disfigures the "more reality" figured in the representation of a person *who is not* except as a *personage* who is "her" letters. It is this truth that surfaces in the final pages of Auerbach's chapter, less as a guilty conscience, perhaps, than as a guilty unconscious. For as his language—in paraphrasing a letter of Flaubert's—still echoes that which he used to praise Dante ("subjects are seen as God sees them, in their true essence"), this truth without interpretation is not that of the plenitude of lived, historical lives, but rather of "a chronic discomfort, which completely rules an entire life. . . . The novel is the representation of an entire human existence which has no issue. . . . Nothing happens, but that nothing has become a heavy, oppressive something." He insists that, as with Dante, this interpretation is immanent ("The interpretation of the situation is contained in its description"), but he then goes on not in praise, but in a final, mounting tirade: Emma and Charles

> have nothing in common, and yet they have nothing of their own, for the sake of which it would be worthwhile to be lonely. For, privately, each of them has a silly, false world, which cannot be reconciled with the reality of his situation, and so they both miss the possibilities life offers them. What is true of these two, applies to almost all the other characters in the novel; each

> of the many mediocre people who act in it has his own world of mediocre and silly stupidity . . . each is alone, none can understand another, or help another to insight; there is no common world of men, because it could only come into existence if many should find their way to their own proper reality, the reality which is given to the individual—which then would be also the true common reality. . . . [But instead it is] one-sided, ridiculous, painful, and . . . charged with misunderstanding, vanity, futility, falsehood, and stupid hatred.

A "silly, false world" which is not reconcilable with reality and which misses life's possibility; stupidity and nothingness, falsehood and misunderstanding, as "what is true" of the characters; and the absence of "true reality" due to the absence of the character's "own proper reality, the reality given to the individual." This, then, is the fulfillment of Dante's promise of the history of Western realism: representation without reality or so much as the possibility of life; truth as falsehood and nothingness; characters lacking both fulfillment *and* prefiguration of "their own proper reality" except in their figural fulfillment as signifying letters.

Alphabetic characters of inanimate material? Dead letters? *Litterae* as the corpse, the heavy, oppressive nothing of *historia?* When Auerbach attempts to turn, at the end of the paragraph I have been quoting, from his dyspeptic tantrum—"In his book the world consists of pure stupidity, which completely misses true reality, so that the latter should properly not be discoverable in it at all"—he attempts to make this turn with a sudden epiphany: "Yet [true reality] is there; it is in the writer's language, which unmasks the stupidity by pure statement; language, then, has criteria for stupidity and thus also has a part in that reality of the 'intelligent' which otherwise never appears in the book." Auerbach's phrasing here is precisely right even as his meaning is profoundly wrong. The "true reality" that cannot be fulfilled or revealed in realistic representation—for what is revealed is falsehood and nothingness—is nonetheless to be revealed and fulfilled somewhere; but if it is not in the realistic representation, it is not "*in* the writer's language" or "*in* the book" either, as if it were some thematic or semantic representation of meaning to be revealed, fulfilled, and made real in an act of understanding. Rather, it *is* the language and *is* the book: the "true reality" of the letters which unmask—literally, "re-veal"—their representational stupidity and nothingness by their pure statement, as if to say, we are the *littera* and its *figura, historia* and its meaning, which now fulfill and reveal the history of our representations of reality by the pure statement of its stupidity and nothingness—its corpse.

And what can we draw from this "exemplary" case of literary history as the literalization of historical letters? The corpse of Flaubert's language is one thing; as for the language of Auerbach's ***Mimesis,*** I come not to bury, but to honor it. I have tried to demonstrate how the figural model of interpretation and representation structures and operates upon the historical narrative of Auerbach's study of literary realism. Literally the figural model structures, and is operative within, his narrative of the two-tiered triumph of the representation of lived, historical reality in Dante and Flaubert. But figuratively, Auerbach's historiography disfigures the literal narrative and its *figura* by fulfilling them as the letters in a *literary* history, letters that represent the stupidity and nothingness of the real history that thought itself, in this literary mode, to be more real—but is, alas, no more real—than its representation as letters. In its intellectual context, this is a Hegelian allegory: the allegory of historical meaning (as phenomenal appearance) being preserved-and-cancelled, left behind in the uncovering of its truth and yet retained as the mere letter of this significance.

I understand this as one kind of allegory of history, what may be called the allegory of the nihilism of historical meaning: the meaning of historiography being that historical reality is cancelled or annihilated in its fulfillment in literature, including those genres called history and literary history. What this means is that to write and think the historical is to enter into allegory, to enact a literary, and specifically a rhetorical, mode of discourse. It is fortuitous, not merely accidental, that Auerbach's title and object of study is *mimesis,* for the insight that lies therein is the same one that I have tried to expose within the book's historical narrative: history itself is *mimesis,* the representation of the dead past, and the figurative structure that appears when history is done is already implied in the rhetorical structure of its ontology, indeed, of its name. The term names two notions, ontologically opposed as origin and representation, and the confusion between the two unfolds whenever historical narrative is attempted. "History" is literally the past, figuratively its meaning as the history that is thought and written. And this history—what we conventionally intend when we use and think the term—must always reduce history as an ontological object into a dead letter, so that it might be "meaningful," the literal sign for an allegorical meaning.

An alternative allegory of history which suggests itself—Walter Benjamin comes to mind—might then be called the allegory of the *eschatology* of historical meaning: the meaning of historiography being not the *re*presentation, but the *pre*sentation of reality, as and in history, in its ongoing deferral of fulfillment; reality preserved, that is, as signs to be read, preserved as literature to be read, including history and literary history. But to speak of alternate allegories of history is not necessarily to invoke any question of choice in the matter; the meaning of my study of Auerbach's historiography may perhaps be that the letter always grasps, even to the point of throttling, the figure of its own historical life. Rather, the apparent "choice" with which I began lay between nonhistorical literary theory and the possibility of literary history. The senses of the alternate allegories of history—nihilism or eschatology, dead meaning or meaning deferred—might be borne in mind today whenever literary history would be so blithely opposed to the labyrinths of literary theory. (pp. 127-45)

Timothy Bahti, "Auerbach's 'Mimesis': Figural Structure and Historical Narrative," in After Strange Texts: The Role of Theory in the Study of Literature, *edited by Gregory S. Jay and David L. Miller, The University of Alabama Press, 1985, pp. 124-45.*

Margaret Drabble   (essay date 1987)

[*Drabble is an English novelist and critic who is best known for her realistic rendering of gender and class roles in Western society. Her early work investigates a number of feminist concerns by analyzing the limitations and complexities of the home, marriage, and motherhood, while her later work is characterized by broader sociological and political concerns. In the following excerpt, she discusses Auerbach's incorporation of the "world of daily fact" into his understanding of the development of Western literature in* Mimesis.]

The novel has long been hailed as a form with a particularly intimate relationship to the world of daily fact, of external and temporal events, and that relationship is most revealingly described in Erich Auerbach's **Mimesis: The Representation of Reality in Western Literature,** from which I take my theme. This remarkable critical exploration, which surveys Western literature from Homer to Virginia Woolf, from the literary conventions of classical antiquity to those developing in twentieth-century Modernist writing, was itself written under circumstances which add greatly to its emotional power. Auerbach was one of the many scholars obliged to leave Germany in the 1930s: dismissed from his professorship of Romance Philology by the Nazis, he took refuge at the University of Istanbul, where, between 1942-45, he wrote **Mimesis.** In his Epilogue he apologizes for omissions from his wide-ranging work, and comments: "I had to deal with texts ranging over three thousand years, and I was often obliged to go beyond the confines of my own field, that of the romance literatures. I may also mention that the book was written during the war and at Istanbul, where the libraries are not well equipped for European studies. International communications were impeded; I had to dispense with almost all periodicals . . . and in some cases with reliable critical editions of my texts." But, he adds, the absence of footnotes is not wholly to be deplored, for "it is quite possible that the book owes its existence to just this lack of a rich and specialized library. If it had been possible to acquaint myself with all the work that has been done on so many subjects, I might never have reached the point of writing."

Those of us who have profited from the book readily forgo the footnotes. Nor can we fail to feel, in reading it, the pulse of great historical events behind it; the combined pressures of a restricted library, a form of exile, and the spectacle of a war-ravaged Europe have produced one of the great statements of humanist scholarship, one of the great assertions of the human spirit, and a reaffirmation of the value of the individual in a time of mass destruction.

Mimesis, which was published in 1946, is so rich and varied a work that one may read it in many ways, but inevitably it lingers in the novelist's memory as a most telling apologia for the evolution of the realist novel. Auerbach, beginning with passages from the *Odyssey* and the *Old Testament,* and proceeding through Petronius, Tacitus, St. Augustine, and various medieval texts, arrives at Dante, whose realism, through the Christian-figural tradition, embraces the sublime and the grotesque, and whose great art renders human and earthly even the image of eternity.

"The image of man," in Auerbach's words, "eclipses the image of God. Dante's work made man's Christian-figural being a reality, and destroyed it in the very process of realizing it." Elsewhere, in his complementary essay on **"Figura"** Auerbach had demonstrated how the shades of meaning between artistic copy, historical reality and archetype meet in Dante's Beatrice, who is at once the historical, physical Bice Portinari and an incarnation of divine revelation. In *Mimesis* he proceeds to demonstrate that the mingling of styles and the strong humanist tendency of Dante's work may be seen as a prefiguration of the nineteenth-century novel, which slowly emerged from the rigid neo-classicism of the seventeenth century, which claimed the reality of the external world as its domain, which dismissed literary decorum in favor of an audacious exploration of physical nature and economic cause, which set itself up as chronicle, as survey, as scientific research.

The imitation of reality was not abandoned even during the strictest neoclassical period; it survived in some forms of comedy, in low and popular art. But its conjunction with serious, at times tragic purpose in the nineteenth- and twentieth-century novel marked a new phase in the long march of Everyman. And by 1927, when *To the Lighthouse* was published, when *Ulysses* had already been in print for five years (well, in print in Paris, at least), the novel had claimed (or reclaimed) great tracts of territory. Insignificant domestic events, physically intimate events, working-class protagonists, lower middle-class protagonists, marginal characters, all had been admitted to the realm of serious art through the pioneering explorations of Balzac, Flaubert, the Goncourt brothers, Dickens, Lawrence, Dreiser, Zola, Bennett, Woolf and Joyce. Mrs. Ramsay knits a stocking, Leopold Bloom fries a kidney, criminals and courtesans and serving girls jostle and mingle, and Paul Morel, son of a miner, works as a clerk for a firm manufacturing surgical appliances. Gone forever were the days when kings and queens strode the stage; in the drama also, though perhaps more hesitantly, realism had entered, and the smell of frying liver and onions that filled the auditorium on the first night of Arnold Wesker's kitchen-sink drama *Roots* in 1959 marked yet another stage in the representation of reality. (pp. 2-3)

Auerbach discusses at length the literary conventions which, at various historical periods, have inhibited or encouraged the description of the humble or the physically shocking or debasing—with, incidentally, a powerful emphasis on the import of Christ's humble birth and humble death in this context—and he leads us to think again about literary decorum, about levels of style, about admissibility of doubtful subject matter, all questions which consciously and unconsciously preoccupy most novelists. (p. 4)

The gradual admission of new areas of human experience to the general literate consciousness is by no means a negligible program, as Auerbach reminds us, and as he beautifully illustrates in, for example, his tracing of the evolution of the portrayal of the French peasant from the twelfth-century mystery play of *Adam,* through his exclusion from classical tragedy and comedy, his passing appearance in the well-known passage from La Bruyère, and his (as it were) apotheosis in the pages of Zola. Each age annexes

its own new ground, as new writers speak forth. But progress, to the pioneers, is fraught with dangers. We know the legal difficulties against which Joyce and Lawrence battled, we know how much Virginia Woolf, who remained in print an entirely decorous writer, suffered from her own different form of daring. It is true that in the West writers no longer risk imprisonment, at least not for breaches of decorum, but that does not mean that all problems are solved, that we have inherited, ready-made, the means whereby we may represent reality. We can represent reality in Trollope's terms only if we live in a world that Trollope himself might have inhabited, and most of us do not. [John] Osborne's and [Kingsley] Amis's world looks quaint now, and even in its time excluded many of us.

One of the most interesting areas annexed by the post-war novel is the area of the woman's novel. This is new ground, in the sense that it is a new reality. Women today, women writers today, are living lives that are very different from those of their nineteenth-century counterparts, more different than the lives of [C. P.] Snow and Amis from the life of Trollope; they are living lives, as Doris Lessing has said, such as women have never lived before. The New Woman has had to forge a new novel to describe these new experiences. Doris Lessing has been in the vanguard of this exploration, and her attempts to represent (and thereby to help to create) the new reality have been sustained and heroic. Her early novels are cast in a "realistic" mode, in an almost old-fashioned narrative mode: *The Grass is Singing* (1950) and the early novels of the Martha Quest series, although new in their African subject matter and challenging in their political interpretation of that subject matter, are conventional narratives. It was in 1962, with *The Golden Notebook,* that she entered another realm. This complex, experimental, synthesizing work is truly original, and it attempts through its very form to represent the multi-faceted, irreducible, shocking, shifting, contradictory nature of experience itself, in its personal, physical, sexual, political, public, psychological entirety, in its weird jumble of the accidental and the deeply-rooted—an attempt to represent reality without omissions, warts and all, gloomy side included. . . . *The Golden Notebook* is composed of various sections, some conventionally realistic linking passages, some in the form of diary entries, some in the form of chapters of a novel apparently being written by the writer of the diary's entries, herself a novelist called Anna Wulf. (pp. 7-8)

What is the meaning of this multiplicity of styles, this many-pathed approach to subject? Does Lessing need these different modes, these different names, because she feels that any one mode tends to divide the wholeness of our experience, to make us trivial or one-dimensional beings? At the least, she has opened up for other writers, partly through what Anna Wulf calls "a failure as usual," the possibility of including in our literate consciousness more of the everyday experience of every woman, more of those areas which even Freud himself so signally neglected; she has challenged directly one of the lingering vestiges of the old literary doctrine of separation of styles which decrees that some bodily functions are hardly mentionable, and never mentionable in a serious context—a point which is, of course, inseparable from the non-literary doctrine of the separation of the sexes, and of the more extreme unseemliness of the female sex. It is a challenge that may certainly be seen in the light of Auerbach's thesis in *Mimesis,* though it is interesting to note, not quite parenthetically, that perhaps the only dated feature of Auerbach's work is to be found in his sometimes questionable references to female stereotypes in literature. (p. 9)

I have myself a particular affection for the realist tradition of the novel, and that I descry its persistence in perhaps unlikely forms. In Auerbach, I find an apologia which dignifies what at times appears even to myself as an obsessive interest in the details of external reality. I share what Mary McCarthy once described as the novelist's love of empiric fact, sometimes of apparently irrelevant fact, and I distrust fictions that have become so self-reflecting that they cease to reflect the outside world in any recognizable way. I like the humdrum, the everyday, the humble. I like descriptions of clothes and streets and houses, of people cooking meals and eating meals and washing dishes. I delight in the fact that in the novels of Lessing, Wilson, and indeed Mary McCarthy herself one can find descriptions of meals so detailed that one would be able to cook from them as from a recipe book. . . . It was from Angus Wilson's *Late Call* that I learned how to rinse rice, from Edna O'Brien that I learned how to slice, how not to slice carrots. Mary McCarthy, in *The Group,* gives us several evocative paragraphs of hints on how to make meat balls and dress them up with Campbell's tomato soup, on how to fix canned beans with catsup, mustard, Worcestershire sauce and brown sugar. There is, I know, some deep significance in the fact that my battered paperback copy of *The Golden Notebook* has found its resting place in the kitchen, among the cookery books, where its loose yellowing leaves mingle with those of Elizabeth David's classic of a different genre, *French Provincial Cooking.* (The only volume in the house that can rival these two for usage is Dr. Spock.) These novels are not ivory tower novels, they are novels about the way we live now, and they contain and encompass clothes and pot plants, nursery gardens and electric ovens, cats and hats, parties and funerals, the feeding of babies and the sicknesses of the elderly, as well as politics, public affairs, historical perspectives, prophecies. Nothing is too trivial, nothing is too humble, nothing is of itself debased. (p. 12)

Erich Auerbach ends his long enquiry with a hope that the modern novel, with its emphasis on the "unprejudiced and exploratory representation of the random moment" will bring to light "the elementary things that our lives have in common" and will thereby bring us nearer to a "common life of mankind on earth." This is a large claim, and novelists today are understandably wary of large claims. They are self-doubting, self-conscious, self-questioning, ironic. They suffer not only from the uncertainties that besiege all of us, in a relativist, pluralist, post-Freudian age, but also from that kind of professional paralysis that springs from the unprecedented degree of critical and analytical probing to which they are all, as soon as they achieve any success, subjected. And yet, perversely, stubbornly, anachronistically, they continue to write. They take cover, put up smoke screens, produce in some instances immensely complex and sophisticated and devious

distractions for the critic; and behind these defenses they continue, confidently, immodestly, to explore, to imitate, to represent a reality which does have, I believe, some common sense. And may I conclude by saying that, for myself at least, I feel that the writing of fiction is in part a mysterious process of incarnation, and that some strange shiver of fusion takes place when a fictional character catches a nonfictive, common, carnal cold. (p. 14)

> *Margaret Drabble, "Mimesis: The Representation of Reality in the Post-War British Novel," in* Mosaic: A Journal for the Interdisciplinary Study of Literature, *Vol. XX, No. 1, Winter, 1987, pp. 1-14.*

FURTHER READING

Bahti, Timothy. "Vico, Auerbach, and Literary History." *Philological Quarterly* 60, No. 2 (Spring 1981): 239-55.
  Analyzes Auerbach's interpretation of Vico and the two thinkers' respective philosophies of history.

Barrett, William. "Words and Masks." *The Saturday Review* 36, No. 12 (20 March 1954): 21.
  Emphasizes the imaginative scholarship and diverse range of subjects that characterize *Mimesis.*

Carroll, David. "*Mimesis* Reconsidered: Literature, History, Ideology." *Diacritics* 5, No. 2 (Summer 1975): 5-12.
  Theoretical discussion of the relationship between history and fiction in *Mimesis.*

Costa-Lima, Luiz. "Erich Auerbach: History and Metahistory." *New Literary History* 19, No. 3 (Spring 1988): 467-99.
  Develops the connection between the theory of mimetic representation presented in *Dante, Poet of the Secular World* and Auerbach's general conception of the history of Western literature.

Davis, Robert Gorham. "The Imitation of Life." *Partisan Review* 21, No. 4 (May-June 1954): 321-26.
  Comments on the style and methodology that distinguish *Mimesis* from other critical works of its time.

Evans, Arthur R., Jr. "Erich Auerbach as European Critic." *Romance Philology* 25, No. 2 (November 1971): 193-215.
  Review of Auerbach's collected works. Evans traces Auerbach's career from its inception to its end.

Green, Geoffrey. "Erich Auerbach." In his *Literary Criticism and the Structures of History,* pp. 11-82. Lincoln: University of Nebraska Press, 1982.
  Discusses the theoretical foundations and significance of Auerbach's studies of literary history.

Holdheim, W. Wolfgang. "The Hermeneutic Significance of Auerbach's *Ansatz.*" *New Literary History* 16, No. 3 (Spring 1985): 627-31.
  Reviews the multiple meanings of the word "Ansatz" ("index"), in relation to Auerbach's approach to the study and meaning of literature.

Muscantine, Charles. A Review of *Mimesis,* by Erich Auerbach. *Romance Philology* 9, No. 4 (May 1956): 448-57.
> Outlines the history of Western literature presented in *Mimesis.*

Schwartz, Delmore. "The King Asked, 'What Time Is It?'." *The New York Times Book Review* (29 November 1953): 40.
> Discusses Auerbach's emphasis on the relevance of the "everyday" in literature and history.

Tuve, Rosemond. "Reality in Literature." *The Yale Review* 43, No. 4 (Summer 1954): 619-22.
> Exuberantly recounts the realist traditions that Auerbach examines in *Mimesis.*

Wellek, René. "Auerbach's Special Realism." *The Kenyon Review* XVI, No. 2 (Spring 1954): 299-307.
> Criticizes Auerbach's strict adherence to historicism as a critical approach to literature in *Mimesis.*

James Madison Bell

1826-1902

INTRODUCTION

American poet.

Bell gained prominence as an outspoken author of abolitionist writings during the American Civil War. Compared to Frederick Douglass and William Cullen Bryant for his skills as an orator, he read his poems to sympathetic gatherings throughout the United States to rally support for the antislavery movement and later for the civil rights of African Americans. While his poetry has come to be regarded as uninventive, Bell is nonetheless respected for his moral and political convictions.

Born in Gallipolis, Ohio, Bell moved to Cincinnati at the age of sixteen and worked as a plasterer with his cousin while attending a high school established for black students. In 1847 he married Louisiana Sanderline, with whom he raised seven children. In 1854 Bell relocated his family to Ontario, Canada. There he joined the antislavery movement and became a friend of John Brown, helping the radical abolitionist organize his raid on the government arsenal at Harpers Ferry, West Virginia, in 1859. Following Brown's arrest and execution, Bell traveled to California, where he remained for the duration of the Civil War, composing poems that he delivered at antislavery rallies. After the war Bell assumed the role of itinerant poet and lecturer, traveling to such cities as St. Louis, Baltimore, and Atlanta. During the 1870s he served as a delegate to the Republican National Convention and campaigned for various party candidates, including Ulysses S. Grant. A volume of Bell's collected poems was published in 1901. He died the following year.

Bell's best-known writings are long poems composed to celebrate significant events in the abolitionist movement. These works, which were issued as pamphlets, include *A Poem Entitled "The Day and the War": Delivered January 1, 1864, at Platt's Hall at the Celebration of the First Anniversary of President Lincoln's Emancipation Proclamation,* a poetic chronicle of African-American life from the era of slavery to emancipation, and *An Anniversary Poem Entitled "The Progress of Liberty": Delivered January 1, 1866 . . . at the Celebration of the Third Anniversary of President Lincoln's Proclamation,* which recounts the assassination of Lincoln and the beginning of Reconstruction. Bell's most admired work, "Modern Moses, or 'My Policy' Man," is a scathing satire of President Andrew Johnson and his mismanagement of Reconstruction. Several of Bell's shorter poems, such as "The Dawn of Freedom," "The Death of Lincoln," and "The Black Man's Wrongs," reflect the sentiments of his longer works, while others, including "Creation Light" and "Descriptive Voyage from New York to Aspinwall," are devoted to subjects relating to Christianity and nature.

The derivative style and structure of Bell's poems displays his admiration for the works of Alexander Pope, Sir Walter Scott, and Alfred, Lord Tennyson. While Bell's poetry is generally considered inartistic, critics acknowledge that his intent was almost single-mindedly political rather than aesthetic. Recognized as a fervent champion of morality and human rights, Bell has been praised by J. Saunders Redding for giving "freedom and the heroes who had fought for it the poetic salvos he thought so richly appropriate, swelling the final great chorus of crude music that roared out through the dark times of preparation and through the din of the years of war."

(See also *Black Literature Criticism,* Vol. 1; *Black Writers; Contemporary Authors,* Vols. 122, 124; and *Dictionary of Literary Biography,* Vol. 50.)

PRINCIPAL WORKS

A Poem: Delivered August 1, 1862 . . . at the Grand Festi-

val to Commemorate the Emancipation of the Slaves
of the West Indian Isles (poetry) 1862
A Poem Entitled "The Day and the War": Delivered Janu-
ary 1, 1864, at Platt's Hall at the Celebration of the
First Anniversary of President Lincoln's Emancipation
Proclamation (poetry) 1864
An Anniversary Poem Entitled "The Progress of Liberty":
Delivered January 1, 1866 . . . at the Celebration of
the Third Anniversary of President Lincoln's Procla-
mation (poetry) 1866
A Poem Entitled "The Triumph of Liberty": Delivered
April 7, 1870 at Detroit Opera House, on the Occasion
of the Fifteenth Amendment to the Constitution of the
United States (poetry) 1870
A Discourse Commemorative of John Frye Bell, Member
of Hopkins High School, Hadley (poetry) 1874
The Poetical Works of James Madison Bell (poetry)
1901

Bishop B. W. Arnett (essay date 1901)

[The respected leader of the African Methodist Episco-
pal (A.M.E.) Church in Ohio during the late nineteenth
century, Arnett gained distinction in 1885 as the first African-American state legislator to represent a predomi-
nately white constituency. A close friend of Bell, Arnett
encouraged the poet to publish his collected works. In his
introduction to The Poetical Works of James Madison
Bell, Arnett lauds Bell's poetry written for the abolitionist cause.]

The wealth of a nation does not consist alone in its bonds,
gold, silver or lands, but the true wealth consists in the intelligence, courage, industry and frugality of the men, the
intelligence, culture and virtue of its womanhood. Each
generation produces its men and women for the times in
which they live.

If it is war, warriors are produced. In case of law, judges
and others are produced, so that the times, whether of an
individual, family or race, very seldom calls for a man,
that he is not to be found to lead on the armies, to teach
its children, to encourage its people to renewed energy and
effort. Our race is no exception to the general rule of history. During all of our sorrowful and sad history, we have
had men and women when needed. (pp. 3-4)

When the heavens were threatening and many were faint
of heart, then the bow of promise spanned the western sky,
it was during the dark hours of our nation's history, it was
then a new star appeared above the horizon and a new
trumpet sounded, new notes were heard and the vibrations
of the sound reached from ocean to ocean, it was then that
the subject of our sketch came upon the stage and became
a lamp to our feet and a light to our pathway.

James Madison Bell was born April 3, 1826, at Gallipolis,
Ohio. He lived there until he was 17 years of age. In 1842
he removed to Cincinnati, Ohio, and lived with his broth-
er-in-law, George Knight, and learned the plasterer's
trade. Mr. Knight was one of the best mechanics in the
city.

At the time of the arrival of Mr. Bell in Cincinnati, the
subject of education was agitated among the colored and
white people. The school question was one of the living
and burning questions, and had been since 1835. Previous
to that time the schools were private, taught by white men
for white children, but Mr. Wing and a number of others
allowed the colored youth to attend the night schools. (pp.
4-5)

The subject of our sketch was a busy man; he worked by
day and studied by night. He worked at his trade in the
summer and fall and studied in the winter, each spring
coming out renewed in strength and increased in knowledge. It was in these times that Mr. Bell entered school,
and at the same time was indoctrinated into the principles
of radical anti-slaveryism. It was in this school, in connection with Oberlin College, that the sentiment of Uncle
Tom's Cabin was born in Walnut Hills, Cincinnati, giving
an impetus to the cause of human freedom. Thus imbued
and thus indoctrinated, he desired a wider field to breathe
a freer atmosphere where his sphere of usefulness could
be enlarged, which could only be enjoyed under the British flag.

In August, 1854, he moved with his family to Chatham,
Canada, where he lived until 1860.

Mr. Bell was a personal friend of John Brown, of Harper's
Ferry. He was a member of his counsel in Canada and assisted in enlisting men to go upon their raid. He was his
guest while the recruiting was going on in Canada and was
one of the last men to see John Brown when he left Canada
for the United States. He only escaped the fate of many
of John Brown's men by the providence of God.

He assisted in raising money to carry on the work, and is
one of the last men now living who was personally connected with the Harper's Ferry raid. All honor to the men
who gave aid, counsel and support to the hero of Harper's
Ferry.

It was while in his twenty-second year that he courted and
married Miss Louisana Sanderline, and to this marriage
a number of children were born, who became useful men
and women. In Canada he pursued his trade and was very
successful and accumulated some money, but having a desire for a broader field, on the second day of February,
1860, he started for California and landed at San Francisco on the 29th of the same month.

On arriving on the Pacific coast he found the leaders of his
race in an active campaign against the disabilities of the
children and the race in that new country. He immediately
became one of them, and joined hands, heart and brain to
assist in breaking the fetters from the limbs of his race in
California and giving an equal opportunity for the people
to acquire an education. (pp. 6-8)

While in California, some of his most stirring poems were
written. The poems on **"Emancipation," "Lincoln," "The
Dawn of Freedom,"** and the **"War Poems"** were all written while living at the Golden Gate. One of his finest
poems is his **"Valedictory on Leaving San Francisco."** He
left California and came back to the Atlantic states in
1865, just in time to fulfill his mission to the race by encouraging the new-born freedmen in their new duties and
responsibilities.

He returned to Canada to visit his family, and after remaining for a short time he removed to Toledo, Ohio, and brought his family with him. For two years he traveled from city to city and proclaimed the truth and doctrines of human liberty, instructed and encouraged his race to noble deeds and to great activity in building up their newly-made homes.

It was during this period that I met him—and to meet him is to love him—and we became warm and true friends. From that day until now I have been one of his most ardent admirers, by reason of the congeniality of the man, of his intrinsic worth and his ability as a native poet.

His poetry is like the flowing of the mountain spring, the secret of its source is unknown. It was not a well dug or bored, but a natural outflowing of the crystalline stream, which came bubbling, sparkling, leaping, rolling, tumbling and jumping down the mountain side, flowing out over the plain like a silver brook on its journey towards the sea, furnishing water for thirsty beast and man, power for mills and factories, and life for the vegetable world. So it is with the poems of Mr. Bell. They will be read by the inhabitants of the mansion and hut, studied in the school house, college and university, recited in the parlor, lyceum, on the platform, and quoted by pulpit and press.

During the years 1867 and 1868 in Cincinnati, Ohio, night after night I accompanied him in his readings; thence to Lockland, Glendale, Hamilton and other places, where I had the pleasure and satisfaction of witnessing some of the effects of his poems. He read **"Modern Moses"** or **"Andrew Johnson Swinging Around the Circle"** with telling effect.

During these years of instruction, for he was instructing the people of their political and civic duties, they needed a teacher and leader, and no one could have done it better than the manner in which he presented it. It was like the music that comes from the heavenly source. His poems were read in all of the large cities of the North and South, and many a young man who was not an honor to his race and a blessing to his people received the first spark of inspiration for true greatness from hearing the poems of our subject. In Washington, St. Louis, Baltimore, Louisville, Atlanta and Charleston, the people opened their arms and received the words after beholding the star of hope as held out by the readings of our subject.

After traveling for several years he returned to Toledo, Ohio, where his family resided. His star rested over the city on the Maumee, and from that time until now he has been known as the "Bard of the Maumee."

He would follow his trade in the summer and fall, travel and read his poems during the winter—holding the trowel in one hand and his pen in the other. He was one of the best artists in his city and neighboring towns, always busy, calls more than he could fill for artistic work, though he labored hard, yet on going home in the evenings the muse would call him and a poem was born. Many of his brightest gems of thought were born on the scaffold and cradled in his wagon.

I have known him to sit down, and in a conversation some of the most beautiful expressions would come from his lips, thoughts that were crystallized, clothed in silken language, and were marshaled like an army on the battle field. His logic was irresistible, like a legion of cavalry led by Sheridan; troop after troop he would hurl against the logical battery of his opponent, whether in debate or speech, and the conclusion was shouts of victory heard above the music of the heart and the songs of the soul. (pp. 9-11)

[Bell's] life has been one of great activity; his services rendered to his race cannot be measured by any standard that we have at our command. His influences have been one of those subtle influences. Like the atmosphere, it has gone many places, and the people have felt and acted upon it; they have become better and wiser by reason of reading and hearing his speeches.

The honor of presenting an individual to a select company, or to a distinguished audience, is one privilege a man, perhaps, enjoys once in a life time, but the privilege that is now afforded me is of a very high order—the privilege of introducing an author and his book, not to a select company of friends or to a high dignitary, but to the commonwealth of letters, to the reading and thinking men, women and children of the present and future generations. The honor carries with it a responsibility for the character of the individual and the character of the book, therefore I do not fear the consequence of the introduction of so distinguished an individual or so useful a book.

I can endorse both, and feel it an honor to have the privilege of so doing, for if the book is to find its place in the reading circle of the world it will stand on its own merits; it will stand the examination of the most critical, whether friend or foe.

The book is a collection of the man—a busy man, a God-fearing man, a race-loving man, one who has spent the better part of his life in work and in study. The poems are the fruitage of his spare moments. I have long and persistently entreated my dear friend to have his poems collected and published. He has at last consented, and the work of compiling has been one of love and pleasure.

I therefore take great pleasure in introducing to the members of the commonwealth of letters, J. Madison Bell, "The Bard of the Maumee."

It was my pleasure and privilege to give a helping hand to Whitman's "Not a Man and Yet a Man," but in this introduction it gives me greater pleasure than I possess language to express.

In 1884 the general conference of the A.M.E. church adjourned its session in Baltimore and was received at the white house by the President of the United States, Chester A. Arthur. It was my pleasure to present the bishops, general officers and members to his excellency, the President of the United States, an honor enjoyed by few. *This privilege of introducing one of my own race, of my own church and political faith, a man whose poems will stand as his monument from generation to generation, and will give light and joy to the laboring and struggling people for many centuries.*

He will lighten their burden and illumine their pathway,

whether in religion or politics; he will stand and present the **"Banishment of Man from the Garden of the Lord,"** and from all of its effects he will hang the star of hope over the gateway of Eden. To the many under oppression, he will stand to them the day of **"Dawn of Liberty,"** and to those who are fighting the battles of the moral, religious and educational interests, he will present them with the *Triumph of Liberty* or **"Creation Light."** (pp. 12-14)

> Bishop B. W. Arnett, "Biographical Sketch of J. Madison Bell: The Distinguished Poet and Reader," in The Poetical Works of James Madison Bell, *second edition, Press of Wynkoop, Hallenbeck, Crawford Co., 1904?, pp. 3-14.*

J. Saunders Redding   (essay date 1939)

[*A pioneering literary and social commentator, Redding is the author of* To Make a Poet Black, *the first comprehensive critical study of black literature by an African American. Although dismissed during the 1960s by Amiri Baraka and other black critics as assimilationist, Redding has gained prominence for his complex vision of African-American humanities that encourages black artists to transcend racial distinctions and address universal themes while affirming their unique cultural heritage. In the following excerpt from* To Make a Poet Black, *Redding dismisses Bell as a poet.*]

[James Madison Bell] wrote less to accomplish freedom than in praise of it after it had been won. He gave freedom and the heroes who had fought for it the poetic salvos he thought so richly appropriate, swelling the final great chorus of crude music that roared out through the dark times of preparation and through the din of the years of war.

Bell was a rover—a sort of vagabond poet, lecturer, and plasterer—living at various times in Gallipolis and Cincinnati, Lansing and Detroit, and Canada. In this latter place he became friend and counselor to the insurrectionist John Brown, and only "escaped the fate of many of John Brown's men by the Providence of God." On his wanderings, combining the practical and the ideal, he followed his trade of master plasterer, recited his poetry in public gatherings, and "proclaimed the truth and doctrines of human liberty, instructed and encouraged his race to noble deeds and to great activity in building up their new homes." With a full and active life, the "Bard of the Maumee," or the "Poet of Hope" (both of which titles he unblushingly claimed) brings to a close a full and active period.

Most of Bell's verse is of the inspirational kind. He seemed to feel it his especial duty to encourage his people through commemorating events and circumstances, men and opinions that seemed to him noble. His pages thunder with lofty references to Lincoln, Douglass, Day, Garrison, John Brown, and others. Most of his poems suffer from being too long, many of them running to more than two hundred lines and two to more than a thousand. That he had neither the skill nor the power to sustain pieces of such length is evidenced by the steady drop in emotional force and the frequent shifting of metrical form within a poem.

Bell's *Poetical Works* is unusual and therefore interesting. He had read a good many of the "popular immortals" and one can see their influence at work on him. He attempted imitations of Pope and Scott, Tennyson and Bryant. His long, expository narratives are veritable melting pots of styles and treatments:

> This is proud Freedom's day!
> Swell, swell the gladsome day,
>   Till earth and sea
> Shall echo with the strain
> Through Britain's vast domain;
> No bondman clanks his chain,
>   All men are free.
>
> Of every clime, of every hue,
>   Of every tongue, of every race,
> 'Neath heaven's broad ethereal blue;
> Oh! let thy radiant smiles embrace,
> Till neither slave nor one oppressed
>   Remain throughout creation's span,
> By thee unpitied and unblest,
>   Of all the progeny of man.

What Bell attempted in most of his longer pieces is illustrated by the introductory "arguments" of two of them:

> The Progress of Liberty is delineated in the events of the past four years—the overthrow of the rebellion, the crushing of the spirit of anarchy, the total extinction of slavery, and the return of peace and joy to our beloved country.
>
> The invincibility of Liberty is illustrated in the beautiful episode of the Swiss patriot, William Tell, wherein the goddess is personified by an eagle towering amidst the clouds.
>
> The poet claims the full enfranchisement of his race from political, as well as personal thraldom, and declares that the progress of Liberty will not be complete until the ballot is given the loyal freedman.
>
> The noble actions and self-sacrificing spirit of the immortal Lincoln is next sung, and in mournful strains the poet bewails his martyrdom. This concludes with a touching eulogy on our sainted martyr.
>
> The reconstruction policy of President Johnson is reviewed, and, while objecting, he does not wholly condemn his motives, but warns the ruling powers that unless the spirit of rebellion is wholly obliterated and every vestige swept away, it will only slumber to awake again with renewed ferocity.
>
> The poet laments the discord of his harp, and its disuse, until answering Freedom's call he again essays its harmony. He portrays the conflict and gives thanks to God for the dawning day of Freedom. He rejoices that Columbia is free; he eulogizes the moral heroes, and describes how America is "Marching on" in the footsteps of the war-like "Hero John."

It is not known when Bell died, but he lived and died not without honor. In a biographical sketch of him [see excerpt dated 1901] Bishop B. W. Arnett of the A. M. E. Church praised him unstintingly, especially as the poet of liberty. Before Bell's impetuous full song the last of the Negro's bitterness against slavery was swept away, but the "sweetness of the liberty" of which he sang seemed turned to wormwood on the tongues of his successors. Had he lived beyond the first decade of the twentieth century, he perhaps would have been less sure of the uninterrupted progress of Liberty than when he wrote:

> Ride onward, in thy chariot ride,
>   Thou peerless queen; ride on, ride on—
> With Truth and Justice by thy side!
>   From pole to pole, from sun to sun!
>
> (pp. 44-7)

> J. Saunders Redding, "Let Freedom Ring," in his To Make a Poet Black, 1939. Reprint by McGrath Publishing Company, 1968, pp. 19-48.

Joan R. Sherman   (essay date 1974)

[*In the following excerpt, Sherman provides an overview of Bell's poetry.*]

The Progress of Liberty (1866) in about 850 lines reviews the four years of war and peace from 1862, liberty's triumph, and Lincoln's martyrdom:

> Hail! hail! glad day! thy blest return
>   We greet with speech and joyous lay.
> High shall our altar-fires burn,
>   And proudly beat our hearts today.
>
> Liberia has been recognized—
>   Also the Haytian's island home;
> And lo! a Negro undisguised
>   Has preached within the Nation's dome!
>
> For lo! Arkansas doth rejoice,
> And Texas sings with cheerful voice,
> And Mississippi's heart doth swell,
> And hail with joy the rising knell
> Now sounding on her gulf-bound coast—
> The dirge of a departed ghost.

To discuss "the changes of the last decade," Bell's *Triumph of Liberty* (1870) requires over 950 lines. Prefaced as "a statement of facts—not fiction" (which suggests Bell's problem as a poet), the poem takes us again through slavery, John Brown's triumph, the Civil War and its black heroes, and the changing fortunes of Liberty. Frequent variations in metrical and stanzaic form here cannot redeem the narrative from dullness:

> Lift up your hearts, ye long oppressed,
>   And hail the gladsome rising dawn,
> For Slavery's night, that sore distressed
>   And tortured you, has passed and gone!
>
> Hail! hail mighty Land with thy proud destiny!
> Enduring as time, all chainless and free!
> Hail! hail to thy mountains majestic and high,
> Reclining their heads against the blue curtained sky.

The poet similarly hails valleys, prairies, streamlets, oceans, cities, and railroads of the land of liberty. . . . A dozen shorter poems in *Poetical Works* echo the sentiments and language of Bell's major salvos to liberty and racial justice. **"The Dawn of Freedom"** celebrates William Wilberforce and abolition of slavery in the British West Indies; two poems commemorate emancipation in the District of Columbia; and **"The Death of Lincoln," "Triumphs of the Free,"** and two poems for the first of August follow suit. **"Admonition"** warns that men are lords of all creation but not of other men, and it urges humanitarianism and brotherhood. **"The Black Man's Wrongs"** appeals for consistency in judging men:

> Look on the face of men like Ward,
>   Day, Douglas [*sic*], Pennington, and then
> Tell me whether these should herd
>   With beasts of burden or with men.

In the same vein Bell champions the right of contrabands to fight "the war for Freedom"; and in **"Sons of Erin"** he warns Irish-Americans to remember O'Connell and refrain from oppressing blacks as the English had the Irish.

Very few of Bell's poems digress from racial themes. **"Creation Light"** recounts the world's creation from a "shapeless, heterogeneous mass" through the events of Genesis, "Till reason's torch illumined the mind" of man. Night and chaos will return when the world ends, but "God, Jehovah, Deity" will remain changeless. The **"Descriptive Voyage from New York to Aspinwall"** is a tedious journey; Bell's account of the sea and of Aspinwall are typical of his nature description:

> O! Thou eternal mystery,
> Thou grand, sublime, though awful sea,
> Alas, how oft thy fury smothers
> The last fond hope of wives and mothers.
> For rarer fruits and fairer flowers
> Scarce ever bloomed in Eden bowers,
> Than bud and bloom and ripen here
> Through all the seasons of the year.

Two acrostics offer philosophical advice, this to Mary Jane Wilson:

> *W*isdom, bless'd wisdom, she speaks unto all,
> *I*n the summer of life, prepare for the fall.
> *L*ike apples of silver, or pictures of gold,
> *S*o prize the rich moments of youth as they roll.

Outstanding among Bell's poems is **"Modern Moses, or 'My Policy' Man,"** a daring, original, and lively satiric assassination of the character and policies of Lincoln's successor, Andrew Johnson. The reactionary ex-Democrat is lumped with those despised braggart knaves and brainless wights raised to power by other assassins' blows. Worse than the murderer Cain is "My liege of graceless dignity, / The author of *My Policy.*"

> But choose we rather to discant,
> On one whose swaggish boast and rant,
> And vulgar jest, and pot-house slang,
> Has grown the pest of every gang
> Of debauchees wherever found,
> From Baffin's Bay to Puget Sound.

With wit and irony Bell catalogues the treacheries of Reconstruction and lays them at Johnson's door. This modern Judas, "with arrogant unworthiness," had sworn to be the bondsman's friend and Moses. Instead he vetoed the Freedman's Bureau bill:

He next reversed the bill of rights,
Lest all the girls—that is the whites—
Should Desdemonias [*sic*] become,
And fly each one her cherished home,
And take to heart some sooty moor,
As Fathers did in days before.

Would give the matrimonial hand
Unto some swarthy son or other
And some, perhaps, might wed a *brother*.

Bell observes Johnson's "blooming nose," crimson either from drink or his Policy, and his playing "the *knave and clown*" on a national tour which was "the grandest burlesque of the age." Johnson is treasonous and disloyal for his switch to support of Southerners:

For he, to use a term uncivil,
Has long been mortgaged to the Devil;
But the fact which no one knows,
Is why the deuce he don't foreclose.
Perhaps he entertains a doubt,
And fears that Mose might turn him out;
Hence, *His Satanic* Majesty's
Endorsement of *My Policy.*

This memorable political satire draws its vitality from Bell's skillful combination of the rhymed couplet form, concrete topicality, and uninhibited personal (rather than corporate) emotion.

Bell's sincere dedication to Afro-American freedom and rights is unquestioned. Oral delivery of the massive Liberty odes surely stirred audiences to enthusiastic aspiration, as Bishop Arnett claimed. But it is only in recital and to such audiences of the last decades of the century that Bell's poetry could ever seem "like the flowing of the mountain spring . . . bubbling, sparkling, leaping, rolling, tumbling, and jumping down the mountain side" [see excerpt dated 1901]. Bell's poetry, read today, lacks the spontaneity, natural vigor, particularity, and compression of thought and feeling which communicate poetic experience without the poet's physical presence. Artistic merit aside, James Madison Bell was undoubtedly *the* verse propagandist for Afro-Americans in his century. (pp. 84-7)

> *Joan R. Sherman, "James Madison Bell," in her* Invisible Poets: Afro-Americans of the Nineteenth Century, *University of Illinois Press, 1974, pp. 80-7.*

Eugene B. Redmond (essay date 1976)

[*A poet, critic, journalist, playwright, and educator, Redmond is among the prominent literary figures of the Black Arts movement of the 1960s. His works, including* River of Bones *(1971) and* Consider Loneliness as These Things *(1973), draw upon nature, music, and African folklore to interpret contemporary African-American life. In the following excerpt from his critical study* Drumvoices: The Mission of Afro-American Poetry, *Redmond surveys Bell's career, and, while characterizing his poetic talents as limited, praises "Modern Moses, or 'My Policy' Man" as an accomplished satire.*]

[James Madison Bell's strength] lay in his "pleas" and "hope." "Fortunate" enough to witness the Civil War,

emancipation, and "Reconstruction," Bell railed against injustices but primarily expressed hope in his forty years of observing the black struggle. Bell spent most of his adult life delivering eloquent and weighty poetic speeches on freedom, hope, and liberty. He was born in Gallipolis, Ohio, which he left at age sixteen to pursue the trade of plasterer and the avocation of orator-poet. A wanderer, Bell played his part in the overthrow of slavery—soliciting funds and recruiting Blacks for John Brown's 1859 raid at Harpers Ferry. Before the raid, Bell had moved to Canada, where he continued his friendship with Brown and fathered a large family. He later traveled to California, back to Canada, to various cities in Ohio and Michigan, and, finally, spent time in Toledo. During this odyssey Bell appeared at concert halls, churches, and various public gatherings to read his poetry at political and commemorative events. He also took advantage of books and gained considerable understanding of history and literature. His major themes are devotion, inspiration, love, unity, collective strength, and political change. Achieving "something of Byronic power in the roll of his verse" (Kerlin [see Further Reading]), Bell's poems are often too long, too tedious, and lacking in interest. Robinson notes:

> Not to mitigate his obvious technical flaws, it is helpful to remember that Bell is best appreciated as something of an actor, his poems regarded as scripts.

Unashamedly chronicling his journeys, Bell included the following as a full title of *Triumph of Liberty, (1870): A Poem, / Entitled the / Triumph of Liberty. / Delivered April 7, 1870, / Detroit Opera House, / on the Occasion of / the Grand Celebration of the Final Ratification / of the Fifteenth Amendment to the Constitution of the United States.* Consisting of 902 lines, the poem erupts through the use of all the "flourishes and vocal modulations at his experienced command." According to Redding [see excerpt dated 1939], Bell "unblushingly" claimed the titles of "Bard of Maumee" and "Poet of Hope." Typical of Bell's style is his tribute to his friend John Brown (from *Triumph of Liberty*):

Although like Samson he was ta'en,
And by the base Philistines slain,
Yet he in death accomplished more
Than e'er he had in life before.
His noble heart, which ne'er had failed,
Proved firm, and e'en in death prevailed;
And many a teardrop dimmed the eye
Of e'en his foes who saw him die—
And none who witnessed that foul act
Will e'er in life forget the fact.

Approaching something of the stature of Vashon's "Vincent Ogé" and Whitfield's "Cinque," Bell's tribute has all the ring of indebtedness to Scott, Byron, Pope, Tennyson, and other English popular masters with whom he was familiar. However imitative and derivative, though, Bell seemed never to be at a loss for exalting, exhortatory poetical flourishes. In **"Song for the First of August"** he sings a song for "proud Freedom's day":

Of every clime, of every hue,
Of every tongue, of every race,
'Neath heaven's broad ethereal blue;

> Oh! let thy radiant smiles embrace,
> Till neither slave nor one oppressed
>   Remain throughout creation's span,
> By thee unpitied and unblest,
>   Of all the progeny of man.

One of Bell's most ambitious works is his **"Modern Moses, or 'My Policy' Man"** in which—in scalding satire—he assesses the administration of President Andrew Johnson. Johnson (1805-75), who succeeded the assassinated Lincoln in 1865, was born poor and learned to write and figure from his wife. His presidency reached its height in a showdown between a progressive Republican Congress and Johnson, a reactionary Democrat. Once in office, Johnson began reversing his harsh criticisms of the South, giving former rebels a rather free hand at things and vetoing several bills aimed at giving Blacks a better share of things. Upset by the whole thing, Bell wrote a blistering satire—which often collapses as such—wherein, with couplet-fury, he observes:

> And crowns there are, and not a few,
> And royal robes and sceptres, too,
> That have, in every age and land,
> Been at the option and command
> Of men as much unfit to rule,
> As apes and monkeys are for school.

Following poets like Clark and Whitfield, and anticipating "signifying" poets of the 1960s and '70s (such as Baraka, Crouch, Touré, Eckels: "Western Syphillization," and others) Bell compares Johnson to all manner of evils. Johnson is also contrasted to "good" or liberal whites such as Congressmen Charles Summer and Thaddeus Stevens and abolitionist Wendell Phillips. Cynically calling Johnson "Modern Moses," Bell also uses the derisive "*Mose*"—which appears to be a way of reducing him to the level of the stereotype whites reserve for Blacks. . . . One must chuckle somewhat at Bell's claim that Johnson cursed in the White House:

> But choose we rather to discant,
> On one whose swaggish boast and rant,
> And vulgar jest, and pot-house slang,
> Has grown the pest of every gang
> Of debauchees wherever found,
> From Baffin's Bay to Puget Sound.

Only recently have we heard echoes of Bell from journalists, congressmen and old ladies astonished at White House tapes showing that ex-President Richard Nixon cursed in the Oval Room. We have observed, then, that Bell, though a tedious and haranguing poet, is important in a continuing chronicle of the mind and creative development of the Afro-American poet. Bell's works also include *The Day and the War* (1864), dedicated to the memory of Brown; *The Progress of Liberty* (1870), a recollection of the war, praise for Lincoln and black troops, and a jubilant greeting of enfranchisement; and *The Poetical Works of James Madison Bell* (1901). . . . Even though Bishop Arnett claimed that Bell's "logic was irresistible, like a legion of cavalry led by Sheridan" [see excerpt dated 1901], the poet recognized his own limitations when he said (*Progress of Liberty*):

> The poet laments the discord of his harp, and its
>   disuse, until answering Freedom's call he
>   again
>   essays its harmony.

> (pp. 94-7)

Eugene B. Redmond, "Jubilees, Jujus, and Justices (1865-1910)," in his Drumvoices: The Mission of Afro-American Poetry, a Critical History, *Anchor Books, 1976, pp. 85-138.*

FURTHER READING

Brawly, Benjamin. "Poetry and the Arts, 1830-1865." In his *The Negro Genius,* pp. 87-9. New York: Dodd, Mead & Co., 1937.

> Biographical sketch followed by an excerpt from *The Triumph of Liberty* that extols the achievements of John Brown.

Kerlin, Robert T. "The Earlier Poetry of Art." In his *Negro Poets and Their Poems,* pp. 32-5. Washington, D.C.: Associated Publishers, 1923.

> Summary of Bell's career followed by an excerpt from *The Progress of Liberty.*

Joseph Conrad

1857-1924

INTRODUCTION

(Born Teodor Józef Konrad Nałęcz Korzeniowski) Polish-born English novelist, short story writer, essayist, and autobiographer.

The following entry presents criticism of Conrad's novel *Lord Jim* (1900). For information on Conrad's complete career, see *TCLC*, Volumes 1 and 6. For discussion of the novella *Heart of Darkness* (1899), see *TCLC*, Volume 13. For discussion of the novel *Nostromo*, see *TCLC*, Volume 25.

Conrad's best-known novel, *Lord Jim* explores themes which intrigued the author throughout his career: the ambiguous nature of good and evil, the importance and fragility of ideals, the isolation of the individual, and the threat of disaster and failure that looms behind the calm surface of everyday life. *Lord Jim* presents the story of Jim, a young sailor who dishonors himself by abandoning his ship during a crisis at sea and the relationship of this event to his subsequent actions. While the events of the story are exceptional, the protagonist Jim is portrayed as an average individual embodying paradoxical, often inscrutable qualities that make up human nature. Integral to the delineation of the themes and characters in *Lord Jim* is the complex narrative structure of the novel. While the figure of Jim is at the center of the work, his actions—and, more importantly, his motives—are conveyed to the reader through other characters, principally the naval officer Marlow. These second- and third-hand accounts serve to distance Jim's story and assure that all questions concerning his life will ultimately remain conjectural.

At the opening of the story, young Jim, a pastor's son, harbors a romanticized conception of himself as a sailor based on his reading of popular fiction. However, after undertaking a naval career, Jim discovers that he is not as heroic as he had imagined when he finds himself paralyzed with fear and unable to rescue a crewmate who has fallen overboard. Later, Jim is serving as an officer on the *Patna* when it is damaged by floating wreckage and begins to sink. The crew panics and boards the lifeboats even though several hundred passengers are aboard. Although aware of his duty Jim succumbs to his fears and jumps overboard to safety. When the episode is made public, Jim is found guilty of dereliction of duty by a naval court and is dishonorably discharged from service. During the trial he encounters Marlow, who takes an interest in his case and arranges through a friend, the German trader and entomologist Stein, for Jim to emigrate to Patusan, an area in the Malay Archipelago. Jim is eventually accepted into Patusan society, and, after helping the native people defend themselves against attack by raiders and local rivals, acquires the honorific title "Tuan" (the Malay equivalent of "Lord"). He subsequently marries a local woman and

becomes a leader among the people. While Jim has proven his courage and is apparently established in a new life, the specter of his past influences his judgment while on the island. For example, after capturing Gentleman Brown, an English pirate who sought to pillage the Patusan settlement, Jim sets him and his men free after Brown insinuates that Jim must himself have committed crimes in the past to have moved to such a remote and obscure land. Releasing Brown, Jim pledges to the Patusans that he will forfeit his own life if Brown perpetrates further harm on the native community. In a second attempt to invade the Patusan village, Brown murders the son of the local leader and Jim is executed in accordance with his earlier promise.

Jim is often viewed by critics as an embodiment of romantic idealism, and the conflict between romanticism and pragmatism recurs throughout the novel. In what may be the novel's most discussed passage, Stein, alluding to Hamlet's famous soliloquy, comments that Jim's problem is the basic human dilemma: "how to be"; that is, whether to accept the risks entailed in the pursuit of one's dreams or to compromise them in order to live in relative peace. Both choices, he notes, are potentially destructive, but, rather than embracing either side of the issue, Stein leaves the paradox unresolved. Conrad's complex and ambiguous portrayal of Jim is considered by some scholars to be indicative of another significant theme in the novel: that it is impossible for one person to truly know or understand another. Critics have noted that Jim is often described as appearing physically obscured by mist or darkness, an image which they say implies that certain aspects of human nature cannot be conceived or comprehended. Nonetheless, whatever the final implications of Jim's end most critics contend that his character and circumstances are meant to echo those of all people, as indicated by the characters' repeated reference to Jim as "one of us" and Conrad's use of the phrase in his 1917 preface to the novel. Many of the characters who come into contact with Jim find themselves profoundly and inexplicably unsettled by his story: Marlow, after only a brief acquaintance, goes to great lengths to find him employment after his trial; a member of the Court of Inquiry that sentenced Jim mysteriously commits suicide. Critics have observed that Jim's predicament forces the characters to confront an aspect of existence which people spend most of their lives trying to avoid: the fact that most people, under the proper circumstances, would fail their morals, their society, and their ideal visions of themselves.

Many scholars, taking a biographical approach to the work, understand the themes of honor and betrayal in *Lord Jim* as a reflection of guilt on Conrad's part for having emigrated from Poland and having pursued a literary career in a foreign language. The most notable presentation of this argument was made in 1930 by Gustav Morf, a Polish critic who argued that the *Patna* is intended to represent beleaguered Poland, which in Conrad's youth was occupied by the Russian Empire, and that Jim's leap represents Conrad's decision to seek his fortune in another country rather than stay and work for Poland's liberation. In a 1957 essay, the Polish poet Czeslaw Milosz contended that the name *Patna* is meant to echo the Latin *patria* or "fatherland." Indeed, many acknowledge that Conrad, scorned by Polish authors in his lifetime, very likely did feel that he had betrayed his native land and tongue and that this may explain the paramount importance of honor and fidelity in his work. Some have called attention to the fact that Jim is given no surname, arguing that this device reflects Conrad's own sense of severance from his cultural and ancestral roots, while others contend that it simply underscores Jim's status as a universal type.

Upon its publication, *Lord Jim* was praised almost unanimously by reviewers, who commended the work's depth of characterization, and the novel achieved great popularity among readers enticed by its exotic setting and suspenseful plot. As the Scottish poet G. S. Fraser has commented: "It is, in fact, part of the interest and range of Conrad that he appeals not only to the sort of reader who enjoys, say, George Eliot or Henry James but to the sort of reader who enjoys Robert Louis Stevenson, Rider Haggard, or Conan Doyle." In the decades following the death of Conrad the reputation of *Lord Jim* waned, along with that of Conrad's work in general. Since the 1950s, however, the novel has been the subject of extensive study, with many critics exploring it in the light of the psychological theories of Sigmund Freud and C. G. Jung. More recently,

Lord Jim, like several other of Conrad's works, has come under charge of racism by critics who believe it identifies people of color metaphorically with the forces of evil and chaos. The novel continues to receive academic and popular attention; scholar Albert J. Guerard attributed its appeal to the universality and timelessness of its themes. He writes: "nearly everyone has jumped off some *Patna* and most of us have been compelled to live on, desperately or quietly engaged in reconciling what we are with what we would like to be."

(See also *Contemporary Authors,* Vol. 104, 131; *Dictionary of Literary Biography,* Vols. 10, 34, 98; *Major Twentieth-Century Writers;* and *Something about the Author,* Vol. 27.)

The Spectator   (essay date 1900)

[*In the following excerpt, the critic favorably reviews* Lord Jim, *praising the style and originality of the novel.*]

It may be that amongst the hundred and twenty-five novels still awaiting notice on our shelves some work of uncommon talent may reveal itself to gladden the heart of the reviewer; in the meantime, we have no hesitation in pronouncing Mr. Conrad's *Lord Jim* to be the most original, remarkable, and engrossing novel of a season by no means unfruitful of excellent fiction. That it may not strike all readers in this light we readily concede. Mr. Conrad's matter is too detached from "actuality" to please the great and influential section of readers who like their fiction to be spiced with topical allusions, political personalities, or the mundanities of Mayfair,—just now the swing of the pendulum is entirely away from the slums, and almost altogether in the direction of sumptuous interiors. Mr. Conrad, in a word, takes no heed of the vagaries of fashion or of pseudo-culture—he only once mentions an author and only once makes a quotation—he eschews epigrams, avoids politics, and keeps aloof from great cities. His scenes are laid in unfamiliar regions, amid outlandish surroundings. But if you once succumb to the sombre fascination of his narrative—as the present writer did years ago on reading *An Outcast of the Islands*—your thraldom is complete. Several writers have derived literary inspiration from their sojourn in the Malay Archipelago; but Mr. Conrad, beyond all others, has identified himself with the standpoint of the natives, has interpreted their aspirations, illumined their motives, and translated into glowing words the strange glamour of their landscape. Such an achievement, though remarkable in itself, seems to indicate a denationalisation that might inspire a certain amount of distrust. But in the volume before us, though the "noble savage" is once more prominent, the story is half finished before we reach Malaya, and the central figure who rivets our interest throughout, though intensely romantic by temperament, is the son of an English country parson, and throughout all his long exile never loses touch with the sentiment, the ideals, the essential *ethos,* of his race. Jim—"Lord Jim" is merely the translation of the title "Tuan Jim," by which he is known amongst the Malays—is a mate in the merchant service, an engaging, handsome lad, full of confidence in his ability to cope with any emergency, whose career is wrecked at the outset by a sudden act of futile cowardice, unless, indeed, we are to regard it as the result of a temporary mental paralysis. Along with his skipper and the engineers, he deserts what he imagines to be a sinking ship with a freight of eight hundred pilgrims; the derelict is subsequently brought into port, and as a result of the inquiry Jim's certificate is cancelled. A kindly ship's captain at Aden—the narrator of the story—attracted by Jim's frank and engaging personality, bestirs himself in his behalf and procures him a fresh start. But wherever he goes Jim is dogged by the rumour of his past, and he throws up post after post until at last Captain Marlow introduces him to Stein, a trader in the Archipelago, who appoints him his agent at Patusan, an inland village in one of the native States. Here, beyond the ken of civilisation, Jim at last finds the occasion for rehabilitating himself in his own self-esteem. Here, bearing a charmed life, he baffles the plots of the Rajah, overthrows a raiding Arab chieftain, the terror of the neighbourhood, and wins fame by his valour and sagacity. Here also he wins the devoted love of the only white woman in Patusan, the stepdaughter of a Portuguese half-caste, and here, in the words of the narrator, "an obscure conqueror of fame, tearing himself out of the arms of a jealous love at the sign, at the call of his exalted egoism, he passes away under a cloud, inscrutable at heart, forgotten, unforgiven, and excessively romantic." We despair within the limited space at our disposal of conveying any adequate notion of the poignant interest of this strange narrative, the restrained yet fervid eloquence of the style, the vividness of the portraiture, the subtlety of psychological analysis, which are united in Mr. Conrad's latest and greatest work. The wizardry of the Orient is over it all. We can only congratulate him on an achievement at once superlatively artistic in treatment and entirely original in its subject.

> *A review of "Lord Jim," in* The Spectator, *Vol. 85, No. 3778, November 24, 1900, p. 753.*

Joseph Conrad   (essay date 1917)

[*In the following essay, composed as a preface to a 1917 edition of* Lord Jim, *Conrad explains his conception of the novel and responds to criticism of the work.*]

When [*Lord Jim*] first appeared in book form a notion got about that I had been bolted away with. Some reviewers maintained that the work starting as a short story had got beyond the writer's control. One or two discovered internal evidence of the fact, which seemed to amuse them. They pointed out the limitations of the narrative form. They argued that no man could have been expected to talk all that time, and other men to listen so long. It was not, they said, very credible.

After thinking it over for something like sixteen years I am not so sure about that. Men have been known, both in the tropics and in the temperate zone, to sit up half the night 'swapping yarns.' This, however, is but one yarn, yet with interruptions affording some measure of relief; and in regard to the listeners' endurance, the postulate must be accepted that the story *was* interesting. It is the necessary preliminary assumption. If I hadn't believed that it *was* interesting I could never have begun to write it. As to the mere physical possibility we all know that some speeches in Parliament have taken nearer six than three hours in delivery; whereas all that part of the book which is Marlow's narrative can be read through aloud, I should say, in less than three hours. Besides—though I have kept strictly all such insignificant details out of the tale—we may presume that there must have been refreshments on that night, a glass of mineral water of some sort to help the narrator on.

But, seriously, the truth of the matter is, that my first thought was of a short story, concerned only with the pilgrim ship episode; nothing more. And that was a legitimate conception. After writing a few pages, however, I became for some reason discontented and I laid them aside for a time. I didn't take them out of the drawer till the late Mr. William Blackwood suggested I should give something again to his magazine [*Blackwood's*].

It was only then that I perceived that the pilgrim ship episode was a good starting-point for a free and wandering tale; that it was an event, too, which could conceivably colour the whole 'sentiment of existence' in a simple and sensitive character. But all these preliminary moods and stirrings of spirit were rather obscure at the time, and they do not appear clearer to me now after the lapse of so many years.

The few pages I had laid aside were not without their weight in the choice of subject. But the whole was rewritten deliberately. When I sat down to it I knew it would be a long book, though I didn't foresee that it would spread itself over thirteen numbers of *Maga*.

I have been asked at times whether this was not the book of mine I liked best. I am a great foe to favouritism in public life, in private life, and even in the delicate relationship of an author to his works. As a matter of principle I will have no favourites; but I don't go so far as to feel grieved and annoyed by the preference some people give to my *Lord Jim.* I won't even say that I 'fail to understand. . . . ' No! But once I had occasion to be puzzled and surprised.

A friend of mine returning from Italy had talked with a lady there who did not like the book. I regretted that, of course, but what surprised me was the ground of her dislike. 'You know,' she said, 'it is all so morbid.'

The pronouncement gave me food for an hour's anxious thought. Finally I arrived at the conclusion that, making due allowances for the subject itself being rather foreign to women's normal sensibilities, the lady could not have been an Italian. I wonder whether she was European at all? In any case, no Latin temperament would have perceived anything morbid in the acute consciousness of lost honour. Such a consciousness may be wrong, or it may be right, or it may be condemned as artificial; and, perhaps, my Jim is not a type of wide commonness. But I can safely assure my readers that he is not the product of coldly perverted thinking. He's not a figure of northern mists either. One sunny morning in the commonplace surroundings of an eastern roadstead, I saw his form pass by—appealing—

significant—under a cloud—perfectly silent. Which is as it should be. It was for me, with all the sympathy of which I was capable, to seek fit words for his meaning. He was 'one of us.' (pp. 65-7)

> *Joseph Conrad, "Lord Jim," in his* Conrad's Prefaces to His Works, *J. M. Dent & Sons Ltd., 1937, pp. 65-7.*

T. F. Powys (essay date 1929)

[*Powys was an English novelist, short story writer, and essayist who explored issues of morality and spirituality in his novels and fables that characteristically blend allegory and literary realism. In the following excerpt, Powys praises Conrad for combining a knowledge of seafaring with artistic imagination in* Lord Jim.]

In that heavenly dream of Lucian, that seized upon him as he slept in the dead time of night, two women laid fast hold of his hands and contended earnestly for him, each saying that he was hers. The one was a homely, sturdy dame, with her hair ill-favouredly dressed up and her hands overgrown with a hard skin, the other a well-faced wench of comely proportions and handsomely attired. And so Lucian, having been finely beaten for using a carving tool too crudely, chose the dainty maiden to go along with, who promised him all good things with little toil.

The same two women must have appeared to Joseph Conrad—perhaps when he had given himself up to the idleness of a haunted man who looks for nothing but words wherein to capture his visions—the one saying, "I, boy, am that sailor's art. Follow me as one of my family. Thou shalt be maintained in a plentiful manner." And the other, "I, sweet child, am Imagination. By my assistance thou shalt be clad in such a garment as this is"—showing the mantle she wore herself, which was very gorgeous to the eye—"and I will set such marks and tokens upon thee, that all men shall stand gaping to read thee, admiring and wondering at thee, blessing the power of thy pen and thy father's happiness to beget such a son."

Conrad, knowing that Truth itself is One—one for all men and for all occupations—bid the two women, who had each a hand upon him, to buss and be friends, and then kissing each of them upon the lips, invited both the one and t'other to his bed, saying heartily that there was no need for them to fight over him because he belonged to them both.

After he had embraced each of them in turn, he told them—walking up and down his room the while—that no great work can ever be completely a wonder of art, unless each of the two women gives her kindly assistance to it. And so, embracing the pair of them again, he bid them stay with him. And they stayed, ceasing to quarrel, for each took her share, and endowed Conrad with her own qualities, and his love of the fair face of Imagination could never make him unfaithful to the hard and wakeful toil of the sailor's life—for the rougher woman has as good a heart as the other.

Each woman, too, gave to him of her own freewill—for no force will compel either to yield what is hers, unless she is willing—the freedom of her own city. The one the city of toil, the other the city of Glory.

There have been some of the greater writers who have enjoyed the favours of both these wonderful women, but I know of none other besides Conrad—unless, perhaps, it were William Blake—who remained faithful to each until the end. (pp. 65-6)

No book that Conrad has written shows more clearly than **Lord Jim** that both these ladies were his bedfellows. Jim himself is the most significant of Conrad's creations. He loved him—one can feel that plainly enough—not as the old parson in Essex fancied his sailor son, but as himself.

One can get a look at Conrad's soul in this book—generous, full of love for all men, and even ready to give, eyes half-shut, with dull ears, a word of praise.

That Jim pleased Conrad is shown clearly, because Jim is so real a character. We hear his footsteps, we see him beside his girl, while the Patusan sky was blood red, immense, streaming like an open vein.

Conrad's pity rises high in **Lord Jim,** like a huge silent moving wave, that breaks at last with the crash of a final tragedy, leaving behind only a rather shapeless brown-coloured mound, with an inlaid neat border of white lumps of coral at the base, and enclosed within a circular fence made of split saplings, with the bark left on.

The wave, though it breaks and vanishes, rises again—for the fair lady of imagination is immortal—and whoever chooses can view once more the immovable forests, rooted deeply in the soil of everlasting time, soaring towards the sunshine, everlasting in the shadowy might of their traditions.

One cannot wonder that Conrad, sitting silent in his study, should be shocked if brought back too suddenly from some far sea or country, to which his genius had carried him. There he would sometimes find the great peace, where all movement in the world had come to an end, and how hard for him to be broken in upon by a general's daughter!

The deep and silent calm, the everlasting beauty of the sea, together with its uttermost cruelty, go with Conrad where he goes, and so deep and vast a beauty must lead to death.

The faith that guides Jim up that terrible river—where there was no wisdom in thinking that an alligator was a log of wood—leads on to certain destruction. No matter whether 'tis Doramin's hand or Brown's that fires the shot. The child-like face, the Jewel, is death—the sea brings him there. . . .

But Conrad had no wish, as some of us have—overborne by our own sorrows—to tumble the world down into a gulf of nothingness. "The human heart," he says, "is vast enough to contain all the world. It is valiant enough to bear the burden, but where is the courage that would cast it off?"

Of Conrad's devotion to women one might say much. He portrays them as wonderful creatures, beautiful, lonely, and a little idolatrous, and it is hard to believe that Jim's

Jewel wore a chemise. But, whatever underclothes Conrad's young girls wore, and they are nearly always to be seen in white—as Dr. Johnson would have had his harem—they can always be known as Conrad's. He was their father, their spouse, their adorer. And have they not now—the girl in *Lord Jim* was his favourite perhaps—met him to crown him with a garland of leaves and flowers, where no general's daughter can break in to annoy?

I think it likely enough that Conrad found it a lighter task to tell a tale solely of the sea, than to work and pound the mud and clay of the land into a story. The storms and calamities that overtake a ship compel our interest. In a moment one is surrounded by waves like towers, the written words become a great noise and a shouting, and a man in danger there is always a hero. No one who is washed overboard in a storm is dishonoured. A rogue drowned in the deeps is a fine figure and becomes a pearl.

> . . . Nothing of him that doth fade,
> But doth suffer a sea-change
> Into something rich and strange. . . .

Lord Jim will not be forgotten. It goes into the unknown places of the earth, it delves under its obscure surface, showing the horror, the hunger, that is in the soul of man. Always unrest, the wish for some other grave.

And Conrad, when he went, waved his hand, but not sadly, at his stories, as Stein waved his at the butterflies. (pp. 67-70)

> T. F. Powys, "Lord Jim," in A Conrad Memorial Library, *edited by George T. Keating, Doubleday, Doran & Company, Inc., 1929, pp. 65-73.*

Gustav Morf   (essay date 1930)

[*In the following excerpt, Morf discusses* Lord Jim *through a psychoanalytical approach, arguing that the work reflects feelings of guilt on Conrad's part for having left Poland, an act which Morf believes is paralleled by Jim's abandonment of the* Patna.]

Lord Jim is more than a novel, it is a confession. As a confession of a man tortured by doubts and nightmarish fears it must be understood, if it is to be understood at all. Such is, at least, my strong conviction, sprung from a psychological analysis of the novel.

Among the works of Joseph Conrad, *Lord Jim,* in many respects, stands apart. This is so evident that people frequently asked Conrad if it were not the one he preferred most of all. Those who asked the question received (in his "Author's Note" [see excerpt dated 1917]) but an evasive answer.

The method that I am going to employ in the analysis of the novel is based on the psychology of Freud and Jung. For this is a case where no other method would do. If we are ever to solve the riddle which surrounds *Lord Jim,* we must succeed in tracing the unconscious forces guiding Conrad in the choice of his subject and in the development of its theme.

It would take a whole book to give the complete theory (and practice) of what I call the "biology of artistic creation"; let it suffice here to explain its general principles.

If we want to understand fully any given artistic creation (especially if it belong to the "mystic" kind), we must admit that besides the intention to please, there is always, in very variable a degree, the tendency to move, to persuade, to teach, to give to the reader's thoughts a new direction. In other words, besides the æsthetic element which is static, there is a "dynamic" intention. A book, the publication of which did not change just the least bit the face of the world, would be meaningless. The proportion between the two opposites, beauty and force, is not invariable. Sometimes one of them is so strong that the other merely appears to be its servant.

This "dynamic" intention of artistic work can express itself unconsciously or half-consciously. In both cases, the process can be described as follows:

Whatever repressed conflicts, fears, wishes, hopes, or joys there happen to be in the artist's soul will be exteriorised (or *sublimated*) in his work. These unconscious elements constitute so many forces guiding him in the choice of his subject, in the invention of the plots, in the treatment of his characters, and in a hundred small details, thus leading him to treat those problems which he cannot solve in his conscious life. The solution will be symbolical, as in dreams and fairy tales. This is the only possible way, since the conscious mind cannot solve problems to which it attributes insolubility. On the other hand, repressed conflicts must be solved, if they are not to endanger the mental well-being of the person concerned.

The exteriorization (or *sublimation*) of conflicts takes place through the medium that responds most easily. Artistic creation, religious fervour, dreams, a sudden enthusiasm for some ideal or some hobby are the most common of mediums. Goethe explained the secret of his inspiration by the fact that *he was able to express what he suffered.* Beethoven's superhuman greatness is ultimately due to titanic conflicts, the sublimation of which, in a man like him, was only possible in music. The writing of a book or of a piece of music often means, therefore, a relief to the artist, just as church-going ought to be a relief to us who sing: "*Lift up* your hearts. . . . "

It may sound improbable that the repressed part of ourselves, our savage or shameful or childish or insane complexes, the very refuse of our personality, should go into the making of the highest art. Nevertheless it is so. Just as even the finest flowers live on dirty matter, on refuse, so artistic creation draws its force and its inspiration from the otherwise useless or dangerous by-products of our conscious life.

In the whole of modern fiction I could not wish for a better example to illustrate this than *Lord Jim.*

The plot of the novel may be recalled here: A young man ("not yet four-and-twenty"), Jim by name, is suddenly confronted with the temptation of his life while serving as chief mate on board an old steamer. On her way across the Indian Ocean, the ship has touched some floating derelict, and when the engines have been stopped, her condition seems so precarious that the disreputable gang who serve as officers decide to clear out as quickly and noiselessly as possible, under the cover of a dark night, leaving the eight hundred Moslem pilgrims on board to their fate. Jim does not mean to accompany them, but, in a moment of excitement, and urged by a voice in the darkness calling insistingly: "Jump! Jump!" he deserts the *Patna* in the firm belief that she is already sinking under his feet. They are picked up by a ship, and as to the abandoned vessel, it is sighted and towed to Aden by a French gunboat. A court of inquiry is held, and the officers of the ship, Jim included, have their certificates cancelled. From this moment, in spite of the sympathetic support of friends, Jim finds it impossible to "live it down." Wandering from port to port, and chased everywhere by the echoes of a past which he dares not face, he is finally sent to Patusan. In that forlorn corner of the East, his arrival means the beginning of a New Era. He soon exercises a great authority over the natives. He lives for some time in the illusion of having mastered his fate, of having forgotten his past.

Jim's illusions are shattered by the arrival of a white outcast, "Gentleman Brown." It would be easy for Jim to disarm him and to send him away, or, in case of resistance, to let him die of starvation. But Jim does nothing. Overcome by a curious weakness, he remains passive. When making off, Brown shoots some volleys into a camp of Jim's Malays, and Jim, feeling that his attitude is responsible for the tragedy, delivers himself up to the relatives of the victims, who kill him.

Lord Jim has often been called a psychological novel, because the source of the conflict resides within the tortured soul of the hero, but those who bestowed this epithet upon the book expressed only very vaguely the nature of Conrad's psychology, and seemed to ignore altogether the important fact that *Lord Jim* is eminently autobiographical and symbolical, that it is built up of the same elements as a dream.

Before discussing the symbolical bearing of the novel, a preliminary point must be made clear. It is the influence of Brown upon Jim which brings about the final tragedy. Before Brown's arrival, Jim was living in an atmosphere of faith and trust. His past was forgotten. Nothing reminded him of what he had done. He was the undisputed king of Patusan. But then, as if to prove that such an ideal state of affairs could not last long, Brown appeared. In the eyes of the natives, he is Jim's rival. The more they fear Brown, the less they will respect Jim. Brown's apparition is Jim's supreme test. A duel fought with spiritual weapons must ensue. If Jim wins, he is for ever the master of hearts and arms in Patusan, but if he loses, it will be a proof that he did not deserve the high situation he had acquired.

And Jim loses. To him, Brown is the embodiment of that unforgettable and unforgiving past which stands up against him in the very moment when he expected it least. Brown, on the other hand, realizes Jim's situation with a remarkable intuition. He understands at once that Jim's past is the weapon that will give him the final victory over his adversary.

Already, at the first of his meetings with Brown, Jim is disarmed by an allusion to his past:

> "Who are you?" asked Jim at last, speaking in his usual voice. "My name's Brown," answered the other, loudly; "Captain Brown. What's yours?" and Jim after a little pause went on quietly, as if he had not heard: *"What made you come here?"* "You want to know," said Brown, bitterly. "It's easy to tell. Hunger. *And what made you?"*
>
> *"The fellow started at this,"* said Brown . . . *"The fellow started at this and got very red in the face. Too big to be questioned, I suppose."*

In their second meeting, Brown pushes his point much farther. The following is his own account:

> "We aren't going into the forest to wander like a string of living skeletons dropping one after another for ants to go to work upon us before we are fairly dead. Oh! no!————" "You don't deserve a better fate," he said. *"And what do you deserve,"* I shouted at him, "you that I find skulking here with your mouth full *of your responsibility, of innocent lives, of your infernal duty? What do you know more of me than I know of you?* I came here for food. D'ye hear?—food to fill our bellies. *And what did* YOU *come for? What did you ask for when you came here?* We don't ask you for anything but to give us a fight or a clear road to go back whence we came————" "I would fight with you now," says he, pulling at his little moustache. "And I would let you shoot me and welcome," I said. *"This is as good a jumping-off place for me as another.* I am sick of my infernal luck. *But it would be too easy. There are my men in the same boat— and, by God, I am not the sort to jump out of trouble and leave them in a d——d lurch,"* I said. He stood thinking a for a while and then wanted to know what I had done ("out there," he says, tossing his head downstream) to be hazed about so. *"Have we met to teach each other the story of our lives?" I asked him. "Suppose you begin. No? Well, I am sure I don't want to hear. Keep it to yourself. I know it is no better than mine. I've lived—and so did you, though you talk as if you were one of those people that should have wings so as to go about without touching the dirty earth. Well—it is dirty. I haven't got any wings. I am here because I was afraid once in my life. Want to know what of? Of a prison. That scares me, and you may know it, if it's any good to you. I won't ask what scared you into this infernal hole,* where you seem to have found pretty pickings. That's your luck and this is mine. . . . "

Brown is obviously feeling his way better and better. By an extraordinary piece of luck (it is just his "infernal luck"), he hits upon the very words which will paralyse Jim's will-power. His allusion to "a jumping-off place," to the "men in the same boat" whom he is not going to "leave in a d——d lurch," his well-assumed indifference to the story of Jim's life, bring back to Jim a past which had to remain buried if he were to live. Jim falls silent with the silence of guilt.

It may seem unnatural that Jim should at first want to know what Brown had done "out there," for to touch Brown's past is to touch his own. It seems that the initiative to speak of the past ought to come from Brown alone. I think that what makes Jim really ask this last question is fear, and what may be called "the fascination of fear." There are things which attract because they are dangerous.

When Brown started to talk with Jim, he did so without much hope, just to gain time. To his great surprise, he was to find an adversary whom he could easily impress and even frighten. Just like his "infernal luck!" Feeling that he is becoming the master of the situation, Brown goes straight ahead, *alluding only to what* is common to them both, and leaving out whatever enormous differences exist between them.

> When he [Brown] asked Jim, with a sort of brusque despairing frankness, whether he himself—straight now—didn't understand that when *"it came to saving one's life in the dark, one didn't care who else went—three, thirty, three hundred people"*—it was as if a demon had been whispering advice in his ear. "I made him wince," boasted Brown to me. *"He very soon left off coming the righteous over me——*. He just stood there *with nothing to say,* and looking as black as thunder—not at me—*on the ground."* He asked Jim *whether he had nothing fishy in his life to remember that he was so damnedly hard upon a man trying to get out of a deadly hole by the first means that came to hand—and so on,* and so on. And there ran through the rough talk *a vein of subtle reference to their common blood, an assumption of common experience; a sickening suggestion of common guilt, of secret knowledge that was like a bond of their minds and of their hearts—.*

Jim's final and deadly mistake, the permission to let Brown and his men go away *in possession of their arms,* is due to the paralysing influence of this identification. Jim's attitude reminds us of that of Hamlet who cannot bring himself to avenge the murder of his father, and who does not know "why yet I live to say 'This thing's to do,' sith I have cause, and will, and strength, and means, to do't."

After this mistake, Jim's fate is settled. His past has proved stronger than his will to live. "Henceforth events moved fast without a check, flowing from the very hearts of men like a stream from a dark source."

When identification becomes as complete as in the case of Jim and Brown, there is neither choice nor free will. We find an illustration of this not only in *Lord Jim,* but in the tale **"The Secret Sharer,"** which is one of Conrad's best psychological tales. It is really the story of the identification between the "captain" (he is obviously Conrad himself) and a murderer, Legatt, whom the captain gives the hospitality of his cabin for some time. There is another example of an identification in Shakespeare's *Hamlet. . . .* Hamlet's will-power is completely paralysed by his identification with his uncle, who appears to him as a sort of lower self. Their "common bond" is their common love

for the queen. In all cases of identification, the unconscious wish becomes the master of men's lives and deeds. Jim's unconscious wish is to see Brown (i.e. himself) go off free and powerful, the captain's is to see the murderer Legatt escape, Hamlet's to see his uncle live and enjoy the fruit of his crime. Brown is Jim's other self as certainly as Legatt is the captain's "secret self" or "own reflection" or "double." It might be Jim speaking of Brown when the captain says of Legatt: "He appealed to me as if our experiences had been as identical as our clothes" (*'Twixt Land and Sea: Tales*), and "a mysterious communication was established already between us two."

Identification is characterized always by an extraordinary indulgence for the second self, an indulgence which must of necessity remain incomprehensible to any other person. When we feel a profound sympathy with or pity for somebody, we identify ourselves always *more or less* with the person who inspires us with these feelings, but the identification hardly ever becomes so complete that the subject loses himself in the object. Jim is an extreme case, a neurotic, while the captain in **"The Secret Sharer"** is a more normal character.

Jim's indulgence for Brown is typical. He simply cannot resist the evil *because the evil is within himself.* Being acutely aware of his own sins, he cannot throw stones at Brown. To a question of Jewel, if Brown was a very bad man, he gives, "after some hesitation," the answer: "Men act badly sometimes without being much worse than others," a definition which is evidently so formulated as to fit himself as well as Brown. Of necessity, he cannot think of Brown's past without thinking of his own, nor judge Brown without judging himself. To condemn the outcast would be to condemn himself. His effort in excusing Brown is a last desperate attempt to save his own moral integrity, one of those fifth-act attempts that are doomed to fail. And so Jim dies ultimately of this identification with Brown, that is, he dies of the mistake of his life, for that mistake alone explains why the first outcast coming along and greeting him as a brother on grounds of their common experience, appears to him fatally as his own hideous self.

A person acting under the influence of a strong identification is incapable of giving the true reasons for his or her behaviour. To themselves, their acts seem inexplicable but absolutely compelling and obeying a logic of their own, to their environment they seem inadequate and foolish, if not downright mad. Everybody thinks that Hamlet is mad, the crew in **"The Secret Sharer"** suspect their captain of drunkenness, and wonder at his violent temper. In *Lord Jim,* the natives cannot understand Jim's sudden partiality for a handful of common robbers. The reasons which Jim gives for his decisions are strangely inadequate. His declaration (that the robbers are not to be disarmed) naturally produces an "immense sensation." Tamb' Itam, Jim's most faithful servant, is "thunderstruck" at his master's folly. Had Jim been at all capable of listening to common sense then, these unmistakable signs of dissent would have enlightened him. But he did not want to know better. Following a dark and compelling impulse, he did not care, just as Hamlet did not care. "His fate, revolted, was forcing his hand."

It is not without interest to discuss the resemblance between the young man who served as a model to Jim and the hero of the novel. Conrad states himself (in his "Author's Note"): "one sunny morning in the common-place surroundings of an Eastern roadstead, I saw his form pass by—appealing—significant—under a cloud—perfectly silent." But this statement, made in reply to critics who had called Jim "a figure of the Northern mists," proves or disproves singularly little. [Gerard Jean-Aubry] has identified the young man as a certain Jim Lingard (the same who served as a model to Tom Lingard in Conrad's Malay novels) and has come to the conclusion that "the real Jim Lingard and the Lord Jim of the novel have nothing in common except their name and physique."

What was Lord Jim's physique then? He was tall ("an inch, perhaps two, under six feet"); powerfully built; had a youthful ("boyish") face, and enjoyed marvellous good health. All these qualities, Jim Lingard may have possessed, but that is not as interesting as the fact that these very qualities Conrad *had not.* Joseph Conrad was rather little, he looked in his youth considerably older than his age . . . , and his health, after the Congo adventure, was always rather precarious. As far as his figure, his youthfulness, and his health were concerned he must have often experienced a feeling of inferiority, and the fact that he chose as a model for Jim a fellow who had in a remarkable degree those qualities in which he was lacking, may be put down to his unconscious wishes for compensation. Men

Conrad (above center) with five apprentice sailors aboard the Torrens, on which Conrad served as first mate.

with youthful faces are exceedingly frequent in Conrad's books.

(That Conrad experienced a feeling of inferiority with regard to tall men is shown in the following anecdote reported by F. M. Hueffer:

> Over and over again he related how overwhelming *with his small stature,* he found negotiations with heavy spars, stubborn cordage and black weather. He used to say, half raising his arms: "Look at me . . . . How was I made for such imbecilities?")

A man with Jim's physique is, moreover, not unfit to undergo a psychological tragedy. Hamlet is also a strong and healthy young man. It is a fact of everyday experience that tall, well-built men have often a character curiously delicate and introvert.

Using the psychoanalytical terminology, it may be said that *physically* Jim is the projection of Conrad's unconscious wishes for compensation. Mentally or morally, he is, on the other hand, the projection of Conrad's repressed fears.

The novel ***Lord Jim*** is eminently symbolical. The circumstances leading up to Jim's "jump" are modelled on those leading to Conrad's naturalization as a British subject. Jim's father is a parson. We know that in Conrad's writings a clergyman easily stands for a man believing too blindly in Providence. Apollo Korzeniowski [Conrad's father] belonged to that very type. He was . . . a great religious idealist. Of Jim we read that "after a course of light holiday literature his vocation for the sea had declared itself." We recognize in this sentence the slightly ironical tone Conrad uses when speaking of himself. Jim's youth is but a humorous version of his own. In fact, his readings, and not the sight of the sea nor the call of any family or national tradition, awoke in him the desire to become a sailor. Jim is sent to a training ship. Conrad's relations wanted first to send him to the Austrian Naval School at Pola, but they finally decided to let him go to Marseilles.

Jim's first voyage to the East takes place in very much the same circumstances as surrounded Conrad's early voyages. Jim was "not yet four-and-twenty," Conrad's age was respectively twenty-one and twenty-three when he made his first two voyages to Australia. Jim is disabled by a falling spar and has to lie for weeks in an Eastern hospital: it is Conrad's accident on board the *Highland Forest.* Jim's library, like that of Joseph Conrad, consists mainly in a green one-volume set of Shakespeare's works. And similar to Conrad, Jim is reckless, without fear, and sometimes "a regular devil for sailing a boat." The smuggling adventures of Dominic and Conrad, the dangerous manœuvres of the Captain in **"The Secret Sharer"** and Conrad's Torres Straits episode, as related in **"Geography and Some Explorers" (*Last Essays*),** belong to the same order. F. M. Hueffer says that he knows from several officers who sailed with Conrad that he "would indulge in extremely dangerous manœuvres, going about within knife-blades of deadly shores." The natives of Patusan called Conrad's hero *Tuan Jim,* "as one might say—Lord Jim," just as the Polish peasants and servants must have called the young Conrad *Pan Józef,* an expression meaning literally *Lord Joseph!* Jim had particular reasons to use only his Christian name and to drop his surname. The same was true of Joseph Conrad Korzeniowski. One may or may not admit the significance of these facts; it is interesting to note the extreme shyness with which Conrad mentioned his real name. When about to arrange the journey to Poland in 1914, according to Mrs. Conrad "he had forgotten some important formality as to the date of his naturalization, and he had omitted to put his full name, Korzeniowski." It is true that Conrad signed his *Polish* letters always with his full name, only, in these, he appears distinctly as a Pole, not as an Englishman.

Finally, when Jim asks himself so anxiously whether public opinion will back him up, whether the sanction of his foreign friends will be absolute enough to absolve him in his own eyes, we again recognize in Jim Conrad himself. Jim's authority over the "natives" stands really for Conrad's success in the English-speaking world.

In spite of his origin and of his careful education, Jim "jumps." In all probability, he would not have done it, had not his very superiors urged him to go, and had not the ship been sure to sink the next moment. This is exactly what happened to Joseph Conrad. *The sinking ship is Poland.* The very names are similar. *Patna* is the name of the ship, and *Polska* the (Polish) name of Poland. *Poland* (i.e. polonity) is doomed to disappear in a short time. There is, rationally speaking, no hope whatever for her. Such was at least the opinion of Jim's superiors, i.e. of Conrad's uncle and guardian, T. Bobrowski. The machines have been stopped, i.e. the independent Polish Government has ceased to exist. At this moment, Jim's superiors advise him to "jump," but Jim did not want to for a long moment. As a matter of fact, Conrad's uncle *urged him during more than seven years* to become a British subject. And finally, Jim yielded and jumped, i.e. Conrad became a British subject.

But then, the ship is successfully towed to Aden by a French gunboat. This is the expression of the repressed hope that every genuine Pole ever cherished at the bottom of his heart . . . , the hope that the day would come when Poland would be saved. That is why of all things it is a *French gunboat* that rescues the *Patna.* Ever since the rise of Napoleon, the Poles have expected their help to come from France. The Polish national anthem "Poland is not yet lost" is a song which originated in the Polish legions serving under Napoleon.

These are the facts of Conrad's life, and his wishes and fears which underlie the first part of *Lord Jim.* The second part of the book (from chapter 19 onwards) is not less symbolic than the first. But while the first part is the representation of a real state of affairs, the second part is the expression of Conrad's fear that the desertion of his native country might ultimately prove a fault by which he had forfeited his honour. The final destruction of Jim consecrates the author's triumph over the guilt-complex. Tuan Jim's defeat is Joseph Conrad's victory. A man who, like Jim, has suffered so much, and who has paid off his debt with his death, is no longer guilty. His death adds much to the poignancy of his fate, it really makes him *a hero.*

If we did not regret Jim's fate (though feeling its inevitability), the novel would have missed the mark. This is the reason why *Lord Jim* must of necessity have what is called "an unhappy ending." In fact, Jim's death is the only satisfactory closing note. Now we can absolve Jim entirely. His memory will be that of a man of unstained honour. This ending is also logical, since Conrad assumes from the very beginning that the conflict is insoluble.

R. Curle made (in his *Joseph Conrad,* 1914) a remark which is strangely inadequate, when he wrote that Jim is "not an Englishman at all, but a passionate and melancholy Pole." Jim, like Hamlet, is the personification of that brooding part which every introvert possesses, and which will govern him if he does not govern *it.* All the difference between a normal person and a neurotic is that the former can keep that part in its proper place, that, unlike Jim (but very much like Conrad), he masters his fate. That is why Jim is not a Pole, but simply a neurotic and, as such, a perfectly true and convincing character. There are thousands of English men and women like him, thousands whose lives are obscured and sometimes destroyed by guilt-complexes. They do not, as a rule, die in such romantic circumstances as Jim or Hamlet, but end by suicide or in a lunatic asylum. Their fate may be less pathetic because it is not grasped and expressed by the mind of an artist, but it is just as real.

Lord Jim is unique amongst Conrad's books. It is perhaps not his best, but his most intimate. It is a book in which he tells us more about the darker sides of his personality than in **A Personal Record** and the **Mirror of the Sea** put together, for in these two books Conrad has taken great care that no "Conrad en pantoufles" (to use his own expression) should appear before the public. In *Lord Jim,* Joseph Conrad exteriorized, in a symbolic form, the deepest conflicts that arose from the dualism Polish-English within himself.

Lord Jim is more than a psychological novel, it is a psychoanalytical novel written before psychoanalysis was founded. It appeared in 1900, the very year when Freud published his first book *Interpretation of Dreams,* which indirectly helps us to explain the novel. Both books, one in a subjective, the other in an objective form, threw light upon "that side of us which, like the other hemisphere of the moon, exists stealthily in perpetual darkness, with only a fearful ashy light falling at times on the edge" (*Lord Jim*).

It was only in the nature of things that Conrad should dislike Freud intensely, as he disliked Dostoievski. Freud was in possession of the same truths as himself, but he appeared to him as a too crude, a too explicit double of himself. (pp. 149-66)

> *Gustav Morf, in his* The Polish Heritage of Joseph Conrad, *1930. Reprint by Haskell House, 1965, 248 p.*

Dorothy Van Ghent   (essay date 1953)

[*In the following essay, Van Ghent delineates parallels between* Lord Jim *and Greek tragic drama.*]

Marlow's last view of Jim, on the coast of Patusan, is of a white figure "at the heart of a vast enigma." Jim himself is not enigmatic. The wonder and doubt that he stirs, both in Marlow and in us, are not wonder and doubt as to what *he* is: he is as recognizable as we are to ourselves; he is "one of us." Furthermore, he is not a very complex character, and he is examined by his creator with the most exhaustive conscientiousness; he is placed in every possible perspective that might help to define him. The enigma, then, is not what Jim is but what we are, and not only what we are, but "how to be" what we are.

Jim's shocking encounter with himself at the moment of his jump from the *Patna* is a model of those moments when the destiny each person carries within him, the destiny fully molded in the unconscious will, lifts its blind head from the dark, drinks blood, and speaks. There is no unclarity in the shape that Jim saw at that moment: he had jumped—it is as simple as that. But because the event is a paradigm of the encounters of the conscious personality with the stranger within, the stranger who is the very self of the self, the significance of Jim's story is *our own* significance, contained in the enigmatic relationship between the conscious will and the fatality of our acts. Jim's discovery of himself was a frightful one, and his solution of the problem of "how to be" was to exorcise the stranger in a fierce, long, concentrated effort to be his opposite. The oracle spoke early to Oedipus, too, in his youth in Corinth, telling him who he was—the man destined to transgress most horribly the saving code of kinship relations—and Oedipus's solution of the problem of "how to be" was the same as Jim's: he fled in the opposite direction from his destiny and ran straight into it.

Jim is one of the most living characters in fiction, although his presentation is by indirection, through Marlow's narrative; that indirection is itself uniquely humanizing, for we see him only as people can see each other, ambivalently and speculatively. He is nevertheless an extraordinarily simplified *type*, obsessed with a single idea, divested of all psychological attributes but the very few that concretize his relationship with his idea. The simplification is classical; it is a simplification like that of Aeschylus' Orestes, possessed by the divine command, and like that of Sophocles' Oedipus, possessed by his responsibility for finding out the truth. Conrad is able thus to imply a clear-cut formal distinction between the man and his destiny (his acts), even though he conceives destiny as immanent in the man's nature and in this sense identical with him. Here is Jim, "clean-limbed, clean-faced, firm on his feet, as promising a boy as the sun ever shone on," and there are his acts—the destruction of his best friend, the destruction of himself, the abandonment of the Patusan village to leaderlessness and depredation. Similarly Orestes and Oedipus, human agents simplified to a commanding ethical idea, are analytically separable from their destinies, the *anakē* or compelling principle fatally inherent in their acts. This subtle but tangible distinction between the human agent and his destiny allows the classical dramatists to orient clearly what we may call the metaphysical significance of the hero's career, the universal problem and the law of life which that career illustrates. We see the hero as an ideal human type (literally "idealized" through his devotion to an idea of ethical action); but his fate is pitiful and terrible—a fate that, if a man's deserts were to be suited to his conscious intentions, should fall only on malicious, unjust, and treasonable men; and the problem, the "enigma," thus raised is the religious problem of the awful incongruity between human intention and its consequences in action, between ethical effort and the guilt acquired through such effort; and the law—if a law appears—will be the law that justifies, to man's reason and feeling, that appearance of awful incongruity. Conrad's treatment of Jim's story is classical in this sense, in that he sees in it the same problem and orients the problem in the same manner.

"In the destructive element immerse," Stein says, voicing his own solution of the problem of "how to be." There is no way "to be," according to Stein, but through the ideal, the truth as it appears, what he calls "the dream," although it is itself "the destructive element." "Very funny this terrible thing is," Stein says,

> "A man that is born falls into a dream like a man who falls into the sea. If he tries to climb out into the air as inexperienced people endeavour to do, he drowns—*nicht wahr?* . . . No! I tell you! The way is to the destructive element submit yourself, and with the exertions of your hands and feet in the water make the deep, deep sea keep you up. So if you ask me—how to be? . . . I will tell you! . . . In the destructive element immerse."

Stein's words are but one outlook on the universal problem that is Jim's, but it is the outlook dramatized in Jim's own actions. It is that dramatized by Sophocles also. Oedipus "submitted" himself to his ideal of the responsible king and citizen, self-sworn to the discovery of the truth. It was the "destructive element," bringing about the terrible revelation of his guilt. So also Jim submits himself to his dream of heroic responsibility and truth to men, fleeing from port to port, and finally to Patusan, to realize it. And, again, the ideal is the "destructive element," bringing about the compact with Brown (a compact made in the profoundest spirit of the dream) and inevitably, along with the compact, destruction. The irony is that Jim, in his destructiveness, was "true." This is the classical tragic irony: the incongruity and yet the effective identity between the constructive will and the destructive act.

Whether Conrad goes beyond that particular tragic incongruity to the other ancient tragic perception, of ennoblement through suffering, is doubtful. The "enigma" that Marlow finds in Jim's career has this other dark and doubtful aspect. When, at the end, after receiving Doramin's bullet, "the white man sent right and left at all those faces a proud and unflinching glance," is he really fulfilled in nobility in our sight? Has his suffering, entailed in his long and strenuous exile and his guilt and his final great loss, given him the knowledge, and with the knowledge the nobility, which is the mysterious and sublime gift of suffering? The answer is doubtful. We need to bring to bear on it the fairly inescapable impression that the only character in the book in whom we can read the stamp of the author's own practical "approval" is the French lieutenant who remained on board the *Patna* while it was being towed into port. The French lieutenant would not have acted as Jim did in the last events on Patusan—indeed is inconceivable in the Patusan circumstances. If, in Conrad's implicit evaluation of his material, the French lieutenant represents the ethically "approved" manner of action and the only one, Jim can scarcely support the complete role of the tragic hero of the classical type, the hero who achieves unique greatness through suffering. (The French lieutenant suffers only for lack of wine.) For our notion of what constitutes a "hero" is thus surely divided: if the French lieutenant's heroism is the true heroism, Jim's is not, and conversely. No doubt the division—and it seems to be real in our response to the book—is associated with a division of allegiance on Conrad's part, between emotional allegiance to Jim's suffering and struggling humanity, in all its hybristic aspiration, and intellectual allegiance to the code represented by the lieutenant, in all its severe limitation and calm obscurity. With this division in mind, it is impossible to identify the "view of life" in the book as a whole with Stein's view of life, impressive as Stein is in his broad and enlightened sensitivity: for the French lieutenant knows nothing of a "destructive element," and if he did—which he could not—would doubtless think that to talk of "submitting" oneself to it was sheer twaddle.

What intervenes between Conrad's ambivalent attitude toward Jim's story and the attitudes of Aeschylus and Sophocles toward their subjects is modern man's spiritual isolation from his fellows. Jim's isolation is profound, most profound and complete at that last moment when he "sent right and left at all those faces a proud and unflinching glance": here his aloneness in his dream—his illusion—of faith to men is unqualified, for the material fact is that he has allowed a brigand to slaughter Dain Waris and his party, and that he has left the village open to ravage. Moral isolation provides a new inflection of tragedy. Orestes freed Argos from a tyranny, and Oedipus freed Thebes from a plague. Their guilt and suffering had a constructive social meaning; they had acted for the positive welfare of the citizens; and that social version of their heroism, internal to the dramas in which they appear, is the immediate, literal basis of our (because it is the citizen-chorus's) appraisal of their heroism. But Jim—to use parallel terms—destroys his city. Thus there is nothing structurally internal to Jim's story that matches the positive moral relationship, in the ancient dramas, between the social destiny and the hero's destiny, the relationship that is presented concretely in the fact that the hero's agony is a saving social measure. There is nothing to mediate, practically and concretely, between Jim's "truth" and real social life, as a benefit to and confirmation of the social context. Jim is alone.

And yet one asks, is his last act, when he "takes upon his head" the blood-guilt, an atonement? If it were so, it would be atonement not in quite the same sense that the madness and exile of Orestes and the blinding and banishment of Oedipus were atonements, for these involved the restoration of community health, whereas Jim's final act brings about (projectively) the destruction of the community—but in the necessary modern sense, necessitated by the fact of the disintegration of moral bonds between men: an atonement for that social sterility, a sacrifice offered in the name of moral community. If it were so, Jim would

still be, metaphorically speaking, the savior of the city. No doubt Sophocles, civic-minded gentleman, did not "approve" of Oedipus: when parricide and incest occur in the leading families, what are the rest of us to do? how is the world's business to be kept up decently? what model shall we look to? But the Greek cities were said to have carried on quarrels over the burial place of Oedipus, for his presence brought fertility to the land. So also the story of Lord Jim is a spiritually fertilizing experience, enlightening the soul as to its own meaning in a time of disorganization and drought; and Conrad's imagination of Jim's story has the seminal virtue of the ancient classic.

In James's *The Portrait of a Lady* we watched the creation of a self. In Conrad's austerely pessimistic work, the self stands already created, the possibilities are closed. Again and again, and finally on Patusan, a "clean slate" is what Jim thinks he has found, a chance to "climb out," to begin over, to perform the deed which will be congruent with his ideal of himself. "A clean slate, did he say?" Marlow comments; "as if the initial word of each our destiny were not graven in imperishable characters upon the face of a rock." The tension, the spiritual drama in Conrad, lie in a person's relation with his destiny. The captain in **"The Secret Sharer"** acknowledges his profound kinship with a man who has violently transgressed the captain's professional code (the man has murdered another seaman during a voyage, and murder at sea is, in Conrad, something worse than murder; whatever its excuses, it is an inexcusable breach of faith with a community bound together by common hazard); but by the acknowledgment he masters his own identity, integrates, as it were, his unconscious impulses within consciousness, and thereby realizes self-command and command of his ship. In contrast with the captain of **"The Secret Sharer,"** Jim repudiates the other-self that has been revealed to him; at no time does he consciously acknowledge that it *was* himself who jumped from the *Patna*—it was only his body that had jumped; and his career thenceforth is an attempt to prove before men that the gross fact of the jump belied his identity.

James works through recognitions; the self-creating character in James develops by taking into consciousness more and more subtle relations—"seeing" more in a world of virtually infinite possibilities for recognition, and thus molding consciousness, molding himself. Conrad works through epiphanies, that is, through dramatic manifestations of elements hidden or implicit in the already constructed character. The difference of method is suggestive of the difference of world view: in James, the world ("reality" as a whole) being, as it were, an open and fluid system, essentially creative; in Conrad, a closed and static system, incapable of origination though intensely dramatic in its revelations. (Paradoxically, the environments in James's open world are the closed environments of city and house, while those in Conrad's closed world are those of the open, the mobile sea.) The word "epiphany" implies manifestation of divinity, and this meaning of the term can serve us also in analyzing Conrad's method and his vision, if we think of the "dark powers" of the psyche as having the mysterious absoluteness that we associate with the daemonic, and if we think mythologically of a man's destiny both as being carried within him, and, *in effect*—since his acts externalize his destiny—as confronting him from without.

The sunken wreck that strikes the *Patna* is one such epiphany in **Lord Jim,** and this manifestation of "dark power" is coincident with and symbolically identifiable with the impulse that makes Jim jump, an impulse submerged like the wreck, riding in wait, striking from under. Outer nature seems, here, to act in collusion with the hidden portion of the soul. But Conrad's supreme mastery is his ability to make the circumstance of "plot" the inevitable point of discharge of the potentiality of "character." The accident that happens to the *Patna* is not merely a parallel and a metaphor of what happens to Jim at that time, but it is the objective circumstance that discovers Jim to himself. The apparent "collusion" between external nature and the soul, that gives to Conrad's work its quality of the marvelous and its religious temper, is thus, really, only the inevitable working out of character through circumstance.

Another major epiphany is the appearance of Brown on Patusan. The appearance of Brown is, in effect, an externalization of the complex of Jim's guilt and his excuses for his guilt, for he judges Brown as he judged himself, as a *victim of circumstances* (the distinction is radical) rather than as a character exposed by circumstances, at least to be given that benefit of doubt which would discriminate intention from deed, ethos from the objective ethical traits to be seen in a man's actions. Therefore he gives Brown a "clean slate," a chance to "climb out"—from himself! But Jim's compact with Brown is more than a compact with his own unacknowledged guilt; it is at the same time, and paradoxically, a lonely act of faith with the white men "out there," the men of Jim's race and traditions, the men upon the sea whose code he had once betrayed, the "home" from which a single impulse of nerves had forever exiled him. Brown is the only white man who has appeared on Patusan to put to test Jim's ethical community with his race and his profession, and in "taking upon his head" responsibility for Brown's honor, he is superbly "true" to that community. But his truth is, effectively, betrayal; it is "the destructive element." Since only a chance in thousands brings Brown to Patusan, again outer nature seems to have acted in collusion with the "dark power" within Jim's own psyche, in order to face him once more with his unacknowledged identity when he is in the full hybris of his truth and his courage. But again the apparent collusion is only the working out of character through circumstance.

The impossibility of escape from the dark companion within leaves a man more perfectly alone in this world because he has that companion—who is always and only himself. The physical settings of Jim's career concretize his isolation. In constant flight from the self that he reads on men's lips but that he refuses to acknowledge except as a freakish injustice of circumstances, and, as he flees, pursuing the heroic ideal which would reconstitute him in the ranks of men where his salvation lies (for, as Conrad says, "in our own hearts we trust for our salvation in the men that surround us"), he comes finally to Patusan, ascends the river to the heart of the island, unarmed (why carry a loaded revolver when it is only oneself that one

must face?)—ascends, that is, the dark paths of his own being back to its source: "thirty miles of forest shut it off."

The first description that Marlow gives of the interior of the island is of a conical hill that is "split in two, and with the two halves leaning slightly apart," and in his reminiscences he returns frequently to the image of the hill (it is, indeed, the hill up which Jim hauled the cannon, in his first great exploit when he won the faith of the natives and became their protector), particularly to a scene of moonlight when the moon is rising behind the fissured mass.

> On the third day after the full, the moon, as seen from the open space in front of Jim's house . . . rose exactly behind these hills, its diffused light at first throwing the two masses into intensely black relief, and then the nearly perfect disc, glowing ruddily, appeared, gliding upwards between the sides of the chasm, till it floated away above the summits, as if escaping from a yawning grave in gentle triumph. "Wonderful effect," said Jim by my side. "Worth seeing. Is it not?"
>
> And this question was put with a note of personal pride that made me smile, as though he had had a hand in regulating that unique spectacle. He had regulated so many things in Patusan! Things that would have appeared as much beyond his control as the motions of the moon and the stars.

On Marlow's last night on the island he sees the same spectacle again, but the mood is different, oppressive.

> I saw part of the moon glittering through the bushes at the bottom of the chasm. For a moment it looked as though the smooth disc, falling from its place in the sky upon the earth, had rolled to the bottom of that precipice: its ascending movement was like a leisurely rebound; it disengaged itself from the tangle of twigs; the bare contorted limb of some tree, growing on the slope, made a black crack right across its face. It threw its level rays afar as if from a cavern, and in this mournful eclipse-like light the stumps of felled trees uprose very dark, the heavy shadows fell at my feet on all sides . . .

Together Jim and Marlow watch "the moon float away above the chasm between the hills like an ascending spirit out of a grave; its sheen descended, cold and pale, like the ghost of dead sunlight." Carried to the mind by the image of the fissured hill, with the suspiciously ghostlike moon floating out of the chasm, is the relentless solitude of Jim's fate. He is not only an outcast from his kind but he is also an outcast from himself, cloven spiritually, unable to recognize his own identity, separated from himself as the two halves of the hill are separated. And the rebounding moon, in which he has so much pride, "as though he had had a hand in regulating that unique spectacle," remains in the mind as a figure of the ego-ideal, even that ideal of truth by which, Marlow says, Jim approached "greatness as genuine as any man ever achieved": its illusionariness, and the solitude implied by illusion. At the end, after all— when the silver ring that is the token of moral community falls to the floor, and through Jim's "truth" his best friend has been killed and the village under his protection betrayed—Jim is only what he has been; he is of the measure of his acts. To be only what one has been is the sentence of solitary confinement that is passed on everyman. It is in this sense, finally, that Jim is "one of us."

Since Jim is "one of us," the truth about Jim will be—within the scope of the expressiveness of Jim's story—a truth about life; and in view of this responsibility, Conrad's task of evaluation demands that *all* the accessible evidence be presented and that it be submitted to mutually corrective hypotheses of its meaning. There are Jim's actions, which are concrete enough and simple as the concrete is simple. But the significance of action is significance in the judgments of men, which are various; and as soon as judgment is brought to the act, the act becomes not simple but protean. *What,* then, *is* the act? The question defines Conrad's method in this book, his use of reflector within reflector, point of view within point of view, cross-chronological juxtapositions of events and impressions. Conrad's technical "devices," in this case, represent much more than the word "device" suggests: they represent extreme ethical scrupulosity, even anxiety; for the truth about a man is at once too immense and too delicate to sustain any failure of carefulness in the examiner.

The omniscient early chapters give briefly the conditions of Jim's upbringing, his heroic dreams, two incidents in his sea training, the *Patna* voyage up to the moment when the submerged wreck strikes, and the courtroom scene with Jim in the dock: that is, the first chapters take us up to the point where the accused is placed before us and the processes of judgment have to begin. From here, Marlow takes over. Marlow is unofficial attorney both for the defense and the prosecution. He selects, objectifies, and humanizes the evidence on both sides, but he lets it—intensified and set in perspective through his intelligent, freely roaming curiosity—speak for itself. Marlow is the most familiar narrative mechanism in Conrad's work; and in this particular book *Marlow has to exist.* For Jim's "case" is not an absolute but a relative; it has a being only in relation to what men's minds can make of it. And Marlow provides the necessary medium of an intelligent consciousness, at once a symbol of that relativity, a concretization of the processes by which just judgment may be evoked, and—through his doubt and reverence—an acknowledgment of the irony of judgment of the relative.

The few particulars that are given of Jim's home environment are all we need to give the word "home" potency for this chronicle: there is the parsonage, its decency, its naïveté, its faith, its sterling morality, its representativeness of "the sheltering conception of light and order which is our refuge." In the thirty-fifth chapter, where Marlow takes final farewell of Jim, and Jim says,

> "I must stick to their belief in me to feel safe and to—to" . . . He cast about for a word, seemed to look for it on the sea . . . "to keep in touch with" . . . His voice sank suddenly to a murmur . . . "with those whom, perhaps, I shall never see any more. With—with—you, for instance."

The parsonage home, as well as the community of men upon the sea, contains the "those" with whom Jim must keep in touch through faithfulness in word and act. "Home" is the ethical code which enables men to live together through trust of each other, and which, in so binding them, gives them self-respect. The exclusiveness and naïveté of the parsonage background interpret the symbol of "home" in all its own relativity, its merely provisional status in the jungle of the universe. When we close the book, the symbol of "home" is as ghostlike as the moon over Patusan. But it is the only provision for salvation, in the sense in which Conrad uses the word salvation when he says, "In our own hearts we trust for our salvation in the men that surround us."

The two incidents in Jim's early sea training, the storm in Chapter 1, when he was "too late," and, in Chapter 2, his disablement at the beginning of a hurricane week, when he "felt secretly glad he had not to go on deck," counterpoint his belief in himself with actualities of frustration. A certain distinct polarity is already established, between his dreams and the "facts"; and when, in Chapter 2, Jim suddenly decides to ship as mate on the *Patna,* it is as if we saw a bar magnet curved into a horseshoe and bent until its poles closed, sealing personal will and the fatality of circumstances in a mysterious identity that is the man himself; for his unexplained choice of the *Patna* is in more than one sense a choice of exile. He could have gone back to the home service, after his convalescence; but he throws in his lot with the men he has seen in that Eastern port (and disdained) who "appeared to live in a crazy maze of plans, hopes, dangers, enterprises . . . in the dark places of the sea," and with those others who had been seduced by "the eternal peace of Eastern sky and sea," who talked "everlastingly of turns of luck . . . and in all they said—in their actions, in their looks, in their persons—could be detected the soft spot, the place of decay . . . " Moreover, on the *Patna* he is in a special sense a man alone, alone with a dream that is unsharable because he is among inferiors: the third chapter presents "the *Patna* gang" from Jim's point of view—"those men did not belong to the world of heroic adventure . . . he rubbed shoulders with them, but they could not touch him; he shared the air they breathed, but he was different . . . " Is his choice of the *Patna* a measure taken to protect his dream from reality? Is it thus significant of his "soft spot"? There is no choice but reality, and actually none but the single, circumscribed, only possible choice that is one's own reality—witnessed by Jim's jump from the *Patna,* as by his shipping on the *Patna* in the first place.

When Sophocles, in his old age, wrote of Oedipus again, he had Oedipus assert his innocence and curse those who had banished him; for Oedipus had acted in ignorance of the circumstances, and therefore could not be held guilty for them. Jim puts up a fight as Oedipus did, and the causes involved are the same: is the self deducible from circumstances? is one guilty for circumstances? is one guilty for oneself when one has no choice but to be oneself? Is one guilty for oneself when one is in ignorance of what oneself is? if, with lifelong strife, one refuses to acquiesce in the self, is one guilty for the self? who has a right to pronounce this judgment?

Obviously from this point another device of presentation

must be used, other than either objective presentation by the author or subjective presentation through Jim, for Jim is too youthful, idealistic, and ingenuous to throw light on himself, and "objectivity"—the objectivity of the camera and the sound recorder—is hopelessly inadequate to the solution of these questions. Marlow has to take up the case, and Marlow—intelligent professional man of the sea, and insatiably curious psychological observer—brings to bear on it not only Jim's own evidence (and his friendship with Jim draws from Jim much more than he could ever say for himself—brings out gestures and tones, situations and impulses, that only sympathy could bring out), and not only the reactions of the judges (and the judges are more in number than those in the courtroom), but also a marvelously sensitive registration of the concrete detail of life, bits of color and form and movement, a chin, a hand, a shuffle, a vase of dry flowers, a striped pajama suit, that could not be admitted as "evidence" in a formal inquiry, but that are nevertheless essential psychological evidence to the sensitive investigator.

The *Patna* gang has to be presented over again, not now from Jim's point of view but from Marlow's. So far as the *Patna* gang is concerned, the question is, is Jim one of them or "one of us"? Marlowe has only to see the group on a street corner to know that Jim is not one of them; but he pushes further—he is around when the fat captain, in his nightsuit, squeezes into the ramshackle gharry and disappears, "departed, disappeared, vanished, absconded; and absurdly enough it looked as though he had taken that gharry with him." It is Marlow's impression of the obscenely ridiculous captain that conveys to us the captain's sur-reality: he is, through Marlow's view, not simply stupid and inferior as he appeared to Jim, but a frightful manifestation of underground evil, as mysterious and unaccountable in its apparition as the captain's vanishing with the gharry is complete; that the captain wears a sleeping suit (like the murderer in **"The Secret Sharer"**) emphasizes the psychological, that is to say spiritual, symbolism of his evil; he is another epiphany, a "showing" from the daemonic underground of the psyche—but he is only that, and the psyche, Jim's psyche, is more than the obscene man in the sleeping suit.

Then Marlow interviews the chief engineer in the hospital, the man with the noble head and the pink toads under his bed. The effort is an effort again to test his perception that Jim is not one of them, but "one of us"; for the initial perception alone is scarcely to be trusted, since Jim, whatever his excuses, had identified himself with the *Patna* gang by jumping from the ship. The pink toads under the chief engineer's bed are a fearful inversion of Jim's own dream: they too are a dream—and the dreamer has a noble head. The pink toads are a horrible degeneration of the dream. They serve as a commentary on the dream that cannot be evaded (no more than can the captain in the sleeping suit). But Jim had stayed for the trial, while the captain had disappeared, the chief engineer had cultivated the d.t.'s, and the second engineer wasn't around (the little man will reappear later, for the act is immortal). It is Jim's dream that makes him stay for the trial, and therefore Jim's dream cannot be identified with the chief engineer's, however identifiable they are in illusionary quality and spiritual po-

tency. Marlow's visit with the chief engineer fixes this judgment of a difference, as well as of a similarity.

These two observations of Marlow's project the question of identity (the question "Who am I?" that is Oedipus' as well as Jim's), that can only be decided by comparison of like things and different things, discrimination of congruences and incongruences. Two identifications of Jim with other persons have been rejected—although even the impulse to distinguish suggests subtle similarities between the objects compared, and we can never forget that Jim was in the lifeboat with the *Patna* gang, though at the other end. The rest of the narrative moves through a devious course of identifications and distinctions. Brierly, the unimpeachable professional seaman, in some astounding way identifies himself with the accused man, Jim, and commits suicide. Is this another version of Jim's "jump"? If so, in avoiding by suicide the possibility of being Jim, Brierly succeeds merely in being what he was trying to avoid; this is Jim's "case" all over again. The loathsome Chester also identifies himself with Jim; Chester instantly spots him as the man for his job—fantastic exile on a guano island; "He is no earthly good for anything," Chester says,—"he would just have done for me"; the man has a "soft spot," and for men with a soft spot, as Jim himself had observed, "death was the only event of their fantastic existence that seemed to have a reasonable certitude of achievement"; for Chester, Jim is "one of us" in a sense that disgusts Marlow, and Marlow's disgust with Chester and therefore with Chester's appraisal of the man helps us to measure Jim: but the fact that Marlow, during those grueling hours in the hotel room when he is writing factitious letters in order to give Jim a chance for privacy with his ordeal, can hesitate between recommending Jim for a decent job and turning him over to Chester still suggests a doubt as to what "one of us" means, whether it has Chester's meaning or Marlow's.

The French lieutenant whom Marlow encounters, though he is a sympathetic man, does *not* identify himself with Jim; and curiously, while the French lieutenant represents the approved ethos of the profession (and not only of the profession of the sea, but of the profession of being human, as the author evaluates his material; for, in that evaluation, being human, as humans ought to be, *is* a profession, with an austere Spartan-like discipline), he is the only person in the book who does not, in some way, identify himself with Jim except for Cornelius and Brown, who hate him as an opposite and as an indictment of their evil (perhaps the captain of the *Patna* and the chief engineer could be included here, but their presentation is more objective and their attitudes less determinable; although the same point would hold): that is to say that the only cases in which subjective identification with Jim does not take place are those of a man—the French lieutenant—who is above Jim's failings by virtue of his mediocrity, and of men who are below Jim's problem by virtue of their psychotic maliciousness. The portrait of the French lieutenant is extremely careful, as all the portraits in the book are done with extreme care, for on the nature of the man who judges depends the validity of the judgment.

> He clasped his hands on his stomach again. "I remained on board that—that—my memory is

going (*s'en va*). Ah! Patt-nà. *C'est bien ça*. Patt-nà. *Merci*. It is droll how one forgets. I stayed on that ship thirty hours . . . "

And just a moment before, we have learned that "all the time of towing we had two quartermasters stationed with axes by the hawsers, to cut us clear of our tow in case she . . . " The French lieutenant's failure to remember even the name of the ship, on which he had stayed for thirty hours *after* Jim had jumped, and the laconic tone of the information about the quartermasters' assignment, are a judgment of Jim in terms of Jim's own dream. The French lieutenant's unconscious heroism is the heroism that Jim had made a conscious ideal; and his witness measures Jim's failure by the painful difference of fact. And yet this damning commentary appears as inconclusive as that of the pink toads under the chief engineer's bed; it is as far from and as near to "the case."

The distinguished naturalist Stein offers another approach. Stein has been a hero of action like the French lieutenant, but he is also a hero of the intellect, and, in his way, a psychologist, a philosopher, and an artist. Stein is able to identify himself with Jim through his own profound idealism (as Marlow does through doubt). But Stein's idealism, so far as we know, has never differentiated itself from his actions; he has the gift of nature which is itself ideal; he had known, Marlow says, how "to follow his destiny with unfaltering footsteps." Stein "diagnoses the case" of Jim, making it quite simple "and altogether hopeless" by framing it in the question: "how to be." "I tell you, my friend," he says,

> "it is not good for you to find you cannot make your dream come true, for the reason that you not strong enough are, or not clever enough. *Ja!* . . . And all the time you are such a fine fellow, too! *Wie?* . . . How can that be? . . . "

> The shadow prowling amongst the graves of butterflies laughed boisterously.

Stein gives Jim his great chance to make his dream come true, by sending him to Patusan. This journey is ambiguous: "once before Patusan had been used as a grave," Marlow reflects; while Stein prowls "amongst the graves of butterflies," Brierly's remark about Jim recurs to Marlow's mind: "Let him creep twenty feet underground and stay there"; and there is the fissured hill at the heart of Patusan, whose chasm is like a "yawning grave," from which the moon (the dream) rises "like an ascending spirit out of a grave . . . like the ghost of dead sunlight." The ancient mythical heroes, Odysseus and Aeneas, made the "journey underground" to Hades in search of wisdom, and brought it back to daylight—the wisdom which was knowledge of their own destinies. And shadowily behind them is the barbarous ritual that made a king by burying him and disinterring him, a surrogate perhaps, or a "story" (mythos), to stand for the killing of an old king and his "resurrection" in a new one. In the grave of Patusan—"the secular gloom and the old mankind"—Jim's dream does come true. But the doubt remains as to whether, like the ancient heroes, he brought back to daylight the wisdom of his destiny—or, in other terms, whether in that

grave an old self was really buried and from it a new one congruent with his dream was resurrected.

The test of daylight, of the bright sea beyond the dark island, offers itself only through Brown. Jim identifies himself with Brown in two ways, through his guilt, and through his honor: Brown is at once the "dark power" in Jim's psyche and his only effective bond with the brightness outside himself, the community of tradition to which "we trust for our salvation." Brown's ambivalence for Jim is Jim's own ambivalence, and it is, in its most extensive sense, the ambivalence that exists in all historical and personal stages of experience where law (the "code") and the self question each other—as well in the Athens of Thucydides and Euripides as in our own time, and as well, we must surmise, in Conrad as in Jim. The tale Conrad prepared to narrate was a tale in the manner of the older classical dramatists, wherein law—whether divine, as with Aeschylus, or natural, as with Sophocles—is justified to the self, whatever its agonies of discovery. But he managed to do a tale that put both the law and the self to question, and left them there. At the end (dated July 1900), Stein does not help:

> Stein has aged greatly of late. He feels it himself, and says often that he is "preparing to leave all this; preparing to leave . . . " while he waves his hand sadly at his butterflies.

> (pp. 229-44)

> *Dorothy Van Ghent, "On 'Lord Jim'," in her* The English Novel: Form and Function, *Holt, Rinehart and Winston, 1953, pp. 229-44.*

Tony Tanner   (essay date 1963)

[*Tanner is an English critic and educator whose works include book-length critical studies of Saul Bellow and Conrad. In the following essay, he examines the thematic conflict in* Lord Jim *between moral idealism, as embodied by Jim, and amoral pragmatism, as practiced by several of the novel's other characters.*]

In *Lord Jim* when the sagacious and tentative Marlow recalls taking Jim's case to the wise merchant Stein he tells his patient listeners that he considered Stein "an eminently suitable person to receive my confidences about Jim's difficulties"; he also tells them, in almost the same breath, of Stein's curious private interest in beetles and butterflies. For Stein is a "learned collector." "His collection of Buprestidae and Longicorns—beetles all—horrible miniature monsters, looking malevolent in death and immobility, and his cabinet of butterflies, beautiful and hovering under the glass of cases of lifeless wings, had spread his fame far over the earth."

We feel, from the start of that crucial interview, a connection between Stein's distinction as a collector and his suitability to appraise Jim, to help him. And of course what we learn is that Stein seems to have an uncanny knowledge of the qualitative extremes of humanity: man as butterfly, man as beetle, he knows them both. Considering that this is an early book the suggestive hints that Conrad weaves into the scene work with an unusually silent and effective tact. Consider, for instance, the way the insects are differently housed. "Narrow shelves filled with dark boxes of uniform shape and colour ran round the walls, not from floor to ceiling, but in a sombre belt about four feet broad. Catacombs of beetles." Not a hierarchy of beetles but a great thick belt of them: and that last short sentence makes just the right sinister impact. "The glass cases containing the collection of butterflies were ranged in three long rows upon slender-legged little tables." It is those slender legs we see—clean, fragile, graceful, and artistic: the appropriate furniture to set off a display of butterflies. The analogy between Jim and the butterflies is pressed still firmer before Marlow has even broached the subject. "I was very anxious, but I respected the intense, almost passionate, absorption with which he looked at a butterfly, as though on the bronze sheen of these frail wings, in the white tracings, in the gorgeous markings, he could see other things, an image of something as perishable and defying destruction as these delicate and lifeless tissues displaying a splendour unmarred by death." While Marlow is *thinking* about Jim, Stein is *examining* a butterfly with great care: we feel that the very quality of reverent attention with which Stein studies his insects somehow qualifies him to make a key assessment of Jim. For the whole inquiry of the book is directed at ascertaining whether there is contained within the perishable "gorgeous markings" of Jim something, some quality, some essence, which will defy destruction, some "splendour" which will remain "unmarred by death." But Conrad is not so simple as to offer a one-to-one correlation between Jim and the butterfly: just as the analogy threatens to become obvious Conrad breaks it:

> "To tell you the truth, Stein," I said with an effort that surprised me, "I came here to describe a specimen . . ."
>
> "Butterfly?" he asked, with an unbelieving and humourous eagerness.
>
> "Nothing so perfect," I answered, feeling suddenly dispirited with all sorts of doubts. "A man."

Leaving the rest of that discussion let us re-examine Jim—bearing in mind the possible metaphor of the butterfly, a creature of beauty, a creature with wings which can carry it above the mere dead level of an earth which beetles crudely hug. Straight away we recall Jim's aversion to dirt. When we first meet him he is "spotlessly neat" and "apparelled in immaculate white from shoes to hat" and this fastidious, scrupulous dazzling whiteness is invested with a slightly mystical quality. For instance when Jim is received by the treacherous Rajah Allang in Patusan, Conrad first of all establishes the fact that the people who have gathered to witness his first appearance among them are "dirty with ashes and mud-stains." By contrast Jim glows with an almost supernatural brightness:

> In the midst of these dark-faced men, his stalwart figure in white apparel, the gleaming clusters of his fair hair, seemed to catch all the sunshine that trickled through the cracks in the closed shutters of that dim hall, with its walls of mats and a roof of thatch. He appeared like a creature not only of another kind but of another essence.

This is not racism, not a belief in white-supremacy peeping through. Jim shows up against the world. Thus when Marlow sees him for the last time:

> He was white from head to foot, and remained persistently visible with the stronghold of the night at his back. . . . For me that white figure in the stillness of coast and sea seemed to stand at the heart of a vast enigma. The twilight was ebbing fast from the sky above his head, the strip of sand had sunk already under his feet, he himself appeared no bigger than a child—then only a speck, a tiny white speck that seemed to catch all the light left in a darkened world. . . . And, suddenly, I lost him. . . .

It is perhaps too easily portentous: the enigma could be anything and the encroaching darkness which finally seems to snuff him out is a touch of cosmic melodrama in the Manichean vein—but the intention is clear. Jim is a creature of "light" threatened by the forces of darkness; he is the creature of purity who stands above the dirty crowd. Throughout the book his characteristic stance is a superior contemplation of a life which goes about its muddled business far below him. As a boy at the marine school he was "very smart aloft. His station was in the fore-top, and often from there he looked down, with the contempt of a man destined to shine in the midst of dan-

James Lingard, the trader on whom Conrad based, in part, the character of Jim.

gers, at the peaceful multitude of roofs cut in two by the brown tide of the stream. . . . " When Marlow visits him in Patusan they stand talking on the top of a hill. "He was like a figure set up on a pedestal, to represent in his persistent youth the power, and perhaps the virtues, of races that never grow old, that have emerged from the gloom." Even at this ignominious trial he stood elevated in the witness-box "and dark faces stare up at him from below." So much is obvious, perhaps too obvious. So perhaps are Conrad's pointers to the vulnerabilities and limitations inherent in Jim's characteristic heroic pose. His incurable taste for romantic day-dreams nourished on fictional situations, his incapacity for self-knowledge, even the physical fact of his being "an inch, perhaps two under six feet" with which the book all too significantly begins, make "the subtle unsoundness of the man" a somewhat less subtle thing than Conrad probably thought. Jim is all too obviously flawed. But his most crucial shortcoming is more interesting. It is hinted at in his first failure to take the opportunity for heroic action which offered itself while he was still a boy at the marine school. While he is indulging in heroic daydreams a real distress signal goes up and the young trainee-sailors have to effect a rescue. But active as he is in his dreams, when confronted by the real thing Jim is paralysed. "He stood still," Conrad uses the phrase twice, "as if confounded." This inability to act is more glaringly revealed on board the refugee ship *Patna*. The nature of the captain and other men who desperately work to lower one lifeboat for themselves with no thought for the hundreds of sleeping refugees is made very clear: they are base, cowardly animals (the skipper particularly is described in the most bestial terms) who, with no thought for dignity or duty, are galvanised into frantic efforts to save their skins. To Jim they are contemptible, loathsome fools involved in scenes of grotesque "low comedy." But Jim himself?—he simply doesn't move. "He wanted me to know he had kept his distance; that there was nothing in common between him and these men—who had the hammer. Nothing whatever. It is more probable he thought himself cut off from them by a space that could not be traversed. . . . " He does not do anything to alert the sleeping passengers, but he does not take part in the almost farcically crude attempts to lower that one shameful life-boat. He does nothing. He is the passive hero who is faced by scenes of macabre low-comedy and doesn't even know how or where to begin. He feels a shuddering contemptuous disdain for the men shamelessly acting on their basest motives—he wouldn't even touch a hammer. (But that hammer betokens action—and the procuring of the hammer was in fact an heroic act even if done for the basest motives.) And yet as Jim tells his story to Marlow it becomes a terrible case of "*qui s'excuse s'accuse.*" He protests too much—that he has nothing in common with these men; yet when the pinch comes, when it seems as though he is really faced by the alternative of life and death, albeit an ignoble life and an heroic death, he suddenly finds that he has jumped, that he is down among those most contemptible of men. The space separating the butterfly and beetle—in men, in one man—can in fact be "traversed"—traversed in an instant. The physical descent is wonderfully apt for this is indeed a classic "fall." The heroic heights are abandoned: the butterfly is suddenly seen sprawling ingloriously among the beetles and an awful question arises. Has Jim at this moment found his true "level"?

We must leave Jim for a moment and consider the other objects of Stein's study—the beetles. Let us regard beetles as ugly earth-bound creatures, devoid of dignity and aspiration, intent merely on self-preservation at all costs: but gifted with a hard shell which serves them well in their unscrupulous will to live—to live on any terms, and capable of great malevolence when that life is threatened. There are hordes of such insects in *Lord Jim.* In fact one could describe the logic of Jim's continual flight as an attempt to escape from the beetles of mankind: and the drama of his travels is generated by the beetles who are continually crossing his path. Apart from the skipper of the *Patna,* who is in some ways the grossest beetle of them all, the most important are Chester, Cornelius, and Brown.

Chester is waiting for Jim after his trial like a morality play tempter. Jim's dishonour is symbolized by the cancelling of his certificate, and the punishment literally staggers him: he walks weakly away from the court. Immediately Chester appears to talk to Marlow—robust, healthy, tough, and contemptuous of all man-made standards.

> He looked knowingly after Jim. "Takes it to heart?" he asked scornfully. "Very much," I said. "Then he's no good," he opined. "What's all the to-do about? A bit of ass's skin. That never yet made a man. You must see things exactly as they are—if you don't, you may just as well give in at once. You will never do anything in this world. Look at me. I made it a practice never to take anything to heart." "Yes," I said, "you see things as they are."

From his conversation it is clear that Chester is a figure of vigour, resourcefulness, and endless energy of action: he is never enfeebled or immobilized by a sickly conscience. "The Lord knows the right and wrong of that story" is his typical comment on the rumor that his accomplice Robinson once indulged in cannibalism. As far as he is concerned, if Robinson ate human flesh to keep himself alive, then that does credit to his realistic turn of mind—he, too, saw things as they were. Chester offers Jim a job of dubious morality and Marlow refuses on Jim's account. Chester shrugs and leaves Marlow with this comment on Jim. "He is no earthly good for anything." Or as we might re-phrase it—he is no good for any earth-bound activity. And so it appears. Jim takes job after job and performs with great efficiency until a beetle turns up, usually with the story of the *Patna* and his own acrid comments on it. At various times Jim is explicitly or unconsciously called a cur, a skunk, a rat—all those repulsive animals with which the butterfly part of his nature least wishes to have anything to do. Cornelius turns up in more unusual circumstances. He is the lazy, sluggish, dilapidated father of the girl Jim loves in Patusan. He wretchedly mistreated his wife so that she died crying, and now he continues his indolent tyranny over the girl. He is a man who has gone morally to seed. But when Jim and the girl fall in love he asserts his odious presence. His base nature is wonderfully intimated in kinaesthetic terms by Conrad. Just to watch the man walk is to know him for what he is:

Cornelius was creeping across in full view with an inexpressible effect of stealthiness, of dark and secret slinking. He reminded one of everything that is unsavoury. His slow laborious walk resembled the creeping of a repulsive beetle, the legs alone moving with horrid industry while the body glided evenly. I suppose he made straight for the place where he wanted to get to, but his progress with one shoulder carried forward seemed oblique. He was often seen circling slowly amongst the sheds, as if following a scent; passing before the veranda with upward stealthy glances; disappearing without haste round the corner of some hut.

He soils the air in which Jim is trying to work out his salvation, and seems to embody a repulsive but ineradicable presence. "He has his place neither in the background nor in the foreground of the story; he is simply seen skulking on its outskirts, enigmatical and unclean, tainting the fragrance of its youth and of its naiveness." But this man has a certain momentum of hate. And from his base perspective he sees the weakness of Jim. He tells his opinion to Marlow. "He is a big fool, honourable sir. . . . He's no more than a little child here—like a little child—a little child." With this insight (and the animus generated by Jim's refusal to give him money for his daughter) he knows enough to set about betraying and destroying Jim. In his own miserable way he *acts*. And Cornelius too has the lineaments of a figure in a morality play. "Somehow the shadowy Cornelius far off there seemed to be the hateful embodiment of all the annoyances and difficulties he [Jim] had found in his path." It is no use Jim's crying out "nothing can touch me" (they are almost his dying words), for somehow such foul presences as Cornelius always loom up to finger with soiled hands the weak spots in his honour. The most notable beetle however is Brown, the man who turns up unexpectedly and is directly responsible for Jim's downfall. As Marlow talks to him on his death bed it becomes clear that Brown feels a profoundly instinctual antipathy towards Jim, a hatred of him which is not accounted for by the narrative facts.

> "I could see directly I set my eyes on him what sort of a fool he was," gasped the dying Brown. "He a man! Hell! He was a hollow sham. As if he couldn't have said, 'Hands off my plunder!' blast him! That would have been like a man. Rot his superior soul! He had me there—but he hadn't devil enough in him to make an end of me."

The revulsion is mixed: Jim's air of moral superiority maddens Brown, as evidence of a superior ethic will always infuriate a man who lives by a baser one, for what Jim sees as a moral mission, his sacred obligation to the natives, Brown can only see as potential "plunder." On the other hand Jim's refusal to fight like a man, his incapacity for diabolical *action*, revolts the man of devilish energy. For Brown, Jim is repulsive because he pretends to be more than a man, and yet in his hollow inactivity he reveals himself to be devoid of all those attributes which make a man man-like. He is, thus, a "fraud." Brown's description of his crucial encounter with Jim brings the issues of the book to a head. Marlow paraphrases Brown's account:

> I know that Brown hated Jim at first sight. . . . he cursed in his heart the other's youth and assurance, his clear eyes and untroubled bearing. . . . And there was something in the very neatness of Jim's clothes, from the white helmet to the canvas leggings and the pipeclayed shoes, which in Brown's sombre, irritated eyes seemed to belong to things he had in the very shaping of his life contemned and flouted.

Brown then recalls the exchange in his own words, an exchange, it should be remembered, which means life or death to Brown. " 'We are all equal before death,' I said. I admitted I was there like a rat in a trap, but we had been driven to it, and even a trapped rat can give a bite. He caught me up in a moment. 'Not if you don't go near the trap till the rat is dead.' " It is a typical answer—Jim still has an incurable distaste for any action which means involving himself with base, dirty people. He doesn't want to take a part in any low-comedy, although we may recall that on one occasion Jim himself was described as a rat. But even as a rat he has no bite to him. Brown pursues his case with an amoral anarchic gusto which has a curious sort of unscrupulous heroism all its own ("a virile sincerity in accepting the morality and consequences of his acts"), and as he makes his points we seem to see Jim withering before our eyes.

> "And I would let you shoot me and welcome it," I said. "This is as good a jumping-off place for me as another. I am sick of my infernal luck. But it would be too easy. There are my men in the same boat—and, by God, I am not the sort to jump out of trouble and leave them in a d—d lurch," I said. . . . "I've lived—and so did you though you talk as if you were one of those people that should have wings so as to go about without touching the dirty earth. Well—it is dirty. I haven't got any wings. I am here because I was afraid once in my life. Want to know what of? Of a prison."

Brown is strong because he can admit to fear without letting it undermine his mainsprings of action: he is strong because his element is the dirt of the world: he is strong because he lives by action (he only fears the arresting walls of a prison), and being a man of action he would never do the one thing which has soured Jim's life, leave his mates, abandon his ship. And Jim finally takes what is to Brown the easy way out and lets himself be shot. On his own terms Brown is "right"—he "sees things as they are" and therefore always acts with a prompt and savage confidence: (he feels the "lust of battle," an emotion foreign to Jim). And because of this he can get through Jim's faulty heroic armature and "shake his twopenny soul around and inside out and upside down." Perhaps Conrad makes the opposition between the two men too clear, but Brown is a convincing figure, the man of dirt who wishes to soil the disdainful immaculateness of Jim, the man of action who wishes to grab hold of that "don't-you-touch-me sort of fellow," the man without wings who yearns to drag down into his element those superior souls who think they can live without touching the earth. He has an Iago streak in him—the basic diabolical compulsion to bring everything to chaos, to reduce fine things to a mess: he has both the irresistible impulse and the requisite satanic insight to puncture the Othellos and Jims of this world. He is the anti-heroic, anti-idealistic supreme: and he is supremely successful because he has an uncanny instinct for attacking just those faults of self-deception and inaction and shame which mar Jim's armour of idealism. The moral to be drawn from Brown's unforeseeable and disastrous appearance in Jim's moral hide-out is not that a bad penny always turns up but that you can never get away from the beetles of this world, their amoral ferocity, and their murderous truth.

Before returning to Jim I want to draw attention to one of Conrad's most notable creations of the beetles of this world. I refer to Donkin in *The Nigger of the "Narcissus."* Once Conrad starts on his description of Donkin he can scarcely control himself. The torrential abuse certainly mars the texture of the book, although it clearly reveals the author's preoccupation with this kind of man. I quote only certain key extracts.

> He looked as if he had known all the degradations and all the furies. He looked as if he had been cuffed, kicked, rolled in the mud; he looked as if he had been scratched, spat upon, pelted with unmentionable filth . . . and he smiled with a sense of security at the faces around.

> His neck was long and thin; his eyelids were red; rare hairs hung about his jaws; his shoulders were peaked and dropped like the broken wings of a bird; all his left side was caked with mud which showed that he had lately slept in a wet ditch.

A broken-winged creature at home in the mud—Donkin is related to Brown.

> They all knew him. Is there a spot on earth where such a man is unknown. . . . He was the man who cannot steer, that cannot splice, that dodges the work on dark nights; that, aloft, holds on frantically with both arms and legs, and swears at the wind, the sleet, the darkness; the man who curses the sea while others work. . . . The independent offspring of the ignoble freedom of the slums full of disdain and hate for the austere servitude of the sea.

Donkin subsumes in his one person all the basest instincts and inclinations of man. He too has a devil of destruction in him, a rancorous feral hate for all the illusions which sustain and dignify mankind.

> He had a desire to assert his importance, to break, to crush; to be even with everybody for everything; to tear the veil, unmask, expose, leave no refuge—a perfidious desire of truthfulness!

That last work comes as something of a surprise, but Conrad means it. This emerges more clearly when Donkin starts trying to sow dissent among the sailors when the voyage gets rough: he complains about everything—discipline, work, pay; he denies the point of all effort. "His picturesque and filthy loquacity flowed like a troubled stream from a poisoned source." But the men listen: his "filthy loquacity" appeals to and elicits a response from all of them. "We abominated the creature and could not deny the truth of his contentions. It was all so obvious." Donkin is in complete command of one kind of truth, the beetle's truth, the truth that asserts that a certificate of duty is a mere piece of ass's skin, that ideals of conduct are "no earthly use," that honour is a fraud. For Conrad this was the abominable truth of the ditch. But it was a truth.

If this is the only kind of truth then Jim is a deluded fool indeed; but for Conrad Jim is something more complex and interesting. In a letter to Edward Garnett written in 1908 Conrad complains of his critics: ". . . there is even one abandoned creature who says I am a neo-platonist. What on earth is that?" Conrad disliked all facile classification, but against that outburst of astonishment we can put an extract from a letter to Sir Sidney Colvin written in 1917.

> I have been called a writer of the sea, of the tropics, a descriptive writer, a romantic writer—and also a realist. But as a matter of fact all my concern has been with the "ideal" value of things, events and people. That and nothing else. The humorous, the pathetic, the passionate, the sentimental *aspects* came in of themselves—*mais en vérité c'est les valeurs idéales des faits et gestes humains qui se sont imposés à mon activité artistique.* Whatever dramatic and narrative gifts I may have are always, instinctively, used with that object—to get at, to bring forth *les valeurs idéales.* Of course this is a very general statement but roughly I believe it to be true.

It is also a letter and must not be taken as a pondered creed—but the reiteration of the notion of "ideal value" is surely significant. Of course Conrad was not a systematic Platonist of any kind, but undoubtedly he had felt an urge to locate and identify a value which lay under the surface of certain people, actions or things, a value inaccessible to the beetles with their relentlessly accurate eye for the surface facts, their diabolical gift for seeing things "as they are." Jim is made a crucial focus of this inquiry, this question of the other truth. Is he just a child, a fool, a coward, a fraud? Or does he embody some sort of ideal value, no matter how debased that ideal may be by an involvement with the mud of the world? This takes us back to Marlow's interview with Stein. Stein habitually talks in ellipses and paradoxes and his speech is full of cryptic lacunae. Thus he mutters: "To follow the dream, and again to follow the dream—and so—*ewig—usque ad finem.* . . . " and more specifically on Jim: "He is romantic—romantic," he repeated. 'And that is very bad—very bad. . . . Very good, too,' he added." Then he throws at Marlow the question of why Jim exists so strongly for him. Marlow searches his mind. "At that moment it was difficult to believe in Jim's existence . . . but his imperishable reality came to me with a convincing, with an irresistible force! I saw it vividly, as though . . . we had approached nearer to absolute Truth, which like Beauty itself, floats elusive, obscure, half submerged, in the silent waters of mystery."

We have been taught to shy at capitalised abstractions in the novel and perhaps rightly—the passage is easily faulted. But it does reveal Conrad's intention, or perhaps we should say Conrad's problem. Jim stands for our best illusions, those exercises of the imagination which we allow to guide our conduct in order to give it purpose, dignity, and, in Conrad's word, glamour. It is our illusions, our ideals, which give us "gorgeous markings" and aspiring wings. Is there anything that can be called truth in them, do these "pure exercises of imagination" contain any of "the deep hidden truthfulness of works of art?" Such seems to be Marlow's line of questioning. Of course to have employed the persona of Marlow is a gesture of detachment, of possibly ironic disengagement on Conrad's part—the narrator examines his character, the author scrutinizes both; but in this early work it is hard to feel that Marlow's tentative Platonic musings are not in fact Conrad's own. When Marlow offers such remarks as: "the truth disclosed in a moment of illusion" or "our illusions, which I suspect only to be visions of remote unattainable truth, seen dimly," we inevitably feel that the author is backing him up to the hilt. Jim reminds Marlow—and, we feel, Conrad—"of those illusions you had thought gone out, extinct, cold": not everybody lives by illusions of course—"it is respectable to have no illusions—and safe—and profitable," but it is also "dull." Illusions redeem life momentarily from its dullness or dirtiness: they are responsible for "that light of glamour created in the shock of trifles, as amazing as the glow of sparks struck from a cold stone—and as short-lived, alas!" Are the illusions true? Marlow is vague—memorably vague: "he [Jim] felt . . . the demand of some such truth or some such illusion—I don't care how you call it, there is so little difference, and the difference means so little." From an author that would be unacceptable—from a genial after-dinner racounteur we let it pass. And we let it pass because a better sentence follows. "The thing is that in virtue of his feelings he mattered." The horizons Jim dreamed of are unattainable, the heroic deeds he imagined to himself he cannot realize in action, life consecrated to an ideal of conduct cannot be lived, not only because of the ungovernable hostility of baser men but also because of the inexpugnable weaknesses in the ideal itself. But the feelings that lie at the root of all these aspirations and ideals—you cannot give the lie to those. Such would seem to be Marlow's point.

And it is because of the unflagging persistence of those feelings, their determination to operate at the highest attainable level, that both Marlow and Stein are inclined to speak of the "truth" of Jim's later life. When Jim's widow complains to Stein that Jim at the end was false, Stein answers with unusual emotion. "No! no! True! true! true!" and Marlow speaks, rather curiously, of "the sheer truthfulness of his last three years of life" as though, like the Great Gatsby, Jim had lived up to "his Platonic conception of himself." As Marlow says early in the book, he was aware of "an obscure truth" in Jim's attitude to life which seemed "momentous enough to affect mankind's conception of itself." Jim's conception of himself is vulnerable and romantic in the extreme and is responsible for culpable failures to act in the right way at the right time. But Conrad is obviously allowing him a poetic gloss, as though

there is something he cannot, dare not, bring himself to utterly condemn. For this reason Marlow's account of Jim tries, at the end, to convince us that "his spirit seemed to rise above the ruins of his existence." But it is a weak gesture, and the last line of the novel has a melancholy ring to it. "Stein has aged greatly of late. He feels it himself, and says often that he is 'preparing to leave all this; preparing to leave. . . . ' while he waves his hand sadly at his butterflies."

One can see **Lord Jim** as Conrad's regretful farewell to the butterflies. Like the actual butterfly which Stein shows Marlow in their first interview, Jim was the last of a dying species as far as Conrad was concerned. "Only one specimen like this they have in *your* London, and then—no more." For the terrible unavoidable truth about Jim is that "he is not good enough"—the worse truth to Conrad is that "nobody, nobody is good enough." Jim cannot triumph over the ugly *facts* (a key word in the novel) though he spends his time trying to: he cannot "lay the ghost" of the ugly fact that he himself embodies and must carry with him wherever he goes. And these ugly facts are beetle facts and together with the brute facts of an indifferent Nature they seem to have the malevolent desire "to annihilate all that is priceless and necessary." But these facts are true—which is why truth is always referred to as "painful" or "sinister" in the later Conrad. Jim, despite the Platonic halo and the author's efforts to shore him up poetically, is not finally true. Or not true enough for the relentlessly penetrating eye of Conrad. The realists have no ideals—thus their lives are ugly. But the idealist has no grip on reality: he cannot live properly at all. **Lord Jim** is a prelude to profound pessimism. Like Winnie Verloc in **The Secret Agent** Conrad came to feel "profoundly that things do not stand much looking into." Unlike Winnie he cannot help continuing to look. And what he comes to see is an abysmal absence of meaning and value in the world. If E. M. Forster is right in saying that "the secret casket of his genius contains a vapour rather than a jewel," that is because Conrad felt that at the center of existence there was only a vapour, and not the much desiderated jewel. There is an arresting passage in a letter to Cunninghame Graham which refers to the last sentence of that writer's preface to *Mogreb-al-Acksa*. The sentence enigmatically implies that there is a safe and meaningful destiny at the end of the road somewhere just to the right of a lone tree on the horizon. Conrad comments:

> Ah! the lone tree on the horizon and then bear a little (a very little) to the right. Haven't we all ridden with direction to find no house but many curs barking at the heels. Can't miss it? Well, perhaps we can't. And we don't ride with a stouter heart for that. Indeed, my friend, there is a joy in being lost, but a sorrow in being weary. . . . But what business have you, O Man! coming with your uncomprehended truth,—a thing less than mist but black, to make me sniff at—the stink of the lamp? Ride to the tree and to the right,—for verily there is a devil at the end of every road. Let us pray to the poor bellied gods, to gods with more legs than a centipede and more arms than a dozen windmills: let us pray to them to guard us from the mischance of arriving somewhere.

Arriving, that is, at the final truth which is "less than mist but black." It seems to me that Conrad reached that last stage of pessimism which very few other writers—Melville is one—have experienced. The stage at which the greatest fear is not that the meaning of life might be evil but that there might be absolutely no meaning at all to be found. It is easy to state it thus glibly: but to have that conviction gnawing at you for the better part of a life time must be a rare and unenviable experience. Which is perhaps why Conrad's letters are among the most anguished any writer has left to us. Such a man may well pray for the grace of non-arrival.

There is no time here for a full study of Conrad's pessimism but the conclusions which it seems to me that Conrad reached, however unwittingly and unwillingly, in **Lord Jim** throw an interesting light on two recurring themes of his work, namely, the experience of total darkness, and the more than nautical significance of "steering." It is commonly agreed that in many of his early works Conrad exhibits a rather facile predilection for melodramatic atmospherics: there is too much ineffable, ineluctable darkness, too much of the "tenebrous immensity" style of writing. But at certain key moments in his books the experience of utter darkness carries a profound moral and psychological significance. Jim really discovers the difficulty of living according to a preconceived ideal not when he makes the fatal jump—he does that in a mood of almost paralysed passivity—but when he is alone with the other base cowards in the complete darkness of the sea. The way he describes the experience is revealing. "After the ship's lights had gone, anything might have happened in that boat—anything in the world—and the world no wiser. . . . We were like men walled up in a roomy grave. No concern with anything on earth. Nobody to pass an opinion. Nothing mattered." And later: "But the lights. The lights did go! We did not see them. They were not there. If they had been, I would have swum back—I would have gone back and shouted alongside—I would have begged them to take me on board. . . . " He is referring to the lights of the abandoned ship, which would have told him that the ship was not sinking after all. But they mean more than that. They are clues to ethical conduct which the external world gives us, the signs which we have to interpret and then act upon, irresistible reminders from the world of men. Conrad is interested in those crucial moments when we are utterly "alone with ourselves," when to all intents and purposes nothing matters, when all the guidance must come from within, when all the lights have gone out. Jim claims that in such circumstances "there was not the thickness of a sheet of paper between the right and wrong of this affair" and "not the breadth of a hair between this and that." Marlow answers, rather mordantly, "It is difficult to see a hair at midnight." Impossible, we might concede. And it is exactly *then* that Conrad wants to know how a man behaves, how a man should behave, how he can find sanctions and supports to resist the insidious gravitational pull towards the base, beetle-like, irresistible argument that "nothing matters." The narrator of **The Shadow Line** goes through a similar experience. During the storm: "I was alone, every man was alone where he stood. And every form was gone, top, spar, sail, fittings, rails; everything was blotted out in the dreadful

smoothness of that absolute night" and then: "both binnacle lamps were out. . . . The last gleam of light in the universe had gone." In such circumstances "the eye lost itself in inconceivable depths," or as we might more crudely put it, the moral eye has nothing to focus on. *That* is the testing time. Darkness is an all too easy short-cut to portentous effects but at certain moments Conrad manages to invest it with a compelling elemental terror and he does so, I think, because it symbolised for him a passionately felt philosophical darkness. At times it [was] as palpable and convincing as "The Cloud of Unknowing" and for similar reasons. Conrad also had an intimate acquaintance with the experience of "the lacking of knowing." This subterranean doubt and scepticism comes very near the surface of some of his letters:

> I have often suffered in connection with my work from a sense of unreality, from intellectual doubt of the ground I stand on.
>
> Everyone must walk in the light of his own heart's gospel. No man's light is good to any of his fellows. That's my creed from beginning to end. That's my view of life—a view that rejects all formulas, dogmas and principles of other people's making. These are only a web of illusions.
>
> My task appears to me as sensible as lifting the world without that fulcrum which even that conceited ass, Archimedes, admitted to be necessary.

The fulcrum he lacks is the fulcrum of faith, the fulcrum of immovable and clarified convictions: "There is no morality, no knowledge and no hope: there is only the consciousness of ourselves which drives us about a world that, whether seen in a convex or concave mirror, is always but a vain and floating appearance." Given this view of the world, any idealism seems as pointless "as though one were anxious about the cut of one's clothes in a community of blind men." And yet Conrad was deeply concerned about a man's moral dress even when he was invisible to the rest of the world. The behavior of the crowd held no interest for Conrad. And to the question, how should one behave in the dark, he had one firm answer—you steer.

Thus extrapolated the idea is vague in the extreme, but let us return to **The Nigger of the "Narcissus"** for a concrete image of this one positive which Conrad fervently believed in. I refer to Captain Singleton's behaviour in the storm during which Donkin whines, complains, and incites the men to abandon a pointless and exacting duty.

> Apart, far aft, and alone by the helm, old Singleton had deliberately tucked his white beard under the top button of his glistening coat. Swaying upon the din and tumult of the seas, with the whole battered length of the ship launched forward in a rolling rush before his steady old eyes, he stood rigidly still, forgotten by all, and with an attentive face. In front of his erect figure only the two arms moved crosswise with a swift and sudden readiness, to check or urge again the rapid stir of circling spokes. He steered with care.

That last telling short sentence (short sentences are rare in Conrad and always used for special emphasis) underlines the simple unquestioning dedication with which Old Singleton does what, in the circumstances, most needs to be done. It makes it seem as though he were acting in unflinching compliance with a categorical imperative. The particularly Conradian aspect of this conception of duty is the fact that he can no longer produce the sanctions and proofs which would justify and enforce the standards of conduct which he nevertheless feels to be "imperative." Singleton steers but without being able to see the final destination. Some people would say that such persistence was futile. Conrad had been in such a situation.

> Sufficient moral tenacity is all I pray for, not to save me from taking to drink, because I couldn't even if I wanted to, but from the temptation to throw away the oar. And I have known good men do that too, saying: "It's no use." Then was my turn to keep the boat head to sea for fourteen solid hours.

Singleton steers (Donkin, we recall, cannot steer): but this is not the kind of steering which Shaw meant when he made Don Juan in hell say: "To be in hell is to drift: to be in heaven is to steer." For Shaw, a social meliorist, meant that men and society should allow themselves to be guided by their best intelligence, the brain, "the organ by which Nature strives to understand itself." Shaw could see, or thought he could, the destination and wanted us to use our heads and hurry up getting there. But for Conrad the mind could be a curse, an inhibitor or interrupter of proper conduct. Cunninghame Graham once wrote to Conrad suggesting he create a Singleton figure with an education added. Conrad's reply is much to our point.

> But first of all—what education? If it is the knowledge of how to live, my man essentially possessed it. He was in perfect accord with life. If by education you mean scientific knowledge then the question arises—what knowledge? How much of it—in what direction? Is it to stop at plane trigonometry or at conic sections? Or is he to study Platonism or Pyrrhonism, or the philosophy of the gentle Emerson? Or do you mean the kind of knowledge which would enable him to scheme, and lie, and intrigue his way to the forefront of a crowd no better than himself? Would you seriously of malice prepense, cultivate in that unconscious man the power to think? Then he would become conscious,—and much smaller,—and very unhappy. Now he is simple and great like an elemental force. Nothing can touch him but the curse of decay,—the eternal decree that will extinguish the sun, the stars, one by one, and in another instant shall spread a frozen darkness over the whole universe. Nothing else can touch him—he does not think.

There is a good deal of the essential Conrad in that paragraph. As he wrote elsewhere: "It is impossible to know anything, tho' it is possible to believe a thing or two." Haunted by the impossibility of knowledge, Conrad could not accept the beetle—Donkin's view of things—and he renounced the fallible, if beautiful, butterfly-Jim conception of life: but he believed in Singleton and the value and necessity of keeping the hands to the wheel, the dignity of standing erect and uncomplaining in the storms of a hostile nature and the darkness of encircling doubt. (pp. 123-40)

> Tony Tanner, "Butterflies and Beetles—Conrad's Two Truths," in Chicago Review, Vol. 16, No. 1, Winter-Spring, 1963, pp. 123-40.

G. S. Fraser (essay date 1966)

[*A Scottish critic, poet, journalist, and translator, Fraser wrote a number of critical works on twentieth-century poets, including Dylan Thomas, Ezra Pound, and Lawrence Durrell. In the following excerpt, he discusses Conrad's treatment of Jim's romanticism in* Lord Jim.]

Conrad's *Lord Jim* came out in 1900. It was his third novel; the first, *Almayer's Folly,* came out in 1895, the second, *An Outcast of the Islands,* in 1896. All three have the same setting, what we now call Malaysia and Indonesia. They are set in a period when these regions were not yet fully colonised, settled only in the coastal regions; the interior was being opened up, slowly, by rather shady merchants and trading agents. If one compares Conrad with his almost exact contemporary Kipling, whose early and some of whose best work is set in the East, one notices a very important difference. Kipling's theme could be called the Romance of Empire: he deals with tragedy, comedy, farce that arises from trying to govern a sub-continent, India, with what is in numbers, compared to the native population, an absurdly small minority of soldiers and civil servants. And Kipling deals also, in his grim little comedies about Simla wives, with what happens to a suburban sort of English society, limited, lower-middle-classish, when you transplant it to a sweaty climate, and suddenly give it the power of the Great Mogul. Kipling's world is a social world, the mess, the club, the gymkhana; his characters come a cropper when they don't fit in with the team.

In Conrad, on the contrary, there is no Romance of Empire. The club and the mess don't come in. Marlow, his great narrator, tells his story in a big hotel, "after dinner, on a verandah draped with motionless foliage and crowned with flowers, in the deep dusk speckled by fiery cigar-ends. The elongated bulk of each cane-chair harboured a silent listener". Conrad's heroes are sea-captains, trading-agents, local representatives of big trading firms. They are not set, like Kipling's, against the background of a great political organism, the Indian Empire. There never was a great Indonesian-Malaysian Empire; archipelagoes, scattered islands, do not lend themselves to that sort of organisation. Conrad's characters breathe a freer and more disturbing air. There is the harbour, there are the lights beyond the harbour. Not so far from the harbour, not so far from the lights, there is the interior, sparsely explored. Up the river, isolated among suspicious Malays, treacherous Rajahs, and cunning Arabs, there is the lonely white man, there not to plant the flag but, like the hero of Conrad's second novel or like Jim himself in the third, because for one reason or another he wants to get away from his fellows.

Again, in so far as it is a white world, the world of Conrad in these early novels is not, unlike Kipling's, a specifically English world; there are as many Dutchmen or Germans as Englishmen and there is not any strong sense of national rivalry. And these men are not "settled", in the sense that Kipling's heroes are. They are mobile though loosely yet intimately linked. Jim flees from his fate or from his shame, round about the Pacific, over a radius of about three thousand miles; yet he is never sure of not meeting somebody who knows his shameful secret.

So, whereas Kipling's heroes are united, one might say, by a sense of group solidarity, Conrad's are united by a sense of common isolation, loneliness calling to loneliness. What Conrad is extraordinarily good at doing—it comes out in **Lord Jim** in the conversation about the *Patna* incident between Marlow and the French naval officer—is revealing the possibility of immediate *rapport* between men, of different languages and cultures, who have shared a similar discipline, a similar suffering, who meet each other quite casually. There is this *rapport* but there is no organisation of bullying, ragging rehabilitation of the black sheep, or odd man out, as in Kipling. For Jim, there is nothing in outer society to prop him up or reclaim him, only Marlow's apparently arbitrary and inexplicable sympathy.

Conrad's world, therefore, though it is a violent and adventurous world, is to quite an extraordinary degree an interior world. All sorts of exciting things happen to Lord Jim but the real drama of his story, the real excitement, is for Conrad what happens inside him. It is something interior, some inner confidence and possibility of self-esteem, that he loses when he jumps off the *Patna;* it is this inner thing that all through the book he is trying to regain or it is the sense of having lost it irremediably that he is for much of the time—in spite of deceptive dreams of redemption for all of the time?—running away from. But, of course, the great paradox of Conrad's narrative art is that with this passionate, central, monotonous obsession with the interior world, the loss or the retention of the sense of honour, he is either quite incapable of doing, or doesn't wish to do, Jim or anybody else "from the inside". There are many monologues in his novels and stories, but they are never interior monologues, but monologues round a table; and they are never monologues by the hero, they are monologues by the extremely intelligent but partly baffled observer. (Decoud's letter to his sister in **Nostromo** might seem to shatter this generalisation, but even Decoud is incapable of talking *to* himself, *about* himself.) Certainly, at least, the generalisation applies to **Lord Jim.**

Thus, though Jim's drama is an interior one, we are never, at any moment in **Lord Jim,** "inside" him; we see him almost all through, except for twenty or so pages of straight summary narrative and preliminary exposition at the beginning, through the eyes of his sceptical protector, Marlow. And, if one is being precise, the drama for the reader is not so much the drama of Jim's inner life as the drama of Marlow's probing, intense, courteous but finally baffled grappling with it, his subtle guesses about its nature, which sometimes seem excessively complicated, over-elaborate.

Marlow, also, all through, is only on the surface telling a very exciting adventure story. More deeply, he is puzzling about what modern philosophers would call a paradigm case. He is very subtly evaluating, evaluating Jim's character and the code of honour that rejects Jim, that drives Jim to desperate lengths, perhaps to immoral, absurd, or insane lengths in the perhaps, by definition, impossible quest of regaining his honour. (The theme, of course, was not a highbrow or an abstruse or unpopular one: as witness the success of a roughly contemporary "good-bad" book, A. E. W. Mason's *The Four Feathers.*) The word "honour" is one of the very important words in **Lord Jim:** so, of course, even more so, is the word "romance". In a key passage, Marlow and his friend Stein (the Mycroft Holmes to Marlow's Sherlock Holmes) hit on the word "romantic" as the key to Jim's character. And both words, though they become overlaid with despairing ironies, are used primarily with a positive admiring force.

Conrad himself was, in a quite ordinary sense of these words, like many of the Polish gentry from whom he sprang, at once a man of honour and a man of romantic sensibilities. He gained his earliest useful experience of seamanship running guns aboard the *Tremolino* for the romantically hopeless cause of Don Carlos in Spain; he ran her ashore, finally, and set fire to her rather than have her fall into the hands of a Spanish gunboat. He fought a duel, too (if that story is true, and not a cover-up for an unromantic attempt at suicide) for the love of a beautiful lady: he made out of these in themselves almost excessively romantic circumstances one of his weakest late novels, **The Arrow of Gold.** And there is, for that matter, a real sense in which one might be tempted to describe **Lord Jim** itself as a romance rather than a novel: in the sense in which *Treasure Island* or *Catriona* is a romance rather than a novel. It has even got pirates in it; and in the preface by Commodore Ivan Thompson to the little Collins Classics edition, one finds this very distinguished seaman regarding it, on the whole, as a rousing and edifying tale of adventure—a decent boy makes one slip, but makes good, and in the end makes the supreme sacrifice—full of knowledgeable seamanship and beautiful descriptions of the sea.

And one is not mocking at Commodore Sir Ivan Thompson. It is, in fact, part of the interest and range of Conrad that he appeals not only to the sort of reader who enjoys, say, George Eliot or Henry James but to the sort of reader who enjoys Robert Louis Stevenson, Rider Haggard, or Conan Doyle. I read lots of Conrad's stories when I was a boy, thoroughly engrossed, and only a little put off, I think, by what seemed to me then Marlow's extraordinarily round-about, backwards-forwards way of telling things. I think, indeed, I first read **Lord Jim** when, at the age of twelve or so, I took it out of the Sunday School library of Craigiebuckler Church in Aberdeen; it held me then, though I think I did skip a bit, and lost the thread sometimes. Very much later, having to lecture on the book to a class at Leicester University, it was extraordinarily interesting to come back to **Lord Jim,** after a gap of close on forty years, and grasp, for the first time, what the thread was.

But one cannot have the thread without, as it were, the labyrinth, or the meaning without the story. Let me summarise the story, as a boy might summarise. Summarised, it feels as if it might make a very good film: yet the film that recently was made had, because of the very nature of the medium, to leave the thread, the meaning, out. Jim, the hero or the central character to be observed in the novel, is the son of a poor country parsonage, who has read many romantic novels about the sea, and who is therefore sent to a training ship. He is an attractive, handsome, alert boy, on the surface neither clever nor excessively complicated, but nourishing his inner life with dreams of gallant acts performed during crises at sea. On the training ship, a man goes overboard, and Jim is just not quick enough to dive into the sea and help to rescue him; he is sure he will be quick enough in future. But on his first voyage out to the East he is disabled by a falling spar and laid up, for a time, in port. He falls in with a set of similar landed seamen who have all gone, in a subtly corrupt way, soft. There is a fine paragraph here which the boy reader, following the story more than the meaning, would not linger on:

> They shuddered at the thought of hard work, and led precariously easy lives, always on the verge of dismissal, always on the verge of engagement, serving Chinamen, Arabs, half-castes—would have served the devil himself had he made it easy enough. They talked everlastingly of turns of luck; how So-and-So got charge of a boat on the coast of China—a soft thing; how this one had an easy billet in Japan somewhere, and that one was doing well in the Siamese navy; and in all they said—in their actions, in their looks, in their persons—could be detected the soft spot, the place of decay, the determination to lounge safely through existence.

And then, after that, there is a short paragraph which is very important, I think, in relation to the final view which Conrad wants us to take of Jim; for Conrad is still speaking not as Marlow who guesses at everything, but as the old-fashioned novelist with his omniscient God's-eye view:

> To Jim, that gossiping crowd, viewed as seamen, seemed at first more insubstantial than so many shadows. But at length he found a fascination in the sight of these men, in their appearance of doing so well on such a slight allowance of danger and toil. In time, beside the original disdain there grew up slowly another sentiment; and suddenly, giving up the idea of going home, he took a berth as chief mate of the *Patna*.

The phrase I would call attention to there is this: "Beside the original disdain *there grew up slowly another sentiment*". Conrad's prose has often a fine un-English floridity, a poetic rhetoric with all the stops pulled out; but he can also, as here, be nobly and considerately reticent, when he has to put his finger on a moral flaw or weakness. The tone here is not quite disgust; it is too severe for regret merely: "There grew up slowly another sentiment . . ." Here, as in the training ship incident, Conrad has planted in us the suspicion that in the charming, decent lad, who might on the surface be a Captain Marryat hero, there is a streak not only of boyish fantasy, of the self-deception

that goes with fantasy, but of softness, of something, if not corrupt, at least corruptible.

Aboard the *Patna,* Jim is given a second chance to realise his romantic dream. It is a pilgrim ship, going to Jeddah. There are only five white men in the crew, the captain a New South Wales renegade German, a fat, gross brute who loves to denounce the tyrannies of Bismarck; the chief engineer, a drunkard; the second engineer, a silly weakling; a donkeyman with a weak heart; and Jim. Loaded with pilgrims, it is a rotten old ship, held together by rust. After a calm voyage, the *Patna* runs into what may be a bit of floating wreckage. A bulkhead is damaged: the probability is that it will stove in, and the *Patna* go down in half an hour or so. The pilgrims are calmly asleep below deck. The whole ship is too rotten and rusted to make any temporary repairs feasible. If the pilgrims are wakened, they will panic, and in any case there are only seven life-boats for eight hundred passengers. The captain, the chief engineer, the second engineer have only one thought: get a boat out, get into it, leave the *Patna* to sink. Jim at first wants to be a hero but his heart is not wholly in it. He refuses to help to lower a boat, but he does not wake and warn the passengers. He keeps thinking—possibly his imagination is Jim's central flaw—of what it would be like to drown, you would choke first. The boat is lowered, the captain and the two engineers keep shouting to the donkeyman, George, to jump; but George has died of heart-strain and Jim is unnerved by tripping into him and sending him sliding. Then, not quite knowing that he is going to do it, not quite knowing why, Jim jumps. The ship seems to have sunk. It has been stopped in the sea, and it slews round so that its lights are invisible. The crew of the lifeboat are picked up, and the German captain makes up a story about making every effort to lower boats and rescue pilgrims, but the ship went down too fast. In fact, the *Patna* remained afloat. In the morning, it is boarded and towed into Aden by a French ship. All its officers have to face a court of inquiry but Jim alone faces the music. His hurt pride, his hurt romantic idea of himself, find a certain assuagement in facing the music.

It is here that Marlow comes in; and it is here, also, that Conrad's richness begins. Jim has to be disgraced, has to lose his certificate. Yet a member of the Court of Inquiry, a proud, unsympathetic sea captain, Brierly, offers Marlow, who has come along as usual as the detached observer, two hundred rupees to give to Jim, to let him skip before the verdict. Brierly says, in a key passage:

> "We are trusted! Do you understand?—trusted? I don't care a snap for all the pilgrims that ever came out of Asia, but a decent man would not have behaved like this to a full cargo of old rags in bales. We aren't an organised body of men, and the only thing that holds us together is just the name for that sort of decency. Such an affair destroys one's confidence. A man may go pretty near through his whole sea-life without any call to show a stiff upper lip. But when the call comes . . . Aha! . . . If I . . . "

And a fortnight later Brierly jumps over the side of his own ship, having given his First Mate unusually elaborate instructions about bearings, course, and so on. Why?

Again we have the fine reticence which so often, as it were, counterpoints Conrad's floridity. Marlow tells us:

> I am in a position to know that it wasn't money, and it wasn't drink, and it wasn't woman. He jumped overboard a week after the end of the inquiry . . .

Why? Captain Brierly, a crack skipper, and a very self-conceited one, had not yet perhaps had his "call to show a stiff upper lip" and yet his whole life and bearing had been tensed, perhaps, with waiting for the call. Anybody who has too rigid an idea of what he is, as well as of what he ought to be, will have vulnerable joints in his armour. The little incident of Captain Brierly underlines a main message of **Lord Jim:** the danger, as well as the necessity, of playing one's role consciously—the awful danger of moving into playing it *self*-consciously, and becoming appalled and paralysed. Marlow makes this clear in his conversation with Brierly's First Mate, poor muddled Jones:

> "You may depend upon it, Captain Jones", said I, "it wasn't anything that would have disturbed much either of us two", I said; and then, as if a light had been flashed into the muddle of his brain, poor old Jones found a last word of amazing profundity. He blew his nose, nodding at me dolefully: "Ay, ay! neither you nor I, sir, had ever thought so much of ourselves".

Here we are near the core of what the novel is about. Jim is not at all like Brierly, except that he is one of those who "think so much of themselves": he can be generous, kind, in the end he manages to be as heroically brave as his ideal image of himself; but it is, egoistically, for that ideal image, and the hope of its reflection in the consciousness of others, that both men brittlely live. Neither man could tell his own story (the man who is always acting a part knows his cues but not the plot of the play). Marlow, for Conrad, is, on the other hand, the ideal story-teller because his overmastering concern is not with his own ideas, or ideal, of himself but with an intuitive groping grasp of the vital situation of others. The guiding interest of Marlow's life is a mingled curiosity and concern, often expressed in practical helpfulness, for those who rouse his attention, combined with a more detached interest, the artist's interest, in "the story in it".

Marlow is in a sense a fatalist; he often talks about fate and about destiny, and that kind of talk, like his talk about romance, can be worrying to readers today. Roughly, his attitude to Jim is this: "This boy, because of certain kinds of illusion, certain kinds of self-deception, of self-absorption, will always run into trouble. I cannot alter his life-pattern, the character that *is* destiny, but when he has come such a cropper already, can I steer him past even worse kinds of reef?" Marlow, in fact, though he lets his irony and his sense of reality play very critically around the romantic idea, is himself, like Conrad himself, a romantic who has been educated by experience but not cured by experience of the primary romantic urge. Jim, flawed and hurt though he is, stands for Marlow for youth, for possibility, for what has been spoiled but can be shaped anew, perhaps wholly redeemed. He is doubtful about whether honour, the first inner spring, can ever be wholly won back. But at least Marlow can stop this handsome wounded boy from becoming a beachcomber, a sponger, a drunkard: can get him work, food, clothes, shelter; and in the end Marlow gets Jim the opportunity both to "get away from it all" and to become, in a world deliberately less real, more dream-like than that of the first half of the novel, genuinely a sort of hero. Yet Marlow is also an ironist; and what he is asking himself, and us, to the end, is whether, even as a sort of hero, Jim ever really *does* escape from what he has done.

There is this passage towards the middle of the novel about what Jim is trying to do:

> There was always a doubt of his courage. The truth seems to be that it is impossible to lay the ghost of a fact. You can face it or shirk it—and I have come across a man or two who could wink at their familiar shades. Obviously Jim was not of the winking sort; but what I could never make up my mind about was whether his line of conduct amounted to shirking his ghost or to facing him out.

Marlow gets Jim job after job, and somebody always turns up who knows the old story. But it may not be "knowing" at all: it may be that someone has merely a way of putting things that, quite unconsciously, for Jim brings it all back. This is rubbed in, a theme with variations. The rogue Chester offers Jim, through Marlow, an appalling job looking after coolies on a rocky island loaded with the rich dung of sea-birds. Chester says:

> "Anyway, I could guarantee the island wouldn't sink under him—and I believe he is a bit particular on that point."

Twenty pages later, Jim, flying from his memories, from his reputation, is a "water-clerk" with a prosperous ship chandler's firm. A visiting sea-captain, without knowing who Jim is, brings up the *Patna* business:

> "Matter, matter!" the old man began to shout: "What are you Injuns laughing at? It's no laughing matter? It's a disgrace to human natur'— that's what it is. I would despise being seen in the same room with one of these men. Yes, sir!"

Bitterly ashamed, Jim decides to leave his good berth. The ship's chandler tells the story to Marlow:

> "Who has been getting at you? What's scared you? Where do you expect to get a better berth?—you this and that." I made him look sick, I can tell you. *"This business ain't going to sink,"* I said. He gave a big jump.

Then there is the final, splendidly ironical springing of the same old trap. Jim's up-river Celebes paradise has been invaded by a horrible Australian pirate, Gentleman Brown. There are two sane ways of dealing with Brown: either to starve him and his men out of their stockade: or, at a certain cost of life, to take the stockade by storm and kill them all.

Jim is away from his village when Brown arrives. He comes back and has a parley with the ruffian. Brown hypocritically asks for leave to depart in peace:

Conrad in 1883.

"And I would let you shoot me and welcome . . . I am sick of my infernal luck. But it
would be too easy. There are my men in the same
boat—and by God I am not the sort to jump out
of trouble and leave them in the damned lurch."

It is that metaphor, that nagging reminder, which persuades Jim to persuade the village chief to let the pirates
go in peace, back to their boat. Jim's vile father-in-law
leads them by a circuitous route to where the son of the
village chief, and other warriors, are guarding the route
of retreat, and there is a massacre. Jim has failed his native
friends. His dearest friend, the chief's son, is dead. And,
unwilling to escape, resisting the protests of his wife, Jim
presents himself before the agonised chief, Doramin, who
shoots him. Marlow's last general comment is this:

> But we can see him, an obscure conqueror of
> fame, tearing himself out of the arms of a jealous
> love at the sign, at the call of his exalted egoism.
> He goes away from a living woman to celebrate
> his pitiless wedding with a shadowy ideal of con-
> duct. Is he satisfied—quite now, I wonder?

It is often said that this second half of the book is a let-
down after the first half, that we move away from a realistic handling of characters, actions, and motives to a sim-

plified world of romance, in which Jim is able to act out
his fantasies of heroism and the esteem of his fellows, as
in a dream. The contrast is there, but it is intended, and
I think that extraordinarily poignant and concentrated
piece of prose I have quoted, ironically romantic, or romantically ironical, so baffingly and beautifully balanced
between celebration and condemnation, underlines a feeling of fulfilment merely in fantasy, a feeling of the dreamlike and precarious, which is meant to grip us throughout
the second part of the novel. Jim wanted high romance,
he is given what he wanted, and in the end the potion is
lethal.

The romantic attitude, its attractiveness and its destructiveness, is, of course, quite explicitly the topic of the most
often quoted part of the novel, the bridge between the "realistic" beginning and the "romantic" end, the conversation about Jim between Marlow and Stein: Stein, a great
collector of butterflies and, like Marlow, of curious cases
of conscience, Mycroft Holmes, as I have said, to Marlow's Sherlock. "I came here to describe a specimen,"
Marlow says. Stein's diagnosis is rapid: "I understand
very well. He is romantic". And Marlow asks Stein:
"What's good for it?" The only final remedy, Stein says,
is death: "There is only one remedy! One thing alone can
us from being ourselves cure". And Marlow sees that:
" 'Yes,' said I, 'strictly speaking, the question is not how
to get cured, but how to live'." Stein agrees: "How to be!
Ach! How to be!"

Jim's problem and the problem of every romantic who
cannot live up to his romantic dream of himself is stated
by Stein sharply:

> "He wants to be a saint, and he wants to be a
> devil—and every time he shuts his eyes he sees
> himself as a very fine fellow—as fine as he can
> never be . . . In a dream . . . "

Jim's strength and weakness both come from the wish to
live in, to live as, the dream of himself, to dodge the insulting reality. What is the answer? Stein, in his broken English, gives it in a passage which is deservedly famous, and
which has been taken as describing the task not only of the
romantic spirit but of the creative imagination in our
wounding and destructive time:

> "Yes! Very funny this terrible thing is. A man
> that is born falls into a dream like a man who
> falls into the sea. If he tries to climb out into the
> air as inexperienced people endeavour to do, he
> drowns—*nicht wahr?* . . . No! I tell you! The
> way is to the destructive element submit your-
> self, and with the exertion of your hands and feet
> in the water make the deep, deep sea keep you
> up. So if you ask me—how to be? . . . And yet
> it is true—it is true. In the destructive element
> immerse . . . That was the way. To follow the
> dream, and again to follow the dream—and so—
> *ewig—usque ad finem!* "

There is a beautiful paragraph on the next page that sums
up the whole book, the glorification of, and yet the doubts
about, the romantic attitude to life, Marlow's own doubts,
beaten down again and again, about Jim also: about
whether Jim, with his soft streak, his self-centredness, ade-

quately embodies the romantic attitude, is really "one of us":

> "He is romantic—romantic," (Stein) repeated. "And that is very bad—very bad . . . Very good, too", he added. "But *is* he?" I queried.

This is our doubt too, the doubt which Marlow's tone sustains throughout the story and even at the end refuses to resolve. A page or two earlier, Marlow has realised that Jim's conduct since the calamity, the jumping overboard from the *Patna,* could be described equally plausibly as that of a moral coward or that of an exceptionally brave man:

> I strained my mental eyesight only to discover that, as with the complexion of all our actions, the shade of difference was so delicate that it was impossible to say. It might have been flight and it might have been a mode of combat.

For Stein (but Stein, as Marlow sees, is very much of a romantic himself) there can be no such fine shades of doubt. He answers Marlow's question about whether Jim is really a romantic, really "one of us", by saying that of course he is (but it is Marlow, not Stein, of course, who really knows Jim):

> "What is it that by inward pain makes him know himself ? What is it that for you and me makes him—exist?"

The implied answer is that the inward pain Marlow and Stein have always felt reaches out, in sympathy, to the inward pain in Jim: and, though Conrad, except for, if his reading was like Axel Heyst's, having read Schopenhauer a little, was not a philosopher or a student of philosophy, we can think of the romantic, or existential, tradition of philosophy, of the *angst* which for Kierkegaard, the *sorge* or care which for Heidegger, the *nausée* or unmotivated disgust which for Sartre is at the very heart of human existence. But it is Conrad's greatness that, drawn so much towards the romantic glamour of a kind of high pessimism, the romanticism of fate and destiny, a romanticism which can be one of subjective self-delusion, unsocial, inhuman, and unjust, he does not surrender. He has also the humane and aristocratic, the classical sense of measure. That comes out, on the very last page, with a saving and realistic irony:

> And that's the end. He passes away under a cloud, inscrutable at heart, forgotten, unforgiven, and excessively romantic! Not in the wildest days of his boyish visions could he have seen the alluring shape of such an extraordinary success! . . .

The irony, of course, is beautifully courteous; a courtesy possibly only to somebody like Marlow (or like Conrad) who was himself "excessively romantic" and who knew, like Stein, that there is no final cure for this condition but death. *Lord Jim* is often dismissed as an early and immature work of Conrad's. In some later works of his which are much admired by critics, *The Secret Agent* and *Victory,* I find either a too frank use of melodramatic devices or a kind of superior relish in human baseness, which do not please me. In Conrad at his best I find a quality of the spirit, a mixture of severity and compassion, of ardour and justice, which seems to me finer than the human spirit exhaled from most novels: a kind of spirit which one associates less with the novelist as such than with the great poet. . . . Perhaps I am "excessively romantic", and incurably so, myself, but I see this fine human spirit very fully and beautifully expressed in *Lord Jim:* for me, not an immature work, but a masterpiece. (pp. 231-41)

> *G. S. Fraser, "Lord Jim: The Romance of Irony," in* Critical Quarterly, *Vol. 8, No. 3, Autumn, 1966, pp. 231-41.*

Ira Sadoff   (essay date 1969)

[*An American poet, novelist, educator, and critic, Sadoff is best known for his poems that characteristically present short, declarative sentences in a manner that has been termed surrealistic, addressing themes of family life, personal experience, and history. In the following essay, he elaborates on the treatment of human responsibility and freedom in* Lord Jim, *stressing elements of the work that presaged Existentialist philosophy.*]

Although a few critics have recognized a relationship between the works of Conrad and the existential philosophers, those comparisons that have been made have dealt with vague, humanistic banalities about "man's condition" rather than with specific works and quotations. As a result, even the most notable of these critics, Adam Gillon, has left us with indefensible abstractions asserting that in Sartre's vision "men have nearly lost their humanity", while Conrad's vision is full of "compassion", and "Sartre's view of man's birth as a wrong that can be righted eliminates happiness", although Conrad's view offers the possibility for the "happiness of self-sacrifice" ["Conrad and Sartre," *Dalhousie Review,* Spring 1960]. If, however, we are going to identify Conrad as an existentialist (or to differentiate him from one) we must avoid such generalities; by contrasting *Lord Jim* with existential works, this paper will deal with the development of Jim from a "lost youngster" to an existential hero, as he confronts the dilemmas of modern man (aloneness, despair, meaninglessness, and guilt), and thereby "masters his fate."

Marlow tells us that Jim is a "lost youngster, one in a million—but then he was one of us; . . . and yet the mystery of his attitude got a hold of me as though he had been an individual in the forefront of his kind, as if the obscure truth involved were momentous enough to affect mankind's conception of itself. . . . " Nietzsche, in *Thus Spake Zarathustra,* said "God is dead. . . . We have killed him, . . . but I come too early, my time has not come yet." In the same way, Jim has come too soon, but he is still a "modern man", "one of us", who is no longer under the higher laws of God or the rigid structure of society.

Conrad continually emphasizes the loss of the ultimate authority, even in his narrative technique. Marlow is not an omniscient narrator; none of the characters in the novel is omniscient. They all present their subjective viewpoints, because they can not enter into Jim's consciousness; they can not give an objective sense of truth. There is, in fact, no truth; there are only multiple points of view because truth, in **Lord Jim,** has become internalized.

If there is no objective truth, no preconception of mankind, Jim must determine his own fate. There is a great gulf between his visions of himself and what he is, in reality. Jim's attempt to change those dreams into reality, his desire to combine the real with the ideal, becomes the thematic conflict of the book. For, as Sartre says [in "Existentialism Is a Humanism"], "there is no reality, except in action . . . man is the sum of his deeds. Existentialism puts everyone in a position to understand that reality alone is reliable; that dreams, expectations and hopes serve to define man only as deceptive dreams, abortive hopes and expectations unfulfilled."

Conrad set up a network of abstract visions for Jim, all of which lead only to his downfall. In the first chapter, when Jim is standing his watch, he thinks of himself as a hero. "He saw himself saving people from sinking ships, cutting away masts in a hurricane, swimming through a surf with a line; . . .—always an example of devotion to duty, and as unflinching as a hero in a book", ". . . he felt sure—he alone would know how to deal with the spurious menace of wind and seas." Conrad uses the subjunctive "would" and refers to Jim as a "hero in a book", not a real man.

What prevents Jim from acting like a hero is his own consciousness, his awareness of the absurdity and chaos of the modern universe. "That man there seemed to be aware of his hopeless difficulty." That sense of hopelessness caused Jim to have "spent many days stretched out on his back, dazed, battered, hopeless, and tormented as if at the bottom of an abyss of unrest." In addition, Jim sees "nothing but the disorder of his tossed cabin." This immobilization is the "fatal shock" that Carl Jung talks about; it is the loss of the sense of order in the universe. This condition is what Sartre calles "abandonment" when he quotes Dostoevski's Kirilov, in *The Brothers Karamazov:* "If God does not exist, everything is indeed permitted." "And man is, in consequence, forlorn, for he can not find anything to depend on, either within or outside himself. He discovers forthwith, he is without excuse." Sartre goes on, "Man is condemned to be free, condemned because he did not create himself, yet is nevertheless at liberty; from the moment he is thrown into the world, he is responsible for what he does." Jim experiences this abandonment after he jumps ship. "When your ship fails you, your whole world seems to fail you; the world that has made you, restrained you, taken care of you. It is as if the souls of men floating on an abyss and in touch with immensity had been set free for any excess of heroism, absurdity or abomination."

Sartre warns us that this abandonment must not lead to quietism, but Jim is at first left helpless by the disorder. "He told me that his first impulse was to shout and straight away make all those people leap out of sleep into terror; but such an overwhelming sense of his helplessness came over him that he was not able to produce a sound." Jim attempts to deny responsibility for himself when he explains, "I had jumped . . . so it seems", but he must reject this attempt, for as Marlow tells him, "If you keep up

this game, you'll very soon find that the earth ain't big enough to hold you—that's all."

If Marlow condemns Jim for running, he understands what Jim is running from and that he, himself, is unwilling to face the same confrontation. Talking about Jim's predicament, he says "This is one of those rare cases which no solemn deception can palliate, which no man can help; where his very Maker seems to abandon a sinner to his own devices." Later in the novel, Marlow talks to Jewel about the inevitability of Jim's leaving her, about the transiency of Jim's power on the island. He says

> It had the power to drive me out of my conception of existence, out of the shelter each of us makes for himself to creep under in moments of danger, as a tortoise withdraws in its shell. For a moment I had a view of the world that seemed to wear a vast and dismal aspect of disorder, while in truth, thanks to our unwearied efforts, it is as sunny an arrangement of small conveniences as the mind of man can conceive.

Marlow's ability to deceive himself relates to Conrad's idea that man constantly deceives himself by remaining unconscious. Sartre calls this self-deception *mauvaise foi,* or bad faith, but both Sartre and Conrad maintain that man can not live his entire life asleep, without consciousness. "Nevertheless", Marlow maintains, "there are few of us who have never known one of these rare moments of awakening when we see, hear, understand so much—everything—in a flash—before we fall back again into our agreeable somnolence."

Jim is not like Marlow or everyone else, because he cannot remain in "somnolence". He is intensely aware of his condition, and so he is responsible for himself and must remain alone. Fifty years before Conrad wrote **Lord Jim,** Søren Kierkegaard explained the concept of aloneness, of man's individual responsibility for himself:

> . . . a crowd in its very concept is the untruth, by reason of the fact that it renders the individual completely impenitant and irresponsible, or at least weakens his sense of responsibility by reducing it to a fraction . . . for a crowd is an abstraction and has no hands; but each individual ordinarily has two hands. . . . For every individual who flees in cowardice from being an individual, such a man contributes his share of cowardliness to the cowardliness which we know as the crowd.

Marlow recognizes Jim's sense of individual responsibility and sees it as an admirable part of his character, although he knows that it also leads to Jim's despair. "Woe to the stragglers! We exist only in so far as we hang together. He [Jim] had straggled in a way; he had not hung on; but he was aware of it with an intensity that made him touching, just as a man's more intense life is more touching than the death of a tree."

The responsibility for Jim is a great one, for, as Sartre says "it puts every man in possession of himself as he is, and places the responsibility for his existence squarely on his shoulders." Marlow's words are not so different when he says "He made himself responsible for success on his own head." We know that Jim will take the responsibility willingly, though, for he says he "knew the truth, and I would live it down—alone, with myself."

The willingness to face himself brings Jim to search for meaning in his own life, a meaning which is personal and internalized. Searching, however, requires the recognition of a temporary vacuum, or as Marlow describes Jim when he arrives in Patusan, he looks "like a lonely figure by the shore of a sombre and hopeless ocean . . . a speck in the dark void. . . ." We also know that Jim has to find his meaning for himself, a meaning within himself. "Once he got in [Patusan], it would be for the outside world as though he never existed. He would have nothing but the soles of his own feet to stand on, and he would have to find his ground at that."

Not only does Jim see the necessity of the search for meaning, but so does Marlow when he finally says

> Each blade of grass has its spot on earth whence it draws its life, its strength; and so is man rooted to the land from which he draws his faith together with his life. I don't know how much Jim understood, but I know he felt, he felt confusedly but powerfully, the demand of some such truth or illusion—I don't care how you call it, there is so little difference, and the difference means little.

Here Marlow shows the necessity for man (in general and Jim in particular) to search for meaning, but the quotation also points up the difference between understanding and feeling, his belief that meaning has nothing to do with intellect; it has to do with emotion.

How does Jim go about finding this meaning? Sartre says "Man is the sum of his deeds", and so it must be Jim's deeds which convert his dream into a reality, which give a meaning to his life. This relates to Conrad's view that it is not Jim's intellect which leads Jim to the acceptance of himself, rather it is his commitment to a life of action. Marlow tells us that Jim has the courage one needs to act: "I mean just that inborn ability to look temptation straight in the face—a readiness unintellectual enough, goodness knows without pose—a power of resistance . . . an unthinking and blessed stiffness before the outward and inward terrors . . . Hang ideas." Toward the end of the book, Marlow remembers Stein's words, "In the destructive element, immerse. . . . To follow the dream, and again to follow the dream—and so—always . . . ." And so it is with Jim. Jim makes his abstract dreams into reality by acting, by following his dream. "How does one kill fear, I wonder?", Marlow remarks to Jewel. "It is an enterprise you rush into while you dream. . . ."

So Jim takes on the dangerous responsibility of leading the people of Patusan. "If I am to do any good here", he tells Marlow, "and preserve my position . . . I must stand the risk." And stand the risk he does. "As he had got the Bugis irretrievably committed to action, and he made himself responsible for success on his own head. . . ." And on Patusan, Jim does not miss his chance. When the crucial battle comes, "he was bound to get on top of that hill and stay there, whatever might happen."

Related to Jim's commitment to action, we see his ability to confront death. Jim's fear of death, in the beginning of the book, is a cause for his immobilization. He sees death as determined by some outside force "which means to sweep the whole precious world utterly away from his sight by the simple and appalling act of taking his life." When he accepts death, though, "everything redounds to his glory; and it is the irony of his good fortune that he, who had been too careful of it once, seemed to bear a charmed life." It is his decision to defy death, which leads him from being "satisfied nearly" to finding fulfillment in life. He gives Brown an opportunity to leave the island, but Brown comes back and the order of the island is consequently destroyed. Jim then knows that he must face death courageously, so "in that very moment he had decided to defy the disaster in the only way it occurred to him such a disaster could be defied." He tells Jewel, " . . . There was nothing to fight for. He was going to prove his power and conquer the fatal destiny itself." And so Jim dies, but he has finally made up for his chance missed.

If Jim dies, why should we not look at his death as a nihilistic outlook on life? In the author's preface, Conrad calls **Lord Jim** a tale of "lost honor." It is exactly that. When Jim regains his honour, his life becomes meaningful. Marlow says "We want a belief in its (life's) necessity and justice, to make a conscious sacrifice of our lives. Without it, the sacrifice is only forgetfulness, the only way of offering is no better than perdition." How do we know that Jim's sacrifice is necessary and gives his life meaning? The French sailor gives a clue when he says "I contend that one may get on knowing that one's courage does not come of itself. . . . One truth the more ought not make life impossible . . . but the honor, monsieur! The honor—that is real—that is. And what life may be worth when the honor is gone, I can offer no opinion . . . I know nothing of it." "And what is the pursuit of truth, after all?" asks Marlow. "And yet, is not mankind itself, pushing on its blind way, driven by a dream of its greatness and its power upon the dark paths of excessive cruelty and excessive devotion?" Here we see why Jim (and modern man) must live on in a seemingly meaningless universe. The pursuit of truth, or the meaning of life, is no greater or smaller than man's dream and the devotion to that dream. As Camus says, "The struggle itself toward the heights is enough to fill man's heart." Man's greatness, then, lies within himself, for he must defy that meaninglessness with the honour within himself, for "There is no fate which can not be surmounted by scorn."

Camus' greatest novel, *The Stranger,* written forty-two years after **Lord Jim,** is the epitome of the existential novel. Yet Meursault, the hero of the book, is not so different from Jim. A comparison between the two books merits a paper in itself, but a few comparisons will serve our purposes well. Meursault is the stranger, the outsider, someone completely alone. He commits an act instinctually, killing an Arab, just as Jim jumps ship without consciousness. Neither Jim nor Meursault (as in the following description of his shooting the Arab) feels responsible for the acts in his own mind.

> I was conscious only of the cymbals of the sun clashing on my skull, and, less distinctly of the

keen blade of light flashing up from the knife, scarring my eyelashes, and gouging into my eyeballs. Then everything began to reel before my eyes, a fiery gust came from the sea, while the sky cracked in two, from end to end, and a great sheet of flame poured through the rift. Every nerve in my body was a steel spring, and my grip closed on the revolver. The trigger gave, and the smooth underbelly of the butt jogged my palm. . . . And each successive shot was another loud, fateful rap on the door of my undoing.

Here, Camus makes several references to the passive act of shooting the Arab, reminiscent of Jim's "I had jumped . . . so it seems." He talks about the trigger *giving,* the butt of the revolver *jogging his palm,* the *fateful* rap, and his own *undoing.*

Meursault is a character who moves from a state of unconsciousness to a conscious awareness of meaning in his own life. He exists outside the social order, has no ambition because he doesn't care if he is promoted or not, cares nothing for marriage, ignores traditional mourning practice for his mother. He, like Jim, exists unto himself, without the social structure; he is totally internalized. He is a "straggler" in the same way that Jim is a straggler, in his aloneness and subjective value system.

What brings meaning to Meursault's life is again the defiance of death. In fact, his death is a matter of honour, the "lost honour" he wins back through defiance. When he is about to be executed, he says, "I laid my heart open to the benign indifference of the universe. To feel it so like myself, indeed so brotherly, made me realize that I'd been happy, that I was happy still. For all to be accomplished, for me to feel less lonely, all that remained to hope for was that on the day of my execution there should be howls of execration." We also notice Jim's remarks about being "satisfied . . . nearly", and recall that the only way he can be satisfied is "by defying the disaster". So, we can answer Marlow's final question, "Is he satisfied quite now, I wonder? We ought to know, he is one of us." Jim is satisfied because his honour has been regained; his final act of defying death makes him accept himself, just as Meursault is fulfilled by his defiance of death.

This brings us to one last comparison, one which can better explain the phrase "he is one of us." Meursault, in the passage quoted above, speaks of feeling "more brotherly" and, earlier in the book when he throws the priest out of his cell, he says

> Every man alive is privileged; there was only one class of man, the privileged class. . . . What difference could it make to me . . . since the way a man decides to live, the fate he thinks he chooses, since one and the same fate was bound to choose not only me but thousands of millions of privileged people, who like him (the priest) called themselves my brothers. . . . All alike would be condemned to die one day; his turn, too, would come like the others.

Meursault, too, is one of us. He is one of the race of modern men, and although he is a stranger, he shares something with the human race; he feels "less lonely" because he is a man among men. Jim, too is a man among men.

We are like Jim and Meursault simply because of [what Sartre terms] the "universality of the human condition." We all face the same fate.

Moreover, Jim's commitment to the people of Patusan and his relationship with Jewel prove his kinship with mankind. He tells Marlow "You take a different view of your actions when you come to understand—when you are made to understand—every day that your existence is necessary to another person." Sartre explains this condition in a different way. "The man who discovers himself directly in the cogito also discovers all the others, and discovers them in the condition of his own existence. . . . Thus at once, we find ourselves in a world that is, let us say, that of inter-subjectivity." We know that Jim wanted a "helper, an ally, an accomplice," and we know that Marlow believes that "in our hearts we trust for our salvation in the men that surround us, in the sights that fill our eyes, in the sounds that fill our ears, and in the air that fills our lungs." Thus, just as Camus says, "It makes of fate a human matter, which must be settled among men." And this is why Jim is one of us, for he has determined his own fate, he has learned to accept himself among men. "This universe henceforth without a master seems neither sterile nor futile. Each atom of that stone, each mineral flake of that night filled mountain, in itself forms a world. The struggle itself toward the heights is enough to fill a man's heart. We must imagine Sisyphus [and Jim] happy." (pp. 518-25)

Ira Sadoff, "Sartre and Conrad: Lord Jim as Existential Hero," in The Dalhousie Review, *Vol. 49, No. 4, Winter, 1969-70, pp. 518-25.*

Vida E. Marković   (essay date 1970)

[*Marković is a Yugoslavian educator and critic. In the following excerpt, she comments on the significance of the repeated references to Jim as "one of us" in* Lord Jim.]

> The human heart is vast enough to contain all the world. It is valiant enough to bear the burden, but where is the courage that would cast it off?

In Conrad's opinion, the novelist should not only make the reader feel, hear, visualize what is presented to him. He should above all make him *see.* Figures in fiction should be more vivid than people in life, since, as is not the case in real life, the reader is initiated into their lives from the inside. Obsessed with man as a conscious being, with an elevated idea of the function of the novelist who deals with man's consciousness and with affairs of conscience, Conrad is determined to make us *see.* But "seeing," for Conrad, has a more complex meaning than merely the physical sense of sight. Conrad saw man and his destiny as preordained in consciousness, and as always at the mercy of consciousness. Man's destiny is governed by his awareness of whether or not he has lived up to its standards. Such a conception of human personality, Conrad thought, could best be expressed in a novel which deals directly with the breach of this inward code of honor and with its consequences.

While writing *Lord Jim* (1900), Conrad was coming into what may be called his early maturity. He had found a means of expressing directly what was revealed to him in the process of creation. His search into the human mind was still so fresh and new that he exulted in the step-by-step process of discovery it was leading to. Stimulated by what was being disclosed to him, he daringly advanced. His profound concentration releasing him from inhibitions, he freely communicated what he discovered. But he had not come to the stage at which this concentration and the artistic discoveries that followed had become an acquired routine. The process of creation and revelation still involved an exhilaration that was to be shared with the reader. He had learned how to make the novel self-contained—the narrator being entirely within the novel—and how by this means to draw the reader more directly into it. The assumed presence of the reader supplies yet another angle of vision which gives the novel verisimilitude. Conrad was discovering the existence of the dark underside of human personality, but he was not himself drawn into it. He would not allow the "heart of darkness" to mesmerize him, to suck him under, the way an exhausted swimmer is pulled down by the ominous whirlpool he can no longer resist. He kept the figure at the center of his vision clear. And indeed in *Lord Jim* the features of the chief character are not blurred. Jim himself retains as unscathed a front as is needed to impress the reader with the external solidity of individual human personality the more to affect him with the tragedy of human fragility lurking beneath.

According to Conrad's own statement, Jim suffers from "the acute consciousness of lost honour." That is all. Out of this Jim's figure grew, out of this the story evolved, from the author's first vision of him as he saw "his form pass by—appealing—significant—under a cloud—perfectly silent" until the last page when the narrator, Marlow, winds up his story, none the wiser after the long exploration into the young figure that had caught his fancy: "And that's the end. He passes away under a cloud, inscrutable at heart, forgotten, unforgiven, and excessively romantic." Conrad's narrator ends as though in despondent hopelessness as to the secret he has tried to unravel. Yet in the foregoing pages he has discovered more about Jim—who is, the author never tires repeating it, "one of us"—than anybody at that time. He has not sought "fit words for his meaning" in vain. (pp. 1-2)

Jim is a young man of good parentage. He comes from the right place. He is "one of us." And yet the moment all this comes to be tested, he fails. The whole of the book is concerned with the author's attempt to explain Jim, not as a special case, for that would have deprived it of its intrinsic significance, but as "one of us." What is Jim? Marlow watches him closely, irresistibly drawn to him as though by magic. Is it because the "knowledge of his weakness . . . made it a thing of mystery and terror—like a hint of a destructive fate ready for all whose youth—in its day—had resembled his youth?" Or did he feel that what brought Jim to the dock is something from which none of us is free? This is implied by his words: "in what was I better than the rest of us to refuse him my pity?" Where is the answer? Gradually as the "yarn" unfolds, the contours

of Jim's ethical being—and this is what the reader is presented with, this is what makes Jim one of the most engrossing characters in modern English fiction—become clearer, not because the author was able to make the walls of Jim's being transparent, but because, while dipping into himself to elucidate his conception, Conrad detected that his own being echoed to that of Jim. It responded to the same vibrations. Not by separating him from mankind and watching him as a being apart, but by treating him as "one of us," identifying himself with him, the author begins to understand him. The answers he formulates are uttered by Marlow. Nothing breaks the emotional continuity: the characters and their shadows, the figure of the protagonist and the commonsense voice of the chorus, are wholly inside the novel. Nothing alien violates its completeness, nothing takes away from Jim's figure. And yet he escapes. It is his elusiveness that probably glues Marlow's eyes to him:

> He was outwardly so typical of that good, stupid kind we like to feel marching right and left of us in life, of the kind that is not disturbed by the vagaries of intelligence and the perversions of—of nerves, let us say. He was the kind of fellow you would, on the strength of his looks, leave in charge of the deck—figuratively and professionally speaking . . . He looked as genuine as a new sovereign, but there was some infernal alloy in his metal.
>
> (pp. 5-6)

Jim is young—he is only twenty-four—and he has a rich imagination. It is his imagination that has made him wish to go to sea; it is also his imagination that has prevented him from acting in accordance with his heroic dreams. The vision of the eight hundred people fighting in terror of death for those seven boats made him take the fatal jump, "into a well—into an everlasting deep hole. . . . " Jim is lacking in that "stiffness" a man on the street unaffected with ideas would have shown in a moment of stress. And Conrad means us to see that this is not only Jim's case. To Marlow it is "as if the obscure truth involved were momentous enough to affect mankind's conception of itself. . . . " Something seems wrong with mankind's conception of itself. Just because he is blessed with a more refined sensibility, Jim carries on his back the special burden of humanity. His mind derives its power from the conscious intellect as well as from the irrational subconscious where imagination begins its flights. He would have acted on the simple natural impulse if there had been nothing between the stimulus and his own naked being. But so would Hamlet: "Thus conscience does make cowards of us all."

Man's is a complicated psychology. Consciousness, conscience—we need both words to intervene against direct reflexive action responding to a motive, a stimulus. Conscious life is guided as much by man's rational being abiding on the surface as by the irrational one hidden within, as unfathomable and immense as the universe around him. Jim lives in a world of dreams and tries, by violence, to adapt the world of reality to it. He is unable to look life in the face and see it as it is. Even after the disaster he persists in his dreams. He insists he "had been trapped." "Everything had betrayed him!" It came on him unexpectedly, on a calm night, and took him by surprise. The concerted powers of a malevolent providence have united against the heroic young man to destroy him. But he will never accept their challenge. He will show the world what he really is. He cannot concede his guilt.

Jim has no courage to look into himself. After the disaster on the sea he may, and he does, develop extreme valor and physical daring, but he never musters enough courage to admit the existence of a dark side to his own personality. Could he but admit it he might have killed the spectre of his past and created a new reality for himself. He need not have abandoned his ideal of chivalrous conduct. But he could not do it. Therefore there is a profound gap in his life, a split in his being, whose very existence depends on internal continuity. The courage he both professes and practices stops at the walls of his external, physical being. Therefore his whole existence stops there, too. This is why nobody can come near him, neither his greatest friends and benefactors, Marlow and Stein, nor his devoted wife, Jewel. He escapes them. When Marlow thinks of Patusan he can remember all the figures, he sees them vividly, but Jim escapes him as though a symbol only and not a physical being.

> The immense and magnanimous Doramin and his little motherly witch of a wife . . . Cornelius, leaning his forehead against the fence under the moonlight—I am certain of them. They exist as if under an enchanter's wand. But the figure round which all these are grouped—that one lives, and I am not certain of him. No magician's wand can immobilise him under my eyes.

To Marlow Jim has been "overwhelmed by the inexplicable . . . by his own personality—the gift of that destiny which he had done his best to master."

Again the tragic necessity of self-knowledge—"gnothi seauton"—is asserted. Jim has ignored this elementary principle imposed on mankind together with the gift of consciousness—and so he is eventually overtaken by his own dark self, whose existence he refused to acknowledge. Symbolically the author often sets him against a dark background, darkness symbolizing the unknown, deeply buried, destructive inner being. Since he cannot reconcile the two elements in his being, he is divided against himself.

Conrad reminds us that this again is universal; "no man ever understands quite his own artful dodges to escape from the grim shadow of self-knowledge." Jim does his utmost to counteract the inward unease by outward assurance. Talking to Marlow about his position in Patusan, he says: "If you ask them who is brave—who is true—who is just—who is it they would trust with their lives?—they would say, Tuan Jim." Referring to the past in the vaguest terms he almost admits: "I talk about being done with it—with the bally thing at the back of my head . . . Forgetting. . . . Hang me if I know!" And then immediately hushes this remote voice: "I can think of it quietly. After all, what has it proved? Nothing." His whole life is a prolonged attempt to conceal himself: "I must go on, go on forever holding up my end, to feel sure that nothing can touch me." On the surface he has found his peace; his life

has become harmonious because his dream, his delusions about himself, seem to have merged with reality. He is the respected "Tuan Jim," the hero, almost more than a mortal. Still, the unadmitted guilt rankles within. He knows that the world he comes from is closed to him and yet he would like that world to know that he is different. He is "like a little child," as though by shutting his eyes he may become invisible to others. He refuses, in effect, to grow out of his youthful daydreams. He does not want to suspect the snake in the bush and so must become its prey.

Jim is human in his rejection of anything less than a complete, integral dream. "A man that is born falls into a dream," as Stein put it, and sinks into it as if into a sea. To this dream that life is, we are to submit ourselves wholly. "Live all you can," as Henry James's Strether advises little Bilham; live as full a life as is offered us, with all our sense exposed to its vibrations. If we don't, if we seek any exemption from the destructive element of life in which we have our being, we are undone. Once Jim had refused to immerse himself, and he paid a high price. The next time he was faced with the same challenge, with the necessity to look into his own darkness and accept himself, was when he was confronted with Captain Brown, the embodiment of the "destructive element" in man himself. Again he refused and missed the chance of getting the spectre of his past by the throat and strangling it. Perhaps this was his opportunity, but it had come veiled and he did not recognize it. Brown gives him a "lesson." His massacre of Jim's people is "a retribution," Marlow says, "a demonstration of some obscure and awful attribute of our nature which, I am afraid, is not so very far under the surface as we like to think."

After Brown had betrayed Jim's trust and so allowed Jim to betray his people, Jim cannot fight for his life because it would lead him the way Brown has gone. It would mean giving in to his dark self, which he stubbornly ignores. The ultimate refusal to accept oneself is tantamount to a rejection of life, an acceptance of death. In Jim's case—as in that of Hamlet—death is a triumph. Hamlet asks Horatio to live in order to tell his story:

> Horatio, I am dead;
> Thou liv'st; report me and my cause aright
> To the unsatisfied.

He does not think he has lived in vain, he is not indifferent to life and the future. Jim's last glance triumphantly runs from face to face as though challenging anyone to call him a coward. He failed in life, but he triumphs in death. Death was his supreme opportunity, it has come to him as "an Eastern bride . . . veiled," but this time he has recognized and followed it.

As though feeling that he has not made it clear enough that, if Jim does represent mankind in its dilemma, his example is not to be followed, Conrad makes him leave "under a cloud." Jewel will not forgive his blindness, his madness in following a dream—she does not know how apt her diagnosis is—and leaving her to whom he has vowed faithfulness. Jim dies to prove that he is true to his pledge, true to his ideal of behavior. Yet those closest to him think him false for this very reason. There again he represents the tragic enigma of life and poses an eternal question. To whom do we owe allegiance in moments of trial? Is it to an abstract conception of human conduct, or to those most closely associated with us?

Conrad's Jim raises fundamental issues of human behavior. Faust, Hamlet, the parables of the Bible, pictures of devils and angels fighting for the possession of man's soul, come to mind. All this has not been casually invented, nor is the tasting of the forbidden fruit in Eden a story without a lasting relevance. Once man has become separated from the rest of the "mute creation" he has taken on the burden of consciousness. He has been evicted from the paradise where he lived without being aware of it, like other living beings, and thrown into a world where he had to control his own life and make his own choices, directed by the consciousness of himself as existing. The consequence is a rift in man's being between what used to be called the "spiritual" and the "physical" elements, or rather the conscious *(ego)* and the unconscious *(anima, id)*. The unconscious is controlled by the conscious and the conscious is governed by the influence of the unconscious. They form a whole, they are inseparable, but they do not easily work together or combine into a harmonious entity. Yet on their fusion depends the possibility of completeness. And it is only a complete man, we think, who can establish a satisfactory relationship with others, with the world he lives in, and accept the universe he is confronted with. Only a man in harmony with himself will be relieved from the curse that follows from self-alienation. Such internal harmony is the *conditio sine qua non* of that "happiness" man is always in search of.

Each of us is prompted by constructive, life-giving urges, just as none is free from destructive, negative ones. There is good and bad in each of us. This a commonplace—as it is also a commonplace to say that we must bring our divided selves into a condition of harmony. But Conrad goes deeper into the matter and sees that man's rational and irrational potentialities, inextricably combined in his being, make him a personality that diverges considerably from the prevailing ideas about man. He has discovered this through watching closely the people around him as they were confronted with the cosmic element of the sea: "Trust a boat on the high seas to bring out the Irrational that lurks at the bottom of every thought, sentiment, sensation, emotion." He has realized the omnipresence of the irrational, which pervades every human being, enters all his pores, all his atoms, his rational, emotional, and sensual being. Conrad had the courage to admit and accept what he saw. The shipwreck of the *Patna* is not the only shipwreck: "there are as many shipwrecks as there are men." (pp. 13-18)

> *Vida E. Marković, "Jim," in her* The Changing Face: Disintegration of Personality in the Twentieth-Century British Novel, 1900-1950, *Southern Illinois University Press, 1970, pp. 1-18.*

Kenneth B. Newell   (essay date 1971)

[*Newell is an American educator and critic. In the following essay, he focuses on the "yellow-dog or 'wretched cur' incident" of chapter six in* Lord Jim, *maintaining that the episode represents the theme of the novel that one person can never truly know another.*]

In chapter 6 of Conrad's **Lord Jim,** the yellow-dog or "wretched cur" incident serves to bring Marlow and Jim together so that Marlow can learn of Jim and his story firsthand. But the incident has a more important function: to serve as one in a pattern of incidents—extending through the novel—wherein the ostensibly malevolent universe reveals its nature, "betrays" Jim, and exposes his essential self. The gale which buffets Jim's training ship introduces this pattern, and the yellow-dog incident helps to develop it. Furthermore, the incident has the function of showing in detail Marlow's initial misunderstanding of Jim. It shows how that misunderstanding is caused, specifically, by Jim's simplicity and desire for self-justification—or generally, by fundamental differences in their qualities of mind and in their assumptions about guilt. Marlow later comes to understand these differences better, but he must admit—even to the end of their relationship and despite his intimate and cumulative knowledge of Jim—that he can never be certain of understanding him. Their fundamental differences, first shown by the yellow-dog incident, obtain in some degree even to the end. And even if their differences did not, the essential unknowability of one man by another (a theme also implied by the incident) would ensure Marlow's uncertainty of ever understanding Jim.

Discussion of the incident must begin not with its occurrence in chapter 6 but with a private allusion to it in chapter 5. Here Marlow had humorously acknowledged the malevolent element in the universe—the "familiar devil" that, by "being malicious," by "devious, unexpected, truly diabolical ways causes me to run up against men with soft spots, with hard spots, with hidden plague spots"—men like Jim. The familiar devil "lets me in for . . . the inquiry thing, the yellow-dog thing—you wouldn't think a mangy, native tyke would be allowed to trip up people in the verandah of a magistrate's court, would you?" From this, Marlow's audience and the reader understand only that, figuratively, Marlow's "familiar devil" ("a mangy, native tyke"—i.e., mischief-maker) was allowed to trip him up by causing him to run up against Jim in the court verandah. The phrase "yellow-dog thing" is here merely a colloquialism in apposition to "the inquiry thing"—the inquiry involving a coward. But Marlow is here also alluding (though forward rather than back) to the yellow-dog incident, which he will relate in the next chapter. Since the incident is not yet known to his audience or the reader, they can be aware only of the figurative meaning of his words. However, as Marlow alone knows, a "mangy, native" dog was literally "allowed to trip up" a casual stranger with whom Marlow was talking "in the verandah of a magistrate's court." And this led to the dog's "tripping up" Jim as well, for the stranger's remark about the dog ("Look at that wretched cur") fooled Jim into giving himself away to Marlow.

When, in the next chapter, Marlow's audience hears (and the reader reads) about the literal incident, its meaning is clear at once, for that meaning has already been provided. It is clear that the malicious, devilish, or "diabolical" powers in the universe are being depicted at work in the incident. Not only do they compel Marlow to attend the inquiry, but they compel him to meet Jim despite a conviction of the uselessness of meeting, they compel Jim to speak to Marlow despite Jim's resolution to the contrary, and they fool Jim into giving himself away to Marlow. In the yellow-dog incident, then, the ostensibly malevolent universe manifests itself, "betrays" Jim, and exposes his essential self. Near the end of the novel, the universe does it still again—this time through Gentleman Brown, that "blind accomplice of the Dark Powers"—and only Jim's death ends the pattern.

During the voyage of the *Patna* there had been an ominous, foreboding atmosphere—a sense in the air that the universe was about to make a revelatory move. This atmosphere was especially present just before the *Patna* was damaged. "The shadow of the coming event" was not visible then, but when the moon "floating slowly downwards had lost itself on the darkened surface of the waters, . . . the eternity beyond the sky seemed to come down nearer to the earth"; and like "a crowded planet speeding through the dark spaces of ether . . . in the appalling and calm solitudes," the ship seemed to be "awaiting the breath of future creations." This ominous atmosphere was then intensified, just before Jim abandoned the *Patna,* by the unobserved approach of a silent black squall (described near the beginning of chapter 9). Now, in the court verandah, this atmosphere exists between Jim and Marlow in the play of expression on Jim's face: "To watch his face was like watching a darkening sky before a clap of thunder, shade upon shade imperceptibly coming on, the gloom growing mysteriously intense in the calm of maturing violence." It is as if the malevolent presence is there and about to "use" Jim, without his being aware of it.

At the time Marlow is not aware of it either. To him Jim's expression signifies only a threat of imminent violence, not a revelation of the malevolent universe. Yet he does understand the situation to be a revelation of Jim—of his true, inner nature. Marlow does not want to witness this revelation, but he is as helpless to stop it as he is to stop Jim's threatening. He protests, he attempts "supernatural efforts of memory" to recall how he may have offended Jim; but Jim increasingly reveals himself and the outbreak of violence comes still closer. The universe had threatened violence before, after the *Patna* had been damaged. And still earlier—when one gale had struck Jim's training ship and another had lamed him—the universe had seemed to threaten total destruction. But on all three occasions the universe had canceled its threat after betraying Jim into self-revelation and thereby had shown that he had revealed himself needlessly. So too, on this occasion, the threat is canceled by Jim's sight of the dog and slow realization of it as an explanation. He now sees as meaningless the incident which before seemed so meaningful. Only a figurehead remains. The dog is merely an "effigy," a "piece of mechanism," and Marlow an innocent bystander. Neither one is the Fate with which Jim yearns to come to grips. And so, as on previous occasions, he is baffled. On the training ship he had stood "confounded" in the gale; disabled on another ship, he had lain "dazed, battered, hopeless"; on the bridge of the stricken *Patna* he

had stood helpless, unable to save the ship or the pilgrims, and at the approach of the silent black squall he had become "maddened" by his helplessness. Now too, after seeing the yellow dog, Jim is helpless to fight back. "Perhaps he looked forward to that hammering he was going to give me for rehabilitation, for appeasement," for "relief," for "effective refutation," but "he had ridiculously failed. The stars had been ironically unpropitious." And now also, according to the manuscript version of the incident, his helplessness maddens him: "He was pained, enraged, and bewildered. For a moment I had every reason to fear I would still have to bear the brunt of that offensive disaster; but even he could see that the thing was without remedy."

On still another occasion Jim's desire to fight back was baffled—when he was in the lifeboat with the other *Patna* officers. Though he dared them (by his remark "Try") to carry out their threat of tossing him overboard, they did not try. The German captain did come at him and Jim cried, "Come on," but the captain stopped short and returned, and Jim was "sorry." For six hours he remained in readiness, gripping a tiller to fight with, but "it was part of the burlesque meanness pervading that particular disaster at sea that they did not come to blows." And now, it is part of the burlesque meanness pervading the yellow-dog incident that Marlow and Jim *almost* come to blows. In the court verandah as in the lifeboat, "it was all threats, all a terribly effective feint, a sham from beginning to end, planned by the tremendous disdain of the Dark Powers."

In Jim's mistake about the "wretched cur" Marlow realizes a significance that Jim does not realize. Jim's movements and speech betray something within himself that feels the insult to be—not "justified," exactly—but natural and expected, though debatable. Jim is threatening violence, yet he is "strangely passive": he shows a "slow and ponderous hesitation." And because it is "with just a faint tinge of bitterness" that he says, "You thought I would be afraid to resent this," he unwittingly acknowledges that he would expect Marlow to have this thought, that the thought is natural. By this "tinge of bitterness" Jim unknowingly disarms his own self-justification, though certainly he does not justify the insult. And by his threat of violence, he protests but protests too much. He intends to fight against the expressed accusation partly because he fights down a similar but unexpressed accusation within himself: he has a "wild hope of arriving in that way at some effective refutation." Marlow senses the nature of Jim's protest: he feels as if Jim had made "some unprovoked and abominable confidence," had been "mercilessly shown up by his own natural impulse." To have "given himself away utterly" was pathetic enough. But, to compound the pathos, Jim had "given himself away for nothing in this case. He had humiliated himself only to be baffled."

Marlow thinks that Jim too realizes how significantly he has revealed himself. Consequently Marlow attributes to Jim a feeling of acute shame: "he was incapable of pronouncing a word from the excess of his humiliation." But Marlow is attributing to him a more extreme emotion than he actually feels. Jim is only acutely embarrassed at his mistake, for he does not realize that he has given himself away and so cannot feel a commensurate humiliation. When Jim runs away from Marlow, he runs away from his disappointment, bafflement, helplessness, and acute embarrassment. Unlike Marlow, he is not aware of the strength of his internal self-accusations and so he cannot realize, as Marlow does, that he is running away from himself.

When, in turn, Marlow shows embarrassment (by stammering), Jim is able to recover and to reply placidly, "Altogether my mistake." At this, Marlow "marvelled greatly." He can now see a great difference between Jim's reaction and his estimate of that reaction, but the difference puzzles rather than enlightens him. Marlow does not yet realize Jim's unawareness at having given himself away. He does not yet realize the difference between their respective levels of insight. And so Marlow wonders greatly at Jim's "courteous placidity": "He might have been alluding to some trifling occurrence. Hadn't he understood its deplorable meaning?" Later, after Marlow knows Jim better, he will be able to believe that, indeed, Jim did *not* understand the deplorable meaning of the occurrence. But at this time Marlow can estimate Jim's inner state only from the outside—from appearance and from the implications of his words—and so he can only conjecture among possible alternatives: Did Jim's placidity argue "an immense power of self-control or . . . a wonderful elasticity of spirits"? And in the manuscript Marlow adds, "Was he a slave to unparalleled stupidity or master of the most consummate dissimulation?" When, soon after, they meet again and Jim seems to have forgotten the incident completely, Marlow wonders whether Jim's continued placidity is "the outcome of manly self-control, of impudence, of callousness, of a colossal unconsciousness, of a gigantic deception [of a monstrous self-deception]. Who can tell!" Marlow repeats here the conjectural terms he used not only when he first met Jim ("self-control or . . . elasticity of spirits," "unparalleled stupidity or . . . consummate dissimulation") but also when he first saw Jim by the harbor office ("I asked myself, seeing him there apparently so much at ease—is he silly? is he callous?") and when he observed Jim in court (his "demeanour . . . suggested gloomy impudence"). Marlow's retention of all his conjectural terms shows that, throughout this period, Jim remains essentially "unknown" to him.

The juxtaposition of all these terms emphasizes the arresting contrasts between them. And it emphasizes the equally arresting fact that such contrasting terms can yet account for the same external behavior by Jim. However, such juxtaposition is not Conrad's way of showing, side by side, several appearances and one reality. Here, rather, is juxtaposition of appearances only. The reality or truth is obscure. But however far any appearance may be from the truth, it yet has a modicum of it. The appearances are not contraries but rather various related aspects or forms of the truth. For Conrad the truth may be too complex to be expressed by any one of the terms and so may be an unexpressed, and probably inexpressible, composite of them. Somewhat later, Marlow will conjecture (in chapter 8) that simplicity and innocence explain Jim's nature. And these two terms may be nearest the truth precisely because Marlow states them after he has come to know Jim better

and *not* when Jim is still "unknown" to him—i.e., in chapter 6. But the terms do not eliminate the possible applicability of nearly all the earlier terms. Simplicity and innocence allow "self deception." And in "self deception" there is an aspect of "unconsciousness," another of "stupidity" (which can lead to "callousness"), and even an implicit necessity for the deception of others—i.e., "dissimulation." Moreover, "self deception" about one's own heroic possibilities can lead to unintentional "impudence."

Before they ever met, Marlow had inferred that Jim was "hopeless." And hopelessness had indicated to Marlow that Jim accepted his guilt. Understandably, such acceptance could make Jim defensive about his guilt, and to Marlow his behavior in the yellow-dog incident did appear unconsciously defensive. But then, when Jim replies placidly, he conveys to Marlow an easy uncaring acknowledgment of guilt or even no acknowledgment at all. This strikes Marlow as inconsistent with the earlier defensiveness. And Jim's next remark only intensifies this apparent inconsistency, for, by it, Jim seems to express a counter-accusation and practically a self-justification: "You may well forgive me. . . . All these staring people in court seemed such fools that—that it might have been as I supposed." Marlow had thought that Jim resented the spoken accusation because of defensiveness; but now it seems possible that Jim resents not just spoken accusation but even unspoken attribution to him of guilt (what the "staring" denotes)—and not because of defensiveness but because of a feeling of self-justification, perhaps even of self-righteousness. The remark gives Marlow his first view of Jim's attempts at self-justification ("this opened suddenly a new view of him to my wonder"), but the view puzzles rather than clarifies.

Several moments before, when he was accosting Marlow, Jim had expressed his resentment of the staring. But at the time Marlow was in no position to note the distinction that Jim was making—a distinction between guilt-attribution in court and outside court:

> "What did you mean by staring at me all the morning?". . . .
>
> "Did you expect us all to sit with downcast eyes out of regard for your susceptibilities?"
>
> "No. That's all right, . . . that's all right. I am going through with that. Only . . . I won't let any man call me names outside this court."

Now, Jim repeats the distinction: "I can't put up with this kind of thing . . . and I don't mean to. In court it's different; I've got to stand that—and I can do it too." Yet, now too, Marlow does not acknowledge the distinction ("I don't pretend I understood him"). Jim accepts the spoken or unspoken attribution to him of guilt as long as that attribution occurs in court, for there it pertains only to his behavior in the *Patna* desertion—behavior that he believes uncharacteristic of him and accidental. But outside of court he resents that attribution and refuses to accept it. He feels that if he did accept it there, it would pertain to his entire life, and he would be accepting his behavior in the *Patna* desertion as characteristic of his nature, innate and predominant. But, as Jim later protests, "What did it prove after all?" He would "wait for another chance—find out." In any case, even if Marlow had noted this distinction, it would still have seemed to him part of Jim's inconsistency.

Moreover, while Jim accepts in court the attribution of guilt as a just punishment, he is also using the trial as an ordeal for testing his courage and stamina—for testing those characteristics in him which the *Patna* affair has called into doubt. Therefore, though the facts reviewed in court would seem to disprove his courage, his facing those facts would prove his courage. But Marlow cannot yet perceive Jim's use of the trial, and if he did, it too would seem to him part of Jim's faulty reasoning.

In the court verandah, when Marlow first realized why Jim was accosting him, he felt that Jim had made "a perfect disclosure of his state." Then when he saw Jim's reaction to the dog, it seemed that Jim's state was no longer perfectly disclosed, but open to theory. He both proposed and questioned several alternative theories which might account for Jim's speechlessness: Perhaps he was speechless from "humiliation. From disappointment too—who knows? Perhaps he looked forward to that hammering he was going to give me for rehabilitation, for appeasement? Who can tell what relief he expected from this chance of a row?" And the manuscript adds, "The eye of man can't follow nor the mind of man can conceive the crooked ways of another man's thought." Then Marlow both proposed and questioned alternative theories which might account for Jim's placidity. But, after further exchange, Marlow must confess even the inadequacy of theory:

> I looked at him curiously and met his unabashed and impenetrable eyes. . . . I don't pretend I understood him. The views he let me have of himself were like those glimpses through the shifting rents in a thick fog—bits of vivid and vanishing detail, giving no connected idea of the general aspect of a country. They fed one's curiosity without satisfying it; they were no good for purposes of orientation. Upon the whole he was misleading.

"Perhaps one could form a theory—but one could not arrive at positive knowledge."

Later, during subsequent conversations, Jim's desire for self-justification will be more apparent, and Marlow will understand it better as he understands the extent of Jim's simplicity and unawareness of inconsistency. Marlow will detect the "subtle unsoundness of the man" and realize how Jim "complicated matters by being so simple . . . —the simplest poor devil." Jim's outlook will then appear "fabulously innocent" and "enormous." But, then and even to the end of their relationship, Marlow will not be sure that he really understands Jim. His unsureness and the difference between their points of view, first shown in the yellow-dog incident, are discernible even to the end; and it is appropriate that they should be, for according to Conrad's point of view no man could ever really know another. "One could form a theory—but one could not arrive at positive knowledge." (pp. 26-33)

Kenneth B. Newell, "The Yellow-Dog Incident

in Conrad's 'Lord Jim'," in Studies in the Novel, *Vol. III, No. 1, Spring, 1971, pp. 26-33.*

Elliott Gose   (essay date 1972)

[*Gose is an American-born Canadian educator and critic. In the following excerpt, he offers an interpretation, based on Jungian psychoanalysis, of major themes of* Lord Jim.]

[Joseph Conrad] was temperamentally self-conscious, obliged to scrutinize motives and methods. The first sentence of the preface to *The Nigger of the "Narcissus"* could be said to stand as a paradigm not only of his aesthetics but of his psychology and philosophy: "A work that aspires . . . to the condition of art should carry its justification in every line." . . . Thematically and artistically, his work was the highest expression of this need to justify. *Lord Jim* seems to me of all these attempts the most ambitious—"the most satanically ambitious" as Conrad confided to a friend. Any work of art is satanic insofar as it attempts to create another universe, especially one operating on laws different from God's. Conrad as a lapsed Catholic would have been well aware of this view. In fact, I would like to suggest that he tried to embody the dilemma in his novel. In the first half of *Lord Jim,* he presented us with an egoist trying to cope with the social world. In the second half, he allowed the egoist to withdraw into himself, satanically to set up his own kingdom. Then he asked, Can such a world of romance stand up on its own terms, transcending the conventional world? Conrad had doubts that he had successfully asked the question or presented the problem. We may therefore expect to have to exert ourselves if we want to understand what is going on in *Lord Jim.*

Our first task is to try to understand the opposed conceptions of the first and second halves of the novel. The *Patna* episode demonstrates that the beliefs men share govern their fate, while the Patusan sequence tests the possibility that one man's imagination can determine his fate. The Western world of the *Patna* is dominated by Marlow's moral principles; the Eastern world of Patusan appears to function according to Jim's application of Stein's romantic prescription. Marlow delivers his code in Chapter 5, immediately after his introduction. Jim, he says, as "one of us" should have "that inborn ability to look temptations straight in the face—a readiness unintellectual enough, goodness knows, but without pose—a power of resistance . . . —an unthinking and blessed stiffness before the outward and inward terrors . . . backed by a . . . belief in a few simple notions."

For Marlow . . . , the central notion is fidelity to "the craft of the sea . . . the craft whose whole secret could be expressed in one short sentence, and yet must be driven afresh every day into young heads till it becomes the component part of every waking thought—till it is present in every dream of their young sleep!" The implications of this statement are far reaching. A good sailor must be alert and conscious of detail. In fact he must reshape his unconscious life to the image of his consciousness of the outside. Formulated in this way, Marlow's belief stands directly opposed to Stein's basic principle that "a man that is born falls into a dream like a man who falls into the sea." Stein, an initiate into the secret lore of adventure, advises living from the dream. Marlow, speaking for responsibility but also for Western materialism, emphasizes the need to understand and master outside reality. Of the situation that precipitated Jim's jump from the *Patna,* Marlow says, "It was all threats, all a terribly effective feint, a sham from beginning to end, planned by the tremendous disdain of the Dark Powers whose real terrors, always on the verge of triumph, are perpetually foiled by the steadfastness of men."

Human solidarity is only one part of Marlow's code; the bond with the visible universe is equally important. Simply, a sailor must be responsive to the elements and to his ship. Jim is unable to give his full attention to them. "He had to bear the criticism of men, the exactions of the sea, and the prosaic severity of the daily task that gives bread—but whose only reward is in the perfect love of the work. This reward eluded him." Instead of showing a concern for the demanding but necessary routine of the ship or for his duty to the passengers, Jim spends his time in daydreams of heroism. These dreams are intensified when he arrives in the East. He is lulled by "the softness of the sky, the languor of the earth, the bewitching breath of the Eastern waters. There were perfumes in it, suggestions of infinite repose, the gift of endless dreams."

Appropriately enough, those who live in the East have

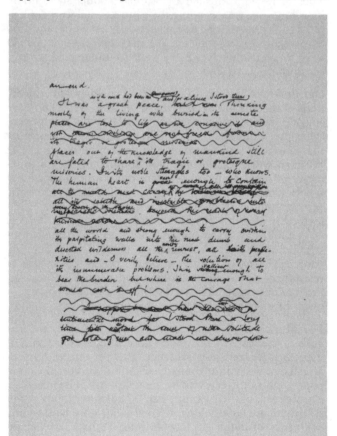

A page from the manuscript of Lord Jim.

evolved a religion which includes this gift of the region. The eight hundred Moslem pilgrims stream on to the *Patna* "urged by faith and the hope of paradise." They journey "at the call of an idea . . . the unconscious pilgrims of an exacting belief." These pilgrims have made the dream their reality. They are as true to it as Marlow is to the demands of his reality and are therefore as successful in achieving their goal. The opposition between Western and Eastern man can be seen initially, then, as the opposition already mentioned between conscious and unconscious. In fact the pilgrims' way of life embodies one version of Stein's philosophy; they have so far submitted to the unconscious as to be identified with the sea. They "spread on all sides over the deck, flowed forward and aft, overflowed down the yawning hatchways, filled the inner recesses of the ship—like water filling a cistern, like water flowing into crevices and crannies, like water rising silently even with the rim." Western man, on the other hand, rises above the sea, as seen in one of several contrasts Conrad makes between the Western and Eastern ways of life. "The Arab standing up aft, recited aloud the prayer of travellers by sea. He invoked the favour of the Most High upon that journey, implored His blessing on men's toil and on the secret purposes of their hearts; the steamer pounded in the dusk the calm water of the Strait; and far astern of the pilgrim ship a screw-pile lighthouse, planted by unbelievers on a treacherous shoal, seemed to wink at her its eye of flame, as if in derision of her errand of faith."

The lighthouse is the epitome of Western man, symbolizing as it does his attempt to penetrate the darkness, to enable himself to steer a safe course through the dangerous unknown, to safeguard the future by rearranging the materials of nature and giving them conscious shape through the light of reason. It winks in derision at the faith of the pilgrims because, where they give themselves up to an inscrutable God (the word *Islam* means "submission"), Western man sets out to subdue the unknown, to impose the light of conscious reason on all dark and treacherous realms.

Balancing the demands of the inner and outer worlds was a preoccupation with Conrad. In 1903, for instance, he wrote to a Polish friend of his artistic aim, "It is difficult to depict faithfully in a work of imagination that innermost world as one apprehends it, and to express one's own real sense of that inner life (which is the soul of human activity)." Conrad believed in human activity, but as something done physically. In his writing he was always concerned to give expression to those patterns of the inner self which are the shaping spirit of such activity.

Jim, from this point of view, has the wrong type of soul to grapple effectively with the problems raised by the crisis on the *Patna*. Conrad therefore presents him with Patusan, a world ordered according to Stein's romantic philosophy. Even Marlow says of Patusan that there "the haggard utilitarian lies of our civilisation wither and die, to be replaced by pure exercises of imagination, that have the futility, often the charm, and sometimes the deep hidden truthfulness, of works of art." As I see Conrad's aim in the second half of ***Lord Jim,*** it was to present a picture of the land of the imagination, to give a true rendering of the large and autonomous forces that reign there.

In fact, I believe that Conrad constructed Patusan on principles strikingly similar to those later used by Jung to analyse the structure of what he called the collective unconscious. Briefly, Jung believed that where psychic energy can not "flow into life at the right time [it] regresses to the mythical world of the archetypes, where it activates images which, since the remotest times, have expressed the non-human life of the gods, whether of the upper world or the lower." Jung saw these images as unconscious personas, "certain types which deserve the name of dominants. These are archetypes like the anima, animus, wise old man, witch, shadow, earth-mother, . . . and the organizing dominants, the self, the circle, and the quarternity, i.e., the four functions or aspects of the self or of consciousness" (*Symbols of Transformation*). As an empiricist, Jung admitted that these figures are a metaphorical way of talking about mental processes, but he also insisted that whether by definition or by observation unconscious processes cannot be known except through metaphor (as they are expressed, for instance, in dreams). In any case, we can see these traditional personified forms as part of a pattern which throws considerable light on Jim's experience in Patusan.

First we should note the presence of a Jungian figure that we have already met, the wise old man. Although *Lord Jim* has a number of helpful, fatherly figures, only one, Stein, fits the following description by Jung:

> Often the old man in fairy tales asks questions like who? why? whence? and whither? for the purpose of inducing self-reflection and mobilizing the moral forces, and more often still he gives the necessary magical talisman, the unexpected and improbable power to succeed, which is one of the peculiarities of the unified personality in good or bad alike. But the intervention of the old man—the spontaneous objectivation of the archetype—would seem to be equally indispensable, since the conscious will by itself is hardly ever capable of uniting the personality to the point where it acquires this extraordinary power to succeed.

Stein sees immediately that Jim is romantic, thinks of Patusan as the place to send him, and gives him the ring which is "the necessary magical talisman" that opens up Patusan for Jim's improbable success. In contrast, Marlow, representing the strength of the conscious mind, comes to realize that, for all his fatherly good intentions, the opportunities he has given Jim were "merely opportunities to earn his bread."

In a letter to Edward Garnett, Conrad voiced agreement with his friend's criticism of *Lord Jim:* "I've been satanically ambitious, but there's nothing of a devil in me, worse luck." In fact, however, Conrad was well aware that he had at least a daimon inside him, an *alter ego* which had long known adventures in the interior world. Patusan seems to me the equivalent of that world, and Stein the magician who makes it come alive for Jim. In the same letter to Garnett, Conrad admitted that he had "wanted to obtain a sort of lurid light out (of) the very events" in

Lord Jim. The word "lurid" is exactly the right word to characterize the tone of the second half of the novel. Conrad's conception of Patusan was, as I see it, intentionally romantic and archetypal. The nature of the action there is thus clearly to be contrasted with, but not necessarily judged by, the more realistic action of the first part of the novel.

As a preliminary to an archetypal analysis of Patusan, let us consider Stein's romantic prescription. "A man that is born falls into a dream like a man who falls into the sea. If he tries to climb out into the air as inexperienced people endeavour to do, he drowns." So "the way is to the destructive element submit yourself, and with the exertions of your hands and feet in the water make the deep, deep sea keep you up." As noted already, this approach is the opposite of Marlow's realistic desire to drive "the craft of the sea" into the minds of young seamen "till it is present in every dream of their young sleep." Marlow would make the inner world over to the demands of the outer; Stein would keep asserting the inner until it works in the outer, "to follow the dream, and again to follow the dream."

Stein's own past offers a good illustration of this process. A hunter of butterflies, he had long looked for a specimen of a certain rare species. "I took long journeys and underwent great privations; I . . . dreamed of him in my sleep," but he never found one until he gave himself over to the life of a native state in which he went as a Western trader. He became a close friend of the ruler, took his sister as wife, and had a daughter by her. Then riding alone he was ambushed by his friend's enemies. Still acting as a man engaged in that life (rather than in the Western one of laws), Stein immersed himself in the destructive element by feigning death, waiting until his attackers drew near, then killing three of them. As he looked at the third "for some sign of life I observed something like a faint shadow pass over his forehead. It was the shadow of this butterfly." It is the rare one, and he catches it.

The parallel with Jim's experience in Patusan is evident. He also gives himself to the life of the native state to which Stein sends him. He conceives a plan to help Stein's old "war-comrade," Doramin, by defeating the destructive force of Sherif Ali. Just after convincing Doramin's followers to follow his plan, he has to face a plot on his life. "Jim's slumbers were disturbed by a dream of heavens like brass resounding with a great voice, which called upon him to Awake! Awake! so loud that, notwithstanding his desperate determination to sleep on, he did wake up in reality." He is warned of the coming attempt on his life by the stepdaughter of Cornelius, the treacherous man with whom he is staying. When he refuses her advice to flee to Doramin, she leads him to the storeroom in which he thinks the assassins may be hiding. At first the room appears empty; then from under the mats emerges a man with a sword; "his naked body glistened as if wet." Confidently, Jim withholds his fire so long that when he shoots the man falls dead "just short of Jim's bare toes." Immediately, Jim finds "himself calm, appeased, without rancour, without uneasiness, as if the death of that man had atoned for everything." Then another assassin crawls out of the mats. " 'You want your life?' Jim said. The other made no sound. 'How many more of you?' asked Jim again. 'Two more, Tuan,' said the man very softly, looking with big fascinated eyes into the muzzle of the revolver. Accordingly two more crawled from under the mats, holding out ostentatiously their empty hands." He takes the three to the river, where (unconsciously) he makes them enact his own earlier desertion of duty. " 'Jump!' he thundered. The three splashes made one splash, a shower flew up, black heads bobbed convulsively, and disappeared; . . . Jim turned to the girl, who had been a silent and attentive observer. His heart seemed suddenly to grow too big for his breast . . . and the calm soft starlight descended upon them, unchecked." Just as Stein has found his treasure after immersing in the destructive element and following his dream where it led him, so Jim under parallel circumstances finds his in the girl to whom he gives a name "that means precious, in the sense of a precious gem—jewel." And Jewel she is called.

This name is responsible for a mistake which illustrates Marlow's comment that the native mind replaces "the haggard utilitarian lies of our civilisation" with "pure exercises of imagination that have . . . sometimes the deep hidden truthfulness of works of art." During a conversation with a man on the coast south of Patusan, Marlow hears about "a mysterious white man in Patusan who had got hold of an extraordinary gem—namely, an emerald of an enormous size, and altogether priceless." More, "such a jewel—it was explained to me by the old fellow from whom I heard most of this amazing Jim-myth . . . is best preserved by being concealed about the person of a woman." If there were such a woman, always close to Jim, "there could be no doubt she wore the white man's jewel concealed upon her bosom." Looking at the "Jim-myth" from a Jungian point of view, Jewel is clearly the anima.

The anima is Jung's term for a conception "for which the expression 'soul' is too general and too vague" ("Aion," *Psyche and Symbol*). For a man it stands as the feminine counterpart of his consciously masculine nature. "The anima personifies the total unconscious so long as she is not differentiated as a figure from the other archetypes. With further differentiations the figure of the (wise) old man becomes detached from the anima and appears as an archetype of the 'spirit' " (*Symbols of Transformation*). The situation which causes these manifestations to appear is lack of inner harmony. Once faced the problem may be resolved. "If this situation is dramatized, as the unconscious usually dramatizes it, then there appears before you on the psychological stage a man living regressively, seeking his childhood and his mother, fleeing from a cold cruel world which denies him understanding" ("Aion"). Since the last part of this statement obviously suits Jim, let us see if the first part about regression toward the mother does.

Conrad certainly goes out of his way to indicate a quality of childishness in Jim in Patusan. Chapter 34 ends with Cornelius' biased comment on him, "No more than a little child—a little child." But Chapter 35 ends with a similar comment by Marlow; as he sails away, Jim appears "no bigger than a child." And earlier, Marlow's description of Jim with Jewel strikes the same odd note. " 'Hallo, girl!'

he cried, cheerily. 'Hallo, boy!' she answered at once. . . . This was their usual greeting to each other." A clue to the reason for such behaviour is also given by Jung; it is that a person regresses, or goes back toward childhood, in order to start again. But before he can start again he must be reborn.

We may see Jim's second chance really beginning just after he makes his two jumps into the real life of Patusan: In the first he goes "like a bird" over the stockade in which he has been a prisoner of the Rajah, and in the second he jumps across the creek which separates him from Doramin, landing "in an extremely soft and sticky mudbank."

> The higher firm ground was about six feet in front of him. "I thought I would have to die there all the same," he said. He reached and grabbed desperately with his hands, and only succeeded in gathering a horrible cold shiny heap of slime against his breast—up to his very chin. It seemed to him he was burying himself alive, and then he struck out madly, scattering the mud with his fists. It fell on his head, on his face, over his eyes, into his mouth. . . . He arose muddy from head to foot and stood there, thinking he was alone of his kind for hundreds of miles, alone, with no help, no sympathy, no pity to expect from any one.

He is wrong, however; as soon as he produces the ring, he is accepted by Doramin and his followers, who give him the sympathy and aid that a helpless child needs. "He was safe. Doramin's people were barricading the gate and pouring water down his throat; Doramin's old wife, full of business and commiseration, was issuing shrill orders to her girls. 'The old woman,' he said, softly, 'made a to-do over me as if I had been her own son. They put me into an immense bed—her state bed—and she ran in and out wiping her eyes to give me pats on the back'." As Jung puts it, "He who stems from two mothers is the hero: the first birth makes him a mortal man, the second an immortal half-god" (*Symbols of Transformation*). On the simplest archetypal level, then, Jim's heroic success-to-come with the assassins, with Jewel, with Sherif Ali's force can all be accounted for by his having found the right way to begin his second chance.

Jim's jump into the mud bears some resemblance to the mythical hero's plunge into darkness as well as to the rejuvenation process of many fairy tales. . . . [The youth in the story "Iron Hans" dips] his hair in the well of purity. In the similar Norwegian tale of "The Widow's Son," as in the Russian "Fire-Bird," the hero plunges into a boiling cauldron and emerges young, fresh, and strong. That Conrad knew of such tales is evident from a letter he wrote Hugh Walpole during World War I. "I have been (like a sort of dismal male witch) peering (mentally), into the cauldron into which *la force des choses* has plunged you bodily. What will come of it? A very subtle poison or some very rough-tested Elixir of Life? Or neither?" (**Life and Letters**). We can find in fairy tales all three of these motifs of magical peering, plunging, and drinking. The latter along with the key word, "elixir," makes an appearance in **Lord Jim,** in an ironic metaphoric description by Marlow of Jim's reaction to the "legend of strength and prowess, forming round his name" in Patusan. "Felicity, felicity—how shall I say it?—is quaffed out of a golden cup. . . . He was of the sort that would drink deep, . . . flushed with the elixir at his lips." But the second motif of "plunging into" is the one that applies best to Jim's jump. If Conrad had plunged Jim in water instead of mud, he would not only have come closer to the conventional model of heroic transformation, he would also have made the incident fit better Stein's prescription, "in the destructive element immerse." Why did he choose this other way?

The most obvious explanation is an experience of Conrad's own. According to his wife, when he was in the Congo, in 1890, he was involved in a terrifying accident. Running a steamboat on the river,

> he had sent his boys ashore to cut wood. . . . After a time he heard shots and sounds of quarrelling. Seizing his rifle—and his whistle, which he hung round his neck, he started to look for them. Almost before he had gone ten yards from the bank his feet sank into a deep bog, he fired all his cartridges without attracting any attention from the two men left on board the steamer, and sank steadily deeper and deeper. He was already as deep as his armpits, when he bethought himself of the whistle. At the third shrill note he saw two men running towards him with boughs and he swooned. His next recollection was finding himself strapped to a chair on the bridge and the steamer already underway. [Jessie Conrad, "Conrad as an Artist," *The Saturday Review of Literature* 2, 1926]

Conrad told the anecdote after Mrs. Conrad found the whistle, still on its string. We might remember that it is on a string round his neck that Jim puts the ring which will save his life in Patusan. Conrad's accident can help to explain the overtones of burial and death noticeable when rebirth is suggested not only in *Lord Jim,* but also in *The Nigger of the "Narcissus"* and in *Heart of Darkness.*

But there is more to this thematic cluster than can be seen in one accident in Conrad's life. The other possibilities come out interestingly in the letter to Edward Garnett on *Lord Jim.* "I admit I stood for a great triumph and I have only succeeded in giving myself utterly away. Nobody'll see it, but you have detected me falling back into my lump of clay I had been lugging up from the bottom of the pit, with the idea of breathing big life into it. . . . The *Outcast* is a heap of sand, the *Nigger* a splash of water, *Jim* a lump of clay. A stone, I suppose will be my next gift to the impatient mankind—before I get drowned in mud to which even my supreme struggles won't give a simulacrum of life" (*Letters to Garnett*). The phrase, "drowned in mud" provides an obvious connection with the accident described by Mrs. Conrad, while the images of birth restore the connection between such an immersion and life. What in Jim's experience is connected with rebirth is in Conrad's connected with creation. Nor is the psychoanalytic correlation far to seek. As the phrases "heap of sand," "lump of clay," and "a stone" indicate, Conrad's gifts to mankind are of an anal nature. Rather than a cause

for outrage, however, we may take that nature as a compliment to his readers. Although one obvious use of anal imagery is aggressive and destructive, another use is also recognized in psychiatry. This second use is creative, perhaps in males a substitute for the female's ability to give birth. As Jung comments, in myths, "the first men were made from earth or clay. The Latin *lutum,* which really means 'mud,' also had the metaphorical meaning of 'filth' " (*Symbols of Transformation*).

If we now look again at Jim's action in the mudbank we can appreciate an important passage not quoted before. Jim made efforts "culminating into one mighty supreme effort in the darkness to crack the earth asunder, to throw it off his limbs—and he felt himself creeping feebly up the bank. He lay full length on the firm ground and saw the light, the sky." Although he then goes on to Doramin's wife still "beplastered with filth out of all semblance to a human being," he has already been born, has thrown off the earth and moved from darkness to light on his own. As Jung notes, in this process of self-transformation into the hero, the individual becomes more intimately connected with the mother, but becomes independent of and equal to the father. In Jungian terms, the hero assimilates the archetype of the wise old man in the process of becoming "his own father and his own begetter" (*Symbols of Transformation*). Where, before, Jim had been grateful for and followed the advice of such father figures as Marlow and Stein, after his rebirth he himself becomes the advice-giver, the planner, the law-giver. He overshadows all fathers: Cornelius ("in-law"), the Rajah (political), Sherif Ali (religious), and even Doramin, whose son becomes Jim's brother.

As we know, however, it is Doramin who shoots Jim at the end of the novel. How are we to treat as a hero someone whose life ends as Jim's does? One answer lies within the archetypal framework through which we have approached his experience. In our analysis so far we have omitted one important figure, the shadow, which in Jung's system stands for all the unfavourable characteristics of an individual which are repressed from conscious knowledge. Rather than disappearing, these unacknowledged dark traits tend to take on a life of their own. "The shadow is a moral problem that challenges the whole ego personality, for no one can become conscious of the shadow without considerable moral effort. To become conscious of it involves recognizing the dark aspects of the personality as present and real" ("Aion"). It is here that Jim's weakness lies. He cannot admit his kinship with the disreputable characters whom he accompanies in deserting the *Patna.* He stands trial in the hope of distinguishing himself from them, but his failure in analysis is precisely moral, in Marlow's opinion. Although Marlow grants that Jim is trying to "save from the fire his idea of what his moral identity should be," he comes to believe that Jim "had no leisure to regret what he had lost, he was so wholly and naturally concerned for what he had failed to obtain." Marlow tries unsuccessfully to make Jim aware of his moral failure. Stein, however, without concerning himself with that side of the problem, simply sends Jim into a situation in Patusan where he can obtain his desired heroism. Jim's success is therefore achieved without his ever coming to terms with his shadow.

According to Jungian theory, this move simply strengthens the shadow. Unrecognized within, it appears without as an *alter ego* which will isolate the individual from his environment. The person who takes on this role in Jim's life is Gentleman Brown. He is obviously a villain, but as Jim's shadow he is able to hit with uncanny accuracy on the words which immobilize Jim and keep him from dealing effectively with that villainy. As Marlow characterizes Brown's verbal approach to Jim, it contains "a vein of subtle reference to their common blood, an assumption of common experience; a sickening suggestion of common guilt, of secret knowledge that was like a bond of their minds and of their hearts." This dark, private bond, which is the inverse of public solidarity, culminates in Brown's act of treachery—which, in Marlow's evaluation, has its inverse morality. "It was a lesson, a retribution—a demonstration of some obscure and awful attribute of our nature which, I am afraid, is not so very far under the surface as we like to think."

In killing Dain Waris, the son of Doramin, Brown disrupts the harmony that Jim created and maintained in his archetypal land. Jim has two choices. He can flee with Jewel and a few followers, or he can maintain the pledge he made to Doramin, to "answer with his life for any harm" that Brown and his men might do if allowed to go free. In keeping his word, Jim has to give up the authority he has exercised in Patusan. He gives it back to Doramin, from whom he had taken it. But what he activates in doing so is a side of Doramin's nature which had lain dormant as long as Jim was in command.

In Marlow's first description of Doramin, we hear that he has a "throat like a bull." When his son's body is brought to him, Doramin is silent until shown Jim's silver ring, which was on the forefinger of Dain Waris because Jim had sent it to him as "a token" of the importance of giving Brown a clear passage down the river. At sight of the ring, Doramin gives "one great fierce cry, deep from the chest, a roar of pain and fury, as mighty as the bellow of a wounded bull." Then when Jim confronts him, "the unwieldy old man, lowering his big forehead like an ox under a yoke, made an effort to rise, clutching at the flintlock pistols on his knees. From his throat came gurgling, choking, inhuman sounds, and his two attendants helped him from behind. People remarked that the ring which he had dropped on his lap fell and rolled against the foot of the white man, and that poor Jim glanced down at the talisman that had opened for him the door of fame, love, and success." In one sense, then, Jim dies a sacrifice to the subhuman side of human nature as represented in Doramin's destructive animality, and in that of Brown, whom Marlow had described as "bowed and hairy . . . like some man-beast of folklore." Since Brown is Jim's *alter ego,* we realize that Jim, the idealist who dresses in pure white, is the victim of his own repressed brute nature.

But, from Jim's point of view, he sacrifices himself to gain the higher goal he has desired. As Marlow puts it, after Brown's act Jim determines that "the dark powers should not rob him twice of his peace." Jim had known such a

state on the *Patna,* the "high peace of sea and sky" which allowed his thoughts to "be full of valorous deeds." In such an atmosphere, "the eternity beyond the sky seemed to come down nearer to the earth, with the augmented glitter of the stars." Conrad had himself experienced this same feeling when he first went to sea: "In my early days, starting out on a voyage was like being launched into Eternity. . . . An enormous silence, in which there was nothing to connect one with the Universe but the incessant wheeling about of the sun and other celestial bodies, the alternation of light and shadow, eternally chasing each other over the sky. The time of the earth, though most carefully recorded by the half-hourly bells, did not count in reality." Earth and its time were exactly what Jim left behind when he dropped the clock he was mending and jumped out of the Rajah's stockade. Here is Conrad's description of the second jump: "The earth seemed fairly to fly backwards under his feet." And here is Marlow's preview of Jim achieving success in Patusan: "Had Stein arranged to send him into a star of the fifth magnitude the change could not have been greater. He left his earthly failings behind him and . . . there was a totally new set of conditions for his imaginative faculty to work upon."

But, when those earthly, animal failings intrude even into this world, Jim chooses to "prove his power in another way and conquer the fatal destiny itself." He must move on to yet another world and find his anima or soul in an eternal realm where no shadows exist. Marlow speculates, "it may very well be that in the short moment of his last proud and unflinching glance, he had beheld the face of that opportunity which, like an Eastern bride, had come veiled to his side."

Like Eustacia Vye [in Thomas Hardy's novel *The Return of the Native,* 1878], Jim may be seen as having found through death "an artistically happy background." But Conrad, like Hardy, felt quite ambiguous about his self-centered hero. Whereas Hardy expressed his reservations in direct comments, Conrad demonstrated his by creating a narrator with an outlook diametrically opposed to Jim's. Needless to say, Marlow's temperament has its effect in the characterization not just of Jim but of Stein and Jewel, and of Patusan. Marlow puts his position most graphically in the form of an opposition between images. In Patusan he watches the moon rise

> like an ascending spirit out of a grave; its sheen descended, cold and pale, like the ghost of dead sunlight. There is something haunting in the light of the moon; it has all the dispassionateness of a disembodied soul, and something of its inconceivable mystery. It is to our sunshine, which—say what you like—is all we have to live by, what the echo is to the sound: misleading and confusing whether the note be mocking or sad. It robs all forms of matter—which, after all, is our domain—of their substance, and gives a sinister reality to shadows alone.

The images present here—"grave" and "ghost," "spirit" and "shadow"—Marlow uses many times to characterize Jim, Jewel, and Stein. The aim of this use is to undercut the validity of Jim's life in Patusan, and of the romanticism which made Jim's heroism possible.

The process of undercutting begins in Marlow's original conversation with Stein. Just before Stein delivers his romantic prescription, Marlow describes him: "His tall form, as though robbed of its substance, hovered noiselessly over invisible things with stooping and indefinite movements; his voice, heard in that remoteness where he could be glimpsed mysteriously busy with immaterial cares, was no longer incisive, seemed to roll voluminous and grave." It is from this recess, "out of the bright circle of the lamp into the ring of fainter light," that Stein discusses the value of the dream. The bright light is equivalent to the sun, the fainter light to the moon of Marlow's allegorical description of Patusan. The opposition between "concrete" and "immaterial" is again emphasized.

It is in such a context that Stein propounds his solution for Jim's problem. And, as he finishes it, Marlow gives us his reaction. "The light had destroyed the assurance which had inspired him in the distant shadows. . . . The whisper of his conviction seemed to open before me a vast and uncertain expanse, as of a crepuscular horizon on a plain at dawn—or was it, perchance, at the coming of the night? One had not the courage to decide; but it was a charming and deceptive light throwing the impalpable poesy of its dimness over pitfalls—over graves." For a third time we have dim light connected with graves. Then Jim is mentioned, and something similar occurs when Stein suggests Patusan as a place to send him. Thinking of Jewel's mother, he says, "and the woman is dead now." Marlow comments, "Of course I don't know that story; I can only guess that once before Patusan had been used as a grave for some sin, transgression, or misfortune. It is impossible to suspect Stein."

When Marlow visits Patusan, he puts quite a bit of emphasis on this grave, and the relation of Jewel and Jim to it. Although the two lovers keep it up well, her mother's grave seems to Marlow to have a sinister appearance in the light of the moon.

> It threw its level rays afar as if from a cavern, and in this mournful eclipse-like light the stumps of felled trees uprose very dark, the heavy shadows fell at my feet on all sides, my own moving shadow, and across my path the shadow of the solitary grave perpetually garlanded with flowers. . . . The lumps of white coral shone round the dark mound like a chaplet of bleached skulls

In view of these associations, it is not surprising that Marlow views Patusan as an unhealthy place for Jim to be, or that his final attitude toward Jim's decision to sacrifice himself is a suspicious one. "We can see him, an obscure conqueror of fame, tearing himself out of the arms of a jealous love at the sign, at the call of his exalted egoism. He goes away from a living woman to celebrate his pitiless wedding with a shadowy ideal of conduct."

If we look back as far as the *Patna* with Marlow's key images in mind, but without forgetting the later "Jim-myth," we can begin to see another possibility of interpreting those images. The sun, which Marlow takes as an image of what man has to live by, is not only present in the *Patna* episode; it is personified.

> Every morning the sun, as if keeping pace in his revolutions with the progress of the pilgrimage, emerged with a silent burst of light exactly at the same distance astern of the ship, caught up with her at noon, pouring the concentrated fire of his rays on the pious purposes of the men, glided past on his descent, and sank mysteriously into the sea evening after evening

This early part of the novel is narrated by an impersonal voice presumably closer to Conrad's own than is Marlow's. In line with Conrad's impersonal philosophy, this voice describes the ship as suffering under the sun "as if scorched by a flame flicked at her from a heaven without pity. The nights descended on her like a benediction." In the night, "the propeller turned without a check, as though its beat had been part of the scheme of a safe universe." Though the universe is not safe, Jim mistakenly identifies with the night world rather than the day, and is betrayed when the *Patna* strikes a mysterious submerged object in the dark.

After he jumps, Jim looks back up at the *Patna*. " 'She seemed higher than a wall; she loomed like a cliff over the boat. . . . I wished I could die,' he cried. 'There was no going back. It was as if I had jumped into a well—into an everlasting deep hole. . . . ' " (ellipses Conrad's). The wall, the cliff, and the hole are all images that reappear in the novel. Marlow picks them up immediately.

> He had indeed jumped into an everlasting deep hole. He had tumbled from a height he could never scale again. By that time the boat had gone driving forward past the bows. It was too dark just then for them to see each other, and, moreover, they were blinded and half drowned with rain. He told me it was like being swept by a flood through a cavern

If we remember that Marlow had described the moon in Patusan as throwing "its level rays afar as if from a cavern," we can realize that in his opinion Jim, unlike Don Quixote, never does get out of the hole; he is buried there. As Jim himself puts it, "after the ship's lights had gone, anything might have happened in that boat. . . . We were like men walled up quick in a roomy grave." The question then becomes whether he can climb out.

Or as Conrad seems to have conceived it: can a man, once he has been buried, reappear *and live*? James Wait [in ***The Nigger of the "Narcissus"***] is rescued from his tomb in the *Narcissus,* but he must die and be committed to the deep before the ship reaches land. Kurtz is taken on board Marlow's ship in ***Heart of Darkness*** more dead than alive. Marlow says, "You should have heard the disinterred body of Mr. Kurtz." Later, "I looked at him as you peer down at a man who is lying at the bottom of a precipice where the sun never shines." Then he really dies, and Marlow is aware that "the pilgrims buried something in a muddy hole." Though Marlow is more intimately involved in the adventures of ***Heart of Darkness,*** Kurtz is a less sympathetic egoist than Jim; we must therefore simply note that a similar problem is posed in ***Lord Jim.***

Before the *Patna* inquiry, we have a picture of Jim passing "days on the verandah, buried in a long chair, and coming out of his place of sepulture only at meal-times or late at night, when he wandered on the quays all by himself, detached from his surroundings, irresolute and silent, like a ghost without a home to haunt." The word "sepulture" should make us aware of the ironic allusion to Christ which is implicit in the experience of Jim, as it was in the rescue of James Wait. At first glance, this reference does not help us solve the problem because, although Christ rose from burial, like Wait and Kurtz, also like them he did not remain on earth long or substantially afterward. Jim does live long, but not, according to Marlow, substantially.

The Christ reference does provide a helpful clue, however, if we wish to connect Conrad's use of the sun with the various father figures in Jim's life. In *The Nigger of the "Narcissus"* Conrad referred to "the immortal sea" which in "its grace" insists that man labour rather than rest in peace. In *Lord Jim* he substitutes the sun as an image of God, but again it is "a heaven without pity." Sea and sun work together, however, in an interesting scene while Jim and the crew of the *Patna* are isolated in the life boat. Marlow reports that even Jim's

> few mumbled words were enough to make me see the lower limb of the sun clearing the line of the horizon, the tremble of a vast ripple running over all the visible expanse of the sea, as if the waters had shuddered, giving birth to the globe of light, . . . I could imagine under the pellucid emptiness of the sky these four men imprisoned in the solitude of the sea, the lonely sun, regardless of the speck of life, ascending the clear curve of the heaven as if to gaze ardently from a greater height at his own splendour reflected in the still ocean

Lack of pity is still evident; it is joined by another characteristic.

The sun gazing "ardently . . . at his own splendour reflected in the still ocean" is presumably acting as the author of nature may. But we have quite a different situation when Marlow very soon after pictures for us a youth like Jim, just starting his career and "looking with shining eyes upon that glitter of the vast surface which is only a reflection of his own glances full of fire." Unlike the author of nature, the youth sees not reality but, according to Marlow, an "illusion" which is very "wide of reality." Although we have to take most of what Marlow reports as good evidence, we do not have to accept his interpretation of it. Accepting his view of the sun, we may ask ourselves whether it has to be the only standard of value. Why can we not see the hero, if he is brave enough and self-sufficient enough, becoming autonomous, born again to a cosmic destiny?

Something like this at any rate is what seems to happen after the sun had risen on the *Patna* lifeboat. Jim describes it. " 'The sun crept all the way from east to west over my bare head, but that day I could not come to any harm, I suppose. The sun could not make me mad. . . .' His right arm put aside the idea of madness. . . . 'Neither could it kill me. . . .' Again his arm repulsed a shadow. . . . '*That* rested with me' " (ellipses and italics Conrad's). He

sums up, "I didn't bother myself at all about the sun over my head. I was thinking as coolly as any man that ever sat thinking in the shade." Jim has outfaced the sun, denied its authority, its right to punish him with the death that he suspects is its penalty for his crime. The result, however, seems to be that he is able to think on his own, "as coolly as any man that ever sat . . . in the *shade.*" In other words, accepting Jim's testimony, we may want to see him as giving off his own light—see him as author, say, of the new life of Patusan. But we should see him as shining in areas not previously illumined, darkness being a figurative necessity for his assertion of authority.

Perhaps, then, we should not try to see Jim getting out of the hole into which he has jumped. Perhaps we should make a virtue of necessity and take the other image Jim offers us, the well, as offering something positive. James Wait was also in such a place; we are told that his rescuers "longed to abandon him, to get out of that place deep as a well" (*The Nigger*). This in itself is only an indication, but from Conrad's other writing it is evident that for him, as for Dickens, the image of the well had a special meaning. Conrad wrote in *A Personal Record* that fiction "after all is but truth often dragged out of a well and clothed in the painted robe of imaged phrases." Some indication of the location of this well came out in an ironic passage of a letter to John Galsworthy. "I shall keep the lid down on the well of my emotions. It's a question whether I even could lift it off. The hot spring boils somewhere deep within" (*Life and Letters*). We have already seen Conrad's contention that it is the artist's duty to "squeeze out" of himself "every sensation, every thought, every image" so that he finishes the day "*emptied* of every sensation and every thought," with "nothing left in" him (*Life and Letters*). I would urge, therefore, that the saying "Truth lies at the bottom of a well" can be taken as a more or less conscious epigraph for Conrad's aim and method as a writer.

To find the truth at the bottom of Jim's well will require, however, a little further digging. A well is often important in fairy tales. In "The Frog Prince" a princess loses her golden ball down a well, and finds there her husband-to-be. In "Iron Hans" . . . a young lad [is] set to guard a well which gilds everything that is dipped in it. Similarly in "The Goose Girl at the Well," its water is associated with her golden hair that shines like sunbeams when she washes at the well. Most common, however, is the use of the well as a means to descend to another world, as in "Toads and Diamonds" or the similar "Mother Holle." In the latter it is again associated with gold, the good girl being showered with gold as she finally leaves this lower world into which she has jumped in despair. All of these tales are in Grimm, as is another common fairy-tale type, the three princesses abducted underground. In "The Gnome" the youngest of three huntsmen is lowered down a well by his two brothers. After defeating three dragons, he has the three princesses raised back up the well, but is treacherously stranded below by his brothers. He finds a flute, and when he blows it some elves appear; they take him back to the upper world where he is finally able to marry the youngest princess.

In *Lord Jim* Patusan is obviously the land at the bottom

of the well where Jim, like the huntsman, can become the hero who rescues and destroys. But we must notice a crucial difference. In the fairy tale, despite serious obstacles, both to the rescue of the three princesses and to his return, the huntsman is able to accomplish both. Jim, however, is able to accomplish only the rescue. In his failure to return from the other world he breaks the pattern of the traditional hero of myth, fairy tale, or epic.

Jim succumbs to the danger expressed by Jung. If "regression occurs in a young person, his own individual life is supplanted by the divine archetypal drama, which is all the more devastating for him because his conscious education provides him with no means of recognizing what is happening, and thus with no possibility of freeing himself from its fascination" (*Symbols of Transformation*). In Marlow's view, this is exactly what happens to Jim. "All his conquests, the trust, the fame, the friendships, the love—all these things that made him master had made him a captive, too. He looked with an owner's eye" at these things, "but it was they that possessed him and made him their own to the innermost thought, to the slightest stir of blood, to his last breath." We have to admit the pertinence of this insight. Not only does "his last breath" push us ahead to Jim's death, but "stir of blood" suggests that we associate that death with an image immediately prefiguring it. "The sky over Patusan was blood-red, immense, streaming like an open vein." Jim's death is a direct result of his giving over authority to one of the archetypal figures in that land. This act can now be seen not only as suicidal (so that in Patusan he is both self-born and self-destroyed) but also as a sacrifice to the sun as the ultimate author of life. For it is the sun which makes the sky "blood-red," the same "western sun" which Marlow claims makes "the coast" of Patusan look "like the very stronghold of the night."

But suppose, being satisfied that Jim fails because he is in some way not strong enough, we are still not willing to take Marlow's analysis at face value. Suppose we feel that a "satanically ambitious" Conrad must have intended a stronger romanticism than Marlow condemns. In that case we must switch our critical perceptions to a closer study of Marlow's own character.

Marlow is aware that his motives for getting involved with Jim were suspect. He hoped through a "miracle" to discover behind the obvious fact of Jim's dereliction of duty some means of meeting "the doubt" it seems to cast on Marlow's own code, "the sovereign power enthroned in a fixed standard of conduct." As indicated by the words "fixed" and "enthroned," Marlow means a standard established and upheld by public authority. His condemnation of Jim for upholding a personal and hence "shadowy ideal of conduct" is therefore understandable. Marlow must, of course, be given high marks for his persistent attempt to be sympathetic while telling Jim's story. But the fact is that he lacks the one quality necessary to a real understanding of Jim. Marlow confesses, "As to me, I have no imagination (I would be more certain about him today, if I had)."

Remembering Marlow's evocation of the sun over the *Patna* lifeboat or the moon over Patusan, we may be inclined to doubt this statement. In fact it brings up the inevitable question of how much of himself an author puts into a narrator. My belief is that much of Marlow's negative imagining (of which we are about to see more) expresses Conrad's own unconscious fears. But I also believe that Conrad consciously characterized Marlow as having an intellectual ability to construct favourable explanations of Jim's conduct which his emotions cannot accept.

In any case, right after denying his own imaginative faculty, Marlow goes on to give what seems to me quite clearly a warning to the reader. "He existed for me, and after all it is only through me that he exists for you. I've led him out by the hand; I have paraded him before you. Were my commonplace fears unjust? I won't say—not even now. You may be able to tell better, since the proverb has it that the onlookers see most of the game." One of the things that makes *Lord Jim* a great novel is the use to which Conrad put that insight, the number of characters whose views we are invited to absorb before coming to our own conclusions. That side of the novel concerns us, however, only as it applies to the principal narrator, Marlow. Conrad has him chivy his conventional listeners, as he did so successfully in *Heart of Darkness.* But in *Lord Jim* Marlow does not gain a deep emotional revelation, as he did in that shorter novel; rather Marlow specifically refuses a chance for involvement and possible enlightenment in the latter part of *Lord Jim.*

On the question of race, religion, and colour, the narrating voice of the early chapters is sympathetic to the dark Moslem pilgrims from the East. Marlow is much less so (as is the friend to whom he writes); he can speak only condescending praise of Jim's friendship for Dain Waris. But he does give us a clue when he mentions Dain Waris' "great reserves of intelligence and power. Such beings open to the Western eye, so often concerned with mere surfaces, the hidden possibilities of races and lands over which hangs the mystery of unrecorded ages." In *Heart of Darkness,* Marlow's active commitment to these "mere surfaces" saves him from "the reality" and "the inner truth, luckily, luckily." Marlow has no direct encounter with the barbaric tribes of the Congo; he learns vicariously through Kurtz. But in *Lord Jim,* the natives are not so barbaric, nor is it their truth which will corrupt Jim. In Patusan, therefore, Marlow's "mere surface" carries less dramatic and thematic weight than it did in the Congo. Marlow's clinging to it is consequently much less of a virtue in Patusan, as the comment on Dain Waris indicates.

The test of Marlow's clear-sightedness comes in his confrontation with Jewel, which is to the second half of the novel what his meeting with Jim is to the first. Ironically, in the first part of the confrontation Marlow may be compared to Jim approaching his destiny, the jump from the *Patna* into his hole. Looking into Jewel's eyes, Marlow seems to see "a faint stir, such as you may fancy you can detect when you plunge your gaze to the bottom of an immensely deep well. What is it that moves there? you ask yourself. Is it a blind monster or only a lost gleam from the universe? It occurred to me—don't laugh—that all things being dissimilar, she was more inscrutable in her childish ignorance than the Sphinx propounding childish riddles to wayfarers." Like Jim, Marlow is offered a chance to find truth at the bottom of a well. And, as in Marlow's relation to Kurtz in **Heart of Darkness**, this chance comes in a vicarious form, through another person. Jewel, like the Sphinx, asks a basic question about her man. Less flattering to Marlow, she propounds an answer, one that upsets him considerably. She suggests that Jim will prove unfaithful to her. Marlow's reaction is to feel insecure. "The very ground on which I stood seemed to melt under my feet."

Although all of Marlow's emphasis is on Jewel's irrational state, the beginning of the scene makes it clear that Marlow has a problem, too. All Jewel has to do is tell him the one reservation she had in giving her love to Jim, and Marlow begins to feel threatened. "I didn't want to die weeping," she says. " 'My mother had wept bitterly before she died,' she explained. An inconceivable calmness seemed to have risen from the ground around us, imperceptibly, like the still rise of a flood in the night, obliterating the familiar landmarks of emotions. There came upon me, as though I had felt myself losing my footing in the midst of waters, a sudden dread, the dread of the unknown depths." The description of the death that Jewel then goes on to give is too much for Marlow.

> It had the power to drive me out of my conception of existence, out of that shelter each of us makes for himself to creep under in moments of danger, as a tortoise withdraws within its shell. For a moment I had a view of a world that seemed to wear a vast and dismal aspect of disorder, while, in truth, thanks to our unwearied efforts, it is as sunny an arrangement of small conveniences as the mind of man can conceive. But still—it was only a moment: I went back into my shell directly. One *must*—don't you know?— though I seemed to have lost all my words in the chaos of dark thoughts I had contemplated for a second or two beyond the pale. These came back, too, very soon, for words also belong to the sheltering conception of light and order which is our refuge.

At least three points here need comment.

First of all, we should notice that the sun has been reduced to a Polyanna adjective connected with "small conveniences." Marlow's irony in doing so is not really confident understatement, as his situation indicates. Second, we should notice that "words," like "light" and "order," have become a "refuge" rather than a means to truth.

And third, we should notice the image Marlow uses to describe his act of seeking refuge from the truth, "as a tortoise withdraws within its shell." This image appears only one other time in the novel, when Jim is in the lifeboat facing the sun. The other three deserters have "crept under" a boat-sail spread on the gunwales. After a while, the captain of the *Patna* "poked his big cropped head from under the canvas and screwed his fishy eyes up at me. 'Donnerwetter! you will die,' he growled, and drew in like a turtle." I don't believe the parallel is fortuitous, but even if it is, the larger parallel of the two incidents will hold. Faced with the threat of sinking in stormy waters or in a panicking sea of "unconscious pilgrims," the officers of

the *Patna* take refuge in a lifeboat. Faced with the possibility of losing his mental "footing in the midst of dangerous waters" and "unknown depths," Marlow withdraws into "that shelter each of us makes for himself to creep under in moments of danger."

The only person to vary the pattern is Jim. He elects to sit outside the shelter, to face the trial, to go to the bottom of the well. He is not interested in "sunny" arrangements and "small conveniences." He is interested in words, light and order, but not as a "sheltering conception." Marlow himself finally puts Conrad's case directly: "The point, however, is that of all mankind Jim had no dealings but with himself, and the question is whether at the last he had not confessed to a faith mightier than the laws of order and progress." Jim's own faith obviously is "mightier" in the sense that he follows it with complete confidence at the end. Conrad expressed his own faith twelve years later in **A Personal Record**: "Only in men's imagination does every truth find an effective and undeniable existence. Imagination, not invention, is the supreme master of art as of life."

We may find it harder to accept Jim's desertion of Jewel. Marlow is willing before the end to face even that. "She had said he had been driven away from her by a dream,— and there was no answer one could make her—there seemed to be no forgiveness for such a transgression. And yet is not mankind itself, pushing on its blind way, driven by a dream of its greatness and its power upon the dark paths of excessive cruelty and of excessive devotion? And what is the pursuit of truth, after all?" The truth Jim is after does not lie in the "mere surfaces" usually scanned by "the Western eye." Rather it lies deep in his own sense of himself. If he discovers a flaw there which calls in doubt the harmony of that order, his decision to abide by the code he has established is at worst equivocal. A minor moral of the novel could certainly be that it is not for those who (like Marlow) are afraid to dip into the well of truth to condemn those who (like Jim) are drowned in the attempt to plumb its depths.

Perhaps Stein's original advice would have been clearer if it had begun "A romantic when he is born falls into a dream. . . ." From this point of view, we can understand why it is necessary for Jim to plunge in, and why it is not necessary for Marlow. We need also to remember that such a plunge was necessary for Conrad. . . . Given a second chance after his misfortunes in Marseilles [at the beginning of his seafaring career], Conrad, like Stein, settled down to the hard business of Western life. Then he gave himself a third chance, allowing the same imaginative faculty that had revelled in the adventures of his youth to create new and more lasting fictional adventures. Conrad's ambition was satanic in more than one way. As a writer who was at once romantic, realist, and impressionist, he aimed to create an ordered and almost tangible world of his own. And in his pride he wished to be honoured for his efforts.

The contrast between the man of action and the man of words was almost second nature to Conrad by the time he began his writing career. The man of action has to know the physical world, its necessities and its recalcitrance. He has to know how to work with other men, how to respect his bond with them. To this substantial world, and to the deserving people who populate it, Conrad naturally paid homage in description and in theme. But, in addition and behind this, in the very act of conception, he attempted "to depict faithfully" in each "work of imagination that inner-most world . . . that inner life (which is the soul of human activity)."

In the light of such a confession, we should not be surprised if in one novel he not only chose a dreamer as his hero, but put him into a dream world to allow him to fight out there the very real conflicts which go on inside all of us. Nor is it improbable that, having chronicled Jim's failure, Conrad should yet have left open the likelihood that his hero had the right to make the choice he did. (pp. 141-66)

> *Elliott Gose, "Lord Jim," in his* Imagination Indulged: The Irrational in the Nineteenth-Century Novel, *McGill-Queen's University Press, 1972, pp. 141-66.*

Richard C. Stevenson   (essay date 1975)

[*In the following excerpt, Stevenson discusses the role of Stein in* Lord Jim.]

> I remember my youth and the feeling that will never come back any more—the feeling that I could last for ever, outlast the sea, the earth, and all men; the deceitful feeling that lures us on to joys, to perils, to love, to vain effort—to death.
> Marlow in **"Youth"**

Most critics agree that Marlow's friend Stein plays a central role in **Lord Jim,** but there is a remarkably wide range of opinion about the significance of that role, especially when it is Stein's oracular pronouncements on "how to be" that are in question. The section of Chapter 20 that contains Stein's famous comments has been called "one of the great passages in all of Conrad's fiction," and yet, if one judges from the critical debate that has stormed over it, the passage might also be called one of Conrad's most obscure. It will be recalled that, having heard the tale of Jim's flight eastward from the *Patna* disaster, Stein attempts to diagnose the human dilemma—that "we want in so many different ways to be":

> "And because you not always can keep your eyes shut there comes the real trouble—the heart pain—the world pain. I tell you, my friend, it is not good for you to find you cannot make your dream come true, for the reason that you not strong enough are, or not clever enough. Ja! . . . And all the time you are such a fine fellow, too! *Wie? Was? Gott in Himmel!* How can that be? Ha! ha! ha!"
>
> The shadow prowling amongst the graves of butterflies laughed boisterously.
>
> "Yes! Very funny this terrible thing is. A man that is born falls into a dream like a man who falls into the sea. If he tries to climb out into the air as inexperienced people endeavour to do, he drowns—*nicht wahr?* . . . No! I tell you! The

way is to the destructive element submit yourself, and with the exertions of your hands and feet in the water make the deep, deep sea keep you up. So if you ask me—how to be?"

> His voice leaped up extraordinarily strong, as though away there in the dusk he had been inspired by some whisper of knowledge. "I will tell you! For that, too, there is only one way." (ellipses Conrad's)

But instead of an affirmative, clarifying vision of the problem, of course, we and Marlow are left with a paradox: " 'And yet it is true—it is true. In the destructive element immerse. . . . That was the way. To follow the dream, and again to follow the dream—and so—*ewig*—*usque ad finem* . . . .' "

The critical debate over Stein's comments has centered most frequently on the image of the sea and its metaphorical connection with the dream or, to use Albert Guerard's term, the "ego-ideal," and the "destructive element." Critics have tended to develop variations of one or the other of two lines of argument, both of which, as I shall explain presently, seem to me to be unsatisfactory. The first argument equates the "destructive element" with the reality principle. Frederick Karl, for example, argues that "Stein . . . suggests reality, control, forethought. His advice that one must immerse in the destructive element . . . conveys his realization of man's limited powers" [see Further Reading]. The greatest problem encountered with this reading is the need to explain Stein's additional equation between sea (destructive element) and dream (ideal). The other argument, and the one that appears now to be quite generally accepted, is that developed by Robert Penn Warren, Dorothy Van Ghent [see excerpt dated 1953], and Albert Guerard [in his *Conrad: The Novelist*, 1958], a reading that in part resolves Stein's paradox by taking literally the connection between the destructive element and the dream. In Guerard's words, then, Stein's advice is "to submit yourself to the 'destructive element' of the ego-ideal; to attempt through action to realize (or live with?) that illusion of self; to 'follow the dream'." As Guerard is fully aware, this reading, while it nicely solves the immediate problem of the multiple equation of dream, sea, and destructive element, raises another: if the sea is equivalent to the ego-ideal, what is the meaning of climbing into air, which ordinarily would be connected with "the ideal as higher . . . , more illusory than water?" One answer proposed by Guerard is tempting—"that Conrad produced without much effort a logically imperfect metaphor, liked the sound of it, and let matters go at that." Robert E. Kuehn [see Further Reading] has taken this line of argument several steps further: Stein's "importance has been greatly exaggerated by some critics, and his tortuously metaphorical prescription of 'how to be' has been analyzed with desperate ingenuity in the hope, no doubt, that it would unlock the mysteries of **Lord Jim.** As far as I know, it has not."

I must agree—but only in part—with both Guerard and Kuehn. First, Stein's pronouncements *are* "logically imperfect," but I take that as part of Conrad's (if not Stein's) point; second, the problem with the "desperate ingenuity" of some critical commentaries on this passage has been precisely that they have tried to "unlock the mysteries of *Lord Jim*" in the sense of de-mystifying the novel. What we tend to forget in our attempts to divest Stein's statements of their paradoxical quality is that his primary function in *Lord Jim* is to sum up the paradoxical nature of human—specifically, Jim's—experience. Stein forces us to perform an intellectual maneuver uncomfortable to western habits of thought—to hold two opposing notions in the mind at once. But it is the tension between these contradictory notions—to state it crudely, the tension between "romantic" and "realist" views—that is responsible for much of the power of *Lord Jim.* Hence it seems to me that our primary critical task in considering Stein's role and its relation to Jim is not one of de-mystification, but one of understanding the mystery as Conrad states it through Stein.

For one thing, it is quite possible to see Stein's statement as a revelation that both the ideal *and* the real are potentially destructive, especially when either is held to exclusively. Thus we have at one extreme Jim's self-destructive idealism and at the other the "realism" of a figure like Chester, the earth-, or better, guano-bound Australian, a man whose dedication to "reality" defines his spiritual deadness: "You must see things exactly as they are—if you don't, you may just as well give in at once. . . . I made it a practice never to take anything to heart." For one who does "take it to heart" like Jim, it is those moments when the ideal and the real come into direct and unavoidable conflict that are the most shattering. Jim's leap from the *Patna* is, of course, one such moment, and his realization that he has betrayed Doramin and Patusan is another. It is at points like these that man is made most conscious of his imperfect nature—of the mutability of his dreams and self in a world geared not to timeless god-like perfection, but to constant flux and movement toward dissolution. As for Stein, his romanticism is defined by his preoccupation with this flux and by his efforts to stay its effects. This preoccupation is most memorably illuminated by the superb collection of butterflies described earlier in Chapter 20, a collection to which Marlow refers repeatedly in connection with Stein, down to the last sentence of the novel. This collection—and one butterfly in particular, which "in solitary grandeur spread out dark bronze wings, seven inches or more across, with exquisite white veinings and a gorgeous border of yellow spots"—is critical to an understanding of Stein, his pronouncements on "how to be," and their connection with the problem of assessing Jim's career.

A number of critics have speculated on ways in which this butterfly illuminates Jim's career. Tony Tanner has pointed out how the butterfly acts as an effective metaphor for Jim's ideal notion of the self: "a creature of beauty, a creature with wings which can carry it above the mere dead level of an earth which beetles [like Chester, Cornelius, or Brown] crudely hug" [see excerpt dated 1963]. Ted E. Boyle has suggested further that the butterfly, as a symbol in Christian iconology of Christ's resurrection, corresponds to Jim's role as messianic hero [in his *Symbol and Meaning in the Fiction of Joseph Conrad,* 1965]. And Donald Yelton has proposed the possible connection between the butterfly and the myth of Psyche. What seems to me

to be of considerable additional significance to the butterfly as symbol is that once captured it no longer exists as a living thing, subject to mutability. With Stein's painstaking aid it has escaped time and become a permanent incarnation of nature's art—"the balance of colossal forces. Every star is so—and every blade of grass stands *so*—and the mighty Kosmos in perfect equilibrium produces—this. This wonder; this masterpiece of Nature—the great artist." Like the marble men and maidens set in perpetual spring on Keat's Urn, the butterfly acts as an emblem of the ideal for which man strives, an emblem frozen in a timeless moment that both enchants man and reminds him of his own subjection to the world of process:

> When old age shall this generation waste,
> Thou shalt remain, in midst of other woe
> Than ours, a friend to man. . . .
> > "Ode on a Grecian Urn"

But just as Keats's address to the Urn as "Cold Pastoral!" brings one up short in reading the "Ode," recalling that the bold lover and his lady are in fact marble and lifeless, so Marlow's ruminations about the butterfly's "delicate and lifeless tissues displaying a splendour unmarred by death" remind one that the possession of this image of beauty "defying destruction" has been achieved only by depriving the individual butterfly of life. In their own ways, then, Jim and the butterfly represent a defiance of earth-bound mutability—but at a cost. Jim's moment of beauty, his "proud and unflinching glance" right and left, is preserved and becomes legend in the collective memory of his audience, but he himself must be physically sacrificed in the process. His "romantic" quest for release from human limitations becomes, finally, a quest for death.

In the cases of both Jim and the butterfly, Stein, like the speaker in Keats's "Ode," acts the part of an ideal audience, at once critical and sympathetic. But Stein is more than a passive onlooker, for he too has experienced a moment of supreme triumph for which the butterfly also acts as an apt symbol. Conrad's narrative sequence here is important. Marlow introduces Stein to the reader at the beginning of Chapter 20 as he gazes intently at the bronze-winged butterfly. Stein is then frozen in his admiration as the narrative stops and Marlow delivers a three-page summary of the collector's life, including his friendship with Mohammed Bonso, his marriage to Bonso's sister, by whom he had a daughter, and the subsequent death of all three within a short space of time. It is after the reader is supplied with this information that the narrative is again set in motion as Stein repeats the word "Marvellous!" He then relates the extraordinary events leading to the moment of his capture of the butterfly—a moment so complete that it left him with "nothing to desire":

> "I had greatly annoyed my principal enemy; I was young, strong; I had friendship; I had the love" (he said "lof ") "of woman, a child I had, to make my heart very full—and even what I had once dreamed in my sleep had come into my hand, too!"
>
> He struck a match, which flared violently. His thoughtful placid face twitched once.

Stein's butterfly acts as the objective correlative of this

Conrad in 1912.

moment, an object of ideal beauty that afterwards can evoke the fullness of heart which, for an instant, gave Stein a sense of god-like completeness. As his quotation of the lines from Goethe's *Torquato Tasso* suggests, the possession of the incomparable butterfly that "had come into my hand," along with friendship, love, and child, seemed to mark an end to striving and imperfection:

> "So halt' ich's endlich denn in meinen Händen,
> Und nenn' es in gewissem Sinne mein."

But the image of the flaring match, like the images of light and darkness so often associated with Jim, reminds the reader abruptly of the transient nature of all human experience, including exaltation:

> "Friend, wife, child," he said, slowly, gazing at the small flame—"phoo!" The match was blown out. He sighed and turned again to the glass case. The frail and beautiful wings quivered faintly, as if his breath had for an instant called back to life that gorgeous object of his dreams.

The perfection of the moment gives way to the forward movement of time. Unlike Jim, however, Stein, with the aid of his butterflies as mementos of past ideal beauty, is able to survive the mutability of his dreams and thus con-

tend with the day-to-day affairs of a less than ideal present. This point—the ability to survive spiritually and physically—is, finally, the most important distinction that can be made between these two "romantics," and it returns us directly to the passage with which we began.

When Marlow asks Stein what is the remedy for a romantic nature like Jim's, Stein's response is to bring his finger "down on the desk with a smart rap." And this "cure," of course, is the one that Jim finally takes. But Marlow then restates his query more practically—"strictly speaking, the question is not how to get cured, but how to live"—and it is to this practical form of the question that Stein addresses himself: "How to be! Ach! How to be." The "real trouble," as Stein puts it, is that one's eyes cannot remain shut: the world as it is—a world premised on transience and mutability—must in some way be reconciled with the timeless world of the imagination. The fact that "you cannot make your dream come true, for the reason that you not strong enough are," is, for Stein, a definition of the human dilemma, a dilemma later explained by Marlow to Jewel in very similar terms: "Nobody, nobody is good enough." Or, as Bruce Johnson has paraphrased Stein's position, "To be human is . . . to be unlike the butterfly, not the precise and peaceful balance of cosmic forces, but the magnificent imbalance of a lust for perfection in a creature aware of his imperfection" [*Conrad's Models of Mind,* 1971].

Stein then proceeds to restate his point with the extended simile of the sea: "A man that is born falls into a dream like a man who falls into the sea." Here, in one sentence, Stein sums up youthful idealism, the period, in the terms of the previous paragraph, when one's eyes are kept shut. As a symbol the sea is most appropriate here, since it provides the perfect setting for expression of the romantic ideal: at this stage, dream and sea are one to the untested sensibility as it "falls" into life. This notion, of course, is a Conradian commonplace. Marlow's remembered bravado in **"Youth"**—"the feeling that I could last for ever, outlast the sea, the earth and all men"—is similar to Jim's. Both, in their ignorance, conceive of the sea as a vague heroic medium in which the laws of mutability and failure play no part. As Marlow notes earlier in *Lord Jim,*

> There is such magnificent vagueness in the expectations that had driven each of us to sea, such a glorious indefiniteness, such a beautiful greed of adventures that are their own and only reward! What we get—well, we won't talk of that; but can one of us restrain a smile? In no other kind of life is the illusion more wide of reality—in no other is the beginning *all* illusion—the disenchantment more swift—the subjugation more complete.

The swiftness of this disenchantment, it seems to me, is precisely the point that is being made in Stein's next sentence. The youthful idealist, having fallen into his dream-sea, must soon open his eyes to discover the true nature of his surroundings. Here Stein deals with the problem of perception—the need to recognize the disparity between what one wants to see and what one does see. His mind moves from sea as the simplified dream vision of the uninitiated to sea as the dangerous medium that one discovers it in fact to be. The reaction of the "inexperienced" to this revelation may be an attempt to close the eyes once more, "to climb out into the air" in a desperate effort to regain the pre-lapsarian state. And it is in this sense that the pursuit of the ideal may be finally destructive. In Stein's terms, by refusing to cope with the sea as it is, by seeking the dream exclusively, the individual allows the sea to *become* the destructive element and—"he drowns—*nicht wahr?*" Stein's prescription, then, seems clear: "The way is to the destructive element submit yourself." Rather than defiance of the world of process, it is active submission that is required for survival, a submission and "exertion" that allows the sea to be a sustainer, rather than a destroyer, of life.

Stein's metaphor suggests a man whose body contends with the sea, but whose head, as a result of his "exertions," is held in the air. The metaphor is "logically imperfect," not simply because Conrad "liked the sound of it," but because it embodies the paradox at the center of the novel: in order to survive spiritually and physically one must at once seek *and* submit. Stein's apparent non-sequiturs do not solve the dilemma—they state it: "And yet it is true—it is true. In the destructive element immerse. . . . That was the way. To follow the dream . . . and again follow

the dream—and so—*ewig*—*usque ad finem.* . . . " Our knowledge that *usque ad finem* was the motto of the author's pragmatic uncle who advised against anything so frivolous as going to sea simply gives the Conradian paradox an added twist.

If my argument is correct—if Stein's pronouncements effectively subsume the complex issues at the novel's center—then what we learn from Stein should play a strategic role in our understanding of Jim's end in Patusan. Our first intimation of Patusan comes just after Marlow has remarked in Chapter 20 that no one could be more romantic than Stein himself; Stein counters by saying that they must "find something practical—a practical remedy—for the evil." As Marlow notes, "For all that, our talk did not grow more practical," but it is on the next morning that Stein first mentions Patusan, which appears to be the "remedy" that he and Marlow seek. Patusan is usually regarded as Stein's gift to Jim of an opportunity to pursue his dream away from troublesome contact with the reality of the outside world—a means to "bury himself in some sort," as Marlow, echoing Captain Brierly, puts it:

> "One doesn't like to do it of course, but it would be the best thing, seeing what he is. "Yes; he is young," Stein mused. "The youngest human being now in existence," I affirmed. *"Schön.* There's Patusan," he went on in the same tone.

Stein says very little in this interchange, but it seems clear that he is intended to have something more in mind for Jim than burial. "He is young" suggests the possibility of growth and change, the possibility, perhaps, that success in Patusan might prepare Jim for renewed contact and accommodation with the outside world and his own shortcomings. Since Stein represents just such an accommodation, he transcends the limited notion of impractical idealism that Marlow seems to associate with the term "romantic." When Stein says at the end of Chapter 20, "Everybody knows of one or two like that," he is referring not only to Jim's failure to "catch" his dream on the *Patna,* but to missed opportunities of his own as well.

Stein has achieved what Wordsworth in the "Intimations" ode called the "philosophic mind," the power to "find / Strength in what remains behind," while Jim, as the "youngest human being now in existence," seeks a return to the "immortal sea" of Wordsworth's child, the state of innocence in which the problem of mutability simply does not exist. Jim's problem at Patusan, of course, is that though he seems to have achieved his quest by becoming Lord Jim, he still carries the dark knowledge of his own fallible humanity within. His effort to share this knowledge with Jewel is the beginning of an attempt at accommodation, an effort to initiate a link between his created world of the imagination and the reality outside Patusan. The fact that Jewel refuses to accept the knowledge that Jim is "not good enough," first from Jim and then from Marlow, indicates the seriousness of Jim's predicament. Once he has created himself as a hero of romance and his audience has refused to admit any alternative, he is left with the delicate task of maintaining what he himself acknowledges to be an illusion.

Gentleman Brown, as the immediate cause of Jim's second

major failure to maintain himself as "great—invincible," has been the subject of some valuable critical discussion. Gustav Morf first pointed out how Brown confronts Jim with what he sees as his darker side, a "second self" for which he shows "an extraordinary indulgence" [see excerpt dated 1930]. Albert Guerard has extended the point by noting how the earlier Brierly episode prepares the way for our understanding of Jim's "suicidal refusal to fight" Brown: the extreme discomfort Brierly experiences in sitting in judgment on Jim is repeated in the later incident—so much so that Jim makes the crucial error of taking Brown, as a fellow "gentleman," on his word of honor. But what strikes me as the central issue in the Patusan episode, as well as in the earlier incident on the *Patna,* is less Jim's failure than the way in which he responds to that failure. Stein's concern, finally, is with precisely this question—the way in which one confronts, or fails to confront, the darker side of the world and of the self. It is in this area that his pronouncements are most useful in assessing Jim's career.

The scenes in **Lord Jim** that most effectively sum up Jim's responses to failure are those with which Marlow's narrative begins and that with which it ends. The first scenes involve Jim's formal confrontation with his actions on the *Patna* before the Board of Inquiry, a trial that is then extended in private before Marlow. The final scene depicts Jim's formal confrontation with his actions in Patusan, a scene in which he acts as both defendant and judge, allowing Doramin the subsidiary role of executioner. In a novel full of intricate preparations and parallels, the correspondences and distinctions between these sections are of special importance to our assessment of Jim. In the first scene Marlow seems to give Jim credit for attending the Board of Inquiry at all; it is an action that distinguishes him from the disreputable—and absent—members of the *Patna*'s crew at the same time that it publicly acknowledges his identification with them. But in spite of Marlow's indulgent tone during and after the Inquiry, Conrad does not allow us to escape certain "facts"—that Jim's concern with the "why" rather than the "how" is, finally, a form of quibbling, that although he does not flee the Inquiry physically, he does mentally, and that this inability to submit to the mutability of his heroic dream is a clear preparation for the retreat eastward that follows. One of the revelations provided Marlow in his interview with the French lieutenant is the simple observation, "And so that poor young man ran away along with the others," to which Marlow mentally responds, "He had made out the point at once: he did get hold of the only thing I cared about. I felt as though I were taking professional opinion on the case." The most important feature of Jim's response to his leap into the destructive element, then, even for the indulgent Marlow, is that of flight.

In this light, the crucial distinction between Jim's first trial and his last is clear: in the latter he does not flee his guilt but instead confronts it directly. What is less clear, judging from critical commentary on the novel's final scene, is how we are to respond to Jim's self-sacrifice. Reactions range from the treatment of Jim's death as pure romantic posturing and resounding failure to the view that his end is a resounding triumph. It seems to me that the force of

Conrad's context—in particular, Stein's comments in Chapter 20 and Marlow's in the novel's last paragraphs—is to discourage this kind of reduction to mutually exclusive polarities, a process which tends to obscure the delicate complexity of Jim's character and situation that has been so carefully developed. Rather, to return to Stein's terminology, Jim's confrontation with Doramin is at once a submission to the destructive element—a courageous assessment of his predicament—*and* a final melodramatic pursuit of the dream, an effort to seize what appears to be his last opportunity for greatness. The problem, of course, is that by this time Jim's options are so severely limited that his action leads not to survival but to certain death. His end, then, is both triumph and failure—triumph in his willingness for the first time to acknowledge the full implications of his past actions, and failure in that, finally, he embraces death rather than life. As Robert Kuehn has said, Jim's end is "self-destructive, wasteful, and yet undeniably fine."

An important corollary to Jim's submission to his guilt is the implicit recognition that flight from Patusan, which is his only real alternative at this point, would be still another attempt to "climb out," an effort, psychologically at least, to continue his retreat "towards the rising sun." In addition, such flight would seem to bear out the truth of Jim's dark kinship with Brown, who is himself in flight at the moment Jim faces Doramin. It is also worth recalling that Jewel, the "living woman" whom Jim leaves for his "shadowy ideal of conduct," has viewed him in the same pre-lapsarian terms of heroic grandeur in which he has previously attempted to view himself. Her earlier refusal to accept a lesser version of him makes clearer, I think, Jim's inability to become a fugitive from Patusan, and all that that implies, in her company.

At the same time, Jim's offering of his own life is the ultimate gesture of atonement and provides a moment of self-transfiguration consistent with his dream. The event itself is carried off in truly spectacular form. And the fact that Jim's expiation of his sins follows the Christian code of his parson father as well as the code of the sea helps to create an effect that strikes one as at once moving and enormously theatrical. If Jim's confrontation with Doramin is Christ-like in its recognition of human fallibility and the fact that a price must be paid, it is also an action derived from the showy heroics of the "sea-life of light literature" that Jim is described reading at the outset. As J. E. Tanner has shown, the rhetoric of Marlow's last paragraphs recalls the world of light romance that is evoked by the omniscient narrator of the novel's first four chapters [see Further Reading]. Even though Conrad's style gently mocks Jim's action, however, it does not invalidate it. His confrontation with his guilt is real, just as surely as the theatricality of his "proud and unflinching glance" is a sign that he is playing his role for all that it is worth. Jim's "hand over his lips [as] he fell forward, dead" may be a last flourish of romantic self-dramatization, but it is also a clear summation of the significance of his final action: he does not present himself to Doramin to make excuses or quibble over the "why" of the disaster. Rather, he comes to accept his own harsh judgment on a life that, until this moment, has pursued the dream so exclusively as to endanger all those close to him. Jim's final action, in its submission to the destructive element that he himself has created, is an act of atonement for his entire career. (pp. 233-42)

Richard C. Stevenson, "Stein's Prescription for 'How to Be' and the Problem of Assessing Lord Jim's Career," in Conradiana, *Vol. VII, No. 3, 1975, pp. 233-43.*

Steven Barza   (essay date 1984)

[*In the following essay, Barza discusses Marlow's role as storyteller, and the social and personal significance of storytelling in relation to the major characters of* Lord Jim.]

In book eight of *The Odyssey,* in a deft reversal of his overall strategy, Homer has the hero salute the story-teller. As the blind harper Demódokos prepares to perform, the warrior Odysseus, disguised and normally wary, ventures broad praise for the minstrels of the world: "All men owe honor to the poets—honor and awe, for they are dearest to the Muse who puts upon their lips the ways of life." Demódokos chronicles the Trojan War with such skill and conviction that Odysseus, overcome, weeps and betrays his identity. Homer intends the scene less as a sly self-commendation than as a claim for narrative's power and as a vivid image of what audience reaction can be.

Joseph Conrad's *Lord Jim,* published in 1900, stands pre-eminently at the beginning of the century's fictional art. The inclusion of a story-teller here serves the same ultimate function as it does in *The Odyssey.* Marlow's role transforms from oral to written, from simple utterance to complex construction, but he remains in essence Jim's minstrel, the "singer" of his deeds. While Jim never hears or commends Marlow's performance, the entire novel asserts its importance. His transmissions show artistry, and his artistry shows purpose—to celebrate virtue, to expand the range of human feeling, to bridge the gap between men.

Conrad came to the artist's calling late in life, not an aspiring adolescent but an adult, with a wide vista, a troubled past, a fully serious set of preoccupations. Though he learned from the French aesthetes, literature could never be for him an aesthetic indulgence. It carried an all-important mission—to overcome the estrangement of exile, expatriation, marginality. "What is a novel," he writes, "if not a conviction of our fellow-men's existence strong enough to take upon itself a form of reality clearer than reality . . . ?" The task is to "move" the reader, to displace him figuratively to the territory of another life. In *A Personal Record* he expresses his initial desires as an artist: "Yes! I, too, would like to hold the magic wand giving that command over laughter and tears. . . . " As a developing writer, he learns the secret: the sweep of the wand must be "conveyed through the senses." It is on this theory that he announces his "task" in the preface to *The Nigger of the "Narcissus"*—"by the power of the written word, to make you hear, to make you feel—it is before all, to make you *see.* " The declaration must be seen in its context, not as a narrow commitment to empiricism, but as part of a broad appeal, by means of sense data, to the emo-

tional life: "If I succeed, you shall find there, according to your deserts, encouragement, consolation, fear, charm, all you demand. . . . " The ultimate goal is to speak "to the latent feeling of fellowship with all creation—to the subtle but invincible conviction of solidarity . . . which binds together all humanity—the dead to living and the living to the unborn." The ultimate goal is to transcend the limits of one's singleness.

"We live," says Marlow in *Heart of Darkness,* "as we dream—alone. . . . " In Conrad's fiction man's innate isolation is compounded by the particular nature of life at sea—a life of shifting relations, of strange ports of call and alien languages, of great and perpetual risk. Still, man connects when he can. Provisional families arise everywhere. Marlow feels comforted when he is slapped on the back by his "youngsters," the students of the sailing craft. Even the narcissistic Brierly remembers to write a reference for his mate before killing himself; the mate in turn remains true to his captain, quitting his job rather than hear him insulted. Even the unscrupulous Chester shows a family loyalty to Robinson. Indeed, their relationship—the one man transmitting the other's story to the world and defending him against negative opinion—offers a perverse parallel to the relationship between Marlow and Jim. There *is* honor among thieves—at least potentially—honor, fidelity, and affection.

And there is curiosity. In *Lord Jim* people crowd the *Patna* inquiry, seeking "some essential disclosure as to the strength, the power, the horror, of human emotions." "This affair," we are told, "seemed to live, with a sort of uncanny vitality, in the minds of men, on the tips of their tongues." As characters fix on Jim's story, Conrad fixes on them, reveals their peculiarities, the dynamic of their lives. Here, as elsewhere, he uses the unusual case, the figure *in extremis,* as a meeting ground for disparate sensibilities. He suggests in these minor characters the pluralistic range and richness of mankind.

The most insistent, most delicate curiosity belongs to Marlow. Jim provokes him from the start: how could someone of his background, appearance, training, and idealism break the seaman's code and abandon ship? This is the tease, the riddle, the propelling question of the book. To solve that riddle, Marlow needs to recreate the incident with all its precise emotional nuance. Only a full and sensitive report can explain how the worthy perform unworthy deeds. And only a sustained study of Jim's career in the years ahead can prove that in fact he *is* worthy, that the jump was a product of freakish circumstance and not a fair reflection of his character.

Likewise Jim, finding circumstances set so perversely against him, desperately needs Marlow to listen, to agree, to believe. "It is certain my conviction gains infinitely, the moment another soul will believe in it." This quotation from Novalis, German Romantic theorist, is a pivotal one for Conrad. He uses it as the epigraph to *Lord Jim,* then summons it again in *A Personal Record.* He is drawn to Novalis's conviction (virtually unique among the Romantics) that the single self is limited, drawn to the ideal of expansion, the notion that the assent of a second self produces an "infinite gain." Note that each time Conrad cites the quote, he enacts the very process that Novalis is describing, providing a seconding belief, multiplying the sentence's validity. Human beings need corroboration; the arts of communication spring up in the effort to obtain it.

The most energized scene in the entire novel takes place in the Malabar House dining room. While waiters and globe-trotters come and go, Jim performs for Marlow, fervently trying to evoke the drama on the *Patna* deck. The incident is still fresh in his mind, and, contrary to his unperturbed manner on the dock, he is reeling with it, first struggling to accept it, then denying it altogether, then fantasizing over the chances for heroism missed. To make his case, to show how "shamefully" he has been tried, he musters detail, dialogue, metaphor, creates atmosphere, traces his own shifts in feeling, achieves at times a rueful, halting, mordantly witty style: "I ought to have a merry life of it, by God! for I shall see that funny sight a good many times yet before I die. . . . See and hear . . . see and hear."

Jim is so driven by the force of what he has to tell that he barely attends to Marlow's responses, barely seems aware of the cautiously weighed replies, the vague demurrals, the stinging retorts. It is enough for him that Marlow is there, listening, nodding, generally sympathetic. "You don't know what it is," he says, "for a fellow in my position to be believed—make a clean breast of it to an elder man." "An elder man," a veteran, an honorable English sailor—Marlow is valuable to Jim as a symbol of the world he fears he has betrayed. "He was not speaking to me," Marlow comments later, "he was only speaking before me."

"Tell them," Jim pleads, and then breaks off, unsure how to finish; "tell them" is what Marlow does. For Jim the jump may be an isolating obsession; for Marlow it serves as a pretext for wider and wider connections. He becomes both author and critic, relating events, exploring their implications, reaching out to others, attempting to create—through their response to Jim's saga—a Community of Feeling Men. He uses his involvement with the outcast as a bridge to other relationships.

Some of these relationships have considerable personal impact. As much as it matters to Jim that Marlow believe his story, it matters to Marlow that Stein believe *his*. For Stein is Marlow's ideal (or perhaps we should say, given his fascination with the depraved Kurtz in *Heart of Darkness,* his *ego* ideal, his *daylight* ideal)—a man of mastery and wide experience, of dramatic action and contemplative thought. Stein's interpretation of Jim's situation is assured and immediate: "He is romantic." Like Marlow, Stein lifts the case out of its specifics, broadens it, recasts it in terms with which *he* can identify. Jim is frustrated, he contends, as all romantics must be, by the gap between dreams and reality. Stein is a romantic too, one who achieved his dream, combined love and high purpose, lived the perfect day—only to have it all stripped away, not by some intractable foe but by a thoughtless whim of destiny.

Conrad's subtlest dramas often go undetected. Stein tells Marlow: the paramount issue is "how to be," how to go on, living with one's loss. The best course, he says, is re-engagement, renewed aspiration, recommitment to the human drama. "In the destructive element immerse. . . . That was the way. To follow the dream, and again to follow the dream—and so—ewig—usque ad finem. . . ." But has Stein followed his own advice? Has he followed the dream, and followed the dream "forever," "until the end"? For years he has restricted his interest to an extraordinary beetle and butterfly collection. Set against his youth, when he was not only a collector but also a husband and leader and fighter, active, vitally connected to others, this obsession with specimens seems a denial of dreams, a turning away from human striving. Now, belatedly, when he hears Jim's story, he "immerses," takes a part, nurses a hope, develops a relationship, turns his attention to the "specimen man."

He develops a relationship not only with Jim but with Marlow. These two elderly ruminators walk in a slow dance-like harmony around Stein's candlelit chambers. Is Jim really a romantic, Marlow asks. "Evident!" cries Stein. "What is it that by inward pain makes him know himself? What is it that for you and me makes him—exist?" "You and me"—Marlow and Stein exist for each other, and we feel them throughout reaching out, touching through their shared involvement in Jim. They become collaborators, join in "practical—practical" action to provide for Jim's future, move from the role of readers to that of writers, creators of a new text.

When Marlow presents Jim's tale to the French Lieutenant, he also waits and watches, hanging on the listener's response. The Lieutenant's response is both shrewd and compassionate. " 'And so that poor young man ran away along with the others.' He had made out the point at once: he did get hold of the only thing I cared about." The Lieutenant understands that Jim is not a lesser man than others, that fear is a universal, that "given a certain combination of circumstances," anyone is apt to run away. Like Stein, he alludes teasingly to incidents in his life when he himself came very close. Marlow thinks he has found another ally, one whose identification and sympathy are as complete as his own. But when he refers to the Lieutenant's "lenient view," the Lieutenant glances sharply, raises his hand, lumbers to his feet. The misfortune might have happened to anyone, but the heart of the matter is that it happened to Jim. As a "reader," the French Lieutenant is emotionally self-protective, demarcating his empathy, refusing to suffer vicariously the defeats of other men. Rather than do so, he breaks off the conversation and sails out of sight, leaving Marlow behind, stung and "discouraged," his invitation for interpersonal merger coldly rejected.

Marlow tells Jim's full story, including his apotheosis in Patusan, as an after-dinner diversion for a group of sated, affluent, luxuriating English gentlemen. Like Demódokos, he is willing to provide the court entertainment, willing to perform his ritual part. But like Demódokos too, he makes of it an occasion to pay a passionate personal tribute. Amid all the ambiguities that he raises, his conviction of Jim's heroism rings clear. "I affirm he had achieved greatness." Marlow thus refutes the French Lieutenant; Jim's dishonor has been redeemed. Greatness must be celebrated, recreated in an oral rendition, whether the culture is advanced or primitive, the subject Jim or a Bugis warrior, the setting an ornate verandah or a clearing with a fire in the jungle.

Marlow's attitude toward his audience has changed since his interviews with the French Lieutenant and with Stein. Now he is authoritarian, purposeful, manipulative; he does not solicit—nor does he need—its approval. In fact, he manages to turn the tables, to confront his audience, to make of its reaction a test of its sensibility and inner value.

His approach is disarming. First he establishes a presumption of like-mindedness, a subtle alliance. Note the generous use of the first-personal plural; the comment "he was one of us" appears with variations eight different times. The community represented by "us" may be as parochial in definition as sailors or white English gentlemen or as broad as mankind. The precise constituency matters less than the idea of "us," the idea of imaginative communal bonding.

Where he does not use first person pronouns, he uses second person pronouns, challenging his audience to respond, to muster long-dormant sensibilities:

> . . . it is respectable to have no illusions—and safe—and profitable—and dull. Yet you, too, in your time must have known the intensity of life, that light of glamour created in the shock of trifles, as amazing as the glow of sparks struck from a cold stone.

Marlow leaves disturbing questions for each listener to decide: Is he a member of the Community of Feeling Men? Has he known the "intensity of life"?

> Our common fate . . . for where is the man—I mean a real sentient man—who does not remember vaguely having been deserted in the fullness of possession by some one or something more precious than life?

Is the listener a "real sentient man"? Has he known the poignancy of loss?

> Yes! few of us understand, but we all feel it though, and I say *all* without exception, because those who do not feel do not count.

Does the listener feel? Does the listener count? The Community of Feeling Men is held together less by toil or by rules of conduct than by emotional identification. Is the listener a part of it? "We exist only in so far as we hang together." Does the listener hang with the rest of his species? Does the listener exist?

In the last section of the novel Marlow writes a long postscript to Jim's tale and sends it to one of the listeners, a member in good standing of the Community of Feeling Men. Though he has resisted Marlow's prognosis of a happy future, a "mastered fate," for Jim, the man has shown a continued interest in the subject, a proper respect for the mystery of another soul. Marlow has recognized a kindred spirit, one as mentally perambulatory as himself. Both reconnoiter other men's minds like exploring scouts.

With basic faith in his audience's receptivity, Marlow can afford a less assertive tone. The provisional certainties of the oral rendition—"I affirm he had achieved greatness"—are abandoned for larger ambiguities—"I affirm nothing." The rambling conversationalism of the after-dinner narrative is abandoned for a tighter prose. Marlow's careful restriction to his own point of view is abandoned too. In the letter, a written text, Marlow takes on the novelist's full prerogative, discloses as he sees fit the consciousness of characters, whether it be the last driving motive of Gentleman Brown or the panic of the ambushed natives:

> A contempt, a weariness, the desire of life, the wish to try for one more chance—for some other grave—struggled in his breast. . . .

> They imagined themselves to be the victims of a vast treachery, and utterly doomed to destruction.

The documents within *Lord Jim* approach, as it ends, the aesthetic status of a novel. They acquire a novel's complexity, its form and care of expression, its omniscient point of view. Marlow's progress, from his first efforts to speak up for Jim to the packets of texts he sends the "privileged man," recapitulates the development of literature.

At the same time the conclusion demonstrates that Stein and Marlow's hope of creating a new "story" for Jim was a noble presumption doomed to collapse. They can offer expert commentary on what *has* happened but cannot shape what will come. Vision does not bestow power. They are not sovereign, cannot detach Patusan from the rest of Jim's experience. And with the failure of their plan their friendship falters too. Stein is devastated, as much by Jewel's tragic misunderstandings as by Jim's death. Once again the distance between minds, even those of lovers, is too great to be bridged. "How uncomprehensible, wavering, and misty are the beings that share with us the sight of the stars," comments Marlow. Nonetheless, he continues to believe in his acts of expression. Younger and more resilient than Stein, he continues to seek relations with others.

If empathy has limits, it also has dangers. Without sufficient mooring, one can be swept up in tides of destructive emotion. Stein "immersed" himself once again, and it cost him whatever precarious repose he had achieved. The French Lieutenant prudently kept Jim's dishonor at a distance, viewing it as a contaminant he dare not touch. When Brierly opened himself to the weakness in Jim, he came eventually to the weakness in himself; his self-image crumbled. Jim's original leap from the *Patna* began, in a sense, with excessive responsiveness. Marlow contends that it sprang from Jim's "heightened" imagination to the peril to the 800 passengers; it sprang as well from a moment's heightened susceptibility to the panic of the German captain and his cronies. Jim is right, in a sense, to assert that he was not himself in that moment. He had lost the primacy of his own instincts; the germ of their fright had entered his system.

A further hazard of empathy is misconception: one can be easily fooled. Even when all parties seek true communication, the transfer of life is imperfect; an irreducible enigma remains. When one of the parties withholds key facts (as Jim does with Jewel), the chances for error multiply. When one of the parties is dishonest or manipulative, the chances for error soar. Jim's second major mistake, his pardon of Brown, who uses his free passage down the river to ambush Dain Waris, is the result of just such distortion. Jim makes the pardon because his initial assumption of moral superiority is brilliantly subverted by Brown and because Jim has no imaginative alternative but to see Brown as an individual like himself—a decent man with bad luck and an imperfect past. "Men act badly," he tells Jewel, "without being much worse than others." But Brown *is* much worse than others—a greedy and vindictive killer. Jim's identification with him is mistaken; Brown has exploited superficial coincidences to establish it in Jim's mind. The error is a comment less on the dangers of empathizing than on the importance of doing it right. Marlow, with his wide-ranging sensitivity, sizes Brown up as a scoundrel at once, distrusts—even on Brown's deathbed—every word the man speaks. But Jim has been self-absorbed for too long; he is a novice at reading the inner character of other men. Empathy in an adult life must be more than quivering openness; it must be trained and disciplined, accompanied by a faculty of realistic appraisal. Jim lacks that faculty, makes the naive errors of a beginning reader, shows a chronic inability to assess people correctly.

The error about Brown is compounded by an error about Cornelius, one just as crucial to the catastrophic ambush that destroys Jim's arduously constructed world. He sends Brown the guarantee of safe passage via Cornelius—Cornelius, Jewel's embittered stepfather, whom Jim replaced, who has been promising vengeance ever since. Now, with opportunity handed him, Cornelius makes his promise good, giving Brown the information that makes the ambush possible. How could Jim blunder so? He is distracted by the prevailing commotion and by the sudden evocation of his past. More importantly, in his innocence he does not realize that evil can co-exist with the ludicrous. He dismisses Cornelius as Thomas Moser does, as a "stock villain," bad comic relief, an unconvincing stereotype. Lurking and whispering, Cornelius may be laughable, but the clown's potential for mischief is real.

Again, an implicit directive is given to the reader. He must discriminate, keep his vision sharp. This was the creed that Conrad maintained as an author, that kept his sentimentality in balance. A critical intelligence, detached and candid, must be consistently applied. In Albert Guerard's terms, sympathy must be consistently tempered by judgment.

Many of the writers at the start of this century explored empathetic connections, the suggestive rapport between the active and the meditative character. In Proust the younger Marcel projects himself into the romantic agonies of the older Swann; in Joyce the older Bloom ruminates on the idealism and impatience of the younger Stephen; in Virginia Woolf the middle-aged matrons—Mrs. Dalloway and Mrs. Ramsay—become intuitive centers for every one in the family cluster (and for some of the strangers, like Septimus Smith, outside), achieving a momentary communion in their ritual gatherings and feasts. These artists shared a common rebuttal to naturalism, to the atomization of the individual: the individual could transcend his isolation through the use of the imagination.

Conrad, however, is distinctive in his wide use of storytelling as a part of the action. Like Homer, he sees that acts of narrative creation used as integral dramatic incidents can imply their creator's ruling aesthetic without disrupting the premise of fictional life. Joseph Conrad, expatriate, solitary wanderer, sailor-turned-novelist, knows how fragile the human relationship is—how fragile and how necessary. He perceives and demonstrates art's essential role in giving that relationship life.

By logical extension, the challenges which Marlow makes to his audience become challenges which Conrad makes to *us*. We, the readers, are in the role of Marlow's listeners; we must summon sensitivity and discernment; we must reappraise ourselves. This is *Lord Jim*'s excitement. It unfolds in slow motion, in complicated stages, expands in a series of concentric rings, from Jim's initial yearning and pain, to Marlow's compassion, to Stein and the French Lieutenant's differing analyses, to the after-dinner audience's mute reception. Then it springs out at us, convinces us that our opinions are germane, that they bear a moral weight. Though Conrad maintains his position behind the screen of his invention, he is constantly commenting on the reader's reactions, urging involvement, warning of risks, bidding for an intense and generous response. (pp. 220-32)

Steven Barza, "Bonds of Empathy: The Widening Audience in 'Lord Jim'," in The Midwest Quarterly, *Vol. XXV, No. 2, Winter, 1984, pp. 220-32.*

FURTHER READING

Aithal, S. Krishnamoorthy. "A Postscript to Criticism on Conrad's *Lord Jim.*" *English Studies* 57, No. 5 (December 1976): 425-31.

Faults past criticism of *Lord Jim* for over-emphasizing the importance of Jim's character rather than focusing on the larger external forces that determine many of his actions.

Bass, Eben. "The Verbal Failure of *Lord Jim.*" *College English* 26, No. 6 (March 1965): 438-44.

Examines points throughout the novel in which Jim has difficulty with language and communication. Bass suggests that this recurrence may be linked to Conrad's alienation as a nonnative English speaker and author.

Batchelor, John. *Lord Jim.* London: Unwin Hyman, 1988, 241 p.

Includes biographical and historical background of Conrad's works, chapters explicating four sections of *Lord*

Jim, and a summary of twentieth-century critical responses.

Berthoud, Jacques. *"Lord Jim."* In his *Joseph Conrad: The Major Phase,* pp. 64-93. Cambridge, England: Cambridge University Press, 1978.
Considers Jim an extreme representation of conflicting and irreconcilable characteristics that exist in all individuals.

Bolton, W. F. "The Role of Language in *Lord Jim.*" *Conradiana* 1, No. 3 (Summer 1969): 51-9.
Contends that Conrad characterizes individuals in *Lord Jim* by means of variations in their use of language.

Bruss, Paul S. "Marlow's Interview with Stein: The Implications of the Metaphor." *Studies in the Novel* 5, No. 4 (Winter 1973): 491-503.
Proposes that Stein, although an admirable character, is "unworthy of the unqualified adulation which the vast majority of Conrad scholars has heaped upon him."

————. *"Lord Jim* and the Metaphor of Awakening." *Studies in the Twentieth Century,* No. 14 (Fall 1974): 69-89.
Traces references to sleep and wakefulness throughout *Lord Jim,* concluding that they mirror Jim's confrontation with his own passivity.

Burstein, Janet. "On Ways of Knowing in *Lord Jim.*" *Nineteenth-Century Fiction* 26, No. 4 (March 1972): 456-68.
Contrasts the manner in which Marlow apprehends the world around him with that of Jim.

Cook, William J., Jr. *"Lord Jim* as Metaphor." *Conradiana* 1, No. 2 (Fall 1968): 45-53.
Examines the images of light and darkness as prominent metaphors, with light representing the personal and universal truths which Jim and Marlow seek and darkness symbolizing confusion.

Cottom, Daniel. "Lord Jim: Destruction through Time." *Centennial Review* 27, No. 1 (Winter 1983): 10-29.
Attributes Jim's downfall to his narcissistic perception of himself as a romantic hero.

Cox, C. B. "The Metamorphoses of Lord Jim." *Critical Quarterly* 15, No. 1 (Spring 1973): 9-31.
Discusses Conrad's use of images of metamorphosis in *Lord Jim.*

Curle, Richard. *"Lord Jim*—1900." In his *Joseph Conrad and His Characters: A Study of Six Novels,* pp. 29-65. New York: Russell & Russell, 1957.
Analyzes five of the principal characters in *Lord Jim.*

Daleski, H. M. *"Lord Jim."* In his *Joseph Conrad: The Way of Dispossession,* pp. 77-103. New York: Holmes & Meier, 1976.
Discusses the complex narrative structure that Conrad employs in his depiction of Jim's downfall.

Drew, Elizabeth. "Joseph Conrad: *Lord Jim.*" In her *The Novel: A Modern Guide to Fifteen English Masterpieces,* pp. 156-72. New York: Dell, 1963.
Provides a summary and explication of *Lord Jim*'s plot.

Engelberg, Edward. "Lord Jim's 'Romantic Conscience'." In his *The Unknown Distance: From Consciousness to Conscience, Goethe to Camus,* pp. 172-85. Cambridge: Harvard University Press, 1972.

Examines Jim's efforts to assuage his feelings of guilt in the context of a study of conscience in literature.

Epstein, Harry S. "*Lord Jim* as Tragic Action." *Studies in the Novel* 5, No. 2 (Summer 1973): 229-47.
Asserts that Conrad intended the structure of *Lord Jim* to render conclusions impossible and thereby more effectively portray existence as unpredictable.

Flamm, Dudley. "The Ambiguous Nazarene in *Lord Jim.*" *English Literature in Transition* 11, No. 1 (1968): pp. 35-7.
Discusses biblical allusions in *Lord Jim,* arguing that repeated references to Jim as "one of us" create parallels between Jim's story and the story of the Fall in Genesis.

Gillon, Adam. "The Eternal Constancy: *Lord Jim.*" In his *Joseph Conrad,* pp. 84-98. Boston: Twayne, 1982.
Examines the thematic importance of betrayal and guilt in *Lord Jim* and criticizes Gustav Morf's theory that the writing of the novel was motivated by guilt stemming from Conrad's emigration from Poland.

Gossman, Ann M. and Whiting, George W. "The Essential Jim." *Nineteenth-Century Fiction* 16, No. 1 (June 1961): 75-80.
Disputes critic Albert Guerard's assertion that there exist inconsistencies in Conrad's characterization of Jim [see Guerard excerpt, *TCLC,* Volume 6].

Haugh, Robert F. *"Lord Jim."* In his *Joseph Conrad: Discovery in Design,* pp. 56-77. Norman: University of Oklahoma Press, 1957.
General overview and analysis of principal characters in the novel.

Heimer, Jackson W. "Betrayal, Guilt, and Attempted Redemption in *Lord Jim.*" *Ball State College Teacher's Forum* 9, No. 2 (Spring 1968): 31-43.
Argues that the various acts of betrayal in *Lord Jim* are meant to impugn idealistic values and ethical codes.

Hewitt, Douglas. *"Lord Jim."* In his *Conrad: A Reassessment,* pp. 31-39. Totowa, N. J.: Rowman and Littlefield, 1952.
Discusses the principal themes in *Lord Jim.*

Hodges, Robert R. "The Four Fathers of Lord Jim." *The University Review* 31, No. 2 (December 1964): 103-10.
Contends that Jim seeks out several substitute father figures, including Marlow and Doramin, in order to recapture the filial bond with his father that he feels was severed after he was publicly attacked for his act of cowardice aboard the *Patna.*

Hoffman, Stanton de Voren. "Burlesque, Parody and Analogue in *Lord Jim:* A Reading of the Novel." In his *Comedy and Form in the Fiction of Joseph Conrad,* pp. 52-95. The Hague: Mouton, 1969.
Argues that there is a strong vein of low comedy in *Lord Jim* and that attention to comic elements is essential to a complete reading of the novel.

Karl, Frederick R. "Early Conrad: From *Almayer* to 'Typhoon'." In his *A Reader's Guide to Joseph Conrad,* pp. 91-144. New York: H. Wolff, 1960.
Concludes that although "*Lord Jim* is more imposing in its parts than as a whole," the story of an individual unable to triumph alone against worldly evil provides a "distressing prophecy for the twentieth century."

Karrfalt, David H. "Accepting Lord Jim on His Own Terms: A Structural Approach." *Conradiana* 2, No. 1 (Fall 1969-70): 37-47.

Contends that *Lord Jim* culminates in the revelation that social and moral codes are based on illusion.

Kirschner, Paul. "Conrad, Goethe, and Stein: The Romantic Fate in *Lord Jim.*" *Ariel* 10, No. 1 (January 1979): 65-81.

Compares *Lord Jim* to the works of Johann Wolfgang von Goethe, arguing that Stein and Jim were conceived in the tradition of Goethe's Romantic heroes.

Kramer, Dale. "Marlow, Myth and Structure in *Lord Jim.*" *Criticism* 8, No. 3 (Summer 1966): 263-79.

Suggests that, through the use of myth in the narrative of *Lord Jim,* Conrad argues that an individual cannot ignore accumulated group wisdom.

Krieger, Murray. "*Lord Jim.*" In his *The Tragic Vision: Variations on a Theme in Literary Interpretation,* pp. 165-79. New York: Holt, Rinehart and Winston, 1960.

Examines Jim's moral conflicts.

Kuehn, Robert E., ed. *"Lord Jim": A Collection of Critical Essays.* Englewood Cliffs, N. J.: Prentice Hall, 1969, 120 p.

Collects a number of previously published and revised essays on *Lord Jim,* along with letters by Conrad concerning his novel.

Malbone, Raymond Gates. " 'How to Be': Marlow's Quest in *Lord Jim.*" *Twentieth Century Literature* 10, No. 4 (January 1965): 172-80.

Views Marlow as the main character of *Lord Jim,* arguing that Marlow's study of Jim informs his quest to learn the proper way to live in society.

McCann, Charles J. "Lord Jim vs. the Darkness: The Saving Power of Human Involvement." *College English* 27, No. 3 (December 1965): 240-43.

Concludes that despite the pessimistic tone of Marlow's narrative *Lord Jim* contains moments of hope.

McCullough, Bruce. "The Impressionistic Novel: Joseph Conrad: *Lord Jim.*" In his *Representative English Novelists: Defoe to Conrad,* pp. 336-48. New York: Harper & Brothers, 1946.

Characterizes the prose style in *Lord Jim* as "impressionistic," citing the fact that "Conrad, like the impressionist painter, sees his subject as somewhat shifting and somewhat illusory."

Miller, J. Hillis. "The Interpretation of *Lord Jim.*" In *The Interpretation of Narrative: Theory and Practice,* edited by Morton W. Bloomfield, pp. 211-28. Cambridge: Harvard University Press, 1970.

Finds that the problem of interpreting *Lord Jim* derives from the subtlety of a narrative which precludes conclusive interpretations.

Milosz, Czeslaw. "Joseph Conrad in Polish Eyes." *Atlantic Monthly* 200, No. 5 (November 1957): 219-20, 222, 224, 226, 228.

Speculates that the name of Jim's steamer, the *Patna,* may connote "patria," referring to the homeland that Conrad abandoned in order to pursue his literary career.

Morf, Gustav. "Lord Jim." In his *The Polish Shades and Ghosts of Joseph Conrad,* pp. 143-58. New York: Astra Books, 1976.

Expands on his influential argument that the themes of abandonment and betrayal in *Lord Jim* reflect Conrad's own sense of guilt about having emigrated from Poland. Morf provides new textual and historical evidence that Jim's leap from the "sinking" *Patna* parallels Conrad's escape from his occupied homeland and cites the work of critics who have affirmed his hypothesis since 1930.

Moseley, Edwin M. "Christ as Tragic Hero: Conrad's *Lord Jim.*" In his *Pseudonyms of Christ in the Modern Novel: Motifs and Methods,* pp. 15-35. Pittsburgh, Pa.: University of Pittsburgh Press, 1962.

Considers Jim to be an archetypal Christ figure who dies at the conclusion of the novel to atone for the moral failings of all people.

Moser, Thomas, ed. *Lord Jim: An Authoritative Text, Backgrounds, Sources, Essays in Criticism.* New York: W. W. Norton, 1968, 486 p.

Includes notes and commentary on the text and a bibliography of secondary sources on *Lord Jim.*

Nelson, Carl. "The Ironic Allusive Texture of *Lord Jim:* Coleridge, Crane, Milton, and Melville." *Conradiana* 4, No. 2 (1972): 47-59.

Discusses allusions in *Lord Jim* to the works of Samuel Coleridge, Herman Melville, and John Milton. Nelson contends that Conrad's repeated literary allusions serve to underscore Jim's romantic conception of himself, which is inspired by heroic figures in literature.

Newell, Kenneth B. "The Destructive Element and Related 'Dream' Passages in the *Lord Jim* Manuscript." *Journal of Modern Literature* 1, No. 1 (1970): 31-44.

Examines early versions of Conrad's manuscript to determine the meaning of the "destructive element" passage, asserting that Stein's speech is not, as is commonly argued, vague or inscrutable, but rather a clear statement of a paradox: that idealism is both hurtful and beneficial.

Newman, Paul B. "The Drama of Conscience and Recognition in *Lord Jim.*" *Midwest Quarterly* 6, No. 4 (July 1965): 351-66.

Discusses fear and the struggle against fear in *Lord Jim.*

Parins, James W.; Dilligan, Robert J.; and Bender, Todd K., eds. *A Concordance to Conrad's "Lord Jim": Verbal Index, Word Frequency Table and Field of Reference.* New York: Garland, 1976, 266 p.

Includes a reproduction of the text marked by line.

Paris, Bernard, J. "The Dramatization of Interpretation: *Lord Jim.*" In his *A Psychological Approach to Fiction: Studies in Thackeray, Stendhal, George Eliot, Dostoevsky, and Conrad,* pp. 215-74. Bloomington: Indiana University Press, 1974.

Describes *Lord Jim* as a "psychological" novel because the interpretation of events, rather than the events themselves, are the central focus.

Phillipson, John S. "Conrad's Pink Toads: The Working of the Unconscious." *Western Humanities Review* 14, No. 4 (Autumn 1960): 437-38.

Discusses the chief engineer's hallucination of pink toads, suggesting that the vision symbolically connotes the desire for escape and the fear of death.

Purdy, Strother B. "On the Relevance of Conrad: Lord Jim

over Sverdlovsk." *Midwest Quarterly* 9, No. 1 (October 1967): 43-51.

> Praises Conrad for advocating the importance of honor and bravery in *Lord Jim.* He contrasts the actions of Jim, who died to regain his honor, with those of U-2 spy plane pilot Gary Powers, who ignored instructions to kill himself if captured.

Reichard, Hugo M. "The Patusan Crises: A Reevaluation of Jim and Marlow." *English Studies* 49, No. 6 (December 1968): 547-52.

> Discusses what Hugo understands as instances of Jim's racism and argues that Jim is a false hero.

Roussell, Royal. "*Lord Jim:* The Search for a New Aesthetic." In his *The Metaphysics of Darkness: A Study in the Unity and Development of Conrad's Fiction,* pp. 80-108. Baltimore: Johns Hopkins Press, 1971.

> Examines instances in *Lord Jim* where Conrad utilizes metaphors of darkness for those facets of life which cannot be represented in art.

Saveson, John E. "The Ambivalence of *Lord Jim.*" In his *Joseph Conrad: The Making of a Moralist,* pp. 165-78. Amsterdam: Rodopi NV, 1972.

> Concludes that Jim seeks moral absolution by winning freedom from externally imposed morality instead of living and dying by his independently conceived code of ethics.

Schneider, Daniel J. "Symbolism in Conrad's *Lord Jim:* The Total Pattern." *Modern Fiction Studies* 12, No. 4 (Winter 1966-67): 427-38.

> Terms *Lord Jim* "a work whose symbolism is particularly dense" and outlines recurring symbols in the novel.

Schultheiss, Tom. "Cornelius the Nazarene: Ambi-Ambiguity in *Lord Jim.*" *English Literature in Transition* 12, No. 4 (1969): 195-96.

> Argues that the numerous sources informing the biblical names of Cornelius "the Nazarene" introduce unnecessary complexity to interpretations of his character.

Schwartz, Daniel R. "The Journey to Patusan: The Education of Jim and Marlow in Conrad's *Lord Jim.*" *Studies in the Novel* 4, No. 3 (Fall 1972): 442-58.

> Contends that Marlow's philosophical perspective is transformed from rational empiricism to subjectivism as Jim progressively influences his thinking.

Sherry, Norman. "That Scandal of the Eastern Seas" and "The Flesh and Blood Individual." In his *Conrad's Eastern World,* pp. 41-64, pp. 65-86. Cambridge, England: Cambridge University Press, 1966.

> Examines parallels between the *Patna* incident in *Lord Jim* and the desertion of the steamer the *Jeddah,* which Conrad is believed to have used as the model for the *Patna.*

Steinmann, Theo. "*Lord Jim*'s Progression through Homology." *Ariel* 5, No. 1 (January 1974): 81-93.

> Discusses similarities between Jim and other characters in the novel, asserting that Conrad uses them to demonstrate elements in Jim's character that remain obscure.

Tanner, J. E. "The Chronology and the Enigmatic End of *Lord Jim.*" *Nineteenth-Century Fiction* 21, No. 4 (March 1967): 369-80.

> Discusses the chronology of *Lord Jim,* contending that although the novel appears to be chronologically disjointed, Conrad's narrative strategy relates the psychological story of Jim in the most logical manner possible.

Tanner, Tony. *Conrad: Lord Jim.* London: Edward Arnold, 1963, 62 p.

> General overview of the plot, characters, and major themes of the novel.

Tennenbaum, Elizabeth Brody. " 'And the Woman Is Dead Now': A Reconsideration of Conrad's Stein." *Studies in the Novel* 10, No. 3 (Fall 1978): 335-45.

> Proposes that Stein, rather than being irrefutable in his judgments as some critics have understood him to be, is actually fallible and beset with doubts.

Wright, Walter F. "Triumph of Lord Jim." In his *Romance and Tragedy in Joseph Conrad,* pp. 107-23. Lincoln: University of Nebraska Press, 1949.

> Contends that Jim's "triumph" resides in having gained an understanding of himself and his existence.

Michael Field

INTRODUCTION

(Pseudonym of Katharine Harris Bradley [1846-1914] and Edith Emma Cooper [1862-1913]. Also wrote under the pseudonyms Arran and Isla Leigh.) British dramatists and poets.

As literary collaborators for more than thirty years, Bradley and her niece Cooper produced over twenty-five dramas and numerous poetry collections under the pseudonym Michael Field. Although initially championed by Robert Browning and other luminaries of English literary society during the late nineteenth century, their works were not as highly regarded in subsequent years. Drawing from Elizabethan forms and subjects, Symbolist techniques, Decadent imagery, and Roman Catholic theology, their plays and poetry are noted for their blending of classical and modern literary methods.

Bradley was born into a wealthy tobacco manufacturing family in Birmingham, England. At the age of sixteen she joined her sister's household to care for her three-year-old niece, Edith Cooper, when her sister was left an invalid following the birth of a second child. Bradley took responsibility for Cooper's education while periodically continuing her own studies at Newnham College, Cambridge, and the Collège de France in Paris. In 1875, under the pseudonym Arran Leigh, Bradley published *The New Minnesinger,* a collection of her poetry that won the praise of the eminent Victorian critic John Ruskin. In 1878 she moved with her sister's family to Bristol, where she and Cooper attended University College. There, the pair began composing verses together while participating in the women's suffrage and antivivisectionist movements.

After they left University College, the personal and literary relationship between Bradley and Cooper intensified. As Bradley wrote: "My love and I took hands and swore / Against the world, to be / poets and lovers evermore." They published their first collaborative effort, the poetry collection *Bellerophôn,* as Arran and Isla Leigh, but, dismayed by reviews that presumed them to be a married couple, chose to publish their ensuing works under the single name Michael Field. *Callirrhoë,* their first drama, earned widespread praise and drew the attention of Robert Browning, who hailed Michael Field as an important new talent. When Browning discovered the actual identity of the authors, Bradley implored him not to divulge their secret, arguing in a letter that "we have many things to say that the world will not tolerate from women's lips. We must be free as dramatists to work out in the open air of nature—exposed to her vicissitudes, witnessing her terrors: we cannot be stifled in drawing-room conventionalities." Eventually, their identities were revealed, however, and the accolades that had initially greeted their work soon subsided. The increasingly unsympathetic perception

of the pair's work was exemplified by the negative reaction to *A Question of Memory,* the only Michael Field drama produced for the public, which closed after one performance in 1893. Bradley and Cooper gradually withdrew from the London literary scene, yet continued to write under their male pseudonym, often composing separate sections of a poem or drama in virtually indistinguishable styles. Toward the end of their lives they converted to Roman Catholicism and their religious fervor dominates their last poems. When Cooper subsequently developed cancer, Bradley nursed her until she died at the age of fifty-one. Less than a year later, Bradley also succumbed to cancer.

Written in the style of Elizabethan verse drama, the plays of Bradley and Cooper are generally based either on classical or European history. For example, *Attila, My Attila* revolves around a willful Roman woman who fantasizes that the conquering Hun will rescue her from her abusive family, while *The Tragic Mary* centers upon Mary Stuart, the cousin and political rival of Queen Elizabeth I. Although most critics have varied little from early estimations of these and other plays as pretentious or dull, some have commended Bradley and Cooper for their subtle dramatic treatment of feminist concerns as well as for their incorporation of Symbolist themes and techniques.

The poetry of Bradley and Cooper has elicited a more favorable critical response than their dramas. *Long Ago,* generally considered their finest work, is a volume of poetry that celebrates female sexuality and lesbian love and is based on the lyrics of Sappho. The pursuit of beauty, a theme that recurs throughout their verse, dominates the poems of *Sight and Song,* a volume that uses famous paintings as its subject matter. The verses of other collections, including *Underneath the Bough* and *Wild Honey from Various Thyme,* have been compared to those of Oscar Wilde and George Moore in their sensuality and rhythmic structure. Their final volumes, *Poems of Adoration* and *Mystic Trees,* are admired for their use of Decadent imagery and thought to express religious themes.

Several critics have attributed the obscurity of Bradley and Cooper to the limited appeal of works produced by writers isolated by their exclusive relationship and by their devotion to art at the expense of accessibility. David J. Moriarity has observed that "in retreating to [their own world] . . . they allowed it to become a Palace of Art and, like Tennyson's 'Lady of Shalott' and the captive women in their own dramas, in seeking to express in their art the experience of life denied to so many women, they became prisoners of their art. Confusing their dramas with the experience of life, their art became their life." Other commentators regard Bradley and Cooper as authors who admirably eschewed societal conventions to pursue their own artistic vision, however narrow. Referring to the two women as one, their biographer Mary Sturgeon commented that "her sanity is evident in the moderation with which she held her feminist sympathies, despite the clamour of the time and the provocation she received from masculine mishandling of her work. Herein too she had removed her self from 'Time's harsh drill,' having too great a reverence for her art to use it for the purposes of propaganda. . . . [She] fulfilled completely her own conception of the poet—as an artist withdrawn from the common struggle to wrestle with a fiercer power, and subdue it to a shape of recognizable beauty."

*PRINCIPAL WORKS

†*The New Minnesinger* [as Arran Leigh] (poetry) 1875
Bellerophôn [as Arran and Isla Leigh] (poetry) 1881
Callirrhoë, and Fair Rosamund (dramas) 1884
The Father's Tragedy, William Rufus, and Loyalty or Love (dramas) 1885
Brutus Ultor (drama) 1886
Canute the Great, and The Cup of Water (dramas) 1887
Long Ago (poetry) 1889
The Tragic Mary (drama) 1890

Sight and Song (poetry) 1892
Stephania (drama) 1892
A Question of Memory (drama) 1893
Underneath the Bough (poetry) 1893; revised editions, 1893 and 1898
Attila, My Attila (drama) 1896
Wild Honey from Various Thyme (poetry) 1908
Poems of Adoration (poetry) 1912
Mystic Trees (poetry) 1913
Dedicated (poetry) 1914
In the Name of Time (drama) 1919
The Wattlefold: Unpublished Poems by Michael Field (poetry) 1933
Works and Days: Extracts from the Journal of Michael Field (journal) 1933

*All works published under the pseudonym Michael Field unless otherwise noted. Drama dates indicate first publication date.

†Published by Bradley alone.

William Butler Yeats (essay date 1892)

[*The leading figure of the Irish Renaissance and a major poet of the twentieth century, Yeats was also an active critic of his contemporaries' works. As a critic he judged the works of others according to his own poetic values of sincerity, passion, and vital imagination. In the following essay, he admires the craft and detailed observation displayed in* Sight and Song, *though he ultimately characterizes the work as an uninspired guide to the art museums of Europe.*]

This interesting, suggestive, and thoroughly unsatisfactory book [*Sight and Song*] is a new instance of the growing tendency to make the critical faculty do the work of the creative. "The aim of this little volume is, as far as may be," says the preface, "to translate into verse what the lines and colours of certain chosen pictures sing in themselves; to express not so much what these pictures are to the poet, but rather what poetry they objectively incarnate." That is to say, the two ladies who hide themselves behind the pen-name of Michael Field have set to work to observe and interpret a number of pictures, instead of singing out of their own hearts and setting to music their own souls. They have poetic feeling and imagination in abundance, and yet they have preferred to work with the studious and interpretive side of the mind and write a guide-book to the picture galleries of Europe, instead of giving us a book full of the emotions and fancies which must be crowding in upon their minds perpetually. They seem to have thought it incumbent upon them to do something serious, something worthy of an age of text-books, something that would have uniformity and deliberate intention, and be in no wise given over to that unprincipled daughter of whim and desire whom we call imagination.

We open the book at a venture, and come to a poem on Benozzo Gozzoli's "Treading the Press."

From the trellis hang the grapes

Purple deep;
Maidens with white, curving napes
And coiled hair backward leap,
As they catch the fruit, mid laughter,
Cut from every silvan rafter.

Baskets, over-filled with fruit,
From their heads
Down into the press they shoot
A white-clad peasant treads,
Firmly crimson circles smashing
Into must with his feet's thrashing.

Wild and rich the oozings pour
From the press;
Leaner grows the tangled store
Of vintage, ever less:
Wine that kindles and entrances
Thus is made by one who dances.

The last couplet has some faint shadow of poetry, perhaps, but as for the rest—well, it is neither more nor less than "The Spanish Gypsey" again. It is impossible not to respect it, impossible not to admire the careful massing of detail, but no man will ever feel his eyes suffuse with tears or his heart leap with joy when he reads it. There are scores of other verses in the book which are as like it as one pea is to another. None of them have any sustained music, for music is the garment of emotion and passion, but all are well put together with carefully chosen rhymes, out of the way adjectives and phrases full of minute observation. Having looked in vain for anything conspicuously better or worse than the lines we have quoted, we open the book again at a venture, and find a poem on Cosimo Tura's "St. Jerome." We quote the first two stanzas:—

Saint Jerome kneels within the wilderness;
Along the cavern's sandy channels press
The flowings of deep water. On one knee,
On one foot he rests his weight—
A foot that rather seems to be
The clawed base of a pillar past all date
Than prop of flesh and bone;
About his sallow, osseous frame
A cinder-coloured cloak is thrown
For ample emblem of his shame.

Grey are the hollowed rocks, grey is his head
And grey his beard, formal and as dread
As some Assyrian's on a monument,
From the chin is sloping down.
O'er his tonsure heaven has bent
A solid disc of unillumined brown;
His scarlet hat is flung
Low on the pebbles by a shoot
Of tiny nightshade that among
The pebbles has maintained a root.

These stanzas do not contain a single commonplace simile or trite adjective, the authors even prefer "osseous" to "bony" in their search for the unexpected. There is intellectual agility in every sentence, and yet of what account are these verses, or any number like them? What new thing do they bring into the world? They are simply unmitigated guide-book.

One regrets the faults of this book the more because they are faults which have for some time been growing on "Mi-

chael Field." *Callirrhoë* had imagination and fancy in plenty, and we hoped its authors would in time get more music and less crudity and at last create a poem of genius. A few years later **Brutus Ultor** came and almost crowned our hopes, but now we have watched and waited for a long time in vain. **Sight and Song,** following as it does **The Tragic Mary,** is enough to make us turn our eyes for ever from the "false dawn" we believed to be the coming day. (pp. 116-17)

> *William Butler Yeats, "Sight and Song," in* The Bookman, *London, Vol. II, No. 10, July, 1892, pp. 116-17.*

The Athenaeum   (essay date 1893)

[*In the following excerpt,* Underneath the Bough *is praised as a welcome compilation of Bradley and Cooper's lyrics that represents the characteristic elements of their craft.*]

Although many of the lyrics in **Underneath the Bough** have long been well known in Michael Field's plays, they are welcome thus reprinted; for the bringing them together in one volume, and together with other lyrics not from the plays, besides making a convenient collection of goodly verse, presents the reader with a compact yet varied view of Michael Field's lyrical impulses and combinations. The intellectual strength and originality—the acquired mannerism—the rich condensed expression—the fine intensity, planned and dominatingly present, yet skilfully kept half concealed—the splendid control of metre, coupled with the inability, or more probably the want of wish, to fascinate by the melody of balanced cadences and with the preference for the grace of quaint and skilful mingled stiffness—are, while always recognizable in any of Michael Field's songs and brief separate lyrics, brought into still stronger prominence as essential characteristics by the close kindred resemblance apparent when these poems are grouped together.

The beauty of thought and phrase in the contents of **Underneath the Bough** is great. So is the beauty of their themes. The two great thoughts, Death and Love—with Sorrow for the inner name of both—are in fact almost the sole inspirations of the whole, but there is no monotony. Michael Field is too masterly to harp on recurrent ideas and jade sentiment to triteness, and the inspirational thoughts pass into new themes, themes with each a varied aspect, if with the same core of life. And while on a first quick perusal one receives the impression of unity— almost as if the poems were irregular stanzas of one work—afterwards, try to find any two poems to pair together as written from exactly the same point of view and you fail. Or if there be an exception to this, it is in the songs of the Third Book—where a supremely sympathetic affection repeats itself in poems which in other respects are diversified. It is in the conceptions of death that shades of difference are most frequent and most marked. In one poem we have death as a kindly annihilation. . . . (pp. 345-46)

In another poem the feeling is of death as a freedom and

an expansion of soul:—. . . . Then here is a tender fancy of death's life—almost like a spiritual allegory:—

> Dream not no darkness bars
> Her world, who in the stars
> Had such delight
> That jealously she turned to slumber;
> Her eyelids now sleep doth not cumber,
> And she, awake all night,
> Helps God to number
> The shining stars.

And still in poem after poem death will be found appearing somewhat other than before—the treatment modified by the immediate theme. Love is set forth in sundry ways—sometimes in conceits, sometimes in utterances of grave poetic earnestness, as adoration, as reproach, as reminiscence—but almost always it is connected in some way with death, and always it is very near sadness or pain.

A peculiarity of these poems is that while they are of antique mould, ancestral not merely in form but in expression, they are in feeling distinctively modern. There may fitly be applied to them their author's words in **"An Invitation,"**

> all the songs I sing
> Welling, welling
> From Elizabethan spring:

but their waters have gathered in the breath of to-day. The sad heart of the nineteenth century speaks through this later Elizabethan. They were cheerier mortals in the era of the Elizabethan race of poets than we are now. They had perils and calamities from which we are exempt; rebellions, plots and rumours of plots, with their consequences of headings and hangings and imprisonments and confiscations—not to speak of religious persecutions and of other rough risks, legal and illegal—would bring sudden storms of misery into many a home, and kept everybody familiar with the thought of the direst tragedies as among the ills incident to human life: but they had more content with life than we have. They took their joys and sorrows separately; they knew the one kind from the other—which we scarcely do—and they understood their sorrow for the downright thing it was, and they were not wistful in their joy. Most likely it was because they lived face to face with troubles of so frankly unmitigated a kind and the contrasts between their fair-weather and their foul-weather experiences were so strenuously marked, they were less unsatisfied and questioning, less burdened by a sense of the pathos of mortal existence, than we who have fallen on stiller days: it is not a tussling period that trains to brooding and lassitude, it is a drifting one. But without searching into the causes of the difference, certain it is that a spiritual, deprecating melancholy, not found in sixteenth and seventeenth century literature, has a deep and pervading influence in the thought, and especially in the poetical thought, of our time. And by this quality Michael Field, however markedly and ably of the school of the more ancient period, is unmistakably dated nineteenth century.

There is a portrait in the Third Book which, besides being of most gracious workmanship, is notably interesting for its statement of a strange poetic unison of two. This is it:—

> A girl,
> Her soul a deep-wave pearl
> Dim, lucent of all lovely mysteries;
> A face flowered for heart's ease,
> A brow's grace soft as seas
> Seen through faint forest trees:
> A mouth, the lips apart,
> Like aspen-leaflets trembling in the breeze
> From her tempestuous heart.
> Such: and our souls so knit,
> I leave a page half-writ—
> The work begun
> Will be to heaven's conception done,
> If she come to it.

The concluding lines, those which describe the dear fulfilment of the older life in the young, are psychologically as well as in expression very beautiful and wise; but to most readers the peculiar interest of the stanza will lie in the suggestion of the two lives, not twin, but with one heart. (p. 346)

> *A review of "Underneath the Bough: A Book of Verses," in* The Athenaeum, *No. 3437, September 9, 1893, pp. 345-47.*

Harold Williams   (essay date 1918)

[*In the following excerpt, Williams provides an overview of the poetry and plays of Bradley and Cooper.*]

Restraint and chiselled beauty of form mark the poems of Miss Bradley and Miss Cooper, who wrote under the pseudonym, Michael Field. A large part of their writing is literary drama in verse. Several of the plays deal with English and Scotch history. *The Father's Tragedy* (1885) is founded upon the story of David, Earl of Rothesay, *The Tragic Mary* (1890) upon the life of Mary, Queen of Scots: and *Fair Rosamund* (1884), *William Rufus* (1886) and *Canute the Great* (1887) are other historical plays written in imitation of the Elizabethans. *Callirrhoë* (1884) and *Brutus Ultor* (1887) have classical themes, but are scarcely classical in feeling. None of these is arresting: they hardly rise above the interest of all fine literary experiment. The supremely beautiful lyrical genius of Michael Field is best seen in shorter poems, and first in the consummate success of *Long Ago* (1889), which attempts the hazardous task of extending the fragments of Sappho. These are each poems of crystalline clearness, of exquisite beauty in form and music. Not less perfect are the nature poems and love-lyrics, nearly all of them very short, of *Underneath the Bough* (1893). These are songs as ethereal in sound as the iridescent colours of sunlight falling upon the glittering spray of the cascade, like snatches of melody heard faintly in the distance. Slight in content as they are, in crystalline purity scarcely any writing of the last three decades will compare with these poems. The influence of Herrick and the Caroline poets is hardly to be overlooked, but the element of imitativeness does not detract from the beauty of the whole.

The poems of *Sight and Song* (1892), an attempt in an exceedingly artificial mode, betray the effort of trying to say something where nothing useful is to be said; and these lyrics, which seek to translate into words the line and colour of some of the world's great pictures, are often laboured, although several, like **"The Birth of Venus,"** in which the picture is of little account save as a suggestion, are among the most beautiful of Michael Field's poems. These three early volumes, printed in limited editions, contain more that is supremely beautiful than any other of Michael Field's books. *Wild Honey* (1908) loses something of the ethereal and indefinable grace of the early lyrics, and *Poems of Adoration* (1912) suffers from the unavoidable limitations of all religious verse. The theme is written up to and upon; it does not spring unsought.

There is little contact with the actualities of everyday life in Michael Field's lyrics and shorter poems. Art, literature, nature and love seen through the haze of literary culture, these are the writers' sources of inspiration. But the gem-like finish and perfection, the harmony of style and thought, the simple directness of these poems lends them a unique beauty. And, if the stress of life is not felt, these brief lyrics are far from empty of matter; if they do not bear the impress of thought and great emotion, they generally express something that was worthy the singing, and always the expression is finely and delicately wrought. No analogy so readily springs to the mind in describing these poems as the image of the clear crystal with sunlight falling upon it. Michael Field marks no tendency. These volumes inherit from the Elizabethan and Caroline poets, they are shaped by a life of seclusion and culture and by the love of all that is best in the world's art. There is here no great writing; but within their own limits Michael Field's lyrics almost reach perfection. (pp. 145-47)

Harold Williams, "The Poetesses," in his Modern English Writers: Being a Study of Imaginative Literature, 1890-1914, *Sidgwick & Jackson, Limited, 1918, pp. 141-51.*

Mary Sturgeon   (essay date 1922)

[*In the following excerpt from her biography of Michael Field, Sturgeon traces the progression of Bradley and Cooper's lyric poetry while referring to the two collaborators by their nicknames for one another—"Michael" for Bradley and "Henry" for Cooper.*]

The lyrical poetry of Michael Field is much smaller in bulk than her dramatic work; yet there are eight volumes of it. On the other hand, it is more perfect in its kind than her tragedies, and yet its chiselled, small perfection cannot approach their grandeur. (p. 65)

Considering the lyrical work as a whole, it is seen to cover Michael Field's poetical career from beginning to end. Not that the lyric impulse was constant (for there were times when the poets' dramatic work absorbed them almost completely); but it never entirely failed. It was, as one would expect, strongest in their early years: it recurred intermittently through the period of the later tragedies, and returned in force when, toward the end of their life, tragic inspiration gave place to religious ardour. Thus, although this poetry is subjective in a less degree than lyrical verse often is, most of the crucial events of the poets' lives are reflected there. The lover of a story will not be disappointed, and the student of character will find enough for his

purpose in personal revelation both conscious and unconscious. Moreover, a spiritual autobiography might, with a little patience, be outlined from these eight volumes; and it would be a significant document, illuminating much more than the lives of two maiden ladies in the second half of the nineteenth century.

Such a spiritual history would be complete, in extent at least, for it would begin with Michael's earliest work in *The New Minnesinger* (that title at once suggesting the German influence in English life and letters at the moment, 1875), with its strenuous ethic of Unitarian tendency based on a creed so wide as to have no perceptible boundary; and it would end only with the devotional poetry of her last written volumes where, with no concern for ethics as such, the poet stands at the gate of the well-fenced garden of the Roman Church with a flaming sword in her hand and a face of impassioned tenderness. But in the interval it would pass through her pagan phase, when she revelled in joyful living—and in the classics, turning their myths into pleasant narrative verse; when in *Long Ago* (1889) she daringly rehandled the Sapphic themes; and when in *Sight and Song* (1892) she tried to convey her intense delight in colour and form by translating into poetry some of the old master-pictures that she loved. More important, however, than those books are in such an autobiography is the human record of joys and loves and sorrows contained in the volume called *Underneath the Bough* (1893); while *Wild Honey* (1908), a collection covering about ten years of her life, brings us down to the epoch of religious crisis and reconciliation with the Church of Rome. Then, with tragic inspiration quelled by Christian hope and submission, all her creative energy flowed into the Catholic lyrics contained in *Poems of Adoration* (1912) and *Mystic Trees* (1913).

One does not pause long on *The New Minnesinger* in this survey of the lyrics, because it was published by Katharine Bradley as Arran Leigh, and is not, therefore, strictly a work of Michael Field. Nor shall we deal with the lyrics in *Bellerophôn,* a volume published by the two poets as Arran and Isla Leigh in 1881. Not that either book is unworthy of study; on the contrary, there are some fine pieces in both. But the poets having elected to leave them in limbo, where one has had to grope for this mere reference to them, there, for my part, they shall remain. Except to note in passing that, following Swift's *Advice to a Young Poet* to "make use of a quaint motto," the poet has inscribed on the front of *The New Minnesinger* the phrase "Think of Womanhood, and thou to be a woman." That has a significance which is elaborated in the name-piece, whose theme is of love and of the woman-poet's special aptitude to sing about it; and where it is insisted that the singer shall be faithful to her own feminine nature and experience. All through the work of the two poets it will be seen that the principle stated thus early and definitely by the elder one ruled their artistic practice; so that we are justified in extracting this, at least, from Michael's earliest book, and noting it as a conscious motive from the beginning.

I think, too, we are entitled to recover from the shades one small song. For, after all, a great literary interest of the work of the Michael Fields is the amazing oneness of the two voices. The collaboration, indeed, deserves much more space than it is possible to give it here. But it is something to the good if we can glance, in passing, at undoubted examples of each poet's work, hoping to see hints of the individual qualities which each contributed to the fellowship. We have already told how, after Henry's death and when Michael knew that she too must soon die, she hastened to gather together certain early pieces by her fellow, and published them, with a poignant closing piece of her own, in the book called *Dedicated* (1914). That closing poem, "Fellowship," closed her artistic life: it is Michael's last word as a poet. But the point for the moment is that she has given us in *Dedicated* the means of recognizing Henry, and distinguishing between the two poets in their youthful work. One may take from *The New Minnesinger,* therefore, as characteristic of the younger Michael, such a piece as **"The Quiet Light:"**

> After the sunset,
> Before the night,
> There comes a season
> Of quiet light.
>
> After the dying,
> Before the death,
> There comes a drawing
> Of quiet breath.
>
> Hush of the daylight,
> O whisper why
> That childlike breathing
> Before we die!

That is a slight thing which does not, of course, represent Michael at anything like her full power; but it does already suggest the emotional basis of her gift, and her lyrical facility. The piece which follows, **"Jason,"** is a luckier choice for Henry, not only in that it gives her greater scope, but in that it is probably a maturer work than the other. The comparison would, therefore, be unfair to Michael if one were judging of relative merits; but we are thinking for the moment only of a difference in *kind* of poetic equipment. And the poem is given for this further fact—it was chosen by Michael herself to read to Father Vincent McNabb a few days before she died, in exultation at her fellow's genius:

> "Upon the sea-beach I diffuse my limbs;
> My wail athwart the harping sea-plain heaves;
> The shards are bitter and the ocean brims
> My sorrow from a fount where darkness grieves;
> I, Jason, by this vessel of my pride,
> Lie, as vain flotsam, 'neath its doughty side.
>
> A wife I had and children—she is gone
> To her own land—but first she waved my feet
> To where my sons, her wrath had fallen upon,
> Lay dead together 'neath their cradle sheet.
> A bride I had, but ere to bed she came,
> Ashes of flame she was, ashes of flame.
>
> And I had comrades in grand years of youth;
> They are all slain or care no more for deeds.
> A golden aim I followed to its truth;
> It is a story now no mortal heeds.
> Once I drove oxen of fire-shooting lips,
> Once I was ruler of a ship of ships." . . .

> The pebbles ground like teeth within a jaw;
> A moan of angry timber thundered forth;
> And the great poop of Argo rolled its maw,
> With a wave's action, from the south to north;
> Earth quaked in fear at glimpse of Jason's doom,
> As slant on him fell Argo as a tomb.

Clearly there are elements here different from those of "The Quiet Light." One feels in this poem a dramatic movement and a sense of tragedy which are not simply given in the data of the noble old story; one sees structural skill in the shaping of the narrative, and recognizes in a memorable line or two—"A golden aim I followed to its truth" and "Ashes of flame she was, ashes of flame"—the final concentration of thought and feeling where great poetry begins.

Perhaps we are not mistaken, therefore, in distinguishing, even so early as these two poems, the contrasting qualities of the two poets which, met in happy union, made so clear a single voice that Meredith was amazed when he discovered that Michael Field was two people. One may define these qualities as emotional on the one side and intellectual on the other. It is, of course, the old distinction between rhetoric and imagination, matter and form; and clearly shows itself again in the two volumes of devotional poetry at the end of their life, where Henry is seen as kin to Herbert and Michael as kin to Vaughan. And though the whole story of the collaboration cannot be contained within any statement so simple as that, its fundamentals are rooted in this complementary relation between the two minds.

Returning to the lyrics, I choose frankly the pieces which throw some light on the poets' lives. And although I do this from an unashamed interest in their story, and without immediate reference to the merits of the verse as poetry, there should be a chance that the poetical values of pieces wrought under the stress of intimate feeling will be not lower but higher than those of others. So, indeed, the event proves; for of the lyrics which may be safely attributed to Michael those are the best which can be called her love-poems. Of love-interest, in the attractive common meaning of the term, there is not a great deal in the work of either poet; and in that of Michael it is mainly comprised in half a dozen songs in *Underneath the Bough.* Sapphic affinities notwithstanding (and imaginary adventures in that region), the two ladies had their measure of Victorian reticence; though that did not decline upon Victorian prudishness. But Michael wrote love-poetry of another kind than the romantic, in a series about her fellow which is probably unique in literature. It will be found in the third book of *Underneath the Bough,* and is supplemented by pieces scattered through later books, notably a small group at the end of *Mystic Trees.* Those poems are a record of her devotion to Edith Cooper, and it is doubtful whether Laura or Beatrice or the Dark Lady had a tenderer wooing. They explain, of course, the slightness of a more usual (or, as some would put it, a more normal) love-interest in Michael's work. But it need not be supposed that there was anything abnormal in this devotion. On the contrary, it was the expression of her mother-instinct, the outflow of the natural feminine impulse to cherish and protect. And this she herself realized perfectly; for there is a passage in one of her letters to Miss Louie Ellis which runs:

> I speak as a mother; mothers of some sort we must all become. I have just been watching Henry stripping the garden of all its roses and then piling them in a bowl for me. . . .

But that Michael was 'normal' in the mere sense of having had love-affairs there is proof enough without recourse to the vulgarity of spying into every lyric for a record of actual experience. Her dramatic instinct would make that pitfall even more dangerous in her case than in most, so that one would not dare to venture in the direction at all without a warrant. But, armed with the poet's confession, one may quote from a tiny sequence which has an almost tropical breath. It tells of a passion that blossomed quickly in hot, bright colour, and died with sudden vehemence.

> Across a gaudy room
> I looked and saw his face,
> Beneath the sapless palm-trees, in the gloom
> Of the distressing place,
> Where everyone sat tired,
> Where talk itself grew stale,
> Where, as the day began to fail,
> No guest had just the power required
> To rise and go; I strove with my disgust:
> But at the sight of him my eyes were fired
> To give one glance, as though they must
> Be sociable with what they found of fair
> And free and simple in a chamber where
> Life was so base.
>
> As when a star is lit
> In the dull, evening sky,
> Another soon leaps out to answer it,
> Even so the bright reply
> Came sudden from his eyes,
> By all but me unseen.
> Since then the distance that between
> Our lives unalterably lies
> Is but a darkness, intimate and still,
> Which messages may traverse, where replies
> May sparkle from afar, until
> The night becomes a mystery made clear
> Between two souls forbidden to draw near:
> Creator, why?
>
> * * *
>
> We meet. I cannot look up; I hear
> He hopes that the rainy fog will clear:
> My cheeks flush him back a hope it may,
> And at last I seek his eyes.
> Oh, to greet such skies—
> The delicate, violet, thunder-gray,
> Behind a spirit at mortal play!
> Who cares that the fog should roll away?
>
> * * *
>
> As two fair vessels side by side,
> No bond had tied
> Our floating peace;
> We thought that it would never cease,
> But like swan-creatures we should always glide;
> *And this is love*
> We sighed.

> As two grim vessels side by side,
> Through wind and tide
> War grappled us,
> With bond as strong as death, and thus
> We drove on mortally allied:
> *And this is hate*
> We cried.
>
> * * *
>
> Go to the grave,
> Die, die—be dead!
> If a Judgment-Angel came and said
> That I could save
> My heart and brain, if I could but will
> For a single moment that you should die,
> I would clasp my hands, and wish you ill,
> And say good-bye.
>
> Go to the grave,
> Die, die—be dead!
> If the Judgment-Angel came and said
> That I could save
> My body and soul, if I could but will
> For as long as an hour that you should die,
> My hands would drop, and my eyes would fill,
> And the angel fly.

If we were concerned with the art of this verse rather than its tale one would be compelled to consider a touch of rhetoric and a violence of gesture which are characteristic of Michael not at her best; but which do correspond with the turbulent youthful emotion out of which the poems were born. Michael's authentic love-story, however, is that which centres upon Henry; and the poems to Henry express a master-passion. There was an element of her nature as strong and as constant as its poetic impulse, and that was her affection for her fellow. Indeed, she was greater as a lover than as a poet; for her life was her finest poem, and Henry was its inspiration. It follows that she was never so happy as when she was engaged upon this theme; and that the sequence I have mentioned is a joyful record of the fellowship. Here is a piece which describes the sealing of the bond between the poets in those early days when they had not yet embarked on their great quest:

> It was deep April, and the morn
> Shakspere was born;
> The world was on us, pressing sore;
> My love and I took hands and swore,
> Against the world, to be
> Poets and lovers evermore,
> To laugh and dream on Lethe's shore,
> To sing to Charon in his boat,
> Heartening the timid souls afloat;
> Of judgment never to take heed,
> But to those fast-locked souls to speed,
> Who never from Apollo fled,
> Who spent no hour among the dead;
> 　Continually
> With them to dwell,
> Indifferent to heaven or hell.

Next we may take a portrait of Henry in her girlhood when the two began to collaborate, this giving incidentally a description of what was, on the testimony of intimate friends (and, indeed, of the poets themselves), their method of work:

A girl,
Her soul a deep-wave pearl
Dim, lucent of all lovely mysteries;
A face flowered for heart's ease,
A brow's grace soft as seas
Seen thro' faint forest-trees:
A mouth, the lips apart,
Like aspen-leaflets trembling in the breeze
From her tempestuous heart.
Such: and our souls so knit,
I leave a page half-writ—
The work begun
Will be to heaven's conception done
If she come to it.

Exactly in that way the two would often cooperate, working together actually on one piece. When it was a question of a big work—of a tragedy or a chronicle-play—there was, of course, a united exploration of the ground and a mapping of it. The two poets would go together to the British Museum or some other great library for the research. The scheme was then fully discussed, ideas were exchanged, conceptions of character formed and tested, and scenes allotted to suit individual taste or aptitude. But the collaboration was even more intimate than that. They would readily interchange their parts; and frequently they would be engaged together upon a page, a speech, or even a single line. It is therefore no poetic licence which declares that the half-written sheet of one would be completed to perfection by the other, but only further proof of the way in which the diverse elements of these two minds were fused in a union so complete that the reader cannot credit a dual authorship, and the poets themselves could hardly distinguish their individual contributions.

There is among the poems to Henry a dainty mock-pastoral in praise of her beauty which might have been written by an Elizabethan songster to his mistress; and a sonnet called **"Constancy"** which speaks with graver passion. . . . (pp. 67-81)

There are pieces which reveal Henry, quieter perhaps, but deeply tender toward her fellow:

My lady hath a lovely rite:
When I am gone
No prayer she saith
As one in fear:
For orison,
Pressing her pillow white
With kisses, just the sacred number,
She turns to slumber;
Adding sometimes thereto a tear
And a quick breath.

There is a short poem in which Michael is thinking about the nature of Henry's genius, and perceives its tragic power as her peculiar gift. . . . And in another piece she compares and contrasts her own gift with that of Henry in imagery as brilliant as its criticism is just:

Mine is the eddying foam and the broken current,
Thine the serene-flowing tide, the unshattered rhythm.
Light touches me on the surface with glints of sunshine,
Dives in thy bosom disclosing a mystic river:

Ruffling, the wind takes the crest of my waves resurgent,
Stretches his pinions at poise on thy even ripples:
What is my song but the tumult of chafing forces,
What is thy silence, Beloved, but enchanted music!

It is evident that Michael knew herself and her impulsive and exuberant Muse, which, to quote one of the irreverent faithful among her friends, would sometimes merely "fizz" into expression. That it could be too facile, and was, by comparison with Henry's depth, superficial, is true. Michael had not the syllogistic mind of her fellow, and arrived at conclusions by an intuitive process rather than by reasoning. She was capable of unintelligent questions and occasional stupid moods that exasperated the critical type of mind which is so much cleverer than that. But she brought a positive contribution to the fellowship, nevertheless, in swift perception, intense ardour, keen sensibility, and above all in the generosity of temper that found its chief expression in devotion to her fellow-poet. Thus the most gracious of her love-lyrics is that in which, after having fostered the younger mind with infinite sympathy, making possible all that it became and achieved, she withdraws herself to cede the higher place to her lover:

Methinks my love to thee doth grow,
And this the sign:
I see the Spirit claim thee,
And do not blame thee,
Nor break intrusive on the Holy Ground
Where thou of God art found.

I watch the fire
Leap up, and do not bring
Fresh water from the spring
To keep it from up-flaming higher
Than my chilled hands require
For cherishing.

I see thy soul turn to her hidden grot,
And follow not;
Content thou shouldst prefer
To be with her,
The heavenly Muse, than ever find in me
Best company.

The love-story of Henry's life was not so frankly revealed; she was never so forthcoming as Michael. Nevertheless, there was such a story, and in outline it seems to have been one of the convergence of kindred minds, of friendship growing to passion, of love declared and reciprocated, but not fulfilled because of some other tie which bound both lover and beloved.

It is not difficult to see how such a crisis might arise in Henry's life. Delicate in health and shy of temperament, she was from her childhood sheltered by Michael, and surrounded by a love which she was accustomed to accept as simply as the air she breathed. Just so unconsciously she would receive the homage offered by their friends, drifting into a closer relation with one of them, both of the lovers cheated by the tranquil air which overlay her depth of feeling, until a sudden surprising passion overtook them. That the awakening for Henry meant renunciation sounds a little old-fashioned to a current philosophy which sees no virtue in the verb 'to renounce,' and demands fulfilment, not only as the highest good, but as the holiest duty of the human creature. But either that modern doctrine is not so new as it sounds, or these two ladies were in advance of their time, for they held it, and (at least in their art) persuasively commended it. They wrote a charming play, *The Cup of Water,* deliberately to claim the woman's right to love, and to demonstrate the cruelty and waste of frustration. And they once said, in a whimsical letter to a friend:

> Doing and being good is all very well in its way; but it is not the same thing as doing and being happy. If the Lord had a lion's mouth (like the one at Venice), how many complaints I should drop into it about his treatment of young women. All the plants have some sunshine: why not some love in each woman's life?

Nevertheless, when it came to the test of action, theory went to the winds, and Henry renounced her lover for her fellow. She held herself bound by every tie of tenderness and gratitude, and no other course was conceivable save to shut the gates of the fortress and bar them against that clamorous joy.

> Speak not, reveal not. . . . There will be
> In the unchallenged dark a mystery,
> And golden hair sprung rapid in a tomb.

Human instinct may rebel at the spectacle of life so baffled; and common sense, in its short way with problems, may deny a valid cause for the sacrifice. But a longer vision is compelled to observe that fulfilment was not, after all, withheld. It came on the spiritual plane, however; for it is safe to say that we owe the finest work of Michael Field to the fact that Henry did not marry her lover:

> Then let a mourner rise and three times call
> Upon our love, and the long echoes fall.

Before leaving the volume called *Underneath the Bough* it is convenient to take examples of lyrics in a different kind from those we have been considering. Thus we may select two or three pieces which an easy label would describe as nature-poems. There are not a great many which answer fully to that description, for although our poets adored the beauty of the physical world, their Muse was too prepossessed by the movement of human life to surrender itself completely to Nature. Yet by certain aspects of Nature they were deeply stirred—great spaces, lofty skies measured by masses of moving cloud, trees blown by the wind—in short, by just those features in which in old Italian painters people have agreed to see the signs of a religious sense. . . . (pp. 81-7)

The two pieces which follow are chosen because they illustrate the touch of fantasy which our poets often added to their nature-poetry—a touch which gives such grace and charm to the lyrics of their earlier plays.

> I will sing what happened to-night on high:
> In the frank, wide sky
> The wind had put the sun to rout,
> The tossed west clouds were floating about;
> From the wreath above me, staid and prim,
> A star looked out,
> Preparing to trim

> Her lamp, and to shine as she had shined
> Worlds out of mind:
> When lo! she felt the wind on her face,
> And for joy of him
> She left the place
> Where she had shined
> Worlds out of mind,
> To run through the frank, wide sky:
> She was veiled by the clouds a moment or two,
> Then I saw her scouring across the blue,
> For joy of the wind.

* * *

> Where winds abound,
> And fields are hilly,
> Shy daffadilly
> Looks down on the ground.
> Rose cones of larch
> Are just beginning;
> Though oaks are spinning
> No oak-leaves in March.
> Spring's at the core,
> The boughs are sappy:
> Good to be happy
> So long, long before!

The volume called *Long Ago* was published as early as 1889: that is to say, four years before *Underneath the Bough* and nineteen years before *Wild Honey.* It is, however, a more perfect work than either of those two, both of which include poems of very various date, circumstance, and merit. *Long Ago* possesses a unity which they lack, and which characterizes the spirit as well as the form of the book. The fact of its having been designed as a whole and wrought to a finish without any long interruption may account for its effect of singleness in impulse and style; but its more satisfying inner unity no doubt arises from the harmony that existed between the poets and their theme, Sappho. Critics notwithstanding, it was not so audacious as it seemed for two Victorian ladies to plunge into the task of rendering Sapphic ecstasy. For, first, the leader of the sally was herself a flame of Dionysiac fire; and the inscription on the banner of her life, from its beginning to its end, was love. There would appear to be a real resemblance between Michael's intensity, her exuberance and quick lyrical impulse, and the legendary Sappho. And this, restrained by Henry's sense of form and deepened by their classical lore in poetry and philosophy, should surely have armed them for the adventure.

There is an ironic flavour now in tasting the comments on the book at its appearance. One of the faithful held up protesting hands at the poets' audacity. Another described the book as a "ludicrous and lamentable attempt." Yet Browning praised it, and marked some of the pieces in the manuscript "Good" and "Good indeed!" Meredith wrote to the poets to express his joy in it. The *Academy* reviewer, in June 1889, predicted that it would some day be described as "one of the most exquisite lyrical productions of the latter half of the nineteenth century"; while Wharton, in the preface to the third edition of his *Sappho,* speaks of the "felicitous paraphrases of Michael Field," and quotes from four of them. The contrast between the two opinions is as amusing as such things are apt to be to those who are not the subject of them; but Michael Field did not see the joke (perhaps her sense of humour *was* deficient), and the severer judgments pained her. They were probably based on an assumption that the poets were trying to recreate Sappho, a project which might have justified brickbats if it had ever been entertained. But their aim was simply to make short dramatic lyrics out of the scenes suggested to their imagination by the Sapphic fragments. The verdict of those most competent to judge the book is, on balance, that they succeeded remarkably well; while as to the average reader, he will surely find something most attractive in the flashing moods of the verse, in its grace and finish, and in its complete harmony. Truly pagan the work is, whether in its sunny aspects or its dark ones, whether in its philosophy or its art. The pursuit of joy, the adoration of beauty, the ecstasy and the pain of love, the gay light and colour of the physical world, its sweet scents and sounds, its lovely shapes and delicate textures, are all here, their brilliance but the brighter for the shadow that flits about them of death and its finality. (pp. 87-91)

To pass immediately from *Long Ago* to the poets' last lyrical works may seem a wilful act, considering the length of time between the books, and their amazing unlikeness. Yet there is a very great interest in the contrast and all that it implies, and a piquancy which one may hope is not too irreverent in the reflection that at the root there is no great difference, after all, between the Lesbian songs and the Christian ones.

The volume called *Poems of Adoration* was published in 1912, and *Mystic Trees* in 1913. They were both signed Michael Field, but the first is all Henry's work with the exception of two pieces, and the second is all by Michael except the poems called **"Qui Renovat Fuventutem Meam"** and **"The Homage of Death."** The two volumes therefore provide material for a useful study from the point of view of the collaboration; and they are a positive lure to a comparison with the devotional poetry of the seventeenth century, notably, of course, with Herbert and Vaughan. One would not go so far as to claim an absolute likeness between Henry and George Herbert, if only because Henry does not spread herself in tedious moralizing nor indulge in *concetti*. To that extent her work is purer poetry and, one would suppose, purer religion than that of the old poet; and she rises oftener to sublimity. But in essentials the two are close akin—in sweetness and strength and clarity, in their sense of form, and in terse, vigorous expression. Between Michael and Vaughan the likeness is even closer, and would tempt one far if it were not that our limits prevent straying. But indeed the human and spiritual values of the two books transcend mere literary questions so greatly as to make those look trivial and even impertinent.

For *Poems of Adoration* was published only a few months before Henry died. Much of the book was composed at dead of night, during great pain, when, as her father confessor has remarked, "most of us would be trying not to blaspheme." The poems are in fact those of a dying woman, and one who had refused herself any alleviating drug. Two of them, **"Extreme Unction"** and **"After Anointing,"** were written when she was at the point of death and had received the last offices of the Church.

Some bear evidence of acute crises of body or soul; and in some the vision of the mysteries of her faith is so vivid that the poet herself is almost overwhelmed. Once or twice, when she has gone to the limit of spiritual sight, she falters; but never does that fine intelligence stumble into the outer darkness. Perceiving that it is coming near the verge of sanity, it draws back in time to leave the vision distinct and credible.

To the strict eye of criticism these poignant facts may appear irrelevant. I cannot bring myself to think that such splendour of soul has no relation to the art that it produced; but those persons who insist on cleaving the two asunder may be reassured as to the technical accomplishment of this poetry. Often cast into something of the poets' earlier dramatic form, its music is sweet, its measures are rhythmical, and its language has force and clarity. It has a majesty which proclaims its origin, and one has no need to know the circumstances of its birth. Imagination rises, swift and daring, to heights which are sometimes sublime, as in [**"Desolation"**]. . . . Here the conception of Christ the wine-treader is treated with magnificent audacity of image and metaphor, while underneath runs a stream of thought which, though it makes great leaps now and then, pouring its strong current into cataract as it goes, yet bears its craft safely up and on. (pp. 94-7)

Mystic Trees, the last book which Michael gave to the world, is more strictly theological than Henry's. Always less the philosopher than her fellow, she took her conversion to Catholicism, in externals at least, more strenuously. She developed, for example, a proselytizing habit which a little tried the patience of her friends, especially those who remembered her as a joyful pagan. That her Christian zeal was as joyful, to her, as her paganism had been did not much console them, or soften the onslaught of her blithe attacks. (p. 101)

[That] over-zeal had a significance for her artistic life too. She wrote in a letter to another friend, "I will pray for Orzie's conversion: *O Louie, be religious! You cannot 'laugh deep' unless you are.*" In the phrase I have italicized Michael is surely confessing, though it may be without intent to do so, that her religion is now awaking in her the same ecstasy which had formerly been awakened by the poetic impulse. To herself it seemed that she had suffered an enormous change, and that she was no longer the old Michael. And it is true that for a time the tragic inspiration of her art was suspended. Perhaps that follows of necessity from the nature of the Christian doctrine, its hope, its humility, its vicariousness, and its consolation. Yet the moment one turns to these religious lyrics one finds the same ecstasy with which the earlier Michael had adored the beauty of the world and had sung the love of Sappho. So, too, in the first work which Michael Field had produced, *Callirrhoë,* the theme is none other than the worship of the god by love and sacrifice. That, in fact, is the meaning implied in nearly all her poetry, as it was the motive force of all her life; and the only change that has occurred when we reach, with *Mystic Trees,* the end, is that the name of the god is altered. But whichever god possessed her had the power to make Michael "laugh deep" in a rapture which, whether of delight or rage or sorrow, was always an intense spiritual joy—which is simply to say, to evoke the poet in her. The exaltation of spirit which in *Callirrhoë* said of Dionysos "He came to bring Life, more abundant life," and declared "Wert thou lute to love, There were a new song of the heaven and earth," is the same as that which wrote to a friend in early days, "We are with the nun in her cell as with the pagan at the Dionysos' feast"; and which affirmed in a letter to another friend that she welcomed inspiration from whatever source, "whether the wind and fire sweep down on us from the mighty realms of the unconscious or from the nostrils of a living God, Jehovah, or Apollo, or Dionysos."

But, as we said, to herself she seemed a new creature; she had found a treasure and must run to share it, even as she had burned to impart the Bacchic fire thirty years before. Thence came the scheme of *Mystic Trees,* which, as Father Vincent McNabb suggested to me, seems to be unique in religious poetry. The book contains a cycle of poems, designed to express the mysteries of the Roman Catholic faith as they are celebrated in the seasons of the Church. The "Trees" of the title are the Cedar and the Hyssop, used as an image of the Incarnation: the great Cedar, the Son of God, becoming the little Hyssop, which, in the lovely cover-design by Mr Charles Ricketts, stands on either side of the Cross with bowed head.

The book is divided into three parts, with a small group of poems added at the end, which Michael wrote while Henry was dying. In the first part, called "Hyssop," the story of the Redemption is unfolded in a series of poems representing the life and death of Christ. (pp. 102-04)

We may take from the second part of the book, called "Cedar" and dedicated to the Virgin, two short pieces which help to illustrate the sweetness of this poetry, its tenderness, its intimacy of approach to divine things, and its innocence.

CALLED EARLY

It is a morning very bright;
Through all the hours of the long starry night
Mary hath not been sleeping: for delight
She hath kept watch through the starry night.

Joseph comes to her quietly:
"A journey I must take with thee,
Mary, my wife, from Galilee."
He saw that she had wept,
And all her secret kept.

UNDER THE STAR

Mary is weary and heavy-laden
As a travailing woman may be.
She calleth to Joseph wearily,
"At the inn there is no room for me,
Oh, seek me a little room!"

Joseph returns. "In a cattle-shed
Hard by, I will make for thee thy bed—
Dost fear to go?
O Mary, look, that star overhead!"
And Mary smiled—"Where the cattle low
My Son shall be loosed from the womb."

From the third part, which is called "Sward" and there-

fore is obviously dedicated to ordinary folk, we need take only the little poem which follows. But we ought to remember the occasion of it, that Michael had been compelled to go alone to Mass because Henry was too ill to accompany her.

Lovingly I turn me down
From this church, St Philip's crown,
To the leafy street where dwell
The good folk of Arundel.

Lovingly I look between
Roof and roof, to meadows green,
To the cattle by the wall,
To the place where sea-birds call,

Where the sky more closely dips,
And, perchance, there may be ships:
God have pity on us all!

Michael said, in a letter to a friend, "*Mystic Trees* is for the young"; and one perceives the truth of that. But I do not think that her word 'young' means only 'youthful,' although children would probably understand the poems readily, and a certain kind of child would delight in them. Nor do I think that they were written with any special audience in mind. But the poet, in reading them afterward, recognized their childlike qualities of simplicity and directness, and their young faith and enthusiasm. Did she realize, one asks oneself, how she had in them recaptured her own youth and its lyrical fervour? She was nearly seventy years old when she wrote them, which is a wonder comparable to Mr Hardy's spring-songs in winter. And though we may accept, if we like, the dubious dictum of the psycho-analyst that every poet is a case of arrested development, that does not make any less the marvel that in old age, after the lyric fire had subsided and the sufferings of her fellow had destroyed the joy of her life, she should have written such poems. For here it is certainly relevant to remember that at this time Henry was dying, and that Michael herself was suffering, silently, the torture of cancer. "Michael has a secret woe of her own," was all that she permitted herself to reveal, in a letter to her closest woman friend. But so stoical was her courage, and so composed her manner, that the hint was not taken, and no one guessed that she too was ravaged by the disease. Before her intimates, as before the world, she kept a cheerful face, in terror lest her fellow should come to know of her state. Her doctor knew, of course, and Father Vincent McNabb. But they were under a bond to spare Henry the added anguish of knowing the truth, and the bond was faithfully kept. Not until her fellow was dead, when Michael had, in fact, laid her in her coffin, did she break silence to the friend who was with her in that ordeal. Two days later a hæmorrhage made it impossible to conceal her condition any longer. "God kept her secret," said Father McNabb, "until the moment when it was no longer necessary"; and without disloyalty to the godhead of the heroic human spirit, we may accept that word from one who brought consolation and devoted friendship to the poets' last sad days.

It was, then, during the closing weeks of Henry's life, and while Michael was suffering that sorrow and great bodily pain, that she wrote *Mystic Trees.* Yet the poems manifestly bear within them a deep creative joy, and breathe sometimes a holy gaiety of spirit; and it is only at the end of the book, in a tiny section containing four short poems, that the poet allows her anguish of body and mind the relief of expression. For that brief space, so rightly named "A Little While," the inspiration to "laugh deep" failed, and stark tragedy overwhelmed her. (pp. 107-11)

> *Mary Sturgeon, in her* Michael Field, *George G. Harrap & Co. Ltd., 1922, 246 p.*

Arthur Symons   (essay date 1923)

[*An English critic, poet, dramatist, short story writer, and editor, Symons first gained notoriety as an English decadent during the 1890s before establishing himself as one of the most important critics of the early twentieth century. His* The Symbolist Movement in Literature *(1899) laid the foundation for much of modern poetic theory. Such celebrated authors as T. S. Eliot, Ezra Pound, and James Joyce benefited greatly from his remarkable gift for defining the elusive qualities of Symbolism and his timely articulation of the aims and techniques of its practitioners. However, a mental breakdown in 1908 adversely affected Symons's writing, and commentators agree that his later criticism lacks the originality and clarity of expression that distinguished his earlier work. In the following excerpt, Symons evaluates the works of Bradley and Cooper as he reacts to earlier critical commentary regarding their achievements.*]

Robert Browning, in his later period, suggests to the intellect, and to that only. Hence his difficulty, which is not a poetic difficulty; not a cunning simplification of method like Shakespeare's who gives us no long speeches of undiluted, undramatic poetry but poetry everywhere like life blood. Not only is he one of the greatest of our poets; he is also one of the most passionate, one of the most dramatic in imagination, and one of the most obscure; therefore, I rank him with John Donne, who stands out of our tradition, who are without ancestors. Nor have I forgotten my first and only meeting with Browning on the 23rd of August, 1889, the year in which he died; I still recall his violence of voice, it had the whole gamut of music in it, it thrilled one, it vibrated one, by certain touches of rare magic in it.

Baudelaire wrote:

> It would be a wholly new event in the history of the arts if a critic were to turn himself into a poet, a reversal of every psychic law, a monstrosity; on the other hand, all great poets become naturally, inevitably, critics. It would be prodigious for a critic to become a poet, and it is impossible for a poet not to contain a critic.

This is one of his sweeping statements; he, himself, was equally infallible as critic and as poet; but that is the case with very few French poets and very few English ones; Browning is no exception to this rule; he was easily carried away by his impulses and by his emotions. So it happened that in the spring of 1885, Browning, at a dinner given by Stopford Brooke, said suddenly: "I have found a new poet," to which several voices responded: "Michael Field."

In 1885 I reviewed their *Father's Tragedy* in *Time,* which I said that *Callirrhoë* proved them to be genuine poets; that this volume was full of the air and the feeling of the forest; that it gave one a sense of the vengeance of the outraged Earth. I made their acquaintance in 1889; I saw them at intervals for several years, at Reigate, at Richmond and in Paris. On the 12th of June, 1890, I took them with me to the Forest of Fontainebleau; we had an expensive lunch at the Restaurant de Franchard. In 1892, I pointed out to them the apparition, the vision, of Paul Verlaine, in Paris, as he came out of a shop on the other side of the road with a huge roll of French bread under his arm. I have never forgotten that vision of Verlaine nor the shop we often frequented, which is still to be seen at one corner of the rue Racine which gives on the Boulevard Saint Michel. In 1886 Katherine wrote to Havelock Ellis saying:

> **The Father's Tragedy,** save Emmeline's song and here and there a stray line, is indeed Edith's work; for the others, the work is perfect mosaic; we cross and interlace like a company of dancing summer flies, if one begins a character his companion seizes it and possesses it; if one conceives a scene or situation, the other corrects, completes.

In the American edition of **Underneath the Bough** I find this note, dated September 8th, 1898.

> For some years my work has been done for the younger generations—not yet knocking at the door, but awaited with welcome. Meanwhile, readers from further England—if they will pardon my so classing them—have given me that joy of listening denied to me in my own island; and to them I offer this book of lyrics, adding such new songs as I count my sweetest to those of "the Old World Series," some of which, I have reason to hope, have won places in their hearts.

Many of those lyrics were written by Katherine to Edith; some of them have outbursts of an almost uncontrollable passion, but for the most part they are tinged with rhetoric and with a violence which is somewhat unreal. (pp. 1584-85)

I do not understand why the writer of the life of Michael Field should have said: "It is doubtful whether Laura or Beatrice or the Dark Lady had a tenderer wooing" [Mary Sturgeon, *Michael Field*]. Verses such as these have the qualities which must soon perish. One sonnet of Shakespeare is as imperishable as one of his Tragedies; Death rendered Beatrice's apotheosis conceivable; and Dante may be said to have re-discovered the Platonic mystery, whereby love is an initiation into the secrets of the spiritual world. It was the initiations of sublime nature into the essence of pure impersonal enthusiasm; there was even too little alloy of earth in Dante's passion for Beatrice. Petrarch's love for Laura was of a different type; the unrest of earthly desire, forever thwarted, but recurring with imperious persistence, and the rebellion against the emotions the lover realized to be lawless, broke his peace. "There is," says John Addington Symonds, "an old Greek proverb that 'to desire the impossible is a malady of the soul.' With this malady in its most incurable form the poet was stricken." (p. 1586)

I cannot find one single lyric which is in any sense perfect in Michael Field's volumes of verses; only, here and there, in a few of the last lyrics written by Edith Cooper, there are startling effects, at once imaginative and pathetic.

Writing in Landor I quoted this sentence of Coleridge, which might almost be applied to the dramas of Michael Field. "What is it that Landor wants to make him a poet? His powers are certainly very considerable, but he seems to be totally deficient in that modifying faculty which compresses several units into one whole. The truth is, he does not possess an imagination in its highest form—that of stamping it *piu nell'uno.*" There is in their verse too careful a search after metaphor and elaborate speech, their method in dialogue is a logical method; the speeches are linked by a too definite and a too visible chain; they do not spring up out of those profound subconscious affinities, which in the work of the great dramatists, mimic Nature with all her own apparent irregularity.

Still, at their finest, there is in them something fierce, subtle, strange, singular—which can become sinister; there is nothing in them which is primitive or elemental, nothing which conveys a sense of that extreme and vehement and violent passion without which no actual tragedy can exist. They have some sense of style, some individuality of their own; they have no vision of great events, no enthralling emotion; but, in the younger one, a rare kind of spirituality which can become exquisite, morbid, intense. Do not look for construction, nor for that "infinite variety" which only great drama must possess; they have but little sense of complexities and of the enormous complexity of our hearts and our passions. There is nothing of that abnormality—they attempted it in the ***Borgia***—that ought violently to stir the senses and awaken our sensations out of their torpor; nothing that startles or suddenly arrests us. They rarely—there are certainly many exceptions—give one a thrill, the thrill of one whose imagination can make beat the hearts of multitudes; who can arouse in our nerves some lurking suspicion of what is hidden in the obscure corners of exasperated minds, who, as they shatter and piece together, after they have shattered it, the little mocking mirror of our existences, fling before our vision those petulent puppets who as they yearn for joys untasted and for desires unsatiated discount their days and accept so inexorably the precious pieces. (pp. 1587-88)

I fail to understand such praise as this "for the genius of Michael Field, uniting as it does the two principal elements of art, Dionysian and Apollian, is therefore, of its nature an illustration of Nietzsche's theory." It is the very acme of absurdity to have said of their sacrelegious attempt or attack on the unsurpassable genius of Sappho in a book named ***Long Ago*** that came out in 1889, that "the leader of the sally was herself a flame of Dionysian fire," and that there would appear to be "a real resemblance between Michael's intensity, her exuberance and quick lyrical impulse, and the legendary Sappho" [Mary Sturgeon, *Michael Field*]. (p. 1589)

What they actually did was to take a few lines from the Greek of Sappho; then to attempt to translate those lines; then to add variations on these themes of their own inventing. One of the most passionate and tragic fragments of Sappho I give in my own rendering:—

> The waning moon out of the sky has vanished,
> The seven Pleiades out of the heaven have gone.
> It is midnight, the hours drag at my heart, banished
> Is slumber from mine eyelids. I sleep alone.

Out of these four lines they made five stanzas of eight lines. This is the last stanza:—

> The moon is gone, yet he delays
> The stars are set, but Sappho stays
> And can it be that death,
> Jealous, be sped
> To suck from me my Phaon's balmy breath?
> I stifle on my heart the funeral moan:
> I do not weel the dead;
> *I lie alone.*

Compared with the Greek these, as well as the other lines are puffed out and enfeebled by alterations, they are colorless and bloodless.

Only two women who ever wrote verse had in them "a flame of Dionysiac fire"; Sappho and Sante Theresa; in both "a flaming heart" burned outward to escape the intolerable pain of its reclusion. (pp. 1589-90)

Again, it is out of the question to compare for one moment Emily Brontë with Michael Field, as in this sentence: "However fully one may recognize the truth that there is no sex in genius, I suppose we shall always be startled at the appearance of an Emily Brontë or a Michael Field." To begin with, the world was not in the least startled by the appearance of either of these; yet, in spite of this, Emily Brontë remains always a woman of unique genius: she is the only woman in whom there has been seen the paradox of passion without sensuousness; in whom passion was alive as flame is alive in the earth; there was in her a passionate great dark unconscious instinct as of primitive nature-worship. (pp. 1590-91)

Now, what shall be said in favor of the Michael Fields? Strangely gifted, had they the creative power of the born Dramatist? Had they any individual genius, any startling originality? Are their characters in any sense vitally alive? It seems to me certain that the younger one who wrote ***The Father's Tragedy*** (1885) assuredly had touches or flashes of genius. It is baneful and full of omens, it is literally the father's annihilation, from the fact that he has let his wild son, David Rothsay, die of starvation in prison. Because he was wanton, he was condemned to die in soul; because of his dishonorable marriage, to die in heart; for his undeserved punishment, to die in body; a triple death, threefold starvation. These prison scenes are terrible; they fill one with a sense of awe and of pity, for so fair a flower of youth to be so rudely plucked from its roots and so left to perish on the mere straw of one naked cell. She naturally gives one none of the unsurpassable agony and mental and physical degradation of Marlowe's *King Edward the Second;* as when he cries:

> Let this gift change thy mind, and save thy soul.

Know that I am a King: Oh, at that name
I feel a hell of grief. Where is my crown?
Gone, gone; and do I still remain alive?
But that grief keeps me waking, I should sleep;
For not these ten days have these eyelids closed.

Yet, in his agony, Rothsay can utter such lines as these:—

Death was a shadow—I myself am Death.
I fed and never knew it; now I starve.
Here is the skeleton I've seen in books!
I am naked now, and Death is not dead;
O, God! he lives in me—in me must die;
And I must watch him with these burning eyes
Like candles set aflare upon my corpse.

(pp. 1591-92)

Arthur Symons, "Michael Field," in The
Forum, *New York, Vol. LXIX, June, 1923, pp.
1584-92.*

Kenneth R. Ireland   (essay date 1977)

[*In the following excerpt, Ireland uses the poems of*
Sight and Song *to examine the relationship between
painting and poetry.*]

"What would the world be without such people as Matthew Arnold, Ruskin, and Michael Field?" This gallant
question by an aging Robert Browning was asked in the
company of Katharine Bradley (1846-1914) and Edith
Cooper (1862-1913), the two poets masked by the pseudonym of Michael Field. That the world has learned to live
without them scarcely needs proof, yet George Saints-
bury's dismissive verdict of "half machine-made verse
which usually comes late in great periods of poetry" [*The
Cambridge History of English Literature*] merits reappraisal, where one collection at least is concerned. In a
joint career of some forty years, between *The New Minnesinger* (1875) and *Dedicated* (1914), *Sight and Song*
(1892) falls chronologically at about the halfway mark
and spiritually into the most individual phase of their poetry. Like many of their contemporaries, they later became converts to Roman Catholicism, but their early enthusiasm is for the world of pagan Greece: fragments from
Sappho act as inspiration in *Long Ago* (1889), and vague,
Anacreontic echoes pervade *Underneath the Bough*
(1893). When *Sight and Song* appeared in 1892, however,
its models were not literary but pictorial, and the wider
implications of this work, affording as it does a "pure"
study of the interrelations between painting and poetry,
underlie this essay.

All thirty-one poems of *Sight and Song* bear titles which
allude to works of art, a subject especially popular since
the early nineteenth century. To derive a whole collection
of verse from this source, however, is rare, and raises important critical issues of general application. The issue of
a coherent structure is foremost, since the selection of
works by some twenty artists would otherwise have little
rationale and would merely represent a random assembly
of favorite paintings. The declared aim of objectivity also
invites discussion, as do questions of authorial intervention and interpretation, and of the ontology and value of
the picture-poem.

One obvious means of creating unity would have been to
select works from a single gallery or museum, as Rilke did
with the celebrated Unicorn Tapestries in his *Malte
Laurids Brigge* (1910). This strategy, however, cannot operate in *Sight and Song,* since no "natural" order exists in
works culled from many different galleries. Although the
first and last paintings in the book are in the Louvre, other
works from the same holding are scattered throughout in
no very clear arrangement. Movement from poem to poem
between the National Gallery, London, and the Venice
Accademia, between the Uffizi and the Dresden Staats-
galerie, seems at best haphazard, ruling out any methodical or geographical survey of European masterpieces.
Shifts in the ownership of paintings since 1892, moreover,
such as the dispersal of Lord Dudley's collection, would
have destroyed any geographical symmetry.

Having discounted the location of the paintings as one
possibility of poetic arrangement, we must look at the
works themselves. Less than one-quarter of the paintings
are hung in Italian galleries; the rest are housed north of
the Alps—despite Michael Field's attraction to the South,
Italy's boundless artistic wealth, and the provenance of
the paintings. With the single exception of the eighteenth-
century French master, Watteau, all of the artists are Italian, were active between 1450 and 1550, and represent the
Renaissance style. Jakob Burckhardt, Gottfried Semper,
and Walter Pater are among the nineteenth-century figures who revived an interest in the life and culture of this
period. Browning's own enthusiasm for Italian Renaissance themes undoubtedly communicated itself to Michael Field. But the absence of any contemporary, nineteenth-century art and a clear bias towards the Great Masters is insufficient to establish one specific period of painting as governing the structure of *Sight and Song.* Indeed,
the conceptual and stylistic differences between the Renaissance art of Florence and Venice, whose painters predominate in the collection, necessitate closer study.

Apart from two drawings by Leonardo and Sodoma, the
works are oil-paintings. They range in size from Watteau's
tiny *L'Indifférent,* which opens the set, to large canvases
by Tintoretto. Throughout, artist and poet alike stress the
value of significant detail and chromatic nuance; for instance, in the closing allusion to a cattleherd no larger
than the saint's thumbnail, in Cosimmio Tura's *Saint Jerome in the Desert,* sharpness of eye and realization of poetic potential are most apparent. Correggio and Botticelli
each inspire four poems, Watteau three, Giorgione, Leonardo, Tintoretto, and Bartolommeo Veneto, two apiece.
It might be noted, however, that Botticelli's *Spring* is
treated twice, as tableau and in close-up, and that paintings by the only non-Italian master represented open and
close the set. The refinements of color and touch in Watteau's *L'Embarquement pour Cythère* [sic] are transferred
to the poem, an appreciation of decorative values manifested again in the choice of Fiorenzo di Lorenzo's "*A
'Sant' Imagine,*" where aesthetic elements dominate a traditional scene. The overall tone is lyrical or elegiac—less
than a quarter of the paintings convey dramatic tension—
while the "scientific calligraphy" of Leonardo at one extreme and the somber piety of a *Pietà* by Crivelli at the
other mark the poles of the tonal register.

An examination of formal aspects of the poetry for principles of unity reveals that very few pieces employ fixed forms. Among several fourteen-line stanzas, only the anonymous **"Mettus Curtius"** and **"Saint Katharine of Alexandria"** (Veneto) approach the strict sonnet form, and even there different sestet rhymes occur in sonnets of irregular meters and enjambment. Two similar five-rhyme sonnets compose the second version of the Botticelli, **"The Figure of Venus in 'Spring',"** but the sestets of these differ, an imbalance of rhyme scheme matched, intriguingly enough, by an imbalance of parts in the first version of the same painting. By contrast, **"Saint Sebastian"** (Correggio) and **"The Blood of the Redeemer"** (Bellini) use harmonious combinations of rhyming couplets and triplets in stanzas of equal length. The Tintorettos are also evoked in couplets, but **"Marriage of Bacchus and Ariadne"** employs regular tetrameters throughout, while **"The Rescue"** exploits suspended rhyme and wide fluctuations of line length and stress. It is difficult, therefore, to perceive any overall structure in the outward characteristics of the verse, but it is clear that forms relate to thematic content.

The poems may be broadly classified into secular and sacred, the former dealing with human, allegorical, or mythological topics, the latter Biblical or hagiographical. Two-thirds of the collection belongs to the first group, and the secular paintings—Watteau's *L'Embarquement* and Giorgione's *Sleeping Venus,* principally—receive the lengthiest poetic treatment. Even so, the average number of lines for secular and sacred poems alike more than quadruples the total in the sonnet form preferred by most earlier practitioners of the picture-poem. Michael Field's expansive, flexible approach indicates that thematic fruitfulness rather than formal rigor is the criterion, and pictorial models like Timoteo Viti's *The Magdalen* or Crivelli's *A Pietà* demonstrate that scenic activity bears little relation to poetic extent. As the discussion of tonal register indicated, few violent events are depicted, Correggio's *The Faun's Punishment* and Tintoretto's *The Rescue* notwithstanding. Other paintings, *Mettus Curtius* or Tura's *Saint Jerome,* for instance, anticipate the climax of the action, but most of the paintings have static subject matter: portraits, Holy Family groups, figures meditating or sleeping, bound or dead. Temporality, the suspension or negation of time, rather than chronology, promises most in the search for structure. Venus' appearance, for example, in Correggio's *Venus, Mercury and Cupid* precedes her genesis four poems later in Botticelli's *The Birth of Venus,* and a similar chronological inconsistency obtains in placing Crivelli's *A Pietà* before Lorenzo di Credi's *The Virgin, Child and St. John.* Season and time of day are emphasized in nearly half the poems. The focus upon early months and hours, spring and summer, morning and noon corresponds with the predominant age of the figures on canvas: the age of youth.

Some thematic connections are less obvious: the allusion to "a toe / As light as Mercury's" in **"L'Indifférent"** (Watteau), is taken up by the title of the second poem, **"Venus, Mercury and Cupid"** (Correggio); pastoral mood joins **"A Fête Champêtre"** (Watteau) to **"A Shepherd-Boy"** (Giorgione), while the latter is associated with **"Saint Sebastian"** (Antonello da Messina) biographically

(the martyr once tended sheep). Technical links, such as shared chromatic values, exist in paintings by the Venetians, Giorgione and Bellini, and Apollo's staff in Perugino's *Apollo and Marsyas* is echoed in Christ's cross and a pagan standard in Bellini's *The Blood of the Redeemer.* Some links require extra-poetic insights for full effect. Tintoretto's *Marriage of Bacchus and Ariadne* forms part of a cycle, in the Ducal Palace at Venice, representing Concord, while Michael Field's **"Triumph of Bacchus and Ariadne"** interprets the theme on a non-pictorial level to express the beauty and happiness of youth. Benozzo Gozzoli's *Treading the Press (La Vendemmia di Noè),* the inspiration of another poem, is one of the frescoes at the Campo Santo in Pisa. These frescoes aroused the interest first of Keats and later of the Pre-Raphaelites, whose leader preceded Field in exploring crosscurrents of painting and poetry. A further literary analogue casts a different light upon the theme, however, when much later, in **"Desolation,"** the lonely bloody figure treading the grapes turns out to be Christ. Autobiographical material, finally, clarifies the links between some poems. One of the poetic partners seeks relief from fever by thinking of the figure in Antonello's *Saint Sebastian:* "his virile, reproachful face reared against the blue heavens—his eyes asking, "Why am I denied what I was made for?' " (**Works and Days**). A diary comment reveals the most significant feature of Giorgione's *Sleeping Venus,* which prompts one of the longest poems in the set: "that ideal sympathy between woman and the land, which nations have divined when they made their countries feminine" (**Works and Days**).

The element of the feminine, in fact, is manifest in Michael Field's choice of painters. Correggio and Perugino, Botticelli and Giorgione are preeminently the masters of grace and charm, poets of female beauty and dreamlike mood, by contrast with more exuberant and energetic "masculine" artists like Michelangelo and Titian. Most of the subjects in **Sight and Song** are female: among individual beauties are Gioconda, Antiope, Veneto's courtesan, Arsinoë, Procris, Leda, and Ariadne; the canvases of Watteau are peopled by elegant queens of society; Venus, the goddess of Love, presides in more than a quarter of the works. Even male characters, like Giorgione's *A Shepherd-Boy,* Watteau's *L'Indifférent,* and the ubiquitous Cupid exude a feminine softness and delicacy. Natural beauty, celebrated in the floral subjects of Leonardo's *Drawing of Roses and Violets,* is linked with the mysteries of woman. The resigned gestures of Bellini's Christ and the passive role of St. Sebastian are closer to the feminine than to the masculine.

Motifs and images from the paintings establish recurrent patterns in the poems of **Sight and Song** and reinforce its chief themes. The senses, for instance, from states of consciousness to unconsciousness, from pain to sleep and death, provide centers for many poems and help to link the physical and the spiritual. An onlooker-voyeur, a god disguised as faun, often accompanies these scenes. In **"Sleeping Venus"** (Giorgione), however, the observer has been painted out: the reader, following the sequence of motifs, dramatically takes over the role and becomes the onlooker-voyeur. Motifs and images also reflect the divided character of the collection. Qualities of softness and transcience, suggested by butterfly and rose, are set off by flint and marble, representing solidity and permanence. The nightshade and daphne, appearing in **"Apollo and Marsyas"** (Perugini), are examples of an ever-present floral symbolism. The torch of love is an instrument of continuity: it is reversed on the ground in **"Antiope"** (Correggio), yet finally borne aloft by the amoretti of **"L'Embarquement"** (Watteau). Alternating between the formality of the same painter's **"L'Indifférent"** and the ecstasy of **"Treading the Grape"** (Gozzoli), the motif of the dance typifies the contrasts of the volume, as do the juxtaposition of physically bound and spiritually free (Sebastian) and of death and life (Procris). Perhaps the most ambivalent image is the arrow, which brings both pleasure and pain and serves both erotic and sacrificial offices, culminating in the figures of Cupid and Sebastian, the former as active imparter, the latter as passive receiver.

A fundamental paradox, emerging from the selection and arrangement of pictorial models, can be traced throughout the volume and seems to underlie the structure of *Sight and Song.* An opening motto from Keats, "I see and sing, by my own eyes inspired" ["Ode to Psyche"], refers to Psyche's butterfly wings, an image of precariousness and fragility used in the first poem (**"L'Indifférent"** [Watteau]) and echoed throughout the collection. Instruction in love (**"Venus, Mercury and Cupid"** [Correggio]) and the eternalization of nature in art (**"Drawing of Roses and Violets"** [Leonardo]) represent affirmative values. Contrasting poems associate female beauty with cruelty: theoretically in **"La Gioconda"** (Leonardo), practically in **"The Faun's Punishment"** (Correggio). Beauty pure in theory (**"The Birth of Venus"** [Botticelli]) and in practice (**"Antiope"** [Correggio]) is viewed alongside the bacchanalian gusto of **"Treading the Press"** (Gozzoli). The underlying sadness of beauty in **"Spring"** (Botticelli) yields to coolness and calculation in **"A Portrait"** (Bartolommeo Veneto). A third of the way into *Sight and Song* another element enters. Divine love is introduced in a group of three poems (**"Saint Katharine of Alexandria"** [Veneto], **"Saint Sebastian"** [Correggio], **"A 'Sant' Imagine"** [Fiorenzo di Lorenzo]) which justify the martyrdom of their subjects and applaud their triumph over death. Secular love reappears, bringing release from physical bondage in **"The Rescue"** (Tintoretto), showing its bankruptcy in **"Venus and Mars"** (Botticelli), and revealing the fatal outcome of jealousy in **"The Death of Procris"** (Piero di Cosimo).

Two other poems examine the implications of sacred Love: **"Saint Jerome in the Desert"** (Cosimo Tura) focuses upon sin and asceticism, and **"Mettus Curtius"** (Unknown) transforms a Roman hero into a Christian knight who rides joyfully to death. Crucially situated at about the two-thirds mark, a pair of poems inspired by Watteau (**"A Fête Champêtre"**) and Giorgione (**"A Shepherd-Boy"**) suggests the transience of secular love and an ideal of beauty and art situated in a Golden Age. Two representatives of Divine Love, a solitary youth (**"Saint Sebastian"** [Antonello]) and a solitary maiden (**"The Magdalen"** [Timoteo Viti]), adopt different attitudes to their fates. Other poems swing to the opposite extreme: **"A Pen-Drawing of Leda"** (Sodoma) evokes the physical union, **"Marriage of Bacchus and Ariadne"** (Tintoretto) the symbolic union of

secular love. A second treatment of a painting (**"The Figure of Venus in 'Spring' "** [Botticelli]) reminds how love foreshadows death. **"Apollo and Marsyas"** (Perugino) illustrates the defeat of human self-love. The climax of the thematic development of the collection comes close to the end in the successive celebrations of Divine Love and secular beauty in **"The Blood of the Redeemer"** (Bellini) and **"Sleeping Venus"** (Giorgione). Field then turns from juxtaposition to contrastive studies of stages in Christ's life (**"A Pietà"** [Crivelli], **"The Virgin, Child and St. John"** [Lorenzo di Credi]). **"L'Embarquement pour Cythère"** (Watteau), a secular pilgrimage to the island of Venus, concludes the set, though, symptomatically, the vision of love and beauty is touched with sadness.

Sight and Song emerges, therefore, as a set of thirty-one variations upon the theme of tension between life and death. On the one side are the forces of love, beauty, and art; on the other, the forces of cruelty, sorrow, and pride. The divided character of the collection reminds us that female beauty both delights and disturbs. The high points of the secular theme are the two works of Giorgione, which infuse the human with the mythological, making it timeless. The sacred theme climaxes with Bellini's masterpiece portraying the supreme sacrifice of the Divine for the human. Its textual position and artistic importance emphasize its value for the collection as a whole. Acting as a framework, the first and final works of the set, both by Watteau, hold a tenuous balance between the forces of life and death. The initial utterance is brief and individual, but the closing statement expands enormously on page and canvas to include a whole community of souls, freed from solitude though not from uncertainty. Poems inspired by Tintoretto (**"Marriage of Bacchus and Ariadne"**) and Perugino (**"Apollo and Marsyas"**) epitomize in the last third of *Sight and Song* the dualistic principle operating throughout: a Bacchus-Dionysus strain of emotion, an Apollonian strain of intellect and harmony. This symbolic pattern, together with the thematic tension between life and death, provide a coherent structure for *Sight and Song.*

The second critical issue, that of objectivity, relates to the declaration of intent in the Preface. The aim of the volume is "to translate into verse what the lines and colours of certain chosen pictures sing in themselves; to express not so much what these pictures are to the poet, but rather what poetry they objectively incarnate." Such an attempt demands, on the part of the gazer, sight refined of "theory, fancies, or his mere subjective enjoyment." Not even Flaubert, it is admitted, could prevent subjective elements from entering his work, yet the effort "to see things from their own centre, by suppressing the habitual centralisation of the visible in ourselves" is valuable, making possible "an impression clearer, less passive, more intimate."

Thus, artistic essence rather than poetic response is the end for Michael Field, and the poet's role seemingly contracts to that of literal mouthpiece for painted artifacts. Yeats's reference to the difficulty of separating dancer from dance is pertinent here, where the express ideal is to fuse performer with performance, poet with poetic object. But the very use of "certain chosen pictures" in preference to others less temperamentally congenial or less suited for the collection involves a degree of artistic preference. The paintings, "objective" models in theory, might equally well in theory be disposed on a random basis; examination of *Sight and Song* has shown that such is not the case, and that the works are rhythmically organized to create particular harmonies, contrasts, and climaxes. Implicit in what has already been said are doubts about sight free from abstract, fanciful, or hedonist tendencies, and about complete identification of viewpoints: a first-person viewpoint, for instance, is never lent to a Sebastian or a Venus.

In other ways, too, the poet's interpretive presence is felt. An immediate initial judgment, "Ah, foolish Procris!," colors the reader's attitude toward the poem inspired by Piero di Cosimo; in **"A Pietà"** (Crivelli), praise of subtle coloring and frank emotional expression leads to an affective response from the poet:

> One is soothed, one feels it good
> To be of this little group
> Of mourners.

Reference in the poem inspired by Lorenzo di Credi to "our English dells" disturbs the unity of mood and place. An undisguisedly personal voice at the close of the Correggio **"Saint Sebastian"** typifies authorial intervention, most noticeable in religious topics:

> Oh might my eyes, so without measure,
> Feed on their treasure,
> The world with thong and dart might do its pleasure!

Elsewhere, rhetorical devices enliven descriptive passages and call attention to the poet's voice. The final stanza of **"A 'Sant' Imagine"** (Lorenzo) directs the reader away from the figure of Sebastian: "And now back to the picture's self we come, / Its subtle, glowing spirit," and it is a self-conscious poet who allows titular echoes to reverberate through the text, as witnessed by the allusion to "all that visits eye and ear" in **"A Shepherd-Boy"** (Giorgione). The movement of the poet's eye over each work is also subjective. In **"The Blood of the Redeemer"** (Bellini), for example, the focus carefully alternates between Christ, architectural stage, angel, and landscape, the role of the latter being an index of artistic and authorial feeling.

Two-thirds of the works, in fact, introduce landscape, the expressive possibilities of which in painting became fully appreciated only around 1470, near the commencement of the Renaissance period to which nearly all the selected paintings belong. Landscape is of particular importance in the second half of the volume, where it acts as commentary on the foreground events; and in its claim to be considered "as more of the emotions than of the intellect" [A. Richard Turner, *The Vision of Landscape in Renaissance Italy*], it again undermines the poet's aim of objectivity. The pathos of **"The Death of Procris"** (Piero di Cosimo) is rendered more poignant by the contrast between the solemn mourners and the uncomprehending indifference of the natural world. In **"Saint Jerome"** (Tura), **"La Gioconda"** (Leonardo), and **"Fête Champêtre"** (Watteau), however, the gray hues and barren forms of the first, the emotional coolness of the second, and the elegiac strains of the last find sympathetic response in their settings. At the close of **"Saint Sebastian"** (Antonello), attention is drawn to the scudding clouds which herald a storm corresponding to the martyr's inner turmoil; the extended triplet harmonies of **"The Blood of the Redeemer"** (Bellini) are visually repeated in a delicate scenic balance of day and night, a symbolic balance of life and death, incapsulating thereby the thematic tension of the volume.

The formal imbalance and gentle melancholy of earlier incarnations of Venus by Botticelli (**"Spring"**) are resolved by means of landscape in the Giorgione **"Sleeping Venus,"** where a calmly reclining figure in deep sleep is matched by a landscape of equal tranquillity; the whole is characterized by an absence of movement and sound, by a harmony of color, line, and feeling, distilling the ideal essence of a Golden Age. Significantly, the more apprehensive vision of **"L'Embarquement pour Cythère"** is placed last in *Sight and Song,* and a modern interpretation of Watteau's painting as an embarkation *from* the island of love adds a certain piquancy to the selection. In an Arcadia which blends elements of actuality and dream, the couples descend to Venus' barque, watched by the goddess' solitary torso. This reminder of sorrow and transience in a landscape of blossom and new life leaves ambiguous, in the final lines of the volume, the harmony of figures and setting, of self and world:

> The waters spread: ere fall of night
> The red-prowed shallop will have passed from
>   sight
> And the stone Venus by herself remain
> Ironical above that wide, embrowning plain.

The third critical issue is the ontology of the picture-poem, and its value and importance for poetry as a whole. Basic to the relationship between picture and poem is the question of scope and the difference of media: the poem can offer a selection of the features present in the painting. Some of the figures on canvas, much of the chromatic spectrum, and often the background setting go unmentioned. In terms of technique, the significance of vertical, horizontal, and circular form, determined by the painting's frame, is absent from the poem, as are notions of overall size and scale and indications of artistic medium and structural form. The investigation of source and influence, of dating and authenticity, the assignment to a specific tradition, critical appraisal—activities all common to art history—find little place in the picture-poem. From an interpretive viewpoint, certain deeper symbolic and aesthetic, sociological and psychological implications are omitted, or receive, at most, brief allusion.

What the poem brings to the picture lies chiefly in its nature as a time-art, contrasted with a space-art. It expands the "frozen moment" by imaginatively lending expression to the thoughts and mental states of depicted figures and giving voice to their unheard conversations, while also generalizing from specific themes and offering comment and summary. Sketching the pre-history and projecting the future course of events, the poem at the same time infuses personal feeling to dramatize the impact of the present. Emphasis upon a figure usually neglected or a detail otherwise missed shows new angles of approach; an inherent ambiguity is rendered unambiguous, a paradox spelled out, a conflict highlighted. Aside from matters of substance, the poem supplements the picture through its own formal techniques. The poetic optic guides and influences the manner in which the gazer "reads" the artwork; the poetic resources of rhyme and meter, rhythm and image, sound and flow are harnessed in the cause of greater suggestiveness and meaning.

Several arguments can be mustered against setting too high a value upon this genre. The question of originality is raised by poems which use existent models rather than pretend to be pure flights of fancy (though the role of convention in the latter case cannot be ignored). Comparing, for example, Field's **"A Pen-Drawing of Leda"** (Sodoma) with Yeats's "Leda and the Swan," one can see that the task of the earlier poet is at once easier, since the subject is given, and more difficult, since the freedom of treatment is limited by the requirement of fidelity to source, which itself must have sufficient potential to sustain the poem. One can claim also that the picture-poem is escapist, seeking refuge in art from the problems of the world outside, removing itself from the sphere of experience (*Erlebnisgedicht*) to that of artifact (*Dinggedicht*). One might argue further that prosaic, at best pedestrian, evocations in one medium expressed in another serve no useful end; a viewer unresponsive to the original painting is unlikely to be converted by its verbal duplication. The difficulty of locating reproductions of art works, if only in monochrome, can lend an exclusive flavor to the genre, which must then of necessity be considered independently of its model. To what extent the picture-poem is ultimately to be judged *qua* poem or according to the faithfulness of its "translation" depends, in the absence of authorial directives, on the familiarity of the reader with the picture.

But several arguments can be advanced for the value and importance of the picture-poem. First, existent models offer the poet a challenge, which in *Sight and Song* is taken up with marked success: the paintings are as if created anew, and Field's poems differ from others' by their length of treatment, their lyrical warmth and chromatic subtleties, and their felicitous blend of concrete details and decorative values. The special worth of the genre lies in its forcing a review and a possible reassessment of the paintings chosen, indeed, of paintings in general, by narrowing the focus from whole rooms and galleries of art down to single works and details thereof, yet linking these with more universal themes. The picture-poem can serve as a critical interpretation, which by a process of historical accretion alters our view of the art work. (pp. 9-19)

To counter the claim that the genre is escapist in its attachment to the world of the artifact, one can argue that the picture-poem in fact represents less an objective phenomenon *per se,* than an objective disguise for personal utterance. In her account of Michael Field, Mary Sturgeon deems *Sight and Song* unimportant to a spiritual biography, yet the evidence suggests that the volume offers very relevant material, expressed obliquely, artistically, and *in nuce.* The same critic concedes the difficulty of stylistically separating the contribution of each poet, though biographical data encourages conjectures based on metrical fluency

and choice of certain subject matter. The essential subjectivity of the volume might be discussed further as a philosophy embracing emotion and intellect, and a poetic partnership of maiden aunt and niece could easily invite psychoanalytical explorations.

A final argument in support of the picture-poem relates to the particular manner of its appearance in *Sight and Song;* no longer bound within the sonnet's "scanty plot," it has expanded into a narrative-descriptive cycle. Whereas symbolic patterns and themes in a volume of verse lacking similar models can be organized by a poet according to his lights, the difficulties of organizing given subjects like paintings are much more acute, since the contents already have their own internal order and cannot be rearranged without destroying the work. The poet's skill in the selection and linkage of the various paintings is thus all the greater, and this cyclical format exhibits the infinite possibilities of unconscious pictorial associations fusing with conscious verbal echoes, of subtle patterning and structural arrangements which, even if declined here, could serve for a future set of picture-poems. Such a format exhibits also a broader dimension of universal validity: the fruitfulness of an extra-literary matrix in the creation of a coherent and variegated poetic world. (pp. 19-20)

> *Kenneth R. Ireland, " 'Sight and Song': A Study of the Interrelations between Painting and Poetry," in* Victorian Poetry, *Vol. 15, No. 1, Spring, 1977, pp. 9-20.*

Lillian Faderman   (essay date 1981)

[*In the following excerpt from her study* Surpassing the Love of Men, *Faderman presents the relationship between Bradley and Cooper as an example of an unconsummated "romantic friendship."*]

[Katharine Bradley and Edith Cooper] were related by blood—Katharine, who was fourteen years older, was Edith's aunt, and the two lived in the same household while Edith was growing up. In 1878 when Edith was sixteen, she joined Katharine at University College, where they studied the classics and philosophy together. They were feminists from their childhood and youth, rejecting the passive, inconsequential roles their society allotted women. As a symbol of this rejection, they seldom used their female names. When she was a child, Edith took the name "Field," presumably because of her love of nature. Once on a visit to Dresden, she had an illness which caused her to lose some hair, and a German nurse dubbed her "little Heinrich," which then became Henry. Katharine matched her with the name Michael. Soon after they began to write together, they combined each nickname into a pseudonym, probably because they guessed that women's work was, even in the 1880's, still not taken entirely seriously. According to some biographers, they were right in their assumption. Their first collaboration, published under feminine or neuter pseudonyms (Arran and Isla Leigh), was virtually ignored. Subsequent volumes of poetry and drama published under the name of Michael Field were quite successful, until it was discovered that Michael Field was two women. Their work then returned to oblivion, though it was highly praised by such contemporaries as Robert Browning and George Meredith.

Since the two women were independently wealthy, however, their lack of success could alter neither their resolve nor their life-style, as they characterized it in a poem of the 1890's, "My love and I took hands and swore / Against the world, to be / Poets and lovers evermore." Although biographers have attributed some brief heterosexual interests to them, it is clear that the major interest in their lives was each other—and inextricably connected with that was the shared excitement in being New Women and poets. Their poetry and their journal both indicate that theirs was a union of love and work—and that love and work were interrelated was a source of great joy to them. In their journal they observed of Robert and Elizabeth Browning. "These two poets, man and wife, wrote alone; each wrote, but did not bless and quicken one another at their work; *we are closer married*" (the italics are theirs). Again they used the language of marriage to describe their method of working together in a May 1886 letter to Havelock Ellis, who wanted to know which of the two wrote a particular piece:

> As to our work, let no man think he can put asunder what God has joined. . . . The work is a perfect mosaic: we cross and interlace like a company of dancing summer flies; if one begins a character, his companion seizes and possesses it; if one conceives a scene or situation, the other corrects, completes, or murderously cuts away.

Their literary productions were bound as closely as their lives for as long as they lived. Even on those rare occasions when one composed a volume separately, it was published under the name of Michael Field, as for example, Edith's *Poems of Adoration* (1912) and Katharine's *Mystic Trees* (1913)—only two poems in the latter are by Edith.

What was the nature of their personal relationship, if even for a moment it can be separated from their professional relationship? Katharine sometimes spoke of her very motherly feelings toward Edith, but some of Edith's journal entries suggest an extremely sensual if not outright sexual interest in Katharine. Their earlier poetry, especially in Book III of *Underneath the Bough,* which is a series of love poems to each other, reveals the all-consuming quality of their bond; for example, **"Constancy"**:

> I love her with the seasons, with the winds,
> As the stars worship, as anemones
> Shudder in secret for the sun, as bees
> Buzz round an open flower: in all kinds
> My love is perfect; and in each she finds
> Herself the goal. . . .

And yet . . . they were generally so completely without self-consciousness in their public declarations of mutual love, that from a twentieth-century perspective it is hard to believe that their love was not—as a Victorian would phrase it—innocent. Although they thought of themselves as aesthetes, unlike their contemporary Oscar Wilde, they would have been shocked to think they were shocking. If they saw something unorthodox about their relationship, they would have been more reticent in their poems to each other.

Their volume of verse, *Long Ago* (1889), inspired by fragments of Sappho's lyrics, gives little hint of any consciousness about the possibility of sexual expression between women; the emphasis in these poems, in fact, is on the heterosexual Phaon myth. It is possible, of course, that Katharine and Edith were not more definite about Sappho's homosexuality because they feared the censors, but it is at least as likely that they treated Sappho's "lesbianism" in a vague manner because they saw it in terms of their own love for each other, which was not as clear-cut as we would see it today. While Sappho's feeling for Phaon is patently erotic, just as it is in Ovid's poem, her love for women is almost impossible to define given our twentieth-century choices. It is sometimes sensual, but the sensuality is usually mixed with strong maternal emotions. Perhaps the poems in this volume which deal with love between women give us the most valuable insight into the relationship between Katharine and Edith, especially from Edith's perspective:

> At this, my darling, thou did'st stray
> A few feet to the rushy bed,
> When a great fear and passion shook
> My heart lest haply thou wert dead;
> It grew so still about the brook,
> As if a soul were drawn away.
>
> Anon thy clear eyes, silver-blue,
> Shone through the tamarisk-branches fine;
> To pluck me iris thou had'st sprung
> Through galingale and celandine;
> Away, away, the flowers I flung
> And thee down to my breast I drew.
>
> My darling! Nay, our very breath
> Nor light nor darkness shall divide;
> Queen Dawn shall find us on one bed.
> Nor must thou flutter from my side
> An instant, lest I feel the dread,
> Atthis, the immanence of death.

While it is hard to pin down exactly how they conceived of love between women, either in their poetry or in their lives, it is certain that they saw it as the single most important factor in their existences. In 1907 it caused them to convert to Catholicism, for the same reason that Alice B. Toklas, a Jew, converted several decades later—because the Catholic religion held out hope of an afterlife where she would be reunited eternally with Gertrude Stein, her beloved. If their poetry is a true indication, Katharine and Edith believed that their religious conversion altered their love only to intensify it. In the poem **"Lovers,"** Katharine wrote: "Lovers, fresh plighting lovers in our age, / Lovers in Christ. . . . / One thing is plain:—that we can never part. / O Child, thou hauntest me in every room; / Nor for an instant can we separate; / And thou or I, if absent in a tomb / Must keep unqualified our soul's debate." In another poem one of them stated: "Beloved, now I love God first / There is for thee such summer burst / Where it was stirring spring before."

The saddest tribute one paid to her love for the other was her inability to outlive her. Edith learned she had cancer in 1912. She lived until December 1913. While nursing Edith, Katharine developed cancer herself—a perfect example to support the theory that the genesis of cancer is related to grief and loss. Katharine kept her own illness a secret from Edith, not wishing to add to her burden, but she outlived Edith by little more than half a year. It was a happier tribute, for her readers at least, that Katharine wrote the most moving poetry of her career at this time, almost all of it relating to her great love and sorrow, as in **"Caput Tuum ut Carmelus"**:

> I watch the arch of her head,
> As she turns away from me. . . .
> I would I were with the dead,
> Drowned with the dead at sea,
> All the waves rocking over me!
>
> As St Peter turned and fled
> From the Lord, because of sin,
> I look on that lovely head;
> And its majesty doth win
> Grief in my heart as for sin.
>
> Oh, what can Death have to do
> With a curve that is drawn so fine,
> With a curve that is drawn as true
> As the mountain's crescent line? . . .
> Let me be hid where the dust falls fine!

Twentieth-century biographers, unable to understand the scope of their commitment to each other and ignoring the autobiographical poem in which they swore to be "poets and *lovers* evermore" (the italics are mine), have observed, like Mary Sturgeon, that Katharine and Edith, "in honouring their vow to poetry, gave life . . . 'a poor second place.'" However, the record they left indicates that in their marriage neither their life nor their work (they would have found it absurd to discuss them as separate entities) was forced to take a second place. (pp. 209-13)

> *Lillian Faderman, "Love and 'Women Who Live by Their Brains',"* in her Surpassing the Love of Men: Romantic Friendship and Love between Women from the Renaissance to the Present, *William Morrow and Company, Inc., 1981, pp. 204-30.*

David J. Moriarty   (essay date 1986)

[*In the following excerpt, Moriarty examines the reaction of male critics to the works of Michael Field.*]

'Michael Field' is the pseudonym used by Edith Cooper and Katherine Bradley, whose unique collaboration amounts to a staggering twenty-five "tragedies," a masque, and eight volumes of verse. In addition, the British Museum collection contains a number of unpublished manuscripts, extensive correspondence, and detailed journals, excerpts of which have been edited and published under the title *Works and Days* by Sturge Moore. Male critics, inclined to note prolific nineteenth-century men writers, regardless of their talents, have ignored or misrepresented these two women more often than not, but what is as disconcerting, feminist critics have ignored them as well, despite the fact that they worked in a genre which is, even today, dominated by men as critics, writers, and producers. Without question Katherine Bradley's and Edith Cooper's experience serves as a protocol for the rediscovery of not only the nineteenth-century woman writ-

er, but all those writing against the accepted societal and cultural grain.

Katherine (b. 1846) and her niece Edith (b. 1862) were born sixteen years apart in the mid-nineteenth century into prosperous Birmingham merchant families, which allowed them the means and the leisure time to pursue their writing, in addition to providing them access to the limited opportunities available to the women of that time for higher education, without which their collaboration would have been impossible.

Neither woman had an early formal education, but Katherine, who acted as her niece's companion and tutor during Edith's formative years, managed to attend the summer session at Newnham College and to go abroad briefly to study at the College de France in Paris, where a love affair with a French friend's brother came to an abrupt end at his untimely death, an experience that propelled Katherine into a state of moral and religious confusion. Upon her return to England, she sought out the counsel of John Ruskin, whose "religion of art" was appealing to those many Victorians afflicted with a similar sense of doubt in such matters.

In the lengthy correspondence between the two that ensued, Katherine addresses Ruskin reverentially as "Master," while Ruskin's salutations progress from being detached and formal to a more familiar and patronizing address, revelatory of his attitude toward women. For example, Ruskin's initial letters begin "My Dear Madam," but this immediately becomes "Dear Miss Bradley," then "My Dear Miss Bradley" and "Dear Miss Catherine [sic]." Indeed, though Ruskin was clearly impressed by her letters and continued the correspondence regularly over many months, eventually welcoming her as a "companion" of the Guild of St. George, a society founded by Ruskin to foster his eccentric economic ideas, his intimacy betrays a patriarchal stance and a refusal to treat Katherine as an adult and an equal. There are many examples of this attitude in the letters. After Katherine had sent him a copy of her first volume of lyrics, **The New Minnesinger** (1876), Ruskin responded, "Some of the best poetry of modern times is by women (Mrs. Browning, Miss Ingelow, Miss Proctor)" but teasingly undercut this a few days later with, "How much too serious my life is to be spent in reading poetry (unless prophetic). But I did accidently open the **Minnesinger** and liked a bit or two of it—and I don't think I threw it into the wastepaper basket." Finally, when Katherine admitted to reading some contemporary "atheistic" philosophers, Ruskin's attitude toward women, an attitude Edith was to characterize years later as "a speckled silliness," comes to the fore as he replies lividly, "you must be called a false disciple. . . . When you called me master—I understood that if in anything you would obey me . . . in the choice of books." Calling Katherine "too stupid" and "a double-feathered little goose" for reading "these miserable modern wretches," Ruskin concluded his letter of December 28, 1877, with a bizarre yet revealing image:

> Suppose a child whom I had sent on a perfectly safe road, deliberately jumped off into a ditch—wallowed there with the pigs without telling

me—got torn by their tusks—and then came to me all over dung and blood—saying, "I didn't care"—what could I do—or say?

Katherine's independent choice of reading matter had severed the master/disciple relationship, and Ruskin, in another letter two days later, sternly excommunicated her from the Guild, "I have at once to put you out of the St. George's Guild—which *primarily* refuses atheists—not because they are wicked but because they are fools," and although Ruskin had tempered his tone but not his attitude when, in another letter less than a fortnight later, he advised, "give up all metaphysical reading at present, be content with history—poetry," the correspondence soon ceased.

In 1878 when the two women went to Bristol to study the classics and philosophy at University College, they championed such causes as antivivisection and women's rights in the Debating Society and adopted the style of the New Woman, aesthetic, colorful, freely flowing, at a time when corsets and bustles were the conventional fashion. Because of their "careless hair and untidy feet," in Mary Sturgeon's phrase [in her study *Michael Field*], they were fascinating figures for those at Bristol, and yet their close personal relationship excluded intimacy with others, a seclusion to be maintained throughout the rest of their lives. It was at Bristol that the women made the decision to live together and collaborate on their art for the remainder of their days, a decision formalized in a dedicatory poem written when Edith was seventeen and Katherine thirty-two. According to Sturgeon, the poem is an exchange of marriage vows, a promise to unite as poets and lovers against the conventional world, "The world was on us, pressing sore; / My love and I took hands and swore, / Against the world, to be / Poets and lovers evermore, / . . . Indifferent to heaven or hell." The radical mission the women set for themselves in the poem is reinforced by the form, since it is an extreme variation of that most conventional of forms, the sonnet.

During the 1880's, after a period of extensive travel in Germany and Italy, the women returned to Bristol and published over the next few years a series of poetic dramas based upon legendary and historical matter. The accession to Ruskin's counsel to concentrate on history and poetry is only apparent here, since each of these plays contains, hidden beneath the historical veneer, a contemporary and feminist message, often inspired by their reading of the "miserable modern wretches" like Nietzsche.

For example, *Callirrhoë* (1884), received with much critical acclaim, though based on an ancient Greek legend quite clearly reveals the influence of Nietzsche's *Birth of Tragedy* as it contrasts the conflict between the Apollonian concept of rational order and what Nietzsche saw as the more modern idea, Dionysian rage, madness, and self-destruction. It was in the legend of Callirrhoë that the women also found a precise metaphor for their mission as tragic poets in the mad priestesses, the Maenads, who officiated at the Dionysian rites.

The volume drew the notice of Robert Browning, and the women wrote divulging their true identities, Edith explaining to Browning in a letter of May, 1884, the unique nature of their collaboration, describing *Callirrhoë* as "like a mosaic work—the mingled, various product of our two brains. . . . if our contributions were disentangled and one subtracted from the other, the amount would be almost even." Katherine, writing a few months later, in a letter dated November 7, 1884, cautioned Browning to keep their identities secret: "we have many things to say that the world will not tolerate from a woman's lips. We must be free as dramatists to work out in the open air of nature—exposed to her vicissitudes, witnessing her terrors: we cannot be stifled in drawing-room conventionalities" [*Works and Days*].

Browning, with good intentions, promoted their work and announced in public at a dinner party in the spring of 1885, attended and reported on by Arthur Symons, in his article "Michael Field," "I have found a new poet." Symon's own curiosity about this 'Michael Field' was aroused, and though he did not meet the women until years later, he almost immediately wrote a favorable review of their work, pronouncing *Callirrhoë* a play that proved them genuine poets. On their most recent volume, containing *The Father's Tragedy* (1885), Symons concluded "that it gave one a sense of the outraged Earth." *The Father's Tragedy,* a play that turns upon the generational clash between father and son, Symons succinctly described as "literally the father's annihilation," a correct assessment of the work, which calls for an end to patriarchal tyranny and for mutual love and understanding between the generations.

The attentions of the likes of Browning and Symons had uncovered the secret of 'Michael Field,' and when it became generally known that it was Katherine and Edith who were writing these plays with themes "the world will not tolerate from a woman's lips," not surprisingly, their subsequent work received more hostile scrutiny. The first to feel the conventional critics' wrath was *Brutus Ultor* (1886), a play couched in the familiar Shakespearian form and delineating the struggle between the noble Brutus, champion of freedom and "the outraged Earth," and the evil Sextus, the aptly named, tyrannical and misogynistic rapist of the piece, which ironically was intended for a wider audience than the previous plays and which contains a more overt feminist message.

For example, the conflict between the protagonist and antagonist is almost coincidental to a discussion of the role of women in the revolutionary process as the idea of women's fulfillment in motherhood is challenged in favor of women's active participation in the overthrow of tyrannous convention. Brutus is eulogized at the close because he has recognized women's potential beyond motherhood: "He felt the wrongs / Of women as they'd natures of their own / And use beyond child-bearing."

The next play, *Canute the Great* (1887), despite the nominal male main character, is most notable for a rather explicit love scene between two women, which forms the core of the drama (Act III, scene iii), and this theme of lesbian love is integral to *Long Ago* (1889), a volume of lyrics in imitation of Sappho. Although the life experience of Katherine and Edith is sufficient to explain their interest in the poetess of Lesbos, Sappho was a fascinating figure for many during the *fin de siècle.* Indeed, a cult of Lesbos had developed at this time, one aspect of a general interest in sexual inversion at the close of the last century, but since most of the followers of this cult were male, the lesbian is most often treated merely as a vehicle for male fantasies.

One must be aware of this to understand Arthur Symons' vehement objections to this work. Symons, one of the instigators of the Decadent Movement in England, found the poems too chaste, "enfeebled by alterations, . . . colorless and bloodless." Though Symons admitted that Edith and Katherine had "at their finest, . . . something fierce, subtle, strange, singular—which can become sinister," in other words "decadent," the women never regarded their love as such. What is strange is that Symons, finding nothing decadent in these love lyrics, chose to denigrate them on false grounds. Calling the work a "sacreligious [*sic*] attempt . . . on the unsurpassable genius of Sappho," Symons objected because "What they actually did was to take a few lines from the Greek of Sappho; then attempt to translate those lines; then to add variations on these themes of their own inventing." This last aspect is what most disturbs Symons, that the women used Sappho's poetry as a departure point to examine "themes of their own inventing," based on their personal experience, rather than limiting themselves to translating the Greek lyrics, which leads Symons to absurdly suggest that Swinburne had come nearer to the essence of lesbian love because he had limited himself to a close translation of Sappho's Greek and had striven "to cast his spirit into the mould of [Sappho]."

The plays the women wrote during the 1890's, from what Symons calls "their second dramatic period—when they were almost ignored—when they came to a certain extent into contact with the so-called Decadent Movement," are among their most significant. Upon close examination they can hardly be termed decadent, and yet Symons persisted in his attempt to make the women conform to the decadent mythology, which requires that the artist be "almost ignored," ignored by the general public while admired by the chosen few.

The Tragic Mary (1890), for example, warrants comparison with Swinburne's treatment of Mary Stuart in his *Bothwell,* in which the character is studied as a decadent witch woman. 'Michael Field,' on the other hand, draws Mary Stuart with a sympathy that humanizes the character, stripping away the symbolic overtones of the *femme fatale* image and allowing the reader to examine Mary as the queen held captive—a figure that recurs often in their dramas. The reality is that Mary, like Shaw's St. Joan, is exploited and finally abandoned by her abusers, becoming the exemplum of the politically exploited woman. This is the tragic irony of the character for the women, not, as it is for Swinburne, that Mary loses her lover Bothwell. Oscar Wilde recognized this when he wrote t ♦ he women, "Your queen is a splendid creature, a live woman to her finger tips. I feel the warmth of her breath as I listen to her. She seems closer to flesh and blood than the Mary of Swinburne's *Bothwell* " [Letter of August 13, 1890, quoted in *Letters of Oscar Wilde*].

Stephania, a Trialogue (1892) is significant on two counts: first, the "trialogue" form and simple suggestive language closely resembles that used by the Flemish symbolist, Maeterlinck, for his innovative *Pelleas et Melisande,* published in the same year, making *Stephania* one of the first examples of a *genuine* symbolist drama produced in England; second, the main character is again without the extremes of idealization and/or harlotry with which the decadents, in their misogynistic vision, usually associated the *femme fatale.* The point of the play is to expose the reality that the symbolic role of the temptress is not congenial to women. Indeed, as Stephania observes, it can be a rather tedious burden:

> O God, how tedious is the harlot's part,
> The mimic vanity, the mimic rage,
> The waiting upon appetite! I loathe
> My gems, my unguents, all the fragrant lights
> I scatter on my hair. To dress for him,
> To garnish infamy, to give one's face
> The vermeil of a flower! I have such need
> Of rest, to lay the cerecloth over him!
> A lethargy falls on me like a hell
> Pressed inward—ah, I have such need of sleep,
> The Change, the peace!

A Question of Memory, performed at the Opera Comique in London on the evening of October 27, 1893, was a singular event in the women's lives. Not only is it their one "realistic" prose drama and their only play produced on stage, but it is the only drama in which the women employed a relatively contemporary setting and common, rather than noble, characters, making it an important departure from the rest of their canon. Staged under the auspices of J. T. Grein's Independent Theatre, which was formed to offer the audience drama not available in the commercial theaters of the day, this play is one of the mere handful of native-born dramas presented by the Independent, a fact that illustrates both the uniqueness of *A Question of Memory* and the bankrupt condition of the British drama at the time.

By employing a stream of consciousness prose for the dialogue, as well as an unconventional ending, where two men and a woman decide to live together, the women upset the critics accustomed to stock dialogue, characters, and the conventional resolution of the common melodramatic fare, and the reviews were either unenthusiastic or patronizing, causing Edith to record in the journal, "We wake to the surprise of finding every morning paper against us. . . . The evening papers are worse than the morning. They are like a lot of unchained tigers. We are hated, as Shelley was hated, by our countrymen, blindly, ravenously."

The review which appeared in the *London Times* [on October 28, 1893] is one of the milder ones. After noting the women's inexperience in "the practical work of the stage," and that the work was unfit for the ordinary theater— strange criticism when one considers the number of women whose plays were performed on stage during the nineteenth century—the *Times* critic continues, "there is a deal of excellent material in it of a somewhat inchoate description, and on the part of the Independent Theatre, . . . its production was a wise measure."

William Archer, credited with popularizing Ibsenism in England, and a critic usually open to the "new drama," began his review as the *Times* critic had ended his, with praise not directed at the women for their daring play, but at the Independent for producing it: "The Independent Theatre would have been false to its mission had it refused its hospitality to such a singular piece." Then Archer went on to express his reservations:

> The authors . . . write a curious short-winded prose. . . .
>
> . . . In the first, second, and fourth acts there is scarcely a single natural sequence of thought, feeling, and expression. The dialogue is always flying off at unexpected tangents, and trying to obtain subtlety by means of incoherence. The authors have observed, quite justly, that feeling *is* incoherent—or rather, that consciousness is like a swirling stream, in which the unexpected and apparently irrelevant objects are always floating to the surface for a moment and then disappearing again, in obedience to laws which we can not formulate. . . . Dialogue . . . is not the dialogue of life, but a world evolved from the playwright's inner consciousness [*The Theatrical 'World' for 1893*].

Archer has defined the stream of consciousness style well, but he has missed the significance of this experiment in adapting it for the drama because he has been conditioned by his taste for Ibsen to expect "the dialogue of life," realistic dialogue, in a play with realistic setting and based on a real occurrence. Archer cannot be excused, however, for his concluding remarks on the unconventional ending— "there is an idea concealed in the . . . casuistry of the last act; but I own it eluded me,"—since anyone familiar with Ibsen's plays should be aware that it was with precisely such "casuistic situations" that he often ended his dramas in order to shock the audience's conventional expectations.

A Question of Memory was beset with problems even before its performance, when friction developed in rehearsals between Acton Bond, the male lead, and the producer, Herman de Lange. As Alice Grein, wife of the theater group's founder, reconstructs the situation, this personality conflict was so severe that the production was in jeopardy, and the women, without any experience in mounting a stage production, were caught in the middle, but when de Lange recommended drastic, and perhaps warranted, alterations in the script, the women resisted and found themselves allied with Bond, at which point Grein himself had to step in to prevent the situation from completely deteriorating.

Grein played his own part in compromising the play's potential for success by choosing François Coppee's *Le Pater* as the second play on the bill. Obsessed with the idea of presenting a play in a foreign language with an English cast, Grein insisted on Coppee's French verse drama, even though, as Alice Grein points out (*The Story of a Pioneer*), "There was admittedly a justification in the complaint of Michael Field, who feared that the impression on the audience might be weakened by repetition" (both plays containing a climactic scene that involved a shooting). Grein's

only concession was to place the women's play first on the program, a departure from the practice of presenting the major production after the curtain raiser, so that their shooting might occur first. According to Alice Grein, "The evening ended with cheers not unmixed with hisses," many of which were directed at the Coppee play that the *Times* critic, quoted above, dismissed tersely and disapprovingly as "on a communistic theme." Given the entire experience, neither Katherine nor Edith, as Alice Grein notes, "were concerned in writing another play for the stage."

The women reverted, instead, to writing closet dramas, with remote historical settings, yet not without contemporary overtones. *Attila, My Attila* (1896) is the first of a series of plays set during the decadence of the Holy Roman Empire. A good part of the play is set in Byzantium, which was associated in *fin de siècle* mythology with the corrupt aristocratic order of the nineteenth century, ripe to be swept away by the invading barbarians, who with their destruction will bring liberation and a new order.

Philippe Jullian, yet another critic who tries to claim the women as decadents, regards this play, along with Yeats's Byzantium poems, as fine examples of the Byzantine style, a style which he points out was popularized by Sarah Bernhardt in various roles that he claims capture "the crimes and splendours of Byzantium" [*Dreamers of Decadance*]. Indeed, the women note in their journal that "Honoria was conceived with Sarah Bernhardt before us all the while."

Honoria, the main character of the play, is, like Byzantium, where East intersects with West, an identity of opposites. She is, in fact, a very contemporary type, that of the "New Woman," which began to emerge in real life and on the stage during the 1890's. The women have cleverly transposed this type from the symbolic intellectual and aesthetic decadence of the late nineteenth century to its source, the last days of the Roman Empire. As they indicate in their preface to the play, "Honoria [who] sought to give freedom to her womanhood by unwomanly audacities . . . [is the] New Woman of the 5th century."

Honoria, of patrician birth, rebels against the boring prospects her status has in store for her, seduces one of the household slaves, and finds herself a pregnant teenager. Upon discovery of her condition, the family is shocked, primarily because she has stooped to the level of a common slave as a means to liberation. The child is done away with; the slave is banished to the salt mines, and Honoria is sent off to the relatives in Byzantium.

The second act begins fourteen years later and reads like a latter-day suburban housewife's nightmare as Honoria, now a mature woman, has been held captive by the relatives through the intervening time, but during this period, she has conjured another fantasy of escape, fantasizing that Attila, that Third World force, will liberate her. The play ends fraught with the irony the authors guaranteed in their preface as the family, heavy-handed throughout and concerned with the conventional proprieties, to discourage Honoria's potential for realizing her latest fantasy, redeems Eugenius from the salt mines and forces her to consummate their marriage. Just as this has been completed, Honoria receives the news that the Hun has been murdered on his marriage bed by a young woman who has been compelled to marry him.

Though the play seems an exercise in the black humor of which the decadents were fond, an ability to mock their own symbols and fantasies, it is not only this. The women have successfully combined this decadent mythology of Byzantium with a satiric view of the nineties' type of the New Woman and her potential for liberation through fantasy. And in the process they have managed to evolve from the old form of tragedy its modern counterpart, black comedy, since Honoria is no tragic heroine in the traditional sense. Too involved in her fantasy of escape and lacking self-realization, Honoria's circumstances do not evoke the conventional catharsis of pity and fear but merely reinforce the reader's own anxiety. In this sense, she is a truly evolutionary and modern character, so caught up in her own self-absorption and self-indulgence, and unable to effect her own liberation, that she represents the modern character in the throes of the contemporary dilemma, paralyzed by self-pity. That this is more precisely a black comedy rather than a traditional tragedy is evidenced by the heavy irony throughout the black humor, emphasized in the outrageous title, *Attila, My Attila.*

A review of the play that appeared in *The Athenaeum* of April 11, 1896 is an odd one. It begins by noting that the characters and matter have been taken directly from Gibbon's *The Decline and Fall . . .* , without "departure from historical fact . . .* , every incident . . . being supported by authority," an important observation for it disarms the reader tempted to dismiss the characters and plot as incredible. Equally important is the reviewer's acceptance of the fact that Honoria is meant to represent the rebellious and contemporary "New Woman." "As a womanly estimate of a woman, the character of 'little Honoria' commands a certain amount of acquiescence," indicates the critic. "We might otherwise be disposed to assign to temperament rather than to mutiny a species of aberration not known among ladies of imperial rank." The suggestion that the play, which the reviewer, lacking our present-day terminology, dubs "an historical ironical tragedy of much power," might be "one on which the Independent Theatre might cast its eyes," reveals this critic's awareness of the ironic and contemporary overtones of the drama. Since the Independent as a rule spurned historical costume drama in favor of more contemporary plays with topical themes and characters, and had, in fact, presented a number of plays in which the New Woman had received serious consideration, the reviewer's comment carries the implication that the group might now be ready for an ironic, satiric treatment of the type.

Though it is difficult to determine if the reviewer is being ironic with such remarks as "in some forms, at least, of dramatic work the competition of women is to be feared," which is immediately undermined by the observation, "There is, however, to speak seriously, much that is genuine and gripping in the play," it is not difficult to discern the sex of the author of such remarks in this unsigned review. Is he being "genuine," a word he uses twice to describe the play, with the contention, "It is a pity that the crudeness elsewhere observable should extend to the language"? Carefully couching his comments in noncommittal either / or phrasing, he puzzles, "We do not know whether to laugh or be shocked when the loving Eugenius addresses to Satyrus, the eunuch, so purely a John Bullish a curse as 'Damn your eyes.' " Is he implying that we should laugh, allowing the women their ribald joke at the expense of the eunuch, the kind of thing often appreciated in a Shakesperean play, or is he indicating that such bawdiness is shocking?

Equally odd is the reviewer's concluding statement, "we do not quite know what to say, except that we think of Aphra Behn, when we are informed in the last act that *coram populo*—the *populus* including ourselves—the marriage of Eugenius and Honoria has been 'consummated.' " Although the consummation seems necessary to develop the play's ironic ending, the reader does not quite know what to think of the reviewer's interesting evocation of Aphra Behn, the accomplished woman dramatist of the bawdy Restoration period, ignored and discredited during the Victorian era for her "coarseness." Is the critic implying an intriguing comparison with Behn's plays, or is he merely objecting that all such untowardness is inexcusable in women playwrights?

By leaving the reader both options, the reviewer is a perfect example of the ambivalent male critic, who, when faced with a work by women, the obvious merits of which can easily be seen, must still accede to his readership, disinclined to accept from women what they might from men. Thus, this critic succeeds, perhaps unintentionally, in damning the play with "feint" praise.

In 1898, persuaded by their artist friends Charles Shannon and Charles Ricketts to move from their "bourgeois house" at Reigate, which they had maintained for ten years, to the more fashionable Richmond, popular with artist and writer types, the women acquired "The Paragon," a small Georgian style house, which they furnished with things "antique," "Japanese," and "aesthetic," a taste cultivated by those in the elite artistic circles of the 1890's. In effect, the move to Richmond served to further insulate the women from the vagaries of the conventional world, which they felt had denied them deserved recognition, and "The Paragon," extensively described by Sturge Moore in his preface to [*Works and Days*], became their refuge from this world, their palace of art.

Though they continued to hold out the hope that their work would be appreciated in another place by another generation, making this hope explicit in a note to the American edition of their earlier collection of poems, *Underneath the Bough* (1898), where they wrote in the singular person of 'Michael Field,' "For some years my work has been done for 'the younger generation'—not yet knocking at the door, but awaited with welcome. Meanwhile, readers from further England—if they will pardon my so classing them—have given me that joy of listening denied to me in my own island," still in private they were bitter and disillusioned, particularly Katherine, upon whom the adverse criticism had begun to take its toll. The spirit of two women against the conventional world, announced in their dedicatory sonnet, had been dampened in Katherine, who wrote to the noted alienist, Havelock Ellis, "want of due recognition is being its embittering, disintegrating work, and we will have in the end a cynic such as only a disillusioned Bacchante can become" [*Michael Field*].

Both women were well aware that the greater part of the cold and negative reception of their later work was due to their gender, and Katherine entered this cynical observation in the journal, "If women seek to learn their art from life, instead of what the angels bring down in dishes, they simply get defamed" [**Works and Days**]. By the end of Victoria's reign, Katherine's cynicism had hardened, as evidenced by her attack on the illusions of the Victorian era, a summation that reveals an abandonment of some of the causes so enthusiastically supported earlier. Reaction had indeed set in when Katherine wrote in 1901:

> The great illusion of the Victorian age is the illusion of progress. . . .
>
> Growth of suburbs, growth of education among the poor, an unmitigated evil—extension of franchise and growth of free trade, unmitigated disasters—the growth of Trade Unions, the damnation of the future.
>
> The growth of sentimentality towards crime; and of sciencecraft (the priestcraft of the Victorian age), insidious, berotting influences.
>
> The synthesis of the reign—Imperialism.
> The great virtue to be cultivated—"hardiness". . . . [**Works and Days**]

Escape from cynicism was afforded when both women converted to Roman Catholicism in 1907. The concept of the sacrificial transubstantiation appealed to conventional mode, their earlier frame of reference for their role as poets, as Maenad priestesses presiding over the creation of tragic poetry through self-effacement and divine madness. The message was now to be translated via Christian mysticism.

After converting, they devoted their efforts to religious verse, though they did publish a number of dramas anonymously, which received a critical respect denied most of their previous attempts, an experience that only reinforced the fact that the hostile reception accorded some of the earlier works was a response to women writing in a genre dominated by male writers and critics.

The rhythm of their collaboration was not even disrupted, in a macabre sense, by death, and Edith, who died of cancer on December 13, 1913, was quickly followed by Katherine, who died of the same disease on September 26, 1914. Of the plays that were published posthumously, *In the Name of Time* (1919) contains, according to Mary Sturgeon, the essential philosophy behind all their work, "a philosophy of change serving a religion of life," as the women project through their protagonist Carloman, in reality the rebel son of Charles Martel but in essence Everyman, their "supreme symbol of freedom." The play combines a call for the loosening of the old bonds with a recognition of the difficult struggle involved. Carloman's mission is to seek what he calls "the Great Reality," and his

life becomes a series of confrontations with the established order, while his quest is marked by failure and futility. Finally, thrown in prison, he discovers that "the Great Reality" consists of "Fellowship, pleasure / These are the treasure," and it is in confinement that he formulates the "philosophy of change serving a religion of life."

> The God I worship. He is just *to-day*—
> Not dreaming of the future,—in itself
> Breath after breath divine! Oh, He becomes!
> He cannot be of yesterday, for youth
> Could not then walk beside Him, and the young
> Must walk with God: and He is most alive
> Wherever life is of each living thing.
> Tomorrow and tomorrow, those todays
> Of unborn generations.

These lines capture for Mary Sturgeon the women's message: "a worship of life, a belief in the joy of fellowship, and a vision of change as the vital principle of living." "It is," Sturgeon concludes, "simply the freedom of love."

Though many major Victorian figures recognized their genius, one finds more recent critics, like Austin Clarke, dismissing the women in ignorance of their work as "two spinster ladies, [who] steadily wrote a series of historical tragedies in five acts and in blank verse" [*The Celtic Twilight and the Nineties*]. Other critics similarly treat the women as freaks when they quibble over whether they were "decadent." If such is not "wholly irresponsible," as Mary Sturgeon contends, it may be irrelevant. . . . Any attempt to make them conform to the myth of decadence, like Symons and Jullian do, is to misrepresent them. Though they employed decadent motifs, they adapted these to "themes of their own inventing," "fellowship," "a worship of life," and "the freedom of love," themes not readily identifiable with decadence.

The superficial trappings of decadence may be present— the unconventional life style, with lesbian overtones; the fascination with Roman decadence; the ultimate submission to the authority of the Roman church—yet much of this must be regarded for what it was, both for them and for their *fin de siècle* counterparts: a pose, a mask, a disguise. In this sense, the women exemplify the "drowning theory" of Annis Pratt, who writes [in *Beyond Intellectual Sexism*], "The drowning effect, . . . to drown out what they are actually saying about feminism, came in with the first woman's novel and hasn't gone out yet." Pratt continues, "Many women . . . have even succeeded in hiding the covert or implicit feminism in their books from themselves. . . . As a result we get explicit cultural norms superimposed upon an authentic creative mind in the form of all kinds of feints, ploys, masks, and disguises imbedded in plot structure and characterization."

If one fails to see through such a disguise, one becomes mired in false paradoxes. Theodore Maynard, the Catholic poet and essayist, senses the paradox of 'Michael Field' when he writes [in his *Carven from the Laurel Tree*] that the women "left a heritage not only of poetry but of paradox. There had been successful literary collaborations before . . . but no collaboration in which the identity of the artists was so completely sunk as in the case of these two ladies. . . ." Maynard, however, goes on to chase the false paradox, so intent on absolving the women as Catholic poets, when he argues, "Here were souls who, though they had been by circumstance and choice decadents of the decadents, never . . . committed in all their lives a really serious sin. . . . "

The real key to the paradox of Katherine and Edith lies not in whether they lived blameless lives, but in their unique collaboration, which for Mary Sturgeon stands "as a robust denial that women are incapable of greatness in art and comradeship," and represents a discovery of "the secret of psychological truth," "a great capacity for life," "an immense love of liberty, and hatred of every kind of bondage," and "a prevailing love of freedom, which takes many forms and is apparent everywhere." All of this is accompanied, according to Sturgeon, by "the fragmentary, the suggestive and often complex wisdom" of the collaboration.

And yet Sturgeon also misses the real paradox and ultimate reason for the women's obscurity, that these poets of liberty never succeeded in breaking through the confines of their passionate devotion to each other. They wrote of their collaboration as a marriage; it is implicit in their dedicatory sonnet and is made explicit by Katherine, whose entry in the journal compares their work with that of the Brownings, each of whom wrote separately. From this Katherine concludes, *we are closer married,"* indicating an even greater exclusivity than that of the conventional monogamous relationship, since it extends through life and vocation to art.

Indeed, this exclusivity encompassed not only their reclusive life, but their art as well. Choosing to write in a genre not often attempted by women, and not popular in an age which preferred prose melodrama, the women discovered the "historical, ironical tragedy," or black comedy, the symbolist drama, and stream of consciousness dialogue. Making their plays "hard reading," in the words of Maynard, who also points out that by publishing their plays in prohibitively priced volumes and in limited editions, they guaranteed themselves "but a few readers" the women again accord with Pratt's "drowning theory." They recognized full well the need for concealment, which explains their use of the male pseudonym, and which gives reason why, after their real identities were known, their work took on a more complex, less traditional, more innovative tenor.

In reference to their art and life, the women often use the imagery of confinement, suffocation, and claustrophobia, images that are related to the captive woman figure that reappears throughout their work. Sandra Gilbert and Susan Gubar, in the Preface to their study of the nineteenth-century woman writer, metaphorically titled *The Madwoman in the Attic,* observe:

> Both in life and in art, we saw, the artists we studied were literally and figuratively confined. Enclosed in the architecture of an overwhelmingly male-dominated society, these literary women were also, inevitably, trapped in the specifically literary constructs of what Gertrude Stein was to call "patriarchal poetry." For not only did a nineteenth-century woman writer

have to inhabit ancestral mansions (or cottages) owned and built by men, she was also constricted and restricted by the Palaces of Art and Houses of Fiction male writers authored. We decided, therefore, that the striking coherence we noticed in literature by women could be explained by a common, female impulse to struggle free from social and literary confinement through strategic redefinitions of self, art, and society.

As early as a letter, dated November 23, 1884, to Robert Browning, Katherine recognized the need to escape from the stifling confines of the conventional Victorian drawingroom and redefine the self, art, and society according to the feminine ideal. Turning her own paradox, she wrote, "We hold ourselves bound in life and literature to reveal—as far as may be—the beauty of the high feminine standard of *the ought to be.* . . . By that I mean we could not be scared away, as ladies, from the tragic elements of life" [**Works and Days**].

Yet it is the tragic element of their own lives that— permitted an economic independence not afforded many Victorian women, which enabled them to escape the stifling drawingrooms for a "room of their own"—they insured their obscurity. In retreating to this room to create their "mosaics," they allowed it to become a Palace of Art and, like Tennyson's "Lady of Shalott" and the captive women in their own dramas, in seeking to express in their art the experience of life denied to so many women, they came to be prisoners of their art. Confusing their dramas with the experience of life, their art became their life. After the performance of *A Question of Memory,* for example, Edith noted in the journal, "I am a woman, and to bring out a play is experience of life—just what women feel so crushingly that they need. You men get it like breathing."

Concurrent with this substitution of art for life experience is the strong identification with one's characters, embodying those fantasies denied one in real life. As Edith reflected toward the end of her life, "I am an artist to the fingertips and I must bring the whole of my life to art, express it in terms of art. . . . I explain the strong physical identification I have with my characters." When such an artist, who has only vicariously experienced life from the tower of art without participating in it directly, is confronted by one who has, there is a feeling of bitter envy, accompanied by the notion that the vicarious experience of life through art is a suffocating existence. Katherine's reflections on Olive Schreiner, the successful novelist of *The Story of an African Farm* (1883), reveal this. Of Schreiner, one who has experienced life first hand in the African territories, Katherine writes [in **Works and Days**]:

> Olive Schreiner home from the Cape, after years of brute, wild life in Africa. The ambassador pays his respects to her, Watts asks to paint her (he is refused), she goes the round of the great. Lovers from Africa come after her—to sink on their knees as soon as they land. . . . Meditating on all this I am filled with jealousy; this woman has been worshipped—she has known solitude—she has walked naked in the open air, she has handled politics, she has set one up and put down another.

I have lived . . . , neither breathing nor being breathed upon.

We are the ones living "those todays / Of unborn generations" envisioned in the final lines of the women's final drama, and it would seem appropriate not to end on a note of suffocation, but upon breathless fantasy. Imagine that we have climbed that difficult stairway and, having knocked on the attic door, we discover that it is opened and that we have been awaited with welcome, we of "the younger generation." Imagine that we are greeted with these, the final lines from **"Fellowship,"** a poem which appeared in the American edition of *Underneath the Bough,* and which, though specifically written by Katherine for Edith, expresses what both women sought to achieve, their image of themselves and their mission, their hope for what they would be for "the younger generation."

> O friends, so fondly loving, so beloved, look up
>   to us,
> In constellation *breathing* [emphasis added] on
>   your errand arduous. . . . Now faded
>   from . . . sight
> We cling and joy. It was thy intercession gave
>   me right
> My fellow, to this fellowship—O Henry, my de-
>   light!
>
> Fellowship, pleasure / These are the trea-
> sure. . . .

(pp. 121-35)

David J. Moriarty, " 'Michael Field' (Edith Cooper and Katherine Bradley) and Their Male Critics," in Nineteenth-Century Women Writers of the English-Speaking World, *edited by Rhoda B. Nathan, Greenwood Press, 1986, pp. 121-42.*

Christine White (essay date 1990)

[*In the following excerpt, White uses the relationship between Bradley and Cooper to refute Lillian Faderman's theory of "romantic friendship" and to propose a more radical conception of nineteenth-century lesbianism. For Faderman's views, see excerpt dated 1981.*]

Katherine Bradley and Edith Cooper were poets and lovers from 1870 to 1913. They lived together, converted to Catholicism together, and together developed the joint poetic persona of Michael Field. As aunt and niece their love was socially structured and sanctioned. As Catholics and Classicists they developed a language of love between women. As Michael and Henry their life together is recorded in the surviving manuscript journals. And as Michael Field they presented themselves to the world as Poets. (The capitalization, and the sense of the importance of this activity, is theirs.) But were they lesbians in any recognizable sense? This question relates to a developing orthodoxy in lesbian history and politics, in particular the influential thesis of Lillian Faderman in *Surpassing the Love of Men* where she discusses Michael Field, an analysis which I will attempt to interrogate in this essay. I want to make an intervention in the interpretative practice employed by Faderman, whereby all loving relationships between women before the 1920s are viewed as romantic

friendships, and not as sexualized or erotic. Through connecting questions of homosexual history, politics, and desire, this essay will suggest a more radical theory of lesbian desire and lesbian history than Faderman's, by focusing on a specific body of writing.

In their relationship and their work, Katherine and Edith typify many of the difficulties in deciphering the meaning and nature of love between women. Faderman's comments are based only on published extracts (a slender volume concerned primarily with their lives as Catholics) from their extensive journals covering the years 1869-1914. The scale of this material is, in fact, enormous: thirty-six foolscap volumes, with several others consisting of correspondence and notes. It is a remarkable resource, but it is neither assimilable to a linear narrative nor capable of being easily represented here. (There is also the problem that some words and phrases are indecipherable.) It would be a mistake, however, to assume that these journals offer anything like a straightforward access to the 'truth' about the relationship or Katherine and Edith's understanding of it, even given all the usual reservations about the mediated status of autobiography. The journals were left with instructions that they might be opened at the end of 1929, and that the editors, T. and D. C. Sturge Moore, should publish from them as they saw fit. It hardly needs pointing out, therefore, that at some point the journals became directed towards publication. When that was, or whom the journals are addressed to, is never clear. There is, I must assume, no truly 'private' record.

There are in the journals and the poetry copious references that may be read as lesbian. These texts are dotted with the words 'Sapphic', 'Beloved', 'Lover' and 'Lesbian'. Although it is possible to infer that such terms indicate a same-sex relationship, Faderman insists that they are not at all sexual. I intend to demonstrate that these references are not simply definable as 'sexual' or 'non-sexual', but have their origins in more diverse sources. Any such analysis must be hedged around by considering the historically specific treatment of the Sapphic and the Lesbian.

Classical Greek literature and culture provided one way for nineteenth-century homosexual writers to talk about homosexuality as a positive social and emotional relationship. These authors appropriated the works of Plato and the myths of male love and comradeship to argue for social tolerance of same-sex love. For homosexual writers, a culture that was in the nineteenth century regarded as one of the highest points of civilization provided a precedent that was both respectable and sexual. This deployment of a Greek cultural precedent appears in Katherine and Edith's volume **Bellerophôn,** published under the pseudonyms Arran and Isla Leigh, in the poem **"Apollo's Written Grief,"** on the subject of Apollo and Hyacinth. This poem may be understood as a homo-political appeal for tolerance and an expression of the search for the right way of conducting a homosexual relationship:

> Men dream that thou wert smitten by the glow
> Of my too perilous love, not by the blow
> Of him who rivalled me.

Apollo's love for his 'bright-eyed Ganymede' is presented as the best option for the boy, since he would otherwise have been consumed by Zephyrus or Zeus 'in greed'. Apollo's love would not have proved dangerous to Hyacinth who, in 'panting for the light' of the sun-god, 'sufferedest the divine / Daring the dread delight'. This poem, therefore, employs the already existing construction and terminology for homosexual love and desire. These myths remained available to readings as homoerotic archetypes or ideals. But where a whole canon of male-male bondings and love exists, women had only one classical equivalent to draw upon for expressions and strategies of female-female love—in the poetry of Sappho. This classical antecedent must, moreover, be recuperated from male appropriations, salaciousness or prurience.

Katherine and Edith wrote at a time when treatments of Sappho's verse were numerous and diverse. There are instances of deliberate suppression of the female pronouns, as in T. W. Higginson's translation published in 1871. In the novels of Alphonse Daudet, Theophile Gautier and Algernon Charles Swinburne, Sappho and Sapphic women were constructed as sadistic, predatory corrupters of innocent women. A standard work on Greek culture describes Sappho as 'a woman of generous disposition, affectionate heart, and independent spirit . . . [with] her own particular refinement of taste, exclusive of every approach to low excess of profligacy'. Alternatively, another academic author declared that there was 'no good early evidence to show that the Lesbian standard was low' (that is, sexual). In other versions, Sappho was portrayed as a woman falling in love with the fisherman Phaon, committing suicide when that love was unreciprocated. The plurality of depictions and appropriations of Sappho indicate the extent to which Sappho became a cultural battleground, much more so than any male homosexual equivalent. Where some writers attempt to recuperate at all costs the great poet from accusations of lewdness, and others concede the love between women, but deny it as being passion of a base nature, Michael Field holds her up as a paragon among women, and puts the passion back into the poet's community of women. Michael Field's 1889 volume *Long Ago,* a series of poems based on and completing Sappho's fragments, explores the heterosexual version of Sappho, alongside poems on passion between women:

> Come, Gorgo, put the rug in place,
> And passionate recline;
> I love to see thee in thy grace,
> Dark, virulent, divine.

This is no sexless romance between friends, but rather a dangerous eroticism. 'Virulent' may relate in part to the appearances of Gorgo in Sappho's poetry. Fragment 44 reads 'I have had quite enough of Gorgo', and fragment 47 '[I cannot bear it;] . . . Archeanassa is Gorgo's lover . . .' Gorgo is a figure in Sappho's poetry who evokes despair and resentment in the poet, not sisterly feelings.

If this is one version of Sappho, there are at least two other Sapphos in *Long Ago.* One is a woman at the centre of a loving community of women, a community which she must keep safe from the intrusions of men. In poem LIV, **"Adown the Lesbian Vales"**, Sappho is in possession of a 'passionate unsated sense' which her maids seek to satisfy.

The relationship between Sappho and her maids is premissed upon a need to keep the women away from marriage: 'No girls let fall / Their maiden zone / At Hymen's call'. The third Sappho is the heterosexual lover of Phaon:

> If I could win him from the sea,
> Then subtly I would draw him down
> 'Mid the bright vetches; in a crown
> My art should teach him to entwine
> Their thievish rings and keep him mine.

This is a possessive heterosexual desire, springing from a manipulative battle to win him in a destructive competition with the fisherman's work at sea.

The second and third versions of Sappho come into conflict over the issue of virginity and poetry. The love of Phaon and the inviolate women of the Lesbian community are combined in poem XVII: 'The moon rose full, the women stood'. Sappho calls to her virginity, her 'only good', to come back, having been lost to Phaon. The inviolate state is 'that most blessèd, secret state / That makes the tenderest maiden great', not the possession of a male's sexual attention. Sappho's loss of virginity effectively puts an end to her poetic gift:

> And when
> By maiden-arms to be enwound
> Ashore the fisher flings,
> Oh, then my heart turns cold, and then
> I drop my wings.
>
> (*Long Ago*)

The connection between poetry and virginity is broached in *The New Minnesinger and Other Poems,* published by Katherine under the pseudonym of Arran Leigh. The title-poem discusses the craft of the woman-poet, 'she whose life doth lie / In virgin haunts of poesie'. The virgin woman poet, by virtue of her freedom from men, possesses the potentiality to be 'lifted to a free / And fellow-life with man'. But whatever 'realm' a woman endeavours to enclose, she must 'ever keep / All things subservient to the good / Of pure free-growing womanhood'. This version of femininity offers an ambiguous challenge to the terms of patriarchal culture. It exists apart from patriarchal dictates, but includes fellowship and equality with men. It embraces the productiveness of womanhood and an all-woman community, but concedes the reality of an attraction to men, destructive as that is.

It is this construction of femininity that makes the Michael Field relationship assimilable to Faderman's model of romantic friendship (or what I will label the Romantic Friendship Hypothesis). However, this construction is more complex than an unequivocal embrace of a nonsexual friendship. Michael Field represents Sappho as a wise old(er) woman who remembers the rejections of youth and deplores the fickleness of younger women and their susceptibility to men. Her constancy to women, 'Maids, not to you my mind doth change' (*Long Ago*, XXXIII), is contrasted with her reaction to the men whom she will 'defy, allure, estrange, / Prostrate, made bond or free'. To her maids she is a maternal or passionate lover, and to men she is manipulative and fickle. (The attitude to men is complicated by virtue of the poems being authored under the name of a man. The 'male' poet relates sexually to both men and women.) The volume concludes with poem LXIX, 'O free me, for I take the leap', where Sappho flings herself from a cliff with a prayer to Apollo for a 'breast love-free'.

Michael Field's Sappho, therefore, is not the denizen of a lesbian or Lesbian idyll. Rather, she is the subject of a contradiction which emerges from those versions described above. On the one hand, Sappho the poet must be defended from accusations of immorality, while, on the other, Sappho the Lesbian must be salvaged from the Phaon myth. The Lesbian community of women is more than a society of friendship, but is also a site of poetic production and, moreover, the production of the Poet identity. Both are threatened by men and heterosexuality. Sexuality is not, therefore, the only interpretative category in play in *Long Ago.* The practice of Poetry is equally as important, and it interweaves with sexuality. In the preface to *Long Ago* there is an ambiguous appeal to 'the other woman'. The volume is jointly authored, yet the voice of the preface is in the first person singular. This prefatorial voice advocates worship for, and the apprehension of, an ideal of the Poet and the lover in the poetry and person of Sappho. There is a direct connection made between Sappho's prayer and the prayer of this first-person voice:

> Devoutly as the fiery-bosomed Greek turned in her anguish to Aphrodite, praying her to accomplish her heart's desires, I have turned to the one woman who has dared to speak unfalteringly of the fearful mastery of love, and again and again the dumb prayer has risen from my heart—
>
> συ δ' αντα
> συμμαχσο εσσο

Here, the Greek is translated as 'you will be my ally'. The 'one woman' is either Sappho, a lover or a writing partner. This ambiguity of identity is central to this volume of poetry. In *Long Ago* Michael Field are writing with Sappho the Poet, and working with Sappho, Aphrodite and the partner in an imaginary alliance. The preface does not specify who that mastery of love is directed to. But perhaps that is the point. In order to speak 'unfalteringly' of woman's love for woman, it is necessary for Michael Field to work in alliance with other women and other women's formulations of such love. The construction in the preface is both strategic and passionate, not a privatized emotion which continues detached from historical and social concerns. It is political, creating changes in the presentation of love between women on the basis of the available cultural models. Finally, Michael Field's appeal to 'the one woman' does not rest upon a strategic image of monogamous romance, which while apparently neutral and ahistorical is intimately connected with bourgeois values and patriarchal family structures, and which lesbianism has the potential to sidestep or remake.

If, in the late twentieth century, contemporary lesbians are determined to write our own dictionary of lesbian love and desire, there appears to be no such imperative behind the writings of Michael Field. Current debates within lesbian politics take two principal forms: first, by reclaiming names that have been used derogatively, such as 'dyke'; second, by developing an entirely new framework of nam-

ing and reference. In *Another Mother Tongue: Gay Words, Gay Worlds,* Judy Grahn begins from a rejection of the so-called expert discourses of science, medicine, and law, and moves on to a rewriting/reinvention of a different, specifically gay cultural dictionary, since 'my little list of taboo words turned out to be keys to knowledge'. Language, and specifically names, are decisive for Grahn in developing a political critique of gay oppression. By contrast, Pat Califia's book *Sapphistry: The Book of Lesbian Sexuality* premisses its development of a lesbian cultural framework upon sexual fantasy and practice. All of these activities are brought under the heading of 'sapphistry', another indicator of the significance of the Lesbian poet for our cultural and political understandings. (pp. 197-202)

Michael Field, rather than inventing a vocabulary with an unmistakable precision of meaning, deploys the language of classical scholarship, the language of love belonging to heterosexuality, the language of friendship (but never noticeably the language of blood-relatives), and later the language of Catholicism. These differing languages represent a series of modulations both chronologically within their *œuvre* and in the different forms of writing they practised. There is no single language which they employ to talk about each other and their relationship. Consequently, there is enough imprecision or ambiguity in the slippage around their words of love and desire for Faderman, misleadingly, to find sufficient material in their writings to call them romantic friends. It is, of course, equally misleading to call them lesbians. Although the term 'lesbian' is historically available, it is not a word they ever used of themselves to indicate a sexual relationship. They did, however, have other terms and metaphors.

In comparing themselves to Elizabeth Barrett Browning and Robert Browning, Michael Field assert *'we are closer married'.* Marriage was an available metaphor or conceptualization for both women to apply to their relationship. Following Edith's death, Katherine invoked the words of the marriage service when making an approach to the literary periodical the *Athenæum* to 'write a brief appreciation of my dead Fellow-Poet, not separating what God has joined, yet dwelling for her friends' delight on her peculiar & most rare gifts'. In the preface to *Works and Days* God is said to have joined Michael Field both as the Poet and as 'Poets and lovers evermore'. And, as a last example, to Havelock Ellis, on the subject of his attempts to discover who wrote which piece, they asserted 'As to our work, let no man think he can put asunder what God has joined.' Faderman refuses any sexual meaning to these statements, insisting that since 'they were generally so completely without self-consciousness in their public declarations of mutual love', their love must have been 'innocent'. In addition to this, Faderman makes the error of deciding that their love for one another *'caused* them to convert to Catholicism' (my emphasis), since this conversion was a way to guarantee being together eternally. These two statements are in contradiction with one another, since if their love were innocent, they surely would not deliberately have planned for a united eternity. Faderman's specious theory appears to be based wholly upon one paragraph in the published journals, written by Edith: 'It is Paradise between us. When we're together eternally, our spirits will be interpenetrated with our loves and our art under the benison of the Vision of God'. Faderman derives the whole of their Catholic experience from this brief extract, which was written when Edith was dying. Moreover, Faderman ignores the evidence of the rest of the journals, which reveal their faith as being a good deal more than a mere instrumentalist insurance policy, and the history and pattern of Catholic conversion at that time, with many literary figures joining the Church and some, notably John Gray and Frederick Rolfe, becoming or attempting to become priests.

Faderman bases the Romantic Friendship Hypothesis on a specific construction of femininity. She presents it as the sole form of the relationship between loving women before the development of a female homosexual identity and pathology through political and scientific discourses, such as the work of the sexologists and the gay rights movements in Germany and France. Consequently, Faderman applies a modern version of relations between women to the late nineteenth century which precludes any consciousness of sexual interest. In doing so, she constructs all female friendships along the lines of the dominant culture. Faderman argues that, since sexual relationships between women were unacceptable to the dominant, and since women were constructed as the passionless gender and ignorant of sex, they could not possibly have had the knowledge, language, or experience of lesbian *desire*. Any Victorian woman, she maintains, would have been profoundly shocked by any such interpretation of their feelings, and therefore every woman's expression of love or passion must of necessity have been free from the taint of homosexual desire. Faderman does not even entertain the possibility that these women, knowing that the dominant culture condemned such feelings and relationships, could have developed their own strategies for talking about and explaining such expressions of sexuality. Instead she presumes that innocence is a superior form of loving compared to sexual experiences between women. She practices the condescension of history, and in doing so attempts to dodge the revelation of her own political agenda. Of course, Katherine and Edith did not have available to them the language, politics, and structures of contemporary lesbianism and feminism. But Faderman's insistence that they could not have known any better rests upon a belief in linear progress from one age to the next. Contemporary lesbians, so the argument goes, are much wiser than their nineteenth-century sisters because they of course can see through the mechanisms used to oppress and limit women. Therefore, by practising this evolutionary politics, Faderman manages to read over the top of all the strategies and devices that Michael Field, among many others, did deploy in order to create a cultural space for themselves. That these strategies did exist is beyond question. . . . (pp. 202-04)

My guess is that in 'romantic friendship' [Faderman] found an analogue to radical lesbian-feminism. She displays yet another methodological error in her making of history into analogues, since this works to deny the material specificity of the past as well as the present. Both romantic friendship and lesbian-feminism are positions distinguished by the desexualized nature of relations between women. This denial of lesbian sexual practice is spelt out by Elizabeth Mavor in *The Ladies of Llangollen: A Study in Romantic Friendship,* a work which in many respects provides the conceptual framework of Faderman's study:

> Much that we would now associate solely with a sexual attachment was contained in romantic friendship: tenderness, loyalty, sensibility, shared beds, shared tastes, coquetry, even passion.

This reading of love declarations between women and accounts of women living together as wholly non-sexual is explained by Faderman as follows:

> Women in centuries other than ours often internalised the view of females as having little sexual passion. . . . If they were sexually aroused, bearing no burden of proof as men do, they might deny it even to themselves if they wished.

Undoubtedly, women internalized the prescriptions of dominant ideology, but the leap from saying they took on board these prescriptions to the assumption that this internalization defined and limited all they believed and practised is quite breathtaking. In particular, it seems hardly credible that simply because women did not have penile erections they would not have recognized how sexual arousal felt and what it meant. Yet this is the outcome of the position adopted by Faderman and Mavor, which argues for a female nature utterly distinct from all things male and masculine. Both writers construct a time that is both more innocent and more separatist than our own. The radical lesbian-feminist position maintains that 'Lesbian separatism is feminism carried to its logical conclusion'. Accordingly, heterosexual feminists are said to be 'sleeping with the enemy', and the aim of every true feminist should be lesbianism, to stop participating in patriarchy by engaging in any way with men and to confront the very basis of society, heterosexuality. Lesbianism is not seen as a matter of sexual preference or political choice, but a political imperative. . . . Lesbian separatists construct lesbianism and lesbians as superior, more creative, more sensitive and more human. Romantic friendship is an expression of lesbian separatism which takes the form of a relationship that is, in Mavor's words, 'more liberal and inclusive and better suited to the more diffuse feminine nature'—not concentrated in an erect penis—and which, according to Faderman, 'had little connection with men who were so alienatingly and totally different'. The prescriptions of lesbian-feminism extend even into what happens sexually between women. Two women together escape the oppression of phallic heterosexuality, but to arrive in a utopian region of non-sexual romance and intimacy they must never behave in a manner which in any way reflects that in which men behave towards women.

Paradoxically, the Romantic Friendship Hypothesis is a celebration of many of the conventional attributes of femininity as it has been constructed by patriarchy, such as passivity, gentleness, domesticity, creativity and supportiveness, and which condemns as irretrievably phallic other characteristics generally labelled masculine, including strength, capability, activity, success, independence and lust. In claiming women-loving women as romantic friends, the hypothesis annihilates from history all those lesbians/lovers who gave histories to (or recognized themselves in the works of) sexologists such as Havelock Ellis, or who, alternatively, formed part of lesbian subcultures based on sexual preference and emotional commitment. Faderman's model consigns lesbian sexual activity to a male fantasy that routinely appears in pornographic writing. She opposes the pornographic image of women's sexuality to the 'true', non-sexual history of women's relationships which, it is claimed, appears in their diaries and writings. Having lighted upon male pornographic images of lesbian sex, Faderman concludes that if men talk about women having sex through a particular discourse, then since that discourse does not appear in women's writings, then women did not have sex together or relate sexually to each other.

I am not arguing that every close relationship between women was a sexual one. Rather, the point is, that the evidence should be looked at without the limitations of lesbian-feminist presuppositions. . . . I want to propose a 'pro-sex' history of lesbianism that gives such women as Michael Field at least some credit for awareness and strategic practice, and which has the potentiality to include within its frame of reference class, race, and power. This pro-sex investigation into lesbian history will reject the lesbian-feminist invention of a realm and an age of harmonious feminity where all women are equal, provided they do not indulge in politically right-off sexual activity.

In order to develop a framework in which to place the pro-sex history of lesbianism, I will now go on to look at the references to desire between women in the works of Michael Field, and examine the plurality of ways in which they talked about their understanding of sexual and emotional love between women. In analysing the treatment of sexuality in Michael Field's journals I will use 'fleshly sin' to denote practice which they did not recognize as having anything to do with their own relationship; and I will refer to 'fleshly love' to describe how they might have organized their understanding of the physical aspects of their relationship. Two instances of fleshly sin and fleshly love between women appear in the journals. Travelling through Europe, Edith fell ill in Dresden, and wrote: 'My experiences with Nurse are painful—she is under the possession of terrible fleshly love [which] she does not conceive as such, and as such I will not receive it.' Clearly the nurse does not recognize her experience. Edith, however, does conceive of this love as fleshly. It is certainly within Edith's conceptual framework to apprehend one woman's feelings of physical desire for another woman. This instance of fleshly love does not belong to the imagination of a pornographer. In the extract, the use of the words 'possession' and 'terrible' cannot be simply read as condemnatory, since any unwelcome sexual attentions may appear to be a terrible possession of the harasser. It is not clear, though, if it is the case that Edith would not accept fleshly love in any context, or that this particular instance is unwelcome.

The second example concerning fleshly sin appears in the manuscript journal for 1908, referring to a painting they saw.

> A man named Legrand—a monstrous charlatan—who can by a clever trick give the infamies of the worldly Frenchwoman—especially in unconscious self-conscious exposure to her own sex . . . [as manuscript] female friends together. What is to be expressed is of Satan—and the means as ugly as the matter. The people round me say 'He must be a Genius'—I answer to myself A Demon-Spawned Charlatan.

I have yet to trace this painting, but it obviously enraged Edith. She can read this picture as false and disgusting. The exposure is apparently to the female gaze, but actually for the male gaze. The prurience of that gaze is expressed through that 'unconscious self-consciousness', a wink at the audience, inviting the viewer in to enjoy the scene. This 'clever trick' is that of the pornographer. Two women apparently exist for their own pleasure, but they are actually on offer as double pleasure for the male viewer. The unreality of the scene is evident to Edith. Her racism is evident in her ascribing of infamies to Frenchwomen (and German women too, as evidenced by her comments on the nurse). The point is, she recognizes that Legrand's painting is a false image of how women behave to one another as 'female friends'. Edith repudiates the way in which patriarchal values frame and perceive relations between women. Legrand is a charlatan; his representation bears no relation to the truth. Yet this rejection is not the same thing as denying the existence of desire between women. However, what that truth is cannot easily be deduced from the writings.

Outside the treatment of Sappho, which is a minefield of interpretative complexity, there is in the journals very little explicit analysis of the relationship between Katherine and Edith. Katherine and Edith's primary concern is always with Michael Field the Poet, and it is the name itself I want to focus on now because it reveals to a large extent how they conceived of their practice as poets. That male-authored publications are usually better received and taken more seriously than female-authored works is a truism. Before the adoption of the joint persona they used the pseudonyms Arran and Isla Leigh, which brought them more favourable reviews than they ever had as Michael Field, and also the assumption that they were either a married couple or a brother and sister. Perhaps this misinterpretation is what led them to adopt the single penname. Although Katherine and Edith used metaphors of marriage to describe their love, it would be surprising if they had wanted to be publicly portrayed as a heterosexual couple. However, 'Michael Field' cannot be regarded as a true pseudonym, since it was widely known in a literary circle that included John Gray, George Meredith, and Oscar Wilde, as well as their friends Charles Ricketts and Charles Shannon, that they were two women. Much of their correspondence is addressed to them both under the heading of Michael Field and they often signed themselves with the joint name. The name contains a compelling contradiction: they both deploy the authority of male authorship and yet react against such camouflage. Michael Field is not a disguise. Nor is it a pretence at being a man.

None the less, they were appalled when they became known to their Catholic congregation as the women behind Michael Field. Edith confronted her confessor Goscommon:

> I say I regret it is known; but that in the same way, I am glad he, as my Confessor, knows, for it will help him to understand some things I feel he has somewhat misunderstood, & also it is for a poet with his freedom of impulse to submit to the control & discipline of the Church.

This anxiety for concealment is in marked contradiction to their previous willingness to be known. Wayne Koestenbaum offers the explanation that 'their aliases gave them a seclusion in which they could freely unfold their "natures set a little way apart" '. Yet that desired seclusion became impossible when they submitted to the authority of the Church. Even though their attempts to develop a framework in which to talk about their love and desires in part depended upon a screen from the world, this effort did not rest wholly upon the use of a male pen-name. Rather, the development of the poetic persona Michael Field gave them another role in which to play out their understandings of their relationship. The persona is distinct from Katherine and Edith, and separate from their pet names Michael and Henry, which were in common currency among friends. Michael Field the Poet is always presented as the highest point of their work.

Complicated shifts took place when they converted to Catholicism. Entering the Roman Catholic Church evokes from Edith the two explicit references to sexuality I have found. In the 1907 volume of the journals she wrote: 'Since I have entered the Holy Catholic Church, I have never fallen into fleshly sin', which presupposes that before she joined she had succumbed to such fleshly temptation. Here fleshly sin may be a reference to masturbation, but I am doubtful, given the second reference in 1908: 'When I came into this Church a year ago [I gave] a gift that was a vow of chastity.' Not practising masturbation may constitute abstinence from fleshly sin, but chastity in this context seems to involve another person. This may be an indication that before conversion there had been a sexual or erotic relationship between Katherine and Edith.

Edith, in one of her last entries before her death, wrote: "We have had the bond of race, with the delicious adventure of the stranger nature, introduced by the beloved father.' Since the word father is not capitalized, I hazard to guess that this is a reference to John Gray, a poet, a convert, a priest, Katherine's one-time confessor and spiritual adviser to them both. He was also the long-time lover of the poet Marc-André Raffalovich. The word 'race' here is intriguing, but again there is the notion of natures that are different. Although they had been in correspondence with Havelock Ellis, there is no evidence in their work of any belief or interest in sexology, inversion and the 'third sex'. That said, these remarks do seem to resonate with the notion of belonging to a 'breed apart'.

Their strategies for making sense of their love do not take the shape of pretending to be or believing themselves to be men, nor of understanding themselves to be romantic friends. In their account of their role as Michael Field and of their love for each other, Katherine and Edith construct a position of opposition against the misapprehensions and prejudices of the world. That opposition relies upon their alliance with one another, and with specific cultural formations that they recognize as expressive or reflective of that alliance. This is the impulse behind their declaration of 1893:

> My Love and I took hands and swore
> Against the world, to be
> Poets and lovers evermore.

The roles of poet and lover are both integral to one another and essential to their rejection of the judgment of 'the world'. This is an implicitly political understanding of women as lovers, rather than a private and personal retreat from the world into romantic friendship.

There is no strategy or organizing principle that they use to define themselves, a point which is demonstrated in the difference between the poem from 1893 and the prefatory poem from the 1875 volume *The New Minnesinger* by Arran Leigh (alias Katherine Bradley). **"To E. C."** refers to the 'mast'ring power' of the other woman's love, and the writer's need of that love which is 'forever voiceless'. The 'lighter passions' will find a way 'into rhythm', and the voiceless need is premissed upon the assertion that 'Thou hast fore-fashioned all I do and think'. This difference marks the shift from a virtual silence about the love to the opening up of a framework in which to talk about that love.

Edith and Katherine's methods of explaining their love and desire are difficult to decipher because they are so unlike our own modes of explanation. But the fact that we have that trouble does not mean that they encountered the same problem. It is, then, necessary to beware of failing or refusing to recognize the complexity of the negotiations these women-loving women made. If we do, as Faderman has done, then all those negotiations made within a hostile dominant culture would lead to a particularly restricted view—a homogeneous and desexualized version—of lesbian and gay history. . . . Much of the history of lesbianism remains to be written, and much of that which has already been written is wrong-headed and dishonest. What I have attempted to do here is to begin the process of mapping out the complicated processes whereby the discourses of lesbianism might have been inscribed in the nineteenth century, and not to fall into a simplistic one-theory-fits-all position. (pp. 204-10)

Christine White, " 'Poets and Lovers Evermore': Interpreting Female Love in the Poetry and Journals of Michael Field," in Textual Practice, *Vol. 4, No. 2, Summer, 1990, pp. 197-211.*

FURTHER READING

Biography

Ricketts, Charles S. *Michael Field*. Edinburgh: Tragara Press, 1976, 12 p.
  Limited-edition biography of Bradley and Cooper by a close friend.

Smith, Logan Pearsall. "Michael Field." In his *Reperusals and Re-Collections*, pp. 85-97. New York: Harcourt, Brace & Co., 1937.
  Personal impressions of Bradley and Cooper by a member of their literary circle.

Criticism

Alexander, Calvert. "Michael Field." In his *The Catholic Literary Revival: Three Phases in Its Development from 1845 to the Present*, pp. 140-49. 1935. Reprint. Port Washington, N.Y.: Kennikat Press, 1968.
  Focuses upon the religious zeal of Bradley and Cooper's later poetry.

Bush, Douglas. "Minor Poets, Mid-Victorian and Later." In his *Mythology and the Romantic Tradition in English Poetry*, pp. 407-09. 1937. Reprint. New York: W. W. Norton & Co., 1963.
  Assesses the writing style of Bradley and Cooper and comments on their use of pagan and Christian themes in the play *Callirrhoë*.

Evans, Ifor. "Minor Poets: II." In his *English Poetry in the Later Nineteenth Century*, rev. ed., pp. 334-35. London: Methuen & Co., 1966.
  Characterizes the plays of Bradley and Cooper as "possibly the most absolute example of the Victorian inability to distinguish between a blank-verse play that is dramatic and an amorphous work decorated with occasional passages of high-sounding verse."

Foster, Jeannette H. "Conjectural Retrospect: 'Michael Field'." In her *Sex Variant Women in Literature: A Historical and Quantitative Survey*, pp. 141-45. New York: Vantage Press, 1956.
  Attempts to characterize the nature of the relationship between Bradley and Cooper.

Massingham, H. J. "Sculpturesque Poetry." In his *Letters to X*, pp. 263-69. London: Constable & Co., 1919.
  Examines the union of classical and romantic elements in the verse of Bradley and Cooper, commenting that such a fusion gives their work "an air of arrested, petrified mobility."

Maynard, Theodore. "The Drama of the Dramatists." In his *Carven from the Laurel Tree: Essays*, pp. 45-50. Oxford: B. H. Blackwell, 1918.
  Focuses on the role of Catholicism in the lives and works of Bradley and Cooper.

McDonald, Jan. " 'Disillusioned Bards and Despised Bohemians': Michael Field's *A Question of Memory* at the Independent Theatre Society." *Theatre Notebook* 31, No. 2 (1977): 18-29.
  Recounts the practical difficulties surrounding the 1893 production of *A Question of Memory* as revealed in the journals of Bradley and Cooper and their correspondence with the Independent Theatre Society, the cast, and the director. This production represents the only staging of a Michael Field play to date.

"Recent Verse." *The Athenaeum*, No. 3402 (7 January 1893): 14.
  Reviews *Sight and Song*, praising its vivid detail, yet ultimately characterizing the work as uninspired.

Sturgeon, Mary C. "Michael Field (Katharine Harris Bradley and Edith Emma Cooper)." In her *Studies of Contemporary Poets*, rev. ed., pp. 347-67. New York: Dodd, Mead & Co., 1920.
  Lauds the work of Bradley and Cooper as passionate and powerful.

James Elroy Flecker

1884-1915

INTRODUCTION

(Born Herman James Elroy Flecker) English poet, dramatist, novelist, short story writer, essayist, critic, and translator.

Flecker is most often associated with the English Decadents of the 1890s, although his entire oeuvre postdates this period. Nonetheless, much of his work, most prominently his poetry and the drama *Hassan,* shares significant traits with the writings of the fin-de-siècle generation: the influence of nineteenth-century French poetry, an emphasis on the aesthetic rather than the ideological aspect of literature, and the frequent use of exotic subject matter. While his works have received criticism for what has been perceived as a consistent lack of strong emotion, they are more usually praised for their display of literary artistry.

Flecker was born in Lewisham, South London. His father was a clergyman and educator who, when Flecker was two years old, moved his family to Cheltenham, where he became headmaster of Dean Close School. Flecker attended Dean Close and Uppingham schools before matriculating at Trinity College, Oxford, in 1902. Although Flecker held a reputation among his peers as a precociously gifted writer and cultured aesthete, his academic performance was adequate at best. One year after his graduation, Flecker published his first collection of poems, *The Bridge of Fire,* which was uniformly dismissed as an imitation of the Decadent poets of the late nineteenth century. In 1908 he attended Cambridge University, where he studied modern and oriental languages with the intention of entering the consular service. Flecker became proficient in Turkish, Persian, and Arabic, translating poetry from these languages. After attaining a graduate degree as an interpreter in 1910, he took a position in the Levant Consular Service; that same year he published a second collection of poems as well as *The Grecians,* a philosophical dialogue that outlines a somewhat idiosyncratic system of education. Soon after assuming his post as vice consul in Constantinople, Turkey, Flecker was diagnosed as tubercular and returned to England for treatment. He spent several months in a sanatorium before resuming his duties in Constantinople. Following a relapse in 1911, he returned to active service as vice consul in Beirut, Lebanon.

Flecker's diplomatic career was undistinguished, and biographers note that he had conflicting feelings about living in the Middle East. On the one hand, exotic cultures appealed to his imagination and served as inspiration for his best works; on the other, Flecker was dismayed by the contrast between his ideal of the "East" and the everyday reality of his life there. Furthermore, some of his poems and letters written during this time express a profound homesickness for England. In the remaining years before his death in 1915, Flecker experienced an increasing de-

cline in health, while at the same time producing his most celebrated works—the poetry collections *The Golden Journey to Samarkand* and *The Old Ships* and the drama *Hassan*—as well as the verse drama *Don Juan* and a novel, *The King of Alsander.* He died at the age of thirty-one in a sanatorium at Davos, Switzerland. *Hassan* was published posthumously in 1922; when performed for the first time the following year, Flecker's drama became one of the most successful theatrical events of its time.

In his preface to *The Golden Journey to Samarkand,* Flecker declared that his foremost literary ambition was "to create beauty." It is this principle that aligns him with the various art-for-art's-sake movements in nineteenth-century literature, including Decadence, Symbolism, and Parnassianism, all of which originated in France and exerted an influence on poetry in England. While critics have observed characteristics of each of these literary schools in Flecker's work, he is primarily discussed as a follower of the Parnassians. Flecker explicitly stated his admiration for this group of mid to late nineteenth-century poets—which included Théophile Gautier, Charles Baudelaire, and José-María de Heredia—and his adherence to their highly formalistic precepts. Rejecting both the emotionalism and the advocacy of ideas that characterize the Romantic tradition, Flecker pursued the strictly formal beauty that has led critics to liken him to a sculptor or gemcutter for the scrupulous craft of his works. Accordingly, Flecker's writings are often viewed as excessively remote from common existence, a quality that is abetted by the exoticism of his subjects in such poems as "The Gates of Damascus" and "Brumana" and the drama *Hassan.*

Inspired in part by tales and characters from *The Arabian Nights, Hassan* combines poetry and prose to relate a story that contains strong elements of both comedy and tragedy. While some critics find that the comic and tragic aspects of the drama are not sufficiently integrated, others consider the work an ingenious amalgam of divergent moods. The heterogenous nature of *Hassan,* commentators conclude, is a reflection of its multiple stages of conception and composition, beginning in 1911 as a short farce and ultimately developing into a five-act play that was completed in 1913, although Flecker continued to revise the work until his death. While *Hassan* is made up largely of prose dialogue interspersed with poems, Flecker so conspicuously crafted his language throughout this work that it is often designated a "verse drama." Along with his poetry, *Hassan* established Flecker's reputation in modern literature as an author whose works continued and advanced the tradition of aestheticism. As Harold Monro wrote: "Flecker is among the 'tragic' figures in literature—the poet who has died young. . . . Few writers have devoted such careful study to their art, and few modern poets realized so truly the necessity for devotion to the art of poetry."

(See also *Dictionary of Literary Biography,* Vols. 10, 19, and *Contemporary Authors,* Vol. 109.)

PRINCIPAL WORKS

The Bridge of Fire (poetry) 1907
The Grecians (dialogue) 1910
Thirty-Six Poems (poetry) 1910; also published as
    Forty-Two Poems [enlarged edition], 1911
The Scholar's Italian Book (textbook) 1912
The Golden Journey to Samarkand (poetry) 1913
The King of Alsander (novel) 1914
The Old Ships (poetry) 1915
Collected Poems (poetry) 1916
Collected Prose (essays and criticism) 1920
Hassan (drama) [first publication] 1922
Don Juan (drama) [first publication] 1925

Douglas Goldring   (essay date 1907)

[*An English novelist and critic, Goldring was a friend of Flecker. In the following review of* Bridge of Fire, *he recognizes Flecker's promise as a poet but finds that this first collection suffers from the influence of the English Decadent writers of the 1890s. Goldring subsequently wrote admiring studies of Flecker's later works (see excerpt dated 1920 and Further Reading).*]

The artistic revival which took place in the latter part of the nineteenth century, and cast *The Yellow Book* and *The Savoy* before a yapping and inappreciative England, has had an influence on the work of many younger poets which can still be easily traced. It has caused them, amongst other things, to see in France the Holy Land of their Art, and to accept Baudelaire and Paul Verlaine as impeccable masters. Thus far its influence has certainly been a good one, but it is a pity that out of all the poets of France it has brought two into special prominence whose poetry, whilst being extraordinarily fascinating, is also very dangerous to imitate. Much of the most interesting verse which has appeared of late years (saving that which hails from Ireland) has suffered considerably from having derived from one or other of the writers mentioned. Our poets, in too many cases, have loved to pose as Pierrot babbling to the moon, smiling cynically to conceal a broken heart and unutterable desires; and Mr. James Flecker, whose verse is before us, is no exception. He acknowledges Baudelaire as his master, and *pour épater le bourgeois* (rather a commonplace thing to attempt nowadays) he has chosen to make a translation of "Les Litanies de Satan," thus paving the way for the poem at the end of the book, in which he describes his attitude towards life. Says he:

> Know me the slave of fear and death and shame.
> A sad Comedian, a most tragic Fool—

and describes himself, with evident gusto, as the "lean and swarthy poet of despair." This factitious despair is a little absurd, and Mr. Flecker does not imitate his master with very much success. Here and there, however, we can discover in his work sufficient traces of a personal note to make us regret that they are so few. The feeble dedicatory poem at the beginning of this book, and the following self-revealing lines:

> Do I remember tales of Galilee,
> I who have slain my faith and freed my will?
> Let me forget dead faith, dead mystery,
> Dead thoughts of things I cannot comprehend.
> Enough the light mysterious in the trees,
> Enough the faithful friendship of my friend . . .

indicate a whole set of thoughts and emotions which might have been developed, and could not fail to have been more interesting than exercises, however clever, in Gallic modes.

When Mr. Flecker forgets to pose, and is content to be sincere, he is sometimes curiously effective, as in the following lines:

> We that were friends to-night have found
>   A sudden fear, a secret flame;
> I am on fire with the soft sound
>   You make in uttering my name.
>
> Forgive a young and boastful man
>   Whom dreams delight and passions please,
> And love me as great women can,
>   Who have no children at their knees

From the point of view of sheer melody, the best thing in

the book is the poem called **"Pervigilium."** This is a remarkable performance as an exercise in metre, though the theme is, perhaps, a little hackneyed. On the whole, Mr. Flecker's book has been something of a disappointment to us. He has a good ear, his verses are remarkably finished, and he is extremely accomplished; but he seems to have some defect of temperament which wars against his success, and to lack entirely that magic touch which the gods often give (in their perversity) to quite dull and stupid people. It is a pity, because he is very clever. (pp. 33-4)

> *Douglas Goldring, in an originally unsigned review titled "The Bridge of Fire," in* The Academy, *No. 1850, October 19, 1907, pp. 33-4.*

The English Review   (essay date 1910)

[*In the following excerpt, the critic praises the artistry of* Thirty-Six Poems.]

Mr. Flecker is a young man, young enough to play with his art without falling into conceit. It is only the grace of youth that can visit a girl in the Kennington Road, and then, without being offensive, write about it in this fashion:

> The great and solemn-gliding tram,
>   Love's still-mysterious car,
> Has many a light of gold and white,
>   And a single dark red star.

It is only a very good workman who plays in this way with his tools; and we begin to realise that Mr. Flecker's charming skill is not an accident of youth when we come to **"The Ballad of Hampstead Heath,"** which describes with a marvellous economy of words a visit to London of young Bacchus and his crew. Mr. Flecker is indeed an artist. In **"The Ballad of Camden Town"** he handles the same metre and Camden Town of all places without a hint of jingle or vulgarity; we rather imagine roses twining round the Cobden statue. And in **"The Ballad of the Student in the South"** there is a poignant sweetness and a scholarly simplicity. For Mr. Flecker knows instinctively what two centuries of English poets have often forgotten, that emotional value depends largely on perhaps only apparent simplicity and that any inversion of the natural order of words is sudden death to any lyrical poem: therefore he is direct and personal, and his love of melody and of a beautiful choice of words does the rest. Not that he deals in those single words that are beautiful in themselves; he does not decorate his best work with "maunds of apples" or "habergeons" or "cramoisy" jewels that sparkle in a verse with their own light: but rather finds his effect by grace of design, by the perfect phrase. He has, in short, the virtue rare in English poets of being an artist, not an amateur. (pp. 767-68)

> *A review of "Thirty-Six Poems," in* The English Review, *Vol. 5, July, 1910, pp. 767-68.*

J. C. Squire   (essay date 1916)

[*Squire was an English man of letters who, as a poet, lent his name to the "Squirearchy," a group of poets who struggled to maintain the Georgian poetry movement of the early twentieth century. Typified by such poets as Rupert Brooke and John Drinkwater, Georgian poetry was a reaction against Victorian prolixity, turn-of-the-century decadence, and contemporary urban realism. Squire and the Georgians wished to return to the nineteenth-century poetic tradition of William Wordsworth and the Lake Poets, concerning themselves primarily with the traditional subjects and themes of English pastoral verse. Squire was also a prolific critic who was involved with many important English periodicals; he served as literary and, later, acting editor of the* New Statesman, *founded and edited the* London Mercury, *and contributed frequently to the* Illustrated London News *and the* Observer. *His criticism, like his poetry, is considered traditional and good natured. In the following excerpt from his introduction to Flecker's* Collected Poems, *which was first published in 1916, Squire examines the prominent characteristics of Flecker's poetry.*]

[The] most numerous and, on the whole, the best of his early poems are translations. And this is perhaps significant, as indicating that he began by being more interested in his art than in himself. Translating, there was a clearly defined problem to be attacked; difficulties of expression could not be evaded by changing the thing to be expressed; and there was no scope for fluent reminiscence or a docile pursuit at the heels of the rhyme.

In 1900-1, *æt.* 16-17, he was translating Catullus and the *Pervigilium Veneris,* and amongst the poets he attacked in the next few years were Propertius, Muretus, Heine, Bierbaum, of whose lyrics he translated several, one of which is given in this volume. This habit of translation, so excellent as a discipline, he always continued, amongst the poets from whom he made versions being Meleager, Goethe, Leconte de Lisle, Baudelaire, H. de Régnier, Samain, Jean Moréas, and Paul Fort. In the last year or two his translations were mostly made from the French Parnassians. What drew him to them was his feeling of especial kinship with them and his belief that they might be a healthy influence on English verse.

He explained his position in the preface to **The Golden Journey to Samarkand.** The theory of the Parnassians had for him, he said, "a unique attraction." "A careful study of this theory, however old-fashioned it may now have become in France, would, I am convinced, benefit English critics and poets, for both our poetic criticism and our poetry are in chaos." Good poetry had been written on other theories and on no theories at all, and "no worthless writer will be redeemed by the excellence of the poetic theory he may chance to hold." But "that a sound theory can produce sound practice and exercise a beneficent effect on writers of genius" had been repeatedly proved in the history of the Parnasse.

> The Parnassian School [he continued] was a classical reaction against the perfervid sentimentality and extravagance of some French Romantics. The Romantics in France, as in England, had done their powerful work and infinitely widened the scope and enriched the language of poetry. It remained for the Parnassians to raise the technique of their art to a height which should

enable them to express the subtlest ideas in powerful and simple verse. But the real meaning of the term Parnassian may be best understood from considering what is definitely not Parnassian. To be didactic like Wordsworth, to write dull poems of unwieldy length, to bury like Tennyson or Browning poetry of exquisite beauty in monstrous realms of vulgar, feeble, or obscure versifying, to overlay fine work with gross and irrelevant egoism like Victor Hugo, would be abhorrent, and rightly so, to members of this school. On the other hand, the finest work of many great English poets, especially Milton, Keats, Matthew Arnold, and Tennyson, is written in the same tradition as the work of the great French school: and one can but wish that the two latter poets had had something of a definite theory to guide them in self-criticism. Tennyson would never have published "Locksley Hall" and Arnold might have refrained from spoiling his finest sonnets by astonishing cacophonies.

There were, he naturally admitted, "many splendid forms of passionate or individual poetry" which were not Parnassian, such as the work of Villon, Browning, Shelley, Rossetti, and Verlaine, "too emotional, individual, or eccentric" to have Parnassian affinities:

> The French Parnassian has a tendency to use traditional forms and even to employ classical subjects. *His desire in writing poetry is to create beauty: his inclination is toward a beauty somewhat statuesque. He is apt to be dramatic and objective rather than intimate.* The enemies of the Parnassians have accused them of cultivating unemotional frigidity and upholding an austere view of perfection. The unanswerable answers to all criticism are the works of Hérédia, Leconte de Lisle, Samain, Henri de Régnier, and Jean Moréas. Compare the early works of the latter poet, written under the influence of the Symbolists, with his *Stances* if you would see what excellence of theory can do when it has genius to work on. Read the works of Hérédia, if you would understand how conscious and perfect artistry, far from stifling inspiration, fashions it into shapes of unimaginable beauty. . . . At the present moment there can be no doubt that English poetry stands in need of some such saving doctrine to redeem it from the formlessness and the didactic tendencies which are now in fashion. As for English criticism, can it not learn from the Parnassian, or any tolerable theory of poetic art, to examine the beauty and not the "message" of poetry.

> It is not [he said] the poet's business to save man's soul but to make it worth saving. . . . However, few poets have written with a clear theory of art for art's sake, it is by that theory alone that their work has been, or can be, judged;—and rightly so if we remember that art embraces all life and all humanity, and sees in the temporary and fleeting doctrines of conservative or revolutionary only the human grandeur or passion that inspires them.

His own volume had been written "with the single intention of creating beauty."

Though many of his own poems show the "tendency to use traditional forms and even to employ classical subjects," Flecker did not, it must be observed, dogmatize as to choice of subject or generalize too widely. The Parnassians were not everything to him, nor were those older poets who had resembled them. It was as a corrective that he recommended the study of this particular group to his English contemporaries. It is arguable that most of his major contemporaries—one might instance Mr. Bridges and Mr. Yeats—are anything but chaotic, extravagant, careless, or didactic. References to "the latest writer of manly tales in verse" and "formlessness" might certainly be followed up; but formlessness and moralizing are not so universal amongst modern English writers as Flecker, making out his case, implied. It does not matter; there is not even any necessity to discuss the French Parnassians. Flecker had an affinity with them. He disliked the pedestrian and the wild; he did not care either to pile up dramatic horrors or to burrow in the recesses of his own psychological or physiological structure. He liked the image, vivid, definite in its outline: he aimed everywhere at clarity and compactness. His most fantastic visions are solid and highly coloured and have hard edges. His imagination rioted in images, but he kept it severely under restraint, lest the tropical creepers should stifle the trees. Only occasionally, in his later poems, a reader may find the language a little tumultuous and the images heaped so profusely as to produce an effect of obscurity and, sometimes, of euphuism. But these poems, it must be remembered, are precisely those which the poet himself did not finally revise. Some of them he never even finished: **"The Burial in England,"** as it appears, is the best that can be done with a confusing collection of manuscript thoughts and second thoughts. He was, as he claimed, constitutionally a classic; but the term must not be employed too rigidly. He was, in fact, like Flaubert, both a classic and a romantic. He combined, like Flaubert, a romantic taste for the exotic, the gorgeous, and the violent, with a dislike for the romantic egoism, looseness of structure, and turgidity of phrase. His objectivity, in spite of all his colour, was often very marked; but there was another trend in him. Though he never wrote slack and reasonless *vers libres,* the more he developed the more he experimented with new rhythms; and one of his latest and best lyrics was the intensely personal poem **"Stillness."** He ran no special kind of subject too hard, and had no refined and restricted dictionary of words. A careful reader, of course, may discover that there are words, just as there are images, which he was especially fond of using. There are colours and metals, blue and red, silver and gold, which are present everywhere in his work; the progresses of the sun (he was always a poet of the sunlight rather than a poet of the moonlight) were a continual fascination to him; the images of Fire, of a ship, and of an old white-bearded man recur frequently in his poems. But he is anything but a monotonous poet, in respect either of forms, subjects, or language. It was characteristic of him that he should be on his guard against falling into a customary jargon. Revising **"The Welsh Sea"** and finding the word "golden," which he felt he and others had overdone, used three times (and not ineffectively) in it, he expunged the adjective outright, putting "yellow" in the first two places and "slow green" in the third. His preface on

Parnassianism was whole-hearted; but any one who interpreted some of his sentences as implying a desire to restrict either the poet's field or his expression to a degree that might justifiably be termed narrow would be in error. In one respect, perhaps, his plea was a plea for widening; he did not wish to *exclude* the classical subject. And his declaration that poetry should not be written to carry a message but to embody a perception of beauty did not preclude a message in the poetry. His last poems, including **"The Burial in England,"** may be restrained but are scarcely impersonal, may not be didactic but are none the less patriotic. He need not, in fact, be pinned to every word of his preface separately. The drift of the whole is evident. He himself, like other people, would not have been where he was but for the Romantic movement; but he thought that English verse was in danger of decomposition. He merely desired to emphasize the dangers both of prosing and of personal paroxysms; and, above all, to insist upon careful craftsmanship.

This careful craftsmanship had been his own aim from the beginning. "Libellum arida modo pumice expolitum" is a phrase in the first of the Catullus epigrams he translated at school; and, whilst the content of his poetry showed a steadily growing strength of passion and thought, its form was subjected to, though it never too obviously "betrayed," an increasingly assiduous application of pumice-stone and file. His poems were written and rewritten before they were printed; some were completely remodelled after their first publication; and he was continually returning to his old poems to make alterations in single words or lines—many of his recent MS. alterations are now incorporated for the first time. His changes at their most extensive may be seen in the development of **"The Bridge of Fire,"** in that . . . of **"Narcissus,"** and in that of **"Tenebris Interlucentem."** As first published this ran:

> Once a poor song-bird that had lost her way
> Sang down in hell upon a blackened bough,
> Till all the lazy ghosts remembered how
> The forest trees stood up against the day.
>
> Then suddenly they knew that they had died,
> Hearing this music mock their shadow-land;
> And some one there stole forth a timid hand
> To draw a phantom brother to his side.

In the second version, also of eight lines, each line is shorter by two syllables:

> A linnet who had lost her way
> Sang on a blackened bough in Hell,
> Till all the ghosts remembered well
> The trees, the wind, the golden day.
>
> At last they knew that they had died
> When they heard music in that land,
> And some one there stole forth a hand
> To draw a brother to his side.

The details of this drastic improvement are worth studying. The treatment of the first line is typical. The general word "song-bird" goes, the particular word "linnet" is substituted; and the superfluous adjective is cut out, like several subsequent ones. **"Gravis Dulcis Immutabilis"** was originally written as a sonnet; the **"Invitation to a Young but Learned Friend"** was considerably lengthened after an interval of years; and the poet's own copies of his printed volumes are promiscuously marked with minor alterations and re-alterations. One of the most curious is that by which the sexes are transposed in the song printed first as **"The Golden Head"** and then as **"The Queen's Song."** The last four lines of the first stanza originally ran:

> I then might touch thy face
>   Delightful Maid,
> And leave a metal grace,
>   A graven head.

This was altered into:

> I then might touch thy face
>   Delightful boy,
> And leave a metal grace,
>   A graven joy.

The reasons for the alteration are evident. The sounds "ace" and "aid" are uncomfortably like each other; the long, lingering "oy" makes a much better ending of the stanza than the sound for which it was substituted; and the false parallelism of "metal grace" and "graven head" was remedied by eliminating the concrete word and replacing it by another abstract one on the same plane as "grace." Such a substitution of the abstract for the concrete word, sound enough here, is very rare with him; normally the changes were the other way round. He preferred the exact word to the vague; he was always on his guard against the "pot-shot" and the complaisant epithet which will fit in anywhere. With passionate deliberation he clarified and crystallized his thoughts and intensified his pictures.

He found, as has been said, kinship in the French Parnassians: and, though he approached them rather as a comrade than as a disciple, traces of their language, especially perhaps that of de Régnier and Hérédia, may be found in his later verse. A reading of Hérédia is surely evident in the **"Gates of Damascus"**: in

> Beyond the towns, an isle where, bound, a naked
>   giant bites the ground:
> The shadow of a monstrous wing looms on his
>   back: and still no sound.

and the stanzas surrounding it. An influence still more marked is that of Sir Richard Burton. Flecker, when still a boy, had copied out the whole of his long *Kasidah,* and its rhythms and turns of phrase are present in several of his Syrian poems. It was in the *Kasidah* that Flecker found Aflatun and Aristu, and the refrain of "the tinkling of the camel-bells" of which he made such fine use in *The Golden Journey.* The verse-form of the *Kasidah* is, of course, not Burton's, it is Eastern; and the use Flecker made of it suggests that an infusion of Persian and Arabic forms into English verse might well be a fertilizing agent. He always read a great deal of Latin verse: Latin poetry was as much to him as Greek history, myth, and landscape. Francis Thompson, Baudelaire, and Swinburne were all early "influences." He learnt from them but he was seldom mastered by them. He did not imitate their rhythms or borrow their thought. The Swinburnian **"Anapæsts"**—in [*The Bridge of Fire*]—written in a weak moment, were an exception. In Flecker's printed copy the title has first, in a half-hearted effort to save the poem whilst repudiating its second-hand music and insincere sentiments, been changed to "Decadent Poem"; and then a thick pencil has been drawn right through it. (pp. xviii-xxviii)

In the Envoy to **The Bridge of Fire** he speaks of himself as "the lean and swarthy poet of despair." It meant nothing; the first poem in the same book, with its proclamation that "the most surprising songs" must still be sung, and its challenge to youth to turn to "the old and fervent goddess" whose eyes are "the silent pools of Light and Truth" is far more characteristic of him, first and last. "Lean and swarthy poet" may stand; but not of despair. The beauty of the world was a continual intoxication to him; he was full, as a man, if not as a poet, of enthusiasms, moral and material, economic, educational, and military. Neither the real nor the spurious disease of pessimism is present in his verse and in his last autumn he was writing, with an energy that sometimes physically exhausted him, poems that blazed with courage, hope, and delight. Like his **"Old Battleship,"** he went down fighting. (p. xxx)

> *J. C. Squire, in an introduction to* The Collected Poems of James Elroy Flecker *by James Elroy Flecker, edited by J. C. Squire, Alfred A. Knopf, 1921, pp. ix-xxx.*

Walter de la Mare   (essay date 1916)

[*An English poet, novelist, short story writer, dramatist, and critic, de la Mare is considered one of modern literature's chief exemplars of the romantic imagination. His complete works form a sustained treatment of romantic themes: dreams, death, rare states of mind and emotion, fantasy worlds of childhood, and the pursuit of the transcendent. Best remembered as a poet and writer of children's verse, de la Mare is also recognized for his novel* Memoirs of a Midget *(1921), a study of the social and spiritual outsider, a concern central to de la Mare's work. In the following excerpt, he offers a positive assessment of Flecker's poetry.*]

To those poets whose fortune it has been to die young, and so at least escape the tragic survival of their own genius, only the last awakening of all has brought what we call fame. Fame, of course, is a relative thing, a kind of genial grace long after the meal of a would-be generous and grateful humanity is over. In promising or anticipating it we merely bequeath to posterity the virtue of our own good taste. None the less it is some sort of a happy ending to a romantic tale, and the poet who leaves a few lyrics behind him that will outlive the passing fashion of his time has won a fair reward in this curious world, though it is quite certain that every true poet would have worked none the less enthusiastically without the least hope of it.

James Elroy Flecker was such a poet. Even in a translation from Catullus, made when he was sixteen, there falls a cadence that makes the sentiment his own:—

> Wherefore to you, my friend, I dedicate
> This so indifferent bookling; yet I pray,
> Poor as it is—"O goddess of my fate,
> Let it outlive the writer's transient day!"

Much later, again, in words and measure now all his own, he invokes a poet of "a thousand years hence":—

> O friend unseen, unborn, unknown,
> Student of our sweet English tongue,
> Read out my words at night, alone:
> I was a poet, I was young.
>
> Since I can never see your face
> And never shake you by the hand,
> I send my soul through time and space
> To greet you. You will understand.

One's contemporaries are more hard of hearing; and Flecker is not yet so well known, perhaps, as are other poets even of our own day—as Rupert Brooke, for instance, who was a good many years younger than himself. His achievement is unlikely to occupy the industrious commentator, or to become the esoteric nucleus of a learned society. If it live, it will be because beauty created in words cannot easily die. It is too rare, and men treasure it for the sake not only of memory, but of hope. Flecker's one desire, indeed, was to create beauty, and because he would not, it may be too because he could not, follow other lures; when he wins his desire, he wins all. When he fails of it, the husk is of little value. (p. 457)

[Flecker], his whole life long, was an exile. Mysteriously woven into his nature and imagination was a passion for all that an untravelled mind means by the East. "In days long gone," he wrote in **"Pavlovna in London,"**

> Have I not danced with gods in garden lands?
> I too a wild unsighted atom borne
> Deep in the heart of some heroic boy
> Span in the dance ten thousand years ago,
> And while his young eyes glittered in the morn
> Something of me felt something of his joy,
> And longed to rule a body, and to know.

That recurrent "finest story in the world" may not seem even to a Western mind "all moonshine." But experience proved that no earthly East was Flecker's true goal. He delighted, with a tense, almost violent excitement, in colour and sensuous beauty, in times and places remote, in names and men and relics romantic and bizarre. His desire was always for the strange. But a direct acquaintance with Mahomedanism served only to illuminate Christianity. Greece he loved, and one of his last fragmentary poems is a tribute to its "glory."

> Yet still Victorious Hellas, thou hast heard
> Those ancient voices thundering to arms,
> Thou nation of an older younger day
> Thou hast gone forth as with the poet's song.
> Surely the spirit of the old oak grove
> Rejoiced to hear the cannon round Yannina,
> Apollo launched his shaft of terror down
> On Salonica. . . .

How strangely these lines, written perhaps not two years ago, fall upon the ear just now! But, though Greece was his devotion, Flecker actually confessed to Mr. Savery that "he had not greatly liked the East." As time went on a more personal element welled into work that is for the most part singularly and deliberately devoid of it. Memory and desire in **"Oak and Olive"** carry his thoughts back from Athens to Charing-cross and "a hall in Bloomsbury," to Gloucester lanes and Painswick-hill. He was happiest, like most of us, in the place where he was not; never will seem the world so fair as on our last earthly morning. Absence enkindled his imagination. But seldom indeed have romantic dream and actuality, the strange and the familiar, been so closely reconciled, with so generous and balanced an ardour, as in the poem which he was still working on at the last, **"The Burial in England."** The war broke in upon his isolation and inflamed his love for the old familiar things. It made him England's heart and soul; but this in no sense entailed any sacrifice of his poetic ideal. By a delightful paradox the poet of that witty fantasia **"The Hammam Name,"** wherein "a Turkish lady" deliriously records the charms of her "Winsome Torment" taking his morning bath—"Bitterness was born of beauty; as for the shampooer, he Fainted, till a jug of water set the Captive Reason free"; the poet also of that delicate, fainting sigh of languor and loveliness, **"Yasmin,"** and of "the Chief Grocer's" catalogue of Oriental delicatessen, lived long enough to spend his time and skill, when little time was left to him, on a revised version of the National Anthem. Popular taste will probably remain loyal to Henry Carey, but Flecker had learned much of his craftsmanship in the translation of his favourite Latin and French poets, and of such translations this out of the English was unquestionably his boldest masterpiece.

But though the later work reveals Flecker as a poet heart and soul with those thoughts and aspirations which we all hold in common just now, he was none the less never instinctively a sociable poet. He was a solitary, and in some men home-sickness antedates even childhood. Unlike, therefore, the majority of poets, he did not transform the common into the miraculous, nor web in primrose and skylark with charmed and tender analogy and metaphor, nor merely accept from nature and humanity what poetic imagination may find in them to delight in. He left all this for the most part unheeded, and pressed on into the virgin region of fantasy; he laboured to make the singular unique, the romantic magical, and the rare unparalleled. The beauty he hungered for is indeed past mortal capture and perilous in pursuit. It cheated or beguiled him on, and ever on. When Lord Arnaldos, gone a-hunting, entreated the sailor of the little ship on the green and shallow sea for God's sake to interpret the song he was singing at the helm, the sailor made answer, "I only tell my song to those Who sail away with me." One at least of the merchants in **"The Golden Journey"** was in quest of impracticable merchandise—

> We travel not for trafficking alone:
> By hotter winds our fiery hearts are fanned:
> For lust of knowing what should not be known
> We make the Golden Journey to Samarkand,

and the Watchman in vain endeavours to console the women mournfully indignant at dreams unshackled by "thoughts of us"; "What would ye, ladies? It was ever thus. Men are unwise and curiously planned," and voices fainting into the distance chaunt on, "We make the Golden Journey to Samarkand." On Iskander, too, and his crew, eighty days after voyaging past the flat Araunian coasts "Inhabited, at noon, by Ghosts," and three score and ten after seeing the land of Calcobar, where men not

only drink blood, but "dye their beards alizarine," sink beneath the horizon, storm fell "And drave them out to that Lone Sea Whose shores are near Eternity." A Ship of Dreams, silken and silver, an exquisitely fresh and beguiling replica of their cankered, warped, and rotting poop, is sighted, and Aristotle and Plato, who (under a seductive and Oriental *alias*) have been "impressed" by the Sultan Iskander, are very much at odds concerning her:—

> "And lo! beside that mainmast tree
> Two tall and shining forms I see,
> And they are what we ought to be,
> Yet we are they, and they are we."
>
> He spake, and some young Zephyr stirred,
> The two ships touched: no sound was heard;
> The Black Ship crumbled into air;
> Only the Phantom Ship was there. . . .

It is an old and tragic, yet consoling parable, and one that Flecker never wearied of enriching and enhancing. The beauty of the world to him was not, as it is to some men, an anodyne, or merely a mystical symbol, but "a continual intoxication." Yet out of his passion for the strange came the sense of mystery that was to haunt his later years. Phantasms ("tall stone men") that recall the poems of Blake for an instant gaze out of his verse and are gone. The silent throng about him. A poem called **"November Eves"**—one of the very few clearly and definitely recorded remembrances of his childhood—is tinged with this "otherness." **"The Pensive Prisoner"** is the tormented expression of an experience that defied even his mature skill and power wholly to reveal:—

> My thoughts came drifting down the Prison where I lay—
> Through the Windows of their Wings the stars were shining—
> The wings bore me away—the russet Wings and grey
> With feathers like the moon-bleached Flowers—I was a God reclining:
> Beneath me lay my Body's Chain and all the Dragons born of Pain
> As I burned through the Prison Roof to walk on Pavement Shining. . . .

When thought becomes as instant and close as this, it is reality that dangerously faints into dream. So, too, there is a thin edge to sensibility which even music itself, as distinguished from words, can hardly express. **"The Blue Noon"** is such an ecstatic vision—of light and colour, air and space, wherein this solid globe is merely an iridescent bubble that may at any moment vanish away, leaving the consciousness free in a bodiless yet sensuous delight. Even if it be fever and malady which admits these experiences, sound sanity, just our commonplace selves, can test their truth, and maybe in so doing realize a foretaste of a life beyond the grave. But fear stands in the way, and in **"Stillness"** the door of the imagination which Flecker had always left lightly ajar for his own escape is forced open by a menacing, unendurable ingression from "the other side." Here he can no longer cloak the strange—which, it is prudent to remember, is never far out of calling of the sinister—with a fantastic humour, or elude its gravity with an airy, inconsequent wit, or deck it up, as he sometimes does, to look very much like a solemn and irresponsible nonsense. This extreme revulsion of feeling, however, evokes from him one of the tenderest and loveliest, as well as "strangest," things in all his poetry:—

> When the words rustle no more,
> And the last work's done,
> When the bolt lies deep in the door,
> And Fire, our Sun,
> Falls on the dark-laned meadows of the floor;
>
> When from the clock's last chime to the next chime
> Silence beats his drum,
> And Space with gaunt grey eyes and her brother Time
> Wheeling and whispering come,
> She with the mould of form and he with the loom of rhyme:
>
> Then twittering out in the night my thought-birds flee,
> I am emptied of all my dreams:
> I only hear Earth turning, only see
> Ether's long bankless streams,
> And only know I should drown if you laid not your hand on me.

Like Keats, like Stevenson, Flecker fought a brave fight against an insidious enemy, and, as Mr. Squire remarks emphatically [see excerpt dated 1916] . . . Flecker was never the "poet of despair." It is true he once said he was—and "lean and swarthy" to boot—but that was merely a little self-indulgence common to the youthful and fervent. He wrote **"No Coward's Song":**—

> I am no coward who could seek in fear
> A folk-lore solace or sweet Indian tales;
> I know dead men are deaf and cannot hear
> The singing of a thousand nightingales. . . .

But did he know it? Was not the thought merely one of those objective, intimidating hints which the body at times deems it prudent to "palm off" upon the spirit? "Yet is not death the great Adventure?" he cried almost jovially on the young English patriots of 1914, many of whom have now faced it, while he himself was to embark but a few weeks after. He was sure what "True Paradise" would satisfy his longing: "We poets crave no heav'n but what is ours," a familiar world re-fashioned, without "Man's and Nature's pain":—

> Grant me earth's treats in Paradise to find.
> Nor listen to that island-bound St. John.
> Who'd have no Sea in Heaven, no Sea to sail upon!

Notes of exclamation are rare in Flecker's verse, and in a volume that contains **"The Old Ships," "The Old Warship Ablaze," "Santorin,"** and **"The Ballad of Iskander"** that particular one must be given an unusual emphasis. Of the joys of that romantic heart none excelled that of ships and the sea and the "talkative bald-headed" mariners that go down upon it. Where else should he discover such beauty and agedness and wonder?—

> It was so old a ship—who knows, who knows?
> —And yet so beautiful I watched in vain
> To see the mast burst open with a rose,

And the whole deck put on its leaves again.

It was certainly as much man's imagination as his soul which Flecker was convinced it is the poet's business to make worth saving. His "single interest," it may be repeated, was "to create beauty"—a beauty as indisseverable from its form as that of a piece of consummate craftsmanship in stone or metal. The will, alas! must be inherent in the deed. Unlike the majority of English poets, he had an æsthetic theory which he enforced in his practice. It was not less his own because he learned it from the French Parnassians. He disapproved of the customary plump and variegated British nosegay in verse culled more or less at haphazard from the gardens of delight; he sought for a poetic attar distilled in the imagination. Such essences are not rare in English lyric; other poets than Flecker have studied alchemy—Keats, Milton, Herrick, and many more; but Britons, whether they write in verse or in prose, object to being slaves (or even "in service") to any particular theory. Yet though a man is born a poet, he must make himself an artist. If poetry, like love and faith, is the first-fruits of an instinctive impulse in a man, art, like chivalry and courtesy and conduct, is a manifestation of character. By sheer, hard, ardent work Flecker became an artist.

Not least of the delights of [*The Collected Poems of James Elroy Flecker*] is to watch his gradual but sure progress, year by year, towards a technical mastery. He sought for the strange and marvellous in life; he sought for the precise yet uncustomary word and phrase that would recreate, embody it. He scorned, says Mr. Squire, "the potshot." Search for what we may long enough, it will come at last of its own free natural will. So it was with him. In his earlier work bizarre epithets stick out like gems on a turban. In his later the tissue is uninterrupted, of a piece. Serene and happy in the apparently unlaboured expression of dream, feeling, fantasy, and truth, we no longer exclaim at mere "felicities." A hardness and sharpness may be the frigid defect of such work. Concision, pure outline, clarity, and a lovely detachment like that of some flower, curiously flawless and exotic, burning in the quiet solitude of a wood, are its imperishable virtues. We must not ask of such poetry what it does for us, but what it does *to* us. We cannot, so to speak, detach from it ideas, "beauties," apophthegms, fine feelings, as we mercilessly smoke bees out of a hive. It is not intentionally helpful or instructive or edifying. At its best it is honey of Hymettus in the cell, to be enjoyed not because it is wholesome or nourishing, but because it is delicious. When he died Flecker's imagination was turning homewards, like some high-pooped, "overpeering" Elizabethan argosy, slow in the water for its burden of apes, spices, ivory, and Orient pearl. We can only guess at further voyaging into the might have been. Enough that he has transported us—even though such travellers must bear the heavy burden of themselves on their backs, even though the poet himself chaunted a dirge to sweet illusion:—

> Oh shall I never never be home again?
> Meadows of England shining in the rain
> Spread wide your daisied lawns; your ramparts green
> With briar fortify, with blossom screen
> Till my far morning—and O streams that slow

And pure and deep through plains and playlands
        go,
For me your love and all your kingcups store,
And—dark militia of the southern shore,
Old fragrant friends—preserve me the last lines
Of that long saga which you sang me, pines,
When, lonely boy, beneath the chosen tree
I listened, with my eyes upon the sea.
O traitor pines, you sang what life has found
The falsest of fair tales.
Earth blew a far-horn prelude all around,
That native music of her forest home,
While from the sea's blue fields and syren dales
Shadows and light noon-spectres of the foam
Riding the summer gales
On aery viols plucked an idle sound.
Hearing you sing, O trees,
Hearing you murmur, "There are older seas,
That beat on vaster sands,
Where the wise snailfish move their pearly tow-
        ers
To carven rocks and sculptured promont'ries,"
Hearing you whisper, "Lands
Where blaze the unimaginable flowers."

                                        (pp. 457-58)

*Walter de la Mare, in an originally unsigned
essay titled "James Elroy Flecker," in* The
Times Literary Supplement, *No. 767, September 28, 1916, pp. 457-58.*

Holograph manuscript of an early version of "The Old Ships."

Robert Lynd   (essay date 1919)

[*Lynd was an Irish journalist and critic. In the following
excerpt, he summarizes Flecker's achievement as a
poet.*]

[Flecker] was one of those poets whose genius is founded
in the love of literature more than in the love of life. He
seems less an interpreter of the earth than one who sought
after a fantastic world which had been created by Swinburne and the Parnassians and the old painters and the
tellers of the *Arabian Nights.*

"He began," Mr. J. C. Squire has said, "by being more interested in his art than in himself" [see excerpt dated
1916]. And all but a score or so of his poems suggest that
this was his way to the last. He was one of those for whom
the visible world exists. But it existed for him less in nature
than in art. He does not give one the impression of a poet
who observed minutely and delightedly as Mr. W. H. Da-
vies observes. His was a painted world inhabited by a
number of chosen and exquisite images. He found the real
world by comparison disappointing. "He confessed," we
are told, "that he had not greatly liked the East—always
excepting, of course, Greece." This was almost a necessity
of his genius; and it is interesting to see how in some of
his later work his imagination is feeling its way back from
the world of illusion to the world of real things—from
Bagdad and Babylon to England.

His poetry does not as a rule touch the heart; but in **"Oak
and Olive"** and **"Brumana"** his spectatorial sensuousness
at last breaks down and the cry of the exile moves us as
in an intimate letter from a friend since dead. Those are
not mere rhetorical reproaches to the "traitor pines"
which

        sang what life has found
    The falsest of fair tales;

which had murmured of—

        older seas
    That beat on vaster sands,

and of—

        lands
    Where blaze the unimaginable flowers.

It was as though disillusion had given an artist a soul. And
when the war came it found him, as he lay dying of consumption in Switzerland, a poet not merely of manly but
of martial utterance. **"The Burial in England"** is perhaps
too much of an *ad hoc* call to be great poetry. But it has
many noble and beautiful lines and is certainly of a different world from his mediocre version of **"God Save the
King."**

At the same time, I do not wish to suggest that his poetry
of illusion is the less important part of his work. The perfection of his genius is to be sought, as a matter of fact,
in his romantic eastern work, such as **"The Ballad of Iskander," "A Miracle of Bethlehem," "Gates of Damascus,"** and **"Bryan of Brittany."** The false, fair tale of the
East had, as it were, released him from mere flirtation with
the senses into the world of the imagination. Of human
passions he sang little. He wrote oftener of amorousness

than of love, as in **"The Ballad of the Student of the South."** His passion for fairy tales, his amorousness of the East, stirred his imagination from idleness among superficial fancies into a brilliant ardour. (pp. 112-14)

Flecker is anything but a monotonous poet. But the image of a ship was almost an obsession with him. It was his favourite toy. Often it is a silver ship. In the blind man's vision in the time of Christ even the Empires of the future are seen sailing like ships. The keeper of the West Gate of Damascus sings of the sea beyond the sea:

> when no wind breathes or ripple stirs,
> And there on Roman ships, they say, stand rows
> of metal mariners.

Those lines are worth noting for the way in which they suggest how much in the nature of toys were the images with which Flecker's imagination was haunted. His world was a world of nursery ships and nursery caravans.

"Haunted" is, perhaps, an exaggeration. His attitude is too impassive for that. He works with the deliberateness of a prose-writer. He is occasionally even prosaic in the bad sense, as when he uses the word "meticulously," or makes his lost mariners say:

> How striking like that boat were we
> In the days, sweet days, when we put to sea.

That he was a poet of the fancy rather than of the imagination also tended to keep his poetry near the ground. His love of the ballad-design and "the good coloured things of Earth" was tempered by a kind of infidel humour in his use of them. His ballads arc the ballads of a brilliant dilettante, not of a man who is expressing his whole heart and soul and faith, as the old ballad-writers were. In the result he walked a golden pavement rather than mounted into the golden air. He was an artist in ornament, in decoration. Like the Queen in the **"Queen's Song,"** he would immortalize the ornament at the cost of slaying the soul.

Of all recent poets of his kind, Flecker is the most successful. The classical tradition of poetry has been mocked and mutilated by many of the noisy young in the last few years. Flecker was a poet who preserved the ancient balance in days in which want of balance was looked on as a sign of genius. That he was what is called a minor poet cannot be denied, but he was the most beautiful of recent minor poets. His book, indeed, is a treasury of beauty rare in these days. Of that beauty, **"The Old Ships"** is, as I have said, the splendid example. And, as it is foolish to offer anything except a poet's best as a specimen of his work, one has no alternative but to turn again to those gorgeously-coloured verses which begin:

> I have seen old ships sail like swans asleep
> Beyond the village which men still call Tyre,
> With leaden age o'ercargoed, dipping deep
> For Famagusta and the hidden sun
> That rings black Cyprus with a lake of fire;
> And all those ships were certainly so old—
> Who knows how oft with squat and noisy gun,
> Questing brown slaves or Syrian oranges,
> The pirate Genoese
> Hell-raked them till they rolled
> Blood, water, fruit and corpses up the hold.

> But now through friendly seas they softly run,
> Painted the mid-sea blue or shore-sea green,
> Still patterned with the vine and grapes in gold.

That is the summary and the summit of Flecker's genius. But the rest of his verse, too, is the work of a true and delightful poet, a faithful priest of literature, an honest craftsman with words. (pp. 114-16)

> *Robert Lynd, "James Elroy Flecker," in his* Old and New Masters, *Charles Scribner's Sons, 1919, pp. 112-16.*

Douglas Goldring   (essay date 1920)

[*In the following excerpt, Goldring offers an overview of Flecker's poetry and prose. For additional commentary by Goldring, see excerpt dated 1907.*]

Flecker's entire output of verse and prose during his lifetime, not counting unpublished work and contributions to periodicals, was limited to seven or eight small volumes, one of which, his admirable **Scholar's Italian Book,** is clearly in a class by itself. He made two attempts at prose fiction, an amusing undergraduate effort called **"The Last Generation,"** and his solitary novel, **The King of Alsander.** This last has always seemed to me an unsatisfactory and unequal performance. It has flashes of wit here and there, a few good passages of rather mannered prose, and many slabs of "fine writing." But as a *jeu d'esprit* it is distinctly heavy and overweighted; and the high spirits are only intermittent. The majority of the reviewers praised the book immoderately on its appearance, but I don't think Flecker himself was much impressed by their eulogies.

Within its narrow compass, the little-known "Dialogue on Education" called **The Grecians** is perhaps the most perfect of Flecker's prose works. I do not think any one who has not read this book can get a proper appreciation of his mind and outlook, for of all his work it is, in some ways, the most intimately self-revealing. The "Dialogue" enshrines the conversation of two schoolmasters—Hofman, the scientist, and Edwinson, the classic—who, while on a visit to Bologna, fall in with a beautiful youth and join with him in a discussion on educational reform. Each gives his view of the questions at issue, until finally the beautiful youth sums up the argument and launches forth into a dissertation on the ideal school. "Keeping clear before me all the danger I run of turning my pupils into dilettanti, I am going to teach them to be as far as possible universal in their comprehensions and admiration of the mysteries and beauties of life. Our Grecians, when they leave us, will have seen, as it were, from a height suddenly, the whole world of knowledge stretching out in rich plains and untraversed seas."

The picture is delightful; but one cannot have things both ways, I suppose, and certain doubts inevitably drift into one's mind. With their eyes dazzled by this radiant vision of "Knowledge" how should the little Grecians learn to pursue Understanding, that elusive shadow? But the passage reveals Flecker to us, reveals him in a characteristic and very attractive light. He himself was a rare scholar, not so much in regard to his actual attainments (though they were considerable) as from the fact that his scholarship really enriched him, coloured his whole outlook, made the world a lovelier place for him. His mind was so steeped in the atmosphere of the classic poets that he saw life and all the world as it were through rose-tinted spectacles. Out of the loveliness which met his gaze he has recreated for us in his poetry a fairyland in which it is an enchantment to wander. Yet it must be admitted that these spectacles to some extent restricted his vision and limited its range: his fairyland has walls. This perhaps explains why his poetry is at its best when he deals with subjects which are obviously "poetic." His was never the genius to find poetry in the raw material of ordinary existence, as, for example, is the way with Mr. D. H. Lawrence. Even when he writes of London his hand is unsteady; and of all his poems the **"Ballad of Camden Town"** is the only one which is unconsciously absurd. **"The Burial in England,"** the last great poem which he wrote, and a fine piece of work in the "big bow-wow" style, is another illustration of this point. The European War stirred Flecker deeply, and though he planned and carried through a grandiose war poem, he did not treat his theme with any real conviction. **"The Burial in England"** is full of ingenious epithets, rich in poetic "ornament," and so wonderful and complicated in its technique that a superficial reader might easily mistake it for a masterpiece. But once strip it of its jewelled phrases, of its beauties of craftsmanship, and it will appear as devoid of true inspiration and originality of thought as the average leading article.

As a critic, Flecker was distinguished by a great capacity for enthusiastic appreciation—a quality far too rare and valuable to be despised. Almost any one can pick holes in another's work: it requires a finer sensibility to appreciate and reveal excellence. Unfortunately his enthusiasms, if infectious, were apt to carry him off his feet, apt to lead him into extravagant praise of writers whom he admired, and extravagant denunciation of writers whom he didn't admire. One got the impression that for him the poets were divided into those who were "magnificent" and those who wrote "Godforsaken muck." But his preferences were founded in the main on knowledge and sound judgment. He was innocent of literary snobbishness; he was not ashamed of admiring Tennyson, and even Kipling; he never descended to the fashionable vulgarity of abusing the Victorians.

Flecker's first volume of verse, *The Bridge of Fire,* though it contains indications of his future powers, still seems to me to have in it much that is poor or merely imitative, and a few pieces, like the dismally unfunny **"Ballad of Hampstead Heath,"** which are frankly bad. Most of the best poems in this book were much worked over—not always with happy results—before they reappeared in the later volume. The beautiful **"Tenebris Interlucentem"** was vastly improved, almost recreated, in its later version; but some of the alterations to other pieces are not so successful. In the little poem called **"We That Were Friends,"** for example, he has made a change in the first verse without improving it, while leaving in the second the unfortunate line, "Whom dreams delight and passions *please.*" (Whatever passions may do it is difficult to think of them as "pleasing" anybody—except perhaps a fish, to whom a

passion might be a "pleasing" surprise.) Another alteration which some of those who possess *The Bridge of Fire* will regret, is in the last verse of the poem called **"The Ballad of the Student in the South."** The first line of this verse originally ran: "We're of the people, you and I." In the version contained in the *Collected Poems* this has been changed to, "For we are simple, you and I"—a much weaker and more "literary" way of saying the same thing.

It was with his *Forty-Two Poems* that Flecker definitely established his position among the poets of his time. Many of us will not forget the excitement of first reading that marvellous **"Ballad of Iskander"**; and in such poems as **"The Masque of the Magi,"** and **"Joseph and Mary"** he showed the same clearness of outline and almost pre-Raphaelite vividness of colour which distinguish *The Golden Journey to Samarkand.* Almost all the finest of Flecker's poetry is to be found in the *Forty-Two Poems* and in *The Golden Journey to Samarkand.* Of the later work included in the *Collected Poems* there are not perhaps more than three pieces which are equal to the best which these volumes contain. These three, however, are of particular interest. I think no other poem of Flecker's is quite so moving as the exquisite piece called **"Stillness,"** with its wonderful last verse—

> Then twittering out in the night my thought-
> birds flee,
> I am emptied of all my dreams:
> I only hear Earth turning, only see
> Ether's long bankless streams,
> And only know I should drown if you laid not
> your hand on me.

This poem seems almost to make clear that had Flecker lived he would ultimately have shed his Parnassian theory, and allowed himself, more often, to be subjective. Among all his poems it seems to me to be in a place by itself. Of the other pieces issued for the first time in book form in the *Collected Poems,* **"The Old Ships"** and **"The Pensive Prisoner,"** with its strange, haunting music, are perhaps the most beautiful. But apart from these three poems, the most important of the *Collected Poems* are those which were originally published under the title of *The Golden Journey to Samarkand.* It was not until Flecker went to the Levant, and found in travel in Turkey and Greece and among the islands of the Ægean the greatest inspiration of his life, that he really came into his own. *The Golden Journey to Samarkand* is the book of his maturity, in which all his finest poetic qualities are displayed to the full, all his weaknesses expunged. Considered as a book, it marks as great an advance on *Forty-Two Poems* as did the *Forty-Two Poems* on *The Bridge of Fire.* Not only is his own description of the Oriental poems as being "unique in English" fully justified, but few poems in our literature show a more passionate love of England than those which he wrote in Syria and in Greece. What Englishman can read the opening lines of **"Brumana,"** for example, and remain unthrilled?

> "Oh shall I never be home again?
> Meadows of England shining in the rain
> Spread wide your daisied lawns: your ramparts
> green
> With briar fortify, with blossom screen

Till my far morning—and O streams that slow
And pure and deep through plains and playlands
    go,
For me your love and all your kingcups store,
And—dark militia of the southern shore,
Old fragrant friends—preserve me the last lines
Of that long saga which you sung me, pines,
When, lonely boy, beneath the chosen tree
I listened, with my eyes upon the sea.

It was fortunate for Flecker that the kind of poetry which by temperament, by intellectual equipment and by the circumstances of his birth and upbringing he was most capable of writing seems to have been just the kind which he most wanted to write. In this respect his career, short as it was, was singularly happy. He followed no literary wild-goose chase. He was not, apparently, dissatisfied with his manner, only with his workmanship, which never satisfied him. At least a part of his genius seems to have lain in a realisation of his exact capacities. He seldom gropes after things which are too high for him. I think it can nowhere be said of him that he "wrought better than he knew"; and, to judge from his constant emendations, he seems to have had an almost exaggerated distrust of what Mr. Arthur Symons has somewhere called "the plenary inspiration of first thoughts." In some ways he was more typically a French than an English poet, and his description of the Parnassians in the Preface to **The Golden Journey to Samarkand** applies to himself almost exactly. Like them he loathed romantic egoism and aimed at "a beauty somewhat statuesque"; like them he had a fine sense of language, using words and epithets with the nicest scholarship and taste; and, again, like them he derived his inspiration from the classics, from history, from mythology, from beautiful names, from places, and, indeed, from anything rather than from life. It was hardly ever life—either in its "ordinariness" or in its strangeness—which Flecker succeeded in transmuting into poetry. His work is an escape from life, rather than an interpretation of it. And here and there, in his less-inspired moments, one feels that it is only its technical brilliance which saves it from having too limiting a flavour of "Oxford College." His poetry is usually rather cold, and it cannot be claimed for Flecker that he was remarkable for originality of thought. His emotional range is limited, and his greatest strength lies in his power to create pictures compact, clear in outline, and rich in colour, and in the haunting music of which he had the secret. "Emaux et Camées" would not have made a bad alternative title for his collected work; and there are times when he strikes one as being an artificer with imagination, or rather when his art seems to resemble that of the jeweller or worker in precious metals. His poems, although never rising to the highest imaginative level, are yet hammered and worked till they attain a hard, indestructible perfection. It is difficult to believe that verse of such a character will be quickly forgotten, for it seems to possess all the qualities necessary for permanence.

Flecker's poetry depends on nothing transitory for its interest; it contains no message to grow stale; and the extraordinary amount of work put into his verses gives them an impressive solidity. It must always be remembered of Flecker that in an age of anarchy in verse he took the trouble to become a master of technique; in an age of formless-

ness he upheld the finest traditions of form. What was beautiful two thousand years ago is beautiful still; and, as Flecker has told us himself, it was with the single object of creating beauty that his poems were written. Who can read them and imagine for a moment that he failed in his object? One cannot think that the glowing visions which his poems bring before the mind will prove any less enchanting to readers in the centuries to come than they are to-day. (pp. 25-34)

> *Douglas Goldring, "James Elroy Flecker: An Appreciation and Some Personal Memories," in his* Reputations: Essays in Criticism, *Thomas Seltzer, 1920, pp. 1-35.*

The Times Literary Supplement   (essay date 1922)

[*The essay below is a review of the publication of Flecker's drama* Hassan, *which was first performed the following year.*]

Hassan is in the curious position of a work which has been preceded by its own reputation. Arrangements were all but made for its performance five or six years ago. Flecker's principal collection of lyrics, **The Golden Journey to Samarkand,** was named after a poem which was more or less widely known to be taken from a play, and justified high hopes. His output had been small, but of steadily increasing merit; and he had written a dozen or more lyrics which had established his position among good judges. The rumour went about that the play when it appeared would prove itself the veritable work of the author of these masterpieces. Flecker himself was an enthusiastic believer in its virtues: "If it [the last scene] doesn't give the public shivers down the back when it is acted," he confided to a friend, "I'll never write again."

There can be no doubt at all about those shivers, unless it be that the public will have shivered so frequently before that great setting out of the pilgrims along their Golden Road, and will have shivered at times with so much bitterness of abject pity and horror, that the finer, the more æsthetic, shiver required of them at last may be refused by an exhausted organism. **Hassan** is a marvellous piece of reading, and, being the work of a man who is essentially an artist, it is all through written to be played. Every scene moves to an event, and all converge upon the climax; nor is there question at any time but that the things that are happening transcend all that the characters can find to say about them: it is with actors, not with talkers, that we are confronted. And yet what memorable things they contrive to say. Is that not, after all, the secret of dramatic writing, to find the situations for which the only appropriate language is—poetry?

Hassan was a poet-confectioner of Baghdad, in the days of the renowned Caliph Haroun Al Raschid; and the first motive of the drama is his despondent, romantic love for the voluptuous and mercenary Yasmin, which ends in his receiving a bucket of water on his head, her comment of brutal disdain upon his sentimental passion. The treatment of this episode is all but farcical; and something of the boisterous frivolity that marks it remains in later scenes, intended, it may be, to serve as a relief to our feelings against the excessive strain which otherwise falls upon them. Flecker had remarked in his preface to ***The Golden Journey to Samarkand*** that it was the poet's business to "make beautiful the tragedy and tragic the beauty of man's life"; and in ***Hassan*** he has specially addressed himself to the second part of the task. As to the revelation of beauty through tragedy, who would not agree? The poet, so conceived, is the reconciler whose vision pierces the hard surface of life and reveals the abiding and compensating truth. It is otherwise when we are told, and told in the same breath, that the poet must make beauty tragic. To say this is to say that the chasm between the desires of the soul and their fulfilment is ultimate, and that we are strangers in the world. Flecker is of those who are inclined to scout the idea that poetry must have its "message," that it is anyway concerned with social and moral problems; and if he means that didacticism is unpoetical, he has a simple case. But if he imagined that the poet can avoid a morality, evoking images of beauty from a life with which except as beautiful he has nothing to do, his own poetry belies him, and his own theory too. For to believe all beauty tragic and to present it so is at once morality and message.

Never, surely, was that message delivered with grimmer resolution than by Flecker in ***Hassan.*** Its climax is the decision of two lovers who have incurred the revengeful wrath and jealous fury of the Caliph to die in torture together rather than accept the ignominy of life and freedom on the terms he offers. The terrible scene of their death passes, half veiled, upon the stage; and afterwards, a second climax added to the first, their ghosts rise and assure us that there is no consolation beyond the grave. Tragic beauty touches its height when the ecstatic Pervaneh, who has all the time been her lover's inspiration and spiritual strength, cleaving still to faith and defying evidence, herself still, as it were, a flame even while she dwindles to extinction, cries out to the souls of the Unborn, "Why, Life. . . . is sweet, my children." The tortures are over, the thought of happiness in another world is vanishing away, and still the abandoned soul, in its last pulsings of remembrance, remembers sweetness.

There is, it would seem, a certain weakness in the constitution of art which predisposes it to pessimism, and which it is as well for us to reckon with when we estimate the validity of an artist's experience or of his account of it. Its appeal is to feeling and emotion; it presents the rare tensions of life rather than its normalities and equable course, and therefore tends to attach meaning to what has brilliancy and to separate the light on the surface of things from their sustaining substance. The artist has a preference for negation, sorrow, catastrophe, because these are dividing agencies, because they cut life into fragments and surround these fragments with a background of gloom. Beauty is made more beautiful by loss, because loss throws it into relief, or drives it to the heart in the quivering arrow of poignancy. Worshipping beauty, therefore, and believing as he always must that what is beautiful is true, the artist slips into the belief that loss is final and irrevocable, because he recognizes in it this intensifying power and finds the crown of the significance of things in the exquisite pathos of our farewell to them. It may be that he has merely

forgotten that intensification of this kind is not applicable to life as a whole; the part shines against an encompassing darkness; the value of the whole cannot be heightened, but remains to be estimated for what it is. No doubt the history of the world, with all its cruelties and indifferences, may be taken on many grounds to support the despairing view; and yet the tradition of the greatest poetry of the world and of our own poetry above all points on the whole in a different direction. The greatest poets dwell on the permanence of beauty rather than on the passing show, and believe that a life moulded by the vision of it is in harmony with the creative spirit of all.

We need to fortify ourselves with some such reflections as these, if we are not to find ***Hassan*** unbearable. For presentment on the stage it is perhaps unbearable essentially; we cannot imagine what loophole of escape there may be for the luckless audience imprisoned with its menacing pitilessness, unless the sense of dismay be stifled somewhat by the unreality necessarily belonging to Arabian emotions depicted by an English hand—and, since that too must be added, acted by English actors. It may be that the high poetry of the piece will struggle in vain against the depressing associations of our theatre, and that the climax will only not be cruel because it does not convince. Yet we cannot easily renounce the hope of experiencing the appeal of its exuberant vitality in direct impact upon every sense. The public of the theatre is wider than the public which reads poetry; and there is intoxication in the thought of words like these falling upon a house so thrilled and shaken that it would have no choice but to receive them:—

> CALIPH. In poems and in tales alone shall live the eternal memory of this city when I am dust and thou art dust, when the Bedouin shall build his hut upon my garden and drive his plough beyond the ruins of my palace, and all Bagdad is broken to the ground. Ah, if there shall ever arise a nation whose people have forgotten poetry or whose poets have forgotten the people, though they send their ships round Taprobane and their armies across the hills of Hindustan, though their city be greater than Babylon of old, though they mine a league into the earth or mount to the stars on wings—what of them?
>
> HASSAN. They will be a dark patch upon the world. . . . Allah made poetry a cheap thing to buy and a simple thing to understand. He gave men dreams by night that they might learn to dream by day.

Flecker's conception of poetry and his exemplification of it in ***Hassan*** is reactionary, in its relation to the general current of our literature. But that general current is so powerful and secure that it has everything to gain from his bold and splendid opposition. We may compare the position of ***Hassan*** in our drama to that of FitzGerald's translation of Omar among English lyrics. It leaves us and travels beyond the Mediterranean, to come back with a reproof. The dramatic workmanship is hardly less perfect than FitzGerald's in his verses. Every character is at once a type and an individual; every scene has its direct and its ulterior meaning, every utterance its gesture and its life.

Though the medium is prose, the substance is therefore always poetry; and when, from time to time, the rhythm and the decoration of verse are applied, we have the sensation that a bird has opened its wings or a smooth-gliding ship set sail. Its peculiar vision of beauty confronting death, beauty intensified by its conflict with the unheeding, the hostile, the swiftly annihilating world, whatever we may think of its ultimate and universal truth, has singular pathos in the work of a young poet whose abounding enthusiasms were menaced before he had tasted the fullness of his gift and who has left behind him this great work, a work that will not quickly be forgotten, yet a work which to him while he lived was a hope unrealized. We may think of him saying in the words of his own Hassan:—

> O rose of evening and O rose of morning, vainly for me shall you fade on domes of ebony and azure. This rose has faded, and this rose is bitter, and this rose is nothing but the world.

"Flecker's 'Hassan'," in The Times Literary Supplement, *No. 1079, September 21, 1922, p. 597.*

John Middleton Murry   (essay date 1923)

[*Murry is recognized as one of the most significant En-*

A scene from the 1923 production of Hassan.

glish critics of the twentieth century, noted for his studies of major authors and for his contributions to modern critical theory. Perceiving an integral relationship between literature and religion, Murry believed that the literary critic must be concerned with the moral as well as the aesthetic dimensions of a given work. In addition, he considered the critic's primary duties to be the differentiation between greater and lesser artists and the creation of a hierarchical delineation of those worthy of further study. Anticipating later critical opinion, Murry championed the writings of Marcel Proust, James Joyce, Paul Valéry, and D. H. Lawrence in numerous books and essays, and while his critical approach led some commentators to question his ability to render objective assessments of the authors he discussed, his essays are nevertheless valued for their originality and insight. In the following excerpt, Murry unfavorably reviews a performance of Hassan.]

Hassan.—Yes, it's all very sumptuous, and it's all been done regardless. I look backward and the array of dress-shirts is positively alarming. Quite certainly it is the thing to do; and I feel a certain satisfaction in having done it, and a real curiosity to see what it is that all the noise has been made over—because I have read **Hassan** and found it in reading a confused pattern with threads of real beauty, an effort of a genuine poet to say something beyond his own immature capacity of utterance, and to say it in a form over which he had manifestly no control. At its best the quality of **Hassan** is dreamlike and intangible; but the quality is not wrought into the substance, it is superimposed. In the poet's mind the act of fusion between the symbol and the thing symbolized is never accomplished. Therefore he never attains a true simplicity; he is by turns elaborate and naïve, and not seldom both at once.

No, I was not precisely bored; I had a comfortable seat, and no impulse to leave before the end. I was content to watch and wait—to wait for something that never came, some moment when the whole sumptuous pageant should take life and be real; mean something, thrill me, transform me into something more than a well-fed occupant of a much more expensive seat than I usually frequent.

But the moment was denied: in spite of Mr. Ainley, whose acting fascinated me. (If Mr. Ainley cannot make a play real, I concluded, nothing can.) The elaborate diction, endurable, faintly enjoyable even, on the printed page, falls flat before the phrases are finished on the stage, droops broken-winged in the intervening air. Not one of the actors can make anything of these phrases. Mr. Leon Quartermaine's lucid voice gropes helplessly for some non-existent rhythm; the others' for some non-existent point. Mr. Ainley alone succeeds in taming them into plausible human utterance, by making them functions of himself, Mr. Ainley, but of no created character at all. He can subdue them, at a price: the price is that he should remain the gifted Mr. Ainley conquering the unconquerable, instead of Hassan uttering himself. But nobody else succeeds at all.

There is music, there are costumes, there are ballets—of these, anon—there are scenes, there is lighting, there is, in a word, Production. Voice-production, stage-production, play-production. Oh, whatever there is to produce, is produced; there is no doubt about that. But the thing that is noticeably not produced is a play. There are effects: stage-effects, music-effects, colour-effects, but one has been forgotten, a dramatic effect. It may be a low-class weakness of mine; but I miss these elements, and I can't help thinking that the audience, although it is *on ne peut plus* boiled-shirt and sacramentally determined that what is The Thing shall be The Thing, misses them a little, too. Those pallid smiles, that unenraptured applause, are not all that could be desired. But the audience, which is high-class enough to know that when you are seeing The Thing, you are supposed to behave in front of it, will never let on. I am low-class, and I will. (pp. 619-20)

> *John Middleton Murry, in a review of "Hassan," in* The Adelphi, *Vol. I, No. 7, December, 1923, pp. 619-21.*

Ashley Dukes   (essay date 1923)

[*Dukes was an important English dramatist and drama critic during the first half of the twentieth century. He is most noted for his writings on modern European theater, particularly poetic drama. He had a broad knowledge of continental drama and, both as a translator and as the manager of his own theater, introduced English audiences to the work of several important French and German dramatists, including Ernst Toller, Georg Kaiser, and Lion Feuchtwanger. In the following essay, Dukes praises Flecker's delineation of the title character of* Hassan.]

James Elroy Flecker met the classical fate of the lyric poet. While he lived his work went begging, and he sold his verses for a song. He fell ill, lay for a while among the groves of Lebanon, and died in the cold sunshine of Davos, where youth winters in the bloom of health and sickness declines from summer to autumn. Now his memory is honoured, his early editions are prized, and managers give his Eastern play a setting of magnificence. When they have done their work, and done it well, *Hassan* remains—the play that Flecker wrote to please himself and not to please the public; the play that grew as a tree grows, sprung from a seed of thought and nourished by the sap of fantasy. We can trace its original form of episodic conceit, the dew-draught of character, the branching inventions of intrigue, the putting forth of the sensitive shoots that form the secondary motive, the storm of cruelty—and horror that shakes the boughs, the burgeoning and blossoming of the whole in the spring that blows from Samarkand. Such work must confound all dull instructors in the craft of play-making. This poet masters the stage intuitively; he has the dramatist's pair of hands. With him the art of presentation comes first. Hassan the confectioner—how likeable, how fanciful, how moving, but above all how *presentable* a character! In two minutes we know the man, in three we vow comradeship with him to the end of the tale. His modesty, his humour, his love of beauty enter into all these scenes of Bagdad, with their crumbling white walls and painted pavilions and golden palaces. The spectacle of the play itself is a procession that passes before his eyes. Simpler settings may be devised by future producers, but the presence of this character alone ensures that pageantry

shall never overweight drama. He commands respect for the muse.

Hassan is fine-grained, though coarse of presence. His passion is fine-grained, though coarse of utterance. For him a soul lives in a woman behind the almond paste of flesh that the confectioner justly esteems; and if he cannot find it the woman is naught. It is a convention that the fair shall favour the prosperous and love the rich. Is it not the convention of half our entertainments? Hassan, obscure and cumbersome, is scorned by his mistress; but when he is raised to the Caliph's favour she drops a rose at his feet. The heroine of our latest musical comedy may do as much, and be little blamed for it. But to Hassan's mind the rose is poisoned. "Last night I baked sugar, and she flung me water; this morning I bake gold, and she flings me a rose. Empty, empty, I tell you, friend, all the blue sky." It is this same fine-grained nature that makes him rebel against the cruelties and tyrannies of the Caliphate, though his own good citizen's inclination is always to bow the knee to the Commander of the Faithful. His silence is eloquent in the trial scene when he sits at the despot's right hand. It is this nature that impels him to seek in others a passion finer than his own, and to defend it loyally—to stand sentinel over the pair of condemned lovers, to intercede for them, to protest against their torture, to forfeit all his new-won dignities, and in the end to take the "golden road" that leads pilgrims as well as merchants away from the reeking walls of Bagdad into the open country and the unknown.

When this epic of character is unfolded on the stage, shall we talk of literature or pageantry? No, this is drama, if the word have any meaning; and the beauty of scene and music and costume is all of it treasure laid at the feet of Hassan, as the slaves of the Caliphate laid carpets and ornaments. A slovenly, unlovely figure of a man, quick in thought, slow in speech, firm in friendship, a fountain of integrity, a well of humour; he will surely live in the history of our theatre, and actors in years to come will number him among their classical parts. (pp. 156-59)

> *Ashley Dukes, "Poets and Historians," in his* The Youngest Drama: Studies of Fifty Dramatists, *Ernest Benn, Limited, 1923, pp. 141-77.*

Cornelius Weygandt   (essay date 1937)

[*A historian and critic, Weygandt was one of the first American scholars to examine contemporary Irish drama, introducing its major practitioners to American readers in his* Irish Plays and Playwrights *(1913). In the following excerpt, he focuses his discussion on Flecker's best-known poems.*]

The bulk of the poetry of James Elroy Flecker loses substance and significance with each rereading. It is all of it nearly always impeccable verse, the work of an artist in words, but most of it is no more than that, save for an image here and there. Only **"The Golden Journey to Samarkand"** and **"The Old Ships"** have the right hardness of material and execution to weather the years. These two poems are finely graven things of that Parnassian fashion that he thought it well his fellow-poets should follow, too.

All his critics point to his obligations to Gautier, Leconte de Lisle and Heredia, but there are obligations, too, to English poets, to men as different as Fitzgerald and A. E. Housman.

Of the two poems of Flecker that any anthology of twentieth-century verse would have to include, the one is of the desert and the other of the sea. **"The Old Ships"** begins with a slow music that we have too little of in English poetry:

> I have seen old ships sail like swans asleep
> Beyond the village which men still call Tyre.

A part of the effect of these lines is due to a succession of syllables that must be accented to bring out the meaning, and that drag the verse as you do so accent them. Another part of the effect is due to the alliteration. The lines are of like sort with "The lone and level sands stretch far away" of the Shelley Flecker so admired. **"The Old Ships"** is one of his poems that is what Flecker's theory declared all poems should be, a succession of clear and beautiful images from A to Z. The ships with which it is concerned at its outset are so old that they may have been attacked by Genoese galleys. From them we pass to "a drowsy ship of some yet older day," perhaps that very one on which Ulysses sailed from Troy.

"The Golden Journey to Samarkand" has appeared in a good many forms since it was first published in 1913, in a volume to which it gave title. As we have it now it is the end of Act V of his play *Hassan* (1922), and an assuagement, in its great beauty, of the Oriental cruelty of the earlier part of that act. This is, I think, the best version. It has thirteen stanzas of four lines each, a few of them broken up into dialogue, but most of them printed as quatrains. There is about the poem the lure of the desert, one of the most romantic of all the lures there are in the infinite variety of beautiful phases of the world. This lure is one of the elemental lures, like the lure of mountains, or of the sea; of jungle, or of tundra; of pine forests, or of prairie; of upland pastures, or of lakes; of little rivers, or of heaths; of salt marsh, or sand-dunes above the beach. This lure of the desert has found voice in English literature before it found voice in Flecker, in Kingsley's *Hypatia* (1853); in Burton's *Pilgrimage to El Medinah and Mecca* (1855); and in Doughty's *Arabia Deserta* (1888). It has found expression, with very great beauty, since Flecker, in Dunsany's *Tents of the Arabs* (1914).

It is "blazing" moonlight, at a city gate of Bagdad, when we meet **"The Golden Journey to Samarkand"** at the close of *Hassan*. All manner of people are waiting to make up the caravan when the watchman shall open the gate. The merchants raise the chant first:

> Away, for we are ready to a man!
> Our camels sniff the evening and are glad.

One and another of the crowd join in, the chief draper, the chief grocer, the principal Jews, the master of the caravan, Ishak the minstrel, a woman and an old man who would have all stay in the city, Hassan himself, and the watchman. It is to Hassan that the great moment of the poem belongs. He is given the lines that sum up the magic of the desert:

> Sweet to ride forth at evening from the wells,
> When shadows pass gigantic on the sand,
> And softly through the silence beat the bells
> Along the Golden Road to Samarkand.

Those lines and the opening lines of **"The Old Ships"** are Flecker at his best, a best that might have risen to even better things had not tuberculosis first debilitated him and then cut him off at thirty.

There are other poems of some power to Flecker's credit. There is **"The Ballad of the Student in the South."** This chronicles a chance romance of travel of a kind usual in Symons, in a manner that is developed from a study of the narratives of Housman. It has in it one of the few readings of life in Flecker:

> Why should we think,
> We who are young and strong?

There are those, no doubt, who would dismiss this as a declaration facile and cheap, but it is the inevitable outcome of the preachment of Meredith that thought is the beginning of sorrow. **"The Ballad of Camden Town"** is a fellow to **"The Ballad of the Student in the South."** There is a naïveté, a simplicity, an everyday sort of air about both that are very winning, but they alike fall short of the poignancy that you feel they should have. **"The Ballad of Camden Town"** comes the closer of the two to this poignancy. It all but reaches it in the lines that recall the days with Maisie:

> I have so little to forgive,
> So much I can't forget.

It is not because this poem is akin to *vers de société* that it misses poignancy, but because, somehow or other, you just don't believe the story. It seems to be gotten-up stuff, invention of the wrong sort, and not a record of a memory.

Two other poems of Flecker, both lyrics, are all but up to his best work. They are **"Stillness"** and **"November Eves."** Both are indoor poems and both studies of fear. **"Stillness"** recurs to the image that ends **"Tenebris Interlucentem."** There it was a ghost in Hell that "stole forth a hand / To draw a brother to his side," and here in **"Stillness"** it is the poet himself who knows that he should drown "if you laid not your hand on me." The consumptive has often a warning of death long before it comes. It was more than four years, in Flecker's case, from the time of his first attack to his death, and for the last eighteen months he must have known that he was fighting a losing struggle. In those years he felt as a child feels in the dark, that it cannot stand the fear unless there is a strong hand to hold to. **"No Coward's Song"** puts one phase of the matter, but there is better poetry in the memories of childish fears recorded in **"November Eyes."** (pp. 372-75)

Flecker has a place in English poetry, a place as sure as that of his friend Rupert Brooke, but he is, I am afraid, like Brooke, an overrated man to-day. To paraphrase his own phrase, his "golden sentences," despite their artistry, often leave you cold. Flecker is not a poet of many poems, but **"The Old Ships"** and **"The Golden Journey to Samarkand"** ought to keep him known to men through their place in the anthologies. (p. 376)

Cornelius Weygandt, "The Last Romantics," in his The Time of Yeats: English Poetry of To-Day against an American Background, *D. Appleton-Century Company, Inc., 1937, pp. 363-85.*

G. Wilson Knight   (essay date 1944)

[*One of the most influential of modern Shakespearean critics, Knight helped shape the twentieth-century reaction against the biographical and character studies of the nineteenth-century Shakespeareans. In the following essay, he analyzes symbol and theme in* Hassan.]

Flecker's **Hassan** appears at first a strange and colourful bird of the tropics among the thrushes and blackbirds of Twentieth Century English drama. Its rich colours have been compared to the feathers of a parrot. Yet it is not simply the lively extravaganza some have supposed: it is no *Kismet*, still less a *Chu Chin Chow*. The setting was a sincere enough poetic medium for one who was himself an Orientalist of distinction, as well as giving opportunities for a richness of colour most helpful in expression of certain essences hard enough for a modern dramatist to master. That is, Flecker uses his Bagdad setting somewhat as Shakespeare uses his Italy or Egypt. Moreover, a transcription of oriental phraseology leads to a richness of colloquial utterance that serves the purpose of Synge's and Masefield's rustic dialect, though itself in its stilted metaphoric formation perhaps nearer to the similes of Euphuism. Exquisite effects are attained. Here are some: 'Plunge not the finger of impertinence into the pie of enquiry, O my uncle'; 'Shall I then drop the needle of insinuation and pick up the club of statement?'; 'For the pen of happiness hath written on thy face the ode of gratitude'; 'The mill of his heart still grinds the flower of life.' **Hassan** is a unique result of happy convergences.

Hassan, the hero, is a bourgeois undistinguished type with a philosophic and contemplative strain. His desire for Yasmin—a very sensuous affair—brings him sharply up against his own limitations. He is fooled and scorned by his confidant Selim, now his rival. Yasmin mockingly emphasises Selim's youth:

> How can I thank thee, O my Uncle, for sending
> me this strong and straight young friend of thine
> to console my loneliness and desolation?

They shout 'Go home, old fellow,' calling him a 'wearisome old fool.' Inferiority and jealousy together madden him: the depicted agony is excruciating, not unlike that of Troilus. His love, from the start partly lust, is now inverted to a lustful revenge:

> I will have you both whipped through the city
> and impaled in the market place, and your bo-
> dies flung to rot on a dung heap.

He faints. This is, as it were, the end of a prologue movement. When Hassan wakes in a new setting and dressed, like Christopher Sly, in new clothes, he, and we, are already plunged into the central action. But observe how that action is to dramatise scenes not unlike his own experience of lust and thoughts of revenge. He is, as it were,

forced to see himself, to attend a patterned and objectified explication of the love-lust-blood complex in his own soul. The main action is his purgation. The simple tradesman-recluse, so fond of carpets, is introduced now to watch in the wider design of human life a reflection of himself. He faints by a fountain; later he is to wake by one. Thereafter we have an epilogue movement to balance this prologue: they frame the central incidents.

The world Hassan sees is gorgeous. Indeed, the whole play is remarkable for its richness. Hassan is himself a confectioner and his trade often the occasion of literary fervour. The final Samarkand poem is loaded with impressions of taste, smell, sight. Between, there is a heavy atmosphere of scented sensualism. Straight sexual desires are unashamed, slave-girls spoken of as shown naked on sale, there is Hassan's delightfully naive desire for a Circassian, his original lust, the Caliph's harem: and all support a central theme of sensuous passion.

But we find not only healthy lusts: there is also what appears a sadistic and perverted lust, not only in certain of the people but in the play as a whole. Hassan's original threat can be taken to set its note; there is Rafi's hideous design on the Caliph (observe that Rafi is far from a sweet lyric hero); grim threats of minor officials; and the towering interest of the Caliph's studied revenge leading to the torture of Rafi and Pervaneh, with Yasmin's underlined enjoyment of that torture. Cruelty is all but sexual, colourfully and sensuously impregnated, associated pleasingly with human nakedness in the Procession of Protracted Death. The actual torture is done and its sounds faintly heard off-stage with rich violin music not so much as accompaniment as suggestive symbolism. You can call this a way of rendering the horror bearable; but it is also a way of making it enjoyable. The utterly un-Shakespearian mechanism of rich music=torture is here throughly organic. A subtle interaction and blend of love, lust, and torture (remember a complex of these in Hassan preludes it all) is intrinsic to the mesh of associations continually. There is a frequent suggestion, for example, of dark red. This may have two directions, continuous rather than contrasted: (i) for roses, with passionate love-thoughts generally, and (ii) for blood and torture. We have 'great red roses, passionate carnations' and kindred images. But this may blend into a blood-lust as in:

'Are not my lips two rubies drenched in blood?' Yasmin, smelling the negro's blood-stained limbs, murmurs passionately 'Thou dark Masrur.' Again,

> YASMIN. How you smell of blood!
> MASRUR. And you of roses.

Blood holds here an erotic perfume, and is exactly used, as I shall show, with reference to the main symbols of the carpet and the fountain. Dark red light is similarly powerful, as in 'When the dark red eye of day is level with the lone highway' from Hassan's love-poem; when in the prison 'the wall reddens' warning the lovers that their decision is due; and with the torture procession silhouetted against a 'deep red afterglow,' suggesting blood and agony. Music, like the colour red, has similar various, yet related, directions: accompanying the human love of Hassan's exquisite serenade; the main torture; and the spiritual resolution of the Samarkand epilogue; with indeterminate uses that refer to war and revenge, in the War Song of the Saracens ('pale Kings of the Sunset') and the dance-music of the Beggars of Bagdad. The play's various rich substances, however ethically questionable, are all continually being assimilated and integrated into a close æsthetic unity.

In this sense you can undoubtedly call it 'sadistic'; yet its sadism is, with equal certainty, worked into an artistic success of a high order. The imaginative logic is faultless, with no confusions of the Marlovian type. Torture is a matter of naked bodies, barbaric music, and dark red; it is richly felt. But it is not associated with cosmic and universal excellences such as accompany Pervaneh's ecstasies of love. Marlow's Helen 'fairer than the evening air clad in the beauty of a thousand stars' opposed by 'Christian' damnation, or Milton's Comus urging all cosmic glories in his own support, are as far from Flecker as from Shakespeare. The associations are all consistent within the play. Here a potential attractiveness in torture is accepted, seen for what it is without fear, and next ordered imaginatively. The nearest equivalent is perhaps Webster's steady equation of murderous horror with a positive and pleasing ritualistic dignity. In *Hassan* the cruelty is more physical, its attraction more colourful, but there is no overthrowing of human dignity comparable with Bajazet's cage or the team of bitted kings behind Tamburlaine's whip. The Procession of Protracted Death against sunset, the silhouettes of wheel and rack and whip, the naked torturer and victims, the Websterian coffin, all have a certain dignity and colourful, if devilish, attraction. The love and bodies of Pervaneh and Rafi are as a perfumed offering, a sacrificial food, their agony partly at least an objective delight. 'Agony' says Ishak 'is a fine colour': and in such a play as this, Pervaneh and Rafi are in one sense highly honoured by being chosen to provide that colour. It will be seen that *Hassan* steers, technically, and ethically, a most delicate, tightrope, course. One slip, and the result would be fearful; but the slip never occurs.

This world is kinged by the Caliph. This enables the poet to follow an age-old dramatic tradition and ease his technique. Such a figure becomes, within the dramatic limits, almost a microcosm of God felt as Power. As a man, the Caliph conforms to a Renaissance type, nearer Webster's villains than any modern; and, indeed, the Renaissance blood and revenge motifs—which it would be rash to consider out of date to-day—are clearly very much alive here. The Caliph is an artist in cruelty, resembling Iago and Bosola; or God as imagined by Browning's Caliban. Ishak tells us how he 'plays the artist with the lives of men.' Here is a fine description:

> ISHAK. Have you not seen the designer of carpets, O Hassan of Bagdad, put here the blue and here the gold, here the orange and here the green? So have I seen the Caliph take the life of some helpless man—who was contented in his little house and garden, enjoying the blue of happy days—and colour his life with the purple of power, and streak it with the crimson of lust: then whelm it all in the gloom-greys of abasement, touched with the glaring reds of pain, and edge the whole with the black border of annihilation—

> HASSAN. He has been so generous. Do not say he is a tyrant! Do not say he delights in the agony of men!

> ISHAK. Agony is a fine colour, and he delights therein as a painter in vermilion new brought from Kurdistan. But shall so great an artist not love contrast? To clasp a silver belt round the loins of a filthy beggar while a slave darkens the soles of his late vizier is for him but a jest touched with a sense of the appropriate.

Observe how close the Caliph might seem to a particularisation of God himself; how much of this speech might apply to those reversals of fortune so insistent a burden in Greek, Mediæval and Renaissance readings of man's universal destiny under the hand of just such a creator-artist as this. Notice too the fine use of the carpet as a generalising symbol, which I shall return to shortly; and the precise manœuvre of imagination by which, in this play where love, lust, and cruelty are entwined, the Caliph is both kindly and cruel with equal enjoyment; while in the imagery of Ishak's words 'crimson' is the colour for normal lust while agony is given 'glaring reds' or 'vermilion,' again pointing the agony-lust complex I have been emphasising. (Observe that the orange and gold are *not* associated with the Caliph: this has important reference to the play's conclusion).

The Caliph shows an exquisite sensibility and says the most delightful things: as his remark to Hassan, 'Thy impudence has a monstrous beauty, like the hind quarters of an elephant'; or his cool reply to Pervaneh's intense pleading, 'Thou hast metaphysic, but hast thou logic'? His mind shows a perfected symmetry and consistency. Asked if his eyes that love flowers can bear to see a human body desecrated, his ears that love poetry listen to the gasps of the tormented, he answers:

> I shall not honour Rafi with my attendance: I shall be far from sight and sound.

Indeed, though the main agent of cruel action, he seems himself unmoved by crude lust. We dramatically enjoy his calm intellectual cruelty, and he thus contributes indirectly to the sadistic tone; but he is, as it were, himself above the action, not lustfully involved in it. His pleasures range coldly and serenely. He is calm and courteous. Called a 'hideous tyrant, torturer from Hell,' he answers: 'You surprise me.' He is a perfect gentleman, the more terrible in that he shows no insensate brutality: he understands perfectly well what he is doing and all those emotions in others with which he plays. Against his actions we must not forget, however, that Hassan himself, though in words only, and Rafi, in firm intention, were both set on a similar cruelty, swayed each by lust for revenge brought on by love. The Caliph has an inhuman dignity in that he is beyond such passions. His revenge is logical rather than passionate since, holding supreme power, he need suffer no emotional disturbance. It is, however, directly related to his horror of the torment Rafi meant for himself: the thought of which certainly occasioned some early outbursts of fury, when his power was temporarily lost. For the rest, he enjoys scientifically, like Bosola, his victim's suffering: 'Let him talk. I have found a man who does not flatter me. Let me study the hatred in his eyes.' It is the dispassionate interest a tragic poet might feel for his own *dramatis personae,* the good and evil antithesis being resolved in terms of intellectual cruelty rather than Spinoza's intellectual love. Probably his extreme horror of Rafi's threat to bury him alive reflects his delight in all sense-pleasures of a refined sort. But he is also like a god, with something of the insentient mystery of Hardy's First Cause about him; while we may recall how Hardy's conception is used by Powys' in *A Glastonbury Romance* to be specifically related there to the more human sadism of Mr. Evans.

There is, too, a strong love-idealism. The lovers' suffering typifies man's universal destiny, while their choice of love with torture reflects that acceptance on which the racial survival depends. For, ultimately, it is love which urges man in face of agony to procreation. The choice here shows the race willing its own continuance, its acceptance of love, that is of life, at the cost of agony and death: it condenses dramatically the most poignant of human problems. That such universal thoughts are not entirely a matter of interpretative expansion is clear when the frail ghost tells the children yet unborn that 'life is sweet.' Indeed, we feel sometimes that the Caliph's rule is a nightmare dream and love alone real:

> We have walked with the Friend of Friends in
> the Garden of the Stars and He is pitiable to
> poor lovers who are pierced by the arrows of this
> ghostly world.

This is called both 'heresy' and 'most dangerous to the state': which raises some pretty modern problems. But note that whereas the Caliph-as-God is at the most associated with the control of human affairs from a somewhat limited and material view (I shall shortly show how the carpet-symbol supports this statement), love is backed by the mysterious Friend of Friends, and the stars. So in the prison scene the universe itself hangs on the result. The 'air,' 'mountains,' and 'pines' demand the sacrifice:

> We are in the service of the world. The voice of
> the rolling deep is shouting: 'Suffer that my
> waves may moan.' The company of the stars sing
> out: 'Be brave that we may shine.' The Spirits of
> children not yet born whisper as they crowd
> around us: 'Endure that we may conquer.' . . .
> Hark! Hark!—down through the spheres—the
> Trumpeter of Immortality! 'Die lest I be
> shamed, lovers. Die lest I be shamed!'

This is spoken by Pervaneh. Flecker follows the usual tradition in making the woman love's spokesman, and, indeed, far more courageous in love's ecstasy than the man. We may recall Shakespeare's differentiation of Antony's death from Cleopatra's.

Which, we may ask, is the true God—the Caliph, whose artistry is at once the artistry of Creator, dramatic poet, and carpet-designer? Or the Friend of Friends accompanied by a glorious nature in a universe gemmed with stars? Or both? And what is the exact relation of Flecker's scheme to Christian belief? This can be answered, if at all, only by close attention to the symbolism.

Hassan offers two fine examples of the binding symbol: a symbol, I mean, which acts as a metaphysical heart, radiating through the whole and in-knitting the art-form's organic life.

Such is Shakespeare's use of the handkerchief in *Othello:* where, for a domestic theme, a domestic object is endued with supernatural sanctity. More often, as with the Severn Bore in Masefield's *Nan,* some aspect of nature is endued with an almost personal and active force. Both sorts exist significantly together in ***Hassan.*** They are (i) the carpet and (ii) the fountain.

Our most detailed and striking use of the carpet to suggest the patterns of human fortune I have already quoted at length. Hassan at the start possesses an old but choice carpet, symbolising his simple life. His love of carpets exceeds his other contemplative interests—poetry, music, pictures. The ugly carpet he dislikes in the House of the Moving Walls seems to symbolise the ugliness of Rafi's revenge-plot. Carpets are continually mentioned: 'Great, rich, soft carpets from Persia and Afghanistan'; a 'carpet like a meadow,' a 'Bokhara good carpet,' the 'carpet of execution.' An interesting metaphor drives in the carpet-human relation: 'I make allowance for the purple thread of madness woven in the camel-cloth of your character.' Hassan on his advancement is given a fine carpet, corresponding to his gorgeous fortune, with its design significantly including a Prince, leopards, stags, three tigers, and an elephant's head. Hassan, however, dreams of it drenched with blood; and the torture is later mercilessly performed on this very carpet of Hassan's success; that is, performed on, or in, himself, his soul. The carpet is elsewhere related to agony:

> ISHAK. The poet must learn what man's agony
> can teach him.
>
> HASSAN. Is it then not better not to be a poet?
>
> ISHAK. Allah did not ask me that question when
> he made me a poet and a dissector of souls. It is
> my trade. I do but follow my master, the exalted
> Designer of human carpets, the Ruler of the
> world. If he prepared the situation, shall I not
> observe the characters? Thus I corrupt my soul
> to create—Allah knoweth what—ten little
> words like rubies glimmering in a row.

Is the 'master' here the Caliph or God? Notice the close reference of poetic interest in agony to a wider scheme for which the poet is not responsible: similarly you might say the sadist only partakes consciously of some instinct already deep-planted in creation. Ishak's speech also recalls Keats' 'only the poet venoms all his days,' and his description of Shakespeare as the 'miserable and mighty poet of the human heart.' The Caliph, in his mysterious office, causes the agony: Ishak, professionally, and Hassan, for his purgation, attend its working out.

The carpet is, however, a static space-pattern; in its way specifically material; an earth-pattern almost. That is why it blends naturally with thoughts of the Caliph or God as ruthless power; a materialistic, Caliban-theology, a scientific theology, omitting finer intuitions. Therefore,

> When you tread on a carpet you drop your eyes

to earth to catch the pattern; and when you hear a poem, you raise your eyes to heaven to hear the tune.

Our other main symbol, the fountain, more nearly resembles that tune. It splays up in mist and makes an arified soft music: 'On a night like this, does not the very fountain sing in tune, and enchant the dropping stones'? Ishak the poet loves 'the water splashing in the fountain,' 'the hour of silence, when we hear the fountains.' Again, from Hassan, 'How clearly the fountain sounds outside with its little splash.' It is always moving; always new; like music, a thing of time rather than space. So the carpet and fountain balance each other: 'I see blood on my walls, blood on my carpet, blood in the fountain, blood in the sky.' Observe the rising material-spiritual sequence. The carpet is more earthly, susceptible to intellectual examination; the fountain more spontaneous and emotional, at once fluid and ethereal. It symbolises the up-gushing life-force, the life-source, and may be related to instincts of sex and power. Hassan at one point would 'taste the ecstasy of power' and 'drink of the fulness of life,' though his kindly nature finally refuses. We may provisionally consider the carpet-design to symbolise a conscious understanding; and the fountain, unconscious instinct. The Carpet, remember, is associated with the Caliph's ruthless artistry. But whatever our *thoughts* about the universe we cannot *live* by belief in such a God.

Hassan's early disillusion is acted in 'The Street of Felicity by the Fountain of the Two Pigeons': the pigeons having ethereal and love connotations, and, maybe, serving some suggestion of duality relating to my following arguments. Under Yasmin's taunts, Hassan clasps his head, crying 'The fountain, the fountain! O my head, my head!' The centre of his agony, that is, closely concerns the fountain. It is a fertility and love symbol associated in this scene with 'the swelling plain,' an Ethiopian watering roses, a lamp 'between the columns where the incense of love is burned.' Yasmin's pouring of water on him to quench his sexual thirst may be allowed to continue the symbolism. But, as he threatens torments, Hassan sees 'blood dripping from the wall,' a contrast to the fountain's water; he is, like Troilus, 'splitting in twain' since Yasmin is (i) 'so beautiful' and (ii) 'so brutal': which mixture of the beautiful and the agonising is the play's very heart. The condensed poignancy here is remarkable. Hassan's speech both compresses and unlocks the whole following action. He faints, falling 'under the shadow of the fountain.' And, as he wakes in a strange room, he murmurs: 'Just now I was in Hell, with all the fountains raining blood.' That phrase expresses our central psychology of sex-instincts in perverted agony and lust. The association of the carpet with suffering we accept; but the *fountain itself* running blood is as a new, more hideous, *sadistic,* horror. During the trial a couple of speeches shadow further this significance:

> CALIPH. Is not the sight of his beloved to the victim of separation like the vision of a fountain to him who dies of thirst?

> HASSAN. But if that fountain be a fountain whose drops are blood?

During Hassan's conversation with the Caliph in his garden we meet again an actual fountain. 'What a beautiful fountain,' says Hassan, 'with the silver dolphin and the naked boy': again the fountain possesses its pair of minor symbols with erotic suggestion. Then follows the story of its making and the Caliph's father's ruthless cruelty to the artist, drawing from Hassan the cry: 'O fountain, dost thou never run with blood?' After the horrors of the lovers' torture and execution, the garden 'is alive' with ghosts. Ishak finds Hassan, exactly as he found him before, unconscious, 'beneath a fountain,' the fountain of his own life. So Ishak murmurs, 'His life is rhyming like a song: it harks back to the old refrain.' These two incidents frame the central nightmare of the main action: a dream formation is thus delicately implied. Hassan mutters of 'swans that drift into the mist,' dreaming of the pure, the watery, the ethereal; he would sail in a coffin-ship down the river and out to the sea of death, where there shall be *'no red fish.'* But instead Ishak offers him the *golden* journey, 'a desert-path as yellow as the bright sea-shore.' The caravan bells are sounding. Hassan's simple life and innocence have been ruthlessly desecrated, but he will forget his new gaudy carpet now soaked in blood, and instead take again the old well-loved carpet of his former life. With him Ishak, leaving his office of court poet, will try now the 'barren road,' and listen for a new voice. But before they leave, the last horror occurs, making for the first time actual what has been for long a dominating impression:

> HASSAN. The fountain—the fountain!

> ISHAK. Oh! alas! it is pouring blood! Come away.

And in the garden 'the ghost of the Artist of the Fountain rises from the fountain itself in pale Byzantine robes.' He is the creative life-force: desecrated, slaughtered, mystically alive.

The lovers die for the created universe seen as glory and love: it is a romantic calvary. We cannot altogether follow their subjective experience within death. Objectively, from the view of the created world, they are now frail ghosts. The Artist of the Fountain himself cannot unveil the final mystery. 'Life is sweet,' the spirit of Pervaneh calls to the children unborn. And then the wind comes, and the ghosts are cold, and Rafi's answers to Pervaneh become weaker, till he forgets even himself: 'Rafi, Rafi, Who was Rafi?' But even at this moment the bells ring out, bells, as Charles Lamb called them, the 'music nighest heaven,' summoning to the desert path. The dreams are dispelled, the ghostly unreality grows more unreal as this new immediacy, like the nearing Horn in *Nan,* swings into our consciousness:

> Away, for we are ready to a man!
>   Our camels sniff the evening and are glad.
> Lead on O master of the Caravan,
>   Lead on the Merchant Princes of Bagdad.

With what a bell-note purity and clarion strength Flecker's skill in clear-cut images ('when shadows pass gigantic on the sand') now crowns and domes our play. How the sharp sense-impressions of taste, smell, and sight; the jams 'meticulously jarred,' such as the Prophet himself may eat in Paradise; the carpets 'dark as wine,' manuscripts with peacock decorations; the 'mastic and terebinth and oil and spice'—how all is newly taut, the rhythms tense, including yet *mastering* all rich essences to shame by contrast the earlier enervate sensuousness, its lust and loves alike. Now for the first time is bravery and purpose. The Caliph and Rafi, under stress of circumstance, showed fear, Hassan was a lovable weakling throughout; only Pervaneh was strong with a strength not hers, but love's. But the Shakespearian energy is now felt, with a strangely recaptured Shakespearian feeling for merchants and merchandise. It is a spiritual pilgrimage, too; though a 'desert' journey, an ascetic state being implied, yet it is bright and purposeful; a dawn of the soul, though set in evening; a setting out beyond both lust and love, blood and water, across deserts, mountains and seas:

> We are the Pilgrims, master; we shall go
> Always a little further: it may be
> Beyond that last blue mountain barred with
>   snow
> Across that angry or that glimmering sea.
>
> White on a throne or guarded in a cave
> There lives a prophet who can understand
> Why men were born: but surely we are brave,
> Who take the Golden Road to Samarkand.

'Golden': as against the reds of lust, the purple of power. As in *Nan,* our final movement is flooded with gold—'a desert path as yellow as the bright sea-shore.' A golden asceticism. As with the gold rider in *Nan,* there is athletic movement, leaving sensuous luxury, 'girls and garlands,' eunuchs and Syrian slaves; there is an 'excess' of spiritual ambition beyond all natural desires. It recalls the darker quest of Ahab in *Moby Dick:* like that it is essentially masculine, leaving women behind. So they go 'for lust of knowing what should not be known.' The interweaving of actual and symbolic, merchant caravan and pilgrim search is masterly. Both categories are locked in 'Samarkand,' used somewhat as Yeats used Byzantium. Flecker's choice of the name is admirable: sharp definition and detonation of line and word mark his vigorous conclusion throughout.

The play penetrates very deep. Hassan himself leaves the 'garden of art for the palace of action'; it is a purgatory of self-discovery—as when he finds himself unable to slay Yasmin; and at the conclusion he and Ishak, who has *broken his lute,* move beyond both art and action. But the whole play's statement must be faced. Remember Yasmin's enjoyment of the torture—'I laughed to see them writhe'; her love of the 'dark Masrur,' with the smell of blood and roses; Masrur's drinking of Rafi's veins associated with his drinking of Yasmin's body; the pouring of her lover's blood on Pervaneh's eyes. The horrors are hideously attractive. The scene between Masrur and Yasmin has a dangerous, insistent, beauty. And yet the sadistic tone cannot be disposed of in terms of pathology. An identity of cruelty with love is, or seems, intrinsic to creation, and such perversion may, under poetic mastery, be an approach to the perennial force and meaning of many mysteries, the Crucifixion for one, though this is perhaps to touch ourselves the 'lust of knowing what should not be known.' Anyway the fearless artistic facing of such substances is the precise condition of that ringing victory at the close. Put otherwise, the poetic consciousness that so exquisitely orders the earlier symbolism and action *is precisely the consciousness shadowed by the Samarkand epilogue:* since all poetry aims, with Ishak, to pass beyond itself. Something very dangerous is fearlessly faced, ordered, and mastered, and the reader or spectator is invited to a corresponding initiation. Moreover, the obvious health of the play's recurrent humour (e.g. the exquisite second Guard)—and nowhere will the essentially mean or inhuman show itself more swiftly than in humour—marks our intuitive recognition of basic sympathy. Remember how Hassan, the human norm of the whole, whose lust for revenge preludes our action, nevertheless finds himself unable to hurt Yasmin when occasion offers.

Tyranny and social injustice are part of the design, but the protagonist is a shop-keeper and merchants get a fine, almost glorified, showing at the end: those who care to may call the play *bourgeois.* The main issues are psychological and spiritual. The insistent revenge interest recalls the Elizabethans, just as the Caliph is a Renaissance figure. Besides the carpet and fountain, numerous impressions enrich the design. The impressionistic subtlety recalls Webster. Yet, since this never impedes the straightforward movement of a simple action, Shakespeare is perhaps the better comparison. At first sight the attraction seems too sugary and easy, the language too thin, with entertainment and lyric value rather than any profundity. But this is a superficial and purely linguistic judgment: the structure of the whole, the manipulation of symbol and action, the interweaving of emotions and colours, is masterly, and the searching of human instincts profound. The play is moreover metaphysically complex. There are primary and secondary orders of dramatic reality; and the slightly ambiguous nature of the whole middle action, its dreamlike quality with respect to Hassan, its dramatic subordination to his central story, most subtly enables the poet to balance death at its ghostly worst against a dispelling of that nightmare by a daylight strength. (pp. 93-103)

> *G. Wilson Knight, "The Road to Samarkand," in* The Wind and the Rain, *Vol. II, No. 3, Winter, 1944, pp. 93-103.*

Herbert Howarth   (essay date 1951)

[*In the following excerpt, Howarth considers the significance of the Middle Eastern culture in Flecker's life and works.*]

Probably, as the phase of revaluation of the work of the first decade of this century comes round, James Elroy Flecker's rating will rise and he will be seen more clearly along with contemporaries of his like Rupert Brooke. Whatever the final estimate of his poetry may be, it has its own compelling idiom: it has always had its devotees, and one or or two of his poems have steadily held their places in the popular anthologies throughout the more than thirty-five years since his death. As a figure he has special interest for those who would gain insight into the inner problems of a man born of a mixed marriage, in whom two strains meet and seek for a common purpose.

Flecker was born in London in 1884, the son of an English

Christian clergyman and a Jewish mother. He grew up in Gloucestershire on the Cotswold Hills, had the routine English upper-class schooling at Uppingham, followed by Oxford. His university career was not academically distinguished, but he made a mark as a poet, a dandy with a genius for the higher kind of bawdy, and a person of independent ideas. For a time he felt he would like to know the working people—it was the era of the Fabians, and Rupert Brooke at Cambridge was thinking along similar lines—and he would nostalgically haunt the drabber parts of London, and he devoted one long vacation to tramping the Bordeaux district of France, drawn there by a rising of the vineyard workers. In his first play, **Don Juan,** which earned praise from Bernard Shaw, he oddly mixed a craving for the betterment of the industrial poor, an ardor for Britain and the Empire, and a passion for romantic love and magic. "The worst scene," Shaw wrote to him about it, "is the argument of Don Juan with the labor leader, which is not knowledgeable." And then—"You had better go on making a fool of yourself for ten years or so and see what will come of it."

Actually Flecker had less than four years of life left. In these he found, as his travels had taught him, that his best creative source was the eastern Mediterranean. He had spent two years at Cambridge preparing himself for the Levant consular service; and so out to Turkey and Syria. The writing of poetry had always been easy to him, but too easy. During his spell in Syria he sometimes succeeded in breaking free of glibness and finding new heights and depths. He produced there a number of lyrics, and one superbly wrought play, **Hassan,** based on a story from the *Arabian Nights.* Then he began to succumb to a chronic tuberculosis. Early in 1915 he died in a sanatorium in Switzerland. So much for the external facts of his life.

Flecker and his generation grew up in the shadow of the work of the great archetype of Victorian romanticism, Sir Richard Burton, today best remembered for the most full-blooded translation of the *Arabian Nights,* but in his own time renowned for his spectacular journeys in the Orient and Africa, for his prolific writing about them, and in particular for his *Kasidah,* a poem of Arab life. At the beginning of the 19th century English poets had to go no further than the Mediterranean where it touched France, Corsica, and Italy, to find color and nationalism and primitive vigor sufficient to activate their powers. Fifty or sixty years later the world was smaller, and Europe more homogeneous, or at any rate more familiar; the imagination had to range further to make contact with the exotic. Laurence Oliphant wandered the world and spent the close of his life largely in the Near East; Fitzgerald hammered out, almost without knowing what he did, his quatrains paraphrasing the Persian Omar Khayyam; Doughty was trekking the desert, and he completed *Arabia Deserta* in the year of Flecker's birth; Wilfred Blunt, growing interested in the people of Egypt, had begun his heroic single-handed contest against Lord Cromer, the British Resident in Cairo. The 20th-century names are as well known: those who found their arena in the Near East, like T. E. Lawrence and Gertrude Bell and Flecker, and those who had to go further, to India and China, like E. M. Forster and Arthur Waley.

What turned them all East? T. E. Lawrence claimed that in boyhood he read *By the Waters of Babylon,* and that made him dream of restoring to life a great dead empire of the Near East. Flecker while still a boy came across Burton's *Kasidah* and transcribed it whole. One is tempted to say that in neither of these cases could the reading have *planted* the ideas that grew from them, but that rather it awakened deep congenial impulses. For certainly, what happened to the Englishmen who went out to the Orient was that they made their chosen regions a focal point for solving their deepest and most personal problems.

Lawrence projected on to Arabia all the opposing Napoleonism and nihilism, the ambition and the despair, of his being. Flecker brought to Syria a no less disruptive complex of dualities. Like Burton, he was peculiarly responsive to the Orient and its fascination, and peculiarly and painfully aware of its evils. T. E. Lawrence, having made himself master of the contours of the desert and the structure of Syrian castles and the nomad Arab mind, could brood most profoundly on the gardens and moat of an old English cathedral town, and for his favorite music choose the "ghost-harmonies" of the essentially English Elgar. A similar tug between place of birth and place of choice characterizes Flecker. In his poem **"Oak and Olive,"** beginning "I was born a Londoner and bred in Gloucestershire," he goes on to tell how the scenes of London and the Cotswolds all were transformed by the mind's eye, as he walked among them, to scenes of the longed-for Aegean:

> Have I not chased the fluting Pan
>   Through Cranham's sober trees?
> Have I not sat on Painswick Hill
>   With a nymph upon my knees,
> And she as rosy as the dawn,
>   And naked as the breeze?

But then, he tells, as soon as he is actually in Greece, his thoughts alter every scene to the shape of the England he has left:

> But when I walk in Athens town
>   That swims in dust and sun
> Perverse, I think of London then
>   Where massive work is done,
> And with what sweep at Westminster
>   The rayless waters run.

With such a sentiment uppermost in his feeling, Flecker seems to be saying that no place possesses the quality of "here," but everywhere tends to become "elsewhere." T. E. Lawrence was in such a plight, too, but he had several loopholes into reality, made available by his pleasure in practical problems, by his interest in machinery, and so forth. Flecker had few such loopholes, and thus was more at the mercy of the opposing pulls. Just as he oscillated between England and the Orient, unfree to be happy in either because the other always preoccupied him, so he was torn between reality and dream: and between a concern, dictated by conscience, with the poor and the drab, and an appetite for the exotic and rich.

Flecker's interest in the East may have been parallel with that of other Englishmen of his generation, but there were also some sharp differences. Most Englishmen who practiced the romantic cult of the Orient asked: "Where can I find vitality? Where will my energies be spurred and my dreams find scope to be lived?" Flecker at least once claimed that this was the shape of his question too: in the first section of his poem **"Ideal,"** there's a dialogue between the poet and an old man who, though only half-drawn, is a queer and disturbing image of skepticism. The poet sings of the nobility of life. The old man mocks him and points to the degeneracy of the city people moving around them. The poet answers that whatever is wrong with London, where folk have "hearts of stone," there are other climates where greatness may yet flourish:

> Said I: "In London fades the flower
> But far away the bright blue skies
> Shall watch my solemn walls arise,
> And all the glory, all the grace
> Of earth shall gather there, and eyes
> Shall shine like stars in that new place. . . . "

But the old man, answering him again, and with an ambivalent comment, puts a different light on the matter, and marks Flecker off from other Orientalizing Englishmen:

> Said he: "Indeed of ancient race
> Thou comest, with thy hollow scheme."

In a way typical of the working of poetry and of the honesty it forces on the poet even when he seems bent on striking a pose, this turn aptly shows the special difficulties facing Flecker. In his case, we see that this young poet's search for a new animating realm involves quite separate personal issues. The translation of his question is no longer merely "Where vitality?" but also, and first of all, "Who am I? Where do I truly belong?"

Before a man can escape he must at least first know where he is trying to escape from. (The man who is torn between two worlds is often trying to escape from both of them, yet all his contortions only carry him backwards and forwards along the groove between.)

Soon after his arrival at Oxford, the poet had taken a step the very triviality of which indicates how much the matter of self-identification was worrying him. Herman Elroy Flecker was his registered name. To be more English he decided to drop Herman and become James. He retained Elroy. Why? There are three possible reasons. He was called "Roy" at home, and could not abandon it. He knew that his mother had wished him to have a Hebrew name (*El roï:* "a God of seeing"), and he would not forsake the one she had chosen. By false etymology he associated it with kingliness. Any or all these thoughts may have decided him. In any case he felt, in a rather primitive way, that his name was important, and must be an expression of himself. By pairing James and Elroy he declared himself simultaneously a modern Westerner and a personality linked with the East and the past.

When he looked into the history of his father's family he found a link with the East even there. The Reverend Flecker's father had been a schoolmaster for a time in Constantinople. A part of the past was sympathetic to the enlightening mission of the teacher; and significantly enough, when he himself reached Constantinople he published **The Grecians,** a study of the principles of education in the form of a modern Platonic dialogue. But in his university period, when he was so nervously and urgently trying to discover himself, he wanted to find somewhere in his family history a more direct contact with a much deeper past, and if possible a contact that would justify his conviction that he was "an aristocrat by nature." Inevitably he now looked to his mother's side of the family. I once asked Arthur Waley, who had been a friend of his, whether he thought Flecker had been influenced by Jewish memories reaching him through his mother. Mr. Waley replied, "A good deal more than that. After all, he himself looked strikingly Oriental and I think this, as much as anything, made him feel he did not belong here. He had a short phase of interest in his mother's ancestors and made up his mind that she was descended from some kind of Maccabean chief or irredentist. . . . "

It is strikingly appropriate to the English poetic tradition that when Flecker at last locates his kingly origins, he places them in a context that is also revolutionary. Associating himself with militant leaders of the past, the English writer often thus lays bare his secret hope that destiny intends him for militant leadership in the future. "I was the true, the grand idealist," Flecker cried in the person of Don Juan:

> Noble on earth, all but a King in Hell,
> I am Don Juan with a tale to tell.

Don Juan is, in some of its unequal parts, a study in his own identity. It has one luminous and crucial scene pivoting on the idea that a man must be interpreted through his maternal ancestors. The Leporello of the play is a South Welshman, Owen Jones, and at the psychological climax he changes from a cringing valet to an agent of magical compulsion, dominating his master and enforcing on him the memory of the procession of the ages: "Who was your mother, O my master? She was some mighty Jewess, I dare say, robed in a leopard's skin, who knew the deep secrets of Persia and wrote them in a book." Again the paradox operates that, by facing inwards on himself and groping about his memories for all that is most *alien* in him, he becomes powerfully associated with a major *English* tradition—the tradition of *faery,* in which the primitive and the magical are apprehended in terms that movingly mix good and evil. So with Melville's Captain Ahab; so with Mr. Kurtz in Conrad; so in Malory's chapter—a chapter that often recurred to the imagination of T. E. Lawrence—when Lancelot begat the world's purest knight on a woman who came secretly to his bed. To know himself Flecker had to dare to peer into clefts of the past and see there the ancient ambiguous symbols; and he had to go to the East in order to be confronted by the landscape of old past-haunted caves and clefts, like the Dravidian cave in Forster's *Passage to India.*

In an essay on pleasures denied to the complacent, Flecker tells how the imagination can be activated by the scenery of Asia, when the past—formidable, dark, pregnant—is glimpsed suddenly there: "He might have walked beneath heavy Indian skies and understood in a flash, standing in the monstrous shadow of an ancient god, the secret of all Empires." T. E. Lawrence knew these apocalyptic moments; they came to him in childhood at Oxford, and when his expeditions to the desert began they came, as one night among the diggings at Carchemish when a storm lit up the figure of a colossal god. To Lawrence they came as a spur to action, and at the same time as the eternal criticism of all action. To Flecker they were rather his marrow, his innards, his dreams, his kingdom, awakening all he had forgotten in himself. The power that Walter Pater found in Mona Lisa, and that D. H. Lawrence wanted to see in the Etruscans and Aztecs, the power that it is sometimes supposed might be available in a primitive integration of good and evil, this Flecker was at moments on the point of seizing from the memory of his mother's ancestors.

"What if the Jews are an older race than we and know old forgotten secrets?" he makes Hassan meditate. The momentary flashes of intuition answered his question "Who am I?" by lighting up the Asiatic side of himself; by accepting that answer he was to write his best poetry; yet he could never accept it permanently and wholeheartedly, and the more he learned of either side of himself, the more passionately he was inclined to cling to the other.

Writers whose intuitive life is lived in one tradition but who are also molded in another tradition by the language they use are not infrequent. Considerable contributions to English literature have been made by them: by such Irishmen as Yeats, or by a Pole like Conrad. Sometimes great sticklers for the "correct" and the formal, yet they impose their difference on the old forms or on the fashions in vogue among their contemporaries, and bring a special originality into their work. Flecker can be counted with these. He gave a new flavor to English. Some readers find it over-sweet; all admit it to be singular. He made a unique literary success out of the current vogue of traveling East to escape the pressure of personal problems. But in his case this escape to the Orient had a special exquisite value: it provided the cleverest of all evasions, the surest of all escapes from oneself. Flecker took a leap right into the area of his ancestral origins, the last place any man would be expected to use as a hide-out from his ancestry.

It must have been clear to the critic in him—he was a good critic of poetry, and his early critical essays still make tolerable reading—that such verse as he had written in a professedly British and patriotic vein showed his differences from England rather than his likenesses. They were over-British. They had, for instance, none of the odd ironies of Kipling, with whom he would have liked to compare himself. T. E. Lawrence describes him [see Further Reading] as "furiously British: a patriotic 'God Save the King' exile, nostalgic, and knowing himself landless, clinging desperately to fiction," and tells how he tried to transcribe this into life by knocking a German down in the Deutscherhof Pension in Beyrouth. These pugnacious exertions might succeed in life, but not in poetry, and it is not surprising that when Flecker realized this he turned to the diametrically opposite maneuver of overtly exploiting his Oriental side in order to dissimulate it. To a man in love with his own gifts and his own dexterity, as he frankly was, this must have been highly gratifying: to adopt a fashion; to use it as an escape from himself through himself; to be the

excelling master of it; and so, secretly, to find himself even while he escaped.

Flecker's writing did in fact become masculine, rounded, truly original only when he reached the Orient and started to exploit the local forms, scenery, traditions. After two or three years he was able to say that he had created the best Oriental poems in the English language, and that he could, at call, improve on Fitzgerald's "Omar Khayyam." He really understood the Aegean and the Fertile Crescent, he claimed, and the best judges admitted his claim. Natural linguist he was (T. E. Lawrence stated that he knew all the great Old World cultures except Russian, and actually he had some interest in Russian too), but his understanding of the Arabs went further than their language. The secrets of Turkish and Arabic poetry were in his grasp. He found the right, provoking English names for the sensuous data of his region:

> Take to Aleppo filigrane,
>   and take them paste of apricots,
> And coffee tables botched with pearl,
>   and little beaten brassware pots:
> And thou shalt sell thy wares for thrice
> The Damascene retailers' price,
> And buy a fat Armenian slave
> Who smelleth odorous and nice. . . .

To these sensuous catalogues he added the strange moral echoes, legacies of the problems of the deserts and the desert religions, which give depth to Arabic poetry. And to this in turn he added a living critique of the eulogistic tradition of the Arabs, showing how when a great poet worked in it he had no option but to accept its distasteful duties, yet continued, watching for the moments when he could suddenly insert truth in it. The output in which Flecker actually does all this is not voluminous, but it is sufficient to show that the "bright blue skies" to which he had come from gray England were as vital as he had hoped.

What was this "flair" that delivered the Orient into his grasp? Was it not the act of recognition of his own identity, made possible, as he had foreseen, by contact with an ancestral landscape? From the moment when this contact was made in 1910 he burned feverishly through a series of conflicting reactions. His tuberculosis was reawakened, and he had to go home for a spell of treatment, but he came back again, and again the tuberculosis and the poetry advanced rapidly abreast of each other.

Love of the Orient; hatred of the Orient; poetry of the Orient; illness demanding a withdrawal from the Orient: these four factors collide, struggle, obtain momentary fusion in Flecker in the short period between 1910 and his retirement to a Swiss sanatorium in 1914. His writing often failed even amid this internal excitement; and it was of the sort that when it was not good was atrocious. But in a few things, notably in the play *Hassan,* he worked at a level of perfection. In doing so he also came close to resolving his disparate trends, the split between his feelings for the poor and his love of richness, between a weakness for dreams and a largely compulsive acknowledgment of the claims of reality.

There are two themes in *Hassan:* the story of a humble

and profoundly humane confectioner who wins the Caliph's favor by accident and loses it with a day by criticizing tyranny; and the story of the mistake of Pervaneh, when she induces her lover, Rafi, to elect for a joint death with her instead of life apart. Into this second theme, the debate between love and life, Flecker projects something of his lifelong fluctuation between dream and reality.

He had in several earlier poems displayed his conscious fear of death:

> O, I'd rather be
> A living mouse than dead as a man dies.

By this criterion all real life is worth living; it does not have to approximate impossible dreams to be good. But some of his poems do try to turn life into impossible dreams. One of his own favorites, a paraphrase from the Turkish *Saadabad,* thus pictures the poet enjoying love as the greatest glory in the world.

In the choice confronting Pervaneh and Rafi, Flecker passes judgment on the dream of *Saadabad,* and makes dreams the synonym of death. "I die for love of you," says the ecstatic Pervaneh, but Rafi cries "Comfort me, comfort me! I do not understand thy dreams." This harrowing prison scene rings the death knell of 19th-century romanticism. In choosing love deified and distorted by poetry, the two choose wrong. They should have chosen life with its incomparable realities.

With no less dramatic conviction, in the person of Hassan the poet solved the problem of presenting poor people in poetry for the first and only time. All the efforts to make "songs of the people" in proletarian London or peasant France had failed. Even though he had tried to write ballads claiming "We're of the people, you and I," as long as he was in the West Flecker seemed unable to bear the common people except at a distance. (His friend Douglas Goldring has recorded that when he actually came close to them it was disastrous, as he found one night when, by a chance of Bohemian life, he was at supper with a little Cockney girl called Gertie. He loved to hear himself make dinner conversation, but she repeatedly bludgeoned him into silence with innuendos connecting his swarthiness with neglect of bathing.) Always retaining an affection for his London working-class poems, he republished one or two later on, yet he probably knew they were misfires. The poetry of the industrial tenements could not be written till Eliot came with a new technique, a sense of the appropriate elusive new forms, whereas Flecker's skill lay in the flexible and surprising use of old chant forms.

Now in the Near East Flecker found that these difficulties of making touch with the people vanished. He could go and meet them and listen to them. That was what he had hoped for from the Orient. One of the poems specially scored in his copy of Thalasso's *Anthologie de l'amour asiatique* was a Baluchistan "Song of the People." When he toured the Aegean islands with his Athenian wife he heard a peasant tell her, "That man married a siren," pointing out the man. Here were the peasants speaking, and what they said was what he had been long telling himself he wanted to hear. He heard from them "the songs of the people, which are better than mine."

His use of what he heard, then, reaches its best point in *Hassan.* Hassan, the confectioner, and Ishaq, the Caliph's poet, both spring from the people. When the Caliph admires the beauty of Hassan's common speech, he asks "Where did you learn poetry, Hassan of my heart?" and the answer comes

> HASSAN. In that great school, the Market of Bagdad. . . . All the town of Bagdad is passionate for poetry, O Master. Dost thou not know what great crowds gather to hear the epic of Antari sung in the streets at evening. I have seen cobblers weep and butchers bury their great faces in their hands!
>
> THE CALIPH. By Eblis and the powers of Hell, should I not know this, and know that therein lies the secret of the strength of Islam. . . .

Hassan, like Ishaq, is lifted into the Caliph's favor, and the brief splendor teaches him that a king is rich because a people is poor, that in an empire even culture is only a function of general misery.

Elroy Flecker had long cherished an image of himself as a king-to-be. When he moved from Athens on the last step of his entry into the Levant he had said, "I do a Waring," thinking of Browning's Londoner who left the West and its drabness to rule among waiting primitive peoples:

> "So I saw the last
> Of Waring?" You! O, never star
> Was lost here but shone out afar.
> In Vishnu-land what avatar!

But actual experience of the East extinguished his Waring image. To be a king in a society based on the servitude and ignorance of millions, that might be tolerable either to a Waring or a Kurtz, but not to a living Flecker. The king becomes the tyrannical Caliph of Bagdad. Because of the Caliph's ways Ishaq says, "I have broken my lute and will write no more *qasidahs* in praise of the generosity of kings. I will try the barren road, and listen for the voice of the emptiness of the earth."

This is a splendid program that Ishaq announces, but not one easy to carry out. The play ends with the Golden Journey to Samarkand, along a road traveled not by the poor of the earth, but sensuous people who handle sensuous goods:

> THE CHIEF DRAPER
> Have we not Indian carpets dark as wine,
> Turbans and sashes, gowns and bowls and veils,
> And broideries of intricate design,
> And printed hangings in enormous bales?
>
> THE CHIEF GROCER
> We have rose-candy, we have spikenard,
> Mastic and terebinth and oil and spice,
> And such sweet jams meticulously jarred
> As God's Own Prophet eats in Paradise.

In fact there is no successful sequel to Ishaq's decision. The character Hassan is the achievement most nearly related to it. Flecker had planned to make Ishaq—a poet and so a projection of himself—the center of his play. When imagination had done its work, Ishaq, for all his admirable qualities, fell into second place, and in the center revolved the fat, poor, middle-aged, humane confectioner. He is no mere piece of autobiography. He is an invention, full and rounded, with a soul where taste and humanity merge, where what Fletcher loved and what he felt he ought to love are reconciled. Ishaq, like Flecker, makes poems. Hassan, like the ideal common man, is a poem.

After this play, finished in the summer of 1913, a rapid physical disintegration set in and Flecker found he could no further perform Ishaq's promise to try the barren road. It was as though in life he had already made a different, a wrong choice with Pervaneh and Rafi, and had seen his mistake only when he was a ghost blowing on the wind. The pang of doubt in all his exuberance, injected by the difficulties of the question "Where do I belong?" had long made him interested in the "Parnasse" school of French poetry and its wormwood tinctures, so unlike the profuse Arabic literary colors. In picturing the lovers' ghosts bleakly evaporating after the execution, Flecker used the palette of the Parnasse with great effectiveness, and was rightly pleased with himself for it. But as he succumbed to illness in his last year, he tended to a wholesale adoption of the Parnassian doctrine, which then began to enfeeble his work.

Once more he turned to dreaming and away from reality. One of his last pieces of writing, a review of Paul Fort's *Vivre en Dieu,* says "The divine function is to dream. . . . All lives dream each other into existence." Against the anemia of some of these last thoughts only two positive indications can be set, a note on Milton as a masculine figure in English poetry, and the idea of a play on Judith; also, just before his thirtieth birthday his fever subsided for a moment and he had his "only mystic vision," an imaginary poem about Jerusalem new and old.

Looking again at the course of his creative life, one feels that there is a sudden sharp rise in it, followed by an equally sudden fall. The rise begins when he goes to live in the Orient. It reaches its upper limit with **Hassan,** and at this point all the problems of his life come together and, interacting dynamically and productively, are within an ace of being resolved and leading to a new phase of work. But that lies just beyond his power. Then the tensions which have been beneficial for an inspired moment become utterly destructive. He sinks and dies. He is never able to follow the kindly, cynical, worldly wisdom of Bernard Shaw, put to him in the letter about **Don Juan:** "Do, for Heaven's sake, remember that there are plenty of geniuses about, and that the real difficulty is to find writers who are sober, honest, and industrious and have been for many years in their last situation."

Like Burton as revealed in the famous *Kasidah,* Flecker found himself, by the test of experience, both lover and hater of the Orient. And unlike Burton and the other Englishmen who made this discovery about themselves, Flecker felt bound to accept a measure of responsibility for what he met in the Orient, since to a part of him these lands were home. Out of this intimate connection with two geographical and cultural extremes came both his creative and physical fevers. Partly he belonged to the East, yet it was hard to agree to belong to a region which was "malig-

nant" in that it weakened the will. The will to what? To live history and accomplish change.

At Candilli on the Bosphorus he watched the ships dim away eastwards down the Black Sea in the evening and retrospected on the armies that had used the junction of the two continents, and wrote how from all this "a light fever distracts the dreamer's body, and his mind longs for some coercive chain, and he begins to understand why men in the East will sit by a fountain from noon to night and let the world roll onward."

He perceived a relationship between the politics and the geography of Asia, and traced to it the prolonged submission during the last centuries to squalor and corruption. And perceiving it he recoiled. "I am a modern civilized man," he cried out. To Catholic friends Flecker wrote that if they were attracted by medievalism they should investigate it in the sordid present of the Near East.

So while his faculties flowered in the Levant, he resented and criticized the stagnant beauties that fertilized him. This man whose stage properties were ornate lattices and friezes—

> We shall watch the Sultan's fountains
>   ripple, rumble, splash and rise
> Over terraces of marble,
>   under the blue balconies,
> Leaping through the plaster dragon's
>   hollow mouth and empty eyes.

—this man was off the stage an apostle of the sanitation and functional architecture of the new West. The places he praised were, for instance, the Berlin of 1905, "where there is, indeed, no taste for art, but, better still, there are no slums." His criterion was the newest of America. "We shall build," he wrote in **The Grecians**—"for comfort and utility, and obtain our beauty not from the added ornamentation of an antique style, but from the principles of symmetry and design. Indeed, I imagine we shall build our school after the American manner with iron and reinforced concrete. Of all methods of construction this is the strongest, for the San Francisco earthquake itself could not shake down the slimmest buildings wrought of this material. Therefore we shall build our school with straight and simple harmonious lines; and in doing so we may, perhaps, be advancing into a new architectural style, some day to be reckoned great. . . . "

For the first years of the century this is a live manifesto, indicating Western values of a conspicuously progressive nature. When he yearned from Brumana for England—

> Oh shall I never never be home again?
> Meadows of England shining in the rain
> Spread wide your daisied lawns: your ramparts
>   green
> With briar fortify, with blossom screen
> Till my far morning

—his characteristic decision to give the title "home" to the place where he is not living at that moment was probably influenced by a concurrent judgment on the quality of housing and living and leisure standards in the West as compared with the East. His images do somewhat suggest the fronts of smug villas, but included in this vision of the

English downs is possibly also le Corbusier's vision, a healthy knitting of nature and town.

Thus at the date when his genius still supported his inner tensions and made literature out of their opposing pulls, there was a constant critical descant, sustained by one song. By a paradox it added the richness of an astringent doubt to his sensuousness, doubled his emotions by coupling each with its obverse, brought form with it. This is true of **Hassan** above all. Describing the play in a letter, Flecker himself adumbrates the point: "It's utterly Oriental externally, but I hope the flash of the little European blood I possess gleams through its seraglio atmosphere from time to time."

The European conscience, which had worried him and sent him wandering round working-class London and peering through windowpanes there, had never been able alone to guarantee him poetry; it had even misled him many times; yet his best work was done when he let it penetrate his elected Eastern material as a corrective antidote.

T. E. Lawrence wrote that with Flecker passed "the sweetest singer" of the pre-war world. That is true, but that is not his significance, for even in his own day sweetness of song was becoming a less prized achievement, and Hardy was showing that infelicity might be an asset to those who had a contemporary message. His significance lay in his treatment of his problems. Lawrence, devoted to the Semitic mind, also said of him: "It is restless, is life, for the man whose blood mates North and South (NW and SE)."

Flecker was restless and he used his restlessness. Repose was not possible to him because illusion was not possible. The other Englishmen who went abroad went to something that was truly different and strange to them, but he went to something that he knew in his blood; and thus he found, more quickly than they did, the things that were wrong, and that urgently needed the attentions of both king and schoolmaster, the poet and the rebel, the Oriental and the Westerner. All these personalities were inherent in him, and had found shadowy, tentative expression in his early writing. To develop them, keep them balanced, integrate their work—that was the aim imposed on him by his crucial contacts with the East. It was perhaps outside any man's strength, but in making the effort, he won his triumph as well as slew himself, and earned the right, which he once claimed in a lyric, to be read by poets a thousand years hence:

> Since I can never see your face,
> And never shake you by the hand,
> I send my soul through time and space
> To greet you. You will understand.

(pp. 449-57)

Herbert Howarth, "Flecker: The Poet and His East," in Commentary, *Vol. 11, No. 5, May, 1951, pp. 449-57.*

John M. Munro   (essay date 1976)

[*An English educator and critic, Munro has written ex-*

tensively on Middle Eastern culture. In the following excerpt, he provides a survey of Flecker's prose writings.]

Flecker's prose is more interesting for the light it throws on his personality and on his poetry and drama than it is in itself. It consists of critical essays, travel sketches, a textbook for students of Italian, some visionary fantasies, translations, a dialogue on education, and a romantic novel, *The King of Alsander.* Most of this work is not especially significant, and the novel must be considered a failure. Among the critical essays included in the *Collected Prose* are two on John Davidson; others on A. E. Housman, W. J. Courthope and Arthur Symons, Paul Fort, **"The Public as Art Critic";** and one which amounts to a critical evaluation of the Parnassians, being the preface to *The Golden Journey to Samarkand.* Though not distinguished, none of these essays is of poor quality; and the earlier ones are quite remarkable if one considers Flecker's youthfulness when he wrote them.

The earlier of the Davidson pieces, for example, **"John Davidson: Realist,"** was written while Flecker was still an undergraduate at Oxford. It is an enthusiastic encomium to a poet who, wrote Flecker, provided "an antidote to our quiet, self-satisfied, ill-founded idealism"; and, though inclined to overpraise him and to elevate the stature of works which most readers would be inclined to ignore, Flecker does make clear why Davidson appealed to him and puts forward a plausible case in support of him. Davidson was an iconoclast, a man who wished to sweep away hypocrisy and humbug; and these anarchic tendencies recommended themselves to Flecker, who at the time the essay was written was rebelling against the restrictive influence of his pious, morally conventional home. Davidson, claims Flecker, had gone even farther in breaking conventions than Ibsen: Ibsen "urged the overhauling of all our social machinery; he attacked with terrible precision the shoddy idealism and the prudish self-complacency that still pervades modern life"; Davidson, however, urges one "to live as if convention, as if Christianity, as if thirty centuries of literature had never existed."

In **"John Davidson,"** Flecker's later critical estimate of the poet, he is more temperate and does not allow his enthusiasm for the man to influence his judgment of the work. Previously, he had praised Davidson's turgid farce *Smith,* with which, Flecker had said, "something vital" came into English literature; and he had had also much admiration for the long, blank-verse "testaments." Now, however, Flecker, who has Davidson's literary achievements more clearly in perspective, admits that, though Davidson was certainly the greatest poet of his age, his was not an especially glorious age. He selects for special mention Davidson's ballads, and he now denigrates the testaments—critical judgments with which most modern readers would agree. Finally, in seeking an explanation for Davidson's comparative failure as a poet, Flecker states that, though he was a man of genius, he was also a man of great ambition; and "his ambition ruined his genius" by causing him to become assertive, shrill, and rather vulgar.

The Davidson essays tell more about Flecker's rebellious tendencies than about his literary taste, but an unfinished

Flecker and his wife, Hellé, in Lebanon.

piece entitled **"The New Poetry and Mr. A. E. Housman's 'Shropshire Lad',"** written while Flecker was at Cambridge, gives insight into Flecker's criteria for poetic excellence and, incidentally, makes a series of critical judgments with which most modern readers would agree. He observes that many people are ready to insist that poetry is dead, but what they really mean is that the "older poetry," that "splendid connected dynasty" from Coleridge to Swinburne, is dead. But, he continues, this is no real cause for regret because, in estimating the worth of poetry written in the "old" tradition, one is apt to confuse grandeur with worth, noble sentiments with poetic ability—a confusion which has led some people to overestimate the value of this kind of writing, particularly with respect to such modern followers of the old tradition as Stephen Phillips and William Watson. What Flecker admires is simplicity, the spare, clear diction of parts of Oscar Wilde's "Ballad of Reading Gaol"; he likes also the characteristic language of the verse of Robert Bridges, Thomas Hardy, W. B. Yeats, and, most notably, A. E. Housman, who uses "pure spoken English with hardly any admixture of poetic verbiage."

In another essay, **"Two Critics of Poetry,"** Flecker praises Arthur Symons at the expense of W. J. Courthope.

Courthope, writes Flecker, estimates poets by their "influence" rather than by their "merit"; and, since he has an evident enthusiasm for "verse which he considers patriotic and healthy," he dismissed Keats and Blake as "conceited asses with a spark of genius" because neither of them, he says, were much interested in politics and society. Symons, on the other hand, who "prefers poetry to politics," is good on the Romantic poets; he is inclined to underestimate Alexander Pope and his contemporaries; but he is, writes Flecker, a much sounder critic than Courthope. According to Flecker, Symons is the better critic because he focuses attention on the poetry and arrives at his judgments on the basis of a clear-sighted, sensitive appraisal of the words the poet has written. Symons considers poetry as poetry, not merely as a means of expressing something which might perhaps be better expressed in prose.

With the exception of the earlier Davidson essay, the idea that poetry should be criticized simply as poetry is a theme which runs throughout Flecker's literary criticism, but it is expressed most forcefully in **"The Public as Art Critic"** in which he enumerates the qualities that the perfect critic should have. He should know all about the technical aspects of writing verse, but he should avoid being pedantic about them. Most important of all, he should have "a deep experience of life," that will enable him to judge without puritanism and prejudice:

> He must not condemn poems because they are morbid, profane, or deal with what the Manchester Watch Committee . . . would call unpleasant subjects. He will know that art is divided, not into decadent and healthy, classic and romantic, but into the two mighty divisions of Good and Bad, and that these divisions alone hold true. One great dogma alone he must hold—that human life is passionately interesting in all its phases, that over the filthiest by-ways the sky of night must stretch its flowery mantle of stars. The critic must be of purer mould than the poet himself. He must have a profound love for man, not the vague enthusiasm of the humanitarian, but a vivid delight in all the men in the world, men sinful, men splendid, men coarse, or cowardly, or pathetic. And in all the phenomena of nature, sordid or shining, the background to our tragedy, he must admire, if not the beauty, then the force, the law, the cruelty, and the power. And with this enthusiasm in his soul he will bitterly condemn dullness, weakness, bad workmanship, vulgar thought, shoddy sentiment as being slanders on mankind; and in this sense and this sense only—that is the glory of man—great art is moral.

Finally, conscious that he may have created an impossible ideal against which few critics could measure themselves, Flecker carefully indicates that he is not saying that art is only for the elect. On the contrary, there is the "spark of the divine in us all"; therefore, it is quite possible that "thousands honestly and genuinely enjoy, admire, and love certain works of art which they know to be considered great." Nevertheless, in spite of this concession to the masses, Flecker really does believe that the public is, by and large, philistine. Art lives on, it is true, but in noble retirement:

> The artist hears all around him infinite rubbish talked about his art, and imagines for the moment that the middle classes are sincere, and will be willing at least to hear his symphony or read his book. You soon undeceive him, you middle classes. You, who have let, are letting, and will let your poets die of hunger, continue to buy your poetry editions of the classics and to frame photographs of the "Sistine Madonna" over your mantel-shelves. You know quite well that vital art bores you and you have never understood it.

Apart from the early Davidson essay, Flecker's literary criticism is a conventional enough expression of the "art-for-art's sake" point of view, reflecting the theory which lies behind most of his verse. Even the early piece about Davidson forecasts Flecker's later development because, in his insistence on that poet's "objectivity," he has written the prelude to his more fully orchestrated praise of the allied doctrines of Parnassianism and "art for art's sake."

More important than Flecker's literary criticism are his visionary fantasies, most notably **"The Last Generation"** which was originally published in *The Best Man* while he was still at Oxford. In this story about a revolt led by a young poet-prophet, Joshua Harris, who is distressed by the ugliness of the modern world, decides to assume control of it. The revolt succeeds; a proclamation is issued; and the important part of it relates to the sterilization of women as a deliberate means of bringing the human race to an end. As the population declines, a group of young people of "taste," the "last generation," forms a club, the Florentine League, and withdraws to a garden, determined "to live apart from the rest of the world" like "that merry company of gentlefolk of Boccaccio's *Decameron* who, when the plague was raging at Florence, left the city, and retiring to a villa in the hills, told each other enchanting tales."

The young people, who read poetry and cultivate the arts, remain in the garden until their thirty-seventh year; then most of the members decide to commit suicide rather than join the ugly world outside, as they are forced to do by a rule established by the league's founders. Eventually, only one remains; but, just as he is about to take poison and join his dead companions, the cup is wrenched from his hand by a "terrific blast," and "a wave of despair and loneliness" sweeps over him, causing him to exclaim: "What am I doing among these dead aesthetes? Take me back to the country where I was born, to the house where I am at home, to the things I used to handle, to the friends with whom I talked, before men went mad. I am sick of this generation that cannot strive or fight, these people of one idea, this doleful, ageing world. Take me away." Whereupon the wind wafts him over the wall of the garden, back to the crude outside world. There he finds that the majority of those still alive have become depraved; there is scarcely a face that "was not repulsively deformed with the signs of lust, cunning and debauch," and soon the last survivor of the Florentine League finds himself at one with them. Gradually, the human race dies out, the buildings crumble, but life remains, "myriads of brown, hairy, repulsive little apes" emerging from the ruins, "one of them building a fire with sticks."

Although **"The Last Generation"** is something of a *jeu d'esprit*, very much the sort of thing a clever Oxford undergraduate of the early 1900s might be expected to write, it does have serious undertones: it serves as another reminder that, though Flecker may have subscribed to the doctrine of art for art's sake, he was far from being one of its more extravagantly melancholic, nihilistic exponents. Inspired by Max Nordau's *Degeneration* (1895), a somewhat hysterical, pseudoscientific diatribe against the art-for-art's-sake movement, and perhaps influenced by reading Samuel Butler's *Erewhon* (1892), a book very much in vogue at Oxford while Flecker was there, **"The Last Generation"** draws attention to the futile consequences of an existence devoted to art rather than to life. To withdraw from life may provide a pleasurable escape from the ugliness of one's surroundings, but such an act is ultimately self-defeating. Life goes on just the same. This Flecker knew; and, though he died young, his realization of the futility of withdrawal saved him perhaps from the fate of such people as Ernest Dowson and others of that group referred to by W. B. Yeats in his *Autobiography* as "the tragic generation."

In another of Flecker's visionary fantasies, **"N'Jawk,"** the Esthetes appear rather better than they do in **"The Last Generation."** The story, such as it is, is about Peter Puxley, who "believed neither in Inspiration nor in Immortality, nor even in . . . sweet Idealism," but his rationalist bent had not had a deleterious effect on his morals for "his character was steady and firm." He enters the church, but dies from a fit of cholic while still young. His soul, propelled through infinity, becomes entangled with the ghost of Slimbert, an Esthete poet and the author of "an exquisite volume of verse in the Doreskin Library of Modern Masterpieces" and of several unsigned essays on "How to make money by writing," published in *Tit-Bits* and *Pearson's Weekly*. The two souls succeed in extricating themselves from one another, but they are captured and transported to an Oriental palace where they are ushered into the presence of the god N'Jawk who, finding Puxley has never done anything to honor him, orders that he be made into porridge. Meanwhile, Slimbert, by dint of extravagant flattery and hypocrisy, avoids Puxley's fate; and he is allowed to spend the rest of eternity with the young ladies of N'Jawk's court.

Though shorter than **"The Last Generation," "N'Jawk"** is somewhat similar; it was also influenced by Samuel Butler, this time by his *Erewhon Revisited* (1901), whose Chapter XVI on the dangerous limitations of rationalism seems to have left its mark. Puxley's name is clearly derived from the names of two eminent Victorian thinkers, Thomas Henry Huxley and Edward Bouverie Pusey, the former associated with the Rationalists and the latter with the Anti-Rationalists. Obviously, there is a little of both Huxley and Pusey in Flecker's creation; but one should not assume that Flecker is mounting a serious attack against these two men and the beliefs they stand for. Rather, Flecker's intention seems to have been to ridicule both the rational and the antirational approach to religion, for it is quite possible that there is no God at all; or, if there is, he may be quite different from what one imagines him to be, in which case all those agonizing, self-engrossing nineteenth-century controversies about faith and morality are rather ridiculous. Survival will be granted to the clear-sighted opportunists.

Another prose piece belonging to this group is **"Pentheus,"** also written from the freethinker's position. The story derives from Euripides' *Bacchae,* specifically Gilbert Murray's rhymed translation of the play, in which were included several notes concerning the cult of Dionysus that refer to the resurrection of the god and the affinity of this event with the coming of Christ. Flecker's fantasy describes how Pentheus, "a harsh and surly tyrant," is alarmed by the revelry encouraged by Dionysus, especially after learning that his own mother has fallen under the god's spell; and he decides to attack him. He fails; and, before being torn limb from limb, he is made to appear ridiculous by performing "a drunken parody of the divine exaltation" which characterizes Dionysus' true followers. Pentheus, however, finds immortality; and at a later date the ancient confrontation between Pentheus and Dionysus is re-enacted. This time Dionysus, not Pentheus, meets disaster; but the god rises again and Pentheus, having had the worst of the exchange, endeavors to make friends with

him and stipulates "that the dancing should be more private, and that the Maenads and Satyrs should be less eccentrically clothed." He also insists that the mystic feasts to the god be relegated to the seventh day when the initiants should be taught their duty to Pentheus; during the remaining six days, they are to be kept "at the bitter loom." Pentheus succeeds in turning religion into support of his own power, and the joy that once characterized Dionysian worship entirely disappears.

Then, continues Flecker, some time later a new god of liberty and war comes on the scene; and he destroys Pentheus; but, like Dionysus, Pentheus also proves to be indestructible. Rather more affable than previously, he has lived on in a new guise, that of a respectable, moral idealist. Unfortunately, his well-meaning philanthropy is just as much a grim parody of divine goodness as his tipsy jollity was a mockery of divine exaltation; and, though "his humdrum days may be pleasant or painful, he has never tasted of our purple grapes of heavy sorrow, our golden grapes of super-human joy. Alas, poor Pentheus!"

The meaning of this fantasy is clear. It is a paean to holy joy at the expense of Puritan conscience, an indictment of the pietistic, well-washed idealism of the Victorian bourgeoisie, and a plea for "life" over morality. It is also a declaration of faith in the kind of life Flecker himself wished to lead, as well as an attack on the moral and spiritual values associated with his father. Together with **"The Last Generation"** and **"N'Jawk," "Pentheus"** reflects the most appealing side of Flecker's personality, his vitality and his enthusiasm for the world in which he lived, an enthusiasm, moreover, which transcended even the claims of art.

Flecker's vitality and enthusiasm are also reflected in his dialogue on educational theory, **The Grecians,** and in his textbook for the study of Italian, **The Scholar's Italian Book;** but in both works their presence mitigates the effectiveness these books might have had as serious educational documents. The latter was composed while Flecker was at Constantinople, and he at first jocularly proposed to call it *Italian for Gentlemen.* Evidently written in a spirit of gay condescension, facetiousness is never far away; and the amused, faintly contemptuous tone of the preface, however refreshingly original, must have alienated a number of schoolmasters who might have considered using the book. Flecker says his object in the book is "to enable any intelligent student who knows some Latin and French to learn with the minimum of labour to read a great literature"; then, making an ironic thrust at previous compilers of Italian grammars, he suggests that they have been "tormented by the dire necessity of filling up a large book on a simple subject." Finally, he says, "I express the hope that some Headmasters may find this book a useful recreation for a sixth form exhausted by successful labours in scholarship hunting."

The main part of the book is divided into two sections: the first, a brief review of Italian grammar; the second, an anthology of passages followed by translations into English. [In her *Life of James Elroy Flecker*] Geraldine Hodgson insists that Flecker was keenly interested in his Italian textbook, but one wonders whether his interest extended beyond the translations themselves. Flecker enjoyed translating, much as he enjoyed writing poetry: both were agreeable exercises of the imagination and the intellect. It is possible, therefore, that, having rendered a number of pieces of Italian prose and verse into English, Flecker decided to make them the core of an Italian language manual and to add the brief review of grammar in an attempt to give his book both organic unity and functional purpose.

On the other hand, this view may be unjust because Flecker was interested enough in education to write a book on educational theory, one in which he establishes as his ideal the humane, aristocratic spirit which informs the gifted amateurism of *The Scholar's Italian Book.* The contempt for "scholarship-hunting" is present, and the educational program he recommends is the kind in which his Italian language manual might be used.

The Grecians, cast in the form of a Platonic dialogue, contains, in fact, Plato's theory of education as developed in *The Republic* but brought up to date. There is, however, an essential difference between Plato's notion of the function of education and Flecker's. Plato wishes to educate men to discover and appreciate truth; Flecker wishes to educate men to appreciate beauty. Plato's dialogue is the work of a philosopher who also happens to be a poet; Flecker's is that of a poet who tries hard to be a philosopher. The epigraph for *The Grecians* could have been taken from Flecker's preface to *The Golden Journey to Samarkand:* "It is not the poet's business to save a man's soul, but to make it worth saving." If one substitutes educator for poet, one has the philosophical basis on which Flecker's dialogue is constructed. Throughout his treatise, the emphasis is on the cultivation of the mind and the body as a way to appreciating the glory and beauty of the world; only passing attention is paid to moral education or preparation for a professional career.

Following Walter Pater in the conclusion to *The Renaissance,* Flecker relegates philosophy to a relatively minor role, noting that "we may find a pure philosopher very deficient in his appreciation of the joy of life," and "the joy of life is the heritage of those who have unlocked the secret door that leads into the garden of the senses." Some boys, Flecker concedes, are incapable of appreciating "the mysteries and beauties of life," and these will be given a special kind of technical training. As for those of "the most refined intelligence," Flecker proposes an unashamedly elitist form of education, designed to produce cultivated aristocrats: "In an ideal state these boys would not have to earn their living: they would automatically become rulers of the State, or else be subsidised to live in leisure as artists or critics. In our actual England we can give this complete education only to the sons of the rich, and to those few boys which our school funds enable us to support, not only here but afterwards. To give a boy this complete education, we must keep him until he is at least twenty-one."

Curiously, however, Flecker is not in favor of allowing such students to absorb the education they receive, free from the petty tyranny of examiners:

> An examiner may be stupid and set worthless papers; but provided the papers be well set, examination is the sole adequate test of a boy's capacity. For we have no sympathy with Cecil Rhodes, nor with the cheerful, popular, and chiefly ignorant crowds who come to Oxford under his fantastic testament: we do not like this democratic selection of the prize favourites: we pin our faith to a written and evident intellectual superiority. We mistrust the boy who is said to be 'very good at work really, but no use at exams.' Such a boy is either morally deficient that he cannot rise to a crisis and concentrate his energy and ideas—and far be it from me to admit such a one to be a Grecian—or else it means that he is incapable of literary composition or self-expression; or else that his thoughts and facts are so confused that he cannot write them down. There is a great deal wrong with boys who fail at examinations.

These are strong words from a man whose career was punctuated by a series of failed examinations!

Flecker's superior students would be required to devote their days "to the culture of the mind"—to be schooled most intensively in "literature, representation and music." Contrary to Edwardian practice, Flecker would not have his students devote the greater part of their time studying the Classics, and he would not overburden them with grammar. "Three hours a week for three years" he regards as sufficient for both Latin and Greek, and he suggests that Classical instruction not be given to students before they are sixteen, at an age, in short, when they may be expected to "obtain a fuller understanding of the classic spirit than those to whom Latin and Greek are a ceaseless drudgery and evil." If the Classics are taught in this way, Flecker believes, students will learn, "no less than others have learnt, from these time-honoured studies, that calm and even fervour of mind, that same and serene love of beautiful things, that freedom from religious bigotry and extravagance which marks the writings of the Greeks, and that seriousness, decorum, and strength, that sense of arrangement and justice which marks the writings and still more the history of the Romans."

The main reason for learning a language, Flecker believes, is not to converse or write in it but to read its literature. After all, he says, "any German clerk . . . any cosmopolitan or Swiss innkeeper, any half-breed dragoman can gabble six or seven tongues, and sometimes gabble them correctly; and the dreariest lady student from Russia can speak beautiful French and passable German, and yet not have in her head a single Russian not to speak of German or French, idea." Students should strive for a level of linguistic proficiency which will enable them to read literature swiftly and with pleasure.

Flecker's choice of literary works for study is somewhat unconventional. Not surprisingly, considering his Parnassian inclinations, Leconte de Lîsle's *Poèmes barbares* is strongly recommended; Corneille and Racine are ignored—after all, one would not expect "to interest a Frenchman in English by presenting him with *Paradise Lost*"; but Honoré de Balzac and Anatole France are given special commendation. Among German literary works, *Faust,* Book I; Heine; Sudermann; and Nietzsche are all recommended; in Italian, he would have his boys read "a great deal of Dante, a little of Petrarch," some

Boccaccio, Matteo Bandello, Masuccio of Salerno, Carlo Goldoni, and Gabriele d'Annunzio, as well as several lesser known writers.

In emphasizing the representative arts, Flecker considers doing so his most revolutionary proposal. He wishes to train his students "to notice things in pictures"; "to regard nature from an artistic point of view"; and "to represent things for themselves." The true end of art education, he says, is to make students realize that the great picture is not necessarily one which portrays a heroic or pathetic subject, for technique should be the sole criterion. He would have his students draw and paint, however clumsily, not merely for the purpose of making exact copies of objects or other paintings, but for the sheer joy of "inventing for himself or imitating nature." He would also expose them not only to great art (not merely that which is generally acknowledged to be great) but also to the French Impressionists, to examples of Japanese prints, to Persian miniatures, and to Indian bronzes.

Flecker admits that his enthusiasm for music is less than his enthusiasm for the representative arts, but he would have his students understand "the aim and structure of classical music." As for history, mathematics, and science, these should be relegated to subsidiary status. History he finds a "specious substitute for liberal education in the arts"; but he acknowledges that it could be "most useful as a pleasant and instructive afternoon diversion for those not very intelligent boys who are working to enter a trade or profession." Unlike Plato, Flecker thinks little of mathematics, suggesting that his "Grecians" be compelled "to learn sufficient mathematics to prevent their being put to shame in the affairs of life, and no more, unless they specially desire it." However, what he says about the teaching of mathematics would find sympathy among the advocates of "new math," because, since he deplores the laborious working out of mechanical exercises, he suggests that a good mathematics teacher should endeavor to interest his class in "the delight he himself takes in mathematical problems, by selecting the most fascinating and important examples of mathematical method." As for the natural sciences, these "if unaccompanied by other studies [are] poor training for the mind"; therefore, Flecker does not believe that his students should be "expected to do more than attend two weekly lectures delivered in non-technical language on scientific laws." There should be a museum at the school, but it should not be cluttered with exotic novelties; it should be a "neat and systematic collection of local flora and fauna."

The school itself should be situated near the sea, preferably on the Hampshire Downs. The buildings should not be "Splendid Gothic," the traditional design of most educational establishments, but should be "after the American manner"—constructed with an eye for "comfort and utility," their beauty deriving "not from the added ornamentation of an antique style, but from the principles of symmetry and design." Physical exercise would be encouraged, not by forcing the children into team sports, but by allowing them to pursue the athletic activity in which they show the most proficiency. Corporal punishment would be allowed because, says Flecker, "I consider the sentimentalist more poisonous than the flagellant," and sexual intimacies among the boys should be discouraged by having each boy possess "a book on the subject" that contains "the exact truth without exaggerating dangers or threatening hell."

The Grecians proposes an impractical system of education; and, though many modern educators would doubtless agree with Flecker's views about school-building design and about physical exercise, they would hardly agree with his emphasis on the humanities at the almost total exclusion of the pure and applied sciences. An interesting document, it is, perhaps, something of an apologia for Flecker's conspicuous lack of academic success; and, as Douglas Goldring has pointed out [see Further Reading], its main interest lies in the fact that it throws considerable light on the man who wrote it. In *The Grecians,* Flecker describes a system of education calculated to produce a humane dilettante with decidedly nonconformist proclivities, rather than a useful, disciplined, industrious member of society—to produce, in fact, a man very like Flecker himself. In other words, what Flecker seems to have unconsciously sought to achieve in *The Grecians* is moral and theoretical justification for his own behavior and way of life.

As a child, Flecker was constantly at odds with the restrictive routines of the schools he attended; and he was always running into trouble as a result of his inability to conform to the corporate discipline of these institutions. He had little respect for members of the teaching profession; he compares them in *The Grecians* with businessmen to the latter's advantage. In the same book he describes their appearance at a special service held in a certain public school. There they were, writes Flecker, "some two hundred head and assistant masters. A more tragic sight I have never seen." "Usually," Flecker continues, "schoolmasters are surrounded by boys and one does not notice what a sorry sight they are, but *en masse* they look positively ill." So it was, in this congregation, they made a depressing sight: "I saw men who had failed, whose lips were hard, and their faces drawn and sallow, [and] when I remarked the imbecile athletes who taught football and puny scientists who expounded the dark mystery of nature, the sapless scholars who taught Plato and Catullus by the page and hour, the little wiry-bodied men in spectacles who trained their pupils in *King Lear* for the Cambridge Locals, I shuddered and felt faint."

This description was too much for Flecker's long-suffering parents, and his father refused to discuss *The Grecians* with his son, "seeing in it nothing but a jeer," an understandable if unjust estimate of the dialogue when one realizes that the congregation which Flecker had described was one which he and his father had attended at Cheltenham. That Flecker should have included this passage is evidence of his tactlessness and bad taste; more important, however, it strongly suggests that his integrity as an educational theorist is questionable since one cannot help feeling that *The Grecians* was as much occasioned by Flecker's desire to attack his father and all the educational values he stood for, as it was by a desire to propound a serious, sincerely held educational philosophy. It is almost as if Flecker wrote his dialogue in an attempt to embarrass his father and, at the same time, to provide himself with an alibi to account for his failure. "Look," he appears to be saying "how could you have expected me to achieve anything worthwhile, considering the unenlightened education you gave me."

The King of Alsander, though not a successful novel, is Flecker's most ambitious prose work. A curious, picaresque tale which mixes high romance and social commentary, it is awkwardly constructed, uncertain in tone, and inconsistent in its characterization; the style wobbles uncertainly between purple prose and undergraduate facetiousness. The hero of the novel, Norman Price, is the son of a country-town grocer; and one day, while working in his father's shop, he meets an old man who enjoins him to run away from home and visit the wonderful land of Alsander. Norman steals some of his father's money for his journey, and he soon arrives at his destination where he meets a charming young girl called Peronella. The two fall in love, much to the chagrin of Peronella's present lover, Cesano; and Norman takes up lodging in her house under the watchful eye of her widowed mother. One day Norman visits the Royal Castle and learns of the recent history of Alsander. It seems that a previous monarch, King Basilandron, much addicted to revelry, one day staged an elaborate Bacchic orgy, and the neighboring state of Ulmreich seized this occasion to invade Alsander. Alsander retained its independence, but its power declined; and, under the reign of Basilandron's successor, King Andrea, who was insane, the country degenerated even more, thanks largely to the corrupt Regency of Duke Vorza, who governed Alsander less for the welfare of its people than for personal gain and enjoyment of a ruler's prerogatives.

During this time Norman appears on the scene and is drawn into a conspiracy by the so-called Society for the Advancement of Alsander which aims to place Norman on the throne instead of the mad Andrea, whom nobody has seen because he is locked up in his own castle. Encouraged by a young man called Arnolfo, Norman works to overthrow Vorza; the plot succeeds; Norman becomes king and pretends to be Andrea, miraculously cured after treatment in England; and a chastened Vorza is bought off by being made Lord Chamberlain. After the coronation, Arnolfo reveals that he is not really a young man, but a girl who is really the exiled Princess Ianthe and who has determined to make Norman her husband. Meanwhile, Peronella discovers a letter which clearly reveals that Norman is an imposter; when she brings it to the attention of Vorza, a counterplot is begun to depose Norman and restore Andrea. There is a battle during which both Vorza and Andrea are conveniently killed, and Norman triumphs, marries Princess Ianthe, and begins to rule Alsander with justice and intelligence. Peronella disappears from Alsander, never to be seen again.

The King of Alsander was probably begun while Flecker was still at Oxford, and it was completed only a few months before his death. In 1906, Douglas Goldring heard Flecker read parts of it; and, under the spell of Flecker's personality, he thought the novel to be remarkably good,

an opinion he later modified considerably. In the summer of 1906, Flecker lost the first three chapters of the manuscript while on his way to Paris; and, though he managed to rewrite most of what he had lost, he admitted in November, 1907, in a letter to Frank Savery that "the novel goeth slowly." Early in 1908, he completed a first draft; and, for a while, it seemed as though John Dent would publish it. The publisher evidently rejected the manuscript for in January, 1912, Martin Secker had agreed to publish it, subject to extensive revision. The revision Flecker found a "dreadful trial," and he was soon convinced that only the first two chapters had some merit. "Nothing in God's earth," he wrote to Frank Savery, "can infuse any reality into the tale; so I confine myself to polishing and writing it up less heavily and hope it may be a popular success."

Flecker's first revision was not acceptable to Secker, and he asked him to revise the manuscript again, which Flecker did; but, by the time the revision had been completed, Secker had lost interest in the novel. In June, 1913, Flecker wrote to Douglas Goldring to ask if he should take Secker to court and to solicit his aid in finding another publisher. By this time, Flecker had convinced himself that *The King of Alsander* was really "a very jolly and fantastic work," and Max Goschen also seems to have felt it had merit because he eventually agreed to publish it. The novel appeared early in 1914, some months before Flecker's death.

Considering the long and unfortunate history of the novel's composition, its several false starts and revisions, it is not surprising that *The King of Alsander* is, in Goldring's phrase, "a patchy affair." But, even if the novel's passage into print had been smoother, it is doubtful whether Flecker would have been able to create an organic work of art since he seems to have derived his plot from a number of existing literary sources rather than from his own imagination, and the separate influences are clearly traceable. The idea of a conspiracy to substitute a young Englishman for a native monarch is reminiscent of Anthony Hope's popular novel *The Prisoner of Zenda* (1894); but, unlike Hope, Flecker never expects the reader to take his outrageous plot seriously. The most obvious influence, however, is Apuleius' *Golden Ass,* "that mysterious wonder-story" written in a "glittering precious style" which Norman takes with him on his travels. From this work Flecker appears to have derived the notion of an episodic narrative which enables the main character to satirize some of the vices and follies of humankind. Moreover, the endings of the two works are remarkably similar: the miraculous appearance of the "white woman" in *The King of Alsander* recalls the intervention of the goddess Isis who restores Apuleius to human form. *Zuleika Dobson* (1911), Max Beerbohm's amusingly told tale of the devastating effects of a young adventuress on the students at Oxford, also seems to have been an influence, as well as Voltaire's *Candide.* Few of the characters involved in Flecker's plot linger in the memory with the possible exception of the eccentric consul, who was probably drawn from life in spite of the author's disclaimer that all the characters in *The King of Alsander* are "purely fictitious." The others are cardboard caricatures, reminding one of the characters of a Ruritanian musical comedy.

For many readers the most interesting feature of the novel is the insight it provides into Flecker's likes and dislikes, his attitudes and views about literature and life in general. For example, one learns that the author thinks highly of Joseph Conrad's *Youth;* that Damascus is "a very filthy town with electric trams and no drains"; that in "no tale since *Tom Jones* have we had an honest Englishman who makes love because it is jolly and he doesn't care."

"There is also a highly revealing digression on the excellence of whipping." Here Flecker once more returns to a subject which exerted a powerful, if unhealthy, fascination for him. In [his poem] **"Taoping,"** he describes a flagellation scene; in *Hassan,* Pervaneh and Rafi are whipped; in his essay *The Grecians,* he advocates judicious flogging in the upbringing of young boys.

However, nowhere else in Flecker's writing is flagellation treated so extensively as it is in *The King of Alsander.* Flecker considers the role of the whip in Spartan and Roman times, in the East, and then moves on to consider the literary aspect of whipping, concluding that there is "no great book without its whipping." He admits that he would rather see adults whipped than children, and the episode concludes with a description of Norman's experience when the executioner lays on "steadily and evenly" until the back of the future king of Alsander "looked like a sheet of music paper."

That Flecker's interest in flagellation was more than theoretical is apparent from his having had a lengthy, intense discussion on the subject with T. E. Lawrence, when he came to visit the Fleckers in Areiya. More pointedly, from Flecker's correspondence with his wife it is clear that caning and being tied up and caned formed an essential part of his married love-making. Thus, in one of Flecker's letters to Hellé from Smyrna shortly after his engagement, he presses her to lose no time in coming to stay with him, adding that he will "keep the little black strap" and make "the loveliest red marks" on her when she comes. Whenever she may be displeased with him, he adds, she "could tie him up and have a glorious revenge." As for *The King of Alsander* there is little in it to recommend itself to most readers. The narrative runs along briskly enough; there is the occasional amusing comment or turn of phrase, as for example the old man's remark that he is quite unimpressed by Norman's "Watts-Dunton talk" after hearing that his dreams are his best friends. But it is difficult to justify a novel's worth in these terms; and, while it might have seemed moderately impressive coming from an undergraduate, it is not especially noteworthy from a supposedly mature man of letters.

Flecker's prose as a whole does little to enhance his reputation. His literary criticism is intelligent but not especially distinguished; his visionary fantasies and treatises on education are interesting mainly for the light they throw on his ideas and personality; and *The King of Alsander* would have been forgotten entirely if it had not been written by a man who had attracted attention as a poet and as a dramatist. Flecker was a writer who enjoyed manipu-

lating words and meters for their own sake, and his genius found its most effective expression in verse; his prose has its merits, but only an ardent Flecker enthusiast would claim that it deserved more than passing attention. (pp. 77-93)

> *John M. Munro, in his* James Elroy Flecker, *Twayne Publishers, 1976, 143 p.*

FURTHER READING

Biography

Booth, Martin. *Dreaming of Samarkand.* New York: William Morrow and Co., 1989, 333 p.
　　Novel based on Flecker's life in the Middle East and his relationship with T. E. Lawrence.

Hodgson, Geraldine. *The Life of James Elroy Flecker.* Boston and New York: Houghton Mifflin Co., 1925, 288 p.
　　Includes a lengthy epilogue discussing the influence of the Parnassians and other nineteenth-century French poets on Flecker's works.

Mercer, T. Stanley. *James Elroy Flecker: From School to Samarkand.* Thames Ditton, Surrey: The Merle Press, 1952, 56 p.
　　Biographical essay and descriptive bibliography of Flecker's works.

Sherwood, John. *No Golden Journey: A Biography of James Elroy Flecker.* London: Heinemann, 1973, 237 p.
　　Biography by Flecker's nephew based on family papers not available to earlier biographer Geraldine Hodgson.

Criticism

Birrell, Francis. "On Getting Muddled." *The Nation & The Athenaeum* 33, No. 26 (29 September 1923): 816.
　　Review of *Hassan.* Birrell finds the drama problematic in both its form and subject, stating: "It is difficult to know what to make of it. Is it a farce? Is it an ironical poetic drama? Is it a wracking tragedy? In a way it is all these things, because Flecker could not make up his mind which side of his nature he should call into play, and we see them all being requisitioned successively."

Bosworth, C. E. "James Elroy Flecker: Poet, Diplomat, Orientalist." *Bulletin of the John Rylands University Library* 69, No. 2 (Spring 1987): 359-78.
　　Examines Flecker's career in the Levant Consular Service and assesses his knowledge of Middle Eastern culture as reflected in his writings.

Chesterton, Mrs. Cecil. "Hassan." *Bookman* (London) 65, No. 385 (October 1923): 7.
　　Positive review of *Hassan* in performance.

Cranmer-Byng, L. "Flecker's *Hassan.*" *The Poetry Review* 14, No. 1 (January-February 1923): 33-5.
　　Descriptive review.

Cunliffe, John W. "James Elroy Flecker." In his *Modern English Playwrights: A Short History of the English Drama from*

1825, pp. 196-200. New York and London: Harper & Brothers, 1927.
> General discussion of *Hassan* and *Don Juan,* with an account of their critical reception.

Davis, Mary Byrd. *James Elroy Flecker: A Critical Study.* Salzburg: Universität Salzburg, 1977, 264 p.
> Surveys Flecker's poetry, prose, and dramas.

Fairchild, Hoxie Neale. "Nothing Very New." In his *Religious Trends in English Poetry, Vol. V: 1880-1920,* pp. 195-221. New York and London: Columbia University Press, 1962.
> Finds little evidence of religious thought or feeling in Flecker's poetry.

Gillanders, Ronald A. *James Elroy Flecker.* Salzburg: Universität Salzburg, 1983, 458 p.
> Major study of Flecker's life and works.

Goldring, Douglas. *James Elroy Flecker: An Appreciation, with Some Biographical Notes.* London: Chapman & Hall, 1922, 200 p.
> Biographical and critical study by a friend of Flecker.

Grigson, Geoffrey. "The Creation of Beauty: James Elroy Flecker and the East." *The Bookman* (London) 79, No. 472 (January 1931): 244-45.
> Review of *Some Letters from Abroad of James Elroy Flecker,* rehearsing the facts of Flecker's life in the Middle East.

Kidd, Timothy. *"Hassan:* The Road to Haymarket." *Theatre Research International* 4, No. 3 (May 1979): 198-213.
> Account of the composition and stage production of *Hassan.*

Knight, G. Wilson. "Edwardian." In his *The Golden Labyrinth: A Study of British Drama,* pp. 308-41. New York: W. W. Norton & Co., 1962.
> Praises *Hassan,* remarking that it "is of those rare dramas which make an important epoch live. The courts of oriental potentates were admired and copied by the Italian princes of the Renaissance, whose culture did so much to inspire our dramatic tradition. Flecker's imaginative ground is well chosen and he adds territory since won to enrich the composition."

Lawrence, T. E. *An Essay on Flecker.* London: Corvinus Press, 1937, 10 p.
> Reminiscence of Lawrence's visit with Flecker in Lebanon.

Lucas, F. L. "Ah, Did You Once See Shelley Plain?" In his *Authors Dead and Living,* pp. 147-58. New York: Macmillan Co., 1926.
> Positive review of *Hassan, The Collected Prose of James Elroy Flecker,* and *The Life of James Elroy Flecker,* by Geraldine Hodgson.

McCormick, Virginia Taylor. "Let Us Talk of Flecker." *The Personalist* 3, No. 2 (April 1922): 85-94.
> Effusive appreciation.

Macdonald, Alec. "James Elroy Flecker." *The Fortnightly Review,* no. 115 (1 February 1924): 274-84.
> Appreciation that concludes: "The death of Flecker at the age of thirty-one is unquestionably the greatest premature loss that English literature has suffered since the death of Keats."

Markowitz, J. "J. E. Flecker—The Role of Tuberculosis in English Poetry." *The Canadian Forum* 17, No. 195 (April 1937): 20-2.
> Speculates that the "intoxication" of tuberculosis may account for the "lyrical ecstasy" of *Hassan.*

Monro, Harold. "James Elroy Flecker." *The Egoist* 2, No. 3 (1 March 1915): 38-9.
> Obituary tribute.

Morgan, A. E. "More Poets: Flecker." In his *Tendencies of Modern English Drama,* pp. 295-97. New York: Charles Scribner's Sons, 1924.
> Positive appraisal of *Hassan.*

Palmer, Herbert. "James Elroy Flecker." In his *Post-Victorian Poetry,* pp. 146-57. London: J. M. Dent & Sons, 1938.
> Laudatory appraisal of Flecker's works.

Phelps, William Lyon. "Brooke, Flecker, de la Mare, and Others." In his *The Advance of English Poetry in the Twentieth Century,* pp. 124-56. New York: Dodd, Mead and Co., 1925.
> Praises Flecker's skill as a poet.

Price, J. B. "James Elroy Flecker." *Contemporary Review* 191, No. 1093 (January 1957): 31-5.
> Overview of Flecker's work, asserting that "modern poets are by no means reluctant to experiment in their language, but there are very few who unite boldness and good taste in so happy a proportion as Flecker."

Routh, H. V. "James Elroy Flecker (1884-1915)." In his *English Literature and Ideas in the Twentieth Century: An Inquiry into Present Difficulties and Future Prospects,"* pp. 79-80. New York: Longman, Green & Co., 1948.
> Emphasizes Flecker's technical skill as a poet.

Shanks, Edward. "James Elroy Flecker." In his *Second Essays on Literature,* pp. 84-105. 1927. Reprint. Freeport, N.Y.: Books for Libraries Press, 1968.
> Survey of Flecker's poetry, fiction, and drama.

Shipp, Horace. "The Triumph of *Hassan." The English Review* 37 (November 1923): 653-55.
> Criticizes the stage production of *Hassan* and the play itself as excessively artificial.

Sutton, Graham. "Not Forgetting: A Pair of Spectacles." In his *Some Contemporary Dramatists,* pp. 202-08. 1925. Reprint. Port Washington, N.Y.: Kennikat Press, 1967.
> Compares *Hassan* with other dramas of the time that were set in the Middle or Far East.

Swinnerton, Frank. "Pre-War Poets: James Elroy Flecker." *The Georgian Scene: A Literary Panorama,* pp. 270-71. New York: Farrar & Rinehart, 1934.
> Concludes that the "brilliance of [Flecker's] skill with words does not always cover the limitations of his interest; the poetry is never excessive in its ambition; but what Flecker knew and felt he could tell in such a way that he sang it separately to every reader."

Thouless, Priscilla. "James Elroy Flecker." In her *Modern Poetic Drama,* pp. 30-9. 1934. Reprint. Freeport, N.Y.: Books for Libraries Press, 1968.
> Contends that *Hassan* combines traits of Romanticism and Parnassianism.

Waugh, Arthur. "James Elroy Flecker." In his *Tradition and Change: Studies in Contemporary Literature,* pp. 116-23. London: Chapman and Hall, 1919.

Reprinted review of *The Collected Poems of James Elroy Flecker.* Waugh states that the "untimely death of James Elroy Flecker, at no more than thirty years of age, unquestionably robbed modern poetry of one of its brightest and most hopeful spirits."

Wolfe, Humbert. "James Elroy Flecker and the Red-Man." In his *Portraits by Inference,* pp. 9-22. London: Methuen, 1934.

Reminiscences of Flecker at Oxford.

Alain Locke

1886-1954

INTRODUCTION

(Full name Alain Leroy Locke) American philosopher, critic, and editor.

A lifelong advocate for African-American arts and letters, Locke is best known as the editor of *The New Negro,* one of the earliest anthologies of works by authors associated with the Harlem Renaissance, an important cultural movement of African-American artists and writers. Locke's aesthetic theories concretized the role and objectives of many African-American artists of the 1920s and were a virtual manifesto for artists involved with the Harlem Renaissance, while his writings on the relationship between culture and aesthetics continue to act as a catalyst in African-American art and literature today. Insisting on the intimate relationship between aesthetics and ethics, Locke based his writings on the sociopolitical relevance of the reclamation by the African-American community of the right to self-representation, a task best achieved, according to Locke, through literary expression.

Born in Philadelphia, Locke attended Central High School and the Philadelphia School of Pedagogy before commencing his undergraduate studies at Harvard University in 1904. While a student at Harvard, he studied under such notable educators as the psychologist and philosopher William James, the author and critic Charles Eliot Norton, and the philosopher George Santayana. A recipient of the Phi Beta Kappa award in his junior year at Harvard, Locke graduated in 1907 and was the first African-American to be awarded a Rhodes Scholarship for study at Oxford University. Locke further distinguished himself by becoming the first African-American to graduate from Oxford with a bachelor's degree in literature. After completing his studies in England, he traveled to Berlin in 1910 in order to pursue his interest in the philosophical movement known as the Austrian School of Value, which comprises the works of the philosopher Franz Brentano and the psychologist Alexius von Meinong. Locke later studied at the Collège de France in Paris, where he attended lectures by the French philosopher Henri Bergson.

In 1912 Locke returned to the United States and was appointed assistant professor of philosophy at Howard University. He returned to Harvard in 1916 and completed his dissertation entitled "The Problem of Classification on the Theory of Value." In 1918 Locke was appointed professor of philosophy at Howard University, where he was active in the organization of curricula and the development of cultural programs until his retirement in 1952. While at Howard, Locke was instrumental in fostering the careers of African-American scholars, artists, and politicians, including the diplomat and Nobel Prize winner Ralph Johnson Bunche. In addition to his responsibilities at Howard

University, Locke taught at universities throughout the United States and the Caribbean as a visiting professor. A resident of Washington, D.C., and an avid traveler, Locke nevertheless focused his attention on African-American cultural developments in Harlem, an area that he viewed as a microcosm representing the changes that had occurred in the African-American community in the years after the Civil War. Locke was involved with several literary journals in New York City, notably the magazine of the National Urban League, *Opportunity,* edited by the sociologist Charles S. Johnson; *Crisis,* edited by the writer and activist W. E. B. Du Bois; and *Survey Graphic,* where, as a contributing editor, Locke first published the material that would later become *The New Negro.* In addition to his book-length studies of African-American culture and literature, Locke published numerous annual literary reviews and critical essays in these and other journals. He died in 1954.

Locke's cultural criticism and philosophy are based on the premise that a necessary relationship exists between aesthetics and ethics. His best-known work, *The New Negro,* outlines his critical methodology. Based on Locke's belief that African-Americans needed to focus attention on self-representation, self-determination, and self-reliance, *The New Negro* is a theoretical and practical prolegomenon for the achievement of these concerns through artistic expression and an analysis of their sociological relevance. *The New Negro* includes works from numerous authors of the period, including Countee Cullen, Langston Hughes, Jean Toomer, Claude McKay, Jessie Fauset, James Weldon Johnson, and Zora Neale Hurston. In the introduction to *The New Negro* and in the other essays that he contributed to the volume, Locke outlined his value-relative philosophy, which opposes dogmatism and absolute values and advances the cause of cultural pluralism. Locke's philosophy rejects all authoritarian and absolutist principles, whether political or philosophical, in favor of a value-relative system that privileges the experiences and beliefs of the individual. Locke writes in "Values and Imperatives": "The effective antidote to value absolutism lies in a systematic and realistic demonstration that values are rooted in attitudes, not in reality, and pertain to ourselves, not to the world. Consistent value pluralism might eventually make possible a value loyalty not necessarily founded on value bigotry." Locke's value relativism developed in tandem with his staunchly democratic beliefs, which are best explained by the phrase "unity in diversity," a principle that encourages individual pursuits that refer to the needs of the community and which he includes in the title of his 1931 essay "Unity through Diversity: A Baha'i Principle." His description of the constituents of Harlem, which is included in the introduction to *The New Negro,* illustrates Locke's vision of a democratic community: "The peasant, the student, the businessman, the professional man, artist, poet, musician, adventurer and worker, preacher and criminal, exploiter and social outcast. Each group has come with its own special motives and for its own special ends, but their greatest experience has been the finding of one another." The list alludes to the catalogues of occupations that pervade Walt Whitman's poetry in *Leaves of Grass* (1855), a work that Locke often lauded for its celebrations of democracy. Locke's emphasis on the individual in value relativism led to his studies of the historical and cultural factors that contribute to the experiences of African-American artists. Locke stressed the importance of relating African history and culture to the experiences of contemporary African-Americans, a process that has been labeled "ancestralism." Locke's *Negro Art: Past and Present* explains "ancestralism" as the study of the continuities and discontinuities between African-American and African culture and history with particular reference to the disruptions caused by slavery and colonialism.

Concomittant with his role as a cultural critic, Locke was also a proponent of "art for art's sake" who believed that critics must utilize aesthetic rather than racial standards in assessing works of art. However, Locke's philosophy, which stresses the intimacy of art and identity, considers race a factor in all aesthetic categories. Thus, throughout his works Locke produced socially engaged and aesthetically discerning discussions of politics and art, such as the "The Dilemma of Segregation" and "The Contribution of Race to Culture." Locke's later career is characterized by

works that qualify his early idealist belief in the power of a few privileged artists, the "talented tenth," to revolutionize the thinking of the masses. "The Social Responsibility of the Scholar" reveals a change of tone in the work of the once indefatigable proponent of high art: "I, too, confess that at one time of my life I may have been guilty of thinking of culture as cake contrasted with bread. Now I know better. Real, essential culture is baked into our daily bread or else it isn't truly culture. In short, I am willing to stand firmly on the side of the democratic rather than the aristocratic notion of culture and have so stood for many years, without having gotten full credit, however. I realize the inevitability of such misunderstanding: what price Harvard and Oxford and their traditional snobbisms!"

Locke's instrumental role in the Harlem Renaissance, his writings on "ancestralism," and his commitment to the study of African-American literature and history have been praised by critics for the direction that they donated to twentieth-century African-American art and literature. However, some commentators have consistently criticized what they perceive as Locke's almost exclusive attention to the "talented tenth" of the African-American community. Because he directed his work towards intellectuals and artists rather than to the general public, critics charge that his elitism obfuscated his understanding of the issues facing most African-Americans and revealed the overwhelming influence of Western European cultural traditions on his thinking. While some critics contend that Locke was politically naive, others praise his cultural standards, vision, and attention to sociopolitical issues, including racism, social equality, and cultural pluralism. Receiving both credit and blame for the success and eventual demise of the Harlem Renaissance, Locke is remembered today as a critic and philosopher who applied his thinking to a variety of fields and whose works continue to contribute to current issues concerning the nature and function of an African-American aesthetic.

(See also *Black Writers; Contemporary Authors,* Vols. 106 and 124; and *Dictionary of Literary Biography,* Vol. 51.)

PRINCIPAL WORKS

The New Negro [editor] (criticism) 1925
Four Negro Poets [editor] (criticism) 1927
Plays of Negro Life: A Source-Book of Native American Drama [editor with Montgomery Gregory] (criticism) 1927
A Decade of Negro Self-Expression (criticism) 1928
The Negro in America (criticism) 1933
The Negro and His Music (criticism) 1936
Negro Art: Past and Present (criticism) 1936
The Negro in Art: A Pictorial Record of the Negro Artist and of the Negro Theme in Art [editor] (criticism) 1940
When People Meet: A Study in Race and Cultural Contacts [editor with Bernhard J. Stern] (criticism) 1942

W. E. B. Du Bois   (essay date 1926)

[*An American educator and man of letters, Du Bois is considered one of the most outstanding figures in twentieth-century American history. A founder of the National Association for the Advancement of Colored People (NAACP), Du Bois edited that organization's periodical, the* Crisis, *from 1910 to 1934. Considered the "dean" of the Rear Guard intellectuals whose works initiated the Harlem Renaissance in the 1920s, Du Bois deplored the movement on account of its representations of sordid aspects of African-American culture, believing that the duty of the African-American writer was to depict exemplary characters who would counterbalance past stereotypes. In the following essay, he praises the scholarly apparatus that Locke prepared for* The New Negro *but questions the political viability of Locke's aestheticism.*]

[*The New Negro*] in many ways marks an epoch. It is in many respects sprawling, illogical, with an open and unashamed lack of unity and continuity, and yet it probably expresses better than any book that has been published in the last ten years the present state of thought and culture among American Negroes and it expresses it so well and so adequately, with such ramification into all phases of thought and attitude, that it is a singularly satisfying and inspiring thing.

It has, too, more than most books, a history. The well-known magazine, *The Survey,* which represents organized social reform in America, has always been traditionally afraid of the Negro problem and has usually touched it either not at all or gingerly. Even last year one of the editors at a great meeting of social workers in Los Angeles succeeded in talking over an hour on the social problems of America, dividing and examining them exhaustively both geographically and qualitatively, and yet said no word on the race problems.

Notwithstanding this *The Survey* has grown and developed tremendously in the last few years. I remember vividly being asked by *The Survey* to furnish it for the New Year 1914 a statement of the aims of the N. A. A. C. P. I did so and said among other things:

> Sixth—Finally, in 1914, the Negro must demand his social rights. His right to be treated as a gentleman when he acts like one, to marry any sane, grown person who wants to marry him, and to meet and eat with his friends without being accused of undue assumption or unworthy ambition.

No sooner had the editors of *The Survey* read this than they telephoned frantically to some of the directors of the N. A. A. C. P. and they found easily several who did not agree with this statement and one indeed who threatened to resign if it were published. *The Survey* therefore refused to publish my statement unless this particular paragraph were excised. The statement was not published.

Since then much water has flowed under the bridge and it happened last year that the editor of *The Survey* was sitting next to Mr. A. G. Dill, our business manager, at a dinner given to Miss Fauset in honor of the appearance of her novel, *There Is Confusion.* The editor looked at the company with interest and Mr. Dill began to tell him who they

were. It occurred to the editor of *The Survey* that here was material for a *Survey Graphic;* still he hesitated and feared the "social uplifters" of the United States with a mighty fear. But he took one step which saved the day: He got a colored man to edit that number of the *Graphic,* Alain Locke, a former Rhodes scholar and a professor at Howard University. Locke did a good job, so good a job that this Negro number of the *Survey Graphic* was one of the most successful numbers ever issued by *The Survey.*

It was a happy thought on the part of the Bonis to have the material thus collected, arranged and expanded, combined with the painting and decoration of Winold Reiss and issued as a book which states and explains the present civilization of black folk in America. Mr. Locke has done a fine piece of editing. The proof reading, the bibliographies and the general arrangement are all beyond criticism.

With one point alone do I differ with the Editor. Mr. Locke has newly been seized with the idea that Beauty rather than Propaganda should be the object of Negro literature and art. His book proves the falseness of this thesis. This is a book filled and bursting with propaganda but it is propaganda for the most part beautifully and painstakingly done; and it is a grave question if ever in this world in any renaissance there can be a search for disembodied beauty which is not really a passionate effort to do something tangible, accompanied and illumined and made holy by the vision of eternal beauty.

Of course this involves a controversy as old as the world and much too transcendental for practical purposes, and yet, if Mr. Locke's thesis is insisted on too much it is going to turn the Negro renaissance into decadence. It is the fight for Life and Liberty that is giving birth to Negro literature and art today and when, turning from this fight or ignoring it, the young Negro tries to do pretty things or things that catch the passing fancy of the really unimportant critics and publishers about him, he will find that he has killed the soul of Beauty in his Art. (pp. 140-41)

> *W. E. B. Du Bois, in a review of "The New Negro," in* The Crisis, *Vol. 31, No. 3, January, 1926, pp. 140-41.*

William Stanley Braithwaite   (essay date 1955)

[*Braithwaite was an American poet and critic who was a colleague and friend of Alain Locke. He is best known as a popularizer of annual review collections of poetry. In the following excerpt, which was first delivered as an address before the Alain Locke Memorial Committee in New York in 1955, he reviews the development of African-American literature in the nineteenth and twentieth century and Locke's role in the advancement of African-American artists.*]

[Alain Locke] was a scholar in philosophy in which he took for his chief concept the theory of values. The doctrine of values, which Thoreau pursued with such dismay to the Puritan skeptics, has always seemed to me the keystone of philosophic thinking, for if the function of philosophy is to estimate and appraise the worth and inevitability of human thought and action, then it is only by determining values can standards be established for the guidance and operation of human conduct and relationships. These standards serve the interests of society, interchangeable as they are with heritage and tradition which are the props of conformity; but it is the individual that counts in the maintenance of standards, for out of reason and emotion, the imagination and intuition, with their interactions of reality and illusion, is compounded the kind of society that prevails in one era or another. I never have been able, though I confess that better Hegelian minds than mine can, to separate aesthetics from philosophy—philosophy to my belief being the science of Truth, if I may use the term science as connoting method rather than formula or finality, and aesthetics being the science of Beauty. Thus we have the two motivating energies, as Henry Adams would say, sustaining the spirit of man.

How, one may ask, do these observations concern Alain Locke's relationship to Negro authorship? Very decidedly, and effectively, I would reply. And to confirm the reply, we will have to glance cursorily, as the limitation of time and occasion imposes, at the history of Negro authorship.

From the beginnings in the 1760's to the ante-bellum period there was produced some verse, verse of moral reflections and indignant protest against the conditions of slavery, in techniques wholly imitative of English models; there were slavery songs which we call "spirituals," and work songs which gave vocal expression to the unremitting and exploited labor on the plantations of the South. These spirituals and work songs are the first genuine folk-expression in America. From Eighteen Hundred to the close of the Civil War, there was a continuous stream of prose writings, crowned with the unique production of slave narratives, autobiographical records of fugitive bondsmen, out of which materials of harrowing and dramatic escapes were fashioned the first attempts at creative expression, the novels of Martin R. Delany, Frank J. Webb, and William Wells Brown. One cannot read the narratives of Gustavus Vassa, Frederick Douglass, and William Wells Brown, the most impressive among the large body of these writings, without deep respect and admiration for the character and spirit of a handicapped people who for two centuries and a half had been assimilating slowly and agonizingly the mores of Western civilization. It was more truly during this period than at any later period that the Negro passed *per aspera ad astra,* and reached that glory through the sheer and indomitable exercise of his will.

As a contemporary historian, Richard Bardolph, of the University of North Carolina, says of this period, from 1831 to 1865:

> [It was] in the nation's social history preeminently the time of the rise of the common man, effectuated by wide-ranging reform efforts increasingly channeled into the anti-slavery movement. The Negro leadership adjusted itself easily to this formula and, convinced of the futility of slave-revolts on the Turner model, worked now in close association with a growing army of northern folk who espoused positive programs.

Through this period, not in single and isolated instances, but in a group consciousness the Negro expressed and gave clearance to the articulated impulse of his nature as a human being. That consciousness was wholly dominated and tempered by the institution of slavery and its far-reaching influence upon the civil, political, and social character of American life both in the North and the South. The spirit of the Negro was fueled but from one source, Christianity, in whose hope lay the single promise of his escape from the suppressions and discriminations hedging in his participation as a member of a democratic society. In his effort to escape he wrote furiously and voluminously, and created a body of discursive and subjective literature out of a natural aptitude for self-expression. Indeed, the period historically may be compared to the Saxon period in Britain, when the conversion to Christianity was the all-absorbing inspiration for literary expression. It is true there were no alliterative verse Beowulfs or Caedmons, but the prose writers to whom I have just referred were inspired by the hope of freedom as the Saxon writers were the fertile soil in which Chaucer flowered, just as surely as the slave narratives were the fertile soil in which flowered the talents of Dunbar.

The name of Dunbar brings us to the third period of Negro authorship—the period from 1896 to the death of Dunbar in 1906—with a scattering of minor and ineffectual rhymsters revolving satellites in orbits of the major figures, Dunbar and Chesnutt. In Dunbar and Chesnutt were first expressed the sensibility of an aesthetic form in Negro authorship that found evocation in the adequate techniques of specific artistic mediums. It was this matter of form that up to the second decade of the Twentieth Century was the undiscovered continent for Negro authorship. The Negro, however, has not been alone in regarding form as the structure of language in all its variations of prose and verse; or in the plastic arts, modelling of clay as it is cast into bronze or polished in marble, as exemplified by a Phidias or a Rodin, or in the pictorial arts as exemplified by a Raphael or a Rubens, by a Picasso or a Matisse. Form is a compound of abstract elements that make up the thoughts and feelings of mankind—his desires and dreams, his joys and sorrows, his hopes and despairs, and which imbue the materials of his experiences, as the spirit imbues the flesh and makes of those experiences a manifest in the materials and techniques serving as a witness to man's troubled or serene consciousness.

The literature of the Negro that I have alluded to in the foregoing was a legacy handed down to serve as a springboard for re-conversion for some perceptive Twentieth Century mind. Please be reassured that what I am about to say is wholly in the aesthetic sense. There was, indeed, this flood of literature, a body of splendid content; but it lacked a soul, and again, I remind you that I am speaking in the aesthetic sense. The mind that gave it a soul was Alain Locke's. At first it was a timid soul, either unaware of, or a bit mistrustful of, its sanctions. But it developed with confidence and conviction under his gentle and encouraging urgency. And suddenly, at the end of the first quarter of this Century it blossomed in *The New Negro* that he fathered. Negro authorship had come of age and received the inheritance his wise mind and transcendent idealism had prophesied.

That evolutionary work—and mind you, I do not call it revolutionary—was the expression of a mind and spirit that had been tutored in the universal law of humanity—that law of "unity in diversity," as Locke called it. A law whose highest doctrine, he adds, may be, to quote him, "carried out to a practical degree of reciprocity." This was the demand that Locke made of Negro authorship, and along with it, the concomitant demand for its recognition by the white world. We can interpret the writings as contained in *The New Negro* as specifically of literary interest, and, perhaps, its greatest importance lies not always directly on the surface, but indirectly in the potentiality of a new literary concept in the intellectual and imaginative development of the Negro in authorship. For Locke's discerning spirit elevated the worth and significance of Negro life, and he included in the work essays dealing with the subjects of social, economic, artistic and civil importance woven into the fabric of human relations which give design to the patterns of American democracy.

One of the essential requisites for an emancipated Negro authorship, was, as I have hinted, the possession of a soul. Locke did not demand, nor would he have had any sympathy with, the divorce of Negro authorship from the interest of Negro life. He repeatedly extolled the richness and variety of Negro life and character, but his passionate concern was that the Negro as an artist should treat them on the same high level of interpretation and execution as the best artists of other races. One of Locke's great masters was G. Lowes Dickinson, the English Platonist, who had declared in his Ingersol Lecture at Harvard that there was no difference between the races of man, except in the growth of the soul. And that affirmation was echoed by Locke, particularly in its application to Negro life when he stated in his Foreword to *The New Negro,* that "Negro life is not only establishing new contacts and founding new centers, it is finding a new soul."

With this acquisition of a new and developing soul, there is another observation which Locke made, of tremendous importance to Negro authorship. His leadership in cultural aspiration, in the breaching of barriers that obstructed the paths to a full participation in the aesthetic expression of Negro authorship was established inevitably with this assertion:

> It was rather the necessity for fuller, truer self-expression, the realization of the unwisdom of allowing social discrimination to segregate him mentally, and a counter-attitude to cramp and fetter his own living—and so the "spite-wall" that intellectuals built over the "color-line" has happily been taken down.

In this, the refusal to be segregated mentally, and in a counter-attitude, to be cramped and fettered, he previsioned a result that was the main responsibility of Negro authorship. It laid a difficult, but not impossible, burden upon that authorship.

That Locke was confident Negro authorship was capable of bearing the burden is attested to time and again in his

writings. Unlike any of his contemporaries, he knew that the roots of the American Negro's imagination were fertilized in the primitive arts of Africa. All the Negro intellectuals were stirred only by the political and economic significance of Africa and deplored often in undisciplined invectives her exploitation by the European overlords. But Locke discovered a cultural heritage that may have given the American Negro his basic attributes for artistic expression. The heritage as a factual record of continuity was severed by slavery. Wrote Locke:

> We will never know and cannot estimate how much technical African skill was blotted out in America. The hardships of cotton and rice-field labor, the crudities of the hoe, the axe and the plow reduced the typical Negro hand to a gnarled stump, incapable of fine craftsmanship even if the materials, patterns, and artistic incentives had been available. But we may believe there was memory of beauty; since by way of compensation, some obviously artistic urges flowed even with the peasant Negro toward the only channels of expression left open—those of song, graceful movement and poetic speech.

The memory of beauty! What an exalted declaration of a heritage that was to sprout impoverished as a plant for nigh three centuries, until under some miraculous bestowal of fertilization it was to blossom and flower—and that flowering due largely to the beneficial spirit of Alain Locke.

That is too much to claim for this man, you will think, whose memory we are this day honoring. But show me another who had the intensified and cultural dedication to exercise the shaping influence that was his. In saying this, I do not intend to minimize the knowledge and the desire of many who sought to encourage and inspire their compatriots, but their efforts ran in less exalted channels, channels that ran through the temporary realities of material things and affairs. Locke's was that enduring field of the imaginative representation of human emotions and actions, symbolized and pictured in narrative and rhythm, which constitute a flowering of the human soul that approaches nearest to the divine. Behind all this was the shadowy tapestry of a race whose most assertive identities were tangled in a wave of civilization that would distort and devalue its most precious self-expansion of physical growth and an imposed delusion of spiritual serenity. The transient and confused conditions of human life make it imperative that some transcendent quality of faith be found, above the routine practice of prayer and sacrament, to assure man of his spiritual integrity, of his collaborative sense as a child of nature. Beyond his physical observation and relationship exist a realm of immeasurable, abstract, and everlasting Reality. It has been the unceasing aspiration of man, both in the mood of reverence and defiance, in all ages, and by all peoples, however divergent in racial origins, to penetrate that realm by some measurement of his consciousness. The most effective effort has been made through man's imagination. The border-line of that penetration exists in Sir Arthur Eddington's dictum that the greatest thing in the physical universe is the brain of man. But this is only an arrival at the bourne. To cross it we must accept the concept of that rebellious Puritan, and great American novelist, Nathaniel Hawthorne, in all of whose romances was pursued one imaginative doctrine, the throwing of man's soul against Eternity. Here was a measurement, however infinitesimal, of man's worth and destiny, adumbrating his inheritance both as a child of God and of nature.

What a circuitous way, may well be your charge, that I have taken to declare that this was Alain Locke's profound purpose in his philosophic-aesthetic writings and promptings on Negro authorship: that the soul of the Negro be thrown against Eternity!

In an essay Locke wrote on the **"Orientation of Hope"** for the *Baha'i World*, he set down this pregnant phrase: "For those of us who are truly dawn-minded." In its context it has an application to his attitude towards Negro authorship. Further, in the same essay he wrote this: "It is the occasion and opportunity of convincing many who were skeptical because they could not see the impending failure of the old order." Here in a differing concern was Locke's re-affirmation of his insight into the literary progress that was to function freely without psychological restrictions, when the "spite-walls" were demolished, and the mentality of the Negro artist was uncramped and unfettered by the wasteful intensity of a counter-attitude.

This dawn-mindedness of Locke's broke the new day of Negro authorship. It was he who introduced the phrase that described the first group-flowerings of writings by Negro authors. It was the "heralding sign," an "unusual outburst of creative expression," which enabled him to say in the final sentence of his Foreword to **The New Negro** that, "Justifiably, then, we speak of the offerings of this book embodying these ripening forces as culled from the first fruits of the Negro Renaissance."

It was a period of enlightenment, too, this proclaimed Renaissance of creative expression, of which Locke was the propelling spirit as surely as was Erasmus the propelling spirit of the Northern Renaissance in the early Sixteenth Century. Locke glowed with the same humanism which made Erasmus quicken the thirst of optimism and faith among the multitude. As with Erasmus humanism ceased to be the exclusive privilege of the few, so with Locke his humanistic philosophy was based on the common acquaintance and appreciation of the Negro's creative works by his own as well as by the peoples of other races.

There is one more principle in the hierarchy of Locke's program for the liberation and recognition of the Negro author, which he insisted upon as essential, and to which I shall refer briefly. In a sense it was the most important, for it was the keystone of the aesthetic edifice he built in all his writings and teachings. This was the doctrine of objectivity. He was aware, and painfully so, as many of us have been, of the physical proscriptions of Negro life—he had himself tasted them in spite of his intellectual triumphs—and it was his passionate devotion to the effort that the Negro artist should not be depressed and hindered by mental and emotional proscriptions. How many times in the old days of our association and discussions when he visited me at Arlington did he with that delicate but penetrating dialectic and logic of which he was a master insist that the Negro author, if he was to become fully emancipated, must of necessity work in a mood of objectivity. And what, pray, did he mean by being objective? Simply, the release from self-pity, from the illogical conviction that the Negro was the only people to suffer indignities, that the need for sympathy should be made imperative by the exposure of sore wounds, rather then by the therapeutic healing by the inner spirit, and that the imagination alone, however encased in the shell of ethnic varieties of human flesh, was subject to the same determinations. This objectivity of Locke's demand for the Negro author reminds me of the quintessential summation made by dear old Colonel Thomas Wentworth Higginson, when he solved the whole racial problem, and especially for the enlightenment of the American nation, by declaring that like all other people "the Negro was intensely human." This was what Locke meant by the objective mood, and through its exercise and manifestation by the Negro author the latter could destroy the stereotypes and produce instead of lifeless automatons and clichéd experiences a vitality of characterization and the mutations of human experience.

In this way would the Negro author, especially in his fiction, achieve a comedy of manners. The models were a Jane Austen, a William Dean Howells, an Edith Wharton, or an E. M. Delafield. Jessie Fauset in four novels, published a quarter of a century ago, was an example of the unity in diversity which was Locke's artistic credo for the new era. In Miss Fauset's *There Is Confusion, Plum Bun, The Chinaberry Tree,* and especially in the devastatingly ironic *Comedy: American Style,* was Locke's credo practiced with distinction. I mention this author and these novels because they fulfill the aesthetic theories Locke preached for the spiritual marriage of race and art. And I shadow the mention with the regretful knowledge that they stand alone in this particular genre of the Negro's literary activity.

I want to close by bringing to your attention an episode in a novel by Wallace Thurman, entitled *Infants of the Spring,* because it shows how directly Locke announced, in one instance, and to those most concerned, his gospel of aesthetic liberation. In brief outline, the story is this: A Negro lady of intelligence and means, without gifts of artistic expression herself, but devoted to the cause of Negro culture, gave her somewhat pretentious home to a group of poets, musicians and composers, painters and novelists, where they could live and work in freedom from economic pressures. The group was inter-racial, lived a free Bohemian life, and in all things of cultural intent regarded themselves as intellectual reformers. The dwelling was called Niggeratti Manor. They were drifting aimlessly upon a springtide of emotion, each with his or her individual idiosyncrasy of dream and idealism, without as a community being grounded in the virtuous fundamentals of life and art. One of the members heard of a man whom he thought could bring them a message of enlightenment and confidence, and they invited him to come to New York and address them. This man was a Dr. Parkes, who had achieved a notable reputation in the inner circles of both white and Negro intellectualism, and also in the academic world of both races. Dr. Parkes was a thin, but palpable disguise of Alain Locke. Of this there is no doubt when you read the novelist's description of Dr. Parkes' personality:

> He was a mother hen clucking at her chicks. Small, dapper, with sensitive features, graying hair, a dominating head, and restless hands and feet, he smiled benevolently at his brood. Then in his best continental manner, which he had acquired during four years at European universities, he began to speak.

And what, this commentator asks, did he say? There were some things that his audience of Negro artists did not like, and particularly about their psychological roots in Africa by virtue of a remembered beauty. Here is what Dr. Parkes said:

> "You are the outstanding personalities of a new generation. On you depends the future of your race. You are not, as were your predecessors, concerned with donning armor, and clashing swords with the enemy in the public square. You are finding both an escape and a weapon in beauty, which beauty when created by you will cause the American white man to reestimate the Negro's value to his civilization, cause him to realize that the American black man is too valuable, too potential of utilitarian accomplishment, to be kept downtrodden and segregated.

> "Because of your concerted storming up Parnassus, new vistas will be spread open to the entire race. The Negro in the South will no more know peonage, Jim Crowism or loss of ballot, and the Negro everywhere in America will know complete freedom and equality.

> "But," and here his voice took on a more serious tone, "to accomplish this, your pursuit of beauty must be vital and lasting. I am somewhat fearful of the decadent strain which seems to have filtered into most of your work. Oh, yes, I know you are children of the age and all that, but you must not, like your paleface contemporaries, wallow in the mire of post-Victorian license. You have too much at stake. You must have ideals. You should become . . . well, let me suggest your going back to your racial roots, cultivating a healthy paganism based on African traditions."

The reference to the African traditions brought forth a volley of protest and rejection from the assembled artists. "What old black pagan heritage?" asked one. "How can I go back to African ancestors when their blood is so diluted and their country and times so far away?" another questioned. And this sentiment was unequivocally affirmed by one who said flatly, "I ain't got no African spirit!"

"I think you have missed the point," responded Dr. Parkes. "I mean you should develop your inherited spirit."

What Alain Locke in the guise of Dr. Parkes was trying to tell this group of young hopefuls was that Western civilization and culture were the fruits of the remembered beauty of the Greeks—a people who had also known slavery—and that similarly, the literature produced by the Negro in modern America should be leavened by the remembered beauty bequeathed by primitive Africa. He did not demand, or even remotely suggest, that the mores, nor the landscape, of primitive Africa be used as materials for the body or framework of literature by Negro authors; but that modern life, all its tragedies and comedies, all its romances and social complexities, and racial dramas, was at hand to be informed and made lustrous by the spirit of a remembered beauty.

And that spirit of beauty which was Alain Locke is before us today leading, as a ball of fire by night and a pillar of cloud by day, to the promised land of literary fulfillment, that we may add a new glory to American culture! (pp. 166-73)

> *William Stanley Braithwaite, "Alain Locke's Relationship to the Negro in American Literature," in* The Phylon Quarterly, *Vol. XVIII, No. 2, Second Quarter, 1957, pp. 166-73.*

H. M. Kallen   (essay date 1957)

[*Kallen was a German-born American critic and educator. The author of numerous books on philosophy and education, Kallen is best known as one of the founders of the New School for Social Research, a university committed to materialist and economic analyses of society. In the following excerpt, he examines the way in which Locke's experience, particularly his encounters with racism, influenced his philosophy as outlined in the essays* "Values and Imperatives" (1935) *and* "Pluralism and Ideological Peace" (1947).]

The expression "cultural pluralism" must now be familiar. . . . It has figured in the public prints. It has come to denote one of the alternatives of foreign policy for our State Department. Even members of the Security Council and the General Staff are reported as talking about the importance of the Bill of Rights and the intercultural relations which the Bill of Rights implies as against those implied by totalitarian creeds. It is not possible to implement any of the propositions of our American Bill or of the Universal Declaration of Human Rights of the United Nations without assuming the primacy and the irreducible plurality of the cultures of mankind and their impact on one another.

As an expression in the American language "cultural pluralism" is about 50 years old. I used it first around 1906 or 1907 when Alain Locke was in a section of a class at Harvard where I served as assistant to Mr. George Santayana. It has taken these two generations for the term to come into more general use and to figure in philosophical discourse in this country. Locke, you may remember, refers in one of his philosophical essays to a book by F. C. S. Northrop of Yale, entitled *The Meeting of East and West,* and indeed since the First World War the expression has recurred in public discussion more and more frequently and more diversely.

In my mind, here is what it fundamentally signifies: first, a concept that social science and social philosophy can and do employ as a working hypothesis concerning human nature and human relations; second, an ethical ideal—an article of faith which challenges certain prevailing philosophical conceptions about both. Those conceptions are fundamentally monistic. There persists in the sciences of man and nature and in philosophies as they have developed in our country, a disposition to assert and somehow to establish the primacy of totalitarian unity at the beginning, and its supremacy in the consummation, of all existence. It is, of course, conceded that multitude and variety seem pervasive, always and everywhere. But it is denied that they are real. It is the One that is real, not the Many—whether we regard many things or many men. Men come and go but Man goes on forever, and it is in their eternal and universal Manhood that all men are brothers. That this brotherhood involves the blood rivalry of Cain and Abel perhaps much more commonly than the relationship between David and Jonathan seems not to affect this monist creed, nor the cliché regarding the fatherhood of God and the brotherhood of Man, which is one of its commoner expressions. A better word for what is intended by "brotherhood" is the word "friendship." For this word carries no implication of an identical beginning and common end that are to be attributed to the event that two persons or two peoples or a thousand peoples who are different from each other and must perforce live together with each other, seek such ways of togetherness as shall be ways of peace and freedom.

Now, the expression "Cultural Pluralism" is intended to signify this endeavor toward friendship by people who are different from each other but who, as different, hold themselves equal to each other. By "equal" we commonly mean "similar" or "identical." Cultural Pluralism, however, intends by "equal" also parity of the unequal, equality of the unlike, not only of the like or the same. It postulates that individuality is indefeasible, that differences are primary, and that consequently human beings have an indefeasible right to their differences and should not be penalized for their differences, however they may be constituted, whatever they may consist in: color, faith, sex, occupation, possessions, or what have you. On the record, nevertheless, human beings continually penalize one another for their differences. This is how they exemplify the brotherhood of man and the fatherhood of God; how the South Africans are brothers to their dark-skinned victims, the Chinese to the Koreans, the Arabs to the Israelis, and the Russians to non-Communist mankind. Each demands of his sibling, "Agree with me, be my brother—or else! And so that you may become completely a brother, you must offer up your own different being to be digested into identification with mine. You must replace your purposes with mine, your ways and means with mine. Unless you do this you refuse brotherhood." Contrast this requirement with the requirement of friendship, which says to the other fellow not "Be my brother" but *Be my friend.* I am different from you. You are different from me. The basis of our communion is our difference. Let us exchange the fruits of our differences so that each may enrich the other with what the other is not or has not in himself. In what else are we important to one another, what else can we pool and share if not our differences?" The valuations here postulated should be obvious. If for example, in coming here today, we had expected merely a repetition of what we already know and feel, it is unlikely that even our reverence to a notable friend and beautiful character would have brought us. We expect something somehow still unknown and unpossessed. We do not care to seek what we already sufficiently have. We want what we don't yet have. This is how we achieve spiritual abundance, which consists in the free and friendly barter of different things and thoughts and neighborly relations. It lives in untrammeled communication between the different on all levels. It signalizes the idea of civilization that the expression "cultural pluralism" denotes.

Now this is what Alain Locke envisioned from the time that he became reconciled to himself. He became a cultural pluralist. It took him some time.

In 1935 Sidney Hook and I got out a collection of essays by younger United States philosophers entitled, *American Philosophy Today and Tomorrow.* Alain Locke contributed to this collection a paper on the theme, **"Values and Imperatives."** Each contributor accompanied his essay with a short autobiographical note. I will read you Locke's note which, I suspect, is not as familiar to his friends as it should be, and then ask what it postulates *en philosophe.* How did the author get this way? How came Locke—a proud and sensitive man who was penalized by "whites" for his darker skin, in matters of spirit an incidental difference—to give up the idea of equality as identification, as sameness with whites, and to urge equality as parity in and of his difference from the whites; hence to see the human enterprise as free, friendly, creative intercommunication between differents and their reciprocal enrichment thereby?

> I should like to claim [he wrote] as life-motto the good Greek principle, *"Nothing in excess,"* but I have probably worn instead as the badge of circumstance,—*"All things with a reservation."* Philadelphia, with her birthright of provincialism flavored by urbanity and her petty bourgeois psyche with the Tory slant, at the start set the key of paradox; circumstance compounded it by decreeing me as a Negro a dubious and doubting sort of American and by reason of the racial inheritance making me more of a pagan than a Puritan, more of a humanist than a pragmatist.
>
> Verily paradox has followed me the rest of my days: at Harvard, clinging to the genteel tradition of Palmer, Royce and Münsterberg, yet attracted by the disillusion of Santayana and the radical protest of James: again in 1916 I returned to work under Royce but was destined to take my doctorate in Value Theory under Perry. At Oxford, once more intrigued by the twilight of aestheticism but dimly aware of the new realism of the Austrian philosophy of value; socially Anglophile, but because of race loyalty, strenuously anti-imperialist; universalist in religion, internationalist and pacifist in world-view, but forced by a sense of simple justice to approve of the militant counter-nationalisms of Zionism, Young Turkey, Young Egypt, Young India, and with reservations even Garveyism and current-day "Nippon over Asia." Finally a cultural cosmopolitan, but perforce an advocate of cultural racialism as a defensive counter-move for the

American Negro, and accordingly more of a philosophical mid-wife to a generation of younger Negro poets, writers, artists than a professional philosopher.

Small wonder, then, with this psychograph, that I project my personal history into its inevitable rationalization as cultural pluralism and value relativism, with a not too orthodox reaction to the American way of life.

Locke presents himself here with the passions and powers of his individuality. His singularity is evident, and he gives hints of his idiosyncrasy. But he accepted neither, although he couldn't reject them. He felt, in sense and intellect, a human being the same as other human beings, especially white ones who denied the sameness. He knew that in his ideals, his intentions, and his works and ways he was not inferior, nor otherwise different from those people who held themselves to be better than he was, and there were intervals—one was certainly his undergraduate days at Harvard—when he did not appear to live under any penalty for his difference. He seems not to have in Philadelphia. I know that at Oxford—I was there at the time—he was penalized. There were among the Rhodes scholars at Oxford gentlemen from Dixie who could not possibly associate with Negroes. They could not possibly attend the Thanksgiving dinner celebrated by Americans if a Negro was to be there. So although students from elsewhere in the United States outnumbered the gentlemen from Dixie, Locke was not invited, and one or two other persons, authentically Americans, refused in consequence to attend. You might say it was a dinner of inauthentic Americans. Now, the impact of that kind of experience left scars. The more so in a philosophic spirit. For the dominant trend among philosophers is always to prove unity and to work at unifications—to assert *one* humanity, *one* universe, *one* system of values and ideals which somehow is coërcive of the many and somehow argues away the actualities of penalization for one's being oneself into unimportant appearances, without in any way relieving the feelings of dehumanization, the pain and the suffering; and without lessening the desire never again to expose oneself to them. There were times that year when Locke thought never to return to the United States. In fact, he deeply wanted not to. He was at ease in Europe. The penalties for "color," especially in France and on the continent, were not apparent. They were not as apparent in England as they are today. But however or wherever the penalties were laid, Locke felt he could not expose himself to their indignities. As a human being with an individuality of his own, he knew that no commitment or obligation could be laid on him heavier than anybody else's, and that the necessities of vindicating his integrity and realizing his own potentialities in his own way had the first claim and the last.

It took him some time to find his way to that acquiescence in unalienable right to his difference, which became the core of his value-system. This acquiescence is not primarily defensive, not a struggle for political or economic or other form of equalization. It expresses itself in affirming the integral individuality of one's person, of taking on freely the obligations that go with it; of insisting not on becoming *like* anybody else, but on having one's singularity recognized and acknowledged as possessing a title equal with any other's to live and grow.

Now this sort of self-acquiescence is the personal premise—whatever be the pattern of grouping—for the group belongingness, the group identification for which one name is cultural pluralism. Alain Locke made this choice as a grown man, just as Walter White made this choice as a boy in Atlanta, when he experienced the violence of a mob of whites.

For Locke's disposition had been first monistic or universalist. Pluralism and particularism imposed their reality upon him by the exigent harshnesses of experience. It is these which convinced him of the actuality of difference, which brought him to recognize that difference is no mere appearance, but *the* valid, vital force in human communication and in human creation.

The transvaluation had never seemed to me to be quite complete. As you can see from his "psychograph," Locke chooses to speak of it as a rationalization. He would have preferred reality to be basically a One and not a Many, and human relations to be expressive of this Oneness. His preference interposed an active reservation to the actuality of the plural. It long kept him from completely committing himself. Philosophically, it led him at last to the concept of ideological peace.

I have spoken of Locke's essay, **"Values and Imperatives."** There is another he wrote and, apart from his doctor's thesis, I don't know of any more philosophical studies by him. The second he called, **"Pluralism and Ideological Peace."** As I read the essay, which he contributed to a collection entitled, *Freedom and Experience,* edited by Sidney Hook and Milton Konvitz, "ideological peace" again involves an association of the different which requires our making a distinction between unity and union. The import of Unity is liquidation of difference and diversity, either by way of an identification of the different, or by way of a subordination and subjection of the different to the point where it makes no difference. *Per contra,* the import of Union is the teamplay of the different. Union resides in the uncoërced, the voluntary commitment of the different to one another in free coöperation; and ideological peace, as Locke had expounded it in this essay, is a conception denoting fundamentally this free intercommunication of diversities—denoting the cultivation of those diversities for the purpose of free and fruitful intercommunication between equals.

To the American Negro it presents the idea of an authentic Negro cultural community sensitive not only to the positive values of all the present, but aware also of the immemorial African past and rendering it presently a living past. Of course, this past is not in the memory of any living American Negro. He must needs create that memory, by means of exploration and study, as Locke did and just as every white must; indeed, as the record shows, identification with African cultures and arts can be more passionate and more complete among white men than among Negroes. To many, perhaps to most, the import of the term "Afro-American" is unwelcome. For Negroes tend to reject such an identification because they perceive themselves to be penalized on account of this same African difference. So long as a person thinks of himself as being penalized as African, so long as he is not self-acquiescent, just so long will he resist identification with those presumed sources or conditions of his imposed inequality. The hyphen represents a bondage, not a resource or power. Let him absorb and digest the condition, turning it from a limiting handicap into a releasing endowment, and he frees himself.

This, it seems to me, is what Locke did. And hence, in his discussion of the New Negro, Locke was able to talk about the Negro problem as a creation of non-Negroes which they imposed on the Negroes. As anybody knows who has lived through the abominations of Senator Eastland's Mississippi in the past few months, Locke's analysis is correct.

The Negro, Locke held, is not a problem. The Negro is a fact, an American fact, but not merely because he has lived and labored in America since Colonial times. He is American in virtue of his commitment, in common with non-Negro Americans, to the essential American Idea, the idea that human beings, all different from each other, are equal to each other in their inalienable rights to life, liberty, and the pursuit of happiness, and owe each other participation in the joint endeavor "to secure these rights" on which the institution of government rests in free societies. All "these rights" may be comprehended as the right to be different without penalty, without privilege, and with each of the different maturing its own excellence, the excellence expressive of its individual or associative singularity in willing coöperation with all. Believing this, Alain Locke gave expression to his own commitment to the Negro fact by undertaking to disclose to Americans, especially to Negro Americans, the Negro, not the problem. He made himself the philosophical midwife to a generation of younger Negro poets, writers, artists.

However it is a very delicate and difficult undertaking to separate any existence from the problems of this existence. This challenge confronts all communities everywhere, not alone the American Negro community. And it is far harder to effect this separation where a community is penalized for merely existing. Hence, one cannot be sure that Locke succeeded. But one can be sure that, without the affirmation of Negro as Negro in terms of what cultural and spiritual production Negro as Negro can achieve, without the manifestation of inner strength based on self-knowledge, developing without tutelage from anybody, the Negro cannot begin to accept himself as a fact instead of a problem to himself. One can be sure that where such a process eventuates, the Negro problem transvalues into a white problem, both south and north. And one may observe that the problem "gets liquidated" wherever communities of diverse identity do thus accept themselves. An orchestration of their diversities follows, a teamplay of their differences. The concept "race" wouldn't apply to these differences since any species whose members can breed together may be said to belong to the same race. First and last the differences are the specific differentiations of personal and group existence that make cultures, that make systems of ideas, creeds and codes about which

human beings fight. "Race" is one such fighting word. Color constitutes no problem when it is not appraised in racist terms. Transactions between peoples of different colors in the same culture and different cultures in the same color, and different colors and cultures have gone on freely enough throughout recorded time. Alain Locke urged that they can go on here at home. He held that they would have to be postulated on what he called ideological peace. In his essay on **"Values and Imperatives"** he urged that this peace might be attained by the conceptions and the methods of science. There is, he declared in that essay of 1935, "an objective universe," whose unity is broken up into a pluriverse by human behavior.

I think that in the twelve years between the first essay in 1935 and the second in 1947, he decided that primarily there is a pluriverse, and that ideological peace is the endeavor to establish a universe, not as a unity, but a union. His pluralism reshaped into a primary, a fundamental pluralism—a value pluralism, a metaphysical pluralism, and the reshaping may have involved something like a religious conversion. As he believed, it is a way of changing your own attitude toward yourself, and your own attitude toward the different. First one needs to recognize the integrity and autonomy of difference; then perhaps one can also peaceably do business with it. In point of fact, Locke had already done so in *The New Negro,* although his philosophic realization seems to have come later.

There are two current words which signify ideas that have a present bearing on this notion of free coöperation of the different, or ideological peace. One of these words, signifying an American policy, is "containment." And what does "containment" mean? It means forcefully holding back the different. Why did we have to have a national policy of containment? Because of Communist aggression against what is not Communist. Perforce it is to be held back, and unless the resistance were equally strong or stronger it could not be held back. Outer containment depends on inner moral and material strength. Whether or not we achieve the political end, it continues morally and culturally on the agenda for the American people, and of our Negro fellow-Americans *vis-a-vis* certain categories of non-Negroes.

The second word is a word that came into vogue after "containment" had become a policy. The word is "co-existence." There are different ways of co-existence. There is the co-existence of cold toleration signalized as balance of power; here powers stand over against each other at alert and ready to shoot—the way the South Koreans had to stand against the North Koreans, the Israelis stand against the Arabs, and the entire West stands against the Soviet and its satellites.

In another phase, co-existence signifies passive toleration. Each existent says to the other: You're there and I've got to recognize you are there, but I don't like you and I won't have anything to do with you. You may be a brother, but you're no neighbor and no friend.

In still another phase, co-existence signifies what we now usually mean by toleration—that is, not an inimical endurance or suffering of the different, but a recognition that the different can live and let you live and that you can live and let the different live. Co-existence means live and let live.

The mature phase of co-existence comes whenever existents pass from this sort of *laissez-faire* into a free, a voluntary coöperative relationship where each, in living on, also helps, and is helped by, the others in living. This is the co-existence that cultural pluralism signifies. It is the consummation of the system of ideas and the philosophic faith that Alain Locke became a notable spokesman for. (pp. 119-27)

H. M. Kallen, "Alain Locke and Cultural Pluralism," in The Journal of Philosophy, *Vol. LIV, No. 5, February 28, 1957, pp. 119-27.*

Eugene C. Holmes   (essay date 1963)

[*In the following excerpt, Holmes discusses Locke's essays in* The New Negro *as a manifesto for the Harlem Renaissance.*]

The rise of a genuine New Negro Movement was fostered and encouraged by one person, Alain Leroy Locke, who became its creative editor and its chronicler. It may be true that the term Renaissance, as Sterling Brown has so perceptively pointed out, is a misnomer because of the shortness of the life span of the Harlem movement. Also, the New Negro writers were not centered only in Harlem, and much of the best writing of the decade was not always about Harlem, for most of the writers were not Harlemites. Yet Harlem was the "show window," the cashier's till, though it is no more "Negro America" than New York is America. The New Negro had temporal roots in the past and spatial roots elsewhere in America and the term has validity only when considered to be a continuing tradition.

It may be argued that the so-called Negro Renaissance held the seeds of defeat for a number of reasons, among them being the general anti-intellectualism of the new Negro middle class. But it was, by every admission, a representation of a re-evaluation of the Negro's past and of the Negro himself by Negro intellectuals and artists. For the rise of the New Negro Movement coincided with an ever increasing interest in Negro life and character in the twenties. American literature was being re-evaluated and overhauled as a revolt against the genteel tradition and the acquisitive society of the last decades of the nineteenth century.

Charles Johnson characterized Alain Locke as "the Dean of this group of fledgling writers of the new and lively generation of the 1920's." Johnson wrote, "A brilliant analyst trained in philosophy, and an esthete with a flair for art as well as letters, he gave encouragement and guidance to these young writers as an older practitioner too sure of his craft to be discouraged by failure of full acceptance in the publishing media of the period" [*The New Negro: Thirty Years Afterward*, 1955]. Johnson referred to Alain Locke as "an important maker of history" of a "dramatic period in our national history." Locke had this to say about these young writers being launched on their careers: "They

sense within their group—a spiritual wealth which if they can properly expound, will be ample for a new judgment and re-appraisal of the race." This, then, is only a part of the backdrop of what has been called the Negro Renaissance. What Charles Johnson referred to as "that sudden and altogether phenomenal outburst of emotional expression unmatched by any comparable period in American or Negro American history."

No one, not even the older Du Bois, could have been better equipped to have been the architect of the New Negro Movement and maker of history. Philadelphia, Locke's birthplace, was the one city where one could speak of a culture. Negro artists were encouraged and Negro literary, musical and painting groups were encouraged. Young Locke was aware of this personally and always kept these artists in mind as reminders of the awakening of Negro art in America. The literary movement had many of its origins in Philadelphia, but, because of social, economic and political reasons, it flowered in New York. For a racial dilemma in Negro art, a racial solution was necessary. This came in the mid-twenties from the inspiration of the New Negro Movement with its crusade of folk expression in all of the arts, the drama, painting, sculpture, music and the rediscovery of the folk origins of the Negro's African heritage.

The racial dilemma was a distinct carryover from the same dilemma encountered by the Negro writers of the late nineteenth century. In most of these writers, there was to be found the same tendentious, pedestrian and imitative style as observed in many of the painters. There was the dialect poetry of Dunbar and his later English poems in which he was the exponent of the romantic tendencies which were to be decried by the next generation of Negro poets. There were the propaganda novels of Frances Harper, Martin Delany, Frank Webb and William Wells Brown. The novels of Charles Chesnutt were outstanding for their genre, style and impact. The political essays, the pamphleteering, the autobiographical slave accounts, the polemical essays were all to be merged with and channelized into that renascence which came to be known as the New Negro Movement.

As a burgeoning critic and student of Negro life in Philadelphia, in Boston and New York, at Howard University where he had gone to teach in 1912, Locke had been working in his way, in concert with many friends, to help lay to rest the mawkish and moribund dialect school of poetry. William Stanley Braithwaite, Locke's friend and mentor while he was at Harvard; William Monroe Trotter, the editor; W. E. B. Du Bois, all helped in hastening the demise of Negro dialect poetry. Friendly critics such as Louis Untermeyer also helped by labeling the traditional dialect as "an affectation to please a white audience." And, along with James Weldon Johnson, who had genuine poetic talent, this critics' coterie saw that dialect poetry had neither the wit nor the beauty of folk speech, but was only a continuation of the stock stereotypes about gentility, humility and buffoonery, and an evasion of all of the realities of Negro life.

One counteraction, however, to this dialect poetry was a conscious reverting to Romanticism and neo-

Romanticism which reflected a middle-class recognition of Europeanized esthetic values. In some ways, this was a result of the rejection of the minstrel-buffoon stereotype. In addition, as the middle class Negro became better educated, there was an increase in his desire to share in the legacy of general culture, to participate in it, even though in a lesser fashion. As Sterling Brown put it, in too many instances "these poets were more concerned with making copies of the 'beauty' that was the stock-in-trade of a languishing tradition." These imitators were, for the most part, only too anxious to avoid any mention of a Negro tradition or to look into their own experiences as Negroes. The result, in their poetry, was escapist, without vitality or understanding.

Along with this counteraction there developed in the same period, the movement which assisted in the Negro writer's spiritual emancipation. As Locke himself put it in his last published account (1952) of the movement: "For from 1912 on, there was brewing the movement that in 1925, explicitly became the so-called Renaissance of the New Negro. The movement was not so much in itself a triumph of realism, although it had its share of realists, but a deliberate cessation by Negro authors of their attempts primarily to influence majority opinion. By then, Negro artists had outgrown the handicaps of allowing didactic emphasis and propagandist motives to choke their sense of artistry. Partly in disillusionment, partly in newly acquired group pride and self-respect, they turned inward to the Negro audience in frankly avowed self-expression."

Langston Hughes, one of their number, thus phrased this literary declaration of independence:

> We younger Negro artists who create now intend to express our individual dark-skinned selves without fear or shame. If white people are pleased, we are glad. If they are not, it doesn't matter. We know we are beautiful. And ugly too. If colored are pleased, we are glad. If they are not, their displeasure doesn't matter either. We build our temples for tomorrow, strong as we know how, and we stand on the top of the mountain, free within ourselves.

Once again, there was a common denominator between the advance-guard elements of the majority and the minority. The anti-slavery collaboration had forged a moral alliance; this was an esthetic one, which spelled out a final release from propaganda and its shackling commitments both for Negro materials in American art and literature and for the Negro artist and writer. And from 1925 to the present, realism and Southern regionalism on the one side, and the promotion of racial self-expression on the other, have informally but effectively combined to form a new progressive atmosphere in American letters. (pp. 293-96)

No one could have been better equipped for the leadership and sponsorship of the New Negro Movement than Locke, who described himself "more of a philosophical midwife to a generation of younger Negro poets, writers and artists than a professional philosopher." For years he [encouraged] . . . artists and musicians to study the African sources at first hand. He was an avid collector of Africana. He wrote expertly about the lost ancestral arts of Af-

rica and traced the influence of African art on European artists in the early twentieth century. He knew a great deal about African influences in Haiti and other Caribbean islands and he consistently pointed out African influences on the Negro American, both before and after the abolition of slavery.

Alain Locke did not make many original researches into American Negro history or into the golden lore of African history, but he grew in stature as he learned more and more of this history. It taught him that the Negro scholar's ability to withstand the infirmities of the American scene is a dialectic phase of the democratic process. And this dialectic must necessarily aid in bringing into fruition the dream of a community of Negro scholars. This was his sensitivity about American history and it led him to an identity with the great leader, the self-taught Frederick Douglass, about whom he wrote a biography. Locke was deeply appreciative of Du Bois' scientific approach to history and Carter G. Woodson's pioneer scientific work in the history of slavery and the Negro past. His contributions to the New Negro Movement always turned out to be re-evaluations of Negro history as it affected the Negro writer, the Negro scholar, and the lives of all sensitively aware Negroes.

As an author, Locke knew that the story of the Negro writer had to be told, because of the social history involved. He came to see that the position of the Negro in American culture had come to mean a great deal more than merely the artistic activity of the Negro minority. It came to mean for him a pointing toward a goal of a "natively characteristic national literature as being one of the crucial issues of cultural democracy." And this had to be evaluated against the slavery and anti-slavery background from which this literature emerged.

The harsh effects of slavery had to be viewed as contributing to the recognition of the Negro's role as participant and contributor to American culture. "Just as slavery may now (1952) in perspective be viewed as having first threatened our democratic institutions and then forced them to more consistent maturity, the artistic and cultural impact of the Negro must be credited with producing unforeseen constructive pressures and generating unexpected creative ferment in the literary and artistic culture of America. In cutting the Negro loose from his ancestral culture, slavery set up a unique and unprecedented situation between the Anglo-Saxon majority and the Negro minority group. The peculiar conditions of American slavery so scrambled Africans from the diverse regions and culture of our entire continent that with the original background culture, tribal to begin with, neither a minority language nor an ancestral tradition remains. The American Negro was left no alternative but to share the language and tradition of the majority culture" [*The Negro in American Literature, New World Writing,* 1933].

The Negro had never set up separate cultural values, even though he had been forced on many occasions to take on defensive attitudes of racialism, "an enforced, protective, counter-attitude, stemming the worst of proscription and discrimination." Locke believed that, despite historical interludes, the Negro's values, ideals and objectives, have always been integrally and unreservedly American. He wrote, "The crucial factors in group relationships are social attitudes and literature—recording and reflecting these in preference even in social fact—becomes the most revealing medium."

Locke wrote more than a dozen books and articles since 1921 on Negro art, music and literature, tracing these developments from the earliest times, from 1760 up to 1920. He began with the first Negro poets, essayists and novelists, showing that the earliest indictments of slavery from the articulate free Negro displayed signs of a strong race consciousness. He showed that if slavery had molded the emotional and folk life of the Negro, that also it was the anti-slavery movement which developed the intellect of the Negro and pushed him forward to articulate, disciplined expression. The edifice of chattel slavery was shaken to its foundation by the combined efforts of the literary and oratorical efforts of Negro leaders and self-taught fugitive slaves. The emergence of the "slave narrative" supplied the incandescent spark, to be added to the abolitionist tinder.

In making America aware of the Negro artist and his work, an important part was played by the *Harlem Number* (1925) of the *Survey Graphic* which was edited by Locke. This issue of the *Survey* contained a hundred pages. There were twenty contributors, fifteen Negro and five white and twelve belonged to the Harlem group. Among the articles were, "Enter the New Negro," "The Making of Harlem," "Black Workers and the City," "Jazz at Home," "Negro Art and America," "The Negro Digs Up His Past," "The Rhythm of Harlem," and many others appertaining to Harlem. This issue of the *Survey* had the largest circulation of any in its history. Several editions had to be run off before the demand was satisfied. In *Black Manhattan,* James Weldon Johnson in 1926, wrote, "It was a revelation to New York and the country. Later the symposium, somewhat enlarged, was brought out as a book, entitled **The New Negro,** under the editorship of Alain Locke. It remains one of the most important books on the Negro ever published."

The movement, for a while *did* thrive in Harlem. Then the "influence of Locke's essays and of the movement in general, spread outward over the country, touching writers in Missouri, Mississippi, in Boston, Philadelphia and Nashville and Chicago" [*Negro Caravan,* eds. Sterling Brown, Arthur P. Davis, Ulysses Lee].

Unknowingly, there was being cultivated a middle class nationalism within the protective folds of the capitalist ethos. The majority did not rebel, but rather hearkened to the voice of bourgeois authority. American capitalism had prospered in the redivision of the profits and spoils of the war. In too many instances, the "New Negro" had served in too large a measure as a means of amusement, to be fawned upon and idolized. Many of the New Negroes were unwilling victims of an inverted racialistic nationalism, looking upon themselves as having arrived, and priding themselves that they could sing, paint and write as well as their white-skinned patrons.

But, the movement was a true "renaissance" in another sense—the antiquity which Negroes wanted to revive from a "lost" African past. However they might share in the leavings of their new found prosperity, if they were to rediscover their racial souls, they had to go back, at least mentally, to the African past. There were the successes and the failures of Du Bois' leadership in the 1921, 1923 and 1925 Pan-African Congresses. The efforts of Locke to instill in the younger poets, artists and musicians, some sense of this African heritage bore fruit in the work of Toomer, Cullen, McKay and Hughes.

The most developed poet and literary figure of the New Negro movement, Langston Hughes, wrote on all manners of subjects and always movingly of Africa. In 1926, *Weary Blues* and in 1927, *Fine Clothes to the Jew,* Hughes displayed his artistry of particular power and beauty pursuing his own course more than any other of the New Negroes. Hughes' antecedents were bound up in a family tradition where the struggle for freedom was always a strong memory and inspiration. A grandfather died fighting beside John Brown. An uncle was a Reconstruction Congressman and the first Dean of the Howard Law School. Even Hughes' blues, melodious and rhythmic are full of African feeling as in *Homesick Blues:*

> De railroad bridge's
> A sad song in de air
> Every time de trains pass
> I wants to go somewhere.

The black world of America and Africa came to have a new meaningful nationalistic pride for so many of these poets. It was not always very deep or couched in any scientific anthropological understanding, but no matter, there was precious little understanding at the time for anyone. What mattered was that this flowering was a true renaissance of feeling, a prideful evocation of the dark image of Africa, germinated from a fructified seedbed but one which took on a new form and content.

The Harlem Renaissance, substantively, transformed the Negro as subject and as artist from the old stereotype into the New Negro, militant, no longer obsequious, more of a paragon because he had shown that he was nearly on equal terms with his white counterpart. He won coveted prizes, fellowships, he was being published and he won his spurs the hard way in creative writing. These artists were not organized but theirs was a strong spirit of cohesion, a bond of group consciousness, toward some goal of achievement which would make the Negro artist proud of his work. It was a self-confidence which grew and proliferated into an outburst of emotional expression, never matched by any comparable period in American history. The new generation of writers began to carve out a niche in the hitherto impermeable walls of American literary culture. Hence the self-confidence, the self-assurance and the pride of craftsmanship.

The New Poetry Movement embraced every facet of Negro experience from lyricism, African heritage, social protest, folk song and blues, Negro heroes and episodes, lynchings, race riots; treatment of the Negro masses (frequently of the folk, less often of the workers), and franker and deeper self-revelation, social injustice and intolerance. Claude McKay's famous *If We Must Die* became the

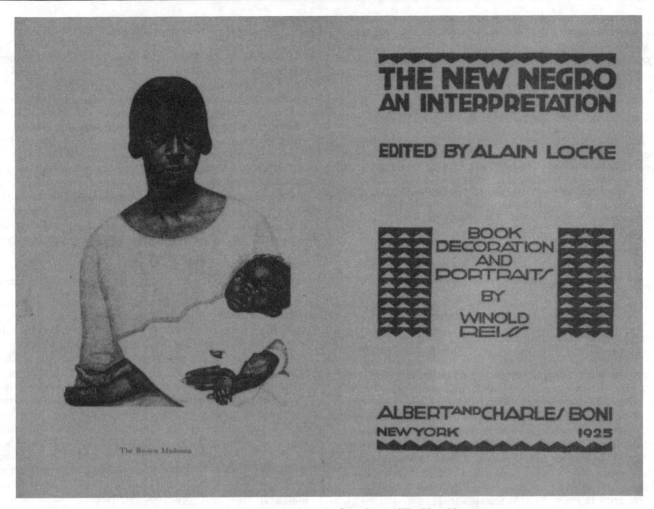

The Brown Madonna

Frontispiece and title page from the first edition of The New Negro.

touchstone for the dynamics of the social forces and conflicts of the twenties. His was an answer to the growing crescendo of race riots and lynchings which characterized the times. Toomer's eloquent outcries in *Cane* were race conscious and challenging. In Cullen's *Shroud of Color,* his sense of race is one of loyalty, pride and group consciousness, "almost the tone of a chosen people."

> Lord, I would live persuaded by mine own
> I cannot play the recreant to these:
> My spirit has come home, that sailed the doubt-
>   ful seas.

Hughes' *Brass Spittoons* tells of the distasteful tasks of menial labor:

> Hey, Boy!
> A bright bowl of brass is beautiful to the Lord
> Bright polished brass like the cymbals
> Of King David's dancers
> Like the wine cups of Solomon.

These poets, in their different ways, were all influential in the twenties and thirties, influencing an entire generation of younger poets. Cullen and Toomer in New York and all over America, Hughes in New York and all over the world, McKay in New York and the socialist world, Ster-

ling Brown at Howard and all over the south, all expressing ideas that were representative of the Negro movement. In *Strong Men,* Brown pens:

> They dragged you from your homeland,
> They chained you in coffles
> They broke you in like oxen
> They scourged you
> They branded you
>   You sang:
>   Keep a-inchin' along
>   Lak a po' inch worm . . .
>   You sang:
>   Walk togedder, chillen,
>   Dontcha get weary
> The strong men keep a comin' on
> The strong men get stronger.

After Frederick Douglass' fictionalized *Madison Washington* and the short stories of William Wells Brown and Chesnutt, the Negro as short story writer could only emerge from a vacuum even though the short story as literary genre had taken creditable form in America. Negro writers were unable to gain any entree into the magazines. Charles Chesnutt's experiences in 1887 with the *Atlantic Monthly* when the editors did not wish to publicize his racial identity was an infamous blot on American literature. Chesnutt's story *The Goophered Grapevine* was accepted by Walter Hines Page and later Page accepted *The Wife of His Youth,* and only belatedly admitted that the author was a Negro, claiming to the editor of the magazine *Critic* that he did not want to do damage to the author's reputation. Dunbar's stories were popular because of the plantation tradition of his dialect style and they did not offend.

In the late twenties, Langston Hughes faced the problem when *Esquire* published *A Good Job Gone.* Hughes wrote about this in *Fighting Words:*

> Here are our problems: In the first place, Negro books are considered by editors and publishers as exotic. Negro material is placed, like Chinese material or Bali material into a certain classification. Magazine editors will tell you, "We can use but so many Negro stories a year." (That "so many" meaning very few.) Publishers will say, "We already have one Negro novel on our list this fall."

> When we cease to be exotic, we do not sell well.

These have been the circumscriptions placed on the Negro short story writer on all sides in the publishing world.

When the Negro writer published in either *Crisis* or *Opportunity,* the pay was paltry and the stories were typed. The stories were concerned with lynchings, race riots, race praise or passing. Rudolph Fisher's *High Yaller* won the first prize in the 1925 *Crisis* contest. Later in the same year, *Atlantic Monthly* published his story, *The City of Refuge.* Many other new writers of the Movement wrote well constructed stories which won *Crisis* and *Opportunity* prizes—Arthur Huff Fauset, John Matheus, Eugene Gordon, Marita Bonner, Edwin Sheen and Jean Toomer. Unlike Fisher, most of these writers did not continue their careers of writing. Eric Walrond's *Tropic Death,* Langston Hughes' *Ways of White Folks* came close to penetrating into the innermost workings of Negro life which were overlooked by the racial idealists who wrote cloyingly of the new Negro middle class escapists.

Perhaps the novel as an art form was grist to the mill of the Negro writer at any time or place, whenever he began to write about his own experiences or those of others. The earliest Negro novelists, William Wells Brown and Martin Delaney, wrote as pleaders for a cause and as Sterling Brown wrote, "their successors have almost followed their example." The inferior propaganda novels such as Frances Harper's *Iola Leroy* or *Shadows Uplifted* and Dunbar's four conventional novels were not comparable to Chesnutt's novels of social realism.

James Weldon Johnson's *Autobiography of an Ex-Coloured Man* was a purpose work, the first "passing novel," Du Bois' *Quest of the Silver Fleece* had virtues but it was not artistic. Nella Larsen's *Quicksand,* Jessie Fauset's *Plum Bun* and Walter White's *Flight,* all written in the twenties, were "passing" novels. White's *Fire in the Flint* had the virtue of being the first anti-lynch novel written by a Negro in the twenties. Du Bois' *Dark Princess* (1928) part fantasy and part fiction, called for a union of the darker nations and also criticised the weaknesses of the Negroes' struggles for freedom and America's handling of the race problem.

The New Negro Movement produced the first really competent novelists—Fisher, Walrond, Cullen, McKay, Thurman and Hughes. The forefield of this New Negro literature was an artistic awakening. Publishers may have had only one Negro on their lists, but as the late E. Franklin Frazier pointed out, the audience was not Negro, but white. These writers were very important in the development of the Negro novelist as a craftsman. With these new writers there was great fire and enthusiasm, a creative dynamism of self-conscious racialistic expression which at the time was a healthy manifestation of the problems which beset the Negro people. Thurman, in *Infants of the Spring* satirized the exaggerations and Bohemian aspects of the movement. Fisher, a physician, the first Negro to write a detective story and a writer of social comedy, in *Walls of Jericho,* wrote of Harlem jive, a socially intelligent satire of the foibles of the new Negro middle class.

The Negro had come to stay as a novelist and the novelists of the New Negro Movement prepared the way for all of those who were to come later. The genius of Wright burgeoned out of the thirties. Many, like Ellison, relied heavily on the New Negro novelists' experiences. The writers of the Federal Writers Project of the thirties looked back only a decade to their New Negro precursors. As Sterling Brown wrote in his essay, *The New Negro in Literature (1925-1955),* "Negro authors of the thirties, like their compatriots, faced reality more squarely. For the older light-heartedness, they substituted sober self-searching; for the bravado of false Africanism and Bohemianism, they substituted attempts to understand Negro life in its workaday aspects in the here and now. . . . Alert to the changing times, a few critics—Alain Locke among them—charted new directions."

In 1930, James Weldon Johnson in *Black Manhattan* wrote: "Harlem is still in the process of making. It is still new and mixed; so mixed that one may get many different views—which is all right so long as one view is not taken to be the whole picture. This many-sided aspect, however, makes it one of the most interesting communities in America. But Harlem is more than a community, it is a large-scale laboratory experiment in the race problem and from it a good many facts have been found."

And Alain Locke, more prophetic and Cassandra-like than he could have ever known, in the last article written before his death said, "It is to this mirror that I turn for the salient changes of majority attitudes toward the Negro, and equally important, for a view of the Negro's changed attitude toward himself. For the Negro seems at last on the verge of proper cultural recognition and a fraternal acceptance as a welcome participant and collaborator in the American arts. Should this become the realized goal, the history of the Negro's strange and tortuous career in American literature may become also the story of America's hard-won but easily endured attainment of cultural democracy." (pp. 298-306)

Eugene C. Holmes, "The Legacy of Alain Locke," in Freedomways, *Vol. 3, No. 3, Summer, 1963, pp. 292-306.*

W. D. Wright   (essay date 1974)

[In the following excerpt, Wright examines the way in which Locke's cultural criticism addressed the issues of integration and equality.]

While Alain Locke was interested in and was trying to help Blacks develop an esthetic culture, and using it to stimulate racial consciousness and to help create racial unity, he was also interested in and was trying to use this same esthetic culture to help Blacks integrate into American society.

Locke believed that Blacks were not only Blacks, but also Americans. They had a dualistic identity. Accepting this dualistic identity, propagating it, made it possible to discuss the role art or esthetic culture played in helping Blacks to achieve their rights and equality in society.

It was very important for Black artists to recognize and accept their dualistic, American identity. Failure to do this meant that they could not make full use of their cultural efforts in behalf of the race. They could help Blacks achieve racial unity and racial consciousness, and help Blacks develop their internal separate life, but they would not be able to use these efforts to help Blacks integrate into American society, which was also one of their important goals.

Recognizing and accepting their *American* identity was also important in another way, because it gave Black artists a greater perspective on Black esthetic culture itself. This culture was Black, had its roots in Black history and in Black social life. But, at the same time, it had its roots in American history and American social life, and was just as much American as it was Black. Black art drew on the American experience, reflected that experience and translated it, though, perhaps, in a peculiar way:

> Separate as it may be in color and substance, the culture of the Negro is of a pattern integral with the times and with its cultural setting. [*The New Negro,* 1925]

It was impossible for Black culture to escape being influenced by the larger American surroundings. Even the spirituals, which were having great vogue at the moment and were regarded as definitely Black, were not completely Black in their genesis. Those who wrote them, or devised them, initially, borrowed from the religious music (white protestant religious music) around them, giving that music a peculiar racial and cultural stamp that made it distinctively different, but also, at the same time, distinctly American. As Locke said: the spirituals were unique, but "at the same time deeply representative of the soil that produced them."

The view that Black esthetic culture was also American esthetic culture was echoed by J. A. Rogers, historian and social critic, who said that jazz itself was influenced as much by the American background as anything which was taken from the African continent. A close look at the music showed that " . . . With its cowbells, auto horns, calliopes, rattles, dinner gongs, kitchen utensils, cymbals, screams, crashes, clanking and monotonous rhythm it bears all the marks of a nerve-strung, strident mechanized civilization. It is a thing of the jungles—modern man-made jungles" ["Jazz at Home," *The New Negro,* 1925].

Black artists had to understand, as Black people in general had to understand, that Blacks were a minority group, and their effectiveness in using their cultural creativity in a social and political way demanded that they both make the proper identification. "The Negro mind reaches out as yet to nothing but American wants, American ideas. But this forced attempt to build his Americanism on race values is a unique social experiment, and its ultimate success is impossible except through the fullest sharing of the American culture and its institutions. There should be no delusions about this" [*The New Negro*].

Acceptance of the American identity would also help Black artists, and Black people in general, to understand the kind of role they had to play in American society. That role, as Locke saw it, was a cultural one. America was dependent upon Blacks for its own cultural development. Whites going off in different directions in American society, following different lines of endeavor, were not readily able to make such a contribution:

> It is obvious . . . that the main line of Negro development must necessarily be artistic, cultural, moral and spiritual . . . in contrast with the predominantly practical, and scientific trend of the nation. . . . Although he must qualify in all the branches of American life and activity, the Negro can be of more general good in supplementing Nordic civilization than through merely competitively imitating or extending it along lines in which it is at present successful and preeminent. ["**Negro Contributions to America**," *The World Tomorrow,* 1929]

In the 1930's, Locke provided an additional rationale for his view that Blacks had a cultural role to play in America. In 1933, in a short interpretation of the cultural history of Black Americans, he observed that the structure and evolution of American society had molded Blacks into this role. The functioning of American society had simply destroyed the possibility for other groups in the society to play the cultural role: "Many other cultural traditions richer and more developed than the Negro's have been transplanted to the American continent. But too many of them have gone literally to the melting pot and lost their cultural distinctiveness and identity" [*The Negro in America,* 1933].

This did not happen to the Black man in the same degree. Segregation, oppression, and a considerable amount of isolation from American society had made it possible for Blacks to retain much of their cultural identity and distinctness: "Persecution, suffering with their greater discipline and pressure, have intensified the Negro heritage and caste prejudice has isolated it from the powerful standardizing process in American life." This meant, to Locke, that the Black folk heritage, the Black folk spirit, had not been inundated by America's mechanized and standardizing civilization. Thus, there were a distinctness and vitality to the Black subculture which provided Black artists with a springboard to create high art and to play a cultural role in American society.

The American acculturation and assimilation processes had virtually destroyed all ethnic-national cultures or had, at least, destroyed their vitality. They also had the effect of dissolving the majority of the American population into a white racial group. This, then, left American society comprised mainly of two racial groups (especially, since whites had virtually eliminated the Indian and his subculture). Of the two racial-social groups, Blacks were the ones who had maintained their cultural distinctness, and whites would have to borrow from them, as the American cultural base, to build a national esthetic culture, which was feverishly being attempted by whites in the post-War period.

The First World War, Locke observed, had destroyed many western values and social and cultural patterns. There was an interest in America (as there was in Europe) to rebuild the national esthetic culture on a different value base. In America, there was even an interest to build a national esthetic culture, which would be free from European influence and inspiration. In order to build this distinctive national esthetic culture in America, Locke held that whites would have to make use of the Black subculture ["**American Literary Tradition and the Negro**," *The Modern Quarterly,* 1926].

In America, white youth (as well as younger white artists) were rebelling against the American Puritan tradition. They were rejecting this tradition with its severe restrictions placed on sexual behavior, its emphasis on utilitarian values, and on economic and/or occupational success. The young wanted to loosen up their lives, to loosen up the American culture: "This seems to me to explain why current literature and art for the moment are so preoccupied with the primitive and pagan and emotional aspects of Negro life and character and why suddenly something almost amounting to infatuation has invested the Negro subject with interest and fascination."

Locke detested the caricature of Black life done by so many white and even Black artists, and the great emphasis being placed on "low" Black life. James Weldon Johnson was moved to speak of the situation in what has to be described as amused contempt:

> On occasions, I have been amazed and amused watching white people dancing to a Negro band in a Harlem cabaret, attempting to throw off the crusts and layers of inhibitions laid on by sophisticated civilization; striving to yield to the feel and experience of abandon; seeking to recapture a taste of primitive joy in life and living; trying to work their way back into that jungle which was the original Garden of Eden; in a word, doing their best to pass for colored. [*Along This Way,* 1933]

Although Locke objected to the way most white artists denigrated Black cultural life, he felt they had a right to interpret that life. He developed a concept of cultural equality, and one aspect of that concept was that whites and Blacks both should have access to the Black experience, to portray it in art. "From the Negro," he said, "[we expect] the most complete and sustained effort and activity" ["**Beauty Instead of Ashes**," *The Nation,* 1928]. But whites should have an equal opportunity to portray Blacks artistically. Indeed, it was important that whites did so. Whites taking an interest in Black life and, especially, if they portrayed it honestly, could only help the efforts being made by Blacks to use esthetic culture as one of the means to help themselves integrate into American society. But, it was also necessary for whites to deal in race materials, to give an artistic interpretation of Black life, so that Black artists, Black people in general, could see themselves as others saw them.

Locke felt there were some whites who did a good job of interpreting the Black existence. These were primarily fiction writers. Unlike W. E. B. Du Bois, he had great praise for Carl Van Vechten's *Nigger Heaven.* He found it artistic and honest, although, at times gross. There were Southern writers, working in Black folk materials, who were doing an excellent job in interpreting Southern Black folk life. Locke was very impressed with the artistic skill and insight of DuBose Heyward and Julia Peterkin, whose novels, *Scarlet Sister Mary,* and *Bright Skin,* he praised favorably.

A New South was emerging in this period. Southern white writers were extensively probing and making use of Black folk materials, to try to gain new values with which to give the New South a new direction. Locke saw similarities between the concept of the New South and the New Negro:

> The New Negro and the New South have more than interesting parallelisms, they have many ideals, loyalties and objectives in common. Each seeks an emancipation from the old obsessions of the Southern traditions—a revolution of mind and social attitude sought as a necessary preliminary to any really vital reform; each demands a change of leadership based on concrete constructive programs . . . each strives to raise a stagnated but richly endowed folk tradition to the level of free-flowing and creative expression; each hopes to freshen and purify brackish group emotions through new, dynamic processes of cultural and spiritual release. ["**Welcome The New South**," *Opportunity,* 1926]

Although Locke felt that Black artists were the ones who would do the best job of portraying Black life, he still posited, as another aspect of his concept of cultural equality, that Blacks had to prove that they were capable of producing cultural works equal to those of whites. He rejected any and all notions that Blacks were intellectually inferior to whites. Any retardation in Black intellectual, artistic, or social life was due to the oppressive environmental conditions in which Blacks had to live. Freed from these conditions, Black intellectual and cultural ability would be vibrant and productive.

But Locke felt that Blacks had already produced intellectual and artistic geniuses. In this connection, he spoke of W. E. B. Du Bois and William Stanley Braithwaite. There were a number of artistic geniuses around. Locke mentioned persons such as singer Roland Hayes, Paul Robeson, Countee Cullen, Langston Hughes, James Weldon Johnson, Jean Toomer, Claude McKay, Jessie Fauset, Rudolph Fisher, Eric Walrond, and others. These were artists equal to any whites in the country.

These geniuses of the race were symbols which others of the race could be proud of, and also whom they could rally around. Locke also felt that these individuals, by their stellar achievements, should immediately be admitted into American society on the basis of equality with whites. Locke, an elitist, one of the "Talented Tenth," wanted individual and/or talented Blacks to be integrated into American society first; also because he felt only a few Blacks would be integrated at a given time anyway. But these talented individuals could become the key to the process of integration of the rest of the race:

> By recognizing the talent and the representative types among Negroes, an easing and vindicating satisfaction can be carried down to the masses, as well as the most quickening and stimulating sort of inspiration that could be given them. Their elite would then become symbols in advance of expected justice and of a peaceful solution. ["**Should the Negro Be Encouraged to Seek Cultural Equality?**" *The Forum,* 1927]

Thus, Black cultural power would work a slow matriculation of Blacks into American society. First would be admitted the intellectual and artistic Talented Tenth. The public recognition and acceptance of these Blacks, as equals, would have an effect of further softening racist attitudes. This would permit other Blacks to then enter American society.

American society had to be aware of some of the problems it could create for itself if it did not recognize the intellectual and artistic ability of these elites, and did not accord them rights and equality:

> The dilemmas of non-recognition become correspondingly deeper. Apart from the injustice and reactionary un-wisdom, there is a tragic irony and imminent social farce in the acceptance by "White America" of the Negro's cultural gifts while at the same time withholding cultural recognition—the reward that all genius . . . requires. ["**Should the Negro Be Encouraged to Seek Cultural Equality?**"]

But there were even more serious consequences to contemplate. Genius was transportable. Gifted Blacks could leave the country: "Genius is the most fluid social capital. Ideas are not subject to embargoes. Negro genius,—as witness Roland Hayes and Henry Tanner,—will bid for recognition and will receive it."

There could even be more serious political difficulties: "The balked intelligence of such a group, thrown back upon the repressed masses, invariably comes forward within another generation's time in the uglier form of radical leadership. As with the Jewish intellectuals of Russia, subverted social light may readily become revolutionary fire."

Locke was no revolutionary. His preference was for a peaceful and even slow process of Blacks integrating into American society. He had a vision of what America would look like if it were free of racism, and Black and white were able to live harmoniously together. It would be an "open" society. Open for what?

For making possible free and unbiased contacts between the races on a selected basis of common interests and mutual consent, in contrast with what prevails at present,—dictated relations of inequality based on caste psychology and class exploitation. . . . Instead of leaving society open at the bottom, as it now is, for the economic and sex exploitation of the weaker and less desirable elements of Negro life, it means the opening of society at the top for equal and self-respecting intercourse as warranted by mutual gain and common interests.

The cultural outpouring of Blacks after the First World War established in the minds of Blacks as well as whites that Blacks were a people capable of artistic and cultural achievement. Doubts which had hitherto existed with respect to these capabilities were now severely challenged, if not cleared up. It was owing to the likes of intellectual leaders and critics such as Alain Locke that Black artists were induced and encouraged to explore and sharpen their artistic talents. There were those artists, such as Claude McKay, who [in his *A Long Way From Home,* 1937] objected to cultural leaders attempting to use Black art as a political weapon. But Locke and these other leaders did not feel that art and politics were incompatible. Locke felt that art which had quality, which was beautiful and which conveyed the truth, and which was produced by an oppressed minority within a country, unavoidably had political implications. What he as well as other cultural leaders wished was simply for Blacks to be able to gain as much socially and politically from their cultural efforts as they were able to gain artistically and esthetically. (pp. 42-9)

> *W. D. Wright, "The Cultural Thought and Leadership of Alain Locke," in* Freedomways, *Vol. 14, No. 1, First quarter, 1974, pp. 35-50.*

Ernest D. Mason   (essay date 1979)

[*In the following essay, Mason analyzes several of Locke's essays on race and culture in order to stress the fact that his philosophy addressed political issues at the same time that it was concerned with culture and aesthetics.*]

As in the cases of so many of his ideas, Alain Locke's thinking on race and race relations is not always clearly understood. A typical example of misunderstanding is provided by literary critic George Kent, who, though praising Locke for his critical and practical services during the Harlem Renaissance, speaks of Locke's "essentially middle-class sensibility and somewhat simplistic integrationist orientation" ["Patterns of the Harlem Renaissance," *Black World,* 1972]. In view of the current ambiguity of the words *middle-class* and *integration,* this statement, while not actually wrong, is most unfortunate since it obscures the deep differences that separate a man like Locke from others who cherish middle-class values and call themselves integrationists in an attempt to deny their own racial and cultural heritage. It seems reasonable then to apply the labels primarily to those who prefer them, and not to Locke who was more concerned with race than with class and who constantly referred to himself as a cultural pluralist, as opposed to an integrationist.

Locke's interest in the idea of race stems primarily from his attempt to combat notions of national, racial, and cultural superiority. In one of his earliest writings, **"The Concept of Race as Applied to Social Culture"** (1924), Locke expresses the urgent need to shift from the anthropological perspective, with its emphasis on the biological and physical aspects of race, to the ethnological perspective, with its emphasis on social and historical factors. "If," he says,

> instead of the anthropological, the ethnic characters had been more in the focus of scientific attention, . . . Race would have been regarded as primarily a matter of social heredity, and its distinctions due to the selective psychological "set" of established cultural reactions. There is a social determination involved in this which quite more rationally interprets and explains the relative stability or so-called permanency that the old theorists were trying to account for on the basis of fixed anthropological characters and factors. [**"The Concept of Race as Applied to Social Culture,"** *Howard Review,* June, 1924]

When we speak of race in the social or ethnic sense, a theoretical reversal takes place. Instead of culture being viewed as expressive of race, as certain anthropological theories would have it, race itself becomes a sociocultural product. The practical implication of this shift, in terms of cultural and racial relations, is that each individual should be considered as a product of his or her culture and judged accordingly. This means, specifically, that in relating to individuals of a different race, we should make an honest attempt to understand the social and historical factors that determine that race's "stressed values which become the conscious symbols and traditions of the culture. Such stressed values are themselves factors in the process of culture making, and account primarily for the persistence and resistance of culture-traits."

One of the many social consequences of the refusal to adopt the sociocultural interpretation of race is the idea of biracialism or racial segregation. In a debate with Locke concerning equality in 1927, Lothrop Stoddard, then a teacher at Harvard, argued for biracialism in the following manner:

> The basic reason for White America's attitude and policy toward the Negro is,—not belief in the Negro's inferiority,—but the fact of his difference. True, most whites today believe the Negro to be their inferior. On the contrary, it springs largely from realization of racial difference and all that it connotes. White Americans feel that to incorporate the many millions of this widely differing stock into our racial life would profoundly change our national character, temperament, and ideas. And since these matters are supremely cherished, we do not propose to jeopardize them, either for ourselves or for unborn generations who have an indefeasible right to their racial heritage. ["The Impasse at the Color Line," *Forum,* 1927]

What is at stake, according to Stoddard, is the preservation of the purity of the white race: "Therefore, if we desire to perpetuate *our* America, we white Americans must absolutely refuse to countenance the spread through our stock of racial strains so different and so numerous that they would undermine our ethnic foundations. In other words, we are dealing, . . . with an imperative urge of self-preservation. And self-preservation is the first law of nature." Locke, in response, points out that the person who argues that race prejudice is primarily the instinct of race preservation and that intimate relations between blacks and whites pose a danger to white America is the very same person

> whose social regime and life most depend upon close personal relations with Negroes,—in familiar and household relations at that,—and whose chief delight is to be instantly and widely familiar with Negroes provided he can protect sentimentally his caste pride and personal egotism, to which, as a matter of fact, such relations are the chief sustaining foil. It is this type of man who in open or clandestine relations, by the sex exploitation of the socially and economically unprotected Negro women, has bred a social dilution which threatens at its weakest point the race integrity he boasts of maintaining and upholding.
>
> In the light of this active contradiction of its own social creed by its own social practice, White orthodoxy on the race questions becomes not a consistent creed of race superiority and inner conviction, but the social self-defense of a bad conscience, the hysterical ruse of a self-defeatist vice. It fumes about keeping society closed at the top and insists on keeping it viciously open at the bottom. It claims to eliminate social contracts between the races, but actually promotes race mixing. Under conditions and habits such as these contradictions have bred, a rabidly "White America" can not refuse to recognize the Negro and long remain White. [**"The High Cost of Prejudice,"** *Forum,* 1927]

Furthermore, adds Locke, blacks themselves have no desire to be mixed racially with whites. "Race fusion," he says, "is in our minds too tainted with the assumptions of White dominance and aggression, too associated with the stigma of inferiority rather than equality, for race amalgamation to be the social ideal and objective of an intelligent and self-respecting race consciousness such as we are now developing. In brief, the progressive Negro of today wants cultural opportunity and cultural recognition, and wants it as a Negro."

Stoddard's doctrine of biracialism aims at separating the races not only physically but culturally as well. Yet cultural fusion is inevitable. As Locke states it:

> What is "racial" for the American Negro resides merely in the overtones to certain fundamental elements of culture common to white and black and his by adoption and acculturation. What is distinctively Negro in culture usually passes over by rapid osmosis of the general culture, and often as in the case of Negro folklore and folk music and jazz becomes nationally current and

representative. The Negro culture product we find to be in every instance itself a composite, partaking often of the nationally typical and characteristic as well, and thus something which if styled Negro for short, is more accurately to be described as "Afro-American," . . . there is little if any evidence and justification for biracialism in the cultural field, if closely scrutinized and carefully interpreted. [**"The Negro's Contribution to American Culture,"** *Journal of Negro Education,* 1939]

At the bottom of Locke's attack on biracialism lies his conviction that race, culture, politics, and equality are all intimately related. At one point he writes: "Ultimately a people is judged by its capacity to contribute to culture" [**"The Ethics of Culture"**]. Elsewhere he states: "there is no way of putting a social premium upon a product and at the same time putting a social discount upon its active producers. . . . The man who contributes to culture must fully participate in its best and most stimulating aspects [**"The High Cost of Prejudice"**]. Such statements clearly explain why Locke devoted so much of his energy to cultural and artistic problems—it was his way of fighting the social and political battle:

> Cultural recognition, . . . means the removal of wholesale social proscription and, therefore, the conscious scrapping of the mood and creed of "White Supremacy." It means an open society instead of a closed ethnic shop. For what? For making possible free and unbiased contracts between the races on the selective basis of common interest and mutual consent, in contrast to what prevails at present,—dictated relations of inequality based on caste psychology and class exploitation.

Locke's rejection of biracialism also helps to explain why he favors DuBois's position as opposed to the views of Booker T. Washington.

> Never [says Locke], up to the time of his death in 1915, was he [Washington] able completely to disavow the interpretation put upon his program as an acceptance of the principle of opportunism and of the policy of biracial segregation. The equal rights reformist wing of the Negro thought under the leadership of DuBois so interpreted it; and later, reactionary and conservatively halfway white opinion seized upon the same interpretation, with approval, for condoning separatism, the double standard of unequal treatment, claiming the endorsement of an outstanding Negro leader. [*The Negro in America,* 1933]

The tension between Washington and DuBois is, in Locke's view, one between the

> necessity for practical compromise and radical assertion of rights and principles. In one phase you have a person like Booker T. Washington attempting a practical program which manifestly is a compromise with an unfavorable situation and in another a person like Dr. DuBois who, as an intellectual and crusader, comes out foursquare for what he knows is right in principle, what everybody admits is right, but what he and everybody also knows is not going to be immedi-

ately conceded by a majority that is in power, and that has back of it a tradition of discrimination. [**"The Negro Group,"** *Group Relations and Group Antagonisms,* ed. R. M. MacIver, 1944]

At a time when blacks were living in abject poverty and being lynched daily, it had to be, according to Locke, one's heart and sense of justice that dictated the rejection of accommodation. Although fully aware of the dangers, Locke insists that blacks "be taught to see and regard as paramount the long-term interests, which is another way of saying that principle rather than expedience must decide if constructive progress is to be made" [**"The Dilemma of Segregation,"** *Journal of Negro Education,* 1935]. In making this statement, Locke acknowledges that suffering and even death are sometimes the price of equality and freedom. Although Locke called himself a pacifist and favored legal pressure through the courts, he was not so unhistorically minded or blind to the limitations of legal action to see that violence might be necessary to produce significant changes in race relations. It is, in fact, Locke's recognition of the limitations of legal action that leads him to reject the theory of "gradualism" in race relations:

> Nothing is more contrary to fact than the rather widespread policy and program of gradualism. This theory of slow accumulative growth, of the slow reform of public opinion, of "the education of public sentiment" is a fallacy; the lines of social reform are not smooth gradual curves but jagged breaks, sudden advances and inevitable setbacks of reaction. . . . There may be a period for the gradual extension of a right, but not for the creation of a right or its recognition; this holds both for races and classes. Even though the values may exist for others, a revolutionary introduction or vindication of them as applying to the new group is always or usually the case. [**"The Negro Group"**]

The essence of Locke's critique of gradualism lies in his distinction between the "extension" of a right which is already in existence for at least some members of an exploited race or class and the "creation" of a right for that race or class. It is a distinction which discloses an important element of the relations between means and ends. Specifically, Locke argues that the creation of rights often requires radical or militant means:

> The compromise phase makes its characteristic gains, the militant phases make certain other gains. It is a matter of temperament as to which you interpret as the more important. I myself (and I think in this I speak for a goodly section of Negro thinkers at this time) believe that we have made more substantial gains in militant phases than in others. In other words, we regard the anti-slavery and Civil War period as a period of great permanent gain. . . . We regard the civil rights, equal rights movement of the first decade of the nineteen hundreds that has been carried on in organizations like the N.A.A.C.P. . . . as another phase of militancy calculated to recover lost ground and gain fresh advances. We regard the after-World-War reaction as another period of militancy on a cultural and to an extent a social front, . . . And we re-

gard the stage when the New Deal measures of social reform began to link up with the Negro cause, as the beginning of another phase of militancy and reform which probably is at its peak today in the Second World War. [**"Values and Imperatives,"** *American Philosophy Today and Tomorrow,* eds. Sidney Hook and Horrace Meyer Kallen, 1935]

To speak of the militancy of the N.A.A.C.P. and the New Deal is hardly to speak of violence. But notice that Locke also considers the Civil War period to have been a "great permanent gain" and both World Wars instrumental in producing militant phases of great social value. Thus the question is not whether or not Locke himself advocated war, racial or otherwise, but whether or not he condoned it as a means of reinforcing the legal or political efforts to achieve racial equality. As a genuine pacifist he could not possibly do so, but as a value relativist he could.

Although Locke defends blacks wholeheartedly, he is by no means blind to the dangers of excessive racialism. He was confronted with this problem most directly in his efforts to make blacks aware of the international dimension of their struggle. Given that race interest on an international scale is an essential factor in the development and survival of a culture, should one deliberately emphasize and perpetuate racial unity at the risk of more chauvinistic prejudice and sectarianism? As Locke himself states the matter, "if we argue for raciality as a desirable thing, we seem to argue for the present practice of nations and to sanction the pride and prejudice of past history. Whereas, if we condemn these things, we seem close to a rejection of race as something useful in human life and desirable to perpetuate" [**"The Contribution of Race to Culture,"** *The Student World,* 1930]. In an effort to solve this dilemma, Locke attempts to avoid the extremes of both universalism and race chauvinism by way of emphasizing their interrelation. His alternative is stated most clearly in his article **"Jingo, Counter-Jingo and Us"** (1938). Here, in response to an article by Benjamin Stolberg, Locke makes clear the nature of minority jingo:

> Like Mr. Stolberg, I also say: "Good Lord deliver us from jingo!" But unlike him, yet like a philosopher, I must begin with the beginning. And "minority jingo" isn't the beginning, and so, not the root of the evil, evil though it may be. Minority-jingo is counterjingo; the real jingo is majority jingo and there lies the original sin. Minority jingo is the defensive reaction, sadly inevitable as an antidote, and even science has had to learn to fight poison with poison. However, for cure or compensation, it must be the right poison and in the right amount. And just as sure as revolution is successful treason and treason unsuccessful revolution, minority jingo is good when it succeeds in offsetting either the effects or the habits of majority jingo and bad when it reinfects the minority with the majority desease. . . . The minority is entitled to its racial point of view provided it is soundly and successfully carried through.

Concluding, Locke says,

> As I see it, then, there is the chaff and there's the

wheat. A Negro, or anyone, who writes African history inaccurately or in a distorted perspective should be scorned as a "black chauvinist," but he can also be scotched as a tyro. . . . Or the racialist to whom group egotism is more precious than truth or who parades in the tawdry trappings of adolescent exhibitionism is likewise to be silenced and laughed off stage; but that does not invalidate all racialism. There are, in short, sound degrees and varieties of these things, which their extremisms discount and discredit but cannot completely invalidate. I am not defending fanaticism, Nordic or Negro, or condoning chauvinism, black or white; nor even calling "stalemate" because the same rot can be discovered in both the majority and the minority basket.

It should be clear then that, for Locke, minority chauvinism need not be a necessary consituent of race pride. Rather, it must be understood as a position which is forced upon minorities because of majority pressures. It is precisely because counter-claims of minority jingoism are externally determined that Locke concludes in favor of minority jingoism, provided of course that it is reasonably held. In his article, **"Unity through Diversity: A Baha'i Principle"** (1931), Locke poses and answers the following question: "Can anyone with a fair-minded sense of things, give wholesale condemnation to the partisanship of Indian Nationalism, or Chinese integrity and independence, of Negro proletarian self-assertion after generations of persecution and restriction? Scarcely,—and certainly not at all unless the older partisanships that have aroused them repent, relax, and finally abdicate their claims and presumptions" [**"Unity through Diversity**: A Baha'i Principle, *"Baha'i World,* 1931]. In other words, "we feel and hope in the direction of universality, but still think and act particularistically."

Locke's interest in the problem of race and race relations throughout the world has led some of his commentators to a number of false conclusions. In *The Mind and Mood of Black America,* S. P. Fullinwider, for instance, maintains that

> Locke was unique in that he was able to turn his critical faculties to things other than the race question—it was not his all-consuming passion. In fact, he tended to see the solution of the Negro's problem in the broader terms of curing the ills which trouble Western civilization. DuBois had plenty to say about the ills of Western civilization but it was always with the Negro as the referent—to solve the Negro's problem would solve the problems of civilization. For Locke it was rather the other way around: the problems of his race were part of the larger problems of modern civilization.

Fullinwider is somewhat off the mark in stating that Locke "tended to see the solution of the Negro's problem in the broader terms of curing the ills which trouble Western civilization." For according to Locke, the ills which trouble Western civilization are precisely those ills created by the race question in America, namely, the lack of respect for racial and cultural differences. In his own words,

I think the Negro situation has perpetuated the psychology, the social habit of discrimination and that other minorities have indirectly suffered from its presence. It seems to me, as I study it, that the psychology of prejudice—that the habit of social group discrimination—is a very infectious and vicious thing which, if allowed to grow, spreads from one group to another; and I also feel that in talking against American racial prejudice we are at the same time talking against religious prejudice, cultural prejudice of all kinds, and even social class prejudice to a certain extent. The same psychology seems to feed them all. ["**The Negro Group**"]

On the surface, it may appear that the distinction is a trivial one. Its seriousness emerges only when we realize that Fullinwider's interpretation gives the false impression that Locke subordinated the social, economic and political struggles of black Americans to his concern for international affairs. Such an interpretation is perhaps merely the outgrowth of Fullinwider's conviction that Locke "reflected the inability of the middle class truly to empathize with the city masses." "Much derision," he continues,

> was directed at Locke by Renaissance poets and writers—as often as not he was set up as a symbol of what the writers were in revolt against. . . . He did not try to hide the polish usually associated with a Rhodes Scholar and Harvard Ph.D. In short, he was easily stigmatized as—"dicty"—he stood apart from the masses—by those writers who were in a great lather to escape from that category themselves.

It is true that Locke, like DuBois, was a strong advocate of a "talented tenth" and felt little could be expected, politically, from the economically deprived masses. Thus one is likely to encounter in his writings such expressions as "exceptional few," "nationally representative classes," "leaderless masses" and "vulgar crowd." For example, [in] **"The High Cost of Prejudice"** he writes: "Both as an American and as a Negro, I would so much prefer to see the black masses going gradually forward under the leadership of a recognized and representative and responsible elite than see a frustrated group of malcontents later hurl these masses at society in doubtful but desperate strife." In no way, however, do such statements prove that Locke had contempt for the masses or that he deliberately sought to distance himself from them. On the contrary, Locke's "elitism" and advocacy of the "talented tenth" represents a devotion to the causes of the black masses, and he esteems elitism only insofar as it furthers political, economic and cultural net gains:

> By recognizing the talent and the representative types among Negroes, an easing and vindicating satisfaction can be carried down into the Negro masses, as well as the most quickening and stimulating sort of inspiration that could be given them. Their elite would then become symbols in advance of expected justice and of a peaceful eventual solution. They would be literally an investment in democracy. . . . Not only great satisfaction, but great social incentive can be created for the masses in the recognition of the outstanding few,—*as a group representative*, howev-

er, and *not* with the reservations to which Negro talent of a previous generation had to submit, namely, of being regarded as a prodigy, a biological sport. [my italics]

The clear inference is that to bridge the gap, to bring the level of the masses' sense of appreciation and understanding closer to the consensus of the best qualified opinion, to stop claims of black inferiority, and to eventually stop racism were Locke's only intentions in advocating a black elitism. This education in appreciation and understanding is, for Locke, most essential:

> As a race group we are at the critical stage where we are releasing creative artistic talent in excess of our group ability to understand and support it. Those of us who have been concerned about our progress in the things of culture have now begun to fear as the greatest handicap the discouraging, stultifying effect upon our artistic talent of lack of appreciation from the group which it represents. . . . Here is our present dilemma. If the standard of cultural tastes is not rapidly raised in the generation which you represent, the natural affinities of appreciation and response will drain off, like cream, the richest products of the group, and leave the mass without the enriching quality of its finest ingredients. This is already happening: I need not cite the painful individual instances. The only remedy is the more rapid development and diffusion of culture among us. ["**The Ethics of Culture**"]

It should be stressed, by way of conclusion, that it is Locke's understanding of the nature of man and of the nature of culture—rather than the "middle-class sensibility" so often attributed to him—that leads him to take the position he does on the nature of race and race relations. Specifically, it is his view that cultural interchange enables people to come together in ways mutually stimulating and functional that determines the direction of his thinking. Such an interchange should in no way result in the weakening of a race's cultural traditions and values, but rather in a more profound consciousness of them. Race, says Locke,

> seems to lie in that peculiar selective preference for certain culture-traits and resistance to certain others. . . . And instead of decreasing as a result of contacts this sense and its accumulative results seem on the whole to increase, so that we get accumulative effect. It intensifies therefore with contacts and increases with the increasing complexity of the culture elements in any particular area. A diversity of culture types temporarily at least accentuates the racial stresses involved. ["**The Concept of Race as Applied to Social Culture**"]

Locke's thinking on race and race relations seems to me to be both sound and healthy. Those who wish to maintain that his position is faulty cannot adequately do so by merely pointing to his personality or lifestyle; they must show the untenability of one or more of the views on which his position depends. So far this has not been done. (pp. 342-50)

Ernest D. Mason, "Alain Locke on Race and

Race Relations," in PHYLON: The Atlanta University Review of Race and Culture, *Vol. XL, No. 4, December, 1979, pp. 342-50.*

George Hall   (essay date 1982)

[*Hall is an American educator and critic. In the following essay, he discusses Locke's critical methodology, compares his aesthetic theories to those of W. E. B. Du Bois, and reviews Locke's reaction to several writers associated with the Harlem Renaissance.*]

For Alain Locke, propaganda was the slanted rhetoric that he cautioned the Negro writers of the Harlem Renaissance to avoid. Being a Negro, he knew the harmful effects the contented slave stereotype of a Thomas Nelson Page, the buffoonery of an early Roark Bradford, and the savage beast in the works of Thomas Dixon had on his race. He knew that the works of these authors, aside from presenting such insulting and distorted images, neither had verisimilitude nor were they great literature. Difficult as it would be for a black writer to observe the world around him without wishing to cry out in rage at the injustices heaped daily on himself or his people, Locke cautioned a restraint and an attention to craft for black authors.

In 1925, Locke, the mentor to the young writers of the Harlem Renaissance, looked with optimism on the future. "The intelligent Negro of today is resolved not to make discrimination an extenuation for his shortcomings in performance, individual or collective; he is trying to hold himself at par, neither inflated by sentimental allowances nor depreciated by current social discounts. For this, he must know himself and be known for precisely what he is, and for that reason welcomes the new scientific rather than the old sentimental interest." This was an extremely difficult position in the wake of discrimination, but the Negro writer was to adhere to the Socratic dictum and create despite the psychological and social persecutions inflicted on him. The purpose of this essay is to show that Alain Locke's ideal of a Negro literature of truth and beauty was in reality an honest propaganda stripped of its negative connotations. In this context, honest propaganda denotes any work of fiction with objectivity, sincerity, clarity, and balance.

This honest propaganda was discussed briefly by W. E. B. Du Bois in 1926, when he reflected upon Locke's *New Negro*:

> With one point alone do I differ with the editor. Mr. Locke has newly been seized with the idea that beauty rather than propaganda should be the object of negro literature and art. His book proves the falseness of this thesis. This is a book filled and bursting with propaganda, but it is for the most part beautifully done; and it is a grave question if ever in this world in any renaissance there can be a search for disembodied beauty which is not really a passionate effort to do something tangible, accompanied and illuminated and made holy by the vision of eternal beauty. [W.E.B. Du Bois, Review of *The New Negro, Crisis,* 1926]

In essence, both Locke and Du Bois agreed about what constituted good art. It was the function of art on which they did not agree. Du Bois doubted if one could really have a disembodied art or beauty; but Locke was not seeking for the Negro writer a disembodied beauty. He expected "tangible" results from the Negro knowing himself through his folk cultural experiences, particularly given the Negro's special circumstances as an American citizen within the wider American cultural tradition.

From the 1920s, during the heyday of the New Negro, to his death in 1954, Locke reviewed the works of young writers in his annual retrospective reviews of the literature of the Negro in *Opportunity* and *Phylon*. He realized that the literature of the young writers was becoming hackneyed; that is, he felt that the young Negro writers, wooed by white patronage, were not developing their talents in the direction of great art but were promoting, in some instances, new versions of old stereotypes. Locke expressed relief when the stock market crash of 1929 ended the glorification and exploitation of the writers both by whites and by themselves in trading their art for sensationalism and exhibitionism.

In 1928, on the eve of the Great Depression, Locke wrote about the effects of negative propaganda on an audience: "Artistically it is one fundamental question for us today—art or propaganda . . . my chief objection to propaganda, apart from its besetting sin of monotony and disproportion, is that it perpetuates the position of group inferiority even in crying out against it. For it leaves and speaks under the shadow of a dominant majority whom it harangues, cajoles, threatens or supplicates. It is too extroverted for balance or poise or inner dignity and self-respect." Locke believed that propaganda caused the Negro writer to return to a negation of his own self-image. Reiterating his theme of the renaissance, Locke exhorted writers to strive for objectivity, to repress their personal bias or hatred and create a balanced work, free of negative propaganda and with a serious purpose. "Negro things may reasonably be a fad for others; for us they must be a religion. Beauty, however, is its best priest and psalms will be more effective than sermons."

To the Negro writer this "religion" had always been an added burden, the burden of either writing what white publishers dictated or, many times, not publishing at all. Although the Negro artist had gained much recognition during the renaissance, the conditions of social prejudice and discrimination had not substantially changed in his daily struggle with the white world. Certainly, Locke tried to nurture and bring to bloom the young Negro writers of the renaissance, but he was also aware of the discrimination the Negro faced and urged the young writers to make great literature their protest and their propaganda.

There were works by writers of the renaissance which came close to Locke's ideal of a positive propaganda: Jean Toomer's *Cane* (1923), Rudolph Fisher's *Walls of Jericho,* and much of the poetry of Countee Cullen, Langston Hughes, and Claude McKay. But many of these artists, Locke felt, had not written as objectively as they were capable of doing. Writing in a 1928 retrospective review, Locke reminded the Negro artist to get down and write— the fad was over. He saw this as "a time to discriminate between shoddy and wool-fairweather friends and their supporters, the stockbrokers, and the real productive talents." His remedy for the literary excesses of the renaissance was "an introspective calm; a spiritually poised approach, a deeply matured understanding, for no true and lasting expression of Negro life can come except from these more firmly established points of view."

But some of course did not agree with Locke's approach, or what Allison Davis referred to satirically as "our Negro school of hearty and pure emotion," in his review of Du Bois' novel, *Dark Princess.* Locke in his own review had said of the novel, "It fails the acid test for propaganda while the author falls an artistic victim to his own propaganda ambushes." Davis, deploring the "catch-word" *propaganda,* wrote of Du Bois' *Princess:* "He has spoken to both our spirits and our intellects. There have been both fire and light in him. Propaganda . . . is his case, the bringing to the people inspiration and energy ordinarily beyond their reach." Davis went on to say that Du Bois may have had to sacrifice some artistry for the inspiration, which, of course, is the crux of the propaganda-truth-beauty role of the artist. The idea to be emphasized is that Locke believed that imagination and cultural advancement would come precisely because of, and not in spite of, a propaganda-free literature; that a work such as *Cane* and Langston Hughes's first novel, *Not Without Laughter* (1934), were both sincere presentations without special pleadings or negative propaganda. Although neither work escaped Locke's constructive criticism, he felt that each work had elements of truth and beauty. He wrote that *Cane* has "a phenomenally earthy 'universal particularity'. . . . Although the novel is Negro through and through, it is deeply and movingly human. . . . To wish for more than this is to ask that the transmitting quality of expert craftsmanship be combined with broad perspective or intuitive insight, one or the other." Of *Not Without Laughter* he wrote, "As it is, despite immaturity of narrative technique, this novel is one of the high water marks of the Negro's self depiction in prose."

At the time, Negro literature turned away from what Locke referred to as the "exhibitionism" and "Romanticism" of the renaissance, to a social realism in the works of southern whites such as William March, Lillian Smith, Erskine Caldwell, and William Faulkner. Locke was encouraged that in Negro fiction, particularly Richard Wright's collection of short stories, *Uncle Tom's Children,* the promise of the renaissance was on its way to being fulfilled. He believed Negro fiction to be approaching the mainstream. He hoped for a universal art of the Negro writer, with racial themes but empty of false propaganda, and for much more than a reportorial realism or narrow proletarianism. It was never the schools of literature that Locke protested; for him, the question was the balanced treatment of situation, character, and theme. It remained a literary problem. If one wrote to achieve social justice, let him also do justice to his characterization; if the Negro had rid himself of old stereotypes, let him not repeat similar stereotypes in his own works. Balance was all.

Nevertheless, lest one believe that Locke preached a truth and beauty for Negro literature only, one must read his essay **"Jingo, Counter Jingo and Us,"** in which he answers Benjamin Stolberg's article in *Nation* (October 23, 1928). Stolberg had used a review of Benjamin Brawley's *Negro Builders and Heroes* as a platform from which to cry out against minority jingo. Locke, as foe of all jingoism and chauvinist prattle in fiction or nonfiction, called jingo a necessary evil as an antidote to the jingo of the white majority against minorities. His greatest fear was that the minorities would be infected with the majority disease. But Locke repeated his belief that "Good art is sound and honest propaganda, while obvious and dishonest propaganda is bad art."

It must have been difficult for Locke continually to experience the social discrimination around him and to keep insisting that Negro fiction, if it were to become great, should thrust aside invective in favor of balance and poise. But he generally chose to leave the invective to the majority. His province was art, and only if invective could be incorporated adequately and fairly in the writer's work could it become honest propaganda and, consequently, good art. Ralph Ellison's novel *Invisible Man* was considered by Locke to be one of the truly significant novels of the twentieth century written by a Negro. In 1945, Ellison supported Locke's statement that honest propaganda was good art: "I recognize no dichotomy between art and protest. Dostoevski's *Notes From the Underground* is, among other things, a protest against the limitations of nineteenth century rationalism; *Don Quixote; Man's Fate; Oedipus Rex; The Trial.* All these embody protest even against the limitations of human life itself" ["The Art of Fiction," *Paris Review,* 1945].

Locke felt that the Negro artist would eventually, through a sensitive interpretation of his own folk roots and culture, move into the mainstream of American literature, as artists from other ethnic groups had done. Since the Harlem Renaissance, many white critics have judged the literature of Afro-Americans according to a double standard for artistic excellence. In many cases the works have been judged as great art on the basis of their being "raceless" rather than their value as works of art. The works, therefore, have been regarded as "Negro" literature rather than as literature of Afro-American artists. It matters little whether a literature of truth and beauty, which Locke advocated through the years, has been recognized on its merits by white critics. Even when such a novel as Ellison's *Invisible Man* was praised by white critics as one of the best novels of the twentieth century, it was extolled for its "racelessness." David Littlejohn, reviewing the book in his *Black on White,* epitomizes this double standard: "He [Ellison] achieves his extraordinary powers through objectivity, irony, distance. He works with symbol rather than with act. He is at least as much an artist as a Negro."

Littlejohn's assessment is a major example of the double standard of judgment that Locke believed would eventually vanish. However well meaning Littlejohn's "as much an artist as a Negro," it implies that until Ellison wrote, only whites were artists, and what a happy surprise to discover that some Negroes can be artists as well. In the evaluation of other Negro authors of the 1960s, Littlejohn finds very few protest-free or raceless works. But no one has used racial symbolism, folk stories, the spirituals, and the whole American Negro cultural experience more than Ellison did in *Invisible Man.*

The double standard that white academicians and other critics used in judging the fiction of Negroes has a dimension that Locke hoped would disappear. Locke wanted the writer to be judged individually on the merit of his art, and he trusted the "guardians" of the Anglo-American literary tradition to be fair. A fairness may or may not be present in many white American critics, but the Negro artist will probably continue to have his problems because of the peculiar preferences of critics who have not made a thorough study of the history, art, or folk culture of the Negro. Perhaps a narrow-minded emphasis on the values of Western culture, assumed to be the highest culture, and on the Afro-American as an inferior one is a reason for the critical double standards. Alain Locke understood this could be a prblem, but in the late 1970s, he would probably react with surprise at the slow development of the consciousness of many white critics.

A lack of understanding and fairness toward the Afro-American writer is one of the reasons that young black artists began in the late 1960s developing the black aesthetic. They eschew the Western tradition of a white truth and beauty and demand that "literature be an aesthetic grounded in Afro-American culture. Many of these new critics insist that, to have value, black literature must contribute to the revolutionary cause of black liberation; not merely in polemics against white oppression but also in reinterpretation of the black experience. All the new critics agree that the literature should not be judged good or bad according to the tastes of Europeans, but according to its presentation of the styles and traditions stemming from African and Afro-American culture" [Darwin T. Turner, "Afro-American Literary Critics," in *The Black Aesthetic,* Addison Gayle, 1972].

The importance of the black aesthetic movement, as Darwin Turner perceives it, is that these younger writers are explaining theory, not merely commenting on practice, whereas in the past, Afro-American critics assumed that the desirable standards were those favored by the white establishment. Whether or not those black writers such as John Killens, Larry Neal, Imamu Amiri Baraka, Nikki Giovanni, and others will continue to pursue the black aesthetic seems auspicious for American literature as a whole.

Locke would probably say that the black aesthetic, with its themes and symbols of Negro culture, had been with us in the renaissance. It was, but literature still was judged good art according to a white tradition, which included white tastes and prejudices. Now, the truth and beauty are black. Urging the Negro to write out of his experience, using his racial background and the American cultural tradition, Locke assumed that the literature would be accepted or rejected on the artist's individual merits. Many of the novels, stories, and poems of Negroes have found this fair evaluation and acceptance, but the big three are still Wright, Ellison, and Baldwin.

The civil rights movements of the fifties, sixties, and seventies; the deaths of Martin Luther King, John and Robert Kennedy; and the Vietnam War—all have occurred since Locke's death and have affected both black and white American writers alike. But unlike Locke, who continually directed the young black writers of the Harlem Renaissance and after to put aside bitterness and militant rhetoric and to produce art, not propaganda, the new black writers have been urged to channel their anger to the cause of black nationalism; to exploit their blackness in their work by demonstrating in their music, art, literature, and themselves that they rejected completely the white aesthetic and the so-called mainstream of American literature; to enhance new themes, symbolism, and imagery unique to their Afro-American experience. Consequently, the new black writers have not accomplished what Locke envisioned. Rather than being immersed in the mainstream, they have stuck to their roots in the rural South and in urban society, and in their music, literature and art. Although Locke's dream for the Afro-American did not materialize, much progress has been achieved. The experience of the Afro-American is unique in America's pluralistic society, and I believe that the Afro-American writer in particular will lose his vibrancy, style, and perhaps his integrity if he does not continue to eschew the mainstream and follow the black aesthetic.

In the meantime, white America has grown and I believe continues to grow in its appreciation of Afro-American culture. For the Afro-American writer to become immersed in the mainstream would create a blandness where there was previously a richness of Afro-American truth and beauty. (pp. 91-9)

> *George Hall, "Alain Locke and the Honest Propaganda of Truth and Beauty," in* Alain Locke: Reflections on a Modern Renaissance Man, *edited by Russell J. Linnemann, Louisiana State University, 1982, pp. 91-9.*

Paul Joseph Burgett (essay date 1985)

[*Burgett is an American critic and educator who has written articles on various aspects of classical and popular music. In the following excerpt, which was first presented as a paper at the 1985 conference "Heritage: A Reappraisal of the Harlem Renaissance," he analyzes the persistent comparisons between African-American musical forms such as jazz and the spiritual and Western European classical traditions in Locke's* The Negro and His Music.]

The concept of vindication is a persistent theme in Locke's writings about the music of black Americans and an examination of this theme is instructive of certain early thinking on the issue of a Black Aesthetic.

An initial observation in this matter holds that the Negro intelligentsia, from the Civil War through the Negro Renaissance, according to [Clare Bloodgood] Crane, were essentially elitist in relation to the black population. The individuals comprising the Negro Renaissance, by virtue of their education and cosmopolitanism—many of them had spent time abroad and their interactions at home were expanded to include a wide-ranging interracial spectrum of people—made up a new class of persons who did not have, to use Nathan Huggins's words, "a grass roots attachment." This elitism remained an intact principle despite certain philosophical differences among disparate perspectives—for example, DuBois's devotion to a referential or propaganda theory of art in contrast to Locke's espousal of a more absolutist perspective, i.e., art for art's sake.

Despite such differences, there clearly was a tendency among the black intelligentsia that sought the cultural transformation of black folk culture into a formal or high culture. Huggins points out [in his *Harlem Renaissance,* 1971] that most "aspired to *high* culture as opposed to that of the common man, which they hoped to mine for novels, poems, plays, and symphonies." Huggins observes further that, except for the poet Langston Hughes, none of the Harlem intellectuals took jazz seriously. While people like James Weldon Johnson and Alain Locke respected jazz as an example of folk music, their greatest expectations lay in its transformation into serious music of high culture by some race genius in the tradition of a Dvorak or a Smetana.

The theme of vindication in Locke's thinking can perhaps best be seen and understood by looking briefly at Afro-American music as he saw it and by analyzing the philosophical perspective that emerges from that framework. The framework, developed by Locke, and reported, essentially, in his book *The Negro and His Music,* is embodied in three categories of musical history, all derived from folk origin, which embrace both sacred and secular types.

The first is folk music. Produced without formal musical training or intention, Negro folk music is fundamentally a product of emotional creation. This type, according to Locke, ". . . has produced the most characteristic Negro musical idiom,—sad but not somber, intense but buoyant, tragic but ecstatic . . . a unique and paradoxical combination of emotional elements." The second type is derived from original folk music. It is, however, a diluted form, "imitatively exploited by both white and Negro musicians, [which] has become the principal source and ingredient of American popular music." The third type, according to Locke, is strictly a formal or classical type of music, which can be "properly styled Negro music only when obviously derived from folk music idioms or strongly influenced by them."

Incidental to these three categories is another type of music composed by blacks, which Locke mentions only in passing. It is what he calls music in the universal mode without trace of folk idiom or influence. It is, to use Locke's words, "in the general mainstream of cosmopolitan or classical music." According to Locke, music of this sort, composed by Negro musicians, can in no sense be called "Negro music."

It is the original black folk music, the spirituals and the secular songs, which Locke uses as a base in developing his views of Afro-American musical development. Several observations about his views of black folk music deserve further development here.

First of all, despite Locke's insistence on the general worth of this music, one senses that its value for him was directly related to its potential for some "higher" development. In other words, folk music is valuable at a specific level. Its value, however, increases when elements of this music can be used to influence the music of some higher level. For example, Locke makes the statement that the spirituals received the "highest possible recognition" when they were used as thematic material for symphonic music in Dvorak's symphony *From the New World.* Specifically, he points to the theme of the slow movement as expressing the true atmosphere of a "Negro spiritual," and he says of the Scherzo movement that it was "nose close to jazz, for Dvorak took his rhythms and tone intervals from the shout type of Negro dance." Locke asserts that Dvorak chose spirituals to represent the atmosphere of America. Because of this symphony, Locke goes on to say,

> . . . the spiritual and even the secular Negro folk melodies and their harmonic style have been regarded by most musicians as the purest and most valuable musical ore in America; the raw materials of a native American music. So gradually ever since, their folk quality and purity of style have been emphasized by real musicians.

It is important to pursue this particular example because the findings establish important implications for Locke's theories about black music.

Despite claims by Locke and others that Negro folk tunes as well as American Indian tunes were used in the symphony to represent American atmosphere, Dvorak himself indicated that this was untrue. In a letter to a friend, he states:

> I send you Kretzschmar's analysis of the symphony but omit that nonsense about my having made use of "Indian" and "Negro" themes— that is a lie. I tried to write in the spirit of those American folk melodies.

Furthermore, and again by Dvorak's own admission, any suggestion of the Negro spiritual idiom in the symphony is actually original material created by the composers [John Clapham, *Antonin Dvorak,* 1966].

There is no doubt that Dvorak heard and was influenced by spirituals. Harry T. Burleigh, a black singer and student at the National Conservatory of Music in New York at the time Dvorak was its director, was known to have sung spirituals for Dvorak on several occasions.

A curious and somewhat ironic aside which concerns Burleigh is Locke's condemnation of black composers' abuse of the spirituals by affecting their settings with too much influence from formal European idioms and mannerisms. He cites Burleigh as one composer responsible for such abuses. (pp. 142-45)

Despite the fact that the composer used no specifically Afro-American melodies, his own or the original, there can be no doubt that the black folk idiom, at times, permeates the symphony [*From the New World*] very subtly. (p. 147)

[It] seems to me that to subscribe to Locke's suggestion of the presence in the Dvorak symphony, *From the New World,* of the spiritual "Swing Low Sweet Chariot" or his sense of an inspiring Afro-American influence in the English horn melody of the second movement, or insisting as he does on the presence of jazz rhythms in the scherzo is to belabor what are, at best, tenuous theories.

Disproving the theories of Locke and others in this instance is, however, not the central issue. Had Dvorak literally employed Negro spirituals in the symphony, the issue would be no less obscured. The real issue seems to involve an attitude about black music. In this instance, that attitude is reflected in Locke's attempts to vindicate the value of black folk music, especially the spirituals, by pointing out their use in a musical form not endemic to the spiritual's culture of origin but, rather, in a highly valued form of Western European culture, i.e., the symphony, by a renowned and respected composer.

There are two other points to be made in relation to Locke's ideas about black folk music. One senses that, for him, the Negro spirituals hold a position of superior value over the secular music. Locke describes the former as

> . . . the most characteristic product of Negro genius to date. The spirituals are its great folk-gift, and rate among the classic folk expressions in the whole word because of their moving simplicity, their characteristic originality, and their universal appeal.

Locke does assign the secular folk songs the status of folk classics but he refers to them as being "second . . . to the spirituals."

The second point relates to the musicians mentioned in Locke's discussion of the Dvorak symphony. He asserts that "most musicians" regard black folk music as the purest and most valuable musical ore in America. Further, he maintains that the folk quality and purity of style of black folk music have been emphasized since the twentieth century by "real musicians." The musicians of whom he speaks are clearly not those engaged in the creation of folk music.

The second category of black music which Locke treats is derived from original folk music. He calls it a diluted form, "the petty dialect," as opposed to the great dialect of the spirituals. It is this second type of black music that served as the principal ingredient of American popular music including minstrelsy, ragtime, and jazz. For Locke, this type of black music spanned a significant period of history—from about 1850 to 1936, the year *The Negro and His Music* was published.

It is in his treatment of jazz, especially, that one obtains a clearer picture of the vindication theme in Locke's treatment of the music of this second category. He asserts that jazz eventually took up more or less permanent residence in two places. "Chicago became the reservoir of the rowdy, hectic, swaggering style of jazz that has since become known as 'hot jazz'." Locke devotes relatively little attention in his writings to the "hot jazz" of Chicago.

"New York (and Paris and London)," on the other hand, "has furnished the mixing bowls for the cosmopolitan style of jazz notable for stressing melody and flowing harmony known as 'sweet jazz'." Locke clearly places much greater emphasis on this style. Of the early New York school of jazz (1905-1915), he singles out four Negro musicians for special consideration. The four, Ford Dabney, James Reese Europe, Will Marion Cook, and W. C. Handy, are called "arrangers of genius" by Locke, because they "organized Negro music out of broken, musically illiterate dialect and made it a national and international music with its own peculiar idioms of harmony, instrumentation, and technical style of playing."

As Locke saw it, the chief common contribution of these men was the "vindication" of black music. These four men were the "ambassadors who carried jazz to Europe and the haughty citadels of serious music." Because New York jazz was polished and sophisticated in contrast to its Chicago counterpart, which was comparatively crude, Locke felt that it was more appropriate and fortunate that the New Yorkers' "smoother, more mellow jazz was the first to become world famous and to have international influence." Further contributions of these men included the "vindication" of black music as the preferred dance vogue on the American stage.

The activities of the early New York jazz people culminated in an event of significant historical proportions. In May 1912 a concert was held at Carnegie Hall in which a jazz orchestra of 125 black musicians under the direction of James Reese Europe presented a concert of black music. Locke's comments about this event are worth reporting:

> The formal coming-out party was at Carnegie Hall, the audience, the musical elite of New York, the atmosphere and the comparison challenged that of any concert of "Classical music," and the compositions conducted by their own composers or arrangers . . . that night the Cinderella of Negro folk music found royal favor and recognition and under the wand of Negro musicians put off her kitchen rags. At that time ragtime grew up to full musical rank and the golden age of jazz really began.

Locke's perspective on the role of white jazz performers is especially important here. In his view, the musical techniques of early jazz, rooted as they were in a distinctive black style of technical performance, were capable of being imitated, making jazz the property of a universal audience. To quote Locke:

> . . . white performers and arrangers and conductors had learned the new tricks and were feverishly and successfully competing in carrying jazz style to a rapid perfection.

> . . . the white musicians studied jazz, and from a handicap of first feeble imitation and patient hours in Negro cabarets listening to the originators finally became masters of jazz, not only rivaling their Negro competitors musically but rising more and more to commercial dominance of the new industry.

Locke observes finally that although jazz is basically Negro, "fortunately, it is also human enough to be universal in appeal and expressiveness." Such an extraordinary statement and those which precede it establish Locke's democratic views regarding aesthetic experience; that in the matter of black musical materials, he allowed for no distinctions in perception based on race.

The third of Locke's three categories of black music is what he calls strictly formal or classical type. This category actually includes three types: jazz classics, classical jazz, and modern American music. The first two types are what Locke calls "worthwhile jazz as distinguished from the trashy variety." The latter refers primarily to the commercial efforts of Tin Pan Alley. A jazz classic is a work which, "rising from the level of ordinary popular music, usually in the limited dance and song-ballad forms, achieves creative musical excellence." The jazz classics were products of the jazz orchestras that were emerging in the late 1920s. Locke admits as principal figures in the creation of these classics such big-time black figures as Fletcher Henderson, Earl Hines, Luis Russell, Claude Hopkins, "Fats" Waller, Cab Calloway, Louis Armstrong, Don Redman, Jimmie Lunceford, and, of course, Duke Ellington. White bands singled out for recognition include those of Jean Goldkette, Paul Whiteman, Ben Pollack, Red Nichols, Ted Lewis, The Casa Loma Orchestra, Jimmy Dorsey, and Benny Goodman.

Locke saw one of the major efforts, indeed responsibilities, of these musicians as the exploitation of black folk materials. In the hands of these skilled musicians, jazz was to be "harnessed and seriously guided . . . to new conquests." It was the black musicians, especially, who had the greater responsibility. Jazz, says Locke, is the spirit child of the black musician, and its artistic vindication rests in its sound development by these musicians.

It was Duke Ellington whom Locke viewed with greatest critical admiration. Of Ellington, Locke says:

> . . . in addition to being one of the great exponents of pure jazz, Duke Ellington is the pioneer of super-jazz and one of the persons most likely to create the classical jazz toward which so many are striving. He plans a symphonic suite and an African opera, both of which will prove a test of his ability to carry native jazz through to this higher level.

Locke saw the work of Ellington as especially important to the placing of intuitive music under control, as restraining and refining crude materials. In Locke's words, "Someone had to devise a technique for harnessing this shooting geyser, taming this wild well."

In making his distinction between jazz classics and the "trashy variety" of popular music, Locke had decisively steered black music out of the progressive stages of a maturing folk music onto the early plane of what he would call "art" music, the universal and timeless quintessence of the composer's creative efforts.

Classical jazz, the second type of Locke's third category, is music "which successfully transposes the elements of folk music, in this case jazz idioms, to the more sophisticated and traditional musical forms." Classical jazz and modern American music are related types, if not the same thing. They represent yet a further development upward of black music. The most obvious medium for the development of classical jazz was what Locke refers to as symphonic jazz—a form derived from but ultimately divorced from dance jazz and popular song ballads.

It is not altogether easy to understand clearly just what symphonic or classical jazz is. By his own admission, Locke calls it "a somewhat unstable and anaemic hybrid." It does seem to be inclusive of all sorts of symphonic music. The works Locke discusses include Gershwin's "Rhapsody in Blue," "Porgy and Bess," William Grant Still's "Afro-American Symphony," Edmund Jenkins's "Charlestonia: A Negro Rhapsody for Full Orchestra," and William Dawson's "Negro Folk Symphony." Locke saw the work of these composers as pioneering efforts in elevating jazz to the level of the classics.

There is a curious comment which Locke makes regarding such cultural elevation in the work of the black composer, Florence E. Price. Concerning her symphony in E minor and her piano concerto, Locke says:

> In the straight classical idiom and form, Mrs. Price's work vindicates the Negro composer's right, at choice, to go up Parnassus by the broad high road of classicism rather than the narrower, more hazardous, but often more rewarding path of racialism. At the pinnacle, the paths converge, and the attainment becomes, in the last analysis, neither racial nor national, but universal music.

Locke does not offer many clues about what he means but he concludes his discussion of black music with some observations about the ultimate achievement of black music.

He suggests first that "Negro idioms will never become great music nor representative national music over the least common denominators of popular jazz or popular ballads that are in common circulation today." Locke goes on to say that "neither America nor the Negro can rest content as long as it can be said: 'Jazz is America's outstanding contribution, so far, to world music'."

He speculates that classical jazz may indeed itself be no more than a transitional stage of American musical development. "Eventually," says Locke, "the art music and the folk-music must be fused in a vital but superior product." Locke was not specific about what this superior product would be because he himself did not know. He did point to appropriate prototypes elsewhere in the world that have successfully blended the folk with the formal.

Locke cites Russian, Hungarian, and Bohemian composers who were confronted with this problem and who

> . . . widened the localisms of their native music to a universal speech; they were careful, in breaking the dialect, to reflect the characteristic folk spirit and preserve its unique flavor. What Glinka and his successors did for Russian music, Liszt and Brahms for Hungarian music, and Dvorak and Smetana for Czech music, can and must be done for Negro music.

Because of his desire for cultural reciprocity, it is clear that Locke sought to fashion an aesthetic alliance between European culture and black American culture. Central to this alliance was the vindication of black musical materials. Essential to vindication was the use of these materials as inspiration in European musical monuments such as the symphony, opera, and ballet.

It is difficult to understand fully what Locke's real motivation was in urging these efforts at vindication. On the one hand, his language suggests a psychological undercurrent of cultural inferiority about black music. His statement, "fortunately, [jazz] is also human enough to be universal in appeal and expressiveness," raises serious questions about how Locke really felt about the value of jazz. His observations about the use of black materials in the Dvorak E minor symphony reveal a pitiable straining for respectability. Locke's reliance on white arbiters of taste is revealing when he cites the following critics of "jazz of the better sort" as names "certainly authoritative enough": Kreisler, Rachmaninoff, Koussevitsky, and Stokowski. Other white critics of jazz whom Locke cites as among the most authoritative include Henri Prunières and Robert Goffin of Paris, Constant Lambert of England, and Hughes Panassie, author of *Le Jazz Hot* (1934).

Locke's aesthetic perspective invites comparison with the efforts of the late nineteenth-century nationalist composers but it was in fact quite different. It was affected to some extent by a vindication syndrome. In fact, the disturbing thread of cultural inadequacy implied in Locke's language about black folk music suggests the strong influence on him of Western monism, which, despite its uncompromisingly racist posture, simply may have been too irresistible in the end.

An alternative interpretation, however, treats the issue of vindication from another perspective. Perhaps Locke was absolutely convinced of the value and greatness of black music and was equally convinced of the efficacy of its integration, on an equal basis, within the white cultural mainstream. However, music of the Negro, as well as black culture generally, was viewed by the white and much of middle-class black American culture as inferior. Considering the strong anti-black sentiment that prevailed within the American mainstream about black folk music materials, the use of these materials or even the suggestion of their use, for example, by so eminent a composer as Dvorak, must have seemed to Locke a significant step forward toward the goal of greater recognition and use by "serious" composers, black and white. It may have been that vindication was essential—not in the sense that black folk music needed such exploitation to prove its worth but rather to suggest that such use was the only way the worth of this music would ever be recognized. In other words, Locke's perspective may have been politically motivated. He understood only too well the powerful hegemony of Western European tradition over American culture. He also understood the racist posture of American culture, and that as a black American and philosopher, he could not expose himself to the indignities of the dehumanization, the pain, and suffering wrought by Western monistic thought. . . . (pp. 147-54)

The Negro Renaissance was a phenomenon of another time. In order to be understood fairly and correctly, Locke must be viewed not from the perspective of the 1980s but from the perspective of his own time. To that end, as Huggins has observed, the historical analyst's task, when nego-tiating the efforts of the men and women of that era, requires "a humanism, that will modulate . . . his own ego and self-consciousness enough to perceive theirs."

The thinking of Alain Locke and other members of the Negro Renaissance was, in its day, startlingly new and considered even radical by many. Within this context, the theme of vindication, whatever criticism it might sustain, was supported by its own special and not uncomplicated logic, and was an appropriate response to conditions of the time. In whatever light this thinking may be viewed today, criticism of Locke's efforts needs to be tempered by the humanity of which Huggins writes. (pp. 155-56)

> *Paul Joseph Burgett, "Vindication as a Thematic Principle in Alain Locke's Writings on the Music of Black Americans," in* The Harlem Renaissance: Revaluations, *Amritjit Singh, William S. Shiver, Stanley Brodwin, eds., Garland Publishing, Inc., 1989, pp. 139-57.*

FURTHER READING

Bibliography

Tidwell, John Edgar and Wright, John. "Alain Locke: A Comprehensive Bibliography." *Bulletin of Bibliography* 42, No. 2 (June 1985): 95-104.
    Most extensive bibliography of primary sources, with selected secondary sources.

Biography

Brewer, W. M. "Alain Leroy Locke." *The Negro History Bulletin* 18, No. 2 (November 1954): 26, 32.
    Obituary that discusses Locke's personal and professional lives.

Holmes, Eugene C. "Alain Leroy Locke: A Sketch." *The Phylon Quarterly* 20, No. 1 (Spring 1959): 82-89.
    Documents Locke's educational and professional history and notes any autobiographical influences in his works.

Criticism

Chapman, Abraham. Introduction to *Black Voices: An Anthology of African-American Literature*, edited by Abraham Chapman, pp. 21-49. New York: New American Library, 1968.
    Discusses the development of African-American literature with particular attention to the importance of identity in the poetry, fiction, and prose of African-American authors.

Davis, Arthur P. "Alain Leroy Locke." In his *From the Dark Tower: Afro-American Writers, 1900-1960*, pp. 51-60. Washington, D.C.: Howard University Press, 1974.
    Discusses Locke's interaction with authors of the Harlem Renaissance, and examines Locke's essays in *The New Negro* (1925) and his writings on African-American

drama in *Plays of Negro Life: A Source-Book of Native American Drama* (1927).

Fullinwider, S. P. "The Sociological Imagination." In his *The Mind and Mood of Black America,* pp. 92-122. Homewood, Ill.: The Dorsey Press, 1969.

Analyzes Locke's philosophical and sociological thought and compares these with the thinking of other cultural critics of the time.

Harris, Leonard. "Rendering the Text." In *The Philosophy of Alain Locke: Harlem Renaissance and Beyond,* edited by Leonard Harris, pp. 3-27. Philadelphia: Temple University Press, 1989.

Discusses Locke's intellectual development, the major influences on his thought, and aspects of his philosophical system and provides a bibliography of Locke's works and a comprehensive bibliography of secondary sources.

Helbling, Mark. "Alain Locke: Ambivalence and Hope." *Phylon* 40, No. 3 (September 1979): 291-300.

Examines the influence levied by Locke's philosophical thinking, which is concerned with values, pluralism, and aesthetics, on his success in organizing and encouraging the artists involved with the Harlem Renaissance.

Holmes, Eugene C. "Alain Locke—Philosopher, Critic, Spokesman." *The Journal of Philosophy* 54, No. 5 (28 February 1957): 113-18.

Analyzes Locke's 1935 essay "Values and Imperatives" in his discussion of Locke's philosophical interest in value relativism and his support for cultural pluralism.

Linnemann, Russell J., ed. *Alain Locke: Reflections on a Modern Renaissance Man.* Baton Rouge: Louisiana State University Press, 1982.

A collection of essays that discuss the works and thinking of Alain Locke. Included in the collection are considerations of Locke's philosophical proposals, his music criticism, his sociological and political writings, his literary criticism, and a seclected bibliography of Locke's major works.

Long, Richard A. "Alain Locke: Cultural and Social Mentor." *Black World* 20, No. 1 (November 1970): 87-90.

Discusses Locke's concept of "ancestralism," which advocates the integration of African cultural influences into African-American art, and reviews Locke's achievements as a critic of drama, music, and culture in furthering public and scholarly awareness of African-American artists.

———. "'Keystone' of a Literary Movement: The Genesis of Locke's *The New Negro.*" *Black World* 25, No. 4 (February 1976): 14-20.

Reviews the publishing history and reception of *The New Negro,* from its inception as a special issue of the magazine *Survey Graphic* to the appearance of the book edition.

McLeod, A. L. "Claude McKay, Alain Locke, and the Harlem Renaissance." *The Literary Half-Yearly* 27, No. 2 (July 1986): 65-75.

Discusses the rancorous relationship between the poet Claude McKay and Locke and utilizes Locke's purported misunderstanding of McKay's artistic intention as evidence of his failings as a literary critic.

Stewart, Jeffrey C. Introduction to *The Critical Temper of Alain Locke: A Selection of His Essays on Art and Culture,* by Alain Locke, edited by Jeffrey Stewart, pp. xvii-xx. New York: Garland Publishing, Inc., 1983.

Reviews the major characteristics of Locke's aesthetic and cultural theories and how these changed and developed throughout his career.

Story, Ralph D. "Patronage and the Harlem Renaissance: You Get What You Pay For." *CLA Journal* 32, No. 3 (March 1989): 284-95.

Examines the necessary but often difficult role that patronage played in the lives of several artists associated with the Harlem Renaissance and the ways in which Locke's role as a middleman between artist and patron was ultimately detrimental to his relationship with several artists.

Thurman, Wallace. *Infants of the Spring,* pp. 233-45. 1932. Reprint. Carbondale, Ill.: Southern Illinois University Press, 1979.

A fictional account of the Harlem Renaissance that satirically portrays Alain Locke as the intellectual and highly cultured Dr. A. L. Parkes.

Washington, Johnny. *Alain Locke and Philosophy: A Quest for Cultural Pluralism.* Contributions in Afro-American and African Studies, No. 94, by Alain Locke, edited by Johnny Washington, pp. 227-37. New York: Greenwood Press, 1986, 246 p.

Examines Locke's major essays on philosophy, education, and political issues and includes the most comprehensive bibliography available of Locke's works.

George Meredith

1828-1909

INTRODUCTION

English novelist, poet, and critic.

The following entry presents criticism of Meredith's novel *The Egoist: A Comedy in Narrative* (1879). For a discussion of Meredith's complete career, see *TCLC,* Volume 17.

The Egoist is considered Meredith's greatest literary achievement and is celebrated as a major work in the history of the British novel. A comedy of manners that centers on the young, narcissistic baronet Sir Willoughby Patterne, *The Egoist* also presents Meredith's learned insight into psychology, sociology, and Social Darwinism in a highly refined and stylized prose. While the moralizing tone, materialist philosophy, and positivist analyses of society are representative of the Victorian novel, the style and narrative technique of *The Egoist* anticipate innovations usually associated with Modernism.

Meredith began work on *The Egoist* in June 1878, and by early 1879 he had delivered the manuscript to his publisher, Charles Kegan Paul. Before bringing out the three-volume book edition, Kegan Paul, against Meredith's wishes, arranged serialization of the novel in *The Glasgow Weekly Herald.* Meredith understood the novel as conceptually and artistically unified and thus the division of the novel into parts, a practice that was used primarily for popular literature, ran counter to his intentions. Meredith conceived of *The Egoist* as a realization of his theoretical interest in comedy, as presented in his *Essay on Comedy and the Uses of the Comic Spirit,* an analysis of English and French comedy in which he also defined the mechanics and function of comedy as a literary genre. Using comedy to reveal personality flaws in individuals and using characters as allegories for the social order, Meredith was the first to replace an elaborate plot structure with careful psychological analyses of characters, an innovation that would greatly influence the modern novel. The focus of *The Egoist* is Sir Willoughby Patterne, and, as Meredith explained to his friend Robert Louis Stevenson, who presumed that the baronet must have been fashioned on himself, the character of Willoughby was taken "from all of us, but principally from myself." Authors and critics in England and throughout Europe immediately praised *The Egoist* as a literary masterpiece and, as was the case with the majority of Meredith's works, the novel gained its first popular renown in the United States, where Meredith enjoyed great success throughout his career.

Subtitled a "comedy in narrative," *The Egoist* is based structurally and thematically on drama rather than fiction and reflects Meredith's understanding of comedy as a means of criticizing society and analyzing the individual. Deriving many of his thoughts on comedy from the works of the seventeenth-century French dramatist Jean-

Baptiste Molière, Meredith was particularly influenced by Molière's *Tartuffe* (1667), and *The Egoist* uses such theatrical devices as demonstrative outbursts from characters, the unities of time and place, and an emphasis on character rather than plot.

Sir Willoughby Patterne, the egoist of the title, was raised by two doting maiden aunts who nurtured his narcissism by encouraging his early proclamations that he was the "sun of the house," a reference to the *roi soleil* ("sun king"), Louis XIV, who believed that he formed the central point of the universe. Ostensibly, *The Egoist* is about the trials that Willoughby experiences in his quest for a socially acceptable wife. His first fiancée, Constantia Durham, abandons him three weeks before the wedding; the second, Clara Middleton, grows to abhor the cynosure, leaving Willoughby to court Laetitia Dale, the daughter of a cottager on the Patterne estate, whom Willoughby had once renounced as being below his station. The matrimonial drama is presented from several different perspectives, using indirect discourse, interior monologue, first-person reflections by the narrator, and a dialogue that is at once witty and presented with all of the interruptions and non sequiturs associated with actual conversation. In addition to the multiplicity of perspectives, Meredith employed metaphor and motif to reveal the ideological bases of the novel. While *The Egoist* is primarily concerned with the nature of egoism, it is also a study of marriage, gender, class, and sexuality. Underscoring the extent to which he conceived of the novel as a topos for the discussion of contemporary issues and general philosophical questions, Meredith once commented "narrative is nothing. It is the mere vehicle of philosophy. The interest is in the idea which action serves to illustrate."

Criticism of *The Egoist* generally utilizes the theoretical outline presented in *An Essay on Comedy and the Uses of the Comic Spirit*, which defines comedy as a corrective to the ills of society. Interpretations of Willoughby Patterne have ranged from Robert Louis Stevenson's, which asserts the reader's unavoidable identification with the egoist, to less sympathetic readings of the baronet as the embodiment of male aggression and the personification of the imperialist ruling class of England. While early reviews of the novel were ultimately favorable, nineteenth-century critics often found that Meredith's elaborate prose style created what one reviewer called "an indigestion of epigram" and prompted Oscar Wilde in "The Decay of Lying" (1889) to comment: "As a writer [Meredith] has mastered everything except language: as a novelist he can do everything, except tell a story: as an artist he is everything except articulate." Later critics have praised Meredith's awareness of language as artifice, citing his influence on both James Joyce and Paul Valéry. Meredith's erudition and his impatience with accepted literary forms contributed to the originality of *The Egoist* and led W. E. Henley in an early review of the novel to write that Meredith "is one of the wittiest men of his generation and an original humorist to boot; he has a poet's imagination and he is a quick observer; he has studied human nature and human life, and he is a master of his native tongue."

(See also *Contemporary Authors*, Vol. 117 and *Dictionary of Literary Biography*, Vols. 18, 35, 57.)

W. E. Henley (essay date 1879)

[*Henley was an English critic and poet. As an important figure in the counter-decadent movement of the 1890s and the leader of an imperialistic group of young British writers—including Rudyard Kipling, H. Rider Haggard, and Robert Louis Stevenson—he stressed the relevance of action, virility, and inner strength over alienation, effeminacy, and despair, the latter being characteristics attributed to the Decadents. A prolific and energetic critic, he was editor of the* National Observer *and the* New Review, *where he was an early defender of works by such writers as H. G. Wells, Thomas Hardy, and Bernard Shaw. In the following excerpt, he weighs the comic and imaginative merits of* The Egoist *against what he calls Meredith's "foppery of style," a reference to his arcane and often verbose narrative style.*]

Mr. Meredith is one of the worst and least attractive of great writers as well as one of the best and most fascinating. He is a sun that has broken out into spots innumerable. The better half of his genius is always suffering eclipse from the worse half. He writes with the pen of a great artist in his left hand, and the razor of a spiritual suicide in his right; for, like certain others of his age and temper, he is the owner and the victim of a monstrous cleverness which will neither be suppressed nor admonished, and will not permit him to do things as an honest, simple person of genius would. As Shakspeare, in Johnson's phrase, lost the world for a quibble, and was content to lose it, so does Mr. Meredith discrown himself of the sovereignty of contemporary romance to put on the cap and bells of the professional wit. He is not content to be plain Jupiter; his lightnings are less to him than the fireworks he delights in; and his pages so teem with fine sayings, and magniloquent epigrams, and gorgeous images, and fantastic locutions, that the mind would welcome dulness as a glad relief. He is tediously amusing; he is brilliant to the point of being obscure; his helpfulness is so extravagant as to worry and confound. This is the secret of his unpopularity. His stories are not often good stories and are seldom well told; his ingenuity and intelligence are always misleading him into treating mere episodes as solemnly and elaborately as a main incident; he is ever ready to discuss, to ramble, to theorize, to dogmatize, to indulge himself in a little irony, or a little reflection, or a little artistic misdemeanour of some sort. But other novelists have done these things before him, and have been none the less popular, and are actually none the less readable. None, however, has pushed the foppery of style and intellect to such a point as Mr. Meredith. Not unfrequently he writes page after page of English as ripe and sound and unaffected as heart could wish; and you can but impute to wantonness and recklessness the splendid impertinences that ensue elsewhere. To read him at the rate of two or three chapters a day is to have a sincere and hearty admiration for him, and a devout anxiety to forget his defects and make much of his merits. But they are few who can read a novel on such terms as these; and to read Mr. Meredith straight off is to have an indigestion of epigram, and to be incapable of distinguishing good from bad, the author of the parting between Richard and Lucy Feverel—which appears to us to be the highwater mark of novelistic passion and emotion—from the creator of Mr. Raikes and Dr. Shrapnel, who are two of the most flagrant unrealities ever perpetrated in the name of fiction by an artist of genius.

It is greatly to be hoped that ***The Egoist*** will be read and studied as it deserves, for it is as good in its way as ***Richard Feverel*** itself. It is described by Mr. Meredith as a comedy in chapters; and those who do not know what comedy is had better procure them a Molière at once and read, ere they attempt ***The Egoist.*** Just as Molière, in the figures of Alceste and Tartuffe, has summarized and embodied all that we need to know of indignant honesty and the false fervour of sanctimonious animalism, so in the person of Sir Willoughby Patterne has Mr. Meredith succeeded in quintessentializing the qualities of egoism, as the egoist appears in his relations with women and in his conception and exercise of the passion of love. Between the means of the two authors there is not, nor can be, any sort of comparison. Molière is brief, exquisite, lucid; classic in his union of ease and strength, of purity and sufficiency, of austerity and charm. In *The Egoist* Mr. Meredith is even more artificial and affected than is his wont; he bristles with allusions, he teems with hints and side-hits and false alarms, he glitters with phrases, he riots in intellectual points and philosophical fancies; and though his style has never yet become him so well, his cleverness is yet so reckless and indomitable as to be almost as fatiguing here as elsewhere. But in their matter the great Frenchman and he have not much to envy each other. Sir Willoughby Patterne is a "document on humanity" of the highest value; and to him who would know of egoism and the egoist the study of Sir Willoughby is indispensable. There is something in him of us all. He is a compendium of the Personal in man; and if in him the abstract Egoist has not taken on his final shape and become classic and typical, it is not that Mr. Meredith has forgotten anything in his composition, but rather that there are certain defects of form, certain structural faults and weaknesses, which prevent one from accepting as conclusive the aspect of the mass of him. But the Molière of the future (supposing such a product to be possible) has but to pick and choose with discretion to find in Mr. Meredith the stuff for a worthy companion figure to Tartuffe, Alceste, and Célimène.

> Comedy [says Mr. Meredith] is a game played to throw reflections upon social life, and it deals with human nature in the drawing-room of civilized men and women. . . . Credulity is not wooed through the impressionable senses, nor have we recourse to the small circular glow of the watchmaker's eye to raise in bright relief minutest grains of evidence for the routing of incredulity. The comic spirit conceives a definite situation for a number of characters, and rejects all accessories in the exclusive pursuit of them and their speech.

These three sentences are the first in *The Egoist,* and they explain Mr. Meredith's idea of the Comic and the apparent method of his book. It is, however, by no means certain that the book is a proof that he has put his theory altogether into practice. That is not so clear. The plot of *The Egoist* is comic, and some of its personages are comic also; and both plot and personages are comic in the best and highest sense. But has Mr. Meredith rejected "all accessories in the exclusive pursuit" of his characters and their speech? Has he verily refrained from having recourse "to the small circular glow of the watchmaker's eye" to rout the incredulity of himself and the public? Unluckily there is much that is superfluous in *The Egoist;* its personages are scarcely all comic personages; much of their speech—though all of it is representative—is too trivial to be typical, and so to take rank as comic speech. Mr. Meredith's personality, in fine, has proved too irrepressible to allow him to consummate his effort by giving to it the fine finish he has taught us to expect in a work of perfect comic art; and though his matter is unexceptionable, he has not been able so to fuse and shape it as to produce the effect he foresaw and intended. There is infinitely too much of statement and reflection, of aphorism and analysis, of epigram and fantasy, of humours germane and yet not called for; so that in the end the impression produced is not the impersonal impression that was to be desired, and the literary egoism of the author of Sir Willoughby Patterne appears to overshadow the amorous egoism of Sir Willoughby himself, and to become the predominating fact of the book.

To object thus much to Mr. Meredith's work we have had to judge him by the highest possible standard. His book is so strikingly original, so astonishingly able, that it is a hard matter to keep ourselves from condoning what seem to us its vices in favour of its virtues. Its minor personages are one and all of rare significance and value; its dialogue is surprisingly sustained and apt; there are pages in it of analysis and deduction that open up new views and fresh vistas on human character and the human mind; there are chapters of an imaginative truth so vivid and intense as to be discomforting. Mr. Meredith has not succeeded in doing exactly what he wished to do; perhaps it would be fairer to say that he has succeeded in his intent, and succeeded for himself alone. But all this to the contrary, there is no question but *The Egoist* is a piece of imaginative work as solid and rich as any that the century has seen, and that it is, with *Richard Feverel,* not only one of its author's masterpieces, but one of the strongest and most individual productions of modern literature. (pp. 555-56)

> *W. E. Henley, in an originally unsigned review of "The Egoist," in* The Athenaeum, *No. 2714, November 1, 1879, pp. 555-56.*

Margaret Oliphant   (essay date 1880)

[*Oliphant was a prolific nineteenth-century Scottish novelist, critic, biographer, and historian. A regular contributor to* Blackwood's Magazine, *she published nearly one hundred novels, many of them popular tales of English and Scottish provincial life, including her best-known work, the series of novels known as the* Chronicles of Carlingford (1863-76). *In the following excerpt, she discusses what she considers general stylistic and thematic faults in* The Egoist.]

The author of *The Egoist* holds an exceptional position in literature. He is not a favourite with the multitude, but if that is any compensation, he is a favourite with people who are supposed to know much better than the multitude. His works come before us rarely; but when they do come, there is a little tremor of expectation in the air. The critics pull themselves up, the demigods of the newspapers are all on the alert. It is understood that here is something which, though in all probability caviare to the general, it will be a creditable thing and a point in a man's favour to admire. Like Mr. Rossetti's pictures, there is a certain ignorance, a certain want of capacity involved in the absence of appreciation. Not to know Mr. Meredith is to argue yourself unknown; and *The Egoist* has been regarded with a great deal of respectful admiration. It is a book which sets out with very high pretensions, and claims to represent to us the leading qualities of the human race in an exceptionally clear and animated way. It is a "comedy in narrative," challenging comparison with the masterpieces in that different branch of art; and even among these masterpieces, a certain selection must be made to justify the comparison, for the unity of its sentiment indicates such comedies as the *Avare* and the *Misanthrope,* rather than the livelier works of mingled interest with which (not to speak of Shakespeare) Goldsmith and Sheridan have furnished us. This, it will be seen, is rather an appalling ordeal for a book in three large volumes, with scarcely an incident from beginning to end, all turning upon the question who is to marry Sir Willoughby Patterne, and occupied with the exhibition of that gentleman's character to the world. Mr. Meredith informs us in his prelude, which ought to have been called the prologue, that in order to elucidate the Book of Earth, the lore of human self-estimation and wisdom, Art is the specific.

> The chief consideration for us is [he says] what particular practice of Art in letters is the best for the perusal of the book of our common wisdom, so that with clearer mind and livelier manners we may escape, as it were, into daylight and song from a land of fog-horns. Shall we read it by the watchmaker's eye, in luminous rings, eruptive of the infinitesimal, or pointed with examples and types under the broad Alpine survey of the spirit born of our united social intelligence, which is the comic spirit? Wise men say the latter. They tell us that there is a constant tendency in the book to accumulate excess of substance; and such repleteness obscuring the glass it holds to mankind, renders us inexact in the recognition of our individual countenances: a perilous thing for civilisation. And these wise men are strong in the opinion that we should encourage the comic spirit, who is after all our own offspring, to relieve the book. Comedy, they say, is the true diversion, as it is likewise the key of the great book, the music of the book. They tell us how it condenses whole sections of the book in a sentence, volumes in a character; so that a fair part of a book, outstripping thousands of leagues when unrolled, may be compassed in one comic sitting.

After this prelude and promise the author goes on, as we have said, to three huge volumes, made up of a thousand conversations, torrents of words in half lines, continued, and continued, and continued, till every sentiment contained in them is beaten to death in extremest extenuation, and the reader's head aches, and his very bones are weary. The first volume is fine, the second tedious, the third beyond all expression wearisome. Sir Willoughby Patterne is an egoist of the sublimest type. How he makes everybody and everything subservient to him, keeping in hand a mild and gentle worshipper who lives close by, and is always ready to burn incense to him, while he engages himself to marry, one after the other, two younger, richer, more beautiful heroines; how he pets and applauds a humble hero in the Marines, who has glorified the name of Patterne in a far-off war, but says "not at home" when that hero appears in the shape of an elderly and shabby lieutenant; how he permits his poor cousin to take the expenses of that lieutenant's boy, and himself administers half-crowns and crowns, but will take no responsibility for the little dependent; how he disgusts the beautiful young heroine who has hastily pledged herself to accept him, so that she struggles through two long volumes in her attempts to get free from him before the eyes of his worshippers, till one by one they fall away, and even the romantic and poetical Letitia has her eyes opened; how at last he is cast upon

the compassion of this first love, a poor diminished creature, found out on all sides; and how even Letitia refuses, and will only consent to have him on the most unrelenting and continued pressure. This is the story. If it had been made a comedy of, in three moderate Acts, instead of three large volumes, it might have been, with the amount of power expended, a fine one. But to tell us of an art which "condenses whole sections into a sentence," and volumes in a character, and afterwards to serve up this slender story in about a thousand pages of long-winded talk, is the most curious and barefaced contradiction. We do not think we ever found ourselves astray in such a tangle of conversation in all our experience: true, the action of a comedy is conducted by conversation, but not, ye gods! in such bucketsful. To have the lively successions, the rapid movement, the clear cut lines of a good comedy suggested to us, and then to read, and read, and read, till the brain refuses further comprehension, and only a spectrum of broken lines of print remains upon its blurred surface, is cruel. For a week or two after we complete the book we find ourselves haunted with that shadow of conversations, thus—

> "She will not be bridesmaid to me."
>
> "She declines? add my petition, I beg."
>
> "To all? or to her?"
>
> "Do all the bridesmaids decline?"
>
> "The scene is too ghastly."
>
> "A marriage?"
>
> "Girls have grown sick of it."
>
> "Of weddings?—We'll overcome the sickness."
>
> "With some—"
>
> "Not with Miss Darleton? You tempt my eloquence."
>
> "You wish it?"
>
> "To win her consent? certainly."
>
> "The scene?"
>
> "Do I wish that?"

But this is an easy specimen. It is like silly verse without the rhyme; the talk in which each speaker occupies a line and a half is more painful still. Even now, at a happy distance from our first reading, we have but to think of the book, and lo! the air is marked all over with those adumbrations, with all manner of jerks and dashes, and notes of interrogation added on.

At the same time, we cannot but allow that the entire self-absorption of Sir Willoughby Patterne has a certain sublimity in it. If there was but half of it, and still better if there was but a third part, it would be powerful. A man who is his own law, and who never deviates from one magnificent principle of self-reference, can scarcely be without a certain force. The incident of the lieutenant's visit referred to above, will be as good a specimen as any of the manner of man. Sir Willoughby, on hearing of the marine's gallantry, had sent him a present and a complimentary letter, being intent on taking for himself and his name all the credit possible. He went so far as to invite the unknown cousin to Patterne Hall. But one day, while he is walking on the stately terrace with his betrothed and various other fine people, he sees in the distance "a thickset stumpy man" advancing to the door of the hall.

> His brief sketch of the creature was repulsive. The visitor carried a bag, and his coat-collar was up, his hat was melancholy. He had the appearance of a bankrupt tradesman absconding: no gloves, no umbrella. As to the incident we have to note, it was very slight. The card of Lieutenant Patterne was handed to Sir Willoughby, who laid it on the salver, saying to the footman, "Not at home."

> He had been disappointed in the age, grossly deceived in the appearance, of the man claiming to be his relation in this unseasonable fashion; and his acute instinct advised him swiftly of the absurdity of introducing to his friend a heavy unpresentable senior as the celebrated gallant Lieutenant of Marines, and the same as a member of his family. He had talked of the man too much, too enthusiastically, to be able to do so. A young subaltern, even if passably vulgar in figure, can be shuffled through by the aid of the heroical story, humorously exaggerated in apology for his aspect. Nothing can be done with a mature stumpy marine of that rank. Considerateness dismisses him on the spot without parley. It was performed by a gentleman supremely advanced at an early age in the art of cutting. Young Sir Willoughby spoke a word of the rejected visitor to Miss Durham in response to her startled looks. "I shall drop him a cheque," he said, for she seemed personally wounded, and had a face of crimson. The young lady did not reply.

This is Sir Willoughby at the sublime point; but by-and-by, when he quotes page upon page in a wordy attempt to convince his second betrothed lady (Miss Durham having saved herself abruptly by a runaway match) that the release she asks is impossible, all the grandeur of his attitude is lost, and the merest stupidity of unreason takes hold upon the self-seeker. Even pride does not take fire. It is roused by the revolting idea that any one should wish to be free from him, but only into exasperating attempts to ignore the lady's meaning, or endless adjurations on the subject of fidelity. As for Clara Middleton, his *fiancée*, she is almost equally wearisome in the perpetual twitter and flutter of her wings, as she struggles for the release which he will not give: she half runs away, then returns again, and talks, talks—in the library, in the laboratory, to half a dozen confidants, to her father, and to Sir Willoughby himself, protesting that she will not marry him, but never venturing to break the bond for herself. The first effort for freedom was made in the first volume; but it is not till the very end of the third, and after arguments and discussions innumerable, that the bond is broken and Clara is allowed to go free. All the devices of the man who will not acknowledge to himself that he is not the idol of all his world, to save his own pride, fatigue us hugely before we are done with them. Mr. Meredith has fallen into the reverse error from that of those novelists who blacken all

their secondary characters in order to have an intense white light of perfection upon their hero or heroine. All the people surrounding Patterne House and all the guests in it, and even the two meek aunts, Eleanor and Isabella, see through the hero and all his little motives, and the centre of self in which he lives and moves, before we are done with him. His dependants are not taken in by his profound self-worship. He is "jilted" twice. Letitia Dale, who began by worshipping, accepts his hand, only, so to speak, by force, declaring that she does not and cannot love him. This seems to us as little true to nature as the existence of one black swan among a multitude of crows. The Egoist who takes nobody in is a most feeble specimen of his kind. In a general way, even the worst specimens impose more or less upon their surroundings, and it is very rare indeed where there is not one out-and-out believer to keep the self-worshipper in countenance. But Sir Willoughby has not a creature left to stand by him. The stupidest of his retainers sees through him—even his old aunts. Mr. Meredith, indeed, partly justifies this by promising us, in his high-flown prelude, the pathos without which he says "no ship can now set sail." The Egoist surely inspires pity, he says. But the universal abandonment of the hero is too much. A man who makes so ineffable a fool of himself, who disgusts everybody, and exposes himself to be kicked all round by every humiliating toe that chooses to point itself at him, is by far too poor a creature to be raised to the eminence of a pattern egoist. He is in reality after the first volume, a very poor counterfeit, not worthy in any way of his *rôle*.

And it is hard to have to repeat to a writer of such reputation as Mr. Meredith, and one who is the favourite of the clever, the pet of the superior classes, *goûté* above all by those who confer fame,—what it is so common to say to all the poor little novelists (chiefly female) who are rated in the newspapers about the devices to which they are driven to furnish forth their third volume,—but unpleasant as the duty is, we must fulfil it. Had the author of **The Egoist** been superior, as he ought to be, to that tradition, his book would have been infinitely better. Had he confined it to one volume, it might have been a remarkable work. As it is, it will do no more than hang in that limbo to which the praise of a coterie, unsupported by the world, consigns the ablest writer when he chooses to put forth such a windy and pretentious assertion of superiority to nature and exclusive knowledge of art. Weakness may be pardonable, but weakness combined with pretention is beyond all pity. Mr. Meredith's fault, however, is perhaps less weakness than perversity and self-opinion. He likes, it is evident, to hear his own voice—as indeed, for that matter, most of us do. If "the water were roasted out of him," according to the formula of the great humorist whom he quotes in his prelude, there might be found to exist a certain solid germ of life and genius; but so long as he chooses to deluge this in a weak, washy, everlasting flood of talk, which it is evident he supposes to be brilliant, and quaint, and full of expression, but which, in reality, is only cranky, obscure, and hieroglyphical, he will do that genius nothing but injustice. (pp. 401-04)

Margaret Oliphant, in an originally unsigned review of "The Egoist," in Blackwood's Edinburgh Magazine, *Vol. CXXVIII, No. DCCLX-XIX, September, 1880, pp. 401-04.*

Robert Louis Stevenson   (essay date 1887)

[*Stevenson was a Scottish novelist and poet. His novels* Treasure Island *(1883),* Kidnapped *(1886), and* Dr. Jekyll and Mr. Hyde *(1886) were considered popular literary classics on publication and firmly established his reputation as an inventive stylist and storyteller. In the following excerpt, he explains the relevance* The Egoist *has had for his own life and work, including Meredith's novel in his list of books that have most influenced him.*]

The most influential books, and the truest in their influence, are works of fiction. They do not pin the reader to a dogma, which he must afterwards discover to be inexact; they do not teach him a lesson, which he must afterwards unlearn. They repeat, they rearrange, they clarify the lessons of life; they disengage us from ourselves, they constrain us to the acquaintance of others; and they show us the web of experience, not as we can see it for ourselves, but with a singular change—that monstrous, consuming *ego* of ours being, for the nonce, struck out. To be so, they must be reasonably true to the human comedy; and any work that is so serves the turn of instruction. (p. 76)

[*The Egoist*] is art, if you like, but it belongs purely to didactic art, and from all the novels I have read (and I have read thousands) stands in a place by itself. Here is a Nathan for the modern David; here is a book to send the blood into men's faces. Satire, the angry picture of human faults, is not great art; we can all be angry with our neighbour; what we want is to be shown, not his defects, of which we are too conscious, but his merits, to which we are too blind. And *The Egoist* is a satire; so much must be allowed; but it is a satire of a singular quality, which tells you nothing of that obvious mote, which is engaged from first to last with that invisible beam. It is yourself that is hunted down; these are your own faults that are dragged into the day and numbered, with lingering relish, with cruel cunning and precision. A young friend of Mr. Meredith's (as I have the story) came to him in an agony. 'This is too bad of you,' he cried. 'Willoughby is me!' 'No, my dear fellow,' said the author; 'he is all of us.' I have read *The Egoist* five or six times myself, and I mean to read it again; for I am like the young friend of the anecdote—I think Willoughby an unmanly but a very serviceable exposure of myself. (pp. 85-7)

Robert Louis Stevenson, "Books Which Have Influenced Me," in his Essays in the Art of Writing, *Chatto & Windus, 1905, pp. 75-90.*

Hannah Lynch   (essay date 1891)

[*In the following excerpt, Lynch praises the pathos and substance in Meredith's study of egoism and underscores the importance of* The Egoist *as a book that subtly and realistically represents female characters and differences.*]

If *Richard Feverel* was an original and bewildering canter along the highway of fiction, *The Egoist* may be described as a breathless charge into the unknown, a direct and forcible challenge of the unsuspected. Here we see mercilessly unveiled civilized man, as he thinks and feels, in the person of a handsome young squire enjoying every advantage of nature, fortune and birth. Nothing in him courts rejection of our sympathies. He is not a villain, and he is a polished, perfect gentleman, well informed, well mannered, well groomed, and exceedingly well mounted for a more than spirited ride through the plains and over the hills of experience. Such a man as Sir Willoughby Patterne, of Patterne Hall, in command of a rent-roll of £20,000, the ordinary novelist, or even our old friends, the great Immortals, could only conceive as playing a successful and a triumphant part through life. Why, in fact, should punishment and humiliation of the lightest nature pursue a youth in whom no vicious taste, no fixed vice, is pronounced? And who but a dissector so utterly merciless as Mr. Meredith could find courage to drive his dissecting-knife straight to the heart of the conventional system, and qualify the unrevealed disease of this graceful ornament of county society by the ugly name of egoism? the malady of the Ego? Who else but this captain of woman could draw us maidens bold enough to read the man and reject him, in spite of the big social bribes he carries in his hand? Ah, this is Mr. Meredith's great and original note, once he has relieved his youthful soul of the romance of *Richard Feverel.* Woman is his study, especially young militant womanhood, and what a study he has made of her! Upon this theme not a single male writer, living or dead, since Shakespeare, can approach him, and to it he brings modern subtle penetration added to Shakespeare's purely natural instinct. Not only has he caught the bloom and poetry of womanhood, and made her visible to us to the soul—this were the achievement of the poet and the artist of very exquisite perceptions; but he has got at the very root of her nature—quite another thing. Women reading him gasp at his revelations, such as they would never dare to make or dream, so completely hedged round are they by the conventionalities of fiction. When they take to writing stories, they either set themselves limitations in the portrayal of their female characters stricter than their brothers, or to hide their own ignorance of themselves (a mystery for us as much as for men) set off at a galloping pace into the realms of improbability.

In all fiction there is not another girl so enchanting and healthily intelligent as Clara Middleton—none described like her. In addition to the attractions of birth, breeding, and beauty which the writer thoroughly relishes, are those of sensibilities that can be delicate without affectation, a delightful wit untainted by smartness, singular good taste and tact, and honesty of soul. Here is a sparkling young woman as clear as daylight, as fresh as the morning dew, beautiful to look upon, as Meredith's women always are, sweet and bewitching without any shabby tricks of mind or habit, who at the same time thinks for herself, a rare virtue in the male novelist's heroine. She is all warm blood and variable moods, as befits her age and sex, but never once untrue to the finest instincts of maidenhood, and unerring in her judgment. She is not perfect, her accomplishments are not enumerated, we never find her playing Beethoven or reading the stars, and somehow, without one word having been said upon the subject, we get the impression that she is a young woman of intellectual resources, and qualified to pronounce upon subjects that engage the minds of sages and artists, while the music of youth runs blithely through her veins, and her feet are nimble in a race with a schoolboy. It is her struggle with her lover, the Egoist, that completes the interest of the book.

Here we have Mr. Meredith purified, polished, complete, without any break in the unity of his work, or any awkward twist in the even flow of narrative, based solely upon subtle and most delicate analysis. The durability of such work is quite as obvious as that of the best that has already withstood the test of centuries, and when to-day's literature comes to be old-fashioned, *The Egoist* will still hold its place as a lasting monument of psychological diagnosis.

Of the story itself little need be said, as it hangs upon a single situation unfolded in one act after a short prologue introducing us to the chief *dramatis personæ*. And can one possibly hope to explain how this situation is worked and twisted and unfolded—how illuminated and ransacked to its most hidden depths for the undiscovered clue of self, for the unrevealed spring which prompts even our everyday 'yea' or 'nay'? To endeavour to do so would be to undertake a task only second to that of the writing of *The Egoist.* Meredith, I should imagine, would shrink from it. It is simply an analysis of the Ego. The universal Ego takes the polished and affable form of a young English squire, the pink of perfection, and highly commendable to ladies of fastidious tastes, the eye of whose soul is turned ceaselessly upon self. There he walks and sits and talks before our newly-illuminated vision, naked to the soul, each beat of the heart discovered without its protection of flesh or garment; not one single young man whom we meet and part with in fiction, but the large pervading personality of human existence crystallized to one permanent shape—not Sir Willoughby Patterne, of Patterne Hall, but the soul of selfishness endowed with a form that might just as well have been yours or mine or our next-door neighbour's. This is Meredith's most absolute triumph of art, to which he brought all the resources of his scientific knowledge of humanity—his powerful phraseology and marvellous metaphor.

Other writers have drawn us pictures enough of selfish men and selfish women. They abound in the literature of all races, selfishness being one of our commonest defects. But Meredith has given a heart and soul and mind to the vice; in fine raiment and graceful proportions, smiled upon by the undiscerning, he makes it tread the boards of our common experience, with the blood and nerves and muscles of manhood. This is an achievement of which even a man of such singular genius as his may be proud. Other writers are happy when they succeed in drawing a type—in immortalizing a single character; but this one has done something greater, more unique and more imperishable still. Into space he enables us to stare, marvelling, at something hitherto barely suspected, now a tangible form with familiar lineaments and unforgettable tones of voice, a something that we dimly understand rises up with us and lies down with us, gives the stamp of meanness to our best endeavours, and misleads us in our noblest aspirations. Sir Willoughby is the personality of self that floats subtly

round us and centres all our thoughts. It takes a masculine shape because the course of the world, both civilized and barbaric, is directed by the wheels of male selfishness. Feminine selfishness has quite another direction. It affects the domestic circle, the persons and interests immediately within its scope. It may bring added discomfort to the immediate victims, but it leaves the world without merrily indifferent, conscious of superior strength that can always laugh it down, with a vitality that cannot be sapped and a confidence in laws that form a barrier against its encroachments. Not so male egoism. This makes straight for the whole race of women, mercilessly potent by reason of physical force, and backed by all the laws, written and unwritten, of its own making.

It is this crushing exposure of the widespread plague, the extension and mingling of its fibres, the crudity and coarseness of its very refinement and super-fastidiousness, that gives *The Egoist* a scientific as well as an artistic value, and commands for it in English literature a place apart.

As a work of art, it is, indeed, the most complete and perfect thing that Meredith has done—a flawless masterpiece without any of the writer's eccentric deviations and mannerisms. Perhaps oppressively witty, though much less so than *Diana,* striking none but the delicately comic chord, and turning to pathos upon the point of a smiling curl of the lip, it carries us through a few weeks' comedy at a pleasant canter to the accompaniment of fanciful humour and polished irony. If we come upon an occasional odd effect—a queer simile, a bit of isolated poetry lapsed into prose, a bar of pure melody dropped into speech—we recognise with pleasure and delight the author of *Richard Feverel,* and we greet him with a cordial smile. This other writer is new to us, but not the less welcome—less serious, more polished and more fanciful; and while less of a poet, he is more of an artist—less philosophic, he is much more scientific. The play of wit is less sparkling and more penetrative. It shines, a soft luminous light, with undiminished radiance throughout the book, lending itself less easily to quotation, baffling even the memory by the quality of the flying phrases. Upon all subjects of daily life has he something original to say, and he can even be poetical and fresh, and compel our senses to delighted thrills upon the worn-out theme of woman's dress—a theme that wrecks other writers and leaves them dismayed by the dulness and insipidity of their own description. Read those lines in *The Egoist,* upon Clara's dress in a breeze.

The characters, as I have said, are few. Clara, the heroine, described by Vernon Whitford, that scholar and student of equable temper, as 'a mountain echo'—an idea that still lingers with us when we have closed the book as the sum of her sweetness, wholesomeness and natural charm—and by Mrs. Mountstuart less felicitously as 'a dainty rogue in porcelain.' Here we gather an added something of her exterior, and *look* at a mountain echo with the eyes of fashion, just as we see through the same sharp and unimaginative eyes 'the sunken brilliancy of the lean long-walker and scholar in a Phœbus-Apollo turned fasting friar,' and the poetess, Lætitia Dale, upon her vivid stroke, 'coming with a romantic tale upon her eyelashes.' This is one of Meredith's tricks—the uttering of pointed phrases by the tongues of sharp, clever women. Sometimes they are far-fetched; always are they too carefully trimmed and edged, as hasty phrases have not often the felicity of being edged. In general it is the fault of his characters to talk too brilliantly, and he forgets that men and women in their commonplace moods are not habitually metaphorical and literary.

As the essence of self-made man, it may be thought that Sir Willoughby is meant to represent an unpleasant and an unusual type. Not so at all. If it had not been for Meredith, he might have gone tranquilly down to the grave, and not even his worst enemy would have had very obvious cause to scent the wolf within him. We meet him first upon his majority—a very fascinating and fastidious young Englishman whom we gradually understand is the letter 'I' vivified and made human, mentally as well as physically straightened to its erectness, and as uncompromisingly personal. We heedlessly learn of his dallying with Lætitia Dale, of the silent and unexacting worship of this soft rhyming representative of 'starving women who endure their hunger uncomplainingly, and are too proud to offer themselves for the sensational pity of a world ever in demand of dramatic situations. We enjoy a secret satisfaction in his discomfiture when Constantia Durham leaves him in the lurch and runs off with the more cheerful military figure, and yet we still hardly realize what manner of man he is when he in turn plants Lætitia and seeks distraction in three years' travel. Meredith makes us understand that he is a youth of spurious niceness, who objected to his betrothed talking freely about male cousins and friends, and considered the pursuit of competing admirers a stain upon her. Cloistral purity was his demand in the market; woman emerging from an egg-shell, 'somewhat more astonished at things than a chicken . . . and seeing him, with her sex's eyes, first of all men.'

How much we thank Meredith for showing us the 'infinite grossness' of this demand! And how we relish his quiet laughter at Sir Willoughby's loathing of the 'dust of the world' touching the privileged object of his choice. We conclude that Miss Durham was a young person of spirit and sense when she ran off with Captain Oxford, and heartily wish her good luck upon her wedding-tour, while Sir Willoughby abroad is holding an 'English review of his Maker's grotesques.' What a delightful stroke that is against the British tourist! Thackeray never matched it. If you would measure it fully, you have but to stand apart and watch the faces and listen to the criticisms of our fellow-countrymen abroad. Everything that is not British is grotesque.

As the Creator is just as responsible for foreign countries and foreign races as for Great Britain, these criticisms, as Meredith wittily points out, comprise a review of His grotesques. It is in such light and inimitable pen-strokes, to be found on every page, that he shows us the man made bare to the very heart. All his social virtues are ruthlessly traced to the meanest source: his wish for cloistral purity in woman, his regarding the presence of competing admiration as a soil, to its true Oriental origin, the monster egoism of his prayer that even beyond death his bride should be his alone, and of his desire to shape her character to the feminine of his own, without any consideration for her natural and healthy preference to be herself. All young men who think it part of the poetry of love to wish to see the unhappy maiden of their choice reduced to ashes or incense, and transmuted by love until they literally become 'the man they are to marry,' cannot do better than study the Egoist, and see for themselves the manner of man they are. The study will fill them with a sense of horror of themselves and of the accepted notion of the infinity of love which Clara, listening gravely, conceived as 'a narrow dwelling where a voice droned and ceased not.' In her sharp apprenticeship as the betrothed of this amiable young squire she learned to become an attentive listener. Little else was expected of her. But it was the destiny of this intelligent and impulsive girl to give Sir Willoughby many a rude lesson in the sex she represented, that left Constantia's elopement and free talk of male cousins and friends in the shade as minor offences against taste and cloistral reserve. After the preliminary descriptive pages, the book is completely given up to Clara's struggle for freedom and her lover's desperate efforts to retain her, fearful of ridicule and the ignominy of a second jilting. She rashly compromises herself with a brilliant Irishman, while unconsciously her heart is given to the Phœbus Apollo turned fasting friar to whom Sir Willoughby, meditating revenge, intends to hand her over upon granting her the freedom she claims, rejoicing privately in the fact that his own choice had irredeemably spotted her for another. There is something pathetic in the poor Egoist's delusion, and while we heartily despise him, we are against our judgment forced to pity him when in the strife his true character is exposed even to his life-long silent worshipper, Lætitia, and we see the unhappy gentleman upon his knees to that discarded devotee imploring her to marry him, so that the county should not say that he had been despised and rejected by three women, one of them poor and his inferior. His misfortune and abasement are contemptible in their cause, and contemptibly borne, nevertheless the something in us which responds to this terrible monster within him begets the pity of brotherhood. Degraded, shrunken, stripped of the glory of success, we see in him a monstrous image of ourselves, of all mankind, so that we are afraid to turn from him and wring hands with the wretch in a kind of shamed sympathy. We readily admit the pure comedy of this sublime absurdity in human form reduced to such shabby dimensions and exposed for the ridicule of posterity, but we cannot laugh very joyously at the exposure. There is too much truth in it for the comic muse, and the pathos is too apparent. (pp. 118-35)

Hannah Lynch, in her George Meredith: A Study, *Methuen & Co., 1891, 170 p.*

Richard Le Gallienne   (essay date 1905)

[Le Gallienne was an English poet, essayist, and novelist who was associated during the 1890s with the Decadent movement of that period. In the following excerpt, he reviews the way in which character, chance, and comedy contribute to the plot and "perfection" of The Egoist.*]*

[The] plot of **The Egoist** grows as the outcome of character, instead of being manipulated according to the will and pleasure of the novelist. The novelist watches and records, but never interferes. It is, of course, the difference between men and women and "wooden puppetry." "The catastrophe" comes "pat" as a mathematical result, and one has the satisfaction of that complete artistic whole, which, I should say, is, generally speaking, more within the reach of so-called "subjective" than of "objective" drama. This question of plot is indeed an easier one to settle in the case of the former than of the latter, what happens *in* a man is less a question for the arbitrary invention of the novelist than what happens *to* him; and I think this is felt when one comes to compare the ending of **The Egoist** with the ending of **Richard Feverel** or **Beauchamp's Career.** There is an element admitted into the working out of the two latter stories, which, of course, is operative in the subjective world as well, but hardly as constantly or as volcanically—that of Chance. That it is no unimportant element of life we know, but how and when it is to be introduced into art is the question, one which is as old as it seems unanswerable. Our modern method of dealing with it would seem to be, that the particular chances to which the *dramatis personœ* are subjected shall be such as are not unlikely to arise out of their characters. Then, of course, there are various degrees of chances in our lives, some so frequent as to be usual and unsurprising . . . and such are not, therefore, disturbances in art. But to be struck by lightning on the way home to dinner is another degree of chance, no less unusual than disagreeable. That Beauchamp should die by drowning as he did was, of course, quite a possibility in the case of a man so unselfish and intrepid, but in spite of the fine note of tragic irony such as is life's own so struck, one feels no such inevitability about his end as comes with the last chapter of **The Egoist.** It does not seem of the same colour with the rest of the book, but merely a wilful darkening of the woof. Beauchamp might have been so drowned on his way home to wife and happiness, but the chances were a thousand to one against it.

In **Richard Feverel** we are confronted with a similar perplexity, and though I doubt if, to set matters right, it would now be any one's choice to lose a scene drawn with such vividness of power as that of Richard's terrible parting from his wife, yet as a part of a whole, I, for one, cannot feel it homogeneous. If one could have been prepared for these catastrophes by some manner of undefined foreshadowing, they might very likely have impressed one as fit; and, if it be retorted that life gives no such warnings, one can only answer that, after all, Art is but a compromise.

Mr. Meredith names **The Egoist** a "comedy in narrative," but in doing so he uses the word comedy with a significance which is rarely respected, and of which it will be necessary to speak further in the next chapter. Suffice it here to say that mere satire, humour, or any species of fun-making, are all very distinct from, however related to, that significance. These but result from the working of the comic spirit which in itself is merely a detective force; they are, of course, included in this present comedy, but they are far from all. When one comes to consider Sir Willoughby one realises how far. He is Mr. Meredith's great

Drawing of Meredith by the Pre-Raphaelite painter Dante Gabriel Rossetti.

study in that Comic Muse which he invokes in his first chapter, and yet he hardly keeps the table on a roar. At least, laughter is not the only emotion he excites; tears and terror rainbowed by laughter might figure our complicated impression. A tragic figure discovered for us through the eye of comedy. It is certainly comic, in the customary sense, to see that great-mannered sublimity, that ultra-refined sentimentalism reduced to paradox by the exposure of its springs; but the laugh is only at the inconsistency, it can hardly face the fact. And to see Sir Willoughby on his knees vainly imploring that Laetitia, who has all through served but as an "old-lace" foil for Clara, and with utter difficulty at last winning her, not for her sake either, but for fear of the world, the east wind of the world, and no longer the worshipful Juggernaut Laetitia of old, but Laetitia enlightened and unloving,—all this is comic of course; to see tables turned is always comic, but we must not forget that life is before them, and, as Hazlitt says, "When the curtain next goes up it will be tragedy"— if the situation on which it falls can be called anything else.

Sir Willoughby indeed inspires that greatest laughter which has its springs in the warmth and the richness of tears. If he is Mr. Meredith's greatest comic study, he is, at the same time, his most pathetic figure. Of course, his pathos is not of the drawing-room ballad order, any more, indeed, than his comedy would "select" for a "library of humour"—those fields are full, Mr. Meredith rarely strives there, possibly for the same reason that Landor strove not. But those for whom he has any appeal must feel with his creator that "he who would desire to clothe himself at everybody's expense, and is of that desire condemned to strip himself stark naked, he, if pathos ever had a form, might be taken for the living person. Only he is not allowed to run at you, roll you over and squeeze your body for the briny drops. There is the innovation." The pathos, as everything else in the book, is *essential*. That is, of course, why *The Egoist* is so pre-eminently Mr. Meredith's typical book, and Sir Willoughby his typical characterisation; and there could hardly be a more victorious justification of a method. One great wonder, that before reading might well have been a great fear, is that, despite the endless dissection of Sir Willoughby, the revelation of every "petty artery" and tissue, he still keeps his outline and remains whole and living to our eyes, when he might so easily have resulted in an anatomical diagram, where one cannot grasp the whole for the parts, and the human form disappears beneath nets of veinwork and muscle. If it were otherwise, it would be impossible to understand how such a monster could be tolerated in any society, but as it is, while we have the fullest knowledge of his ghastly inner constitution, we are yet able to see him as those about him did; the courtly gentleman, generous to, if a little exacting from his dependents, with many charms that might well keep that something twisted in him, the existence of which he himself suspected as little as any one, from exposure, save under stress of the very closest relations.

Besides his primary importance as one more great addition to Art's "men and women," Sir Willoughby has another significance as a satire on masculinity; he is the type of it, "the original male in giant form"; and though a world-wide type, especially does he stand for the British male, at once, perhaps, the finest, and certainly the most obnoxious representative of his sex. His silly airs of omnipotence, his dull-eyed numb conceit, his ridiculous solemnities, his boorish exclusiveness, his spurious niceties and sham moralities, his utter fundamental earthiness and vulgarity and all the various too-well-known characteristics that rear an ass's head upon the paws and haunches of the national lion; these that it is to be feared satirists will continue to satirise without sending a ray of awakening into his dull self-satisfied head, these Mr. Meredith has satirised with a laughter that surely would reach the ears of the creature, if they were but as sensitive as they are long. In all his books Mr. Meredith has amused himself with this ridiculous John Bull, whose good qualities, let us not forget, he can embody with no less vigour; but not even in *Diana,* where he strikes so manfully for womanhood against that masculinity incarnate, the British Bench, has he dealt him such a blow.

Of the other characterisations in the book, each so firm and living, of the dialogue that made James Thomson exclaim upon it as the greatest ever written in the English tongue, of the wit and the poetry of style, of these space forbids writing here, though I hope to refer to them, in a general way, later on. One perfection, however, should be here noted, the artistic unity of the whole book; an unity which perhaps no other of Mr. Meredith's books, except *Rhoda Fleming,* achieves, though probably in the opinion

of most *Diana* would be a third. But, speaking for myself, and much as I cherish *Diana,* the conclusion somehow troubles me. I cannot read it without incongruous reminiscence of the last line in *The Angel in the House.* **The Egoist,** however, excites no such feelings, the colours all blend, and the "composition" is perfect. Dramatic grouping so fit, action so organic, and, as I have said, a *dénoûment* so related, is surely a high bid for perfection in the novelist's art. (pp. 29-36)

Richard Le Gallienne, " 'The Egoist,' 'Richard Feverel,' and the Novels Generally," in his George Meredith: Some Characteristics, *revised edition, John Lane, 1905, pp. 14-49.*

Orlo Williams   (essay date 1926)

[*In the following excerpt, Williams analyzes the characters, style, theme, and structure of* The Egoist *in order to assert that the stylistic excesses and philosophic complexity of the novel result from Meredith's understanding of the narrator as artist and moralist.*]

Some critics of to-day would, I believe, register scorn on hearing that any novel of George Meredith's could be reckoned under the head of enchantment, and one might go so far with them as to admit that the effect which Meredith counted upon issuing from the stroke of Comedy was something more robust and intellectual; but scorn for George Meredith's work in general only rebounds upon the scornful. The literary fortunes of such a writer are bound to vary with successive currents of taste and opinion, but that they will ever approach bankruptcy is certainly not to be thought of.

To his readers of any particular moment, whether they be few or many, Meredith's reputation may safely be left. He demands of them education, the faculty of steady reflection, an interest in ideas rather than incidents and a somewhat abnormal promptitude in following metaphor. He gives them a great deal in return. If it be true that the psychological effect of great art is the organisation of good impulses in the percipient, then Meredith's art is great, for the impulses which it organises are those of liberty, enthusiasm, healthy-mindedness, alertness, self-discipline and wise laughter at folly. He was a penetrating reader of human motives and a keen critic of outworn dogmas. Tyranny, pedantry and sloth of mind or body were abhorrent to him, and it was to lashing these and encouraging their opposites that he united his analytical power and his poetic vision. In the name of Comedy he was a moralist, but he gave his morals the form of art. Many of the causes for which he fought have triumphed since his day: in fact, the state of society which excited his irony is as extinct as the Austrian domination of Italy. Yet the art remains, with its shining virtues and its obvious defects—the art of *Vittoria* no less than that of *The Ordeal of Richard Feverel, Evan Harrington, Harry Richmond, Diana of the Crossways, Beauchamp's Career* and *The Egoist.*

His defects may repel, but there is surely enough in this list—of his major works alone—to outweigh, if not to cancel, any just repulsion. His frequent over-emphasis and boisterous flights of a peculiar fancy, his exaggerated dislike for the obvious and the trite, his faulty ear for the cadences of English prose, an occasional grossness or want of fine taste, and a technique in dialogue which produces an effect of unreality, even, sometimes, of absurdity—these are the main heads of legitimate blame. We need not blink them, if we remember that George Meredith, like Carlyle, like Charles Lamb and—one might truly say—like Shakespeare, was so compounded as necessarily to be a mannerist. His mental progresses were abnormal, to an extent of which he, of course, was quite unconscious. He did not willingly torture our English tongue, nor deliberately intend to daze our minds with fantasias of elliptical imagery and irritate us with that somewhat garish verbal repartee which figured for him as "wit," preferably Celtic. The very gifts which gave him originality and an individual coign of critical vantage made him also, at times, volcanically obscure, bombastic and difficult of comprehension. However much we may regret his projection of his peculiar self into his work, it is of little use to protest against it or state it as a flat condemnation. It was inevitable. Moreover, if Meredith's prose is often involved, difficult and inharmonious, his thought is not obscure. A little patience will always find the thread, which is never trivial nor unworthy. But he was a rhapsodist as well as a thinker, and one must hear and see the rhapsodist. The face and the voice of George Meredith, if we had known them, would have made many a rough place smooth.

I may, perhaps, confess a personal preference for *The Egoist* without defending my preference in detail. A general vote would place it high, in any case. In one of his letters Meredith said that it contained but half himself and that his friend would like *The Amazing Marriage* better. His meaning is clear. In *The Egoist* he suppressed, or tried to suppress, the rhapsodist, the gargantuan humours, the imaginative acrobatics. He used the eagle's eye but pinioned its wings. He constrained himself, like his Muse of Comedy handling the great Book of Earth, to "condense whole sections in a sentence and volumes in a character": he focussed his gaze upon a narrow scene and a short span of time. His concentration was not in vain: it gave firmness to his construction, ease to his narrative, brilliance to his portraiture and finality to his argument. Perhaps that is why *The Egoist* lasts so well, in spite of its faded Victorian setting. The tophats and strapped trousers, the shawls and veils and ample skirts, the heavy dinner-parties, the riding hacks, the barouches, the secluded park-existence have passed away; men have no rights, women no reticences, and both sexes, having no taste for elegant verbal fence amid suave avenues, frankly pound one another with hard-hit tennis balls. The circumstances that compounded a Willoughby Patterne are already legendary, and he himself appears almost as preposterous as a Polynesian image in a museum, yet the essential comedy remains to engage our emotions as freshly as ever, because Meredith has made Willoughby's self-delusions and discomfitures the symbol of that eternal comedy which is played by the dominating impulses of man. *The Egoist* has a lasting effect upon an intelligent reader, stimulating new emotions, arousing recognitions, untangling confusions in his mind and thus working in him a change which may outlive any particular memories of it. This is the unfailing quality of art upon high levels.

The story of *The Egoist* is a very simple one in outline. Sir Willoughby Patterne, a young baronet, wealthy, handsome, witty, who has grown up amid the effusive adulation of his county, is concerned to find a wife and mistress of Patterne Hall. He had been jilted once by a girl, who had fled from his too dominating embraces straight into the arms of another husband. He himself had jilted Laetitia Dale, his constant adorer, who still lived and still adored under her invalid father's roof, which was in the park of Patterne. These are preliminaries. The real action opens with the capture by Sir Willoughby from among many admirers of the young, beautiful and spirited Clara Middleton, daughter of a pedantic old scholar. Clara has begged for six months' grace before marriage, but has consented to a solemn plighting of troth. She and Dr. Middleton come to spend three weeks before the wedding at Patterne Hall. In all the circumstances that minister to Sir Willoughby's intense self-love Clara sees the glamour which had won her fall off and reveal a distasteful tyrant. She is resolved to escape, but finds the tenacity of Sir Willoughby overpowering. Her desperate efforts only succeed when they have driven him, in his acute fear of wounds to his vanity from the world's derision, to indulge in double-dealing, which a chance discovers. Sir Willoughby's plan, when he found the rebel incorrigible, had been to marry his adoring Laetitia after all, and practically to force Clara upon his cousin and secretary, the scholar Vernon Whitford. What happens is that he is compelled to release Clara unconditionally, but to sue on his knees for a new Laetitia who has learned to see him as he is, and who lashes him painfully with her opinion of him before she consents to become, without love, his wife and helper. Clara and Vernon Whitford, who had unconsciously become lovers, pair off with their creator's blessing as two who have nobly come through their ordeal.

This theme of a young girl, entrapped in her ignorance into an engagement which she soon finds repulsive and forced into desperate flounderings to regain her liberty, has nothing surprising or uncommon about it. Any novelist might adopt it, and we can almost imagine how a given novelist would treat it. Thackeray's drama, for instance, would have been one of innocence escaping from corruption, with Clara as the lovely, honest and rather stupid dove, Sir Willoughby as the brilliant falcon with a slight odour of disreputability holding his victim in his claws amid the sniggers of worldly and corrupt society, and Vernon Whitford as the lowly and steadfast lover of romance, whose flame is ignored by his mistress till the day of deliverance. Henry James, again, would have been tempted to make Clara an American damsel, some bright-souled but ignorant Milly from New England, who had yielded her hand in an ardour of enthusiasm for the Old World, mysterious, enchanting, the scene of legend and romance, of venerable beauty, state and ceremony. She would have plighted herself simply and modestly yet with secret passion in what Henry James called the "American Scene," against which the figure of Sir Willoughby, sauve and debonair, would have stood out as a deliverer rescuing a parched maiden from a desolation of mere modernity. She would have come to Patterne Hall under the wing, not of a pedant father, but of a rigid and less impressionable aunt or confidant, to find that Europe held poison in its powerful spell. Gradually, punctuated by agonising debates and hesitations, the truth would be driven into her unsullied heart that underneath all the inexpressible loveliness of ancient towers, smiling parks, exquisite villages, deference, courtliness and perfect social amenity there was something rotten and miasmic to which the natives were accustomed, but against which she, bright, simple Milly, had not been inoculated. She would be like a fly caught in a web—a web which Henry James's imagination could weave with extraordinary mastery. Every morning would bring her against some fresh bewilderment, some moral assumption or some supple action which, in her light of the New World, could only appear doubtful and degrading. And then at last she would fly, with a lovely resignation, back to her less complicated home, another victim to the unhealthy fascination of ancient Europe. And it would have been through the eye of Vernon Whitford, an American anglicised and toughened like Henry James himself, that he might have projected the whole drama, with infinite and protracted sympathy for both points of view, and with a tendency to suggest the moral that Patterne's magnificent ease and splendour only just compensated for its want of Milly's honest simplicity. It would have been left vague whether Vernon, having seen Milly off at Southampton, remained unrepentant in Kundry's garden, or, issuing unostentatiously by the back-door, returned himself, after a decent interval, to be purified and marry Milly-Clara in the bright New England air.

Anybody can translate the theme of *The Egoist* into other guises ranging from the purely romantic to the most recent psychoanalytical, and it will not be entirely a waste of ingenuity to do so if, in the light of the process, George Meredith's own treatment of his theme is thrown into relief. The clash between Clara and Sir Willoughby, as he sees it, is certainly not one of mere sentiment, nor a conflict between mere goodness and badness picturesquely staged to excite emotion. Clara is not an angel and Sir Willoughby is anything but a villain: indeed, Meredith is at pains to display his hero as a thoroughly admirable person when judged by common worldly standards, and at no less pains to admit, while excusing, the danger that a girl of Clara's temperament, "not pure of nature" but "pure of will," may overstep the bounds of delicacy in desperate situations. On the other hand, it is not purely the situation—what Henry James called the "case"—which interested Meredith: he did not concentrate all his imagination and enthusiasm on heightening by cunning suggestion and constructive artifice the opposition between what Clara and what Sir Willoughby respectively "stood for," just to leave it there for the spectator's benefit as a work of art triumphantly "done." He was not the artist alone, but moralist and judge as well. He was profoundly concerned with the issue, since he had stated the case as an example: he analysed and condemned the human motives and social practices which caused the crime before devising a punishment to fit it. He treated his material with the touch of an artist, but he chose it with the eye of a philosopher.

In Meredith's novels it is the artist who constructs, paints and occasionally embroiders, but it is the moralist who meditates and directs: and the moralist, like Dr. Middleton in a happy mood, not seldom overpowers his compan-

ion. The blend of these two impulses, if not always perfect in practice, was Meredith's ideal and his peculiar virtue as a novelist. In his brilliant prelude to *The Egoist,* as in his longer *Essay on Comedy,* he personified this ideal in the Comic Spirit, the corrector of pretentiousness, dulness, and rawness, "the ultimate civiliser, the polisher, a sweet cook." Meredith's comedy is no libidinous spirit of La Dive Bouteille, much less an airily tripping Good-Humoured Lady, laughing unconcernedly over the confusion of a company of masks. She is something of a governess; she wields a birch rod; she insists upon the laughter of reason; she illuminates and epitomises the biggest book on earth, the Book of Egoism. Her spectacles and her rod instil some portentousness into her laughter, yet we would not have her otherwise. She is real, she is unique, and she has all the merits with which Meredith endowed her. Of this all his work is proof, but *The Egoist* above all.

> The Egoist surely inspires pity. He who would desire to clothe himself at everybody's expense, and is of that desire condemned to strip himself stark naked, he, if pathos ever had a form, might be taken for the actual person. . . .
>
> You may as well know him out of hand, as a gentleman of our time and country, of wealth and station; a not flexile figure, do what we may with him. . . .
>
> Aforetime a grand old Egoism built the House. It would appear that ever finer essences of it are demanded to sustain the structure; but especially it would appear that a reversion to the gross original, beneath a mask and in a vein of fineness, is an earthquake at the foundations of the House.

These passages from the last page of the Prelude give the essence of the case as Meredith stated it. His misdemeanant is not the egoist in general, but an egoist whom the refinement of civilisation should have purged of his grossness. He indicts his Sir Willoughby, an outwardly exquisite production of breeding, education and fortune, for relapsing into the state of cave-primitiveness in his behaviour to women. Moreover, as a radical patriot, he is moved to tilt at the conditions of country-gentlemanhood, as being the hotbed of a retrograde and unworthy self-love, of stiff-necked conservatism, pompousness and injustice. He pictures the gentleman as beset by imps, ready to plague him into an antic dance on the first outbreak of his almost inevitable folly. The dance which his imps led Sir Willoughby is the gist of his novel, and it gains its power from the fact that in Sir Willoughby's capers, remorselessly described, each of us recognises some figures in the particular tarantella to which his own vanity is prone to sting him.

Meredith presents his story as a satirical comedy of society, which was to be swift and lucid, full of brilliant dialogue and rich in dramatic surprises. Throughout the book, from his boisterous fantasia on Mrs. Mountstuart Jenkinson's remark that Willoughby had "a leg" to the scene at the end where a drawing-roomful of characters is held for inordinate length at cross purposes, one continually catches him figuratively rubbing his hands at his enthusiastic view of the coruscation which he fanned with an endearing but irritating assiduity. (pp. 84-97)

It must be put down as a weakness of Meredith's that he was apt to get more fun out of his comic characters than he managed to give his readers; and in *The Egoist,* in spite of touches which are truly comic, we must write down most of Dr. Middleton, the pedantic bear, timorous of women and fond of port, Dr. Corney, another purveyor of Celtic wit, the impossible conversation at luncheon where Lady Culmer and Lady Busshe are mystified by de Craye and the final delirium in the drawing-room round poor, dazed Mr. Dale, on the side of this weakness. These are not Comedy but a kind of elevated buffoonery, which is out of tune. Mrs. Mountstuart Jenkinson would have hit the mark if she had said of her creator, "he has an uncertain ear." Capable of exquisite beauty and true wit, Meredith too often fell short of both by striving too mightily for them, like the tenor in Balzac's story, who, in a supreme effort to surpass his own art for his mistress's ear, made, in effect, the most painful noises.

Nevertheless, when these lapses and overinsistences are eliminated, there remains a residue that may worthily be called High Comedy. The preparation for the main action—apart from the leg-fantasia—is swift and pointed. Willoughby is admirably introduced, and the episode of Constantia, and of Willoughby's wooing of Laetitia on the rebound, but only to jilt her, are presented to us with a light hand and easy mastery. The essentials of Willoughby, though a trifle over-satirised, are in our minds before Clara arrives on the scene. We see him pampered and selfish, capable of brutal rudeness to a kinsman, painfully sensitive to the world's tongue, and obstinately retentive of a woman's heart, Laetitia's, which he insists on holding without paying for it. The account in the fourth chapter of Willoughby's voyage and of his ecstatic greetings to Laetitia on return, with the final picture of a constant woman, disappointed but adoring, is one of the most effective passages that Meredith ever wrote. (pp. 99-100)

Yes, there is Comedy enough in *The Egoist,* both in its conception and execution; there is much happy—as well as unhappy—dialogue, notably that of Clara with Laetitia and with Vernon; there is a light grace of youth in Crossjay and even poetry in the description of Clara advancing over the lawn, "a sight to set the woodland dancing, and turn the heads of the town." Yet, if Comedy were all, one would have to say it was Comedy got singularly out of hand and flouting all the canons of comic proportion.

Fifty chapters is a long run for a Comic Spirit which "conceives a definite situation for a number of characters, and rejects all accessories in the exclusive pursuit of them, and their speech." There are two audiences to every dramatic presentation, the fictitious audience of the characters themselves and the real audience of the spectators or readers. Meredith, with his ebullient imagination and his passionately communicative mind, could never peg himself down to that economy which ensures that the amount of explanation sufficient to prime the fictitious audience with its necessary intelligence of the action shall also be sufficient for the real audience. Being a philosopher and a moralist, his eye was fixed upon his real audience, whom he

suspected, not without some reason, of having an intelligence and a power of seizing illuminating connections of ideas far below his own. He felt himself bound to enlighten them, like the *conférencier* in a *revue,* with comments on the inner meaning of the passing show and disquisitions upon human nature, as exemplified in his drama. That is why the skirts of his Comedy are so voluminous; he puffs them out continually with the wind of his own spirit.

These philosophical or analytical interpolations are the things which, above all, give Meredith's novels their particular character. Not to appreciate them is not to appreciate Meredith, for they are the essential distillations of his mind; and though they hamper the dash and velocity with which, in his intention, the action should have been endowed, they enrich immeasurably the content of the whole work, giving it massiveness, durability and a hold upon the higher regions of the mind. *The Egoist* would be only a pale ghost of itself without these typical contributions from its author, and there are few of them that we could wish away. Who, for instance, would willingly expunge the wisdom with which the classic fourteenth chapter— "Sir Willoughby and Laetitia"—opens? "In the hundred and fourth chapter of the thirteenth volume of the Book of Egoism it is written: Possession without obligation to the object possessed approaches felicity." The brilliant enlargement upon this text, which reveals at once the acuteness and amplitude of Meredith's vision, is both an admirable piece of philosophy in itself and a good preparation for the ensuing dialogue. Chapter XXIII, again, calls a protracted halt, but not a halt without profit. The disquisition upon the human delusion that good fruit will come of the union of temper and policy, and the penetrating analysis of Willoughby's form of the delusion, if it is an excrescence upon pure form, is exhilaratingly shrewd. In how many injured minds is not Willoughby's day-dream of magnanimous triumph over a discomfited and too late repentant Clara most accurately repeated? And who has more eloquently chastised his sex's weakness than Meredith in the concluding pages of this chapter, with his picture of Willoughby "flaming verdigris" and his rebuke to primitive masculinity? "Women have us back to the conditions of primitive man, or they shoot us higher than the top-most star. But it is as we please. . . . They are to us what we hold of best or worst within. By their state is our civilisation judged: and if it is hugely animal still, that is because primitive men abound and will have their pasture." A similar long halt is called at the thirty-ninth chapter—"In the Heart of the Egoist"—which is a notable sermon on egoism full of arrows that fly to the conscience of every man. It shows Willoughby, in an agony of self-pity, deciding that Clara must be given up and planning with a dark diplomacy how she shall be so given up as to appear discarded; and, in parenthesis, Meredith reflects upon primitive man and society in striking metaphors which do not conceal his unerring intelligence, pointing to primitive man as the prime egoist and presenting Willoughby as the socialised development of this elementary being, who has discovered a "greater realm than that of the sensual appetites."

"He slew imagination"—what a lightning stroke, and how it hits each man of us! Who can lay his hand on his heart and say that, in converse with a woman, he has never "dragged her through the labyrinths of his penetralia" and wilfully, insistently, slain imagination?

There are other and slighter passages of this kind in *The Egoist* which hold the quintessence of Meredithianism. The reader knows them or can find them for himself. It is to be noted that they are not sheer digressions in Sterne's Shandean manner, but, though they may include some moralisation in general, they are in the main an illumination of character, especially of the leading character, Willoughby and Clara.

And this consideration leads us to a closer view of those two characters, as Meredith so fully presented them to us. Nobody, of course, can read *The Egoist* without experiencing a deep and lasting impression of Willoughby and Clara. They are types which we know to be true, and peculiarly English, in essentials, if not in every detail. So vivid, indeed, are both of them that many a reader, by a natural process of mind, is drawn to think of them as real, to estimate their characters and react emotionally to their vicissitudes as if they were historical personages or his own acquaintances. These estimates and these reactions are coloured by the reader's own personality, for it is by ourselves, and not by impersonal standards, that we judge all people, especially our friends and our enemies. We cannot help ourselves in this respect, and the novelist encourages us; for it is an unsuccessful narrator who does not stimulate his hearers to adopt these personal and emotional attitudes towards the figments of his brain. His success is the quality which we call vividness. Yet, after all, this vividness, in a novel, is the creation of one mind and not life itself; and therefore the greater the vividness of the characters, the more interesting it is, if possible, to hold our personal reactions in abeyance for a moment and to observe exactly how and with what intention, with what felicities and what inconsistencies, our novelist has presented them. It is a task for second or third reading, and often attended with surprises, convicting us not seldom of inattention and unfounded prejudice. Such an observation of those interesting characters, Sir Willoughby Patterne, Clara Middleton and Laetitia Dale, could only be elaborated in writing at unpardonable length: but one or two notes may, perhaps, be attempted as instances of these observations—let us not call them analysis, which is an ugly word, savouring of coldness, chemistry, and glamour dissipated. Truly they are not dissections of dead bones but researches into the secrets of intense life.

Meredith presented his leading characters in two ways—from the outside, by recounting their speech and actions, and from the inside by placing us, he playing Virgil to our Dante, inside the tortuous passages of their minds, to observe at length the thoughts and passions and fancies working within them. His minor characters are presented from the outside only; and it is an interesting, though rather baffling, light upon Vernon Whitford that Meredith hardly ever takes us inside his mind, and then but briefly. If this is why Vernon seems an oddly flat and angular character, one wonders why Meredith so presented Clara's successful lover. Yet the effect is undeniable: the shy, awkward, intellectual, scrupulously honest scholar,

singularly obtuse to a woman's meaning and distrustful of emotion, is wonderfully vivid seen in his two dimensions against the full three dimensions of Willoughby and the two ladies. Of Willoughby and Clara, however, is it not true that, whereas the external presentation of the former—a necessarily satirical presentation—is exaggerated even to absurdity while the internal presentation is profound and convincing, with the latter it is just the reverse? Meredith's Clara, as seen and heard, wins every heart, but when he takes us into her mind, our mentor becomes overpowering, for so impressed is he with the confusion of a young and spirited girl's thoughts that he must make the confusion worse by his flood of metaphors.

Willoughby has often been thought preposterous; and so he is, if you only regard his conversation. Meredith wished to present him as a man of brilliant gifts and impressive personality, as one not unworthy of the neighbourhood's admiration; yet if you read aloud the speeches put into his mouth from the very beginning, it is impossible to give them an intonation which makes them seem other than comic. They are the speeches of a "character" part, of an intolerably pompous and stilted fellow whose absurdity no Mrs. Mountstuart Jenkinson would have missed for an instant. Hear him when he greets Laetitia after his return from a long voyage.

> He sprang to the ground and seized her hand. "Laetitia Dale!" he said. He panted. "Your name is sweet English music! And you are well?" The anxious question permitted him to read deeply in her eyes. He found the man he sought there, squeezed him passionately, and let her go. . . .

These few lines epitomise the whole contrast between the two presentations of Willoughby. By his words he stamps himself an affected nincompoop; and then follows the thrust of Meredith's true wit. "He found the man he sought there, squeezed him passionately, and let her go." It is the biting presentation of the inner Willoughby, of masculine egoism dramatised, which makes him an individual work of art, ever living, ever true. One could follow this contrast in detail throughout the book; it is the contrast between the work of an imperfect ear and an unerring mind. When the external Willoughby is before us we sympathise with Clara far more than Meredith intended, for who, on reading any of his dialogues with Clara—such a speech, for instance, as that beginning: "Whenever the little brain is in doubt, perplexed, undecided which course to adopt, she will come to me, will she not? I shall always listen,"—does not find his heart charged, like Sir Toby's when observing Malvolio's posturings, with opprobrious expletives? Yet, no sooner is the glass turned inwards than Willoughby takes on another stature. He no longer "has a leg," but becomes an embodiment of human passions and disquietudes. As we see him, say, in Chapter XXIX, restlessly pacing his chamber in first astonished presentiment that things are mysteriously going against him, or at the end of Chapter XXXI suddenly complacent at having drawn tears from Laetitia, or at the close of Chapter XXXVII—a wonderful passage—deliberately creating a beautiful image of the faded Laetitia to satisfy his vanity, Willoughby swells to heroic proportions. Without recognising these proportions we cannot estimate Meredith's creation truly, for only by submitting ourselves to its element of poetic greatness can we justly criticise its imperfections.

Clara Middleton is one of that bevy of enchanting young women in the creation of whom Meredith expressed his ardent but, from modern standpoints, moderate feminism. His mastery in presenting these characters has been justly praised, and there is no need to enlarge upon the brilliance, the virginal freshness, the seductiveness and the generous burning spirit with which he has endowed Clara. The effect of her physical beauty, perfectly apparent, is more striking for the absence of fleshliness: the agony of her situation is all the sharper for the rigid exclusion of pathos. (pp. 103-12)

But in the internal presentation of Clara, acutely penetrating though it is, we hear too strongly the accents of Meredith, which drowned the confused murmurs of a perplexed girl's heart. Meredith's feminism was of the kind which demanded for women, not so much liberty of action as liberty of mind and will; and in his great women heroines it is the treasures and high qualities of their spirit which he displays and insists on. In *The Egoist,* when he envisages the possibility of a real fugue on Clara's part, with de Craye or any other man, he becomes quite anxious and apologetic on her behalf; while in supporting the claims to self-determination of her swift and vigorous spirit he is a bold and scornful challenger of repressive, masculine "Turkishness."

His difficulty, as a novelist, however, is always how to photograph in words the workings of a woman's mind. He cannot do it, in fact: he comprehends, but cannot reproduce, and has therefore to fall back upon the reasonings and images of his own man's mind as his only means of expressing the directly inexpressible. Chapter XXI of *The Egoist,* entitled "Clara's Meditations," is a good example of this insufficiency. Dr. Middleton, under the influence of old port, has gone back on his promise to take her away, and she is tossing in sleepless fury at the disappointment, and giving a free rein to her passionate desire to escape somehow, anyhow, from the toils in which she is caught. Meredith's method of describing her thoughts, half narrative, half a vicarious introspection, is not happy: we understand, but the voice of the novelist, wrestling in rhetoric and metaphor, comes between us and Clara. At the time when Clara, alone in her bed, is being simple, naïve, elemental, Meredith, with an air of having drawn the bedcurtains, yet of peeping in, now and then, to note characteristic movements, orates with brilliance and complication on the hearthrug. A woman in the toils was his darling theme, and he invariably adorned it with acutest observations, but not invariably with dramatic power or vivid characterisation. He is best, then, when he is frankly moralising, and his Clara for the moment no more than a philosophic instance, as here, when the question whether other men were like Willoughby shoots through Clara's mind. (pp. 114-16)

Were these notes not already too long, much might be said of Laetitia Dale. As a perfectly finished and never exaggerated character she is, perhaps, better than any. More than any other she keeps the Comedy at its high level, when the overdone pomposities of Willoughby or the fizzling fireworks of de Craye threaten to let it down. And no incident is more dramatic than the change in her view of Willoughby which began when he "fluted exceedingly" to her at midnight in the drawing-room—a delicious scene—and culminated in her remorseless flaying of him in the presence of his protesting aunts. Meredith did not always find the just intonation for his delicate yet spirited perception of true Comedy, but the character of Laetitia Dale proves that he could do so on occasion, and then triumphantly. Also, a complete account of Meredith's feminism would need to include some observations upon Laetitia, for his view of her as a fading flower, cheated unfairly of her gatherer, points to its limitations. There was a remarkable absence of nambi-pambiness in Meredith's idealism, and he would never have hesitated to offend the extremer champions. When he pointed out to his own generation that its attitude to women was an outrage to Nature, he meant Nature and not an ideological abstraction; and he grieves, rather than exults, that in the solitude of a Laetitia and a Diana, Nature was, in some measure, thwarted. There was a solid robustness at the bottom of Meredith which kept him from ever "fluting exceedingly," for all his exuberance, or from posturing, like Sir Willoughby as the "gauntleted Knight attempting the briny handkerchief." Indeed, it is curious that in Meredith the airy balloonings of the wit among dullards, of the Celt prodding Saxons and of the Radical twitting Tory backwardness are firmly anchored to the earth by a sheer dead-weight of English yeoman common-sense. He could toss it about, as he tossed his iron "beetle" in his garden, but he could not fly away with it. And this, no doubt, is one reason for confidence in the durability of Meredith's art: it is grafted upon a stock so sturdy that only a cataclysm could blow it away. (pp. 118-19)

Orlo Williams, M.C., "The Egoist," in his Some Great English Novels: Studies in the Art of Fiction, *Macmillan and Co., Limited, 1926, pp. 84-119.*

Robert D. Mayo   (essay date 1942)

[In the following excerpt, Mayo discusses the significance of the "Blue Willow Pattern," a popular china pattern in the nineteenth century, in relation to the character of Willoughby Patterne and in the plot structure of The Egoist.*]*

No one has yet pointed out the full significance of Sir Willoughby Patterne's name in *The Egoist.* It has, in the first place, an obvious association with *pattern,* and tends to recall Sir Willoughby's exemplary traits as a wealthy young land-owner—"a picture of an English gentleman," and a model of excellence and eligibility. This is the effect intended in such passages as that in which he is contrasted with his cousin, Vernon Whitford:

> But one was a Patterne; the other a Whitford. One had genius; the other pottered after him with the title of student. One was the English gentleman wherever he went; the other was a new kind of thing, nondescript . . .

Here Meredith is matching Sir Willoughby's name with one of his dominant characteristics, and is following the old tradition of satirical comedy. But from a number of other passages in the novel it is clear that the name is meant to arouse other associations, less obvious, but none the less intentional. To the alert reader Sir Willoughby Patterne is supposed also to suggest *Willow Pattern,* as a close inspection of the novel will bear witness. It is this view of *The Egoist* which seems to have escaped previous commentators, although to overlook it is to obtain an incomplete picture of the book's design.

The blue Willow Pattern, named for the willow tree which figures in its center, is undoubtedly the most popular single design ever to be employed on English earthenware. The pattern originated about 1780 at the Caughley porcelain factory in Shropshire, where it was adapted from conventional forms on Chinese porcelain. It was widely copied by other manufacturers of English china, and soon attained an extraordinary popularity. According to a writer in 1849, "the sale of the common blue plate, known as the 'willow-pattern' exceeds that of all the others put together." References to "Blue Willow" are fairly common in nineteenth century writings, but a surer mark than these of its popular favor is the number of nursery verses referring to it which were current during the middle and late years of the century. In Meredith's day, as in our own, Willow-ware was undoubtedly the best known variety of English china.

Early in its history a romantic legend became associated with the Willow Pattern, and owing to the great popularity of the latter, acquired a considerable currency in England. The legend itself is probably not oriental in origin, but merely represents an attempt to explain the scenes on the universally familiar blue willow-plate. The story was told in some detail in the first volume of *The Family Friend* (1849), but it is likely that this is but an elaboration of what had already circulated for some years before. In December, 1851, the Willow story formed the subject of an extravaganza presented at the Strand Theatre in London, entitled *The Mandarin's Daughter; or, The Willow Pattern Plate.* From April 19 to July 3, 1875—four years before the publication of *The Egoist*—another version of the same story, by F. C. Burnand, was offered as a German Reed entertainment at St. George's Hall, London, and some years later the tale was made the subject of a Savoy opera. In naming his hero Sir Willoughby Patterne, therefore, and in duplicating certain features of the Willow legend, Meredith was not presuming acquaintance with totally unfamiliar material.

The Willow story is variously told, but practically all versions agree in outline. According to most of these the rich and influential mandarin who inhabited the stately mansion depicted on the right in the design was a widower possessed of a lovely daughter named Koong-see. He intended to marry his daughter to a wealthy suitor of high degree, but the maiden opposed her parent's wish. She had chosen for her lover a poor and honorable man serving as her father's secretary and had exchanged vows with him in clandestine meetings under the blossoming trees of the Willow Pattern. Suspecting his daughter's defection, the

mandarin imprisoned her in a pavilion in his garden, and commanded her to marry the husband of his choice when the peach tree should be in blossom. Here Koong-see pined for her freedom, and prayed that she might find release. Her chosen lover found means to communicate with her, invaded her prison, and carried her off, while her father feted the promised bridegroom in the banquet hall. The lovers were hotly pursued by the mandarin (in some versions by Ta-jin, the rejected suitor), but they escaped over the Willow bridge. After further adventures the gods turned them into birds in token of their fidelity.

It is this romantic tale, curiously, which seems to have provided Meredith with the groundplan of *The Egoist.* The resemblance between the two is obvious, but the triumph of true love over parental veto is a theme so common to fiction that the likeness might escape notice had the novelist not drawn particular attention to it by the name he gave his hero. In his relation to Clara Middleton, Sir Willoughby Patterne, the representative of a great country family, and in spirit (we are told) "a despotic prince," assumes the double role of tyrannical father and frustrated lover (although in Dr. Middleton's support of his suit, and in their *rapprochement* over the wine cups there may be an echo of the original relationship). Like Koong-see Clara resolves to escape from a seemingly brilliant match because it promises to fetter her to a man she

"Meredith Destroying Literary Form," cartoon by E. T. Reed in Punch, *28 July 1894.*

does not love. Her captivity is hardly physical, no more than Sir Willoughby's "despotism," but her struggle is no less real and leads to one abortive attempt at flight. Like the maiden of the Willow story, also, she takes for her lover a dowerless scholar and secretary. In *The Egoist,* it is true, the sequence is reversed, and Clara makes her bid for freedom before she and Whitford are acknowledged lovers. The reasons for Clara's revolt occupy Meredith's interest more than her new love—here there has been a shift of accent—but Vernon is no less her liberator from "dolorous bondage," and she assures Sir Willoughby before he releases her that she could marry no one else. In "Vernon's Holy Tree," in fact, the soaring "double-blossom wild cherry," under which Clara first awakens to a serious interest in Whitford, we may find a reflection of the lush floral background of the Willow love story.

In view of these parallels, which from his later references to the Willow Pattern, Meredith evidently intended us to recognize, we are able to attach new significance to Mrs. Mountstuart Jenkinson's enigmatical reference to Clara as "a dainty rogue in porcelain." This phrase, which figures recurrently in the narrative, both puzzles and displeases Sir Willoughby, who objects that "rogue and mistress of Patterne do not go together." But to his repeated query of "why rogue?" his friend cryptically answers that "porcelain explains it," and declines to clarify her meaning further. "Like all rapid phrasers," says Meredith, "Mrs. Mountstuart detested the analysis of her sentence. It had an outline in vagueness, and was flung out to be apprehended, not dissected." May not the elusive meaning be a reference to the independent action of Clara's prototype in the Willow story? Sir Willoughby, we are told, "detested but was haunted by the phrase," and with his progressive dissatisfaction with Clara's attitude towards himself, he came to feel that he could glimpse something of her "roguishness"—that is her self-willed determination to maintain her integrity of spirit against his "Egoist ideal of a waxwork sex."

> She certainly had at times the look of a nymph that has gazed too long on the faun, and has unwittingly copied his lurking lip and long sliding eye. Her play with young Crossjay resembled a return of the lady to the cat; she flung herself into it as if her real vitality had been in suspense till she saw the boy. Sir Willoughby by no means disapproved of a physical liveliness that promised him health in his mate; but he began to feel in their conversations that she did not sufficiently think of making herself a nest for him. Steely points were opposed to him when he, figuratively, bared his bosom to be taken to the softest and fairest.

Once introduced by Mrs. Mountstuart, the "rogue-in-porcelain" motif is caught up like a musical theme, and repeated, alluded to, and periodically re-scrutinized by the principal characters through the greater part of the book. The figure, furthermore, is pursued beyond mere recapitulation. Now Clara is "prettily moulded in a delicate substance"; later she is one of those "delicate vessels" that "ring sweetly to a finger nail"; and, after her struggle for freedom, she looks "like a bit of china that wants dusting"—until as we approach the end of the story we feel, like Clara, that we have been "overdone with porcelain" and are constrained to exclaim with Mrs. Mountstuart "Porcelain again!" and "*Toujours le porcelaine!*"

In addition to the frequent recurrence of what might be termed Clara's *leitmotif,* it is important to recall that Meredith has twice carried over the "porcelain-idea" into the plot itself. both incidents are skillfully linked with the "rogue-in-porcelain" theme and must represent a conscious attempt on his part to extend his original conceit to another plane of the narrative. The arrival of Colonel De Craye at Patterne Hall marks a decisive stage of Sir Willoughby's relations with his bride-to-be, in providing him with a definite focus for his discontent. In Chapter 17, entitled "The Porcelain Vase"—which begins, significantly, with a reversion by Mrs. Mountstuart and Sir Willoughby to the subject of the "rogue in porcelain"—the Colonel's appearance is signalized by the arrival of a carriage bearing, not the guest, but the fragments of a porcelain vase. This was to have been De Craye's wedding gift to his friend, but it has been broken through an accident on the road which has abruptly brought Clara and the handsome Colonel together. Here Meredith is employing the "thematic material" symbolically, suggesting the shattering of his hero's earlier illusion of a perfect match.

"Well, now the gift can be shared, if you're either of you for a division," Mrs. Mountstuart declares, returning to the subject of their earlier conversation. "At any rate, there was a rogue in *that* porcelain"—"What was meant by Clara being seen walking on the highroad alone?" queries the novelist. "What snare, traceable ad inferas, had ever induced Willoughby Patterne to make her the repository and fortress of his honour!" And the next moment he brings Clara into the scene, "chatting and laughing with Colonel de Craye . . . a dazzling offender; as if she wished to compel the spectator to recognize the dainty rogue in porcelain."

> . . . the broken is the broken, sir, [exclaims Dr. Middleton to Vernon Whitford later] whether in porcelain or in human engagements: and all that the one of the two continuing faithful, I should rather say, regretful, can do, is to devote the remainder of life to the picking up of the fragments . . .

After Clara's mutiny the remainder of *The Egoist* is devoted to Sir Willoughby's regretful gathering of the fragments.

In the second half of the novel, again, it is Lady Busshe's wedding present—likewise porcelain—which becomes the center of converging lines of interest. The gift, a porcelain service—which Clara archly terms "another dedicatory offering to the *rogue* in me!"—becomes the occasion for a battle of wits at Patterne Hall. For Lady Busshe, with her "passion to foretell disasters," it provides a means of testing her suspicion of a rift between Sir Willoughby and his bride; for Clara, "incapable of decent hypocrisy," it presents an obstacle to her resolve to add no further tie to those which already bind her; to Sir Willoughby it offers a threat to his desire to present to the world a serene, unbroken facade. In the dinner scene which follows, one of the most brilliantly comic in the book, Sir Willoughby scarcely succeeds in concealing his predicament from Lady Busshe. Her victorious trumpeting is thus communicated by Mrs. Mountstuart:

> " 'I shall have that porcelain back,' says Lady Busshe to me, when we were shaking hands last night: 'I think,' says she, 'it should have been the Willow Pattern.' And she really said: 'he's in for being jilted a second time!' "

> Sir Willoughby restrained a bound of his body that would have sent him up some feet into the air. He felt his skull thundered at within.

Lady Busshe's parting thrust, typically Meredithian in its obliquity, acquires meaning only with reference to Koongsee's jilting of Ta-jin in the Willow legend. The extravagance of Sir Willoughby's horror is not otherwise explainable. Mrs. Mountstuart may translate for emphasis Lady Busshe's gibe into more direct terms, but she does not need to explain the pun. Like other Meredithian characters, Sir Willoughby has a hypersensitive ear for overtones, hints, and side-hits, and is acutely aware of her meaning in raising at this juncture the name of Willow Pattern. "In her bitter vulgarity, that beaten rival of Mrs. Mountstuart Jenkinson for the leadership of the county had taken his nose for a melancholy prognostic of his fortunes; she had recently played on his name: she had spoken the hideous English of his fate." It is this portentous linking of his plight with that of the jilted suitor of the sentimental Willow story which goads Sir Willoughby into a course of action that eventually gains Clara her freedom. Alarmed by the possibility of losing face a second time in the county's eyes he admits the alternative of marrying Laetitia Dale and relinquishing his promised bride to Vernon Whitford.

> He was bound to marry: he was bound to take to himself one of them: and whichever one he selected would cast a lustre on his reputation. At least she would rescue him from the claws of Lady Busshe, and her owl's hoot of "Willow Pattern," and her hag's shriek of "twice jilted."

The Willow legend thus becomes a factor in the *dénouement* of **The Egoist** and an integral part of the book's design. If we may judge from the evidence collected, moreover, it provided Meredith with a rough outline for his novel, which he consciously held in mind from the outset. Though he never explicitly identifies his "source," it is implied by a wealth of allusion from the moment Sir Willoughby makes his first appearance to the time when Lady Busshe utters her "owl's hoot of 'Willow Pattern.' " But beyond providing Mrs. Mountstuart with a topic for conversational skirmishing and Lady Busshe with an armour-piercing taunt, it is difficult to assign to the Willow "theme" any very important function in the novel. The resemblance between the two stories is too much obscured by indirectness to heighten appreciably our feeling of *pattern* or *form* in the narrative, or to serve effectively as an ironic augury of Sir Willoughby's fate. Meredith's unsuccess in these respects is shown by the failure of readers to respond to his hints. The link between the name "Willoughby Patterne" and "rogue in porcelain" is lost on most of his audience, who pass over Lady Busshe's pun as mere freakishness. Even when rescued from obscurity the Willow "theme" seems a superfluous piece of ingenuity. It cannot be said to illuminate in any essential way the relationship of Clara to her father or her two lovers, or—apart from revealing the intensity of Sir Willoughby's humiliation—throw light on the springs of action. Notwithstanding Meredith's pronouncement in the "Prelude" to **The Egoist,** that "the Comic Spirit conceives a definite situation for a number of characters, and rejects all accessories in the exclusive pursuit of them and their speech," this device would seem to be more an *accessory* than anything else. He was rarely content to occupy himself with the "exclusive pursuit" of any story. In his abiding anxiety to avoid the hackneyed and the obvious, he was impelled to dazzle his readers with feats of virtuosity. This the use of the Willow story certainly is—an exercise in adroitness, an elaborate conceit which adds to the effect of quaintness and artificiality in the novel, but advances nowhere. It is in some degree the artifice for artifice's sake of a writer who, as Paul Elmer More says, like Mrs. Mountstuart was "mad for cleverness." (pp. 71-8)

> Robert D. Mayo, " 'The Egoist' and the Willow Pattern," in ELH, Vol. 9, No. 1, March, 1942, pp. 71-8.

Lord Dunsany   (essay date 1946)

[*Dunsany was an Irish novelist, dramatist, poet, and critic. Best known for his popular dramas and supernatural fiction, his criticism includes literary assumptions and judgments that are reminiscent of nineteenth-century critical methods. In the following essay, he discusses the poetic quality of Meredith's prose style in* The Egoist.]

Probably the first impression that any reader of Meredith will have of him is one of his remoteness from the ways of the people of whom he tells; but, when one reflects that his job is that of a philosopher and an observer, one sees the necessity for this remoteness. People like Mrs. Mountstuart Jenkinson and Lady Culmer and Lady Busshe, in [**The Egoist**] do their own recording only in conversation, and the more permanent record of their lives is usually done from outside. There is something of Watteau in Meredith, Watteau peering through a garden hedge at families of the French nobility; though in all Watteau's paints there was no acid, and he idealized what he saw on the distant lawns, which the satiric Meredith certainly does not do for the people of Patterne Hall. But the evidences of Meredith's remoteness are all little trifles, while evidence of his nearness to the hearts of the people whom he observes is to be found in every paragraph, and one may read him for his insight into the human heart; but particularly one may read him for the vividness with which he sketches his characters. And this vividness comes from the medium in which he sketches them, which is an unusual medium. For writers usually show their heroine with words that are trying to do the work of watercolours. They tell the colour of her eyes and hair and complexion, the shape of her face and eyebrows, the length of her eyelashes, her height and the form of her figure; and, when they have done, one cannot have as clear a picture of her as one would even get from one of those illustrations reproduced from a watercolour sketch, such as one sometimes sees in books, often facing the wrong page. But Meredith gives us far grander pictures, done in a nobler medium, for the medium in which he paints his characters is always poetry. For instance he describes the heroine of *The Egoist* as 'sunny in her laughter, shadowy in her smiling', and, elsewhere in the book, as 'a heavenly soul with half a dozen of the tricks of earth'. But a character in a book needs to be sketched only once, while moods may be illustrated on every page, and with pictures of these *The Egoist* scintillates. Here for instance is one of those lovely little pictures: 'She walked back at a slow pace and sang to herself above her darker-flowing thoughts, like the reed-warbler on the branch beside the night-stream; a simple song of a light-hearted sound, independent of the shifting black and grey of the flood underneath.'

On another occasion he says of the same girl: 'Powder was in the look, to make a war-horse breathe high and shiver for the signal.' And of another look this time on the face of the Egoist, he says: 'Sunrays on a pest-stricken city, she thought, were like the smile on his face.' For he can describe phases of the mind, and the outer appearance of them, as poetically as he can describe women. 'Deaf misunderstanding,' he says also somewhere in this book, 'may be associated with the tolling of a bell.'

Anybody that may be denied the opportunity, which is always an illuminating one, of hearing fresh metaphors daily, newly minted upon the lips as they are required, may be sure of finding an ample store of them in Meredith. To be altogether without metaphors is to be without any comparison for the vaguer things that one thinks of, or hears described, with the known objects of the world around us. And there is an even worse thing than to be without metaphors, and that is to be where withered old phrases are used which were once good metaphors, but which no longer have any meaning, because they are no longer understood, dead things like 'the blue riband of the turf'. And, even still worse than this, one may find oneself sometimes among people who use phrases that never had any meaning at any time, but which are accepted as doing well enough for a metaphor where a metaphor may seem to be required. These are more harmful to the mind than no metaphors at all, as decayed food is worse for the body than nothing to eat. For such a state of things Meredith is an admirable antidote. When Meredith writes that 'she went downstairs like a cascade; and like the meteor observed in its vanishing trace she alighted close to Colonel De Craye and entered one of the rooms off the hall', nobody has to write to the papers to explain that this is a metaphor in use among actors and used to mean this, that, or the other; the meaning is vivid and clear on the face of it, and no metaphor has any value where it is not. And a picture is given of the girl by the imagination of Meredith, that shows more brightly in the reader's imagination than any reproduction of a portrait in watercolour would be likely to do in his eyes. His metaphors are clear at each end, as metaphors must be. He does not describe a young girl coming downstairs without having seen one with his keen poet's eye, and he does not compare her to a cascade and to a meteor without having observed these things.

Sometimes he gives us sheer description, mere pictures of the beauty of the earth lying about us, a beauty to which poets are always dwelling near, and by which perhaps they were made what they are, as for instance where he describes a cherry in bloom in spring: 'She turned her face to where the load of virginal blossom whiter than summer cloud on the sky, showered and drooped and clustered so thick as to claim colour and seem, like higher Alpine snows in noon-sunlight, a flush of white. From deep to deeper heavens of white, her eyes peered and soared. Wonder lived in her.' But lovely pictures such as these are not mainly the raw material of his work, they are rather left in his mind to adorn his imagination, and there they serve for comparisons with whatever he may observe. Thus, when Meredith observes a girl walking or thinking, he is immediately able to show a parallel or reflection from among the beauties of nature with which his imagination is stored, so that we see her with the same clarity with which we should see her if a master painter had stood beside her with brush and palette in hand and rapidly sketched her at that moment. And when I compare Meredith to a painter, I would rather compare him to a Japanese painter, to one of those artists that lived so close to the birds and flowers and insects and mountains and sea, until they looked too suddenly westwards and tried to copy our machines and got their fingers caught in one of them. Indeed, Meredith himself suggests in this book a comparison between the methods of the painter and his own, where describing his heroine as 'a sight to set the woodlands dancing' he discusses what a jury of art-critics might say of her, and then goes on to give his own description with those illuminating parallels that he found in nature: 'See the silver birch in a breeze,' he says: 'here it swells, there it scatters and it is puffed to a round and it streams like a pennon, and now gives the glimpse and shine of the white stem's line within, now hurries over it, denying that it was visible, with a chatter along the sweeping folds, while still the white peeps through.'

I think I have quoted enough of Meredith to show, what the reader of [*The Egoist*] will see in a very few pages, that the sketches of those that move through it are made by a poet, and one in whose mind the countryside shines with a bright clear light. And across the landscape of that countryside his characters are led wherever his plot takes them, and are all of them brilliantly described. To describe the plot of a novel as a kind of airy canvas on which an artist paints is not to do it sufficient justice, and in the case of Dumas it would fall so far short of a just description, that the canvas with some outlines in charcoal were evidently the picture itself, for he employed what among some writers is known as a 'devil' to put on the paint; but with Meredith one need not regard the plot as very much more than the medium that was to hold the glittering splendour of his words. Of course it is good stout canvas, able to hold our attention, but, when it has done that, the plot does not seem to go very far beyond its obvious duty; and when, in this book, all the characters get at cross purposes on account of their inability to be sure on whose behalf the hero of the book is making proposals to two different young ladies, the reader has to be careful to keep his interest from being lost, itself, among those cross-purposes. A plot is, I take it, Meredith's excuse for telling a story and, to drop the metaphor of the canvas, is perhaps what the telegraph wire is to the September swallows, the clothes-line to the washing, or the thread to the necklace of pearls. It may be of more importance than any of these wires and threads and strings, but, if so, I cannot see it, dazzled by the beauty of what he strings upon it. Another thing that [*The Egoist*] very obviously contains, besides the plot, is the study of character, of the Egoist with his egoism, and the brilliant Dr. Middleton, ready to sacrifice his daughter's happiness, not for port; that would be unfair to him; but for a special vintage of port. To me, however, the study of character is not equal in value to poetry, and perhaps not the study of anything; and I can look at Meredith's study of the Egoist as I could admire the picture of a man in a tall hat, without being greatly interested in the height or make of the hat, but perhaps fully satisfied with the painting. For with the same delightful touch with which Meredith describes cherry-trees, flowers, and mountains, he describes the characters of men and women, and the moods that ruffle them as passing winds ruffle the water and grasses. He has looked at characters until he has understood them, but at nature he has looked even longer, so that he has gone beyond understanding and come to a unity with it, such as we lose as the race grows older and more sophisticated. It is this sympathy of his with nature that gives him his great charm, and whatever he describes among us he is able to describe somewhat as a faun might describe it, who had never seen a factory and who only looked at our doings to sing of them idly at evening. (pp. v-ix)

> Lord Dunsany, in an introduction to The Ego-
> ist: A Comedy in Narrative *by George Mere-
> dith, 1947. Reprinted by Oxford University
> Press, London, 1956, pp. v-ix.*

Dorothy Van Ghent   (essay date 1953)

[*In the following excerpt, Van Ghent considers the response of twentieth-century readers to* The Egoist *and compares Meredith's narrative and themes to those found in Henry James's* Portrait of a Lady.]

[Meredith's *The Egoist* presents a critical problem.] That is the problem offered by a writer of recognizably impressive stature, whose work is informed by a muscular intelligence, whose language has splendor, whose "view of life" wins our respect, and yet for whom we are at best able to feel only a passive appreciation which amounts, practically, to indifference. We should be unjust to Meredith and to criticism if we should, giving in to the inertia of indifference, simply avoid dealing with him and thus avoid the problem along with him. He does not "speak to us," we might say; his meaning is not a "meaning for us"; he "leaves us cold." But do not the challenge and the excitement of the critical problem as such lie in that ambivalence of attitude which allows us to recognize the intelligence and even the splendor of Meredith's work, while, at the same time, we experience a lack of sympathy, a failure of any enthusiasm of response?

The difficulty is not that the Meredithian prose places too much demand upon the reader's attentiveness. There is no "too much" of this kind that a work of art can require of

us. *Tristram Shandy* requires as much or more. Even *Pride and Prejudice,* for all its simplicity of surface, asks that we read with as alert an attentiveness to the word. Henry James offers more sinuous verbal paths than Meredith, paths that demand more of concentration inasmuch as they may be marked only by commas or question marks or dots that signify a suspension or attenuation of the track of communication, where Meredith would set up crusty substantives for the mind's grasp to help it around corners. "The enjoyment of a work of art," James said,

> the acceptance of an irresistible illusion, consti-
> tuting, to my sense, our highest experience of
> "luxury," the luxury is not greatest, by my con-
> sequent measure, when the work asks for as little
> attention as possible It is greatest, it is delightful-
> ly, divinely great, when we feel the surface, like
> the thick ice of the skater's pond, bear without
> cracking the strongest pressure we throw on it.

And, indeed, it seems to be precisely where Meredith offers the toughest stylistic going that we enjoy him the most. This is true at least of *The Egoist,* if not of later work. Curiously, our very sense of a *virtue* of excrescence in the style is symptomatic of that failure of thoroughly significant communication which we feel in Meredith. It is symptomatic, but let us insist that it is not the failure itself; for to be felt as excrescence, even fine excrescence, style must be related to *something else* in the work to which it seems to be perilously appended—just as building ornament is sensed as excrescent only as we see it in relation to the building.

Nor is the difficulty a lack of sensitive craft and pattern. *The Egoist* is a beautifully planned novel. Its pace is assured and powerful; from the opening incident, when Willoughby, on the terrace with Constantia Durham, snubs the marine lieutenant and tosses off, "I'll send him a check," to the last, when he deliciously misfires his revenge in all directions at once, events march their complicated route with a large inevitability. The spatial, or plastic, conception of the book is as fine as its movement in time: Willoughby's fantastic rigidity is set around, like a Maypole, with a gay and urgent dance on ribbons; the flat-footed, muscle-bound, blown-jowled monolith of his self-importance is host to a lawn festival of delicate searchings, bright scurryings, mobile strategies of the intelligences whose living occasions he has tried to halter at his center.

Nor should we confuse Meredith's failure with his deliberate limitation of the comic drama to the scope of a lawn festival, or, as he says, in his "Prelude" on the Comic Spirit, to

> human nature in the drawing-room of civilized
> men and women, where we have no dust of the
> struggling outer world, no mire, no violent
> crashes . . .

In this "Prelude," he merely puts into manifesto a limitation which Jane Austen made; . . . [we need not] bring any question against a novelist on the grounds that he confines his interest to "human nature in the drawing-room." Human nature is as human there as anywhere else, its opportunities as full and as menacing as in a slum or a coal mine or a dust bowl or a snake pit. (pp. 183-85)

Mr. Wilson Follett, in his introduction to the Modern Library edition of **The Egoist,** approaches Meredith's dwindled reputation in another way, from the point of view of certain vast generational changes in philosophical and psychological assumptions as to the nature of personality. He says,

> The central fact, the change behind all changes, is the modern annihilation of the Will, both as a valid concept and as a working tool. Up to our own generation man had embraced the belief . . . that he was at least partly the master of his own fate; and, acting on that belief, he had often made his conviction actually work. It had the important pragmatic sanction that it made him feel at home in his world, a world of moral choice. It is among the ruins of that world that we now grope. We see ourselves as lost and rootless in a universe without meaning—victims of malevolently blind forces, in and outside ourselves, that predetermine our actions and reduce our will and our vaunted reason to mere delusive reflexes, behavioristic phenomena. Meredith represents a world of Will, a society of lives modifiable by Will; and that fact alone is enough to give our time the sensation of being divided from him by a span computable in nothing less than light-years.

How, then, are we to understand the fact that George Eliot's universe, where moral choice traces its significant reign, is not similarly divided from us? Or, to use a modern example, how are we to justify our response of excited intelligence and conviction to a book like Albert Camus's *La Peste,* where the vocation of man, even man in despair, is seen as altruistic *willing?* It might, indeed, be argued that, in a world denuded of values and meanings, dramas in which the will is an operative factor would have a greater poignancy of significance—at least potentially—than they could have in a world which took for granted the measurable effects of willing. It might be argued that, as the conception of the will has become more complicated, complicated by our knowledge that we act under "blind forces" which are our will while yet we will against them, dramas of human relationships under the aspect of personally willed modification would have a more intense interest for us because we would find in them a more complex significance, a greater ambiguity, than would be possible if the personal will were thought of as morally univocal and psychologically undivided. The fiction that has attracted us most in an "absurd" world whose expressive signature is the concentration camp is fiction in which the will, though viewed variously, is still the moral center of the composition: this is true—to take extreme cases—of those fictions in which the personal will is defeated, "absurdly" defeated, as in Kafka and Hardy; it is true of Hemingway's fictions, where the very meagerness of the area within the Nothing where the will can operate is the sign of its tragic nobility; it is true of those fictions that explore the possibilities of self-knowledge (knowledge of what it is that we "will," or of the will's capacity for modification, or of its need for reteaching by experience of the emotions and instincts it has neglected or denied), as in Conrad and James and much of Thomas Mann; it is true of those that explore the epic corruption of the will, as in Melville and Dostoev-

ski. Generational changes in assumptions as to what the will is, how it works, whether it is practically operative or not, do not explain our distance from Meredith, for—so far as moral significance in fiction is concerned—our interest is still intensely in the concept of the will. It is probable that indifference to a work of art (after we have considered the work well) is never explained by the *kind* of "world view" or "life view" that it holds, no matter how alien from our own, but only by the lack of self-substantial coherency of that view of things as represented in the aesthetic form.

In connection with Meredith's view of the human world as a place where choices made by the personal will perceptibly affect reality, **The Egoist** offers, in its major elements, special reasons for a rapport with the modern reader which is nevertheless lacking. There are, in the book, two chief modes in which the effective will appears, represented by Willoughby's immalleable self-will, aspiring to a simplification of the universe on his own measure, and by Clara Middleton's delicate, mobile, searching will, aspiring to air, opportunity, multiplicity. As for Willoughby's effectiveness,

> Through very love of self himself he slew,

as his epitaph has it—certainly a pronounced victory of volition. The "comic drama of the suicide" illustrated by Willoughby's career is a drama that, in clinical rather than in English country-house materials, is fairly obsessive to modern interest. It is a drama that Dr. Karl Menninger has traced, uncomically, in *Man against Himself.* We find the note of it in W. H. Auden's poem "September 1, 1939."

> The windiest militant trash
> Important Persons shout
> Is not so crude as our wish:
> What mad Nijinsky wrote
> About Diaghilev
> Is true of the normal heart;
> The error bred in the bone
> Of each woman and each man
> Craves what it cannot have,
> Not universal love,
> But to be loved alone.

Of the craving "to be loved alone" Meredith's Willoughby makes the necessary conversion into self-love, since we cannot be loved alone by anybody but ourselves. With Clara,

> He dragged her through the labyrinths of his penetralia, in his hungry coveting to be loved more and still more, more still, until imagination gave up the ghost, and he talked to her plain hearing like a monster.

Willoughby is the fetus in full panoply, clothing himself "at others' expense," enjoying, or seeking to enjoy, "without incurring the immense debtorship for a thing done," possessing "without obligation to the object possessed." These phrases are Meredith's description of the sentimentalist, Willoughby being the prime example; they are also descriptive of an embryo. Willoughby is the monster of the womb, imposing on drawing room and lawn his unearned adulthood, his fetal vaporousness supported by name, wealth, and "a leg," and his demands for osmotic nourishment as if society were but one huge placenta designed for his shelter and growth. With Willoughby we *should* have the utmost rapport, for we have learned fiercely to understand him, through our so broadly ramified education in the fetal and infantile proclivities of the adult.

Willoughby must be delivered, but unfortunately not as in a normal birth, from the womb to the world, for he has been wearing the world as a custom-made womb. His delivery is the delivery of other people from him, from the extravagance of their courtesy in allowing him to occupy them. Willoughby is the difficult occasion for other people to dis-entrail themselves, by the exercise of intelligence, from a strangling, homomorphic Cause; he is the occasion in revolt against which individuality and variety of will are realized. By courtesy, faith, habit, and social exigency Clara Middleton and Vernon Whitford and Laetitia Dale find themselves in the kissing arms of this octopus, fanned on by the aunts, by Dr. Middleton's taste in port, and by a society of submarine fantasies and chattering twilight expectations. They extricate themselves, with difficulty, by learning to recognize meaning in experience and by acting on the recognition. "The drama of Meredith's characters," Ramon Fernandez says [in his *Messages*],

> is always and essentially the drama of an exacting sensibility. They begin by going straight ahead, in the direction of life, along the road of action. Their first acts, however rich and generous they may be, are simple, normal, not to say conventional . . . Since they can live only by acting, they act at first in perfect harmony with the circle in which tradition has caused them to be born. But then sensibility, at the first collision, is awakened. They feel confusedly that they can no longer live in the conditions which at first they accepted. And there they are, thrown back upon themselves, attentive, on the alert, seeking anxiously among the echoes of experience the key to the enigma which shall deliver them. To live for them is to seek to think, but to think in order to be able afresh to breathe, act, and bloom.

The nobility, the interest, the viability of this conception of character we cannot but acknowledge, and we make the acknowledgment the more readily as Meredith's view of life touches off with electric irony, and almost as if allegorically, certain grim features, both psychological and political, of our own condition.

Why, then, do we find ourselves indifferent? "Not a difficulty met," James said of Meredith, speaking as a novelist about a novelist,

> not a figure presented, not a scene constituted— not a dim shadow condensing once into audible or visible reality—making you hear for an instant the tap of its feet on the earth.

This is perhaps to go too far, particularly between novelists who are so much akin—in respect at least of stylistic elaboration, the social setting, the delicate development of a consciousness of values—as James is to Meredith in *The Egoist.* But it is indicative. Willoughby is a victim in wax model, Virginia Woolf said, not flesh and blood: he "is

turned slowly round before a steady fire of scrutiny and criticism which allows no twitch on the victim's part to escape it"—a process that, on description, looks as unfair as other destructive magical rites, as unfair as torture for confession. The fact is that Willoughby is treated as a perfectly lonely aberration, a freak; nobody (neither we as readers nor anyone in the book) knows how he came about, how he happened, what he is for, what connection there might be between his psychological peculiarities and the human soul at large. We do not really supply the connections when we say, "There is a Willoughby in each of us," for though the statement seems valid enough, its validity lies outside the book and not structurally within it: *within* the book there are no Willoughbys except Willoughby. Meredith makes similarly extraneous statements about Willoughby's human representativeness, but they remain dogmatic, without internal aesthetic corroboration. From the earliest note we have of his youth,

> When he was a child he one day mounted a chair, and there he stood in danger, would not let us touch him, because he was taller than we, and we were to gaze. Do you remember him, Eleanor? 'I am the sun of the house!' It was inimitable!

he is uncaused, a prodigy; and his career in maturity has only an external relatedness—a relatedness of exploitation—to other people; he is an obstacle to them, an ingratiating and portentous obstacle, but quite definitively outside of them, not inside. That we are not, *aesthetically,* given any insight as to what subtle internal bonds there might be between Willoughby and society—what, in the social soul, was itself Willoughby in order to fertilize this monster—or as to what taint of identity there might be between the soul of Willoughby and the soul of anybody else, makes us restless with his image, powerfully as that image is drawn, for he has evidently much too important a symbolic potential to be left so without spiritual relations, so unproliferative of the possible meanings he might have either for the constitution of the body politic or for that of the private psyche.

Like the giant of *Jack and the Beanstalk,* he is an external menace only, not a suffered portion of self or of the cultural conditions of self. That giant's feet did not touch the earth, because, after the scramble of escape, the stalk was cut down at a single blow. At the end of *The Egoist,* a dozen people—all the world—take whacks with free conscience at the beanstalk. Jane Austen's Mr. Collins, in *Pride and Prejudice,* is a monster quite in the fetal style of Willoughby, but Mr. Collins has the spiritual support of a society of other monsters with common economic causes, and the menace that he offers is one that, graded from grotesque obviousness to inconspicuous subtlety, is distributed through the social organism, pervasive in the private soul, providing the common stuff of the very language—thus truly dangerous because unconsciously environing. Mr. Collins—that is, the representative qualities of Mr. Collins, the complacencies of egoism backed by desperations of economic footing and caste, in a culture contracted to their measure—cannot really be escaped, even by happy marriages and removals, but must be dealt with alertly at every moment as the condition of existence.

Henry James's Osmond, in *The Portrait of a Lady,* also affords parallels with Willoughby, and again the difference in treatment is significant of Meredith's failure to give his egoist a spiritual context. *The Egoist* is of the year 1877; *The Portrait of a Lady,* 1881. We should not wish to force an unwarranted meaning upon these dates, but they do provide a curious comment on the parallels between the two books, particularly in view of James's opinion of Meredith. Health, wealth, and beauty are the qualifications Willoughby demands in his bride; she must also

> come to him out of cloistral purity . . . out of
> an egg-shell, somewhat more astonished at
> things than a chick . . . and seeing him with her
> sex's eyes first of all men.

It is a note sounded also by Osmond, in James's *Portrait,* and we hear in it almost the same comic exaggeration. He asks, concerning Isabel, who has been suggested to him as a possible bride,

> "Is she beautiful, clever, rich, splendid, univer-
> sally intelligent and unprecedentedly virtuous?
> It's only on those conditions that I care to make
> her acquaintance."

Contempt for "the world" is the breath of life to both Willoughby and Osmond; their need to scorn it and set themselves and their possessions apart from it is the inspiration of their existence, on the principle that "the world" must admire where it is scorned and pay to the scorner the tribute of its own helpless vulgarity. For Willoughby,

> The breath of the world, the world's view of him,
> was partly his vital breath, his view of
> himself . . . [He was] born to look down upon
> a tributary world, and to exult in being looked
> to. Do we wonder at his consternation in the
> prospect of that world's blowing foul upon him?
> Princes have their obligations to teach them they
> are mortal, and the brilliant heir of a tributary
> world is equally enchained by the homage it
> brings him . . .

And for Osmond,

> To surround his interior with a sort of invidious
> sanctity, to tantalise society with a sense of ex-
> clusion, to make people believe his house was
> different from every other, to impart to the face
> that he presented to the world a cold original-
> ty—this was the ingenious effort of the person-
> age to whom Isabel had attributed a superior
> morality . . . under the guise of caring only for
> intrinsic values Osmond lived exclusively for the
> world . . .

These parallelisms—and others—almost suggest that James deliberately used the pattern conceived by Meredith. But how much more he discovered in it! The difference lies in a sense of spiritual context. Willoughby appears without "internal relations" with the society he dominates or with the individuals whose self-development he attempts to suffocate; he is, moreover, personally value-less, a formal abstraction of conceit without any other palpable qualification than a "leg." (pp. 185-91)

The prose style of *The Egoist,* intensely nervous and packed, constantly inventive, has somewhat the same sta-

tus of an abnormal and eccentric growth as does Willoughby, and in this sense Siegfried Sassoon's remark that the phraseology of the book "is an artifice which seems appropriate" has an unintended rightness. The style is beautifully wrought, as is the figure of Willoughby himself; we cannot deny it its qualities of virtu. Again and again the vivid and witty image concretizes a state of mind. There is Willoughby's agony over the threatened defection of Clara.

> The fact that she was a healthy young woman
> returned to the surface of his thoughts like the
> murdered body pitched into the river, which will
> not drown, and calls upon the elements of disso-
> lution to float it.

Or the quality of his pathos with Laetitia:

> As his desire was merely to move her without an
> exposure of himself, he had to compass being pa-
> thetic as it were under the impediments of a
> mailed and gauntleted knight, who can not easi-
> ly heave the bosom, or show it heaving.

Or his torments of decision:

> Laocoon of his own serpents, he struggled to a
> certain magnificence of attitude in the muscular
> net of constrictions he flung round himself.

It is of this kind of stylistic virtuosity that Ramon Fernandez speaks when he says that Meredith's "artifice" consists

> in representing the most concrete possible equiv-
> alent for a mental movement . . . Meredith fills
> in the intervals of the action with little symboli-
> cal actions because he is anxious above all not to
> let his thought and that of the reader lose their
> dramatic rhythm.

His images, Fernandez says, thus constitute "a defense system against abstraction." Since the definitive and suicidal characteristic of the egoist is his abstraction from the living world, a style so full of concrete images and tough little verbal dramas has its peculiar logic here, for it keeps the egoist within our ken; he might otherwise lose his liveliness and dissolve into his own sentimental vapor. Yet, attractive as is this rationalization of style, one asks if there is not a fallacy in throwing so much of the burden of concreteness upon style and if the concreteness most necessary to fiction does not lie in that spiritual *contextualism* of lives which we have noticed as lacking in *The Egoist.* Where such context strongly exists and style subserves it, is not the concreteness there too—the concreteness that makes the created world of a novel excitedly meaningful "for us"? Where it does not exist, and style is called upon to substitute for it by energy and picture, is not style forced into an unnatural position where it figures as a kind of "egoist" itself—a separated, self-willed, self-regarding element? In what is surely one of the most abstract vocabularies in fiction, and one of the least "image-making" of styles, Jane Austen evoked a concrete world that is meaningful "for us" because, like a world, it exists in the autonomy of its own internal relations.

On Meredith's style is imposed a somewhat desperate function of keeping author, characters, and reader in a state of awareness, not so much of what is going on, but of each other, a function of keeping us awake to the fact that we are reading a brilliant book by an exceptionally intelligent author about highly burnished characters—all of which the style makes us ever so ready to admit. One thinks of Milton here, for Meredith's style has its brilliance as Milton's has its "grandness," and in reading Milton one has to hang on by the words and the astonishing verbal manipulation if sometimes by nothing else. What Desmond McCarthy said of Meredith might be said of Milton: "It must be remembered in reading Meredith that half his touches are not intended to help you to realize the object so much as to put power into the form." The statement applied to Meredith makes only a fumbling kind of sense, inasmuch as it divides the "form" from the "object," and what we see as failure in Meredith is just this division of form and object, the division of the elegant pattern and splendid style of the book from potential meaning, from potential relationships between characters and thus potential relationships with ourselves. Applied to Milton, it has a good deal more sense, and the difference lies here. One feels that, in a highly special and deeply meaningful way, the Miltonic style *is* "the object"; one feels that the verbal manipulation is the mind's desperate exhibition of its independence and strength, working on the plastic stuff of the word in a frightful vacuum of other stuff adequately tough to reward the worker's gift and exertion—the mind is with its "back to the wall," so to speak, in the position of Lucifer; one feels that this is the moral kinetics which, in Milton, is profoundly "the object," and that the "power" of Milton's language is the same as that satanic power which moved a causeway through empty space from hell to earth. We cannot say so much of Meredith. Style is here a brilliant manner, and, with some embarrassment—for we would not be without the pleasures Meredith provides—we would quote Dr. Middleton on style in the author's own admirably intelligent style:

> You see how easy it is to deceive one who is an artist in phrases. Avoid them, Miss Dale; they dazzle the penetration of the composer. That is why people of ability like Mrs. Mountstuart see so little; they are bent on describing brilliantly.

(pp. 192-94)

Dorothy Van Ghent, "On 'The Egoist'," in her The English Novel: Form and Function, *Holt, Rinehart and Winston, 1953, pp. 183-94.*

Charles J. Hill   (essay date 1954)

[*In the following excerpt, Hill discusses the influence of John Stuart Mill's essay* On the Subjection of Women *(1869) on Meredith's "feminism" and his representation of women in* The Egoist.]

It is generally acknowledged that *The Egoist,* published in 1879, represents the quintessential Meredith. Nowhere else in his analysis of motives more penetrating, or his idea of comedy more steadily exemplified. Moreover, in dealing with the predicament of Clara Middleton, Meredith comes to grips with the position of women in Victorian society, a theme which was to figure, in one way or another,

in all of his later books. In fact, the subjection of women in a world governed in the interests of men becomes, inevitably, a salient theme in the author's remorseless exposure of the masculine ego. Inseparable from the central theme of egoism, it has in the final analysis an almost equal importance. For the significant action of the story is all related to Sir Willoughby's efforts to bind the woman of his choice, and Clara's struggle to break her engagement. It is illuminating to discover how the repetition of appropriate imagery assists the development of these themes in the carefully ordered structure of the novel.

In the presentation of Sir Willoughby Patterne, Meredith gives us not only the character of an individual but the portrait of a type. The dignity of the Egoist is sacred. Not only must he think well of himself, but he must have the approval of others. Sir Willoughby holds the most exalted opinion of himself, because all his life he has been nourished upon adulation. He has a sensitiveness extremely tender, is "fiercely imaginative" in whatever concerns himself. It is characteristic of the Egoist that he is perpetually looking at himself, perpetually listening to himself, and that he must have his environment minister to his ideal conception of himself. Sir Willoughby expects his relatives and his friends to serve as satellites, who will give him back his own image and make him shine the brighter by their subservient admiration. And what Sir Willoughby demands in a wife, it is made unmistakably clear, is one who will be an obedient slave, a fixed star, one who will read and reverence him, one who will be as faithful to him as a mirror or an echo.

It is precisely because Clara Middleton comes to see that marriage with him would in fact be "marriage with a shining mirror, a choric echo," that she resolves to make her fight for freedom. Clara cannot bring herself to sink her identity in his. She is determined not to "reduce herself to ashes, or incense, or essence, in honour of him, and so . . . literally be the man she was to marry." But to Sir Willoughby betrothal means possession, complete, exclusive, and eternal; and the extreme of his vanity is displayed when he begs her, in the event of his death, to promise him a worshipful widowhood! Clara listens to him gravely, "conceiving the infinity as a narrow dwelling where a voice droned and ceased not." Though she has much to endure before she is liberated, this is the beginning of the end.

The egoism represented by Sir Willoughby is related to Meredith's serious thinking about man in society. His view of man, as everybody is now aware, had its basis in the evolutionary theory which was the outstanding contribution to the scientific thought of his time and which he adapted after his own fashion. In a word, Meredith looked upon egoism as a reversion to primitive brutishness. The primitive in modern man may be subtly disguised, for the civilized egoist is a sophisticated animal, skilled in concealing his predatory motives, but he is animal nonetheless.

This conception of egoism as a survival of primitive brutishness becomes, indeed, the informing idea in Meredith's novel. It inspires not only a number of important statements but an impressive body of interpretive imagery. We encounter, for example, the direct pronouncement:

> The Egoist is our fountain-head, primeval man; the primitive is born again, the elemental reconstituted. Born again, into new conditions, the primitive may be highly polished of men, and forfeit nothing save the roughness of his original nature . . . he has become the civilized Egoist; primitive still, as sure as man has teeth, but developed in his manner of using them.

The Egoist's sentimental idea of women, demanding of them ("to be named innocent") cloistral purity and ignorance of the world they live in, is seen by Meredith as a "voracious æsthetic gluttony," a refinement of the gross original instinct of the predatory male to possess. Whether women "distinguish the ultra-refined but lineally great-grandson of the Hoof in this vast and dainty exacting appetite, is uncertain. They probably do not; the more the damage." "The devouring male Egoist," Meredith goes on to say, wants women fashioned as "precious vessels . . . for him to walk away with hugging, call his own, drink of, and fill and drink of, and forget that he stole them." Here the idea of the Egoist as rapaciously possessive is related to the position of women in Victorian society, and the image of the "devouring male Egoist" is supported throughout the narrative by many related images drawn from eating and drinking.

Clara Middleton once speaks in terms which echo the words of her author just now quoted. "Men who are egoists," she says in an important conversation with Laetitia Dale, "have *good* women for their victims; women on whose devoted constancy they feed; they drink it like blood." Thus, to Sir Willoughby, Laetitia is a "feast," which he snatches at "hungrily if contemptuously." Her eyes give him the "food" that he enjoys. It is notable that the Egoist wishes to keep the woman he would consume as a morsel reserved for himself. Therefore Sir Willoughby had resented the fact that Constantia Durham had had many suitors: "She had been nibbled at, all but eaten up," while he waited. "He wished for her to have come to him out of an eggshell, somewhat more astonished at things than a chicken, but as completely inclosed before he tapped the shell." By contrast, he somehow rationalized that he had caught Clara from the crowd before she had been contaminated. She was not like other girls who "run about the world nibbling and nibbled at, until they know one sex as well as the other."

Sir Willoughby covets her as "fresh-gathered morning fruit . . . warranted by her bloom," and tastes in imagination the felicity that she promises. But when he becomes vexed and frightened by her his emotions are quite different. Then he would like to "burn and devour her." In his annoyance he makes "devouring exclamations"; he suffers from a "gnawing jealousy," and Meredith speaks of the "jaw-chasm of his greed." Clara thinks of herself as being caught and consumed, but the images which come most frequently to *her* mind are those of the hunted quarry and the captive.

Women are in the position of inferiors, she once observes to Laetitia Dale. "They are hardly out of the nursery when

a lasso is round their necks." Clara admires Vernon Whitford because he does not flatter her or "practice the fowler's arts." But Sir Willoughby is "a falcon," and Clara's case is likened to that of "a captured wild creature" crying for help. She feels her position as the betrothed of Sir Willoughby palpably, "as a shot in the breast of a bird." She sees herself trapped, caught in "the jaws of her aversion." Willoughby's house is a "cage," a "dungeon" in which she appears fated to spend a "life-long imprisonment." The imagery of devouring is joined with the figure of the prison when Clara conceives of herself as "fixed at the mouth of a mine," condemned to descend into it daily, "to be chilled in subterranean sunlessness . . . in those caverns of the complacent-talking man."

Now it was with *The Egoist* that Meredith began to make the marriage problem a major issue. The predicament of Clara Middleton, plighted to a despot from whom she must be liberated, is as much his concern as is the anatomy of Sir Willoughby's egoism; and Meredith is frequently moved to generalize from Clara's particular case. "What of wives miserably wedded?" he exclaims in a crucial passage. "What aim in view have these woeful captives?" "Clara," he writes, "had shame of her sex. They cannot take a step without becoming bondswomen: into what a slavery!" But Meredith was no facile generalizer. He knew that not every man is an egoist and that many women of his day enjoyed a rational and companionable partnership with their husbands. He was acutely aware, nevertheless, of the limitations and the taboos imposed upon the sex in regard to education and opportunity, and of all the consequences for women arising out of their dependence in the married state. The position of women, in fact, seemed to him to be not only a test of men but a measure of the society in which they live.

> Women have us back to the condition of primitive man, or they shoot us higher than the topmost star . . . They are to us what we hold of best or worst within. By their state is our civilization judged; and if it is hugely animal still, that is because primitive men abound and will have their pasture.

It is significant that in this highly characteristic utterance the imagery associated with "the devouring male egoist" should reappear.

If Meredith's conception of egoism as a reversion to primitive brutishness is related to his "evolutionary philosophy," his thinking about the dependence of women and the marriage problem owes much to the essay of John Stuart Mill on "The Subjection of Women." Meredith had read this essay when it appeared, in 1869, and his wholehearted acceptance of Mill's arguments is reflected not only in the substance of *The Egoist* (and elsewhere) but in the very language of that novel. Indeed, the correspondences are so striking that it is strange they have not been noticed, since Meredith's appreciation of Mill has long been common knowledge. What Meredith has done in *The Egoist* is to dramatize the ideas of Mill, and since the thematic material of the novel has already been examined, the parallels with the essay can be quickly pointed out.

It is notable in the first place that Mill describes the legal dependence of women as "the primitive state of slavery" which has not lost "the taint of its brutal origin." Women are in the situation of bond-servants, educated to accept their captive state. "Men do not want solely the obedience of women, they want their sentiments," Mill writes, expressing the thesis of *The Egoist* precisely. "How many are the forms and gradations of animalism and selfishness, often under an outward varnish of civilization and even cultivation!" he exclaims in a voice that could as well be Meredith's. "There is nothing which men so easily learn as this self-worship," he is observing a little later, and to all that Mill has to say about the effect upon men and women alike, and upon the harmony of their relations in the state of marriage, which the inferiority imposed upon women is bound to produce, Meredith is in fullest accord. Mill's contention that women cannot expect emancipation, or be expected to devote themselves to gaining it, "until men in considerable number are prepared to join with them in the undertaking," must also have made a deep impression upon him. *The Egoist,* which reads almost as if it were a document in the campaign, shows the extent to which Meredith was already committed to the cause and the debt which he owed to Mill.

From this time to the day of his death, Meredith was to be counted a champion of women. The novels that followed *The Egoist* all treat some aspect or other of the marriage problem, and Meredith was frequently solicited for support of the feminist cause. "Women who read my books," he wrote to a female correspondent, "have much to surmount in the style, and when they have mastered it and come to the taste, I am well assured of their having discovered in me one who is much at heart with them." (pp. 281-85)

> *Charles J. Hill, "Theme and Image in 'The Egoist',"* in The University of Kansas City Review, *Vol. XX, No. 4, Summer, 1954, pp. 281-85.*

V. S. Pritchett (essay date 1969)

[*Pritchett is a highly esteemed English novelist, short story writer, and critic. Considered one of the modern masters of the short story, he is also considered one of the world's most respected and well-read literary critics. Pritchett writes in the conversational tone of the familiar essay, a method by which he approaches literature from the viewpoint of a lettered but not overly scholarly reader. A twentieth-century successor to such early nineteenth-century essayist-critics as William Hazlitt and Charles Lamb, Pritchett employs much the same critical method: his own experience, judgment, and sense of literary art are emphasized, rather than a codified critical doctrine derived from a school of psychological or philosophical speculation. In the following excerpt, he examines character, theme, and style in* The Egoist.]

Sir Willoughby Patterne is a gentleman, a sort of Darcy in his pride in his family or House. He is rich. He is a snob. England, says Meredith, is over-full of such amateurs. They receive the education of princes. They do not go into public life or serve their country. Their allegiance is to themselves and their estates. A great number hunt the fox.

They like sport. But Sir Willoughby is not a barbarian; for reasons of prestige (for he likes to condescend to the intellect), he is an amateur scientist. Sir Willoughby's aim is to be regarded as the most civilised of men, the most excelling. His concept of high civilisation is that it is as detached from the world at large as an unassailable mountain peak. The view is both metaphysical and—solely in his own interests—practical. His name is an intended pun: he is the pattern of a sterile concept of the civilised life. Move him into D. H. Lawrence's generation and he will be the famous tree with its roots in the air. There is no doubt that he is an authentic character and a particularly English one for he has the peculiar native weakness for being a personage. His estate, his friends, his servants, and the women he falls in love with are mirrors in which he regards his own beauty and virtue. So that he is more than a gentleman; he is an idea *in excelsis,* a gentleman who has every moment to act out the part before an audience. What he cannot stand is loss of audience. To people who cross him he is lofty, cold and dismissive. His idealism is self-love. So, as a lover he is a Narcissus, who looks for absolute purity in women, absolute faith. In this department Meredith says of him:

> He was a Social Egoist, fiercely imaginative in whatsoever concerned him. He had discovered a greater realm than that of the sensual appetites.

In marriage, he looks for heirs who will ensure the status of the House; in love, unquestioning adoration.

Here Meredith has found his ideal subject, the chance to fulfil the requirements he laid down in his *Essay on the Comic Spirit.* What had eluded him so often was the discipline of a form that would make his disparate gifts consort: the romantic, the lyrical, the epigrammatic, the analytic, the grotesque, the fantastic and the histrionic, so that they melt together and do not fall apart into anti-climax and incredibility. He had found such a form in the great romantic adventure-narrative of *Harry Richmond* by following the lesson of Fielding. In *The Egoist,* he saw that he must be stricter; that the subject needed unity of place; and that his Idea would be most intensely seen if he went to the theatre, to Molière and Congreve, and gave his novel the artifice of a play. English Egoism, for him, must be a theatrical subject; because its imagination is theatrical. His rapid scenes must be stated, reversed, re-stated, reversed again, so that Willoughby—the pattern—could be examined from all angles. The theme is the egoist's ordeal. He must slowly be reduced in his pretensions and the comedy will lie in the ruthlessness he brings to his self-defence when he begins to lose. There must be no sight of the struggling outside world. The thing must not sprawl; it is the business of comedy, Meredith holds, to condense. And to be perfect, the women must be equal in brains to the men. For it is part of Meredith's didactic purpose to show that the woman who marries the perfect gentleman will be his prisoner and subject; his pride will be more important than her love.

As usual, we see Meredith opting for a theory and for examining people in connection with it; and this brings the disadvantage that Meredith himself will be talking all the time and he will seem dangerously like Sir Willoughby in person as Clara Middleton found him:

> Miss Middleton caught her glimpse of his interior from sheer fatigue in hearing him discourse of it. What he revealed was not the cause of her sickness—women can bear revelations—they are exciting: but the monotonousness. He slew imagination.

As a novel *The Egoist* has the monotony of a work of animated criticism and it can be objected that Sir Willoughby is a "still" portrait moralised by an essayist. But all Meredith's turns before the curtain about Egoism are good, because there is really no curtain. We see the important notion that Egoism is more than a trait: it is a faith, is personalised and shown not flatly but ironically in action in the following passage:

> Consider him indulgently: the Egoist is the Son of himself. He is likewise the father. And the son loves the father and the father the son. . . . Are you, without much offending, sacrificed by them, it is on the altar of mutual love, to filial piety or paternal tenderness.

Meredith's irony is less a moralisation than an intended dramatic intrusion on the scene. He does not comment from outside, but seems to stop the actors, come up on the stage and show them what they are doing.

Meredith had two important strokes of luck in writing this novel. He had the luck to think of the boy Crossjay, the ardent, mischievous imp, to make him work as a nuisance and also to give him a heart. Meredith himself—one would suspect—had no adult heart; perhaps the loss of his mother, or the disaster of his first marriage, had killed it. But he retained a young pre-adult heart, rather as Dickens did.

The most refreshing things in *The Egoist* after the superb opening scene are the glimpses we have of Crossjay's and Clara Middleton's tender attachment to each other—a boy of ten's feeling for a young woman not yet twenty. Crossjay is one of the most engaging young schoolboys in English romance, at any rate in a scene so restricted as a gentleman's park. And there is a very serious background to the portrait: he is caught between two hostile theories of education. Education is always in Meredith's mind: how are we to be trained and for what? Crossjay brings surprise, a young animal's spontaneity, the love of action, the tenderness of Nature on to the scene; and Meredith has seen that the role of the young boy in such a novel is not comic relief; he will be a necessary, unconscious, light-footed messenger, a Puck without knowing it, in a stiff intrigue. The boy also draws out the romping or roguish side of the young girl who is being dragged too fast into the marriage system, which is her fate; but he also makes her think. The attraction of all Meredith's women is that they think. It is delightful to see Clara Middleton getting the courage to think for herself; to think her way through Sir Willoughby's formidable armour, to think her way into not being carried off by de Craye, the Irish gallant, without ceasing to be amused by him. Her quickness will cheer up the moralising Whitford who, rather to our regret, she will marry. She brings in all the good scenes of the out-of-

doors—the famous cherry blossom scene, the excellent flight in the rain to the railway station: Meredith at his happiest. She brings the balancing touch of nature to a comedy which is necessarily artificial; and in the final conflict with Sir Willoughby, Meredith gives her a conscience. I am thinking of the moment when, after he has been caught proposing to Laetitia before he is "off" with Clara, he escapes by the casuistry that he was merely proposing on Whitford's behalf. He hands her over to Whitford and this has been thought psychologically impossible. I do not think so for it is the essence of Egoism to deny that control has ever left one's hands. And the comic point is well made: Sir Willoughby is given the escape-clause by which he, perpetually self-centred, can save his face and tell the world that he arranged it all; but *she* knows she has won. And has won, moreover, on his ground. He has done what he has said he never does—broken his word; and in going through the proper forms of asking for release, shows him, not without irony, that she is morally more scrupulous. The twists of the comedy are fine, but they are opportunities for further observation.

The last two chapters of *The Egoist* are excellent and the end is not one of the suicides of his talent. He has to avoid the conventional happy-ending, although Clara will be allowed it, of course, and like so many of his lovers will have an energetic courtship in the Alps where, as he writes, "Sitting beside them the Comic Muse is grave and sisterly". For the rest of the cast things will not be quite so easy. He goes on in the final sentence:

> Taking a glance at the others of her late company of actors, she [the Comic Muse] compresses her lips.

Willoughby has to take a final lashing from his future wife's tongue, for Laetitia has suffered much; she is seen trying to purge herself of bitterness. She had been a beautiful, healthy young girl like Clara; now she is in poor health. The scene in so many earlier Victorian novels would have been one of high-flown dramatic challenge and surrender; but Meredith sees to it that we are genuinely moved by this hard-headed woman:

> "Privation [she says] has made me what an abounding fortune usually makes of others—I am an Egoist. I am not deceiving you. That is my real character. My girl's view of him has entirely changed; and I am almost indifferent to the change. I can endeavour to respect him, I cannot venerate."

It is rather too pat (I have often thought) to make Laetitia an Egoist also. And surely, you will say, here *is* another suicide, this ending in a loveless marriage. No, because Willoughby is given his due: once he has his way, he is generous and recovers some of his incurable glow and Meredith, with one of his customary intrusions as if he were wryly introducing his personal life into the story, says:

> But he had the lady with brains! He had: and he was to learn the nature of that possession in the woman who is our wife.

Our wife! Meredith's personal story can never quite be

kept out. So many of the lacerating and penetrating passages seem to come with force from that: those describing Willoughby's jealousy which echoes the jealousy described in *Modern Love:*

> the lover who cannot wound has indeed lost anchorage; he is woefully adrift: he stabs air, which is to stab himself.

Some words must be said about Meredith's dialogue. Up to his time, the rule has been that the chief characters [in English comedy] speak in the voice useful to the novelist, and the minor characters—particularly the comics and the lower classes, are given natural idiomatic speech. The exception is Jane Austen, that superb technician who commanded several kinds of dialogue—formal or literary or natural. Meredith's dialogue brings in the modern wave. It is brisk, abrupt, allusive and born to its moment, for he builds his novels out of moments. He goes in for catching natural talk in snatches in the big chapters of rumour, and also for rapid epigrammatic stage repartee. In these interchanges, for the most part, the characters use only his brains. This can be exhausting; but, at its best, it is nimble. (pp. 112-19)

> *V. S. Pritchett, in his* George Meredith and English Comedy: The Clark Lectures for 1969, *Random House, 1970, 123 p.*

Donald R. Swanson (essay date 1969)

[*Swanson is an American critic and educator. In the following excerpt, he discusses the relationship between technique and theme in* The Egoist *and clarifies the function of stylistic and narrative devices that are used in the novel.*]

The Egoist, perhaps Meredith's most successful novel in integration of technique and theme, is above all a poet's novel depending upon imagery, allusion, and patterns of language for its effect rather than upon the traditional narrator and the relatively unambiguous language of prose narative. The plot of the novel is transparently simple; almost too simple, one would think, for a long novel: a country gentleman, engaged to a young girl who wants to break their engagement, finally permits her to do so, and turns to another woman whom he has known since childhood. This simplicity, however, allows the novelist to expand the complexity of character and image in a way that would be far less possible if the plot were more elaborate. It is in a later novel, *One of Our Conquerors,* that Meredith seeks to combine his complexity of style with complexity of plotting. The result has baffled many critics who have been offended more by the unusualness of Meredith's technique than by the "obscurity" of which they accuse him. Present-day readers are likely to find *One of Our Conquerors* old-fashioned rather than too experimental. Some of Meredith's techniques anticipate those of later writers; some are unique to himself, although they have both antecedents and progeny.

In spite of Meredith's frequent assertion that he does not make a plot, his novels are usually very carefully arranged. This is most clearly true of *The Egoist,* where every incident is necessarily interwoven with every other incident.

Thus, though the "plot," in the [Aristotelian] sense of "the arrangement of the incidents", is very simple, it is of the kind that Aristotle calls "Complex", wherein "the change is accompanied by . . . Reversal, or by Recognition" which arises "from the internal structure of the plot". The events in Meredith's novel not only reveal the Egoist, but reveal him in relation to the world around him. This world, composed of individual people in contact with each other, is itself constantly changing, since its components are changing both in themselves and in their relationships with each other. By shifting his focus from one of these people to another, Meredith manages to portray the world in which Sir Willoughby Patterne, the Egoist, lives; this is the world that he fears and contemns while he looks to it for worship and praise.

The central focus, which in the early part of the novel is on Sir Willoughby, gradually shifts to Clara Middleton, whose struggle to free herself from her engagement to Willoughby is a major external conflict in *The Egoist.* Focus is not limited, however, to these two characters: it centers upon each character in turn, including the most minor ones. The effect is as if the reader, knowing several persons distantly, is suddenly thrown into intimate contact with each in turn, and is thus made aware of the multiplicity of worlds in which they live. In this manner he is made acutely aware of the limitations of the Egoist, whose fear of the "World" makes him unable to enter into intimacy of any kind with any member of it. Clara's sexual coldness towards Willoughby, her real physical revulsion when he touches her, occurs only after she has begun to be aware of his inability to love anyone but himself: he wants only to absorb her, to make her merely an extension of himself. When he looks into her eyes, he wants to see reflected there the image of the man he loves.

Point of view in *The Egoist* is complicated not only by these patterns of focus but also by Meredith's use of several kinds of narrative interwoven, and by his use of choral voices and fictive documents that make general comments about society and the human psyche, often in terms of complex metaphors and images. The imps of the Comic Spirit sometimes descend like the Elemental Spirits of "The Rape of the Lock", and the "Book of Egoism" is cited by volume and chapter. The whole effect is to keep the reader aware of the artifice, and at the same time to see in the artifice a reflection of a part of the real world.

Meredith is always conscious of the importance of his speaker, and of the relationships between different kinds of narration. Sometimes the story proceeds headlong, the narrator maintaining at least a rough chronology as he proceeds from one event to another; sometimes forward motion is arrested in a scene, in which characters themselves present the story through their speech and actions; sometimes action is stopped altogether, while ideas related to the events are discussed at length, sometimes by more than one speaker. Meredith's early remark that "After a satisfactory construction of plot, when to dramatize and when to narrate, is the novelist's lesson" might, if he were to apply it to his own work, be expanded to include when to make general comments on the ideas underlying the action and narration.

Irony is always active in narration, comment, and scene. The narrator who thinks of Sir Willoughby as "one of us" is himself often the prey of the Comic Spirit, when his subject is the Egoist. The narrator adapts readily to the mind and language of the person with whom he is for the moment principally concerned. In the few pages that constitute the first chapter of *The Egoist,* for example, the language is, until the very end, that of Sir Willoughby, and the evaluations are his. When a "Lieutenant Crossjay Patterne" of the Marines is cited for bravery, Sir Willoughby's condescension to so lowly a creature determines the attitude of the narrator: "The man is a Marine, but he is a Patterne." As Sir Willoughby grows proud of his heroic relative, the puffed-up narrator can say that "We are a small island, but you see what we can do." The absurdity of the pompousness becomes apparent when the lieutenant actually appears—at Sir Willoughby's request—only to be snubbed by the young baronet, who is already skilled in the art of "cutting". The idealized young hero turns out to be "a mature and stumpy Marine" who is poorly dressed and obviously lower-class. Though the reader has been carried through the action by a narrator in sympathy with Sir Willoughby, the momentary scene with which the narration ends is so presented that the reader is made to see the action from the outside, and as Miss Durham sees it, even though her feelings are only implied by her silence and her appearance. The chapter ends with the introduction of the imps of the Comic Spirit, as chorus, in a comment of which the speaker is clearly not in sympathy with the Egoist:

> Dating from the humble departure of Lieutenant Crossjay Patterne up the limes-avenue under a gathering rain-cloud, the ring of imps in attendance on Sir Willoughby maintained their station with strict observation of his movements at all hours; and were comparisons in quest, the sympathetic eagerness of the eyes of caged monkeys for the hand about to feed them, would supply one. They perceived in him a fresh development and very subtle manifestation of the very old thing from which he had sprung.

The "very old thing from which he had sprung" is not "egoism" only, but more basically his primitive animal nature, uncorrected by conscious self-knowledge. The narrator can appear both impersonal and intensely personal at the same time, and such subtle shifts in point of view as are constantly occurring in Meredith's writing require an attentive reader with a properly attuned sense of irony.

Another characteristic of Meredith's novels, and one that can be seen clearly in *The Egoist,* is that physical motion, towards or away from certain geographical points, has special symbolic significance. In *The Egoist* frequent mention is made of the patterns of the dance: at first, everyone and everything gravitates towards Willoughby, who is also metaphorically the "sun". Later, when Clara begins to break away from him, she becomes another center towards which others move. Willoughby and his satellites remain at Patterne Hall, while those who have broken free of him move towards the Alps, one of Meredith's constant symbols of freedom, both physical and psychological.

The Egoist begins with a Prelude, which, like a musical prelude, presents the dominant themes of the work to follow. Meredith's Prelude consists, in fact, of several variations on a theme. In it he uses several narrative voices, which he repeats with variations in the novel, and which allow him to show several different sides of the same idea. It explains the author's purpose and method in writing comic fiction, while it illustrates in itself many of the qualities of his method—his complex prose style, his use of extended metaphor, his quotation from fictive documents and persons and his maintenance, even in the essay, of a multiple point of view. The attitudes towards art and science expressed in the Prelude are reflected in the novel that follows, and the social function of comedy, made explicit in the Prelude, is clearly implied in the developing relations between the characters. Image is piled upon image, but all cluster around a single central one, the "Book of Egoism", whose leaves are seen rolling off to the poles on the surface of an earth that the reader, following the narrator, sees as from a great distance.

"Comedy", Meredith says at the beginning of the Prelude, "is a game played to throw reflections upon social life, and it deals with human nature in the drawing-room of civilized men and women." The game is an important one because, as Meredith points out here and elsewhere, it helps to advance the course of civilization. The essential quality of comedy is its ability to shed light where nothing else can. The instrument through which the light is shed is the "Comic Spirit", Meredith's personification of the ability to stand off at a distance and view one's self, and one's society, in the light of Reason.

Man's major malady, which causes him to "wax out of proportion", is Egoism, as important to the Meredithean scheme of things as the sin of Pride is to Milton: both Pride and Egoism are necessary qualities in man, but in excess both are punishable offences, one by Hell-fire and the other by the Imps of the Comic Spirit. Yet the pricking of the Imps is corrective; they are the instruments not of damnation but of enlightenment.

It is characteristic of Meredith's writing that he does not distinguish in it between metaphor and fact. The Comic Spirit is treated as a real deity, and "Dame Gossip", the "Philosopher", and other such external commentators in the novels are treated both as characters (who do not appear) and as real persons who exist outside the works, whose comments are quoted by the narrator. Meredith's use of narrators sometimes helps to obscure the line between metaphor and event.

The central narrator of the Prelude to *The Egoist* (for Meredith never speaks to the reader directly in his own voice) does not, he says, appeal to the incredulous; they may be the subjects, but they are not the audience, of comedy. Comedy, Meredith says, is not life but art, and like all art it depends upon conventions. "Life, we know too well", says Meredith in his *Essay on Comedy,* "is not a Comedy, but something strangely mixed; nor is Comedy a vile mask". Comedy, like tragedy, selects only certain aspects of life, and deals with them within limits imposed by the nature of the materials and their arrangement. The supernatural events that occur in *The Shaving of Shagpat* could not occur in a work like *The Egoist,* where violent

Meredith in old age.

death would be a violation of tone. A work of art must have a selective consistency within itself—a quality that life does not have.

The Prelude to *The Egoist* suggests to the reader what he can expect from the novel:

> The Comic Spirit conceives a definite situation for a number of characters, and rejects all accessories in the exclusive pursuit of them and their speech. For, being a spirit, he hunts the spirit in men; vision and ardour constitute his merit: he has not a thought of persuading you to believe in him.

One of the first principles of Meredith's comedy is a unity of tone, which allows for sudden and complex shifts in point of view, and long digressions in which the "vision" of the Comic Spirit is allowed wide play. Meredith does not insist upon the total believability of the narrator, which would, to his way of thinking, destroy the objective detachment that he insists the civilized reader should have. In *Sandra Belloni,* Meredith answers the objection to the intrusive narrator by making his principal narrator object to "this garrulous, supersubtle, so-called Philosopher" who intrudes into the action of the story to comment upon the general significance of the action. This Philosopher, says the narrator,

points proudly to the fact that our people in this comedy move themselves,—are moved from their own impulsion,—and that no arbitrary hand has posted them to bring about any event and heap the catastrophe. In vain I tell him that he is making tatters of the puppets' golden robe—illusion: that he is sucking the blood of their warm humanity out of them.

The reader knows full well that both the "narrator" and the "Philosopher" are creations of the author, but Meredith takes care to make this explicit in order to prevent the "illusion" from allowing the reader to turn comedy into melodrama. Meredith constantly reminds the reader that what he is viewing is not life but art, and that the characters in his comedy are not whole people but essences: "the spirit in men".

Comedy, for Meredith, is more concerned with the qualities of a person's mind than with his physical appearance, and the description of physical detail is irrelevant unless it tells something about these qualities. "You see he has a leg", tells more about Sir Willoughby (and incidentally about the person who makes the remark) than any amount of description would, and the implications of Mrs. Mountstuart Jenkinson's remark on the occasion of Sir Willoughby's coming of age, explicated at length and from several different points of view, are reflected throughout *The Egoist.*

The central metaphorical device in the Prelude is the "Book of Egoism", which is commented upon by several "persons". The primary narrator, who quotes the others, introduces the theme on which the subsequent variations are based:

> Now the world is possessed of a certain big book, the biggest book on earth; that might indeed be called The Book of Earth; whose title is the Book of Egoism, and it is a book full of the world's wisdom. So full of it, and of such dimensions is this book, in which the generations have written ever since they took to writing, that to be profitable to us the Book needs a powerful compression.

It must be remembered that the style of this passage, like that of the rest of the Prelude, is parody: the tone, the parallel repetitions, the alliteration, the central mythic device are intended to suggest the style of a contemporary author. But the passage also figures forth the idea that Meredith wishes the reader to entertain, to visualize; and it helps to characterize the narrator who goes on to quote "authorities". The Prelude as a whole serves to introduce the reader to the "dominant idea" before the characters are presented in action.

Meredith departs from the English comic tradition in his insistence upon the intellectuality of comedy. He also differs in the kinds of comic characters he creates; they are not only his central characters, but they develop as well. English comic characters are usually static: it is the tragic, or at least the serious, ones that develop. Sir Willoughby can develop and still remain comic because, in spite of the changes that have taken place in him, he remains unable to divest himself of his egoism, even when he begins to see it, however dimly.

The narrator of the Prelude elucidates the idea of egoism by means of quotation and paraphrase of "wise men" and "the notable humourist", whose style is clearly different from that of the narrator himself:

> Who, says the notable humourist, in allusion to this Book, who can studiously travel through sheets of leaves now capable of a stretch from the Lizard to the last few poor pulmonary snips and shreds of leagues dancing on their toes for cold, explorers tell us, and catching breath by good luck, like dogs at bones about a table, on the edge of the Pole? Inordinate unvaried length, sheer longinquity, staggers the heart, ages the very heart of us at a view.

In order not to miss the irony inherent in the selection of point of view here, it is necessary to remember that for Meredith 'humour' is of a lower order than comedy: emotional, rather than intellectual. In the *Essay on Comedy* he says that

> Humourists touching upon History or Society are given to be capricious. They are, as in the case of Sterne, given to be sentimental; for with them the feelings are primary, as with singers. Comedy, on the other hand, is an interpretation of the general mind, and is for that reason of necessity kept in restraint.

Since it is "a piece of humour to puzzle our wits", the narrator of the Prelude undertakes to translate the humourist's remarks into understandable language. Thus the same idea is presented from two different points of view—that of the "humourist" and that of his interpreter. These involve different language, different images, different evaluations, and even different things to evaluate. It is not the humourist, but the narrator, who comments upon "Realism" and "Science".

The Prelude is not only an introduction to the novel, a comment upon the nature of comedy and of egoism, and a justification of comedy. It is also a comment on other ways of viewing the world and on narrative methods other than those employed in *The Egoist.* Comedy and life are not the same, and to attempt to treat comedy realistically would be to destroy the comedy. Realism, according to the Prelude, is an enemy of comedy because it is not properly selective:

> . . . the realistic method of conscientious transcription of all the visible, and a repetition of all the audible, is mainly accountable for our present branfulness, and for that prolongation of the vasty and the noisy, out of which, as from an undrained fen, steams the malady of sameness, our modern malady.

Realism buries essentials under a mass of irrelevant detail in order to achieve verisimilitude, and it lacks "the inward mirror, the embracing and condensing spirit" that shows more of men than can be seen from externals. It thus blinds man to Reason, and prevents him from seeing his own egoism.

Neither can science give us more than facts about the physical world, which have no meaning until we select and arrange them. It gives us information, not insight, and with our information we can remain just as blind to our own natures as we were without it:

> We drove in a body to Science the other day for an antidote; . . . and Science introduced us to our o'er-hoary ancestry—them in the Oriental posture: whereupon we set up a primaeval chattering to rival the Amazon forest nigh nightfall, cured, we fancied. And before daybreak our disease was hanging on to us again, with the extension of a tail. . . . We were the same, and animals into the bargain. That is all we got from Science.

Meredith is often looked upon as a supporter of modern science, and particularly of the theory of evolution. That he accepted the Darwinian Hypothesis as true he makes clear in many places in his writing, but he just as clearly points out that in his view it does not much matter once the facts are known.

Meredith is concerned not with biological evolution but with the evolution of man in society: man has passed beyond the stage of unconscious "natural selection" to the stage where all of his choices are capable of being conscious ones, and thus man can to a large extent determine the course of his own future evolution. Man has, in other words, a considerable degree of free will. Education is extremely important, since it makes man better able to make wise choices, but he is in any case responsible for his actions up to the limit of his capacity for understanding. Richard Stang has pointed out that "The science of Meredith's day, mechanistic physics and Darwinian biology, in denying man's humanity, also denied his freedom, and any psychology which relied on science would do the same thing " [*The Theory of the Novel in England, 1850-1870,* 1959]. But Meredith rejects this kind of "science"; he holds man to be a conscious agent, and thus morally responsible for his own actions. He holds also that "man is not as much comprised in external features as the monkey" [*The Shaving of Shagpat*], that his mind is an essential part of him and thus ought to be portrayed in fiction. "We have little to learn of apes, and they may be left", Meredith continues in the Prelude. Apes are, nevertheless, useful mirrors of human qualities. They have long been associated with the baseness in man: Shibli Bagarag in *The Shaving of Shagpat* can see himself in the old monkey who would be a king and who became a monkey as a result of his own free choice. In *Evan Harrington,* published shortly after Darwin's *Origin of Species,* and in which Meredith plays with Darwinian terminology, the monkey in the tailor's shop does little more than "ape" the human characters in a traditional fashion.

Darwinian evolution is purely an animal matter; the evolution that is important to man is the social. There are, for Meredith, higher and lower forms of society; and societies, like men, are constantly changing. The lower can evolve into a higher, but likewise, a higher can regress into a lower. The measure of a civilization can be gauged by the prevalence of the "Comic idea", which can exist only in a society where there is some social equality between men and women: " . . . there never will be civilization where Comedy is not possible", Meredith says, "and that comes of some degree of social equality of the sexes". The egoist fancies himself a "conqueror" of the inferior sex; his intellect has not yet evolved to the stage where he can conceive of sexual equality.

Art can show man to himself in a way that science cannot, since art involves the organization of facts from a human point of view, and of the practice of art in letters, comedy "is the best for the perusal of the Book of our common wisdom". Meredith believes that "the duty of the poet and novelist is to reaffirm human freedom in the face of scientific determinism and show man that he can control his own actions through knowledge" [Stang, *The Theory of the Novel in England, 1850-1870*]. The Comic Spirit, which is "born of our united social intelligence", is needed if man is to be civilized: it is both a product and a cause of civilization. Comedy "proposes the correcting of pretentiousness, of inflation, of dulness, and of the vestiges of rawness and grossness to be found among us. She is the ultimate civilizer, the polisher, a sweet cook." Comedy is opposed to "sentimentalism", the counterfeit of emotion, but not to "romance", with which Meredith associates genuine and unselfish love of another, and in which pretense is absent.

The laughter of comedy is the laughter of Reason; laughter without the light of Reason, that is, without a clear sight of the world and of one's self, is mere animal sound, "a low as of the udderful cow past milking hour!" Reasonable laughter also allows for pathos, which is necessary to some degree in comedy because "The Egoist surely inspires pity". Too much pathos works against Reason to produce sentimentality, but total lack of it blinds one to the Comic Spirit:

> Contempt is a sentiment that cannot be entertained by comic intelligence. What is it but an excuse to be idly minded, or personally lofty, or comfortably narrow, not perfectly humane. If we do not feign when we say that we despise Folly, we shut the brain.

To be contemptuous is to be, like Sir Willoughby, a supreme Egoist.

The Egoist, then, is the prime subject of comedy. Like Dostoyevsky's Underground Man, he denies humanity to other people: people, except for the Egoist himself, are merely things. The Egoist is wholly bound up in himself, in his own feelings. He it is who is unable really to see himself from a distance by the light of Reason and in relation to other people: that is, the subject of comedy is he who lacks the Comic Spirit. He is to be laughed at for his absurdity, yet he must be pitied, too; and the audience that views him is invited to see its own reflection in him. And the audience that sees is capable of advancing the development of its own civilization yet a step further. (pp. 32-42)

> *Donald R. Swanson, in his* Three Conquerors: Character and Method in the Mature Works of George Meredith, *Mouton, 1969, 145 p.*

Gillian Beer   (essay date 1970)

[*In the following excerpt, Beer examines Meredith's use and understanding of comedy, analyzing, specifically, the role of the comic spirit in* The Egoist.]

[*The Egoist* is] an exploration of the boundaries beyond which comedy cannot venture. 'Life, we know too well, is not a Comedy, but something strangely mixed', [Meredith] wrote in [*An Essay on Comedy and the Uses of the Comic Spirit*]; *The Egoist* ranges beyond what Meredith had earlier declared to be the province of comedy: social follies rather than man's inescapable nature. 'Do not offend reason', enjoin *Essay* and Prelude but as soon as Meredith is dealing with human figures he shows a heightened consciousness of how narrow is reason's power in human conduct; and he sees further that since the flouting of reason is the root of comedy, comedy may have a tragic issue in the lives of human beings. . . . Although tragedy is not in question, the special emotional edge of *The Egoist* comes from a sense of poignancy held at bay.

The narrative language represents the characters' active inner life and sets it off against their elaborately controlled dialogue exchanges. (pp. 124-25)

Meredith says in the *Essay* that comedy does not deal with 'periods of fervour' but in the novel both Clara and Willoughby are in a state of ferment, swelling beneath the glossy surface of polite interchange in which a raised eyebrow is the only possible representation of rage. The basis of the novel is the struggle between the instinctual demands of a man or woman's nature and the social forms they adopt by demand or as disguise. The struggle is not judged easily: Meredith believes in civilisation and evolution. What he shows is that a man like Willoughby may use the forms of civilisation to disguise from himself an uncontained and animal voraciousness, and that the same civilised forms may prevent a woman like Clara from responding in her own full identity because they present her with a model of what a lady should feel and be—a model which is static and anti-evolutionary.

The clash takes its crucial form in the disparity between the pre-ordained conventional patterns of fiction and actual existential feeling. Sir Willoughby Patterne is a 'model' gentleman ('He has a leg', as Mrs Mountstuart cryptically observes). He is the ideal hero of popular Victorian fiction—handsome, intelligent, wealthy, generous, and admired by all about him. Clara, the girl to whom he is engaged, seems to have all the qualities of a typical novel heroine: she is pretty, absolutely 'pure' and inexperienced sexually, with means of her own and the only daughter of an elderly scholar-gentleman. Everyone is preparing for a conventional courtship and wedding. But this is an anti-conventional novel which takes the easy expectations of society and the plot judgments of fiction and turns them askew. Thus, Clara who has been swept off her feet by Willoughby's romantic whirlwind courtship begins to realise that whirlwind courtships may be a form of aggression and a prelude to annihilation. She comes to understand (all unwillingly) that Sir Willoughby's ideal of marriage is not partnership but absorption. The narrator interprets Willoughby's view of it thus:

She would not burn the world for him; she would not, though a purer poetry is little imaginable, reduce herself to ashes, or incense, or essence, in honour of him, and so, by love's transmutation, literally be the man she was to marry. She preferred to be herself, with the egoism of women! She said it: she said: 'I must be myself to be of any value to you, Willoughby.'

He uses everyone to act as a flattering mirror for himself and is incapable of dialogue:

'So entirely one, that there never can be question of external influences. I am, we will say, riding home from the hunt: I see you awaiting me: I read your heart as though you were beside me. And I know that I am coming to the one who reads mine! You have me, you have me like an open book, you, and only you!'

'I am to be always at home?' Clara said, unheeded, and relieved by his not hearing.

Meeting his faithful first love, Laetitia, after a journey abroad of three years, this is how he greets her:

'Laetitia Dale!' he said. He panted. 'Your name is sweet English music! And you are well?' The anxious question permitted him to read deeply in her eyes. He found the man he sought there, squeezed him passionately, and let her go . . .'

Clara's growing dislike of Willoughby's possessiveness develops into a sullen physical antagonism. She cannot bear him to kiss her.

The gulf of a caress hove in view like an enormous billow hollowing under the curled ridge.

She stooped to a buttercup; the monster swept by.

These passages show the range of strategies by which the reader is led to judge Sir Willoughby; the representation of his consciousness in which his thoughts and the narrator's overlap; direct speech; motives imputed to him by an epitomising commentator; mock-heroic aggrandising metaphor. Willoughby is indeed pursued. (pp. 127-29)

[Although] our sympathy is in the main invited for Clara, Meredith is too subtle an observer to refuse a measure of fellow-feeling to Willoughby or to suggest that he has a monopoly of egoism. 'The love-season is the carnival of egoism, and brings the touchstone to our natures.' Meredith is showing the workings of egoism in *all* his characters and particularly in Clara, and in this way he suggests that egoism is common to us all. (p. 132)

Laetitia's declaration at the end of the book, 'I am an Egoist', is a declaration of growth as well as of hardening. Her timid self-abnegation has given way to independence. Clara's egotism is inextricable from her discovery of her self, which includes her sexual self—and *The Egoist* is exceptional among Victorian novels in the closeness and intensity with which it suggests sexual revulsion (just as *The Tragic Comedians* is exceptional in the ferocity with which it depicts sexual obsession). Clara realises 'the tragedy of the embrace' which will come to her if she dutifully fulfils her engagement and 'the clash of a sharp physical

thought: "The difference! the difference!" told her she was woman and never could submit.' In this struggle 'physical pride' and 'incandescent reason' unite to affirm her distinctness—while at the same time they lead her to understand how essential love is to her.

With her body straining in her dragon's grasp, with the savour of loathing, unable to contend, unable to speak aloud, she began to speak to herself, and all the health of her nature made her outcry womanly:—'If I were loved!'—not for the sake of love, but for free breathing; and her utterance of it was to ensure life and enduringness to the wish, as the yearning of a mother on a drowning ship is to get her infant to shore.

To Willoughby the essentially feminine is 'a parasite—a chalice': Clara's twistings, false starts, half lies have, in contrast, the hectic serpentine movement of the hunted. She is saved from Willoughby's portentous self-absorption not only by her capacity to love but by her humour. Meredith's language to describe her is similar to his description of the comic spirit: 'her equable shut mouth threw its long curve to guard the small round chin from that effect; her eyes wavered only in humour.' But her close resemblance to the spirit of the work ('that slim feasting smile, shaped like the long-bow') does not protect her from the consequences of her human complexity.

The book is an intricate account of the duel between Willoughby and Clara: neither of them is a particularly scrupulous fighter. Both are fighting defensively to preserve the same thing: their identity. Willoughby *cannot* release Clara from her engagement because his love for her is intimately entangled with his assurance of his own worth—if she goes he will no longer be Sir Willoughby Patterne, cynosure of the county, but a twice-jilted man. Clara *cannot* marry Willoughby to be absorbed by his voracious love. Although the original cause of his dispute with Clara is his vaunted wish to 'banish the world' and live in total absorbed intimacy with her, he is really entirely dependent on the world's estimate of him. He exists to himself only through the mirror image it reflects of him, and his relationship with Clara was to have been a rosy and enlarging mirror—extending his image beyond death.

Clara 'was the first who taught him what it was to have sensations of his mortality.' The concerns of the book are lofty and the suffering of the characters is allowed its full stature and inwardness. We *realise* the experience of Willoughby's self-pity through the imagery:

This was the ground of his hatred of the world: it was an appalling fear on behalf of his naked eidolon, the tender infant Self swaddled in his name before the world, for which he felt as the most highly civilised of men alone can feel, and which it was impossible for him to stretch out hands to protect. There the poor little loveable creature ran for any mouth to blow on; and frost-nipped and bruised, it cried to him, and he was of no avail!

(This is strikingly close to the imagery used by Clara, in the passage quoted above.) The mingling of parental tenderness and infantilism measures both the intensity and the inadequacy of Willoughby's capacity to love. The ultimate thinness and repetitiveness of his characterisation is seen to represent the actual thinness and repetitiveness of egotism.

The book is long (about 600 pages): it may seem an excessive length for the breaking of an engagement—even so solemn a betrothal as Willoughby has enforced. Until two-thirds of the way through there is little physical action. This is partly because Willoughby owns everything within sight except the railway; Clara's flight to the railway station is in itself an assertion of freedom. Her vision of the Alps is the only glimpse of a free world beyond the confines of the book. In contrast to the lush, privately-owned landscape of the home-counties is set the crystalline freedom of the mountains. The length of the book corresponds to the density of the emotional life described: it is swift, not leisurely, but 'The slave of a passion thinks in a ring, as hares run: he will cease where he began.' The claustrophobia of the relationship between Willoughby and Clara, which is the cause of its dissolution, also makes it almost impossible to dissolve.

In order to underline the claustrophobic effect Meredith follows a form of three unities: the action is continuous, in one place, and never moves out of its narrow range of emotions, chief among which is frustration (Laetitia, Vernon, Clara and Willoughby are all frustrated). He adds the further, fictive, unity that the book is seen largely from a single point of view, that of Clara. He does, however, allow us to know Sir Willoughby's thoughts: he transcribes them apparently quite straightforwardly and often without commentary. But the mind of the reader scrutinises them. In this way he allows us to make the same discoveries about Sir Willoughby as Clara does, by a means additional to, and to some extent independent of, hers. At times it seems scarcely believable that Sir Willoughby should fail to recognise his motives for what they are, so clearly does he state grossly selfish ideas to himself; but it is precisely the failure to take that final step to self-consciousness which involves self-criticism which makes Sir Willoughby what he is. By making us share Sir Willoughby's stream-of-consciousness, Meredith further suggests that we all think, quite lucidly, many more thoughts than we dare scrutinise.

His observation of the two principal characters is scrupulously exact. For example the deliberately uncharming account of the way Clara desperately annexes confidants: first Laetitia, then Vernon, then Mrs Mountstuart (it is important for our estimate of her that she only *seems* to have confided in Horace de Craye). This series of incidents is both a comic exaggeration of the conventional role of the confidante (a role found in French neo-classical *tragedy*) and a representation of the hysterical urge to be understood and justified which is common to most of us in emotional crises. This realism and inwardness (which reaffirms the emotional meaning of literary conventions) is seen also in the picture of Laetitia. It combines uneasily with the extremely formal dramatic structure of the last part of the book, in which all the devices of high comedy are deployed: the hidden listener, Crossjaye, who unintentionally hears Sir Willoughby's midnight proposal to Laetitia; the chapter headings from stage directions; the comic

chorus of county ladies; the crowding of all the characters onto the stage for the scintillating untying of knots.

The delight of the book's conclusion (as well as its drop in intensity) comes because the solutions imposed derive from a more familiar literary world. Willoughby has been made to look ridiculous (to the reader, but not entirely to the other characters). His victories may be hollow, but they clothe his nakedness—and for him this preserves his identity, which is vested in appearances. (His favourite image of himself is as *le roi soleil*.) Clara has won her battle—but at the end of the book is a little withdrawn, so that she seems again just an ordinary young woman.

The sense of comic release at the end of the novel is in part a sense of release from the stringency of Meredith's comic vision. He said himself that the book contained 'only half myself'; the tart rationality of the scrutinising Comic Spirit cannot fully contain the emotional force of the characters. The comic imps are not our representatives. They come from a different world. They inhibit our involvement with the characters, but we are not like them. It is a situation akin to the fourth book of *Gulliver's Travels:* we cannot comfortably identify ourselves with either group. Comic imps and Houhyhynyms, however admirable, are ineffacably different from us. At times the primness of the narrative insistence on folly seems limited in the face of the characters' suffering, whether or not the suffering is self-imposed. We are not kept at the 'point fixe' of comedy: we move into the characters, then very far away, to where they seem like comic china ornaments caught in grotesque attitudes. The emotional energy of the book is such that at times the rigid comic form is almost shattered. (pp. 132-37)

> *Gillian Beer, in her* Meredith, A Change of Masks: A Study of the Novels, *The Athlone Press, 1970, 214 p.*

John Goode   (essay date 1971)

[*Goode is an English nonfiction writer and critic. In the following excerpt, he examines the philosophical, social, and psychological factors that contribute to Meredith's understanding of egoism and the import of the word in nineteenth-century England.*]

Criticism is a game played to throw reflections on the literary work in order to exhibit the way in which it deals with human nature. But *The Egoist* seems to be an inward mirror: it throws its own reflections, so that, for example, to discover that the willow pattern or the symbolic status of hands are important is to do no more than restate what the author, and, indeed, his protagonists, tell us. How do we muscle in on a game of patience? The novel states its own terms, works itself out in perfect accord with those terms, and the critic either paraphrases . . . , makes doubtful analogies with life . . . or becomes something else, a metacritic questioning the terms themselves.

Thus Gillian Beer. She measures the achievement of *The Egoist* against works not so committed to a specific aesthetic, notably *The Tragic Comedians,* and she sees it finally as a *parenthetical* work in which Meredith works out schematically the role of authorial distance before he moves on to the later novels, 'in which Meredith shows an enhanced tenderness toward his characters and a willingness to move through the emotions and not only through the head'. I don't really know what *The Egoist* 'moves' through if it is not the generation of an emotional commitment (think only of the way in which Meredith links Clara, Crossjay and the wild weather). But, more importantly, Gillian Beer's placing seems to me to demolish the novel altogether. She sees it as an experiment in a deliberately enclosed form: 'in contrast with *The Egoist, The Tragic Comedians* derives from real life, not from literature.' It explicitly is such an experiment, of course, but the enclosure has no point unless it enables the novel to relate more vividly to life. It invokes 'the embracing and condensing spirit', and thus to argue that it derives, more than most other literary artefacts, from 'literature', is to condemn it outright. Meredith is claiming a definite social role for art in the Prelude ('Art is the specific'), so that the only way we can evaluate the novel is to evaluate its terms and the claims those terms make to offer a meaningful impression of the actual.

The very title [*The Egoist*] seems to reduce the 'original psychological notation' which is the most recognizable development in later-nineteenth-century fiction, to a simple moral typology. George Steiner's history of the words 'egoism' and 'egotism' concludes that, on the whole, they 'betray the survival of a neo-classical façade long after Rousseau and Romanticism had subdued the feelings which had originally animated these words'. If he is right, and if *The Egoist,* therefore, is merely the elaboration of a pre-Romantic psychology, its theme is anachronistic, and its extensive exploration within the formal terms of the novel is gratuitous. For the most successful realizations of pre-Romantic characterization depend precisely on their allusive brevity. We are alerted to the complexity of Atossa, for example, because we recognize that the moral framework of *The Moral Essays* demands a rhetorical process of typification through epigram and pictorial fixity. *The Egoist* seems to be trying to create a profound world out of that highly achieved surface.

But Steiner is inaccurate, at least about the latter half of the nineteenth century. He fails to make any real distinction between 'egotist' and 'egoist', and yet the *N.E.D.* would have told him that *The Saturday Review* saw Meredith's use of the French orthography as an adoption of 'the current slang'. Although the word was used in the eighteenth century as a philosophical term, the most extensive use of it in the 1870s in that way was by Henry Sidgwick, who was concerned to take it seriously as a possible moral attitude, so that he hardly conceals a neo-classical anti-individualism. Its most important use, however, is as a biological/psychological term, with, to be sure, moral implications, by Spencer and Comte. 'Egoism' belongs to a technical context, and we can gauge how technical if we note that whereas Comte himself uses the word in a fairly general way (it does, of course, have a consistent history in French) when he says, for example, *'Le Positivisme conçoit directement l'art moral comme consistant à faire, autant que possible, prévaloir les instincts sympathiques sur impulsions égoistes',* the English translation renders this last phrase as 'selfish instincts' and uses 'egoistic' in the specific context of the section on biology. What I am emphasizing is that 'egoist' re-enters the English language between the mid-fifties and mid-seventies with a renewed connotative force—linking it with the attempt to find a basis for human conduct in empirical scientific discourse. And with this renewed force, it is connected not with attempts to resurrect pre-Romantic attitudes, but with attempts to find post-Romantic ideas, ideas which would cope with that aspect of human experience which is not coherently explained in terms of individual consciousness. Such an attempt dominates the speculative thought of the mid-Victorians. It pervades, for example, Leslie Stephen's *Thought in the Eighteenth Century,* in which he speaks for the generation reflected in Meredith's novel when, commenting on Hartley, he writes: 'The purely selfish solution . . . has a terrible plausibility, especially when all philosophy is obliged to start from the individual mind, instead of contemplating the social organism.' 'Egoism', through its links with Comte and Spencer, becomes involved with the movement to create sociology—that is, to confront fully the romantic self and to transcend it in social terms. Positivism is the most influential system to cater for this desire, but Bradley, in his own terms, was also engaged in affirming extra-personal forces which motivate individuals as social beings. We shall see that *The Egoist* needs to be referred to all these contexts, and that, consequently, it is at the pulse of its own epoch.

The Prelude rejects the scientific description of human nature, but to reject it is not to dismiss it. *The Egoist* echoes in its title and in the connotations of its theme Comte's biological account of human emotion, the theory of cerebral functions. Comte analyses the cerebral functions in terms of a progressive scale moving from egoism to altruism, a scale which exists statically in the mind of every individual and dynamically in individual growth and social evolution. The fundamental law of the scale is that 'cerebral functions are higher in quality and inferior in force as we proceed from behind forwards'. He categorizes the egoistic functions in three stages, moving progressively towards the individual's awareness of and involvement in society. At the base are the defensive instincts—self-preservation and procreation; above them are the instincts which make for self-improvement, military (destructive) and industrial (constructive). Intermediary between these purely egoistic instincts and the social affections are pride (which is defined as love of power) and vanity (love of approbation). Both of these 'are essentially personal, whether in their origin or in their object. But the means through which these instincts are to be gratified give them a social character, and render their tendencies far more modifiable'. One final relevant point is made by Comte, and that is that the organism which provides the bridge between egoistic instincts and social affections is the family:

> If, on the one hand, domestic life is that which prepares us best to feel the charm of living for others, on the other hand it places us in the situation that best enables each of us to abuse this power over others . . . For Society continually acts in purifying the leading characteristics of Family.

The Egoist is not, of course, a Positivist manifesto; on the contrary, as we shall see, much of its didactic impetus is directed against Comte's seductive and dangerous complacency. Nor does it reflect Comte schematically: it is rather that it is saturated with the Comtist ambience. The implicit way it tends to find itself in the novel is best exemplified in the episode of the rumour about the widow 'who had very nearly snared him'. It requires an aggressive act on the widow's integrity in order to quash it:

> Sir Willoughby unbent. His military letter I took a careless glance at itself lounging idly and proudly at ease in the glass of his mind, decked with a wanton wreath, as he dropped a hint, generously vague, just to show the origin of the rumour, and the excellent basis it had for not being credited.

Marriage at this point is an act of self improvement: 'His duty to his House was a foremost thought with him' and he has moved in 'his admirable passion to excel' from hunting to the pursuit of Constantia Durham. The constructive act of building the new generation has to be preceded by the military training of the hunt (which Meredith explicitly links to a stage in society in which the State demands no personal service, just as Comte makes the modification of egoism dependent on the ability of society to exert its influence), and it is thus natural that, in this description of Willoughby's exertion to the destruction of the threatened snare, he should use Comte's adjective 'military'. Comte is important for *The Egoist,* not because of a deliberate commitment to or confrontation with that philosopher in particular, but because the general tenor of his thinking pervades so much English thought in the 1870s (the decade of the official translation and the heyday of figures like Beesly and Harrison).

In a general way, therefore, the structure of egoism in the novel has to be related to this biological scheme. The most important point (and this is true as well of Herbert Spencer) is that Comte maintains an air of moral neutrality about the word—egoism is the starting-point of what transcends it. Up to a point, which we shall have to define precisely, *The Egoist* shares this neutrality. The Book of Egoism is the Book of the Earth. 'The Egoist is our fountainhead, primeval man' and thus, without irony, Meredith can go on to say he is 'a sign of the indestructibility of the race'. This is why it is a grand old Egoism that built the house: it is not endorsed in absolute terms, but it is granted its role: man's instinct for self-preservation, which Comte defines as nutrition and which is both affirmatively and ironically imaged in the novel as Crossjay's appetite and Dr Middleton's gastronomic vulnerability, is what has created the society whose finest manifestation is the Comic Spirit. The primitive force which determines Willoughby is a potential for good, and Clara's own rebellion begins with a necessary self-assertion: 'She preferred to be herself, with the egoism of women'. It is those who deny themselves for Willoughby's sake who are the perpetrators of the social ill-health which enables him to remain unexposed—the Patterne ladies, Lætitia and, to a very large extent, Vernon. For Willoughby is a *degenerate* egoist essentially. What he seeks in love is not self-preservation, but something more, 'the pacification of a voracious aesthetic *gluttony*'. This implies that in one sense he is retarded, so that, for example, the procreative instinct is perverted to a narrower appetite: 'Miss Middleton was different: she was the true ideal, fresh gathered morning fruit in a basket, warranted by her bloom'. But equally he is, in the Comtist perspective, highly advanced, a *social* egoist whose main motives are pride and vanity, which, as Comte says himself, are the most difficult to modify for two reasons: first, they are in 'perpetual antagonism' with each other, and, second, the most developed society has a tendency to stimulate both.

Egoism ceases to be a morally neutral word in Meredith's novel as soon as it becomes involved with a social structure, particularly that of the family. In the first place, it becomes linked to competitiveness—Willoughby uses a Darwinian vocabulary of natural selection about Flitch or Vernon (they are 'extinct' if they thwart him). Secondly, its involvement with property—property that is not built, but inherited and used as an instrument of power and a claim to applause (this emerges in Willoughby's patronage of Vernon)—provides not a modification of the beast, but a protective cover. Willoughby's jealousy is defined as 'the primitive egoism seeking to refine in a blood gone to savagery under apprehension of an invasion of rights'. George Woodcock, in his excellent Introduction to the Penguin edition of *The Egoist,* says that Meredith may have been aware of Stirner (and that Stirner was known in England at this time is confirmed by F. H. Bradley's use of him to admonish Henry Sidgwick). And if that is the case, he would have read (I'm quoting here from Woodcock's book, *Anarchism*):

> He who, to hold his own, must count on the absence of will in others is a thing made by those others, as the master is a thing made by the servant.

Certainly Willoughby, because of his competitive and property-based sensitivity, is finally exposed as a thing, a leg, we may say, whose life consists of dancing to the tunes and leaping the obstacles provided by those over whom he has power.

But this makes the novel a very radical challenge to Comte's version of social evolution. For in so far as Willoughby grows away from primitive egoism, he clearly grows not towards society, but towards a more inexorably alienated relationship to it. Comte's assertion that pride and vanity require social *means* is endorsed by the novel, but that this makes them more accessible to modification is exposed as absurd. In fact, the very title implicitly attacks the Comtist (and equally Spencerian) biological/ethical relation through the concepts of egoism and altruism. Strictly speaking, for Comte, though there is egoism, there can be no Egoist, for egoism is merely a part of the pattern which is in all of us at various phases of growth: it is an element in an evolutionary process, and hence cannot be a fixed attribute. That Meredith should use the phrase 'social egoist' and make his consummate example embody not so much the basic features of egoism, but the intermediary features, pride and vanity, is a direct challenge to Comte's social faith. For what the 'scientific' explanation of ethics fails to account for is the divorce between self and self-communication. The Carlylean clothes image is invoked only briefly in the Prelude, but it is enough to alert us to the special claims of insight which art makes in the face of sociology (and this is one reason why we have little to learn of apes). Self-consciousness, which is what differentiates pride and vanity from the other egoistic instincts, is not the same as self-awareness. Art offers an 'inward mirror'. It is the psychology of the social egoist that matters, not just his position in the evolution of society.

We should recall here that one of the earliest uses of the word 'egoist' in England was by Thomas Reid, and that Reid used it in an epistemological framework to describe those (unspecified) philosophers who were trapped in a post-Cartesian solipsism. In the 1870s it is Henry Sidgwick who devotes most coherent attention to the egoist world-view, this time within a discourse on ethics. Both Reid and Sidgwick assume that 'egoist' defines a tenable and permanent *attitude*. Meredith could hardly have been unconscious of Sidgwick at least (and if he was, Stephen would have sufficiently evoked self-interest as a possible consciously held attitude). He commits himself neither to the simply biological nor to the overtly ideological uses of the word, but the coexistence of the two demands psychological dramatization of the interaction of biologically enforced will and ethically based idea. It is the rationalization of the first by the second which becomes the most obvious theme of the novel, and it is this that commits him to take account of egoism at precisely the point where it accounts for itself in terms of 'the world', in pride and vanity.

Willoughby himself uses the word 'egoist' in a traditional pejorative sense. Nevertheless, his most explicit *idea* is hatred of the world: 'up in London you are nobody,' he says, ' . . . a week of London literally drives me home to discover the individual where I left him'. His enemy is the world, but this means only, of course, that the world has to be continually squared. This is the simplest paradox of the novel, and Clara rapidly recognizes it. In Comtist terms it should make Willoughby ripe for modification, but the novel sees the psychology of self-consciousness primarily in terms of reflection and therefore of enclosure. Given the epistemological and ethical connotations of the word, it becomes possible for pride and vanity to become motives which not only use society as a means of personal gratification, but which attempt to transform the means themselves into functions of the egoistic mind. This is why to be a social egoist is to be 'arcadian by the aesthetic route'. The golden world of grand old egoism (Meredith is, of course, using 'arcadian' with ironic undertones) is recovered through the assimilation of the outer world into personal images. The dominant motif of the novel has to do with mirrors (which are servants both of vanity and art): 'In his more reflective hour the attractiveness of that lady which held the mirror to his features was paramount'. The image undergoes many repetitions and variations until it enters explicitly into his calculations about Lætitia, with an almost insanely obsessive intonation: 'It would be marriage with a mirror, with an echo; marriage with a shining mirror, a choric echo. The point is that pride and vanity, so far from being intermediate in the

evolution from egoism, are its terminus ad quem; they formulate, as long as they are not completely antagonistic to each other, an enclosed world from which there is no escape. Thus Meredith uses the motif to encapsulate an immediate reflex action springing from an apparently selfless concern:

> He sprang to the ground and seized her hand. 'Lætitia Dale!' he said. He panted. 'Your name is sweet English music! And you are well?' The anxious question permitted him to read deeply in her eyes. He found the man he sought there, squeezed him passionately, and let her go. . . .

It is a reflex, but it is the reflex of the reflective man. Most of his reflections, it is true, are mediated by sentimental stereotypes: he accuses Clara of seeing the world through popular romances, but his hilarious projections of the ruined and penitent Clara are, of course, all highly literary, and Meredith makes it quite explicit 'as his popular romances would say'. The mirror works both ways: in order that society should reflect Willoughby, Willoughby has to shape himself to society. Comte is ironically half right. But the primary concern is with the process of reflection itself, so that the mirror motif enters into his carefully chosen language: 'You hit me to the life' he says to Lætitia, and, later: 'Where I do not find myself—that *I* am *essentially* I—no applause can move me'. It is because he seeks a mirror that he is so anxious to reveal himself first to Clara and later to Lætitia: 'But try to enter into my mind; think with me, feel with me'.

The image is linked, as a phrase such as this suggests, to another motif which equally embodies the enclosed psychology of social egoism, and which manifests itself in terms of the imprisonment of the reflected image. At the end of ch. ix, Willoughby reflects with a systematic aesthetic gluttony which looks forward to that of Will Brangwen, on the physical beauties of Clara. In the following chapter he makes a decisive bid to appropriate her mind by 'revealing' his fault in a way which makes him into a Darwinian natural force and a 'fallen archangel'. Clara realizes that she is now in 'the inner temple of him'. He rejects the bid Vernon is making for independence because it threatens the walls of 'our magic ring'. 'One small fissure,' he says, 'and we have the world with its muddy deluge'. Later in the chapter Willoughby supplies his own title, and by the end of the episode Clara feels herself trapped:

> The idea of the scene ensuing upon her petition for release, and the being dragged round the walls of his egoism, and having her head knocked against the corners, alarmed her with sensations of sickness.

The temple, externalized as the house itself, becomes an image of the reflective mind, again making for an extreme scepticism about Comte's theory. For this image finds a parallel on a narrative plane, when Willoughby, to secure Dr Middleton, Clara's social guardian, takes him to the inner cellar of Patterne Hall. On this level, the procedure works. Pride is able to exploit social means to its own end. What prevents it ultimately from asserting domination is not society, but the opposing *self* of Clara's egoism—

courage to be dishonourable. Mirror and cave are total defences against the social world they respond to. What happens, of course, is that the enclosed, reflective mind destroys itself. The key image modulates from mirror to web: 'And this female, shaped by that informing hand, would naturally be in harmony with him, from the centre of his profound identity to the raying circle of his variations'. This image has overtones both of mirror ('raying') and web. Once Clara has broken out of the house, Vernon has placed him with the zoological image:

> His insane dread of a detective world makes him artificially blind. As soon as he fancies himself seen, he sets to work spinning a web, and he discerns nothing else. It's generally a clever kind of web; but if it's a tangle to others it's the same to him and a veil as well.

Willoughby is no longer in an inclusive world of self: there are other spiders, and Clara's flight makes him feel 'as we may suppose a spider to feel when plucked from his own web and set in the centre of another's'. Pride and vanity are henceforth at war.

These images are not substitutes for the dramatic realization of the process. The gyrations Willoughby gets caught in in the attempt to preserve the mirror-cave are manifest in the outstanding moments of the novel—the interviews with Lætitia, the pursuit of Clara and the struggle with Clara for Dr Middleton's mind. What the images do is to transpose the biological source of egoism into a psychological drama growing out of an ethical and epistemological commitment. It is not biological growth that transforms egoism; it is a fundamental intellectual error that exposes it—through very love of self himself he slew. Sidgwick argued that empirical hedonism (which is the 'method' of egoism) was likely to be self-defeating, and went on to say 'that a rational method of attaining the end at which it aims requires that we should to some extent put it out of sight and not directly aim at it . . . [is] . . . the "fundamental Paradox of Egoistic Hedonism" '. Stephen made a similar, slightly positivized point in his commentary on Bishop Butler. The comedy of *The Egoist* grows out of the 'twists of the heart', the ironic contradictions which are inherent in the relationship between the idols of the tribe and the idols of the den, and it is given moral depth by the careful placing of moral discriminations at the point at which the human mind, in its self-realization, is confronted with a choice between being directed outwards towards love or turning in on itself to form a cave of possession in which there is no fissure. (pp. 205-14)

> *John Goode, " 'The Egoist': Anatomy or Striptease?" in* Meredith Now: Some Critical Essays, *edited by Ian Fletcher, Barnes & Noble, Publishers, 1971, pp. 205-30.*

Donald David Stone   (essay date 1972)

[*Stone is an American educator and critic whose works include several studies of late Victorian literature. In the following excerpt, Stone reviews the stylistic innovations that make Meredith's works "built for immortality" and, through his analysis of Willoughby and Clara, em-*

phasizes the relevance of the relationship between style and character in The Egoist.]

After hoping in novel after novel for a critical and popular success, Meredith apparently felt that he had not put enough ingredients into his new book [*The Egoist*]. Writing to Robert Louis Stevenson, he doubted "if those who care for my work will take to it at all . . . It is a Comedy, with only half of me in it, unlikely, therefore, to take either the public or my friends." Modesty aside, Meredith indeed limited the scope of his design and disciplined his energies in the new novel, making *The Egoist* the most manageable of Meredith's works. Characters and plot and themes do not swarm out of control, as they do in his usual novels. If *The Egoist* was not the popular success that *East Lynne* had been or *Robert Elsmere* would be, it was eagerly read at Oxford and Cambridge, and it confirmed Stevenson, among others, in the belief that Meredith was "built for immortality." . . . Meredith's portrait of Everyman as an irrationalist is one of the triumphs of the English novel; in attacking egoism in an embodied form, he made his most lasting contribution to modern mythology. Henley, who wrote four separate reviews of the novel, saw in Willoughby "a compendium of the Personal in man."

In Victorian England egoism was seen as more than a comic butt; it was a philosophical, a political, a social threat. Matthew Arnold had presented culture as the necessary bulwark against anarchy, the unenlightened egoism of all classes; for him, the guardian of culture was criticism. With considerably more optimism, Meredith envisaged the possibility of an enlightened civilization, "a society of cultivated men and women," whose watchword would be harmony—a reconciliation of all the warring claims of the nineteenth century—and whose guardian would be the Comic Spirit. In a famous passage from the lecture on comedy, Meredith personified the Spirit as at once a lofty and a faun-like deity, imbued with the best of heaven and earth and concerned with men's "honesty and shapeliness in the present":

> whenever they wax out of proportion, overblown, affected, pretentious, bombastical, hypocritical, pedantic, fantastically delicate; whenever it sees them self-deceived or hoodwinked, given to run riot in idolatries, drifting into vanities, congregating in absurdities, planning shortsightedly, plotting dementedly; whenever they are at variance with their professions, and violate the unwritten but perceptible laws binding them in consideration one to another; whenever they offend sound reason, fair justice, are false in humility or mined with conceit, individually, or in the bulk—the Spirit overhead will look humanely malign, and cast an oblique light on them, followed by volleys of silvery laughter.

Sir Willoughby Patterne is the most conspicuous example in the novel of the comic overreacher, the emblematic menace to society and all that society stands for, but the other major characters are all egoists too, in one respect or another. Once Clara and Vernon and Laetitia can see themselves for what they are, however, they can choose to change if they wish. Laetitia, it might be argued, becomes an intensified egoist by the end of the novel so that she may be a perfect match for her husband, Willoughby. Clara and Vernon, on the other hand, achieve full perspective and are last seen high in the Alps. "Sitting beside them," Meredith observes, "the Comic Muse is grave and sisterly."

The novel moves on at least two separate planes of development: from the closed drawing rooms and laboratory of Patterne Hall to the enlightened freedom of the mountains, as far as Clara is concerned, and from the autocratic freedom to roam the world at will toward the status of mastered master of a provincial backwater, in Willoughby's case. Accordingly, half of the novel takes place on the level of a drawing room comedy; the tone for such scenes is as theatrical as the Prelude to the novel intimates:

> Comedy is a game played to throw reflections upon social life, and it deals with human nature in the drawing-room of civilized men and women, where we have no dust of the struggling outer world, no mire, no violent crashes, to make the correctness of the representation convincing . . . The Comic Spirit conceives a definite situation for a number of characters, and rejects all accessories in the exclusive pursuit of them and their speech.

The heavy use of dialogue—and its functional use in representing members of a society who are active only verbally—does point toward James's novel in dialogue, *The Awkward Age.* But *The Egoist* is still another of Meredith's hybrid books, keeping to the drawing room at times but often extending outside of Patterne Hall into magnificent scenes in nature. What would have served as theatrical set pieces, like the dinner at Lady Mountstuart Jenkinson's, are occasionally only obliquely described by the characters afterward. Although the novel contains the most unified of Meredith's plots, the study of character and characters remains his principal interest. It might be argued that the novel is built on a series of stylistic levels, each appropriate to the particular character's point of view. Thus Willoughby is seen very early as a Restoration prince and wit; it is only appropriate that his place in the novel be confined to that of a character in a comedy. His comical poetic justice results from his inability to put off theatricalizing. Like Richmond Roy, he becomes the slave of his own rhetoric, and histrionics becomes second nature to him. In a strict sense, Willoughby and Clara belong to different literary genres. Hers is a discovery of the poetic truth of life, which enables her to see through the masquerade at Patterne Hall, just as Laetitia's discovery is of life's cold prose, which enables her to live with Patterne Hall.

Like James, Meredith is a master of the use of point of view in the novel. Whereas James preferred more often to confine the angle of vision to a single character for the sake of artistic coherence, however, Meredith capitalized on the differing points of view of his characters to make a thematic point. In this respect James's atypical *The Bostonians* is similar to *The Egoist,* where the theme and method are united to give a comic picture of human incomprehension. More generally in James, however, a single character, like Isabel Archer or Lambert Strether, grows in comprehension to the point where his or her angle of vi-

sion is not only the single one that the reader is given, it is also the *right* way of comprehending the experience undergone. At the end of *The Bostonians,* however, it is evident that none of the characters have seen the light. Such comic incomprehension allows James to make a negative philosophical point: in all likelihood neither the characters in *The Bostonians* nor the readers of the novel will attain the author's own point of view. In light of the subsequent critical haggling over the novel, James's point was well taken. In *The Egoist* all the major characters but Willoughby have gained a sense of perspective, and although he towers above the others as a symbolic menace, in terms of the immediate plot he is socially contained.

Unable to see himself as others see him, Willoughby is unable to see beyond his own conception of himself. Early in the novel we are told that, while looking into the then adoring eyes of Laetitia Dale, "He found the man he sought there, squeezed him passionately, and let her go." The reader's impression of Willoughby, for the first third of the novel, is both terrifying and misleading. He is presented as the absolute lord of his domain, admired by the surrounding world. From Clara Middleton's point of view, it at first seems perverse that she should want to break her engagement to such a man, even though she is terrified that she will be sacrificed to him against her wishes. The security of Willoughby's position is delusive, however. Having been jilted once before, he fears that the same thing will happen again, that the world will point an accusing and mocking finger at him. The "world," as it turns out in a succession of brilliant anticlimatic chapters, is no more than the prying Ladies Busshe and Culmer, and it is to impress them that he manages to bargain for a loveless marriage with Laetitia. Willoughby *Tyrannus* accordingly metamorphoses into the figure of a slave to his illusions, "enchained by the homage" of what he has defined for himself as the world; he becomes an actor forced to do what his audience expects from him.

A recent admirer of *The Egoist,* Louis Auchincloss, has explained Willoughby, in Dostoevskian terms, as a man with tragic problems: "He cannot love—one is almost tempted to see his drama as a tragedy of impotence" [*Reflections of a Jacobite,* 1961]. But if hell, for the Russian novelist, is the inability to love, such a condition, for Meredith, is the occasion for comedy. In the context of the novel Willoughby is a comic creation, a comic threat to himself as well as others. One is relieved that Meredith did not yield to the temptation of tracing a comic pattern to its logical tragic conclusion, as he did in the case of Beauchamp, or of Purcell Barrett in *Sandra Belloni.* Instead of diffusing his interests, Meredith channeled them into an exclusively comic direction. A compressed comic character, with suggestions of a humors figure like Sir Epicure Mammon, Willoughby is amazingly suggestive. A "flat" character, unlike Clara or Vernon or Laetitia, he is a vivid example that such fixed beings may be more vital and memorable than most three-dimensional beings. The danger of egoism, as Meredith realized, is that it reduces the individual to a personality. To develop, one needs a supple mind; Willoughby's limitation of mind necessarily leads to a limitation of his own freedom. The novel, as J. Hillis Miller has noted [in his *The Form of Victorian Fic-*

tion, 1961], "is a sophisticated investigation of the theme of self-fulfillment in a world where the individual needs other people, but also needs to be free to develop according to his own nature . . ." Clara has the dilemma of choice in the novel because she is confronted by the examples of Willoughby's egoism and Vernon Whitford's individualism. The egoist is of necessity a performer, not an individual who can choose for himself and thereby change.

Willoughby's most conspicuous addiction is to sentimental rhetoric—that "sentiment," in Thomas Love Peacock's phrase, "which is canting egotism in the mask of refined feeling." The donning of human masks, a major Meredithian concern, is demonstrated in the unconscious theatricalizing of Willoughby's thoughts and feelings. In one of the chapters devoted to his attempts at soul-unsearching, Willoughby grimly envisages what the loss of Clara will mean to his pride:

> Ten thousand furies thickened about him at a thought of her lying by the roadside without his having crushed all bloom and odour out of her which might tempt even the curiosity of the fiend, man.

He moves from this monstrous image to a sentimental staging of a future dialogue between the magnanimous hero and the repentant Clara. He imagines her, eternally cast off, in the act of reading from the script he has prepared for her:

> "My friend—I call you friend: you have ever been my friend, my best friend! Oh, that eyes had been mine to know the friend I had!—Willoughby, in the darkness of night, and during days that were as night to my soul, I have seen the inexorable finger pointing my solitary way through the wilderness from a Paradise forfeited by my most wilful, my wanton, sin. We have met. It is more than I have merited. We part. In mercy let it be for ever. Oh, terrible word! Coined by the passions of our youth, it comes to us for our sole riches when we are bankrupt of earthly treasures, and is the passport given by Abnegation unto Woe that prays to quit this probationary sphere. Willoughby, we part. It is better so."
>
> "Clara! one—one only—one last—one holy kiss!"
>
> "If these poor lips, that once were sweet to you . . ."
>
> The kiss, to continue the language of the imaginative composition of his time, favourite readings in which had inspired Sir Willoughby with a colloquy so pathetic, was imprinted.

Never far from the rhetoric of Willoughby is the inner sensualist; the thought of the "last" kiss immediately brings out the inner beast in him, and he refuses again to relinquish possession of Clara.

"The love-season is the carnival of egoism," Meredith observes, "and it brings the touchstone to our natures." In Willoughby's case, the ordeal is devastating. The idea of courtship to him is demonstrated to be an extension of fox hunting: his pursuit of Constantia Durham and Clara is described in metaphors drawn from the chase. Willoughby coats the essentially primitive nature of his action in an absurd rhetoric of lovemaking. When he tries to persuade Clara to withstand the "world" with him and to be his "beyond death," Willoughby attracts our disgust as well as hers. But when he repeats the same kind of rhetoric to Laetitia, many pages later, the effect is comic. Clara has changed in viewpoint, Laetitia is changing, and we have changed; Willoughby, however, is indefatigable: "We two against the world!" he recites from his lovers' litany, and so on. "If Willoughby would open his heart to nature," as Clara muses in another context, "he would be relieved of his wretched opinion of the world." Instead, he is the victim of his rhetoric, a provincial pseudo-Byron, who achieves unknowingly, and by reason of his unknowingness, the stature of comic touchstone to the other characters. Willoughby has been criticized by mechanistic students of the novel for being "given" to the reader rather than adequately explained, but, in the first place, what is given is an anthropological prototype, and, in the second place, he exists to "explain" the other characters' development. "Miss Middleton owed it to Sir Willoughby Patterne that she ceased to think like a girl," as Meredith points out. To know him is a liberal education.

Set in opposition to him is Clara, who learns from his example and, ironically, from his own words, "Beware of marrying an Egoist," while she avoids becoming one herself. If Willoughby ranks with Richmond Roy as Meredith's greatest mythic achievement, Clara Middleton is surely his best human figure. For Stevenson, she was "the best girl ever I saw anywhere," and it is still not impossible to echo the sentiment of Meredith's early admirers that her only equals in literature are Shakespeare's heroines. In explaining a sudden infatuation, the unfortunate hero of Forster's *The Longest Journey* appeals to his friend to "read poetry—not only Shelley. Understand Beatrice, and Clara Middleton, and Brunhilde." Clara's progress in the novel, like that of the heroine of *A Room with a View,* is linked to the development of her heart and brain. For both young ladies, the outcome calls to mind Forster's final chapter title, "The End of the Middle Ages." Personal development is equated with social progress. When, early in Meredith's novel, Willoughby presents his rhetorical dream to her that, "by love's transmutation," she might "literally be the man she was to marry," she replies that she prefers "to be herself, with the egoism of women!" Clara's discovery of her fiancé's selfishness initially enforces a desire to act on her own authority. She wants to sever the bonds of the engagement simply to be free, but it is at the moments when Clara feels herself trapped that she is most conventional. "Dreadful to think of!" she is shocked to discover, "she was one of the creatures who are written about."

Arguing with herself that she must be herself, Clara expresses to Laetitia her fear of the confines of Patterne Hall: "I chafe at restraint; hedges and palings everywhere! I should have to travel ten years to sit down contented among these fortifications. Of course I can read of this rich kind of English country with pleasure in poetry. But it seems to me to require poetry. What would you say of human beings requiring it?" If Laetitia, the amateur poetess, changes during the course of the novel into a practical, prosaic woman, Clara moves in the opposite direction toward poetry, toward a life imbued with the poetry of earth. In one of the best scenes of the novel, a scene with obvious affinities to, and more crucial differences from, the chapter devoted to Isabel Archer's all-night meditation in James's *The Portrait of a Lady,* Clara contemplates all night the problem of her difficult situation and that of women in general. "Can a woman have an inner life apart from him she is yoked to?" she wonders. But whereas Isabel finds refuge ultimately in the fact of her individuality, Clara detects the first hint of an answer in nature. She watches, in the early morning, the activities of the birds:

> The lovely morning breathed of sweet earth into her open window and made it painful, in the dense twitter, chirp, cheep, and song of the air, to resist the innocent intoxication. O to love! was not said by her, but if she had sung, as her nature prompted, it would have been. Her war with Willoughby sprang of a desire to love repelled by distaste. Her cry for freedom was a cry to be free to love.

Clara is unsure as yet of the meaning of her discovery; she thinks more in terms of loving "unselfishness and helpfulness" at this time, but she soon discovers that these qualities are embodied in the figure of Vernon Whitford.

Clara's first instinct is to run away from her predicament, but she learns in time that to do so would be to succumb to the same unreasoning rashness by which she became engaged to Willoughby in the first place. "I have seen my own heart," she can tell Laetitia at the end of the novel. "It is a frightful spectre. I have seen a weakness in me that would have carried me anywhere." Clara learns, unlike Willoughby, "to be straightforwardly sincere in . . . speech" as well as in action. When she first articulates this wish to Laetitia, while explaining her repugnance toward her fiancé, Clara complains of her lack of "power to express ideas" in the manner of that accomplished poetess. "Miss Middleton, you have a dreadful power," replies Laetitia, whose own eyes have begun to open.

Meredith chooses to describe his developing heroine in terms of the poetry of nature, just as he invests Willoughby with theatrical trappings. The two rhetorics can be seen side by side in the episode where Clara attempts, metaphorically and really, to escape one of Willoughby's threatening bursts of sentiment:

> "You are cold, my love? you shivered."
>
> "I am not cold," said Clara. "Someone, I suppose, was walking over my grave."
>
> The gulf of a caress hove in view like an enormous billow hovering under the curled ridge.
>
> She stooped to a buttercup; the monster swept by.

Like Diana Warwick, Clara can be defined as "deeply a woman, dumbly a poet." One must distinguish between the poetic rhetoric and the theatrical rhetoric in Meredith; the one tries to embody the natural, the other succeeds in concealing the natural. If the Alps come to stand for intellectual freedom, the symbol for harmony with nature in the novel is the double-blossomed wild cherry tree. Immediately after Clara discovers her fiancé to be an "immovable stone-man," she finds a source of refuge in Vernon, who represents "the world taken into her confidence." In need of his rational guidance, she comes upon him sleeping under the cherry tree:

> She turned her face to where the load of virginal blossom, whiter than summer-cloud on the sky, showered and drooped and clustered so thick as to claim colour and seem, like higher Alpine snows in noon-sunlight, a flush of white. From deep to deeper heavens of white, her eyes perched and soared. Wonder lived in her. Happiness in the beauty of the tree pressed to supplant it, and was more mortal and narrower. Reflection came, contracting her vision and weighing her to earth. Her reflection was: "He must be good who loves to lie and sleep beneath the branches of this tree!"

Clara's history in the novel is summarized in the movement from wonder to reflection, from her first awareness of the poetry of earth to her ability to articulate it and her identification of it with Vernon. Once she is united with him, she has begun to learn how to reconcile the earth and the transcendental wonder. However, it is beyond the reach of the novel to articulate the final achievement satisfactorily. The problem arises that although Vernon can be accepted as a symbol, he never seems a sufficiently human mate for Clara.

The heroes of the late Meredith novels—Vernon, Redworth in *Diana of the Crossways,* Dartrey Fenellan in *One of Our Conquerors,* Matey Weyburn in *Lord Ormont and His Aminta,* Gower Woodseer in *The Amazing Marriage*—are alike in their supposed ability to reconcile instinctive with intellectual reason, in their manliness, and in their common sense. Each of the heroes undergoes, or has undergone, an unfortunate experience with an ill-matched woman—a motif frequent in Meredith's works, no doubt suggested by his own unhappy first marriage. The author wishes them to embody such an impossible form of perfection that they fail to be credible literary characters. Having shown in *Beauchamp's Career* how a brilliantly endowed protagonist would of necessity not succeed in a human sphere, Meredith turned to a succession of symbolic victors, embodiments of his own views. While Vernon does fit the role called for in the scheme of the novel, at times he fails to convince the reader that such an embodied Meredithian symbol could survive beyond the limits of the book. And, as a representative of vitality, he is notably less vital than his cousin Willoughby.

Meredith contrasts the cousins very early in the novel, as they travel around the world together. We are informed of the liveliness of Willoughby's letters, and of the straightforwardness and absence of irony in Vernon's. Willoughby projects his personality wherever he goes; Vernon absorbs what he sees and hears. "One was the English gentleman wherever he went; the other was a new kind of thing, nondescript, produced in England of late, and not likely to come to much good himself, or do much good to the country." Despite this ironic modesty on Meredith's part, Vernon does embody for Clara the principle of useful, selfless work. A hiker and mountain climber, as well as a scholar, Vernon was partly intended as a tribute to Meredith's friend Leslie Stephen; his best scene in the novel, his pursuit of Clara through the woods during a rainstorm, suggests the best side of Stephen: "Let him be drenched, his heart will sing."

While Clara's "power" to express herself first reveals to Laetitia that her idol has feet of clay, it is Willoughby who turns Laetitia into a female egoist. In the chapter ironically entitled "Sir Willoughby Attempts and Achieves Pathos," the male Egoist tries to see if he still exerts power over his longtime worshiper by indulging in inflated, self-pitying histrionics. The result, which he is unable to detect, is that "He had, in fact, perhaps by sympathetic action, succeeded in striking the same springs of pathos in her which animated his lively endeavour to produce it in himself." Laetitia collapses in a fit of self-pity, realizing the painful waste of her years and energy. When Willoughby seeks her hand in the attempt to escape from the probable scorn of the "world" after Clara abandons him, he finds to his horror that she has changed, that her illusion has been destroyed and, with it, her career as a sentimental poetess.

When he finally coerces her into accepting him, it is at the very cost that had prompted Clara to break away from him: the prospect of a loveless marriage to an egoist. Not even General Ople has the discomfiting future that Willoughby faces with one who warns: "I am hard, materialistic; I have lost faith in romance, the skeleton is present with me all over life. And my health is not good. I crave for money. I should marry to be rich. I should not worship you. I should be a burden, barely a living one, irresponsive and cold. Conceive such a wife, Sir Willoughby!" But the addiction to rhetoric has become second nature to him, and he retorts, "It will be you!" Laetitia promises to be his "critic" and confesses that she has become, as a result of privation, a willful "Egoist." If Clara and Vernon are perfectly mated in theory, Willoughby and Laetitia are the perfect pair in fact: the unconscious and the conscious egoist. "But he had the lady with brains!" Meredith notes. "He had: and he was to learn the nature of that possession in the woman who is our wife."

For the purposes of the novel, at least, Willoughby is socially contained, and the set of marriages brings the comedy to its inevitable conclusion. Despite those satisfactions of the demands of society and fiction, Meredith hints at a number of disturbing issues that are beyond the scope of a comic novel and are taken up in his subsequent works. "If one must go through this," Clara wonders, "to be disentangled from an engagement, what must it be to the poor women seeking to be free of a marriage?" Later the author openly philosophizes on the "Condition of Woman" question, a matter most memorably argued by John Stuart Mill in the late 1860's and exemplified in the treatment of Meredith's own heroines. "They are to us what we hold of best or worst within," he says, from an enlightened male viewpoint. "By their state is our civilization judged." He had similarly argued in the lecture on

comedy that the advancement of women is both a prerequisite for and a theme of comedy. In *One of Our Conquerors* he illustrates what happens when a sensitive woman is overpowered by an egoistic mate. That *The Egoist* occupies Meredith's consistently comic attention does not obscure the potentially grave underlying problems. Willoughby is another of Meredith's versions of the devil, a comic counterpart to Shakespeare's Richard III or Milton's Satan. It is a sign of Meredith's affirmative, societal philosophy that he felt such a being could be contained by social barriers, an "army of unalterable law." Modern readers, however, may very well decide that Willoughby is horrendously and delightfully unchangeable and may choose to disbelieve in either the corrective powers of comedy or the rational sanctions of society. Willoughby is at once an Arnoldian Barbarian and a Darwinian prehistoric man, who reminds us that the irrational not only survives in life, but poses a danger if unexposed. (pp. 121-33)

> *Donald David Stone, "The Last Victorian: Meredith in the 1880's," in his* Novelists in a Changing World: Meredith, James, and the Transformation of English Fiction in the 1880's, *Cambridge, Mass.: Harvard University Press, 1972, pp. 116-72.*

Maaja A. Stewart   (essay date 1978)

[*In the following excerpt, Stewart discusses the literary tradition and social significance of the English country house and relates the economic realities of Patterne Hall to Willoughby's egoism, or his incessant projection of his identity onto other individuals and things.*]

The ideals that buttress the house of Sir Willoughby Patterne in *The Egoist* are built out of literary symbols gathered around the English country house for more than two centuries. Meredith's dissection of the individual egoism of Sir Willoughby merges with his dissection of the country house ideals. Throughout the novel the hero's self-deceptions and his real power over the characters surrounding him reverberate with allusions to one of the most stable images of community in English literature. The failure of Sir Willoughby as a man is also a failure of one dream of an ideal life within a changing historical reality: both sentimentalize practical endeavors of the past to infuse the present with romance. In the "Prelude" to the novel Meredith envisions the comic imps waiting for centuries around a great house:

> They dare not be chuckling while Egoism is valiant, while sober, while socially valuable, nationally serviceable. They wait.
>
> Aforetime a grand old Egoism built the House. It would appear that ever finer essences of it are demanded to sustain the structure: but especially would it appear that a reversion to the gross original, beneath a mask and in a vein of fineness, is an earthquake at the foundations of the House. Better that it should not have consented to motion, and have held stubbornly to all ancestral ways, than have bred that anachronic spectre.

In the novel both Willoughby and the ideal of the country house, which his society seeks to sustain, are divorced from vital civilization. The sentimental English, Meredith says in his [*Essay On Comedy*], "live in a hazy atmosphere that they suppose an ideal one." The Patterne estate, recalling through statement and symbols earlier literary celebrations, provides for Meredith a concrete image through which to examine this "hazy atmosphere" of comic delusions. The vision of humanity clinging to outmoded ideals is, as Jacob Loewenberg has so well noted, central to Meredith's idea of comedy: comedy deals with the follies and foibles of mankind, but "its tragic import lies in the fact that the things we laugh at are things once sacred, and that what we deride as absurd belongs to some of the fairest visions of the human spirit" [*Dialogues from Delphi,* 1949].

The conversion of a pastoral, even edenic, vision into a localized dream had become a compelling part of English literature and life between the sixteen hundreds, when Ben Jonson wrote "To Penshurst" and Andrew Marvell "Upon Appleton House," and the latter part of the eighteenth century when numerous English novelists retired their men of sensibility and culture to country estates. It is especially striking that in a neoclassical age to which civilized life mattered profoundly, the literary habitation for such a life was not London but the country estate: the "good men" in popular novels almost invariably found their resting place in Paradise or Bramble Hall, or on Grandison's estate; the urbane Alexander Pope spent the best part of his life perfecting Twickenham and using it as an ideal against which to measure the corruptions of the city and its inhabitants; a minor poem such as John Pomfret's "The Choice," dated 1700, was popular throughout the century, because, as Samuel Johnson said [in his *The Lives of the Most Eminent English Poets,* 1781], it sketched "a system of life adapted to common notions, and equal to common expectations" by accommodating the country house ideals to even moderate fortunes. In the latter half of the nineteenth century, Henry James, that fascinated observer of English ways, still speaks of the actualities of English country house life in terms reminiscent of the ideals celebrated in literature:

> Of all the great things that the English have invented and made part of the credit of the national character, the most perfect, the most characteristic, the only one they have mastered completely in all its details, so that it becomes a compendious illustration of their social genius and their manners, is the well-appointed, well-administered, well-filled country house [*English Hours,* 1905].

Willoughby attempts to create and project a self which transcends his limited personal being by drawing on a spacious mythical identity provided him by the vocabulary and assumptions of this idealized tradition. The myth supplies him with poses which can express his deepest egoism in a variety of ways. The images of enclosure, completeness, harmony, and stability gather around both Willoughby and his house throughout the novel, recalling earlier literary celebrations of country houses which associate this "ideal life" with Eden or the Golden Age. This pastoral image merges with various secular visions of power, in which the master of the house becomes the absolute center of society. At various times Willoughby's poses recall the total economic and social relatedness of feudalism; the patrician hero of the eighteenth-century novels, who with his benevolent authority is able to pull disparate human passions into a harmony around himself; the grandly eloquent memory of the grace and charm of the courts of Restoration Charles and of the French Sun King. Meredith's comic treatment of Willoughby and his society strips these associations of their potential ethical implications, leaving us with a decadent vision of a society and a man who seek a life of pure aesthetic pleasure. Unlike the masters of houses whom poets and novelists had extolled for two centuries, Willoughby is not sustained for the moral good of society, but "for the pleasure of the imagination"; he answers the "aspiration after some form of melodious gentlemanliness which is imagined to have inhabited the island at one time." He is nurtured as the "lord of the Hall, the feast, and the dance," as a "splendid young representative island lord." He provides a holiday from moral concerns by being an unchanging reference point to others. As men worship gods they can endure, so they also make heroes to systematize and immobilize their aspirations in necessarily limited human beings.

Such heroes can be dangerous or, at the very least, disappointing beings if they insist on their own mobility; they become ridiculous if they do not. Herein lies the comic center of the novel. The casual spectators to the drama of Willoughby's courtships realize they are playing a game whose terms they have defined: for them the index of civilization lies not in moral action or spiritual awareness but in the grace and charm of a world of sleek surfaces. Mrs. Mountstuart, for instance, draws no distinction between the aesthetic reverberations of Willoughby's loves and losses and her attempt to group the characters into a harmonious melody during her dinner party. Living and compelling ideals require the strenuous effort, constant readjustment, and mobility possessed only by Clara, Vernon, and Laetitia in the novel. The comic society around Patterne Hall, lazy and bored, casually substitutes idols for ideals. Heavy, immobile, changeless—these demand nothing but carefully defined admiration. Underneath this idolatry lies a hardheaded practicality and an acceptance of the severe limitations of life, as Mrs. Mountstuart confides to Clara: "His wife must manage him. . . . You look down at the idea of managing. It has to be done. . . . We must be moderately slavish to keep our place; which is given us in appearance; but appearances make up a remarkably large part of life, and far the most comfortable, so long as we are discreet at the right moment."

Willoughby, however, tries to merge the appearances and the necessarily more complex psychological reality by internalizing these carefully defined admirations and by assuming a definition of his essential being built on the literary images provided him. This constantly threatens to turn him into a caricature, a parody of the image society wants. The ladies guard against this potential: they have "the desire to feel that so prevailing a gentleman was not in any degree pitiable." Clara's initial distaste brings this potential into actuality in her mind: "He was handsome;

so correctly handsome, that a slight unfriendly touch precipitated him into caricature. . . . She tried to look on him as the world did." Ironically, her struggle to view him with society's eyes occurs when Willoughby tries to convince her that their love must separate itself from the world to retain its intensity and meaning. Only as a drawing-room entertainer, when Willoughby is surrounded by the ladies whose admiration supports his ideal self-image, can Clara see him as "a productive creature. . . . He had even a touch of the romantic air which Clara remembered as her first impression of the favourite of the county." In her growing awareness she is able to see that the aesthetic surface of life is sharply at variance with an ethical and spiritual life, which Willoughby tries to subsume under aesthetic terminology.

The social history of his house hints at the disparity between Willoughby's ideal image and actuality. The "grand old Egoism" that built his house does not belong to the Edenic, feudal, or patrician worlds Willoughby likes to recall, but to a wholly commercial world of the middle class, which reduces everything to the category of property. To appreciate the deep originality of Meredith's variation of the nouveau riche theme in **The Egoist** we have only to consider his **Sandra Belloni** in which the younger Poles anticipate Willoughby in trying to skip over bourgeois realities into an idealized country-house setting. Unlike Willoughby, however, the Poles cannot easily dispense with their own concrete memories of the London commercial world; they remain unsettled, dreaming of leaving Brookfield and moving into the more aristocratic Besworth Castle. Willoughby, living within an inherited security, uncomplicated by hectic social climbing and disparate personal memories, can more easily substitute a changeless nonhistorical vision for historical reality. Meredith, by briefly sketching the historical context in which Willoughby should be viewed, underlines his self-delusion and his decadence. Since he is the fifth in descent from the lawyer Simon Patterne, the house was probably established in the eighteenth century when a new capitalist order had thoroughly found its way into the country-estate business. According to Raymond Williams, an "estate was calculated as an opportunity for investment, carrying greatly increased returns. In this development, an ideology of improvement—of transformed and regulated land—became significant and directive. Social relations which stood in the way of this kind of modernization were then steadily and at times ruthlessly broken" [*The Country and the City,* 1973]. Lawyer Patterne exemplifies this ruthlessness in his skill "in the art of cutting" excess branches off the family tree. The raising up of a family by concentrating all its wealth on one member is a familiar enterprise in eighteenth-century bourgeois families, as dramatized in Samuel Richardson's *Clarissa.* Crossjay and his seven hungry siblings at home constantly recall the fate of the lopped branches of earlier generations. Other human casualties to the centralized power of Willoughby's house can be guessed at: numerous unmarried and thus undowered daughters, like the ladies Isabel and Eleanor, who humbly accept their socially reduced selves that can be exiled from their beloved house merely to satisfy the new bride's whim; numerous marriages of convenience, like the "strictly sagacious" one made by Willoughby's father.

"Patternes marry money: they are not romantic people," states Lady Busshe. Thus the description of Simon Patterne is deliberately ironic: as John Goode points out, Meredith "draws attention to the Hobbesian reality behind the Burkeian affirmation of an organic society (the tree prospers by pruning)" ["*The Egoist:* Anatomy or Striptease?" in *Meredith Now: Some Critical Essays,* ed. Fletcher].

Outside the family, the Patterne estate grew great, we can safely speculate, by driving out smaller men through the engrossing and enclosing activities prevalent during its existence. Meredith's choice of a lawyer rather than a merchant for the founder of the house evokes the cash-nexus society whose symbol is the middleman handling paper currency rather than goods. Furthermore, for a reader of eighteenth-century literature, like Meredith, a lawyer who amassed enough wealth to join the landed gentry might suggest a figure like the notorious Peter Walters, so often the target of Swift's, Pope's, and Fielding's satire. Meredith directly expresses his relish for the irony inherent in such a situation in **Sandra Belloni** in which the movement from city to country does depend on illegally appropriated funds. Perhaps Willoughby's strong propensity to forget the distinction between *meum* and *tuum* as he tries to claim the souls of others is a psychological refinement of his heritage. Nevertheless, the "grand old Egoism," though certainly not pleasant, was, unlike Willoughby, openly and practically selfish in exploiting men and materials to build its house. Furthermore, Lawyer Patterne's activities were part of the social, philosophic, and economic individualism important to the beginning of the capitalist society: they reflected what Ian Watt has called "the dynamic tendency of capitalism itself, whose aim is never merely to maintain the *status quo,* but to transform it incessantly" [*The Rise of the Novel,* 1957]. The "grand old Egoism" also reflected the paradoxical relationship between self-love, even self-indulgence, and social good, which fascinated eighteenth-century writers as different as Defoe, Mandeville, and Pope.

Unlike his ancestor, Willoughby is an "anachronic spectre" who fears change and tries to bolster the status quo by imposing feudal attitudes on nineteenth-century reality. Like Meredith's Jocelyn, Romfrey, and Fleetwood, who live in idle loftiness within the security of inherited wealth, Willoughby restricts his actions to those which help to keep his self-image intact. He builds a laboratory which serves not as a place to work but as a retreat and a convenient conversation piece. Like Romfrey, he uses Darwinian terminology of the survival of the fittest to support his feudal attitudes as he looks back to the generations of his forebears consolidating wealth and power. He plans to enter Parliament because this is what gentlemen do, but he needs Vernon's help even in his position as a justice of the peace. He can dismiss the possibility of serious economic disasters besetting his country by speaking of "soup at the Hall-gates, perhaps; licence to fell timber in one of the outer copses, or some dozen loads of coal." He enjoys military bravery vicariously through Lieutenant Crossjay and is ready to become the lordly patron to the "Patterne in the Marines" until he finds that the man will not fit into his drawing room. His own fighting, as

Flint cottage, Box Hill, Meredith's home and model for the Patterne mansion in The Egoist.

Goode comments, is restricted to the hunting field, until he gives that up for "building," which consists of finding a suitable lady for his house.

Meanwhile, his idealized vision of himself and of the changeless patrician social order is threatened by the events taking place around him. As G. M. Trevelyan says [in his *Illustrated English Social History*, 1953]: "The greatest single event of the 'seventies, fraught with immeasurable consequences for the future, was the sudden collapse of English agriculture," due largely to the policy of free trade and the "American cousins" who force even Willoughby to speak of them "respectfully and pensively, with a tail tucked in" after his brief contact with their "greatness". While the country houses would still flourish, they would lose their socially and economically unified meaning; they "were less than ever supported by agricultural rents, which American imports lowered and brought into arrears. The pleasures of the country house and the business of the estate were now financed by money which the owner drew from industry and other investments, or from his income as ground landlord of more distant urban areas. He was still a country gentleman, but he paid for himself by being other things as well" [Trevelyan].

Meredith's allusions to earlier eulogies of country house ideals, which are not reflected by the reality of the Patterne estate, suggest that Willoughby, though financially intact, lives emotionally and spiritually on counterfeit currency. His ruthless exploitation of others for the sake of an "art of life" he seeks to exemplify does not sustain the inward spirit of his "intimates," nor do his actions reverberate outward with ethical meaning. Meredith's description of Clara's position after the initial formal courtship is over also serves to delineate Willoughby's more complex emotional position as an heir to the traditions of the house:

> Now men whose incomes have been restricted to the extent that they must live on their capital, soon grow relieved of the forethoughtful anguish wasting them by the hilarious comforts of the lap upon which they have sunk back, insomuch that they are apt to solace themselves for their intolerable anticipations of famine in the household by giving loose to one fit or more of reckless lavishness. Lovers in like manner live on their capital from failure of income: they, too, for the sake of stifling apprehension and piping to the present hour, are lavish of their stock, so as rapidly to attenuate it: they have their fits of intoxication in view of coming famine: they force memory into play, love retrospectively, enter the old house of the past and ravage the larder, and would gladly, even resolutely, continue in illusion if it were possible for the broadest honey-store of reminiscences to hold out for a length of time against a mortal appetite.

Willoughby's sweetest "honey-store of reminiscences" is a variation of the old pastoral formula of withdrawal from the contamination of the outer world. As a traditional idealist, a man seeking to preserve his integrity and independence, he views the country house as an alternative to the existing city with its ignoble strife, worldly ambitions, and destructive passions of fear, envy, and greed. Early in his career, Willoughby "abandoned London, he loathed it as the burial-place of the individual man.". . . Most pathetically, in his courtship first of Clara and then of Laetitia, Willoughby expresses the vision of Patterne estate as an ideal place, where pastoral simplicity merges with the high culture of "practical poetry" and pursuit of science, which in the nineteenth century had become a popular substitute for the "pure delights of literature." He also presents his house as the only place where the patrician hero can develop the life of the spirit by withdrawing from the large disillusioning world to refine communal living to a fine art through domestic virtues. "The art of life," he tells Clara, "is to associate [with] a group of sympathetic friends in our neighbourhood." He plans his life by repeatedly stressing an abstract vision of aesthetic coherence and stability. The actual ingredients of this vision are amusingly limited: his house is to be decorated by his French cook and two English scholars, a wife who forms a companion picture to himself before the world, an old love who pines in a cottage in one corner of his park, and a chorus of admiring aging ladies of the neighborhood.

Throughout the novel, Willoughby self-consciously tries to keep all these human ingredients "intoxicated" in various ways with their illusions to support the illusion of his own aesthetic life. For those who casually surround him, this can be done through a simple formula: "Among gentlemen he was the English gentleman; with ladies his aim was the Gallican courtier of any period from Louis Treize to Louis Quinze." (pp. 420-29)

[Willoughby's] refusal to think sincerely, to see himself without delusions, forces him in the end to give himself fully to the world of appearances: in his scramble to marry Laetitia, he suffers the fate of the sentimentalist described by James Russell Lowell: "He is under the wretched necessity of keeping up, at least in public, the character he has assumed, till he at last reaches that last shift of bankrupt self-respect, to play the hypocrite with himself" [*Among My Books,* 1870]. (p. 441)

> *Maaja A. Stewart, "The Country House Ideals in Meredith's 'The Egoist',"* in Nineteenth-Century Fiction, *Vol. 32, No. 4, March, 1978, pp. 420-41.*

J. Hillis Miller   (essay date 1981)

[*Miller is an American critic and educator who has successfully applied several critical methods to literature, including New Criticism, which examines a literary work as an object complete in itself through a close analysis of symbol, image, and metaphor; the existential phenomenology of Georges Poulet, which views an author's work as the product of a unique individual consciousness; and deconstructionism. Based on the thought of French critic and philosopher Jacques Derrida, Deconstructionism asserts that the structure of language complicates the issue of authorial intention and that a multi-*

plicity of meanings are encoded in any simple statement. Opposing the traditional critical view that the study of literature is defined as the search for stable meaning, ideas, and truths in a text, deconstructionists concentrate solely on the linguistic and semiotic elements in a text, denying the representational function of words and delineating instead the way in which a work is constructed of verbal forms. Language is the common denominator in all works of literature, and it is on the complexity, ambiguity, and etymology of the written word that deconstruction places a consistent emphasis. In the following excerpt, Miller presents a reading of the character of Clara Middleton and emphasizes the interconnectedness of gender and language in Meredith's representation of a female subject.]

Among examples of the presentation of female characters in Victorian fiction, Clara Middleton in George Meredith's *The Egoist* is one of the most important. Certainly *The Egoist* presents a strong sense of "living characters"—of Willoughby, the egoist himself, of Clara, of Vernon Whitford, of the cranky and garrulous narrator whom the reader first encounters in the celebrated "Prelude." The prelude maps egoism "from the Lizard to the last few pulmonary snips and shreds of leagues dancing on their toes for cold, explorers tell us, and catching breath by good luck, like dogs at bones about a table, on the edge of the Pole." The method of *The Egoist,* the prelude tells the reader, is a form of mapping. It is a presentation of the unimaginable complexity of the geography of egoism in a schematic outline, according to a reductive code, small-scale matching large-scale, part for whole. This is a version of synecdoche which assumes that the structure or grain of the example corresponds cunningly to the structure or grain of the whole from which it is taken. For this reason, "art is the specific," "the inward mirror, the embracing and condensing spirit," which can "give us those interminable mile-post piles of matter . . . in essence, in chosen samples, digestibly," "so that a fair part of a book outstripping thousands of leagues when unrolled [the great Book of Earth or the Book of Egoism, the record of all man's social intelligence over the generations], may be compassed in one comic sitting."

The reader will note a crucial feature of Meredith's theory of the novel. Meredith recognizes that a novel is necessarily based on a figure of speech. Rather than merely containing "illustrative" figures, it *is* a figure of speech. A novel is not merely in itself, *in toto,* a figure, a vast synecdoche. It is a figure of a figure. It does not represent a nontextual reality in a textual condensation but condenses one enormous book, the Book of Earth, in another compendious, shorter one. The social world is already a written record. The verbal art of comedy is a précis of that record. It is not a mimesis in language of something nonverbal but a synecdochic "specific," a homeopathic cure of language by language.

This image is reinforced within the body of the novel by many uses of the conventional figure of speech whereby one person's understanding of another is his "reading" of him. This metaphor is more than merely conventional in *The Egoist.* It defines another person's character as visible in somewhat enigmatic characters which must be deciphered, for example, when Willoughby seems to Clara "an obelisk lettered all over with hieroglyphics, and [she condemned to] everlastingly [hear] him expound them, relishingly [renew] his lectures on them," or when, in a crucial paragraph in the chapter "Clara's Meditations," the narrator generalizes, apropos of Clara's "reading" of Colonel De Craye, about the situation of unmarried women in Victorian society, in their deciphering of the characters of men:

> Maidens are commonly reduced to read the masters of their destinies by their instincts; and when these have been edged by over-activity they must hoodwink their maidenliness to suffer themselves to read: and then they must dupe their minds, else men would soon see they were gifted to discern. Total ignorance being their pledge of purity to men, they have to expunge the writing of their perceptives on the tablets of the brain: they have to know not when they do know. The instinct of seeking to know, crossed by the task of blotting knowledge out, creates that conflict of the natural with the artificial creature to which their ultimately-revealed double-face, complained of by ever-dissatisfied men, is owing.

Meredith here reads Clara's reading of De Craye. He takes it as a synecdoche for those pages of the Book of Earth that record all those innumerable maidenly decipherings of men. The discourse of the narrator of *The Egoist* is, so to speak, a marginal commentary on the main text. It is an interpretation of the Book of Social Wisdom, working, as does all interpretation, by way of detailed explication of samples, examples which are taken as fair representations of the whole.

What specific form does Meredith's cure of language by language take in its presentation of character? I have said that *The Egoist* creates a strong sense of the presence of specific characters. Meredith matches any Victorian novelist in conveying to his readers sharply etched configurations for each character. The reader knows each character as the presence of a consciousness to itself. Moreover, each of these characters is presented as defined in its essence by its awareness of itself in relation to other people. I am aware of myself, I *am* myself, to the degree that I am aware of the psychic pressure upon me of the psyches of other people. These other psyches are like breaths disturbing the flame of my self-consciousness. At the same time they feed that flame. They are necessary to its subsistence. I am conscious of myself as conscious of the consciousness of others. This is the general law of selfhood for characters in Victorian novels, but Meredith, especially in his remarkable late novels, beginning with *The Egoist* and continuing through *Diana of the Crossways, One of Our Conquerors, Lord Ormont and His Aminta,* and *The Amazing Marriage,* excels in presenting intimately, from within, the subtle pressures that the presence of the consciousness of another presents to the self-presence of a given character. If art is the specific by being an "inward mirror," Meredith's characters are mirrors within that mirror. Each lives by speculation, by his reflection of the lives of others in himself, or by seeing himself reflected in the mirrors of others, according to that law admirably formulated in Shakespeare's *Troilus and Cressida:*

> The beauty that is borne here in the face
> The bearer knows not, but commends itself
> To others' eyes; nor doth the eye itself,
> That most pure spirit of sense, behold itself,
> Not going from itself; but eye to eye opposed
> Salutes each other with each other's form;
> For speculation turns not to itself.
> Till it hath travelled and is married there
> Where it may see itself.

This need by each mirror of another mirror is extreme in Willoughby; it is the ultimate weakness which makes him the slave of others in spite of his satanic "generalship" in deceiving and dazzling the eyes of others. "The breath of the world, the world's view of him, was partly his vital breath, his view of himself."

Equally shrewd is Clara's dependence on others. Her unwitting enslavement of herself to Willoughby and her struggle to free herself honorably make up the main action of the comedy. It is apropos of her exacerbated sensitivity to the effect on her sense of herself of what might be called Willoughby's psychic aura, the magnetic field of the forceful will to appropriation with which he surrounds himself, that many of the admirably subtle notations of the law that self-awareness is awareness of others is made. An example is the scene in which Willoughby tries to embrace his fiancée as they stroll through his estate:

> The gulf of a caress hove in view like an enormous billow hollowing under the curled ridge.
>
> She stooped to a buttercup; the monster swept by.

The Egoist, so it appears, presupposes and powerfully presents the existence of spiritual entities called selves. Each has its own sharp configuration, different from all others. Each is present to itself and to other such spiritual entities as force, as presence. These are merely mediated, described, or interpreted by language. Such figures as are used in these descriptions are expressions of something other than themselves. Key terms in Meredith's psychology of character are "self," "mind," "feeling," "will," and "nature." All these terms presuppose the notion of a prelinguistic fixed character: "She was to do everything for herself, do and dare everything, decide upon everything. He told her flatly that so would she learn to know her own mind"; "But decide at once. I wish you to have your free will"; "It's a dispute between a conventional idea of obligation and an injury to her nature. . . . [H]er feelings guide her best. It's one of the few cases in which nature may be consulted like an oracle"; "She was not pure of nature . . . : she was pure of will; fire rather than ice."

What is Clara's "nature," this fixed, extralinguistic self which she must protect from Willoughby's base invasions and appropriations? Chapter 21, "Clara's Meditations," is an extraordinary moment in *The Egoist,* an extraordinary moment even in the Victorian novel generally. It is the moment of the dissolution, from within, as a "lived experience" (but the notions of "life" and "experience" are transformed in this moment too), of the presupposition that each man or woman has a fixed character with definite hieroglyphic outlines which may be figured truly, for example in his or her physiognomy or in the figures of speech with which he or she may be described in language. Since this presupposition is the one on which *The Egoist* as a whole, with its vivid presentation of the intersubjective battle of character with character, is based, since it is the presupposition on which Victorian fiction or even, *mutatis mutandis,* the European novel as a whole appears to be based, much is at stake in these pages. The whole chapter should be read, but extracts will indicate its main outlines:

> She was in a fever, lying like stone, with her brain burning. Quick natures run out to calamity in any little shadow of it flung before. Terrors of apprehension drive them. They stop not short of the uttermost when they are on the wings of dread. A frown means tempest, a wind wreck; to see fire is to be seized by it. When it is the approach of their loathing that they fear, they are in the tragedy of the embrace at a breath. . . .

> The false course she had taken through sophistical cowardice appalled the girl; she was lost. The advantage taken of it by Willoughby put on the form of strength, and made her feel abject, reptilious; she was lost, carried away on the flood of the cataract. . . .

> Thank heaven for the chances of a short life! Once in a net, desperation is graceless. . . .

> She was now in the luxury of passivity, when we throw our burden on the Powers above, and do not love them. The need to love drew her out of it, that she might strive with the unbearable, and by sheer striving, even though she were graceless, come to love them humbly. It is here that the seed of good teaching supports a soul; for the condition might be mapped, and where kismet whispers us to shut eyes, and instruction bids us look up, is at a well-marked crossroad of the contest.

> Quick of sensation, but not courageously resolved, she perceived how blunderingly she had acted. For a punishment, it seemed to her that she who had not known her mind must learn to conquer her nature, and submit. She had accepted Willoughby; therefore she accepted him. . . .

> She was almost imagining she might imitate him [Vernon Whitford, who has submitted to Willoughby], when the clash of a sharp physical thought: "The difference! the difference!" told her she was a woman and never could submit. Can a woman have an inner life apart from him she is yoked to? She tried to nestle deep away in herself: in some corner where the abstract view had comforted her, to flee from thinking as her feminine blood directed. It was a vain effort. The difference, the cruel fate, the defencelessness of women, pursued her, strung her to wild horses' backs, tossed her on savage wastes. In her case duty was shame: hence, it could not be broadly duty. That intolerable difference proscribed the word.

> But the fire of a brain burning high and kindling everything, lit up herself against herself:—Was one so volatile as she a person with a will?—Were they not a multitude of flitting wishes, that she took for a will?—Was she, feather-headed that she was, a person to make a stand on physical pride?—If she could yield her hand without reflection (as she conceived she had done, from incapacity to conceive herself doing it reflectively), was she much better than purchaseable stuff that has nothing to say to the bargain?

> Furthermore, said her incandescent reason, she had not suspected such art of cunning in Willoughby. Then might she not be deceived altogether—might she not have misread him? . . .

> She reviewed him. It was all in one flash. . . . An undefined agreement to have the same regard for him as his friends and the world had, provided that he kept the same distance from her, was the termination of this phase, occupying about a minute in time, and reached through a series of intensely vivid pictures. . . .

> [For one in her condition] the brain is raging like a pine-torch and the devouring illumination leaves not a spot of our nature covert. The aspect of her weakness was unrelieved, and frightened her back to her loathing. From her loathing, as soon as her sensations had quickened to realize it, she was hurled on her weakness. She was graceless, she was inconsistent, she was volatile, she was unprincipled, she was worse than a prey to wickedness—capable of it; she was only waiting to be misled. Nay, the idea of being misled suffused her with languor; for then the battle would be over and she a happy weed of the sea, no longer suffering those tugs at the roots, but leaving it to the sea to heave and contend. . . .

> Issuing out of torture, her young nature eluded the irradiating brain, in search of refreshment, and she luxuriated at a feast in considering him—[Colonel De Craye, who would tempt her to elope]—shower on a parched land that he was! . . .

> She would have thought of Vernon, as her instinct of safety prompted, had not his exactions been excessive. He proposed to help her with advice only. She was to do everything for herself, do and dare everything, decide upon everything. He told her flatly that so would she learn to know her own mind. . . .

> Her war with Willoughby sprang of a desire to love repelled by distaste. Her cry for freedom was a cry to be free to love: she discovered it, half-shuddering: to love, oh! no—no shape of man, nor impalpable nature either; but to love unselfishness, and helpfulness, and planted strength in something. Then, loving and being loved a little, what strength would be hers!

This admirable sequence is one of the high-water marks of the Victorian novel, indeed of realistic fiction in Europe generally. Here the procedures of realism dismantle themselves by being systematically exploited, taken to their limits, transported to that hyperbolic point where they reverse themselves and become something else. That something else undermines the conventions of storytelling which at the same time make the passage and the novel of which it is a part possible in the first place. This is according to that law which says conventions and assumptions of any mode of writing contain the seeds of their own destruction if they are carried far enough, not very far, actually.

George Meredith has in this passage accepted the implicit charge made to the realistic novelist: represent in words, among other things, what actually goes on from moment to moment within consciousness. In one sense, the passage succeeds in this magnificently. It creates the vivid illusion that there was a person named Clara who went through this experience. The reader is led to reexperience this experience from within, sharing it again, in the renewal made permanently possible, over and over again, by the words of the narrator as Meredith has invented them. The reader dwells not only within Clara's thoughts and emotions but even within her intimate bodily feelings and sensations. As Ramon Fernandez long ago recognized [in his *Messages, première série,* 1926], Meredith's "realism" is based on an assumption of the overlapping, if not quite coincidence, in inextricable copresence of body, "feelings" (in both senses), mind, external physical world, and the bodies and minds of other people. Things outside are apprehended by things inside, mind and body working together. The "incandescent reason" appropriates, often in spite of itself, in "sharp physical thought," both material objects, such as double-blossomed wild cherry trees, and other persons, such as that Vernon Whitford who lies under the tree for Clara to behold. In this feeling for the inextricable inmixing, though not quite identity, as of wine and water or of oil homogenized in water, of realms kept by some philosophers and by some novelists more strictly separate, Meredith anticipates such a "phenomenological" philosopher of our own day as Maurice Merleau-Ponty. There would be room for a systematic interpretation of Meredith's work both in fiction and in poetry along the lines initiated by Fernandez's brilliant essay.

At the same time, this passage, when it is read more carefully, can be seen to lay bare its own machinery of representation and thereby to put in question the validity, as mimesis, of both its conceptual and its figurative terminology. It even puts in question the validity of the distinction between conceptual and figurative, as well as those "phenomenological" assumptions Fernandez formulates so brilliantly and ascribes to Meredith.

In her sleepless, all-night meditation, in Willoughby's house, on her plight in having solemnly engaged herself to marry him, Clara discovers, under the pressure of that situation, that the structure of assumptions presupposed in that promise to marry was false. Basic to this structure was the presupposition that she had a solid character on the basis of which promises could be made and kept. Clara's "nature," on the contrary, is an anonymous and shapeless energy which cannot be outlined. It must be compared, incoherently, to fire, to liquid, to the formless wind, to a featureless desert, or to unshaped stone. It changes from moment to moment. It has no permanent

shape as yet, for "the tempers of the young are liquid fires in isles of quicksand." Vernon Whitford is right in seeing that Clara's "character was yet liquid in the mould, and that she was a creature of only naturally youthful wildness provoked to freakishness by the ordeal of a situation shrewd as any that can happen to her sex in civilized life." Of Clara it must be said that "her needs were her nature, her moods her mind." Her "nature" is her "currents of feeling." "Nature," "character," "mind" are here dissolved, liquified. They cease to be anything solid on which a promise or a commitment might be based. Self becomes evanescent tempers, feelings, needs, moods, currents of water or fire without permanent shape. Currents? Water? Fire? What is the status of these figures if the entities for which they are figures—mind, character, and so on—have no literal existence as persisting things but are themselves figures for the unfigurable? To say that Clara is "liquid fire in isles of quicksand" is in this case the same as to say that Clara is her moods or her mind or her character, since she is no characterable character representable by some fixed hieroglyph or seal. *Character* in this case, if it is to have any meaning, must be distorted from its dictionary meaning as a permanent brand impressed on the psyche and mirrored in doubling characters in features, gestures, physiognomy. The word *character* here becomes a figure for what Clara is, namely, "her whims, variations, inconsistencies, wiles; her tremblings between good and naughty, that might be stamped to noble or to terrible; her sincereness, her duplicity, her courage, cowardice, possibilities for heroism and for treachery," in short, for her liquid, fiery, or airy mobility. The words *will, nature, feelings, mind, self,* and *character* are not names, in this case, for a stable entity or for its faculties. When applied to Clara, they are figures drawn from an archaic psychology to be used tropologically to describe what has no proper name, since it flits away from any attempt to pin it down. The enterprise of the "realistic representation" of human psychology here reaches a point where it overreaches itself, goes beyond its own boundary lines, in the attempt to fulfill its project completely. Realism dissolves itself in the multiplicity of its notations and in its recognition of its dependence on a figurative language for which there is no possibility of substituting proper terms. What is there to be named does not have a consistence or permanence compatible with literal names.

The double assumption on which that aspect of realism which involves the mimesis in language of states of mind rests is the following: that there is a prelinguistic self or character and that this in its modes may be expressed, mirrored, or copied without distortion in language. Walter Pater, for example, praises Rossetti for choosing the right "term" "from many competitors, as the just transcript of that peculiar phase of soul which he alone knew, precisely as he knew it" [*Appreciations,* 1889]. *The Egoist,* especially in the "transcription" of Clara's meditations, puts this double assumption in question. The putting in question is accomplished in part by overt thematic statement ("Was one so volatile as she a person with a will? Were they not a multitude of flitting wishes that she took for a will?"), in part by the manifest role of incoherent figures in the transcription.

The theory of figure implicit in the practice of transcription here is made explicit elsewhere in Meredith, for example in a passage in *One of Our Conquerers:* "It is the excelling merit of similes and metaphors to spring us to vault over gaps and thickets and dreary places. . . . Beware, moreover, of examining them too scrupulously: they have a trick of wearing to vapour if closely scanned"; or in the following striking formulation in *Diana of the Crossways:* "The banished of Eden had to put on metaphors." Metaphors, one can see, are peculiar. On the one hand they are an essential covering, a web or integument of language which serves as a bridge over places where the continuity of language would otherwise break and tumble us into a crevasse or into a copse of undergrowth. I take it this means that metaphors name the unnamable, present the unpresentable, and thereby serve simultaneously as decent covering, as revelation or unveiling, and as a making continuous of a cloth of language which otherwise would be rent, would fail to reach from here to there in a sequential narrative. Covering of what? Unveiling of what? The second passage makes explicit what is implicit in the first. The function of metaphors is to cover the pudenda of all the daughters and sons of Eve and Adam. Since the fall literal, naked language has been impossible, shameful. Certain things, the genitalia, in fact, have been namable only indirectly, in names displaced from other less shameful places. These figures are fig leaves to cover the gaps and thickets where proper naming is no longer proper.

This metaphorical naming contains the aporia inherent in all acts of simultaneous unveiling and veiling. Such metaphors when closely scanned have a trick of wearing to vapor. They are not appropriate names for those gaps and thickets in dreary places. Their inappropriateness is appropriate to their function as veils. When they wear to vapor and vanish they then best function as veils, since they have revealed nothing, told no secrets. At the same time, their function as sewing, as darning threads crisscrossed over a gap in the discourse, is no longer fulfilled. The gap is revealed, the abyss which disrupts or breaks the smooth texture of the text, for example, the assumption that the characters in a narrative have characters, are proper selves. The cloth of the veil becomes gauze, transparent and insubstantial as vapor, a weaving of clouds. The phallic thicket becomes a vaginal gap. If the metaphors hold, then they have named that gap, revealed it, and the text is once more broken. Is the thicket, however, unambiguously phallic? An impenetrable underbrush in a dreary place seems more like an interlaced integument, a weaving or a veil once more, pubic hair which may hide something or may hide an absence. Weaving, the psychoanalysts tell us, is said to have been invented by women, to have been devised, according to this myth, in the plaiting of pubic hair to make a mock phallus. This weaving was the hiding of an absence and a phantasmal pseudo revelation. At the same time it was a metaphor claiming the existence of what is not there, so covering the fact that the phallus is not there. Between revealing and hiding, the metaphors vibrate, fleeing one extreme, total opacity, as revealing but revealing nothing, a misleading sham revelation claiming substance where there is none, but finding the other extreme, total transparency, coming to the same thing. Far from springing us to vault over gaps and thick-

ets and dreary places or covering the indecent with decency, the improper with propriety in fallen man or woman, a metaphorical text is made of gaps and thickets. That is to say, it is made of metaphors, which comes to the same thing, since the gaps and thickets are the metaphors.

It is no accident that so many male novelists in the Victorian period—Thackeray, Dickens, Trollope, or Meredith himself—so often project into a female protagonist the dramatization of that question fundamental to the novel, Can we or can we not believe that human beings, male or female, have fixed selves? The female protagonist has a lesson to teach us men. The assumption that ontologically substantial characters do exist cannot be detached from the logocentrism or phallogocentrism which underlies it and of which it is a version. The fixed hieroglyphic of character here plays the role of the logos or phallus, the head meaning which is the source and guarantee of all the derivative meanings and configurations of the self: moods, feelings, wiles. Only if Clara is indeed the reflex and mirror image, the choric echo, of the phallic and upright Willoughby, that obelisk covered all over with hieroglyphs, can she be said to have a self: "In walking with her, in drooping to her, the whole man was made conscious of the female image of himself by her exquisite unlikeness. She completed him, added the softer lines wanting to his portrait before the world." Clara's discovery in the chapter of her meditations is that she has no central column of self charactered over with permanent emblems of her character. She therefore cannot reflect back to Willoughby his conception of himself as, in promising to marry him, she has tacitly undertaken to do. Instead, there is a gap there around which flow or burn or blow her evanescent moods, whims, wiles, inconsistencies.

This discovery is also an unsettling revelation for Willoughby. He has depended on Clara to give him a stable female image of himself and finds that he must do without such mirroring. It is a discovery also for the narrator and for the novelist behind the narrator. They have peered into the mirror of an invented female character to seek their own images and to put to the test thereby the phallogocentric assumptions presupposed in the notion of character. The reader, too, male or female, according to my hypothesis about the function of "realistic" fictions, puts his or her own assumptions about character, about his or her own character or self, to the test when he or she reads such a novel. The integument of metaphor in the passage cited above is a thin covering over the sexual issue it more or less directly treats, "the difference! the difference!" Clara is unable to bring herself to fulfill her bargain by consenting to submit herself physically to Willoughby's appropriation of her as a "chalice," as an "inanimate overwrought polished pure-metal precious vessel." She does not have the solidity or consistency to be such a vessel, the reversed image of the obelisk, glove for his hand. The man—lover, narrator, or reader—who looks into Clara as mirror to find confirmation of his sense of his own character finds only unfixable volatility. This volatility is both revealed and hidden by the network of figures which the novelist must use to name it, in a fluid or vaporous parody of the chalice "overwrought" with designs. The chalice is the obelisk turned inside out, the hollow reflex of the Apollonian sunray turned to stone and carved all over with the secret hieroglyphic speech of the sun fixed in legible characters for those who have the interpretation of them, as Willoughby pretends to read himself. From obelisk to chalice to vaporous integument of metaphors, each model deprives of substantiality the one before, in a movement toward the "truth" that there is no truth except in metaphor.

Though this passage of Clara's meditations conveys, to me at least, an entirely persuasive sense of having lived through the vacillations of Clara's "physical thinking," from moment to moment, this following through is impossible without the figures of fire, ocean, storm, stone, wild horses on savage wastes, mapped crossroads, brain raging like a pine torch, and so on. Clara exists as these figures, both in the sense that the reader's phantasmal illusion of her real existence is created by Meredith only with the aid of these figures and in the sense that if we move through the looking-glass to take her as a real "person" being described in elaborate, temporalized notation by the narrator, she exists, in herself, not as a substantial character but as a sequence of figures, fleeting, evanescent, each succeeded by another which contradicts it, as an image of fire contradicts one of water, an image of wind the other two, and so on. In this flow of figures, the conceptual words, *mind, will, nature,* and so on, and the literal words for parts of the body, *brain, blood, head, hand, face,* are also redefined. They are volatilized, vaporized, and become themselves part of the sequence of figures.

In this volatilization a complex system of presuppositions is simultaneously insubstantiated. The self becomes not something fixed but a multitude of fleeting wishes, feelings, thoughts. The distinction between extralinguistic and linguistic, on which mimetic realism is based, breaks down. The self and any society of selves exist as the signs for them. These signs are governed by no fixed columnar head sense. The distinctions between literal, figurative, and conceptual collapse. They are replaced by different versions of catachresis, words transferred from some other realm to name improperly what has no proper name and comes into existence in the improprieties of that strange figure. The temporal continuity of the self, finally, essential presupposition of the connectedness of storytelling, dissolves into the sequence of these pictorial emblems, noted so carefully by the narrator: "An undefined agreement to have the same regard for him as his friends and the world had, provided that he kept at the same distance from her, was the termination of this phase, occupying about a minute in time, and reached through a series of intensely vivid pictures." Internal time consciousness in *The Egoist* is the dimension of discontinuity between one moment and the next, of the noncoincidence of mental image and what it images, and of the absence of identifiable origin or end. The moment of beginning or source of a given thought, conviction, or penchant of the feeling mind can never be certainly identified. On the example of Clara's physical distaste for Willoughby the narrator generalizes: "Sweeping from sensation to sensation, the young, whom sensations impel and distract, can rarely date their disturbance from a particular one." Much later, trying to explain to Mrs. Mountstuart how and when she came to find that she did not love Willoughby, Clara can express herself only in what might be called a temporal oxymoron: "By degrees, unknown to myself; suddenly." There was a time when she intended to marry Willoughby, in fact when she came on her visit to Patterne Hall she did, and then, later, there was a time when she did not, as Mrs. Mountstuart sardonically observes: "And *gradually* you *suddenly* discovered, since you came here, that you did not intend it, if you could find a means of avoiding it." Though the change was a fact of consciousness, it did not occur at a time when consciousness was distinctly conscious of it as a fact different from the previous fact of a different intent. She changed her mind or the intention of her mind both suddenly and gradually, in a fashion not compatible with any image of regular temporal continuity. In any case her change of mind did not take place in her mind, but unknown to herself. Choosing, intending, and promising are performatives which depend on the mind's continuity and on the mind's constant presence to itself for their efficacy, but Clara neither constantly knows her own mind clearly nor is able to keep it constant to itself. The aetiology of her choices, intentions, and promises cannot be identified. Their validity is thereby nullified: "And she could vehemently declare that she had not chosen [when she first promised to marry Willoughby]; she was too young, too ignorant to choose . . . . to call consenting the same in fact as choosing [as Vernon has done], was willfully unjust." The chapter "Clara's Meditations" is her most acute experience of this discontinuity, this failure of the mind to be present to itself, either in the moment or in the moment's awareness of its origins, in its connection to some past moment. The moment of Clara's greatest self-clarification is the moment when she is most opaque to herself. (pp. 98-113)

If Clara cannot maintain her continuity with herself, if she does not remain the same person from moment to moment, well enough to be said to have a character or a will, how can the reader be expected to hold together in one coherent interpretation the text which records the discontinuities and intermittences of her heart, always and necessarily faithless to itself?

Nevertheless, *The Egoist* has a "happy ending." Clara frees herself from her "promise" to marry Willoughby and gives herself freely to Vernon Whitford in a meeting which takes place outside the boundaries of the book, "between the Swiss and Tyrol Alps over the Lake of Constance." Their meeting occurs on the border between Switzerland and Austria, not quite in one country or the other, and in a landscape which is both rock and water, mountain and lake, "over the Lake of Constance." How can this happy ending be prospectively believed? How can the narrator plausibly promise that such a meeting and such a betrothal will take place, or has already taken place to his retrospective eye? How can he plausibly promise that the marriage of Vernon and Clara will be a happy one, based on unshakable love and fidelity? What constancy can Clara promise Vernon by the Lake of Constance if she has no character to guarantee and underwrite her fulfillment of any promise, no stable signature to allow her to sign her name to a marriage contract, if she exists only as a multitude of fleeting and inconsistent wishes? The answer lies in an alternative theory of character and of promising which emerges in *The Egoist*, out of the wreckage left by the deconstruction, in "Clara's Meditations," of traditional theories of character and of promising. The tracing out of the outlines of this alternative theory of character must, however, be done in another essay and in another place. (pp. 121-22)

> *J. Hillis Miller, " 'Herself against Herself':
> The Clarification of Clara Middleton," in* The
> Representation of Women in Fiction, *edited
> by Carolyn G. Heilbrun and Margaret R. Hi-
> gonnet, The Johns Hopkins University Press,
> 1983, pp. 98-123.*

Carolyn Williams   (essay date 1985)

[*In the following excerpt, Williams discusses the relationship between the comic genre and the female gender
and challenges previously held notions about Meredith's
"feminism."*]

In an *Essay on Comedy and the Uses of the Comic Spirit*
Meredith makes his famous equation between the status
of women and the quality of comedy in a given culture.
These two generalized manifestations of civilization—the
organized arrangements of gender and genre—evolve together, claims Meredith, in an argument that is no less intriguing for being somewhat circular as to causal relations.
But whether comedy is to be regarded as cause or as effect
of a progressive civilization, Meredith defines cultural
progress as the growth of social equality between women
and men:

> There has been fun in Bagdad. But there never
> will be civilization where comedy is not possible;
> and that comes of some degree of social equality
> of the sexes.

The "fun" that Meredith places "in Bagdad" alludes to
the uncivilized, "eastward" version of sexual inequality,
a certain male "pride of inflammability" which is expressed in the practice of keeping women behind the veil
so that their faces cannot disrupt "civilized" behavior.
Meredith uses this anecdote of the Arab to expose the connection between national pride and male sexual bravado.
Though Meredith's own national pride gleams through
the cosmopolitan urbanity of his prose from time to time
as he assesses the state of comedy in modern western civilization, for the most part his essay is a relentless, teasing
attempt to educate the tastes of his own countrymen and
women. Especially the women:

> I am not quoting the Arab to exhort and disturb
> the somnolent East; rather for cultivated women
> to recognize that the comic Muse is one of their
> best friends. They are blind to their interests in
> swelling the ranks of the sentimentalists. Let
> them look with their clearest vision abroad and
> at home. They will see that, where they have no
> social freedom, comedy is absent; where they are
> household drudges, the form of comedy is primi-
> tive; where they are tolerably independent, but
> uncultivated, exciting melodrama takes . . . a
> sentimental version of them.

This exhortation to the cross-cultural study of a literary
genre appeals to the interests of women, but not precisely
to women themselves, who remain the object of the exhortation ("they" or "them"), the pivot-point of a return in
Meredith's argument from "the somnolent East" to western culture. Women must be taught by "one of their best
friends" to understand their own best interests; it is they
who need to be civilized so that comedy may flourish in
the central civilization of the west.

But perhaps, on the other hand, comedy does the cultivating, for comedy "lifts women to a station offering them
free play of their wit, as they usually show it, when they
have it, on the side of sound sense." Though the very possibility of wit in women seems to be in some doubt within
this nest of rhetorical qualifications, the destiny of that
somewhat hypothetical womanly wit is certain. The
higher station to which women may be "lifted" is the station of equality with men, figured here as identification:

> The comic poet dares to show us men and
> women coming to this mutual likeness; he is for
> saying that when they draw together in social
> life their minds grow liker; just as the philoso-
> pher discerns the similarity of boy and girl, until
> the girl is marched away to the nursery.

The "daring" enterprise of the comic poet is precisely to
display this process of gender uplift and assimilation; this
particular philosopher is asking the perpetually frustrated
question—"Why can't a woman be more like a man?"—
but with a difference. Meredith sees that it would be helpful to liberate women from the mysterious East and the
nursery, even while he freely (though ironically) re-
associates them. He is able, to a remarkable extent, to see
the punitive ironies inherent in the disparity of education
between men and women, even from a certain stance of
benevolence in which the male casts himself as educator
of women (or children, or "somnolent" orientals) for the
good of western civilization in general. The portrait of
Willoughby Patterne in *The Egoist* has seemed to most
critics convincing evidence that Meredith fully perceived
such patriarchal benevolence as the worst form of male
Egoism. In that novel he represents male Egoism as a mutually reinforcing system of gender, class, and national
pride, and he shows it perpetuating itself from generation
to generation while subtle, almost invisible progressive
shifts in the balance of power nevertheless take place behind the scenes. But it seems to me that Meredith's very
insight about this engine of social reproduction is often
blinded or compromised when he presents himself most
programmatically as a feminist, for in those cases his feminism takes the stance of benevolence he elsewhere discrim-
inates with such finesse.

The most celebrated passage in an *Essay on Comedy* is
usually quoted only in part. Usually the quoted part trails
off at the climactic capstone of Meredith's argument:
where women have achieved a degree of social equality
with men, "there . . . pure comedy flourishes. . . ." But
I will quote it here in full, with its anticlimactic continuation:

> [W]here women are on the road to an equal foot-
> ing with men, in attainments and in liberty—in

what they have won for themselves, and what has been granted them by a fair civilization—there, and only waiting to be transplanted from life to the stage, or the novel, or the poem, pure comedy flourishes, and is, as it would help them to be, the sweetest of diversions, the wisest of delightful companions.

It goes without saying, perhaps, that this last turn does not present women in the role of social equality, nor even of assimilated identification, with men. Comedy itself is figured here as the benevolent educator, helping women to become "the sweetest of diversions, the wisest of delightful companions"—companions, one must suppose, for deserving men, perhaps for the daring comic poet or novelist.

It would be illuminating to tease out the threads of intersection that weave the benevolent late nineteenth-century male feminist into the same social fabric with the "benevolent" colonialist and anti-feminist, but this essay will take a different turn. Only in a tangential sense will my argument be an attempt to expose Meredith's feminism in the contradictions of its own historical time and place. The "tangential" sense in which this essay will nevertheless have a historicizing anchor involves my claim that Meredith's particular version of social evolution blinded him to some of the contradictions within his feminist stance, ambivalences that we can now easily see; but this dimension of my argument will not take place in concretely contextualizing terms. Instead, this essay will explore the mechanics of Meredith's feminism at work in one particular comic form, the feminist comedy of manners in narrative that Meredith wrote two years after an *Essay on Comedy, The Egoist* (1879). In that novel I want to examine representations of power and voice, cultivation and self-culture, women and men, in order to ask several questions about Meredith's association of the female gender with the comic genre. George Meredith once told Foster Watson that his novels kept two aims always in view: education and the emancipation of women. But how are these two aims related to one another in the web of necessity and possibility that is the comic plot? Does education result in emancipation for the woman at the center of this web? How does Meredith manipulate the precise "degree of social equality of the sexes" represented in *The Egoist*? Does the movement of the narrative enact a transformation of that "degree" from lesser to greater? or are the same old Patternes simply re-inscribed at closure? In other words, is Meredith's comic plot progressive or conservative?

The answer is decidedly "both," for an inherent ambivalence lies at the heart of Meredith's attempted integration of progressive, feminist goals with comedy as a genre; or, in other words, the choice to cast his feminist program of education in the form of comedy forecloses from the beginning many of its progressive possibilities. As a presiding mode or style, Meredith's Comic Muse does encourage expansiveness, wit, flexibility, play, and the loosening of traditional ties; but in its dimension as a genre, comedy presses toward a closing affirmation of social stability and order that by definition conserves and recuperates the status quo. A progressive social comedy, then, is in a fundamental sense an oxymoronic, paradoxical blend, a slightly unstable compound, a genre well-suited to expressions of ambivalence. Meredith's evolutionism allows him to avoid the difficulties of this contradiction in terms. For Meredith seems to have believed that social change is accomplished in such incremental, gradual stages that its effects would not necessarily be seen in the span of one lifetime. His belief in progress, together with his sense of the long stretches of post-Darwinian evolutionary time, amounted, therefore, to a faith in things unseen; and according to that faith, shifts in the structure of social relations would not have to be visible for Meredith to believe that change had taken place in spirit. His faith—in a kind of social change that is inexorable and yet so gradual as to be almost invisible at any given moment—permits him to leave unasked the questions that we now raise.

Meredith opens *The Egoist* with a "Prelude" which continues the theoretical argument of an *Essay on Comedy* in an oblique, allusive, self-reflexive pastiche of styles. The "Prelude" introduces the comic "game" to follow, but in addition to its pre-ludic function, it also reflects on the nature and rules of the game. Here Meredith conceptually poises the genre of comedy between sentimentalism and realism; comedy deflates the pretensions and unrealities of sentimentalism while maintaining an anti-realistic level of illustrative generalization or typicality. The first sentence of his "Prelude" opens the novel with Meredith's argument against the conventions of realism:

> Comedy is a game played to throw reflections upon social life, and it deals with human nature in the drawing-room of civilized men and women, where we have no dust of the struggling outer world, no mire, no violent crashes, to make the correctness of the representation convincing.

How is "correctness of representation" to be achieved, then, without the dust, mire, and violent crashes of the "outer world," or without the accretive texture of detail appropriate to the conventions of empirical observation? Meredith's "Prelude" argues equally against "violent crashes" and against "infinitesimal" observation. Instead, it argues for a narrative "pointed with examples and types under the broad Alpine survey of the spirit born of our united social intelligence, which is the Comic Spirit." Meredith's Comedy is the genre of generalization. "Correctness of representation" here, in other words, involves programmatically exemplary types, illustrative or representative representations, *patterns*. But what may we expect from such a narrative spirit, so explicitly born of "our united social intelligence"? Given the doubleness of "reflection"—metaphorically linked both to the intellectual and the mimetic, to the activity of illuminating new views of its object as well as to the activity of mirroring or reproducing the object—given that doubleness, if comedy is a "game played to throw reflections upon social life," isn't it likely to be caught up in reproducing the very patterns it purports to be reaching beyond? rewriting them, reforming them, rather than truly struggling free?

But Meredith further complicates the metaphorical figuration of genre. If comedy is a "game played to throw reflections," it is also a mode of reading those reflections. In figuring comedy as a way of reading—as opposed to a way of writing—Meredith partially circumvents the problem of whether (or how much) social change can actually be expected to occur, for the figure of reading carries with it the implication of passivity to the "outer world." In other words, comedy as a genre "reads" the general shape of things; it does not take a social or aesthetic responsibility for shaping them. Meredith's strategy of defining this genre as a way of reading correlatively figures the object to be represented as a prior text that must be read, and this imaginary pre-text Meredith calls the "Book of Earth whose title is the Book of Egoism." As the Book of Egoism, the pre-text seems to be social life; as the Book of Earth, its scope seems broader, including Nature as well as Culture. But, as J. Hillis Miller has pointed out, the novel "does not represent a nontextual reality in a textual condensation but condenses one enormous book . . . in another, compendious, shorter one. The social world is already a written record" [*The Representation of Women in Fiction,* Heilbrun and Higonnet, eds., "The Clarification of Clara Middleton," 1983]. Nature is conceived here as the extralinguistic; everything under consideration is already text, the already-written or enculturated. The existence of a prior, extralinguistic force so vast and chaotic that it must be organized by the comic spirit in order to be read is both presupposed and premised as unspeakable. Comedy's "broad Alpine survey" establishes an aesthetic distance toward the Book, enabling social life to be seen reflected in compressed, general forms, "examples and types" distilled from the chaos of "infinitesimal" observation into intelligible, recognizable shapes, the shapes, moreover, of "our" own faces:

> there is a constant tendency in the Book to accumulate excess of substance, and such repleteness, obscuring the glass it holds to mankind, renders us inexact in the recognition of our individual countenances: a perilous thing for civilization.

In Meredith's theoretical introduction, "Comedy" names the functions of distance and compression that make it possible for the already-written to be read, the operations that bring the already-textualized "outer world" into the drawing-room as recognizably "*human* nature."

The glass "it" holds to "mankind," however, is really the glass *she* holds to kind men, for this civilizing, linguistic function is introduced as distinctly female. Here an "enthusiast," one of the "wise men;" who serve in the "Prelude" as ventriloquists for "our united social intelligence," expounds the virtues of Comedy:

> Comedy he pronounces to be our means of reading swiftly and comprehensively. She it is who proposes the correcting of pretentiousness, of inflation, of dulness, and of the vestiges of rawness and grossness to be found among us. She is the ultimate civilizer, the polisher, a sweet cook.

This epistemological and sexual division of labor seems obvious. The role of Comedy cast as "a sweet cook" in the "Prelude" resonates with the role of woman, after being comedically educated, cast as "the sweetest of diversions" in an *Essay on Comedy.* But the genre has changed genders. In an *Essay* comedy was "one of their best friends,"

lifting women to the status of equal companionship with their educators; but here the genre is personified as a female engaged in "woman's work," polishing and cooking, both figured as analogies for preparing a text to be read, making it digestible by making a "digest." The "household drudge" here is not the uncultivated woman who appreciates only primitive comedy, but Comedy herself. Her particular form of "correctness" in narrative representation entails no dust, no mire, no loud noises. Her text is the text that remains after the angel has been cleaning the house of fiction.

The agent casting these female roles remains resolutely behind the scenes. A certain devaluation implied in the analogy to housekeeping, for example, threatens to undercut its other term, reading; but Meredith has been careful to put these words in the mouth of "an enthusiast," so that the association of comedy and the female still shimmers in an ironic haze, as in *An Essay on Comedy* it remained suspended at the distance of objectification. Figured as benevolent educator in the "real" or "struggling outer world," comedy remained distant from its female object, the women in need of its edification; but figured here as the civilizer of the house of fiction, comedy is simultaneously represented as woman, reader, editor, and domestic—as subject not object, but a subject with relatively limited powers, the powers of response and rectification in relation to a male text, but not the powers of textual production. Certainly the assignment of *reading* to the function designated "female" must be marked as having a devaluative valence in a text *written* by a male. Comedy as sweet cook is at best a re-writer or revisionist, even though the indigestible pre-text, by the implications of this gendered logic, is correlatively rendered male and in some sense devalued also. (pp. 45-51)

> *Carolyn Williams, "Unbroken Patternes: Gender, Culture, and Voice in 'The Egoist',"* in Browning Institute Studies, *Vol. 13, 1985, pp. 45-70.*

FURTHER READING

Auchincloss, Louis. "Meredith Reassailed." In his *Reflections of a Jacobite,* pp. 85-94. Boston: Houghton Mifflin Company, 1961.
> Considers the merits of Meredith's novels and reviews both negative and positive assessments of the works before reflecting on what Auchincloss considers the "genius of Meredith" as exemplified by the "superlative narratives" in *Diana of the Crossways* and *The Egoist.*

Bailey, Elmer James. "The Master Workman." In his *The Novels of George Meredith: A Study,* pp. 133-47. New York: Charles Scribner's Sons, 1907.
> Outlines the thematic and stylistic innovations that Meredith forged in *The Egoist* and compares the novel to George Eliot's *Daniel Deronda* and Henry James's *Portrait of a Lady.*

Baker, Robert S. "Sir Willoughby Patterne's 'Inner Temple': Psychology and 'Sentimentalism' in *The Egoist*." *Texas Studies in Literature and Language* 16, No. 4 (Winter 1975): 691-703.

Examines the issues of sexuality and sensuality in *The Egoist* and provides a psychoanalytic interpretation of Willoughby Patterne based on his relationships with various women in the novel.

———. "Faun and Satyr: Meredith's Theory of Comedy and *The Egoist*." *Mosaic* 9, No. 4 (Summer 1976): 173-93.

Contests the emphasis placed on the literary nature of comedy in most readings of Meredith's *Essay on Comedy* and recuperates the psychological and philosophical significance of the *Essay* by stressing its influence on the thematic and stylistic construction of *The Egoist*.

Beach, Joseph Warren. "The Egoist." In his *The Comic Spirit in George Meredith*, pp. 123-41. New York: Longman, Green, and Co., 1911.

Discusses Meredith's understanding of egoism and his characterization of Willoughby Patterne, stressing that both contribute to the satire found in *The Egoist*.

Belkin, Roslyn. "According to Their Age: Older Women in George Meredith's *The Egoist*." *International Journal of Women's Studies* 7, No. 1 (January-February 1984): 37-46.

Examines the relationship between elderly female characters and Willoughby Patterne, highlighting the impertinence shown by Willoughby, and likewise by critics of *The Egoist*, towards the "old maids" in the novel.

Booth, Thornton Y. "The Triumph of His Realism: *The Egoist*." In his *Mastering the Event: Commitment to Fact in George Meredith's Fiction*, pp. 46-55. Logan: Utah State University Press, 1967.

Observes the type of realism specific to Meredith's fiction, finding that Meredith was able to create characters with whom the reader is compelled to identify, an example being Willoughby in *The Egoist*.

Bowers, Neal. "Prelude as Theory and Scenario in *The Egoist*." *Ball State University Forum* 24, No. 2 (Spring 1983): 3-8.

Analyzes the relationship between the "Prelude" to *The Egoist* and the main body of the novel and discusses the similarities between the "Prelude" and Meredith's *Essay On Comedy and the Uses of the Comic Spirit*.

Buchen, Irving H. "Science, Society, and Individuality." *The University Review* 30, No. 3 (March 1964): 185-92.

Discusses Willoughby's interest in science in relation to Meredith's philosophy of society, sexuality, and gender.

———. "The Egoists in *The Egoist*: The Sensualists and the Ascetics." *Nineteenth Century Fiction* 19, No. 3 (December 1964): 255-69.

Examines the sexual aspect of the characters, symbols, and themes in *The Egoist*.

Conrow, Margaret. "Meredith's Ideal of Purity." *Essays in Literature* 10, No. 2 (Fall 1983): 199-207.

Contrasts Meredith's romantic idealism as expressed through his conception of sexual purity with recent critical assessments of *The Egoist* that stress the modern style and tone of the novel.

Craig, Randall. "*The Egoist*, Don Juan, and Language." *English Literary History* 56, No. 4 (Winter 1989): 897-921.

Investigates the language of *The Egoist* in relation to the characters and narrator, identifying various types of discourse in the novel.

Crees, J. H. E. "The Comic Spirit—The Sentimentalist." In his *George Meredith*, pp. 17-34. Oxford: B. H. Blackwell, 1918.

Claims that character "gives *The Egoist* its unique place in literature" and advances the thesis that the efficacy of Meredith's comedy results from the realistic rendering of characters in the novel.

Curle, Richard H. P. "On Egoism, Sentimentalism, and their Relationship." In his *Aspects of George Meredith*, pp. 216-28. New York: E. P. Dutton and Co., 1908.

Recounts Meredith's definition of egoism as found in *The Egoist* and defines the similarities and differences between the sentimentalist, or one who is "self-conscious and perfectly awake to . . . his aims," and the egoist, who is a "product of nature" and therefore "unconscious of his egoism."

Ellis, S. M. "*The Egoist. The Tragic Comedians.*" In his *George Meredith: His Life and Friends in Relation to His Work*, pp. 255-67. New York: Dodd, Mead & Co., 1920.

Reviews biographical information relevant to the composition of *The Egoist* and presents the early publishing history of the novel.

Foster, David. "The 'Golden Key': Imagination and Reason in *The Egoist*." *Journal of English and Germanic Philology* 79 (October 1980): 541-54.

Analyzes the relationship between morality and imagination in *The Egoist* with reference to the definition of the ego and egoism in Victorian England.

Gindin, James. "Meredith." In his *Harvest of a Quiet Eye: The Novel of Compassion*, pp. 57-77. Bloomington: Indiana University Press, 1971.

Provides a general overview of the literary merits and weaknesses in *The Egoist* and compares the novel to other works by Meredith.

Gretton, Mary Sturge. *The Writings and Life of George Meredith: A Centenary Study*, pp. 131-41. Cambridge: Harvard University Press, 1926.

Stresses the importance of the minor characters in *The Egoist* and examines the way in which Meredith's meticulous investigation of Willoughby's psyche aided his characterization of Vernon Whitworth, Crossjay, and Dr. Middleton.

Haley, Bruce. "The Athlete as Barbarian: Richard Feverel and Willoughby Patterne." In his *The Healthy Body and Victorian Culture*, pp. 227-51. Cambridge: Harvard University Press, 1978.

Discusses the Victorian interest in health and considers how issues of sexuality and class emerge out of the symbolism surrounding and treatment of the body in *The Egoist*.

Halperin, John. "George Meredith." In his *The Language of Meditation: Four Studies in 19th Century Fiction*, pp. 98-115. Elms Court, England: Arthur H. Stockwell, 1973.

Analyzes the chapter entitled "Clara's Meditations" in order to draw attention to the importance of the interior monologue as a vehicle of self-discovery and a dramatic device and briefly compares Meredith's style to that of George Eliot and Jane Austen.

Hudson, Richard B. "Meredith's *The Egoist* as a Play." *Modern Language Notes* 109, No. 3 (March 1944): 165-68.
Discusses Meredith's role in the dramatic adaptation of *The Egoist* and considers the weaknesses of the drama in relation to the novel.

————. "The Meaning of Egoism in George Meredith's *The Egoist*." *The Trollopian* 3, No. 3 (December 1948): 163-76.
Examines Meredith's understanding of egoism by relating the comic novel *The Egoist* to the more somber considerations of the topic in Meredith's poetry.

Jedrzejkiewicz, Maria. "The Exposure of Literary Conventions in *The Egoist* by George Meredith." *Studia Anglica Posnaniensia* 5, Nos. 1-2 (1973): 185-91.
Examines Meredith's manipulation and satirization of several literary devices, most importantly melodrama and sentimentality.

Kelvin, Norman. "The Rational Compromise: The 1870's." In his *A Troubled Eden: Nature and Society in the Works of George Meredith*, pp. 72-113. Stanford: Stanford University Press, 1961.
Discusses the narrator of *The Egoist* as both dramatist and moralist and reviews the influence of rationalist philosophy on Meredith's thinking.

Landis, Joseph C. "George Meredith's Comedy." *Boston University Studies in English* 2, No. 1 (Spring 1956): 17-35.
Relates the types of irony operating in *The Egoist* to those outlined in Meredith's *Essay on Comedy and the Uses of the Comic Spirit.*

Lindsay, Jack. "The Egoist." In his *George Meredith: His Life and Work*, pp. 238-44. London: The Bodley Head, 1956.
Provides a Marxist interpretation of *The Egoist* by discussing the similarities between the egoist in Meredith's novel and the alienated bourgeois individual in Victorian England.

Mannheimer, Monica. "Middle Novels: Towards Self-Reliance." In her *The Generations in Meredith's Novels*, pp. 155-65. Stockholm: Almqvist and Wiksell, 1972.
Discusses the character Clara Middleton and Meredith's promotion of women's rights in *The Egoist.*

Maxwell-Mahon, W. D. "The Pattern of Egoism: A Comment on George Meredith's Major Novel." *Unisa English Studies* 10, No. 3 (September 1972): 21-35.
Discusses style and theme in *The Egoist* in order to explicate the careful construction of the novel and prove that it remains Meredith's "major achievement."

McCullough, Bruce. "The Comic Spirit—George Meredith: *The Egoist.*" In his *Representative English Novelists: Defoe to Conrad*, pp. 215-30. 1946. Reprint. Freeport, N.Y.: Books for Libraries Press, 1972.
Reviews the similarities and differences between Meredith's use of comedy in *The Egoist* and that found in other eighteenth- and nineteenth-century British novels.

Millett, Kate. "The Sexual Revolution, First Phase: 1830–1930." In her *Sexual Politics*, pp. 91-214. New York: Avon Books, 1971.
Feminist reading of *The Egoist* that emphasizes the importance of the character Clara Middleton and highlights instances of sexuality and sensuality in the novel.

Moffatt, James. "*The Egoist.*" In his *George Meredith: A Primer to the Novels*, pp. 255-743. London: Hodder and Stoughton, 1909.
Recounts the plot of *The Egoist*, analyzes passages that illuminate the style of and themes in the novel, and proposes that the highly wrought style and crafted dialogue that set *The Egoist* apart from other novels of the day are features of the novel's artistry rather than a superfluous indulgence on the part of Meredith.

Moses, Joseph. "*The Egoist* and the Comedy of Limited Character." In his *The Novelist as Comedian*, pp. 164-83. New York: Schocken Books, 1983.
Examines the relationship between theme and character in *The Egoist* and evaluates previous critical assessments of the novel.

Parrill, Anna S. "Portraits of Ladies." *Tennessee Studies in Literature* 20 (1975): 92-99.
Discusses the similarities and differences between the characters of Isabel Archer in Henry James's *Portrait of a Lady* and Clara Middleton in *The Egoist.*

Priestley, J. B. "His Attitude: The Comic Spirit." In his *George Meredith*, pp. 112-43. New York: Macmillan Company, 1926.
Analyzes Meredith's writings on comedy and attributes the substance and complexity of the characters and themes in *The Egoist* to Meredith's understanding of the "Comic Spirit."

Sassoon, Siegfried. "First Meeting with Stevenson—*The Egoist.*" In his *Meredith*, pp. 139-54. New York: Viking Press, 1948.
Recounts biographical information relevant to the composition of *The Egoist* and the critical comments that shaped the early reception of the novel.

Sawin, Lewis, ed. Introduction to *The Egoist: A Play*, arranged for the stage by George Meredith and Alfred Sutro. Athens: Ohio University Press, 1981.
Provides the history of the dramatic adaptation of *The Egoist.*

Smirlock, Daniel. "Rough Truth: Synechdoche and Interpretation in *The Egoist.*" *Nineteenth Century Fiction* 31, No. 3 (December 1976): 313-28.
Discusses Meredith's use of synechdoche in the narrative of *The Egoist* and notes the artistic and philosophical achievements of the novel.

Stevenson, Lionel. "The Comic Spirit." In his *The Ordeal of George Meredith: A Biography*, pp. 220-33. New York: Charles Scribner's Sons, 1953.
Highlights autobiographical elements and stylistic achievements in *The Egoist.*

Stevenson, Richard. "Laetitia Dale and the Comic Spirit in *The Egoist.*" *Nineteenth Century Fiction* 26, No. 4 (March 1972): 406-18.
A character study of Laetitia Dale, who, according to Stevenson, functions as the "comic spirit," or savvy and perceptive critic, in the novel.

Stewart, Maaja A. and Casal, Elvira. "Clara Middleton: Wit and Pattern in *The Egoist.*" *Studies in the Novel* 12, No. 3 (Fall 1980): 210-27.
Traces Clara's progressive intellectual development in *The Egoist* and proposes that she is important not as an example of Meredith's "feminist" politics but as a char-

acter who offers a "different perspective" that is integral to the social satire in the novel.

Sundell, Michael C. "The Functions of Flitch in *The Egoist.*" *Nineteenth Century Fiction* 24, No. 2 (September 1969): 227-35.

Proposes that the character of Flitch lends interpretive continuity to the themes and plot in *The Egoist.*

Watson, William. "Fiction—Plethoric and Anæmic." *The National Review* 14, No. 80 (October 1889): 167-83.

Reviews the failings of Meredith as a novelist, commenting that *The Egoist* "is the most entirely wearisome book purporting to be a novel that I ever toiled through in my life."

Wilkenfield, Roger B. "Hands Around: Image and Theme in *The Egoist.*" *English Literary History* 34, No. 3 (September 1967): 367-79.

Examines the symbolism of the hand and hand-holding in *The Egoist.*

Williams, David. "Egoism and After." In his *George Mere-dith: His Life and Lost Love,* pp. 149-70. London: Hamish Hamilton, 1977.

Discusses relevant biographical information relating to the composition of *The Egoist* and reviews the major themes and characters in the novel.

Williams, Ioan, ed. "*The Egoist* (1879)." *In Meredith: The Critical Heritage,* pp. 202-39. London: Routledge and Kegan Paul, 1971.

Reprints reviews and criticism of *The Egoist* that were written during Meredith's lifetime.

Wilt, Judith. "The Hunting of the Egoist." In her *The Readable People of George Meredith,* pp. 147-79. Princeton: Princeton University Press, 1975.

Analyzes the narrative strategies, characters, and comic tone in *The Egoist.*

Wright, Walter F. "Comedy at Patterne Hall." In his *Art and Substance in George Meredith: A Study in Narrative,* pp. 60-78. Lincoln: University of Nebraska Press, 1953.

Reviews Meredith's investigation of egoism and his uses of comedy and psychology through an analysis of the major characters and motifs in *The Egoist.*

Martin Andersen Nexø

1869-1954

INTRODUCTION

Danish novelist, short story writer, travel writer, essayist, poet, autobiographer, and dramatist.

An author who wrote prolifically in several genres, Nexø is primarily known for his novel cycles *Pelle erobreren* (*Pelle the Conqueror*) and *Ditte menneskebarn* (*Ditte: Girl Alive; Ditte: Daughter of Man; Ditte: Towards the Stars*) which depict the struggles of the lower class in industrialized, capitalist society. In all of his writings Nexø strove to present his characters as both individuals and as universalized representatives of their social group in order to reveal the hardships faced by the poor in modern society. Despite his overt social commentary, critics praise Nexø's works as both artistically and ideologically significant, finding that in them he gives voice to the working class throughout the world without advancing doctrinaire social or political agendas.

Nexø was born in the slums of Copenhagen. In 1877 his family moved to a rural area on the island of Bornholm, his father's birthplace. Nexø thrived in the open air of the country and eventually gained employment as a herdboy. In 1884 he moved to Rønne, a large city on the island, to apprentice as a shoemaker. During his six years in this position, Nexø read widely and associated with contemporaries who were interested in literature and socialist ideals. He began writing between 1891 and 1893 while attending the Askov Folk High School, an institution of liberal education for adults. After teaching from 1893 to 1894, during which time he also published his first poems and newspaper articles, Nexø developed tuberculosis and was forced to give up his teaching position to recuperate. For the next two years he journeyed throughout Spain and Italy and wrote travel essays for Danish periodicals. Traveling on limited funds, Nexø lived among the poorer classes, and his impressions of proletarian conditions in these countries greatly affected him as he realized that poverty, so apparent in Denmark, was an international concern. In 1896 Nexø returned to Denmark, where he began teaching again, and two years later published his first volume of short stories, *Skygger*. By 1901 he chose to forego his teaching career and earn his living solely through writing, issuing several volumes of short stories as well as novels and travel essays. The majority of his works during this period display the influence of late nineteenth-century Decadent literature in their antibourgeois themes and egocentric protagonists. The publication of his novel *Dryss* in 1902 marked a transitional period for Nexø, who observed that "through that book on sickly individualism (egoism), I had found the common, natural being: the worker, the proletarian."

After the completion of his most successful work, *Pelle the Conqueror,* Nexø joined the Social Democratic party in

1910, becoming an ardent and highly popular supporter of the worker's cause; however, with the advent of the First World War and the Social Democrats' subsequent advocacy of increasingly radical tactics, Nexø broke away from the Party. After a visit to the Soviet Union in 1922, he composed *Mod dagningen,* a travel book that glorified the Soviet state. Nexø continued to support Soviet communism despite the unpopularity of such a viewpoint in his homeland, and in 1923 he moved to Germany, where he remained in self-exile for seven years. With his return in 1930 and the publication of his memoirs between 1932 and 1939, Nexø again achieved popularity in Denmark for the compelling reminiscences of his early life. After Germany invaded Denmark in 1941, Nexø was arrested as a Communist and jailed for a brief period. Two years later he again faced incarceration under the increasingly repressive Nazi occupation, but was able to escape to Sweden. Following World War II Nexø was honored by the Danish Author's Association for his literary efforts and his resistance to oppression. Subsequently, however, he was harshly criticized for his condemnation of Social Democrats and his support of communism, views that were conspicuously expressed in the first volume of his novel cycle *Morten hin røde* and his letters. Nexø moved to Dresden in what was formerly East Germany in 1951 and was at work on the last volume of *Morten hin røde* when he died in 1954.

Nexø's literary reputation rests on his novel cycles *Pelle the Conqueror* and *Ditte menneskebarn,* which are highly regarded for their epic qualities and vivid depictions of proletarian life. In *Pelle the Conqueror* Nexø traced the life of Pelle from his youth as a farmhand on the island of Bornholm under a near feudal system, to his rise as a labor leader in the industrialized city of Copenhagen at the turn of the century. Described as a work of "imaginative realism," *Pelle* closely reflects circumstances in Nexø's own life, and several commentators recognize his blending of fact and fiction. Throughout the novel, Pelle grows increasingly aware of the hardships and injustices of life among the working class, yet most of the story invokes a strong sense of optimism based upon the solidarity of the masses. Pelle is the embodiment of all workers, although Nexø's delineation of his protagonist's unique strengths and weaknesses makes Pelle more than a character type. Contributing to the epic quality and artistry of *Pelle the Conqueror* are Nexø's use of biblical symbolism and his allusions to Danish folklore, a device that serves to unify the thoughts and actions of the workers. Critics note that Pelle's role is similar to that of a prophet leading the masses toward a "promised land" through his utopian dream of a cooperative society. According to Faith and Niels Ingwersen the impact of the novel resides in Nexø's effective use of mythology and a collective folk heritage, and they assert that "readers of *Pelle the Conqueror,* even if they can pinpoint ideological flaws, can hardly fail to grasp the fact that it was—and is—a very effective political weapon: it is an inspiring, optimistic battle hymn to the workers' cause."

Nexø's novel cycle *Ditte* is far less optimistic than *Pelle,* delineating the life of the eponymous female protagonist and her early death from overwork. Ditte, like Pelle, is raised amid rural poverty and eventually migrates to the city in search of employment; however, Ditte is not propelled by the need to change the worker's condition, but instead falls victim to those who would exploit her willingness to serve and nurture. Nexø dedicated the novel to his mother, and critics note that in many ways Ditte represents motherhood and selfless devotion to the service of others. The Ingwersens posit that the first three volumes of the cycle contain fairy-tale motifs wherein characters parallel magical helpers, princes, witches, sorcerers, and trolls, a structure that corresponds to Ditte's childlike belief in a life in which goodness triumphs over evil. Depicting Ditte's later life, the last two volumes evoke her gradual decline and death.

Nexø's planned final novel cycle, *Morten hin røde* (which may be translated as "Morten the Red"), continues the saga of the proletariat from the perspective of Morten, a character who appears in both *Pelle* and *Ditte.* A Marxist writer whose radical socialist beliefs mirror Nexø's own, Morten serves as the mouthpiece for Nexø's ideology during his later years. In *Pelle* Morten vows to record Pelle's life in a novel of the proletariat, although he expresses doubt that Pelle's optimistic vision will bring about the tri-umph of the cause of the workers. In *Ditte* Morten vacillates between desiring a worker's revolution and realizing that a revolt would be ineffective at the time. In this last work Morten, a defeated and estranged Communist, neither conveys the idealism of Pelle nor elicits the sympathy of Ditte, and the novel is generally not as highly regarded as Nexø's earlier efforts, principally because his emphasis on social philosophy is considered detrimental to character development and narrative artistry. Nexø, however, strongly preferred that his works be judged for their depictions of social events in history rather than by aesthetic criteria. Nevertheless, he is best remembered for the artistic merit of his novels and is credited with achieving a form of realism in which he infused a sense of idealism into the harsh lives of his characters as a means to enlighten as well as inspire working-class readers. Contrasting *Pelle the Conqueror,* "the classic proletarian novel," with the fairy tales of Nexø's countryman Hans Christian Andersen, Harry Slochower asserted: "Nexø resolved to tell of the effort [of the proletariat] to turn the fairy-tale to reality, the story of man's attempt to conquer the social obstacles that prevent his dreams of freedom from becoming actuality."

PRINCIPAL WORKS

Skygger   (short stories)   1898
Det bødes der for   (short stories)   1899
En moder   (novel)   1900
Muldskud   (short stories)   1900
Familien Frank   (novel)   1901
Dryss   (novel)   1902
Soldage   (travel essay)   1903
    [*Days in the Sun,* 1929]
Muldskud: Anden samling   (short stories)   1905
Pelle erobreren.   4 vols.   (novel)   1906-10
    [*Pelle the Conqueror* (Translated in four volumes:
    Pelle: Boyhood, 1913; *Pelle: Apprenticeship,* 1914;
    Pelle: The Great Struggle, 1915; and *Pelle: Daybreak,*
    1916)]
Af dybets lovsang   (short stories)   1908
Barndommens kyst   (short stories)   1911
Bornholmer noveller   (short stories)   1913
Lykken   (short stories)   1913
Under himmelen den blaa   (short stories)   1915
Ditte menneskebarn.   5 vols.   (novel)   1917-21
    [*Ditte* (Translated in three volumes: *Ditte: Girl Alive!*
    1920; *Ditte: Daughter of Man, 1921; Ditte: Towards
    the Stars,* 1922; also published in 1931]
Dybhavsfisk   (short stories)   1918
Folkene paa Dangaarden   (drama)   1919
Undervejs   (short stories)   1919
De tomme pladsers passagerer   (short stories)   1921
Muldskud.   3 vols.   (short stories)   1922-26; also pub-
    lished as *Samlede fortællinger,* 1926
Mod dagningen: Skildringer fra Rusland   (travel essay)
    1923
Digte   (poetry)   1926; also published as *Digte: Anden
    forøgede udgave* [revised and enlarged edition], 1951
Midt i en jærntid   (novel)   1929
    [*In God's Land,* 1933]

Erindringer. 4 vols. (memoirs) 1932-39
  [*Under the Open Sky: My Early Years* (partial translation), 1938]
To verdener: Tanker og Indtryk fra en Ruslandsrejse (travel essay) 1934
Morten hin røde. 3 vols. (unfinished novel) 1945-57
Taler og artikler. 3 vols. (speeches and essays) 1954-55
Breve fra Martin Andersen Nexø. 3 vols. (letters) 1969-72

*This work includes *Et lille kræ, Under aaben himmel, For Lud og koldt vand,* and *Vejs ende.*

Martin Andersen Nexø (essay date 1906)

[*In the following excerpt from the preface to the 1906 Danish edition of* Pelle the Conqueror: Boyhood, *Nexø introduces the character of Pelle.*]

It would be futile to wander around looking for the literary father of this brave lad whom I am sending out into the world here, newly confirmed and full of appetite. For twelve years I have coddled him in my own way, and all of his joys and sorrows have resounded in myself since the time I could crawl—in my mind, in my guts, down my backbone. He is my own to the highest degree, and has every right—like the sons in the sagas when they left home—to demand a parting word from me. It will be easy enough for other people to notice all of his faults, but there is no one who knows him as well as I do.

Although he was not created with the wave of a hand, he still demands a lot of space—the account of Pelle the Conqueror's struggles and victories takes up four volumes. But that should not frighten off anyone in this country, where we are trained to handle the heftiest tomes right from the cradle.

And he ought to be accompanied by great throngs of people! *Pelle the Conqueror* is supposed to be a book about the proletariat—that is, about human beings themselves—who, naked and equipped only with good health and appetite, enlist in the service of life; about the bold stride of the worker across the earth on his endless, half-unconscious journey toward the light! No other social class has such a vast background for its path in life as does the peasantry, or such significant destinies—where the proletarian fights, it is always for fundamentals; *he* still remains a martyr to the most basic demands for justice.

Pelle will have his turn too. The second volume depicts his apprenticeship years in the little provincial town with its traditional artisan hierarchy; in the third volume he travels across the sea as a young journeyman—toward the King's Copenhagen—and becomes part of the rise of the workers; the last volume takes place in Copenhagen as it is today, thoroughly organized and controlled by the hands of the workers—*the people's Copenhagen.*

Fine fellow that he is, Pelle gets involved in all of it. And everything is intended to be echoed in him: in his footsteps resound the endless steps of the many who want to struggle forward; *his* sorrows and joys should serve as a foundation for their happiness in life. (p. 241)

> *Martin Andersen Nexø, in his* Pelle the Conqueror, *Vol. 1: Childhood, edited by Tiina Nunnally, translated by Steven T. Murray, Fjord Press, 1989, 244 p.*

The New York Times Book Review (essay date 1913)

[*In the following review of the English translation of the first volume of* Pelle the Conquerer, *the critic offers a favorable appraisal of the work.*]

Is the very long novel—the novel in several volumes—becoming once more the fashion? It is only a short while ago that the last portion of *Jean Christophe* was published; Compton Mackenzie's new book is avowedly but the opening part of his hero's story, and now in *Pelle the Conqueror* we have a novel in four volumes, of which this one, containing the account of Pelle's boyhood, is the first. According to the introduction by Prof. Otto Jespersen, much of the story is autobiographical, and we can well believe that this is true, for it reads, not like fiction, but like an exceptionally vivid record of actual events; events commonplace enough—as commonplace as life itself. When we first meet Pelle and his father Lasse they have but just arrived at the island of Bornholm in the Baltic, whither they have come from their native Sweden, seeking employment. Or, to be accurate, Lasse is seeking employment, for Pelle is only a very little boy, much excited over this, his first journey. Lasse is at last hired by the bailiff of Stone Farm, where he takes care of the cattle, Pelle being expected to pay for his board by running errands and later acting as herd boy. The book tells of their daily life during the years at Stone Farm and ends when Pelle, having been confirmed by the parson and "equipped with the Prophets, the Judges, the Apostles, the Ten Commandments, and one hundred and twenty hymns," leaves the farm to seek his fortune in the town which he has never seen.

It is all related with the utmost simplicity. Pelle is a real boy, full of energy and fun, ready to play or fight and loving to tease the schoolmaster, but tender-hearted and devotedly attached to his father. All the happenings upon the big farm—the constant toil, the quarrels, and the love making, sickness, and holiday joys, birth, and death—we see through the child's eyes. They are a rough and primitive people among whom his lot is cast, but not so brutal as those of whom we have read in other novels. Many of them are kindly, and there is a quite unconscious readiness for self-sacrifice in Kalle and his wife and the old grandmother, who, despite privation and grief, had found life very good. Living close to the soil, superstitious, humble before the master and mistress, who seemed to them creatures belonging almost to another world, grumbling sometimes, but usually content with little, they represent an old order whose first faint stirrings of change appear in the boy Pelle and in his father's desire that he shall learn to read and write, for then, Lasse thinks, he may become anything, even a clerk or a schoolmaster.

Lasse is perhaps a more appealing because a more pathetic character than Pelle, the son of his old age. His bravado, whose futility he knows so well, his pitiful attempts at self-assertion, which end in nothing; his desire to keep his role of Providence to the boy who believes in him utterly, his frustrated endeavors to clutch at the manhood he feels is fast slipping from him, the trick Fate plays him at the end, when peace and comfort seem almost within his grasp, above all his devotion to his only child, make of him a memorable figure. He does nothing spectacular. During the thrilling scene of the shipwreck he, like the reader, is a mere looker-on, yet one remembers him after the hero of that dramatic episode is forgotten. Lasse is a Père Goriot, who reaps love instead of ingratitude.

However, it is the boy Pelle about whom the whole revolves—Pelle, who was often cold, frequently overworked, and occasionally abused, yet found time for play, and could feel on looking back upon it that he had had a happy childhood. That childhood is here presented neither in rosy nor in very dark colors; there is neither the false sentiment which gushes over the delights of penury, nor that other, equally false, which makes no allowance for habit or temperament, but a genuine realism which shows the mingling of pleasure and sorrow, the joys of play and the brook during Summer, the hardships of the long, dark Northern Winter. And we feel and see it all—the barns and outhouses, the broad fields, with sand dunes beyond, and beyond them again the sea. And the homely folk, dairy maids and laborers, the headman upon whom there fell so terrible a calamity, the young fisherman, who expiated his sin with his life—we know them every one. There is no straining after effect; it is all natural, seemingly spontaneous.

So far as one may judge who is unable to read it in the original Danish, the book seems well written and the translation excellent. Certainly, the construction is good, and though the plot is simplicity itself, the narrative never drags. The character-analysis, moreover, is done with a line here, a few words there—and the individual stands before us, a live human being. Pelle himself is of course portrayed more at length than are any of the others; his ideas—the half-pathetic, half-comic and often wholly grotesque ideas of a child—his feelings toward those around him, his unconscious centering of all his little world about himself, the gradual, barely perceptible change of his attitude toward his father, from one of utter dependence to one almost protective, are alike skillfully and naturally drawn. We leave the book anxious to know what sort of a man this boy will make, and certain that he will become one worth hearing about. Martin Andersen Nexø is not destined long to remain, so far as the American reading public is concerned, an unknown author. All those who care for good work should and doubtless will hasten to make his acquaintance.

"Martin Andersen Nexø's Novel 'Pelle the Conqueror'," in The New York Times Book Review, *December 7, 1913, p. 720.*

The Nation   (essay date 1917)

[*In the following review of the English translation of the fourth and concluding volume of* Pelle the Conquerer, *the critic summarizes the novel cycle.*]

Now that the fourth and last volume of **Pelle** is before him, the English reader may well feel moved to reread the earlier volumes, which have appeared at considerable intervals, in order to test or to refresh his impression of the work as a whole. The very fact that each of these volumes taken by itself showed uncommon stability and definition—was, in a sense, a "complete story"—may have tended to obscure its place in the tetralogy. *Jean-Christophe,* with which **Pelle** challenges comparison in several respects, is only intelligible in the light of its conclusion; its division into parts, whether the ten parts of the original or the four parts of the English version, is arbitrary. The work as a whole has no recognizable form or comeliness. **Pelle,** on the other hand, not only hangs together as a whole, but represents a series of distinct phases in the career which we are following. As with *Jean-Christophe,* it is a career of experiment, of search for the meaning of life—and a successful search. Rolland chose a genius, an "artist," for his protagonist: Nexö has chosen one to whom life is a thing distinct from art and infinitely more important.

To this final volume is appended a note about the author by Professor Jespersen of the University of Copenhagen. It seems that Nexö was very little known in Denmark when the first part of **Pelle the Conqueror** appeared, some ten years ago. He was a teacher in Copenhagen who had done a little travelling and a little writing—chiefly some short stories which a few people had recognized as exceptional. Copenhagen was the place of his birth (1869); its circumstances were of the humblest. The knowledge of slum life shown in his pictures of "the Ark" and its mean and filthy surroundings was evidently gained at first hand. So was his knowledge of rustic squalor, since most of his boyhood, like Pelle's, appears to have passed upon the island of Bornholm in the Baltic. His very name is taken from the town of Nexö on that island, where, like Pelle again, he became a shoemaker's apprentice and made his first ardent and awkward experiments in the direction of happiness. There was other work for his hands, chiefly as a bricklayer, before he won the schooling which prepared for his work as a teacher. It was all a preparation for his work as a writer. The story of Pelle is the story of a manhood struggling with all sorts of obstacles, often thrown down and trampled upon, yet making its way steadily and with unquenchable confidence, towards a mastery of life. The test of character, after all, is not that we should be always sure where we are going, but that we should never doubt ourselves to be "on our way." When Pelle first sets out townwards and fortunewards, leaving poor Father Lasse on his dunghill, his high-heartedness belongs to youth and health merely—or might have so belonged. And he is in real peril of losing it, as he faces the rough world of the town and passes from boyhood along the dangerous bridge of adolescence. There are times when even the safeguard of his egotism fails him. The world is all a muddle. The poor are the helpless victims of the rich, for example, and he is merely one of the poor; therefore he may as well drown his pain in the gutter. But even at his lowest spiritual ebb there remains the seed of something fine and valiant in him; and more than once there is a woman to remind him of it, and to spur him back to himself.

By degrees, it will be recalled, his husk of youthful selfishness is stripped away, and zeal for the service of his kind takes its place: for his kind in a narrow sense, perhaps—his fellow-workers as against those who employ and profit by them. He becomes the champion and leader of the work-people in a long struggle. It culminates in a phase of violence which results in defeat at the hands of authority and Pelle's imprisonment for a term of years. Meanwhile, as the result of his devotion to the cause, his family have nearly starved, and he discovers that his wife has sold herself to feed them and him. So the third part ended, on a note of apparent defeat and despair. The fourth, which is now before us, opens on the day when Pelle is released from prison and goes forth to face the world again. He has served a sort of martyrdom, and has some vague expectation of being received with enthusiasm by the people whom he has led. He finds that the cause has made progress, that the work-people are in better case than formerly, but that he himself is half-forgotten. Moreover, his own point of view has changed, and when the chance comes to assert himself once more as a leader he finds little to say, and nothing at all in the old militant vein. His wife at least has welcomed him, he has forgiven her, and we are to see their imperfect mating become as nearly perfect as the difference in their natures permits. But for a long time he remains unaroused to further efforts at leadership. There is hard going at home. He takes to his old trade of cobbler and so manages a bare living. Meanwhile he is not unhappy, his spirit broods and bides its time; his old confidence remains somewhere in the background of his consciousness. Presently, through the perfecting of his friendship with a member of the class which he has despised, the fresh impulse to action comes. Once more, but this time no longer in single-handed self-sufficiency or in a spirit of conflict, he takes up the burden of the workers and modestly initiates, in the character of employer, a system of coöperation which is to prove the basis of a new and happier social order. There is less of the panoramic in the concluding part of the narrative than in its predecessors. But this is natural, since Pelle has to lay the foundation of his broader usefulness in the establishment of just relations with the intimate few. We see him here learning to be a husband and a father and a friend, and by this very process confirming his manhood and fitting himself for wider service. Every member of the little surrounding group which contributes to his growth is painted with extraordinary vividness and thoroughness: his wife Ellen first of all; then Brun, the old librarian and born aristocrat whose pure love of humanity finally wins Pelle from his pride; Johanna, the desolate and yet not altogether hopeless child-victim of social wrong; Morten the writer, who is to find in Pelle and what he stands for a solider inspiration than in all the books upon Brun's shelves. Such a work of imagination as this, with its deep humor, its deep humanity, brings home to us, as nothing else can, the artificial nature of those boundaries which language and custom set between one race and another. It is a book for the world; one cannot lay it down without a sense of quickened emotion and enlarged vision. (pp. 241-42)

"A Career of Experiment," in The Nation, *New York, Vol. CIV, No. 2696, March 1, 1917, pp. 241-42.*

Joel M. Johanson   (essay date 1919)

[*In the following excerpt, Johanson analyzes* Pelle the Conqueror, *praising the universality of the work and the characterization of Pelle, which Johanson maintains contribute to the novel's stature as an "epic of labor."*]

Pelle the Conqueror, a four-volume novel by Martin Andersen Nexö, appeared a few years before the outbreak of the war. Its author was probably quite unknown to American readers until the translation of his novel was completed. Then his work began to be favorably compared with Rolland's *Jean-Christophe,* which had caused such a stir a short time before, and its author to be considered in the first rank among contemporary novelists. The deluge of ephemeral and partisan literature loosed by the war soon eclipsed his name. But now that the reconstruction time has come his work will no doubt regain its former interest. This is the more likely because it represents in living terms the collapse of the competitive system of industry and the groping for some substitute, which ends in a steady drift toward the coöperative. In Denmark, it will be remembered, the coöperative organization had progressed farther than anywhere else in Europe before the war. During the war the movement advanced rapidly everywhere in Europe, and now it has reached the United States, not only in the form of propaganda but in the practical programme of such a party as the Non-Partisan League in the western states. A review of the Danish work, which presents the antecedent chaos, the tentative beginnings, the successful organization, and the prospective triumph of coöperation, is therefore peculiarly opportune.

Pelle the Conqueror is not doctrinaire. The idea of coöperation is not its hero. It is the vivid transcript of a Swedish immigrant boy's life in Denmark. Doctrine and opinion may be made out of this boy's experiences just as practical wisdom is formed out the experiences of life.

The four volumes of the novel deal with four phases of its hero's development: boyhood, apprenticeship, the struggles of maturity, and the victory.

The first volume [*Boyhood*] is one of those realistic studies of boyhood in which modern realistic literature abounds. Pelle and his aged father come from Sweden to the Danish island of Bornholm in the Baltic and seek employment as farm-workers. They are domiciled on Stone Farm, which is owned by the Kongstrups, reputed to be the island's severest taskmasters. Since the father is too old and the son too young for full wages, they receive together a trifling wage. The unfolding of the boy's intelligence in the environment of the farm, while he herds cattle in the meadows in summer and cares for them in the stables in winter, and as he tries to establish himself among his playmates on the farm and in the little religious school, is a remarkable record of imaginative realism. After his confirmation he is considered ready to shift for himself and goes to the neighboring seaport town, where he is apprenticed in the shoemaker's trade.

The second volume [*Apprenticeship*] continues the story of the boy's development as an apprentice in the hard school of the city. The curiosity about the life around him which characterized his farm experiences here has a larger field for exploration; and there is little about the town and its inhabitants that he does not have an opportunity to learn while he serves his apprenticeship. The difficulties of orientation are much greater; but in the attempt to find himself in his surroundings his character gains in strength and stability. At length his curiosity about that life beyond the narrow town horizon, which sends him strange intimations from time to time, attracts him away from Nexö to the capital before his apprenticeship is fully served.

The third volume, called *The Great Struggle,* is concerned with the period of young manhood in Copenhagen. There he finds himself at the very heart of a problem that had come to him in mysterious hints and perplexing suggestions on the farm and in the town. He sets himself to solve this in the same way in which he had learned to face and overcome the smaller problems of his adjustment to his simpler youthful environment. His method is to throw himself with great energy into the labor movement, of which he becomes eventually the leader. This is not a volume on labor unionism; it is still the life of a strong and magnetic personality. The bitter conflicts between his loyalty to a cause and the needs of his own life—his loves, wife, and family—give the account an intimately personal impression. At the height of his success as a labor leader, just when he has won a great general strike, he is sent to prison on a false charge of forgery.

The last volume recounts his attempts, after his release from prison, to rehabilitate himself and to reëstablish his family life, broken up even before his imprisonment through his devotion to the labor cause. Henceforth his interest in the labor problem takes the form of attempting to organize a coöperative shoemaking industry in the capital. This enterprise involves him in endless struggles with the manufacturers' association, but he gradually succeeds and extends his coöperative principle into other activities. His personal fortunes are improved and his family happily reunited and established on a country estate known as Daybreak. *Daybreak* is the title of the last volume. Different from the realistic novels of the day, this ends with a note of optimism.

Although the novel is thus primarily an account of Pelle's personal life, this is deftly interwoven into a report of conditions that have a wide economic and historical significance. Certain well-known problems are here shown as they are viewed from their centre. *Boyhood* presents the centralizing tendency in competitive agriculture, with its accompanying maladjustments. The better farms of the island are being acquired by the wealthy farmers while the barren plots are being left for the poor. A miserable existence must be eked out by occasional labor in the stone quarries. The independent peasantry is being transformed into a proletariat. The young men and women stream away from the dismal prospect on the land to a deceptively hopeful future in the towns, and their places are in turn occupied by immigrants. Pelle migrates with them to the town.

There he observes the same centralizing tendency in the trades. These are coming under the control of the masters, who succeed by exploiting the toil of their apprentices. The masters themselves are being forced to the wall by the competition of machine-made goods from the larger industrial centres. The apprentices, when their service is finished, finding no work at their trades, drift, like the peasants, into the ranks of the proletariat. The problem of increasing unemployment and acute poverty, recurring each winter, begins to attract an uneasy curiosity. Since the prospects in a trade are after all no better than they were in the country, Pelle gives up his service and is caught up in the drift toward Copenhagen, still seeking "the promised land."

The capital is the centre toward which all the blind forces of life converge. Here all the evils of town and country are aggravated. There are crowded tenements, hideous slums, sweated labor, monopoly, usury, drunkenness, disease, desperate poverty, and all that familiar category. A new phenomenon is labor grown rebellious and refusing to work when conditions become intolerable. Out of this attitude grow unionism and its accompaniments: strikes, lockouts, mediations, parleyings, protocols, mutual hatred, and suspicion. The sanguine immigrant from Sweden has come, after many chances, to this end. It seems that another emigration is his only hope. But he concludes that emigration would bring him merely a repetition of his Danish experiences; it would be another course from pillar to post. Therefore, if "the land of promise" is not to be found abroad, it must be made at home. So he becomes an active member in the labor agitation, finally leads it, and brings it to preliminary success. Thus labor wins the right to organize and respect for its organization. Pelle's imprisonment at this juncture is an omen little understood by triumphant unionism. Between the conditions revealed in Denmark and those in any other industrial country there is little real difference; they are everywhere the same. All the phenomena of sociological investigation are recorded as the incidents of the central figure's life.

The fourth volume presents a phase of the problem that is relatively new in America. It suggests that unionism, now recognized and respectable, has not obtained the results it struggled for. There is as much poverty and unemployment as before. It further suggests that the new aspect of the movement, the parliamentary and political, will yield no more acceptable results. Then it points a way of escape through the organization of coöperative industries to be owned by the laborers themselves. Pelle leads this new movement, both by the object-lesson of his own coöperative equal-sharing shoe factory, and by active propaganda. The new principle progresses against all the obstacles that competitive industry can contrive for it until it controls certain trades, highly organized from the soil to the consumer. The capital for the first venture comes from outside his class, an expedient that Pelle is reluctant to accept. He becomes reconciled to it by the reflection that labor must constructively employ in its proposed new order all those instrumentalities that the two groups, capital and labor, had hitherto used against each other. Thus he goes about making his promised land at home.

In this review it is seen that the hero of the novel, the completely realized character, reveals through his life the fortunes of the laboring class. This class Disraeli once dignified by the name of nation. When he looked out upon the civil discord and strife of England he spoke of his country as being "divided into two nations." More and more since his time does it become apparent how well he understood the situation; every industrial country is divided into two nations contending with each other for power and position. Pelle represents the consciousness of one of these nations in Denmark, and similarly in the entire western world where the same conditions exist. The novel is intimately personal in its realism, but it is not that isolated and exceptional experience that is recorded in so many modern investigations into the individual soul. It acquires an epic sweep and significance because of the universal nature of this one individual. The background upon which the pattern of his life is traced has been made completely familiar to us by countless social researches in the last generation. In the respect that the hero rises to be a leader in the most significant of modern movements the epic quality is heightened and maintained. The book is therefore similar to the great national epics, in which the personal fortunes of the hero are indeed, as in **Pelle the Conqueror,** of primary interest, but acquire a greater significance by their intimate union with their people's destinies. The heroes of the Iliad and the Odyssey are the builders of the Greek states. Beowulf's magnificent combats establish a people in security. Æneas founds Rome. The hero must be an autonomous individual as well as representative of national or universal destiny.

If the hero is made a symbol, or is governed by purposes beyond his control, or serves some abstract idea, so that the spontaneous expression of his personality is thereby limited, the epic loses one of its distinguishing qualities. The Æneid is therefore an inferior epic, since its hero is felt to be rather the high destiny of imperial Rome than a self-governing personality. Like the Æneid in this respect are those interesting works, *The Adventures of Gargantua and Pantagruel* and *Don Quixote,* which are, of course, not epics, although they present wide-sweeping views of life. They are the works of reflective and skeptical men, the summaries of discredited cultures, presented in a burlesque and farcical imitation of that epic manner which would have been appropriate before the cultural unity of the time they satirize had been destroyed. To continue a swift historical sketch, the romances of roguery return simply to the realities of contemporary life among the commons, with however light a purpose. Upon these realities, more seriously considered, the enduring works must eventually be built. In the "history" of Tom Jones there are realism, unity, and characterization seriously directed. But Tom Jones remains an interesting type of one kind of Englishman; he does not represent the fate or fortunes of England. In such a work, on the other hand, as Hugo's *Les misérables,* which, it may be observed in passing, is an obvious inspiration for the Danish novelist, there is found a wider significance in the life of the hero without his reduc-

tion to a symbol. The epic impression is impaired, however, by Hugo's characteristic lyrical gift, and his attempted realizations are not sufficiently objective.

To come quickly to the present (if that distant time before the war may be called the present) *Jean-Christophe,* the well-known novel by Romain Rolland, summarizes the civilization of Europe just turned into the new century, as reflected in the life of a master-musician. It is not a national novel; it is frankly cosmopolitan. But cosmopolitanism has unfortunately not yet arrived as a reality in the world,—although Erasmus could avow himself a cosmopolitan with some show of truth, since he represented a universal power and spoke in an international language. Art was once said indeed to be limited by no national barriers; and musicians may have been the true internationals before the war. But now that notion has vanished. In any event it is difficult to think of an artist, intent upon self-realization in pure artistic expression, as representing the simple realities of the workaday world. During the war the author of *Jean-Christophe* issued from his Swiss retreat a pamphlet explaining his attitude as *Above the Conflict.* This attitude during the past crisis will explain why there is a lack of vital consistency between the life of Jean and the author's interpolated reflections on European civilization as seen from a high intellectual eminence. The novel is in the tradition of *Wilhelm Meister,* whose cosmopolitan author considered the cultural development of his hero with Olympian detachment in the midst of troublous times.

The Danish novel is the true epic of labor. It is simple, for it is the story of the simple told by themselves. It is unified, for it is the story of the multitudinous obscure, conveniently known as that single entity, "the masses." It is universal, "for ye have always the poor with you." It marks the clear emergence of the laborer as self-sufficient hero, and the final articulate realization of his dignity. There have been many side-references to the life of the humble, many bird's-eye views of the ancient lowly, but hitherto probably no work that views life from the laborer's centre, interprets it by his philosophy, and attempts to construct the world upon his principles.

The wisest have always been known to seek counsel; and in these times even statesmen, caught in the whirl of events, acknowledge the need of guidance. Institutions are in a plastic condition and may be rationally moulded, or passively allowed to fix again into their former dangerously rigid shapes. If they are to be rationally moulded, there must be a more general understanding of labor; its miseries, its blind struggles, its *almost* infinite patience, its slow coming to self-consciousness, and its growing determination that competition must yield to something kindlier. "The poor hath hope, and iniquity stoppeth her mouth." He who would understand labor could scarcely do better than to study the life of Pelle. (pp. 219-26)

Joel M. Johanson, "Pelle, the Conqueror: An Epic of Labor," in The Sewanee Review, *Vol. XXVII, No. 2, Spring, 1919, pp. 218-26.*

Carl H. Grabo   (essay date 1928)

[*Grabo was an American educator and critic. In the following excerpt, he considers* Pelle the Conqueror *and* Ditte menneskebarn, *focusing on Nexø's use of naturalistic narrative techniques.*]

Pelle the Conqueror has rather more pattern than [Romain Rolland's] *Jean-Christophe.* The inter-relations of characters are more completely depicted, the group is more coherent. There is, in short, some plot; though not enough to give an impression of rigidity, of life cramped and forced into moulds, yet sufficient to create expectation and suspense. Surely suspense is legitimate in the most rigorous realism, for there is suspense in life itself. Experience, even though it falls into no single pattern, is separable into a series of broken inconclusive patterns which the novelist may, for emphasis, accentuate and complete. This Nexö has done, with the result that the story is more memorable than *Jean-Christophe* and the fable with its chief episodes is more vividly recalled—one test of good craftsmanship.

Nexö's greatest power lies in the perfect frankness and naturalness with which he records the most homely, sordid, and even bestial facts of human experience. No novelist, unless it be Hamsun, is so wholly unforced and undramatic in the depiction of facts in themselves disagreeable but which in his large scene are no more than details. These Scandinavian realists accept life more wholly, more sanely, one feels, than do we, with our taboos and our obliquities. James Joyce in *Ulysses* is no less frank, but his swaggering emphasis, his deliberate bravado, is the unwholesome display of one to whom life is revolting and who vacillates between the extremes of sensuality and asceticism. Nexö portrays life unflinchingly but with a casualness, a freedom from false emphasis, which is wholly disarming. He is no more coarse nor prurient than a textbook on physiology. No citation divorced from its context can do justice to this quality in Nexö, his wholly unemphatic acceptance of all experience, however coarse and brutal. The brief excerpt from *Ditte,* which follows, is not exceptional; yet the revolting character of the tenement house to which this description is incident could not be half so well conveyed in a more exclamatory and sympathetic manner. To the children, whose experience this is, the manner of life is not revolting but interesting:

> When they were sitting by the window it was possible to have it open; otherwise they had to keep it shut—because of the rats. They were walking along the roof-gutter, appearing suddenly out of a drain pipe as if it were the top of a staircase—right in front of one's nose— walking the whole round, bustling and sniffing the air, looking ever so funny. When the rain drove the children out of the yard they took possession of the roofs of the outhouses and gambolled about down there. But in the night-time it was still worse. When the moon shone into the yard one could see them literally lying in wait in the entrances to the cellars; and no sooner had the baker put his sheets of bread out to cool on the roofs of the outhouses than the rats were at it, before he'd even had time to turn away. Old Rasmussen had seen it when she sat up with the women of the building who were expecting babies. One could actually see the rats getting their noses burned on the hot rolls. Then they'd whirl round, squealing and rubbing their noses with their paws.

The sufficient if not elaborate design of *Pelle* and of *Ditte* and the unforced character of the realism, technical excellences both, spring from a philosophy which provides a selective principle. Nexö accepts all of life because life to him has meaning, because all experience, even the most bestial, contributes to the growth of soul. The particularity of detail, the unflagging factual quality of his work, is not an end in itself but a means to the development in his hero and his heroine of those spiritual qualities which enable them to find themselves and achieve a fit place in society. Their experiences have both an individual and a social bearing. Surely peasant life has never been so graphically portrayed as in the first volumes of *Pelle* and of *Ditte,* nor has the thesis been elsewhere so powerfully proclaimed that from the coarsest physical surroundings character may spring, and the finest spiritual qualities have their roots in muck. The mystical enlargement of soul which is Jean-Christophe's achievement seems vague and thin beside an idealism so robust as this.

Although it is the fictional biography of its hero, *Pelle,* unlike [Samuel Butler's] *The Way of All Flesh,* does more than depict an individualistic morality, or, like *Jean-Christophe,* record the development of genius. Its theme is a larger one, the discovery of the self in its social relations. Pelle's experiences have a twofold purpose, individual and social. It is only at the last, when he is happy in his work as a labor leader, that the conflict of ideals is resolved. In this fusion of individual and social morality, the naturalistic technique falls into line with the traditional purpose of the novel. The emphasis is upon Pelle, but background is more constant, more important, than in a novel like *Jean-Christophe.* Minor characters, too, loom larger; their development, though minimized, is not overlooked, and they persist longer in the action. Thus, for instance, Pelle's wife, his adjustment to her and hers to him, is sufficiently depicted, for it is a step in his adjustment to society. Plot in the old rigidly predetermined sense there is not, but the mesh of social relationships is complex. We have here more than the story of a single life.

Neither Rolland nor Nexö is in his philosophy of life, strictly speaking, a naturalist. The heroes of each have an individual endowment which is more than the product of inheritance played upon by environment. Neither author accepts a mechanistic philosophy; to both, human life is more than an experiment in animal behavior. Yet each employs a technique derived from the naturalistic method of Zola. A more rigidly naturalistic technique than theirs is productive, I think, of less interesting fictional results. For the purpose of art it is necessary to predicate of humanity an incalculable factor. If life is no more than a chemical formula, why write realistic fiction at all? Novels for entertainment, merely as anodynes to the pain of existence, there will always be. But the serious novelist would be better occupied with experimental psychology than with fiction. Fiction on the mechanistic formula, as a hand-maiden to science, cannot, I think, endure.

Naturalism as practised by Nexö, though it returns, in a sense, to the traditional purpose of the novel to portray the life of an individual in relation to society, does so with a difference. The old picaresque novel followed the fortunes of a single character. It portrayed the seamy side of the social fabric, but uncritically. The biographical novel of a later development, such as *David Copperfield,* depicted the individual in his pursuit of wife and fortune and left him at last ensconced in his comfortable niche. In neither form was the hero put through any course of questionings as to his social adjustment. That was wholly a material thing, a matter of rank, fortune, and family relationships. Structurally speaking this adjustment was wholly a matter of plot, the resultant of a series of complicated incidents working out to a predetermined end. The naturalistic fiction of our day, as exhibited in the work of Nexö, takes neither the individual nor society so much for granted. It questions both and is satisfied with no passive relation of the one to the other. It breathes the air of inquiry. Product of the scepticism of experimental science it seeks in its fictive instances to find new answers, a new morality, individual and social, to replace what science has destroyed. It builds new hypotheses by means of a new method which, while indebted to science, is not science but art. (pp. 265-70)

> *Carl H. Grabo, "Actualism," in his* The Technique of the Novel, *1928. Reprint by Gordian Press, Inc., 1964, pp. 250-323.*

Clara Madsen   (essay date 1932)

[*In the following essay, Madsen studies Nexø's social philosophy.*]

As early as 1906 the author of **Pelle the Conqueror** and **Ditte: Daughter of Man** struck a new note in fiction, the note envisioning the proletariat as the carrier of future development. At that time the proletariat "had turned the King's Copenhagen into the people's Copenhagen" [Nexö, preface to **Pelle erobreren**]. And Nexö defines the proletariat as a "fixed entity, sprung from the loins of the bourgeoisie" [*St. Louis Post Dispatch,* 9 December 1928] who took their high place following the French Revolution.

Nexö maintains that "no social class or rank can make powerful cultural progress without possessing a culture." And the culture of the proletariat is solidarity. By this Nexö means that as a man among men, the proletarian fulfills his human duties to the best of his ability, staking his share for the community. And although he owns nothing but his ability to labor, his fresh content of ideas carried out through his actual participation in the struggle will make the new era, "an era of getting together and one in which human beings do not aim to knock each other but to work loyally hand in hand. Whereas, monopolies in land and machines mean a determination by the few to lower relative wages."

It seems highly requisite to an understanding of Nexö as an author to try to discover the constructive forces and powers in the proletariat that are to establish certain basic principles in the new social order. Nexö is idealistic enough in his presentation to warrant an approach from the point of view of literature. It is through his art, that Nexö goes deeper down than the social order. He goes to universality.

Mr. Johanson in the *Sewanee Review* explains why **Pelle** is an epic, and he compares it with *The Illiad* and *The Odyssey* [see excerpt dated 1919]. Like Achilles and Odysseus, Pelle's "personal fortunes are intimately united with the destiny of his people," the laboring class. "Like Achilles and Odysseus, and unlike Aeneas, Pelle is a self-governing personality." And although **Boyhood** represents the centralizing tendency in competitive agriculture, **Apprenticeship** the antecedent chaos of the factory system, **The Great Struggle** the successful organization, and **Daybreak** the prospective triumph of co-operation, one is wholly unaware of any labor doctrines while reading. Pelle is too human and Nexö is a literary artist.

In all of Nexö's work one is able to discern the effects of his own congenital poverty in which he gradually acquired his reverent respect for honest toil and living ideals; for he came in contact with strong and magnetic personalities whose forces and elements of character were worthy of becoming the constructive forces in a new social order. He has won fame telling their story. And like Pelle, Nexö is "one who is too loyal to turn his back on those among whom he has been happy" [**Pelle: The Great Struggle**].

Martin Andersen Nexö was born into poverty June 26, 1869, in one of Copenhagen's oldest and poorest working quarters. His father was a stone mason, but he had come from a line of farmers in Bornholm. His mother was the daughter of a smith. She went about town with a little wagon, selling fish and pot-herbs to aid in the livelihood of the family. Martin was the fourth child, and as soon as he could walk alone, he sold papers, gathered shingles to sell, and watched the younger children. "All the poor man's joys and sorrows have sounded in myself from the time I could crawl . . . in my mind, in my stomach, and on my back" [preface to **Pelle erobreren**].

After he was twenty years of age, Nexö had the opportunity of going to high school for three winters. He was then able to start teaching and writing, supremely happy among children and books. On July 10, 1893, *Fyns Tidende* published his first literary achievement, a picture of a Bornholm guild feast. At the same time, he also wrote a poem, **"For de Faldne,"** concerning some drowned fishermen, in which he pictured the dangers of their livelihood. But the strain of writing after a day's teaching was too great for Nexö. He contracted pneumonia and was forced to give up his position. Madam Molbach, his benefactress, came to the rescue with four hundred kroner and sent him on a trip through Southern Europe to regain his health. While fighting death in 1894, he wrote **"Min Svanesang."**

Nexö returned to Denmark in the summer of 1896, determined to fight for the poor. He had not then decided upon a social scheme for their salvation. Neither did he pretend to literary aspirations. Against his will, his work now belongs to the *belles lettres* of Denmark. He has always maintained that he knows more of life than he does of writing. Words are not enough. He wants "stuff" and "bread," and his definition of bread is one that makes Luther's "pale into insignificance." It includes "everything, from the very dust to the highest heavens—for everybody. The only promise not contained in it is that of becoming a millionaire" [*St. Louis Post Dispatch*].

This contact with sterling qualities led to Nexö's clear comprehension of their ineffectiveness in a capitalistic state. It impelled him to fight for a reorganization of society. In doing it, he first attacked Christianity. He observed that taking one's trouble to God made an individual submissive and easily controlled. Therefore, religion was a tool of the capitalistic state instead of a living, constructive philosophy.

He likewise disparages education. Rather than as the instrument which he believes should "afford one opportunity to square himself with Eternity and Infinity" he sees it thus [in **Pelle: Daybreak**]:

> One could never be sure of what those above one told one and yet all teaching came from them. No, the people ought to have had their own schools, where the children would learn the new ideas instead of religion and patriotism. Then there would long ago have been an end to the curse of poverty.

And [in the same volume] he scorns patriotism in similar terms.

> People used to go about saying that the Germans were the hereditary enemy, and that the Fatherland was taking the lead of all other countries. But now the employers were sending to Germany for troops of hirelings, and were employing them to drive their own countrymen into a state of poverty. All that talk of patriotic feeling had been only fine words. There were only two nations—the oppressors and the oppressed.

The writer asked Nexö, "Is there any definite check on the wealthy class in your philosophy?" He answered, "When we proletarians reign there will no longer be wealthy and poor classes—and no bourgeoisie!"

Nexö has always taken an active part in social and political reforms. He belonged at first to the Danish party of Social Democrats, an organization that was victorious in the general election of April 11, 1924, and was supported by the trade unions. But Nexö did not remain a Social Democrat. He thought this party lost its salt and joined the Communist movement. He is now a member of *Samara Sovjet*.

Nexö himself is clearly identified with two of his characters besides Pelle. They are both called Morten, and they are both writers for the working man. The Morten in **Pelle: Daybreak** goes to Spain and Southern Italy overjoyed to see "for once poor people who aren't cold!" In **Ditte: Towards the Stars,** Nexö pictures himself more accurately.

"You are Morten," she whispered with difficulty. "I know you. I have never had time to read anything of yours; but you have made many men happy. They say you write so beautifully of us. And do you believe yourself in all you attribute to us?"

In his [article in the *St. Louis Post Dispatch*] he says, "We do not perceive ourselves as raw material for some intellectual prodigies or monsters. We are hearts and souls, and the heart and soul are to us the most precious thing about man—not the brain."

Yet intelligence gives Pelle an armor for life which Father Lasse and Ditte do not have. It is only after Pelle has learned to read that he becomes fully aware of society as a class struggle. He gains his perspective through Darwin's *Origin of Species* when he sees that his idea of union, which he has arrived at blindly, is a law of nature itself. He sees the tide of co-operation is evolution. And "his system of profit-sharing must be the starting-point for a war between Labour and Capital."

Nexö's doctrine that man is innately good and that poverty is the root of all evil is, of course, open to question. Time after time he traces the bad in his characters back to something definite, and that something is always colored by poverty. All his women characters turn prostitutes, for in dire necessity that is their only way of securing food, usually for the family. There is Hanne and Marie and the girl in the "Ark" who dared not summon the father of her child before the magistrate for fear of being dismissed from her place. Ferdinand becomes a professional thief, hunted all his life, because he has had to steal when a youth. Then there is Karl, one of the three children in the "Ark." He, so innately sweet and lovable, loses a hand in the unprotected machinery. As a result of his consequent failure to aid in the support of the three, he becomes sullen and desperately despondent. Every failure is a tragedy, because Nexö shows us that everyone would have been good if poverty had not made him corrupt.

> He was not fond of using great words but at the bottom of his heart he was convinced that everything bad originated in want and need [**Pelle: Daybreak**].

As for Western culture he denounces it by saying, "I have nothing to contribute to West European culture. I was born a revolutionary proletarian." He commits himself farther:

> It redounds to the shame of the older culture that it can state the weight of sun, moon, and stars with precision down to the pound, but can not weight out bread to mouths that are hungry [*St. Louis Post Dispatch*].

Yet there is hope in his tragic spectacle of life. In the last volume of **Ditte** the proletarian, who had suffered and fought through the many terrible years, comes to Ditte's deathbed and speaks to her:

> There is no one who can conduct the law suit out there like you and tell the soul how good we are and how undeservedly we suffer, and that we are dumb. It is for you we have been looking, God, our Father, and I [**Ditte: Towards the Stars**].

In Russia, Nexö received his stimulating world perspective. He calls it "the wide perspective." He was a personal friend of Lenin's and after several personal invitations from him, Nexö went to the "Proletarian's Fatherland" for four months in 1923 to observe conditions there. *Toward Dawn* is the enthusiastic account of his impressions of the place where he learned the true significance of the Orient as well as saw his principles in practice, for it is evident that Nexö's principles are in harmony with the principles of Marx's although Nexö declares in a letter to the writer that the only work of Marx's he has read is *The Communist Manifesto*.

In his book [*Mod dagningen*] Nexö writes, "England has a right to be nervous about Soviet Russia. The Jews and the East are experiencing a renascence in Russia. When they do, England will no longer remain the economic ruler in the East." He also quotes Hoover's advice to Russia, given when he was administering Russian relief:

> Russia's reconstruction (through the aid of foreign capital) will be possible only when Russia will give quittance to her big industry and go entirely over to agriculture.

Nexö explains this opposition as the result of America's fear of Russia's promising industrial competition with the whole world. He credits America, "swimming in capital" with having no higher motives for refusing Russia a loan than had England.

"Is a revolution bloodier than a war?" Nexö asks. He cites Carlyle's statement that the biggest revolutions have taken fewer lives than the smallest wars. He further cites Arthur Ransome in the *Manchester Guardian* who writes that the toll of the Soviet rising was ten thousand lives, but that four thousand of them were robbers and murderers. And also Albert Rhys Williams in his book *Through the Russian Revolution* writes that, "the four months it took the Soviet to secure power cost only one tenth the number of lives that the Civil War cost in America."

Yet, Nexö does not justify revolutionary conspiracies. He shows their futility and he propagandizes for a peaceful world revolution all the way through. Peter Dryer's attempt to spur a brigade of threatening unemployed to violent action ended only in his death. It was Pelle who saved the situation by turning the sullen crowd back to the peaceful movement. He revived hope in the discouraged group and showed them the folly of violent methods. Morten in *Pelle* concentrates only upon theories of anarchism and syndicalism. His impatience is as ineffective as is Peter Dryer's.

Nexö notes all the fundamental principles underlying the Soviet economic organization in his idealistic way. They are means to the realization in his dream of beauty and are justified in so far as they have contributed to this spiritual awakening in the masses. The socialization of productive forces has resulted in better housing that has meant comfortable quarters and richer living. The electrification has meant lighter work as well as destruction of monopoly. He cannot ignore the economic situation, for as [John Dewey in *Impressions of Soviet Russia*] puts it:

> The secret lay in the fact that they could give to the economic and industrial phase of social life

the central place it actually occupies in present life.

The aims of her educational system are especially admirable. They are its chief merit. The whole foundation of the school rests upon the idea. "The school must be freed from the State's chains." Discipline is clarified in the one sentence: "See to it that the child is interested. Then attention will take care of itself." The cultural aim is to "show each child his place in the large association and to unfold his innate skill and talent."

But the Russian Revolution means more than an overthrow of an old economic system to Nexö. It is the breaking through to youth for the whole human race, an Utopia beckoning from the wilderness to "a life that is tiresome and dull and far too well known." Then only does Nexö believe, can the conflict about human interests begin.

> The Red Flag is the dawn rays. Some day the proletariat will see that and understand that that color is also the color of their own heart-blood. Some day the proletarians will swing Russia's red flag around the world, and then the Proletariat's Fatherland will include all mankind.
>
> (pp. 1-8)

> *Clara Madsen, "The Social Philosophy of Martin Andersen Nexö," in* Scandinavian Studies and Notes, *Vol. 12, February, 1932, pp. 1-9.*

Harry Slochower   (essay date 1937)

[*Slochower is an Austrian-born American psychologist and professor of German and humanities whose critical works combine literary criticism and psychology. In the following excerpt, he summarizes the four volumes of* Pelle the Conqueror, *examining thematic content, symbolism, and characterization.*]

Pelle the Conqueror is the epic story of labor in harness and poverty, of its awakening and struggle for social freedom. More specifically, the novel reproduces labor's conflicts, as they took shape in Denmark under a semi-feudal and guild system and under modern industrial conditions in the city of Copenhagen. Although the book appeared before the War, it still towers as the classic proletarian novel.

Martin Andersen Nexö knows the lot of the workingman. "All the poor man's joys and sorrows," he writes in the Foreword to the first volume of *Pelle,* "have sounded in myself from the time I could crawl." He was born on June 26, 1869, and lived in the oldest and poorest sections in Copenhagen. His father came from a line of farmers in Bornholm and later worked as a stone-mason. His mother was the daughter of a smith. Nexö spent his boyhood on the island Bornholm in the Baltic, as a herd-boy. Bornholm lies near the town Nexö, from which the name of the author is derived. Here, he worked as a shoemaker's apprentice. As Tretyakov has pointed out, there is a similarity between the first steps of Nexö and Gorky. Both started at the very bottom, both were attracted by the romanticism of the bold and cynical lumpenproletariat and both came to the socialist idea. Nexö's countryman, Hans

Christian Andersen, too, had known poverty, was the son of a poor shoemaker. Andersen's way took the form of his celebrated fairy-tales. Nexö resolved to tell of the effort to turn the fairy-tale to reality, the story of man's attempt to conquer the social obstacles that prevent his dreams of freedom from becoming actuality.

Boyhood, the first book of *Pelle* deals with country-life. The comparison with [Sigrid] Undset's work suggests itself. In Undset, the land belongs to the protagonists of the story and the events are seen from the angle of the master. The "heroes" of *Boyhood* own no land and the story is told from the viewpoint of the serf. Correspondingly, Nexö's prose is molded by a firm, realistic idiom as against the Biblical, archaic technique that characterizes Undset's novel.

Although capitalism had won the freedom of the market by about the middle of the nineteenth century, vestiges of feudalism were still to be found on the Danish island, Bornholm, in the late nineteenth century. To be sure, the farm-hands are not owned, have the right to hire themselves out or to leave, and also receive pay. However, their wages are extremely low and paid out in small installments; hours are not fixed. The laborer is "free" to leave; actually, he is bound to stay. But the agrarian system is dying. It does not have the stability of the older paternal order in [Undset's] *Kristin Lavransdatter;* here, the owner must enforce his social superiority in his personal relationship to the laborers, having recourse even to physical punishment.

The land of Bornholm is poor and the natives struggle to wrest a scant sufficiency out of its stony soil. Stone Farm, the scene of Pelle's boyhood, is owned by the Kongstrups, who have acquired the best soil by buying up the neighboring land which the small cottars were unable to maintain. After selling their land to the Kongstrups, many of them stay on to work as farm-hands. The farm has thus become the symbol of all the ills and discomforts that brooded over the poor man's life in Bornholm.

The book opens with the arrival of Pelle and his father Lasse in Bornholm at dawn on the first of May, 1877. Lasse is a landless Swedish peasant, an elderly, work-worn, bent little man. After a full life-time of hard work, he has nothing to show except a green sack of personal belongings. He represents the most suppressed of the landless class in the hey-day of landed and commercial private property, with the prejudices and superstitions of the feudal serf. "It doesn't become us," he tells his little son, "to find fault with our betters." To the young boy, Father Lasse is the foundation for his existence, the real Providence, the last great refuge in good and ill. Nexö has drawn this father with unstinted warmth. Old Lasse is lovable and touching in his feebleness and courage. But for him, it can only be the end. For his son, it is the beginning. And in this first book, we get a sense of the hope and promise in Pelle. As yet, however, Pelle is but a boy of eight or nine, and he has promised himself great things from this new world.

> Pelle was perfectly well aware that even the poorest boys there always wore their best clothes, and ate bread-and-dripping with sugar

> on it as often as they liked. There money lay like dirt by the roadside, and the Bornholmers did not even take the trouble to stoop and pick it up. . . . The whole world would become theirs, with all that it contained in the way of wonders.

He and his father are hired to work for the Kongstrups and both have to labor from morning to night. The first book tells of their life on the farm, and ends with Pelle leaving the semi-feudal country for the town.

Work on the farm proves to be long and hard. By their combined efforts, father and son can barely make ends meet. There was little liberty; yet few complained. Vestiges of feudal psychology tend to foster this attitude. The exploited laborers are in awe of their masters, who "lived their life under great conditions, beings, as it were, halfway between the human and the supernatural." There is fear of the bailiff; there is the tradition of the master's special privileges to approach the female farm-hands. But Pelle is not discouraged. At this stage, the lad sees himself as the center of the universe, which seemed to be the playground for his infinite yearnings. The world is all raw matter to him, out of which he would fashion his own objects at will. In his youthful pantheism, Pelle merges himself with the whole scheme of nature. This dreamy unity with the All, together with the comforting nearness of his father provide little Pelle with an unquestioning feeling of security and safety. And over his forehead, his hair waved in a "cow's lick," said to mean good fortune, and he ever felt the confidence of victory.

As Pelle grows up, he receives some rude shocks. He is ridiculed by the agricultural pupil of the farm and when Lasse does not kill the pupil, does not even thrash him, the father's omnipotence begins to fade and Pelle is led to seek the means of protection in himself. One day, he fights with a boy who is bigger and stronger than himself and holds his own. Here, he learns his first lesson:

> If you wanted to fight, you had to kick wherever it hurt most. If you only did that, and had justice on your side, you might fight anybody.

Later, he saves his father from a bull. He grows strong and healthy and moves along as carelessly happy as if the world were his.

In the first book, Nexö introduces two basic motifs that run through the entire novel: conservatism and rebellion. The first is here represented by those who work on the farms (or stone-quarries). They are the firm, stolid peasants who find satisfaction in minor conquests made over nature or man, content with the narrow circle of their static existence. The other is embodied in the free life of the sailors who roam in the open world with drink, dissipation and a girl in every port. But the extremes meet. This life is as barren, as circular as the other. The sailors return to the home-port at regular intervals. Their freedom is lacking in direction.

This polarization is approximated by the Kongstrups. Kongstrup's wife exhibits the stout perseverance of a farmer. She is obsessed with a property psychology, wants to own everything and own it absolutely. This mania of hers is concentrated on her husband. He, on the other hand, is reckless and "free," especially in his sexual habits. Fru Kongstrup castrates her husband—the only way she can succeed in holding him: an example of the passion for private property doing violence to that which it desires.

Kalle and Erik offer similar contrasts. Kalle, the brother of Lasse, owns a small piece of rocky land. Although constantly in want, he never grumbles. Kalle is sheer, peaceful good-naturedness. His spirit is that of complete, smiling acceptance. He accepts the fact that his wife has had an illegitimate child by the master of the farm; he swallows the fact that his daughter fares similarly with the master's son. Like the soil, to which he clings with pure sensuousness, he works untiringly, season after season, without revolting. Yet Kalle possesses the basic elements of social consciousness. He is kind as a father, husband, friend, son and touching in his generous relationship to his blind grandmother. There is a promise in the goodness and the remarkable fertility of the Kalles.

Erik, his counterpart, is blind rebelliousness. He is the big, strong giant of the Kongstrup farm, whose pugnaciousness is most in evidence when the master is not around. One day, Erik attacks the bailiff, his immediately felt oppression, and suffers the fate of "the hairy ape." He is struck down by a whiffle-tree, reduced to semi-idiocy and thereafter follows in the bailiff's footsteps. Erik's rebellion is brute, unguided, physical force. He acts alone and without understanding. His insanity is only an extension of the disharmony between his physical power and mental dullness. The working class lacks, as yet, plan and theory. Erik's individualistic rebellion only lands him in the enemy's camp.

Such is the division among the laborers. But this is only the beginning. And Pelle already gives indication of a unity between stability and freedom, shows promise of combining Kalle's warm humanity with Erik's strength and resistance. In the meanwhile, his young body is opening its pores to sun and soil, gathering power for his coming struggles. Although he is compelled to clean dung-heaps, grease boots and run errands, Pelle grows strong through the earthy life he leads. Nexö has enveloped the story of the daily routine on the farm, among the cattle in the fields and the woods with a sweet and peaceful homeliness, giving this first book a spring-like, lyrical warmth and simplicity. To be sure, the feeling of contentedness is limited mainly to the hours when the day's labor is over, or when there is a lull in the work. But in these moments, it felt

> so good to be here, and the feeling sank gently over Pelle every time a cow licked herself. Every sound was like a mother's caress, and every thing was a familiar toy, with which a bright world could be built.

The strength of elemental life streams through this book. The individual has greater play in this preindustrialized community and Nexö describes with colorful detail the herding of the cattle in the meadows during the summer, Pelle's school days and swimming hours, the pranks of the men and women, the merry festival on the Common on Midsummer Eve. From the sensual contact with the earth, from its smells and sounds and warmth, Pelle draws strength and power.

The feudal order in Bornholm is in dissolution. The farmhands do not quite accept their lot. Lasse and Pelle stay out of the fights. "They felt themselves too weak." But when Pelle watches Erik go down, he begins to jump, "as if he had St. Vitus' Dance," a symptom which recurs whenever Pelle comes across acts of injustice about which he feels he can do nothing.

As Lasse's discontent grows, they decide to run away and steal out in the night. But neither of them has any plans as to where they might go, and when the green chest becomes too heavy for him, Lasse decides to go back: "I'm afraid I'm not able to tread uncertain paths." Life has passed old Lasse by.

But Pelle is young. He wanted to be something great and there was no possibility of that in the country. He decides to leave for the town. His childhood had been happy; at any rate, only pleasant memories "gleamed toward him through the bright air. . . . Nothing had harmed him." Pelle had derived much simple happiness from the country. One day, under different conditions, he will return to it. On the first of May, Pelle leaves the country, the world of feudal servitude and acceptance. Once, his father had told him:

> You must always, always remember, laddie, not to set yourself up against those that are placed over you. Some of us have to be servants and others masters.

But Pelle had something better to do than listen to this. He was sound asleep and dreaming that he was Erik himself and was thrashing the bailiff with a big stick.

As little Pelle wanders out from Stone Farm, he dreams again of the infinite possibilities that lie before him in the great world beyond Bornholm. But he has made no plans whatsoever. A driver whom he meets on the road has heard that shoemaker Jeppe Kofod needs an apprentice. Pelle finds a place in Master Jeppe's workshop.

Just as the Danish country-side had retained remnants of the feudal order, so had the smaller towns kept some of the characteristics of the guild economy. In the shop, where Pelle is apprenticed, there is the "Master," Jeppe, representative "of the old days" and rigidly opposed to everything new. There is Andres, his son, the young master. Under them, are the "Apprentices," bound to the Master for board and lodging. Among them, a definite order of rank obtains; the younger apprentice must submit to the wax-ordeal, walk behind his superior, carry his bundle and may not address him on the street. After an apprentice has served his time, he is made to sit all alone in the master's room for a week, working at his journeyman's task—a pair of sea-boots. These are then tested and if found satisfactory, the apprentice is declared a journeyman, who might travel. To the older men, this order of things seems part of the eternal pattern of nature. Once, they discuss the question as to what is the "greatest power." One believes that woman, another that the sun, a third that the sea is the greatest power. None of them think of man, as an element in molding conditions. They regard their way of life as fixed and determined by cosmic forces.

The probation period is a trying time for Pelle. The lad from the country was not comfortable in the smelly, dark workshop, and he offered a tempting target for the pranks of the town-youngsters. Pelle was continually running into the sharp edges and corners of the unfamiliar town life. And, for the first time, he was alone without the protection of Father Lasse. Gripped with misery and loneliness, one evening, Pelle steals out and sets off on a run to Stone Farm. He arrives there in the middle of the night, only to find that Lasse has left. Pelle returns the very same night to the town. The desire for the primitive farm-life, to which Knut Hamsun's characters yield, is soon dissipated in Nexö's character.

But the guild system is in process of disintegration. Machine production has been introduced into the cities and one market after another is being closed to the Master-guilds. The handicraft is condemned to death. The decay of the old guild order finds its reflection in the infiltration of new social doctrines. They have heard about something called "sosherlism." The older men are unreservedly against it, quite convinced that the socialists "want to overthrow everything" and, what is worse, "they want to abolish the king."

Throughout the whole of the second book *Apprenticeship,* there is an atmosphere of aimlessness and drifting, characteristic of developing, adolescent youth. Cut off from his moorings, Pelle is bewildered by the town, where lamp-posts grow, instead of wheat (his manner of recognition that the town is not directly self-supporting). Pelle's state is seen here mainly through the minor characters.

We have already mentioned the sturdy Master Jeppe. In his son, there is little left of the strength of the old order. Master Andres is lame and consumptive, has romantic longings for a journey to the North Pole and the stars. He does not own a shop, but is forced to work with his father. The new social ideas that trickle through from the mainland attract him and he shows an inarticulate understanding of Pelle who loves his young master.

A more grotesque form of romanticism growing out of the town's dingy enclosures is that of Wooden-Leg Larsen. He wears his old pilot-coat, a reminder of the time when he was a sailor, before an accident deprived him of his leg. By various devices, by music (produced with his barrel-organ) and boastful talk, he helps to offset the morbidity and depressiveness of town-life.

Anker, Jeppe's cousin, is a watchmaker who believes that he was appointed to create the new "Time." In his youth, (it was the period about 1848), Anker had come in contact with a revolutionist. He then began to ponder the question of poverty and it resulted in his "losing his wits." Now, he goes about talking strangely of a time of happiness for all the poor. Father Lasse, Pelle recollects, also had dealt with the same subject; so Anker could not altogether be crazy. In Anker, Nexö has drawn a picture of the emotional social idealist with "fixed" ideas, who envisions the classless society, but is lacking in the physical qualities required for coping with the practical tasks. As a stevedore

Portrait of Nexø as a young man.

aptly remarks, Anker has "the millennium on the brain." One day, he is attacked by foreign seamen, and kicked about brutally. Jörgensen, the "Great Power" appears, throws the sailors aside, sets Anker "on his legs again" and takes him home.

"The Great Power," one of the most impressive symbols in the novel, is the Erik of the guild system, the latent power of the working class, undaunted, unpredictable, elemental.

> It was said that in his youth he had strolled into town from across the cliffs, clad in canvas trousers, with cracked wooden shoes on his feet, but with his head in the clouds as though the whole town belonged to him. . . . He behaved like a deity of the rocks.

Not long afterwards, everybody in town turned against him. They accused him of brushing aside long-established experience and introducing "novel methods of work which he evolved out of his own mind." Worse than that, he refused to submit to "those who were born to ride on the top of things." Jörgensen had cut a lion out of granite, in honor of Liberty, a task of which a famous sculptor had despaired. But when Jörgensen demanded, beside the money, the honor of the work, difficulties were put in his way so that he lost his little home and was forced to re-move to the poor quarter of the town. Jörgensen becomes a common laborer, working on the very scheme he has evolved, consoling himself with drink "to keep his ener-gies in check." In Larsen, the old sailor and in Jörgensen, the stonecutter, Nexö has ingeniously reversed the sym-bols of revolt and submission, showing how the two meet in their extreme forms.

A more striking contrast to the Great Power is the Italian shoemaker Garibaldi. Like Jörgensen, Garibaldi is a supe-rior worker in his craft. He knows that with the coming of machinery, his trade is doomed. Like the Great Power, he is not a member of a guild. But, while Jörgensen re-mains on his native grounds, learning the class-struggle from personal experience, Garibaldi wanders about, gath-ering his ideas from travels in France and Germany. The Great Power has the physical strength to revolt, but doesn't know how; Garibaldi is class-conscious, knows what needs to be done, but does nothing. Jörgensen falls to drinking only in distressing moments; for Garibaldi, drink is part of his daily nourishment. The first is a silent man; but he engages in gigantic projects, such as changing the course of a river, and "striking" against the entire town. The other is garrulous, romantically boastful; he loudly calls on the shoe-apprentices to strike and the next day has disappeared, seeking new adventures.

Pelle admires both and again, he is destined to unite in himself the striking force of Jörgensen with the adaptive skill of Garibaldi. As yet, he is only vaguely conscious that the "rich" are the obstacle to his progress. But his appren-ticeship is a step forward. As Pelle is forced to walk behind his journey-man (whom he proudly imitates at first), he becomes aware of the artificiality of social superiority and its dark results.

Amidst it all, the boy grows to be a youth. He learns of death. Jörgensen's little daughter, Karen, drowns herself, exhausted by her work as a servant-girl. And Pelle learns of love for the first time. One day he is alone with Manna, one of the girls he often played with in the yard. "A new knowledge arose in him, and impelled him to embrace her violently." Pelle is overwhelmed by his Spring's awaken-ing.

> His mind had resolved the enigma, and now he discovered the living blood in himself. It sang its sufferings in his ear; it welled into his cheeks and his heart; it murmured everywhere in number-less pulses so that his whole body thrilled. Mighty and full of mystery, it surged through him like an inundation, filling him with a warm, deep astonishment.

Powerful forces are unleashed and deep longings stir with-in him. The mighty sea itself becomes the symbol for his restless yearnings, as

> the song in all men's hearts . . . the roving-ground of life's surplus, the home of all that was inexplicable and mystical.

Nexö has merged, with great artistic effectiveness, the theme of death, love and the sea, a combined suggestion of man's infinite attachments, boundless longings and mysterious beginning and end.

But Pelle is not driven to melancholy dreamings. These thoughts wake in him a desire for action.

Pelle had now spent five years in Jeppe's shop. The other apprentices, after they had become journeymen, forsook their calling. Pelle saw his own fate in theirs. Old Jeppe, forced to the wall by the introduction of machine-made shoes, sells the business, with apprentices and all. But "Pelle did not wish to be sold." Although he still had a year of his apprenticeship before him, he leaves Jeppe's work-shop, thoroughly discouraged. His dream was dead. Pelle is tempted to let himself drift.

> He was so tired. Why not let himself sink yet a little further. . . . There would be a seductive repose in the acts, after his crazy struggle against the superior powers.

He wanders into a church. Here, the poor are promised their part in the millennium. In the midst of the service, a child's voice cries out "Mother, I'm hungry." The Preacher takes this cry as his text and points out that "the poor are God's chosen people." Their "mere hunger for bread" would be purged by God and become "the true hunger of the soul for eternal happiness." Pelle's life has taken on an unsettled, roving character; he is in danger of becoming a lumpenproletarian. But he is roused from his lethargy by the fate of the Great Power and Father Lasse.

The Great Power had been robbed of his ideas and home. When soon afterward, his little girl drowns herself, Jör-gensen breaks out. One day, he is down at the harbor, threatening to blow it up. He brings the whole works to a standstill, enforcing an involuntary "strike" on the part of the two hundred workmen. This was no delirium. The Great Power had touched no drink since the day they had carried his daughter home. "No; it was the quietest revo-lution imaginable . . . the harbor belonged to him!" The town-people are bitterly arraigned against him.

> They must have peace from this fellow, who couldn't wear his chains quietly, but must make them grate like the voice of hatred that lay be-hind poverty and oppression.

They are about to shoot him down, when his old mother appears. She seizes him by the ear and draws him away—an unforgettable scene in the book. Soon afterward, in an effort to rescue a traveling shoemaker from danger, Jör-gensen is blown up by a dynamite explosion. A group of workers are standing at his bed. One of them ventures the question: "I don't understand why all the poor folks don't make a stand against the others." An old stonemason re-plies:

> If one of the gentlemen only scratches our neck a bit, then we all grovel at his feet, and let our-selves be set on to one of our own chaps. If we were all like the Great Power, then things might have turned out different.

The Great Power dies. His energies had run away like brook-water into the sea. Here was physical power, no "millennium on the brain"; but he acted alone, above the heads of the oppressors and the oppressed, without direction. The Great Power goes to his death among the rocks whence he sprang. Still, he marks an advance over Erik. He was more clearly aware of his actual enemy, he did not waste his energies in brawls, did not fight the foreman-underling, but attacked Monsen, the ship-owner. And while Erik ends a tool of the Kongstrups, Jörgensen dies in an attempt to save a fellow-worker. He is blown up by a force greater than Monsen, by the dynamite of which he was a part and which he did not know how to use. His life has not been in vain. He has set the poor artisans thinking and he spurs Pelle on to new efforts. The very day of Jörgensen's death, Pelle abandons the stone-quarries, at which the Great Power had labored to tragic end. He goes tramping. On the road, he meets Father Lasse.

Lasse had also "revolted," had left Stone Farm and become a landowner. "Dry bread tastes better to me at my own table than—yes, by God, I can tell you, it tastes better than cake at any other body's table!" But the land on which he had settled was rocky and overrun with heather and juniper scrub. He could not pay the last installment and so lost his farm. Pelle meets him on the road, carrying all his possessions in a sack. Lasse's fate is an eloquent commentary on the Back to Nature gospel of the agrarians.

These two events do not crush Pelle but rather stir his fighting spirits. Pelle determines to abandon the town for the city.

> He was leaving this world of poverty, where life was bleeding away unnoticed in the silence.

Sure of victory, he leans over the steamer's rail, smiling broadly at Father Lasse. "He had forgotten all that lay behind him." But not quite. While working in Jeppe's shop, Garibaldi had walked in one night and shouted:

> What, still sitting here? In other parts of the world they have knocked off work two hours ago. What sort of slaves are you to sit crouching here for fourteen hours? Strike, damn it all!

He was like a falling star and filled Pelle's blood with the desire to wander. One word remained in Pelle's mind: "Strike!" What it meant, he did not know. But, once, when Pelle was on his way to the town hall to be flogged for beating a rich man's boy, he had a fleeting vision that he and the Great Power had allied themselves to banish poverty from the world.

Pelle has abandoned both the country and the town. He has left the "island," the ground where people acted in isolation and in confusion. He is coming to the "mainland" where he can plant his feet on firm ground. His way takes him to Denmark's industrial capital, Copenhagen. Pelle's development parallels the historic evolution of labor. The Reformation, the English reforms of 1644 and the French Revolution had banished the feudal order. With the industrial revolution, capitalism supplanted the guild system. It likewise parallels the history of Denmark, where there was a strong movement in the seventies and eighties from the country to the towns and the cities. In coming to the capital, Pelle entered a social system from which no further migration was possible. Here, he had to make his final stand. It is the last quarter of the nineteenth century, the time when international labor began to organize.

His last migration was once again an expression of his dreaming, as well as of his "recklessness," a product of his youthful longing for the Promised Land. As he enters the city, Pelle still disports himself in fairy-like musings.

But the city offered, for the time, crowded tenements, slums, sweated labor, poverty; and the machine had been introduced. Pelle's skill at handicraft shoemaking, and the tools he had brought with him, counted for little. The machine was owned, but not by those who produced. Those who worked possessed only their labor capacity. The worker was free from his feudal master and he was "freed" from the land. But he owned none of the means of production. He had but one choice: to work for wages. He was free—not to work; this meant to be free to starve. Since production was for profit, the worker's wages were always less than the market-price of the goods he made. The worker could not therefore buy the total product of his labor. The machine necessarily put out goods at a faster rate than they were bought. This resulted in glutting of the market and brought unemployment. The worker was at the mercy of organized capital with regard to working conditions, wage-scale and employment. Here, Pelle finds himself at the very heart of the problem that had come to him in hints on the farm and in the town.

At the opening of the third book, *The Great Struggle,* we find Pelle living in the Ark, a tremendous structure of rotting timbers and labyrinthine passages and chambers. Inside, the air hung clammy and raw in the greenish, dripping darkness. Its black, smelly interior contained all the tragedy and humor of poverty. Its inmates never planned for the future, began to worry about food only when they sat down to table and discovered there wasn't any. The Ark is the retreat of light-shy creatures, of sickly women and children, of little old men "waiting for death." Here, lived the dregs of society, the lumpenproletariat.

The children whose faces are marked with the scars of scrofula, play at a game, called "Glory":

> You turned your eyes from the darkness down below, looking up through the gloomy shaft at the sky overhead, which floated there blazing with light, and then you suddenly looked down again, so that everything was quite dark. And in the darkness floated blue and yellow rings of color, where formerly there had been nothing but dustbins and privies. This dizzy flux of colors before the eyes was the journey far out to the land of happiness, in search of all the things that cannot be told.

This game of make-believe is the fantastic way of the shipwrecked, drawing down beauty from the heavens to compensate for hunger. It is Hanne's game.

Hanne is the beautiful Princess of the Ark, the resplendent and tragic embodiment of the Glory game. Her father had drowned himself in a sewer; her mother lived by mending soldiers' trousers. Hanne's world is dismal and cheerless. Her desire for life and happiness finds expression in her illusions and fantasies, her feeling that "something" has got to happen. Hanne "belongs" to the Ark, as dreams and fairy-tales belong with unbearable conditions. Hanne smiles and flirts, laughs, muses and hums softly to herself. In her ears, there is an almost constant singing. Where there are old barks, she sees great ships, manned by adventurous men from foreign parts.

Pelle is attracted by Hanne's beauty and by her charming child-like ways—but only, when he is tired. On the farm and in the town, the people had, on the whole accepted their conditions submissively. Here, Pelle finds a different spirit. The workers of the city did not beg for what they wanted.

> An awakening shudder was passing through the masses. They no longer wandered on and on with blind and patient surrender. . . . Even the simple ventured to cast doubts upon the established order of things. Things were no longer thus because they must be; there was a painful cause of poverty. . . . Their fingers itched to be tearing down something that obstructed them— but what it was they did not know.

Pelle finds that in the capital, the workers are closer to one another. As he watches them marching and hears the thousands of voices break out into song, he has a feeling "as though a door within him has opened, and as though something that had lain closely penned within him had found its way to the light." Erik and the Great Power had acted alone, and strong as they were, their isolation brought defeat. But there was strength in going with the others. As he stood amidst the mass of workmen,

> Pelle was no longer the poor journeyman shoemaker. . . . He became one . . . with that vast being; he felt its strength swelling within him. . . . A blind certainty of irresistibility went out from this mighty gathering, a spur to ride the storm with.

However, the burning restlessness of the masses had, as yet, not crystallized into a definite plan of action. They had not yet solved the crucial problem of organization and they lacked leadership. At this point of their development, Pelle enters the city.

The collective consciousness of an industrial order is re-created by Nexö with great skill. Not that the third book is lacking in individual characterizations. But the immensity of the common problem, the collective nature of the class struggle reduces the relative importance of the purely personal. No longer is a worker a single human being, as he was under the feudal and guild system. The productive unit is now the factory. Each product is made in coöperation with other laborers. *The Great Struggle* thus becomes primarily the story of the mass movement of the proletariat.

Pelle is the embodiment of this movement. The Ark brings home to him the great injustice wrought by poverty. Here, dreams are frustrated and energy is thwarted. He finds a little boy tied fast to the stove. His mother is a factory girl without means to get some one to look after her son. Pelle sets the child loose and at once he goes storming up and down, revelling in his freedom. In his loneliness, the boy

had not learned how to speak; but now speech comes quickly to him.

Pelle himself had found social coöperation in the Ark. The "Family" consisting of three orphans, had been the first to help Pelle when he came to the city and was robbed of his last penny. Marie, the oldest of the three, is particularly attached to Pelle. This "Family" is not ruled by a sense of private property. As the children help Pelle, so they help one another. Through this family, Pelle comes in contact with a spirit of altruism that results in mutual good. It came to embody for him the physical nucleus of the socialist pattern.

At this time, Pelle conceives the plan for a "coöperative business":

> A number of craftsmen should band together, each should contribute his little capital. . . . The work would be distributed according to the various capacities of the men, and they would choose one from their midst who would superintend the whole. In this way the problem could be solved—every man would receive the full profit of his work.

Pelle's conception had not sprung from pure reflection, but from his concrete experiences with the labor problem. The idea forced itself on him, as a natural and necessary consequence of the difficulties he had encountered. He had come to a socialistic solution of the worker's problem under capitalism.

While he lives in the Ark, Pelle stirs the hope and courage of the poor. But he knows that there was no prospect for the present to save these storm-beaten people. Pelle meets the Stolpes and falls in love with their daughter Ellen. He marries, and removes from the Ark.

Stolpe is an old and tried Social-Democrat. He believes that the workers need only gain a parliamentary majority to solve their economic problems. "God pity the poor man if he takes the law into his own hands!" Ellen was brought up in this atmosphere.

Pelle was happy. Ellen loved him deeply. Pelle had awakened love in her and it took the shape of a perpetual need of giving. They now had a home and a family. Slowly, Pelle develops a sense of private property and the maintenance of the household leaves him little time for outside activities. He refuses the offer to assume the leadership of the labor organization, stops going to meetings. Ellen's rich love more than makes amends.

> He was conscious of a sense of inexhaustible liberality, such as the earth had suddenly inspired in him at times in his childhood; and an infinite tenderness filled his heart.

Later on, Pelle translates this liberality into a social framework. For the time being, however, he succumbs to the temptations which Goethe had fought off at Sesenheim. Pelle has found his Friderike and does not flee. He yields to the lure of a cozy and comfortable family life, to the psychology of the middle class person, who in rising above his station, forsakes his fellow worker. Pelle is happy in his individualism.

The human and artistic qualities of this proletarian novel become apparent in this instance. The "anti-revolutionary" direction of Pelle is not ridiculed away, but presented in all the force and conviction it carries. If a victory is to be gained, it will not be over a strawman.

But Pelle is destined to devote his powerful energies to the working class. Morten, the son of the Great Power rouses him from the lull of his idyllic family life. Morten is a writer of proletarian prose and poetry. He tells Pelle about the misery he had recently come to know and points out the false psychology of the worker who would rise above his own class. Scarcely one in a thousand can come out on top.

> We want to stay precisely where we are, shoe-makers and bakers, all together! But we must demand proper conditions!

The meeting with Morten is followed by the tragic accident to Peter, Marie's brother, whose fingers are cut off, while working at the machine. He is only a child and an invalided worker already. This accident arouses Pelle's slumbering resentment. Over Ellen's silent protest, he throws himself head and shoulder into the movement.

There follows the dramatic account of the workers' conflict with organized capital. In its course, Pelle grows to heroic proportions until he becomes the symbol of the militant international working class itself. Pelle's leadership and strategy grow, not from theoretical conjectures, but from the inherent, concrete course of the labor problem itself. The actual conditions of labor make of him a "labor agitator."

Pelle assumes the presidency of the shoemakers' union and succeeds in welding it into a powerful organization. The Court shoemaker visits Pelle and tries to bribe him by a lucrative offer. But Pelle is now beyond the lure of "success." He conceives the idea of a National Federation of Unions. It issues from his realization that one kind of work depended on another and that poverty was not local to one kind of worker, but was national and international. The employers attempt to destroy the Federation by declaring a general lockout. It is mid-winter, but the workers decide to strike.

The lockout works untold hardship on the masses. At home are the wives and children shivering in the cold and crying for bread. Some workers lose heart and go back as strike breakers; others walk the streets in a stupor. Nexö depicts these counter-currents faithfully, almost sympathetically, as growing out of human situations; they are factors to be reckoned with.

To Pelle, the general lot of the working class makes itself felt in three personal tragedies, involving Hanne, Father Lasse and Ellen.

The "Princess" had found her prince. He was Albert Karlsen, the son of the owner of Stone Farm. He was only a sailor, but to Hanne, he stood for strange adventures, untold promises and glories. She follows him as in sleep. But her dream has a rude awakening; Hanne becomes a mother. Her nature had completed its airy flutterings. Her child has no father to care for the poverty-stricken family, and

Hanne has to apply to the public soup kitchens. On the way home, she goes into a shop and asks for some warm cast-off things. Instead, the "Princess" is given a light summer dress. It is cold in the Ark and they go to bed early. Hanne has not eaten anything, but her eyes are blazing like fire and she feels so light. Suddenly she gets up and puts on the summer dress. It has grown warm for Hanne and she wants to dance. She runs out into the street, meets Pelle and begs him to take her to the dance hall, "The Seventh Heaven." Inside, there is little merriment, for most of the dancers are unemployed workers. But Hanne brings with her the fire of a magic flower. It is no longer winter.

> Warmth lies like fleeting summer upon her bare shoulders, although she has come straight out of the terrible winter, and she steps with boldly moving limbs, like a daughter of joy.

And now Hanne begins her dance, her feverish dance that drives away the cold and the hunger and the misery, Hanne's beautiful and desperate dance, born of hopelessness, signifying her complete but dignified capitulation to an unbearable lot, and withal expressive of her burning hunger for life—Hanne's dance of death. Nexö rises in this scene to his greatest imaginative realism, so rich—as to suggest several shades of symbolism.

> Hanne dances with a peculiar hesitation, as though her joy had brought her from far away. Heavily, softly, she weighs on the arms of her partners, and the warmth rises from her bare bosom and dispels the cold of the terrible winter. . . .

> Now the room is warm once more. Hanne is like a blazing meteor that kindles all as it circles round; where she glides past the fire springs up and the blood runs warmly in the veins. . . . Those who cannot dance with her must slake the fire within them with drink. The terrible winter is put to flight, and it is warm as in Hell itself. . . .

> They say she has not had a bite of food for a week. The old woman and the child have had all there was. And yet she is burning! And see, she has now been dancing without a break for two whole hours! . . . Hanne dances like a messenger from another world, where fire, not cold, is the condition of life. . . . How lightly she dances! Dancing with her, one soars upward, far away from the cold. One forgets all misery in her eyes.

> But she has grown paler and paler; she is dancing the fire out of her body. . . . Now she is quite white. . . . But Hanne . . . is only longing for the next pair of arms—her eyes are closed. She has so much to make up for! And who so innocent as she?

> Hanne grows red, redder than blood, and leans her head on (Pelle's) shoulder. Only see how she surrenders herself, blissful in her unashamed ecstasy! She droops backward in his arms, and from between her lips springs a great rose of blood, that gushes down over the summer-blue dress.

Throughout, Hanne has maintained what was the soul of her life,—her dream of the beautiful. Not once during her miserable life in the Ark, as an unmarried mother, did she lose her dignity. Hanne's dance is her supreme and final effort to withstand the forces she is unable to engage in direct struggle. Hanne is the winter-flower of the proletarian battle-field.

Father Lasse's attempt to live on his own land failed, as we have seen. He follows Pelle into the city, and so as not to fall a burden on Pelle, becomes a scavenger and sings in courtyards in his hoarse, quavering voice. One day, Pelle finds him in a cellar. Pelle takes him home, but Father Lasse is dying.

When Pelle was a child, Lasse used to feel his face in the dark; it became a mark of the father's protectiveness over his son. Even now, when he is dying, Lasse tries to get out of bed to see that Pelle had something over him in the cold. As Pelle watches over his sick father, his memory drifts back to the past, to his childhood-days.

> Like a deep, tender murmur, like the voice of the earth itself, Lasse's monotonous speech renewed his childhood; and as it continued, it became the never-silent speech of the many concerning the conditions of life. Now, in silence, he turned again from the thousands to Father Lasse, and saw how great a world this tender-hearted old man had supported. . . . Like the Heavenly Father Himself, he had encompassed Pelle's whole existence with his warm affection, and it would be terrible indeed when his kindly speech was no longer audible at the back of everything.

As Lasse toiled on year after year, he had a dream that he might spend his last days in comfort with his son. Lasse now realizes that for most proletarian fathers of today, it is a hopeless dream. Long ago, on Stone Farm, he had impressed on Pelle not to find fault with "our betters." But in the cellar he had met a mason "who had built one of the finest palaces in the capital, and he hadn't even a roof over his head." Father Lasse has come to recognize class divisions and the danger of pious acceptance. He lay there whispering. "Hand in hand we've wandered hither, lad, yet each has gone his own way. You are going the way of youth, and Lasse—but you have given me much joy." Father Lasse dies.

> Then the loving spirit, which for Pelle had burned always clear and untroubled amid all vicissitudes, was extinguished. It was as though Providence had turned its face from him; life collapsed and sank into space, and he found himself sitting on a chair—alone. All night long he sat there motionless beside the body, staring with vacant eyes into the incomprehensible, while his thoughts whispered sadly to the dead of all that he had been.

Death is a universal phenomenon, part of the necessary order of nature. Lasse's death was unavoidable, but the conditions under which he lived, which drove him to his particular death, were not.

Toward the end, Lasse's figure rises to greatest human heights. The old peasant who had stood for the past order, develops, despite his age, until he can cast aside his life-long beliefs. Throughout his discouraging struggle with poverty, Lasse maintains his dignity and sense of tact. At the time of the strike, Lasse lives in a cellar, releasing Pelle from all obligations as son, that he might be father to millions of Lasses to come.

Hanne's and Lasse's fate were crushing blows. But still another was to descend on Pelle.

The strike had sapped all of his means. As hunger stares into their faces, Ellen resorts to selling herself. The wives of the proletariat are being forced into the streets. She was making this sacrifice because she loved Pelle and the children. Like Father Lasse, Ellen silently acts to make Pelle's struggle easier. Pelle is stunned by this blow, and leaves his home. But his private grief only spurs him on to greater efforts in the social struggle.

Hitherto, he had advised a passive fight. Now, he urges a general strike that is to involve the necessities.

> Why should we bake their bread? We, who haven't the means to eat it! Why should we look after their cleanliness? We, who haven't the means to keep ourselves clean! Let us bring the dustmen and the street-cleaners into the line of fire! And if that isn't enough we'll turn off their gas and water!

Pelle's tactics meet with success. The strike is won; the right of union organization is recognized. Pelle, filled with gladness over the victory is on the way to see his old friends in the Ark, whose lot he has not forgotten. He sees, as in a vision, the time when there will be no Arks:

> A dream floated before him, of comfortable dwellings for the workers, each with his little garden and its well-weeded paths.

But the Ark is burning! Pelle plunges into the blazing structure to rescue a child. (Kristin endangers her life on a similar mission; but her aim is to save the soul of a corpse.) As the Ark burns, "the grime and poverty and the reek of centuries were going up in flames." But to those who lived there, the Ark, as it was, constituted their home, their sole possession.

> Like homeless wild beasts they whimpered and rambled restlessly to and fro, seeking for they knew not what. Their forest fastness, their glorious hiding-place, was burning! What was all the rest of the city to them?

It is the first of May, once again. But this time, Pelle is not going to Stone Farm, nor is he on his way to Jeppe's workshop. This time, he is leading the march of thousands of workers through the capital, celebrating their victory. The people are going forth and Pelle is conscious of one thing only:

> The rhythmic tread of fifty thousand men! As a child he has known it in dreams, heard it like a surging out of doors when he laid his head upon his pillow. This is the great procession of the Chosen People, and he is leading them into the Promised Land! And where should their road lie if not through the capital?

The weird, hungry and unkempt have risen to take possession of the highway. Their "Promised Land" (Nexö, time and again, employs theologic symbols) lies not in death and communion with the Absolute, but in coöperation with the living. They march onward, imperturbably, despite the wounds that must yet be smarting. A vast, intoxicating power has descended upon them. And it is intoxicating to walk in the ranks. It fills one with strength and joy. The individual has merged himself with the mass and has thereby become greater than himself. As they come into the market-place, the forbidden flag of the working class suddenly rises in the air, "slashed and tattered, imperishable as to color." The procession is taken by surprise at this daring act. But, only for a moment:

> Then they begin to shout, until the shouts grow to a tempest of sound. They are greeting the flag of brotherhood, the blood-red sign of the International.

The strike has been won. But Pelle must go to prison. In the midst of the strike, when his family was suffering privations, Pelle had once sketched a ten-kroner note. The authorities were looking for a trumped-up charge against Pelle. They search his home and find the sketch. Pelle decides to give himself up.

On his way to the court-house, he meets Marie. She begs him: "Wait till tomorrow! All the others are rejoicing over the victory tonight—and so should you! . . . Come with me, Pelle . . . I owe nothing to any one but you." She had helped Pelle when he first entered the city in need, and now, when he was once more alone and in need, Marie came again to give herself to him, she, who never enjoyed anything by herself.

> No, she owed nothing to any one, this child from nowhere. . . . Beautiful and pure of heart she had grown up out of wretchedness as though out of happiness itself and where in the world should he rest his head, that was wearied to death, but on the heart of her who to him was child and mother and beloved?

In prison, Pelle takes stock. During long, lone hours, he reads, and, for the first time, ponders about the fundamental nature of things. He becomes aware of extra-temporal issues, of inner loneliness and individual isolation. He reflects how costly the victory had been. Hanne had burnt up; Father Lasse was dead, the Family crushed. And he lost Ellen. Pelle had left the house when he discovered her "unfaithfulness." But in his cell, he begins to realize how high Father Lasse and Ellen towered above him as human beings. Both had sacrificed themselves out of love for him and the movement, while he, in his social zeal and enthusiasm, had neglected them. In prison, Pelle's heart widens to include such "enemies."

Pelle is like a sturdy plant that is only strengthened by storm and wind. Like Garibaldi, he had been migrating, but unlike him, Pelle has learned something from each experience and like the Great Power, he will now stay on the ground on which he has toiled.

As Pelle emerges from prison, setting out the fourth time to conquer the world, he meets Ferdinand. Ferdinand once defended a poor boy who was being cheated by a grocer. He struck a policeman who wanted to arrest the boy, had a merry time evading the police, but is caught and sent to prison. The door of the prison proclaimed:

> *I am the threshold to all virtue and wisdom; Justice flourishes solely for my sake.*

When Ferdinand comes out, he proceeds at once to deprive a little boy of two krones. The prison has turned him into a thief and robber. He urges Pelle to join him, pointing out that it is a question of robbing or allowing yourself to be robbed. Pelle advises him to try and get some honest employment again. Ferdinand retorts:

> You'd like me to look after a bloated aristocrat's geese and then sit on the steps and eat dry bread to the smell of the roast bird, would you?

Ferdinand is the blind rebel against bourgeois authority. "It wouldn't matter if you could only get a good hit at it all." In the more mechanized system of capitalism, the Ferdinands, however, are even less effective than were the Eriks and Jörgensens.

When Pelle returns home, he finds Ellen waiting for him, finds that she is caring for "Boy Comfort," Marie's child. Pelle learns that Marie died giving birth to the child and that he is the father. Ellen never reproaches him for it. "Her unfailing mother-love was like a beautiful pulse that rose from the invisible and revealed hidden mystical forces. . . . She was nearer to the springs of life than he."

Marie's fate lay like a shadow over Pelle's mind. Again poverty had claimed its victim. And there were still others.

One day, a young, pale girl comes to Morten. She had been living in the timber yards and made a living by going from one to another of the bigger lads. The boys enticed men out there and sold her, taking most of the money themselves and giving her drinks. Johanna is only eleven or twelve and already accustomed to pay for every kindness with her weak body. Her fate is a parallel to that of Morten's own sister Karen. At times, Johanna shows softness; at other times, she displays spite, suspicious of the motives behind any kindness shown her. This meanness was not due to her "nature"; it originated in want and misery.

> Distrust and selfishness came from misusage; they were man's defense against extortion.

They discover that the child is Hanne's daughter. She had her mother's whimsical, dreamy nature, and had run away from her grandmother to meet the wonderful. Hanne's story was being repeated. As Johanna stands there before him, Pelle sees in her the picture of "an unfulfilled promise of beauty." She is the tragic and ugly consequence of her mother's romantic dreamings. Morten has taken it upon himself to care for the poor girl. The public institutions are not calculated to foster life in the downtrodden proletarian children. Morten wants to bring happiness to Johanna, to show that misery can become health and joy under the sunshine of kindness. In his writings, Morten was trying to reveal the hidden hunger for love in the masses and here an actual case was offered him in which this might be concretely demonstrated. If only he could disclose "how beautiful we are down here when the mud is scraped off us." But Johanna dies, dies despite the love heaped on her by Morten and later by Pelle and Ellen. The Lower Depths cannot be rescued in our time. She dies, "a fluttering soul that had been trodden in the mire beneath heavy heels—a poor crushed fledgeling that could neither fly nor die."

Pelle finds the capital greatly changed. The machines have come to stay. His apprenticeship was definitely of no use and the tools he owned were worthless. To become a master now, required capital and credit. Pelle found that the workers were well organized and wages were higher. But everything had become dearer and they still lived from hand to mouth. The social development had not kept pace with the mechanical. Social laws prevented starvation only, making of the workers a kind of politically kept proletariat. What had they done about all this? The ballot was being used to gain seats in Parliament. A bureaucratic spirit had settled. People were satisfied with formal gains, selling their birthrights for petty trinkets. He misses the former anxiety, the fundamental undertone of the movement.

> They were voting, confound it, with all their might. They were positively perspiring with parliamentarianism, and would soon be doing nothing but getting mandates. And what then? Did any one doubt that the poor man was in the majority—an overwhelming majority? What was all this nonsense then that the majority were to gain? No, those who had the power would take good care to keep it; so they might win whatever stupid mandates they liked!

Pelle begins to read. The prison solitude had taught him to like books. Now after the experience of the Great Struggle, theoretical analysis proves revealing. The proletariat must begin to seek the meaning of it all. It surprised him to find how little history had concerned itself with the working class. But this was now changing. Pelle reads Karl Marx and Henry George. One day he comes upon Darwin's *Origin of Species*. He notes, upon reflection, that the doctrine of the survival of the fittest through the struggle for existence has been translated from the natural into the social order. Pelle rebels against the implication that the survival of the capitalist class was fixed by nature. But Pelle is also opposed to the alternative interpretation that the proletariat might become "fittest" to survive, if it used militant methods.

> A new age must come, in which all that was needed in order that they might share in it— kindness of heart, solidarity—was predominant.

Pelle works out the plan of coöperatives in industry. It was nothing else but the simple idea of the home carried out so as to include everything. Ellen and Marie had taught it to him.

> They did not brood over the question as to which of the family paid least or ate most, but gave to each one according to his needs, and took the will for the deed. The world would be like a good loving home, where no one oppressed the other—nothing more complicated than that.

To build his coöperatives, Pelle needs capital. At this point, Nexö introduces a kind of *deus ex machina,* the rich and benevolent Brun.

Brun, the last descendant of an old and wealthy family has renounced his bourgeois past, refused to take over his father's business and turned to books. But Brun is saved from the decay of Thomas and Hanno Buddenbrook. He meets Pelle, hears of his scheme and life begins to interest him for the first time. His line ends, but Pelle comes in where he goes out. Brun has read and thought a good deal and has an insight into the technique which his own class resorts to, knows that

> the workmen are not in want because they're out of work, as our social economists want us to believe: but they are out of work because they are in want.

With the help of Brun's capital, Pelle proceeds to put his coöperative idea into practice. Pelle's venture is in the nature of the experiments made by the Utopian Socialists. More directly, it reflects the coöperative movement in Denmark. Pelle's idea is an attempt to translate the coöperative principle from agriculture to industry. His coöperatives deal directly with the consumer. Profit is divided equally among the workmen, hours are reduced.

Pelle and Ellen move out to the country where Brun joins them. Here, in a simple worker's home of harmony and cheer, the last branch of an aristocratic family finds a renewal of life. Brun wills his entire fortune to Pelle and Morten. "It was made by all those who work, and gathered together by a few; my giving it back is merely a natural consequence."

The last part of *Pelle the Conqueror* appeared in 1910. By that time, it had become clear that the cooperative movement in Denmark and elsewhere had failed in its essential and final aim. And, indeed, there are indications in this book that Nexö was conscious of the weakness of Pelle's experiment.

In *Daybreak* (the title of the last book), Pelle does not evince the fire and verve that characterize him in the first three books. In prison, he has learned "patience." As a boy he had left Stone Farm, because he had felt that life there was narrowing. Pelle now moves back to the country; but the elemental quality of *Boyhood* is lacking. His venture has a Utopian character. It is based on the support of a millionaire's capital, on the good will of Pelle himself who is the owner of the coöperative works and it is confined to the economic sphere. Moreover, his enterprise is a tiny island in a sea of capitalistic competition, in no position to compete against large monopolies, which can underbid and force him out.

The ideological weaknesses of the last book have their counterpart in its artistic limitation. *Daybreak* lags far behind the other books in technical craftsmanship and power, ending on a weak note: Morten declares he will write a novel dealing with the proletariat and it shall be called "Pelle the Conqueror." In this way, Nexö the artist confesses his own lack of conviction in Pelle's experiment.

The character of Peter Dreyer is strikingly revealing in

this connection. Dreyer works for Pelle, but is the severest critic of his scheme. Nexö suggests that Dreyer and his followers were "taking the whole thing up from the bottom." What does Peter Dreyer stand for? He is not a Social-Democrat, for he believes in revolution. But he is not a consistent social revolutionary, for he holds that the machines in themselves are the cause of unemployment. Nor is he a clear-cut anarchist, since, at times, he urges mass-action. Peter Dreyer is a kind of unorganized, permanent revolutionary, inwardly torn by his impatience to eliminate human suffering. Withal, Dreyer is a confused character. And it seems to me that he is Nexö's (perhaps unwitting) confession of his own confusion and misgiving with respect to the coöperative movement. Nexö is not always satisfied with Pelle:

> Was it the prison life—or was it perhaps the books—that had transformed this young man, who had once gone ahead with tempestuous recklessness, into a hesitating doubter who could not come to a decision?

In *Ditte,* which appeared later, Nexö refers to Pelle disparagingly. It should also be noted that Nexö succeeds in presenting Pelle as a "conqueror" by disclosing a minimum of the opposing class forces against which he struggles. Only in *Apprenticeship* do we get to see the power of the "enemy."

There is another unproletarian note in Nexö's work. It consists in the rôle which women play in his novels. Hanne never comes near to the labor movement. Marie, full of understanding and loyalty, dies, undone by the fervor of a night. And Ellen, despite the fact that her father is an active unionist and her husband the leader of the workers, never quite understands their social passion. In *Ditte,* Nexö tells the story of a proletarian girl. But Ditte only suffers; she is never roused to social consciousness and dies pitiably. Nexö suggests that woman's irrational nature is worth more than "a thousand sensible reasons." Women are "like beautiful flowers, whatever people said about their being man's equal."

The first part of Pelle appeared in 1906 and the last part in 1910. The novel's shortcomings are historically conditioned. Pelle's method and outlook, his reliance on the wealthy librarian, Brun, correspond roughly to the ideology of Danish Social-Democracy at that time. The War and the Russian Revolution have led Nexö to fully embrace the socialist idea. Today, he is fast coming to be recognized as belonging, together with Gorky, to the leading representatives of the proletarian novel. He was deservingly hailed at the Writers' Congress in Paris. He has been and doubtless will continue to be an inspiration to proletarian novelists everywhere.

Pelle the Conqueror is the artistic precipitate of a passionate conviction that social freedom is the basis for human freedom. It combines masterly technique, revolutionary ardor with steeled patience. Nexö draws the bitterness out of the worker's lot, without veiling its stark character, renders suffering tolerable, without making it acceptable, avoids the extremist errors of a heroic Utopia and of a defeatist, depressing reality. The scope of *Pelle* is wider than that of any other proletarian novel. And it derives its greatest glory from the circumstances that it succeeds in weaving into an organic whole the human with the social factors that go to make up the life of the worker. While he creates the sense of group unity, Nexö has drawn convincing individuals. The symbolic nature of the characters does not extinguish their flesh and blood individuality. The collectivistic milieu never drowns out the uniqueness of personality. Artistic justice is done to human variations. Nexö's characters are rich and alive, precisely because they do not fall into a closed class-groove. The work combines the best features of Dos Passos' collectivistic novels, and of Malraux's individualistic emphasis.

In his basic note, Nexö sounds the dignity of labor and the worker's lovable characteristics, thereby widening the range of the proletarian novel to include such "enemies" as Father Lasse and Ellen. They form the elemental ground from which Pelle draws strength and confidence. Without their love, the *Great Struggle* and *Daybreak* would not be possible. Nexö touches here on the recurrent motif of the Fathers and Mothers producing the warmth and love which socialism aims for and which it needs even as it works to establish them.

In the last book, Nexö writes most eloquently of this spirit, now drawn from Pelle's life with Ellen in the country. Like the contact with soil and sun, Ellen's love recreates and invigorates him for the struggle. There is a deep symbol in the spectacle of nature's eternal rebirth. Nexö's art rises to lyrical rhythms in the last pages, wherein the phenomenon of spring's coming suggests the ever-rising vigor of the proletariat.

> It is spring once more in Denmark.
>
> It had been coming for a long time. . . . It rushed along with messages of young, manly strength, and people threw back their shoulders and took deep breaths. . . . And deep down the roots of life begin to stir and wake, and send the sap circulating once more. . . . Men stand and gaze in amazement after the open-handed giant, until they feel the growth in themselves. All that was impossible before has suddenly become possible, and more besides.

Nexö is foreshadowing what may be considered the ideal social set-up: union of soil and factory. Pelle returns to the soil, drawing energy from it which he uses toward working out ways by which the machine might be made to produce for human use. Farmer and worker unite. The sea, too, is no longer a symbol of adventurousness as it was at the beginning, but acts as a link between the workers of the various countries.

Pelle is at once the symbolic bearer of the eternal spring of the labor movement, as well as of human development. "He seemed to have existed since the morning of time." There burns in him a sacred fire that cannot be extinguished. "He could not be conquered now; he drew strength from infinity itself." *Pelle* speaks both to the worker in harness, as well as to the worker as a human being. It expresses the way and will of the many:

We come from the darkness and we go toward
the light and no one can hold us back.

(pp. 108-44)

Harry Slochower, "Socialist Humanism: Martin Andersen Nexö's 'Pelle the Conqueror'," in his Three Ways of Modern Man, *International Publishers, 1937, pp. 105-44.*

Lawrence S. Thompson (essay date 1954)

[*Thompson was an American educator, translator, and critic whose publications include* Norse Mythology: The Elder Edda in Prose Translation *(1974). In the following essay, he surveys Nexø's literary works and discusses his socialist ideology.*]

If Martin Andersen Nexø is identified more readily as a Communist apologist than as a free and independent writer, it is the result of his own militant stand on the side of the Soviet Union and the Communist Party. Even though Nexø was a writer who saw and thought clearly in his prime, he was devoted to socialism from youth, and after World War One he became formally attached to Communism and one of the West's leading defenders of the U.S.S.R. In 1951 he chose to make his home in East Germany, and last spring he passed away in Dresden.

It would be no more proper to pass over Nexø as a mere Communist propagandist than it would be to dismiss Haldór Laxness as a literary agitator. Throughout Nexø's work there is a humane occidental tradition which, in many respects, is as dissimilar to the prevailing ideology of the Soviet Union as is Laxness's devotion to his native island. In Nexø we find Grundtvigian idealism (inculcated at the folk high schools in Bornholm and Askov), not a few traces of the influences of Zola, Pontoppidan, Strindberg, and other nineteenth century western European authors, a deep-seated belief in the goodness of the individual, and a sense of humor that is heretical beyond the Pripet Marshes. Nevertheless, Nexø maintained throughout life a firm belief in the righteousness of the proletarian revolution, and in *Morten hin røde* he reflects his own ideas when he says:

> Morten was firmly convinced that a man's immediate attitude to the Russian Revolution was an unmistakable sign indicating whether he was basically liberal or reactionary. That was the final test to ascertain definitely what was gold and what was merely gilded brass!

Nexø tells the story of his early years in four autobiographical volumes: *Et lille krae* (1932, covering 1869-77 in Copenhagen); *Under aaben himmel* (1933, covering 1877-83 in Nexø, Bornholm); *For Lud og koldt vand* (1937, covering 1883-91, apprenticeship as shoemaker and mason); and *Vejs ende* (1939, covering 1891-95, studies at Askov, tuberculosis, and travels to Spain and Italy). Not unlike Pelle the Conqueror, Nexø had a difficult life, and childhood scenes from Bornholm left an abiding impression on him, reappearing constantly in his later work. He was the fourth of eleven children of a laboring man, whose troubles were not too different from those of Lasse, Pelle's father; it is not surprising to find that Pelle's ideas about

the social order grew from the same circumstances that were responsible for Nexø's own thinking. What is significant, however, about Pelle and his creator is that they grew beyond the brutish resentment of the underprivileged working man. The spirit of Grundtvig which permeated the folk high schools tempers Nexø's thinking with a humanity that is quite foreign to ideas prevalent beyond the Iron Curtain.

In 1893 Nexø taught in Odense, and there he contracted not only tuberculosis but also an ineradicable yearning for authorship. Fortunately he recovered from the former but not from the latter. The widow of the poet Christian Molbech made it possible for Nexø to take a trip to Italy and Spain (1895-96) to recover from his sickness, but his desire to write was only intensified. *Soldage* (1903) is the first of Nexø's travel books, and it reflects his intense interest in the Spanish working man that was to reappear in another travel volume, *Spanien,* with the significant publication date of 1937.

After three years of teaching in Copenhagen (1898-1901) Nexø decided to devote his full time to writing. He had made some efforts to write lyric poetry in the traditional manner during the Askov period, but by 1893 he had found the subject matter that was to dominate his mature production, the life and the struggles of the working man. In 1894 he wrote "Lotterisvensken," a tale set in Bornholm, and in 1898 he published his first significant work, *Skygger,* a collection of short stories dealing with the lives of workers and peasants in a vivid and lively style. Subsequently Nexø published *Det bødes for* (1899) and *En moder* (1899), novels in which currently stylish pessimism was the dominant note. *Muldskud* (I-II, 1900-05) is a collection of tales of folk life, and in 1902 came Nexø's first major Bornholm novel, *Dryss,* a penetrating psychological interpretation of a middle-class academician.

The four volumes of *Pelle the Conqueror* (1906-10) won Nexø world fame, and his subsequent reputation is largely based on this work. Nexø himself said that *Pelle* is "the novel of the first organized stage of labor's development," and he made no effort to present Pelle as anything but the reformist labor union leader. The author was not content with the current literature portraying the degeneration of the middle class, and he wanted to show that there was a positive even if latent vitality in the great mass of humanity. Thus, he did not present an amorphous mass of working men and women with the single purpose of perpetuating the class struggle, but rather a carefully distinguished group of individuals representing many facets of human personality. In *Pelle* Nexø reveals all his superior ability in character portrayal, the effective use of social backgrounds, a strong, sure style.

In 1917-21 came the five volumes of *Ditte menneskebarn,* the tale of "the *mater dolorosa* of the capitalist era," as the author describes the little servant girl. Ditte, even more than Pelle, is the product of a social environment that breeds revolution and discontent; but unlike many daughters of the proletariat, Ditte has no ambitions for the cheap comforts of lower middle class life. Nexø makes Ditte the symbol of millions of workers who were to protest their lot not by revolution, but by an appeal for honest human sympathy.

Both Pelle and Ditte were conceived before the October Revolution of 1917 and as such are excellent case studies of pre-Soviet socialist thinking in Western Europe, unhampered by the conventions and formal restrictions that have made truly creative work difficult in the U.S.S.R. After World War One Nexø went to Germany, a country whose life in the Twenties he portrays effectively in *De sorte fugle* (1930); but the overwhelming influence on him during this period was the U.S.S.R. which he visited in 1922 (see *Mod dagningen,* 1933) and subsequently on frequent occasions, notably 1931 and 1933 (reported in *To verdener*) and 1944 (see *Breve til en landsmand,* 1945). That he has been a loyal and, to a great extent, doctrinaire member of the Communist Party since 1922 is a fact which he has stated on countless occasions, but up to the end he maintained his literary independence, for his works were published in a free country in which honest criticism of the social order is welcome. Had Nexø published in the Soviet Union or even East Germany, he might well have encountered some difficulties.

Nexø's two masterpieces are *Pelle* and *Ditte.* He continued to write successful short stories and full-length fiction until his death, but none were equal to his two great novels. *Midt i en jaerntid* (1929, translated as *In God's Land*) is an amusing satire on the Danish peasant and his lack of vision in World War One. *Morten hin røde* and *Den fortabte generation* (1945-48) were written after imprisonment by the Nazis in World War Two and subsequent escape to Sweden; and while they are intended as continuations of *Pelle* and *Ditte,* they lack the brilliance, the humor, even the humanity of their predecessors.

Martin Andersen Nexø is a literary child of one of the most violent periods of social and political change in modern times. At best, he has portrayed the social processes he knew so intimately with an inspiration and a genius that have found no home in the totalitarian states produced by these changes. In Denmark his work has not been without influence in promoting the social adjustments of the Twenties and Thirties that have made that sturdy nation virtually Communist-proof. Perhaps the core of Nexø's thinking and art lies in the simple fact that men and women like Pelle and Ditte could rise from the drabness and hopelessness of their backgrounds, and here is the ethical justification for Nexø's whole life work. If Ditte and Pelle are socialists, it might not be out of order to apply to their variety of socialism the same test that Lincoln proposed for U. S. Grant's brand of whiskey. (pp. 423-24)

> *Lawrence S. Thompson, "Martin Andersen Nexø, 1869-1954," in Books Abroad, Vol. 28, No. 4, Autumn, 1954, pp. 423-24.*

Faith Ingwersen and Niels Ingwersen (essay date 1984)

[*Faith Ingwersen is an American educator and critic of Scandinavian studies; Danish-born American Niels Ingwersen is also an educator and critic of Scandinavian studies. In the following excerpt from their full-length analysis* Quests for a Promised Land: The Works of Martin Andersen Nexø, *they examine Nexø's conception of the nature and purpose of literature and discuss the humanist vision conveyed in his works.*]

In 1906, Nexø wrote his colleague Johan Skjoldborg and thanked him for his most recent novel but added that it was not "artistically" on a par with his earlier production: "Here in *Sara* [1906] you give us too often that conclusion which the reader should reach on his own." That sort of aesthetic advice from the author of *Pelle the Conqueror* is not surprising. Similarly, in a letter to Josef Kjellgren, written in 1944, Nexø admonished his young colleague, "let them [dramatic human destinies] work on the reader, so he in turn is also allowed to build! If you have suggested and sketched your world correctly, he will then construct it in all its details for you—and he is thankful that he is permitted to share the labor. Nothing annoys the competent reader more than being presented with a fully completed work." Curiously enough, since Nexø was then composing *Morten the Red,* it was not a piece of advice that he himself followed.

Although Nexø maintained that he never worked with his style and often reiterated that he preferred practical work to that at his desk, the author's protestations must be taken with a grain of salt. If an author is criticized for allowing tendentiousness to weaken his art, he may become understandably defensive and then take the offensive by declaring himself completely indifferent to aesthetics. Nexø espoused the view that the artist was not an outstanding individual, as he was assumed to be by the dying bourgeois culture, but an exponent of the constructive forces among the masses.

Despite that proclaimed attitude, Nexø was visibly irritated when critics claimed that he was influenced by other authors, such as Zola, Dostoevsky, and Gorky. Nexø emphasized that he read little, in fact, that he had to catch up on reading his supposed models. His inspiration, he pointedly remarked, lay in the experiences of his own life and in that of his class; but since his articles often reveal a knowledge of both classical and contemporary social literature, it seems fair to suggest that, from quite early in his career—ever since the success of "Pelle" had allotted him a public role—Nexø was engaged in projecting an image. That image is of a proletarian who fights with his pen for the cause of his people; thus, it is an image that, although predominantly true, downplays the artist in favor of the crusader. As the years went by, Nexø's impulse increasingly to belittle art eventually became detrimental to his own art.

The name of one accomplished artist—that of Cervantes—could nonetheless have been invoked as an influence upon Nexø without stirring up his wrath. Nexø's article on Cervantes from 1904 suggests that he identified with both the author and the hero of *Don Quixote.*

The impoverished Spanish nobleman knew both the plight of the poor and the reality of persecution, and in Nexø's opinion, "three hundred years ago Cervantes created with his *Don Quixote* the first social novel." It is tempting to suggest that, in the roving knight who was always in quest of a cause, Nexø found a kindred anarchistic spirit. Don Quixote rejected an unsatisfactory reality, and since he was an accomplished dreamer, he fought to create a world that would fulfill those dreams, no matter how foolish they may have seemed. When chastised for setting free the inmates of a prison, he replied, "For me it was sufficient that they were suffering; I did not ask what their crimes were."

For Nexø, *Don Quixote* was a portrayal of the crusading artist. Although Don Quixote might be called a fool, Nexø had nothing against being classed with those whom the establishment scorns as foolish defiers of rules and regulations. In 1934, when Nexø answered an inquiry as to how he had become an author, he cited in his reply, **"Yes, how?" ("Ja, hvordan?")**, his solidarity with the proletariat as the major impetus to his writing.

The highlight of Nexø's reply is a brief, but marvelous, analysis of Hans Christian Andersen's "Clod Hans" ("Klods Hans," 1855). Nexø reminds his readers that the artist may often appear to be like the seemingly unintelligent child who does not absorb the learning offered by officialdom and who thus must go to a remedial class. Such children tend to find joy in life's discarded odds and ends, and thus they can actually educate themselves quite well. Andersen's Hans is such a fellow; in contrast to his utterly bourgeois brothers, who have absorbed the knowledge proper to society, he overcomes all obstacles and wins the princess. On his way to the castle, he gathers what others consider to be junk: a broken wooden shoe, a dead crow, and handfuls of mud—all of which come in handy at the castle. There, Hans's impertinent responses gain the interest of the rather bored princess, who lustily applauds him when he slings mud at the head bureaucrat.

"The one who drew the best picture of the artist was Hans Christian Andersen—with Clod Hans," stated Nexø; and thus he declared his love for those wise fools who, like Hans and Don Quixote, through their actions challenge and change a repressive society. Both Cervantes and Andersen were consummate artists—as were their heroes—and Nexø identified with them. Nexø would hardly have objected if, when approaching his works, one were to keep in mind Don Quixote's idealism and Hans's irreverence.

Many of Nexø's mature works are filled with an infectious feeling of expectancy toward life. He voiced the optimistic conviction that a healthy culture was just on the brink of replacing one that was outworn but bitterly clinging to its hegemony. Nexø intended his works to be one of the means of impelling that necessary and inevitable transition. In the preface to *Pelle the Conqueror* Nexø unequivocally expresses a simultaneously mundane and lofty vision of the future: "*Pelle the Conqueror* was to be a book about the proletarian—that is, about the human being itself—who naked, equipped only with health and appetite, enrolls in the ranks of life; about the worker's broad strides across the world in his endless, half-unaware wandering toward the light!"

In an examination of the contours of, and the ideological forces behind, Nexø's vision, his choice of genres is important, for he was undoubtedly aware that the use of a given literary form—if only to transform it—was an ideological decision.

Although the older Nexø may not have read much, he had periodically read voraciously in both youth and early manhood. As [Børge] Houmann suggests [in his *Martin Andersen Nexø og hans samtid*], Nexø's acquaintanceship with works of some of the great entertainers of the nineteenth century—Eugene Sue, Fenimore Cooper, Captain Marryatt, Karl May, and Jules Verne—may have given him that sense of plot, even of melodrama, which sometimes fortunately marks and sometimes unfortunately mars his fiction. Nexø's later reading in Ibsen, Bjørnson, and Strindberg may well have sharpened his sense of literature as a forum for the vigorous debate of social problems. As Nexø prepared to become a teacher, he became quite well versed in the Danish classics, and according to a former student, he was an inspiring teacher of older Danish Literature. In short, the proletarian writer had a fairly solid literary ballast.

When Nexø was asked what he intended to accomplish with *Pelle the Conqueror,* he placed the book within the context of literary history as precisely as could any academic critic. Nexø pointed out that most works depicting the fates of heroes had grown increasingly individualistic and pessimistic during the nineteenth century, and he declared that his novel was meant to be an antidote to that development.

Although *Pelle the Conqueror* is meant to be the harbinger of a new consciousness and a new age, the form that Nexø used to present his vision was the traditional one of the nineteenth-century *Bildungsroman.* Through that choice he registered his opposition to the pessimistic novel of his own era, for in the latter—in contrast to the earlier *Bildungsroman*—the hero no longer had the power to determine his own fate. Pelle, however, is still a hero who, through personal growth, finds his rightful position within society.

With *Pelle the Conqueror* Nexø thus employed and transformed a humanistic, bourgeois paradigm and created a socialistic *Bildungsroman.* The book's variance from the traditional genre is, however, noticeable and significant, for the classical *Bildungsroman* tends to be individualistic and static in its view of history, whereas Nexø's novel, with its faith in the social progress of the proletariat, promotes a dynamic view of the historical process. Although such optimism may seem less evident in Nexø's later works, most of them—whether fiction or nonfiction—officially share the same function and outlook.

The reader familiar with the tradition of the novel of *Bildung* will recall that the genre presents the view that existence is basically ordered and meaningful and that the human being who makes the correct choices during life's decisive moments will achieve harmony and fulfillment. In Nexø's memoirs, he firmly asserted that, through his writing, he had tried to combat chaos. Order to Nexø may appear to mean a specific political system, but his vision is based primarily upon a humanitarian and humanistic dream of social and spiritual decency. In a speech delivered in 1913, he emphasized the conviction that proletarian striving is motivated by more than economic demands, since the common people desire human dignity beyond all else. For Nexø, as for such later civil-rights proponents as Mahatma Gandhi and Martin Luther King, a movement of liberation seemed meaningful only if material and spiritual values were fused.

With such lofty dreams of an ideal society, Nexø did not escape being labeled a utopian. The advent of the Soviet Union, which seemed to prove to him that utopia could be a tangible reality, supported his vision of individual and societal *Bildung.* To Nexø, the development in Russia was not an example of extremism, but the natural rise of the long-suffering proletariat. In 1942, when Denmark was occcupied by the Nazis, he called Marxism "the golden mean," and in **Morten the Red,** written a few years later, the protagonist informed an incredulous bourgeois radical that "Goethe was the first Marxist." As Børge Houmann insists, Nexø was, at heart, a "socialist-humanist."

Nexø was also a radical rationalist, for his works are a persistent and at times exasperated call to reason. Nexø saw the exploitation by both feudal and capitalistic systems as utterly unreasonable, and he believed that eventually innate reason would triumph over all ignorance and prejudice. Like the educators of the Enlightenment, Nexø basically held that the human being is good by nature and is capable of growing, a belief that could be found in such disparate camps as those of the writers of the bourgeois *Bildungsroman* and writers of anarchist manifestoes.

Not only the preeminence that Nexø gives to actual experience over theory, but also the belief he vests in evolution would seem to echo the Enlightenment. As critic Johan de Mylius has ascertained, in Nexø's adamant rejection of Darwinism he did not deny the concept of evolution, but only the liberalistic version of it, which legitimized the exploitation of the masses ["Ideologiske mønstre i *Pelle erobreren,*" *Edda,* 1975]. Nexø shared the rationalist's conviction that historical development was bound to carry humanity to hitherto unknown heights of culture.

Although Nexø may be called a utopian writer, he is very firmly grounded in social reality, and his vision, even if it may strain some readers' sense of credibility, is a mundane one that is served by his Realistic technique. It is a very tangible world with very palpable problems that one encounters in Nexø's *oeuvre.* In his anti-individualism Nexø distances himself from both psychological and philosophical pondering, a tendency that may explain why, until recently, scholarship has avoided him.

Such an assessment of Nexø as an author is nonetheless inadequate, since he often, more or less obviously, transcended the mimetic mode of writing. Whether one confronts one of Nexø's works of fiction, an article, or a speech, it becomes strikingly evident that he relies heavily on a mythically inspired rhetoric, sprinkled with a generous quota of metaphors. He readily admitted that, in order to exert control over his amorphous material and bring out the essence of his vision, he had to resort to a symbolic technique. Although Nexø invented symbolism when it was called for, he primarily utilized the symbols that age-old traditions made available to him through oral-

formulaic narrative, myth, and the Bible. He was relying on the "literary" heritage of his proletarian milieu.

That usage of inherited elements should not be considered to be merely a technical strategy, for Nexø's *oeuvre* shows that he thought of the world in terms of the mythically charged figures and structures of the narratives that had been for centuries integral to the *almue's* ["peasant's"] perception of life. In much of Nexø's fiction, from the epic novels to the briefest sketches—and even in many articles and speeches—one finds striking touches of parable, fable, fabliau, and particularly of religious legend and folktale.

The last genre is the embodiment of the dreams and hopes of the proletariat. Innumerable tales relate the severe hardships suffered by some poor youth who, through passing the tests of endurance and ingenuity, earns his or her right to the ultimate social reward: a royal spouse and half the kingdom. The tale captures the poor's desire to rise to incredible social heights and to obtain tangible, material rewards. That desire thus symbolizes the proletariat's dream of *lykke,* that magnificent fortune which repressive social systems had consistently denied it.

Nexø seemingly found the tale quite attractive, in spite of its individualism: one person rises to the pinnacle of success but leaves his or her class behind in its former misery. That traditional view of the tale cannot be dismissed, but it warrants modification, for the final phrase of many a tale, "and then they lived happily ever after," can be seen in a dual light. *They* may refer not only to the happy prince and princess, but also to all the people of the realm, for the former pauper has liberated them from a curse. The kingdom was ruled by evil powers, and rightful authority, usually represented by an old king, was powerless. It may therefore not be farfetched to see the arrival of the protagonist as that of a mythical liberator or savior, who slays a monstrous evil, inherits the realm, and thus grants everlasting happiness to all.

Whether or not such a reading can be applied to the majority of known tales is a moot point in this context, for (as **Pelle the Conqueror,** in particular, suggests) it was Nexø's. Pelle—as well as Poor Per, the hero of several parables and articles—is a rebel with the determination to overcome suppressors. To Nexø, his own tales echoed the folktales' age-old, stubborn protest against suppression.

It may seem startling that in **Pelle the Conqueror** Nexø relied both on the *Bildungs* paradigm, which was bourgeois in origin, and on the folktale, which was, he felt, proletarian in origin. Actually, however, the fusion of the two genres is quite effortless: in the final analysis, the novel of quest seems to derive from the tale of quest. Their structural similarities are striking, and although the tales tend to focus on a material reward, some of them clearly show that the protagonists may earn their material reward only if they have gained that self-knowledge which can be termed maturity. Such tales imply the spiritual dimension that is central to the process of *Bildung:* the actual reward lies in finding one's identity not only as an individual, but also as a social being. Both genres imply the marvelously optimistic message that the enlightened human being is the master of his or her own fate. A similar optimism permeates many of Nexø's works, and only the most doctrinaire Social Realist would object that such mythical aspects detract from Nexø's Realism. In fact, the East German critic Erika Kosmalla praises Nexø for having used, and given a new content to, the religious symbolism of the common people. In the same vein, Georg Lukács finds that Nexø brought a new vigor to literature precisely by relying on the lore of the masses, a lore that was the vessel of their dream of *lykke.*

As a Realistic writer, Nexø intended, of course, to give his readers a glimpse of a utopia—of a life blessed by good fortune—and not surprisingly, he turned to the age-old culture he had left behind. In the *almue,* the common peasantry, who for centuries had tilled the soil, Nexø found a non-individualistic culture that, nonetheless, granted the poverty-stricken individual a profound sense of meaning and satisfaction in life. Although Nexø might deplore the fatalism of that class as a direct hindrance to social progress, he realized that the ability of the poor to resign themselves patiently to hardships enabled them to endure and persevere. Fatalism and optimism were inextricably intertwined, and that union was a guarantee—as Nexø made clear in his *Memoirs*—that the spirit of the class could not be broken.

As [Anker] Gemzøe has argued [in his *"Pelle erobreren": En historisk analyse*], Nexø met modern technological development with suspicion and sought solace and inspiration in the rural past. The older, seasoned protagonist of **Pelle the Conqueror** perceives the city as a monster that entraps the masses that have come to it from the countryside, so he attempts to create a model garden-city with ties to a rural way of life. Although Gemzøe emphasized the prominent role in Nexø's thinking that this culturally time-honored preference for nature over culture played, it must be added that Nexø's ideal was a reconciliation between nature and culture, that is, land tamed and made fruitful by the busy farmer. In Nexø's memoirs, he wrote, "For me the most exquisite kind of activity has always been to work with pickaxe and shovel at a piece of wasteland: to crack stones, tear up thornbushes, transform it into fertile ground. . . . I know nothing more beautiful than a home that has been wrested from the rocks or the heath."

The most explicitly harmonious picture of that past way of life is found in **Pelle the Conqueror.** Pelle and his father, Lasse, visit the latter's cousin, Kalle, who owns a piece of land on the rocky heath of Bornholm. Pelle and Lasse put in long, hard, unsatisfying hours at a feudally run farm, whereas Kalle, his wife, and children joyously cultivate their own land and reap the results of their labor.

It is Kalle's blind old mother-in-law who gives voice to Nexø's mythically ideal vision. As she lies dying, she reminisces about her youth and marriage and, thus, conjures up a world of spontaneity, sensual beauty, and happiness. Her husband would wake her early in the mornings, and together they would delight in the daybreak and make love under the open sky. That remembrance is a testimony to an authentic relationship not only between the sexes, but also between nature and culture, for throughout their life together—in lovemaking as well as in hard, but satisfy-ing, work—those two human beings were at one with a beautiful and bountiful nature.

Perhaps the best term to capture the special quality of those two individuals is that of *homo ludens.* Both wife and husband were mature, hardworking people, but in spite of their toil, they could frolic like children and meet life with an exuberant playfulness that testified to their spiritual strength. After such a fulfilling past, the old woman faces death with complete peace of mind. She entertains no notion of an afterlife but meets the unknown without fear, longing, or sentimentality. In this mythically charged portrayal of a woman of the old culture, Nexø made concrete the ideal, but earthy, human being of his vision.

A reconciliation between nature and culture is both a physical and a spiritual ideal, and that fact is brought home by the story **"Good Fortune"** (**"Lykken,"** 1907). After a stonecutter meets with an accident, his family seems headed for destitution; but thanks to a newly enacted law, the stonecutter is granted economic compensation and can move from the rocky hills to a fertile valley. As the story closes, the family is happily working its fields.

In spite of the story's stark Realism, **"Good Fortune"** has a mythical frame of reference. In its first pages a masterful personification of death appears: he seems to be an educated, but spiteful, man who—since the poor do not fear him—harbors a deep antipathy for them and therefore attempts to break their tenacity and will. Death is associated not only with that barren landscape in which the family initially resides, but also with that fatalistic state of mind which refuses to entertain any hope for the future. The latter deadly impulse is defeated by cultural intervention through social legislation; thus, the story in a concrete manner reflects the ancient death-to-rebirth pattern.

In **"Good Fortune"** and in many of Nexø's other works one recognizes a by-no-means unique equation between barren nature and sterile culture. Numerous metaphors suggest that, to Nexø, the wasteland also mirrored a mental and a societal reality, since senseless violence, selfish sexuality, excessive individualism, the lust for power, and the horrors of war—all are as inimical to humanistic culture as that wilderness which always lies ready to claim the cultivated land.

Nexø's depiction of nature, of even the wilderness, may nevertheless have a strongly pantheistic touch or, as Ejnar Thomsen puts it, pan-erotic overtones. Although Nexø had no patience with that barrenness which is cultural in origin, he responded with a mixture of awe and fear to primordial nature, be it nature inimical to humanity, humanity's own urge to violence, or feminine sexuality's supposed tendency toward predacity. The author, who proclaimed that first and foremost his work was meant to create order, was deeply fascinated with that chaos which actually posed a threat to his vision. His ambivalence added texture and vitality to his works but unfortunately waned as the author grew older and increasingly less willing to admit to the possible existence of an insurmountable chaos.

In Nexø's movingly unpretentious introduction to his

memoirs, he confessed that his personal attempt at *Bildung* might not have been entirely successful: "When I look back, it seems to me that my life has been a struggle against chaos, an endless combat to shape a somewhat acceptable whole from a heap of odds and ends. . . . My own need to turn over and over various phenomena is deeply connected with my lack of harmony and peace of mind. One cross-examines phenomena in order to find a basis for a middle ground, in desperate attempts to find peace."

The same restlessness and inconclusiveness can also be found in **Morten the Red;** Morten has admitted that he had "much trouble with himself in the long-lasting battle to force his sensations and his way of feeling onto a common human level and to reach that stage where he could incorporate ordinary humanity's longings, hopes, and sufferings within himself and represent them in his works. To him that seemed the highest an author could achieve, and that was exactly why at times he was subject to a feeling of having pitifully failed." Passages like the above, which suggest both the author's and his fictional alter ego's personal uncertainty and even discordance, may be said to recall stages that are past, but such conflicts seem to have been intentionally dismissed, rather than overcome.

In spite of Nexø's undeniable potential for soul-searching, he resisted the impulse. The critics Poul Houe and Jørgen Elbek regret that the author did not live up to his early literary promise for probing into the psyche. But Nexø, like his contemporaries Knut Hamsun (1859-1952) and Johannes V. Jensen (1873-1950), seemingly chose to sustain a healthy extroverted attitude that would prohibit an exploration of the self. In a sense that choice enabled Nexø to create his best known works, but even in these, the limitations that such a choice imposes briefly surface. There are moments in which neither Pelle nor Ditte can deal with inner demons. Although such situations are authorially dismissed as temporary aberrations, their being so quickly glossed over seems to cause them to linger in the mind of the reader. It seems as if Nexø's staunch anti-individualism eventually became directed not only against the bourgeois world, but also against the characters within his own fiction.

Nexø's complexity, often engendered by inconsistency, has been mentioned briefly in the discussion of the nature-culture dichotomy, but his work's other complexities, springing from similar inconsistencies, also deserve attention. In 1918, the author Marie Bregendahl (1867-1940) made the astute observation that Nexø's early works contained more homicides than all Denmark had witnessed during his lifetime. Nexø, who otherwise tended in his speeches to be a spokesman for the use of peaceful means in the social struggle, replied by espousing the view that "revolution means cutting to the roots; one cannot have a revolution and let the old remain." In many of Nexø's short stories and intermittently in his novels, violence is viewed as both necessary and cathartic.

In Nexø's reply to Marie Bregendahl, he states that he "loves people who are absolute" and that "murder, death are merely symbols for not stopping halfway." So they may be, but it is significant that homicidal acts and violent deaths are chosen as objective correlatives for the absolute spirit. Although many savage moments are expressions of social protest, in some cases it seems to be the acts themselves that count, not their results. Nexø often focuses on the kind of mind that, in its peculiar logic, has lost all connection with societal norms and that thus asserts itself through violence.

Nexø's fascination with the grotesque individual fate may call into question his frequently repeated admiration for commonplace humanity. When he conjures up images of workers with their little homes, neat gardens, and happy—and very traditional—family lives, the reader can hardly object to that vision of blissful normality, but at the same time the reader cannot suppress doubts as to its validity. One well understands that an author who has known devastating poverty as well as the curse of liquor in family life might advocate a mundane utopia, yet one wonders whether Nexø, who testified to the human being's reluctance to settle for the ordinary, was not censoring his own writing. To what extent that censorship was consciously or unconsciously imposed is difficult to ascertain, but at times the implied author and the actual author seem undeniably at odds.

That ambivalence is felt most strongly in Nexø's depiction of women, for female sexuality remains veiled in a haze of mystery. He describes both the child and the old woman with touching, unsentimental tenderness, but the sexually tempting woman emerges as an intriguing and an elusive figure. Even Ditte, who—though she experiences a number of sexual relationships—may seem to contradict this statement, is basically the heroine of a mythically charged legend.

Female sexuality, as mentioned earlier, is linked with beautiful, barren—even deadly—nature. Nexø, in keeping with his sense of cultural mission, had to bring such a force under control. His answer to the threat of female sexuality is, unstartlingly, the institution of marriage. That bourgeois institution tames the excessive individualism of sexual desires and gives them cultural direction. Consequently, the woman who refuses to accept the role of the traditional housewife, but who insists however dimly upon realizing her own dreams is given short shrift in Nexø's works. Once again, however, a certain inconsistency sheds an ironic light on Nexø's vision, for some of those doomed women (for example, Marie in **In an Age of Iron**) gain in their independence and frustration a stature that is denied others who gladly live life as appendices to their men. Nexø espouses the virtues of the proverbial "doll house," but the implied author knows better.

Although deciding where the borderline lies between conscious and unconscious self-irony in Nexø's works is nearly impossible, the presence of such self-ironic elements not only supports Børge Houmann's suggestion that Nexø thus gave voice to many of his own personal conflicts, but also compels one to add that many of them remained unresolved. The modern reader may wish that Nexø would have permitted himself more room for an exploration of those psychological and ideological contradictions. Nonetheless, a thorough self-questioning—such as was common among the authors that preceded Nexø—very likely would have weakened not only the infectious optimism and strength of Nexø's vision, but also the epic power of his best narratives. Perhaps the combination in Nexø's works of an overriding authorial single-mindedness with an implied ambivalence is one that will attract both the reader who craves a meaningful, life-giving vision and the reader who demands an *oeuvre* of a dialectical nature.

Nexø, who so ardently wanted to destroy bourgeois myths that were detrimental to the proletariat and who spent most of his life deflating such myths, was himself a powerful mythmaker. He dissolved myths very effectively, but in that very act he created others. By necessity a vision of his scope—happiness for all humanity—requires myth. One may charge that he simultaneously preserved bourgeois—or even pre-bourgeois—myths, but as critics Anker Gemzøe and Aage Rønning have pointed out, a man who was so passionately engaged in the historical struggle of his times could hardly help being held captive by some of the contradictions of his age.

Since Nexø's works are so strongly charged both politically and ideologically, proffered advice as to how he should be read may fall on deaf ears. His prejudices as well as those of his readers may well be prohibitive to an appreciation of a masterly, if flawed, body of works. Readers are nevertheless advised to approach Nexø's *oeuvre* in terms of its simultaneous demythification and mythification of the world. (pp. 17-28)

> *Faith Ingwersen and Niels Ingwersen, in their* Quests for a Promised Land: The Works of Martin Andersen Nexø, *Greenwood Press, 1984, 156 p.*

FURTHER READING

Ouida
1839-1908

INTRODUCTION

(Pseudonym of Maria Louise Ramé; also Marie Louise de la Ramée) English novelist, short story writer, and critic.

A popular and prolific writer during the latter half of the nineteenth century, Ouida is best known for her melodramatic adventure and romance novels. Noted for their improbable plots, exotic settings, and opulent descriptive style, these works appealed to the public's fascination with the affairs of high society. Notorious among her contemporaries for her unconventional style of living, Ouida remains of interest primarily for her fanciful depictions of nineteenth-century life among wealthy Europeans.

Born in Bury St. Edmunds, in West Suffolk, Ouida was the only child of an English mother and a French father. As a young girl, she mispronounced "Louise" as "Ouida" and later adopted this as her pseudonym. Ouida took classes in needlepoint, painting, and deportment at a "young lady's seminary," and studied history, mathematics, and literature with her father, who was thought by some to be an agent of Louis-Napoléon and who eventually abandoned the family. In 1857 Ouida moved to London with her mother and grandmother. There she was introduced to William Harrison Ainsworth, a popular historical novelist and the influential editor of *Bentley's Miscellany*. Ouida's first short story, "Dashwood's Drag; or, The Derby and What Came of It," was published in *Bentley's* in 1859. After a number of her short stories were published in various periodicals, her first novel, *Granville de Vigne*, was serialized in the *New Monthly Magazine* between 1861 and 1863 and later published as *Held in Bondage*. The commercial success of her subsequent novels, including *Strathmore* and *Under Two Flags*, enabled Ouida to move into a fashionable London hotel, where she held parties primarily attended by young military officers and male celebrities. Accounts of Ouida's flamboyant life-style and unusual personal habits were widely reported and discussed, especially her penchant for dressing entirely in white, her love of dogs, and her highly conceited opinion of her own writing. In 1871 Ouida left England, eventually settling in Italy, where she resided for the rest of her life. During the 1890s the popularity of her novels began to decline, and her remaining years were marked by financial hardships and legal difficulties. Ouida died of pneumonia in 1908.

In *Granville de Vigne,* Ouida introduced the character type featured in her best-known novels—the attractive and adventurous young guardsman. *Under Two Flags,* which is generally considered her most enduring work, centers on Bertie Cecil, an aristocratic youth who accepts the blame for a forged check written by his brother and joins the French Foreign Legion as a private. After several misadventures, Bertie is sentenced to death for striking an officer. He is ultimately saved by Cigarette, a young singer who obtains a reprieve for him but arrives too late to deliver it to the authorities and throws herself in front of the guns of the firing squad at the last moment. *Under Two Flags* was successfully adapted for theater and film productions, as were her novels *Strathmore* and *Moths* and two of her widely read children's stories, "A Dog of Flanders" and "The Nürnberg Stove." Ouida's later novels, including *Pascarel, Friendship, A Village Commune,* and *In Maremma,* often feature Italian settings and characters and have been praised for their depictions of local Italian politics during the 1870s and 1880s. In addition, her study of the novels of the Italian writer Gabriele D'Annunzio has been credited with bringing his works to the attention of English readers.

Most criticism of Ouida's work has focused on her novels. While these works have been praised as engaging, they have more often been derogated for what some critics view as their false erudition, overwrought style, and implausible plots. Early reviewers frequently protested what they considered the immoral content of Ouida's novels and her excessive fascination with material wealth, yet some commentators credit the notoriety of these early works with establishing the widespread interest in her novels that continued throughout most of her career. While acknowledging her more obvious faults as a writer, several noted critics have nevertheless praised her work as absorbing entertainment. As Frederic Taber Cooper observed: "[Ouida's] genius is of an erratic type that is most likely to have justice done it by those who do not stop to measure and weigh and analyse, but simply read straight on, yielding themselves to the magnetism which, for some readers, she undoubtedly possesses."

(See also *Dictionary of Literary Biography*, Vol. 18, and *Something about the Author*, Vol. 20.)

PRINCIPAL WORKS

Held in Bondage (novel) 1863
Strathmore (novel) 1865
Chandos (novel) 1866
Idalia (novel) 1867
Under Two Flags (novel) 1867
Tricotrin (novel) 1869
Cecil Castlemaine's Gage, and Other Novelettes (short stories and novellas) 1870
Puck (novel) 1870
Folle Farine (novel) 1871
A Dog of Flanders, and Other Stories (short stories) 1872
Pascarel (novel) 1873
Two Little Wooden Shoes (short stories) 1874; also published as *Bebee; or, Two Little Wooden Shoes, 1896*
Signa (novel) 1875
In a Winter City (novel) 1876
Ariadne: The Story of a Dream (novel) 1877
Friendship (novel) 1878
Moths (novel) 1880
Pipistrello, and Other Stories (short stories) 1880
A Village Commune (novel) 1881
*Bimbi: Stories for Children (short stories) 1882
In Maremma (novel) 1882
Frescoes: Dramatic Sketches (essays) 1883
Wanda (novel) 1883
Princess Napraxine (novel) 1884
Othmar (novel) 1885
A Rainy June (novel) 1885
Don Gesualdo (novel) 1886
A House Party (novel) 1886
Guilderoy (novel) 1889
Ruffino, and Other Stories (short stories) 1890
Syrlin (novel) 1890
Santa Barbara, and Other Tales (short stories) 1891
The Tower of Taddeo (novel) 1892
The New Priesthood: A Protest against Vivisection (pamphlet) 1893
The Silver Christ, and A Lemon Tree (short stories) 1894
Two Offenders, and Other Tales (short stories) 1894
Toxin (novel) 1895
Views and Opinions (essays) 1895
Le Selve, and Other Tales (short stories) 1896
An Altruist (novel) 1897

The Massarenes (novel) 1897
Street Dust, and Other Stories (short stories) 1899
La Strega, and Other Stories (short stories) 1899
The Waters of Edera (novel) 1899
Critical Studies (essays) 1900
Helianthus (unfinished novel) 1908

*This collection contains the short story "The Nürnberg Stove."

L. Mallette Anderson (essay date 1878)

[*In the following excerpt, Anderson praises Ouida's prose style while criticizing the "immoral" content of her works.*]

Louise de la Ramee, better known as "Ouida," a *nom de plume* under which she writes those brilliant, caustic, much-condemned, but at one time much-sought-after novels, is an eccentric woman of acknowledged genius.

"Ouida" is her pet name; and she says the world has no business with any other. She evidently carries this point further, and believes, in addition, that the world has no business with anything she does, or that concerns her. For, if the accounts we have of her be true, she pursues her recklessly independent course of life according to her own peculiar views, utterly regardless of the opinion that may be formed of her, and in many respects in open defiance of the laws of propriety and the established rules of social life as recognized and observed by less gifted and more ordinary women. . . .

Much has been written and told concerning her, but after all, little is definitely known about her. It is not even decided whether she is married or single, Madame or Miss; and, of course, leading the free uncontrolled life she does, she is freely criticised; and in absence of facts, inquisitive people learn what they can of her doings, surmise and conjecture, and then weave a story to suit their fancy, which they color according to taste, and finally give out as a true version.

Notwithstanding all the stories afloat as to the kind of woman she is, her habits of life are simple. She loves nature, and lives mostly in the open air, and for that reason she enjoys the Italian climate. In fact, from the early spring days when the tender green firs soften with emerald tint the outline of hill and vale, until after the purpling grapes have been gathered by brown-eyed peasants, and cold winds sweep the land, she lives out of doors; among vine-clad hills, in a beautiful garden flooded with sweetest perfume from countless blossoms and nerites, to the song of birds in the early morning, when the light falls upon opening bud and ripening fruit, and the gold-fish glistening in the near pond. And in winter she writes in one of her beautiful rooms, upon a table of cinque-cento work, with her favorite dog, a deerhound, at her feet, and scattered around are treasures of art of priceless value, and all about her a profusion of flowers, for she is passionately fond of flowers, and loves dogs and horses. (p. 284)

But no one would suppose from "Ouida's" books that her habits of life were so simple, for they are permeated with false views, artificial feeling, morbid sentiment, exaggerated characters, and overwrought. And the fact of her being an English woman makes her and her novels more incongruous. If she was a French woman, she could be dealt with more leniently, as a French woman is not supposed to be just as either English or American women are.

Judged from our standpoint she shocks and surprises, both by her vices and extravagancies in everyday life, as well as by her novels. Her books are not only suggestive; but vice and licentiousness, after the manner of more than one novelist, are rendered absolutely fascinating. Judged as we judge George Sand, these vices and discrepancies would be passed over; but as she is not French, and has great gifts, we can but deplore the misdirection of her genius; and wish that she was otherwise.

In judging "Ouida" it is only fair to take into account her early training. She was educated by her father, who was a man of fine intellect, but who had wasted his talents. He trained his daughter to masculine modes of thought and culture, in a different way altogether from what is considered the proper thing for girls. With such training and under the influence of such a father, with the natural bent of her mind and temperament, imagination easily and reasonably supplies the end. She more than likely travelled with her father, for she was his companion always, and saw the world as he saw it, viewed the scenes he viewed, knew the men and women he knew, learned to think as he thought, and at last became, what any impassionable, impulsive being would become, under the circumstances—a world-wise, cynical, even *blase* woman, a term scarcely to be applied to one of her sex. Added to this, there has been undoubtedly some love affair in her own life as tragic as any of which she writes, and which, instead of softening and purifying her soul, laid a withering blight upon her moral nature; for wormwood and gall are scarce bitter enough to dip her pen in when writing of love. In all her books, love is the theme which seems to turn into bitterness all the sweet of her woman's nature. And they leave us no hope that she is other than a cold, misanthropical, bold woman, whose natural warmth of affection and intensity of feeling under happier circumstances would have made of her an impetuous, imprudent woman likely, but a warm-hearted, loving, generous one.

Authorship was always a natural impulse to her. It is said that at four years old she wrote in printed characters a child's story. She writes rapidly and without mental or bodily fatigue, and she never erases what she has written until it comes to her in proof, and she corrects very little. Her handwriting is very peculiar and unfeminine, "and her manuscript looks like Greek manuscript."

A late writer says of her: "Anything like moderation is despised; good workmanship is regarded as the plodding of stupidity, and all chance of cultivating what talent she has as a writer, is thrown out to find place for strong effect." "Ouida" has her faults, and glaring ones too; but it is hard to agree to so severe a criticism. But she does not care whether she pleases the world or not by her books, and is never displeased in the least when told that her books do not meet with the approbation of the English reading public; for she despises English criticism, both in literature and in art.

In some of her later works there is a very perceptible, though a scarcely defined regret, that, notwithstanding her gaslit, absinthe-drinking, flower-strewn, jewel-decked world which she pictures in her books, and in which she has lived, but which has long since been freedom to her, she would much rather dwell in a dingy paradise as it were than therein. It is as if in her freedom, amid her treasures, and the glare and impurity with which she has for the most part surrendered herself to, that she remembered a time when she was a different being; a better woman, nay, a pure blossom herself; and as if the remembrance of that time and all she had lost, was to her agony almost maddening at times, which stings her conscience, and makes her harsh and ruthless.

Ruskin said of Doré, "Bad, with an awful power," and the same may be said of "Ouida." For she is to the literature of the day what Gustave Doré is to the new school of French art. She like Doré fascinates when she repels, charms when she shocks, and so we may say of her, "bad, with an awful power."

One critic says: "Her work is like scene painting; but if a man prefers gazing at a chromolithograph rather than the gems of the Pitti Gallery, he cannot be talked at for his tastes."

"Ouida" is known and recognized as a demoralizing power, and occupies just the position she merits in the literary world. But when her books are found side by side on the library shelves, *Idalia* with *John Halifax,* we know what *John Halifax* is; know it to be healthy in sentiment, pure in tone, and that it teaches a moral lesson. But *John Halifax* is put back on the shelf and *Idalia* or *Folle Farine* is chosen instead, and taken home to be enjoyed, likely in secret, as would be a daintily spiced dish or a deleterious drink which is known to be hurtful. Nevertheless it is a trial, especially to women; and for awhile they live in a new world, in an atmosphere of perfumed air, odor of violets and roses, where there are handsome wicked men, lovely, sinful women—in that nether world, that land of Bohemia, a knowledge of which is forbidden pure women, of which wives and daughters know little, but of which they desire to know more; naturally, because forbidden, and likely because their husbands and brothers find it so delightful a world.

In her books they catch a glimpse of Pheyne and Lois, abandoned, voluptuous, beautiful women, sinful and stained with vice; yet as there seen, graceful, fascinating beings, whose lives are filled with the pleasures of the world which "Ouida" paints so bewitchingly. This with the smooth sentences, rich and glowing imagery and her unrivaled descriptive powers, render her style irresistibly fascinating, and her books masterpieces of rhetoric.

Were it not that she possesses this charm of style, she would have but few readers among the higher classes. Her books, divested of her rare imaginative power and gorgeous rhetoric, and her sentiments less bare, would be so coarse and revolting, that none but vulgar minds could enjoy them.

They are as unlike any other books as our common dirt is like hăsheesh. For as in a hăsheesh vision, time, space, and country all are forgotten, and therein mingle voluptuous forms, beautiful lost women, amorous sighs, handsome, faithless, brave wicked men, lustrous eyes, gleaming bare shoulders, snowy curving arms, soft thrilling hands, swelling busts, faint lights, heavy perfumes, all so adroitly set before the eager mind, that it is no wonder that they are read with burning cheek and bated breath.

The moral of her books, or rather the immorality of them, the licentiousness and that fascinating melancholy which is not at first set down as morbid sentiment, does not impress the reader at once; but after the book is finished and laid aside, the acrid taste lingers.

These are the books which are dangerous, which while the bad effect is plainly felt, are yet written with such force, such brilliancy, such a fascination of style, that they hold the fancy spellbound, while the judgment condemns. They are *dragées* apparently, but are sugar-coated pills only, delightful to the taste most surely, and as a sweet morsel we roll them under the tongue, or as a glass of rich cordial or Curaçoa wine the reader slowly sips these books, first with languid feelings of pleasure, then with avidity and abandonment, till the intense sweet palls upon the literary palate. Then comes the disrelish, the sweet first, the bitter afterwards. The cynicism, the cold analysis of all things, for she picks to pieces all human feeling as a botanist does a flower, or as an anatomist the human body; the ultra disbelief in any sincerity, any truth, or goodness, or purity, the doubting of every motive under the sun, all this forces itself upon the mind afterwards, leaving the reader very often, with every effort to think or judge kindly of human nature, completely paralyzed for the time being at least.

It is claimed by some that any one who reads "Ouida's" books is as bad as she is; by others that it is impossible to read them without being affected by them, for the mind, chameleon like, partakes of the hue of whatever it rests upon. Another, that they are so delightful, he wishes that he had never read one of them that he might still have the pleasure of reading them.

Many acknowledge her to be a woman of genius, versatile, and a brilliant writer, whose pages burn with imagery the most glowing; still, to them she is odious, and they declare all she writes bad; and could hardly be persuaded that any good could possibly emanate from such a source. Some few could read her books without detriment—general readers—for it is said that he who reads all books no book hurts; but they who read but few books should read only good ones, under which head "Ouida's" do not come. And they are certainly not the best of books to give young imaginative girls, for obvious reasons.

No one surpasses her in individuality of conception, or in delineation of certain phases of character. She is too "the best illustrator of fiction of the purely romantic type, and the affectation of short sentences and incessant paragraphing, of quick characterizations, is a natural part of her general plan of construction. She creates her characters,

moreover, outrightly, neither stealing, begging nor borrowing from her contemporaries, and whatever merit there is in originality, aside from intrinsic merit, is certainly hers."

All of her books bear the same characteristics of gorgeous coloring, biting sarcasm, elegance of diction, almost rhythmic form of language, and exaggerated portraiture of character. She is original and purely romantic, but persistent in her types. The characters are creatures who live in a world of romance, and have nothing in common with us; but their individuality is clearly defined, "and the romantic ideal is carefully elaborated into an artistic consistency in which a niceness of literary skill, modeled upon the French school, is constantly displayed."

But at the last comes the trail of the serpent over all; love without the sweet, and with all its bitterness; the wine of life turned to gall in the drinking, and all else turned to ashes in the eating, is the key-note of all. Consequently she has never written a healthy story; they are all morbid, cold, cruel. How can she write any other when she thinks that "the only motive power and the sole key note of all creation is cruelty in some form or another." Even her loves love with analytical cruelty, which destroys, soul and body, the object loved. According to her view "Love kills everything and then dies itself, or perhaps it does not die; then it is a flame, always burning, burning, burning, till the body and the heart are cracked, empty, shrunken potsherds. That is love." And again, "love lends a fire divine to human souls only by burning all their world to waste. And when love is dead, there is no God."

After all is said, "Ouida's" books are dangerously seductive; for while one class might read them for the sake of a beautifully told story, without taking in any of the false philosophy, cynicism and ultra contempt for purity, as they would a sugar-plum, ignoring the poisoned color, testifying only to the pleasant and agreeable sweetness, heedless of the internal detriment, which they recognize by a craving for more of the same sort of ambrosia, accompanied by a distaste for any solid healthy literary food, another class of readers would seize upon them with eagerness, read with relish, revel in them, absorb them, and even soil their lips with quotations from them. A small number would read with discernment, winnow out the really beautiful thoughts, accept them, and cast aside the tares. And a very few would throw them aside with disgust, unread.

Latterly she has written what might be termed art-novels. *In a Winter City* and *Ariadne* are both rendered delightful by her criticisms and opinions on art, and her descriptions of some of the masterpieces of sculpture and painting, and of rare works of art, scattered, or rather gathered in princely homes throughout Italy, to which she seems to have the "open sesame" that admits her into the sacred precincts of some of the finest private art collections in Italy not usually open to foreigners. *Ariadne* is one of the grandest in conception of all her stories. It is a pæan of triumph, a song of praise to Rome the eternal,

> Where you at least learn your own littleness and
> that of gods and men; Rome, which has seen
> Zeno and Aidoneus pass away, and come to be

words upon the mouths of men; Rome, which has beheld Olympus fade away like a dream of the night; Rome, which killed the Nazarene and set Borgia and Aldobrandini up in his likeness to reign over the earth and heaven; Rome, which has seen nations perish leaving no sign, and deities die like moths, yet lives herself and still conjures the world with the sorcery of an irresistible and imperishable name.

The art-novel is a delightful branch of literature, and "Ouida" possesses the true love of art, and it is to be hoped that she will yet give to the reading world a work of that kind which will enrich English literature, be worthy of her culture, and bear the impress of her genius without the defects which mar her former books, and thus prove to the captious that she is not altogether superficial. (pp. 285-88)

> L. Mallette Anderson, " 'Ouida' and Her Novels," in Potter's American Monthly, *Vol. XI, No. 79, July, 1878, pp. 284-88.*

Harriet Waters Preston (essay date 1886)

[*In the following excerpt, Preston appraises Ouida's novels in the context of the romantic tradition in literature.*]

It is no light thing to be a popular writer; and when one has been a popular writer for twenty-five years, more or less, and, under whatever variety and severity of protest, is quite as much read as ever at the end of that time, the phenomenon is undoubtedly worthy of attention. So much I take to be strictly true of the indefatigable novelist who calls herself by the curious name of Ouida. Everybody reads her twenty or thirty books. The critic reads with a shrug, and the moralist with a sigh; the grave student with an apology, and the railway traveler with an ostentatious yawn; the school-girl (I mean, of course, the modern, unfettered school-girl) with bated breath and shining eyes, and the bank clerk and the lady help with nameless thrills of envious rapture. The professional translators must watch, one would think, every stroke of this industrious lady's pen, and quarrel, among themselves, for the privilege of extending to the remote barbarian the boon to which the English-speaking races alone are born. And still there are no symptoms of failure in the abundant fountain (it would be more correct, perhaps, to say soda-fountain) from which these highly colored and sharply effervescent waters are drawn. Crowds always come to quaff the sparkling beverage, asking no questions, for conscience' sake, about the chemistry by which it is produced. The old sip for a wonder, and the young for a sign. Let us try and discover why and for what end.

I will premise that this inquiry is going to be, primarily and chiefly, a search for merits, rather than a citation of defects. There is very much reason to believe that this is in all cases the true method of criticism: to get inside of a subject, and then work outward; to fathom the character of the mind, if one can, before endeavoring to judge the production. It may not be altogether easy for a plain mortal, with no finer implement than a steel pen, to put herself in Ouida's place, but it ought, by all means, to be attempted.

And first it may be remarked that in the general type of her tales she is really the heir, and the legitimate heir, of very high traditions. She is by nature a flagrant romanticist; but so was Scott a romanticist, and Dumas père and De la Motte Fouqué, and Lord Lytton and Lord Beaconsfield, and George Sand and Victor Hugo, and Jane Porter and the authoress of Thomas Thyrnau, and eke G. P. R. James. To be classifiable with such names, even to be at the foot of such a class, is to be a member of no mean school. Walter Scott is of course the master, as he was, in time, the precursor, and he must ever remain, by virtue of his historic divination, his glorious humor, and his healthful and virile moral sense, far and away the noblest Roman of them all. But there are traces of his method and reflections of his spirit in every one of the writers I have named, and in a good many others, less than the least of these, who have, nevertheless, been able, for a moment each, to catch the popular ear. They are all free, and profess to make their readers free, of a world of ardent love and furious war; of vast riches and dazzling pomp; of heroic virtues and brutal crimes; of consummate personal beauty, flower-like, fairy-like, god-like, as the case may be; of tremendous adventures, enormous windfalls, crushing catastrophes, and miraculous escapes. High color, strong contrasts, loud music, and thrilling sensations ("I can do the big bow-wow style myself with any now going," says Scott, in his gallant and charming tribute to Jane Austen) are the common properties of them all, and there can be no question that the average human reader has a natural relish for such things, which is bound to gratify itself even when, as happens at the present moment, they are decidedly out of the literary fashion. We smile at the perfumed baths and jeweled hairbrushes of Ouida's young guardsmen; at the cataracts of diamonds which descend from the shoulders of her heroines when they go to the ball, and the curtains of rose-colored Genoa velvet, edged with old Venice point, which the valet or the maid will draw noiselessly aside, in order to let the noontide sun steal in upon her jaded revelers on the morning after a festivity. But Chandos himself is not more expensive in his habits than Lothair, and the ecstatic sibilation, like that of a child over a stick of candy, with which Ouida dilates on the luxuries which surround her favorites is paralleled, to say the least, by the solemn rapture of the great statesman before the stock-in-trade of a fashionable jeweler. The worship of wealth is vulgar and demoralizing, yet it is not absolutely and entirely vulgar. It is a possible root of all evil, but it is not the one, sole root, and even the apostle never meant to say that it was. It *marches,* as we used to say of the boundaries of a country, with very noble things, the supreme splendors of art, the possibilities of a vast beneficence. The transference of wealth from one person to another is apt to be dizzying to him who gains no less than acutely uncomfortable to him who loses, but it is a natural, healthful, inevitable process. The absolute annihilation of wealth in fire, flood, or siege is a universal calamity. Riches—mere giddy, golden riches, such as Ouida and the romanticists generally so constitutionally dote upon—have always played a great part in the moral development of mankind, and were probably intended, from the beginning, so to do. They are for the possession of the few and the edification of the many; and whoever succeeds, whether by argument or parable, in reconciling the minds of men to the fact that wealth *must be* where civilization is, but cannot be for all; whoever helps the many, in their need, to acquiesce in the abundance of the few, will have done more for his kind than all the socialists. The conception of Ouida as a moralist of this magnanimous type is doubtless a humorous one, and any good she may do in this direction will probably be indirect and involuntary. The great, uninteresting middle class comes in for very little of her consideration; but of the lot of the extremely poor—the positively or possibly suffering poor—she is not ignorant nor forgetful, as I shall have occasion to show, by and by.

Meanwhile, it may be observed in her favor that at least she shows herself a better political economist than the far greater writer with whom we have just compared her. She does set some limit to the wealth even of her most opulent hero. After having handsomely endowed him with "home estates as noble as any in England, a house in Park Lane, a hotel on the Champs-Élysées, a toy villa at Richmond, and a summer palace on the Bosphorus," beside a yacht, "kept always in sailing order, and servants accustomed to travel into Mexico or Asia Minor at a moment's notice," she does, nevertheless, own him subject to the law which entails pecuniary ruin upon the man whose expenditure is exactly four times as great as his income; and he starves, when the time comes, with as much distinction as he had previously squandered. For Lothair, as for Monte Christo, no ruin is possible. Their investments are in the infinite. But then Disraeli and Dumas were not romanticists, merely, but idealists, while Ouida's imagination, vigorous though it be, and prolific, seldom rises to really poetic heights.

It is genuine imagination, however, and takes one well away from the "stuffiness" of the mere society column, which is all the small-fry of the later school seem to aspire to. Let us take as a fair illustration of her earlier manner—of the period when she was wholly untrammeled by probability, and unvexed, apparently, by more than the very slightest experience of life, or a superficial knowledge of books—*Idalia.* In the first place, we have for a hero the penniless Scotch lord, in his mouldering tower: a man of kingly stature and falcon eye, of indomitable pride and immeasurable descent, and of unparalleled prowess in the pursuit and slaughter whether of beasts or men. A coarse variation upon Ravenswood, indeed, but infinitely better than that daft creature Macleod of Dare, in that he lives and breathes, has wits and uses them. It was a rather happy thought, also, to name him Ercildoune, after the Rhymer; and though we are half tempted to abandon him in disgust, when we meet him in a Paris café, "wringing the amber Moselle from his long mustaches," yet we are willing to believe, what is in itself a tribute to her creative power, that the vulgarity is the author's rather than her hero's, and we decide, upon the whole, that we would like to know more about him. And we are sincerely glad that we have done so, when it comes to following the gallant Scot in his wild night ride, as bearer of dispatches down the lonely Roumanian pass, and in that Homeric fight of his with the men who lay in ambush for him behind the fallen pine. The whole thing is magnificently described,

and carries the reader along with something like the breathless credulity of his most tender years, up to the point where the queen's messenger flings his precious papers into the foaming stream, and bares his bosom to the bullets of six thoroughly armed foes. How could he have escaped death, since they all fired, *à bout portant?* But escape he did, of course, though left for finished by his cowardly assailants; for are we not still in the first half of the first of the three mystic volumes? The dazzling creature, robed in Eastern silks and blazing with Golconda gems, who found him, and had him conveyed for treatment to the skillful sisters of the white convent upon the mountain side, was no Valkyria, come to unlock the warrior's paradise, but a living woman, very handsome, naturally, and altogether most interesting and extraordinary. I must confess to a weakness for Idalia. As the ubiquitous genius of the Revolution in Europe a generation ago, the airy and beautiful head-centre of countless republican plots, with millions at the beck of her fairy fingers, luring peoples to revolt, and nerving individuals to the most enthusiastic self-sacrifice, she seems to me far more boldly and successfully conceived than the renowned Mary Ann of the author of *Lothair.* Just what manner of woman Idalia was, personally, the author has been at such elaborate pains to tell us that it is somewhat difficult to determine. Here are a few of her "precious indications:"—

> The reverse of Eugénie de Guérin, who was always hoping to live and never lived, she had lived only too much and too vividly. She had had pleasure in it, power in it, triumph in it; but now the perfume and the effervescence of the wine had evaporated. There was bitterness in the cup, and a canker in the roses that crowned its brim, for she was *not free.* Like the Palmyrean queen, she felt her fetters underneath the roses. . . . At last she rose; she knew how many would visit her during the day, and she was, besides, no lover of idle dreams and futile regret. Brilliant as Aspasia and classically cultured as Héloïse, she was not one to let her days drift on in inaction. . . . No days were long for her, even now that she rebelled against the tenor and purport of her life.

The riddle of the Sphinx can have been nothing to that of a lady who is comparable, in the same breath, to Eugénie de Guérin, Zenobia, Aspasia, and Héloïse. Yet, somehow, as in the case of Ercildoune, with whom she is fairly and, in the end, happily matched, the creature is so instinct with life and emotion that we believe in her, in spite of this pompous and foolish description. The suggestion, for instance, that she was "not free" is proved, by the event of the story, to do her gross injustice. It is a particularly vile suggestion, in this case, and may serve as text for a few disagreeable remarks which must inevitably be made, sooner or later, by any one attempting a fair appreciation of Ouida. Her ideal of vice is as fantastic and exaggerated as all her other ideals. She appears to have the same sort of diseased *fancy* for it which some people have for strong and foul odors. She would seem early to have adopted into her theory of life the following principle, which she enunciates clearly enough somewhere in *Chandos,* and which contains just the grain of truth calculated to make it thoroughly pernicious:—

> The age rants too much against the passions.
> From them spring things that are vile, but with-
> out them life were stagnant and heroic action
> dead. Storms destroy, but storms purify.

Starting from this premise, and accompanied erelong, it must be confessed, by a goodly number of those who claim to constitute "the age," she proceeds to a sort of glorification of sensuality. She has the honor of having, to some extent, anticipated Zola. She is eager to inform us that all her very noblest heroes, even one who, like Chandos, is made capable of sparing and forgiving a most malignant foe, have been at one time or another "steeped" in degrading indulgence. Nor is ordinary sensuality sufficient for her. Adultery is often too pale, and she must needs hint at something worse. She makes Idalia consent to pass for the mistress of her own father, and alarms Chandos with the ghastly idea that he may have been making love to a daughter of his. Doubtless her vaulting ambition to portray these ecstasies of crime o'erleaps itself, and suggests the idea that she may really be as ignorant of the world of men as she must be of that of letters, when she talks of poems "half Lucretian and half Catullan," and is reminded how Dante walked the streets of Florence "five hundred centuries ago." The apologists of Lord Byron have sometimes made a similar claim for him, namely, that his worst passages, his most utterly infamous intimations, were rather the freaks of a diseased fancy than the record of disgusting facts; but far distant be the time when it shall not seem specially monstrous for a woman to call for this kind of defense.

Let *Idalia* stand as the type of the half dozen voluminous tales which belong to the period when Ouida was a romanticist *pure et simple*. It is the ablest, upon the whole, although there may be those who prefer the buoyant and beaming naughtiness of **Under Two Flags** to the rather reckless display of lofty sentiments and grand heroics which marks the earlier volume. Taken altogether, these books reveal a truly remarkable wealth of invention and no mean constructive power; an ability, which may well challenge our admiration, to conceive an almost endless variety of striking figures and picturesque situations, combined with an independence of conventionalities, whether moral or literary, which moves one to something like awe. These books have, moreover, beside their intrinsic qualities, a certain interest in the history of fiction, as constituting, along with *Lothair* and perhaps *My Novel* and *What Will He Do with It?* as well as the earlier efforts of Ouida's direct imitators, Miss Braddon, Mrs. Wood, etc., the very last of the strictly romantic novels which can have been written in entire good faith upon the author's part. The times were changing rapidly in the years when these tales appeared, and it was inevitable that a mind as active and impressionable as Ouida's should change its tune and method in them. She was born, like all the restless and imaginative souls of our day who remember the "forties," to the ardent and confident belief in a *cause:* and that was the cause of civil freedom, the propagation of the American idea, the emancipation of "Europe's oppressed peoples" from the supposed tyranny of their effete kings,—the cause of which Kossuth and Mazzini were the prophets, Lamartine the poet-laureate, and Garibaldi the doughty champion. That cause was by no means lost, still less was it admitted by its adherents to be lost, at the time when Ouida began to write. The "clouds of glory" which the century had "trailed" from its tumultuous infancy were still faintly rosy, but they were destined to be pretty thoroughly dissolved in the "light of common day" during its sixth and seventh decades. France kissed the rod of the unprincipled oppressor, and settled down, under her handsome new chains, to a season of material prosperity and physical comfort which she has secretly regretted ever since it came to its inevitable end. Hungary, the haughty and intractable, also seized her opportunity to sign, on advantageous terms, a compact with her mortal foe. Italy alone had apparently remained true to her vivid colors, had broken her yoke and ousted her foreign invader, and set up for a free and united nation, vowed to modern ideas. Incidents of the war of Italian independence are very effectively worked in with the *dénoûment* of several of Ouida's earlier and more exuberant romances, **Idalia** among them. The authoress had, by this time, elected to make Italy her home, and in some sort of very sincere fashion, albeit with much music and parade, had formally given her heart and plighted her troth to that endearing country. I believe the love which this queer genius bears to Italy to be an entirely genuine and disinterested sentiment,—as much so, perhaps, as any of which she is capable. Those books of hers which, like **Pascarel, Signa,** and **In Maremma,** may be classed under the head of Italian idyls do really teem with something resembling the large, lawless, unkempt, and yet impassioned beauty of the land itself, while the chronic and patiently borne misery of a large proportion of the Italian population fires her with a sort of wrathful pity, which in its turn moves her reader to honest sympathy with herself. Moreover, she feels the *picturesque* of Italy in every fibre; and if she is open to the charge of always writing more or less bad Ruskinese when she essays to depict it, which of us who were brought up on the Modern Painters can cast the first stone? There are real artistic verity and poetic feeling in such pictures as this of the Blue Grotto at Capri:—

> Perfect stillness, perfect peace, filled only with
> the low and murmuring sound of many waters;
> a beauty not of land nor of sea, sublime and spiritual as that marvelous azure light that seemed
> to still and change all pulse and hue of life itself;
> a sepulchre and yet a Paradise, where the world
> was dead, but the spirit of God moved on the
> face of the waters.

And this, of the olive:—

> For the olive is always mournful. It is, amid
> trees, like the opal amid jewels. Its foliage, its
> flowers, its fruits, are all colorless. It shivers softly, as though it were cold, even on those sunbathed hills. It seems forever to say, "Peace,
> peace," where there is no peace, and to be weary
> because that whereof it is the emblem has been
> banished from the earth,—because men delight
> in war.

And this, on the never-to-be-hackneyed subject of Rome:—

> Rome is terrible in her old age. It is the old age

of a mighty murderess of men. About her there is ever the scent of death, the abomination of desolation. She was, in the days of her power and sorcery, a living lie. She called herself the mother of free men, and she conceived only slaves. The shame of her and the sin cling to her still, and the blood which she has shed makes heavy the air which she respires. Her head is crowned with ashes, and her lips, as they mutter of dead days, breathe pestilence.

And this, of the region round Signa, and the stern aspect of winter upon the Tuscan hills:—

There is wild weather in winter at Signa. The mountain streams brim over, and the great historic river sweeps out in full flood, and the bitter Alpine wind tears, like a living thing, over the hills and across the plain. Not seldom the low-lying fields become sheets of dull, tawny water, and the little hamlets among them are all flooded; and from the clock-towers the tolling bells cry aloud for succor, while the low, white houses seem to float like boats. In these winters, if the harvest before have been bad, the people suffer much. They have little or no bread, and they eat the raw grass, even, sometimes. The country looks like a lake when the floods are on; only for ships there are churches, and the light-houses are the trees, and, like rocky islands, in all directions, the village roofs and the villa walls gleam red and shine gray, in the rain. It is only a short winter, and the people know that when the floods rise and spread they will find compensation, later on, for them in the doubled richness of grass and measure of corn. Still, it is hard to see the finest steer of the herd dashed a lifeless, dun-colored mass against the foaming piles of the bridge; it is hard to see the young trees and the stacks of hay whirled together against each other; it is hard to watch the broken crucifix and the cottage bed hurled like dead leaves on the waste of waters; it is hardest of all to see the little curly head of a dead child drift with the boughs, and the sheep, and the empty hen-coop, and the torn house-door, down the furious course of the river. . . . There are beautiful hills in this country, steep and bold, and formed chiefly of limestone and sandstone, covered all over with gum-cystus and thyme and wild roses and myrtle, with low-growing laurels, and tall cypresses, and boulders of stone, and old thorn-trees, and flocks of nightingales always, and the little sad-voiced owl that was beloved of Shelley. Bruno's farmstead was on one of these hills; half the hill was cultivated and the other half was wild, and on its height was an old, gray, mighty place, once the palace of a cardinal, and where there now dwelt the steward of the soil on which Bruno had been born. His cottage was a large, low, white building, with a red roof and a great arched door, and a sun-dial on the wall, and a group of cypresses behind and a big walnut-tree before it. There was an old well, with some broken sculpture; some fowls scratching under the fig-boughs; a pig hunting for roots in the bare, black earth. Behind it stretched the wild hillside, and in front a great slope of fields and vineyards; and far below them, in the distance, the valley

and the river, and the bridge, with the high crest of upper Signa and the low-lying wall-towers of the Lastra on either side of the angry waters. . . . When, now and then, a traveler or painter strayed thither, and said that it was beautiful, Bruno smiled, glad because it was his own country,—that was all.

But Italy was destined to do more for Ouida, as an artist, in the larger sense of the word, than to satisfy her ideal of the beautiful in landscape. An experience was reserved for her there, or, more probably, a series of experiences, which vastly enlarged her knowledge of living men and women, and corrected, rudely perhaps, but effectually, her notions of civilized human society in the nineteenth century. Whatever one may think of the spirit in which it is conceived, there can be no doubt that the book which goes by the sarcastic name of *Friendship* marks a distinct intellectual advance on the part of the author. In it she clears at one leap the bounds which divide the romantic from the realistic school, and comes down on her old Pegasus, indeed, and with plumes all flying, among the grim observers of our disillusioned latter day. *Friendship* is indubitably coarse and crude in parts, but there is no part of it which is not preeminently readable, and this is more than can be said of some of the innocuous "idyls." As for the identifications with real people, over which all tongues were busy, for a time, in the city where the scene of *Friendship* is supposed to be laid, the critic has absolutely nothing to do with them. He who will may see a bit of enraptured self-portraiture in the superfine figure of the peerless Étoile. Strictly speaking, the reader is concerned only with the fact that, though the painting is somewhat overcharged, the figure is really one of extraordinary grace; while there is a certain penetration and subtlety in the analysis of Étoile's nature to which, for whatever reason, the author had not previously come near attaining. How profoundly and unsparingly studied, how consummately, if maliciously, painted, are the figures of Lady Joan Challoner and Prince Ioris! Each is almost a new type for the jaded devotee of fiction, and each leaves behind a singularly vivid memory. The intimate mixture of love and scorn with which Ouida seems to regard the entire Italian people is raised to the power of a consuming passion in her portraiture of Ioris: the gentlest and most helpless of aristocrats; the tenderest, falsest, and most worthless of lovers; the refined, sorrowful, indolent clairvoyant,—appealing and exasperating, fascinating and contemptible, representative of a thoroughly exhausted patrician stock. The picture drawn in *Friendship* of the foreign colony in a Continental city, its frivolity and irresponsibility, its meanness, moral and pecuniary, its prostrate subserviency to rank, and its pest of parasitic toadies and busybodies, is without doubt an ugly one: but it does resemble the real thing, alas! and is not *very* grossly caricatured; and if it have power to dissuade one individual, with strong home ties and affections and an appreciable stake in life, one who is not driven away by the positive compulsion of circumstances, from deciding to expatriate himself, it will not have been dashed off in vain.

The note of sound reality, which Ouida touches almost for the first time in *Friendship*, continues to vibrate more or less perceptibly through all her subsequent productions;

checking their extravagance, reducing their feverish temperature, regulating by the laws, at least, of remote probability their often insane and occasionally indecent action, imparting form and unity to her facile and rapid compositions. Enamored of gold and purple she still is, and always will be, but she has evidently learned something of the beauty of *nuances* and the value of alloy. She has by no means ceased to dote upon princes and dukes, but she acknowledges them to be human. She fixes her eyes unwinkingly upon their glories, and dares even to analyze and to judge them. Her Othmars, her Wandas, her Princess Napraxines, endure the limitations and pay the debts of our common humanity. Often entangled in the snares of fine writing, still she succeeds in freeing herself wholly from them at times, and shows herself mistress, for pages in succession, of a clear, nervous, telling style. Omniscience is not quite as much her "foible" as formerly. Her mania for allusive and universal quotation has, plainly, subsided; and her teeming ideas, whether caught from the reviews of books or the hearsay of learned conversation, have become so far clarified and classified that it would no longer be possible for her to write,—

> His eyes dwelt on Trevenna with a strange wistfulness, a look which mutely said, "Is it *thee,* Brutus?"

Or,—

Portrait of Ouida in 1878.

He glanced at his butterflies as he chattered, and saw that *the pin was entering their souls like iron.*

Or,—

> In *physics* he did not believe; he never touched *them.* Air and sea-water were his sole physicians.

Or,—

> When a name is on the public mouth, the public nostril likes to smell a foulness in it.(!)

Yet more notably, however, does this really shrewd and many-sided writer show the corrective touch of an enlarged experience, the worth of serious observation and reflection upon palpable facts, in the development of what may be called her civic instinct; her power of appreciating the economic and political conditions which actually come under her eyes, and of estimating the probable results of their natural evolution. Already, in the flowery *épopée* of **Idalia,** amid the hymns and the *fanfares,* the alarums and excursions, and the generally light, scenic, and, so to speak, decorative treatment of a vast and blind popular upheaval, there had occurred the following bit of acute criticism on one of the time-honored traditions of international policy in Europe. It is when there is a question of pecuniary recompense to the sublime Ercildoune, for having all but lost his own life through saving the Queen's secret, in that fine scene in the Roumanian pass, to which allusion has already been made:—

> "If you'll pardon my saying so, I don't admire that system of *indemnification,*" pursued Ercildoune. "A single scoundrel, or a gang of scoundrels, commits an insult, as in this case, on England, or some other great power, through the person of her representative, or perhaps merely through the person of one of her people. The state to which the rascals belong is heavily mulcted, by way of penalty. Who suffers? Not the guilty, but the unhappy multitude, peasants, traders, farmers, citizens, gentlemen,—all innocent,—who pay the taxes and the imposts. Of an outrage on a great power, if accidentally committed on a traveler by a horde of thieves, you take no notice whatever. If one were obviously done as a political insult, you would declare war. But when the thing happens in a small state, she is punished by an enormous fine, which half ruins her, for a crime which she could no more prevent than you could help, in Downing Street, the last wrecker's murder which took place in Cornwall. Pardon me again, but I fail to see the justice or the dignity of the system; and, for myself, when my own conviction is that the assassins who stopped me were not Moldavians at all, what compensation could it be to me to have the money wrung from a million or two of guiltless people, whose country the cowards chose to select as their field? If you want to avenge *me,* track these dastards, and give them into my power."

This is only a bit of reflex action, to be sure, the gleam of an uncommonly lucid interval, an involuntary cry of common sense; but it foreshadows the powers of sharp insight and independent judgment which Ouida was destined to develop, after her revolutionary revels were ended, and she had settled down to the face-to-face observance of the first results of political emancipation in her beloved Italy. She had expected to assist at an apotheosis; had dreamed of the brilliant exit from its dusty chrysalis of a regenerated and rejuvenated nation; of the triumph, self-decreed, of an entire people; of a procession as long as Italy; and of a laurel crown for her own flowing locks, very likely, upon the Capitol. She found herself partaker in a sordid and dismal disappointment. Loving the Italian lower class, especially in Tuscany,—as who can help loving who has ever lived among or been served by them?—loving them with all their faults, and the better, almost, for the childlike character of a good many of their faults, she could not fail soon to perceive that they, at least, were no great gainers by the change which had transferred them from the mild, hap-hazard surveillance of the amiable last Grand Dukes to the hands of the fussy and rapacious bureaucracy which meddles with all their humble affairs in the name of United Italy. There were indications, both in **Pascarel** and in **Signa,** that her sympathy with these helpless and obscure victims of modern progress might, some day, get the better of her self-consciousness, and sharpen her busy pen to a more stinging point than that, even, which had recorded the treachery of Ioris and the despair of Étoile. Finally, in the **Village Commune,** she brings her formal indictment against the present Italian government, and a tremendous indictment it is. The sad and simple *intrigue* of the book, the story of the poor, insignificant folk, whose minute means of subsistence were destroyed, their hopes crushed, and their lives quite ruined, because their lot happened to lie in the pathway of the big, new governmental machine, is told with great terseness and simplicity, for Ouida. It merely illustrates and is quite subordinate to the political purpose of the **Village Commune,** which is, to say the truth, rather a pamphlet than a novel. Let the reader listen for a little to the erewhile flowery and languishing romanticist, in this new vein of hers. It will at least give him a respectful notion of her versatility.

> Tyranny is a safe amusement, in this liberated country. Italian law is based on the Code Napoleon, and the Code Napoleon is, perhaps, the most ingenious mechanism for human torture that the human mind ever constructed. In the cities, its use for torment is not quite so easy, because where there are crowds there is always fear of riot; and besides, there are horrid things called newspapers, and citizens wicked and daring enough to write in them. But away in the country, the embellished and filtered Code Napoleon can work like a steam-plough; there is nobody to appeal, and nobody to appeal to; the people are timid and perplexed; they are as defenseless as sheep in the hands of the shearer; they are frightened at the sight of the printed papers and the carabinier's sword; there is nobody to tell them that they have any rights, and, besides, rights are very expensive luxuries anywhere, and cost as much to take care of as a carriage-horse.

> The public creates the bureaucracy, and is eaten up by it: it is the old story of Saturn and his sons. Messer Gaspardo was a very insignificant item

of the European bureaucracy, it is true, but he was big enough to swallow the commune of Vezzaja and Ghiralda. . . . Government, according to Messer Nellemane,—and many greater public men have thought the same before him,—was a delicate and elaborate machinery for getting everything out of the public that could be got. The public was a kid to be skinned, a grape to be squeezed, a sheep to be shorn; the public was to be managed, cajoled, bullied, put in the press, made wine of, in a word,—wine for the drinking of Messer Nellemane. He was only a clerk, indeed, with a slender salary, but he had the soul of a statesman. When a donkey kicks, beat it; when it dies, skin it: so only will it profit you. That was his opinion, and the public was the donkey of Messer Nellemane.

> Messer Gaspardo Nellemane stopped, espying, as I have said, that thing whose sight was beatitude and yet exasperation to him,—a *contravention.* He had made a code of little by-laws, all brand new and of his own invention. He thought administration should be persecution. If it did not perpetually assert itself, who would respect it? He had made everything punishable that could possibly be distorted into requiring punishment. Every commune has the right to make its own by-laws, and Messer Gaspardo had framed about three hundred and ninety; and the Giunta, sleepily and indifferently, had assented to them, and the worshipful Syndic Cavaliere Durellazzo had looked them over and said, *"Va bene; va benissimo!"* And so, in Santa Rosalia, all the secretary's regulations had been adopted and had become law. Quite recently, he had incorporated into these regulations the law that nobody should cut reeds in the Rosa without permission of and payment to the commune. *L'état, c'est moi,* and its pocket is mine, too, was always in the thoughts of Messer Nellemane.

> So the fountain became a thing of the past, and the labor for its destruction was entered, for a considerable sum, in the communal expenses, under the head of "Works for the salubrity and decoration of Santa Rosalia." An ugly waste ground, filled with nettles and rubbish, was all the people got in its place; and as for the old stones, some people did say they were reërected in a rich Russian's villa, fifty miles away, Messer Gaspardo knowing the reason why. A gardener of the neighborhood swore to his neighbors that he had seen them there, and that he had heard they were the carved work of a great ancient sculptor. But Messer Nellemane said they had all been broken up to mend the roads, and had been of no value for aught else whatever. And so the subject had dropped, as most inquiries into public wrongs or the expenditure of public money do drop; and though Santa Rosalia mourned for its lost fountain, it mourned altogether in vain, and the Giunta unanimously considered that the piazza looked very much better bare. Both trees and fountain begat humidity, they thought, and why should they not do in Rosalia just what was doing in Rome?

> The law should be a majesty, solemn, awful, unerring, just, as man hopes that God is just; and,

from its throne, it should stretch out a mighty hand to seize and grasp the guilty, and the guilty only. But when the law is only a petty, meddlesome, cruel, greedy spy, mingling in every household act and peering in at every windowpane, then the poor, who are guiltless, would be justified if they spat in its face, and called it by its right name, a foul extortion. . . . The Inquisitors are dead, but their souls live again in the *Impiegati.*

This is a one-sided statement of the case, doubtless, but there is no denying that it is a remarkably able one. It is said to have had the result of adding a decided element of romantic insecurity to the audacious lady's own residence in Signa, and to have so exasperated the powers that be as to make them look back, with unavailing regret, to the summary way, with its assailants, of the *régime* which theirs has displaced. Other liberal-minded foreigners, long resident in Italy, not so sensational and impassioned as Ouida, and better instructed, perhaps, in the countless difficulties of practical administration, will admit that there is too much truth in the **Village Commune,** even while they smile at its extravagance, and point to the fact that if the Tuscan peasant was happy and contented in his poverty under the Grand Dukes, it was because his pet peccadilloes were all blandly overlooked, and none but political offenses were punished at all; while he lent his foolish voice as loudly as any to the *plébiscite* which decreed their expulsion. My own impression is that in the more guarded and temperate re-affirmations of Ouida's appendix to the book in question, we come as near as may be to the real gist of the matter:—

It is irritating to see the foreign press, which knows nothing, actually, of the condition of things, laying down the law on Italian affairs. The English press attributes all the official evils of New Italy to the transmitted vices of the old régimes. Now I did not live during the old régimes, and cannot judge of them, but this I do know, that the bulk of the people regret passionately the personal peace and simple plenty that were had under them. The vices of the present time are those of a grasping, swarming bureaucracy everywhere, and of the selfishness which is the worst note of the Italian character. . . . It is strange that, with the present state of Ireland before their eyes, the whole of the public men of Italy should be as indifferent as they are to the perpetual irritation of the industrious classes at the hands of the municipalities and their organization of spies and penalties. But indifferent they are. Whether Bismarck approve their Greek policy, or Gambetta do not oppose their doings at Tunis, is all they think about. The suffering of a few million of their own people is too small a thing to catch their attention. They think, like Molière's doctor, "Un homme mort n'est qu'un homme mort, et il ne fait point de conséquence, mais une formalité negligée porte un notable préjudice à tout le corps de médicins."

No one can accuse me of any political prejudices. My writings have alternately been accused of a reactionary conservatism and a dangerous

socialism, so that I may, without presumption, claim to be impartial. I love conservatism when it means the preservation of beautiful things, I love revolution when it means the destruction of vile ones. What I despise in the pseudoliberalism of the age is that it has become only the tyranny of narrow minds, vested under high-sounding phrases, and the deification of a policeman.

Impressed, at all events, by the deep feeling and evident candor of the writer, and the almost total absence, in passages like these, of her wonted vanity and parade, we may cordially admit that there is matter here fit to atone for many literary and social sins, and to give this erratic and often reckless story-teller a plausible claim on the immunities promised to him "who considereth the poor."

I have, I think, fulfilled my engagement to say all that can fairly be said in favor of one whose books are in many hands and whose name is on many lips, while it is wholly impossible to dissociate either books or name from a certain persistent odium. Power and variety are two very distinguished qualities in a writer, and these are possessed by Ouida in so large a degree that very few indeed of the female writers now living can rival her. Let it not be supposed, however, that fiction such as hers, even at its best, is claimed to represent the highest type. (pp. 47-57)

> *Harriet Waters Preston, "Ouida," in* The Atlantic Monthly, *Vol. LVIII, No. CCCXLV, July, 1886, pp. 47-58.*

Edgar Fawcett   (essay date 1887)

[*In the following essay, Fawcett appraises Ouida's novels and comments on the essay excerpted above by Harriet Waters Preston.*]

Readers of current literature may have recently observed that two writers of reputation, Miss Harriet W. Preston [see excerpt dated 1886] and Mr. Julian Hawthorne, have been expressing rather pronounced opinions regarding the works of Ouida. Mr. Hawthorne's judgment was brief, and I need only add that it was extremely severe,—far more severe, indeed, than any critical statement which I ever remember to have seen expressed by this writer. Miss Preston's decision took a much ampler form, and occupied nearly twelve pages of the *Atlantic Monthly.* Whatever may have been Miss Preston's intention, she certainly does not appeal to us as one whom the merits of Ouida have more than lukewarmly affected. And yet, at the beginning of her essay, she assumes the attitude of an appreciator rather than a detractor, taking pains to declare that her inquiry regarding the true causes of Ouida's immense popularity shall be "primarily and chiefly a search for merits rather than a citation of defects." With this excellent resolution fully formed, she at once proceeds to draw comparisons between Ouida and such great writers as Scott, George Sand, and even Victor Hugo. This has an encouraging sound enough; we have the sensation that a refreshingly new note is to be struck in the general tone of fierce vituperation by which Ouida has been so persistently assailed for twenty years. The truth about Ouida would be a pleasant thing to hear; we have heard so much facile falsehood. But Miss Preston proceeds to invest her theme with a curiously languid and tepid atmosphere. She finally astonishes all the sincere admirers of Ouida—and their number is today, among intelligent people, thousands and thousands—by saying that her "imagination, vigorous though it be, and prolific, seldom rises to really poetic heights." This is certainly depressing for any one who has taken delight in such exceptional prose-poems as *Ariadne* and *Signa*. Still, a proper avoidance of enthusiasm must always form part of the modern critic's equipment; the fashion is to look at everything imperturbably, from the Sphinx to the Brooklyn Bridge; we somehow only tolerate the exorbitant and the florid when it takes the shape of disgusted invective. For a long period Ouida has endured the latter (not always quite patiently, if some of her retaliatory newspaper letters are recalled), and I confess that we owe Miss Preston a debt of gratitude for breaking the ice at last. None the less, however, do we own to a feeling that the ice might have been assailed by a little heavier and more efficient cleaver. The *Atlantic* reviewer appears, indeed, to be a trifle afraid, not to say ashamed, of her own pioneership. Tradition would seem to be furtively reminding her that she is heading a revolt against it. And there certainly might well seem a kind of literary defiance in any defence of Ouida. She has stood so long as a pariah that to give her boldly a few credentials of respectability, as it were, might in a temperament by no means timid still require some courage. I would not even appear to suggest that Miss Preston has doubted her own assertions concerning this great romancist, whenever they have been of a favorable turn. But it has struck me that she has almost doubted the advisability of her own position as so distinct a non-conformist. One smiles to remember the ridiculous abuse poured upon Ouida in England ever since somewhere about the year 1863. She has probably afforded more opportunity for the callow undergraduate satirist than any author of the present century. I do not maintain that she was at first the recipient of an undeserved ridicule. But afterward this ridicule, because of the radical change in her work, became pitiably tell-tale; it revealed that aggravating conservatism in those who arraigned her which had its root in either a very unjust, hasty, and perfunctory skimming of her later books, or an entire ignorance of their contents. She undoubtedly began all wrong. There are some liberal and high-minded people with whom the follies and faults of such stories as *Granville de Vigne* and *Idalia* have wrought so disastrously that all their future impressions have been colored by these unconquerable associations. It seems to me that Mr. Hawthorne is one of these, and I am certain that the late Bayard Taylor was one. When *Ariadne* appeared, only a year or two before Taylor's lamentably ill-timed death, he wrote concerning that enchanting tale in the New York *Tribune* with a sternness of condemnation most regrettable, as I thought, in so alert and vigorous an intellect. When I expressed to Taylor my surprise that he should have seen nothing beautiful or poetic in *Ariadne*, he frankly declared to me that he saw nothing commendable in any line that Ouida had written. But many of her lovely sketches had already appeared, and that exquisite idyl, **"Bébée, or The Two Little Wooden Shoes,"** with its tearful tenderness and its fiery, gloomy, piercing *finale* of pas-

sion, had given proof of its author's wakening force and discipline.

Miss Preston's chief error, I should affirm, has been her somewhat careless huddling together of all Ouida's works and passing criticism upon them *en bloc*, without more than vague indication of the different periods in which they were produced, or the various stages of development which they exhibit. This talented lady, however she is to be praised for taking Ouida seriously (and that is a fine thing to have done at all, when it meant the flinging down of a gauntlet before disparagement no less insensate than cruel), has still failed in taking Ouida half seriously enough. I read with astonishment in the *Atlantic* review, for example, an extended notice of *Idalia*, while such vastly better work as *Folle-Farine* or *In Maremma* was quietly ignored. Candidly, I hold that Miss Preston's entire consideration of Ouida has been as limited, unsatisfactory, and insufficient as it has been, when all circumstantial points are duly recognized, kindly, generous, and honorable.

I have already expressed it as my conviction that Ouida began very badly. She indeed began as badly as any genius did whose early and subsequent accomplishments in English letters are now known to us and may be read side by side with hers. Byron certainly showed far less power at the commencement of his career than she did at the commencement of her own; and those who possess my own deep veneration for the grandeur of Tennyson's poetry at its highest heights may have read some of the deplorable stanzas, modelled on a sort of hideous German-English plan, which have thus far, I believe, escaped the savage exposures of even his most merciless American publishers. I find myself involuntarily tracing a parallel between the young Ouida and the young poets who preceded her by a few decades more or less. But this tendency easily explains itself, since she is pre-eminently a poet, notwithstanding her great gifts for romantic narration. The rhythmic faculty has been denied her, and for this reason she probably has written so much of that "poetical prose" which the average Englishman has been taught to hold in such phlegmatic contempt. If *Granville de Vigne* had appeared in rhymes as clever and as prolix as Owen Meredith's "Lucile," it would doubtless have won a place far above that bright, hybrid, pseudo-poetic popular favorite. But *Granville de Vigne* has won no place, nor has *Strathmore*, nor has *Idalia*, nor has *Puck*, nor even *Chandos*, pronounced as was the dawning change it exhibited. These works all mean a palæozoic age for Ouida: her extraordinary powers were yet struggling for worthier expression. They are valuable alike in their absurdities and their better revelations, though the latter shone fitful, indeterminate, and often distressingly transient. The superabundance of "color," the weight of adjective piled on adjective, the lavish display of an erudition as voluminous as it was sometimes erratic, the meretricious defects of style, the *collet monté* superfluity of rhetoric, the impossible and ludicrous descriptions of luxury,—all this has become with many of us in a manner comically classic. Ouida's early heroes, with their fleet Arabian steeds, their lordly lineage, their fabulous wealth or sentimentally picturesque poverty, their fatal fascinations for women and their deadly muscular developments for men,—Ouida's early heroes, I say, have grown as representative of the overwrought in fiction as those of Byron have grown representative of like indiscretion in poetry. Nor are these faults of her youth entirely outlived by Ouida. "Fine writing" is still occasionally her bane, though it becomes less and less so with each new book she now produces. Her vocabulary has always been as copious as the sunlight itself, and her style is at present a direct, flexible, and notably elegant one. She has been accused of "cramming," and of making a little knowledge do service for much. But only very illiterate people could believe such a masquerade possible with her. She is indisputably a woman of spacious and most diversified learning, though she has not always known either the art of modestly concealing this fact, or that of letting it speak spontaneously and judiciously for itself. Still, pedantry is not seldom the attribute of a greatly cultivated mind. We have seen this in the case of George Eliot, whose admirers will perhaps feel like mobbing me when they read that I think her genius in many ways inferior to that of Ouida. And yet I grant that to a very large extent she possesses what Ouida was for a long time almost totally without,—taste, artistic patience, and that surest of preservatives, a firm and chiselled style.

Under Two Flags may be said to have recorded a turning-point in this unique writer's career. It was full of the same tinselled and lurid hyperboles which had made so many readers of the extraordinary series hold up horrified hands in the past. But its gaudiness and opulence of language were suited to its Algerian *locale,* and the drowsy palms and deep-blue African skies of which it spoke to us accorded with the tropic tendencies of its phrases. It displayed a wondrous acquaintance, also, with military life in Algeria, and for this reason amazed certain observers of an altered *mise en scène* in a novelist whom they had believed only able to misrepresent the patrician circles of England. But **Under Two Flags** amazed by its perusal from still another cause. It contained one of the most thrillingly dramatic episodes ever introduced into any novel of the school to which such episodes belong, namely, the wild desert-journey of Cigarette, the *vivandière,* bearing a pardon for the condemned soldier whom she loves. Cigarette reaches the place of execution just in time to fling herself upon her lover's breast and save him from the bullets of his foes by dying under them. We are apt nowadays to look askance at such heroic incidents, and the word "unnatural" easily rises to our lips as we do so. Perhaps it rises there too easily. Self-sacrifice of the supreme kind has gone out of fashion in modern story-telling, and by a tacit surrender we have given scenes like this, with all their warm-blooded kinships, to the domain of the theatre. That fiction will ever care to resume her slighted prerogative, the thriving influence of Zola and his more moderate American imitators would lead us to believe improbable. Still, the caprices of popular demand lend themselves unwillingly to prophecy. One fact, however, cannot plausibly be contradicted: the theatre has not invested her gift at any very profitable rate of interest, nor justified her present monopoly of all that is stirring in romanticism.

Tricotrin, if I mistake not, was the first important successor of **Under Two Flags,** and here Ouida gave us the noteworthy proof that she had turned her attention toward ideal and poetic models. I fear it must be chronicled that the chaff in **Tricotrin** predominates over the wheat. The whole story is not seldom on stilts, and we often lose patience with the hero as more of a *poseur* than of the demigod he is described. The entire *donnée* is too high-strung for its nineteenth-century concomitance. We feel as if everybody should wear what the managers of theatres would call "shape-dresses." Ouida still tempts the parodist; the machinery of her plot, so to speak, almost creaks with age, now and then; her personages attitudinize and are often tiresomely sententious. Tricotrin does so much with the aid of red fire and a calcium that his glaringly melodramatic death becomes almost a relief in the end. And yet the book scintillates with brilliant things, and if it had been written with an equal power in French instead of English, might have passed for the work of Victor Hugo. There is a great deal about it that the passionate and democratic soul of the French poet would have cordially delighted in. It belongs to the same quality of inspiration that produced *Notre Dame de Paris, L'Homme qui rit,* and *Fantine.* But there have always been English people who have laughed at Hugo's tales, and in much the same spirit Ouida's countrymen laughed at the itinerant, communistic Tricotrin, with his superb beauty, his pastoral abstemiousness and purity, his altruistic philanthropy, his forsworn birthright of an English earl, his wide *clientèle* of grimy and outcast worshippers, and his astounding range of opportunity to appear just in the nick of time and succor the oppressed. Far more daring license with the manipulation of fact, however, has been taken by the elder Dumas and others. Ouida's book came about thirty or forty years too late for sober critical acceptance in her own country, and it was of a kind that her own country has never permanently accepted. Still, it revealed her perhaps for the first time as an original power in letters. She had struck in it the one note which has always been most positively her own; she had told the world that she was a prose-poet of dauntless imagination and solitary excellence. As an idealist in prose fiction no English writer has thus far approached her. **Tricotrin** would not alone have made her what she is. It remained for her to improve upon this remarkable effort, and to fling up, like some tract of land under convulsive disturbance, peaks that for height and splendor far outrivalled it. The valleys in her literary landscape are sometimes low indeed; a few even have noxious growths in them, and are haunted by foolish wills-o'-the-wisp. Such, I should say, are her first few sustained works, like **Granville de Vigne** and **Strathmore.** Nor has she always clung to the talisman by which she afterward learned to invoke her best creations. At times she has seemed to cast this temporarily away, as in **Friendship** and **A Winter City.** I have now reached, as it were, my one sole conclusion regarding her abilities at their finest and securest outlook. She is an idealist, and that she should have determinedly remained. The foibles of modern society are no subjects for either her dissection or her satire. She has never been any more able to become a Thackeray or a Dickens than they, under any conceivable circumstances, could have become Ouidas. It is an immense thing for a writer to recognize just what he is capable of doing best, and to leave all the rest alone. But Ouida, with a burning uneasiness, has continually misunderstood her own noble gifts. With an eye that could look undimmed at the sun, she has too often grown weary of his beams. Once sure of her wings, white and strong as they proved, she had nothing to seek except the soft welcome of the air for which they were so buoyantly fitted. But no: she has repeatedly folded them and walked instead of flying. Birds that fly with grace do not often walk so. She is a poet, and she has forgotten this truth with a pertinacity which has been a deprivation to the literature of her time. And yet for several years after the publication of *Tricotrin* the idealist was most hopefully paramount in all that she did. If *Folle-Farine* had been her first book instead of her sixth or seventh, it would have made even the English blood that she has more than once declared so sluggish, tingle with glad appreciation of its loveliness. The change in her was for a time absolute and thorough. *Folle-Farine* was the story of a despised outcast girl, ignorant and unlettered, yet with a soul quick to estimate and treasure the worth and meaning of beauty wherever found. It is all something which the realists would pull long faces or giggle at as hopelessly "highfalutin." But then the realists, when they ride their hobby with a particularly martial air, are inclined quite to trample all poetry below its hooves. I don't know how well the story of *Folle-Farine* would please some of Balzac's successors, but I am sure that he himself would have delighted in it. The girl's infancy among the gypsies and subsequent fierce persecution at the hands of her grandfather, Claudis Flamma, as one devil-begotten and loathsome, are treated with an intensity bordering on the painful. But through all the youthful anguish and martyrdom of *Folle-Farine* there flows a charming current of idyllic feeling. Such passages as these, stamped with the individuality of Ouida, meet us on every page:

> In one of the most fertile and fair districts of Northern France there was a little Norman town, very, very old, and beautiful exceedingly by reason of its ancient streets, its high peaked roofs, its marvellous galleries and carvings, its exquisite grays and browns, its silence and its color, and its rich still life. Its centre was a great cathedral, noble as York or Chartres; a cathedral whose spire shot to the clouds, and whose innumerable towers and pinnacles were all pierced to the day, so that the blue sky shone and the birds of the air flew all through them. A slow brown river, broad enough for market-boats and for corn-barges, stole through the place to the sea, lapping as it went the wooden piles of the houses, and reflecting the quaint shapes of the carvings, the hues of the signs and the draperies, the dark spaces of the dormer windows, the bright heads of some casement-cluster of carnations, the laughing face of a girl leaning out to smile on her lover.

This certainly is not what we call compact writing; there is none of that neatness and trimness about it which bespeak the deliberative pen or the compunctious eraser. But what a sensuous and winsome poetic effect does it produce! Few writers can afford the loose clauses, the random *laissez-aller,* of Ouida. She sometimes abuses her assumed privilege, even in her most authentic moments,—those, I mean, of pure imagination. But it is then that the super-

abundance of her diction and its careless yet shining fluency hardly ever lose their attractiveness. It is then that the prolixity to which I have before referred is an attribute we are glad to pardon, and love while we are doing so. The argument of *Folle-Farine* soon ceases to deal with the sufferings of a child. The poor creature's hopeless love for the cold and unconsciously heedless Arslàn, bitter at the world's indifference to those magnificent gods and goddesses that he still goes on painting in his old granary among water-docks and rushes there by the river-side, is portrayed with unnumbered masterly strokes. And afterward, when Folle-Farine tends him as he lies stricken with fever in a Parisian attic, the evil temptings of the unprincipled Sartorian, as they offer life and fame to Arslàn at a price whose infamy cannot be questioned by her who hears them, cloud this whole narrative with a truly terrible gloom. Folle-Farine's immolation of self to save him whom she worships, and her final self-inflicted death amid the peace of the river-reeds, far away from the loud and gilded Paris that she detests, are the very darkest essence of the most absorbing and desolating tragedy. But the poetry of this whole fervid conception is never once lost sight of. We close the book with a shudder, as if we had been passing through the twilight of some magic forest where the dews are death. But we realize how matchless is the sorcery that can so sombrely enchain us, and long after its woful spell has vanished memory vibrates with the pity and sorrow it roused.

Ariadne is another masterpiece, and not unlike the foregoing in the main sources of its excessive melancholy. It is the story of a feminine spirit swayed by an unreciprocated love, as waywardly given as lightly undervalued. The characters are without subtlety, as in all Ouida's prose-poems. They are fascinating or repelling shadows, whom we can name adoration, egotism, fidelity, as we please, but whose eerie juxtapositions, whose pictorial and half-illusory surroundings, may summon sensations not unlike those caused in us by some admirable yet faded fresco. Never was Rome in all her grandeur and desuetude made the more majestic background of a heart's forlorn history. We read of "the silver lines of the snow new-fallen on the mountains against the deep rose of dawn;" of how "shadows of the night steal softly from off the city, releasing, one by one, dome and spire and cupola and roof, till all the wide white wonder of the place ennobles itself under the broad brightness of full day;" of how one can "go down into the dark cool streets, with the pigeons fluttering in the fountains, and the sounds of the morning chants coming from many a church door and convent window, and little scholars and singing-children going by with white clothes on, or scarlet robes, as though walking forth from the canvas of Botticelli or Garofalo." Sculpture forms what one might call the pervading stimulus of this most impassioned story, its young heroine being a sculptor of inspired powers. In the same way music supplies an incessant accompaniment for the glowing words of *Signa.* The youth who gives his name to the book is a musician who possesses something more glorious than mere aptitude. Psychologically it is the reverse of *Ariadne,* delineating the torment of a man who puts faith in the most shallow and vacant female nature. It is just as plaintive, just as haunting, as its predecessor, but it is simpler, less penetrative and less wide-circling, less Dantesque in its mournful dignity and less astonishing through its scholarship. These three prose-poems—*Folle-Farine, Ariadne,* and *Signa*—are the three high alps of Ouida's accomplishment thus far. It is not easy to praise them with full justice, because unrestrained panegyric is never that, and yet the lyrical spontaneity of the works themselves—their evidence of having won their splendid vitality by having been poured from the writer's inmost heart, as warm as that heart's blood—would tempt one who had fully felt their strength, originality, and greatness, to dip his pen in exceedingly rosy ink and then shape with it very ardent encomiums. I am far from calling these memorable undertakings "idyls," as Miss Preston terms them, or in any manner agreeing that *Friendship* "marks a distinct intellectual advance."

Here was a woman who had shown us as no one else, living or dead, ever had shown in precisely the same way, that she could make the sweetest and most impressive poetry do service as the medium for telling the sweetest and most impressive of tales. Mixed with their Gothic fantasy there was something Homeric in these three volumes which I have before named. There were no touches that reminded us at all of the modern novel. Each had its separate æsthetic haze clinging about it, and a golden haze this was, in every case. With only a few changes here and there, the atmosphere of each story might have been made Greek, or even Egyptian. The delights or horrors of life were put most strikingly under our vision; but the details of life, the routine of things *au jour le jour,* the trifling modes and customs of mortality, as it pursues its whims, its vices, its flirtations, its amours, its divorce-suits, all remained remote and unconsidered. The glamour of dream clung to every character and event. The joys and miseries outrolled before us were as abstract and aloof, when viewed with relation to our morning mail or our menaced butcher's-bill, as the loves of Paris and Helen in the *Iliad,* or of Ulysses and Calypso in the *Odyssey.* These three enticing stories no more concerned our bread-and-butter-getting existences of prosaic actuality than they concerned the wash of tides at either pole. We turned their glowing leaves to escape from our own silent quarrel with realities rather than to meet the monotonous recurrence of them either photographed painstakingly or sketched felicitously. In other words, we gave ourselves up to the alternately gentle or stormy wizardries of a poet, contented in the oblivion thus begotten for decorated statistics of the annalist or placid vivisections of the surgeon. I am aware that all such departure from his cherished modern standards must at once be tyrannously cried down as a bore by that self-satisfied arbiter, the average reader of to-day. Perhaps Ouida felt some necessity of propitiating this multiform custodian of profit and loss. It may have been that her publishers told her, with that sincere sadness born of financial depression, how much handsomer had been the "returns" from *Strathmore* and *Chandos* than from *Ariadne* or *Signa.* Be this as it may, Ouida forsook her new gods, and, except in the composition of some exquisite short pieces which recalled the purity, the human breadth, and the past star-like radiance of **"A Provence Rose," "A Dog of Flanders,"** and **"The Nürnberg Stove,"** I do not know of her having ever again hewn her statues from the same flawless Pentelic marble.

But the resumption of her old more materialistic task—that of writing novels which should reflect the doings and misdoings of her own century—she was now prepared to undertake with a much firmer hand and with an unquestionably chastened sense of old delinquencies. The tale *Friendship* may be said to commemorate this unfortunate transition. It marks the third distinct change in Ouida's mental posture toward her public. It is to me a descent and not an elevation, and yet I freely concede that the novelist *rediviva* was in every way superior to the novelist who lived and rhapsodized before. In *Friendship* we see much of the flare and glare once thrown upon every-day occurrences tempered to a far more tolerable light. Deformity often takes the lines of just proportion, and not seldom of amiable symmetry as well. Miss Preston praises *Friendship* as pre-eminently readable in every part, and here I should again differ with her, since in my judgment the book contains a great deal of insufferable tedium. Ouida's worst fault as a stylist is here laid tormentingly bare. She harps with such stress of repetition upon the guilty bondage of Prince Ioris to Lady Joan Challoner that the perpetual circumlocution makes a kind of maëlstrom in which interest becomes at last remorselessly swallowed. It has been stated that incidents and characters in *Friendship* were taken from Ouida's own life, and that Lady Joan Challoner's name conceals one belonging to a foe of the author. Whether this report be true or false, we resent the almost maliciously periphrastic style in which we are told again and again that Lady Joan was the jailer of Ioris and watched him struggle in vain with the gyves of his own sin. To have a nature of the most detestable selfishness described over and over till we are familiar with its meanest impulse, its narrowest spite, resembles being seated by a person of repulsive physiognomy in a chamber lined with mirrors. The reduplications become unbearable to us, till we take the only feasible course for avoiding them: we go into another apartment. Still, in the present case, I did not go into another apartment; I finished *Friendship* and received from it an impression as vivid as disagreeable. *C'est le ton qui fait la musique,* and this story, notwithstanding its eternity of repetitions, appeared to me told in a querulous, railing voice which robbed it of charm. But it evinces a most undeniable improvement in method. The sentences are terser and crisper than in those other adolescent novels, and the syntax is no longer straggling and hazardous. Of a certain redundancy Ouida has never wholly rid herself. The effort to do so is manifest in her later books, but it still remains a weakness with her to tell us the same thing a number of times and with only a comparative alteration of phraseology. Still, no one—not even Balzac himself—has a more succinct, dry, poignant way of putting epigram. It seems to me that she is without humor; her fun inevitably stings as wit alone can do; that soft phosphorescent play of geniality which would try to set its reflex gleam in the stony gaze of a gorgon, appears quite unknown to her. She has been wise, too, in not cultivating humor, for it is something which must fall upon a writer from heaven: he might as well try and train himself into having blue eyes instead of black. But Ouida has trained many of her qualities, and the self-search with which she has done so has betokened the most scourge-like rigors. The novelist in her is to me all a matter of talent vigilantly guarded and nurtured; the poetic part of her—the part to which we are indebted for three supreme achievements—could not have helped delivering its beautiful message. Afterward Ouida remembered that she was somebody quite outside of what one would call a genius,—that she was a woman of enormously versatile information, and that the possibility of her writing novels which would excite a great deal of public attention could scarcely be overestimated. Beyond doubt she had now reached a state of dexterity as regarded mere craftsmanship which thoroughly eclipsed the crudity of former times. But just as she had been raw and experimental in a way quite her own, so was she now adroit, self-restrained, and professional with a similar freshness.

Moths came next, and was a book sought and commented upon, admired and execrated, from St. Petersburg to San Francisco. Of all her novels, this is perhaps the one which has brought her the greatest number of readers in what may be set down as the third period of her singular celebrity. It is filled with the most drastic interest for even the most jaded and *ennuyé* examiner. The story is the perfection of entertainment, of diversion. Its sarcastic scorn of fashionable frailties and flippancies even surpasses that which made *Friendship* notorious. Social life among the most aristocratic people of Europe is drawn so sumptuously and prismatically that without ever having enjoyed the honor of dining or supping with princes and duchesses, we still own to a secret revolt against the verisimilitude of their recorded pastimes and dissipations. In *Moths,* as in all her purely fictional and unpoetic work, Ouida gives us the belief that she is flying her kite entirely too high, that she is too greatly enamoured of the rank and titles of her dukes and earls, that the European *beau monde,* as an idea, has too bewilderingly intoxicated her fancy. As Balzac delighted in letting us know the exact number of francs per annum possessed by almost every member of his *Comédie Humaine,* so Ouida loves to tell us of her grandees' castles and palaces, of their *fêtes* and *musicales,* of their steam yachts and their four-in-hands, of their "private physicians" (it is rarely one simple physician with her), of their multitudinous retainers and servants. Her heroines go to their apartments to dress, and in so doing give themselves up to their "women:" it is seldom that any one of them is humbly enough placed to have merely a single *femme de chambre.* All the horses are blooded animals, all the jewels priceless, all the repasts miracles of gastronomy, all the ladies' toilets royally costly. Saloons and boudoirs and bedchambers are adorned with wonders of modern art, on canvas or in marble, in tapestry or bric-à-brac, in panellings or frescos. Nearly every new book that she writes is a sort of *édition de luxe* of itself. I am by no means sure that she does not smile at the dazzling glories which she evokes, while continuing to spread them before us with a secret conviction that they will allure hundreds and even thousands, though they repel tens and twenties, of those whom they confront. What to many refined observers may have seemed a streak of trivial childishness in her may be, after all, a shrewder cleverness than these accredit her with. For Ouida is superlatively clever; indeed, it may be added by those whom none of her sham glitterings have blinded to the genuineness of her actual

gold, that she is lamentably clever. Had she thought less of a certain transient applause which writers incomparably beneath her may win, she might much sooner have attained that firm fame during her lifetime which her death alone will now create. In *Moths* the cleverness to which I have alluded is everywhere apparent. She has made it a story that the shop-girl or the dry-goods clerk may read with thrills and tears. Vera's horrible misfortune in having been sold by her mother to the brutish Russian prince admits of no misinterpretation. The vast command of wealth and the lofty station which now follow for the dreamy and statuesque heroine are skilfully blended with her love for the brilliant marquis-tenor Corrèze and the distressing captivity of her jewelled chains. There is a strong suggestion of the "penny dreadfuls" in the whole *entourage* of the tale, with Vera's anguished heart beating under robes of velvet and her tortured brain throbbing under coronets of gems. But it is immeasurably above the vulgarity of those gaudy and often mawkish serials. Its pathos is intense, and its continuous intervals of pure poetry undeniable. It is dramatic, too, in the very strictest sense, and its adaptation for the English stage was naturally to be expected. As for what the moralists would call its "lesson," I should affirm that to be exempt from the least chance of misconstruction. Like all these later stories of Ouida's, *Moths* has been denounced as grossly unwholesome for young minds. I do not know about young minds gaining benefit from its perusal; I should imagine that, like many things which minors do not understand, its effect upon them might be harmful, and even noxious. So is the effect of rich dishes and indigestible fruit upon young stomachs, while stronger gastric juices sustain no hurt from their consumption. It is time that this outcry against what is evil in literature for young minds should be silenced by a sensible consideration of how potent or impotent are the defences reared by educators and guardians. It would surely be unwise to cut down all the apple-orchards because in those days which precede autumn's due ripeness multitudes of foraging children have brought on themselves avoidable colics. If the colics sleep in the undeveloped apples, and mischievous little Adams and Eves *will* taste thereof, a stout wall and an ill-tempered dog behind it are the only trustworthy preventives against their temerity. To claim that Ouida's works are not healthful reading for those whose youth makes the mere mention of evil and vice deleterious because in all their bad meanings unexplainable, is to claim, I think, that any author may be misunderstood provided the mentality of his public is sufficiently meagre for his miscomprehension. The decried "immorality" of Ouida I have never at all been able to perceive. I ignore the question of her immoral purport in the prose-poems heretofore treated. There such a discussion wears colors of absurdity; it is almost as if some one should assure me that Milton's Satan was a matter of shame to his portrayer. But with regard to all Ouida's novels of what I have called her third period, the accusation (and it is a very wide accusation) becomes at least worthy of attention. Ouida has no hesitation in referring to relations between the sexes which common conventionality has reprobated and condemned. A great deal of her more modern work deals frankly with this theme. Sometimes it is dealt with in tones and terms of a most scathing irony; again it is handled with mixed disdain and ridicule; and still again it is openly grieved over and deplored. But I fail to find a single instance of the vileness of adultery being either condoned or alleviated. To choose an uncanny subject is very different from handling that subject with the grosser motive of extenuating what is base in it. I should assert that Ouida never—absolutely never—does the latter. There are one or two scenes in *Moths* which have a shocking nudity of candor. But they are never dwelt upon for the purpose of pandering to any despicable taste in the reader. They form a link in the dolorous chain-work of the heroine's ills, and they are introduced for the purpose of rendering her final step of rebellion against the world's legally imposed pressure more pardonably consistent with the whole scheme of her unsolicited mishaps. While revealing what she believes to be low and contemptible in society of to-day, Ouida employs merely the weapons which Juvenal himself made use of. She is never sympathetic with wrong-doing, any more than the Latin poet was in fulminating against Roman decadence. Witness, as an example of this impersonal sincerity, her unsparing denunciations hurled at such characters as Lady Joan in *Friendship* and Lady Dolly in *Moths.* How cordially she seems to detest the artificiality of every *mauvais sujet* she describes! She lays bare alike the sordid and the sensual aim; she pierces with her shafts of wit and hate the adventurer, the hypocrite, the scandal-monger, the titled voluptuary, the mendacious and guileful male flirt, the modest-visaged and still more deceptive *intrigante*. But there is no revelation through all her *danse macabre* of ill-behaved people which may even faintly indicate that she is in any way sympathetic with their indiscreet or reckless caperings. For those who shout Ouida down as abominable because she chooses to touch the abominable, I have no answer. All that point of view merely involves the question of whether the abominable can be touched or not in literature, provided it is so approached and so grasped that the author makes its mirk and stain seem nothing but the soilure and grossness which they really are. I am acquainted with several American men of letters who have told me that they deeply regret the broad public distaste against so-called "indecency" in novel-writing. These men have already written novels of merit and force, but they greatly desire to write novels which may express the full scope and depth of life as they see and feel it. They declare themselves, however, debarred from such performance by the stringent edicts of their publishers and editors. It seems to me that Ouida has quietly contemned the inclinations of her publishers and editors. She has chosen to tell the whole truth,—not as Zola tells it, but as George Sand (whom she resembles in one way as much as she resembles Victor Hugo in another) always chose uncompromisingly to tell it. Her gorgeousness of surrounding has made her perfectly pure and reformatory motive dim to those who cannot eliminate from the scum and reek of a stagnant pool the iridescence filmed there. Ouida has seen the rainbow colors close-clinging to such malodorous torpor in human society, and she has striven to report of them as faithfully as of the brackish waters below. But she has intensified their baleful tints. She has made the ermine that wraps her sinful potentates too white and the black spots which indent this ermine too inky. She is and has always been incapable of saying to her muse what Mr. Lowell says

in his profound and strangely unappreciated poem, "The Cathedral":

> Oh, more than half-way turn that Grecian front
> Upon me, while with half-rebuke I spell,
> On the plain fillet that confines thy hair
> In conscious bounds of seeming unconstraint,
> The *Naught in overplus,* thy race's badge!

No; Ouida determinedly delights in overplus, and when one thinks of her muse at all it is of a harried and over-taxed muse, with feverish imprecations against the wear and tear to which divinity has been heartlessly subjected. When I turn toward the novels which have succeeded *Moths,* I am constrained to declare Ouida a writer more fertile in expedients for disillusioning her most loyal adherents than any other known through the past centuries as one deserving the name of a genius. She is so incontestably a genius, however, that she can go on committing her excesses without alienating her leal devotees. She is like some monarch confident of his subjects' worship while he crowns himself with roses and quaffs wine from gold beakers to the detriment and discontent of throngs waiting at his gates. There are no throngs waiting at Ouida's gates, however; or rather the throngs are her entranced readers, and not by any means those fastidious about the requirements of true royalty. But a few, knowing her grand mind, regret the self-forgetfulness to which it has stopped.

In Maremma startled these few, as if it were a pledge of permanent return among the classic idealisms which have made this author's best right to assert herself one of the greatest figures in contemporary literature. And *In Maremma* is a tale of matchless grace and sweetness. We marvel as we read of the Italian girl who went and dwelt in the Etruscan tomb, loving the dead whom she found buried there, and finally meeting in it, by a most terrible satire of circumstances, him who dealt her a death-wound of passion,—we marvel, I say, as we read of this delicious, free-souled, innocent kinswoman to Folle-Farine and Ariadne, how any human brain could be so multiplex and many-shaded as that of Ouida. What gulfs of difference separate this new heroine of hers from the world-encompassed and society-beset beings whom she has so recently pictured! And yet for a time the novelist has dropped her microscope (often so foolishly misemployed) and the poet has resumed her neglected lyre. The old notes are still struck with dulcet harmony. *In Maremma* is Ouida again at her loftiest and most authentic. She shows in it her old impetuous desire to feel with and for the persecuted and maltreated of the earth. I cannot explain why it should not be ranked with the three great masterpieces to which I have already made such enthusiastic reference. Perhaps it should be so ranked. If there is any excuse for depriving it of a place on this exquisite list, that excuse must be found in its more earthy *raison d'être* when compared with the almost ethereal spirituality of the other books.

Wanda, Princess Napraxine, and *Othmar,* coming afterward with a speed of succession that showed the most earnest industry, have given proof of their author's second return to at least relative realism. But *Wanda* is a romance of inexpressible grace and force. It is the purest romance:

Front cover from a reprint of Ouida's first novel.

to speak of it as highly colored is like calling a particularly rich sunset overfraught with glows and tints. Judging it by the modern methods of the "naturalistic" school is to pronounce it a monstrosity of art. But a great many of the elder Dumas' works would suffer in a like way if so considered, and nearly every prose line of Hugo's would fall under the same ban of disfavor. *Wanda* is a great romantic story. Its mode of telling is one protracted intensity. Its fires burn with a raging and heavy-odored flame. But they spring forth, for all that, with no ungoverned madness. They are kindled by a hand desirous of their heat and curl, but avoidant of their reckless outflow. It is very easy to denounce such a tale as vulgar. In these final years of our dying century all literary fierceness and eagerness of this kind are so denounced. If romanticism is to fade away forever, this volcanic bit of sensationalism is undoubtedly doomed. But its sensationalism is of the sort we think of when we remind ourselves of *Monte Cristo* and *Le Juif Errant.* The haughty Austrian countess, with her prestige of stainless pedigree and her imperial self-esteem,—the Russian serf who has concealed his disgraceful birth under a stolen title,—the Hungarian nobleman of almost kingly rank and unblemished honor, who contemptuously lays bare the shameful brand of imposture in his rival,—the ancestral castle in the Tyrol, with its obeisant swarms of vas-

sals and its regal household administration,—all these are the old materials and manœuvres of **Strathmore** and **Idalia,** but presented with tenfold more adroitness and *savoir-faire.* The secret of reading **Wanda** with the keenest relish for its exuberant ardors must lie in complete forgetfulness of life as it is and pious acceptance of life as it might be. But this is the test by which nearly all romance is tried. I have no space to treat at length of **Princess Napraxine** and its sequel **Othmar;** but if space were broadly allowed me I could state of them no more and no less than I have already stated of **Wanda.** Princess Napraxine herself is a silly and patience-taxing person. Ouida's enemies must have exulted in her as "immoral," which she indeed truly would be were she not so transparently *légère.* The chief pity is that so fine a fellow as Othmar should have done anything except disdain her. But both these two last novels teem with pages of description, reflection, tenderness, sweetness, and pathos which make the fact doubly sad that Princess Napraxine (a pedant, a prig, and a strutting combination of silliness and bad manners) should ever have been summoned to blot and mar them by her paltry charlatanisms.

The isolated position held by Ouida in an age when principles and theories essentially opposite to her own have seemingly captured the world of letters, would of itself point to endowments both rare and sturdy. That she has pushed her way into renown against obstacles which were often all the more stubborn because they were of her own rearing, is a matter for serious inquiry and reflection; but that she should have forced from certain able contemporaries who originally satirized and flouted her, the respect and homage which we pay to transcendent competency, is a still more significant truth. It means that Ouida must mount to her place of deserved state in spite of faults which would shape for many another writer stairways with a wholly different direction. But there has seldom been a writer whose virtues and vices were so inextricably blended. For example, the very people in her stories of fashionable society who conduct themselves with the least lucid common sense perpetually spice their repartees and railleries with a most engaging wit. We may not sympathize with what they say, but we are keenly amused by their modes of saying it. Disraeli, whom I believe Ouida sincerely admires as a novelist, possesses all her love for palatial filigree and porphyry; yet he has nothing of her sprightliness, crispness, and *verve* when telling us of the bores, the simpletons, and the few passably bright people who make up "society."

In more than a single way Ouida is behind her time,—a time over whose rather barren-looking levels of analysis and formulation she flings the one large light of romance now visible. In this latter respect she is, indeed, a kind of glorious anachronism, but from another standpoint her grooves of thought appear painfully narrow. Occasionally she airs a contempt for her own sex which makes us wish that with all her learning she knew a little more of the dispassionate repose taught by science and of its hardy feuds against *a priori* assumptions. Ouida has made declarations about womankind which cause us to wonder how she can possibly have been so unfortunate in her feminine friends, with the thousands of chaste and lovable women now to be met inside the limits of civilization. The *mauvaise langue,* when turned against womanhood, is nowadays classed among effete frivolities. What we forgave at the beginning of the century on this head we now simply dismiss as beneath anything like grave heed. The day has passed when such Byronics of misogyny, however gilt with flashing sarcasms, will either delude or solace. We leave "sneers at the sex" to the idleness of otherwise unemployed club-loungers, whose growls are innocuous. Still, in justice to Ouida, I should deny that her hatred of women ever reached anything like an offensive boiling-point except in the early novel *Puck,* which has probably done as much to feed the spleen of her enemies as any work to which she has given her name. In subsequent novels she has created many women of great sweetness and high-mindedness, as Étoile in *Friendship,* Vera in *Moths,* Wanda in the story of that title, Yseult in *Princess Napraxine,* and Damaris in *Othmar.* Perhaps a depraved and sinful woman is more execrable than a man of the same perverted traits. This is a question open to debate, though Ouida somehow suggests an opposite judgment. It is true that the majority of her very bad people are not men, though she is capable, at a pinch, of some darkly Mephistophelian types.

On the other hand, her love for the helpless and the unfriended, her profound charity toward the down-trodden and destitute and neglected among humanity, is one of the several bonds between her own genius and that of Hugo,—a poet whom she resembles more than I have availed myself of opportunity to indicate.

But I do not claim that these words about Ouida—though I have called them "the truth," and though, as regards my own most sincere faith and equally sincere unfaith, I so insist upon calling them—are in any degree a satisfactory criticism. How this woman's littleness dies into a shadow beside her imaginative greatness, a real critic will hereafter tell. I have already stated in the pages of [*Lippincott's Monthly Magazine*] my fixed belief concerning the scientific method which every critic who at all merits the place of one should infallibly use. For myself, I wish to be thought no more than that purveyor of opinions whom I have previously sentenced with some emphasis. I simply print what I think and believe about Ouida, and I have declared it to be "the truth" only as I see and realize truth. If it be falsehood I shall welcome with gladness any actual critic who so proves it. But to satisfy me of my own errors he must not by any means deport himself in the same arbitrary and downright fashion as I have done. He must bear in mind that if he desires to convince me of my one-sidedness he must not oppose it with *dicta* as unfoundedly hypothetical as my own. He must not be a man who profusely deals, as I do, in unverified declarations. He must logically elucidate to me where I am wrong and why I am right. It occurs to me, with that vanity of all essayists who temporarily have the field quite to themselves, that I am more often right than wrong. But if I am conclusively proved more often wrong than right by that system of acute investigation which only the science-bred critic understands, then I shall still feel that I have been of marked service to the writer thus empirically reviewed; for I shall at least have made myself a means of rousing careful and faithful consideration toward a series of imaginative works thus far either unreasonably contemned or irresponsibly lauded. The scientific tone and poise is so prevailing and favorite a one at the present time in works which a few years ago it rarely invaded, that I cannot help asking myself why the critics, who of all living persons are most easily accredited with the scientific tone and poise, should not more fondly and unhesitatingly employ it. They almost universally fail to employ it, however; and on this account the wandering verbiage of their estimates may be said to be as valueless as the announcements which I now pluck up boldness enough to print. But my boldness has a weak fibre or two of cowardice in it, I fear, after all. I should never have presumed to write of Ouida as I have written, had I not prized her compositions, frankly and *de bon cœur,* far more than I blame them. For this reason I have given my favorable views publicity. Ouida is so internationally popular that I am confident of friendly endorsements which will mitigate for me the necessary agony of being anathematized as her defender. There my cowardice stops—in a certainty of helpers and supporters. For the rest, if I am called names because I pay to a reigning genius what I hold as her rightful tribute, my stolid resignation will be equal to any martyr's. I shall endure the odium, certain of its ultimate destruction. Times change, and I think the day is not far distant when Ouida will be amazed at the sovereign fame which she herself has builded through all these years of failure and triumph, of weakness and power. But perhaps she will not be astonished at all, being dead. Or perhaps . . . But I leave that point for the religionists and the agnostics to fight out between themselves. One gets immortality of a certain kind, now and then, whether *pallida mors* bring to us posthumous beatitude, brimstone or annihilation. And Ouida, I should insist (with deference to the coming scientific critic), has secured this terrene kind of immortality. I don't know whether or not she would rank it as a very precious boon. To judge from a good many passages in her abundant writing, I should be inclined to decide negatively. (pp. 251-70)

Edgar Fawcett, "The Truth About Ouida," in Lippincott's Monthly Magazine, *Vol. XL, August, 1887, pp. 251-70.*

Marie Corelli   (essay date 1890)

[*Corelli was a prolific English novelist whose works were popular during the late nineteenth and early twentieth centuries. In the following essay, she expresses admiration for Ouida's style and characterizes Ouida as a literary genius.*]

There are a large number of self-styled "superior" people in the literary world who make it a sort of rule to treat with vague laughter and somewhat unintelligent contempt the novels of the gifted Mdlle. de la Ramée, known to the reading public as "Ouida." Men, particularly, profess to be vastly amused with the heroes she depicts; the splendid "muscular" types of masculine beauty, the wondrous individuals who "drench" their beards and moustaches with perfume, smoke scented cigars and run through millions of money in no time; and it may readily be admitted that numerous excrescences in the shape of over-floridness, unnecessary exaggeration of character and sensuousness of suggestion, do, to a great extent, spoil works that would, but for these defects, take their place in the highest rank of modern literature.

But, when all is said and done, the fact remains, that "Ouida" is a woman of *genius.* Not Talent, merely, but Genius. In the opinion of many judges, this genius may be considered as a flower growing in a perfect wilderness of brambles and rough fern, yet the flower is there all the same, and the unprejudiced eye will at once discover it. Nothing is so easy as to find fault; everyone can do that, from the little penny-a-liner up to the fullblown, "slashing" swash-buckler critic for the literary Reviews; yet, to read books in the mere spirit of fault-finding, is, I humbly venture to assert, to read them wrongly. To take up a novel, poem or essay with the mental determination to look for its imperfections is the greatest mistake in the world. Imperfections can be found in all the masterpieces of Literature, from Homer and Catullus downwards. We can, if we so choose, sit on our three-legged stool of criticism and sneer at all the gods. Homer is too lengthy—we are bored with his shipping list. Plato is too didactic. Dante and Byron are too personal; they insist on their own private wrongs too flagrantly. Keats is too, too sweet; his honey cloys our lips! Shelley is obscure and full of moonstruck misty vagaries. And Shakespeare—ah! we pause at Shakespeare. What shall we say of him? Well, if we are of the Donelly-ass persuasion, we can bray forth our belief that he was Bacon; if we belong to Mrs. Grundy's school, we can whisper that in certain of his allusions he is decidedly improper! And so with everything and everybody. And because a few reviewers jest lightly, and more or less sneeringly at the "Ouida" social types, we are apt to pass on the sneer and repeat the jest without giving the author whom we condemn the fair chance of our own unbiassed examination. Yet reviewers, though they pose as Oracles, are, after all, only men; and difficult as it may be to believe a fact so bare of chivalry, it is pretty certain that many a male author is ungallantly jealous of a woman's brain that proves in any respect sharper, quicker and more subtle than his own. Hence we find most professional men-critics somewhat contemptuous and intolerant of women's literary attainments (*vide* the largest half of the masculine criticism bestowed on the more highly distinguished female authors, such as Mrs. Barrett Browning, George Eliot, George Sand and others of that calibre); they are more willing to give the helping word of praise to any member of their own sex who makes the mildest and most random "hit" of one season; especially if such an individual happens to have taken club-shares in the "Great Firm of Perpetual Log-Rolling and Press-Favour Limited," which does such excellent business for its supporters. *Women-*reviewers are comparatively few, and when they do take to the reviewing line of business, it is very frequently after they have failed as novelists. Now, to expect feminine non-success to applaud feminine triumph would surely be like asking women to become full-fledged angels at once, without giving them time to grow their wings! As for ourselves, who read, or pretend to read, the books we so glibly chatter about, we too often "skip" through novels; we get a crude idea of the story without for one instant taking the trouble to disentangle the threads of thought on which it is hung. In the case, however, of absolute, turgid, incoherent incomprehensibility, such as is found in Mr. George Meredith's fictionary efforts, and Browning's verse, we are so thoroughly in the dark that a reckless, maddened few of us will actually start "societies" to elucidate the mysteries wherewith we, being only endowed with a little common-sense, cannot sanely and comfortably grapple. True, the "societies" only muddle our brains a trifle more by their explanatory "systems," but then it is a relief to think we can at least shift the burden of trying to understand the non-understandable on somebody else's shoulders, even though that somebody else should, in the end, prove to be as incorrigibly stupid as we are!

Now "Ouida" is not a darkly sybilline writer. No one need puzzle over her utterances, for these are in many respects almost *too* plain for the grimly pious satisfaction of good Mother Grundy! Moreover, no excuse whatever can be found for the perverted view of life this gifted author insists on holding up to the public eye as the *only* prospect possible on our already too dark and sin-clouded human horizon. Bad as society may be, we like to think that there is good lurking somewhere beneath its evil scum; bereft of beauty and desolate as an age of cynicism and gold-gathering selfishness always is, we like to hope that it may prove a mere passing storm-cloud, clearing the sky, perchance, for brighter and more wholesome weather. Why, therefore, "Ouida's" characters of good women should, as a rule, be foolish, and come to a miserably undeserved end, while her characters of courtesans and *cocottes* should nearly always be triumphant, is a question that only "Ouida" herself can answer. Recognizing as I do, with respect, the force of her inspiration, it is a matter of both wonder and regret to me that her brilliant pen has so often been used for the depicting of social enormities and moral sores; but while deploring the fact I still assert: Genius, Genius—not mere talent—is in this woman. And it is my habit to honour Genius, as a lightning-message from the gods, whereever and however it flashes across my path. I have never met Mdlle. de la Ramée; I have never even corresponded with her. And certain well-intentioned persons have assured me that should I ever venture into her presence, I should probably meet with a rough reception, "as," say the gossips, "she hates her own sex." This may be, or it may not; but as I never pin my faith on rumour, I am inclined to give "Ouida" the benefit of the doubt. At all events, no *brusquerie* on her part would alter or pervert in the least the current of a certain homage on mine. I cannot for example, withhold my honest admiration from the woman who wrote the following passage on the world's greatest poet, Shakespeare. It is taken from the fine story of *Ariadnê:—*

> Can you read Shakespeare? You think Dante greater. Of course you do, being an Italian. But you are wrong. Dante never got out of his own narrow world. He filled the great blank of the Hereafter with his own spites and despites. He marred his finest verse with false imagery to rail at a foe or flaunt a polemic. His Eternity was only a millpond in which he should be able to drown the dogs he hated. A great man!—oh, yes!—but never by a league near Shakespeare.

Sympathy is the hall-mark of the poet. Genius should be wide as the heavens and deep as the sea in infinite comprehension. To understand intuitively—that is the breath of its life. Whose understanding was ever as boundless as Shakespeare's? From the woes of the mind diseased, to the coy joys of the yielding virgin; from the ambitions of the king and the conqueror, to the clumsy glee of the clown and the milkmaid; from the highest heights of human life to the lowest follies of it—he comprehended all. That is the wonder of Shakespeare. No other writer was ever so miraculously impersonal. And if one thinks of his manner of life it is the more utterly surprising, With everything in his birth, in his career, in his temper, to make him cynic and revolutionist, he has never a taint of either pessimism or revolt. For Shakespeare to have to bow, as a mere mime in Leicester's house!—it would have given any other man the gall of a thousand Marats. With that divinity in him, to sit content under the mulberry trees, and see the Squires Lucy ride by in state,—one would say it would have poisoned the very soul of St. John himself. Yet never a drop of spleen or envy came in him; he had only a witty smile at false dignities, and a matchless universality of compassion that pitied the tyrant as well as the serf, and the loneliness of royalty as well as the loneliness of poverty. That is where Shakespeare is unapproachable. He is as absolutely impartial as a Greek Chorus. And thinking of the manner of his life, it is marvellous that it should have bent him to no bias, warped him to no prejudice. If it were the impartiality of coldness, it would be easy to imitate; but it is the impartiality of sympathy, boundless and generous as the sun which shines upon the "meanest thing that lives, as liberally as on the summer rose!" That is why Shakespeare is as far higher from Dante, as one of Dante's angels from the earth.

Now, the men-critics, who, as soon as a novel of "Ouida's" comes in for review, murmur, "Ouida! oh, she's always good game!" and scratch off at once a half column of "smart" gibing, would be cleverer than they are ever likely to be, if they could write such a passage of pure, fluent, eloquent English as this; nay, if a man instead of a woman *had* written it, he might (and would!) be proud. Men are far more conceited concerning their literary efforts, than women. And though I do not wish to claim for "Ouida" any position that she is not, in the opinion of more experienced literary judges, entitled to possess, I *do* claim for her simple justice. Justice my lords and gentlemen!—pause and consider, before falling foul of "Chandos" and his exaggerated masculine beauty, whether there is not an incisive truth, firmness and fineness of delineation in the character of Chandos's half-brother "John Trevenna," the wily, cruel, cunning, pitiless creature whose actions all spring from self-interest and the inherited thirst of vengeance? You will search in vain through the effeminately pretty stories of William Black, the slow wordiness of Marion Crawford, the wearyful commonplaces of W. D. Howells, or any loftily-named "Saga" of Hall Caine's for so powerfully drawn a *human* type as this "Trevenna," who *lives* in the printed page, as absolutely, as breathingly, as any one of Balzac's heroes. Turn to *Tricotrin,* and if you are thoroughly matter-of-fact, pass over all the idealistic wanderings of the self-disinherited man; "skip" his concealed, but infinitely tender and romantic passion for the spoilt child "Viva"; but read—every word of it mind!—read the scene with the wreckers on the coast of Spain. If such a passage as that had been found in one of Walter Scott's or Dickens's novels, it would have been quoted in every "Elegant Extract" book and "Penny Reader" in the kingdom. There is certainly no *living* novelist in whose works can be found a more thrilling, nobly-drawn word-picture of storm, darkness and terror. Again, take the story of *In Maremma.* It is improbable, you say? So is *She* over which the public went mad some short time since. But *In Maremma* is a perfect Love-Poem in prose; and *She,* with every respect for its author's imaginative power of creating flesh-creeping horrors, is very, very far from being in the least poetical. Yet Love and Poetry *exist;* they are rare but not impossible things, thank Heaven!—while the idea of *She* is entirely out of all possibility. Hence "Ouida" deals with a beautiful *fact,* while Mr. Rider Haggard deals with a ghastly *fancy;* result,—a blatant burst of enthusiasm for the ghastly fancy—a smile, sneer, and doubtful shrug at the beautiful fact. One cannot, of course, pretend to account for the tastes of reviewers—but certain it is that the pitiful love of poor "Musa" the heroine of *In Maremma,* is to the full as touching and pathetic as any of Bocaccio's far-famed stories, and as probable in all points as any of the legends of poetic love and passion in all ages, while the style in which it is written is exquisite, delicate and scholarly to a degree, unsurpassed by any modern *male* or female writer of to-day's fiction.

It is the fashion just now among certain critics to rave over the performances of Robert Louis Stevenson, whose *Master of Ballantrae* has in some quarters been called a "classic." If it is "classical" to be hopelessly dull, then I agree with this verdict, but I venture to doubt whether the Press-eulogised author thereof, has any touch of the perceptive delicacy needed to carve out for us such a finished cameo-study as "Ouida's" **"Umiltà."** This is a short story which few people seem to know, yet it is quite perfect of its kind. Not a word too much—not an exaggeration—not a single blot of over-colouring; pathetic, yet simple as a mountain melody—a mere village incident raised to the dignity of a poem by the matchless way in which it is treated. The portrait of the fair, pure, proud, unjustly-accused **"Umiltà"** stands out like a white statue in full sunlight, a flawless thing and beautiful; and the same hand that called it into being wrote *Moths!* Yes, I know! but neither I nor anyone else can presume to account for the changing moods and phases of the writing temperament. Why did Byron write *Don Juan?* Why did Shelley touch the repulsive subject of the *Cenci?* An author endowed with the restless Protean-like quality of genius cannot be always at the same dead level of placable equanimity. Talent, like that of Mr. Andrew Lang, who, sitting on his little bibliographic dust-heap, discourses pipingly on "Was Jehovah a stone Fetish?" is, we know, at the beck and call of every subject on which it is paid to write; but Genius is wilful, often exceedingly irritating in its capricious changes of humour, and never exactly what the world would have it be. Thought, like Time, has its sweet and bitter seasons. In the happiest hours of her imagination I can imagine "Ouida" writing such stories as **"Umiltà,"** or that most touching of all child-romances **"Moufflou,"** which can be read many times yet never without a sense of tears in the throat, or **The Dog of Flanders, Two Little Wooden Shoes,** or that *whitest* of all her works, if I may use such a term, **Wanda.** But all hours are not happy ones, and when bitterness creeps into some natures, why, naturally, bitterness will *out.* And random, reckless, and sometimes pointless though her shafts may be, because of the sheer haste with which she flings them, there is often a terrible sting of *truth* in "Ouida's" assertions. Take the following examples:

> A cruel story runs on wheels, *and every hand oils the wheels as they run.*

> Some people hold that a life that rises from obscurity to triumph should look back in grateful obligation to *those who, when it was in obscurity, did their best to keep it there!*

> Popularity has been defined as the privilege of being cheered by the kind of people you would never allow to bow to you. Fame may be said to be the privilege of being slandered at once by the people who *do* bow to you, as well as by the people who do *not!*

> Perhaps nobody can comprehend how utterly *uneducated* it is possible to be, who has not lived entirely with the *educated classes!*

There is no faltering feminine weakness in these expressions; they are as pointed, as ruthless, as witty, as any sayings of Rochefoucauld. A Man might have written them—ye gods! think of it—the Nobler Creature might have penned such lines and smiled complacently at his own cleverness afterwards!

Let it not be imagined that I, or any of us for that matter, seek to defend "Ouida's" system of morals as set forth in her books. Not at all. Bad morals are bad everywhere, whether served up to us at breakfast in our morning-paper accounts of the latest divorce case, or in the widely-discussed novels of Tolstoi and Emile Zola, or in the *Poems and Ballads* of Swinburne, or in the amazingly absurd social plays of Ibsen. The popularity of *As in a Looking Glass* does not make the moral of that book any better, while, unlike "Ouida's" productions, it has not a saving gleam of poetic treatment about it to redeem its quality. Cannot the public discriminate aright? What is it they really admire? *Sandford and Merton? The Wide Wide World? Goody Two-Shoes?* This is not apparent in the spirit of the time. Myself, I think the wildest of "Ouida's" flights into romance, **Idalia**— which we, being prosy folk, must acknowledge as too highly exaggerated—is still far more wholesome and preferable to the repulsive suggestiveness of the work entitled *A Romance of the Nineteenth Century,* written by a *man,* distinguished and clever enough to have known what he was about when writing it. "Ouida" has never sinned to such a nauseous extent of mind-pollution as *that.* Her faults are those of reckless impulse and hurry of writing; being a woman, she has all that warm and often mistaken *ardour of the pen* which a man, unless he be very young, very gifted, and very enthusiastic,

generally lacks. Taking up her descriptive palette, she mixes her brilliant colours too rapidly, and the male beings she draws, beautiful as gods and muscular as Homer's sinewy warriors, become the laughing-stock of men generally; especially of the ugly and wizened ones who compose the majority! Her lovely women are *too* lovely, and invariably start a feeling of discontent in those members of the fair sex who are unable to spend a fortune on gowns. Love is the chief *motif* of all her novels; and love such as she depicts, arising mainly from the attraction of sex to sex is, *of course,* impossible and absurd and—*wicked!* It does not exist, in fact! We love and marry because it is highly respectable so to do, especially where there is plenty of money to live upon. The "strong bent of Nature," as Emerson hath it, the "immortal hilarity," the "rose of joy"—no! really, really! this will not do, though Emerson declares it will; it is wrong, quite wrong! The nineteenth century will not permit us to *love* any more; we are requested to *scheme* instead. And when our scheming is successful, and we are once married and established in a comfortable social position, we can have what some Theosophists call "soul-affinities." This is very nice and very romantic, very "moral" and very pretty;—and in such an exalted state of virtue we naturally reject the "Ouida" novels with scorn, especially that bitter, biting one called **Friendship!**

But though we need not praise the "Ouida" morals, or endorse the "Ouida" exaggerations, we must, if we are not blind, deaf and obstinate, admire the "Ouida" eloquence. There is no living author who has the same rush, fire and beauty of language; we are bound to admit this if we wish to be just. There are plenty of authors, though, who think it no shame to steal whole passages from her books, and transplant them bodily word for word into their own productions, and in the works of one third-rate lady novelist whom I will not name, I have discovered more than twenty prose gems taken sentence for sentence out of "Ouida" without a shadow of difference! However, it is a strange but true fact, that the deliberate robber of other people's ideas never secures the fame he or she attempts to steal. Imitation may be the sincerest form of flattery, but it is nearly always suicide to the imitator. The original conception triumphs in the end; it remains, while its feeble *replicas* perish; and the most painstaking labour can never compass even a paraphrase of one line of sheer *inspiration.* This gift of *inspiration* which cannot be bought, or sold, or taught, "Ouida" possesses, not in a small, but in a very large and overflowing degree, though, for all I know, it may not be as perceptible in her new book about to be published, as it has been in her previous works. That is a question in abeyance as yet. Her faults, judged by the strictest rules of criticism, *may* be manifold, but it should always be remembered that she is a writer of *romance,* and that she deals with the supposed romantic side of social life. One cannot but think her recent article on Shelley a mistake; yet it is only the result of her unbridled enthusiasm for the *poet,* that makes her write such "wild and whirling" words as that a "hundred thousand" girls might esteem themselves happy to be sacrificed as a holocaust to Shelley's passion—"hundred thousand" being in this instance a mere *façon de parler.* It is the reckless expression of impulse, and, rash as it may be, is more commendable than the cold-blooded casuistry of Mrs. Mona Caird, who has recently made what seems like a deliberate and dispassionate magazine-appeal for universal polygamy! Probably the worst that can be said for "Ouida" is that she is a *romancer,* and an answer to that accusation is best given in her own eloquent way:

> When the soldier dies at his post unhonoured and unpitied, and out of sheer duty, is that *unreal,* because it is noble? When the sister of charity hides her youth under a grey shroud and gives up her whole life to woe and solitude, is that *unreal* because it is wonderful? A man paints a spluttering candle, a greasy cloth, a mouldy cheese, a pewter can, "how *real!*" the people say. If he paints the spirituality of dawn, the light of the summer sea, the flame of arctic nights, of tropic woods, they are called *unreal,* though they exist no less than the candle and the cloth, the cheese, and the can. All that is heroic, all that is sublime, impersonal or glorious, is now derided as *unreal.* It is a dreary creed; it will make a dreary world. Is not my Venetian glass with its hues of opal as *real* every whit as your pot of pewter? Yet the time is coming when everyone, morally and mentally at least, will be allowed no other than a pewter pot to drink out of under pain of being "writ down an ass." It is a dreary prospect!

True, oh "Ouida!" Pitifully, deplorably true! Our age is one of Prose and Positivism; we take Deity for an Ape, and Andrew Lang as its Prophet! (pp. 362-71)

> Marie Corelli, "A Word About 'Ouida'," in
> Belgravia: A London Magazine, *Vol. LXXI,*
> No. 282, April, 1890, pp. 362-71.

G. S. Street   (essay date 1895)

[*In the following essay, Street considers the strengths and weaknesses of Ouida's novels, particularly addressing charges of false characterization and lack of stylistic control.*]

The superfluous champion is a foolish being, but his superfluity lies, as a rule, not in his cause, but in his selection of adversaries. In a world of compromises and transitions there is generally much to be said on both sides, and there are few causes or persons for whom a good word, in a fitting place and time, may not be spoken. I acquit myself of impertinence in stating what I find to like and to respect in the novels of Ouida. For many years, with many thousands of readers they have been popular, I know. But ever since I began to read reviews, to learn from the most reputable authorities what I should admire or avoid, I have found them mentioned with simple merriment or a frankly contemptuous patronage. One had, now and then in boyhood, vague ideas of being cultivated, vague aspirations towards superiority: I thought, for my part, that of the many insuperable obstacles in the way of this goal, this contempt of Ouida's novels was one of the most obvious. I enjoyed them as a boy, and I enjoy them now; I place them far above books whose praise is in all critics' mouths, and I think I have reason for the faith that is in me.

One may write directly of "Ouida" as of a familiar institu-

tion, without, I hope, an appearance of bad manners, using the pseudonym for the books as a whole. The faults alleged against her are a commonplace of criticism: it is said that her men and her women are absurd, that her style is bad, that her sentiment is crude or mawkish. It is convenient to make those charges points of departure for my championship.

Everybody has laughed at Ouida's typical guardsman, that magnificent creature of evil life and bitter memories, sumptuous, reckless, and prepared withal to perform heroic feats of physical strength at a moment's notice. Nobody, I admit, has met a guardsman like him; I admit his prodigality to be improbable in its details, and the insolence of his manners to be deplorable. But if you can keep from your mind the unlikenesses of his superficial life, you come upon an ideal which is no doubt falsely elaborated, but which, too, is the reverse of despicable. With all his faults, Ouida's guardsman is a man, and a man of a recognisably large nature. The sort of man whom Ouida has set out to express in him, often with unhappy results, is a man of strong passions and a zeal for life. He grasps at the pleasures of life, and is eager for all its activities; he will endure privations in the cause of sport and discomforts in the cause of friendship and risks in the cause of love. His code of honour may not keep him out of the Divorce Court, but, except in that connection, it saves him from lying and trickery. His social philosophy, that of the essential male in a position of advantage, is not enlightened, and his sense of humour is elementary; but his habit of life is clean and active; he is ready to fight, and he does not swagger. His one affectation is, that if by chance he has done something great in the ways of sport or war, he looks as if nothing had happened. There are things in life which he puts before the main chance. Such, more or less, is the sort of man in question, virile certainly, and one whom only the snobbery of intellect can despise. His is not a very common type in a materialised age, when even men of pleasure want their pleasure, as it were, at store prices, and everybody is climbing pecuniary and social ladders; it is a type that, I confess, I respect and like. At least it is indisputable that such men have done much for our country. Now Ouida, as I have admitted, has made many mistakes in her dealings with this type of man: who has altogether avoided them? They are many who find the pictures of him in Mr. Rudyard Kipling, superficially at least, far inferior to Mr. Kipling's "natives," and his three immortal Tommies. Ouida has made him ridiculously lavish, inclined to translate his genuine emotions into terms of sentimentalism, and to say things of his social inferiors which such a man may sometimes think, but is careful not to say. To affirm that the subject is good and the treatment of it bad, would be to give my case away. My contention is that the treatment, with many imperfections, leaves one assured that the subject has been, in essentials, perceived.

But her guardsman belongs to Ouida's earlier manner, and it is most unfair, in estimating her, to forget that this manner has been mellowed and quieted. In *Princess Napraxine* and in *Othmar*—the two most notable books, I think, of her later period—there are types of men more reasonably conceived and expressed more subtly. Geraldine, the cosmopolitan, but characteristic Englishman; Napraxine, the amiable, well-bred savage; Des Vannes, the calculating sensualist; Othmar himself, the disappointed idealist, these are painted, now and then, in somewhat glaring colours, but you cannot deny the humanity of the men or the effectiveness of their portraits. And when you remember how few are the male creations of women-writers which are indubitable men, you must in reason give credit to Ouida for her approximation.

I submit that it is not an absolute condemnation to say of Ouida's women that they are "hateful." There are critics, I know, who deny by implication the right of an author to draw any character which is not good and pleasant. That there may be, at one time or another, too pronounced a tendency to describe only people who are wicked or unpleasant, to the neglect of those who are sane and healthy and reputable, is certain; but the critics should remember that there is no great author of English fiction who has limited himself to these. One may regret that any writer should ignore them, but only stupidity or malevolence refuses to such a writer what credit may be due to him for what he has done, because of what he has left undone. Of Ouida's women much the same, *mutatis mutandis,* may be said, as has been said so often of Thackeray's: the good women are simpletons or obtuse, only the wicked women interesting. That criticism of Thackeray has alway seemed to me to be remarkably crude, even for a criticism: it argues surely a curious ignorance of life or lack of charity to deny any "goodness" to Beatrix Esmond or Ethel Newcome. But of Ouida it is tolerably fair. There *is* an air of stupidity about her good and self-sacrificing women, and since there is nobody, not incredibly unfortunate, but has known women good in the most conventional sense, and self-sacrificing, and wise and clever as well, it follows that Ouida has not described the whole of life. But perhaps she has not tried so to do. It is objected occasionally, even against a short story, that its "picture of life" is so-and-so, and far more plausibly can it be objected against a long tale of novels: but I have a suspicion that some of the writers so incriminated have not attempted the large task attributed to them. Granted, then, that Ouida has not put all the women in the world into her novels: what of those she has?

Certainly her best-drawn women are hateful: are they also absurd? I think they are not. They are over-emphasised beyond doubt, so much so, sometimes, that they come near to being merely an abstract quality—greed, belike, or animal passion—clothed carelessly in flesh. To be that is to be of the lowest class of characters in fiction, but they are never quite that. A side of their nature may be presented alone, but its presentation is not such as to exclude, as in the other case, what of that nature may be left. And, after all, there have been women—or the chroniclers lie sadly—in whom greed and passion seem to have excluded most else. The critics may not have met them, but Messalina and Barbara Villiers, and certain ladies of the Second Empire, whose histories Ouida seems to have studied, have lived all the same, and it is reasonable to suppose that a few such are living now. One may be happy in not knowing them, in the sphere of one's life being too quiet and humdrum for their gorgeous presence, but one hears of such women now and then.

They are not, I think, absurd in Ouida's presentment, but I confess they are not attractive. One's general emotion with regard to them is regret that nobody was able to score off or discomfit them in some way. And that, it seems, was the intention of their creator. She writes with a keenly pronounced bias against them, she seeks to inform you how vile and baneful they are. It is not a large-hearted attitude, and some would say it is not artistic, but it is one we may easily understand and with which in a measure we may sympathise. A novel is not a sermon, but *sava indignatio* is generally a respectable quality. I am not trying to prove that Ouida's novels are very strict works of art: I am trying to express what from any point of view may be praised in them. In this instance I take Ouida to be an effective preacher. She is enraged with those women because of men, worth better things, who are ruined by them, or because of better women for them discarded. It would have been more philosophical to rail against the folly of the men, and were Ouida a man, the abuse of the women might be contemptible—I have never been able to admire the attitude of the honest yeoman towards Lady Clara Vere de Vere; but she is a woman, and "those whom the world loved well, putting silver and gold on them," one need not pity for her scourging. It is effective. She is concerned to show you the baseness and meanness possible to a type of woman: at her best she shows you them naturally, analysing them in action; often her method is, in essentials, simple denunciation, a preacher's rather than a novelist's; but the impression is nearly always distinct. You may be incredulous of details in speech or action, but you have to admit that, given the medium, and the convention, a fact of life is brought home with vigour to your sympathics and antipathies. You must allow the convention— the convention between you and the temperament of your author. As when in parts of Byron a theatrical bent in his nature, joined with a mode of his time, gives you expressions that on first appearance are not real, not sincere, you may prove a fine taste by your dislike, but you prove a narrow range of feeling and a poor imagination if you get beyond it; so I venture to think in this matter of Ouida's guardsman and her wicked women, the magnificence, the high key, the glaring colours may offend or amuse you, but they should not render you blind to the humanity that is below the first appearance.

And if the hateful women are unattractive, is there not in the atmosphere that surrounds their misdeeds something—now and again, just for a minute or two—vastly and vaguely agreeable? I speak of the atmosphere as I suppose it to be, not as idealised in Ouida's fashion. It is not the atmosphere, I should imagine, of what in the dear old snobbish phrase was called "high life"—gay here and there, but mostly ordered and decorous: there is too much ignored. It is the atmosphere, really, of a profuse Bohemianism, of mysterious little houses, of comical lavishness, and unwisdom, and intrigue. I do not pretend—as one did in boyhood—to know anything about it save as a reader of fiction, but there are moments when, in the quiet country or after a day's hard work in one's garret, the thought of such an atmosphere is pleasant. We—we others, the plodders and timid livers—could not live in it; better ten hours a day in a bank and a dinner of cold mutton; but fancy may wander in it agreeably for a brief time, and I am grateful to Ouida for its suggestion.

I do not propose to discourse at length on Ouida's style. As it is, I do not admire it much. But I cannot see that it is worse than the average English in the novels and newspapers of the period. It is crude, slap-dash if you will, incorrect at times. But it is eloquent, in its way. It does not seem to have taken Swift for an ideal; it is not simple, direct, restrained. But it is expressive, and it is so easy to be crude, and slap-dash, and incorrect, and with it all to express nothing. There are many writers who are more correct than Ouida, and very many indeed who are a hundred times less forcible, and (to my taste) less tolerable to read. It may be true that to know fully the savour and sense of English, and to use it as one having that knowledge, a writer must be a scholar. I do not suppose that Ouida is a scholar, but I am sure that the scholarship that is only just competent to get a familiar quotation aright is not a very valuable possession. In fine, I respect an unrestrained and incorrect eloquence more than a merely correct and periphrastic nothingness. I would not take Ouida's for a model of style, but I prefer it to some others with which I am acquainted.

Perhaps to be a good judge of sentiment one should not be an easy subject for its influence. In that case nothing I can say on the question of Ouida's sentiment can be worth much, for I am the prey of every sort of sentiment under heaven. If I belonged to a race whose males wept more readily than those of my own, I should be in a perpetual state of tears. Any of the recognised forms of pathos affects me with certainty, so it be presented without (as is sometimes the case) an overpowering invitation to hilarity. In these days, however, if one does not insist on sentiment all day long, if one has moods when some other emotion is agreeable, if one is not prepared to accept every profession for an achievement of pathos, one is called a "cynic." At times the pathos of Ouida has amused me, and I too was a cynic. But, as a rule, I think it genuine. Despised love, unmerited misfortunes, uncongenial surroundings—she has used all these motives with effect. The favourite pathos of her earlier books, that of the man who lives in a whirl of pleasure with a "broken heart," appeals very easily to a frivolous mood, and may be made ridiculous to anybody by a touch, but its contrasts may be used with inevitable effect, and so Ouida has sometimes used them. Dog-like fidelity, especially to a worthless man or woman, can be ridiculous to the coarse-grained only. Love of beauty unattainable, as of the country in one condemned to a sordid life in a town, can hardly be made absurd. But the mere fact of unrequited affection, being so very common, requires more than a little talent to be impressive, even to a sentimentalist, in a novel, and Ouida, I think, has made this common fact impressive over and over again, because, however imperfect be the expression, the feeling, being real, appeals without fail to a sympathetic imagination.

The two qualities, I think, which underlie the best of Ouida's work, and which must have always saved it from commonness, are a genuine and passionate love of beauty, as she conceives it, and a genuine and passionate hatred

of injustice and oppression. The former quality is constantly to be found in her, in her descriptions—accurate or not—of the country, in her scorn of elaborate ugliness as contrasted with homely and simple seemliness, in her railings against all the hideous works of man. It is not confined to physical beauty. Love of liberty, loyalty, self-sacrifice—those moral qualities which, *pace* the philosophers, must in our present stage of development seem beautiful to us—she has set herself to show us their beauty without stint of enthusiasm. Nobody can read her tales of Italian peasant life without perceiving how full is her hatred of inhumanity and wrong. In a book of essays recently published by her this love and hatred have an expression which in truth is not always judicious, but is not possibly to be mistaken. They are qualities which, I believe, are sufficiently rare in contemporary writers to deserve our attention and gratitude.

In fine, I take the merits in Ouida's books to balance their faults many times over. They are not finished works of art, they do not approach that state so nearly as hundreds of books with a hundred times less talent spent on them. Her faults, which are obvious, have brought it about that she is placed, in the general estimation of critics, below writers without a tenth of her ability. I should be glad if my appreciation may suggest to better critics than myself better arguments than mine for reconsidering their judgment. (pp. 167-76)

G. S. Street, "An Appreciation of Ouida," in The Yellow Book, *Vol. VI, July, 1895, pp. 167-76.*

Stephen Crane   (essay date 1897)

[*Crane was a prominent American novelist and short story writer whose works have been credited with marking the beginning of modern American Naturalism. His Civil War novel,* The Red Badge of Courage *(1895), is a classic of American literature that realistically depicts the psychological complexities of fear and courage on the battlefield. In the following essay originally published in* Book Buyer *in January 1897, Crane praises* Under Two Flags.]

Most of us forget Ouida. Childhood and childhood's different ideal is often required to make us rise properly to her height of sentiment. The poetic corner in the human head becomes too soon like some old dusty niche in a forgotten church. It is only occasionally that an ancient fragrance floats out to us, and then, usually, we do not recognize it. We apply some strange name and grin from the depths of our experience and wisdom. Perhaps it is rather a common habit to mistake a sort of a worldly complacence for knowledge.

For my part I had concluded that I had outgrown Ouida. I thought that I recognized the fact that her tears were carefully moulded globules of the best Cornish tin and that her splendors were really of the substance of shadows on a garden wall. And yet a late reading of **Under Two Flags** affected me like some old and honest liquor. It is certainly a refreshment. The characters in this book abandon themselves to virtue and heroism as the martyrs abandoned themselves to flames. Sacrifice appears to them as the natural course. Pain, death, dishonor, is counted of no moment so long as the quality of personal integrity is defended and preserved. Certainly we may get good from a book of this kind. It imitates the literary plan of the early peoples. They sang, it seems, of nobility of character. Today we sing of portières and champagne and gowns. *Under Two Flags* has to me, then, a fine ring in the gospel of life it preaches. I confess, of course, that I often find Beauty's perfections depressing. We men of doleful flaws are thrown into moods of profound gloom by the contemplation of such a bejewelled mind. We grow solemn and sad, and feel revengefully that we might like to touch a match to the hem of Beauty's sacred bath-robe, and see if we couldn't incite him to something profane and human— something like a real oath, or, at least, a fit of perfectly manly ill-temper.

Cigarette is finer. In Ouida's drawing of this secondary character we detect something accidental. With Cigarette the novelist did not take so much pains. She never intended Cigarette to be splendid, and perhaps this is why the girl appears to some of us as really the best character in the book. She is a figure of flesh among all these painted gods. She has imperfections, thank heaven, and it is very nice to come upon a good, sound imperfection when one has grown surfeited with the company of gods.

Nevertheless, with all the cavilling of our modern literary class, it is good to hear at times the song of the brave, and *Under Two Flags* is a song of the brave. To the eye of this time it is, of course, a thing of imperfect creation, but it voices nevertheless the old spirit of dauntless deed and sacrifice which is the soul of literature in every age, and we are not growing too tired to listen, although we try to believe so. (pp. 233-34)

> Stephen Crane, "Ouida's Masterpiece," in Stephen Crane: Uncollected Writings, *edited by Olov W. Fryckstedt, Uppsala, 1963, pp. 233-34.*

Max Beerbohm   (essay date 1897)

[*Although he lived until 1956, Beerbohm is chiefly associated with the fin de siècle period in English literature, more specifically with its lighter aspects of witty sophistication and mannered elegance. His temperament was urbane and satirical, and he excelled in both literary and artistic caricatures of his contemporaries. "Entertaining" in the most complimentary sense of the word, Beerbohm's criticism for* The Saturday Review—*where he was a long-time drama critic—everywhere indicates his scrupulously developed taste and unpretentious, fairminded response to literature. In the following essay, which was originally published in the* Saturday Review, *Beerbohm comments on critical responses to Ouida's novels and describes his fascination with her works.*]

The Democracy of Letters will exasperate or divert you, according to your temperament. Me it diverts merely. It does no harm to literature. Good books are still written, good critics still criticise, in the old, quiet way; and, if the good books are criticised chiefly by innumerable fools

hired to review an imponderable amount of trash, I do not really see that it matters at all. The trash itself is studied, now and again, by good critics and so becomes a springboard for good criticism, and it were unfair as it were useless, therefore, to shield good books from the consideration of ordinary reviewers. You may call it monstrous that a good writer should be at the mercy of such persons, but I doubt whether the good writer is himself aggrieved. He needs no mercy. And, as a matter of fact, the menaces hurled by the ordinary reviewers, whenever something new or strange confronts them, are very vain words indeed, and may at any moment be merged in clumsy compliments. A good critic—and by that term I mean a cultured man with brains and a temperament—may at any moment come by, and, if he praise, the ordinary reviewers, most receptive of all creatures, will praise also. I was glancing lately through a little book of essays, written by a lady. At the end of the book were printed press-notices about a volume of this lady's book of verse. Among these gems, and coruscating beyond the rest, was one graven with the name of Mr. William Sharp: "In its class I know no nobler or more beautiful sonnet than 'Renouncement;' and I have so considered it ever since the day when Rossetti (who knew it by heart), repeating it to me, added that it was one of the three finest sonnets ever written by women." Such a confession as Mr. William Sharp's is not to be found in the ordinary press-notice, but that is merely because the ordinary reviewer is of a less simple and sunny disposition than our friend, and speaks not save as one having his own authority. Nevertheless he is in no wise more clever than Mr. Sharp (or Captain Sumph), and very likely he did not even know Rossetti. Whether Mr. Sharp liked this sonnet before he met it under high auspices, is a point which may never be made clear, but there can be no doubt that the method of the ordinary reviewer is to curse what he does not understand, until it be explained to him. The element of comedy becomes yet stronger if the reviewers be subsequently assured that the explanation was all wrong. Who shall forget the chorus of adulation that rent the welkin for the essays of this very lady whose sonnet Mr. Sharp "so considered"? Two great writers had greatly praised her. I, humble person, mildly suggested that their praise had been excessive, and gave some good reasons for my opinion. Since then, the chorus has been palpably less loud, marred even by discordant voices. I do not pride myself particularly on this effect; I record it only because it gives a little instance of a great law.

Simpler, more striking, and more important, as an instance of reviewers' emptiness, is the position of Ouida, the latest of whose long novels, *The Massarenes,* had what is technically termed "a cordial reception"—a reception strangely different from that accorded to her novels thitherto. Ouida's novels have always, I believe, sold well. They contain qualities which have gained for them some measure of Corellian success. Probably that is why, for so many years, no good critic took the trouble to praise them. The good critic, with a fastidiousness which is perhaps a fault, often neglects those who can look after themselves; the very fact of popularity—he is not infallible—often repels him; he prefers to champion the deserving weak. And so, for many years, the critics, unreproved, were ridiculing a writer who had many qualities obvious to ridicule, many gifts that lifted her beyond their reach. At length it occurred to a critic of distinction, Mr. G. S. Street [see essay dated 1895], to write an "Appreciation of Ouida," which appeared in the *Yellow Book.* It was a shy, self-conscious essay, written somewhat in the tone of a young man defending the moral character of a barmaid who has bewitched him, but, for all its blushing diffidence, it was a very gentlemanly piece of work, and it was full of true and delicate criticism. I myself wrote, later, in praise of Ouida, and I believe that, at about the same time, Mr. Stephen Crane wrote an appreciation of his own in an American magazine [see excerpt dated 1897]. In a word, three intelligent persons had cracked their whips—enough to have called the hounds off. Nay more, the furious pack had been turned suddenly into a flock of nice sheep. It was pretty to see them gambling and frisking and bleating around *The Massarenes.*

Ouida is not, and never was, an artist. That, strangely enough, is one reason why she had been so little appreciated by the reviewers. The artist presents his ideas in the finest, strictest form, paring, whittling, polishing. In reading his finished work, none but a few persons note his artistic skill, or take pleasure in it for its own sake. Yet it is this very skill of his which enables the reviewers to read his work with pleasure. To a few persons, artistic skill is in itself delightful, insomuch that they tend to overrate its importance, neglecting the matter for the form. Art, in a writer, is not everything. Indeed, it implies a certain limitation. If a list of consciously artistic writers were drawn up, one would find that most of them were lacking in great force of intellect or of emotion; that their intellects were restricted, their emotions not very strong. Writers of enormous vitality never are artistic: they cannot pause, they must always be moving swiftly forward. Mr. Meredith, the only living novelist in England who rivals Ouida in sheer vitality, packs tight all his pages with wit, philosophy, poetry, and psychological analysis. His obscurity, like that of Carlyle and Browning, is due less to extreme subtlety than to the plethoric abundance of his ideas. He cannot stop to express himself. If he could, he might be more popular. The rhapsodies of Mr. Swinburne, again, are so overwhelmingly exuberant in their expression that no ordinary reader can cope with them; the ordinary reader is stunned by them before he is impressed. When he lays down the book and regains consciousness, he has forgotten entirely what it was all about. On the other hand reticence, economy, selection, and all the artistic means may be carried too far. Too much art is, of course, as great an obstacle as too little art; and Pater, in his excessive care for words, is as obscure to most people as are Carlyle and Browning, in their carelessness. It is to him who takes the mean of these two extremes, to that author who expresses himself simply, without unnecessary expansion or congestion, that appreciation is most readily and spontaneously granted.

Well! For my own part, I am a dilettante, a *petit maître.* I love best in literature delicate and elaborate ingenuities of form and style. But my preference does not keep me from paying due homage to Titanic force, and delighting, now and again, in its manifestation. I wonder at Ouida's novels, and I wonder still more at Ouida. I am staggered when I think of that lurid sequence of books and short sto-

Lithograph of a Life Guardsman, 1860.

ries and essays which she has poured forth so swiftly, with such irresistible *élan.* What manner of woman can Ouida be? A woman who writes well never writes much. Even Sappho spent her whole life in writing and rewriting some exquisite, isolated verses, which, with feminine tact, she handed down to posterity as mere fragments of her work. In our own day, there are some ladies who write a large number of long books, but I am sure that the "sexual novel" or the "political novel," as wrought by them, must be as easy to write as it is hard to read. Ouida is essentially feminine, as much *une femme des femmes* as Jane Austen or "John Oliver Hobbes," and it is indeed remarkable that she should yet be endowed with force and energy so exuberant and indefatigable. All her books are amazing in their sustained vitality. Vitality is, indeed, the most patent, potent factor in her work. Her pen is more inexhaustibly prolific than the pen of any other writer; it gathers new strength of its every dip into the ink-pot. Ouida need not, and could not, husband her unique endowments, and a man might as well shake his head over the daily rising of the indefatigable sun, or preach Malthusianism in a rabbit-warren, as counsel Ouida to write less. Her every page is a riot of unpolished epigrams and unpolished poetry of vision, with a hundred discursions and redundancies. She cannot say a thing once; she must repeat it again and again, and, with every repetition, so it seems to me, she says it with greater force and charm. Her style is a veritable cascade, in comparison with which the waters come down at Lodore as tamely as they come down at Shanklin. And, all the while, I never lose interest in her story, constructed with that sound professional knowledge, which the romancers of this later generation, with their vague and halting modes, would probably regard as old-fashioned. Ouida grips me with her every plot, and—since she herself so strenuously believes in them—I can believe even in her characters. True, they are not real, when I think of them in cold blood. They are abstractions, like the figures in early Greek tragedies and epics before psychology was thought of—things of black or white, or colourless things to illustrate the working of destiny, elemental puppets for pity or awe. Ouida does not pretend to the finer shades of civilized psychology. Her men and women of Mayfair are shadows, as I see when I am not under the direct spell of her writing, and she reproduces real life only when she is dealing with childish or half-savage natures—Cigarette the *vivandière,* Redempta the gipsy, Italian peasants, dogs and horses. She cares for the romance and beauty and terror of life, not for its delicate shades and inner secrets. Her books are, in the true sense of the word, romances, though they are not written in Wardour Street. The picturesqueness of modern life, transfigured by imagination, embellished by fancy, that is her *forte.* She involves her stock-figures—the pure girl, the wicked woman, the adorable hero and the rest—in a series of splendid adventures. She makes her protagonist a guardsman that she may describe, as she alone can, steeplechases and fox-hunts and horses running away with phaetons. Or she makes him a diplomat, like Strathmore, or a great tenor, like Corèze, or a Queen's messenger, like Erceldoune, or something else—anything so that it be lurid and susceptible of romance. She ranges hither and thither over all countries, snatching at all languages, realising all scenes. Her information is as wide as Macaulay's, and her slips in local colour are but the result of a careless omniscience. That she should have referred to "the pointing of the *digito monstrari,*" and headed one of her chapters with the words "Thalassis! Thalassis!" and made the Queen present at a Levée, and thrown one or two false side-lights on the Oxford Eights Week, may seem very terrible to the dullards who think that criticism consists in spotting mistakes. But the fact remains that Ouida uses her great information with extraordinary effect. Her delight in beautiful things has been accounted to her for vulgarity by those who think that a writer "should take material luxury for granted." But such people forget, or are unable to appreciate, the difference between the perfunctory faking of description, as practised by the average novelist—as who should say "soft carpets," "choice wines," "priceless Tintorettos"—and description which is the result of true vision. No writer was ever more finely endowed than Ouida with the love and knowledge of all kinds of beauty in art and nature. There is nothing vulgar in having a sense of beauty—so long as you have it. Ouida's descriptions of boudoirs in palaces are no more vulgar nor less beautiful than her descriptions of lakes and mountains.

With their fair, silken moustachios and their glengarries and their velvet jackets, Ouida's guardsmen, pegs for luxury and romance, are vastly stimulating. I should like to have peered through the cloud of "Turkish" that did always involve them, and have seen Lord Vaulerois tossing aside a pile of millefleurs-scented notes and quaffing curaçoa, as he pondered the chances of Peach-Bloom for the Guards' Steeplechase, or the last mad caprice of Léla Liette! Too languid, as he lay there on his divan, to raise the vinaigrette to his nostrils, he was one who had served his country through more than one campaign on the boiling plains of the Sahara; he who, in the palace of a *nouveau riche,* had refused the bedchamber assigned to him, on the plea that he could not sleep under a false Fragonard, had often camped *à la belle étoile* in the waste places of Central Asia; thrice he had passed through the D. C. as calmly as he would swim the Hellespont or toss off a beaker of rosy Comet-Wine; with his girlish hands that Duchesses envied he had grappled lions in the jungle, and would think nothing of waiting for hours, heedless of frost and rain, to bring down some rocketer he had marked in a warm corner at Crichel or Longleat. Familiar with Cairene Bazaars as with the matchless deer-forests of Dunrobin, with the brown fens round Melton Mowbray as with the incomparable grace and brilliance of the Court of Hapsburg; *bienvenu* in the Vatican as in the Quirinal; deferred to by Dips and Décorés in all the *salons* of Europe, and before whom even Queens turned to coquettes and Kings to comrades; careless, caressed, *insouciant;* of all men the beloved or envied; inimitable alike in his grace of person and in the perfection of his taste; passing from the bow-windows of St. James's to the faded and fetid alleys of Stamboul, from the Quartier Bréda to the Newski Prospect, from the citron-groves of Cashmere, the gay fuchsia-gardens of Simla, to the hideous chaos of Illinois, a region scorched by the sirocco, swept by inextinguishable prairie-fires, sepultured in the white shrouds of remorseless blizzards, and—as though that were not enough—befouled with the fumes and crushed with the weight of a thousand loathsome cities, which are swift as the mushroom in their growth, far more deadly than the *fungus fatalis* of the Midi—it was here, passing with easy nonchalance as the foal passes from one pasture to another, with a flight swifter than the falcon's, luxurious in its appurtenance as a Shah's seraglio; it was here, in these whirling circles of intrigue and pleasure and romance, and in this span of an illimitable nomady, that flew the nights and days of Philip, nineteenth Marquis of Vaulerois, as the world knew him—"Fifi" of the First Life.

I am glad that in her later books Ouida has not deserted "the First Life." She is still the same Ouida, has lost none of her romance, none of her wit and poetry, her ebullitions of pity and indignation. The old "naughtiness" and irresponsibility which were so strange a portent in the Medio-Victorian days, and kept her books away from the drawing-room table, seem to have almost disappeared; and, in complement of her love of luxury for its own sake, there is some social philosophy, diatribes against society for its vulgar usage of luxury. But, though she has become a mentor, she is still Ouida, still that unique, flamboyant lady, one of the miracles of modern literature. After all these years, she is still young and swift and strong, towering head and shoulders over all the other women (and all but one or two of the men) who are writing English novels. That the reviewers have tardily trumpeted her is amusing, but no cause for congratulation. I have watched their attitude rather closely. They have the idiot's cunning and seek to explain their behaviour by saying that Ouida has entirely changed. Save in the slight respect I have noted, Ouida has not changed at all. She is still Ouida. That is the high compliment I would pay her. (pp. 103-15)

> Max Beerbohm, "Ouida," in his More, fourth edition, 1921. Reprint by Books for Libraries Press, Inc., 1967, pp. 101-15.

Frederic Taber Cooper   (essay date 1903)

[*An American educator, biographer, and editor, Cooper served for many years as literary critic at the* Bookman, *a popular early twentieth-century literary magazine. In the following essay, he examines the reasons for the decline in popularity of Ouida's novels.*]

On a recent rainy day, the usual noonday crowd that loiters before a certain Ann Street book shop was missing. The bargain counters were shrouded in waterproof covers; the better class of books had been withdrawn indoors from the weather. Only the penny box remained exposed, a pile of tattered magazines idly fluttering their leaves in the wind and absorbing the water that dripped from an ineffectual awning. On the top of the pile lay a bedraggled copy of the Seaside Library, the front cover torn across, exposing the title *Syrlin,* by "Ouida," Author of *Under Two Flags, Signa,* etc. To one whom these words reminded of an early and forgotten enthusiasm, it seemed but a pious act to rescue an old acquaintance from its fallen state.

The incident would not be worth chronicling, if it were not in a measure typical of Ouida's own changed fortunes. Twenty years ago she enjoyed a vogue somewhat analogous to that of Marie Corelli to-day in this country, or of Georges Ohnet in France. It seems rather curious now to recall the avidity with which she was read, although not one reader out of twelve had the candour to acknowledge openly the fascination of her original, perverse and at times rather hysterical style. To-day she has literally declined to the penny box; she is relegated to the garret and the second-hand dealer, along with the old coats and hats and other fashions of yesterday. In the early eighties, critics thought it worth while to inveigh against her false ethics and dangerous morals; anxious mothers were careful to shield their daughters from the corruption of *Moths* and *Puck* and *Friendship.* To-day such anxiety would be superfluous. The younger generation does not read Ouida. It finds her style as tediously verbose, as hopelessly out of date, as *Clarissa Harlowe* or *Sir Charles Grandison.* For every ten young women of to-day who can tell you that Blanche Bates made a capital Cigarette and rode a real horse, there is scarcely one who thinks it worth remembering that *Under Two Flags* was originally written by Ouida.

But to revert once more to that dilapidated old copy of *Syrlin,* the really interesting thing about it is the critical discernment shown upon the title-page. Whoever formulated it, whether author or publisher, hit upon the two volumes which of all that Ouida wrote best deserve to be remembered and preserved. *Syrlin* itself was not, even rela-

tively, a significant work. It practically brought to a close the long series of novels which began with *Granville de Vigne* and contain some of the best, as well as some of the worst, elements of sensational fiction that the latter half of the nineteenth century has produced. There is probably no other writer of her generation who so deliberately alienated his literary birthright, so openly prostituted a talent of uncommon worth to pander to a perverted taste for sensationalism. No one can read *Under Two Flags* without feeling that the woman who could write that story possessed at least some grains of that leaven with which the world's great stories of adventure have always been leavened—that she was one of those authors who not only create a little world of their own, but believe in its reality; who look into their brains as into a magic mirror, and record all the phantasmagoria that they see passing there, with a conviction that is contagious, especially if one brings youth and enthusiasm to the reading of it. Anatole France once confessed, with characteristic whimsicality, that the best novel he ever read was a half-forgotten old romance, read while a schoolboy surreptitiously "between the pages of a Greek Lexicon," but that he had been careful never to read it again. *Under Two Flags* is a rather exceptional book; in a large measure it is free from Ouida's besetting faults; and the story is carried to a finish with a verve and an audacity which somehow compel admiration. But aside from this story, it may be taken as an axiom that if any one remembers having read Ouida at twenty with a quickened pulse, he will be wise to follow the example of Anatole France and not reread her at forty.

The reason for the decline of Ouida's popularity is not far to seek. It is not merely because she was outside of the literary movement of her time that she founded no school and leaves no successor. It is not because her creed was a romanticism that was French rather than English—a romanticism that was already going out of fashion in France when she began to write. Many another writer has lived to see the death of his own popularity. There is no better instance than that of Paul de Kock, the spoiled child of a whole generation of readers. And yet De Kock still lives after a fashion, because he pictured the life of his time— the *bourgeois* life of Paris half a century ago—with a thoroughness not to be found elsewhere. Ouida's cardinal sin is the inherent falsity of her portrayal of life; and it is due partly to ignorance, but chiefly to an obliquity of mental vision, a sort of intellectual astigmatism which results in a view of the world at large so distorted that at times it approaches caricature. Throughout her books it is a question which is the more surprising characteristic, her superficiality or her self-assurance. The idea of restraining her plots within the bounds of her own knowledge and experience of life seems never to have occurred to her. There is no tangle of passions so intricate, no situation so extravagant, no human tragedy so grim and gruesome, but what she essays to paint it, with the proverbial courage and complacency of ignorance. Her description of a field hospital during the Crimean war, with its heaped-up dead and dying, is a thoroughly characteristic instance:

> There they lay, packed as closely together as dead animals in a slaughter-house; some on the floor that was slippery with blood like a sham-

ble; some on pallets, saturated with the stream that carried away their life in its deadly flow; some on straw, crimson and noisome, the home of the most horrible vermin; some dead, hastily flung down to be out of the way, black and swollen, a mass of putrefaction, the eyes forced from their sockets, the tongue protruding, the features distended in hideous grotesqueness; others dead, burned and charred in the explosion, a heap of blanched bones and gory clothes and blackened flesh, the men who but a few hours before had been instinct with health and hope and gallant fearless life. Living men in horrible companionship with these corpses, writhing in torture which there was no hand to relieve, no help from heaven or earth to aid, with their jagged and broken limbs twisted and powerless, were calling for water, for help, for pity; shrieking out in wild delirium or disconnected prayer the name of the woman they had loved or the God that had forsaken them.

Now it needs no special perspicuity to realise that writing of this sort is not real art; that Ouida had no clear-cut picture of the scene she was trying to describe, no definite memories from which to draw, and that she supplied their place with a tempestuous whirlwind of ugly words. In all that mass of generalisations there is not a single specific, concrete fact that stands out in clear relief, not a single detail of personal observation of the sort that helps one to see. Such writing needs no visit to a battlefield or hospital; it may be concocted at ease by one's own fireside with the help of a vivid imagination and a riotous vocabulary. These gifts Ouida certainly has in full measure. Word follows word and sentence follows sentence, an unchecked torrent, an inexhaustible flood of comparisons and superlatives, redundant, superfluous, wearisome. She seizes upon an idea and rings the changes upon it until its possibilities are exhausted. Redundancy has no terrors for her. She compels attention by the very insistence of her iteration. Her description of her characters, even minor characters, will often run through two or three pages—and even then the subject is not necessarily closed, but may be reopened a chapter or so later, with a few supplementary paragraphs of comparisons. None of her personages is ever a simple, average human being, just passably good or bad, like the casual person in real life. All of them, men and women alike, have the attributes of at least a score of ancient gods and modern heroes. When she wishes to tell us that Chandos, for instance, had a high forehead, fair hair, contemplative eyes and a selfish mouth, she writes instinctively that "The brow was magnificent, meditative enough for Plato's; the rich and gold-hued hair bright as any Helen's; the gaze of the eyes in rest thoughtful as might be that of Marcus Aurelius; the mouth, insouciant and epicurean as the lips of a Catullus." Similarly, the Princess Vera, a minor character in *Friendship,* is not merely fair and graceful. She is "one of the loveliest women that ever brightened a court;" she has "a face like the Cenci, a walk like a young Diana's; a smile like a child's, a grace like a flower's, eyes like a fawn's, fancies like a poet's, and a form that Titian would have given to Venus."

There is another character who plays an important rôle in

Friendship, the Lady Joan Challoner, whose description is worth quoting at some length, for all unconsciously it forms a capital satire upon Ouida herself:

> She has some odds and ends of real art and real history jumbled together in her brain, like the many-coloured snips and shreds in a tailor's drawer in Spain. But they were all tumbled about pell-mell, and the wrong colours came up at the wrong time. . . . All her fiddles are Cremonas; all her sprigged china is Saxe, all her ugly plates are Palissy, all her naked people are Michael Angelo's, all her tapestries are Gobelin; all her terra cottas are Pentelic marbles. Now that is a mistake, you know; the world is too little for so very much treasure. She forgets that she makes her diamonds as cheap as pebbles.

Here in a few clever phrases we have two of Ouida's chief offences: She, too, makes her diamonds as cheap as pebbles, and piles on her historical colouring pell-mell. She ostentatiously spreads a cheap veneer of erudition over all she writes; her pages bristle with italics, with French and German and Italian, Latin and Greek; with the names of strange people and strange towns. They give the impression of having been written with a Baedeker in one hand and a biographical dictionary in the other. She piles up the names of dead and gone philosophers and poets and statesmen as though they had been the chosen comrades of her early years. She flings in references to half the capitals of Europe, with the familiar, half-patronising air of a weary, much-travelled citizen of the world. On the whole, the great wonder is that, with all these hit-or-miss references to history, science and art, she makes comparatively so few egregious blunders. The casual reader is seldom aware over what dangerously thin ice she glides. It is only now and then that she ventures a step or two beyond the limits of her classical phrase-book or her dictionary of biography and stumbles into such blunders as in *Chandos,* where she writes gravely: "Other men had for their motto *pro patria,* but he took for his *pro ego*"—apparently construing *ego* as an ablative singular of the first declension. Similarly curious are her ideas about the death of Petronius, about whom every reader of *Quo Vadis* could give her useful information. "It could have been no fun for Nero to torture him," she makes Chandos remark. "The old fellow never once winced."

Usually, however, Ouida covered up her limitations with a good deal of skill, as far as facts and dates and acute accents are concerned. It was in the broader generalities of life that she betrays herself. When she chose to write of the places she loved and the people she really knew, her mental vision was sufficiently clear. When she pictured Florence and the Maremma and the hills above the Arno, when she laid her scenes among the simple peasantry of Italy, she wrote pages that are pleasant even now to linger over, on account of their straightforward sincerity. But she perversely chose for the most part to write of a life that she obviously did not know—the most exclusive and aristocratic circles of London and Paris, Rome and St. Petersburg. From Trouville to Monte Carlo, from the Riviera to the Tyrol, she painted the same distorted, corrupt, fantastic picture of an opéra-bouffe aristocracy, wearing their vices openly, like a flamboyant suit of motley. Her lords and barons and dukes are usually bores and libertines and gamblers, who "spend the night over cards and wine, and gaze with hot, rcd eyes upon the rising sun." Her favourite heroes are combinations of cad and prig. Worse even than her men are her women, her titled ladies who are demimondaines in all but name, or else cold icicles of virtue, potential nuns who have somehow missed their vocation. Her young girls marry in babe-like ignorance of fundamental physical facts, and spend the rest of their lives in shuddering and "hoping that God will let them die soon." Society is a cesspool, virtue one of the lost arts, truth is forgotten at the bottom of her well, love and friendship mere figments of speech. To know Ouida at her worst, one must read *Granville de Vigne,* the book that first brought her into notice, and that later was published under a changed title, *Held in Bondage.* Ouida has always posed as something of a socialist, a bohemian, a foe of the upper classes. Yet it is obvious that she was proud of her De Vigne. He must be taken as representing her conception of what a true gentleman, an aristocrat of purest lineage, ought to be. In his student days, De Vigne is responsible for the ruin of a farmer's daughter, a casual occurrence mentioned not as being derogatory to her hero, but as showing the unreasonableness of the girl in expecting a De Vigne to stoop to marry her. The incident counts for so little with him that when he meets her again, five years later, he fails to recognise her and is tricked into a marriage; but learning his mistake too late, leaves her at the altar. Years later he meets another woman whom he learns to love—a young girl whom he is bound in honour to respect and protect. Concealing the fact that he is a married man, he urges his suit until he discovers that another man is entertaining designs as dishonourable as his own. As De Vigne is a model gentleman, it is interesting to learn what Ouida thinks he should do under these circumstances. Meeting the other man casually, he takes him by the collar, shakes him, thrashes him with his riding whip "as a man would thrash a cur," lifts him and throws him with care and precision down the entire length of a long flight of stone stairs, and then deliberately walks down after him and kicks him when he lies on the ground. And the incident is retailed afterward by admiring friends at his club as the fitting action of a finished gentleman.

It would be unfair, however, to judge Ouida by this first raw, crude effort. Its faults are in a measure the faults of her work as a whole, but it lacks the redeeming qualities of her later books. Ouida's novels group themselves conveniently into three classes, of which *Under Two Flags, Moths* and *Signa* may be taken respectively as representative novels. The first group includes mainly her earlier stories, all characterised by their extravagance of plot and multiplicity of adventure. The hero is usually a wanderer, a self-made exile, meekly bowing to the hard decree of Fate or voluntarily assuming the burden of another's sin. In *Granville de Vigne* he is fleeing to India to escape the memory of his wretched marriage; in *Chandos* he is stripped of his inheritance and driven out, a penniless wanderer, through the malignity of a secret enemy, who proves in the end to be a bastard brother. In *Under Two Flags,* also, it is a brother's sin, the forgery of a cheque, that drove Bertie Cecil to sacrifice his inheritance and bury himself alive in the ranks of the Chasseurs d'Afrique.

In *Wanda,* it is a patrician wife's discovery of her baseborn husband's parentage that sends him from her only to come creeping back and live the life of an outlaw, hiding in the mountain caverns of her estate merely for the joy of knowing that he is near to her. In *Tricotrin* the motive for exile is so slight, so flimsy, that one feels it is less a motive than a pretext. The hero is a born nomad, an Ishmaelite by choice. It was not because while a lad he was unjustly accused of theft that he abandoned a fortune and a title, but because the rôle of a modern Wandering Jew was one that appealed to him. *Tricotrin,* it may be added parenthetically, is in a measure a transition work. It has in certain chapters much of the simplicity, the sympathy for the peasantry and the love of nature that characterise Ouida's Italian stories *Signa* and *Pascarel* and *In Maremma;* and on the other hand, the development of the character of Vera, Tricotrin's waif, classes it in the second general group of her novels, stories that Ouida probably flattered herself were psychological studies of women.

This second group contains the volumes which called forth the greatest amount of protest at the time of their appearance. In forming a revised estimate of them from the vantage-ground of a score of years, what one regrets chiefly is that such good material was sacrificed to such a faulty method. The plots of books like *Moths, Guilderoy, Princess Napraxine, Syrlin* are full of opportunity. At the hands of a Bourget or a Prévost, they could have been developed into character studies worthy to take rank with *Mensonges* or *L'Automne d'une femme.* As it is, they are marred by the obvious falsity of all that the characters say or do. It is all so palpably evolved, not from real life, but from Ouida's inner consciousness. Besides, she disqualified herself for serious consideration as an exponent of her own sex by the deliberate extravagance of her whole attitude toward women:

> Useless as butterflies, corroding as moths; untrue even to lovers and friends, because incapable of understanding any truth; caring only for physical comfort and mental intoxication; kissing like Judas, and denying in danger like Peter; tired of living, yet afraid of dying; believing, some in priests and some in physiologists, but none at all in virtue; sent to sleep by chlorodine and kept awake by raw meat and dry wines; cynical at twenty and exhausted at thirty, yet choosing rather to drop dead in the harness of pleasure than fall out of the chariot race for an instant; taking their passions as they take sherry in the morning and bitters before dinner; pricking their sated senses with the spices of lust or jealousy, and calling the unholy fever love; having outworn every form of excitement except the gambler's, which never palls, which they will still pursue when they shall have not a real tooth in their mouths nor a real hair on their heads, the women of modern society are, perhaps, at once the most feverish and the most frivolous, the basest and the feeblest, offspring of a false civilisation.

In *Moths,* the volume in which this curious tirade is to be found, there is the case of a young girl, all idealism and innocence, forced by a mother's ingenious lies to marry a bestial Russian before she even knows the significance of what she is made to do. "She abhorred him, yet she accepted him. No mere obedience could account for that acceptance without some weakness or some cupidity of nature. It hardened him against her; it spoiled her lovely, pure childhood in his eyes; it made her shudder from him seem half hypocrisy." Here is a situation that needs the keenest intuition, the subtlest understanding of a woman's nature. Ouida handles it in a way that makes cheap melodrama. No woman ever lived before who was quite so chaste as Vere, no mother quite so heartless as Lady Dolly, no husband so brutal as Zouroff, no lover so seductive as Corrèze, the tenor whom Zouroff shoots through the throat, and who ultimately elopes with the heroine. There is a staccato note throughout the book, a superlative tone that constantly reminds one that these are not real living, breathing human beings, but puppets symbolising the extremes of human virtues and vices. *Princess Napraxine* is meant to be a study of a woman too cold and selfish ever to give real happiness to any man. She is true to her husband, not through virtue but indifference. She will not elope with the man who loves her and whom at times she half believes she loves, because she is sure that within six months she will be tired of him. And so Othmar out of pique marries a young girl who, unhappily for herself, really loves him, and two deaths must needs intervene before Princess Napraxine finds out that love is at least worth the trouble of a trial. If she were a shade less stereotyped, if she did not always move just so languidly and smile just so cruelly, if, in short, she ever showed herself capable of being swayed seriously by any emotion, good or bad, other than selfishness, she would be one of the most interesting of Ouida's whole gallery of women.

Freda Avillion, in *Syrlin,* is a near cousin to Nadine Napraxine—another of those women whom Ouida paints in sheer scorn of her sex. Lord Avillion's infidelities are notorious, yet his wife is not troubled by them, nor by the knowledge that the world, her world, knows them, and knows, too, that she knows them. The one thing which would trouble her would be the necessity of dropping the mask and owning her knowledge to the world. There is a singer in the story, Syrlin—another of those irresponsible, Bohemian characters like Corrèze and Tricotrin and Pascarel, whom Ouida likes to paint, because she can make them her mouthpiece to denounce the follies of a sinful world. Syrlin loves Freda, and so long as his love is a discreet, respectful homage she allows her heart to soften toward him. But Syrlin does not understand her world nor her code. He thinks to please her by avenging her husband's faithlessness by an insult so subtle, so studied, yet so unmistakable, that it brings upon her the very notoriety which she would have given her life to avoid. It is the one unpardonable offence, and Syrlin, when he realises his blunder, promptly executes his own death sentence. Taken separately, Ouida's studies of women are not without discernment and interest. But it is a mistake to read too many of them at once. Their burden is essentially the same— "there is not one feminine thing in a thousand that can love truly." And when that one is found she squanders her love upon a Guilderoy, who wearies of her; a Prince Ioris, who would have her share him with another, as in *Friendship;* an Este, who forgets her, as in *In Maremma.*

Whether Ouida's Italian stories are of greater or less literary value than her other works is a matter of individual opinion. Certainly they have a flavour of their own, so distinct and individual that it is difficult to realise that *Signa* and *Under Two Flags* were written by the same hand. It is worth while to speak of *Signa* at some length, for it is a comparatively little known volume, and yet one which might be read with pleasure by all who have ever come under the spell of Florentine skies or felt the poetry and the mystery of the Etruscan hills that overlook the Arno. Ouida knows every inch of the ground covered in this book, and loves it, too, the quaint old hillside town of Signa and the simplicity and industry and bitter poverty of its peasant population. The story concerns the life of a young musical genius, a peasant lad, who promises to become a second Mozart. The opening scene stands out with special vividness. Two brothers, Lippo and Bruno, come upon the dead body of Pippa, their missing sister, beside the Arno on the night of the flood. It is years since Pippa had disappeared from home, and now in her hour of need she has struggled back to die almost at the threshold, her nameless child, still living, in her arms. The brothers save the child, but they let the floods of Arno bear off poor Pippa and the family shame with her. Bruno, a sullen, solitary, plodding farmer, with an honest heart, faithfully pays year after year one-half his earnings to his cringing, lying, smooth-mannered brother for the maintenance of little Signa, until he learns how the little lad is being systematically beaten and starved and neglected. Then he takes the boy to his own home and gradually learns the novel charm of having some human creature to love and protect. Bruno's dream for the boy is to make him a farmer like himself, a well-to-do farmer with a bit of land of his own; but Signa has other and loftier dreams; there are voices constantly singing in his ears, music sweeter than the songs of the people or the voices of birds. He must go away to the big cities, where he may study and become great. And Bruno, dully comprehending, yet questioning the wisdom of it, lets him go. His fame is that of a meteor, a brief blaze of triumph, ending in the ruin wrought by a female thing who is as false as she is fair. And Bruno is guilty of the crowning blunder of thinking that the fundamental problems of life may be solved with a few inches of cold steel. What one remembers as long as anything else in the book is the closing sentence, which gives in epitome much of Ouida's philosophy of life:

> Signa can count her age by many centuries. Before the Latins were she knew Etruria; but, many as be her memories, she remembers no other thing than this; there is no justice that she knows of anywhere. Signa is wise. She lets the world go by, and sleeps.

It is too early to declare whether any considerable number of Ouida's novels are likely to live. Judged by the standards of to-day, there is many a novelist with better prospects of immortality, who might be more easily spared. Her genius is of an erratic type that is most likely to have justice done it by those who do not stop to measure and weigh and analyse, but simply read straight on, yielding themselves to the magnetism which, for some readers, she undoubtedly possesses. It is comparatively easy to pick flaws in her style, her ethics and her plots—far easier than to explain why she now and then takes the most sceptical reader captive and sweeps him along in the whirlwind and torrent of her descriptions, thrills him with impossible standards of faith and trust and honour, and makes him accept with the credulity of a little child adventures that his sober judgment tells him are a tissue of grotesque impossibilities. Such deeds of bravery and devotion and self-sacrifice as are recorded in *Under Two Flags* are not to be met with in real life. Yet there is something rather splendid about the very audacity of the book. It is full of scenes not easily forgotten—the spirited horserace of the early chapters, the scene of the accusation when Bertie, charged with forgery, realises the truth that the forger is his own brother; the whole sequence of scenes between Bertie, the obscure, unknown Chasseur d'Afrique, and the French officer who hates him—that prolonged and silent duel of clashing will powers between the colonel who is a boor and the private soldier who, through misery and loneliness and degradation, cannot forget that he is a gentleman. Finally, the insult offered to the woman he loves, the avenging blow in the face of his superior officer—man to man at last, just for that one instant—the arrest, the sentence, and then Cigarette's wonderful quest for a reprieve; the mad daring of her race against time to deliver it; and in the moment of triumph, the death that she herself would have chosen—a soldier's death for the girl whose proudest titles had been those of "Child of the Army" and "Soldier of France." It is good now and then to meet with books that stir one's pulses and awaken an enthusiastic thrill, even if they do sin against logic and probability and established literary canons. Such books are so few and far between that the world will not willingly let them die. And that is why it is safe to predict that so long as Ouida is remembered at all she will be remembered as author of *Under Two Flags.* (pp. 153-59)

> *Frederic Taber Cooper, "Ouida—an Estimate," in* The Bookman, *New York, Vol. XVII, April, 1903, pp. 153-59.*

Carl Van Vechten   (essay date 1921)

[*Van Vechten, an American critic and novelist, was one of the first established white authors after William Dean Howells to take a serious and active role in studying and promoting the works of black writers, musicians, and artists. Noted during the early 1920s for his sophisticated novels about New Yorkers, Van Vechten's most famous work is* Nigger Heaven (1926), *a novel set in Harlem. In the following excerpt, originally written in 1921, he offers a high opinion of Ouida's literary achievement.*]

Many of my literary liaisons have been belated. A number of my favourite books have been other men's mistresses before they have become mine. More than once I have blushed for my comfortable failure to keep up with the times, even the old times, although, occasionally, I remind myself with some pride that I read Daudet's Sappho before the prescribed age of twenty. This, however, was an exceptional performance. I can always look back and discover a new face. At ninety I expect to sit before my fire, dallying amorously with some overlooked masterpiece.

Sometimes (and with what delight!), I hit upon an entirely new name. That is a real experience in a wanton career of bibliophilic amours. More often, however, not only have I long been aware of the existence of the future beguiler of my intimate moments but also a volume or two by this author has snoozed patiently on my shelves, silently waiting the magic hour when its pages may begin to call to me with the voice of seduction. Certainly I cannot say that I remember ever having been ignorant of Ouida, but in some hazy way her work was associated in my mind with that of the Duchess, Laura Jean Libbey, and Bertha M. Clay. Little by little, however, I became conscious that this name fell frequently from the lips of intelligent people. It was borne in upon me, insistently if slowly, that I had missed something, just what was not too apparent, but something important beyond any manner of doubt. Joseph Hergesheimer had read Ouida; Max Beerbohm had read Ouida, and not only devoted an essay to her [see essay dated 1897] but also invented his most celebrated dedication in her honour; Edgar Fawcett had read Ouida; so had Stephen Crane, Vernon Lee, G. S. Street, and Arthur Symons. Wilfred Scawen Blunt and Auberon Herbert read and admired her. G. K. Chesterton, reader for Fisher Unwin in 1899, wrote in his report of *The Waters of Edera,* "Though it is impossible not to smile at Ouida, it is equally impossible not to read her."

In the course of time, my curiosity was aroused. It behooved me, I began to believe, to follow in the footsteps of this illustrious, if somewhat incongruous, company. My mood was excellent for the enterprise. I was weary of modern fiction, tainted with Freud and Fabre, weary of James Joyce and Dorothy Richardson and D. H. Lawrence, weary of Romain Rolland and his quest for a perfect world; what better opportunity to sample the simpler diversions of a novelist who had given as much pleasure to ingenuous chambermaids as she had to the recondite author of *The Happy Hypocrite?* (pp. 47-8)

Now those who have preceded me in this adventure, I discover, applaud Ouida for qualities she undoubtedly possesses: her passionate hatred of injustice, her love for animals, her feeling for beauty, and her skill in evoking the atmosphere of Italy. Indubitably, she assimilated and reproduced in a remarkable manner the spirit of this country. Even Henry James has given his grudging admiration to her handling of the Italian scene. Her sympathy for the peasant is responsible for many a nice piece of prose. In her review of the work of F. Marion Crawford, for example, she contradicts his assertion that the Italians are lacking in imagination: "This is but partially true; I am not sure that it is true at all. Their modern poetry is beautiful, more beautiful than that of any other nation. Their popular songs are poetic and impassioned as those of no other nation are, and one may hear among their peasantry expressions of singular beauty of sentiment and phrase. A woman of middle age, a contadina, said to me once, 'So long as one's mother lives, one's youth is never quite gone, for there is always somebody for whom one is young.' A rough, rude man, a day-labourer, who knew not a letter and spent all his life bent over his spade or plough, said to me once, one lovely night in spring, as he looked up at the full moon, 'How beautiful she is! But she has no heart.

She sees us toiling and groaning and suffering down here, and she is always fair and calm, and never weeps!' Another said once, when a tree was hard to fell, 'He is sorry to come away, it has been his field so long.' And when a flock of solan geese flew over our land, going from the marshes to the mountains on their homeward way, and descended to rest, the peasants did not touch them: 'They are tired, poor souls,' said one of the women; 'one must not grudge them the soil for their lodging!' " Her humanitarianism included a horror of war, oppressive taxation of the poor, vivisection, Joseph Chamberlain, and the German Emperor. She was a warm admirer of Georges Darien, the French anti-militarist novelist, the Barbusse, the John Dos Passos of the Franco-Prussian war. She deplored the desecration of the Tuscan country-side and the vandalism prevailing in Italian cities. While I am by no means blind to these æsthetic and moral virtues in her well-rounded work, I lay my wreath on another altar. My joy in Ouida is more akin to that of the chambermaid: I take an unfeigned delight in her reports of the pleasant lives of the idle rich. (pp. 49-50)

She described the homes of the rich to the last marble staircase and the Aubusson carpeted pavilion where the guests indulged in wicked merrymaking; she counted every pearl on the throat of her adventuress and, having added them, poured them over her pages, prodigally, by the bucketful. Exotic flowers, priceless jewels, orphic baubles, elaborate toilets, and unparalleled foods are carted past the eye until the vision is surfeited, but it is only for the purpose, Ouida almost convinced herself, of showing the reader how empty is the life of the very rich. She has not convinced one reader. Ouida wrote of a life she hungered to enjoy, she catalogued precious stones she wanted to wear, she painted portraits of men she desired to embrace. Nor was this merely the unintelligent envy of the outsider. She was enough on the inside to observe the objects of her jealous attention at close range and she has set down their existence with an idealization of its power and fascination which, even when she most moralizes over its fatal rottenness, has almost persuaded me that the life of the idle English is the life for me.

Unrequited affection was another subject which obsessed her. . . . At the age of fourteen Ouida began to fall in love with any man who treated her with ordinary politeness and believed him to be equally in love with her. Later, in her womanhood, an Italian Marchese became the embarrassed object of her attentions, and there is circumstantial evidence that she even felt amorously inclined towards Mario, for she always kept a picture of the tenor on her desk in her villa at Scandicci, and she tenderly represented him as Corrèze in her novel, *Moths.* Never, however, was her affection for a man reciprocated. In *Ariadnê,* she depicts the real artist as always unhappy, always suffering, unless he can give himself wholly to his art and eschew human love.

It has long been a contention of mine that middle-class life is as dull in art as it is in reality. Ouida, seemingly, agreed with me. Her novels deal with the aristocracy or the peasantry or the artist class, never with the middle-classes, except in the guise of nouveaux riches, whom she was never weary of ridiculing (classic examples are the Masserencs and Fuchsia Leach in *Moths*). In her report of the world that interested her, her imagination and her vitality were unflagging. There is something Homeric in her sweep and carrying power, something almost Balzacian, or at least Sandian, in the superb manner in which she crowded a stupendous canvas with figures. Max Beerbohm, indeed, has asserted that Mr. Meredith was "the only living novelist in England who rivals Ouida in sheer vitality." I like to think of her, attired in a Worth velvet gown, her hair loose and flying down her back (so she wore it on all occasions long past middle age), superbly ugly in her eccentric splendour, surrounded by her dogs which, Henry G. Huntington informs us, had none too clean habits, dashing off in her broad hand, which wrote, perhaps, sixty words to the page, her ecstatic romances. The unnumbered sheets were permitted to flutter to the floor. Later they were pieced together. Correction was deemed supererogatory; verification of references, unheard of. Has any other creator ever worked like this, directly from the imagination, save such geniuses as Gautier and Balzac and George Sand? "Her prodigality," Ambrose Bierce once wrote (and whatever one may say of the author of *The Devil's Dictionary,* one cannot deny that he was a judge of intellect), "was seen chiefly in her expenditure of intellectual force, of which she wasted enough to have made a half-hundred better novelists than herself. Almost any contemporary worker at her trade would have profited as a dog under her intellectual table."

Never, except in some of her shorter stories, did Ouida rid herself entirely of her vice of redundancy. Her method of composition was largely responsible for this flaw. But how delightful to read an author that one may skip occasionally! (pp. 52-5)

Mademoiselle de la Ramée struck her pace in her first novel, *Granville de Vigne,* or *Held in Bondage.* Other of her romances, possibly, are written with more care and with more art, but, with Max Beerbohm, I agree that Ouida was always Ouida. True lovers of this novelist will not concur with the hesitant and belated opinions of those who suddenly and condescendingly discovered the importance of the change in her style and manner with the publication of *The Masserenes,* which Ouida herself admitted was "worth 10,000 Trilbys." The change in style and manner are certainly to be noted, but the congenital frenzied glamour which made her what she was that day, just as certainly was apparent in *Granville de Vigne.* For some, perhaps, there may be too much glamour, but as Mr. Street has sensibly remarked, "You must allow the convention—the convention between you and the temperament of your author."

In *Granville de Vigne,* Ouida introduces us to the first of her daring, intrepid, ultra-raffiné, wasp-waisted guardsmen, the fascinating Vivian Sabretasche:

> They said he was deucedly dangerous to women, and one could hardly wonder if he was. A gallant soldier in the field, a charming companion in a club or mess-room, accomplished in music, painting, sculpture, as in the hardier arts of rifle and rod, speaking eight continental languages with equal facility, his manners exquisitely ten-

der and gentle, his voice soft as the Italian he loved best to speak, his face and form of unusual beauty, and to back him, all that subtler art that is only acquired in the eleusinia of the boudoir— no marvel if women, his pet playthings, did go down before Vivian Sabretasche.

It is from this book, too, that I have culled what is, perhaps, all things considered, my favourite passage in all fiction, that descriptive of Constance Trefusis, the first of Ouida's wicked, wicked women:

> Magnificent she looked in some geranium-hued dress, as light and brilliant as summer clouds, with the rose tint of sunset on them, and large white water-lilies in her massive raven hair, turned back à l'impératrice off her low brow, under which her eyes shot such Parthian glances. One could hardly wonder that De Vigne offended past redemption the Duchess of Margoldwurzel, ruined himself for life with his aunt, the Marchioness of Marqueterie, annoyed beyond hope of pardon the Countess of Ormolu, the five baronesses, all the ladies in their own right, all the great heiresses, all the county princesses-royal, all the archery-party beauties, and, careless of rank, right, or comment, opened the ball with—the Trefusis.

If, among this prolific writer's books, there is one for which I hold a particular affection, it is, I fancy, *Idalia,* that romance of a rich and powerful superwoman, patriot, and revolutionist, the devastating Countess Vassilis who, in her implications, occasionally reminds one of both Sandra Belloni and the Princess Casamassima. This novel vividly suggests an opera to me, with Mary Garden as Idalia, "the lady of his dreams," as Ouida would have called the book but for the intervention of Harrison Ainsworth, editor of the *New Monthly Magazine,* in which the story first appeared; it is easy to imagine Mary Garden in her torn domino, having been forcibly dragged from the masked ball, confined in the monastery, confronting with chaste contempt the vicious Monsignore Villaflor. As a matter of fact, the novel was dramatized almost immediately after publication and the play seems to have met with success in London, but either in opera or drama it is impossible to dream of a satisfactory embodiment of the brave and beautiful Sir Fulke Erceldoune.

In one of his letters Flaubert asserts, "Very great men often write very badly, and so much the better for them." Many sermons might be preached from this text. A convenient, if somewhat arbitrary, manner of dividing creators of fiction is to classify them as geniuses and artists. Dostoevsky, for example, was a genius, and Turgeniev, an artist. The comparison may be conveyed into the realm of painting: Whistler was an artist, Cézanne, a genius. . . . It is possible, of course, to be both, but the combination is rare and in most cases arguable. What, for instance, would George Moore be without his art? What, Theodore Dreiser, without his genius? In the case of Ouida, there can be no dispute. Ouida was not an artist, but just as surely she was a genius.

Remy de Gourmont once remarked, "Le style, c'est de sentir, de voir, de penser, et rien plus." If this be true,

Ouida assuredly has style. She feels her characters; she has observed their milieu. Indeed, it is one of her most typical faults that she has too much feeling. *Friendship,* that roman à clef which relates her side (was there another?) of her eccentric love affair with the Marchese Lotteringhi Della Stufa, whom Ouida met in 1871 and for whom she conceived the one grand passion of her life, would have benefited by the exercise of a colder pen. The background, however, here as elsewhere, is carefully studied. Street caught the truth when he remarked that the essentials are there and Max Beerbohm has pointed out that Ouida's lavish descriptions of interiors are not clichés, in the manner, say, of Mrs. Alexander McVeigh Miller [authoress of *The Bride of the Tomb; or, Lancelot Darling's Betrothed*]; they are actuated by her real love of beauty and are meticulously observed and recreated. Baudelaire exclaimed of Théophile Gautier, "Homme heureux! homme digne d'envie! il n'a jamais aimé que le Beau!" This apostrophe might just as reasonably have been addressed to Ouida. (pp. 55-8)

In her report of the world, . . . Ouida may have been a trifle inaccurate, but she found no difficulty in creating a world of her own, a world which, to some extent at least, has existed since she created it. Ouida's society is a little wickeder, a little gayer, a little richer than the real thing, but heaven knows that society since her day has done its best to live up to her specifications. Lanky guardsmen with their wasp-waists, the vampire of the silver screen, these we owe to Ouida's imagination.

There is still another phase of Ouida's talent that deserves a passing reference, her essays in criticism. Ouida was an excellent critic, clear-sighted, unshackled, fearless. She formed independent judgments and said what she thought. Naturally, however, her opinions were frequently deeply coloured by her ferocious prejudices. (p. 61)

Ouida's study of D'Annunzio, the first to appear in England, is rather remarkable, and stands up well today, even when it is compared with Henry James's criticism of the Italian writer. It is a pity that she did not turn her attention more frequently to this branch of writing. *Critical Studies,* although it contains her diatribe against Joseph Chamberlain and papers on subjects dear to her heart such as the ugliness of modern life, humanitarianism, and the decadence of the Latin races, is made up for the most part of essays on the novel, or essays on novelists, in which she often expresses her views on the writing of fiction. It is entirely characteristic of this lady that she frequently saw in others the faults she never saw in herself. In her essay on D'Annunzio, she writes, "The tendency of redundancy is not his fault alone; it is that of his time." In this paper she continues to be unconsciously brutal to herself: "There is unhappily an absolute absence of wit, of mirth, of humour." Ouida was gifted with a certain type of wit, but she was entirely lacking in humour. "He does not trust enough to the power of suggestion," is another of her boomerangs, and she takes Bourget to task for using foreign words! In *Ariadnê* there is a eulogy of Shakespeare which does the author's sensibility much credit; she finds in the poet's work "never a drop of envy or spleen." This from the malicious author of *Friendship,* a novel which cost her

her position in English society in Florence. In *Frescoes* may be found her celebrated paper on **"Romance and Realism,"** which contains her cri de cœur: she asks her readers to remember that the passion-flower is as real as the potato. She seems to have held the opinion that realism was a matter of subject and not of method. A comparison of Laura Pearl in **Puck** with Zola's Nana will prove that even passion-flowers may be dealt with in two distinct manners.

As I have remarked earlier in this paper, everybody reads Ouida, but only such men as Joseph Hergesheimer and Max Beerbohm are not ashamed to admit it. G. S. Street observes, "Her faults, which are obvious, have brought it about that she is placed, in the general estimation of critics, below writers without a tenth of her ability" [see essay dated 1895]. "The world takes its revenge on us for having despised it," she wailed to Wilfred Scawen Blunt. I think that some of the inhibitions of the world and its critics in regard to Ouida are due to the printing and binding of her novels. In America, their most elaborate dress is the red or green volumes stamped with gold, issued by Lippincott in Philadelphia. The reprints of Chatto and Windus in London are even worse, bound in tomato red and printed in small type from carious plates. Indubitably, a new edition of Ouida, on good paper, handsomely printed and bound, with prefaces by a few of her more illustrious admirers, would do much to dispel the current illusion which has it that in reading Ouida one is descending to the depths of English literature. I suspect, indeed, that if Ouida were suitably printed and bound she would begin to rank not very much below Dickens and Thackeray and considerably above the turgid George Eliot. (pp. 62-4)

> *Carl Van Vechten, "Ouida," in his* Excavations: A Book of Advocacies, *Alfred A. Knopf, 1926, pp. 47-64.*

Bonamy Dobrée (essay date 1932)

[*A highly regarded English historian and critic, Dobrée distinguished himself both as a leading authority on Restoration drama and as a biographer who sought, through vivid depiction and captivating style, to establish biography as a legitimate creative form. Dobrée is also known for his editing of* The Oxford History of English Literature *and the* Writers and Their Work *series. In all his writings, Dobrée's foremost concern was to communicate to the reader his aesthetic response to the work under discussion. In the following essay, he focuses on the reasons for Ouida's popularity during the Victorian era and the subsequent neglect of her works.*]

In the 'seventies, a dashing woman of about thirty-five might have been seen driving about the neighbourhood of Florence in an equipage of high style, usually accompanied by her mother, and surrounded with a menagerie of animals. She was fair, with a thin, oval face; masses of golden-brown hair overhung large, dark-blue eyes, while her body terminated in small hands and feet. A charming woman; but, unfortunately, she had 'a voice like a carving knife'. This was Maria Louise (de la) Ramée, better known as Ouida, who, born in 1839 enjoyed a period of resounding popularity, with its consequent wealth, but who faded

from public favour and died in poverty in 1908, barely subsisting on a Civil List pension obtained for her only the year before.

Yes, she was enormously read, but her books were not allowed to lie about on drawing-room tables. She was too glamorous; she was, they said, 'unwholesome'; but then that was part of the thrill, for she was in rebellion against rigid Victorian conventions, current moral, religious, and domestic ideals; and the worst of it was that, in the light of her burning vision, these ideals did, after all, appear a little mean. If she was 'flashy', the ideals were tawdry. No, one must not confess to reading her, except to mock at her absurd mistakes, her 'diverting inaccuracies'—did not the critics with their fastidious taste pick ever so many holes in her? (till two of the most fastidious, Mr. G. S. Street [see essay dated 1895] and Mr. Max Beerbohm [see essay dated 1897], came to the rescue)—why, one could no more confess to liking her than today one can confess, except as a sign of being very, very highbrow, to liking thrillers. For thrillers was exactly what she did write; not simply physical thrillers, but moral and emotional ones, in which we abandon ourselves to moral and emotional sensation just as we do to excitement over physical thrills in the sensation novels of today; her wicked are so deeply wicked, her good so extravagantly good, the issues between them so strenuously fought out, that one abandons any hankering after analysis, probability, subtlety, and floats, even now, deliciously on the great wave of her exuberant, superabundant vitality.

The difficulty is not to account for her old popularity, but for her neglect at the present day; indeed we feel that, could Ouida arise again, she would only have to change her idiom a little, and she would catch us all once more; indeed that best-seller, Mr. P. C. Wren's *Beau Geste,* is only **Under Two Flags** written in a different language. What we really resent in Ouida today is her lavishness; lavish is the word one would choose to describe her predominant quality. Beauty is heaped on perfection, vileness is flung on the top of degradation, in a manner repugnant to our weaker digestions, and all in an immense torrent of words. But then the Victorians revelled in such spates of language, even in their best literature—think only of Carlyle and Browning—and that we do not so revel is not necessarily to our credit, for what may masquerade as restraint may really be thinness. No doubt, however, it is over-luxurious to relish such phrases as this from Ouida's **Strathmore,** written with such obvious delight in its alliteraton: 'threw his ermine over his emptiness, covered all cancans with his coronet, and hushed all whispers with his wealth'. But then this luxury, not only in words, but spread over everything, making scenery better than it ever was in real life, turning a boudoir into a paradise, and infecting souls and bodies with a super-humanity which dazzles (where it does not stun)—how refreshing! what a delicious escape! what a haven, what an orgy of what the modern psychologist would call 'wish-fulfilment'! Take the opening portrait of Tricotrin, set in the most gorgeous wine-harvest scenery you can imagine, add 'the women-faces its tranquil pools had mirrored', and remember 'the sun breaking through the foilage above in manifold gleams and glories that touched the turning leaves bright red as fire':

> It was a beautiful homeric head; bold, kingly, careless, noble, with the royalty of the lion in its gallant poise, and the challenge of the eagle in its upward gesture; the head which an artist would have given to his Hector, or his Phoebus, or his God Lycœus. The features were beautiful too, in their varied and eloquent meanings; with their poet's brows, their reveller's laugh, their soldier's daring, their student's thought, their many and conflicting utterances, whose contradictions made one unity—the unity of genius.

If we already know what an Ouida hero is like, we are not surprised to learn immediately that he had the genius of a Mozart (he possessed a 'Straduarius'), the eloquence of a Mirabeau, the sagacity of a Talleyrand, and that, had he wished, he could have been the most famous painter of his age, as indeed he was the foremost. Naturally—one says 'naturally' when one is steeped deep enough in the atmosphere—he was an English peer who had nobly given up his heritage, and, as naturally, was capable of muscular feats which any athlete would envy. They are all like that, her heroes, except that they are usually more languid: their lily hands can strangle lions, their unutterable boredom is relieved only by deeds of heroism in battle, their taste, and often their performance, in the arts is beyond reproach. And the spirit does not belie the body, as a rule: the endurance of these men, their self-control (exceptionally broken down by wild passion), their loyalty, their un-

tarnishable honour, prove that they are no mere whited sepulchres; often they are men of staggering ability. The wicked, of course, are unspeakably vile.

Her women, alas, are rarely so perfect; outside, yes, they are so overwhelmingly lovely that princes fawn at their feet, statesmen throw away their careers for a kiss, lesser mortals dare death for the dimple of a smile. But inside— ah!—cruel, cunning, cold (Ouida's style is infectious), without hearts: filled only with social ambition and the love of feminine power, they are demons who batten on revenge, as described by this great castigator of her sex. Not that all, by any means, are like that. The Princess Souroff is as spotless as any of Ouida's heroes; the girl in **The Massarenes** is as honest a piece of womanhood as you would meet anywhere. But the picture in the main is flattering to males, and for that reason men would read the novels; and women might perhaps read them to meet in them the perfect man. And moreover, there is Cigarette, the *vivandière* of **Under Two Flags,** to appeal to both sexes, the charmingly romantic loyal heroine, who met her death because she loved too well, and whom only the sternest would blame because she had loved too often.

There already, perhaps, are enough elements to give popularity, but to that you must add Ouida's immense variety of personages and scenes. Her heroes can be statesmen, guardsmen, Bohemians, singers, King's Messengers: her women can be real or sham noble, or poverty-stricken peasants, or gypsy fortune-tellers; because she deals in extremes she rarely touches on the middle classes. Her

Scene from the 1936 film adaptation of Under Two Flags.

scenes take us roaming all over Europe and some of Africa, and besides, within the geography, what places! Palaces, hovels, haunts of virtue or vice high or low, courts and galleys, wild woodlands, suffocating deserts, mountains or coasts; and who dare say that her descriptions of interiors or exteriors are not vivid, even if wordy, and do not give the mind other places to dwell in, abundantly, lavishly (these epithets recur), for the reader's ease, satisfaction, or excitement? And then, on the whole, she manages the story so well; we are all agog to know what is going to happen next; it is difficult even now to put one of her books down. We shall skip, no doubt, run our eye swiftly down the page, refuse, perhaps unwisely, the trimmings of the ample dish. Usually her books are well constructed, though it has happened to me to read *Moths,* omitting the middle third, without finding that it mattered much. This will not do, however, with most of her books. There is, indeed, too much detail, repetition even; but the truth is that she was in love with life, and though it may be easy to make fun of her art, at least it makes us also in love with life, even with her fantastic vision of it. And since we ourselves are thrall to her, how shall we be surprised that the Victorians fell easy victims?

And then there are two aspects which we can well imagine more attractive to the Victorians than to us: the first is the characters themselves, the second what they imply. We do not today care so much for types, we prefer the analysis of a personality, and Ouida's persons are types, or rather, they are what used to be called 'humours'; they represent qualities, such as good or evil, heroism or vileness, courage, cruelty and so on; and, here is the appeal, when she depicts good qualities, physical or moral, they are those which most of us, at some time of our lives, if generally in very early youth, wish to acquire. And, believing in her heroes so thoroughly as she does, we believe in them too, at least while we read her, and it is probable that the Victorians, simpler-minded than we are, believed in them more easily than we can. There then were the people one would give anything to be, and, since one believed in them, one could identify one's self with them for the moment. What more rapturous experience could there be?

And it is again because we are not so simple-minded as the Victorians (apparently) were—we have become horridly adult, what our forebears would call cynical—that we probably cannot so whole-heartedly enjoy the other aspect, her moral vision. She had values; her novels were, at least, about something, and those values were, undoubtedly, right, though many would today call them sentimental; but not the thousands who cherish *Beau Geste*. She was all for honesty, loyalty, self-sacrifice, stoic endurance, not from a sense of duty, but—and here the Victorians spied the serpent—from love. And above all she admired generosity, generosity of life, in living, in giving of self. Her hatred of injustice showed itself especially in her stories of Italian peasant life, and it is not for nothing that the memorial erected at her birthplace, Bury St. Edmunds, is flanked by statuettes labelled 'Sympathy' and 'Generosity'. She was all whips and scorpions for those who sacrifice the profounder emotions to the tinsel of fashion or success; she hated all meanness, all self-seeking. Her novels are in a way nonsense, yes; the whole thing is far

too highly-coloured, flaunting, improbable, not to say impossible; everything is at an unattainable pitch, but the materials are the right ones, if not for truth as we have come to see it, at least for a flamboyant beauty. In reading her it is not possible to think of her as anything but popular: she gives life and its glamour with both hands. Her work is always over-full, her language often incorrect, her excursions into foreign tongues, dead and living, sometimes unfortunate. Her work will not stand the test of actuality, but it will stand that of an undisciplined imaginative truth. Of course she was read, of course she was loved; and it would not be surprising if a new cheap edition of **Under Two Flags** should sell its thousands. Other books of hers no doubt require a more recondite taste, the taste that is content to abide a mass of flummery for the sake of a few pearls, the taste that can see virtue in abundance, even if it is over-abundance. 'Her every page', Mr. Beerbohm remarks, 'is a riot of unpolished epigrams and unpolished poetry of vision': and those qualities were more appreciated in her day than they are now. Most significant, however, is the fact that Mr. Beerbohm dedicated *More* 'To Mlle. de la Ramée, with the author's compliments, and to Ouida with his love'. That, perhaps, is the final explanation of her popularity. (pp. 193-98)

> *Bonamy Dobrée, "Ouida," in his* Milton to Ouida: A Collection of Essays, *Frank Cass and Co. Ltd., 1970, pp. 193-98.*

V. S. Pritchett   (essay date 1950)

[*Pritchett is a highly esteemed English novelist, short story writer, and critic. Considered one of the modern masters of the short story, he is also one of the world's most respected and well-read literary critics. Pritchett writes in the conversational tone of the familiar essay, a method by which he approaches literature from the viewpoint of a lettered but not overly scholarly reader. A twentieth-century successor to such early nineteenth-century essayist-critics as William Hazlitt and Charles Lamb, Pritchett employs much the same critical method: his own experience, judgment, and sense of literary art are emphasized, rather than a codified critical doctrine derived from a school of psychological or philosophical speculation. His criticism is often described as fair, reliable, and insightful. In the following excerpt from an essay originally published in the* New Statesman and Nation *in 1950, Pritchett discusses the influence of Ouida's life on her literary works.*]

It was like a visit to the theatre or the waxworks. One walked into the Langham Hotel out of the London daylight and was shown, at last, into a large, darkened apartment twinkling with candles. Heavy black velvet curtains were drawn over the windows; masses of exotic flowers were banked against them and, enthroned in an enormous bed in the midst of all this, sat the genius: a small, ugly, dank-eyed woman with her hair down her back, scratching away fast with a quill pen on large sheets of violet-tinted paper and throwing each sheet on to the floor when it was done with. A large dog guarded the morning's work from the visitor's touch. One had gone to have one's head bitten off either by Ouida or her dog.

Ouida would be under thirty at this time, a woman with her father's excessive nose and a rude grating voice. Already conceit, indeed megalomania, had settled on a theatrical character. She is not the first novelist to have delusions of grandeur—Scott had his Abbotsford, Balzac had coronets put on his luggage—for when one is dealing in fantasy, it is not unnatural to help oneself. In the secret room of Ouida's life, where the shames of her childhood in Bury St. Edmunds were hidden, there must have been a shrewd, hard, frightened being which stiffened its chin and told her that she had earned the right to folly and exorbitance. She had become the most famous novelist then living in the world when she was hardly out of her teens; she had slaved as only the best-sellers can; she had raised her unhappy mother from poverty to wealth; she had proved that the "realities" so meanly admired in a gossiping provincial town were despicable. She was original. The day-dreams of an adolescent girl had been imposed successfully upon herself; they were triumphantly imposed upon the world. How was it done? At the end of her life when she lay dead of neglect in a wretched Italian tenement, her maid reverently placed two of her mistress's quill pens on the table at the foot of the bed. The quill which had flamed over the violet paper in the gloom of the Langham, which had tossed ahead of the sprawling cavalry charge of Ouida's prose, had once more proved itself mightier than the reviewer's bitter pen. (pp. 223-24)

The daydreams of Bury St. Edmunds where her plausible French father came to fill her head with nature lessons, tall stories of international plots and the dazzling intrigues of European courts, were the day-dreams of the whole of middle-class England and America. Liberal democracy was bored with its routine. The aristocracy and idle rich with their Turkish tobacco and their tremendous sins—how these haunted the heads of Victorian wives and their hard-working husbands. It did not matter that Ouida was ignorant of the fashionable world; all the better could she describe what the fashionable *ought* to look and sound like. The fashionable world itself, so childishly romantic and sentimental underneath its brisk airs and its levity, rather wished it like that, too. Her novels were the fantasies of the outsider, of those who have to keep their station in life, of those who, obeying all the rules and calculating all the main chances, keep one corner in their minds for visions of an insouciant and gorgeous race which performs such non-interest-bearing acts as wrecking a career "to save a woman's name from the breath of slander", and lives with heroic and insolvent melancholy in recklessly furnished rooms. "Beauty", the guardsman,

> had the drawing-room floor of a house in Kensington Gore, well-furnished and further crowded with crowds of things of his own, from Persian carpets bought on his travels to the last new rifle sent home only the day before. . . .

A setter, a retriever and a couple of Skyes

(Ouida was always crowded with crowds of dogs)—

> were on the hearthrug (veritable tiger skin). Breakfast in dainty Sèvres silver stood on one table sending up an aroma of coffee, omelettes and devils; the morning papers lay on the floor,

a smoking cap was hung on a Parian Venus; a parrot, who apparently considered himself master of the place, was perched irreverently on a bronze Milton, and pipes, whips, pistols and cards were thrown down on a Louis Quinze couch, that Louise de Kérouaille or Sophie Arnould might have graced. From the inner room came the rapid clash of small-swords, while "Touché, touché, touché! Riposte! Holà!" was shouted, in a silvery voice, from a man who, lying back in a rocking chair in the bay window of the front room, was looking on at a bout with the foils that was taking place beyond the folding doors.

Snobbery is often a form of romanticism; it is the chastity of the perfectionist. But on Ouida's level romance is not romance until it is snobbish; and not, we may say, as we look back upon the Victorian novel, on her level alone. One of the better rumours about Ouida's novels was that they were the secret work of the not very nice George Eliot; and do not George Eliot's heroines unfailingly go up in the world as they become more refined by moral struggle? Are there not pages of Tennyson that look like Debrett put into verse? And are there not, indeed, modern novels in which souls are brought humbly to the Faith by the glamorous sight of an earl on his deathbed? The material luxury of Ouida's early novels, with their crammed marble halls and their general air of being expensive bazaars of history, is the expression of an expansive society becoming every year richer on colonies and luxurious colonial wars. And is it far-fetched to see in the hysterical dialogue of her books something of the repressed emotional violence of Victorian society? Why else this taste for melodrama and the smell of sulphur:

> "Your lips were mine," she cried, laughing still in that mocking mirth, "their kisses must poison hers. Your hand slew him! its touch must pollute hers. Oh, lover, who lived on my smile! Did you not know the dead love would rise and curse the new?"

There can be no doubt when one has read Miss Bigland's account of Ouida's painful and ludicrous love affair with the Marchese della Stufa in Florence, that she herself felt in phrases of this operatic violence. And underlying it is her curious, rather seductive melancholy, the fervid not unintelligent Byronism which her French father must have brought over to Bury St. Edmunds from the Continent. (What happened to him? "Only the Emperor knows.") It was a sadness all the more romantic for being decked out with shrugs, floods of ungrammatical French and Bohemian cynicism; and it was also the inevitable undertone of the day-dreamer's life as, exhausted, she wakes up from her drug. (pp. 224-26)

What takes one's breath in nearly every detail of Ouida's life is her boldness, her huge guzzling confidence in her powers, her ability to impose her life, as if she herself were a work of the imagination and not a human being. One is aware of a gusher. There is an appalling vitality which is undistracted by self-criticism or unstayed by the existence of any other person. She plays up shamelessly to the men. She had, for the purposes of her work, an extraordinary speed of assimilation, a greed for more facts to be turned into more dreams. Her so-called immorality—Miss Bigland has no difficulty in showing that Ouida was a prudish woman whose sensual desires had been sweepingly sublimated—enabled her to break conventions and, for example, to give dinners "for Guardsmen only" which were very useful in supplying her with local colour as well as giving her the best kind of publicity: the scandalous. A word or two about the Foreign Legion, a skirmish, an Arab café, and men who wish "to forget", would soon be transfigured by her reckless imagination. She saw the thoroughbreds crushing the skulls of the enemy; she threw in an abduction. Her tragedy (some thought) was that she was a *grande amoureuse* who was too ugly to find a lover. One suspects that her only "lover" had been that elusive refugee, her father. Though she may be said to have been continually in love all her life with one man after another, there are no signs that her love was anything more than a terrifying and possessive hallucination and often known to herself alone; if disclosed, it drove every man to horrified flight. He had seen the octopus and it wore white satin.

Ouida was an actress who never settled to her role. Now she was a foreign aristocrat, now the great political figure, now the humanitarian defending the virtuous poor against the wicked rich, now the cynic as wilful as her one remarkable creation, the Cigarette of *Under Two Flags;* now the misunderstood artist, who will not sell her soul to a public of hucksters. They were the leading roles of an internal drama. (pp. 226-27)

There are some apologists for the novels of Ouida. She is said to have been an influence, though it is surely unkind to see it extending to Lawrence, as Miss Bigland does. We must agree, however, that she raises an early peacock wail of passion in the Victorian novel. *Pascarel* (which is admired) seems to me watery and unreadable stuff. The studies of the lives of the Italian poor are more interesting; they indicate a break with the earlier English preoccupation with Italy and, indeed, Ouida with a social conscience is a sentimental but bold writer. As Miss Bigland justly says, the reviewers who brought academic guns to bear on her fiction were themselves a little ridiculous in their solemnity. I have read only two or three of her novels and of these I prefer the unredeemed like *Under Two Flags* and *Strathmore* to the more respectable ones; the cigars, the passionate riding crops, the Rhenish of her country houses, the shooting women of her Algerian camps and the overproof Cognac of her Parisian Avernus, to the trite Italian works of her reformed period. I confess I have not read *In Maremma* which is praised for its landscape. Shockingly repetitive as she was, wild in her skiddings across drawing-rooms and deserts, she was not without shrewdness. She had an eye for raffish character. One responds to the tidal wave of her awful vitality, the terrific swamping of her prose. One would have given anything to go to her parties in Florence. Mr. E. M. Forster has told us that it is the novelist's duty to "bounce" us. Ouida does that with all her might; so hard, indeed, that her novels bounce high out of sight into that luscious upper air—somewhere between Mayfair and the moon—where the super ego practises its incredible scales and beats its frightful bosom. In its way, her stuff is more honest than the worst of Disraeli or Bulwer Lytton from which it derives; and more genial than the Barclay and Corelli for whom she prepared the way. (p. 228)

V. S. Pritchett, "The Octopus," in his Books in General, *Chatto & Windus, 1953, pp. 223-28.*

Kenneth Churchill   (essay date 1980)

[*In the following excerpt, Churchill discusses the use of Italian settings and history in Ouida's fiction.*]

The most significant English novelist to write on Italy in the 1870s was Ouida. After occasionally using purely conventional Italian scenery in a very minor way in some of her earlier novels (*Chandos,* 1866; *Idalia,* 1867; and *Puck,* 1870), she fell in love with the country on her first visit there in 1871, settled in Florence, and thereafter looked constantly to Italy for her literary material.

Ouida takes up the fictional potential of Italy where T. A. Trollope left off; the more so since she shared with him a common model for the treatment of Italy in her deep admiration of George Sand. Like Trollope's, Ouida's Italian novels were for the most part thoroughly sentimental love stories narrated with a minimum of psychological insight and prose quality and a maximum of local colour for padding. But despite the general superficiality of her work she does at times respond to Italy more deeply than Trollope's novels had done, and can offer her reader two new kinds of feeling towards the country, both of which, after she had introduced them, go on to culminate in important aspects of Lawrence's Italian work.

The first is a particular stress in her treatment of the attraction of Italy to the northerner, the attraction which has meant that 'the atmosphere of Italy has been the greatest fertiliser of English poetic genius.' England seems to Ouida to be stultifying to the creative imagination. 'All lands are soulless where the olive does not lift its consecrated boughs to heaven'; and they are soulless because they have lost contact with any roots they may have had in the past in a sensuous, pagan enjoyment of life. The olive is the symbolic point of contact between modern man and the ancient pagan civilisations which flourished in the 'dryad-haunted groves' of the Mediterranean; and it is this contact which particularly delights Ouida in Italy. Her favourite city, Florence,

> is always half a pagan at heart—she, the daughter of Hercules, who saw the flying feet of Atalanta shine upon her silvery hills, and heard the arrows of Apollo cleave her rosy air.

> The past is so close to you in Florence. You touch it at every step. It is not the dead past that men bury and then forget. It is an unquenchable thing; beautiful, and full of lustre, even in the tomb, like the gold from the sepulchres of the Aetruscan kings that shines on the breast of some fair living woman, undimmed by the dust and the length of the ages. (*Pascarèl*)

Throughout the novels references to the Etruscan past abound whenever Ouida wishes to evoke the graceful and joyous response to life which seems to her to be the most valuable thing that Italy has to offer the visitor from the north. Most of the novels are set in that part of Tuscany which is redolent of the ancient civilisation; and in *In Maremma* (1882) there are even scenes set in an Etruscan tomb on the Tuscan coast. The constant assertion and reminder of the continuity of a joyous celebration of life going on in the Italian countryside over thousands of years is an attempt to give depth and significance to an admiring attitude towards Italian peasant life which nevertheless remains, like Trollope's, purely sentimental. Ouida relies too simply on the use of the word 'Etruscan' as a magic charm without ever making any serious attempt to explore and portray, for example, what precisely these 'Etruscan' qualities are and how they can relate to the lives of her readers. Her uncritical enthusiasm contrasts painfully with the pre-occupations of the work which James was producing at the same time as her own. But she does have the distinction of having first rendered explicitly in the novel that connection between modern Italian life and the attractions of pagan antiquity which was implicit in contemporary work on the Renaissance, and was to become a substantial theme of the English novel during the next forty years.

However, there was another side of modern Italian life which was distinctly not derived from the Etruscans and was, indeed, threateningly antagonistic to all that was best in the Italian character. Hitherto, English writers had often expressed their support and admiration of the Italian people in their struggle against the Austrians and the temporal power of the Church; and Ouida's own first Italian novel, *Pascarèl* (1873), concerns a hero of the fight against Austria. But living in Italy during the first years of unification, Ouida became the first English writer to chronicle the sense of growing disillusion with the actual achievement. For the end of the political and military struggle had not produced the expected flowering of the magnificent potential of Italy, but a sadder and more devastating series of attacks on that potential than had ever been seen under the old régime.

Ouida identified two major factors contributing to this attack. . . . [Charles] Lever, in *The Daltons,* had suggested that English residents in Florence were involved in dubious financial speculation in Italian affairs. In the 1870s, with the new nationalistic government, Italy offered unprecedented opportunities to such speculators to launch schemes which would ostensibly bring benefit and glory to Italy, but in reality merely bring profit to their own pockets; and it is against this that the first part of Ouida's attack is directed. *Friendship* (1878) takes up Lever's criticisms of English society abroad in a sustained and strident attack on all Ouida's real or imagined enemies in Florence, the chief of whom, Lady Joan (based on Janet Ross), is accused of many kinds of dishonesty, but denounced for nothing so bitterly as for her constant involvement in fraudulent speculation.

Such activities were made all the easier by the second factor to which Ouida attributes Italy's sorry plight in the early years of independence: the creation of a bureaucracy invested with tyrannical powers and utterly devoid of moral principle and of any sense either of duty or compassion. Throughout the country brutal men had been able suddenly to seize dominating positions in the local political and administrative structures, whence they could bully and exploit their neighbours. A central event in the short story 'The Marriage Plate,' in *Pipistrello & Other Stories* (1880), which Ouida presents as characterising the new state of affairs in Italy, is the shock of a poor peasant on discovering that his beloved dog, which he has left guarding his pony and trap in Florence, has been viciously dragged away by the police because of a new law against leaving dogs unchained in the streets of the city. The people who had been promised freedom through independence find, bewilderingly, that there is only a worse tyranny than before.

Ouida combines both these elements of contemporary Italy in her finest novel, *A Village Commune* (1881). The village of Santa Rosalia is described as representative of the autonomous petty tyrannies which the Risorgimento has created all over Italy. The system is personified by the Syndic's brutal secretary, Nellemane. He himself has written the by-laws of the community, which are carefully designed to line his own pocket by making every inhabitant constantly liable to be fined, since even the most ordinary and inevitable events of daily life can be found to contravene one or other of the provisions of the wretched man's personal criminal code. By a combination of brute force and manipulation of the law, he and his henchmen terrorise the village and create an atmosphere of fear and hatred; while at the same time the whole countryside is being laid waste by the speculative building of railways, tramways and steam-mills. The villain Nellemane naturally has an interest in such profitable enterprises, and is in a position to give full scope to their development in the area under his control. His own pet scheme is a plan to convert the Roman catacombs into an underground railway, a plan whose palpable absurdity is only a striking exaggeration, and not a misrepresentation, of the scandalous nature of many such projects which were actually in the air at the time. (Ouida provides an appendix guaranteeing the authenticity of her material.) Eventually, Nellemane is rewarded for his administrative zeal by being made a Deputy.

All this was new food for thought for the English reader interested in Italy. If what was needed to rejuvenate industrial society was a return to the essence of paganism, then Italy was evidently the place to establish contact; and if contact was to be made, it must be made quickly, for the Italian people and the Italian country seemed daily to be losing some of their charm and beauty in the face, precisely, of the encroaching industrialisation and brutalisation of modern life. Despite the prevalent sentimentality and superficiality of her work, Ouida had indicated the area in which much subsequent literary interest in Italy was to lie, and had contributed one significant novel to the tradition of English writing about Italy. (pp. 162-65)

Kenneth Churchill, "Italy and the English Novel, 1870-1917," in his Italy and English Literature, 1764-1930, *Barnes & Noble Books, 1980, pp. 162-81.*

FURTHER READING

Biography

Allan, William. "Ouida." In *The British Eccentric,* edited by Harriet Bridgeman and Elizabeth Drury, pp. 88-97. New York: Clarkson N. Potter, 1976.

> Biographical discussion focusing on Ouida's eccentricities.

Bigland, Eileen. *Ouida: The Passionate Victorian.* London: Jarrolds, 1950, 272 p.

> Biography of Ouida. Bigland comments that "By the sheer vitality of her writing, the astonishing tempo she maintained throughout her books, her passionate fights for lost causes, her intense awareness of beauty and atmosphere, she assuredly did a very great deal for those [writers] who came after her."

ffrench, Yvonne. *Ouida: A Study in Ostentation.* New York: D. Appleton-Century Co., 1938, 191 p.

> Study of Ouida and the era in which she lived. According to ffrench: "Although [Ouida] was in advance of many of her contemporaries—a fact proved by her intelligent political and social insight—the dawning of Edwardianism put an end to her great literary vogue. A new public had arisen: a public that refused to be fobbed off with impossible romances and situations of far-fetched idealisms. A public that demanded, above all, realism and plain, everyday characters; commodities that Ouida was both unable and unwilling to supply."

Lee, Elizabeth. *Ouida: A Memoir.* London: T. Fisher Unwin, 1914, 336 p.

> Early biography that includes extensive excerpts from Ouida's letters.

Macaulay, Rose. "Eccentric Englishwomen: IV. Ouida." *The Spectator* 158, No. 5680 (7 May 1937): 855-56.

> Discusses Ouida's residence in Florence, Italy, her fondness for dogs, her habit of dressing entirely in white, her elevated opinion of herself as an author, and her "strange" social habits.

Phillips, Celia G. "Ouida and Her Publishers: 1874-1880." *Bulletin of Research in the Humanities* 81, No. 2 (Summer 1978): 210-15.

> Focuses on Ouida's financial relationships with her publishers.

Stirling, Monica. *The Fine and the Wicked: The Life and Times of Ouida.* New York: Coward-McCann, 1958, 223 p.

> Biographical discussion of Ouida. Stirling concludes: "Passionate and ludicrous, prejudiced and brave, this talented woman may not have been what she herself called a thoro'bred—but she had the royal touch."

Williamson, G. C. "Ouida." In his *Behind My Library Door: Some Chapters on Authors, Books, and Miniatures,* pp. 1-14. New York: E. P. Dutton, 1921.

> Reminisces about Williamson's visit to Ouida as a publisher's agent and his subsequent correspondence with her.

Criticism

"Ouida: An Estimate." *The Academy* n.s. 51, No. 1307 (22 May 1897): 549-50.

> Discusses the popular appeal of Ouida's novels, focusing primarily on *Moths* and *The Massarenes.*

Calverly, Mary. "Ouida's Knowledge of Italian Life." *The Contemporary Review* 40 (October 1881): 564-69.

> Criticizes Ouida's portrayal of Italian life and language in *A Village Commune.*

Chang, Charity. " 'The Nürnberg Stove' as an Artistic Fairy Tale." *Children's Literature: Annual of the Modern Language Association Group on Children's Literature and The Children's Literature Association* 5 (1976): 148-56.

> Examines the short story "The Nürnberg Stove" from Ouida's 1882 collection *Bimbi: Stories for Children.* Chang explains: "In her creation of 'The Nürnberg Stove,' Ouida has used the familiar motives of a dangerous journey and the achievement of a near-impossible goal to convey her own personal vision of the relationships of people to themselves and to each other."

Elwin, Malcolm. "Ouida." In his *Victorian Wallflowers,* pp. 282-312. London: Jonathan Cape, 1934.

> Biographical and critical study of Ouida.

Schroeder, Natalie. "Feminine Sensationalism, Eroticism, and Self-Assertion: M. E. Braddon and Ouida." *Tulsa Studies in Women's Literature* 7, No. 1 (Spring 1988): 87-103.

> Argues that "Braddon's and Ouida's novels reflect Victorian women's attempts to rebel against the conventional feminine ideal. . . . Though the authors were forced to bow to convention and punish aggression and self-assertiveness, the predominantly female reading audience was regaled with woman's potential for power, a power that ironically flourishes in a patriarchal society."

Tappe, E. D. "Ouida's *Idalia:* The Source of Its Moldavian Scenes." *Notes and Queries* 6, No. 7 (July-August 1959): 285-86.

> Traces Ouida's description of Moldavia in *Idalia* to an article by Laurence Oliphant in *Blackwood's Magazine.*

"Ouida's Novels." *The Westminster and Foreign Quarterly Review* 49 (1 April 1876): 360-86.

> Examines the characters, scenery, and plots of Ouida's early novels. The critic concludes: "Taking a comprehensive view of these novels, we are struck by the evidence of great power, carelessly wielded in most instances, and a not infrequent predilection for *bizarre* incidents and melodramatic situations, when natural treatment is imperiously demanded."

Virginia Woolf

1882-1941

INTRODUCTION

(Born Adeline Virginia Stephen) English essayist, novelist, critic, short story writer, diarist, and biographer.

The following entry presents criticism of Woolf's essays. For discussion of Woolf's complete career, see *TCLC*, Volumes 1 and 5; for discussion of her novel *Mrs. Dalloway*, see *TCLC*, Volume 20; for related commentary, see the entry on the Bloomsbury Group in *TCLC*, Volume 34.

Woolf is one of the most prominent literary figures of the twentieth century, and her essays contain some of her most respected prose. Throughout her life she wrote book reviews, biographical and autobiographical sketches, social and literary criticism, personal essays, and commemorative articles treating a wide range of topics. Because of Woolf's renown as an innovative novelist, in particular for her contributions to the development of stream-of-consciousness narrative technique, commentary on her essays at first focused on the insight they afforded into her own fiction. In recent years, however, Woolf's essays have received attention for their perceptive observations on nearly the entire range of English literature, as well as on many social and political concerns of the early twentieth century.

Woolf was the daughter of the eminent literary critic and historian Sir Leslie Stephen and his second wife, Julia. While Woolf received no formal education, she was raised in a cultured and literary atmosphere, receiving her education from her father's extensive library and from conversing with his friends, many of whom were prominent writers of the era. Woolf's mother died in 1895, and, following the death of her father in 1904, Woolf settled in the Bloomsbury district of London with her sister, Vanessa, and her brothers Thoby and Adrian. Their house became a gathering-place where such friends as J. M. Keynes, Lytton Strachey, Roger Fry, and E. M. Forster congregated for lively discussions about philosophy, art, music, and literature. A complex network of friendships and love affairs developed between various participants, serving to increase the solidarity of what became known as the Bloomsbury Group. Here Woolf met Leonard Woolf, the author, politician, and economist whom she married in 1912.

Woolf flourished in the unconventional atmosphere that she and her siblings had devised. The freedom afforded by the Bloomsbury milieu was conducive to her literary inclinations, and the need to earn money led her to begin submitting book reviews and essays to various publications. Her first published works—literary reviews for the most part—began appearing anonymously in 1904 in the *Guardian,* a weekly newspaper for Anglo-Catholic clergy. Subsequently Woolf published reviews and essays in a

number of other periodicals, including the *National Review, Cornhill,* and the *Times Literary Supplement.* Bruce Richmond, who edited *TLS* from 1902 to 1938, assigned novels, biographies, histories, and travel books for her to review, and provided thoughtful editing of Woolf's submissions. She later credited Richmond with helping to shape her style as an essayist: "I learnt a lot of my craft writing for him: how to compress; how to enliven; and also was made to read with a pen and notebook, seriously." Woolf's letters and diaries reveal that her journalism occupied much of her time and thought between 1904 and 1909. By the latter year, however, she was becoming absorbed in work on her first novel, eventually published in 1915 as *The Voyage Out.* Although she attained great renown as a novelist and short story writer thereafter, she continued to write and publish essays throughout her career.

Woolf maintained that the purpose of writing an essay was to give pleasure to the reader, and she endeavored to do this with witty, supple prose, apt literary and cultural references, and a wide range of subjects. Aiming to identify closely with her audience, she adopted a persona she termed "the common reader": an intelligent, educated person with the will and inclination to be challenged by what he or she reads. While the majority of Woolf's essays are devoted to literary matters, some of her most highly regarded nonfiction writings are topical and occasional essays that treat such subjects as war and peace, feminism, life and death, sex and class issues, her own travels, observations of the contemporary scene, even the death of a family pet. She addressed social and feminist concerns in greatest depth in *A Room of One's Own* and *Three Guineas,* discussing the cultural and economic pressures that hinder women's scholarly pursuits and exploring the underlying causes of war.

As a literary critic, Woolf undertook the appraisal of a wide range of authors. She reviewed and wrote extended critical commentary on her literary contemporaries, including Rupert Brooke, E. M. Forster, Henry James, Rudyard Kipling, and D. H. Lawrence; the great Victorian and Romantic poets and novelists; major figures of the eighteenth century and the Elizabethan age; and many lesser-known literary and historical characters. Her literary criticism is largely appreciative and impressionistic, containing little that can be called objective or analytical. Woolf's commentary on works by authors of the past usually includes a full consideration of the society in which the work originated, and critics have found these essays among her most effective. One of the best and most famous of her literary essays is *Mr. Bennett and Mrs. Brown,* in which Modernist fiction—which Woolf's own works exemplify—is contrasted with the Realist-Naturalist tradition represented by H. G. Wells, John Galsworthy, and Arnold Bennett. In a few deft paragraphs, Woolf provided a vivid character sketch of an old woman in a train compartment, and then parodied the methods of description that would be used by the trio of Edwardian novelists. Their polemical approach to fiction, Woolf charged, would leave no room for the character and sensibility of the fictional Mrs. Brown to take shape. Commentators have occasionally found Woolf's assessments of her contemporaries faulty: her early published criticism of D. H. Lawrence, for example, was severely critical and has been assessed as unperceptive. However, her notebooks reveal that she eventually revised her opinion of Lawrence, expressing appreciation of his literary achievement. Scholars stress the value of studying Woolf's private papers together with her published criticism in order to arrive at a true estimation of her literary opinions. In fact, her notebooks, diaries, and letters often reveal more acute critical estimations than those found in the literary reviews.

During her lifetime Woolf collected and edited only two volumes of her essays, *The Common Reader* and *The Common Reader: Second Series.* After her death, her husband published a number of others, including *The Death of the Moth, The Moment, The Captain's Death Bed, Hours in a Library,* and *Granite and Rainbow,* as well as a four-volume edition, *Collected Essays.* In this collection, Leonard Woolf included all the essays that Woolf herself had prepared for book publication and a number of others that had not been reprinted since their initial periodical appearance. He divided the essays into two groups, "literary and critical" and "biographical," and arranged them chronologically by subject. Critic Andrew McNeillie

noted that "to the reader interested in the author's development and the context in which her professional life was lived, how it began, and how she regarded it, Leonard Woolf's editorial approach offered no assistance." In 1986 McNeillie began preparing a new edition of the essays, researched in conjunction with information made available through published editions of Woolf's diaries, letters, and reading notebooks. Projected to encompass six volumes, this collection is expected to provide a valuable resource for scholars and readers.

(See also *Dictionary of Literary Biography,* Vols. 36, 100; *Contemporary Authors,* Vols. 104, 130; and *Short Story Criticism,* Vol. 7.)

*PRINCIPAL WORKS

Mr. Bennett and Mrs. Brown (essay) 1924
The Common Reader (essays and criticism) 1925
A Room of One's Own (essay) 1929
The Common Reader: Second Series (essays and criticism) 1932; also published as *The Second Common Reader,* 1932
A Letter to a Young Poet (essay) 1932
Three Guineas (essay) 1938
The Death of the Moth, and Other Essays (essays) 1942
The Moment, and Other Essays (essays) 1947
The Captain's Death Bed, and Other Essays (essays) 1950
A Writer's Diary: Being Extracts from the Diary of Virginia Woolf (diary) 1953
Hours in a Library (essays) 1957
Granite and Rainbow (essays) 1958
Contemporary Writers (criticism) 1965
Collected Essays. 4 vols. (essays, criticism, and journalism) 1966-67
The London Scene: Five Essays (essays) 1975
The Letters of Virginia Woolf. 6 vols. (letters) 1975-80
Books and Portraits (essays and criticism) 1977
The Diary of Virginia Woolf. 5 vols. (diaries) 1977-84
Moments of Being: Unpublished Autobiographical Writings (autobiographical essays) 1976; also published as *Moments of Being,* rev. ed., 1985
Virginia Woolf's Reading Notebooks (notebooks) 1983
The Essays of Virginia Woolf. 3 vols. (essays) 1986-88
A Passionate Apprentice (journals) 1990

*This list includes Woolf's nonfiction works. For a complete list of Woolf's major writings, see *TCLC,* Vol. 5.

Solomon Fishman   (essay date 1943)

[*In the following essay, Fishman discusses the relationship between Woolf's professional interest in the novel genre and her critical views on fiction as expressed in her essays.*]

The views of a critic who has made his mark in one of the branches of imaginative literature have a special claim upon our attention mainly because we feel that he has greater access to the mysteries of his craft than the curious outsider. In our own time we have come to expect the most acute criticism of poetry from the poets themselves. The novelists have not displayed an equal volubility concerning the exercise of their art; hence the extraordinary interest which attends the commentaries of Flaubert and James on their own novels and on fiction generally. In the present century only a few novelists of first rank have seriously occupied themselves with the criticism of fiction, among them Virginia Woolf. One should expect from the novelist an illumination of the actual making of novels and a greater intimacy with the problems of the craft than one obtains from the lay-critic. Mrs. Woolf disappoints us in this. Inhibited by the scruple that the "agony" of creation can be of moment only to the creator, she deliberately severs her critical writings from her novels. The discontinuity is illusory, of course, and her disguise as lay-reader never quite succeeds. Despite preliminary disavowals of specialized knowledge, the **Common Reader**s do not really mask a writer who was one of the boldest innovators in fiction and an artist highly sensitive to technique and significance.

Impressionism afforded her the freedom which would have been denied by a rigorous analytical method, and no doubt was more responsive to her particular gift as stylist. Without deprecating the achievement of her critical essays, some of which are unsurpassed in style and finish in the whole field of English letters, one regrets Virginia Woolf's silence on a subject into which she must have had great insight—the means by which the novelist transforms the conceptual and general into the concrete and specific. But if she waived the task of elucidating her own experience, she was always curious about this experience in other novelists. Unconsciously, perhaps, she sought in the masterpieces of the past and recent past a verification of her aims in fiction. Her professional interests, therefore, are sublimated but never wholly submerged; in the long run they alone endow her criticism with relevance and value. They enable her to look at a novel squarely, neither as a mirror of social influences, nor as an accretion of the author's psychic predicament. Awareness of historical and psychological facts in the genesis of the novel is not absent from her criticism, but origins are consistently subordinated to value. Almost exclusively her criticism was an attempt to locate the virtues which differentiate greatness in fiction, and to establish a scale of values.

In the realm of aesthetic speculation there is no task more redoubtable than the formulation of standards in fiction. The major dilemmas which baffle the critic of poetry are magnified for the critic of fiction by the absence of landmarks which at least indicate the alternatives—the *loci critici* of an Aristotle, Coleridge, T. S. Eliot, or I. A. Richards. It is no wonder that in coping with fiction the critic resorts to impressionism, to the vague and unscientific. E. M. Forster has said that "Principles and systems may suit other forms of art, but they cannot be applicable here," and Virginia Woolf concurred. Her criticism operated by intuition without the mediation of method; she had a flair for "profound general statements which are caught up by the mind when hot with the friction of read-

ing," which was reinforced by temperamental aversion to systems and conclusions, whether metaphysical or aesthetic. Her critical gift flourished in an encounter with a particular novel or novelist but was diminished when it attempted the statement of principles. We cannot hope, therefore, to discover in her writings a rationale of fiction, but only a series of insights and perceptions which may, when coördinated, adumbrate an aesthetic.

Here is one of her ventures in generalization, a statement as remarkable for its diffuseness as for its honesty.

> Life escapes, and perhaps without life nothing else is worth while. It is a confession of vagueness to have to use such a figure as this, but we scarcely better the matter by speaking as critics are prone to do, of reality. Admitting the vagueness which afflicts all criticism of novels, let us hazard the opinion that for us at this moment the form of fiction most in vogue more often misses than secures the thing we seek. Whether we call it life or spirit, truth or reality, this, the essential thing has moved off, or on . . .

In it we recognize a critic who was not easily deflected from the main task, the search for the "essential thing." One might construe the failure in definition as a concomitant of loose thinking; it would be more benevolent to regard it as an admission of defeat on the part of one who had pursued certain lines of inquiry to an ultimate impasse, to an idea so volatile that it cannot be conveyed except in hypostatic terms. Obviously, isolated from its total context, the statement has little value. It is necessary to work back from it, to trace the strands of speculation which point toward it and are implicated in it. The terms employed are provocative: *truth* and *reality* are crucial in the discussion of imaginative literature and can disclose a great deal about the critic's position if we can determine their referents. Since their ambivalence proceeds from the imitative character of literature, they may relate to either of two entities, the imitation itself or the thing imitated; or they might be made to refer to the connecting link which unites both entities. Upon the critic's understanding of these terms is predicated a philosophic and an aesthetic judgment of literature, and beyond them an aesthetics in which philosophical and critical views are subsumed.

The epistemological cleavage inherent in the terms *truth* and *reality* corresponds to the familiar division of critics into formalists and moralists. It is not easy to assign Virginia Woolf categorically to either camp. A novelist is less inclined than a poet to grant an autotelic existence to literature, yet Mrs. Woolf was not vehement in rejecting that view. At most she was willing to concede that "fiction is like a spider's web, attached ever so lightly perhaps, but still attached to life at all four corners." When confronted by unequivocal aestheticism, however, she took a firmer stand, protesting Roger Fry's notion that "everything must come out of the matière of prose and not out of the ideas and emotions he [the writer] describes." While she trusted Fry's judgments on painting, she refused to follow him when he carries them over into literature. Yet we cannot ascribe to her the alternative of a naïve utilitarian or moralistic conception of literature, for nothing irritated her more than a doctrinal novel or a novelist who labors his narrative with elevating discourse or instruction.

Virginia Woolf's critical approach precluded a dualistic interpretation of literature; it focused sharply on the point at which "life and something that is not life" are fused, rather than on the differences which separate art and life. Her real preoccupation was with what Mr. Blackmur calls "the formal means by which the poet can convey an illusion of actuality." This may not be apparent on the surface of her criticism, for it contains few explicit references to form, just as it renounces the whole question of technique. The omission is striking, but fortunately the lacuna has been filled by other writers, notably Percy Lubbock, whose *Craft of Fiction* is almost everything her criticism is not—a controlled, analytic, coherent study of technique in fiction. But Lubbock's work, although essential, is preliminary, and overcautious in withholding the act of evaluation until the novel as an *object* is disengaged and held to the light. For, as Virginia Woolf maintains, if a book is an object, it is capable of producing an effect; and although an understanding of how the book was made may explain the effect, the latter is what is of primary concern to both novelist and critic. At any rate, this is the only logical motive I can perceive for her treatment of the problem of form in terms of theory rather than of technique. Form interests her not as the subject of clinical scrutiny, but only as an aspect of the novelist's power—the power "to force us along [his] road, make us see what [he] sees."

The impulse which governs the direction of Virginia Woolf's criticism is the effort to resolve the polar tensions of philosophic and aesthetic criteria in literature. In her words, "a novel starts in us all sorts of antagonistic and opposed emotions. Life conflicts with something that is not life. . . . The whole structure, it is obvious, thinking back on any famous novel, is one of infinite complexity, because it is thus made up of so many different judgments, of so many different kinds of emotion."

If we examine the philosophical criteria which she applied to fiction, we find them to be conventional enough, and we can pass over them rapidly. She demanded that it present a significant account of man's experience in relation to his fellows, to the external world, and to that abstraction which "for want of a more precise term we call 'life itself'." There are degrees, furthermore, by which the writer's philosophic contribution may be measured. First, delicacy and fineness of perception—the quality which Jane Austen exhibits more perfectly than most novelists. "Think away the surface animation, the likeness to life, and there remains to provide a deeper pleasure, an exquisite discrimination of human values." Then, breadth and inclusiveness, evinced in the compass of a mind like Tolstoi's, of whom she says that "nothing seems to escape him. Nothing glances off him unrecorded. . . . Even in a translation we feel that we have been set on a mountaintop and had a telescope put in our hands." Surpassing these in her scale is the dimension of depth, which is founded upon insight and compassion, on understanding of the soul and the "knowledge of what is most persistent . . . in human nature." Profuse in these qualities, the Russian writers, particularly Tchekov and Dos-

toievsky, made a powerful impression on Virginia Woolf, and left her with an acute sense of the inadequacies of the English novel. "The novels of Dostoievsky are seething whirlpools, grating sandstorms, waterspouts which hiss and boil and suck us in. They are composed purely and wholly of soul. Out of Shakespeare there is no more exciting reading."

This passage demonstrates how criticism can deteriorate into effusion. Virginia Woolf's best, that is, her most original and discerning criticism occurs not when she is describing philosophical attributes, but when she engages in the more difficult phase of the critic's task, the discrimination of aesthetic properties, of what makes a novel a novel, and what causes one narrative to act with so much greater effect than another. And when she is so engaged she is almost willing to throw overboard philosophic considerations. Ideological criticism founders upon a novel like *Wuthering Heights.* "We are given every opportunity of comparing *Wuthering Heights* with a real farm and Heathcliff with a real man. How, we are allowed to ask, can there be truth or insight or the finer shades of emotion in men and women who so little resemble what we have seen ourselves? But even as we ask it we see in Heathcliff the brother that a sister of genius might have seen: he is impossible, we say, but nevertheless no boy in literature has so vivid an existence as his." There is no trace in the book of the power of observation, nor of speculative curiosity concerning the problems of life; instead of breadth of view, there are only "impressions close packed and strongly stamped between . . . narrow walls." Lacking virtually all of the equipment which ordinarily marks the competence of a novelist and the gifts which have attracted to the novelist the widest of audiences, Emily Brontë has nevertheless weathered the test of time, and her reputation is intact.

Obviously if Virginia Woolf regarded *Wuthering Heights* as representative of greatness in fiction, the terms *truth* and *reality* as they appear in the context of her criticism cannot be construed in the primary or literal sense. They cannot be equated with fidelity to fact or with realism. Since her terms fail to provide their own gloss, we must arrive at their meaning obliquely by examining further critical utterances. In the same essay on the Brontës, we read that "It is the suggestion of power underlying the apparitions of human nature, and lifting them up into the presence of greatness that gives the book its huge stature among other novels."

The idea of power provides a clue to the critic's apperception of the nature of the aesthetic process. *Wuthering Heights* was well chosen to illustrate it because it is so patent a specimen of the novel in which power triumphs over a host of inadequacies. It embodies for Virginia Woolf the essence of what differentiates all great novels, from *Robinson Crusoe* to *La Recherche du Temps Perdu,* from the unleavened mass of mediocre books which attempt no more than a mere transcript of life. On the basis of this distinction she consigns the bulk of contemporary fiction to limbo.

> No age can have been more rich than ours in writers to give expression to the differences

which separate them from the past and not to the resemblances which connect them with it . . . the most casual reader can hardly fail to be impressed by the courage, the sincerity, in a word, by the widespread originality of our time. But our exhilaration is strangely curtailed. Book after book leaves us with the same sense of promise unachieved, of intellectual poverty, of brilliance which has been snatched from life but not transmitted into literature.

I think it will be evident from the foregoing that the novelist's power is the power of transmitting one sort of reality into another sort; that is, the power of imagination, or "esemplastic" imagination, as Coleridge conceived it. Coleridge's nomenclature is reserved for poetry, but its relevance to prose narrative is explicitly provided for. We may assume then that the novelist's power does not differ generically from the poet's. It would be a rough axiom, though a fundamentally correct one, to declare that a great novel is *ipso facto* great poetry. Virginia Woolf does so on more than one occasion. We are informed, for example, that " . . . we read Charlotte Brontë not for exquisite observation of character . . . not for comedy . . . not for a philosophic view of life . . . but for her poetry."

But the difficulty of formulating a critique of fiction is not solved by substituting the word *novel* for the word *poetry* in authoritative critical documents: the problem is first to locate the common ground of poetry and fiction and then to stake out the territories which do not coalesce; in other words, to discover what elements of poetic composition are compatible with narrative and how poetic elements get into the novel. It is manifest that the technical procedures of the poet and novelist are widely divergent. The novelist lacks the manifold advantages of the poet in the mechanics of composition—compression, the norms of established formal patterns, the manipulation of language on two planes, aural and semasiological. For no matter how hard he may kick against the traces of "representation", no novelist can abandon himself to metaphorical discourse throughout the length of a narrative; unless, of course, he is the author of *Finnegans Wake*. Yet ultimately, both poet and novelist are impelled by the same necessity of transmuting the materials of experience—thought, feeling, observation, language—into something different and more valuable than had existed before.

Virginia Woolf's examination of fiction is singular in its emphasis on the relationship of poetry and narrative, but again her indiscriminate terminology leads to confusion. "One wonders," David Daiches is prompted to ask in *The Novel and the Modern World,* "if Mrs. Woolf's conception of fiction in terms of poetry is not an excuse for remaining in her study. The lyrical mood has many disguises, but its basis like that of the metaphysical mood is egotism." Mr. Daiches' strictures are justified perhaps if they refer to her conception of fiction as incarnated in her novels, for her work reveals a progressive abandonment of the idiom of prose and an increasingly lyrical style. It is true that the novelist sometimes appropriates the technique of poetry, especially so when "like the Brontës, the writer is poetic, and his meaning is inseparable from his language, and itself rather a mood than a particular observation." But there is no indication that Virginia Woolf aligns herself with those who would achieve a synthesis at the expense of the dissolution of forms. Whatever aim informs the lyricism of her novels, her critical writings make it clear that the novelist assimilates the method of the poet at his own peril. The conscience of the novelist speaks in the observation that "Meredith and Hardy were imperfect novelists largely because they insisted upon introducing qualities of thought and poetry, that are perhaps incompatible with fiction at its most perfect."

Yet in another place she appears to contradict herself flatly by the statement that "fiction will be much the better for standing cheek by jowl with poetry and philosophy." The two statements can scarcely be reconciled unless we understand *poetry* to signify different things in each context. In the first instance it denotes *genre;* in the second it has the much broader application of her remark apropos of Aeschylus: "To understand him it is not so necessary to understand Greek as to understand poetry. It is necessary to take that dangerous leap through the air without words. . . . There is an ambiguity which is the mark of the highest poetry; we cannot know exactly what it means." By *poetry* is signified poetic capability, which, as she pointed out, is most fully realized in Shakespeare, less perfectly in Dostoievsky. It is, therefore, not restricted to metrical composition, but common to all types of imaginative literature. Its characteristic, it will be noted, is ambiguity; what she meant by the ambiguity inherent in literature of high order, is the impossibility of ever reducing it to a conceptual paraphrase. We cannot know exactly what it means because the manner in which it is said is part of the meaning and inseparable from the meaning.

Unless we accept this reading of her notion of poetry, we must assume that she believes the poet or novelist to be an irresponsible agent whose chief purpose is mystification. It is no doubt true that Virginia Woolf exhibits a marked predilection for the problematic and fantastic; witness her admiration for Sterne with his "light attachment to the accepted reality, this neglect of the orderly sequence of narrative." This is corroborated to some extent by her own work, **Orlando** particularly, which leads E. M. Forster to bracket her with Sterne as a fantast. "There is even the same tone in their voices—a rather deliberate bewilderment, an announcement to all and sundry that they do not know where they are going." However, and this is of paramount importance, they actually do know where they are going. The ambiguity of literature is unpredictable, but not accidental; it is willed by the maker. If this were not so, literature would cease to have value for Virginia Woolf.

Poetic power, as she conceives it, is independent of ideology and equivalent to the capacity for evoking ambivalent meanings. The ambivalence exists because literature is compounded of life and "something that is not life." In transmuting the one into the other, the writer is compelled to make some sort of selection from the mulifarious items of experience; further, he must juxtapose the items selected in such a manner that they will best express his intention. Selection and arrangement imply design, which in turn is controlled by a master principle. If we grasp the principle, we come close to perceiving the nature of poetic power. The following provides a key—"the meaning of a book, which lies so often apart from what happens and what is said and consists rather in some connection which things in themselves different have had for the writer, is necessarily hard to grasp." "Connection of things in themselves different" suggests Coleridge's description of the synthetic imagination as revealing itself in "the balance and reconciliation of opposite or discordant qualities." From Coleridge's complicated system I. A. Richards distils a single term *myth,* perhaps the most useful of all terms in the critique of fiction. Myths, he writes, "are no amusement or diversion to be sought as a relaxation and an escape from the hard realities of life. They are these hard realities in projection, their symbolic recognition, coördination, and acceptance. The opposite and discordant qualities in things in them acquire a form. . . . "

By consciously juxtaposing things not ordinarily associated in "real" life the writer creates something new which is no less real. The symbol-making propensity of the writer, then, is what gives literature its ambiguity, in that symbols, unlike "things" permit infinite possibilities of interpretation. "Thus Defoe, by reiterating that nothing but a plain earthenware pot stands in the foreground, persuades us to see remote islands and the solitudes of the human soul. By believing fixedly in the solidity of the pot and its earthiness he has subdued every other element to his design; he has roped the whole universe to his harmony." Besides describing symbol, Virginia Woolf here demonstrates its law: The more concrete and particularized the symbol, the greater its projection and its range of reference. Hence the essential "irony" of imaginative literature.

Since the creation of symbol is to some extent arbitrary, a single act of fusion may produce a brilliant image, startling by virtue of its daring or novelty; but it is obvious that great literature is more than a constellation of discrete acts of imagination. Whether we are dealing with a quatrain or a trilogy, we require, in the first place, that the symbol-making process be sustained; in the second, that it be consistent. The act of "recognition," the primary stage in symbol formation is now submitted to, or subsumed in a process of coördination; in brief, it acquires form and order.

When we apply the concept of myth to the writer of fiction, we perceive that not only must he be capable of breaking the mold of passive observation, but that, in view of the physical properties of the novel, he must sustain this power over a considerable extent of space and time. This constitutes the architecture of the novel. In the essay **"How Should One Read a Book"**, Virginia Woolf suggests that the quickest way to grasp the elements of the art of fiction is not by reading, but by writing.

> The thirty-two chapters of a novel . . . are an attempt to make something as formed and controlled as a building; but words are more impalpable than bricks; reading is a longer and more complicated process than seeing . . . make your own experiment with the dangers and difficulties of words. Recall, then, some event that has left a distinct impression on you. . . . But when you

attempt to reconstruct it in words, you will find that it breaks into a thousand conflicting impressions. Some must be subdued; others emphasised; in the process you will lose probably all grasp upon the emotion itself. Then turn from your blurred and littered pages to the opening pages of some great novelist—Defoe, Jane Austen, Hardy. Now you will be able to appreciate their mastery. It is not merely that we are in the presence of a different person . . . but that we are living in a different world.

The novelist, we perceive, creates a world; from a thousand conflicting impressions he convokes an ordered picture of reality which by virtue of order gives the illusion of completeness. Or, according to Mr. I. A. Richards, he fashions from the incongruity and disorder of experience on the pragmatic level, he fashions a myth which has wholeness and unity. The idea is contained for Mrs. Woolf in the word *vision*—"a vision such as we get in a good novel where everything contributes to bring the writer's conception as a whole before us." Vision makes for wholeness; it also provides unity. "Yet different as these worlds are, [Hardy's, Austen's, Defoe's] each is consistent with itself. The maker of each is careful to observe the laws of his own perspective, and however great a strain he puts upon us, he will never confuse us, as lesser artists frequently do, by introducing two different kinds of reality into the same book." She is willing to allow the novelist much latitude in the method of selection. The transmutation of reality may be so radical or so bizarre that it produces, in her words, an agony in the reader who attempts to adjust the novelist's perspective to his own. Sometimes, in the instance of Emily Brontë, the writer takes extreme liberties in the matter of verisimilitude; sometimes, as with Hardy, he wrenches the fable to the point of mawkishness. Such departures from the norm of narrative practice are tolerated inasmuch as they are subordinated to the greater achievement of vision.

Despite her protest of indifference to origins in fiction, Virginia Woolf finds it impossible to ignore them altogether. As we have seen, she is much occupied with the quality of mind which can produce a succession of images so integrated and sustained in effect that they compel the reader to cede his own perspective and acquiesce, for the time being, in another vision. The creative mind exhibits dual tendencies—a polarity of intensity and restraint. Coleridge's "more than usual state of emotion with more than usual order" is apposite; one might go farther and say that mythopoeic power is characterized by both the rational and the demonic.

"Symbolic recognition and coördination" are functions of the rational; "symbolic acceptance," of the demonic. Poetic invention is not the result of mere receptivity to stimuli; it demands, first of all, intense concentration; and second, the courage to keep faith with the symbol after having conjured it. This courage Virginia Woolf calls "integrity." "What one means by integrity, in the case of the novelist, is the conviction that this is the truth. Yes, one feels, I should never have thought that this could be so; I have never known people behaving like that. But you have convinced me so it is, so it happens."

A great deal has been written to prove that art is "artificial", that the making of symbol is a wholly capricious exercise. Virginia Woolf does not hold with this view. Truth in literature, defined by Mr. Daiches as "proper selection combined with the proper handling of symbols," far from being fabricated or contrived, must issue from two sources; from the personal conviction of the writer—"a single person with a single sensibility," and from what Mr. Blackmur terms "anterior conviction." The whole problem, as Mrs. Woolf sees it, is one of utmost subtlety: "For the vision of a novelist is both complex and specialized; complex, because behind his characters and apart from them must stand something stable to which he related them; specialized because since he is a single person with one sensibility the aspects of life in which he can believe with conviction are strictly limited."

The problem of belief is no less pressing for the poet than for the novelist, but it taxes him less heavily. Within the compass of a single poem symbol-making most frequently requires the discovery of "objective correlatives" of emotions and ideas, whereas the novelist is charged with the discovery of the correlatives of the inner and outer lives of men and women in relation to each other and to the world. Yeats has simply to name "the holy city of Byzantium" and a symbolic recognition is made. The novelist sometimes uses this sort of correlative, as in *Les Faux-Monnayeurs* when the false coin is tossed onto the table, but generally his symbols are more extended: Think of the rôle of Mynheer Peeperkorn in *The Magic Mountain,* or an even more complex instance, the figure of Joseph in Mann's latest work. Since the novelist is committed to dealing with experience in terms of portraiture and plot, the symbol, or rather the configuration of symbols called myth, derives its validity from the tensions which exist between the individual and the universal. When a novel is wholly successful, individual and universal, fable and myth, are so continuous that one can no longer distinguish, in Mr. Austin Warren's phrase, "whether the type incarnated itself or the individual implied a typicality." Virginia Woolf perceives this when she writes that "nobody can deny Hardy's power—the true novelist's power—to make us believe his characters are fellow beings driven by their passions and idiosyncrasies, while they have—and this is the poet's gift—something symbolical about them which is common to us all."

The essay **"Modern Fiction"** was written in 1919; perhaps in that year Mrs. Woolf was justified in denying mythopoeic power to her contemporaries. (It is worth noting then in writing of the twentieth century novelists she deviates more widely than elsewhere from her rôle of guide to the lay-reader.) The charges she prefers are devastating, but not inapposite. "So then our contemporaries afflict us because they have ceased to believe. The most sincere of them will only tell us what it is that happens to himself. . . . They cannot tell stories because they do not believe the stories are true. They cannot generalize. They depend on their senses and emotions, whose testimony is trustworthy, rather than on their intellects whose message is obscure." Against the modern she posits the writers of a former age—a Scott, Wordsworth, or Jane Austen.

They have their judgment of conduct. They know the relations of human beings toward each other and the universe . . . for certainty of that kind is the condition which makes it possible to write. To believe that your impressions hold good for others is to be released from the cramp and confinement of personality. . . . It is also the first step in that mysterious process in which Jane Austen was so great an adept. The little grain of experience once selected, believed in, and set outside herself, could be put precisely in its place, and she was then free to make of it, by a process which never yields its secrets to the analyst, into that complete statement which is literature.

She does not explicitly attribute lack of faith or disintegrity to Bennett, Galsworthy, and Wells, who are singled out for attack. Rather, their novels are "materialistic", "concerned not with the spirit but the body." They devote splendid gifts to the task of making the "trivial and transitory appear true and enduring." This is a curious statement from one who delighted in Sterne's notion that a girl might be more interesting than a cathedral and a dead donkey more instructive than a philosopher. It is unfortunate that *important* and *trivial* appear with such lack of precise reference in this context, for they detract from its penetration. That she does not propose to establish a scale of values for the materials of narrative is evident, for in the same essay we read that the "proper stuff of fiction does not exist; everything is the proper stuff of fiction, every feeling, every thought; every quality of brain and spirit is drawn upon, no perception comes amiss."

The materialism of the Georgians consists, not in their subject matter, but in their inability to submit the "little grain of experience" to the catalyst of symbolic transformation, whereby it becomes free of the author and is ready to take its place in a transcendental reality. The real basis of her animadversions is form. Indeed, all of the focal terms of her critical apparatus—truth, poetry, vision, integrity—are seen to be aspects of form if we agree that form means the angle at which the poet's sensibility converges upon the object in the act of transforming it into symbol. Her real quarrel with Bennett, Wells, and Galsworthy concerns their method, not their ideologies. They rely on observation rather than on insight; their purview is not a poetic vision of life; instead of fashioning symbols they depend upon outworn formulas. Here she reveals the principle which governs her own method: "Life is not a series of gig-lamps symmetrically arranged; but a luminous halo, a semi-transparent envelope surrounding us from the beginning of consciousness to the end."

It is the spirituality of James Joyce which sets him apart from the others. We are told, furthermore, that his "spirituality" consists precisely in his method; for has not Joyce, like herself, depicted the semi-transparent envelope which surrounds consciousness? But granting the spirituality of his method, granting also that "Any method is right, every method is right that expresses what we wish to express if we are writers; that brings us closer to the novelist's intention if we are readers," she is constrained to withhold total praise, and consigns *Ulysses* to a rank below that of the best novels of Hardy and Conrad. She is not reactionary;

she does not cavil at the book's obscurities, nor its technique. The flaw of *Ulysses* is in its method, or rather in the aims of its method: "Is it due to the method that we feel neither jovial nor magnanimous, but centered in a self which, in spite of its tremor of susceptibility, never embraces or creates what is outside itself and beyond?"

It adds to Virginia Woolf's stature as a critic that she was able to perceive the regulative idea which underlies the structure of *Ulysses* when the book was only partially revealed in the installments appearing in *transition;* namely the effort to produce an autonomous piece of literature, a novel so complete, so hermetic, that it becomes an object entirely, and so independent of the author, in Mr. Daiches' phrase "as to make judgment and comparison impossible." Or one might say that Joyce attempts to endow symbol with only one dimension, intensiveness, and to suppress its extension or projection, thus depriving it of "ambiguity."

Although the most cogent of Mrs. Woolf's theoretical statements pertain to form, she does not consent to the notion that the ends of criticism are accomplished by defining the "ontological effect" of a novel. The concept of form is valuable for her insofar as it differentiates literature from what is not literature, but it cannot serve alone as a measure of value. Otherwise, the qualities of magnanimity and joviality which she finds lacking in *Ulysses* could hardly be relevant. The reservations voiced concerning the greatness of *Ulysses* derive from her aesthetic rather than from her theory of criticism.

The views of Joyce and Mrs. Woolf are diametrically opposed at their source. Joyce's aesthetic is expounded in *The Portrait of the Artist:* art, according to Dedalus-Joyce, tends toward the achievement of *stasis,* which implies a state of contemplation, of detachment from the *kinesis* of life. In such a state, "the personality of the artist refines itself out of existence"; the work of art is automatically released from all obligations except the obligation to the exigencies of its own existence, which is its form. I am not sure that Mrs. Woolf would have rejected entirely the Thomist basis of Joyce's aesthetic. Certainly she affirms the non-utilitarian condition of literature and denies its function as propaganda or incitement to action. Writing of *Antigone,* she observes that when the curtain falls we sympathize even with Creon.

> This result, to the propagandist undesirable, would seem to be due to the fact that Sophocles . . . uses freely all the faculties that can be possessed by a writer; and suggests that if we use art to propagate political opinions, we must force the artist to clip and cabin his gift to do us a cheap and passing service. Literature will suffer the same mutilation that the mule has suffered, and there will be no more horses.

The Joycean versions of *integras* and *consonantia* are not far from her own notions of vision and integrity; however, *claritas* (Joyce translates *radiance*) would have meant for her something quite different. The difference is one of emphasis, perhaps, but nonetheless radical. Her aesthetic has at its core the concept of the dynamic of literature. The aesthetic experience does not consist in the capture of the

object, thereby guaranteeing a cessation of future emotion or activity. The object of art is conceived not as a receptacle but as an agent capable of disclosing to the beholder a constantly expanding realm of experience. Imaginative literature is a potential: "an idea presented by a great writer explodes and gives birth to all kinds of other ideas, and that is the only sort of writing of which one can say that it has the secret of perpetual life." The motif appears again and again: Great literature sets us free, it releases us from the cramp and confinement of individual experience, it serves as a stimulus rather than as terminal experience—"the reading of these books [*Lear, Emma, La Recherche du Temps Perdu*] seems to perform a curious couching operation on the senses, one sees more intensely afterwards; the world seems bare of its covering and given an intenser life."

The emphasis is on intellectual response, not on active or emotive reflexes. The essay on George Gissing is particularly pertinent. She finds him, on the whole, a painful writer, lacking virtually all the natural gifts of the novelist. He has never mastered a perspective which excludes his own petty grievances; he is devoid of poetic ability; he has never learned to manage language with grace. One virtue, and that alone, redeems his work. "With all his narrowness of outlook and meagreness of sensibility, Gissing is one of the extremely rare novelists who believes in the power of the mind, who makes his people think. They are thus differently posed from the majority of fictitious men and women . . . the brain works and that alone is enough to give us a sense of freedom. For to think is to become complex; it is to overflow the boundaries, to cease to be a 'character', to merge one's private life in the life of politics or art or ideas. . . . "

We note here the insistence on impersonality as an attribute of aesthetic experience. Not that the importance of personality in literature is underrated. Vision and integrity are, after all, to a large extent, products of personal conviction. But in creating symbol or myth, the writer transforms his perception into something which transcends the individual. The personal element in literature is always a source of power, but one that entails great risk: "the self which, while it is essential to literature, is also its most dangerous antagonist. Never to be yourself and yet always—that is the problem." Joyce devoted tremendous effort to achieve the plane of pure drama, in which the work of art is released from its dependence on personality; yet to Virginia Woolf, *Ulysses* appears "centered in a self which . . . never creates what is outside itself and beyond." The source of her inability to accept *Ulysses* is to be sought in their respective aesthetic systems. Joyce's has its origins in a theology which values contemplation as highest in the order of human occupations. Hers is rooted in the rationalist and humanist tradition which reaches back to Montaigne—the Montaigne of her paraphrase: "Movement and change are the essence of our being; rigidity is death; conformity is death. . . . For nothing matters except life; and, of course, order."

Virginia Woolf was probably not ill-advised in choosing the amateur rather than the technical approach to literature. It gives her criticism equilibrium, rescues it from the aridity of doctrine unsupported by example, and steers it clear of the adventitious. In closing with the work itself, she dismisses the antecedent and peripheral: "However we may wind and wriggle, loiter and dally in our approach to books, a lonely battle awaits us at the end. There is a piece of business to be transacted between writer and reader before further dealings are possible. . . . Our first task . . . is to master his perspective. Until we know how the novelist orders his world, the ornaments of that world, which the critics press upon us, the adventures of the writer, to which biographers call attention, are superfluous possessions of which we can make no use."

Since Mrs. Woolf practised criticism in the traditional mode of the nineteenth century, its theoretical aspects elude formulation. One might very well appropriate her comment on Hazlitt to her own work: "since in his view, it was the duty of a critic to 'reflect the colours, the light and shade, the soul and body of a work,' appetite, gusto, enjoyment were far more important than analytic subtlety or prolonged and extensive study." The implication here is that the critic may miss a great deal if he wields too sharp a tool. In reducing the intuitive perceptions of such a critic to formula, and by imputing to them a coherence which does not actually exist, one is likely to commit the error of over-simplification, if not of distortion. However, the components of a system are there, if only potentially, and they invite reconstruction, if only a hypothetical one. The effort to provide her theory with pattern has necessarily excluded a description of the quality and texture of her criticism. Her essays will be read, I feel, because they reflect an independent mind, confident of its judgment and tastes; owing no tribute to authority or convention, but not intimidated by the obvious any more than by the esoteric and obscure. There is a great deal of the flâneur in Virginia Woolf, which sometimes leads her far afield from the main stream of letters, but we are thereby rewarded by an increase of breadth and sympathy. Her essays unite the gusto of the amateur with a devotion to literature which is not surpassed in contemporary letters. One of the few positive beliefs which her scepticism allows her is the conviction that man fulfils himself most completely in the reading and writing of good books. One may argue that this is an excessively narrow point of view; but if it attenuates her scope and limits her powers, it also gives her criticism its peculiar vitality. According to her a novel should be an experience, not a document; there are other attitudes towards literature, but hers is logically unassailable. (pp. 321-40)

> Solomon Fishman, "Virginia Woolf on the Novel," in The Sewanee Review, *Vol. LI, No. 2, Spring, 1943, pp. 321-40.*

Mark Schorer   (essay date 1943)

[*Schorer was an American critic and biographer who, in his essay "Technique as Discovery" (1948), argued that fiction deserves the same close attention to diction and metaphor that the New Critics had been applying to poetry. For Schorer, criticism must examine "achieved content," or form, as well as content. In the following review of* The Death of the Moth, and Other Essays, *he discusses the value of Woolf's criticism in providing insight into her fiction writing.*]

Since Virginia Woolf's unhappy death—that great crime of our world, murderous in so many ways which still elude tribunal—a curious tendency to invert the relationship between her fiction and her literary criticism has asserted itself. Mr. David Daiches's handbook on the subject discussed her criticism with wholly disproportionate length and solemnity; Mr. William Plomer has said that she is more of a novelist in her criticism than in her novels, which, if it does not overestimate the criticism, at least denigrates the novels; still others have made the extreme judgment that she was first of all a critic, and then a critic writing fiction. [*The Death of the Moth, and Other Essays,* a] collection of short pieces posthumously prepared by her husband, substantiates, both in its examples and in its precepts, the older view, which is also the view of Mr. E. M. Forster's attractive essay: "It is as a novelist that she will be judged." What one means to say is only that her general essays, like her criticism, are finger exercises, drills—even when full-dress—for the novelist's sensibility, preliminary and exploratory essays wholly subordinate to the novels, and as such by her regarded.

The general essays—the first seven pieces in the book—are forms of reverie of the sort with which her novels abound; here she utilized the convenient amorphousness of the nineteenth-century familiar essay (even then an anomaly, now an anachronism) in order to manipulate images and other impressions which, when ordered within the frame of fiction, gave the old, outworn type a useful, original function. The essays on general literary subjects, like the famous *Mr. Bennett and Mrs. Brown,* are no less clearly related to the novels. The last seven selections in this book are of that order; and all are the means either of clarifying the novelist's own problems, intellectual and technical, or of justifying her conception of the function of the novelist, most particularly, of the woman novelist in an incompletely liberalized society, Virginia Woolf herself.

Her literary criticism—the twelve central selections— gives the argument its main support. "Say nothing about the learning and the industry, the devotion and the skill which have created these two huge volumes, and . . . record merely such fleeting thoughts as have formed in the mind," she writes of the Yale Edition of the Walpole-Cole correspondence; of Sara Coleridge's autobiography— "She said many things in those twenty-six pages, and Mr. Griggs has added others that tempt us to fill in the dots"; an imaginary letter to the antiquary, William Cole, opens imperiously: "In my opinion you are keeping something back"; and of the life of Gibbon she says, "But as we run over the familiar picture there is something that eludes us." These remarks reveal the active and aggressive temperament of the novelist, nothing of the critic. For the desire to comprehend experience directly (whether Walpole's or one's own) without intermediaries between the object and the sensibility; the desire to complete experience by giving it form, that is, to fill the dots of life, which is no less fragmentary than Sara Coleridge's slice of it; and finally, the desire to find a clue which will make experience cohere, to wring from life that "something" which it eternally keeps back, to seize at last upon that "something that eludes us"—all these are the motive of the novelist. And they have nothing to do with the critic, who is learned, who is concerned with the hard facts of literary discipline and technique rather than with the mysteries of experience, and who comes to literature with objective standards, not to life with a question.

Her literary criticism is subordinate to Mrs. Woolf's fiction in still another way; illuminatingly, she writes: "For we are incapable of living wholly in the intense world of the imagination. The imagination is a faculty that soon tires and needs rest and refreshment. But for a tired imagination the proper food is not inferior poetry or minor fiction . . . but sober fact, that 'authentic information' from which . . . good biography is made." Hence her passion not only for biography but for history as well; her interest in correspondence, "the humane art"; the irrepressible impulse of her criticism to move from a text to the manners of the age which produced it, as from an author's work to his life. All this was the nourishment of her fiction, and the result provides an interesting paradox. For while Virginia Woolf, perhaps more than any writer of stature in the present century, insisted—and with her wonderful sensitivity, should have—upon seizing on life directly, and actually, in doing so, gave sensuosity a value which it had never had before in the English novel—in spite of all this, half the time she approached her material through literature, and in at least three ways. Her novels are crowded with literary echoes—that is to say, with borrowed modes of feeling—echoes which exasperated and finally alienated many readers. Most of her characters seem to be literary people, who approach *their* experience with the benefit of Mrs. Woolf's own exquisite sensibility and with the more dubious benefit of the artist's preconceptions and preoccupations generally. Finally, at least two of her books, **Orlando** and **Between the Acts,** derive their very structure from the history of English literature. What one reads is no less a portion of one's experience than any other activity; of present point is the fact that Virginia Woolf approached her reading, in her criticism, as she approached the whole of experience in her novels: with aggressive curiosity, a refined sensibility, but an exaggerated sense of the relevance of impression (which last Mr. Forster seems to regard as a property "essentially poetic," a gross error). What is lacking, finally, is the sense of value.

For what is that "something" which old William Cole held back? He may have been in love with a Miss Chester. And what is the "something that eludes us" in the life of Gibbon? Under the austerity and the learning, he was really—yes—lonely. Are these points worth making? All of us, in our time, have been in love with a Miss Chester and have lost her, and loneliness is the universal condition. This is a kind of sentimentality which overtakes even the most exquisite mind if it prefers to operate without objective values; and it was so that Virginia Woolf habitually wrote her criticism. The result is that it always tells us more about Virginia Woolf than about the text or the man in question; and it tells us important things about Virginia Woolf, the novelist.

In her novels as in her criticism she confused "value" with "theory," and that is a grave mistake. She finds the intel-

Virginia Woolf.

lectual overtones in the novels of E. M. Forster a deficiency: "Exerting ourselves to find out the meaning, we step from the enchanted world of imagination, where our faculties work freely, to the twilight world of theory, where only our intellect functions dutifully." The artist must not "make his theories fit too tight to accommodate the formlessness of life," she wrote in **The Second Common Reader.** This is perfectly obvious, if they *are* theories; how but by values, however, can we "accommodate the formlessness of life" at all, how, that is, make the fragments of a world which our impressions give us cohere, how, indeed, come by that famous "something"? Mr. Forster makes a distinction in his little book which is interesting, if superficial: "There seem to be two sorts of life in fiction, life on the page and life eternal." The first, he says, Virginia Woolf had—her characters never seem unreal; the second she did not have—one does not remember them. Many people will not accept this judgment; and the critic cannot accept the distinction as final. It is again the question of the writer with objective values and the writer who declines them; and thus a novelist of relatively inferior equipment and trashy tastes, like Dickens, may succeed at precisely the point where Mrs. Woolf, with her remarkable equipment and impeccable tastes, fails. Another problem is involved. It was the great achievement of Proust and of James, for example, to derive philosophical weight from their impressions, and to give back to us whole and ordered worlds; it was the great achievement of Virginia Woolf, whose impressions did not transcend the value of psychology, to give back to us whole and ordered, if infinitely fragile worlds in at least three novels, including her last, *Between the Acts.* "The illusion is upon me," says Bernard at the end of *The Waves,* "that something adheres for a moment, has roundness, weight, depth, is completed." It is nothing short of extraordinary that, armed only with her sensibility and a zealous devotion to writing for the sake of writing (which Mr. Forster properly emphasizes), Virginia Woolf managed in at least three of her ten novels to put the illusion of completeness upon us. To observe that sensibility preening its feathers, as it were, has always been an excitement, in the present as in earlier volumes of non-fiction. And this book, as a matter of fact, would be invaluable to Mrs. Woolf's admirers if only for one passage, an estimate of George Moore, which follows:

> Not one of his novels is a masterpiece; they are silken tents which have no poles; but he has brought a new mind into the world; he has given us a new way of feeling and seeing; he has devised—very painfully, for he is above all things painstaking, eking out a delicate gift laboriously—a means of liquidating the capricious and volatile essence of himself . . . and that, whatever the degree, is triumph, achievement, immortality. If, further, we try to establish the degree we shall go on to say that no one so inveterately literary is among the great writers; literature has wound itself about him like a veil, forbidding him the free use of his limbs; the phrase comes to him before the emotion; but we must add that he is nevertheless a born writer, a man who detests meals, servants, ease, respectability or anything that gets between him and his art; who has kept his freedom when most of his contemporaries have long ago lost theirs; who is ashamed of nothing but of being ashamed; who says whatever he has it in his mind to say, and has taught himself an accent, a cadence, indeed a language, for saying it in which . . . will give him his place among the lesser immortals of our tongue.

A perhaps too reverent account of Moore; but was she, by that time, really thinking of Moore at all? One may say of Virginia Woolf, who was wonderful in more ways than she was vulnerable, that she had the power, and the poise, to compose so perfect an estimate of herself. Can one think of another who could, today? (pp. 377-81)

> *Mark Schorer, "Virginia Woolf," in* The Yale Review, *Vol. XXXII, No. 2, Winter, 1943, pp. 377-81.*

Desmond Pacey   (essay date 1948)

[*Pacey was a New Zealand-born Canadian educator, critic, and author of children's verse. In the following essay, he identifies the principal standards of judgment in Woolf's literary criticism.*]

She was a born critic, and a critic whose judgments were inborn, unhesitating. She is always referring her impressions to a standard—hence the incisiveness, the depth and the comedy that make those spontaneous statements so illuminating. There is nothing naïve about her. She is by no means a simple spectator. Maxims fall

from her pen. She sums up; she judges. But it is done effortlessly. She has inherited the standard and accepts it without effort. She is heir to a tradition, which stands guardian and gives proportion. [*The Death of the Moth*]

Thus Virginia Woolf writes of Madame de Sévigné, and in so doing utters a judgment which is at least as true of herself as of her subject. For Mrs. Woolf was herself a born critic, an impressionist who nevertheless had clear and consistent standards of judgment, a literary experimenter to whom tradition was a real and living force.

From her father, Leslie Stephen, she inherited and acquired an eager interest in literature, and especially in that of the eighteenth century. From first to last she moved among people to whom the high importance of literature and the arts was self-evident, and to whom criticism was a staple of conversation and one of the assumed necessities of daily life. It was almost inevitable, then, that she should seek to refine her impressions, form judgments, and, when she had subjected them to rigorous review and revision, publish them. The product was the two series of *The Common Reader* (1925 and 1932), the critical essays in *The Death of the Moth* (1942) and *The Moment and Other Essays* (1947), and the pamphlets *Mr. Bennett and Mrs. Brown* (1924) and *Letter to a Young Poet* (1932).

Her critical approach is modest and unassuming. Her essays read like conversation which has been purged of redundancy, triviality, and flatulence, but which has retained all its informality, warmth, and verve. Though sometimes maxims fall from her pen, though she does not hesitate to sum up and judge, she does so casually and easily. She never essays the role of pontiff, nor speaks with academic condescension. She is professedly "the common reader," apologizing semi-seriously for her ignorance:

> But before I begin, I must own up to those defects, both real and acquired, which, as you will find, distort and invalidate all that I have to say about poetry. The lack of a sound university training has always made it impossible for me to distinguish between an iambic and a dactyl, and if this were not enough to condemn one for ever, the practice of prose has bred in me, as in most prose writers, a foolish jealousy, a righteous indignation—anyhow, an emotion which the critic should be without. [*Letter to a Young Poet*]

She is impatient of rules—and of schools. "It would appear, then," she writes in an essay on Christina Rossetti, "that there are at least three schools of criticism. . . . This is confusing. . . . Better perhaps read for oneself, expose the mind bare to the poem, and transcribe in all its haste and imperfection whatever may be the result of the impact."

The result of exposing the mind bare to the poem, novel, play, or essay is what Virginia Woolf gives us in her criticism. It is, in other words, impressionistic criticism, though she is not fair to herself when she speaks of its being transcribed in haste and imperfection. One has the sense always that her impressions have been carefully weighed, refined, chastened, clarified, before transcription. They are the impressions, moreover, of an extremely sensitive mind, and of a mind well steeped in literary tradition: the element of the merely private and eccentric is reduced to a minimum. What she seeks always is the heart of a book, its special quality, its distinctive core of meaning, rather than to dazzle us with some private illumination of her own or to prove some pet critical doctrine.

But her impressionism and her impatience with rules do not argue a lack of standards. Though she seldom indulges in abstract theory, though she never obtrudes the standards to which her impressions are referred, the standards are there, in the background of even the slightest essay, and they are maintained with a high degree of consistency.

Chief among these standards is an insistence upon wholeness, upon singleness of vision and effect in a work of art. She informs the young poet that his task is "to find the relation between things that seem incompatible yet have a mysterious affinity, to absorb every experience that comes your way fearlessly and saturate it completely so that your poem is a whole, not a fragment." Discussing the novels of E. M. Forster, she declares "if there is one gift more essential to a novelist than another it is the power of combination—the single vision." George Meredith incurs her disapproval because "he seems to be of two minds as to his intention."

Achievement of this singleness of effect, of course, depends upon the artist's passion for form. "The thirty-two chapters of a novel," she writes, "are an attempt to make something as formed and controlled as a building." She reserves her greatest praise for writers such as Henry James and Jane Austen who were devoted to conscientious craftsmanship. All of James's books have "the final seal upon them of artistic form"; whatever Jane Austen writes "is finished and turned." Of a relatively slipshod artist such as Shelley, on the other hand, she is severely critical: "How are we to account for the fact that we remember him as a great poet and find him on opening his pages a bad one? The explanation seems to be that he was not a 'pure poet.' He did not concentrate his meaning in a small space; there is nothing in Shelley's poetry as rich and compact as the odes of Keats."

Her second great principle is the impersonality of all great art. Gissing is an imperfect novelist because through his books "one sees the life of the author faintly covered by the lives of fictitious people. With such writers we establish a personal rather than an artistic relationship." She makes a similar point about George Moore, but argues it more fully:

> All his novels are written, covertly and obliquely, about himself. . . . But are not all novels about the writer's self, we might ask? It is only as he sees people that we can see them; his fortunes colour and his oddities shape his vision until what we see is not the thing itself, but the thing seen and the seer inextricably mixed. There are degrees, however. The great novelist feels, sees, believes with such intensity of conviction that he hurls his belief outside himself and it flies off and lives an independent life of its own, becomes Natasha, Pierre, Levin, and is no longer Tolstoy. When, however, Mr. Moore creates a Natasha she may be charming, foolish, lovely, but her beauty, her folly, her charm are not hers, but Mr. Moore's. All her qualities refer to him. In other words, Mr. Moore is completely lacking in dramatic power. On the face of it, *Esther Waters* has all the appearance of a great novel: it has sincerity, shapeliness, style; it has surpassing seriousness and integrity; but because Mr. Moore has not the strength to project Esther from himself its virtues collapse and fall about it like a tent with a broken pole.

The same idea pops up again, in an unexpected context, when she is discussing Lord Chesterfield's *Letters:* "It may be that the art of pleasing has some connection with the art of writing. To be polite, considerate, controlled, to sink one's egotism, to conceal rather than to obtrude one's personality may profit the writer even as they profit the man of fashion." Whether this preference for impersonal art accounts for her interest in the literature of the eighteenth century, or merely reflects it, it is impossible to determine; but that there is a close connection between them is obvious.

A corollary of this doctrine of impersonality is her belief that the artist should not obtrude his opinions or regard art as a pulpit. Of Meredith she writes:

> His teaching seems now too strident and too optimistic and too shallow. It obtrudes; and when philosophy is not consumed in a novel, when we can underline this phrase with a pencil, and cut out that exhortation with a pair of scissors and paste the whole thing into a system, it is safe to say that there is something wrong with the philosophy or with the novel or with both. Above all, his teaching is too insistent. He cannot . . . suppress his own opinion. And there is nothing that characters in fiction resent more. If, they seem to argue, we have been called into existence merely to express Mr. Meredith's views upon the universe, we would rather not exist at all. Thereupon they die; and a novel that is full of dead characters even though it is also full of profound wisdom and exalted teachings, is not achieving its aim as a novel.

This idea that the novel's primary function is to display persons rather than to parade opinions occurs quite frequently in her essays. In *Mr. Bennett and Mrs. Brown* she writes, "I believe that all novels . . . deal with character, and that it is to express character—not to preach doctrines, sing songs, or celebrate the glories of the British Empire, that the form of the novel . . . has been evolved."

But for all her passion for form and her conviction that the artist should not thrust his opinions upon us, Mrs. Woolf is no disciple of the art for art's sake school. Art can and should convey a message, provided that it is an organic part of the work and not an applied excrescence, and that it deals with the permanent and universal rather than the temporary and local. What she praises most highly in the work of Henry James is not his craftsmanship, or at least not that as something in and for itself, but the fact that "here, by a prodigious effort of concentration, the field of human activity is brought into fresh focus, revealing new horizons, new landmarks, and new lights upon it of right and wrong." She feels that the surest way for the artist to achieve universality is to eschew the public and political issue in favour of the private and ethical. In ignoring the Napoleonic struggle and concentrating upon the private joys and sorrows of English country people, Jane Austen created something of enduring interest: "she was writing for everybody, for nobody, for our age, for her own." "What she offers is, apparently, a trifle, yet is composed of something that expands in the reader's mind and endows with the most enduring form of life scenes which are outwardly trivial. . . . It has the permanent quality of literature. Think away the surface animation, the likeness to life, and there remains to provide a deeper pleasure, an exquisite discrimination of human values." Chaucer and E. M. Forster afford other examples of her approved treatment of morality in literature. Of Chaucer she writes: "It is safe to say that not a single law has been framed or one stone set upon another because of anything that Chaucer said or wrote; and yet, as we read him, we are of course absorbing morality at every pore." Forster has no great interest in institutions, no wide social curiosity; "his concern is with the private life; his message is addressed to the soul."

What the artist should give us, then, is not a programme but an illumination, not a creed but a renewed sense of values. Yet this stress upon private and moral values was not mere escapism; it arose from Mrs. Woolf's conviction that the private issues were fully as important as the more obvious political ones, and that their successful resolution was a prerequisite for the resolution of the others. This is stated fully and clearly in a paragraph on Shelley:

> Politically, Shelley's England has already receded, and his fight, valiant though it is, seems to be with monsters who are a little out of date, and therefore slightly ridiculous. But privately he is much closer to us. For alongside the public battle rages, from generation to generation, another fight which is as important as the other, though much less is said about it. Husband fights with wife and son with father. The poor fight the rich and the employer fights the employed. There is a perpetual effort on the one hand to make all these relationships more reasonable, less painful and less servile; on the other, to keep them as they are. Shelley, both as son and husband, fought for reason and freedom in private life, and his experiments, disastrous as they were in many ways, have helped us to greater sincerity and happiness in our own conflicts. The Sir Timothys of Sussex are no longer so prompt to cut their sons off with a shilling; the Booths and the Baxters are no longer quite so sure that an unmarried wife is an unmitigated demon. The grasp of convention upon private life is no longer quite so coarse or quite so callous because of Shelley's successes and failures.

It is in this context that her most famous single critical pronouncement, the oft-quoted essay on **"Modern Fiction,"** can be most fully appreciated. Her attack on the Edwardian social realists—Arnold Bennett, H. G. Wells, and John Galsworthy—is not the expression of a mere private grudge, or simply the reaction of a member of a new generation against the ideals of the previous one. It is a carefully considered rejection based on a theory of art which runs

through all her critical writing. She is, to put it rather differently, appealing to tradition as well as to experiment; she is weighing their aims and achievements not only against her own but against those of Chaucer and Jane Austen. When she charges that the Edwardians "write of unimportant things; that they spend immense skill and immense industry making the trivial and the transitory appear the true and enduring," or pleads with us not to take it for granted that "life exists more fully in what is commonly thought big than in what is commonly thought small," she is not merely defending her own work against the charge of triviality but also expounding her conviction that it is the issues of private life which are really fundamental and universal. The true task of the novelist is to display the inner life of his characters, "to convey this varying, this unknown and uncircumscribed spirit, whatever aberration or complexity it may display, with as little mixture of the alien and external as possible."

She saw that this effort to "reveal the flickerings of that innermost flame which flashes its messages through the brain" would involve the disregard of many of the conventional signposts of fiction, and this brings us to another of her permanent principles, the necessity for literary experiment. When experiment ceases, literature dies. "Death in literature," she writes, "comes gracefully, smoothly, quietly. Lines slip easily down the accustomed grooves. The old designs are copied so glibly that we are half inclined to think them original, save for that very glibness." She expresses her readiness to welcome any experimental technique which achieves its effect: "Any method is right, every method is right, that expresses what we wish to express." Elsewhere she extends this welcome of novelty to the whole of life: "Movement and change are the essence of our being; rigidity is death; conformity is death. . . . For nothing matters except life; and, of course, order."

That final clause serves to remind us that Mrs. Woolf's acceptance of experiment does not extend to anarchy or to irresponsible eccentricity. She has too strong a sense of the past, too great a respect for tradition, for that. She is critical of some of the more extreme manifestations of the experimental spirit in the twentieth century, though she recognizes the conditions which have prompted them: "At the present moment we are suffering, not from decay, but from having no code of manners which writers and readers accept as a prelude to the more exciting intercourse of friendship. The literary convention of the time is so artificial . . . that, naturally, the feeble are tempted to outrage, and the strong are led to destroy the very foundations and rules of literary society. Signs of this are everywhere apparent. Grammar is violated; syntax disintegrated. . . . " And with that we have reached what is perhaps the heart of the problem of criticism for Mrs. Woolf, the point to which she returns again and again: how may the contemporary writer come to grips with the contemporary world?

For that he must come to grips with the world of his own time she is fully convinced. "Literature, if it is to keep us on the alert through five acts or thirty-two chapters must somehow be based on Smith, have one toe touching Liverpool. . . . " She remarks approvingly of Chaucer that "he never flinched from the life that was being lived at the moment before his eyes." She declares that Elizabeth Barrett "was inspired by a flash of true genius when she rushed into the drawing-room and said that here, where we live and work, is the true place for the poet." But how can the writer of the twentieth century achieve any satisfactory relationship with a society in disintegration? The difficulties are immense. There are the restraints of prudery: "Chaucer could write frankly where we must either say nothing or say it slyly." There is the bewildering multiplicity of substitutes for the old patron: "There is the daily Press, the monthly Press; the English public and the American public; the best-seller public and the worst-seller public; the high-brow public and the red-blood public; till now organized self-conscious entities capable through their various mouthpieces of making their needs known and their approval or displeasure felt." We suffer from a peculiar cultural isolation: "We are sharply cut off from our predecessors. A shift in the scale—the war, the sudden slip of masses held in position for ages—has shaken the fabric from top to bottom, alienated us from the past and made us perhaps too vividly conscious of the present." We enjoy such a mass of accumulated knowledge that there seems little point in adding to it: "Collectively we know so much that there is little incentive to venture on private discoveries."

But the chief deficiency of the present age, according to Mrs. Woolf, is its lack of certainty, of assured beliefs. We cannot produce great essays because we have none of that "obstinate conviction which lifts ephemeral sounds through the misty sphere of anybody's language to the land where there is perpetual marriage, a perpetual union." We contrast unfavourably with the eighteenth century: "If the world was smaller it was also more compact; it knew its own mind; it had its own standards. Its poetry is affected by the same security. When we read *The Rape of the Lock* we seem to find ourselves in an age so settled and so circumscribed that masterpieces were popular." Even the early nineteenth century possessed relative stability. Writing of Wordsworth and Scott, Mrs. Woolf says:

> We feel ourselves indeed driven to them, impelled not by calm judgment but by some imperious need to anchor our instability upon their security. . . . From what, then, arises that sense of security which gradually, delightfully, and completely overcomes us? It is the power of their belief—their conviction, that imposes itself upon us. . . . In both there is the same natural conviction that life is of a certain quality. They know the relations of human beings towards each other and towards the universe. Neither of them probably has a word to say about the matter outright, but everything depends upon it. Only believe, we find ourselves saying, and all the rest will come of itself.

Faced with this contemporary confusion, she vacillates between determination to master it and despair that anything worth while can be accomplished. In the latter mood, she writes: "It is an age of fragments. A few stanzas, a few pages, a chapter here and there, the beginning of this novel, the end of that, are equal to the best of any

age or author. But can we go to posterity with a sheaf of loose pages, or ask the readers of those days, with the whole of literature before them, to sift our enormous rubbish heaps for our tiny pearls?" And in another place she observes: "We must reconcile ourselves to a season of failures and fragments. We must reflect that where so much strength is spent on finding a way to tell the truth the truth itself is bound to reach us in rather an exhausted and chaotic condition." But on the whole it is the note of determination which prevails, the note which is so clearly sounded in this passage from *Letter to a Young Poet:*

> But how are you going to get out, into the world of other people? That is your problem now, if I may hazard a guess—to find the right relationship now that you know yourself, between the self that you know and the world outside. It is a difficult problem. No living poet has, I think, altogether solved it. And there are a thousand voices prophesying despair. Science, they say, has made poetry impossible; there is no poetry in motor cars and wireless. And we have no religion. All is tumultuous and transitional. Therefore, so people say, there can be no relation between the poet and the present age. But surely that is nonsense. These accidents are superficial; they do not go nearly deep enough to destroy the most profound and primitive of instincts, the instinct of rhythm. All you need now is to stand at the window and let your rhythmical sense open and shut, open and shut, boldly and freely, until one thing melts into another, until the taxis are dancing with the daffodils, until a whole has been made from all these separate fragments.

"A whole . . . from . . . fragments"—again we see Virginia Woolf insisting upon what is, to her, the cardinal principle of art. The wheel has come full circle; we have made our survey of the principles which inform, and the problems which agitate, her literary criticism. What is the value of her criticism? In the first place, it serves as an enlightening commentary upon her own creative work. Knowing her stress upon wholeness and form and her distrust of a detachable philosophy in fiction, we shall look in her novels for pattern and design rather than for a message in the usual sense. Aware of her distaste for thinly disguised autobiography in fiction, we shall not make the mistake of equating Mrs. Dalloway or Mrs. Watson with Mrs. Woolf, or of attributing to the author opinions which she puts into the mouths of her characters. Conscious of her preference for the private rather than the public issue, we shall read her novels not for political or economic commentary but for a sharpened sense of life, an enrichment of experience, a renewed consciousness of the complexity of persons and their relationships. Having seen with what frankness and earnestness she wrestles, in her criticism, with the problem of the artist in the contemporary world, we shall approach her own efforts to catch the distinctive rhythms of modern life, and to combine tradition with experiment, with greater sympathy and understanding.

But her criticism, I believe, has value in itself, not simply in relation to her novels. She has a genius for summing up a writer's essential quality in a brief, vivid, and metaphorical sentence. Here are some examples, and the writers to whom they refer:

> (Hazlitt)   Sentence follows sentence with the healthy ring and chime of a blacksmith's hammer on the anvil; the words glow and the sparks fly; gently they fade and the essay is over.

> (Coleridge)   As we enter his radius he seems not a man but a swarm, a cloud, a buzz of words, darting this way and that, clustering, quivering and hanging suspended.

> (Henry James)   It is the half light in which he sees most, and sees farthest.

> (Hakluyt)   Hakluyt is not so much a book as a great bundle of commodities loosely tied together, an emporium, a lumber room strewn with ancient sacks, obsolete nautical instruments, huge bales of wool, and little bags of rubies and emeralds.

> (Dostoevsky)   The novels of Dostoevsky are seething whirlpools, gyrating sandstorms, waterspouts which hiss and boil and suck us in.

> (Horace Walpole)   His letters have a fine hard glaze upon them that preserve them, like the teeth of which he was so proud, from the little rubs and dents of familiarity.

> (Gibbon)   We seem, for hours on end, mounted on a celestial rocking-horse which, as it gently sways up and down, remains rooted in a single spot. In the soporific idleness thus induced we recall with regret the vivid partizanship of Macaulay, the fitful and violent poetry of Carlyle.

The temptation to go on quoting such passages is almost irresistible. They are the product, obviously, of a mind which responds with unusual sensitivity to the essential quality of a writer, and which has a high capacity for the enjoyment of literature.

And that, I believe, is Virginia Woolf's greatest contribution as a critic. As the chief, or almost the chief, representative of impressionistic criticism at a time when scientific and historical criticism have dominated the field, she serves to remind us that literature is above all something to be enjoyed. On the whole, the impact of scientific and scholarly methods on literary criticism has been salutary: it has swept away much empty rhetoric and discredited the fuzziness and irresponsible subjectivism into which romantic and impressionistic criticism is prone to degenerate. But scientific and scholarly criticism is also prone to degenerate, in the hands of its less able exponents. One finds in much contemporary criticism a certain pedantic humourlessness, a puritanic austerity, a carping irascibility. From reading it one would gather that the study of literature, far from being a delight, is a painful, even an agonizing, process. What is needed is a renewed emphasis upon the enjoyment of literature, and to that renewal Virginia Woolf has contributed her full share. "What he had read he had read with fervour," she says of Hazlitt, and the remark is equally true of herself.

Indeed it is with Hazlitt, of all other critics, that Virginia Woolf's affiliations are closest. She shares most of both his weaknesses and his strengths. Like him, she is occasionally prone to prejudice, especially when dealing with her immediate predecessors and contemporaries. She is less than just, it seems to me, in her attack upon the Edwardians, and she fumbles badly when she comes to James Joyce. It would be difficult to guess the erudition and gusto of the latter from this critique of *Ulysses:*

> It fails because of the comparative poverty of the writer's mind, we might say simply and have done with it. But it is possible to press a little further and wonder whether we may not refer our sense of being in a bright yet narrow room, confined and shut in, rather than enlarged and set free, to some limitation imposed by the method as well as by the mind. Is it the method that inhibits the creative power? Is it due to the method that we feel neither jovial nor magnanimous, but centred in a self which, in spite of its tremor of susceptibility, never embraces or creates what is outside itself and beyond.

On the other hand, it is only fair to point out that she obviously is trying to do full justice to Joyce, and that there is not the slightest basis for suspecting that she wrote out of jealousy or any kind of personal malice.

Mrs. Woolf resembles Hazlitt also in that she cares little for exact scholarship and is only fitfully interested in the historical background of literature. In an amusing little essay called **"Why?"**, which appears in **The Death of the Moth,** she pokes fun at the whole academic approach to literature, questions the value of teaching it in the universities, and pities a young man who has just produced a three hundred page book on the evolution of the Elizabethan sonnet. In her critical essays we find few references to the social and intellectual events and forces which shaped, or helped to shape, the books she is discussing; she does, however, display a lively interest in the domestic manners of the various periods, and she seems to have an intuitive sense of historical atmosphere.

Her essays are less prolix and repetitious than Hazlitt's but they are equally selective in subject and unsystematic in approach. She makes no pretence of covering the whole ground of English literature, and though the essays are arranged chronologically by subject she shows little concern with the historical development of the various literary forms. She will write as much or more on a very minor writer as on a great one, and many of the greatest she scarcely touches at all. Chaucer is there, but not Spenser; the Duchess of Newcastle gets twelve pages, Shakespeare only three.

Her criticism, then, has definite limitations. But it also has definite strengths. She has the humour of Hazlitt, has it indeed more fully and richly. After quoting extensively from Macaulay's eulogy of Addison, she writes: "Whether Addison or another is interred within, it is a very fine tomb." She has great fun with a priggish biography of Miss Mitford: "But how dangerous a thing is life! Can one be sure that anything not wholly made of mahogany will to the very end stand empty in the sun? Even cupboards have their secret springs, and when, inadvertently we are sure, Miss Hill touches this one, out, terrible to relate, topples a stout old gentleman. In plain English, Miss Mitford had a father. There is nothing actually improper in that. Many women have had fathers. But Miss Mitford's father was kept in a cupboard; that is to say, he was not a nice father." In an essay on a certain Archbishop Thomson, she details his climb up the rungs of the clerical ladder, then writes: "It is a matter of temperament and belief whether you read this list with respect or with boredom; whether you look upon an archbishop's hat as a crown or as an extinguisher. If, like the present reviewer, you are ready to hold the simple faith that the outer order corresponds to the inner—that a vicar is a good man, a canon a better man, and an archbishop the best man of all—you will find the study of the Archbishop's life one of extreme fascination. He has turned aside from poetry and philosophy and law, and specialised in virtue." As these selections indicate, Mrs. Woolf has Hazlitt's happy balance of sharp good sense and emotional warmth: her wit holds her back from any mere vague emotional rapture. She has Hazlitt's vigour too—a vigour in her critical writing that will come as something of a surprise to those who know her only by her novels (though they have far more vigour than most critics of them suggest). Above all, she has Hazlitt's gusto. Like him, she writes in a concrete and spontaneous style which communicates to us the full force and flavour of her response to the book under consideration.

There is no doubt that Virginia Woolf will be remembered primarily as a novelist, rather than as a critic. It is not part of the intention of this article to prove that her literary criticism alone would make her a candidate for eminence. But there is value and there is, above all, pleasure in her criticism. Add to that the fact that her critical standards throw much light upon her own intentions as a novelist, and it makes her literary criticism worthy of serious consideration. (pp. 234-44)

> *Desmond Pacey, "Virginia Woolf as a Literary Critic," in* University of Toronto Quarterly, *Vol. XVIII, No. 3, April, 1948, pp. 234-44.*

Diana Trilling   (essay date 1948)

[*Trilling is an American critic and author whose criticism often focuses on the social or political aspects of a work of literature, considering purely aesthetic factors insufficient justification for a work of art. In the following essay, she relates the uncommon outlook in Woolf's literary criticism to Woolf's privileged social position.*]

Probably anyone acquainted with the name of Virginia Woolf is familiar with the remarkable photograph of her which has so regularly appeared along with her work—the long, tense face at once so suffering and so impervious, the large, too-precisely socketed eyes and the full, too-precisely outlined mouth rimmed with humor but also with conscious vanity, the aristocratic nose and the surely troublesome hair dressed in such defiance of whatever fashion. Unmistakably it is the portrait of an extreme feminine sensibility, of a spirit so finely drawn that we can scarcely bear to follow its tracings. But just as unmistakably it is the portrait of a pride of mind a thousand times more imposing than an army of suffragettes with banners. Here without question—we decide merely on appear-

ances—is someone who conforms to the rules of neither the feminine nor the feministic game, someone who demands that we recognize her as a quite special instance of her sex.

And it is indeed as a special instance, both of her sex and her profession, that Virginia Woolf has always impressed herself. It would be difficult to name another modern literary figure who has been handled so carefully, as if she existed in a realm wholly apart from that in which other writers live and breathe and are submitted to the harsh give-and-take of criticism and as if to apply to her work the usual criteria of judgment were only to reveal our own deficiency of refinement.

We ponder what accounts for this history of preferential treatment and it occurs to us that perhaps the most efficient explanation is that most people, artists not excepted, have a strange way of getting pretty much the response they ask of the world. Is it not, after all, in exactly the degree that this delicate lady insisted upon equal consideration in the male world that she always made it extremely difficult to condescend to her as a "mere" woman; in the degree that, despite her pride of intellect and her open feministic protest, she always took her ultimate refuge in female sensibility, that she made it almost impossible to meet her head-on like a man, or with the irony she herself directed against an out-and-out feminist like George Eliot?

And in the matter of her class no less than her attitudes as a woman, we similarly see demand producing its response. Everything in Virginia Woolf's birth and circumstances contributed to the specialness of her social and artistic point of view: she was the daughter of Leslie Stephen and from earliest childhood nurtured among the most civilizing minds of England; her only school was her father's magnificent library; she never struggled for a living. Had the child of this much privilege regarded her social situation as a handicap or limitation of experience, or if she had sorrowed for the large rest of mankind which had never had her advantages, we can guess what would have been the result. Taking her at this diminished estimate of herself, the public would have directed against her the very envy she would be working to propitiate.

But Mrs. Woolf made the charming albeit fantastic assumption that her readers had all of them had the space and time, the physical and emotional conditions for savoring life in terms similar to her own. Or, only a trace less generously, she admitted the possible difference in background between herself and the rest of mankind but yet asked us to pause and consider what we had missed while we were so busy creating our own heritages, educating ourselves, earning and spending our wages. So pause we did, and were no doubt the better for at least momentarily checking the impulse—when, say, she titled her literary essays *The Common Reader*—to cut the common ground from beneath her feet by confronting her with the universe of urgent fact separating the circumstances which governed her approach to books from ours. It was thus not Virginia Woolf alone who projected the Virginia Woolf image, but we too, in conspiracy with her. And together we produced a very notable act of the imagination, which does us all much credit.

And yet, even in the midst of phantasy, we have of course always reserved the right of correction from reality. Even as we have most enjoyed ourselves we have known that some day either we or Mrs. Woolf would have to call a halt to this pleasant game we were playing together. The republication of *The Common Reader*—the first series of essays, originally published in 1925, and the second series, originally published in 1932—and the appearance, as well, of a posthumous volume of previously unprinted or unre-printed essays, *The Moment,* force on us the occasion for reassessment. Freshly we encounter Mrs. Woolf's unique gifts of grace and appreciation. And freshly we test the values, or lack of value, in her cultural position. And what is our surprise, even as we gird ourselves for a new and sterner judgment, to discover what certainly we never ex-pected: that toward her last years she herself became aware that her view of life was not the common one; that, indeed, it was desperately constrained.

It has often been remarked of Virginia Woolf that she was a commentator on literature rather than a critic, more an antiquarian than a literary analyst. Now, as we read the essays with which we are already familiar together with most of the new ones in *The Moment,* this judgment is firmly supported. There is no question but that Mrs. Woolf was at her best, and that her best was superlative of its kind, when she was dealing with little-known figures of the past whom she could re-create out of scraps of letter and journal, out of a remembered morsel of talk here and a flash of scene there, rather than when she attempted to take the full meaning of the work of an established author. The essay **"Geraldine and Jane,"** the **"Rambling Round Evelyn," "The Duchess of Newcastle," "Dr. Burney's Evening Party"**—in these random sketches subject and method are as if created for each other, and Mrs. Woolf's beautifully educated imagination and lapidary precision of language combine to make something as rare as it is charming. The art she practices here is very much a lady's art, decidedly conspicuous in its consumption of culture as well as of leisure. But surely, we decide, so long as we can afford it, it makes a highly desirable decoration of life.

It is when we come to the pieces which concern major lit-erary figures and performances that we begin to miss the firm critical stance and that we see the famous light touch as something less than a benediction, that we become irri-tated by such a strenuous devotion to the niceties of lan-guage. We face the fact that Mrs. Woolf's hand lacks the strength to grip essential truth, that at the very moment when she is most eagerly grasping for that elusive quality, the life in art, it regularly bounces out of her reach. The essay on Montaigne is perhaps the most dramatic exam-ple: Mrs. Woolf's refusal to take a firm hold on Mon-taigne's greatness has, finally, the effect of destruction. The giant form dissipates into nothingness sooner than be held between thumb and forefinger like a prayer bead.

And as we try to understand why someone so gifted in ap-preciation was so little capable of apprehending greatness, inevitably we are returned to the subjective basis of Virgin-ia Woolf's literary attitudes. All of Mrs. Woolf's critical judgments proceed from a formulated aesthetic. Some-times she stated her principles didactically, as in *Mrs. Bennett and Mrs. Brown* or in **"The Art of Fiction."** Al-ways, in every word she wrote, fiction or nonfiction, her aesthetic is clearly implied. Art, Mrs. Woolf felt, must be free of dependence upon material fact. It must not be tied to the common fate of ordinary human beings but must create and celebrate a beauty which is larger than reality. It is a limited and limiting aesthetic, and one whose roots are close indeed to Mrs. Woolf's personal experience. It is an aesthetic of someone whose special circumstances dictated a cruel antithesis between art and life. Mrs. Woolf's picture of life is as of a wild horde of hostile influ-ences beating at the walls of her private sanctuary.

Thus, lest she suddenly find herself among the uninherit-ing, she cannot afford even the comradeship which we should suppose George Eliot claimed from her as an avowed feminist. Commenting on George Eliot's "melan-choly virtue of tolerance," Mrs. Woolf writes: "Her sym-pathies are with the everyday lot, and play most happily in dwelling upon the homespun of ordinary joys and sor-rows. She has none of that romantic intensity which is connected with a sense of one's individuality, unsated and unsubdued, cutting its shape sharply upon the back-ground of the world." And speaking of *Middlemarch* she reports that Dorothea found "one scarcely knows what" in Ladislaw, though who has read the novel and does not know that what Dorothea found was life itself? Or of Dickens she can say: "He lacks charm and idiosyncrasy, is everybody's writer and no one's in particular, is an insti-tution, a monument, a public thoroughfare trodden dusty by a million feet. . . . His sympathies . . . fail him when-ever a man or woman has more than two thousand a year, has been to the university, or can count his ancestors back to the third generation."

She can imagine, what is unimaginable by anyone who, with D. H. Lawrence, thinks of fiction as the "one great book of life," that Madame de Sévigny had the capacities of a fine novelist. And of Lawrence himself, whose *Sons and Lovers* she did not get around to until after his death, she can comment that his prose lacked art because of his low birth. "The thought plumps directly into his mind; up spurt the sentences as round, as hard, as direct as water thrown out in all directions by the impact of a stone. One feels," she concludes, and we suspect a superb stylist has never been better, though so unintentionally, compliment-ed, "that not a single word has been chosen for its beauty, or for its effect upon the architecture of the sentence."

Since the new volume, *The Moment,* is not new in the sense of offering only late examples of Virginia Woolf's work but simply in the sense of bringing together pieces previously unavailable in book form, its dominant vein, expectably enough, is that of the work in *The Common Reader.* There are essays on "The Faery Queen," on Con-greve, on Sterne, on Mrs. Thrale, on Scott and Lockhart. There are a few overtremulous pieces such as the title-piece, the piece **"On Being Ill,"** a piece called **"Pictures."** In other words, if we allow ourselves to be careless we can miss entirely the one or two essays which signalize the vol-ume because they show its author suddenly precipitated into a wholly new consciousness. **"The Leaning Tower"** and **"The Artist and Politics"** are essays which Mrs. Woolf wrote in her very last years. They indicate the awful impact of the war on such a sensibility. Perhaps, almost a full decade earlier, there had already been a faint intimation, in the fact that Mrs. Woolf had been impelled to concern herself with Lawrence, that she was beginning to feel upon her the slight pressure of an ugly contemporaneity. In **"The Leaning Tower,"** a paper dated 1940 and read to the Workers Educational Association of Brighton, the pressure is no longer slight. It is the full impact of contemporary turmoil.

"The Leaning Tower" is a terse, bold, bald, and brilliant statement of the situation in which literature finds itself as Virginia Woolf's life draws to its close. Contrasting the twentieth century with the nineteenth, it tells us how immune England's writers before 1914 were to the wars of their times and how profoundly influenced by the conditions of peace and prosperity. "They had leisure," writes Mrs. Woolf. "They had security; life was not going to change; they themselves were not going to change. They could look; and look away. They could forget; and then—in their books—remember." The writer's tower was steady.

But after 1914, or, more accurately, after 1925, the tower began to lean perilously. The view it gave out upon became all change and upheaval. A new literary generation, sons of well-to-do parents—Auden, Spender, Isherwood, MacNiece—could now look no class "straight in the face; they look either up, or down, or sidelong. There is no class so settled they can explore it unconsciously." Feeling no security of either birth or education, they are filled with pity for themselves and anger at a society which perches them at such an angle. They can do little more than turn their eyes in upon themselves—witness the increase in autobiographical writing—while demanding the classless society which will release them from their precarious position.

And the essay concludes with the hope that this classless society will result from the war. The wistfulness is truly touching with which Mrs. Woolf asserts the promise this change holds for the future. "We shall regret our Jane Austens and our Trollopes; they gave us comedy, tragedy, and beauty. But much of that old-class literature was very petty; very false; very dull." We begin to wince under the anxious, unthinking eagerness with which she tries to prepare for the new dispensation. "Much is already unreadable. The novel of a classless and towerless world should be a better novel than the old novel."

Then comes heartbreak: Mrs. Woolf is giving us her prescription for hastening art's better day. It is that we should all borrow books from the lending libraries and learn to read them wisely—the door shuts forever on the paternal library of her childhood. "Nor," she writes, "let us shy away from the kings because we are commoners. That is a fatal crime in the eyes of Aeschylus, Shakespeare, Virgil, and Dante, who, if they could speak—and after all they can—would say, 'Don't leave me to the wigged and gowned. Read me, read me for yourselves!' . . . Literature is no one's private ground; literature is common ground."

But enough. There are self-confrontations which, coming too late and hard, are too painful to linger over. Could we not almost wish that Virginia Woolf had let it be only us, not herself, who called a halt to the happy game we once played together? (pp. 87-94)

Diana Trilling, "Virginia Woolf: A Special Instance," in her Claremont Essays, *Harcourt Brace Jovanovich, 1964, pp. 87-94.*

Ralph Samuelson (essay date 1965)

[*Samuelson examines Woolf's intellectual preoccupation with gender issues and class concerns, especially as related to matters of authorship.*]

One of the more interesting textural motifs in both Virginia Woolf's novels and her essays is the tension that often arises between the author's insistence on the one hand that women are equal to men and yet on the other hand that they are different and ultimately autonomous. In a way, Virginia Woolf wants both to have and to eat her cake, wants to keep the quality of "intuitive perception" as something surrounding her most interesting characters (Mrs. Ramsay, of *To the Lighthouse,* has a "simplicity" which "fathomed what clever people falsified"), and yet to insist that any attempt by men to see women as *merely* intuitive is snobbery and condescension of the worst sort.

As a novelist, she is willing to have a character in *The Voyage Out* make the interesting critical observation that Jane Austen may be the best woman novelist because she is the only woman novelist who did not "try to write like a man," and yet as a critic Virginia Woolf is willing to develop the idea that the best writers are "androgynous." As it is put in the rather famous passage from *A Room of One's Own:*

> One must turn back to Shakespeare then, for Shakespeare was androgynous; and so was Keats and Sterne and Cowper and Lamb and Coleridge. Shelley perhaps was sexless. Milton and Ben Jonson had a dash too much of the male in them. So had Wordsworth and Tolstoi. In our time Proust was wholly androgynous, if not perhaps a little too much of a woman.

The male and the female parts of the mind must "marry" to produce good, androgynous literature; but on the other hand, in many women writers, there is already too much of an attempt to imitate the style of men, which presumably means that the female and male parts of the mind, at least in some women writers, have come together in a rather bad marriage. Essentially, Virginia Woolf is grappling with the problem of reconciling *equality* and *difference,* with respect to men and women, and in particular men and women writers. While this motif—one should really call it a major theme—figures forth in virtually everything she wrote, including her major novels, it may be of particular interest to look at some of Virginia Woolf's critical writings, and to see there how her preoccupation with the freedom of women (both as women and as writers), in a form direct and outspoken, weaves itself into interests political, literary, and esthetic, often getting her into some rather serious contradictions and inconsistencies.

Virginia Woolf has received a good deal of generalized praise for her work as a critic, which has been a way of both faintly damning her really valuable contributions, and also of glossing over some of her truly serious shortcomings. Her long essay *A Room of One's Own* was compared favorably by *Spectator* to Mary Wollstonecraft's *The Rights of Women* and Mill's *The Subjection of Women;* in fact, it was said to outshine "them both in genius," while the *Yale Review* found its "quiet, demure laughter" delightful. *A Room of One's Own,* like *Three Guineas* and the scores of essays and reviews Virginia Woolf wrote, is certainly an interesting work, but it finally raises more questions about its writer's real beliefs than it presents those beliefs with firmness and consistency.

Along with Virginia Woolf's preoccupation with the problem of equality and difference between the sexes runs an equally strong, but more submerged concern with class; and the two things often get mixed up together. She is a critic who is fiercely proud of both her sex and her upper class, and yet she is a critic, and writer, who tries hard now and then to break out of this double confinement. For example, near the end of *A Room of One's Own* she develops the notion that the ideals of "chastity" and "anonymity," strong in all women, inhibit them as writers. At the same time, her rather careful almost conservative, opinions on much modern literature seem to show in Virginia Woolf herself a strong impulse toward chastity and anonymity, the cursed possessions of which, in women, she blames on men. She is strongly attracted to her two great contemporaries, Joyce and Lawrence, and yet finds curious reasons for rejecting them—reasons based, one cannot help feeling, on their distance from her own sex and class. In her general disapprobation of Joyce and Lawrence she would, presumably, place them below Meredith, George Eliot, Dickens (albeit Dickens has too much of the "male" in him), Thackeray, and Conrad. She dislikes "coarseness," moreover, only in certain writers, normally those rather close to her own period. Thus Gissing gives one problems (*The Common Reader*); while the ability of Chaucer "to speak without self-consciousness of the parts and functions of the body" is to be applauded, as is Juliet's nurse, a creation of that most "androgynous" writer, Shakespeare. Moll Flanders, however, is coarse, because of the advent of "decency" since Chaucer's time. And "Sterne, from fear of coarseness, is forced into indecency," she says, never admitting, or simply not realizing, that Sterne may have rather *enjoyed* indecency for its own sake.

Another aspect of Virginia Woolf's class preoccupation comes out in her double desire to learn more about lower-class life in literature, and yet to more or less reject the very literature that gives her this. She constantly complains that we have little from the lower classes in the way of good literature about the lower classes, and yet Joyce she finds too "angular" (a term meaning too "male," somehow) and Lawrence too coarse. In another essay she snidely remarks that as a poet Lawrence "has moments of greatness, but hours of something very different," and in the same essay calls Joyce's *Ulysses* a "memorable catastrophe." In still another essay she says "it is impossible, it would seem, for working men to write in their own language about their own lives," apparently forgetting again about Lawrence.

Part of the problem with both Joyce and Lawrence, as implied above, is that they are simply too much divorced from "chastity" and "anonymity," as is, presumably, the "sexless" Shelley (could it be that she condemns Shelley so severely for the same reasons that her own Victorian forebears called him a "monster"? for his treatment of Harriet?).

. . . . .

Virginia Woolf really seems interested in a new double standard—a double standard for her own sex. She would like women to be able to hide behind chaste, anonymous skirts when they need to withdraw from a milieu suddenly too "male"—whether in literature or real life—and yet she would like them at the same time to be able, as writers, to indulge in Faustian experiences for the sake of a full expression of their art. And, of course, there is not necessarily anything wrong in this feminist double standard. It is, in fact, a most interesting concept. The trouble is that it fails to emerge honestly from Virginia Woolf's writings, needing instead to be abstracted by the reader himself.

Particularly in the book *Three Guineas,* we can see Virginia Woolf's ambivalent attitude toward her own class. It

Virginia Woolf.

frees her to write, and yet it also restricts her. Thus she can make the interesting point that somehow the daughters and wives of upper-class men have less influence on the world than the daughters and wives of men of the laboring class. She speaks of the normal, "indirect" influence women possess over their husbands, and in a footnote, of the "very subtle kind exerted by Lady Macbeth upon her husband" (did she actually regard Lady Macbeth's influence as *subtle*?). She says that most women, to be of *real* influence, must, of course, approach economic equality with men. In another footnote, she implies that women in the nineteenth century who went in for sports in general (she had been pointing out that few women hunted with guns, that "their appearance in the hunting field was the cause of much caustic comment") may have been considered loose. " 'Skittles,' the famous nineteenth-century English horsewoman, was a lady of easy morals," and it was "probable that there was held to be some connection between sports and unchastity in women in the nineteenth century." But Virginia Woolf never says whether *she* approves of, or would have approved of, "Skittles," because in her essays she has not really seen her way through to the double standard that she constantly moves toward, yet halts just short of. Thus Virginia Woolf *wants* to believe in "easy morals"—whatever they are—and in the vigor of the lower classes, and many other things, but remains, in her criticism, tied pretty firmly to her own class and sex.

Perhaps nowhere is her desire yet relative inability to move outside this double confinement more apparent than in the essay **"Notes on D. H. Lawrence."** The creative artist in Virginia Woolf is intensely attracted to Lawrence's talents, in particular to *Sons and Lovers,* a novel in which there is "astonishing vividness, like an island from off which the mist has suddenly lifted." But there is a "dissatisfaction" in the book which derives from Lawrence's own dissatisfaction at being, like Paul Morel, a miner's son. And this dissatisfaction is the very thing, unfortunately, that one cannot approve of, and that prevents *Sons and Lovers* from being a great novel. Almost knowing she has got herself into the position of saying that Lawrence, despite his genius and energy and education, is fated through his *birth* never to become a great novelist, she says that Lawrence's trouble is that, unlike Proust, "one feels that he echoes nobody, continues no tradition, is unaware of the past, or the present save as it affects the future." This argument is never used on anyone else, so far as I know, not even on Keats. In fact she even attacks the reviewer who once contemptuously called Keats a "cockney." And the essay on Lawrence finishes on a curiously hard note—an attack on Lawrence's sentences, which are awkward, or worse, because of Lawrence's background: "One feels that not a single word has been chosen for its beauty, or for its effect upon the architecture of the sentence."

Quite aside from the fact that Lawrence was indeed aware of a tradition—and that Virginia Woolf might have realized this if she had read *The Rainbow,* with its strong evocation of a tradition of the farm itself, of men working the soil in a pre-industrial England—the essay seems a rather desperate one. She is strongly attracted to Lawrence, yet also obviously dislikes him, and is almost honest enough to realize that she dislikes him for all the wrong reasons.

The essay on Lawrence states that Lawrence himself, like Paul Morel of *Sons and Lovers,* "was a miner's son and [the fact that] he disliked his conditions, gave him a different approach to writing from those who have a settled station and enjoy circumstances which allow them to forget what those circumstances are." It is possible that Lawrence's achievement, in the very teeth of economic and social disadvantages, was a thing Virginia Woolf simply could not accept, so contrary was the fact to her lifelong insistence that women must enjoy an economic room of their own in order to write as well as men.

At the same time, it is worth noting that Virginia Woolf failed to discover certain things that she and Lawrence did in fact have in common. For instance Lawrence, once married to Frieda, never worked steadily at any job but his writing; and Lawrence, like Virginia Woolf, was never hampered by children.

Although it is not fair to judge a writer for what he or she does not discuss, it is unfortunate for us that Virginia Woolf never got around to dealing with Lawrence's *ideas.* For if she had confronted them, tried coming to terms with Lawrence's view of women, for instance, we might have had today a truly formidable critical opinion to hold against Lawrence, as perhaps one kind of ultimate, hard-core measure of some of his most fundamental and cherished beliefs.

. . . . .

The heaviest attacks against Virginia Woolf's nonfiction writings remain, so far as I know, those early *Scrutiny* reviews of the two feminist treatises *A Room of One's Own* and *Three Guineas.* In one *Scrutiny* review, M. C. Bradbrook speaks of the "camouflage" in *A Room of One's Own* which "prevents Mrs. Woolf from committing the indelicacy of putting a case," while Q. D. Leavis, discussing *Three Guineas,* sees the organizational method as a "deliberate avoidance of any argument," thus clearing up any mistaken assumption that Virginia Woolf automatically speaks for all women in this essay.

Of the fiction writings, a new book by Edward Davis (*Readings in Modern Fiction*) may be the most devastating attack yet made on Virginia Woolf, specifically on *Mrs. Dalloway.* After making the point that Mrs. Dalloway (and Virginia Woolf herself) is basically a lady who hates sex, hates life, and accepts only what surrounds her upper-class world and that part of London which makes up "the empire of the snob," Davis speaks of a section of the novel which

> . . . indulges in a purple—a very pale purple—patch about visions of the all-embracing Being, not God, but the mindless material and cosmic Woman of which all life is but a part. This giantess, she hints, beckons to all lonely travellers, to all who are sunk in the drowse of existence. It is in her lap that we sleep. (And what is all this about? . . . At best it is only the exteriorisation of her Mother-Imago; a projection of that distorted image one builds so as to separate what

is foul and fiendish in one's mother from what is good and lovable. And it is linked with Virginia Woolf's feminism. She could never forgive existence for not having made her a man and for not having made men, the gross creatures, women; and so it pleases her, in a very obvious though not—for her—very conscious way to substitute for the image of a masculine God the image of a She).

Davis, like the *Scrutiny* reviewers, reacts angrily not only to the feminist strain in Virginia Woolf but to her class consciousness. And certainly neither area of inquiry can be avoided whether one reads the essays or the novels.

I would, however, submit the following generalization: that the problems that arise in the nonfiction writings very seldom come up in the novels, despite the fact that the novels grind away at very much the same materials. It is partly that in the novels, the problem of *precise belief* on social, economic, or political questions—or the precise interpretation of facts—never obtrudes. In *Mrs. Dalloway,* for instance, a very real, substantial group of people is presented to the reader—people of whom it is seldom, if ever, felt that they "illustrate" either feminist or upper-class ideals. There is the pompous Lady Bruton; the obsequious lackey Hugh Whitbread; the rather empty-headed and bland Richard Dalloway; the tough-minded Peter Walsh; Elizabeth, Clarissa's innocent and naïve daughter; and Septimus Smith, who commits suicide in defiance of the threatened dominance of Sir William Bradshaw the psychiatrist. It would be hard to demonstrate from this novel that any sexual, political, or social line has been taken. Indeed, if there exists in *Mrs. Dalloway* a tendency toward class criticism at all, it seems directed precisely at that upper-class world whose members lead lives empty, obsequious, snobbish, vicious, and uncommitted. Thus the class with which Virginia Woolf closely identifies in so many of her essays comes under rather heavy attack in perhaps the finest of her novels. As an example of this kind of attack upon the values of the British upper class, one may note the following description of Hugh Whitbread, the gentleman who helps Lady Bruton draft her letters to the *Times:*

> He did not go deeply. He brushed surfaces; the dead languages, the living, life in Constantinople, Paris, Rome; riding, shooting, tennis it had been once. The malicious asserted that he now kept guard at Buckingham Palace, dressed in silk stockings and knee-breeches, over what nobody knew. But he did it extremely efficiently. He had been afloat on the cream of English society for fifty-five years. He had known Prime Ministers. His affections were understood to be deep. And if it were true that he had not taken part in any of the great movements of the time or held important office, one or two humble reforms stood to his credit; an improvement in public shelters was one; the protection of owls in Norfolk another; servant girls had reason to be grateful to him; and his name at the end of letters to the *Times,* asking for funds, appealing to the public to protect, to preserve, to clear up litter, to abate smoke, and stamp out immorality in parks, commanded respect.

To the Lighthouse is still another novel in which the irritations that arise in a reader of the essays are likely here to remain at rest. One forgets the issue of both class and feminism in the general study of what is nothing less than an intense, though subdued, power struggle between Mr. and Mrs. Ramsay. And in the "Time Passes" section midway in the novel, we see Virginia Woolf's poetical vision at perhaps its best as it works away at her intellectual preoccupation with the *élan vital:*

> So with the lamps all put out, the moon sunk, and a thin rain drumming on the roof a downpouring of immense darkness began. Nothing, it seemed, could survive the flood, the profusion of darkness which, creeping in at keyholes and crevices, stole round window blinds, came into bedrooms, shallowed up here a jug and basin, there a bowl of red and yellow dahlias, there the sharp edges and firm bulk of a chest of drawers. Not only was furniture confounded; there was scarcely anything left of body or mind by which one could say, "This is he" or "This is she." Sometimes a hand was raised as if to clutch something or ward off something, or somebody groaned, or somebody laughed aloud as if sharing a joke with nothingness.
>
> Nothing stirred in the drawing-room or in the dining-room or on the staircase. Only through the rusty hinges and swollen sea-moistened woodwork certain airs, detached from the body of the wind (the house was ramshackle after all) crept round corners and ventured indoors. Almost one might imagine them, as they entered the drawing-room questioning and wondering, toying with the flap of hanging wall-paper, asking, would it hang much longer, when would it fall? Then smoothly brushing the walls, they passed on musingly as if asking the red and yellow roses on the wall-paper whether they would fade, and questioning (gently, for there was time at their disposal) the torn letters in the wastepaper basket, the flowers, the books, all of which were now open to them and asking, Were they allies? Were they enemies? How long would they endure?

This is the tone and the vision achieved in the best of the novels. In these, we see sensitive but very real women such as Mrs. Ramsay and Mrs. Dalloway moving through an alien world. But the world is not made alien simply by men, or by class predicaments. There is often a sense of the total bafflement of a sensitive protagonist let loose upon what is simply an inscrutable reality. The "transparent envelope" and the "luminous halo," as well as making life worth living, make it often terrifying to Virginia Woolf's most interesting and sympathetic characters—Mrs. Dalloway, Septimus Smith, Mrs. Ramsay.

One might say that the essays try to account by logic for an alien world; the novels, by intuition. And if the logic is torn with inconsistencies, if the essays are not truly prepared to argue their point, one might well ask why we should bother with them at all. What is the point, one might ask, of approaching a critic who has no critical system, a feminist riddled with inconsistencies?

The answer is that the essays and treatises, rich with a leisured education behind them, fascinate by their very na-kedness. They allow us to see the mind of a writer—a writ-er at her best powerful and original—at work with materi-als in which her own really alarming ambivalences con-cerning class and sex, her strong tensions and contradic-tions, are not yet resolved and remade into the substance of her art. In a curious backsided kind of tapestry, we see in these writings a mind grinding away at material that should be grist only for the toughest logician, but yet being prepared, all the same, for an ultimate shaping into some-thing of great beauty by that other Virginia Woolf: the in-tuitive novelist who found for the experiences she came to know within her luminous halo a flexible poetical prose in-side a loose novelistic framework, executed more than once with astonishing success. (pp. 249-56)

> Ralph Samuelson, "More Than One Room of Her Own: Virginia Woolf's Critical Dilem-mas," in Western Humanities Review, Vol. XIX, No. 3, Summer, 1965, pp. 249-56.

Barbara Currier Bell and Carol Ohmann   (essay date 1974)

[*Bell is an American educator and critic who has written on research techniques and feminist literary criticism. Ohmann was an American educator and the author of* Ford Madox Ford: From Apprentice to Craftsman *(1964). In the following excerpt, they evaluate Woolf's subjective, "feminine" approach to literary criticism as a significant departure from the tradition of "mas-cu-line" literary criticism, characterized by analysis and objectivity.*]

[Virginia Woolf's] criticism is less well known than her fiction. It's been neglected, and deserves much more atten-tion than it's gotten. In passing, we might make the guess—we consider it quite a reasonable one—that it has been easier for professional academics to praise, or even only to notice, a woman novelist than it has been to accept a woman critic.

As a critic, Virginia Woolf has been called a number of disparaging names: "impressionist," "belletrist," "racon-teur," "amateur." Here is one academic talking on the subject: "She will survive, not as a critic, but as a literary essayist recording the adventures of a soul among conge-nial masterpieces. . . . The writers who are most down-right, and masculine, and central in their approach to life—Fielding or Balzac—she for the most part left untouched. . . . Her own approach was at once more subterranean and aerial, and invincibly, almost defiantly, feminine" [Louis Kronenberger, "Virginia Woolf as Crit-ic," *The Republic of Letters*]. In other words, Virginia Woolf is not a critic; how could she be? She is a woman. From its beginning, criticism has been a man's world. This is to say not only that males have earned their living as critics but, more importantly, that the conventionally ac-cepted ideals of critical method are linked with qualities stereotypically allotted to males: analysis, judgment, ob-jectivity. Virginia Woolf has had a poor reputation as a critic not merely because her sex was female but because her method is "feminine." She writes in a way that is said to be creative, appreciative, and subjective. We will accept

this description for the moment but will later enlarge on it, and even our provisional acceptance we mean to turn to a compliment.

Virginia Woolf's difference from conventional critics is precisely one reason, we would argue, why she should be praised. She is not "almost defiantly feminine"; she is be-yond a doubt defiantly feminine. She is in revolt against the established terms and tones of literary study. Re-searching for a book on literary history, she had this expe-rience, which she records in her diary:

> Yesterday in the Public Library I took down a book of X.'s criticism. This turned me against writing my book. London Library atmosphere effused. Turned me against all literary criticism: these so clever, so airless, so fleshless ingenuities and attempts to prove—that T. S. Eliot for ex-ample is a worse critic than X. Is all literary crit-icism that kind of exhausted air?—book dust, London Library, air. Or is it only that X. is a sec-ond hand, frozen fingered, university specialist, don trying to be creative, don all stuffed with books, writer? . . . I dipped for five minutes and put the book back depressed. The man asked, "What do you want, Mrs. Woolf?" I said a his-tory of English literature. But was so sickened I couldn't look. There were so many.

Or again, she writes: "[Do not] let us shy away from the kings because we are commoners. That is a fatal crime in the eyes of Aeschylus, Shakespeare, Virgil, and Dante, who, if they could speak—and after all they can—would say, 'Don't leave me to the wigged and gowned. Read me. Read me for yourselves.' They do not mind if we get our accents wrong, or have to read with a crib in front of us. Of course—are we not commoners, outsiders?—we shall trample many flowers and bruise much ancient grass. . . . [But] let us trespass at once. Literature is no one's private ground; literature is common ground" [**"The Leaning Tower"**].

No other twentieth-century critic has approached litera-ture with less explicit "system" and more sympathy than Virginia Woolf. Trespassers, she knew, had to stay aloof from all critical schools, to differ from them all. In her diary, she frequently expressed a wish to break new ground: "I feel . . . at the back of my brain that I can de-vise a new critical method; something far less still and for-mal than [what has been done before]. . . . There must be some simpler, subtler, closer means of writing about books, as about people, could I hit upon it." Although she was never finally satisfied with herself, she did write criti-cism that is truly revolutionary. In what follows, we will try to describe the most significant terms of her revolt.

She solves, first of all, the problem of how to address her readers amiably and unpretentiously, and her solution is crucial to her overall success as a critic. For she is not tra-ditionally authoritarian, not an eminence, not a lecturer in her mode of relationship to her audience. Instead of the stance of omniscience, which is a stance that is often un-congenial to women writers (it never did Charlotte Brontë any good, Emily avoided it, and George Eliot assumed it with success only, perhaps, because her dominant emo-tional tone was one of suffering compassion and hence not altogether at odds with conventional requirements for women)—instead of the stance of omniscience, Woolf invents "the common reader," and employs that persona convincingly. When she says "we," she means *we,* rhetorically asserting the existence of a community, but, in fact, by that rhetoric and the other devices we will note, working to create a community.

"We" are readers, not critics or scholars. "We" are English men and women who read for pleasure and for inspiration when "we" can get it. "We" are tolerant but not permissive; "we" laugh and cry, but "we" are not fickle, "our" sentiments have limits; "we" believe in common virtues; "we" like fantasy in measurable doses; "we" are worldly wise but not world-weary; "we" are of "our" age but ours could be any age; "we" constantly question and argue with writers the minute they assume too much, or pretend wisdom, or get too far from the facts of daily life. "['We' are] guided by an instinct to create for ['ourselves'], out of whatever odds and ends ['we'] can come by, some kind of whole—a portrait of a man, a sketch of an age, a theory of the art of writing" [**"The Common Reader"**]. But "we" do not like labels. "We" do not care about the difference between the pre-Romantics and the post-Romantics, or between a novelist of manners and a novelist of sentiment. "We" may, in the end, accept assumptions, or morals, or fantasies, but not without good reason. "We" are suspicious of books "for we have our own vision of the world; we have made it from our own experience and prejudices, and it is therefore bound up with our own vanities and loves. It is impossible not to feel injured and insulted if tricks are played and our private harmony is upset [**"*Robinson Crusoe*"**]. When we do make a judgment, we make it forthrightly and simply. "[The Edwardians] have developed a technique of novel-writing which suits their purpose; they have made tools and established conventions which do their business. But those tools are not our tools, and that business is not our business. For us those conventions are ruin, those tools are death" [**Mr. Bennett and Mrs. Brown**].

Her "common reader" helps Woolf to produce critical essays that are exceptionally readable, clear, and vivid. Thanks to "us," her essays move smoothly and quickly, for the common reader's reactions seem to dictate most of her commentary, even though the truth, of course, is exactly the opposite: she has shaped or elicited the reactions she posits. Her continual consciousness of the "common reader" is especially useful to Woolf in essays on abstract aesthetic topics. "We" prevent her from becoming too general, or pedantic, or confusing. We ask hard questions like "What is art?" or "How should one read a book?" and demand outright answers. Also, "we" are a source that generates imagery. Woolf, of course, uses a great deal of imagery in her criticism; the fact has been often observed but by no means (or seldom) connected with the common reader. First of all, we like imagery. In an effort to please us, Woolf uses it as liberally as cooks use seasoning. Second, we need imagery. Many of the ideas Woolf puts forth, particularly in the aesthetic essays, are essentially abstruse, and images are the fastest, most concrete, and effective means of explanation—that is, if they are of a certain kind: either simple, or striking, or both.

An essay titled **"The Elizabethan Lumber Room"** will do as an extended example here. It offers an introduction to Woolf's favorite period, discussing the *Zeitgeist,* the quires of poetry, prose, and drama, and their characteristic evolution. It might be a syllabus for a seminar at Columbia or Harvard. But it is more winning than most seminars. It offers a highly imaginative alternative to conventional literary criticism.

The essay is a review of Hakluyt's famous book, *Early Voyages, Travels, and Discoveries of the English Nation.* In her very first sentence, Woolf puts herself on our level by acknowledging, "These magnificent volumes are not often, perhaps, read through." We nod. We have not often, or even ever read through Hakluyt; we do belong in the community that Woolf invokes. Then, Woolf involves us further with her metaphor of the lumber room; it is exactly the simple and striking kind of image we like and need: "[Hakluyt] is not so much a book as a great bundle of commodities loosely tied together, an emporium, a lumber room strewn with ancient sacks, obsolete nautical instruments, huge bales of wool, and little bags of rubies and emeralds. One is for ever untying this packet here, sampling that heap over there, wiping the dust off some vast map of the world, and sitting down in semi-darkness to snuff the strange smells of silks and leathers and ambergris, while outside tumble the huge waves of the uncharted Elizabethan sea."

Hakluyt's expeditions, Woolf goes on to tell us, were manned by "apt young men" who loved to explore and trade for treasure. They told the mysterious and wondrous tales that Hakluyt recorded as truth. Here, knowing our liking not only for imagery but also for narrative, Woolf tells us some of these tales: "The Earl of Cumberland's men, hung up by adverse winds off the coast of Cornwall for a fortnight, licked the muddy water off the deck in agony. And sometimes a ragged and wornout man came knocking at the door of an English country house and claimed to be the boy who had left it years ago to sail the seas. . . . He had with him a black stone, veined with gold, or an ivory tusk, or a silver ingot, and urged on the village youth with talk of gold strewn over the land as stones are strewn in the fields of England." At one level, Woolf is entertaining us, but at another, she is instructing us, for these tales were, after all, a major source for Elizabethan literature. "All this," she writes, "the new words, the new ideas, the waves, the savages, the adventures, found their way naturally into the plays which were being acted on the banks of the Thames." The extravagant spirit that fabricated them is the same extravagant spirit that buoys us up through so many Elizabethan writings. In the words of the essay, "Thus, with singing and with music, springs into existence the characteristic Elizabethan extravagance; the dolphins and lavoltas of Greene; the hyperbole, more surprising in a writer so terse and muscular, of Ben Jonson. Thus we find the whole of Elizabethan literature strewn with gold and silver; with talk of Guiana's rarities, and references to that America . . . which was not merely a land on the map but symbolized the unknown territories of the soul."

The next section of the essay, in which Woolf weighs two

important Elizabethan genres against each other, effort-lessly continues from her opening metaphor. The magic spirit of the lumber room inspired poetry but was bad for prose. She writes, "Rhyme and metre helped the poets to keep the tumult of their perceptions in order. But the prose writer, without these restrictions, accumulated clauses, petered out interminable catalogues, tripped and stumbled over the convolutions of his own rich draperies." From this point, Woolf moves to the next with another image, "The stage was the nursery where prose learnt to find its feet."

Now, having covered prose, poetry, and drama, and hav-ing explained the reason for drama's importance, she be-gins slowly to trace the evolution *out* of Elizabethan litera-ture: "The publicity of the stage and the perpetual pres-ence of a second person, were hostile to that growing con-sciousness of one's self . . . which, as the years went by, sought expression." As necessarily as a pendulum swing, the pressure of the outside world caused writers to reflect upon themselves, but with the old imagery intact. Woolf quotes Sir Thomas Browne: " 'The world that I regard is myself; it is the microcosm of my own frame that I cast mine eye on; for the other I use it but like my globe, and turn it round sometimes for my recreation.' 'We carry with us the wonders we seek without us; there is all Africa and her prodigies in us.' " She leads us to sympathize with Browne: she involves us with her picture of him in the same way she involved us with her picture of Hakluyt, his covers shut before his conclusion. "In short, as we say when we cannot help laughing at the oddities of people we admire most, he was a character, and the first to make us feel that the most sublime speculations of the human imagination are issued from a particular man, whom we can love." Again, we nod; we identify; we fully consent to her use of "we."

At the very end of her essay, Woolf repeats the lumber room metaphor. Only now, instead of being an image for Hakluyt's book—the outside world that so excited Eliza-bethans—it is an image for the mind of Sir Thomas Browne—the inside world that so intrigued writers of the seventeenth century. "Now," she writes, "we are in the presence of sublime imagination; now rambling through one of the finest lumber rooms in the world—a chamber stuffed from floor to ceiling with ivory, old iron, broken pots, urns, unicorns' horns, and magic glasses full of emer-ald lights and blue mystery." The lumber room has served to beguile us in the beginning of the essay, to guide us throughout, and to give us a rich sense of unity at the end. Yet, like the symbols of great poetry, it has never preached to us directly.

Though the "common reader" was Virginia Woolf 's most dramatic critical innovation—and probably the most im-portant to *her*—she made other experiments in criticism to escape tradition. She pushed, for example, a certain kind of biographical criticism to its frontier. "Try to be-come the author," she advises herself, and thinks further, "Were I another person I would say to myself, Please write criticism; biography; invent a new form for both" [*A Writer's Diary*]. Woolf 's search for a new combination of criticism and biography might be thought of as represent-

ing her attachment to that old critical dictum, "The style is the man." In a number of her essays, she personifies the works of a writer; so she presents us not with a series of texts but with some*one,* a man or a woman.

She makes a person, for instance, out of Goldsmith's es-says, and calls the person Goldsmith. "The Citizen [in Goldsmith's volume *The Citizen of the World*] is still a most vivacious companion as he takes his walk from Char-ing Cross to Ludgate Hill. . . . Goldsmith keeps just on the edge of the crowd so we can hear what the common people are saying and note their humours. Shrewdly and sarcastically he casts his eye, as he saunters on, upon the odd habits and sights that the English are so used to that they no longer see them" [**"Oliver Goldsmith"**]. The point is that "Goldsmith," in this passage, is actually Gold-smith's book.

Woolf had sense enough to think about the appropriate-ness of her technique carefully, so that the debate about biographical criticism has been enriched by her thoughts. Considering Henley, a man who, according to her, wrote the most mechanical sort of biographical criticism, she said, "There are times when we would sweep aside all bi-ography and all psychology for the sake of a single song or a single poem expounded and analysed phrase-by-phrase" [**"Henley's Criticism"**]. Finally, in favor of her biographical tendencies, as a critic, however, she said that a writer stops being a writer, even when he does not write, and also that "the pith and essence of [a man's] character . . . shows itself to the observant eye in the tone of a voice, the turn of a head, some little phrase or anec-dote picked up in passing" [**"Sterne"** and **"The New Biog-raphy"**]. If the tiniest, vaguest clues can show a man's es-sence, then Woolf was surely justified in reading from book to author and back again. In her essay **"Personali-ties,"** she analyzes again her brand of criticism, offering the following justification and quite sensible reservation about it: "The people whom we admire most as writers . . . have something elusive, enigmatic, imperson-al about them. In ransacking their drawers we shall find out little about them. All has been distilled into their books. The life is thin, modest, colourless, like blue skimmed milk at the bottom of the jar. It is the imperfect artists who never manage to say the whole thing in their books who wield the power of personality over us." In other words, bringing the life of the writer *to* the work or deducing personality *from* a work may be more or less ap-propriate, more or less revelatory, according to the nature of the biography or the *oeuvre* under scrutiny. Woolf may not have succeeded in inventing a new form in her mixture of biography and criticism: at the least, we remember Johnson's *Lives of the Poets,* Lamb's *Essays of Elia,* or Hazlitt's *Table Talk,* and we may even recall *Hours in a Library,* written by Sir Leslie Stephen, Woolf 's father. She did, however, overtake her rivals in the devotion and the grace with which she practiced it.

Of course, Woolf habitually moved out of criticism cou-pled with biography into pure biography. Many of her es-says review letters, memoirs, autobiographies, biogra-phies. Her interest in these latter stretches further and is a further instance of her revolt against tradition: she writes repeatedly on works outside the standard canon of English literature. She suggests that the word "literature" might well be redefined, as we find it undergoing redefinition today, to include popular or miscellaneous writing of all periods. And she takes women writers quite seriously, going out of the conventional way to notice them and give notice of them. Roughly 20 percent of her published essays are about women writers directly. Roughly the same proportion again are indirectly concerned with the frustrating limits that conventional society places on women's personal and literary lives. An essay on Dorothy Osborne's *Letters,* for example, stresses that the literary talents of women could only begin, historically, to find expression in what we might call "underground" writing. In **"Mme. de Sévigné,"** she looks anew at a famous "token woman"; in **"Sara Coleridge,"** she sketches the difficulties of a literary daughter; and in **"Poe's Helen,"** she emphasizes Helen far more than Poe.

The features of Woolf's criticism we have been concerned with are all, we would argue, strategies in a single campaign: an effort to take books down from library shelves and put them into the hands of her ideal community, the common readers. And to talk about them outside the walls of lecture rooms. And to talk about them, finally, in such a way that they matter, not in literary history, but in our lives.

Woolf has, as we noted at the beginning, been called "subjective," and we accepted the term with its apparently pejorative overtones. But the acceptance was only temporary, and we want now to return to it so as to redefine it.

In 1923, beginning to revise a number of essays for publication in the collection she titled *The Common Reader,* Woolf wrote in her diary, "I shall really investigate literature with a view to answering certain questions about ourselves." Not "myself," but "ourselves." She is not a subjective critic in the sense that she refers to her own life in her critical essays. She does not, for instance, mention that she knew some of the contemporary authors she wrote about; and, as an early biographer remarked, "No one would guess from reading 'The Enchanted Organ' that the woman whose selected letters she was reviewing had been not only Miss Thackeray, Mrs. Richmond Ritchie and Lady Ritchie but also Aunt Annie [the sister of Sir Leslie Stephen's first wife]" [Aileen Pippett, *The Moth and the Star*]. It would be impossible to learn from her criticism about Woolf's daily routine or her friends or her marriage or her mental illness or her work for the Women's Cooperative Guild. Yet her work may be called subjective in this broader sense, that she sees literature as a series of personal transactions, a series of encounters between people writing and people reading, and she urges us to see both literature and popular culture that way ourselves.

Learning, she knows, is by no means necessarily a humanizing experience. In the biography of Dr. Bentley, head of Trinity College, Cambridge, she tells us, Bentley is described as extraordinarily learned, knowing Homer by heart, reading Sophocles and Pindar the way we read newspapers and magazines, spending his life largely in the company of the greatest of the Greeks. And yet, in his life, she says, "we shall [also] find much that is odd and little that is reassuring. . . . The man who should have been steeped in beauty (if what they say of the Classics is true) as a honey-pot is ingrained with sweetness was, on the contrary, the most quarrelsome of mankind" [**"Outlines (II: Dr. Bentley)"**]. He was aggressive; he was coercive; he bullied and threatened his academic staff at Trinity and, beyond a doubt, did the same to students. Did the Society of Trinity College dare to think he spent too much of the college funds on the staircase of his own lodging? Did they perceive that he stole food, drink, and fuel from the college stores? Then let them look to their jobs and their other preferments. And so on and on and on.

Nonetheless, Woolf's essays imply, over and over again, that learning *can* be a humanizing experience. And here we turn back to our beginning. Far from merely recording the adventures of a soul among masterpieces, Woolf's criticism always exerts a standard of judgment, seldom explicit but nonetheless there, informing her essays, evident in the selection of her details as well as the choices of her persona and her rhetoric. In *A Room of One's Own,* she speaks of Shakespeare's mind as a mind without "obstacle," a mind "unimpeded" and "incandescent," free to produce works of art. Such works "seem to stand there complete by themselves," which is to say not only that form and content beautifully accord, but that the works do not break or unseam to show, say, an anger that is only personal or a grievance merely local. And John Paston, reading in Norfolk with the sea to his left and the fen to his right, saw in Chaucer fields and skies and people he recognized but seldom rendered more brightly, more clearly, "rounded and complete." Chaucer's mind, too, was "free to apply its force fully to its object" [**"The Pastons and Chaucer"**]. On the other hand, reading Charlotte Brontë's novels, Woolf finds material not germane to fictional design, not consistent with the predominant point of view and style. There are interpolations of self-defense and interjections of indignation—indignation about, for example, the lot of the English governess. The explanation for these anomalies, Woolf suggests, can be found by moving back beyond the work of art to the mind that made it, and there is the life "cramped and thwarted," pressed into uncongenial services and attitudes that frustrated the impulse of genius to express itself, "whole and entire" [*A Room of One's Own*]. While Woolf's criticism of Brontë is in some ways adverse, it is, nonetheless, basically sympathetic. What was evokes hauntingly the image of what might have been. And more, what should have been. The critical ideal applied to Shakespeare, Chaucer, and Brontë is the same ideal of the free self that Woolf expresses in her novels, a self breaking bonds and vaulting bounds, a self arriving at the furthest intensity of thought and emotion.

In this last sense, then, Woolf's criticism may without injury be called subjective or personal. Its function is to humanize our lives, to urge a liberation and wholeness of self. It is a brilliant and graceful protest against any narrower, more abstract, or merely professional critical purpose. To put the case concretely, as she habitually did, it is a brilliant and graceful protest against one of the pictures she drew in *A Room of One's Own:* Professor von X., engaged in writing a "monumental work." Professor von X. is heavy in build, his eyes are very small, his complexion is red with anger, and he "jabs" with his pen at his paper "as if he were killing some noxious insect." (pp. 362-71)

> Barbara Currier Bell and Carol Ohmann, "Virginia Woolf's Criticism: A Polemical Preface," in Critical Inquiry, Vol. 1, No. 2, December, 1974, pp. 361-71.

Jane Novak   (essay date 1975)

[*Novak is an American educator and critic. In the following excerpt, she discusses ways in which Woolf's literary essays reveal her attempt to reconcile romantic and classical critical perspectives.*]

Virginia Woolf thought Roger Fry an admirable critic because he could make the layman see in a painting the crucial choices of the artist; he pointed out harmonies, patterns, and happy deviations from patterns. What was most significant, he could convey to his audience a sense of the balanced relationships and the inevitable sequences of line and mass that he believed to be the prime source of aesthetic pleasure. In her Roger Fry Memorial Address she describes his lecturing method—seeing, pointing, reasoning, using his own experience as a painter to re-create the canvas in the making. She praised his sensitivity, his honesty, and his avoidance of fixed ideas.

Believing as Fry did that the understanding and enjoyment of art are among the most profound and enduring pleasures that life has to give, Virginia Woolf worked in the same way to make the common reader understand the intricate process of writing a novel. Her view was that of the practicing writer, but she assumed the role of a knowledgeable reader who did not want to fetter a fellow reader's judgment but to open his eyes and to increase his pleasure. She warned him against critical dogmatists and urged his sympathy for the novelist.

Her declared passion for the artist's view was as keen as that of Henry James, and it infused her definition of modern criticism. The modern critic, she says, discards all "barren" laws of art and all "sweeping and sterile" systems in order "to enter the mind of the writer, to see the work of art itself, and to judge how far each writer had succeeded in his aim." She acknowledged that this abandonment of rule was itself a difficult rule, demanding of the critic the highest degree of imaginative flexibility, yet she insisted that he must use his freedom, because "to be free to make one's own laws, and to do it afresh for every newcomer is an essential part of any criticism worth having" ["Mr. Symons' Essays"].

The danger of this empirical individualism, she admitted, was impressionism, which in both art and criticism might meander into irrelevant, egotistical diversions. But she claimed a compensatory gain from the honest admission that the critic's voice is private and fallible, not oracular and final. She described this advantage while scolding Coventry Patmore for making Aristotle responsible for the "oddities" of his own judgment:

> In an impressionistic critic of the school which Patmore condemned you will meet precisely the same freaks of prejudice and partisanship, but with the difference that as no attempt is made to relate them to doctrine and principles, they pass for what they are, and the door being left wide open, interesting ideas may take the opportunity to enter in. But Patmore was content to state his principle and shut the door.

This comment is suffused with her hostility to male figures of authority, but she did believe firmly that only with the door wide open to tentative and experimental ideas could the twentieth-century critic perform his primary duty— "keep the atmosphere in a right state for the production of works of art." Having been an eyewitness to the British public in paroxysms of rage and laughter before the paintings of Gauguin, Cézanne, and Van Gogh in November 1910, she knew that formal experimentation in the arts required for its acceptance a climate of aesthetic open-mindedness.

So desirable was this state to Virginia Woolf that in her address **"How Should One Read a Book?"** she enlisted all those who read for the love of reading in the work of maintaining freedom for the author. Since the common reader shares with the novelist, although in a feebler form, the desire to create, she appealed to him to instruct himself by reading widely and to exert a vigorous influence on literature, a criticism by word of mouth more salutary than that of the press or of academia. Her advice to this imaginary "reader as friend to the writer" was to follow her own method as artist and critic—to yield sensitively and uncritically to the first multitudinous and confused impressions, then to order these impressions, seeing the book as a whole, and lastly, to compare and judge it.

Her essay on how to read is a description of how a critic might re-create the writer's processes in order to bring about a harmony between the insights of his empathetic understanding of the work and his severe judgment. Although she encourages the reading of biographies and memoirs, she warns the reader to ask himself how far a book is influenced by the author's life. Banishing all preconceptions, a reader must begin the work sympathetically. She advises him to be an accomplice of the writer, indeed even to try to quicken his understanding of the writer's problems of choice by writing himself. In reading the novel he must submit himself to the crescendos and diminuendos of emotion that are the form of the work. Then, when he has allowed some time for his subconscious to work upon the first fragmented impressions, he must experience the book's symmetry, judging where it has failed and where it has succeeded according to the laws of its own design. At last, he must sternly compare it with the best of its kind.

Here in this eclectic diversity of approach is historical balance—a romantic interest in the writer's personality and individual mode of expression, a classical interest in the work's self-contained form and its formative values, an aesthetic analysis of its effect and its medium, and a judicial decision as to its rank in its tradition. Yet these critical techniques are all subtly differentiated from the traditions to which they belong by her strong desire to be, like Fry, a critic of the work in the making. All questions are logically included in her fascination with the artist's search for

Woolf painted by her sister, Vanessa Bell.

a technique based on his unique vision—a technique that alone can provide a principle of selection and hold all details in the most powerful emotional relationship. She asks: How and how well does he strike a balance between the randomness of life and the formal principles of his art?

Virginia Woolf's first step, "To enter the mind of the writer," was taken in the spirit of Sainte-Beuve, to whom she paid tribute in an early review ["**Creative Criticism**"]. Though pretending, like Hippolyte Taine, to the analytical detachment of a naturalist of the mind, Sainte-Beuve was more intuitive and less rigid. He advised the critic "to listen to writers long and carefully" and to make his deductions with intellectual tact. Criticism, he said, for all its pretensions to the scientific method, would always require special gifts. He suggested that the critic try "to seize the familiar trick, the telltale smile, the indefinable wrinkle, the secret line of pain hidden in vain beneath the scanty hair." With the same interest in individual character, Virginia Woolf studied the famous dead. Sometimes, in the manner of her father, Leslie Stephen, she made superficial cause-effect inferences about the relationship of the period and the work, but she habitually erected a writer's frame of reference from his writings and a mélange of miscellaneous biographical details. Like Sainte-Beuve, she was often interested in his companions, but for their own sake as personalities rather than influences.

Her interest in the author's life and in his friends was of a piece with a major theme of her fiction—the fascinating

and near insoluble riddle of the human personality. Her talent for vicariousness was well-known to her coterie: she examined the lives of the famous and of the obscure with open, gossipy irreverence. Moved by the charm of idiosyncracy, she reported homely facts about the literary great, which, in their trivial eccentricity, impress upon the reader their human reality. The mundane details from the past, neither reducing nor sentimentalizing the subject's life, create in her literary essays a tone of mingled empathy and irony.

This method, so dependent on her considerable ability to identify with her subject, sometimes failed embarrassingly, resulting in such partisan and disputable assertations as: "No one has ever loved Dickens as he loves Shakespeare and Scott" [*David Copperfield*]. But the belletristic comments were marginal to her purpose. She raised a writer from the dead, not to express her affection for him or to place him in historical context or to explain his works by his days. Rather, she was interested in how his temperament and talent worked upon his experience. She wanted to enter his mind, she explained, as he was stimulated and played upon by the subject matter of his art. She presented an artist's milieu, not as a formative influence, but as a disorder of contradictory details and miscellaneous events—a preliminary view of his world as it looks to him before he arranges and disguises it for the reception of his characters. By reading George Gissing's letters, she says, we can visualize his "world of four-wheelers and slatternly land-ladies, of struggling men of letters, of gnawing domestic misery . . . in a design which we began to trace out when we read *Demos* and *New Grub Street* and *The Nether World*" ["**George Gissing**"].

Believing that the faculty employed at first reading was sensual, she was especially interested in other artists' habits of seeing and feeling and in their struggles to order their sensations into language. Hardy, she observed, knew that the rain "falls differently as it falls on roots or arable"; Dickens knew the "smell and savour of London"; De Quincey saw his surroundings with the diffused vision of "a dreaming pondering absent-mindedness," which made his imagery dreamlike and portentous ["**The Novels of Thomas Hardy**," "*David Copperfield*," "**De Quincey's Autobiography**"]. Her own effort to find words for the look of things was instinctive and continuous.

Her method is always to relate the reader's experience with the work to the facts of the artist's life rather than the other way around. She presents biographical detail as neither necessary to the reader's understanding of the work nor casual to its creation—rather these details help us to enter the writer's mind and to see him as a whole. "A writer is a writer from his cradle; in his dealing with the world, in his affections, in his attitude to the thousand small things that happen between dawn and sunset, he shows the same point of view as that which he elaborates afterwards with a pen in his hand" ["**Sterne**"]. But although his dealings with the world are of interest because he is a man of original talent, she warns the critic that too much preoccupation with his life may cause him to lose his way. The creative power of the writer is often at work transforming and transcending his miseries. For all her curiosity about the artist's experience, she declares that life is not his master; she is always jealous of his independence.

Turning to the next step of seeing "the work itself," she abandons her discussion of the balance between life and art and interests herself in the balance between forms and values. Biographical controversy is extrinsic to this task.

> For the book itself remains. However we may wind and wriggle, loiter and dally in our approach to books, a lonely battle awaits us at the end. There is a piece of business to be transacted between writer and reader before any further dealings are possible, and to be reminded in the middle of this private interview that Defoe sold stockings, had brown hair, and was stood in the pillory is a distraction and a worry. Our first task, and it is often formidable enough, is to master his perspective. [*"Robinson Crusoe"*]

From the visual arts comes her key term "perspective"; like the James phrase "point of view," it is part of the painter's vocabulary and has a double meaning. It stands for what she saw as indivisible in the greatest fiction—the concept of value and the fact of technique. In novelistic criticism it meant to Virginia Woolf both the artist's vision of life in his self-contained fictional world and the principles of selection and proportion by which he created its form. Since perspective provides the rule for the harmony and balance of a classical visual composition, she logically uses visual, even linear metaphor to describe the effects of novels in which the fundamental assumptions about human experience are coherently and emotionally realized. A Peacock novel, although its author delights in distortions, is "so manageable in scale that we can take its measure" [**"Phases of Fiction"**]. Jane Austen, in relating her characters, creates between them "exact distances and accurate measurement" both literal and psychological; the reader sees Hardy's figure "against the earth, the storms, and the seasons" and "in their relations to time, death, and fate," and as a result "they take on more than mortal size." In *A Passage to India,* Forster "builds his model on a larger scale" than in his English novels, including with its more extended physical scene a wider scope of experience for its characters [**"The Novels of E. M. Forster"**]. These are impressionistic metaphors of effect; like Fry, Virginia Woolf is pointing out and bringing to the surface the elements of design and relationship by which effects are realized. She uses visual terms to emphasize that the emotional power of the whole is dependent on a coherent and balanced composition. She says, "A work of art means that one part gets strength from another part" [*A Writer's Diary*].

In her critical vocabulary, "perspective" controls the fictional imitation of reality; it is not merely a thematic principle, although themes are part of its mastering unity. In her **"Phases of Fiction"** novelists are ranged, with appropriate distinctions, not by chronological order or by their common thematic concerns but by like technical problems that stem from similar fundamental assumptions about the life in their imaginary worlds. Proust and Dostoevsky are placed side by side because for both the inner life has a distinct and peculiar beauty; their common problem is

to develop a climactic action true to the workings of this inner existence. If they can imagine a persuasive form, if they can effectively choose, order, and balance details, if they can create emotional high points true to the peculiar reality of the fictional world—in short, if they can realize their perspective—the power of their fiction will temporarily flout and destroy the reader's own sense of life, impose itself upon his imagination and possess it. She offers the masterpiece of *Robinson Crusoe* as a model; its perspective forces us to abandon our large and romantic view of life on a desert island. Defoe's belief in fact, substance, and utility governs the reader's emotion and his glad response to every invention and discovery of Crusoe. Defoe's reality masters the reader because all details relate to the fundamental principles of belief in the novel; the fictional form is in perfect harmony with the fictional values.

Any critic using the word "reality" must define it. Virginia Woolf most often uses it to stand for a mysterious entity that lies behind experience. But in considering the particular historical reality that a writer must realize, she defines it this way, skillfully avoiding abstraction:

> At the outset in reading an Elizabethan play we are overcome by the extraordinary discrepancy between the Elizabethan view of reality and our own. The reality to which we have grown accustomed is, speaking roughly, based upon the life and death of some knight called Smith, who succeeded his father in the family business of pitwood importers, timber merchants and coal exporters, was well known in political, temperance, and church circles, did much for the poor of Liverpool and died last Wednesday of pneumonia while on a visit to his son at Muswell Hill. That is the world we know. That is the reality which our poets and novelists have to expound and illuminate. [**"Notes on an Elizabethan Play"**]

She goes on to contrast the Elizabethan view of reality, which easily encompassed unicorns and ghosts, the extravagant behavior of a Belimperia, and a sense of the presence of the gods. Less vividly, her definition of the reader's reality can be paraphrased as the phenomena of his experience and imagination to which he unhesitatingly attaches meaning and the cause-effect sequences that he accepts or predicts automatically. A novel must enlarge or narrow, light up or darken this view by its own scheme of order and belief. To enjoy and to understand fully, the reader must recognize the writer's perspective rather than impose his own reality on the fiction.

This means he must recognize and temporarily accept the underlying values of the novel. If the foregoing discussion is in the language of ontology, psychology, and literary convention, it is moral as well, although Virginia Woolf sidesteps the word. Discussing the technique of *Emma* in her essay on Greek tragedy, she makes clear that if Jane Austen placed her characters in closest proximity in a world of narrow physical limits, "bound and restricted to a few definite movements," the result was to increase the emotional and ethical leverage of their every act of will. [**"On Not Knowing Greek"**].

But she points out to the common reader that the consistency of a novelist's perspective cannot alone provide the power of his fiction. He must perfectly believe his own fictional view. If a writer develops a technique suited to the order of his convictions and his convictions begin to lose their validity and vitality for him, he is left, as Virginia Woolf believed Conrad was left in his final period, with "old nobilities and sonorities . . . a little wearily reiterated as if times had changed" [**"Joseph Conrad"**]. But believing in his perspective, he must labor so that it perfectly and unobtrusively controls the art of his fiction. Wherever he may be convicted of patently asserting his creed, there is grave weakness. She called Hardy the greatest tragic writer among English novelists, but thought *Jude the Obscure* a failure because it is too often argument rather than impression.

The reader who, in Virginia Woolf's opinion, can exert a valuable influence on literature is the reader who sensitively and appreciatively responds to the novel in which technique and belief are perfectly harmonious. And this reader is one who will take pleasure in the inevitable balance and unity of the form.

Virginia Woolf is not an obviously innovative critic; this is hardly avant-garde aesthetic theory, and her terminology is far from precise. Her critical emphasis on value as formative, on the intellectual and emotional power of harmonia, on the interpenetrating relationship of past and present, on the desirability of authorial effacement, and on literature as a source of wisdom and delight is so plainly from the classical tradition of criticism that it is of interest chiefly because of her fresh examples and her avoidance of such jargon as the foregoing. Her discussion of the magnitude of the action in *Jude the Obscure* might serve as a footnote to Matthew Arnold's "Preface" in his 1853 *Poems;* her observation on the action of *Ulysses*—"that there are not only other aspects of life, but more important ones into the bargain"—is as morally judgmental as Samuel Johnson; her comparison of Hemingway's characters to those of Maupassant and Chekhov, a time-tested critical method, echoes the reminders of Arnold and T. S. Eliot that dead geniuses are always our contemporaries [**"Modern Fiction"**]. But her lack of dogmatism, her respect for the common reader, and her brilliant use of metaphor create a tone and a method that are uniquely her own.

Although a literary essayist with classical loyalties, she was fiercely antitheoretical. Her criticism is never a reasoned, precise, systematic discussion of the problems of art. Her references to the past are in terms of the continuity of human life rather than of literary history. The key statements of her working hypothesis on the nature of balance in fiction come from a wide variety of essays and reviews. Her method was inductive and her principles, developed during the discussion of specific works, ranged in a psychological spectrum rather than in sharp categories. Her major statement of fictional theory, **"Phases of Fiction,"** is largely description of a variety of perspectives as demonstrated by the works of major novelists whom she classifies as romantics, truth-tellers, character-mongers and comedians, psychologists, satirists and fantastics, and poets.

Because she defined "the book itself " as "not form which you can see but emotion you can feel," the descriptions move from considerations of formal problems to Pateresque aesthetic reveries. She was quite aware of the difference between the two critical methods. Quoting, with unmistakable appreciation, from the imagistic reflections of Hazlitt on a dusty folio, she adds: "Needless to say that is not criticism. It is sitting in an armchair and gazing into the fire, and building up image after image of what one has seen in a book. It is loving and taking the liberties of a lover. It is being Hazlitt" [**"William Hazlitt"**]. And of some of her criticism the reader must say, "It is being Virginia Woolf." In part she seems to be obeying Pater's injunction to define the special unique impression of pleasure. Yet surprisingly, her contempt for Sir Edmund Gosse's similar critical goal, which she describes as "to illumine, to make visible and desireable . . . the finished article," is only delicately veiled by her compliments to his learning and his urbanity [**"Edmund Gosse"**]. For her the distinction was between the critic like Gosse who can appreciate the finished article and the critic like Fry who can appreciate the canvas in the making. Her intent was to trace the artist's search, to produce an analysis of the effect more tough-minded and practical, less intuitive and narcissistic than that of Pater. She was interested not only in recording the exact character of her response but in discovering how the artist evoked it. "Although to feel is of the first importance, to know *why* one feels is of great importance, too," she wrote in 1917 [**"Creative Criticism"**]. To know why, one must examine technique, but never with the scientific analysis of academic criticism, which, as Quentin Bell notes, she distrusted altogether.

There is, however, no denying her numerous affinities with the romantic classicist Pater: the admiration of the resources of prose, the emphasis on art's fixing of the fleeting moment, the desire to merge matter and form indivisibly, and the elevation of the intense moment of vision. Even her cautious and undeveloped definition of the relation between ethics and aesthetics is reminiscent of *Marius the Epicurean:* "We cannot help thinking that of the two poems the one with a higher morality is better aesthetically than the one with a lower morality." Most important perhaps is the similarity between her theory of perspective and Pater's assertion that it is not "fact" but the artist's "sense of fact" which reigns in his work.

In reprise, although her literary essays are not systematized criticism, they are part of a critical tradition. They examine the writer's experiences, define his perspective, and attempt to see how he has fused the two into a form with emotional power. They are not precise and exhaustive analyses, but they do not pretend to be. Her essays seek to create an understanding of works in the making written by writers who interest her, and as David Daiches has observed, her taste was remarkably catholic. In addition, with great intuition and sympathy, her criticism dealt with many women writers as they had never been dealt with before. Virginia Woolf's essays are the tributes of a grateful and sensitive reader who understands the intricate processes of writing; they are evocative, urbane, confident, and felicitous.

Her contemporary reviews, however, have a different tone. Their rhetorical position is no longer informed reader to reader but writer to writer. She is no longer talking about household saints but about sibling rivals. There are essential similarities, of course. She still occasionally attempts to guess the source of an author's inspiration, that moment of experience which began the process of his creation, and she is always conscious of the difficult work that follows this flash, but she is no longer greatly confident that her judgment of his work will hold up in the future.

There is no question that she took her reviewing seriously, but for all her scrupulosity she believed that any criticism of one's contemporaries is inevitably flawed by lack of distance and by professional jealousy. "No creative writer can stomach another contemporary," she wrote dogmatically. Indeed, she did not always display the open-minded generosity she recommends in **"How Should One Read a Book?"** but she frankly delineates her biases. In 1918, after fourteen years of reviewing, she writes with characteristic duality in a *Times Literary Supplement* (hereafter *TLS*) review:

> For it is extremely difficult to take the writings of one's contemporaries seriously. The spirit in which they are read is a strange compact of indifference and curiosity. On the one hand the assumption is that they are certainly bad, and on the other the temptation assails us to find them a queer and illicit fascination. Between these two extremes we vacillate, and the attention we grant them is at once furtive and intense. [**"The Claim of the Living"**]

Knowing the damage to a writer's morale, reputation, and purse inflicted by an unfavorable review, and knowing herself pathologically pained by hostile attacks, she recommends in a Hogarth pamphlet, *Reviewing,* that a private diagnostic interview between writer and reviewer is preferable to an abrasive public appraisal. Barring the unlikely realization of such an alternative, she advises all reviewers to adopt the policy of Harold Nicolson who says that he addresses himself to the authors of books he reviews, outlines his likes and dislikes, and trusts that the dialogue will be helpful to the reader.

She describes her own role as that of a consultant, expositor, expounder, a post-factum collaborator, sometimes even a frank competitor. "It is no business of ours to write other people's novels," she writes in a review of a Hugh Walpole volume. "We confess in this case we should like to" [**"The Green Mirror"**]. In fact, her reviews of biographies and memoirs, a frequent assignment for her, are unabashedly miniature works of their own rather than assessments of the work at hand. "How it may be with other readers we know not, but with us the test of a good biography is that it leaves us with the impulse to write it all over again," she begins a review [**"A Character Sketch"**].

Another reason for separating her contemporary reviews from her literary essays on writers of the past is the influence of the practical, commercial, and political conditions of book reviewing that sometimes affect even the most independent critic. As a young reviewer, her work was subject to cutting and to strictures against offending. She complains in a letter that her review of *The Golden Bowl,* over which she had labored five days, making twelve pages of detailed notes, had to be cut in two at the last minute. There is also evidence in her correspondence that some of her kind words were disingenuous, although her own sensitivity to criticism may have been as much of a censor as the editor. She is always free of humbug, but she sometimes gives guarded praise where she might have censured. In a letter to Violet Dickinson she complains violently of Vernon Lee's "watery mind": "I am sobbing with misery over Vernon Lee who really turns all good writing to vapour with her fluency and insipidity—the plausible woman. I put her on my black list with Mrs. Humphry Ward. But although this is as true as truth, as the sage said in the fairy tale, it can't be said in print."

Her reviews were subject to some editorial pressure even after she was fully established and less fearful of giving offense. The editor of *TLS* tactfully but inflexibly insisted that she delete the word "lewd" which she had used as an epithet for Henry James in an essay on his ghost stories. Some light on this astonishing word choice comes from this passage in *Jacob's Room,* which was published the same year as the essay: "Professor Bulteel of Leeds had issued an edition of Wycherley without stating that he had left out, disemboweled, or indicated only by asterisks, several indecent words and some indecent phrases. An outrage, Jacob said; a breach of faith; sheer prudery; token of a lewd mind and a disgusting nature." (If Jacob Flanders' definition of lewdness as reticence on the subject of carnality is to be accepted, the charge might even be made against the fiction of Virginia Woolf. She found Joyce's "indecency" as disgusting as James' hovering reticence.)

Perhaps her low opinion of her own reviews or of their subjects is evidenced by their omission from the ***Common Readers.*** Leonard Woolf included a very few in the posthumously published four-volume ***Collected Essays*** and acted as publisher for forty-six more edited by Jean Guiguet in 1965 *(Contemporary Writers),* but there are still hundreds yellowing in old periodicals from *The Athenaeum* to *Vogue,* from the London *Guardian* to *The Yale Review.* For all the occasional triviality of their subjects, their frankly described prejudices, their disclaimers, and their repetitiveness, they are essentially sound and sensitive views. They show Virginia Woolf imagining the search and judging the success of writers trying to work out problems that are of interest to her.

Of particular fascination are over forty early reviews, heretofore unlisted in Woolf bibliographies, now to be read in the Monks House Papers at the University of Sussex. Most of them are reviews of memoirs and biographies in which she is often taking the editor-biographer to task, either for having been unselective or for having too stringently imposed a pattern on the "loose, drifting stuff of life." These questions were central to her own writing; even as a very young writer she was pondering them.

As an expositor and expounder she frequently analyzes in the novels of her peers two other problems of balance relevant to her own work; the reconciliation of superficial finesse with lifelike action, and the conflict between form and idea in fiction. The first antithesis is discussed most often in her reviews of writers with a practiced facility in plotting and style. She praises the formal perfection of Joseph Hergesheimer's novels, but finds his characters sometimes "chilled by the icy finger of theory"; for all the exquisite fashioning of his fiction, she says it reminds her of "those watches that are made too elaborately to be able to go" ["The Pursuit of Beauty"]. In a similar vein she writes in her diary of the flaws of a popular well-made novel:

> A moving, in its way, completed story. But shallow. A superficial book. But also a finished one. Rounded off. Only possible if you keep one inch below; because the people, like Sainty, have to do things without diving deep; and this runs in the current; which lends itself to completeness. That is, if a writer accepts the conventions and lets his characters be guided by them, not conflict with them, he can produce an effect of symmetry: very pleasant; suggestive; but only on the surface. That is, I don't care what happens: yet I like the design.

Her compulsion to go below the surface and to produce the symmetry and design on a deeper level than that of the conventional outer action is implicit whenever she considers and judges popular fiction.

On the threat of didacticism to art she writes often, since popular fiction often advances current scientific and social theory. Because of her own ardent feminism she was particularly sensitive to unassimilated convictions in fiction. Her moral indignation erupted in pamphleteering, but she worked to make it an implicit emotion in her novels.

Although she did not systematize, a classification of descending order can be inferred from her reviews of fiction that is controlled by ideas. She seems to have believed that a novelist's overriding conviction might affect his novel in one of three ways if he did not succeed in absorbing it into an aesthetic and emotional unity: (1) a strong, independently conceived conviction can create form by establishing points of interest that are intellectual rather than emotional; (2) a strong, independently conceived conviction can inspire digressions that interfere with the artistic form; or (3) a secondhand, intellectually fashionable conviction can rob his work of vitality.

The late-Victorian Samuel Butler and the twentieth-century Norman Douglas are writers whose novels she places in the first category. Douglas, she said, found in *South Wind* a form for expressing the individual character of his mind. She charges Samuel Butler with humoring his ideas until the story stagnates, but praises him for achieving shape by another means than a plot of action:

> At one time we think it is his humour that eludes us, that strange, unlaughing, overwhelming gift which compresses his stories at one grasp into their eternal shape; at another the peculiar accent and power of his style; but in the end we cease to dissect, and give ourselves up to delight in a structure which seems to us to be so entire and all of a piece; so typically English, we would like to think, remembering his force of character, his humanity, and his great love of beauty. ["A Man with a View"]

Why, then, did she assign H. G. Wells to the second class, refusing him the same degree of honor as Butler, although Wells, too, had found a form to express the individual character of his mind? She accuses him of a fatal carelessness for the power of fiction, abandoning emotional force to "talk at" the reader. She calls him a creator with "large and slack and insensitive hands . . . in too great a hurry to be artful"; "he throws off the trammels of fiction as lightly as he would throw off a coat in running a race," ["The Rights of Youth"]. But she makes concessions for the energy and sincerity of his work and patronizingly adds that "with all its crudeness and redundancy, its vast soft billowy mass is united by a kind of coherency and has some relation to a work of art."

Contrasts between her specific comments about Butler and Wells are helpful in understanding the difference between the eternal shape and the billowy mass. Butler, she says, writes fearlessly for posterity with very little regard for the contemporary reader; Wells harangues his contemporary audience. Butler's most successful characters, like Christina Pontifex, are rich and solid, while Wells' Joan and Peter are crude lumps and unmodeled masses. Wells' beliefs cause him to let fiction take care of itself; Butler creates a fictional world that is an aesthetic whole.

The third class of didactic fiction that her reviews imply fell, in her eyes, far below the level of the first two. She believed that the arid fiction of disciples, or "novels which are footnotes to science" are removed from life and removed from human emotion. Commitment to received ideas is a dangerous state for the novelist; "the danger of a cause which has great exponents lies in its power to attract recruits who are converts to other people's reforms but are not reformers themselves" ["The Green Mirror"]. Reviewing Gilbert Cannan's *Mummery* in 1918, she describes the thinking of the writer who echoes secondhand ideas: "When he draws conclusions from what he has seen and becomes the intellectual satirist, he writes as if from habit, repeating what he has learned by heart from writers of what he calls 'the Sturm and Drang period.' . . . The conventions of the intellectual are as sterile as the conventions of the bourgeoisie."

She termed Freudian fiction the by-product of intellectual fashion; she thought a complete acceptance of Freud's principles, particularly in their popularized form, a dangerous oversimplification for the novelist. In any case, although the Hogarth Press published the first English translation of Freud, she sometimes lightly mocks him. And although throughout both *Mrs. Dalloway* and *To the Lighthouse* she makes creative use of Freudian symbolism as it had been commonly interpreted, she deliberately gives objects other simultaneous, nonsexual meanings. "Nothing was simply one thing," is a principle in *To the Lighthouse*.

Reviewing unfavorably a novel that takes a Freudian view, she says that the author, J. D. Beresford, has acted the part of a stepfather to some of Freud's progeny. She judges the novel's unlifelike characters to be the inevitable result of its systematic psychological assumptions. The new insight, she comments, simplifies rather than complicates, detracts rather than enriches ["Freudian Fiction"].

She herself created characters that embody her values, but she constantly feared making "people into ideas," as she judged Aldous Huxley had done in *Point Counter Point,* and she considered the danger of didacticism in her own fiction with apprehension, believing that ideas hold up the creative, subconscious faculty. Although her first notes for the plan of a novel combine form, image, and idea, her next step is to put them aside and to cultivate the subconscious powers. For while she insists "The art of writing has for its backbone some fierce attachment to an idea," she also declares "Art is being rid of all preaching" ["**The Modern Essay**"].

In making these two statements she stands before us in the characteristic, persistent, untiring act of balancing oppositions that are not mutually exclusive but which place the artist in a position of high tension and critical choice. What seems at times to be her inconsistency, even her intellectual and temperamental perversity, characterizes the method appropriate to her single-minded pursuit of equilibrium. She automatically challenges the dogmatic extremes of positions she has seemed to support; she seeks principles and methods that reconcile extremes. Her working methods follow this pattern, and her novels dramatize this view of life as a search for balance. (pp. 35-50)

> *Jane Novak, in her* The Razor Edge of Balance: A Study of Virginia Woolf, *University of Miami Press, 1975, 169 p.*

Mark Goldman   (essay date 1976)

[*In the following excerpt from his* The Reader's Art: Virginia Woolf as Literary Critic, *Goldman examines Woolf's theories regarding the nature and function of literary criticism and the critic.*]

Though Mrs. Woolf refused the title of critic (and scholar) in the preface to the first **Common Reader,** the methodology and severe standards of the essays on the art of reading reveal her in the more characteristic and consistent role of conscious literary critic.

As early as 1916, in an essay entitled **'Hours in a Library'**, Mrs. Woolf celebrated the delights of reading and proclaimed the freedom of the private reader against the authority of the specialist or man of learning.

> Let us begin by clearing up the old confusion between the man who loves learning and the man who loves reading, and the point that there is no connexion whatever between the two. A learned man is a sedentary enthusiast, who searches through books to discover some particular grain of truth upon which he has set his heart. If the passion for reading conquers him, his gains dwindle and vanish beneath his fingers. A reader, on the other hand, must check the desire for learning at the outset; if knowledge sticks to him well and good, but to go in pursuit of it, to read on a system, to become a specialist or an authority, is very apt to kill what it suits us to consider the more humane passion for pure and disinterested reading.

Her own passion for books began at the age of fifteen, when her father, the Victorian scholar and critic Sir Leslie Stephen, gave her the run of his large library. The pains she takes to preserve her amateur standing and independent spirit as a critic are also an inheritance from her father, as she reveals in her essay, **'Leslie Stephen'**. 'To read what one liked because one liked it, never to pretend to admire what one did not—that was his only lesson in the art of reading. To write in the fewest possible words, as clearly as possible, exactly what one meant—that was his only lesson in the art of writing.' In an essay simply called **'Reading'**, Mrs. Woolf again reflects on the strange seductive power of books, this time indulging her impressionist fancy as she rambles over the rich landscape of English literature. Here is the sense of literature as part of the English life and land, as an old house and garden and rolling downs stretching toward the sea where the Elizabethan voyagers took ship and sailed for the new world. The historical progress followed in the first chapter, from the Pastons and Chaucer to the contemporary scene, the sense of tradition traced through history by way of a house and land in *Orlando* and *Between the Acts,* is foreshortened in the pages of a book, read in an armchair by the window with the light slanting over the shoulder and the sounds of summer drifting in.

> These were circumstances, perhaps, to turn the mind to the past. Always behind the voice, the figure, the fountain there seemed to stretch an immeasurable avenue, that ran to a point of other voices, figures, fountains which tapered out indistinguishably upon the further horizon. I could see Keats and Pope behind him and then Dryden and Sir Thomas Browne—hosts of them merging in the mass of Shakespeare, behind whom, if one peered long enough, some shapes of men in pilgrims' dress emerged, Chaucer perhaps, and again—who was it? some uncouth poet scarcely able to syllable his words: and so they died away ['**Reading**'].

But the art of reading is also a critical matter, as Mrs. Woolf demonstrates in the essay concluding the second **Common Reader,** 'How Should One Read a Book?' Originally presented as a talk, the audience must have realized that as readers they were to be created in Mrs. Woolf's image. At the outset, she again admonishes the reader to follow his own critical conscience, in the Cambridge-Bloomsbury tradition of the individual against authority and conformity. To be open-minded, to get rid of all preconceptions about the author and the work when we read, is the first step not merely toward enjoyment but understanding.

> Steep yourself in this, acquaint yourself with this, and soon you will find that your author is giving you, or attempting to give you, something far more definite. The thirty-two chapters of a novel—if we consider how to read a novel first—are an attempt to make something as formed and controlled as a building; but words are more impalpable than bricks; reading is a longer and more complex process than seeing.

The reading process is intensified, then, as we turn to the familiar question of form. What is clearly revealed here, and implicit throughout her essays, is a creative tension in her criticism between the emotional response, the impression, the experience of the work, and its rational explanation and evaluation—on formal grounds and in terms of traditional standards. As a psychological novelist, Mrs. Woolf was committed to the 'unconscious' self, as she describes the creative source, as well as to the equally essential tool for the writer, the critical intelligence. Though her faith in sensibility may also be part of her characteristic feminine protest against masculine, academic authority, the critic's emotional response to the work of art was integral, as we shall see, to the Bloomsbury aesthetic.

Mrs. Woolf's argument is further complicated when the idea of form . . . is associated with feeling or emotion, a point to be explored in connection with the essay **'On Re-Reading Novels'.** In **'How Should One Read a Book?'** she refers again to the idea of perspective, which is also related to the problem of form. If the reader would turn writer, Mrs. Woolf observes, he would realize the difficulty of imposing form on the fleeting impressions of life, of creating art out of the chaos of experience. For the great writers, though they see the world in as many ways as their books suggest, submit to the dimensions of a self-contained, consistent world that is the single work of art. 'The maker of each is careful to observe the laws of his own perspective, and however great a strain they may put upon us they will never confuse us, as lesser writers frequently do, by introducing two different kinds of reality into the same book.' (pp. 85-6)

Mrs. Woolf considers a number of *genres* in the essay on reading a book, and in her discussion of poetry quotes from a series of poems for purposes of comparison. Reading involves comparison, she says, which leads inevitably to the final act of evaluation or judgment. Merely by giving shape to the book, by imposing form on those emotions experienced by the passive reader, one begins to exercise the function of the critic and the judge. 'The first process, to receive impressions with the utmost understanding, is only half the process of reading; it must be completed, if we are to get the whole pleasure from a book, by another. We must pass judgment upon these multitudinous impressions; we must make of these fleeting shapes one that is hard and lasting.' The most difficult task for the reader is the necessity to compare and judge; to read, as it were, without the book in front of him in order to pinpoint the qualities of a work and determine its final worth. He must train himself not only to read creatively, with insight and imagination, but to read critically; to evaluate a work in terms of its internal laws and against the great tradition which was the final standard for Virginia Woolf.

It is interesting to compare Mrs. Woolf's critic as impressionist-judge with her father's view on the function of criticism. Though a follower of Arnold, Leslie Stephen wanted to go beyond the critical touchstone in order to incorporate a body of critical judgments into a kind of literary case-law. Yet even the positivist-minded Stephen reserved a place for the critic's emotional response, as he makes clear in his essay, 'Thoughts on Criticism by a Critic'. 'This vivacity and originality of feeling is the first qualifi-

cation of a critic. Without it no man's judgment is worth having.' And again, from another direction: 'A good critic can hardly express his feelings without implicitly laying down a principle.' A modern humanist critic, Norman Foerster, has also stressed the twofold response to the work of art, even while stating his case for a revitalized ethical criticism. 'He will read it in two ways, first one way and then another, or else in two ways, simultaneously. One way we may speak of as 'feeling the book', the other as 'thinking the book'.' Leslie Stephen and Norman Foerster may be regarded as humanists making some allowance for impressionism; and Virginia Woolf as an impressionist merely acknowledging the judicial function of the critic. Yet the same conflict between impression and judgment, thought and feeling, has been noted in the early essays of T. S. Eliot. The rejection of Arnold and Pater was behind Eliot's attempt, in *The Sacred Wood,* to deny the dichotomy of thought and feeling (dissociation of sensibility), which he felt encouraged impressionism (and abstract scientism). Eliot's position is actually close to Mrs. Woolf's notion of a fusion of critical functions, though his intention is more rigorous and programmatic in the light of his poetic aims, as we can see from the early essays.

> Such considerations, cast in this general form, may appear commonplace. But I believe that it is always opportune to call attention to the torpid superstition that appreciation is one thing, and 'intellectual' criticism something else. Appreciation in popular psychology is one faculty and criticism another, an arid cleverness building theoretical scaffolds upon one's perceptions or those of others. On the contrary, the true generalization is not something superposed upon an accumulation of perceptions; the perceptions do not, in a really appreciative mind, accumulate as a mass, but form themselves as a structure; and criticism is the statement in language of this structure; it is a development of sensibility. ['The Perfect Critic']

Eliot's familiar words echo familiar responses, though we no longer nod our heads so readily in hypnotic assent. We will be discussing Eliot's ideas later, in connection with Virginia Woolf's criticism, and against the background of modern criticism itself. Here we see that in Mrs. Woolf's view, the reader may at last turn to the great writers and critics, to authority, after he has served his apprenticeship in the art of reading. Only then can he profit from the decisions of a great judge, a Coleridge, Dryden, or Samuel Johnson. Virginia Woolf's essays reveal a continual effort to resolve the apparent critical conflict between reason and emotion, the individual and authority, abstract rules and the concrete fact of the work of art. And it is clear from the conclusion of **'How Should One Read a Book?'** that the exacting program for the common reader is essential to her own position as novelist, reviewer, or critic. If the reader is not to be victimized by the ordinary reviewer and his weekly abandonment of criticism for advertising, he must be able to maintain those standards which are the results of the profound discipline described in her essay. She aligns herself once more with the private reader rather than the professional critic, but the kind of reader she envisions is one whose influence will be felt by the writer and thus inevitably by literature itself.

> We must remain readers; we shall not put on the further glory that belongs to those rare beings who are also critics. But still we have our responsibilities as readers and even our importance. The standards we raise and the judgments we pass steal into the air and become part of the atmosphere which writers breathe as they work. An influence is created which tells upon them even if it never finds its way into print. And that influence if it were well instructed, vigorous and individual and sincere, might be of great value now when criticism is necessarily in abeyance; when books pass in review like the procession of animals in a shooting gallery, and the critic has only one second in which to load and aim and shoot and may well be pardoned if he mistakes rabbits for tigers, eagles for barndoor fowls, or misses altogether and wastes his shot upon some peaceful cow grazing in a further field. If behind the erratic gunfire of the press the author felt that there was another kind of criticism, the opinion of people reading for the love of reading, slowly and un-professionally, and judging with great sympathy and yet with great severity, might this not improve the quality of his work? And if by our means books were to become stronger, richer, and more varied, that would be an end worth reaching.

But how does such a faith in the 'uncommon reader', to borrow David Daiches' chapter heading [in his *Virginia Woolf,* 1942], square with the facts or reality of the literary situation today? Malcolm Cowley provides a somewhat sociological view, though from the perspective of an editor or critic, of literary conditions in America [in *The Literary Situation,* 1958]; while Leslie Fiedler gives us a more characteristically apocalyptic and depressing account of the scene in this McLuhan age [in *Waiting for the End,* 1964]. Aside from national distinctions, however, Virginia Woolf wrote for and about a different generation of readers, as T. S. Eliot reminds us in his obituary notice. But Mrs. Woolf was well aware, as we shall see in her essay on reviewing, of the inherent danger in the literary conditions of her own time.

Significant Form

The concern for the reader as critic leads inevitably to a discussion of form, though Mrs. Woolf seems to avoid the dichotomous monster by approaching it from the point of view of the reader rather than the writer. In her essay **'On Re-Reading Novels'**, . . . Mrs. Woolf got at the question of form by way of Percy Lubbock's *The Craft of Fiction.* Reviewing the book when it appeared, she believed it was a step in the direction of a serious aesthetic for the novel, though she disagreed with his visual conception of form. In **'How Should One Read a Book?'**, Mrs. Woolf insisted that reading was a more complex process than seeing. In the essay **'On Re-Reading Novels'** she clarified her point by discussing form as an emotional rather than a visual pattern. To better understand Mrs. Woolf's definition of form and her insistence on that definition, it would be instructive to see the connection between Mrs. Woolf's aes-

thetic and the theories of her Bloomsbury friends, the art critics Clive Bell and Roger Fry.

Clive Bell had formulated his celebrated phrase, 'significant form', in 1914, in a book entitled *Art;* though Roger Fry had suggested a similar idea in 1909, in 'An Essay in Aesthetics'. Both critics base their conception of significant form on the so-called 'aesthetic emotion' which works of art are capable of transmitting. And this emotion is a response to a significant pattern of relations, the form of the work, which is in turn the perfect and complete expression of an idea, an emotion, a 'vision of reality', as Mrs. Woolf would say, in the mind of the artist. In maintaining the balance between form and feeling, Bell, like Mrs. Woolf, tries to avoid the so-called 'affective fallacy' on the one hand, and the 'intentional fallacy' on the other. 'Therefore, when the critic comes across satisfactory form he need not bother about the feelings of the artist; for him to feel the aesthetic significance of the artist's forms suffices. If the artist's state of mind be important, he may be sure that it was right because the forms are right.' In 'An Essay in Aesthetics', Roger Fry defines the same relation between form and emotion. 'When the artist passes from pure sensations to emotions aroused by means of sensations, he uses natural forms which, in themselves, are calculated to move our emotions, and he presents these in such a manner that the forms themselves generate in us emotional states.' Fry repeats his point about the idea, or state of mind, or emotion behind the significant form of the work of art, in 'The Artist's Vision'. When we contemplate a work of art, he says—a Sung bowl, for example— 'there comes to us . . . a feeling of purpose; we feel that all those sensually logical conformities are the outcome of a particular feeling, or of what, for want of a better word, we call an idea, and we may even say that the pot is the expression of the idea in the artist's mind'. We can see from this discussion the relation between what Fry calls, in one of his books, 'Vision and Design'.

Turning again to Mrs. Woolf's essay **'On Re-Reading Novels'**, with Bell and Fry in the background, we can understand Mrs. Woolf's insistence on the emotional significance of form. If her account of the critical (and creative) process is true, there is no possibility, she would maintain, of establishing the classic dichotomy of form and content. Only the imperfect works, she insists, allow us to separate the two. In a great novel, there is a perfect fusion that leaves no 'slip or chink'; nothing is left, in fact, but the form of the work entire in the mind. In answer to Lubbock, she repeats: 'There is vision and expression. The two blend so perfectly that when Mr. Lubbock asks us to test the form with our eyes we see nothing at all. But we feel with singular satisfaction, and since all our feelings are in keeping, they form a whole which remains in our minds as the book itself.' This is of course a classic description of organic form, classically stated by James in 'The Art of Fiction'. [There have been] recent reactions to formalist theories of the novel; and a critic like William Troy, discussing Virginia Woolf, goes so far as to dismiss claims for formal discoveries as being no more, in terms of the novel, than experiments in method, limited even further to the idea of 'point of view':

Despite the number of artists in every field who assume that an innovation in method entails a corresponding achievement in form, method cannot be regarded as quite the same thing as form. For the novelist all that we can mean by method is embraced in the familiar phrase 'the point of view'. As his object is character his only method can be that by which he endeavors to attain to a complete grasp and understanding of that object. 'Method' in fiction narrows down to nothing more or less than the selection of a point of view from which character may be studied and presented. ['Virginia Woolf and the Novel of Sensibility,' *Perspective,* Winter 1954]

[Once] Mrs. Woolf has drawn her distinction between Lubbock's and her own conception of form, she restores the balance between art and emotion. In Bell and Fry, and in her own essays, form is the result of, and results in, emotion. Yet, as Mrs. Woolf has also maintained, form is by definition that controlling, ordering process which we call art. On these terms she is finally willing to agree with Lubbock. By insisting on a twofold definition of form, she seems to be letting in the back door what she has just pushed out the front. But we have noted that her criticism involves a basic counterpoint of form and feeling, art and emotion—saving her from a critical nihilism on the one hand, and a rigid, systematic aesthetic on the other.

Woolf in 1939.

The emotional or impressionistic pattern ascribed to the novel is, of course, analogous to Mrs. Woolf's experimental structure in her fiction. Though a Jamesian in her demands for an aesthetic novel, she is unwilling to accept Lubbock's visual sense of form, which derives from James. In this context, J. K. Johnstone's attempt to trace a direct line from Fry's aesthetic to Virginia Woolf's theory and practice of fiction, while valid to some extent, ignores Mrs. Woolf's skepticism toward any visual conception of form, and toward Fry's plastic approach to the verbal art of fiction [*The Bloomsbury Group,* 1954].

When Mrs. Woolf refers, in her biography of Roger Fry, to his literary criticism, there is a note of professional skepticism in the midst of praise for an astute, persuasive argument.

> As a critic of literature, then, he was not what is called a safe guide. He looked at the carpet from the wrong side; but he made it for that very reason display unexpected patterns. And many of his theories hold good for both arts. Design, rhythm, texture—there they were again—in Flaubert as in Cézanne. And he would hold up a book to the light as if it were a picture and show where in his view—it was a painter's of course—it fell short.

Yet Fry's insistence on form, pattern, design—inherent in his admiration for Cézanne and the Post-Impressionists—undoubtedly reinforced Mrs. Woolf's belief, inherited from James and Flaubert, in the aesthetic novel. Mrs. Woolf also tells us in her biography of Fry that he had a theory of the influence of Post-Impressionism on literature, which he never had time to work out. Fry appears to have incorporated part of this theory in his essay, 'Some Questions in Esthetics', where he attempts to purify painting by purging it of all but plastic values and, at the same time, to create for literature an equivalent purity of form. Since each art, Fry feels, has its own *raison d'être,* its proper criteria for creating and judging it as art, literature should rid itself of those excrescences which Mrs. Woolf deplored in her essays on the Edwardians. Fry refers to A. C. Bradley's statement on the autonomy of poetry, and goes on to say: 'For poetry in this passage we may, I think, substitute the idea of any literature as pure art. The passage at least suggests to us that the purpose of literature is the creation of structures which have for us the feeling of reality, and that these structures are self-contained, self-sufficient and not to be valued by their reference to what lies outside.' Here then is the belief in the autonomy of art, which Mrs. Woolf consistently endorses in her essays. (pp. 86-90)

The Critic as Reviewer

Having observed Mrs. Woolf as the reader turned critic, it would be helpful to consider briefly her role as a reviewer or occasional commentator on books who is similarly changed into a conscious literary critic. Many of Mrs. Woolf's articles were originally written for *The Athenaeum, The Nation and the Athenaeum, The New Statesman, The Criterion, The New Republic, The Atlantic Monthly, The New York Herald Tribune,* and many more. As a steady contributor to the *London Times Literary Supple-*

ment, she wrote at least 154 articles between 1916 and 1937, 138 of these before the publication of the first **Common Reader** in 1925. Only sixteen articles were submitted to *The Times* during the last twelve years, nearly all of them longer essays for the first page of the Supplement. She was writing articles for other periodicals during this time, but the evidence from her contributions to the *TLS* alone seems to indicate a gradual moving away from occasional reviewing to the writing of longer critical essays. There is further evidence in the **Diary** of her dissatisfaction with the role of reviewer and of her intentions and efforts to write only what she considered literary criticism. In writing an essay on the ghost stories of Henry James for the *Supplement,* she even encountered censorship, having used the word 'lewd' to disturb the sensibilities of her editor, Bruce Richmond.

> He made it sufficiently clear not only that he wouldn't stand 'lewd' but that he didn't much like anything else. I feel that this becomes more often the case, and I wonder whether to break off, with an explanation, or to pander, or to go on writing against the current. This last is probably right, but somehow the consciousness of doing that cramps one. One writes stiffly, without spontaneity. Anyhow, for the present I shall let it be, and meet my castigation with resignation. People will complain, I'm sure, and poor Bruce fondling his paper like an old child dreads public criticism; is stern with me, not so much for disrespect to poor old Henry, but for bringing blame on the Supplement. And How much time I have wasted.

But she continued to write for the *Supplement,* devoting the same time and care to her reviews as she did to all her work. Her husband has testified to this dedication, even in the writing of occasional essays, in his preface to the first posthumous collection of her essays **The Death of the Moth.** He tells of finding a typescript for the author of a book reviewed by Mrs. Woolf, which had 'no fewer than eight or nine complete revisions of it which she had herself typed out'. Comparing the critical value of reviews in general with her own efforts, Mrs. Woolf again expresses a desire in the **Diary** to devote herself only to serious criticism.

> When I read reviews I crush the column together to get one or two sentences; is it a good book or a bad? And then I discount those two according to what I know of the book and of the reviewer. But when I write a review I write every sentence as if it were going to be tried before three Chief Justices. I can't believe that I am crushed together and discounted. Reviews seem to me more and more frivolous. Criticism on the other hand absorbs me more and more.

As her reputation grew, she could refuse to write more of the popular biographical sketches which have helped to establish Virginia Woolf's reputation as a writer of accomplished light essays. 'And I have, with great happiness, refused to write Rhoda Broughton, Ouida for de la Mare. That vein, popular as it is, witness Jane and Geraldine, is soon worked out in me. I want to write criticism' [*Diary,* 8 December 1929]. She had begun writing for *The Times* before she had published her fiction, and she was

grateful for the opportunity to learn her craft as a critic and writer, as she declares in her **Diary** just after resigning as a regular contributor to the *TLS*. The passage is significant, since it was also written only a year before she published a long essay on the art of reviewing.

> A letter, grateful, from Bruce Richmond, ending my 30 years connection with him and the Lit. Sup. How pleased I used to be when L. Called me 'You're wanted by the Major Journal!' and I ran down to the telephone to take my almost weekly order at Hogarth House! I learnt a lot of my craft writing for him: how to compress; how to enliven; and also was made to read with a pen and notebook, seriously.

Reviewing appeared first, in 1939, as a pamphlet, with an added 'Note' by Leonard Woolf. Since Mrs. Woolf's essay is really an indictment of reviewing, Mr. Woolf feels compelled, as a publisher and former literary editor (of *The Nation*), to disagree with his wife's conclusions. For Mrs. Woolf, he says, writes from the point of view of the author and critic, and the review is really meant for the reading public. As journalism it serves a real need and is to be distinguished from literary criticism, though the reviewer may at times indulge in what he calls 'true criticism'.

Mrs. Woolf, it is true, clearly approaches reviewing and the reviewer from the point of view of the writer and critic. Though the review was a child of journalism, there was a division of labor, she feels, toward the end of the eighteenth century, whereby the critic—a Dr. Johnson, for example—dealt with principles and the past and the reviewer with the new books that fell periodically from the press. In the nineteenth century this division was even more distinct. 'There were the critics—Coleridge, Matthew Arnold—who took their time and their space; and there were the 'irresponsible' and mostly anonymous reviewers who had less time and less space, and whose complex task it was partly to inform the public, partly to criticize the book, and partly to advertise its existence.' Though the present situation seems to be the same, it is far different, due simply to the greater number of reviews printed and the smaller amount of space allowed the reviewer. The many reviews of the same book cancel one another out and serve neither writer nor reader, and least of all the reviewer who would be a critic. For Mrs. Woolf the only conclusion to be drawn from the evidence is that the reviewer has ceased to be of value to the author or the public and should be abolished. She cites Harold Nicolson's admission that he continually hedges between trying to please the public and judging against the highest literary standards. His only refuge is to speak directly to the author and tell him why he likes or dislikes his book hoping that the reader will benefit from the dialogue. This only confirms Mrs. Woolf's views and she feels free to offer her own remedy for the anomolous situation. Instead of the usual reviewing, she foresees what she calls the 'Gutter and Stamp' process, where one man, the Gutter, will summarize the work, while another—who might be called the 'taster'—will affix a stamp of approval or disapproval. And though the author and reviewer remain to be considered, there is no reason, she adds, why this system will not serve the public as well as the present one.

For the reviewer, the saving grace is that he enjoys telling writers why he likes or dislikes their books. Since the author and reviewer are mutually dependent, the problem is how to preserve what Nicolson calls the 'value of the dialogue'. Mrs. Woolf's serio-comic solution is a private consulting service, with the reviewer-critic as doctor and the writer as patient. Valuable criticism might result, for a fee, from this transaction, which at least dramatizes one of the real functions of literary reviewing.

> Nor is it only the young and needy who would seek advice. The art of writing is difficult; at every stage the opinion of an impersonal and disinterested critic would be of the highest value. Who would not spout the family teapot in order to talk with Keats for an hour about poetry, or with Jane Austen about the art of fiction?

In considering finally what effect the abolition of the reviewer would have upon literature, Mrs. Woolf finds that the public would also benefit from the changed relationship between author and critic. Having gained his privacy and lost his self-consciousness, the writer could concentrate on his work, as the reviewer could attend to the book before him. The Gutter and Stamp system would also eliminate what only passes for criticism and save enough space for longer, more purely critical essays. The new status of the writer would eventually affect the reading public. The unselfconsciousness of the literature of the past might return and result in a new relationship between reader and writer and a new epoch for literature itself.

> A new relationship might come into being, less petty and less personal than the old. A new interest in literature, a new respect for literature might follow. And, financial advantages apart, what a ray of light that would bring, what a ray of pure sunlight a critical and hungry public would bring into the darkness of the workshop.

Though the modern reviewer, according to Mrs. Woolf, is superfluous under the present system, his attempts to deal with current or contemporary literature have always met with difficulty, if not disaster. She cites Matthew Arnold's opinion that even under the most favorable conditions, 'it is impossible for the living to judge the works of the living'. And Mrs. Woolf chooses the case of Lockhart, one of the famous Scotch reviewers, biographer and son-in-law of Scott, as a perfect illustration of the pitfalls lying in the path of the reviewer.

Though a man of taste and learning, experience and sensitivity, he faced the same problems, armed only with the same unlucky weapon—courage—as his modern counterpart. As a reviewer, Mrs. Woolf feels a sympathetic shudder for Lockhart on that fateful day in 1820 when he had to review a new book of poems by John Keats. From what he had heard of Keats, a Cockney friend of the radical Leigh Hunt, it was natural for the aristocratic Lockhart to summon all his prejudices against the unknown poet. It was not to be expected, however, that in judging him he was rushing to his own doom—'the worst that can befall a reviewer. He committed himself violently, he betrayed himself completely. He tried to snuff out between finger and thumb one of the immortal lights of English literature' ['**Lockhart's Criticism**'].

Lockhart's collected criticism clearly reveals the difficulty of judging contemporary writers, since the new work inevitably encourages in the reviewer so many irrelevant reactions. Yet he often agreed with posterity, as in the case of Wordsworth and Coleridge, Borrow and Beckford; though it is true, Mrs. Woolf admits, 'that he predicted a long life for *Zohrab the Hostage,* who has had a short one'. His general average in fact compares favorably with the capable reviewer of any age.

> In short, the case of Lockhart would seem to show that a good reviewer of contemporary work will get the proportions roughly right, but the detail wrong. He will single out from a number of unknown writers those who are going to prove men of substance, but he cannot be certain what qualities are theirs in particular, or how the importance of one compares with the importance of another.

Mrs. Woolf hopes to avoid the normal occupational hazards of reviewing, in '**An Essay in Criticism**', by clearly recognizing them, by admitting her own prejudices and defining the nature and limitations of her critical task. In reviewing a new book of short stories by Ernest Hemingway—*Men without Women*—Mrs. Woolf is both the reviewer and reader as critic: submitting to the demands made by a contemporary work, but attempting to raise such reviewing to the level of criticism by establishing a useful tension between a clear conception of her role and a close analysis of the work at hand. Once more she reacts against authority in the name of the reader (and writer) by resisting the tendency to place too much faith in the critic. It is evident that she has the reviewer-critic in mind as she repeats the point about the difficulty of judging contemporary literature.

> For the critic is rather more fallible than the rest of us. He has to give us his opinion of a book that has been published two days, perhaps with the shell still sticking to its head. He has to get outside that cloud of fertile, but unrealized, sensation which hangs about a reader, to solidify it, to sum it up. The chances are that he does this before the time is ripe; he does it too rapidly and too definitely. He says that it is a great book or a bad book. Yet, as he knows, when he is content to read only, it is neither.

In trying to steer a middle course between the responsive reader and the judicial critic, Mrs. Woolf finds it more difficult, as we have seen, to analyze a contemporary work, where the reader's impressions have not been tested by time or traditional standards. Confessing this from the outset, she hopes to find some tentative truth between the immediate experience and the hardened conclusion. Though she admits to having heard that Hemingway is an avant-garde, expatriate writer in Paris, she soon realizes from reading *The Sun Also Rises* that if he is modern it is not by virtue of his method. In other words, he does not belong to Virginia Woolf's experimental school, though she concedes, as in Chapter Two, that it is foolish to insist always on experimentation, since traditional art has its own *raison d'être.*

> But the critic has the grace to reflect that his de-

mand for new aspects and new perspectives may well be overdone. It may become whimsical. It may become foolish. For why should not art be traditional as well as original? Are we not attaching too much importance to an excitement which, though agreeable, may not be valuable in itself, so that we are led to make the fatal mistake of overriding the writer's gift?

Reviewing his earlier novel, *The Sun Also Rises* (1926), before analyzing the short stories in *Men without Women* (1927), Mrs. Woolf finds that it is Hemingway's subject matter rather than his fictional method that has given rise to the rumor of modernity. She now abandons her analysis of the critic and turns to the work itself.

Though Hemingway presents no new angle of vision, he is faithful to what he sees, working, as he describes the bullfighter in *The Sun Also Rises,* close to the horns of his art. But in proceeding to the more difficult task of comparison and analysis, in order to judge the work more accurately, Mrs. Woolf finds 'something faked', which she distinguishes from his 'absolute purity of line'. That something is his treatment of character, and she turns to the stories in *Men without Women* in order to see if he has developed in depth or merely sharpened the familiar tools of his art. Since Hemingway is writing short stories, Mrs. Woolf suspects that he might concentrate his talent: depending more on the critical moment and a greater use of dialogue, while discarding narrative and description as unnecessary to his spare structure. The writing in *Men without Women* seems to confirm her suspicions, suffering from an inordinate use of dialogue and a lack of proportion detrimental to the short story genre. But Mrs. Woolf is less than objective here, since she is an advocate of Chekhov's inconclusive method, as opposed to the Maupassant school to which Hemingway belongs. In Maupassant, the compressed stories point to a revelatory ending (or, in the current usage, an 'epiphany'), so that 'when the last sentence of the last page flares up, as it so often does, we see by its light the whole circumference and significance of the story revealed'. She does not say which school is better, but from her earlier admission and from other essays (**'Modern Fiction', 'The Russian Point of View'**, etc.), it is clear that her objectivity will stretch just so far. Her conclusion, then, about Hemingway's stories being destroyed by a dexterity that gets in the way of the 'fact', is only further evidence of a bias that is basic to her own art. 'But the true writer stands close up to the bull and lets the horns—call them life, truth, reality, whatever you like—pass him close each time.' Mrs. Woolf's use of the Hemingway metaphor to point up his weakness is ironic, since his art, above all, was dedicated to mastering truth or the fact. Now, of course, we can see Hemingway in a different light. Despite his apparently conventional method, we can appreciate his radical stylistic innovations. Mrs. Woolf misses Hemingway's own merging of fact and vision because her view of reality demands a different kind of experimental novel of sensibility. She knows, however, and her honesty in this essay is proof of that knowledge, that the critic may finally exclude himself only at the risk of avoiding the act of criticism. She concludes an experiment, then, which has told us a good deal about the function of criticism without failing to tell us something about the work criticized.

> Mr. Hemingway, then, is courageous; he is candid; he is highly skilled; he plants words precisely where he wishes; he has moments of bare and nervous beauty; he is modern in manner but not in vision; he is self-consciously virile; his talent has contracted rather than expanded; compared with his novel his stories are a little dry and sterile. So we sum him up. So we reveal some of the prejudices, the instincts and the fallacies out of which what it pleases us to call criticism is made.

The Critic as Contemporary

Mrs. Woolf's ideal republic, or aristocracy, of art would see the reviewers banished or transformed into critics, and a return to traditional standards, but always with a view to the present. In this utopian state the critics would be artists, and the reader, also a critic according to Mrs. Woolf's prescription, would demand nothing from the writer but his art. The ideal reading public described at the end of **Reviewing** becomes the perfect patron or reader in **'The Patron and The Crocus'.**

> He must make us feel that a single crocus, if it be a real crocus, is enough for him; that he does not want to be lectured, elevated, instructed, or improved; that he is sorry that he bullied Carlyle into vociferation, Tennyson into idyllics, and Ruskin into insanity; that he is now ready to efface himself or assert himself as his writers require; that he is bound to them by a more than maternal tie; that they are twins indeed; one dying if the other dies, one flourishing if the other flourishes; that the fate of literature depends upon this happy alliance.

The reader and reviewer become, then, in the person of Virginia Woolf, the artist as critic. But her narrow self-interests serve the wider interests of literature; for the artist, the critic and the reader are interdependent in any age, and especially so, as she demonstrates in **'How It Strikes a Contemporary',** in a transitional one like our own.

Mrs. Woolf had made the familiar distinction between our experience of the classics and the work of our contemporaries in her essay **'Hours in a Library'.** As in the essays on reviewing, she comments on the fact that it is difficult in the case of new books to know which ones are real and what it is that they are saying and so distinguish them from the dead imitations that will disappear after a few years. Since she is a traditionalist, the consciousness of the past, of its presentness, as Eliot would say, is essential to the criticism of modern literature. In **'Hours in a Library',** Mrs. Woolf re-emphasizes the need to understand the past in order to judge the experiments of the present.

> Whatever we may have learnt from reading the classics we need now in order to judge the work of our contemporaries, for whenever there is life in them they will be casting their net out over some unknown abyss to snare new shapes, and we must throw our imaginations after them if we are to accept with understanding the strange gifts they bring back to us.

'How It Strikes a Contemporary' was strategically placed by Mrs. Woolf at the end of her roughly chronological survey in the first *Common Reader* in order to discuss the modern condition from the perspective of the past. This essay . . . represents the convergence of two dominant streams in Mrs. Woolf's critical thinking: her sense of the past and extreme sensitivity to the present. Again she deplores the lack of agreement among the critics of contemporary literature, refusing to accept the fact that this has always been so, and that the reader can do no more than follow his instinct and re-read the classics or masterpieces of literature. Since this has been her own advice as a reviewer-critic, it seems that she is now determined to impose some order on 'the chaos of contemporary literature'. For the great critics of the past, though they were often wrong about their contemporaries, had a stabilizing influence by virtue of their presence on the literary scene. Standards were imposed upon the age by the critics who dominated it, a Dryden, a Johnson, a Coleridge or an Arnold.

> The diverse schools would have debated as hotly as ever, but at the back of every reader's mind would have been the consciousness that there was at least one man who kept the main principles of literature closely in view; who, if you had taken to him some eccentricity of the moment, would have brought it into touch with permanence and tethered it by his own authority in the contrary blasts of praise and blame ['**How It Strikes a Contemporary**'].

For the creation of great literature, Arnold had said, two powers must come together, the power of the man and the power of the moment. Mrs. Woolf feels that society must also be ready before the great critic can emerge. If he is not himself a major poet, he is bred from the 'profusion of the age'. Since much of her essay deals with the fact that ours is an 'age of fragments', Mrs. Woolf seems to be restating Arnold's thesis in 'The Function of Criticism at the Present Time' that the contemporary period (the 'twenties' in this instance) is a transitional one, preparing the way for the great age to come, or Arnold's 'epoch of expansion'. From the nature of her attack on reviewers and academicians, it is again clear that Mrs. Woolf's conception of the critic is inseparable from her image of the artist; her ideal critic must incorporate the qualities of the famous artist-critics of the past.

> Men of taste and learning and ability are forever lecturing the young and celebrating the dead. But the too frequent results of their able and industrious pens is a dessication of the living tissues of literature into a network of little bones. Nowhere shall we find the downright vigour of a Dryden, or Keats with his fine and natural bearing, his profound insight and sanity, or Flaubert and the tremendous power of his fanaticism, a Coleridge, above all, brewing in his head the whole of poetry and letting issue now and then one of those profound general statements which are caught up by the mind when hot with the friction of reading as if they were the soul of the book itself.

Virginia Woolf's commitment to the present is predicated on a faith in the 'moment'. She also finds support for her instinctive optimism in the courage, sincerity, and originality of modern literature. . . . [While the classics] may neglect the modern exploration of the self, they create a profound sense of security stemming from the conviction, the belief, and standards of the past. The modern writer, however, has concentrated on an image of himself; he cannot generalize or create a world because, in Mrs. Woolf's words, he has 'ceased to believe'. Mrs. Woolf returns us here to . . . [a discussion of modernism]; it is necessary to believe 'that your impressions hold good for others' in order to be released from 'the cramp and confinement of personality'. Though she was not, like T. S. Eliot, a conscious classicist, she would agree with him that art is an escape from as well as an expression of personality.

Matthew Arnold made the classic case for criticism during an 'epoch of concentration'. Similarly, Mrs. Woolf felt the need for the writer to be a critic in our time in order to create the necessary conditions for his art. The call for a great critic, for standards, for a return to the past in order to understand and judge the present, is especially significant for a transitional and, hopefully, seminal age. We have already remarked on the tendency of each literary generation to see itself caught in the chaotic present, looking back or ahead to a new age of accomplishment. If ours is only an age of transition, if we cannot yet look for masterpieces, we can still, as Mrs. Woolf has done, see the future in terms of the complex relationship between the past and the present. It is more than ever the task of the critic, then, to achieve a wider perspective, so that, like Lady Stanhope's Messiah, masterpieces may again appear upon the horizon. (pp. 93-100)

> *Mark Goldman, in his* The Reader's Art: Virginia Woolf as Literary Critic, *Mouton, 1976, 142 p.*

René Wellek   (essay date 1986)

[*Wellek's* History of Modern Criticism *(1955-86) is a comprehensive study of the literary critics of the last three centuries. His critical method, demonstrated in* History *and outlined in his* Theory of Literature *(1949), is one of describing, analyzing, and evaluating a work solely in terms of the problems it poses for itself and how the writer solves them. In the following excerpt, Wellek assesses the aims of Woolf's literary criticism and surveys her critical responses to the works of several major novelists of the eighteenth through the twentieth centuries.*]

Almost everyone who has discussed the criticism of Virginia Woolf has labeled her an "impressionist" and has quoted a passage from her essay on **"Modern Fiction"** (1919): life is "a luminous halo, a semi-transparent envelope surrounding us from the beginning of consciousness to the end." The new novelists are exhorted: "Let us record the atoms as they fall upon the mind in the order in which they fall, let us trace the pattern, however disconnected and incoherent in appearance, which each sight or incident scores upon the consciousness." Here she speaks, however, about life and the new novelists including herself, defining her ambition, and not about criticism. Her own criticism, though often metaphorical and even whimsically personal, is wrongly described in terms of "atoms falling on the mind" and even of "patterns scored upon the consciousness." Philosophically, Virginia Woolf was no idealist, no Bergsonian, not even a British empiricist, but a fervent adherent of G. E. Moore, whom she studied with real effort in 1908 and quoted even in her novels. Moore advocated a modern "realism," that is, he distinguishes between acts of consciousness and objects related to but distinct from those acts. Particulars exist outside of the mind. While Virginia Woolf's views must not be pressed into a philosophical scheme, she clearly aims, at least in her criticism, at grasping an object, and she did not and could not approve either of the solipsism implied in Anatole France's "adventures of the soul among masterpieces" or Pater's view of man's imprisonment in his own mind and body or of the imposition of one's ego on works of art demanded by "creative criticism."

Virginia Woolf did not, of course, ignore the share of art in the composition of her essays, deft, well-ordered, well-phrased, nor could she neglect the importance of the practitioner's experience for the critic. She goes very far in denying the value of criticism not nourished by the "excitement, the adventure, the turmoil of creation." The critics "who get to the heart of the matter" are Keats, Coleridge, Lamb, Flaubert, rather than academic professors such as Walter Raleigh—who, she recognizes, actually had a hankering for a life of action and despised criticism—or such a cautious, decorous journalist as Edmund Gosse, who "like all critics who persist in judging without creating forgets the risk and agony of childbirth." Still, Virginia Woolf is entirely aware of the distinction between creation and criticism and often assigns a limited and even humble function to criticism. The critic is to tell us how to read, is himself a "common reader" in a sense in which she deliberately misread Dr. Johnson's "rejoicing to concur with the common reader" in the *Life of Gray*. Virginia Woolf's reader reads for his own pleasure. "He is guided by an instinct to create for himself, out of whatever odds and ends he can come by, some kind of whole—a portrait of a man, a sketch of an age, a theory of the art of writing," all demands quite remote from Johnson's common reader, who is simply a reader "uncorrupted by literary prejudice," free from the "refinements of subtilty [sic] and the dogmatism of learning."

Virginia Woolf does concern herself with the "portrait of a man"—many of her essays are biographical, and she herself practiced the art on a larger scale in her book on **Roger Fry** (1940) and even in **Orlando** (1928), a fictionalized account of the Sackville family over the centuries. She is also concerned with a "sketch of an age," often evoking the social setting and the atmosphere of a bygone period; or she does, on occasion, say something about a "theory of the art of writing," reflecting on the share of consciousness, on what she calls the "undermind," or asserting the importance of "conviction," "a rare gift" she found in Chaucer, "shared in our day by Joseph Conrad in his earlier novels."

Still, she is aware that none of these concerns of the common reader are central to the business of criticism. She can even ridicule the preoccupation with biography. Commenting on Defoe, she complains that the date of his birth, his ancestors, his occupation as a hosier, his wife and six children, his sharp chin can take up much more time than reading *Robinson Crusoe* through from cover to cover. It seems to her a "wise precaution to limit one's study of a writer to the study of his works." Still, she always returns to the view that "somewhere, everywhere, now hidden, now apparent in whatever is written down is the form of a human being." But she envies the Greeks who "remain in a fastness of their own. Fate has been kind there too. She has preserved them from vulgarity. Euripides was eaten by dogs; Aeschylus killed by a stone; Sappho leapt from a cliff. We know no more of them than that. We have their poetry and that is all." "The only question of any interest is whether that poetry is good or bad." Virginia Woolf drowned herself. Her biographer and nephew, Quentin Bell, has not, alas "preserved" her "from vulgarity."

Similarly, she loves to sketch the minutiae of an age, to evoke its peculiar atmosphere, to tell "the lives of the obscure," to speak of the Pastons and their letters as an introduction to Chaucer or of Hakluyt's *Voyages* as the "Elizabethan lumber-room." She often sees writers of the great masterpieces in terms that would have been comprehensible to Hippolyte Taine or her father as "the outcome of many years of thinking in common, of thinking by the body of the people, so that the experience of the mass is behind the single voice." But she reflects that Shakespeare's plays "are of no use whatever as 'applied sociology.' If we had to depend upon them for a knowledge of the social and economic conditions of Elizabethan life, we should be hopelessly at sea." Great art transcends the ages but is rooted in its age. Virginia Woolf did not believe in art existing out of time and place or in *l'art pour l'art,* as she has often been accused of doing. She has a lively historical sense, a feeling for the color of England in different ages, and a feeling, rare at that time, for the changes in the audience of literature and the interplay between author and reader, text and response. Thus she speaks of the early readers of Sidney's *Arcadia:* "Each has read differently, with the insight and the blindness of his own generation. Our reading will be equally partial. In 1930 we shall miss a great deal that was obvious to 1655; we shall see some things that the eighteenth century ignored." A book, she knows, "is always written for somebody to read," for "writing is a method of communication" and "to know whom to write for is to know how to write." The fate of literature "depends upon a happy alliance" between writers and readers.

Several times Virginia Woolf sketches a history of the economic support of English literature, contrasting the single patron, Sidney's Lady Pembroke, with the "vast miscellaneous crowd" of later times, quoting Goldsmith's well-known account of the decline of patronage in the eighteenth century. She worries continually about the role of reviewing in her own time. In an extravagant article she proposes its abolition on the grounds that favorable and unfavorable reviews cancel each other out nowadays. She makes the unpractical proposal to replace reviewing with interviews of the author with a critic who would proffer advice for a fee. The importance of reviewing for the reading public rather than for the writer is hardly considered. She is rather concerned with the writer's declared or implied attitude to his readers. Samuel Butler, George Meredith, and Henry James were still conscious of their "public, yet superior to it." "Each despised the public; each desired a public; each failed to attain a public; and each wreaked his failure upon the public by a succession, gradually increasing in intensity, of angularities, obscurities, and affections which no writer whose patron was his equal and friend would have thought it necessary to inflict." This is merely one example to support the truth that "undoubtedly all writers are immensely influenced by the people who read them." Comparing the readers of Cervantes to those of Thomas Hardy, she thinks that "the reader of today, accustomed to find himself in direct communication with the writer, is constantly out of touch with Cervantes." She doubts that Cervantes felt the tragedy and the satire of *Don Quijote* as we feel them and suspects him, gratuitously it seems to me, of being as callous as was Shakespeare (or, I would correct, Henry V) in dismissing Falstaff. "As for knowing himself what he was about—perhaps great writers never do. Perhaps that is why later ages find what they seek." It is the theme taken up later by the Polish phenomenologist Roman Ingarden, who speaks of "indeterminacy" or even of "empty spots" in a work of literature, which generations of readers are free to fill in their own way.

There is, I would argue, a "structure of determination" which prevents arbitrariness, and Virginia Woolf knows this when she attempts to describe, characterize, and evaluate the world of the novelists she studies. She seems, deliberately, to create a counterpart to the essays of her father, Leslie Stephen, which are also concerned with the world of the English novelists but judged always with the standards of a social morality: Stephen praises them for recognizing the "surpassing value of manliness, honesty, and pure domestic affection" or condemns them for morbidity, cynicism, or cloudy idealism. Virginia Woolf goes about it differently. She wants to master the "perspective," understand "how the novelist orders his world," "the one gift" of the novelist "more essential than another," "the power of combination—the simple vision."

From her essays we could abstract a history of the English novel from Sidney's *Arcadia* to Conrad and Joyce, not in terms of "origin, rise, growth, decline and fall," of the evolutionism of her father and his time which she expressly rejects, but in individual portraits or vignettes which characterize or evoke the particular world of the writer. Sidney's *Arcadia* has a "pictorial stillness," with "verse performing something of the function of dialogue in the modern novel." The characters are like ambling phantoms. Sidney's grasp upon them is so weak that "he has forgotten what his relation to them is—is it 'I' the author who is speaking or is it 'I' the character?" Such a genuinely critical observation makes acceptable the conclusion that "all the seeds of English fiction—romance and realism, poetry and psychology" lie latent in *Arcadia*. We might even admire her saying that "by degrees the book floats away into the thin air of limbo. It becomes one of those half-forgotten and deserted places where the grasses grow over fallen statues and the rain drips and the marble steps are green with moss and vast weeds flourish in the flower-beds. And yet it is a beautiful garden to wander in now and then; one stumbles over lovely broken faces, and here and there a flower blooms and the nightingale sings in the lilac-tree." It is a method now completely out of fashion and generally deprecated, but it has its function and its respectable ancestry in Lamb, Hazlitt, and Pater. (pp. 65-9)

Her favorite eighteenth-century novelist is Laurence Sterne. His world is not, however, "altogether the world of fiction. It is above." Virginia Woolf argues that Sterne is "not an analyst of other people's sensations. Those remain simple, eccentric, erratic. It is his own mind that fascinates him, its oddities and its whims, its fancies and its sensibilities; and it is his own mind that colours the book [*Tristram Shandy*] and gives it walls and shape." Laurence Sterne is the most important character in the book. The other characters "are a race apart among the people in fiction. There is nothing like them elsewhere, for in no other book are the characters so closely dependent on the author. In no other book are the writer and the reader so involved together." In *Tristram Shandy* Sterne seems to her "witty, indecent, disagreeable, yet highly sympathetic." He succeeds in making us "feel close to life" but at the same time, paradoxically, shows us "a life which has nothing in common with what, in the shorthand of speech, one calls 'real life.' " "Shandy Hall, the home of cranks and eccentricities, nevertheless contrives to make the whole of the outer world appear heavy, and dull and brutal, and teased by innumerable imps." Though Virginia Woolf wrote an appreciative introduction to *The Sentimental Journey,* she voices her embarrassment at the display of virtue. "We are never allowed to forget that Sterne is above all things sensitive, sympathetic, humane." She misses "the variety, the vigour, the ribaldry of *Tristram Shandy,* " but even in the *Journey* she finds "a backbone of conviction to support him." Sterne was "a stoic in his way and a moralist, and a teacher," and finally "a very great writer." Still, her essays, perceptive of the man and his world, are disappointing: she has nothing to say about Sterne's main claim to originality, his writing a novel about the novel, his parody of the conventional novel, his handling of time—all those qualities which have since made Sterne a pivotal figure in the history of fiction.

As we move into the nineteenth century, Virginia Woolf 's essays combine more and more judgment with evocation and description. The essay on Jane Austen is almost entirely favorable. Discussing her early story, *The Watsons,* Virginia Woolf finds in it all the elements of Jane Austen's greatness. "Think away the surface animation, the likeness to life, and there remains, to provide a deeper pleasure, an exquisite discrimination of human values." "It is against the disc of an unerring heart, an unfailing good taste, and almost stern morality, that she shows up these deviations from kindness, truth and sincerity which are among the most delightful things in English literature." Virginia Woolf sees Jane Austen's limitations clearly: "She could not throw herself wholeheartedly into a romantic moment. She had all sorts of devices for evading scenes of passion. Nature and its beauties she approached in a sidelong way of her own." Her figures, Virginia Woolf comments elsewhere, "are bound, and restricted to a few definite movements." But that reticence is admirable: "How definitely, by not saying something, she says it; how surprising, therefore, her expressive phrases when they come." Virginia Woolf thinks of Emma saying to Mr. Knightley at the Westons' ball, "I will dance with you," "which though not eloquent in itself, or violent or made striking by beauty of language, has the whole weight of the book behind it." Little is said which could be called aesthetic criticism, though Virginia Woolf alludes to the "more abstract art which, in the ball-room scene [of *The Watsons*], so varies the emotions and proportions the parts that it is possible to enjoy it, as one enjoys poetry, for itself, and not as a link which carries the story this way and that." With her last finished novel, *Persuasion,* Virginia Woolf argues, Jane Austen began to overcome her limitations. The sensitivity to nature is new. An emotion of love (which Virginia Woolf assumes is drawn from her own experience) is expressed for the first time. A new Jane Austen seems to emerge. Virginia Woolf speculates what would have become of her if she had not died at the age of forty-two. "She would have been the forerunner of Henry James and Proust." After A. C. Bradley's essay on Jane Austen (1911) had begun to reestablish her fame, Virginia Woolf's enthusiasm for the writer whom she called "the most perfect artist among women" was, with E. M. Forster's admiration and R. W. Chapman's editions, the main stimulus of the new cult. (pp. 69-71)

George Eliot is seen in the perspective of her biography, "raising herself with groans and struggles from the intolerable boredom of petty provincial society," finally entering into the union with George Henry Lewes which isolated her from society. Virginia Woolf admires *Middlemarch* most as a "magnificent book which with all its imperfections is one of the few novels written for grown-up people." She is, however, troubled by George Eliot's heroines. "They bring out the worst of her, lead her into difficult places, make her self-conscious, didactic and occasionally vulgar." "They cannot live without religion" and have "the deep feminine passion for goodness." George Eliot is equally unable to portray a man, fumbling when she has to conceive a fit mate for her heroine. The emotional scenes like the end of *Mill on the Floss,* with Maggie Tulliver drowned, clasping her brother in her arms, "drag her from her natural surroundings." One wonders what remains of her work except the agricultural world of her remotest past. "The searching power and reflective richness of the later novels," though acknowledged, remains unaccounted for.

Virginia Woolf is even more critical of Meredith. Reading *Richard Feverel,* "we at once exclaim how unreal, how artificial, how impossible" its characters are. The scene may be splendid, the landscape a part of the emotion, but Meredith is not among the great psychologists and his teaching "seems now too strident, too optimistic, too shallow." The later books are even "meretricious and false," "charred bones and masses of contorted wire." Virginia Woolf would have liked a touch of realism—"or is it a touch of something more akin to sympathy?"—"It would have kept the Meredith hero from being the honourable but tedious gentleman that . . . we have always found him." In *The Egoist,* Meredith "flouts probability, disdains coher-

ency, and lives from one high moment to the next." Still, Meredith, she grants, has imagination, has "the power of summoning nature into sympathy with man and merging him in her vastness." Meredith is a "rhapsodist," lyrical in sensibility but "extremely conventional as a mind." He belongs to the great eccentrics like Donne, Peacock, and Gerard Manley Hopkins, not a bad company, we might think.

Hardy is obviously a much greater writer in Virginia Woolf's eyes. She glosses over "an extreme and even melodramatic use of coincidence" in his early novel, *Desperate Remedies,* and merely alludes to the conflict within "a faithful son of field and down, yet tormented by the doubts and despondencies bred by book-learning." When she comes to speaking of *Far from the Madding Crowd,* which "holds its place among the great English novels," she can only lyrically evoke its atmosphere in a long metaphorical passage. "The dark downland, marked by the barrows of the dead and the huts of shepherds, rises against the sky, smooth as a wave of the sea, but solid and eternal," etcetera, etcetera, but then she generalizes sensibly about the types and situations in the novels. "The woman is the weaker and the fleshlier, and she clings to the stronger and obscures his vision." Love is the great fact of human life. "But it is a catastrophe; it happens suddenly and overwhelmingly, and there is little to be said about it." We do not really know Hardy's characters. "His light does not fall directly upon the human heart." Each man is battling with the storm, alone. "We do not know his men and women in their relations to each other, we know them in their relations to time, death, and fate." Virginia Woolf disapproves of "convicting" Hardy of a creed, of "tethering him to a consistent point of view." The reader should know "when to put aside the writer's conscious intention in favour of some deeper intention of which perhaps he may be unconscious." Only *Jude the Obscure* justifies the charge of pessimism. Its "misery is overwhelming, not tragic." Virginia Woolf defends even the violence and melodrama of the books as due to "a curious peasant-like love of the monstrous for its own sake," as part of "the wild spirit of poetry which saw the strangeness of life itself, with no symbol of caprice and unreason too extreme to represent the astonishing circumstances of our existence." She forgives all the shortcomings and failures of Hardy, "the greatest tragic writer among English novelists."

Virginia Woolf has a similar sympathy for Conrad. She admires his vision and his "implacable integrity, how it is better to be good than bad, how loyalty is good, and honesty and courage." She vastly prefers the early books: *Typhoon, The Nigger of the Narcissus,* and *Youth. Lord Jim* falls apart. The second half does not develop satisfactorily from the first. Conrad "sees his people in flashes; it explains what we may call the static quality of Mr. Conrad's characters." An atmosphere of profound and monotonous calm pervades the book. The idea is simple, but the texture is extremely fine. The later fiction, however, fails to come up to her expectations. She reviewed *The Rescue* unfavorably. She misses a "central idea which, gathering the multiplicity of incidents together, produces a final effect of unity." It is just "stiff melodrama." *Nostromo* suffers from "a crowding and suffocating superabundance." The later Conrad was "not able to bring his figures into perfect relation with their background." "He was not sure of the world of values and convictions." She sees a conflict between the seacaptain and the talkative Marlow. There is something "somnolent, stiff, ornate," even "pomposity and monotony" in Conrad, and once she even denies him the honor of being an English writer. "He is too formal, too courteous, too scrupulous," a foreign aristocrat, without intimacy and humor.

The standard of judgment implied in these essays is the preference for the universally human, for the power of generalizing, of creating situations and characters which (like Hardy's characters) persuade us that there is "something symbolical about them which is common to us all." "Imagination is at its freest when it is most generalized." In contrast, two novelists whom she discussed remained subjective, particular. George Gissing uses personal suffering as his only theme. She approves of Gissing's purpose of making us think of the "hideous injustice in the system of society" but considers him "self-centered," limited by "narrowness of outlook and meagerness of sensibility." A very different writer, George Moore, writes also only about himself. He lacks all dramatic power. Not one of his novels is a masterpiece. "They are silken tents which have no poles," she says strikingly. *Esther Waters,* though it has "a shapeliness which is at once admirable and disconcerting," is a failure. The "scenes and characters are curiously flat. The dialogue is always toneless and monotonous." Still, she thinks George Moore "has brought a new mind into the world, he has given us a new way of feeling and seeing." He "liquidates the capricious and volatile essence of himself and decants it in [his] memoirs." But she does not even try to define the nature of this new mind.

Henry James, one would think, must have been very important for her practice as a novelist. She reviewed *The Golden Bowl* carefully and descriptively as early as 1905. But the critical pronouncements show a divided mind. She does not much care for the ghost stories. "The horror of *The Turn of the Screw* is tame and conventional." "Quint and Miss Jessel are not ghosts, but odious creatures much closer to us than ghosts have ever been." "The Great Good Place" is a failure because of James's lack of "visionary imagination." She complains that in *What Maisie Knew* the "characters seem held in a vacuum at a great [re]move from the substantial lumbering world of Dickens and George Eliot or from the precise crisscross of convention which metes out the world of Jane Austen." In *The Wings of the Dove* James becomes "merely excessively ingenious. . . . After all this juggling and arranging of silk pocket handkerchiefs, one ceases to have any feeling for the figure behind. Milly thus manipulated disappears. He overreaches himself." Virginia Woolf likes *The American Scene* ("very quiet and luminous"), and the "wonderful" *Notes of a Son and Brother* even more. We owe to Henry James and to Hawthorne, she says, "the best relish of the past in our literature—not the past of romance and chivalry, but the immediate past of vanished dignity and faded fashions." She alludes to James's "late and mighty flowering" and calls him "English in his humour, Johnso-

nian in his sanity." "The courtly, worldly, sentimental old gentleman" whom she met in 1907 seemed to her, however, something of a figure of fun, to judge from the letter in which she described his convoluted questions, and in a review of Joseph Warren Beach's *Method of Henry James* (1918) some deep hostility comes to the surface. James is called "vulgar, a snob, an American." His characters are "tainted by the determination not to be vulgar; they are, as exiles tend to be, slightly parasitic; they have an enormous appetite for afternoon tea; their attitude not only to furniture but to life is more that of an appreciative collector than an undoubting possessor." She reflects that "one had rather read what he meant to do than what he actually did do." Still, she admits the interest of his later books, "not a plot, or a collection of characters, or a view of life, but something more abstract, more difficult to grasp, the weaving together of many themes into one of them, the making out of a design." She seems to be describing her own procedures. But she did not, publicly, discuss the relation to James beyond these remarks.

She defined her own position most clearly in regard to her immediate predecessors, Arnold Bennett, H. G. Wells, and John Galsworthy. These are her best-known essays, particularly ***Mr. Bennett and Mrs. Brown*** (1924), which is one of a series of articles rehearsing the theme that the novels of the three authors are encumbered by loads of detail, by "bushels of fact." "You cannot," she says [in ***Granite and Rainbow***], "cross the narrow bridge of art carrying all its tools in your hands". But the attacks on Bennett and company surely overshoot the mark. To say that their books leave one with a "feeling of incompleteness and dissatisfaction," that "in order to complete them it seems necessary to do something—to join a society, or, more desperately, to write a cheque," is hardly true of *The Old Wives' Tale, The Man of Property,* or *Tono-Bungay.* The charge that Bennett's ideal is "an eternity of bliss spent in the very best hotel in Brighton" does not apply even to *Imperial Palace,* and Wells can hardly be called "a materialist from sheer goodness of heart," though we may agree with her complaint about "the crudity and coarseness of his human beings." Virginia Woolf resented Arnold Bennett's criticism of her novel ***Jacob's Room,*** which asserted that the work contained "no characters that vitally survive in the mind." She turned the tables on him when she considered him not interested in human nature but in "rents, freeholds, copyholds, and fines." She effectively quotes the beginning of Bennett's *Hilda Lessways,* minutely describing a row of houses, to support the general charge against a fashionable novelist as providing plot and "an air of probability embalming the whole so impeccably that if all his figures were to come to life they would find themselves dressed down to the last button of their coats in the fashion of the hour." Her own novel, on the contrary, "would have no plot, no comedy, no tragedy, no love interest or catastrophe in the accepted style, and perhaps not a single button sewn on as the Bond Street tailors would have it." She pleads that we should tolerate "the spasmodic, the obscure, the fragmentary," even "the failure" of a new novel, for she believed that "we are trembling on the verge of one of the great ages of English Literature." Virginia Woolf proclaims the end of realism and prophesies the age of a novel of sensibility.

She was, however, disappointed with the new experimental novelists. One would expect her to welcome Dorothy Richardson. She praises her for discarding "the old deliberate business" and sympathetically describes her method, which she does not call "stream of consciousness." "The method," she continues, "if triumphant, should make us feel ourselves seated at the centre of another mind, and, according to the artistic gift of the writer, we should perceive in the helter-skelter of flying fragments some unity, significance, or design." She grants that Dorothy Richardson "achieved a far greater sense of reality than that produced by the ordinary means," but she finds herself, after all, "distressingly near the surface . . . never, or only for a tantalizing second, in the reality which underlies these appearances." No doubt Virginia Woolf felt that with similar methods she herself had reached this deeper reality.

D. H. Lawrence upset her profoundly in private, though her only review, of *The Lost Girl* (1920), complains rather that the book is conventional. "We read Mr. Lawrence as one reads Mr. Bennett—for the facts and for the story." Virginia Woolf never alludes to the crucial episode of the book, the story of the heroine Alvina with Cicio in the mountains of the Abruzzi. To say that "little by little Alvina disappears beneath the heap of facts recorded about her," and that "the only sense in which we feel her to be lost is that we cannot longer believe in her existence," sounds as if Virginia Woolf had not read this admittedly incongruous but very Lawrentian part of the otherwise traditional Bennett-like book. Her later **"Notes on D. H. Lawrence"** (1932) profess that up to 1931 "he was known to [her] almost solely by reputation and scarcely at all by experience." His reputation was that of "the exponent of some mystical theory of sex." She disliked "The Prussian Officer," which left no clear impression except "starting muscles and forced obscenity." The two collections of poems, *Nettles* and *Pansies,* seemed to her "like the sayings that small boys scribble upon stiles to make housemaids jump and titter." But now she read belatedly *Sons and Lovers* and found it "clear cut, decisive, masterly, hard as rock, shaped." She admires the "rapture of physical being" evoked, for instance, in the scene in which Paul and Miriam swing in the barn. But she keeps her distance: she sees the dissatisfaction of a man of the common people who wants to get into the middle classes, and, contrasting him with Proust, she thinks that he "continues no tradition, is unaware of the past, of the present save as it affects the future. As a writer, this lack of tradition, affects him immensely." When she read the *Letters* collected by Aldous Huxley (1930), she reacted with abrupt jottings in her **Diary:** "Lawrence is airless, confined. . . . I don't want 'a philosophy' in the least. . . . I don't like strumming with two fingers—and the arrogance." She protests against Huxley's saying that Lawrence is an "artist." "Art is being rid of all preaching. . . . Lawrence would only say what proved something." Similar pronouncements can be found scattered through the **Diary** and the **Letters,** but her shrinking from what seemed to her his aggressive masculinity is clear enough.

Her attitude toward Joyce is somewhat similar. T. S. Eliot praised *Ulysses* in conversation, and Harriet Weaver wanted her to publish the book with the Hogarth Press. Noth-

ing could be done about it, for at that time nobody could have found a printer for *Ulysses* in England. But her own view of the book is far from wholehearted admiration. Publicly she called it "a memorable catastrophe—immense in daring, terrific in disaster." In the **Diary** she is more explicit: "Genius it [*Ulysses*] has, I think; but of the inferior water. The book is diffuse. . . . It is pretentious. It is underbred, not only in the obvious sense, but in the literary sense. A first rate writer, I mean, respects writing too much to be tricky; startling; doing stunts." Elsewhere she complains of "the damned egotistical self which ruins Joyce and [Dorothy] Richardson" and of a "cheap, smart, smoking-room coarseness."

She saw through Aldous Huxley, whom she liked personally, very early. Her review of *Limbo* (1920) recognizes that he is clever, amusing, and far too intellectual and bookish. "It is well to leave a mind under a counterpane of moderate ignorance," she advises him, but she obviously did not take her own advice, at least in her criticism. She was immensely well-read and reviewed even mediocre novels with patience and sympathy. Her reviews of such forgotten novelists as Elinor Mordaunt, L. P. Jacks, W. E. Norris, Leonard Merrick, and the still remembered Frank Swinnerton and Joseph Hergesheimer are extremely indulgent though never without some reservations. She got "tired of being caged with Aldous, Joyce and Lawrence," thought that the new novel had failed to keep its promise, and felt herself to be more and more alone and unappreciated, reacting irritably to satirical attacks against her and Bloomsbury, such as those of Wyndham Lewis, or to disparaging comments in *Scrutiny.*

The two collections of her essays she herself edited, **The Common Reader** (1925) and **The Second Common Reader** (1932), were arranged in the chronological order of the authors discussed. In an article entitled **"Phases of Fiction"** (1929), she classified the English and foreign novelists as if they were present simultaneously in her bookshelves. The apparently detached typology leads, however, to the kind of novel she herself preferred and practiced. She begins with "truth-tellers," Defoe, Maupassant, and Trollope; discusses "the Romantics," Scott, Stevenson, and Mrs. Radcliffe; comments briefly on "Character-mongers and Comedians," Dickens, Jane Austen, George Eliot; on "Psychologists" such as Henry James, Proust, and Dostoevsky; "Satirists and Fantasists," Peacock and Sterne; and finally the "Poets," Tolstoy, Meredith, Emily Brontë, Melville, and again Proust. She concludes, however, with an admission of the inevitability of mimesis. "The novel is the only form of art [she forgets the film] which seeks to make us believe that it is giving a full and truthful record of the life of a real person." It is "inevitable that the reader . . . should go on feeling as he feels in life." But the novelist should control the human sympathy. "Indeed the first sign we are reading a writer of merit is that we feel this control at work on us. The barrier between us and the book is raised higher." "The balance between the power of bringing us into close touch with life" and "style, arrangement, construction" is considered the main achievement of the great novelist who gives us "an epitome" as well as an "inventory" of life. In commenting on Percy Lubbock's *Craft of Fiction* (1921), the book that had expounded the Jamesian concept of the novel most authoritatively, Virginia Woolf admits that novels "bristle with temptations. We identify ourselves with this person or that" and "the book itself, the form escapes," as Lubbock had complained. But she does not care for the term *form,* which she wrongly considers as coming from the visual arts (as if Plato and Aristotle had never lived). It suggests to her the visual and the static. She thinks of the novel as being constituted in "the very process of reading itself," a very modern concept. "It is not form which you see, but emotion which you feel." But she grants that beyond emotion there is "something which though it is inspired by emotion, tranquilises it, orders it, composes it," which "places certain emotions in the right relations to each other," a result which she would not want to call "form" but rather "art."

Many of her judgments of the novelists are based on an answer to the question whether this right balance between life and art is achieved or whether there is a preponderance of one or the other which upsets it. Considering her friendship with E. M. Forster, her review of *Aspects of the Novel* is surprisingly disapproving. She complains that Forster is silent about the novelist's language. He censures patterns she cares for. Beauty is suspect to him. "Fiction is treated as a parasite which draws sustenance from life and must in gratitude resemble life or perish." She concludes, not limiting herself to Forster, that "if the English critic were less domestic, less assiduous to protect the rights of what it pleases him to call life, the novelist might be bolder too. He must cut adrift from the eternal tea-table. . . . The story might wobble; the plot might crumble; ruin might seize upon the characters. The novel, in short, might become a work of art." That is what she wanted to achieve herself, even at a price. Forster, in *Howards End,* "having recorded too much and too literally," wavers between realism and symbolism. "The hesitation is fatal. For we doubt both things—the real and the symbolical," an ambiguity that she considers a failing, even a disaster: she always insists on consistency, coherence, the observance of the writer's perspective, and finds that only "lesser writers introduce two different kinds of reality into the same book." One wonders whether she is not warning herself against the dangers incurred by her own novels.

The balance of life and art is one criterion. Another is the contrast of national types and traditions. Virginia Woolf was acutely aware of the class character of English fiction of the nineteenth century. All the novelists were "fairly well-to-do middle class people." She welcomes the coming disappearance of classes and does not regret that this, very likely, "will be the end of the novel as we know it." It may become extinct like poetic drama. Virginia Woolf waxes satirical about the "nieces of Earls and cousins of Generals" in English fiction. "Our ignorance of the aristocracy is nothing compared with our ignorance of the working classes." There are "no gentlemen in Dickens; no working men in Thackeray. One hesitates to call Jane Eyre a lady." Virginia Woolf can only conclude with a question mark about the "art of a truly democratic age."

Yet she does recommend one remedy against the limits of English fiction: the Russian novel. She belongs to the early

Virginia and Leonard Woolf.

English enthusiasts of the Russian novel and was carried away not only by Turgenev, Tolstoy, Dostoevsky, and Chekhov but also by rash generalizations about the Russian soul, the "entirely new conception of the novel," "larger, saner and more profound than ours." "Could any English novel survive," she asks, "in the furnace of that overpowering sincerity," "their undeviating reverence for truth?" In her well-known essay **"The Russian Point of View,"** the enthusiasm reaches fever pitch and the generalizations become often dubious. "The simplicity, the absence of effort, the assumption that in a world bursting with misery the chief call upon us is to understand fellow-sufferers 'and not with the mind—for it is easy with the mind—but with the heart'—this is the cloud which broods above the whole of Russian literature." It is a cliché to speak of the soul as "the chief character in Russian fiction" and an error to say that in Russian novels "there is none of that precise division between good and bad to which we are used." The contrast she draws between Annabella in Ford's *'Tis a Pity She's a Whore* and Anna Karenina compares the incomparable. "The English girl is flat and crude as a face painted on a playing card; she is without depth, without range, without intricacy," whereas "the Russian woman is flesh and blood, nerves and temperament, has heart, brain, body, and mind." English and Russian fiction seem to her "immeasurably far apart," though, on occasion, she grants the English "a natural delight in humour and comedy, in the beauty of the earth, in the activities of the intellect, and in the splendours of the body," supposedly absent from the Russians.

Fortunately these sweeping generalizations are modified in the many essays on individual authors. She sees the difference between Dostoevsky and Tolstoy and formulates it in the terms derived from Merezhkovsky's antithesis. "Life dominates Tolstoi as the soul dominates Dostoevsky." Virginia Woolf obviously prefers Turgenev, Tolstoy, and Chekhov to Dostoevsky. She admired Tolstoy as "the greatest of all novelists," as "genius in the raw. Thus more disturbing, more 'shocking,' more of a thunderclap, even on art, even on literature, than any other writer." (pp. 72-80)

The English-Russian contrast preoccupied her almost as much as the male-female. There is here no need to speak of her feminism, of **A Room of One's Own,** of her pleas for "leisure, money and room to themselves" so that women could write, not only to vent their grievances in novels which are "dumping grounds for the personal emotions" but also to become writers who could define their own sense of values, even in politics and social criticism, and who finally would achieve a greater impersonality which would "encourage the poetic spirit" and would make them speak out about "our destiny and the meaning of life." Virginia Woolf was acutely aware of the handicaps and restrictions imposed by law and custom on women writers in the past, but she deplored the effects of resentment and self-assertiveness on women writers. "The vision loses its perfect integrity, and with that, its most essential quality as a work of art." But Virginia Woolf was of two minds about femininity in literature. Sometimes she wants a feminine literature, though she has doubts about any common characteristics of feminine writings in the past. "Jane Austen can have had nothing in common with George Eliot; George Eliot was the direct opposite of Emily Brontë." But she also complains (not too seriously, one hopes) about the "sentence made by men; it is too loose, too heavy, too pompous for a woman's use." "Charlotte Brontë, with her splendid gift for prose, stumbled and fell with that clumsy weapon in her hands. George Eliot committed atrocities with it that beggar description." Virginia Woolf praises Dorothy Richardson: "She has invented, or, if she has not invented, developed and applied to her own use a sentence which we might call the psychological sentence of the feminine gender." Fortunately Jane Austen and Emily Brontë were not trying to write like men. Virginia Woolf dislikes overtly, self-consciously virile writers: D. H. Lawrence, Norman Douglas, and James Joyce. In a sharp review of Hemingway's *The Sun Also Rises* she objects not only to his crude and flat characters and conventional technique but also to his machismo. But ultimately she can contradict herself and say "a writer has no sex." "The greatest writers lay no stress upon sex one way or the other." "Any emphasis, either of pride or of shame, laid consciously upon the sex of a writer is not only irritating but superfluous." She quotes with approval Coleridge's saying that "a great mind must be androgynous." At least theoretically and

imaginatively in her books she overcame the division of the sexes.

Virginia Woolf was mainly interested in the novel and in biography. Her interest in poetry, at least in her printed criticism, is limited and somewhat perfunctory. She thinks that "very little of value has been said about poetry since the world began," and she did not add to this slender store. . . . But [her] lack of sympathy with modern poetry, including Yeats and T. S. Eliot, should not obscure her appreciation of narrative poets such as Chaucer or Elizabeth Barrett Browning, whose *Aurora Leigh* she tried to rescue from oblivion, or her admiration for Donne, who "still excites interest and disgust, contempt and adoration." She defends allegory in Spenser's *Faerie Queene:* "Passions are turned into people," are given amplitude and depersonalized. "Who shall say that this is the less natural, the less realistic?" But she dislikes the stanzaic form of the poem. "The verse becomes for a time a rocking horse." We are confined in "one continuous consciousness which is Spenser's." Again and again she voices her preference for the novel and the drama because they require the writer to enter into other people's minds.

This is also her ideal of criticism. "Do not dictate to your author; try to become him. Be his fellow-worker and accomplice." "Everywhere else we may be bound by laws and conventions—there [in art] we have none." Virginia Woolf seems to appeal to the tradition descending from Lamb and Hazlitt via Sainte-Beuve and Pater to her friends. But Virginia Woolf's essay on Hazlitt is extremely critical of his person and mind. He seems to her a divided and discordant mind with "so much energy and yet so little love for his task." His essays are "dry, garish in their bright imagery, monotonous in the undeviating energy of their rhythm." She disapproves of his closed mind—"his own and it is made up"—and gently but insistently rejects the moral and political preoccupations of Macaulay, Matthew Arnold, and her father's "intemperate candour." Her own principle is "simply that the essay should give pleasure." "Not a fact juts out, not a dogma tears the surface of the texture." "It must be pure from dullness, deadness, and deposits of extraneous matter." But surely this passage exalting an ideal of pleasing the reader by a smooth surface of the noncommittal is quite inadequate to her actual practice. In the same review she disapproves of the genteel essayists of her time in vehement terms unusual in her writings. "We are nauseated by the sight of trivial personalities decomposing in the eternity of print." She asks for "backbone," "some fierce attachment to an idea," even for an "obstinate conviction." In praising Coleridge's criticism as "the most spiritual in the language" and his notes on Shakespeare as "the only criticisms that bear reading with the sound of the play still in one's ears," she formulates his power "of seeming to bring to light what was already there beforehand, instead of imposing anything from the outside." Reviewing Spingarn's *Creative Criticism* she can endorse the conception of criticism established "thanks to Sainte-Beuve and others." "We try to enter into the mind of the writer, to see each work of art by itself, and to judge how far each artist has succeeded in his aim," a repetition of Goethe's well-known formulas.

She concludes that criticism is not creation but "an interpretation" of art.

Though she may not have importantly contributed to a theory of literature or even of the novel, Virginia Woolf has accomplished the task of the critic: she characterized many of the main novelists and judged them acutely, blending characterization and judgment, for she knew that judgment arises out of the description and interpretation. Occasionally she may be arbitrary or whimsical, but in her best essays she achieves what she granted that Hazlitt succeeded in doing. "He singles out the peculiar quality of his author and stamps it vigorously." (pp. 81-4)

> René Wellek, "The Bloomsbury Group," in his A History of Modern Criticism: 1750-1950, Vol. 5, *Yale University Press, 1986, pp. 55-91.*

Steve Ferebee (essay date 1987)

[*In the following excerpt, Ferebee contends that Woolf's literary criticism prefigured the late-twentieth-century critical technique of "reader-oriented criticism."*]

Virginia Woolf believed that by describing her reading of a text she could evaluate that text. This belief dominates both her own studies of literature and our reading of her literary essays because in those essays Woolf records her reactions to a text and educates her reader about the open-minded, individualistic manner of reading, which, she says, originated with her father's advice to "read what one liked because one liked it, never to pretend to admire what one did not" ["**Leslie Stephen**"]. Instead of limiting her reader to the reactions she herself has had to a text, Woolf encourages multiplicity by assuming its inevitability. At the same time, however, she explains the objective basis for her subjective reactions. Woolf's literary critical method is to urge the reader to compare his reaction to Woolf's, all the while attempting to understand what in the text causes that response. Like many current literary critics, Woolf finds meaning not only in the text but also in the reader. That her method predates the current flurry of reader-oriented criticism substantiates Virginia Woolf's place in the history of letters.

In an essay she was working on when she died, Woolf names three kinds of readers: the specialized reader, "who attaches himself to certain aspects of the printed words"; "the very large class of perfectly literate people who strip many miles of print yearly from paper yet never read a word"; and, finally, the readers who search for genuine "thoughts and emotions," original content, and style ["**The Reader**"]. It is to this latter class of readers that Woolf addresses her ***Common Reader*** essays. She describes her reader in the preface to the first collection:

> He reads for his own pleasure rather than to impart knowledge or correct the opinions of others. Above all, he is guided by an instinct to create for himself, out of whatever odds and ends he can come by, some kind of whole—a portrait of a man, a sketch of an age, a theory of the art of writing.

The writer's function is to help the reader discover meaning; above all, she says in "**The Leaning Tower**," "in life and in literature, it is necessary to have some means of bridging the gulf between the hostess and her guest on the one hand, and between the writer and his unknown reader on the other." The writer does encode certain aids in the text, but a great deal of literature's success depends on the reader's ability and willingness to work with the writer, to look, as she says in her essay on *Robinson Crusoe,* through the writer's eyes and seek to understand his "perspective." Similarly, Virginia Woolf says that literature is a "piece of business to be transacted between writer and reader." Reading is not a sedentary process; it is, as in writing, an active pursuit of meaning. In the more than two hundred literary essays Woolf wrote over a thirty-seven-year career as an essayist, she often discussed the reader's function, which is to find personal meaning by uncovering interpretive signs in the text.

The power and charm of Virginia Woolf's essays radiate from her conviction that the writer communicates his or her message most rewardingly when the receptor is active and creative. Because readers learn through feeling, they should first read with open minds, allowing any number of impressions to form. But to "get our emotion directly and for ourselves is only the first step. We must go on to riddle it with questions." Both as a reader and as an essayist, then, Virginia Woolf begins with the assumption that each reader reacts differently to a text; in her essays she transforms this reaction into a creative process of comprehension. In "The Thinker as Reader," an article on Wallace Stevens, Robert DeMaria states that "the creation of a reader is a profound critical and theoretical act; the kind of reader a writer imagines indicates both the form that he most often sees literature as taking and the form in which he usually casts his own literary works." Virginia Woolf is a case in point. She speaks directly and personally at the same time because she knows who her readers are. She encourages their sense of individual identity, and she makes use of it in her own essays.

Common Readers Reading

From 1905 until 1941 Virginia Woolf published most of her essays in serious British and United States' journals such as *The Nation, The New Republic,* and *The Yale Review.* When she began writing for the *Times Literary Supplement (TLS)* in 1905, the educated, literate readers of this journal became her most consistent audience until she ceased writing for it [in] 1938. By calling for a "common" reader in her collections of essays, Virginia Woolf was not calling for a lower, less educated audience than that which read the *TLS* or *The Nation.* She took her title from Dr. Johnson's "Life of Gray," in which Johnson says, "I rejoice to concur with the common reader; for by the common sense of readers, uncorrupted by literary prejudices, after all the refinements of subtilty and the dogmatism of learning, must be generally decided all claim to poetical honours." Does her derivative title suggest a relationship between her twentieth-century readers and those of the eighteenth-century essayists?

Readers of eighteenth-century essays and those of Woolf's common-reader essays develop similar relationships with their essayists by growing accustomed to the role in which the essayists cast themselves. Social gossip from eighteenth-century coffeehouses, reported by controlled, but talkative personae, compare with Virginia Woolf's conversational, intimate approach. However, the eighteenth-century essayist adopted a fictitious persona, not the voice of Samuel Johnson or Joseph Addison, but of the *Rambler* or Isaac Bickerstaff, while Virginia Woolf speaks as just another common reader.

This eighteenth-century dramatization of a character establishes a sense of illusion missing in Woolf's essays. The reader hears a character's voice, a mask behind which the eighteenth-century gentleman could criticize his society without fear of censure. Virginia Woolf generates meaning not by the reader's sympathy for and identification with a character, but by her style and content. Virginia Woolf presents rather than dramatizes her personality, and it is her voice which the reader hears. The major difference between eighteenth-century essays and Woolf's is the degree of distance between essayist and reader. The reservation and illusion produced by the fictional setting of an eighteenth-century essay contrast markedly with the intimacy and credibility produced by authenticity of an essay by Virginia Woolf.

Whatever differences there are between the earlier essayists and Woolf, the eighteenth-century writers did create an audience for the informal essay in periodicals. They "firmly established" a large, middle-class body of readers whom they "could easily visualize" [James Sutherland, *English Literature of the Late Seventeenth Century*]. In this tradition of periodical essayists and Dryden's matter-of-fact practical criticism presented in dramatic terms, "the writer presupposed a reader who enjoys talking" [Joan Bennett, *Virginia Woolf: Her Art as a Novelist*]. Furthermore, this audience grew larger during the nineteenth-century; it also became more varied and sure of its expectations. The essayist, whom Woolf calls "the most sensitive of all plants to public opinion," developed methods of encouraging the reader's active participation. In an introduction to *The Spectator* essays, Donald Bond writes, "[B]ecause of the many letters which *The Spectator* received and published, it combined the voice of the author with the widest form of 'audience participation'." But collaboration in the eighteenth-century essay, as in Woolf's essays, consists of more than letters to the editor. "Pray, gentlemen, let us go hand in hand a little," says Defoe's Mr. Review. Besides illustrating Defoe's concern for immediacy and intimacy, this type of direct reference draws the reader into an active conversation with the essayist by appealing to the reader's sense of himself or herself as a participant in the development of Defoe's essay. In "The Writer's Audience Is Always a Fiction," Walter Ong says that Addison and Steele "assumed a fashionable intimacy among readers themselves and between all readers and the writer, achieved largely by casting readers as well as writer in the role of coffeehouse habitués."

The important connection between Woolf and the eighteenth-century essayists is that both cast their readers and themselves in a definite role. Woolf accommodates her modern reader by her colloquial, unpretentious vocabulary, her intimate, friendly tone, and her varied, appealing subjects. But she also "demands the full, intelligent participation of her readers." Woolf's essays, consequently, appeal to a wide variety of readers: scholars, historians, the working man or woman. Virginia Woolf's "common" reader does not mean "average"; it means widespread. In rejecting an academic role for herself, Woolf adopts an associative, personal point of view that allows her to speak as an individual to an individual. In her words, it provides a "code of manners . . . which writers and readers accept as a prelude to the more exciting intercourse of friendship." Woolf learned from the eighteenth-century essayists that the reader is most effectively drawn into the essay if he knows what role he plays; the role of the reader in the Virginia Woolf essay is to be honest, intelligent, committed to learning, and willing to communicate. Woolf also takes this role.

Moments of Meeting

Woolf is careful to explain the role to her reader. As V. S. Pritchett says in a review of Woolf's **Collected Essays,** she talks with her reader in conversation which "flatters" her reader. "When she says 'we,' " Barbara C. Bell and Carol Ohmann point out in a perceptive article, Woolf alludes to herself and "her ideal community, the common readers" [Barbara Currier Bell and Carol Ohmann, "Virginia Woolf's Criticism: A Polemical Preface," *Critical Inquiry*, 1974]. Indeed, Woolf's first-person plural pronouns develop into more than a rhetorical method of distancing herself; they establish the reader's sense of cooperative identity.

On the one hand, Woolf does assume the rhetorical "we" in some literary essays: "according to a theory of ours"; "we cannot help suspecting"; "we may roughly describe." Woolf adopts rhetorical pronouns, as do most writers, to add variety and to create a sense of distance from her subjects. But on the other hand, "we" is also equivalent to the team of essayist and reader: "if we have no novelist in England today"; "let us watch Miss Frend"; "yet let us choose another scene"; "peering over Mr. Sherwood Anderson's shoulder, we see." These pronouns refer to reader and essayist because they give the usually passive reader a definite sense of active participation; the conventional rhetorical distance between essayist and reader disappears as Woolf creates a clear role for the reader.

Consider the sense of reciprocity created by the pronouns used to bridge the gap between essays in the **Common Reader** collections. The first-person plural pronouns in **"The Strange Elizabethans,"** the first essay in the **Second Common Reader,** firmly establish the reader's position in that essay; indeed, they generate identity, unify the essay, and clarify the theme by pitching the Elizabethan's language against "our pronunciation." The essay ends with a "we" which directly refers to the modern reader; this is a personifying pronoun: "When we say that Harvey lived we mean that he quarreled and was tiresome and ridiculous and had a face like ours." Because the "we" and "ours" refer to the essayist and reader, both separated from the Elizabethan Gabriel Harvey, Virginia Woolf draws the reader into her collection. She repeats the device in the next essay with another allusion to the modern reader: "When we think how many millions of words have been written and printed in England in the past three hundred years . . . ". She continues this method in **"The Countess of Pembroke's Arcadia"** ("To draw the blinds and shut the door, to muffle the noises of the street and shade the glare and flicker of its light—that is our desire"); in **"*Robinson Crusoe*"** ("There are many ways of approaching this classical volume; but which shall we choose?"); and throughout the entire collection.

In her essays Virginia Woolf makes the reader feel like a part of the creation of the essay. In her literary essays, particularly, Woolf establishes a communal activity. Besides stressing the first-person plural pronoun, she occasionally refers to the reader: "When the reader, a few pages deep and beginning to feel settled in the new atmosphere, collects himself, his first comment is likely to be that it is a very strange thing that no one has thought of writing this book before." This reference, in a 1917 book review, is typical in that Woolf dramatically portrays the reader in a commonplace setting and gives the reader a reaction to begin comparing with his or her own. Woolf's reader references often portray the reader (to himself) as an attentive, well-read member of a literary community. This type of reference is a fundamental part of Woolf's attempt to nurture her reader's individuality and sense of cooperation with the essayist. For example, in a 1918 *TLS* review of Hugh Walpole's *The Green Mirror*, Woolf assumes that her reader is well educated and interested in modern fiction: "The reader who is acquainted with modern fiction will at this point reflect that he has met these people or their relations already." As V. S. Pritchett says, Woolf seeks to "flatter" her reader, and she does this by assuming a certain base of knowledge about and interest in the many subjects of her essays. This community of exclusivity works especially well with her *TLS* audience, but it never becomes so specialized that other interested readers cannot enjoy her essays. Thus Virginia Woolf creates a literary partnership with the "attentive reader," who discovers, at the same time Woolf points it out in her essay, certain relevant ideas about her subject. Consequently, "we" become more and more substantial, more and more intimate with and attuned to the essayist, because "we" share with her a sincere attempt to discover answers to questions she raises in the essay.

Generally, the reader's role is to be active and to learn. Readers should, Woolf urges, be as strict in their reading as writers should be in their writing. "Don't let writers waste your time," she advises. Indeed, the reader's sense of his or her own importance is connected to what Woolf defines as a responsibility to literature's future. "We have got to teach ourselves to understand literature," she says in **"The Leaning Tower,"** "because in the future we are not going to leave writing to be done for us by a small class of well-to-do young men who have a pinch, a thimble-full of experience to give us. We are going to add our own experience, to make our own contribution." Note the personifying "we" and the emphasis communicated by the imperatives "have got to" and "must become" and by the future tense of "are going to." The reader becomes the protector of English literature who is better equipped for reading than professional readers because the average person has a greater store of experiences with which to judge

literature, whose basis must always be what it teaches about human life. Woolf creates this role for herself and her reader, and she makes it a circular partnership because "the standards we raise and the judgments we pass steal into the air and become part of the atmosphere which writers breathe as they work."

Because she treats the reader as an independent, thinking partner, Woolf as an essayist has the double task of providing sufficient signs in the text and of leaving the reader, at the right moment, to make out a meaning. "The art of writing," Woolf says, "consists of laying an egg in the reader's mind from which springs the thing itself." As Joan Bennett puts it, Woolf's essays leave the reader "in the right frame of mind" to consider her subject in the essay. A book on Samuel Butler, for instance, is important because it guides Woolf, and, by implication, the reader, to reread Butler's books. Woolf suggests that this kind of guidance is what the reader should look for in essays; this is the "piece of business to be transacted between writer and reader." In order to nurture her reader's sense of independence, Virginia Woolf develops an essay style that is meant to affect her reader. She looks for and practices what can be called moments of meeting between essayist and reader.

Each reader's moment will, of course, be unique because each reader is unique. Virginia Woolf sees reading as an experience which stimulates life in that both consist of these moments when people create or change. Accordingly, because "great geniuses make us see in the world any shape they choose . . . we remodel our psychological geography when we read Dickens." Montaigne's essays are successful because his reader suddenly sees himself reflected in those essays. Dostoevsky's power originates from his ability to drop a suddenly familiar idea "into the pool of our consciousness." And in Woolf's literary essays like **"Phases of Fiction,"** we see the essayist's mind grappling with a series of books, continually readapting itself to different expectations and desires. Contemporary writers, Woolf says in a 1916 essay **"Hours in a Library,"** "cast a net," hoping to catch some human truths, and, as readers, "we must also throw our imaginations after them if we are to accept with understanding the strange gifts they bring back to us." Woolf concludes this essay by claiming that "all our faculties are summoned to the task, as in the great moments of our experience; and some consecration descends upon us from their hands which we return to life, feeling it more keenly and understanding it more deeply than before." Successful literature, Woolf believes, changes readers into creators by deepening their understandings of their own lives.

The Practicality of Subjectivity

Many critics claim that Virginia Woolf approached her literary essays only as a novelist; consequently, they view her essays merely as workshops for her novels. However, her approach to all literature is like that of the reader she describes, and it begins with subjective reactions. In fact, "form" for Woolf, as she discusses it in a 1922 essay **"On Re-Reading Novels,"** is the emotion stimulated during the act of reading. "The book itself is not form which you see, but emotion which you feel." Virginia Woolf founded her literary essays upon her belief that reading is a subjective experience. As Mark Goldman stresses with the title of his study of Woolf as a literary critic, *The Reader's Art,* one idea which we must stress is that Woolf always tries to show *what happens* to the reader while he or she is reading. This is why Virginia Woolf thinks "it is necessary to do your reading with your own eyes," and it is why she urges her readers to investigate their reactions to what they read, as she herself does in **"Phases of Fiction"** and other literary essays. From an analysis of the original subjective reaction, the good reader develops objective reasons for that reaction.

In **"Phases of Fiction,"** a series of essays written for the *Bookman* in 1929, there is an object lesson in Woolf's literary criticism. The reading experience itself—what happens during reading and evaluating—is Virginia Woolf's meaning and subject in **"Phases of Fiction."**

A four-paragraph introduction explains the method used in these essays and establishes Woolf's role as a common reader, one which she extends to her readers as well. Let the "professed historian and critic" read "to understand a period or to revise a reputation." The "ordinary" reader is "suspicious of fixed labels and settled hierarchies." In **"Phases of Fiction"** Woolf dramatizes the art of reading by dividing novels into six "appetites": (1) for truth and facts; (2) "for distance, for music, for shadow, for space"; (3) for a "sense of walls and towns about us"; (4) for "the more dubious region" of the psychologists; (5) for satire and fantasy; and (6) for the generalized, diffused picture of human life in novels by "the Poets." Virginia Woolf discusses how various novels satisfy or do not satisfy these appetites; each appetite leads to the next, because part of the basis of Woolf's literary method is comparison. After reading the "truth-tellers," Defoe, W. E. Norris, and Trollope, for instance, she says that "it is not strange that we should become aware of another desire welling up spontaneously and making its way into those cracks which the great monuments of the truthtellers wear inevitably upon their solid bases. A desire for distance, for music, for shadow, for space takes hold of us." She compares Peacock with Sterne, Hardy with Meredith, Proust with Dostoevsky; she says that the satirist's blunt "attitude toward reality" distinguishes his attitude from the psychologist's, in which a "thousand emotional veins and streaks are perceptible in this twilight or dawn which are lost in the full light of midday." What the essayist has done, then, is to "record" an "attempt to show the mind at work upon a shelf full of novels, and to watch it as it chooses and rejects, making itself a dwelling-place in accordance with its own appetites."

The value of such an approach lies in the possibilities which will be revealed about the mind's choices and rejections. In "the Romantics," for instance, the appetite is for "the force which the romantic acquires by obliterating facts. With the sinking of the lights, the solidity of the foreground disappears, other shapes become apparent and other senses are devised. We become aware of the danger and darkness of our existence; comfortable reality has proved itself a phantom." Woolf believes that the reader's mind, which becomes almost a character in this essay, be-

comes satiated with one kind of reading and moves naturally and eagerly to another banquet. After the emotional involvement offered by the psychologists, for example, "the mind feels like a sponge saturated full with sympathy and understanding; it needs to dry itself, to contract upon something hard"; and so it moves to "the Satirists and Fantastics." With her suggestive approach, Woolf emphasizes the fecundity of the novel; and she does so without limiting her reader's imagination with "fixed labels and settled hierarchies." "The most significant proof of this fertility, however, is provided by our sense of feeling something that has not yet been said; of some desire still unsatisfied."

Virginia Woolf pulls her reader into the partnership necessary for her essays by accepting an agreement that common readers are better than professional readers, such as professors or reviewers. And because she also accepts the common reader's role, she puts her "limited, personal, erratic" observations on an equal level of significance with the reader's. Woolf's observations, purposefully subjective, are valid because they show the reader more than what he or she knew about the novels Woolf discusses. This type of literary criticism, which extends to each reader the possibility of discovering a new meaning in the text, was challenged by New Criticism, which claimed that there is nothing outside the text necessary to an understanding of a literary work. This exclusion of the reader's reaction theoretically destroyed the common reader, for literary criticism became the activity of that elite group of professionals which Woolf deplored, not an activity of the entire society. Thus, Virginia Woolf is not taken seriously as a literary critic, because, as Mark Goldman puts it, it seems that she has no system and that she goes beyond the text to the writer's biography or personality. Goldman, however, shows that there is indeed a system, and Virginia Woolf demonstrates that going beyond the text is followed by returning to the text. (pp. 343-57)

Though Virginia Woolf is not as interested as [some later twentieth-century critics, including Stanley Fish and Norman Holland] are in a psychological or sociological investigation of the mind's activities as it reads, she does realize that it is in that process that meaning unfolds and must be sought. She is not a theoretical critic; she practices before she theorizes. And though she does not think the text consumes itself or that the reader writes his own text, when she writes about a literary work she intends to describe what happened to her while reading it and why. As Jane P. Tompkins says in her Introduction to *Reader-Response Criticism,* the assumption that connects the various critics concerned with the reader's part in literature is that "although they never deny [that] the ultimate object of attention is the literary text, they endow the process of reading the text, of receiving it and responding to it, with value." This value forms the heart of Woolf's literary method. During a time when I. A. Richards and T. S. Eliot emphasized objectification of the literary critic in pursuing the meaning of a literary artifact, Virginia Woolf pointed toward a future generation of critics by pursuing a subjective reading experience to arrive at an organic evaluation of a text. (pp. 360-61)

Steve Ferebee, "Bridging the Gulf: The Reader in and out of Virginia Woolf's Literary Essays," in CLA Journal, Vol. XXX, No. 3, March, 1987, pp. 343-61.

FURTHER READING

Bibliography

Kirkpatrick, Brownlee Jean, ed. *A Bibliography of Virginia Woolf.* Rev. ed. Oxford: Clarendon, 1980, 268 p.
　　The standard primary bibliography.

Rice, Thomas Jackson. *Virginia Woolf: A Guide to Research.* New York: Garland Publishing, 1984, 258 p.
　　Primary and secondary bibliographies, including listings of other bibliographies, biographies, memoirs, reminiscences and interviews, book-length critical studies and essay collections, general critical studies, and sections listing criticism on Woolf's principal works.

Biography

Bell, Quentin. *Virginia Woolf: A Biography.* New York: Harcourt Brace Jovanovich, 1972.
　　The standard biography, written by Woolf's nephew and based largely on private family papers. Published in both one and two volumes, the one-volume edition cited retains a two-part structure, with separate paginations and indexes.

Bishop, Edward. *A Virginia Woolf Chronology.* London: Macmillan Press, 1989, 268 p.
　　Provides a chronological outline of Woolf's life and career.

Bond, Alma Halbert. *Who Killed Virginia Woolf? A Psychobiography.* New York: Insight Books, 1989, 200 p.
　　Psychological study that addresses Woolf's reasons for committing suicide.

DeSalvo, Louise. *Virginia Woolf: The Impact of Childhood Sexual Abuse on Her Life and Work.* Boston: Beacon Press, 1989, 372 p.
　　Explores the effect of traditional Victorian child-rearing practices and specific instances of sexual abuse by male relatives on Woolf and their influences on her written works.

Edel, Leon. *Bloomsbury: A House of Lions.* Philadelphia: J. B. Lippincott Co., 1979, 288 p.
　　Biographical study of the Bloomsbury Group, beginning with the members' early lives. Woolf's life is covered to 1938.

Gordon, Lyndall. *Virginia Woolf: A Writer's Life.* Oxford: Oxford University Press, 1984, 341 p.
　　Critical biography discussing Woolf's written works in relation to her life.

Love, Jean O. *Virginia Woolf: Sources of Madness and Art.* Berkeley: University of California Press, 1977, 379 p.
　　Biography covering Woolf's life to age twenty-five, focusing on a portrayal of her familial milieu in order to demonstrate that "by that point, her family and early experiences had made their ineradicable imprint and had determined the paradoxical tendencies of her personality and therefore of her remaining years."

Panken, Shirley. *Virginia Woolf and the "Lust of Creation": A Psychoanalytic Exploration.* Albany: State University of New York Press, 1987, 336 p.
　　Challenges the accepted view, put forward by Leonard Woolf and accepted by many biographers, that periods of mental illness were for Woolf concomitant with the creative process.

Poole, Roger. *The Unknown Virginia Woolf.* 3rd ed. Atlantic Highlands, N.J.: Humanities Press International, 1990, 326 p.
　　New edition of a controversial biography, originally published in 1978, in which Poole disputes the "received version of Virginia Woolf's illness," established by Leonard Woolf and Quentin Bell, that presupposes her to have been insane.

Rose, Phyllis. *Woman of Letters: A Life of Virginia Woolf.* New York: Oxford University Press, 1978, 298 p.
　　Includes some discussion of Woolf's literary career.

Spater, George, and Parsons, Ian. *A Marriage of True Minds: An Intimate Portrait of Leonard and Virginia Woolf.* London: Jonathan Cape, 1977, 210 p.
　　Account of the lives of Virginia Woolf and Leonard Woolf, focusing on their marriage. The authors had access to correspondence (some unpublished), diaries, family documents, and photos not available to earlier biographers.

Trombley, Stephen. *All That Summer She Was Mad: Virginia Woolf, Female Victim of Male Medicine.* New York: Continuum, 1982, 338 p.
　　Considers Woolf's supposed insanity in the context of the views of her doctors on the causes, definition, and treatment of mental illness. Trombley disagrees with the presumption on the part of Woolf's physicians, family, husband, and biographers that she was periodically mad.

Criticism

Bosanquet, Theodora. Review of *Three Guineas,* by Virginia Woolf. *Time and Tide* XIX, No. 23 (4 June 1938): 788, 790.
　　Approbatory review commending Woolf's commentary on women's issues of education and employment.

Burt, John. "Irreconcilable Habits of Thought in *A Room of One's Own* and *To the Lighthouse.*" *ELH* 49, No. 4 (Winter 1982): 889-907.
　　Discusses the feminist content and modernist form of *A Room of One's Own.*

Carroll, Berenice A. " 'To Crush Him in Our Own Country': The Political Thought of Virginia Woolf." *Feminist Studies* 4, No. 1 (February 1978): 99-131.
　　Examines the social and political philosophy expressed in both Woolf's fiction and nonfiction writing.

Collins, H. P. Review of *The Common Reader,* by Virginia Woolf. *The Criterion* III, No. 12 (July 1925): 586-88.
　　Attributes to Woolf's critical essays a profound historical sense and discusses her portrayal of the intellectual

and emotional atmosphere of her subjects' historical epoch in her biographical criticism.

Connolly, Cyril. "The Novelist as Critic." *The New Yorker* XXIV, No. 7 (10 April 1948): 101-02, 105.
Assesses Woolf's essays and criticism as "lighter and easier than her fiction" and commends her as "a critic for those who write as well as for those who read."

Ćwiąkała-Piątkowska, Jadwiga. "The Feminist Pamphlets of Virginia Woolf." *Kwartalnik Neofilologiczny* XIX, No. 3 (1972): 271-79.
Finds Woolf's political experiences and observations acutely expressed in *A Room of One's Own* and *Three Guineas.*

Daiches, David. "The Uncommon Reader." In his *Virginia Woolf,* pp. 122-42. London: Editions Poetry, 1945.
Favorable assessment of Woolf's literary criticism.

Delord, J. "Virginia Woolf's Critical Essays." *Revue des langues vivantes* 29, No. 2 (Jaargang 1963): 126-31.
Acknowledges the common assessment of Woolf's criticism as "impressionistic," and contends that "the value of her critical work lies in her capacity to raise a record of impressions above day-dreaming and to arouse a creative response in her reader."

Fox, Alice. "Literary Allusion as Feminist Criticism in *A Room of One's Own.*" *Philological Quarterly* 63, No. 2 (Spring 1984): 145-61.
Identifies in Woolf's essay literary allusions that mock male supremacist assumptions about women.

Gorsky, Susan Rubinow. "Essays and Criticism." In her *Virginia Woolf,* pp. 28-45. Boston: Twayne, 1978.
Examines Woolf's criticism, reviews, journalism, essays, and pamphlets for insights into her aesthetic views on literary modernism and her attempt to define the functions of art.

Gregory, Horace. "On Virginia Woolf and Her Appeal to the Common Reader." In his *The Shield of Achilles,* pp. 188-93. New York: Harcourt, Brace and Co., 1944.
Commends Woolf's revivification of the familiar essay in the two volumes of *The Common Reader* and *The Death of the Moth,* finding her most effective when providing critical commentary that "appears to be incidental to the portrait of a literary figure."

Guiguet, Jean. "Analysis and Argument." In his *Virginia Woolf and Her Works,* pp. 124-92. London: Hogarth, 1965.
Offers a critical assessment of Woolf's essays and the feminist pamphlets *A Room of One's Own* and *Three Guineas* in order to ascertain Woolf's own attitudes about literature and feminism.

Henig, Suzanne. "D. H. Lawrence and Virginia Woolf." *The D. H. Lawrence Review* 2, No. 3 (Fall 1969): 265-71.
Outlines Woolf's reversal of critical opinion about Lawrence, whom she initially disparaged. Woolf's early published criticism of Lawrence has been assessed as unperceptive; however, private writings reveal that she subsequently attained an understanding and appreciation of his literary achievement.

Hummel, Madeline M. "From the Common Reader to the Uncommon Critic: *Three Guineas* and the Epistolary Form." *Bulletin of the New York Public Library* 80, No. 2 (Winter 1977): 151-57.
Examines Woolf's adaptation of the conventions of epistolary fiction in *Three Guineas.*

Hynes, Samuel. "The Whole Contention between Mr. Bennett and Mrs. Woolf." In his *Edwardian Occasions: Essays on English Writing in the Early Twentieth Century,* pp. 24-38. New York: Oxford University Press, 1972.
Provides an overview of the principal issues raised during the decade of critical dispute between Woolf and Arnold Bennett.

John, K. "The New Lysistrata." *The New Statesman and Nation* n.s. XV, No. 381 (11 June 1938): 995-96.
Review of *Three Guineas* which relates the essay to the feminist concerns of *A Room of One's Own.*

Johnson, Manly. *Virginia Woolf.* New York: Frederick Ungar, 1973, 130 p.
Overview of Woolf's career, focusing on her principal works. The critic includes a chronology and bibliography.

Jones, Frank. "Well-Intentioned/Well-Equipped." *Partisan Review* XV, No. 5 (May 1948): 587-93.
Commends Woolf as an insightful author of familiar essays that presuppose an intelligent readership.

Kreutz, Irving. "Mr. Bennett and Mrs. Woolf." *Modern Fiction Studies* 8, No. 1 (Spring 1962): 103-15.
Evaluates Woolf's critical assessment of Arnold Bennett's fiction in *Mr. Bennett and Mrs. Brown.*

Leavis, Q. D. "Caterpillars of the Commonwealth Unite!" *Scrutiny* VII, No. 2 (September 1938): 203-14.
Hostile review of *Three Guineas* in which Leavis pronounces Woolf intellectually vacuous, overly emotional, self-indulgent, and class-bound.

Lewis, Wyndham. "Virginia Woolf: 'Mind' and 'Matter' on the Plane of a Literary Controversy." In his *Men without Art,* pp. 158-71. New York: Russell & Russell, 1964.
Contends that Woolf presents an inaccurate assessment of Edwardian literary conventions in "Mr. Bennett and Mrs. Brown," rendering her criticism invalid.

Majumdar, Robin, and McLaurin, Allen, eds. *Virginia Woolf: The Critical Heritage.* London: Routledge & Kegan Paul, 1975, 467 p.
Collects significant early reviews of Woolf's principal works. The editors supply an introduction surveying Woolf's critical reception to the time of her death and summarizing later criticism.

Manuel, M. "Virginia Woolf as the Common Reader." *The Literary Criterion* LII, No. 2 (Summer 1966): 28-32.
Suggests that Woolf's two volumes of *Common Reader* essays reflect, not the insights of a "common reader," as Woolf presents herself, but "the workshop criticism of a novelist" addressing other writers.

Marcus, Jane, ed. *Virginia Woolf and Bloomsbury: A Centenary Celebration.* London: Macmillan Press, 1987, 307 p.
Collection of biographical and critical essays delivered in 1982 and 1983 at seminars and gatherings celebrating the centennial of Woolf's birth.

McIntyre, Clara F. "Is Virginia Woolf a Feminist?" *The Personalist* XLI, No. 2 (Spring 1960): 176-84.

Examines Woolf's handling of "the woman question" and feminist issues in her novels and nonfiction writings.

McLaughlin, Thomas M. "Virginia Woolf's Criticism: Interpretation as Theory and as Discourse." *Southern Humanities Review* XVII, No. 3 (Summer 1983): 241-53.

Identifies a theory of fiction and of criticism beneath the informal, impressionistic style of Woolf's essays.

McNeillie, Andrew. Introduction to *The Common Reader, First Series,* by Virginia Woolf, edited by Andrew McNeillie, pp. ix-xv. New York: Harcourt Brace Jovanovich, 1984.

Discusses form as it relates to individual essays by Woolf and her essay collections.

————. Introduction to *The Common Reader, Second Series,* by Virginia Woolf, edited by Andrew McNeillie, pp. vii-xiii. London: Hogarth, 1986.

Provides an overview of Woolf's literary activities at the time she originally compiled, edited, and published this volume of her collected essays, and commends the exuberance, wit, and erudition which characterize Woolf's nonfiction.

————. Introduction to *The Essays of Virginia Woolf, Volume I: 1904-1912,* by Virginia Woolf, edited by Andrew McNeillie, pp. ix-xviii. London: Hogarth, 1986.

Surveys Woolf's career as a literary journalist, discussing her reviews for the *Guardian, National Review,* the *Times Literary Supplement,* and *Cornhill* magazine.

————. Introduction to *The Essays of Virginia Woolf, Volume II: 1912-1918,* by Virginia Woolf, edited by Andrew McNeillie, pp. ix-xx. London: Hogarth, 1987.

Overview of this period in Woolf's life, which included her marriage to Leonard Woolf, the completion and publication of her first novel, the initial publications of the Hogarth press, and two episodes which McNeillie characterizes as "prolonged bouts of severe mental illness." McNeillie notes that during these years "Woolf was evolving, with gathering momentum, her modernist aesthetic."

————. Introduction to *The Essays of Virginia Woolf, Volume III: 1919-1924,* by Virginia Woolf, edited by Andrew McNeillie, pp. xi-xxii. London: Hogarth, 1988.

Surveys Woolf's life and works during the years when she became widely known and celebrated as a novelist, focusing on her critical writing during these years.

Middleton, Victoria. "*Three Guineas:* Subversion and Survival in the Professions." *Twentieth-Century Literature* 28, No. 4 (Winter 1982): 405-17.

Examines Woolf's criticism of patriarchal ideology and its rhetoric in *Three Guineas.*

Morris, Feiron [pseudonym of Vivien Eliot]. Review of "Mr. Bennett and Mrs. Brown," by Virginia Woolf. *The Criterion* III, No. 10 (January 1925): 326-29.

Commends Woolf's analysis of literary technique.

Rosenbaum, S. P., ed. *The Bloomsbury Group: A Collection of Memoirs, Commentary, and Criticism.* London: Croom Helm, 1975, 444 p.

Includes critical, biographical, and autobiographical writings by and about Woolf and other members of the Bloomsbury Group.

Rosenthal, Michael. *Virginia Woolf.* London: Routledge & Kegan Paul, 1979, 270 p.

Critical study that includes chapters devoted to Woolf's theories of fiction-writing, social criticism, and literary criticism.

Ruas, Charles. "An Interview with Nigel Nicolson." *Book Forum* IV, No. 4 (1979): 618-35.

Includes reminiscences by Nicolson, a son of Vita Sackville-West and Harold Nicolson, about his parents' friendship with Woolf and the task of editing her letters.

Schulkind, Jeanne. Introduction to *Moments of Being,* by Virginia Woolf, edited by Jeanne Schulkind, pp. 11-24. New York: Harcourt Brace Jovanovich, 1985.

Maintains that Woolf's autobiographical essays reveal and support the beliefs, values, and sensibility that underlie all of her published works. Schulkind also supplies a preface explaining the addition of new material—a seventy-seven page typescript by Woolf discovered in 1980—to the text, and an "Editor's Note" outlining Woolf's working methods and explaining Schulkind's own editorial processes of selection and organization.

Sharma, Vijay L. *Virginia Woolf as Literary Critic: A Revaluation.* New Delhi: Arnold-Heinemann, 1977, 189 p.

Assesses the validity of Woolf's critical tenets. Sharma pronounces Woolf "that rare critic who not only developed a critical theory of her own but was also armed with intelligence, integrity and life-affirming values."

Silver, Brenda R. " 'Anon' and 'The Reader': Virginia Woolf's Last Essays." *Twentieth-Century Literature* 25, Nos. 3-4 (Fall-Winter 1979): 356-68.

Traces throughout Woolf's letters, notebooks, and diaries her plans for a proposed volume of essays, uncompleted at her death. Several successive drafts of the two essays cited in the title, left in fragmentary form, were reconstructed by Silver based on her research.

————. "Introduction: The Uncommon Reader." In *Virginia Woolf's "Reading Notebooks,"* by Virginia Woolf, edited by Brenda R. Silver, pp. 3-31. Princeton, N.J.: Princeton University Press, 1983.

Pronounces the reading notebooks illustrative of the range and depth of Woolf's literary and social interests. Silver examines ways that Woolf developed ideas for her fiction as well as her critical articles and book reviews in her notebooks.

Steele, Elizabeth. *Virginia Woolf's Literary Sources and Allusions: A Guide to the Essays.* New York: Garland, 1983, 364 p.

Supplies information about the literary sources which Woolf consulted while writing her essays. Steele provides a chart for each of Woolf's principal essays, listing Main Source(s), Supporting Source(s), Important Allusion(s), and Passing Allusion(s).

Twentieth-Century
Literary Criticism

Cumulative Indexes
Volumes 1-43

This Index Includes References to Entries in These Gale Series

Children's Literature Review includes excerpts from reviews, criticism, and commentary on works of authors and illustrators who create books for children.

Classical and Medieval Literature Criticism offers excerpts of criticism on the works of world authors from classical antiquity through the fourteenth century.

Contemporary Authors series encompasses five related series. **Contemporary Authors** provides biographical and bibliographical information on more than 97,000 writers of fiction, nonfiction, poetry, journalism, drama, and film. **Contemporary Authors New Revision Series** provides completely updated information on active authors covered in previously published volumes of *CA.* **Contemporary Authors Permanent Series** consists of updated listings for deceased and inactive authors removed from the original volumes 9-36 when those volumes were revised. **Contemporary Authors Autobiography Series** presents specially commissioned autobiographies by leading contemporary writers. **Contemporary Authors Bibliographical Series** contains primary and secondary bibliographies as well as analytical bibliographical essays by authorities on major modern authors.

Contemporary Literary Criticism presents excerpts of criticism on the works of novelists, poets, dramatists, short story writers, scriptwriters, and other creative writers who are now living or who have died since 1960.

Dictionary of Literary Biography comprises three related series. **Dictionary of Literary Biography** furnishes illustrated overviews of authors' lives and works and places them in the larger perspective of literary history. **Dictionary of Literary Biography Documentary Series** illuminates the careers of major figures through a selection of literary documents, including letters, interviews, and photographs. **Dictionary of Literary Biography Yearbook** summarizes the past year's literary activity and includes updated and new entries on individual authors. A cumulative index to authors and articles is included in each new volume. **Concise Dictionary of Literary Biography,** a six-volume series, collects revised and updated sketches on major American authors that were originally presented in *Dictionary of Literary Biography.*

Drama Criticism provides excerpts of criticism on the works of playwrights of all nationalities and periods of literary history.

Literature Criticism from 1400 to 1800 compiles significant passages from the most noteworthy criticism on authors of the fifteenth through the eighteenth centuries.

Nineteenth-Century Literature Criticism offers significant passages from criticism on authors who died between 1800 and 1899.

Poetry Criticism presents excerpts of criticism on the works of poets from all eras, movements, and nationalities.

Short Story Criticism combines excerpts of criticism on short fiction by writers of all eras and nationalities.

Something about the Author series encompasses three related series. **Something about the Author** contains well-illustrated biographical sketches on authors and illustrators of juvenile and young adult literature from all eras. **Something about the Author Autobiography Series** presents specially commissioned autobiographies by prominent authors and illustrators of books for children and young adults. **Authors & Artists for Young Adults** provides high school and junior high school students with profiles of their favorite creative artists.

Twentieth-Century Literary Criticism contains critical excerpts by the most significant commentators on poets, novelists, short story writers, dramatists, and philosophers who died between 1900 and 1960.

Yesterday's Authors of Books for Children contains heavily illustrated entries on children's writers who died before 1961. Complete in two volumes.

Literary Criticism Series
Cumulative Author Index

This index lists all author entries in the Gale Literary Criticism Series and includes cross-references to other Gale sources. References in the index are identified as follows:

AAYA: *Authors & Artists for Young Adults,* Volumes 1-6
CAAS: *Contemporary Authors Autobiography Series,* Volumes 1-13
CA: *Contemporary Authors* (original series), Volumes 1-133
CABS: *Contemporary Authors Bibliographical Series,* Volumes 1-3
CANR: *Contemporary Authors New Revision Series,* Volumes 1-33
CAP: *Contemporary Authors Permanent Series,* Volumes 1-2
CA-R: *Contemporary Authors* (revised editions), Volumes 1-44
CDALB: *Concise Dictionary of American Literary Biography,* Volumes 1-6
CLC: *Contemporary Literary Criticism,* Volumes 1-68
CLR: *Children's Literature Review,* Volumes 1-24
CMLC: *Classical and Medieval Literature Criticism,* Volumes 1-8
DC: *Drama Criticism,* Volume 1
DLB: *Dictionary of Literary Biography,* Volumes 1-107
DLB-DS: *Dictionary of Literary Biography Documentary Series,* Volumes 1-8
DLB-Y: *Dictionary of Literary Biography Yearbook,* Volumes 1980-1988
LC: *Literature Criticism from 1400 to 1800,* Volumes 1-17
NCLC: *Nineteenth-Century Literature Criticism,* Volumes 1-33
PC: *Poetry Criticism,* Volumes 1-3
SAAS: *Something about the Author Autobiography Series,* Volumes 1-12
SATA: *Something about the Author,* Volumes 1-65
SSC: *Short Story Criticism,* Volumes 1-8
TCLC: *Twentieth-Century Literary Criticism,* Volumes 1-43
YABC: *Yesterday's Authors of Books for Children,* Volumes 1-2

Baker, Elliott 1922- . . . . CLC **8, 61**
See also CANR 2; CA 45-48

Baker, Nicholson 1957- . . . . CLC **61**

Baker, Russell (Wayne) 1925- . . . . . . CLC **31**
See also CANR 11; CA 57-60

Bakshi, Ralph 1938- . . . . CLC **26**
See also CA 112

Bakunin, Mikhail (Alexandrovich)
1814-1876 . . . . NCLC **25**

Baldwin, James (Arthur)
1924-1987 . . . . . CLC **1, 2, 3, 4, 5, 8, 13,
15, 17, 42, 50, 67; DC 1**
See also CANR 3,24; CA 1-4R;
obituary CA 124; CABS 1; SATA 9, 54;
DLB 2, 7, 33; DLB-Y 87;
CDALB 1941-1968; AAYA 4

Ballard, J(ames) G(raham)
1930- . . . . CLC **3, 6, 14, 36; SSC 1**
See also CANR 15; CA 5-8R; DLB 14

Balmont, Konstantin Dmitriyevich
1867-1943 . . . . TCLC **11**
See also CA 109

Balzac, Honore de
1799-1850 . . . . NCLC **5; SSC 5**

Bambara, Toni Cade 1939- . . . . CLC **19**
See also CA 29-32R; DLB 38

Bandanes, Jerome 1937- . . . . CLC **59**

Banim, John 1798-1842 . . . . NCLC **13**

Banim, Michael 1796-1874 . . . . . . NCLC **13**

Banks, Iain 1954- . . . . CLC **34**
See also CA 123

Banks, Lynne Reid 1929- . . . . CLC **23**
See also Reid Banks, Lynne

Banks, Russell 1940- . . . . CLC **37**
See also CANR 19; CA 65-68

Banville, John 1945- . . . . CLC **46**
See also CA 117, 128; DLB 14

Banville, Theodore (Faullain) de
1832-1891 . . . . NCLC **9**

Baraka, Imamu Amiri
1934- . . . . CLC **1, 2, 3, 5, 10, 14, 33**
See also Jones, (Everett) LeRoi
See also DLB 5, 7, 16, 38;
CDALB 1941-1968

Barbellion, W. N. P. 1889-1919 . . . TCLC **24**

Barbera, Jack 1945- . . . . CLC **44**
See also CA 110

Barbey d'Aurevilly, Jules Amedee
1808-1889 . . . . NCLC **1**

Barbusse, Henri 1873-1935 . . . . TCLC **5**
See also CA 105; DLB 65

Barea, Arturo 1897-1957 . . . . TCLC **14**
See also CA 111

Barfoot, Joan 1946- . . . . CLC **18**
See also CA 105

Baring, Maurice 1874-1945 . . . . TCLC **8**
See also CA 105; DLB 34

Barker, Clive 1952- . . . . CLC **52**
See also CA 121

Barker, George (Granville)
1913- . . . . CLC **8, 48**
See also CANR 7; CA 9-12R; DLB 20

Barker, Howard 1946- . . . . CLC **37**
See also CA 102; DLB 13

Barker, Pat 1943- . . . . CLC **32**
See also CA 117, 122

Barlow, Joel 1754-1812 . . . . NCLC **23**
See also DLB 37

Barnard, Mary (Ethel) 1909- . . . . CLC **48**
See also CAP 2; CA 21-22

Barnes, Djuna (Chappell)
1892-1982 . . . CLC **3, 4, 8, 11, 29; SSC 3**
See also CANR 16; CA 9-12R;
obituary CA 107; DLB 4, 9, 45

Barnes, Julian 1946- . . . . CLC **42**
See also CANR 19; CA 102

Barnes, Peter 1931- . . . . CLC **5, 56**
See also CA 65-68; DLB 13

Baroja (y Nessi), Pio 1872-1956 . . . . TCLC **8**
See also CA 104

Barondess, Sue K(aufman) 1926-1977
See Kaufman, Sue
See also CANR 1; CA 1-4R;
obituary CA 69-72

Barrett, (Roger) Syd 1946-
See Pink Floyd

Barrett, William (Christopher)
1913- . . . . CLC **27**
See also CANR 11; CA 13-16R

Barrie, (Sir) J(ames) M(atthew)
1860-1937 . . . . TCLC **2**
See also CLR 16; YABC 1; CA 104;
DLB 10

Barrol, Grady 1953-
See Bograd, Larry

Barry, Philip (James Quinn)
1896-1949 . . . . TCLC **11**
See also CA 109; DLB 7

Barth, John (Simmons)
1930- . . . . . . CLC **1, 2, 3, 5, 7, 9, 10, 14,
27, 51**
See also CANR 5, 23; CA 1-4R; CABS 1;
DLB 2

Barthelme, Donald
1931-1989 . . . . . CLC **1, 2, 3, 5, 6, 8, 13,
23, 46, 59; SSC 2**
See also CANR 20; CA 21-24R, 129;
SATA 7; DLB 2; DLB-Y 80

Barthelme, Frederick 1943- . . . . CLC **36**
See also CA 114, 122; DLB-Y 85

Barthes, Roland 1915-1980 . . . . CLC **24**
See also obituary CA 97-100

Barzun, Jacques (Martin) 1907- . . . . CLC **51**
See also CANR 22; CA 61-64

Bashkirtseff, Marie 1859-1884 . . . NCLC **27**

Basho, Matsuo 1644-1694 . . . . PC **3**

Bassani, Giorgio 1916- . . . . CLC **9**
See also CA 65-68

Bataille, Georges 1897-1962 . . . . . . CLC **29**
See also CA 101; obituary CA 89-92

Bates, H(erbert) E(rnest)
1905-1974 . . . . CLC **46**
See also CA 93-96; obituary CA 45-48

Baudelaire, Charles
1821-1867 . . . . NCLC **6, 29; PC 1**

Baudrillard, Jean 1929- . . . . CLC **60**

Baum, L(yman) Frank 1856-1919 . . . TCLC **7**
See also CLR 15; CA 108; SATA 18;
DLB 22

Baumbach, Jonathan 1933- . . . . . . CLC **6, 23**
See also CAAS 5; CANR 12; CA 13-16R;
DLB-Y 80

Bausch, Richard (Carl) 1945- . . . . . . CLC **51**
See also CA 101

Baxter, Charles 1947- . . . . CLC **45**
See also CA 57-60

Baxter, James K(eir) 1926-1972 . . . . CLC **14**
See also CA 77-80

Bayer, Sylvia 1909-1981
See Glassco, John

Beagle, Peter S(oyer) 1939- . . . . CLC **7**
See also CANR 4; CA 9-12R; DLB-Y 80

Beard, Charles A(ustin)
1874-1948 . . . . TCLC **15**
See also CA 115; SATA 18; DLB 17

Beardsley, Aubrey 1872-1898 . . . . . NCLC **6**

Beattie, Ann 1947- . . . CLC **8, 13, 18, 40, 63**
See also CA 81-84; DLB-Y 82

Beattie, James 1735-1803 . . . . NCLC **25**

Beauvoir, Simone (Lucie Ernestine Marie
Bertrand) de
1908-1986 . . . CLC **1, 2, 4, 8, 14, 31, 44,
50**
See also CANR 28; CA 9-12R;
obituary CA 118; DLB 72; DLB-Y 86

Becker, Jurek 1937- . . . . CLC **7, 19**
See also CA 85-88; DLB 75

Becker, Walter 1950- . . . . CLC **26**

Beckett, Samuel (Barclay)
1906-1989 . . . . . CLC **1, 2, 3, 4, 6, 9, 10,
11, 14, 18, 29, 57, 59**
See also CA 5-8R; DLB 13, 15

Beckford, William 1760-1844 . . . . NCLC **16**
See also DLB 39

Beckman, Gunnel 1910- . . . . CLC **26**
See also CANR 15; CA 33-36R; SATA 6

Becque, Henri 1837-1899 . . . . NCLC **3**

Beddoes, Thomas Lovell
1803-1849 . . . . NCLC **3**

Beecher, Catharine Esther
1800-1878 . . . . NCLC **30**
See also DLB 1

Beecher, John 1904-1980 . . . . CLC **6**
See also CANR 8; CA 5-8R;
obituary CA 105

Beer, Johann 1655-1700 . . . . LC **5**

Beer, Patricia 1919?- . . . . CLC **58**
See also CANR 13; CA 61-64; DLB 40

Beerbohm, (Sir Henry) Max(imilian)
1872-1956 . . . . TCLC **1, 24**
See also CA 104; DLB 34

Behan, Brendan
1923-1964 . . . . CLC **1, 8, 11, 15**
See also CA 73-76; DLB 13

Behn, Aphra 1640?-1689 . . . . LC **1**
See also DLB 39, 80

Behrman, S(amuel) N(athaniel)
1893-1973 . . . . CLC **40**
See also CAP 1; CA 15-16;
obituary CA 45-48; DLB 7, 44

Brown, Rosellen 1939-............ CLC 32
See also CANR 14; CA 77-80

Brown, Sterling A(llen)
1901-1989 .... CLC 1, 23, 59
See also CANR 26; CA 85-88;
obituary CA 27; DLB 48, 51, 63

Brown, William Wells
1816?-1884............. NCLC 2; DC 1
See also DLB 3, 50

Browne, Jackson 1950- .... CLC 21
See also CA 120

Browning, Elizabeth Barrett
1806-1861 .... NCLC 1, 16
See also DLB 32

Browning, Robert
1812-1889 .... NCLC 19; PC 2
See also YABC 1; DLB 32

Browning, Tod 1882-1962 .... CLC 16
See also obituary CA 117

Bruccoli, Matthew J(oseph) 1931- .. CLC 34
See also CANR 7; CA 9-12R

Bruce, Lenny 1925-1966 .... CLC 21
See also Schneider, Leonard Alfred

Brunner, John (Kilian Houston)
1934-..................... CLC 8, 10
See also CAAS 8; CANR 2; CA 1-4R

Brutus, Dennis 1924- .... CLC 43
See also CANR 2; CA 49-52

Bryan, C(ourtlandt) D(ixon) B(arnes)
1936-........................ CLC 29
See also CANR 13; CA 73-76

Bryant, William Cullen
1794-1878 .... NCLC 6
See also DLB 3, 43, 59; CDALB 1640-1865

Bryusov, Valery (Yakovlevich)
1873-1924 .... TCLC 10
See also CA 107

Buchan, John 1875-1940 .... TCLC 41
See also YABC 2; brief entry CA 108;
DLB 34, 70

Buchanan, George 1506-1582 .... LC 4

Buchheim, Lothar-Gunther 1918- .... CLC 6
See also CA 85-88

Buchner, (Karl) Georg
1813-1837 .... NCLC 26

Buchwald, Art(hur) 1925-.......... CLC 33
See also CANR 21; CA 5-8R; SATA 10

Buck, Pearl S(ydenstricker)
1892-1973 .... CLC 7, 11, 18
See also CANR 1; CA 1-4R;
obituary CA 41-44R; SATA 1, 25; DLB 9

Buckler, Ernest 1908-1984........ CLC 13
See also CAP 1; CA 11-12;
obituary CA 114; SATA 47

Buckley, Vincent (Thomas)
1925-1988 .... CLC 57
See also CA 101

Buckley, William F(rank), Jr.
1925- .... CLC 7, 18, 37
See also CANR 1, 24; CA 1-4R; DLB-Y 80

Buechner, (Carl) Frederick
1926- .... CLC 2, 4, 6, 9
See also CANR 11; CA 13-16R; DLB-Y 80

Buell, John (Edward) 1927-........ CLC 10
See also CA 1-4R; DLB 53

Buero Vallejo, Antonio 1916- ... CLC 15, 46
See also CANR 24; CA 106

Bukowski, Charles 1920-.... CLC 2, 5, 9, 41
See also CA 17-20R; DLB 5

Bulgakov, Mikhail (Afanas'evich)
1891-1940 ....TCLC 2, 16
See also CA 105

Bullins, Ed 1935- ....CLC 1, 5, 7
See also CANR 24; CA 49-52; DLB 7, 38

Bulwer-Lytton, (Lord) Edward (George Earle
Lytton) 1803-1873 .... NCLC 1
See also Lytton, Edward Bulwer
See also DLB 21

Bunin, Ivan (Alexeyevich)
1870-1953 .... TCLC 6; SSC 5
See also CA 104

Bunting, Basil 1900-1985.... CLC 10, 39, 47
See also CANR 7; CA 53-56;
obituary CA 115; DLB 20

Bunuel, Luis 1900-1983 .... CLC 16
See also CA 101; obituary CA 110

Bunyan, John 1628-1688 .... LC 4
See also DLB 39

Burgess (Wilson, John) Anthony
1917- ..... CLC 1, 2, 4, 5, 8, 10, 13, 15,
                                22, 40, 62
See also Wilson, John (Anthony) Burgess
See also DLB 14

Burke, Edmund 1729-1797.......... LC 7

Burke, Kenneth (Duva) 1897- .... CLC 2, 24
See also CA 5-8R; DLB 45, 63

Burney, Fanny 1752-1840 .... NCLC 12
See also DLB 39

Burns, Robert 1759-1796............ LC 3

Burns, Tex 1908?-
See L'Amour, Louis (Dearborn)

Burnshaw, Stanley 1906-..... CLC 3, 13, 44
See also CA 9-12R; DLB 48

Burr, Anne 1937- .... CLC 6
See also CA 25-28R

Burroughs, Edgar Rice
1875-1950 .... TCLC 2, 32
See also CA 104; SATA 41; DLB 8

Burroughs, William S(eward)
1914- .... CLC 1, 2, 5, 15, 22, 42
See also CANR 20; CA 9-12R; DLB 2, 8,
16; DLB-Y 81

Busch, Frederick 1941- ... CLC 7, 10, 18, 47
See also CAAS 1; CA 33-36R; DLB 6

Bush, Ronald 19??-................ CLC 34

Butler, Octavia E(stelle) 1947- ..... CLC 38
See also CANR 12, 24; CA 73-76; DLB 33

Butler, Samuel 1612-1680 .... LC 16
See also DLB 101

Butler, Samuel 1835-1902 ...... TCLC 1, 33
See also CA 104; DLB 18, 57

Butor, Michel (Marie Francois)
1926- .... CLC 1, 3, 8, 11, 15
See also CA 9-12R

Buzo, Alexander 1944-............ CLC 61
See also CANR 17; CA 97-100

Buzzati, Dino 1906-1972 .... CLC 36
See also obituary CA 33-36R

Byars, Betsy 1928-............... CLC 35
See also CLR 1, 16; CANR 18; CA 33-36R;
SAAS 1; SATA 4, 46; DLB 52

Byatt, A(ntonia) S(usan Drabble)
1936-.................... CLC 19, 65
See also CANR 13, 33; CA 13-16R;
DLB 14

Byrne, David 1953?-.............. CLC 26

Byrne, John Keyes 1926-
See Leonard, Hugh
See also CA 102

Byron, George Gordon (Noel), Lord Byron
1788-1824 .... NCLC 2, 12

Caballero, Fernan 1796-1877..... NCLC 10

Cabell, James Branch 1879-1958 ... TCLC 6
See also CA 105; DLB 9, 78

Cable, George Washington
1844-1925 .... TCLC 4; SSC 4
See also CA 104; DLB 12, 74

Cabrera Infante, G(uillermo)
1929-.................. CLC 5, 25, 45
See also CANR 29; CA 85-88

CAEdmon fl. 658-680............ CMLC 7

Cage, John (Milton, Jr.) 1912- ..... CLC 41
See also CANR 9; CA 13-16R

Cain, G. 1929-
See Cabrera Infante, G(uillermo)

Cain, James M(allahan)
1892-1977 .... CLC 3, 11, 28
See also CANR 8; CA 17-20R;
obituary CA 73-76

Caldwell, Erskine (Preston)
1903-1987 .... CLC 1, 8, 14, 50, 60
See also CAAS 1; CANR 2; CA 1-4R;
obituary CA 121; DLB 9, 86

Caldwell, (Janet Miriam) Taylor (Holland)
1900-1985 .... CLC 2, 28, 39
See also CANR 5; CA 5-8R;
obituary CA 116

Calhoun, John Caldwell
1782-1850 .... NCLC 15
See also DLB 3

Calisher, Hortense 1911-.... CLC 2, 4, 8, 38
See also CANR 1, 22; CA 1-4R; DLB 2

Callaghan, Morley (Edward)
1903-1990 .... CLC 3, 14, 41, 65
See also CANR 33; CA 9-12R;
obituary CA 132; DLB 68

Calvino, Italo
1923-1985 .... CLC 5, 8, 11, 22, 33, 39;
                                    SSC 3
See also CANR 23; CA 85-88;
obituary CA 116

Cameron, Carey 1952-............ CLC 59

Cameron, Peter 1959-............. CLC 44
See also CA 125

Campana, Dino 1885-1932........ TCLC 20
See also CA 117

Campbell, John W(ood), Jr.
1910-1971 .... CLC 32
See also CAP 2; CA 21-22;
obituary CA 29-32R; DLB 8

Chaplin, Charles (Spencer)
    1889-1977 . . . . **CLC 16**
    See also CA 81-84; obituary CA 73-76;
    DLB 44

Chapman, Graham 1941?- . . . . **CLC 21**
    See also Monty Python
    See also CA 116; obituary CA 169

Chapman, John Jay 1862-1933 . . . . . **TCLC 7**
    See also CA 104

Chappell, Fred 1936- . . . . **CLC 40**
    See also CAAS 4; CANR 8; CA 5-8R;
    DLB 6

Char, Rene (Emile)
    1907-1988 . . . . **CLC 9, 11, 14, 55**
    See also CA 13-16R; obituary CA 124

Charles I 1600-1649 . . . . **LC 13**

Chartier, Emile-Auguste 1868-1951
    See Alain

Charyn, Jerome 1937- . . . . **CLC 5, 8, 18**
    See also CAAS 1; CANR 7; CA 5-8R;
    DLB-Y 83

Chase, Mary (Coyle) 1907-1981 . . . . . . **DC 1**
    See also CA 77-80, 105; SATA 17, 29

Chase, Mary Ellen 1887-1973 . . . . . . **CLC 2**
    See also CAP 1; CA 15-16;
    obituary CA 41-44R; SATA 10

Chateaubriand, Francois Rene de
    1768-1848 . . . . **NCLC 3**

Chatier, Emile-Auguste 1868-1951
    See Alain

Chatterji, Bankim Chandra
    1838-1894 . . . . **NCLC 19**

Chatterji, Saratchandra
    1876-1938 . . . . **TCLC 13**
    See also CA 109

Chatterton, Thomas 1752-1770 . . . . **LC 3**

Chatwin, (Charles) Bruce
    1940-1989 . . . . **CLC 28, 57, 59**
    See also CA 85-88,; obituary CA 127

Chaucer, Geoffrey c. 1340-1400 . . . . . **LC 17**

Chayefsky, Paddy 1923-1981 . . . . **CLC 23**
    See also CA 9-12R; obituary CA 104;
    DLB 7, 44; DLB-Y 81

Chayefsky, Sidney 1923-1981
    See Chayefsky, Paddy
    See also CANR 18

Chedid, Andree 1920- . . . . **CLC 47**

Cheever, John
    1912-1982 . . . . . **CLC 3, 7, 8, 11, 15, 25,**
                                      64; SSC 1
    See also CANR 5, 27; CA 5-8R;
    obituary CA 106; CABS 1; DLB 2;
    DLB-Y 80, 82; CDALB 1941-1968

Cheever, Susan 1943- . . . . **CLC 18, 48**
    See also CA 103; DLB-Y 82

Chekhov, Anton (Pavlovich)
    1860-1904 . . . . . . **TCLC 3, 10, 31; SSC 2**
    See also CA 104, 124

Chernyshevsky, Nikolay Gavrilovich
    1828-1889 . . . . **NCLC 1**

Cherry, Caroline Janice 1942-
    See Cherryh, C. J.

Cherryh, C. J. 1942- . . . . **CLC 35**
    See also CANR 10; CA 65-68; DLB-Y 80

Chesnutt, Charles Waddell
    1858-1932 . . . . **TCLC 5, 39; SSC 7**
    See also CA 106, 125; DLB 12, 50, 78

Chester, Alfred 1929?-1971 . . . . **CLC 49**
    See also obituary CA 33-36R

Chesterton, G(ilbert) K(eith)
    1874-1936 . . . . **TCLC 1, 6; SSC 1**
    See also CA 104; SATA 27; DLB 10, 19,
    34, 70

Chiang Pin-Chin 1904-1986
    See Ding Ling
    See also obituary CA 118

Ch'ien Chung-shu 1910- . . . . **CLC 22**

Child, Lydia Maria 1802-1880 . . . . **NCLC 6**
    See also DLB 1, 74

Child, Philip 1898-1978 . . . . **CLC 19**
    See also CAP 1; CA 13-14; SATA 47

Childress, Alice 1920- . . . . **CLC 12, 15**
    See also CLR 14; CANR 3; CA 45-48;
    SATA 7, 48; DLB 7, 38

Chislett, (Margaret) Anne 1943?- . . . **CLC 34**

Chitty, (Sir) Thomas Willes 1926- . . **CLC 11**
    See also Hinde, Thomas
    See also CA 5-8R

Chomette, Rene 1898-1981
    See Clair, Rene
    See also obituary CA 103

Chopin, Kate (O'Flaherty)
    1851-1904 . . . . **TCLC 5, 14; SSC 8**
    See also CA 122; brief entry CA 104;
    DLB 12, 78; CDALB 1865-1917

Christie, (Dame) Agatha (Mary Clarissa)
    1890-1976 . . . . . . **CLC 1, 6, 8, 12, 39, 48**
    See also CANR 10; CA 17-20R;
    obituary CA 61-64; SATA 36; DLB 13

Christie, (Ann) Philippa 1920-
    See Pearce, (Ann) Philippa
    See also CANR 4; CA 7-8

Christine de Pizan 1365?-1431?. . . . . . . **LC 9**

Chulkov, Mikhail Dmitrievich
    1743-1792 . . . . **LC 2**

Churchill, Caryl 1938- . . . . **CLC 31, 55**
    See also CANR 22; CA 102; DLB 13

Churchill, Charles 1731?-1764. . . . . . . **LC 3**

Chute, Carolyn 1947- . . . . **CLC 39**
    See also CA 123

Ciardi, John (Anthony)
    1916-1986 . . . . **CLC 10, 40, 44**
    See also CAAS 2; CANR 5; CA 5-8R;
    obituary CA 118; SATA 1, 46; DLB 5;
    DLB-Y 86

Cicero, Marcus Tullius
    106 B.C.-43 B.C. . . . . **CMLC 3**

Cimino, Michael 1943?- . . . . **CLC 16**
    See also CA 105

Cioran, E. M. 1911- . . . . **CLC 64**
    See also CA 25-28R

Clair, Rene 1898-1981 . . . . **CLC 20**
    See also Chomette, Rene

Clampitt, Amy 19??- . . . . **CLC 32**
    See also CA 110

Clancy, Tom 1947- . . . . **CLC 45**
    See also CA 125

Clare, John 1793-1864 . . . . **NCLC 9**
    See also DLB 55

Clark, (Robert) Brian 1932- . . . . **CLC 29**
    See also CA 41-44R

Clark, Eleanor 1913- . . . . **CLC 5, 19**
    See also CA 9-12R; DLB 6

Clark, John Pepper 1935- . . . . **CLC 38**
    See also CANR 16; CA 65-68

Clark, Mavis Thorpe 1912?- . . . . **CLC 12**
    See also CANR 8; CA 57-60; SAAS 5;
    SATA 8

Clark, Walter Van Tilburg
    1909-1971 . . . . **CLC 28**
    See also CA 9-12R; obituary CA 33-36R;
    SATA 8; DLB 9

Clarke, Arthur C(harles)
    1917- . . . **CLC 1, 4, 13, 18, 35; SSC 3**
    See also CANR 2; CA 1-4R; SATA 13

Clarke, Austin 1896-1974. . . . . **CLC 6, 9**
    See also CANR 14; CAP 2; CA 29-32;
    obituary CA 49-52; DLB 10, 20, 53

Clarke, Austin (Ardinel) C(hesterfield)
    1934- . . . . **CLC 8, 53**
    See also CANR 14; CA 25-28R; DLB 53

Clarke, Gillian 1937- . . . . **CLC 61**
    See also CA 106; DLB 40

Clarke, Marcus (Andrew Hislop)
    1846-1881 . . . . **NCLC 19**

Clarke, Shirley 1925- . . . . **CLC 16**

Clash, The . . . . **CLC 30**

Claudel, Paul (Louis Charles Marie)
    1868-1955 . . . . **TCLC 2, 10**
    See also CA 104

Clavell, James (duMaresq)
    1924- . . . . **CLC 6, 25**
    See also CANR 26; CA 25-28R

Clayman. Gregory 1974?- . . . . **CLC 65**

Cleaver, (Leroy) Eldridge 1935- . . . . **CLC 30**
    See also CANR 16; CA 21-24R

Cleese, John 1939- . . . . **CLC 21**
    See also Monty Python
    See also CA 112, 116

Cleland, John 1709-1789 . . . . **LC 2**
    See also DLB 39

Clemens, Samuel Langhorne
    1835-1910 . . . . . . **TCLC 6, 12, 19; SSC 6**
    See also Twain, Mark
    See also YABC 2; CA 104; DLB 11, 12, 23,
    64, 74; CDALB 1865-1917

Cliff, Jimmy 1948- . . . . **CLC 21**

Clifton, Lucille (Thelma)
    1936- . . . . **CLC 19, 66**
    See also CLR 5; CANR 2, 24; CA 49-52;
    SATA 20; DLB 5, 41

Clough, Arthur Hugh 1819-1861. . **NCLC 27**
    See also DLB 32

Clutha, Janet Paterson Frame 1924-
    See Frame (Clutha), Janet (Paterson)
    See also CANR 2; CA 1-4R

Coburn, D(onald) L(ee) 1938- . . . . . . **CLC 10**
    See also CA 89-92

Cocteau, Jean (Maurice Eugene Clement)
    1889-1963 . . . . **CLC 1, 8, 15, 16, 43**
    See also CAP 2; CA 25-28; DLB 65

Deighton, Len 1929-...... CLC 4, 7, 22, 46
See also Deighton, Leonard Cyril
See also DLB 87

Deighton, Leonard Cyril 1929-
See Deighton, Len
See also CANR 19; CA 9-12R

De la Mare, Walter (John)
1873-1956 .... TCLC 4
See also CLR 23; CA 110; SATA 16;
DLB 19

Delaney, Shelagh 1939-........... CLC 29
See also CA 17-20R; DLB 13

Delany, Mary (Granville Pendarves)
1700-1788 .... LC 12

Delany, Samuel R(ay, Jr.)
1942-.................. CLC 8, 14, 38
See also CA 81-84; DLB 8, 33

de la Ramee, Marie Louise 1839-1908
See Ouida
See also SATA 20

De la Roche, Mazo 1885-1961 ..... CLC 14
See also CA 85-88; DLB 68

Delbanco, Nicholas (Franklin)
1942-..................... CLC 6, 13
See also CAAS 2; CA 17-20R; DLB 6

del Castillo, Michel 1933- .... CLC 38
See also CA 109

Deledda, Grazia 1871-1936 .... TCLC 23
See also CA 123

Delibes (Setien), Miguel 1920- ... CLC 8, 18
See also CANR 1; CA 45-48

DeLillo, Don
1936- .... CLC 8, 10, 13, 27, 39, 54
See also CANR 21; CA 81-84; DLB 6

De Lisser, H(erbert) G(eorge)
1878-1944 .... TCLC 12
See also CA 109

Deloria, Vine (Victor), Jr. 1933-.... CLC 21
See also CANR 5, 20; CA 53-56; SATA 21

Del Vecchio, John M(ichael)
1947-..................... CLC 29
See also CA 110

de Man, Paul 1919-1983 .... CLC 55
See also obituary CA 111; DLB 67

De Marinis, Rick 1934-........... CLC 54
See also CANR 9, 25; CA 57-60

Demby, William 1922-........... CLC 53
See also CA 81-84; DLB 33

Denby, Edwin (Orr) 1903-1983..... CLC 48
See also obituary CA 110

Dennis, John 1657-1734........... LC 11

Dennis, Nigel (Forbes) 1912-........ CLC 8
See also CA 25-28R; obituary CA 129;
DLB 13, 15

De Palma, Brian 1940-........... CLC 20
See also CA 109

De Quincey, Thomas 1785-1859 ... NCLC 4

Deren, Eleanora 1908-1961
See Deren, Maya
See also obituary CA 111

Deren, Maya 1908-1961.......... CLC 16
See also Deren, Eleanora

Derleth, August (William)
1909-1971 .... CLC 31
See also CANR 4; CA 1-4R;
obituary CA 29-32R; SATA 5; DLB 9

Derrida, Jacques 1930-........... CLC 24
See also CA 124, 127

Desai, Anita 1937- .... CLC 19, 37
See also CA 81-84

De Saint-Luc, Jean 1909-1981
See Glassco, John

De Sica, Vittorio 1902-1974 .... CLC 20
See also obituary CA 117

Desnos, Robert 1900-1945........ TCLC 22
See also CA 121

Destouches, Louis-Ferdinand-Auguste
1894-1961
See Celine, Louis-Ferdinand
See also CA 85-88

Deutsch, Babette 1895-1982 .... CLC 18
See also CANR 4; CA 1-4R;
obituary CA 108; SATA 1;
obituary SATA 33; DLB 45

Devenant, William 1606-1649 .... LC 13

Devkota, Laxmiprasad
1909-1959 .... TCLC 23
See also CA 123

DeVoto, Bernard (Augustine)
1897-1955 .... TCLC 29
See also CA 113; DLB 9

De Vries, Peter
1910-........ CLC 1, 2, 3, 7, 10, 28, 46
See also CA 17-20R; DLB 6; DLB-Y 82

Dexter, Pete 1943-............ CLC 34, 55
See also CA 127

Diamond, Neil (Leslie) 1941-....... CLC 30
See also CA 108

Dick, Philip K(indred)
1928-1982 .... CLC 10, 30
See also CANR 2, 16; CA 49-52;
obituary CA 106; DLB 8

Dickens, Charles
1812-1870 .... NCLC 3, 8, 18, 26
See also SATA 15; DLB 21, 55, 70

Dickey, James (Lafayette)
1923- .... CLC 1, 2, 4, 7, 10, 15, 47
See also CANR 10; CA 9-12R; CABS 2;
DLB 5; DLB-Y 82; DLB-DS 7

Dickey, William 1928-.......... CLC 3, 28
See also CANR 24; CA 9-12R; DLB 5

Dickinson, Charles 1952-......... CLC 49

Dickinson, Emily (Elizabeth)
1830-1886 .... NCLC 21; PC 1
See also SATA 29; DLB 1;
CDALB 1865-1917

Dickinson, Peter (Malcolm de Brissac)
1927-.................... CLC 12, 35
See also CA 41-44R; SATA 5; DLB 87

Didion, Joan 1934-..... CLC 1, 3, 8, 14, 32
See also CANR 14; CA 5-8R; DLB 2;
DLB-Y 81, 86; CDALB 1968-1987

Dillard, Annie 1945-........... CLC 9, 60
See also CANR 3; CA 49-52; SATA 10;
DLB-Y 80

Dillard, R(ichard) H(enry) W(ilde)
1937-..................... CLC 5
See also CAAS 7; CANR 10; CA 21-24R;
DLB 5

Dillon, Eilis 1920-............... CLC 17
See also CLR 26; CAAS 3; CANR 4;
CA 9-12R; SATA 2

Dinesen, Isak
1885-1962 .... CLC 10, 29; SSC 7
See also Blixen, Karen (Christentze
Dinesen)
See also CANR 22

Ding Ling 1904-1986 .... CLC 68

Disch, Thomas M(ichael) 1940-... CLC 7, 36
See also CAAS 4; CANR 17; CA 21-24R;
SATA 54; DLB 8

Disraeli, Benjamin 1804-1881 ..... NCLC 2
See also DLB 21, 55

Dixon, Paige 1911-
See Corcoran, Barbara

Dixon, Stephen 1936-............. CLC 52
See also CANR 17; CA 89-92

Doblin, Alfred 1878-1957........ TCLC 13
See also Doeblin, Alfred

Dobrolyubov, Nikolai Alexandrovich
1836-1861 .... NCLC 5

Dobyns, Stephen 1941-........... CLC 37
See also CANR 2, 18; CA 45-48

Doctorow, E(dgar) L(aurence)
1931-..... CLC 6, 11, 15, 18, 37, 44, 65
See also CANR 2, 33; CA 45-48; DLB 2,
28; DLB-Y 80; CDALB 1968-1987

Dodgson, Charles Lutwidge 1832-1898
See Carroll, Lewis
See also YABC 2

Doeblin, Alfred 1878-1957........ TCLC 13
See also CA 110; DLB 66

Doerr, Harriet 1910- .... CLC 34
See also CA 117, 122

Donaldson, Stephen R. 1947-...... CLC 46
See also CANR 13; CA 89-92

Donleavy, J(ames) P(atrick)
1926-............. CLC 1, 4, 6, 10, 45
See also CANR 24; CA 9-12R; DLB 6

Donnadieu, Marguerite 1914-
See Duras, Marguerite

Donne, John 1572?-1631 ...... LC 10; PC 1

Donnell, David 1939?- .... CLC 34

Donoso, Jose 1924-........ CLC 4, 8, 11, 32
See also CA 81-84

Donovan, John 1928- .... CLC 35
See also CLR 3; CA 97-100; SATA 29

Doolittle, Hilda 1886-1961
See H(ilda) D(oolittle)
See also CA 97-100; DLB 4, 45

Dorfman, Ariel 1942-............. CLC 48
See also CA 124

Dorn, Ed(ward Merton) 1929-... CLC 10, 18
See also CA 93-96; DLB 5

Dos Passos, John (Roderigo)
1896-1970 ... CLC 1, 4, 8, 11, 15, 25, 34
See also CANR 3; CA 1-4R;
obituary CA 29-32R; DLB 4, 9;
DLB-DS 1

Edwards, G(erald) B(asil)
    1899-1976 . . . . **CLC 25**
    See also obituary CA 110

Edwards, Gus 1939- . . . . **CLC 43**
    See also CA 108

Edwards, Jonathan 1703-1758 . . . . **LC 7**
    See also DLB 24

Ehle, John (Marsden, Jr.) 1925- . . . . **CLC 27**
    See also CA 9-12R

Ehrenburg, Ilya (Grigoryevich)
    1891-1967 . . . . **CLC 18, 34, 62**
    See also CA 102; obituary CA 25-28R

Eich, Guenter 1907-1971
    See also CA 111; obituary CA 93-96

Eich, Gunter 1907-1971 . . . . **CLC 15**
    See also Eich, Guenter
    See also DLB 69

Eichendorff, Joseph Freiherr von
    1788-1857 . . . . **NCLC 8**
    See also DLB 90

Eigner, Larry 1927- . . . . **CLC 9**
    See also Eigner, Laurence (Joel)
    See also DLB 5

Eigner, Laurence (Joel) 1927-
    See Eigner, Larry
    See also CANR 6; CA 9-12R

Eiseley, Loren (Corey) 1907-1977 . . . . **CLC 7**
    See also CANR 6; CA 1-4R;
    obituary CA 73-76

Eisenstadt, Jill 1963- . . . . **CLC 50**

Ekeloef, Gunnar (Bengt) 1907-1968
    See Ekelof, Gunnar (Bengt)
    See also obituary CA 25-28R

Ekelof, Gunnar (Bengt) 1907-1968 . . **CLC 27**
    See also Ekeloef, Gunnar (Bengt)

Ekwensi, Cyprian (Odiatu Duaka)
    1921- . . . . **CLC 4**
    See also CANR 18; CA 29-32R

Eliade, Mircea 1907-1986 . . . . **CLC 19**
    See also CA 65-68; obituary CA 119

Eliot, George 1819-1880 . . . . **NCLC 4, 13, 23**
    See also DLB 21, 35, 55

Eliot, John 1604-1690 . . . . **LC 5**
    See also DLB 24

Eliot, T(homas) S(tearns)
    1888-1965 . . . . **CLC 1, 2, 3, 6, 9, 10, 13,**
               15, 24, 34, 41, 55, 57
    See also CA 5-8R; obituary CA 25-28R;
    DLB 7, 10, 45, 63; DLB-Y 88

Elizabeth 1866-1941 . . . . **TCLC 41**
    See also Russell, Mary Annette Beauchamp

Elkin, Stanley (Lawrence)
    1930- . . . . **CLC 4, 6, 9, 14, 27, 51**
    See also CANR 8; CA 9-12R; DLB 2, 28;
    DLB-Y 80

Elledge, Scott 19??- . . . . **CLC 34**

Elliott, George P(aul) 1918-1980 . . . . . **CLC 2**
    See also CANR 2; CA 1-4R;
    obituary CA 97-100

Elliott, Janice 1931- . . . . **CLC 47**
    See also CANR 8; CA 13-16R; DLB 14

Elliott, Sumner Locke 1917- . . . . **CLC 38**
    See also CANR 2, 21; CA 5-8R

Ellis, A. E. 19??- . . . . **CLC 7**

Ellis, Alice Thomas 19??- . . . . **CLC 40**

Ellis, Bret Easton 1964- . . . . **CLC 39**
    See also CA 118, 123

Ellis, (Henry) Havelock
    1859-1939 . . . . **TCLC 14**
    See also CA 109

Ellis, Trey 1964- . . . . **CLC 55**

Ellison, Harlan (Jay) 1934- . . . **CLC 1, 13, 42**
    See also CANR 5; CA 5-8R; DLB 8

Ellison, Ralph (Waldo)
    1914- . . . . **CLC 1, 3, 11, 54**
    See also CANR 24; CA 9-12R; DLB 2, 76;
    CDALB 1941-1968

Ellmann, Lucy 1956- . . . . **CLC 61**
    See also CA 128

Ellmann, Richard (David)
    1918-1987 . . . . **CLC 50**
    See also CANR 2; CA 1-4R;
    obituary CA 122; DLB-Y 87

Elman, Richard 1934- . . . . **CLC 19**
    See also CAAS 3; CA 17-20R

Eluard, Paul 1895-1952 . . . . **TCLC 7, 41**
    See also Grindel, Eugene

Elyot, (Sir) Thomas 1490?-1546 . . . . . **LC 11**

Elytis, Odysseus 1911- . . . . **CLC 15, 49**
    See also CA 102

Emecheta, (Florence Onye) Buchi
    1944- . . . . **CLC 14, 48**
    See also CA 81-84

Emerson, Ralph Waldo
    1803-1882 . . . . **NCLC 1**
    See also DLB 1, 59, 73; CDALB 1640-1865

Eminescu, Mihai 1850-1889 . . . . . . **NCLC 33**

Empson, William
    1906-1984 . . . . **CLC 3, 8, 19, 33, 34**
    See also CA 17-20R; obituary CA 112;
    DLB 20

Enchi, Fumiko (Veda) 1905-1986 . . . **CLC 31**
    See also obituary CA 121

Ende, Michael 1930- . . . . **CLC 31**
    See also CLR 14; CA 118, 124; SATA 42;
    DLB 75

Endo, Shusaku 1923- . . . . . **CLC 7, 14, 19, 54**
    See also CANR 21; CA 29-32R

Engel, Marian 1933-1985 . . . . **CLC 36**
    See also CANR 12; CA 25-28R; DLB 53

Engelhardt, Frederick 1911-1986
    See Hubbard, L(afayette) Ron(ald)

Enright, D(ennis) J(oseph)
    1920- . . . . **CLC 4, 8, 31**
    See also CANR 1; CA 1-4R; SATA 25;
    DLB 27

Enzensberger, Hans Magnus
    1929- . . . . **CLC 43**
    See also CA 116, 119

Ephron, Nora 1941- . . . . **CLC 17, 31**
    See also CANR 12; CA 65-68

Epstein, Daniel Mark 1948- . . . . **CLC 7**
    See also CANR 2; CA 49-52

Epstein, Jacob 1956- . . . . **CLC 19**
    See also CA 114

Epstein, Joseph 1937- . . . . **CLC 39**
    See also CA 112, 119

Epstein, Leslie 1938- . . . . **CLC 27**
    See also CANR 23; CA 73-76

Equiano, Olaudah 1745?-1797 . . . . **LC 16**
    See also DLB 37, 50

Erasmus, Desiderius 1469?-1536 . . . . . **LC 16**

Erdman, Paul E(mil) 1932- . . . . **CLC 25**
    See also CANR 13; CA 61-64

Erdrich, Louise 1954- . . . . **CLC 39, 54**
    See also CA 114

Erenburg, Ilya (Grigoryevich) 1891-1967
    See Ehrenburg, Ilya (Grigoryevich)

Erickson, Steve 1950- . . . . **CLC 64**
    See also CA 129

Eseki, Bruno 1919-
    See Mphahlele, Ezekiel

Esenin, Sergei (Aleksandrovich)
    1895-1925 . . . . **TCLC 4**
    See also CA 104

Eshleman, Clayton 1935- . . . . **CLC 7**
    See also CAAS 6; CA 33-36R; DLB 5

Espriu, Salvador 1913-1985 . . . . **CLC 9**
    See also obituary CA 115

Estleman, Loren D. 1952- . . . . **CLC 48**
    See also CA 85-88

Evans, Marian 1819-1880
    See Eliot, George

Evans, Mary Ann 1819-1880
    See Eliot, George

Evarts, Esther 1900-1972
    See Benson, Sally

Everett, Percival L. 1957?- . . . . **CLC 57**
    See also CA 129

Everson, Ronald G(ilmour) 1903- . . . **CLC 27**
    See also CA 17-20R; DLB 88

Everson, William (Oliver)
    1912- . . . . **CLC 1, 5, 14**
    See also CANR 20; CA 9-12R; DLB 5, 16

Evtushenko, Evgenii (Aleksandrovich) 1933-
    See Yevtushenko, Yevgeny

Ewart, Gavin (Buchanan)
    1916- . . . . **CLC 13, 46**
    See also CANR 17; CA 89-92; DLB 40

Ewers, Hanns Heinz 1871-1943 . . . **TCLC 12**
    See also CA 109

Ewing, Frederick R. 1918-
    See Sturgeon, Theodore (Hamilton)

Exley, Frederick (Earl) 1929- . . . . **CLC 6, 11**
    See also CA 81-84; DLB-Y 81

Ezekiel, Nissim 1924- . . . . **CLC 61**
    See also CA 61-64

Ezekiel, Tish O'Dowd 1943- . . . . **CLC 34**

Fagen, Donald 1948- . . . . **CLC 26**

Fair, Ronald L. 1932- . . . . **CLC 18**
    See also CANR 25; CA 69-72; DLB 33

Fairbairns, Zoe (Ann) 1948- . . . . **CLC 32**
    See also CANR 21; CA 103

Fairfield, Cicily Isabel 1892-1983
    See West, Rebecca

Fallaci, Oriana 1930- . . . . **CLC 11**
    See also CANR 15; CA 77-80

Faludy, George 1913- . . . . **CLC 42**
    See also CA 21-24R

Fante, John   1909-1983 . . . . CLC 60
See also CANR 23; CA 69-72;
    obituary CA 109; DLB-Y 83

Farah, Nuruddin   1945- . . . . CLC 53
See also CA 106

Fargue, Leon-Paul   1876-1947 . . . . . TCLC 11
See also CA 109

Farigoule, Louis   1885-1972
See Romains, Jules

Farina, Richard   1937?-1966 . . . . CLC 9
See also CA 81-84; obituary CA 25-28R

Farley, Walter   1920- . . . . CLC 17
See also CANR 8; CA 17-20R; SATA 2, 43;
    DLB 22

Farmer, Philip Jose   1918- . . . . CLC 1, 19
See also CANR 4; CA 1-4R; DLB 8

Farrell, J(ames) G(ordon)
    1935-1979 . . . . CLC 6
See also CA 73-76; obituary CA 89-92;
    DLB 14

Farrell, James T(homas)
    1904-1979 . . . . CLC 1, 4, 8, 11, 66
See also CANR 9; CA 5-8R;
    obituary CA 89-92; DLB 4, 9, 86;
    DLB-DS 2

Farrell, M. J.   1904-
See Keane, Molly

Fassbinder, Rainer Werner
    1946-1982 . . . . CLC 20
See also CA 93-96; obituary CA 106

Fast, Howard (Melvin)   1914- . . . . . . CLC 23
See also CANR 1; CA 1-4R; SATA 7;
    DLB 9

Faulkner, William (Cuthbert)
    1897-1962 . . . .   CLC 1, 3, 6, 8, 9, 11, 14,
                        18, 28, 52, 68; SSC 1
See also CANR 33; CA 81-84; DLB 9, 11,
    44, 102; DLB-Y 86; DLB-DS 2;
    CDALB 1929-1941

Fauset, Jessie Redmon
    1884?-1961 . . . . CLC 19, 54
See also CA 109; DLB 51

Faust, Irvin   1924- . . . . CLC 8
See also CA 33-36R; DLB 2, 28; DLB-Y 80

Fearing, Kenneth (Flexner)
    1902-1961 . . . . CLC 51
See also CA 93-96; DLB 9

Federman, Raymond   1928- . . . . . . CLC 6, 47
See also CANR 10; CA 17-20R; DLB-Y 80

Federspiel, J(urg) F.   1931- . . . . CLC 42

Feiffer, Jules   1929- . . . . CLC 2, 8, 64
See also CANR 30; CA 17-20R; SATA 8,
    61; DLB 7, 44; AAYA 3

Feinberg, David B.   1956- . . . . CLC 59

Feinstein, Elaine   1930- . . . . CLC 36
See also CAAS 1; CA 69-72; DLB 14, 40

Feke, Gilbert David   1976?- . . . . CLC 65

Feldman, Irving (Mordecai)   1928- . . . . CLC 7
See also CANR 1; CA 1-4R

Fellini, Federico   1920- . . . . CLC 16
See also CA 65-68

Felsen, Gregor   1916-
See Felsen, Henry Gregor

Felsen, Henry Gregor   1916- . . . . CLC 17
See also CANR 1; CA 1-4R; SAAS 2;
    SATA 1

Fenton, James (Martin)   1949- . . . . . . CLC 32
See also CA 102; DLB 40

Ferber, Edna   1887-1968 . . . . CLC 18
See also CA 5-8R; obituary CA 25-28R;
    SATA 7; DLB 9, 28, 86

Ferguson, Samuel   1810-1886 . . . . . NCLC 33
See also DLB 32

Ferlinghetti, Lawrence (Monsanto)
    1919?- . . . . CLC 2, 6, 10, 27; PC 1
See also CANR 3; CA 5-8R; DLB 5, 16;
    CDALB 1941-1968

Ferrier, Susan (Edmonstone)
    1782-1854 . . . . NCLC 8

Ferrigno, Robert   19??- . . . . CLC 65

Feuchtwanger, Lion   1884-1958 . . . . . TCLC 3
See also CA 104; DLB 66

Feydeau, Georges   1862-1921 . . . . . . TCLC 22
See also CA 113

Ficino, Marsilio   1433-1499 . . . . LC 12

Fiedler, Leslie A(aron)
    1917- . . . . CLC 4, 13, 24
See also CANR 7; CA 9-12R; DLB 28, 67

Field, Andrew   1938- . . . . CLC 44
See also CANR 25; CA 97-100

Field, Eugene   1850-1895 . . . . NCLC 3
See also SATA 16; DLB 21, 23, 42

Field, Michael . . . . TCLC 43

Fielding, Henry   1707-1754 . . . . LC 1
See also DLB 39, 84

Fielding, Sarah   1710-1768 . . . . LC 1
See also DLB 39

Fierstein, Harvey   1954- . . . . CLC 33
See also CA 123, 129

Figes, Eva   1932- . . . . CLC 31
See also CANR 4; CA 53-56; DLB 14

Finch, Robert (Duer Claydon)
    1900- . . . . CLC 18
See also CANR 9, 24; CA 57-60; DLB 88

Findley, Timothy   1930- . . . . CLC 27
See also CANR 12; CA 25-28R; DLB 53

Fink, Janis   1951-
See Ian, Janis

Firbank, Louis   1944-
See Reed, Lou
See also CA 117

Firbank, (Arthur Annesley) Ronald
    1886-1926 . . . . TCLC 1
See also CA 104; DLB 36

Fisher, Roy   1930- . . . . CLC 25
See also CANR 16; CA 81-84; DLB 40

Fisher, Rudolph   1897-1934 . . . . TCLC 11
See also CA 107; DLB 51

Fisher, Vardis (Alvero)   1895-1968 . . . . CLC 7
See also CA 5-8R; obituary CA 25-28R;
    DLB 9

FitzGerald, Edward   1809-1883 . . . . NCLC 9
See also DLB 32

Fitzgerald, F(rancis) Scott (Key)
    1896-1940 . . . . TCLC 1, 6, 14, 28; SSC 6
See also CA 110, 123; DLB 4, 9, 86;
    DLB-Y 81; DLB-DS 1;
    CDALB 1917-1929

Fitzgerald, Penelope   1916- . . . CLC 19, 51, 61
See also CAAS 10; CA 85-88,; DLB 14

Fitzgerald, Robert (Stuart)
    1910-1985 . . . . CLC 39
See also CANR 1; CA 2R;
    obituary CA 114; DLB-Y 80

FitzGerald, Robert D(avid)   1902- . . . CLC 19
See also CA 17-20R

Flanagan, Thomas (James Bonner)
    1923- . . . . CLC 25, 52
See also CA 108; DLB-Y 80

Flaubert, Gustave
    1821-1880 . . . . NCLC 2, 10, 19

Flecker, (Herman) James Elroy
    1884-1913 . . . . TCLC 43
See also CA 109; DLB 10, 19

Fleming, Ian (Lancaster)
    1908-1964 . . . . CLC 3, 30
See also CA 5-8R; SATA 9; DLB 87

Fleming, Thomas J(ames)   1927- . . . . CLC 37
See also CANR 10; CA 5-8R; SATA 8

Fletcher, John Gould   1886-1950 . . . TCLC 35
See also CA 107; DLB 4, 45

Flieg, Hellmuth
See Heym, Stefan

Flying Officer X   1905-1974
See Bates, H(erbert) E(rnest)

Fo, Dario   1929- . . . . CLC 32
See also CA 116

Follett, Ken(neth Martin)   1949- . . . . CLC 18
See also CANR 13; CA 81-84; DLB-Y 81

Fontane, Theodor   1819-1898 . . . . . NCLC 26

Foote, Horton   1916- . . . . CLC 51
See also CA 73-76; DLB 26

Forbes, Esther   1891-1967 . . . . CLC 12
See also CAP 1; CA 13-14;
    obituary CA 25-28R; SATA 2; DLB 22

Forche, Carolyn   1950- . . . . CLC 25
See also CA 109, 117; DLB 5

Ford, Ford Madox
    1873-1939 . . . . TCLC 1, 15, 39
See also CA 104; DLB 34

Ford, John   1895-1973 . . . . CLC 16
See also obituary CA 45-48

Ford, Richard   1944- . . . . CLC 46
See also CANR 11; CA 69-72

Foreman, Richard   1937- . . . . CLC 50
See also CA 65-68

Forester, C(ecil) S(cott)
    1899-1966 . . . . CLC 35
See also CA 73-76; obituary CA 25-28R;
    SATA 13

Forman, James D(ouglas)   1932- . . . . CLC 21
See also CANR 4, 19; CA 9-12R; SATA 8,
    21

Fornes, Maria Irene   1930- . . . . . . CLC 39, 61
See also CANR 28; CA 25-28R; DLB 7

Forrest, Leon   1937- . . . . CLC 4
See also CAAS 7; CA 89-92; DLB 33

Gardam, Jane 1928- .... CLC **43**
See also CLR 12; CANR 2, 18; CA 49-52;
SATA 28, 39; DLB 14

Gardner, Herb 1934- .... CLC **44**

Gardner, John (Champlin, Jr.)
1933-1982 .... CLC **2, 3, 5, 7, 8, 10, 18,
28, 34; SSC 7**
See also CA 65-68; obituary CA 107;
obituary SATA 31, 40; DLB 2; DLB-Y 82

Gardner, John (Edmund) 1926- ..... CLC **30**
See also CANR 15; CA 103

Gardons, S. S. 1926-
See Snodgrass, W(illiam) D(e Witt)

Garfield, Leon 1921- .... CLC **12**
See also CA 17-20R; SATA 1, 32

Garland, (Hannibal) Hamlin
1860-1940 .... TCLC **3**
See also CA 104; DLB 12, 71, 78

Garneau, Hector (de) Saint Denys
1912-1943 .... TCLC **13**
See also CA 111; DLB 88

Garner, Alan 1935- .... CLC **17**
See also CLR 20; CANR 15; CA 73-76;
SATA 18

Garner, Hugh 1913-1979 .... CLC **13**
See also CA 69-72; DLB 68

Garnett, David 1892-1981 .... CLC **3**
See also CANR 17; CA 5-8R;
obituary CA 103; DLB 34

Garrett, George (Palmer, Jr.)
1929- .... CLC **3, 11, 51**
See also CAAS 5; CANR 1; CA 1-4R;
DLB 2, 5; DLB-Y 83

Garrick, David 1717-1779 .... LC **15**
See also DLB 84

Garrigue, Jean 1914-1972 .... CLC **2, 8**
See also CANR 20; CA 5-8R;
obituary CA 37-40R

Garvey, Marcus 1887-1940 ...... TCLC **41**
See also CA 124; brief entry CA 120

Gary, Romain 1914-1980 .... CLC **25**
See also Kacew, Romain

Gascar, Pierre 1916- .... CLC **11**
See also Fournier, Pierre

Gascoyne, David (Emery) 1916- .... CLC **45**
See also CANR 10; CA 65-68; DLB 20

Gaskell, Elizabeth Cleghorn
1810-1865 .... NCLC **5**
See also DLB 21

Gass, William H(oward)
1924- .... CLC **1, 2, 8, 11, 15, 39**
See also CA 17-20R; DLB 2

Gates, Henry Louis, Jr. 1950- ...... CLC **65**
See also CANR 25; CA 109; DLB 67

Gautier, Theophile 1811-1872 ..... NCLC **1**

Gaye, Marvin (Pentz) 1939-1984 ... CLC **26**
See also obituary CA 112

Gebler, Carlo (Ernest) 1954- .... CLC **39**
See also CA 119

Gee, Maggie 19??- .... CLC **57**

Gee, Maurice (Gough) 1931- .... CLC **29**
See also CA 97-100; SATA 46

Gelbart, Larry 1923?- .... CLC **21, 61**
See also CA 73-76

Gelber, Jack 1932- .... CLC **1, 6, 14, 60**
See also CANR 2; CA 1-4R; DLB 7

Gellhorn, Martha (Ellis) 1908- .. CLC **14, 60**
See also CA 77-80; DLB-Y 82

Genet, Jean
1910-1986 ... CLC **1, 2, 5, 10, 14, 44, 46**
See also CANR 18; CA 13-16R; DLB 72;
DLB-Y 86

Gent, Peter 1942- .... CLC **29**
See also CA 89-92; DLB 72; DLB-Y 82

George, Jean Craighead 1919- ...... CLC **35**
See also CLR 1; CA 5-8R; SATA 2;
DLB 52

George, Stefan (Anton)
1868-1933 .... TCLC **2, 14**
See also CA 104

Gerhardi, William (Alexander) 1895-1977
See Gerhardie, William (Alexander)

Gerhardie, William (Alexander)
1895-1977 .... CLC **5**
See also CANR 18; CA 25-28R;
obituary CA 73-76; DLB 36

Gertler, T(rudy) 1946?- .... CLC **34**
See also CA 116

Gessner, Friedrike Victoria 1910-1980
See Adamson, Joy(-Friederike Victoria)

Ghelderode, Michel de
1898-1962 .... CLC **6, 11**
See also CA 85-88

Ghiselin, Brewster 1903- .... CLC **23**
See also CANR 13; CA 13-16R

Ghose, Zulfikar 1935- .... CLC **42**
See also CA 65-68

Ghosh, Amitav 1943- .... CLC **44**

Giacosa, Giuseppe 1847-1906 ...... TCLC **7**
See also CA 104

Gibbon, Lewis Grassic 1901-1935 ... TCLC **4**
See also Mitchell, James Leslie

Gibbons, Kaye 1960- .... CLC **50**

Gibran, (Gibran) Kahlil
1883-1931 .... TCLC **1, 9**
See also CA 104

Gibson, William 1914- .... CLC **23**
See also CANR 9; CA 9-12R; DLB 7

Gibson, William 1948- .... CLC **39, 63**
See also CA 126

Gide, Andre (Paul Guillaume)
1869-1951 .... TCLC **5, 12, 36**
See also CA 104, 124; DLB 65

Gifford, Barry (Colby) 1946- .... CLC **34**
See also CANR 9; CA 65-68

Gilbert, (Sir) W(illiam) S(chwenck)
1836-1911 .... TCLC **3**
See also CA 104; SATA 36

Gilbreth, Ernestine 1908-
See Carey, Ernestine Gilbreth

Gilbreth, Frank B(unker), Jr.
1911- .... CLC **17**
See also CA 9-12R; SATA 2

Gilchrist, Ellen 1935- .... CLC **34, 48**
See also CA 113, 116

Giles, Molly 1942- .... CLC **39**
See also CA 126

Gilliam, Terry (Vance) 1940-
See Monty Python
See also CA 108, 113

Gilliatt, Penelope (Ann Douglass)
1932- .... CLC **2, 10, 13, 53**
See also CA 13-16R; DLB 14

Gilman, Charlotte (Anna) Perkins (Stetson)
1860-1935 .... TCLC **9, 37**
See also CA 106

Gilmour, David 1944-
See Pink Floyd

Gilpin, William 1724-1804 .... NCLC **30**

Gilroy, Frank D(aniel) 1925- .... CLC **2**
See also CA 81-84; DLB 7

Ginsberg, Allen
1926- .... CLC **1, 2, 3, 4, 6, 13, 36**
See also CANR 2; CA 1-4R; DLB 5, 16;
CDALB 1941-1968

Ginzburg, Natalia 1916- ...... CLC **5, 11, 54**
See also CA 85-88

Giono, Jean 1895-1970 .... CLC **4, 11**
See also CANR 2; CA 45-48;
obituary CA 29-32R; DLB 72

Giovanni, Nikki 1943- ..... CLC **2, 4, 19, 64**
See also CLR 6; CAAS 6; CANR 18;
CA 29-32R; SATA 24; DLB 5, 41

Giovene, Andrea 1904- .... CLC **7**
See also CA 85-88

Gippius, Zinaida (Nikolayevna) 1869-1945
See Hippius, Zinaida
See also CA 106

Giraudoux, (Hippolyte) Jean
1882-1944 .... TCLC **2, 7**
See also CA 104; DLB 65

Gironella, Jose Maria 1917- .... CLC **11**
See also CA 101

Gissing, George (Robert)
1857-1903 .... TCLC **3, 24**
See also CA 105; DLB 18

Gladkov, Fyodor (Vasilyevich)
1883-1958 .... TCLC **27**

Glanville, Brian (Lester) 1931- ...... CLC **6**
See also CANR 3; CA 5-8R; SATA 42;
DLB 15

Glasgow, Ellen (Anderson Gholson)
1873?-1945 .... TCLC **2, 7**
See also CA 104; DLB 9, 12

Glassco, John 1909-1981 .... CLC **9**
See also CANR 15; CA 13-16R;
obituary CA 102; DLB 68

Glasser, Ronald J. 1940?- .... CLC **37**

Glendinning, Victoria 1937- .... CLC **50**
See also CA 120

Glissant, Edouard 1928- .... CLC **10, 68**

Gloag, Julian 1930- .... CLC **40**
See also CANR 10; CA 65-68

Gluck, Louise (Elisabeth)
1943- .... CLC **7, 22, 44**
See also CA 33-36R; DLB 5

Gobineau, Joseph Arthur (Comte) de
1816-1882 .... NCLC **17**

Godard, Jean-Luc 1930- .... CLC **20**
See also CA 93-96

Godden, (Margaret) Rumer   1907-... **CLC 53**
See also CLR 20; CANR 4, 27; CA 7-8R;
SATA 3, 36

Godwin, Gail   1937-....... **CLC 5, 8, 22, 31**
See also CANR 15; CA 29-32R; DLB 6

Godwin, William   1756-1836...... **NCLC 14**
See also DLB 39

Goethe, Johann Wolfgang von
1749-1832 .... **NCLC 4, 22**

Gogarty, Oliver St. John
1878-1957 .... **TCLC 15**
See also CA 109; DLB 15, 19

Gogol, Nikolai (Vasilyevich)
1809-1852 ..... **NCLC 5, 15, 31; DC 1;**
SSC 4
See also CAAS 1, 4

Gokceli, Yasar Kemal   1923-
See Kemal, Yashar

Gold, Herbert   1924-....... **CLC 4, 7, 14, 42**
See also CANR 17; CA 9-12R; DLB 2;
DLB-Y 81

Goldbarth, Albert   1948-........ **CLC 5, 38**
See also CANR 6; CA 53-56

Goldberg, Anatol   1910-1982 .... **CLC 34**
See also obituary CA 117

Goldemberg, Isaac   1945- .... **CLC 52**
See also CANR 11; CA 69-72

Golding, William (Gerald)
1911- ..... **CLC 1, 2, 3, 8, 10, 17, 27, 58**
See also CANR 13; CA 5-8R; DLB 15

Goldman, Emma   1869-1940....... **TCLC 13**
See also CA 110

Goldman, William (W.)   1931-.... **CLC 1, 48**
See also CA 9-12R; DLB 44

Goldmann, Lucien   1913-1970 ...... **CLC 24**
See also CAP 2; CA 25-28

Goldoni, Carlo   1707-1793 .... **LC 4**

Goldsberry, Steven   1949-......... **CLC 34**

Goldsmith, Oliver   1728?-1774....... **LC 2**
See also SATA 26; DLB 39

Gombrowicz, Witold
1904-1969 .... **CLC 4, 7, 11, 49**
See also CAP 2; CA 19-20;
obituary CA 25-28R

Gomez de la Serna, Ramon
1888-1963 .... **CLC 9**
See also obituary CA 116

Goncharov, Ivan Alexandrovich
1812-1891 .... **NCLC 1**

Goncourt, Edmond (Louis Antoine Huot) de
1822-1896 .... **NCLC 7**

Goncourt, Jules (Alfred Huot) de
1830-1870 .... **NCLC 7**

Gontier, Fernande   19??-.......... **CLC 50**

Goodman, Paul   1911-1972.... **CLC 1, 2, 4, 7**
See also CAP 2; CA 19-20;
obituary CA 37-40R

Gordimer, Nadine
1923-....... **CLC 3, 5, 7, 10, 18, 33, 51**
See also CANR 3; CA 5-8R

Gordon, Adam Lindsay
1833-1870 .... **NCLC 21**

Gordon, Caroline
1895-1981 .... **CLC 6, 13, 29**
See also CAP 1; CA 11-12;
obituary CA 103; DLB 4, 9; DLB-Y 81

Gordon, Charles William   1860-1937
See Conner, Ralph
See also CA 109

Gordon, Mary (Catherine)
1949- .... **CLC 13, 22**
See also CA 102; DLB 6; DLB-Y 81

Gordon, Sol   1923-................ **CLC 26**
See also CANR 4; CA 53-56; SATA 11

Gordone, Charles   1925-.......... **CLC 1, 4**
See also CA 93-96; DLB 7

Gorenko, Anna Andreyevna   1889?-1966
See Akhmatova, Anna

Gorky, Maxim   1868-1936 .... **TCLC 8**
See also Peshkov, Alexei Maximovich

Goryan, Sirak   1908-1981
See Saroyan, William

Gosse, Edmund (William)
1849-1928 .... **TCLC 28**
See also CA 117; DLB 57

Gotlieb, Phyllis (Fay Bloom)
1926- .... **CLC 18**
See also CANR 7; CA 13-16R; DLB 88

Gould, Lois   1938?-............. **CLC 4, 10**
See also CA 77-80

Gourmont, Remy de   1858-1915.... **TCLC 17**
See also CA 109

Govier, Katherine   1948-........... **CLC 51**
See also CANR 18; CA 101

Goyen, (Charles) William
1915-1983 ....**CLC 5, 8, 14, 40**
See also CANR 6; CA 5-8R;
obituary CA 110; DLB 2; DLB-Y 83

Goytisolo, Juan   1931- .... **CLC 5, 10, 23**
See also CA 85-88

Gozzi, (Conte) Carlo   1720-1806 .. **NCLC 23**

Grabbe, Christian Dietrich
1801-1836 .... **NCLC 2**

Grace, Patricia   1937-.............. **CLC 56**

Gracian y Morales, Baltasar
1601-1658 .... **LC 15**

Gracq, Julien   1910- .... **CLC 11, 48**
See also Poirier, Louis
See also DLB 83

Grade, Chaim   1910-1982 .... **CLC 10**
See also CA 93-96; obituary CA 107

Graham, Jorie   1951-.............. **CLC 48**
See also CA 111

Graham, R(obert) B(ontine) Cunninghame
1852-1936 .... **TCLC 19**

Graham, W(illiam) S(ydney)
1918-1986 .... **CLC 29**
See also CA 73-76; obituary CA 118;
DLB 20

Graham, Winston (Mawdsley)
1910- .... **CLC 23**
See also CANR 2, 22; CA 49-52;
obituary CA 118

Granville-Barker, Harley
1877-1946 .... **TCLC 2**
See also CA 104

Grass, Gunter (Wilhelm)
1927- .. **CLC 1, 2, 4, 6, 11, 15, 22, 32, 49**
See also CANR 20; CA 13-16R; DLB 75

Grau, Shirley Ann   1929- .... **CLC 4, 9**
See also CANR 22; CA 89-92; DLB 2

Graves, Richard Perceval   1945- .... **CLC 44**
See also CANR 9, 26; CA 65-68

Graves, Robert (von Ranke)
1895-1985 ... **CLC 1, 2, 6, 11, 39, 44, 45**
See also CANR 5; CA 5-8R;
obituary CA 117; SATA 45; DLB 20;
DLB-Y 85

Gray, Alasdair   1934- .... **CLC 41**
See also CA 123

Gray, Amlin   1946- .... **CLC 29**

Gray, Francine du Plessix   1930-.... **CLC 22**
See also CAAS 2; CANR 11; CA 61-64

Gray, John (Henry)   1866-1934 .... **TCLC 19**
See also CA 119

Gray, Simon (James Holliday)
1936- .... **CLC 9, 14, 36**
See also CAAS 3; CA 21-24R; DLB 13

Gray, Spalding   1941- .... **CLC 49**

Gray, Thomas   1716-1771 .... **LC 4; PC 2**

Grayson, Richard (A.)   1951- .... **CLC 38**
See also CANR 14; CA 85-88

Greeley, Andrew M(oran)   1928- .... **CLC 28**
See also CAAS 7; CANR 7; CA 5-8R

Green, Hannah   1932-......... **CLC 3, 7, 30**
See also Greenberg, Joanne
See also CA 73-76

Green, Henry   1905-1974 .... **CLC 2, 13**
See also Yorke, Henry Vincent
See also DLB 15

Green, Julien (Hartridge)   1900- .. **CLC 3, 11**
See also CA 21-24R; DLB 4, 72

Green, Paul (Eliot)   1894-1981...... **CLC 25**
See also CANR 3; CA 5-8R;
obituary CA 103; DLB 7, 9; DLB-Y 81

Greenberg, Ivan   1908-1973
See Rahv, Philip
See also CA 85-88

Greenberg, Joanne (Goldenberg)
1932- .... **CLC 3, 7, 30**
See also Green, Hannah
See also CANR 14; CA 5-8R; SATA 25

Greenberg, Richard   1959?- .... **CLC 57**

Greene, Bette   1934- .... **CLC 30**
See also CLR 2; CANR 4; CA 53-56;
SATA 8

Greene, Gael   19??- .... **CLC 8**
See also CANR 10; CA 13-16R

Greene, Graham (Henry)
1904- ..... **CLC 1, 3, 6, 9, 14, 18, 27, 37**
See also CA 13-16R; SATA 20; DLB 13, 15;
DLB-Y 85

Gregor, Arthur   1923-.............. **CLC 9**
See also CANR 11; CA 25-28R; SATA 36

Gregory, Lady (Isabella Augusta Persse)
1852-1932 .... **TCLC 1**
See also CA 104; DLB 10

Grendon, Stephen   1909-1971
See Derleth, August (William)

Hardenberg, Friedrich (Leopold Freiherr) von
1772-1801
See Novalis

Hardwick, Elizabeth 1916- .... **CLC 13**
See also CANR 3; CA 5-8R; DLB 6

Hardy, Thomas
1840-1928 ... **TCLC 4, 10, 18, 32; SSC 2**
See also CA 104, 123; SATA 25; DLB 18,
19

Hare, David 1947- .... **CLC 29, 58**
See also CA 97-100; DLB 13

Harlan, Louis R(udolph) 1922- ..... **CLC 34**
See also CANR 25; CA 21-24R

Harling, Robert 1951?- .... **CLC 53**

Harmon, William (Ruth) 1938- ..... **CLC 38**
See also CANR 14; CA 33-36R

Harper, Frances Ellen Watkins
1825-1911 .... **TCLC 14**
See also BLC 2; CA 125;
brief entry CA 111; DLB 50

Harper, Michael S(teven) 1938- .. **CLC 7, 22**
See also CANR 24; CA 33-36R; DLB 41

Harris, Christie (Lucy Irwin)
1907- .... **CLC 12**
See also CANR 6; CA 5-8R; SATA 6;
DLB 88

Harris, Frank 1856-1931 .... **TCLC 24**
See also CAAS 1; CA 109

Harris, George Washington
1814-1869 .... **NCLC 23**
See also DLB 3, 11

Harris, Joel Chandler 1848-1908 ... **TCLC 2**
See also YABC 1; CA 104; DLB 11, 23, 42,
78, 91

Harris, John (Wyndham Parkes Lucas)
Beynon 1903-1969 .... **CLC 19**
See also Wyndham, John
See also CA 102; obituary CA 89-92

Harris, MacDonald 1921- .... **CLC 9**
See also Heiney, Donald (William)

Harris, Mark 1922- .... **CLC 19**
See also CAAS 3; CANR 2; CA 5-8R;
DLB 2; DLB-Y 80

Harris, (Theodore) Wilson 1921-.... **CLC 25**
See also CANR 11, 27; CA 65-68

Harrison, Harry (Max) 1925- ...... **CLC 42**
See also CANR 5, 21; CA 1-4R; SATA 4;
DLB 8

Harrison, James (Thomas) 1937- ... **CLC 66**
See also Harrison, Jim
See also CANR 8; CA 13-16R

Harrison, Jim 1937-......... **CLC 6, 14, 33**
See also Harrison, James (Thomas)
See also DLB-Y 82

Harrison, Tony 1937-............. **CLC 43**
See also CA 65-68; DLB 40

Harriss, Will(ard Irvin) 1922- ...... **CLC 34**
See also CA 111

Hart, Moss 1904-1961 .... **CLC 66**
See also Conrad, Robert Arnold
See also obituary CA 89-92; DLB 7

Harte, (Francis) Bret(t)
1836?-1902........ **TCLC 1, 25; SSC 8**
See also brief entry CA 104; SATA 26;
DLB 12, 64, 74, 79; CDALB 1865-1917

Hartley, L(eslie) P(oles)
1895-1972 .... **CLC 2, 22**
See also CA 45-48; obituary CA 37-40R;
DLB 15

Hartman, Geoffrey H. 1929-...... **CLC 27**
See also CA 117, 125; DLB 67

Haruf, Kent 19??-................ **CLC 34**

Harwood, Ronald 1934-........... **CLC 32**
See also CANR 4; CA 1-4R; DLB 13

Hasek, Jaroslav (Matej Frantisek)
1883-1923 .... **TCLC 4**
See also CA 104, 129

Hass, Robert 1941-............ **CLC 18, 39**
See also CANR 30; CA 111

Hastings, Selina 19??- .... **CLC 44**

Hauptmann, Gerhart (Johann Robert)
1862-1946 .... **TCLC 4**
See also CA 104; DLB 66

Havel, Vaclav 1936-........ **CLC 25, 58, 65**
See also CA 104

Haviaras, Stratis 1935- .... **CLC 33**
See also CA 105

Hawes, Stephen 1475?-1523?........ **LC 17**

Hawkes, John (Clendennin Burne, Jr.)
1925- ...... **CLC 1, 2, 3, 4, 7, 9, 14, 15,
27, 49**
See also CANR 2; CA 1-4R; DLB 2, 7;
DLB-Y 80

Hawking, Stephen (William)
1948- .... **CLC 63**
See also CA 126, 129

Hawthorne, Julian 1846-1934 ..... **TCLC 25**

Hawthorne, Nathaniel
1804-1864 ... **NCLC 2, 10, 17, 23; SSC 3**
See also YABC 2; DLB 1, 74;
CDALB 1640-1865

Hayashi Fumiko 1904-1951 ...... **TCLC 27**

Haycraft, Anna 19??-
See Ellis, Alice Thomas
See also CA 122

Hayden, Robert (Earl)
1913-1980 .... **CLC 5, 9, 14, 37**
See also BLC 2; CANR 24; CA 69-72;
obituary CA 97-100; CABS 2; SATA 19;
obituary SATA 26; DLB 5, 76;
CDALB 1941-1968

Hayman, Ronald 1932-............ **CLC 44**
See also CANR 18; CA 25-28R

Haywood, Eliza (Fowler) 1693?-1756.. **LC 1**
See also DLB 39

Hazlitt, William 1778-1830 ...... **NCLC 29**

Hazzard, Shirley 1931- .... **CLC 18**
See also CANR 4; CA 9-12R; DLB-Y 82

H(ilda) D(oolittle)
1886-1961 .... **CLC 3, 8, 14, 31, 34**
See also Doolittle, Hilda

Head, Bessie 1937-1986........ **CLC 25, 67**
See also BLC 2; CANR 25; CA 29-32R;
obituary CA 119

Headon, (Nicky) Topper 1956?- .... **CLC 30**
See also The Clash

Heaney, Seamus (Justin)
1939- .... **CLC 5, 7, 14, 25, 37**
See also CANR 25; CA 85-88; DLB 40

Hearn, (Patricio) Lafcadio (Tessima Carlos)
1850-1904 .... **TCLC 9**
See also CA 105; DLB 12, 78

Hearne, Vicki 1946-............... **CLC 56**

Hearon, Shelby 1931-............. **CLC 63**
See also CANR 18; CA 25-28

Heat Moon, William Least 1939-... **CLC 29**

Hebert, Anne 1916- .... **CLC 4, 13, 29**
See also CA 85-88; DLB 68

Hecht, Anthony (Evan)
1923- .... **CLC 8, 13, 19**
See also CANR 6; CA 9-12R; DLB 5

Hecht, Ben 1894-1964 .... **CLC 8**
See also CA 85-88; DLB 7, 9, 25, 26, 28, 86

Hedayat, Sadeq 1903-1951........ **TCLC 21**
See also CA 120

Heidegger, Martin 1889-1976 ...... **CLC 24**
See also CA 81-84; obituary CA 65-68

Heidenstam, (Karl Gustaf) Verner von
1859-1940 .... **TCLC 5**
See also CA 104

Heifner, Jack 1946-............... **CLC 11**
See also CA 105

Heijermans, Herman 1864-1924 ... **TCLC 24**
See also CA 123

Heilbrun, Carolyn G(old) 1926-..... **CLC 25**
See also CANR 1, 28; CA 45-48

Heine, Harry 1797-1856
See Heine, Heinrich

Heine, Heinrich 1797-1856 .... **NCLC 4**
See also DLB 90

Heinemann, Larry C(urtiss) 1944- .. **CLC 50**
See also CA 110

Heiney, Donald (William) 1921-..... **CLC 9**
See also Harris, MacDonald
See also CANR 3; CA 1-4R

Heinlein, Robert A(nson)
1907-1988 ...... **CLC 1, 3, 8, 14, 26, 55**
See also CANR 1, 20; CA 1-4R;
obituary CA 125; SATA 9, 56; DLB 8

Heller, Joseph
1923- .... **CLC 1, 3, 5, 8, 11, 36, 63**
See also CANR 8; CA 5-8R; CABS 1;
DLB 2, 28; DLB-Y 80

Hellman, Lillian (Florence)
1905?-1984..... **CLC 2, 4, 8, 14, 18, 34,
44, 52; DC 1**
See also CA 13-16R; obituary CA 112;
DLB 7; DLB-Y 84

Helprin, Mark 1947- ..... **CLC 7, 10, 22, 32**
See also CA 81-84; DLB-Y 85

Hemans, Felicia 1793-1835 ...... **NCLC 29**

Hemingway, Ernest (Miller)
1899-1961 ... **CLC 1, 3, 6, 8, 10, 13, 19,
30, 34, 39, 41, 44, 50, 61; SSC 1**
See also CA 77-80; DLB 4, 9; DLB-Y 81,
87; DLB-DS 1; CDALB 1917-1929

Hempel, Amy 1951-............... **CLC 39**
See also CA 118

Henley, Beth 1952-................ **CLC 23**
See also Henley, Elizabeth Becker
See also CABS 3; DLB-Y 86

Koestler, Arthur
    1905-1983 .... CLC **1, 3, 6, 8, 15, 33**
    See also CANR 1; CA 1-4R;
        obituary CA 109; DLB-Y 83

Kohout, Pavel 1928-.............. CLC **13**
    See also CANR 3; CA 45-48

Kolmar, Gertrud 1894-1943...... TCLC **40**

Konigsberg, Allen Stewart 1935-
    See Allen, Woody

Konrad, Gyorgy 1933-.......... CLC **4, 10**
    See also CA 85-88

Konwicki, Tadeusz 1926-..... CLC **8, 28, 54**
    See also CAAS 9; CA 101

Kopit, Arthur (Lee) 1937- .... CLC **1, 18, 33**
    See also CA 81-84; CABS 3; DLB 7

Kops, Bernard 1926-.............. CLC **4**
    See also CA 5-8R; DLB 13

Kornbluth, C(yril) M. 1923-1958.... TCLC **8**
    See also CA 105; DLB 8

Korolenko, Vladimir (Galaktionovich)
    1853-1921 .... TCLC **22**
    See also CA 121

Kosinski, Jerzy (Nikodem)
    1933- .... CLC **1, 2, 3, 6, 10, 15, 53**
    See also CANR 9; CA 17-20R; DLB 2;
        DLB-Y 82

Kostelanetz, Richard (Cory) 1940- .. CLC **28**
    See also CAAS 8; CA 13-16R

Kostrowitzki, Wilhelm Apollinaris de
    1880-1918
    See Apollinaire, Guillaume
    See also CA 104

Kotlowitz, Robert 1924-............ CLC **4**
    See also CA 33-36R

Kotzebue, August (Friedrich Ferdinand) von
    1761-1819 .... NCLC **25**

Kotzwinkle, William 1938- ... CLC **5, 14, 35**
    See also CLR 6; CANR 3; CA 45-48;
        SATA 24

Kozol, Jonathan 1936-........... CLC **17**
    See also CANR 16; CA 61-64

Kozoll, Michael 1940?-............ CLC **35**

Kramer, Kathryn 19??-............ CLC **34**

Kramer, Larry 1935- .... CLC **42**
    See also CA 124, 126

Krasicki, Ignacy 1735-1801....... NCLC **8**

Krasinski, Zygmunt 1812-1859 .... NCLC **4**

Kraus, Karl 1874-1936........... TCLC **5**
    See also CA 104

Kreve, Vincas 1882-1954 .... TCLC **27**

Kristofferson, Kris 1936-.......... CLC **26**
    See also CA 104

Krizanc, John 1956-.............. CLC **57**

Krleza, Miroslav 1893-1981........ CLC **8**
    See also CA 97-100; obituary CA 105

Kroetsch, Robert (Paul)
    1927- .... CLC **5, 23, 57**
    See also CANR 8; CA 17-20R; DLB 53

Kroetz, Franz Xaver 1946- .... CLC **41**
    See also CA 130

Kropotkin, Peter 1842-1921....... TCLC **36**
    See also CA 119

Krotkov, Yuri 1917-.............. CLC **19**
    See also CA 102

Krumgold, Joseph (Quincy)
    1908-1980 .... CLC **12**
    See also CANR 7; CA 9-12R;
        obituary CA 101; SATA 1, 48;
        obituary SATA 23

Krutch, Joseph Wood 1893-1970.... CLC **24**
    See also CANR 4; CA 1-4R;
        obituary CA 25-28R; DLB 63

Krylov, Ivan Andreevich
    1768?-1844................. NCLC **1**

Kubin, Alfred 1877-1959 .... TCLC **23**
    See also CA 112; DLB 81

Kubrick, Stanley 1928-............ CLC **16**
    See also CA 81-84; DLB 26

Kumin, Maxine (Winokur)
    1925- .... CLC **5, 13, 28**
    See also CAAS 8; CANR 1, 21; CA 1-4R;
        SATA 12; DLB 5

Kundera, Milan
    1929- .... CLC **4, 9, 19, 32, 68**
    See also CANR 19; CA 85-88; AAYA 2

Kunitz, Stanley J(asspon)
    1905- .... CLC **6, 11, 14**
    See also CANR 26; CA 41-44R; DLB 48

Kunze, Reiner 1933-.............. CLC **10**
    See also CA 93-96; DLB 75

Kuprin, Aleksandr (Ivanovich)
    1870-1938 .... TCLC **5**
    See also CA 104

Kureishi, Hanif 1954-.............. CLC **64**

Kurosawa, Akira 1910-............ CLC **16**
    See also CA 101

Kuttner, Henry 1915-1958........ TCLC **10**
    See also CA 107; DLB 8

Kuzma, Greg 1944-................ CLC **7**
    See also CA 33-36R

Kuzmin, Mikhail 1872?-1936...... TCLC **40**

Labrunie, Gerard 1808-1855
    See Nerval, Gerard de

La Bruyere, Jean de 1645-1696...... LC **17**

**Laclos, Pierre Ambroise Francois Choderlos
    de** 1741-1803 .... NCLC **4**

**La Fayette, Marie (Madelaine Pioche de la
    Vergne, Comtesse) de**
    1634-1693 .... LC **2**

Lafayette, Rene
    See Hubbard, L(afayette) Ron(ald)

Laforgue, Jules 1860-1887....... NCLC **5**

Lagerkvist, Par (Fabian)
    1891-1974........ CLC **7, 10, 13, 54**
    See also CA 85-88; obituary CA 49-52

Lagerlof, Selma (Ottiliana Lovisa)
    1858-1940 .... TCLC **4, 36**
    See also CLR 7; CA 108; SATA 15

La Guma, (Justin) Alex(ander)
    1925-1985 .... CLC **19**
    See also CANR 25; CA 49-52;
        obituary CA 118

Lamartine, Alphonse (Marie Louis Prat) de
    1790-1869 .... NCLC **11**

Lamb, Charles 1775-1834........ NCLC **10**
    See also SATA 17

Lamming, George (William)
    1927-.................... CLC **2, 4, 66**
    See also BLC 2; CANR 26; CA 85-88

LaMoore, Louis Dearborn 1908?-
    See L'Amour, Louis (Dearborn)

L'Amour, Louis (Dearborn)
    1908-1988 .... CLC **25, 55**
    See also CANR 3, 25; CA 1-4R;
        obituary CA 125; DLB-Y 80

**Lampedusa, (Prince) Giuseppe (Maria
    Fabrizio) Tomasi di**
    1896-1957 .... TCLC **13**
    See also CA 111

Lampman, Archibald 1861-1899 .. NCLC **25**
    See also DLB 92

Lancaster, Bruce 1896-1963........ CLC **36**
    See also CAP 1; CA 9-12; SATA 9

Landis, John (David) 1950-........ CLC **26**
    See also CA 112, 122

Landolfi, Tommaso 1908-1979... CLC **11, 49**
    See also CA 127; obituary CA 117

Landon, Letitia Elizabeth
    1802-1838 .... NCLC **15**

Landor, Walter Savage
    1775-1864 .... NCLC **14**

Landwirth, Heinz 1927-
    See Lind, Jakov
    See also CANR 7; CA 11-12R

Lane, Patrick 1939-.............. CLC **25**
    See also CA 97-100; DLB 53

Lang, Andrew 1844-1912......... TCLC **16**
    See also CA 114; SATA 16

Lang, Fritz 1890-1976 .... CLC **20**
    See also CANR 30; CA 77-80;
        obituary CA 69-72

Langer, Elinor 1939- .... CLC **34**
    See also CA 121

Lanier, Sidney 1842-1881 .... NCLC **6**
    See also SATA 18; DLB 64

Lanyer, Aemilia 1569-1645 .... LC **10**

Lao Tzu c. 6th-3rd century B.C.... CMLC **7**

Lapine, James 1949-.............. CLC **39**
    See also CA 123, 130

Larbaud, Valery 1881-1957....... TCLC **9**
    See also CA 106

Lardner, Ring(gold Wilmer)
    1885-1933 .... TCLC **2, 14**
    See also CA 104; DLB 11, 25, 86;
        CDALB 1917-1929

Larkin, Philip (Arthur)
    1922-1985 ... CLC **3, 5, 8, 9, 13, 18, 33,
                                        39, 64**
    See also CANR 24; CA 5-8R;
        obituary CA 117; DLB 27

Larra (y Sanchez de Castro), Mariano Jose de
    1809-1837 .... NCLC **17**

Larsen, Eric 1941-.............. CLC **55**

Larsen, Nella 1891-1964 .... CLC **37**
    See also BLC 2; CA 125; DLB 51

Larson, Charles R(aymond) 1938-... CLC **31**
    See also CANR 4; CA 53-56

Latham, Jean Lee 1902-.......... CLC **12**
    See also CANR 7; CA 5-8R; SATA 2

Mayhew, Henry   1812-1887 ...... NCLC 31
See also DLB 18, 55

Maynard, Joyce   1953- .... CLC 23
See also CA 111, 129

Mayne, William (James Carter)
1928- .... CLC 12
See also CA 9-12R; SATA 6

Mayo, Jim   1908?-
See L'Amour, Louis (Dearborn)

Maysles, Albert   1926- and Maysles, David
1926- .... CLC 16
See also CA 29-32R

Maysles, Albert   1926- .... CLC 16
See also Maysles, Albert and Maysles,
David
See also CA 29-32R

Maysles, David   1932- .... CLC 16
See also Maysles, Albert and Maysles,
David

Mazer, Norma Fox   1931- .... CLC 26
See also CLR 23; CANR 12; CA 69-72;
SAAS 1; SATA 24

McAuley, James (Phillip)
1917-1976 .... CLC 45
See also CA 97-100

McBain, Ed   1926-
See Hunter, Evan

McBrien, William   1930- .... CLC 44
See also CA 107

McCaffrey, Anne   1926- .... CLC 17
See also CANR 15; CA 25-28R; SATA 8;
DLB 8

McCarthy, Cormac   1933- .... CLC 4, 57
See also CANR 10; CA 13-16R; DLB 6

McCarthy, Mary (Therese)
1912-1989- ... CLC 1, 3, 5, 14, 24, 39, 59
See also CANR 16; CA 5-8R;
obituary CA 129; DLB 2; DLB-Y 81

McCartney, (James) Paul
1942- .... CLC 12, 35

McCauley, Stephen   19??- .... CLC 50

McClure, Michael   1932- .... CLC 6, 10
See also CANR 17; CA 21-24R; DLB 16

McCorkle, Jill (Collins)   1958- ...... CLC 51
See also CA 121; DLB-Y 87

McCourt, James   1941- .... CLC 5
See also CA 57-60

McCoy, Horace   1897-1955 .... TCLC 28
See also CA 108; DLB 9

McCrae, John   1872-1918 .... TCLC 12
See also CA 109; DLB 92

McCullers, (Lula) Carson (Smith)
1917-1967 .... CLC 1, 4, 10, 12, 48
See also CANR 18; CA 5-8R;
obituary CA 25-28R; CABS 1; SATA 27;
DLB 2, 7; CDALB 1941-1968

McCullough, Colleen   1938?- .... CLC 27
See also CANR 17; CA 81-84

McElroy, Joseph (Prince)
1930- .... CLC 5, 47
See also CA 17-20R

McEwan, Ian (Russell)   1948- ... CLC 13, 66
See also CANR 14; CA 61-64; DLB 14

McFadden, David   1940- .... CLC 48
See also CA 104; DLB 60

McFarland, Dennis   1956- .... CLC 65

McGahern, John   1934- .... CLC 5, 9, 48
See also CANR 29; CA 17-20R; DLB 14

McGinley, Patrick   1937- .... CLC 41
See also CA 120, 127

McGinley, Phyllis   1905-1978 ...... CLC 14
See also CANR 19; CA 9-12R;
obituary CA 77-80; SATA 2, 44;
obituary SATA 24; DLB 11, 48

McGinniss, Joe   1942- .... CLC 32
See also CANR 26; CA 25-28R

McGivern, Maureen Daly   1921-
See Daly, Maureen
See also CA 9-12R

McGrath, Patrick   1950- .... CLC 55

McGrath, Thomas   1916- .... CLC 28, 59
See also CANR 6; CA 9-12R, 130;
SATA 41

McGuane, Thomas (Francis III)
1939- .... CLC 3, 7, 18, 45
See also CANR 5, 24; CA 49-52; DLB 2;
DLB-Y 80

McGuckian, Medbh   1950- .... CLC 48
See also DLB 40

McHale, Tom   1941-1982 .... CLC 3, 5
See also CA 77-80; obituary CA 106

McIlvanney, William   1936- .... CLC 42
See also CA 25-28R; DLB 14

McIlwraith, Maureen Mollie Hunter   1922-
See Hunter, Mollie
See also CA 29-32R; SATA 2

McInerney, Jay   1955- .... CLC 34
See also CA 116, 123

McIntyre, Vonda N(eel)   1948- ..... CLC 18
See also CANR 17; CA 81-84

McKay, Claude
1889-1948 .... TCLC 7, 41; PC 2
See also CA 104, 124; DLB 4, 45, 51

McKay, Claude   1889-1948
See McKay, Festus Claudius

McKay, Festus Claudius   1889-1948
See also BLC 2; CA 124; brief entry CA 104

McKuen, Rod   1933- .... CLC 1, 3
See also CA 41-44R

McLuhan, (Herbert) Marshall
1911-1980 .... CLC 37
See also CANR 12; CA 9-12R;
obituary CA 102; DLB 88

McManus, Declan Patrick   1955-
See Costello, Elvis

McMillan, Terry   1951- .... CLC 50, 61

McMurtry, Larry (Jeff)
1936- .... CLC 2, 3, 7, 11, 27, 44
See also CANR 19; CA 5-8R; DLB 2;
DLB-Y 80, 87; CDALB 1968-1987

McNally, Terrence   1939- ...... CLC 4, 7, 41
See also CANR 2; CA 45-48; DLB 7

McPhee, John   1931- .... CLC 36
See also CANR 20; CA 65-68

McPherson, James Alan   1943- ..... CLC 19
See also CANR 24; CA 25-28R; DLB 38

McPherson, William   1939- .... CLC 34
See also CA 57-60

McSweeney, Kerry   19??- .... CLC 34

Mead, Margaret   1901-1978 .... CLC 37
See also CANR 4; CA 1-4R;
obituary CA 81-84; SATA 20

Meaker, M. J.   1927-
See Kerr, M. E.; Meaker, Marijane

Meaker, Marijane   1927-
See Kerr, M. E.
See also CA 107; SATA 20

Medoff, Mark (Howard)   1940- ... CLC 6, 23
See also CANR 5; CA 53-56; DLB 7

Megged, Aharon   1920- .... CLC 9
See also CANR 1; CA 49-52

Mehta, Ved (Parkash)   1934- .... CLC 37
See also CANR 2, 23; CA 1-4R

Mellor, John   1953?-
See The Clash

Meltzer, Milton   1915- .... CLC 26
See also CLR 13; CA 13-16R; SAAS 1;
SATA 1, 50; DLB 61

Melville, Herman
1819-1891 ...... NCLC 3, 12, 29; SSC 1
See also SATA 59; DLB 3, 74;
CDALB 1640-1865

Membreno, Alejandro   1972- .... CLC 59

Mencken, H(enry) L(ouis)
1880-1956 .... TCLC 13
See also CA 105, 125; DLB 11, 29, 63;
CDALB 1917-1929

Mercer, David   1928-1980 .... CLC 5
See also CANR 23; CA 9-12R;
obituary CA 102; DLB 13

Meredith, George   1828-1909 ...... TCLC 17
See also CA 117; DLB 18, 35, 57

Meredith, George   1858-1924 ...... TCLC 43

Meredith, William (Morris)
1919- .... CLC 4, 13, 22, 55
See also CANR 6; CA 9-12R; DLB 5

Merezhkovsky, Dmitri
1865-1941 .... TCLC 29

Merimee, Prosper
1803-1870 .... NCLC 6; SSC 7

Merkin, Daphne   1954- .... CLC 44
See also CANR 123

Merrill, James (Ingram)
1926- .... CLC 2, 3, 6, 8, 13, 18, 34
See also CANR 10; CA 13-16R; DLB 5;
DLB-Y 85

Merton, Thomas (James)
1915-1968 .... CLC 1, 3, 11, 34
See also CANR 22; CA 5-8R;
obituary CA 25-28R; DLB 48; DLB-Y 81

Merwin, W(illiam) S(tanley)
1927- ...... CLC 1, 2, 3, 5, 8, 13, 18, 45
See also CANR 15; CA 13-16R; DLB 5

Metcalf, John   1938- .... CLC 37
See also CA 113; DLB 60

Mew, Charlotte (Mary)
1870-1928 .... TCLC 8
See also CA 105; DLB 19

Mewshaw, Michael   1943- .... CLC 9
See also CANR 7; CA 53-56; DLB-Y 80

Meyer-Meyrink, Gustav 1868-1932
See Meyrink, Gustav
See also CA 117

Meyers, Jeffrey 1939- . . . . CLC 39
See also CA 73-76

Meynell, Alice (Christiana Gertrude
Thompson) 1847-1922 . . . . TCLC 6
See also CA 104; DLB 19

Meyrink, Gustav 1868-1932. . . . . . TCLC 21
See also Meyer-Meyrink, Gustav

Michaels, Leonard 1933- . . . . CLC 6, 25
See also CANR 21; CA 61-64

Michaux, Henri 1899-1984 . . . . . . CLC 8, 19
See also CA 85-88; obituary CA 114

Michelangelo 1475-1564. . . . . LC 12

Michelet, Jules 1798-1874. . . . . . . NCLC 31

Michener, James A(lbert)
1907- . . . . CLC 1, 5, 11, 29, 60
See also CANR 21; CA 5-8R; DLB 6

Mickiewicz, Adam 1798-1855 . . . . . NCLC 3

Middleton, Christopher 1926- . . . . . CLC 13
See also CANR 29; CA 13-16R; DLB 40

Middleton, Stanley 1919- . . . . CLC 7, 38
See also CANR 21; CA 25-28R; DLB 14

Migueis, Jose Rodrigues 1901- . . . . . CLC 10

Mikszath, Kalman 1847-1910 . . . . . TCLC 31

Miles, Josephine (Louise)
1911-1985 . . . . CLC 1, 2, 14, 34, 39
See also CANR 2; CA 1-4R;
obituary CA 116; DLB 48

Mill, John Stuart 1806-1873. . . . . NCLC 11
See also DLB 55

Millar, Kenneth 1915-1983 . . . . CLC 14
See also Macdonald, Ross
See also CANR 16; CA 9-12R;
obituary CA 110; DLB 2; DLB-Y 83;
DLB-DS 6

Millay, Edna St. Vincent
1892-1950 . . . . TCLC 4
See also CA 103; DLB 45;
CDALB 1917-1929

Miller, Arthur
1915- . . . . . . CLC 1, 2, 6, 10, 15, 26, 47;
DC 1
See also CANR 2, 30; CA 1-4R; CABS 3;
DLB 7; CDALB 1941-1968

Miller, Henry (Valentine)
1891-1980 . . . . CLC 1, 2, 4, 9, 14, 43
See also CA 9-12R; obituary CA 97-100;
DLB 4, 9; DLB-Y 80; CDALB 1929-1941

Miller, Jason 1939?- . . . . CLC 2
See also CA 73-76; DLB 7

Miller, Sue 19??- . . . . CLC 44

Miller, Walter M(ichael), Jr.
1923- . . . . CLC 4, 30
See also CA 85-88; DLB 8

Millett, Kate 1934- . . . . CLC 67
See also CANR 32; CA 73-76

Millhauser, Steven 1943- . . . . CLC 21, 54
See also CA 108, 110, 111; DLB 2

Millin, Sarah Gertrude 1889-1968 . . CLC 49
See also CA 102; obituary CA 93-96

Milne, A(lan) A(lexander)
1882-1956 . . . . TCLC 6
See also CLR 1, 26; YABC 1; CA 104, 133;
DLB 10, 77, 100

Milner, Ron(ald) 1938- . . . . CLC 56
See also BLC 2; CANR 24; CA 73-76;
DLB 38

Milosz Czeslaw
1911- . . . . CLC 5, 11, 22, 31, 56
See also CANR 23; CA 81-84

Milton, John 1608-1674. . . . . LC 9

Miner, Valerie (Jane) 1947- . . . . CLC 40
See also CA 97-100

Minot, Susan 1956- . . . . CLC 44

Minus, Ed 1938- . . . . CLC 39

Miro (Ferrer), Gabriel (Francisco Victor)
1879-1930 . . . . TCLC 5
See also CA 104

Mishima, Yukio
1925-1970 . . . . CLC 2, 4, 6, 9, 27; DC 1;
SSC 4
See also Hiraoka, Kimitake

Mistral, Gabriela 1889-1957 . . . . . . TCLC 2
See also CA 104

Mitchell, James Leslie 1901-1935
See Gibbon, Lewis Grassic
See also CA 104; DLB 15

Mitchell, Joni 1943- . . . . CLC 12
See also CA 112

Mitchell (Marsh), Margaret (Munnerlyn)
1900-1949 . . . . TCLC 11
See also CA 109, 125; DLB 9

Mitchell, S. Weir 1829-1914 . . . . . TCLC 36

Mitchell, W(illiam) O(rmond)
1914- . . . . CLC 25
See also CANR 15; CA 77-80; DLB 88

Mitford, Mary Russell 1787-1855. . NCLC 4

Mitford, Nancy 1904-1973. . . . . CLC 44
See also CA 9-12R

Miyamoto Yuriko 1899-1951 . . . . . TCLC 37

Mo, Timothy 1950- . . . . CLC 46
See also CA 117

Modarressi, Taghi 1931- . . . . CLC 44
See also CA 121

Modiano, Patrick (Jean) 1945- . . . . . CLC 18
See also CANR 17; CA 85-88; DLB 83

Mofolo, Thomas (Mokopu)
1876-1948 . . . . TCLC 22
See also BLC 2; brief entry CA 121

Mohr, Nicholasa 1935- . . . . CLC 12
See also CLR 22; CANR 1; CA 49-52;
SAAS 8; SATA 8

Mojtabai, A(nn) G(race)
1938- . . . . CLC 5, 9, 15, 29
See also CA 85-88

Moliere 1622-1673 . . . . LC 10

Molnar, Ferenc 1878-1952. . . . . . . TCLC 20
See also CA 109

Momaday, N(avarre) Scott
1934- . . . . CLC 2, 19
See also CANR 14; CA 25-28R; SATA 30,
48

Monroe, Harriet 1860-1936. . . . . . . TCLC 12
See also CA 109; DLB 54, 91

Montagu, Elizabeth 1720-1800 . . . . NCLC 7

Montagu, Lady Mary (Pierrepont) Wortley
1689-1762 . . . . LC 9

Montague, John (Patrick)
1929- . . . . CLC 13, 46
See also CANR 9; CA 9-12R; DLB 40

Montaigne, Michel (Eyquem) de
1533-1592 . . . . LC 8

Montale, Eugenio 1896-1981. . . CLC 7, 9, 18
See also CANR 30; CA 17-20R;
obituary CA 104

Montesquieu, Charles-Louis de Secondat
1689-1755 . . . . LC 7

Montgomery, Marion (H., Jr.)
1925- . . . . CLC 7
See also CANR 3; CA 1-4R; DLB 6

Montgomery, Robert Bruce 1921-1978
See Crispin, Edmund
See also CA 104

Montherlant, Henri (Milon) de
1896-1972 . . . . CLC 8, 19
See also CA 85-88; obituary CA 37-40R;
DLB 72

Monty Python . . . . CLC 21

Moodie, Susanna (Strickland)
1803-1885 . . . . NCLC 14

Mooney, Ted 1951- . . . . CLC 25

Moorcock, Michael (John)
1939- . . . . CLC 5, 27, 58
See also CAAS 5; CANR 2, 17; CA 45-48;
DLB 14

Moore, Brian
1921- . . . . CLC 1, 3, 5, 7, 8, 19, 32
See also CANR 1, 25; CA 1-4R

Moore, George (Augustus)
1852-1933 . . . . TCLC 7
See also CA 104; DLB 10, 18, 57

Moore, Lorrie 1957- . . . . CLC 39, 45, 68
See also Moore, Marie Lorena

Moore, Marianne (Craig)
1887-1972 . . . CLC 1, 2, 4, 8, 10, 13, 19,
47
See also CANR 3; CA 1-4R;
obituary CA 33-36R; SATA 20; DLB 45;
CDALB 1929-1941

Moore, Marie Lorena 1957-
See Moore, Lorrie
See also CA 116

Moore, Thomas 1779-1852. . . . . NCLC 6

Morand, Paul 1888-1976 . . . . CLC 41
See also obituary CA 69-72; DLB 65

Morante, Elsa 1918-1985. . . . . CLC 8, 47
See also CA 85-88; obituary CA 117

Moravia, Alberto
1907- . . . . . . CLC 2, 7, 11, 18, 27, 46
See also Pincherle, Alberto

More, Hannah 1745-1833 . . . . NCLC 27

More, Henry 1614-1687. . . . . LC 9

More, (Sir) Thomas 1478-1535 . . . . . . LC 10

Moreas, Jean 1856-1910 . . . . TCLC 18

Neruda, Pablo
1904-1973 ..... CLC **1, 2, 5, 7, 9, 28, 62**
See also CAP 2; CA 19-20;
obituary CA 45-48

Nerval, Gerard de 1808-1855...... NCLC **1**

Nervo, (Jose) Amado (Ruiz de)
1870-1919 .... TCLC **11**
See also CA 109

Neufeld, John (Arthur) 1938- ...... CLC **17**
See also CANR 11; CA 25-28R; SAAS 3;
SATA 6

Neville, Emily Cheney 1919-....... CLC **12**
See also CANR 3; CA 5-8R; SAAS 2;
SATA 1

Newbound, Bernard Slade 1930-
See Slade, Bernard
See also CA 81-84

Newby, P(ercy) H(oward)
1918- .... CLC **2, 13**
See also CA 5-8R; DLB 15

Newlove, Donald 1928- .... CLC **6**
See also CANR 25; CA 29-32R

Newlove, John (Herbert) 1938-..... CLC **14**
See also CANR 9, 25; CA 21-24R

Newman, Charles 1938-.......... CLC **2, 8**
See also CA 21-24R

Newman, Edwin (Harold) 1919- .... CLC **14**
See also CANR 5; CA 69-72

Newton, Suzanne 1936- .... CLC **35**
See also CANR 14; CA 41-44R; SATA 5

Nexo, Martin Andersen
1869-1954 .... TCLC **43**

Ngema, Mbongeni 1955- .... CLC **57**

Ngugi, James (Thiong'o)
1938- .... CLC **3, 7, 13, 36**
See also Ngugi wa Thiong'o; Wa Thiong'o,
Ngugi
See also CANR 27; CA 81-84

Ngugi wa Thiong'o 1938-... CLC **3, 7, 13, 36**
See also Ngugi, James (Thiong'o); Wa
Thiong'o, Ngugi
See also BLC 2

Nichol, B(arrie) P(hillip) 1944-..... CLC **18**
See also CA 53-56; DLB 53

Nichols, John (Treadwell) 1940-.... CLC **38**
See also CAAS 2; CANR 6; CA 9-12R;
DLB-Y 82

Nichols, Peter (Richard)
1927-................... CLC **5, 36, 65**
See also CANR 33; CA 104; DLB 13

Nicolas, F.R.E. 1927-
See Freeling, Nicolas

Niedecker, Lorine 1903-1970.... CLC **10, 42**
See also CAP 2; CA 25-28; DLB 48

Nietzsche, Friedrich (Wilhelm)
1844-1900 .... TCLC **10, 18**
See also CA 107, 121

Nievo, Ippolito 1831-1861 .... NCLC **22**

Nightingale, Anne Redmon 1943-
See Redmon (Nightingale), Anne
See also CA 103

Nin, Anais
1903-1977 ...... CLC **1, 4, 8, 11, 14, 60**
See also CANR 22; CA 13-16R;
obituary CA 69-72; DLB 2, 4

Nissenson, Hugh 1933-........... CLC **4, 9**
See also CANR 27; CA 17-20R; DLB 28

Niven, Larry 1938-................ CLC **8**
See also Niven, Laurence Van Cott
See also DLB 8

Niven, Laurence Van Cott 1938-
See Niven, Larry
See also CANR 14; CA 21-24R

Nixon, Agnes Eckhardt 1927-...... CLC **21**
See also CA 110

Nizan, Paul 1905-1940........... TCLC **40**
See also DLB 72

Nkosi, Lewis 1936-................ CLC **45**
See also BLC 2; CANR 27; CA 65-68

Nodier, (Jean) Charles (Emmanuel)
1780-1844 .... NCLC **19**

Nolan, Christopher 1965-.......... CLC **58**
See also CA 111

Nordhoff, Charles 1887-1947...... TCLC **23**
See also CA 108; SATA 23; DLB 9

Norman, Marsha 1947- .... CLC **28**
See also CA 105; CABS 3; DLB-Y 84

Norris, (Benjamin) Frank(lin)
1870-1902 .... TCLC **24**
See also CA 110; DLB 12, 71;
CDALB 1865-1917

Norris, Leslie 1921-............... CLC **14**
See also CANR 14; CAP 1; CA 11-12;
DLB 27

North, Andrew 1912-
See Norton, Andre

North, Christopher 1785-1854
See Wilson, John

Norton, Alice Mary 1912-
See Norton, Andre
See also CANR 2; CA 1-4R; SATA 1, 43

Norton, Andre 1912- .... CLC **12**
See also Norton, Mary Alice
See also DLB 8, 52

Norway, Nevil Shute 1899-1960
See Shute (Norway), Nevil
See also CA 102; obituary CA 93-96

Norwid, Cyprian Kamil
1821-1883 .... NCLC **17**

Nossack, Hans Erich 1901-1978..... CLC **6**
See also CA 93-96; obituary CA 85-88;
DLB 69

Nova, Craig 1945-............... CLC **7, 31**
See also CANR 2; CA 45-48

Novak, Joseph 1933-
See Kosinski, Jerzy (Nikodem)

Novalis 1772-1801 .... NCLC **13**

Nowlan, Alden (Albert) 1933-...... CLC **15**
See also CANR 5; CA 9-12R; DLB 53

Noyes, Alfred 1880-1958 .... TCLC **7**
See also CA 104; DLB 20

Nunn, Kem 19??-................ CLC **34**

Nye, Robert 1939- .... CLC **13, 42**
See also CANR 29; CA 33-36R; SATA 6;
DLB 14

Nyro, Laura 1947- .... CLC **17**

Oates, Joyce Carol
1938- ..... CLC **1, 2, 3, 6, 9, 11, 15, 19,
33, 52; SSC 6**
See also CANR 25; CA 5-8R; DLB 2, 5;
DLB-Y 81; CDALB 1968-1987

O'Brien, Darcy 1939-.............. CLC **11**
See also CANR 8; CA 21-24R

O'Brien, Edna
1936-.......... CLC **3, 5, 8, 13, 36, 65**
See also CANR 6; CA 1-4R; DLB 14

O'Brien, Fitz-James 1828?-1862.. NCLC **21**
See also DLB 74

O'Brien, Flann
1911-1966 .... CLC **1, 4, 5, 7, 10, 47**
See also O Nuallain, Brian

O'Brien, Richard 19??-............ CLC **17**
See also CA 124

O'Brien, (William) Tim(othy)
1946-................... CLC **7, 19, 40**
See also CA 85-88; DLB-Y 80

Obstfelder, Sigbjorn 1866-1900.... TCLC **23**
See also CA 123

O'Casey, Sean
1880-1964 .... CLC **1, 5, 9, 11, 15**
See also CA 89-92; DLB 10

Ochs, Phil 1940-1976............. CLC **17**
See also obituary CA 65-68

O'Connor, Edwin (Greene)
1918-1968 .... CLC **14**
See also CA 93-96; obituary CA 25-28R

O'Connor, (Mary) Flannery
1925-1964 ... CLC **1, 2, 3, 6, 10, 13, 15,
21, 66; SSC 1**
See also CANR 3; CA 1-4R; DLB 2;
DLB-Y 80; CDALB 1941-1968

O'Connor, Frank
1903-1966 .... CLC **14, 23; SSC 5**
See also O'Donovan, Michael (John)
See also CA 93-96

O'Dell, Scott 1903-................ CLC **30**
See also CLR 1, 16; CANR 12; CA 61-64;
SATA 12; DLB 52

Odets, Clifford 1906-1963 .... CLC **2, 28**
See also CA 85-88; DLB 7, 26

O'Donovan, Michael (John)
1903-1966 .... CLC **14**
See also O'Connor, Frank
See also CA 93-96

Oe, Kenzaburo 1935-.......... CLC **10, 36**
See also CA 97-100

O'Faolain, Julia 1932-........ CLC **6, 19, 47**
See also CAAS 2; CANR 12; CA 81-84;
DLB 14

O'Faolain, Sean 1900- ..... CLC **1, 7, 14, 32**
See also CANR 12; CA 61-64; DLB 15

O'Flaherty, Liam
1896-1984 .... CLC **5, 34; SSC 6**
See also CA 101; obituary CA 113; DLB 36;
DLB-Y 84

O'Grady, Standish (James)
1846-1928 .... TCLC **5**
See also CA 104

O'Grady, Timothy 1951-.......... CLC **59**

Poe, Edgar Allan
  1809-1849 ... NCLC 1, 16; PC 1; SSC 1
  See also SATA 23; DLB 3, 59, 73, 74;
  CDALB 1640-1865

Pohl, Frederik 1919- .... CLC 18
  See also CAAS 1; CANR 11; CA 61-64;
  SATA 24; DLB 8

Poirier, Louis 1910-
  See Gracq, Julien
  See also CA 122, 126

Poitier, Sidney 1924?- .... CLC 26
  See also CA 117

Polanski, Roman 1933- .... CLC 16
  See also CA 77-80

Poliakoff, Stephen 1952- .... CLC 38
  See also CA 106; DLB 13

Police, The...................... CLC 26

Pollitt, Katha 1949- .... CLC 28
  See also CA 120, 122

Pollock, Sharon 19??- .... CLC 50
  See also DLB 60

Pomerance, Bernard 1940-........ CLC 13
  See also CA 101

Ponge, Francis (Jean Gaston Alfred)
  1899-...................... CLC 6, 18
  See also CA 85-88; obituary CA 126

Pontoppidan, Henrik 1857-1943 ... TCLC 29
  See also obituary CA 126

Poole, Josephine 1933-........... CLC 17
  See also CANR 10; CA 21-24R; SAAS 2;
  SATA 5

Popa, Vasko 1922- .... CLC 19
  See also CA 112

Pope, Alexander 1688-1744 .... LC 3

Porter, Gene Stratton 1863-1924 .. TCLC 21
  See also CA 112

Porter, Katherine Anne
  1890-1980 ..... CLC 1, 3, 7, 10, 13, 15,
                27; SSC 4
  See also CANR 1; CA 1-4R;
  obituary CA 101; obituary SATA 23, 39;
  DLB 4, 9; DLB-Y 80

Porter, Peter (Neville Frederick)
  1929-................... CLC 5, 13, 33
  See also CA 85-88; DLB 40

Porter, William Sydney 1862-1910
  See Henry, O.
  See also YABC 2; CA 104; DLB 12, 78, 79;
  CDALB 1865-1917

Post, Melville D. 1871-1930 ...... TCLC 39
  See also brief entry CA 110

Potok, Chaim 1929-....... CLC 2, 7, 14, 26
  See also CANR 19; CA 17-20R; SATA 33;
  DLB 28

Potter, Dennis (Christopher George)
  1935-...................... CLC 58
  See also CA 107

Pound, Ezra (Loomis)
  1885-1972 ..... CLC 1, 2, 3, 4, 5, 7, 10,
            13, 18, 34, 48, 50
  See also CA 5-8R; obituary CA 37-40R;
  DLB 4, 45, 63; CDALB 1917-1929

Povod, Reinaldo 1959-............ CLC 44

Powell, Adam Clayton, Jr. 1908-1972
  See also BLC 2; CA 102;
  obituary CA 33-36R

Powell, Anthony (Dymoke)
  1905-.......... CLC 1, 3, 7, 9, 10, 31
  See also CANR 1; CA 1-4R; DLB 15

Powell, Dawn 1897-1965 .... CLC 66
  See also CA 5-8R

Powell, Padgett 1952-............. CLC 34
  See also CA 126

Powers, J(ames) F(arl)
  1917-.......... CLC 1, 4, 8, 57; SSC 4
  See also CANR 2; CA 1-4R

Powers, John J(ames) 1945-
  See Powers, John R.

Powers, John R. 1945-............ CLC 66
  See also Powers, John J(ames)
  See also CA 69-72

Pownall, David 1938-............. CLC 10
  See also CA 89-92; DLB 14

Powys, John Cowper
  1872-1963 .... CLC 7, 9, 15, 46
  See also CA 85-88; DLB 15

Powys, T(heodore) F(rancis)
  1875-1953 .... TCLC 9
  See also CA 106; DLB 36

Prager, Emily 1952-.............. CLC 56

Pratt, E(dwin) J(ohn) 1883-1964.... CLC 19
  See also obituary CA 93-96; DLB 92

Premchand 1880-1936 .... TCLC 21

Preussler, Otfried 1923-........... CLC 17
  See also CA 77-80; SATA 24

Prevert, Jacques (Henri Marie)
  1900-1977 .... CLC 15
  See also CANR 29; CA 77-80;
  obituary CA 69-72; obituary SATA 30

Prevost, Abbe (Antoine Francois)
  1697-1763 .... LC 1

Price, (Edward) Reynolds
  1933-......... CLC 3, 6, 13, 43, 50, 63
  See also CANR 1; CA 1-4R; DLB 2

Price, Richard 1949- .... CLC 6, 12
  See also CANR 3; CA 49-52; DLB-Y 81

Prichard, Katharine Susannah
  1883-1969 .... CLC 46
  See also CAP 1; CA 11-12

Priestley, J(ohn) B(oynton)
  1894-1984 .... CLC 2, 5, 9, 34
  See also CA 9-12R; obituary CA 113;
  DLB 10, 34, 77; DLB-Y 84

Prince (Rogers Nelson) 1958?- ..... CLC 35

Prince, F(rank) T(empleton) 1912- .. CLC 22
  See also CA 101; DLB 20

Prior, Matthew 1664-1721.......... LC 4

Pritchard, William H(arrison)
  1932-...................... CLC 34
  See also CANR 23; CA 65-68

Pritchett, V(ictor) S(awdon)
  1900-............... CLC 5, 13, 15, 41
  See also CA 61-64; DLB 15

Probst, Mark 1925- .... CLC 59
  See also CA 130

Procaccino, Michael 1946-
  See Cristofer, Michael

Prokosch, Frederic 1908-1989.... CLC 4, 48
  See also CA 73-76; obituary CA 128;
  DLB 48

Prose, Francine 1947-............. CLC 45
  See also CA 109, 112

Proust, Marcel 1871-1922 .. TCLC 7, 13, 33
  See also CA 104, 120; DLB 65

Pryor, Richard 1940-.............. CLC 26
  See also CA 122

Przybyszewski, Stanislaw
  1868-1927 .... TCLC 36
  See also DLB 66

Puig, Manuel
  1932-1990 .... CLC 3, 5, 10, 28, 65
  See also CANR 2, 32; CA 45-48

Purdy, A(lfred) W(ellington)
  1918-................ CLC 3, 6, 14, 50
  See also CA 81-84

Purdy, James (Amos)
  1923-............. CLC 2, 4, 10, 28, 52
  See also CAAS 1; CANR 19; CA 33-36R;
  DLB 2

Pushkin, Alexander (Sergeyevich)
  1799-1837 .... NCLC 3, 27

P'u Sung-ling 1640-1715 .... LC 3

Puzo, Mario 1920-......... CLC 1, 2, 6, 36
  See also CANR 4; CA 65-68; DLB 6

Pym, Barbara (Mary Crampton)
  1913-1980 .... CLC 13, 19, 37
  See also CANR 13; CAP 1; CA 13-14;
  obituary CA 97-100; DLB 14; DLB-Y 87

Pynchon, Thomas (Ruggles, Jr.)
  1937-..... CLC 2, 3, 6, 9, 11, 18, 33, 62
  See also CANR 22; CA 17-20R; DLB 2

Quarrington, Paul 1954?-.......... CLC 65
  See also CA 129

Quasimodo, Salvatore 1901-1968 ... CLC 10
  See also CAP 1; CA 15-16;
  obituary CA 25-28R

Queen, Ellery 1905-1982 .... CLC 3, 11
  See also Dannay, Frederic; Lee, Manfred
  B(ennington)

Queneau, Raymond
  1903-1976 .... CLC 2, 5, 10, 42
  See also CA 77-80; obituary CA 69-72;
  DLB 72

Quin, Ann (Marie) 1936-1973....... CLC 6
  See also CA 9-12R; obituary CA 45-48;
  DLB 14

Quinn, Simon 1942-
  See Smith, Martin Cruz
  See also CANR 6, 23; CA 85-88

Quiroga, Horacio (Sylvestre)
  1878-1937 .... TCLC 20
  See also CA 117

Quoirez, Francoise 1935-
  See Sagan, Francoise
  See also CANR 6; CA 49-52

Rabe, David (William) 1940-... CLC 4, 8, 33
  See also CA 85-88; CABS 3; DLB 7

Rabelais, Francois 1494?-1553........ LC 5

Rabinovitch, Sholem 1859-1916
  See Aleichem, Sholom
  See also CA 104

Author Index

Serpieres 1907-
See Guillevic, (Eugene)

Service, Robert W(illiam)
1874-1958 .... TCLC 15
See also CA 115; SATA 20

Seth, Vikram 1952-.............. CLC 43
See also CA 121, 127

Seton, Cynthia Propper
1926-1982 .... CLC 27
See also CANR 7; CA 5-8R;
obituary CA 108

Seton, Ernest (Evan) Thompson
1860-1946 .... TCLC 31
See also CA 109; SATA 18; DLB 92

Settle, Mary Lee 1918- .... CLC 19, 61
See also CAAS 1; CA 89-92; DLB 6

Sevine, Marquise de Marie de
Rabutin-Chantal 1626-1696..... LC 11

Sexton, Anne (Harvey)
1928-1974 ... CLC 2, 4, 6, 8, 10, 15, 53;
PC 2
See also CANR 3; CA 1-4R;
obituary CA 53-56; CABS 2; SATA 10;
DLB 5; CDALB 1941-1968

Shaara, Michael (Joseph) 1929- .... CLC 15
See also CA 102; obituary CA 125;
DLB-Y 83

Shackleton, C. C. 1925-
See Aldiss, Brian W(ilson)

Shacochis, Bob 1951-............. CLC 39
See also CA 119, 124

Shaffer, Anthony 1926- .... CLC 19
See also CA 110, 116; DLB 13

Shaffer, Peter (Levin)
1926- .... CLC 5, 14, 18, 37, 60
See also CANR 25; CA 25-28R; DLB 13

Shalamov, Varlam (Tikhonovich)
1907?-1982.................. CLC 18
See also obituary CA 105

Shamlu, Ahmad 1925- .... CLC 10

Shammas, Anton 1951-............ CLC 55

Shange, Ntozake 1948-........ CLC 8, 25, 38
See also CA 85-88; DLB 38

Shapcott, Thomas W(illiam) 1935- .. CLC 38
See also CA 69-72

Shapiro, Karl (Jay) 1913- .. CLC 4, 8, 15, 53
See also CAAS 6; CANR 1; CA 1-4R;
DLB 48

Sharp, William 1855-1905 .... TCLC 39

Sharpe, Tom 1928-............... CLC 36
See also CA 114; DLB 14

Shaw, (George) Bernard
1856-1950 .... TCLC 3, 9, 21
See also CA 104, 109, 119; DLB 10, 57

Shaw, Henry Wheeler
1818-1885 .... NCLC 15
See also DLB 11

Shaw, Irwin 1913-1984...... CLC 7, 23, 34
See also CANR 21; CA 13-16R;
obituary CA 112; DLB 6; DLB-Y 84;
CDALB 1941-1968

Shaw, Robert 1927-1978 .... CLC 5
See also CANR 4; CA 1-4R;
obituary CA 81-84; DLB 13, 14

Shawn, Wallace 1943- .... CLC 41
See also CA 112

Sheed, Wilfrid (John Joseph)
1930- .... CLC 2, 4, 10, 53
See also CA 65-68; DLB 6

Sheffey, Asa 1913-1980
See Hayden, Robert (Earl)

Sheldon, Alice (Hastings) B(radley)
1915-1987
See Tiptree, James, Jr.
See also CA 108; obituary CA 122

Shelley, Mary Wollstonecraft Godwin
1797-1851 .... NCLC 14
See also SATA 29

Shelley, Percy Bysshe
1792-1822 .... NCLC 18

Shepard, Jim 19??-................ CLC 36

Shepard, Lucius 19??-............. CLC 34
See also CA 128

Shepard, Sam
1943- .... CLC 4, 6, 17, 34, 41, 44
See also CANR 22; CA 69-72; DLB 7

Shepherd, Michael 1927-
See Ludlum, Robert

Sherburne, Zoa (Morin) 1912-...... CLC 30
See also CANR 3; CA 1-4R; SATA 3

Sheridan, Frances 1724-1766........ LC 7
See also DLB 39, 84

Sheridan, Richard Brinsley
1751-1816 .... NCLC 5; DC 1
See also DLB 89

Sherman, Jonathan Marc 1970?-.... CLC 55

Sherman, Martin 19??-............. CLC 19
Scc also CA 116

Sherwin, Judith Johnson 1936-... CLC 7, 15
See also CA 25-28R

Sherwood, Robert E(mmet)
1896-1955 .... TCLC 3
See also CA 104; DLB 7, 26

Shiel, M(atthew) P(hipps)
1865-1947 .... TCLC 8
See also CA 106

Shiga, Naoya 1883-1971........... CLC 33
See also CA 101; obituary CA 33-36R

Shimazaki, Haruki 1872-1943
See Shimazaki, Toson
See also CA 105

Shimazaki, Toson 1872-1943....... TCLC 5
See also Shimazaki, Haruki

Sholokhov, Mikhail (Aleksandrovich)
1905-1984 .... CLC 7, 15
See also CA 101; obituary CA 112;
SATA 36

Sholom Aleichem 1859-1916 .... TCLC 1, 35
See also Rabinovitch, Sholem

Shreve, Susan Richards 1939-...... CLC 23
See also CAAS 5; CANR 5; CA 49-52;
SATA 41, 46

Shue, Larry 1946-1985............ CLC 52
See also obituary CA 117

Shulman, Alix Kates 1932- ...... CLC 2, 10
See also CA 29-32R; SATA 7

Shuster, Joe 1914- .... CLC 21

Shute (Norway), Nevil 1899-1960... CLC 30
See also Norway, Nevil Shute
See also CA 102; obituary CA 93-96

Shuttle, Penelope (Diane) 1947- ..... CLC 7
See also CA 93-96; DLB 14, 40

Siegel, Jerome 1914- .... CLC 21
See also CA 116

Sienkiewicz, Henryk (Adam Aleksander Pius)
1846-1916 .... TCLC 3
See also CA 104

Sigal, Clancy 1926-............... CLC 7
See also CA 1-4R

Sigourney, Lydia (Howard Huntley)
1791-1865 .... NCLC 21
See also DLB 1, 42, 73

Siguenza y Gongora, Carlos de
1645-1700 .... LC 8

Sigurjonsson, Johann 1880-1919... TCLC 27

Sikelianos, Angelos 1884-1951 .... TCLC 39

Silkin, Jon 1930- .... CLC 2, 6, 43
See also CAAS 5; CA 5-8R; DLB 27

Silko, Leslie Marmon 1948-....... CLC 23
See also CA 115, 122

Sillanpaa, Franz Eemil 1888-1964... CLC 19
See also CA 129; obituary CA 93-96

Sillitoe, Alan
1928- .... CLC 1, 3, 6, 10, 19, 57
See also CAAS 2; CANR 8, 26; CA 9-12R;
DLB 14

Silone, Ignazio 1900-1978 .... CLC 4
See also CAAS 2; CANR 26; CAP 2;
CA 25-28, 11-12R,; obituary CA 81-84

Silver, Joan Micklin 1935- .... CLC 20
See also CA 114, 121

Silverberg, Robert 1935- .... CLC 7
See also CAAS 3; CANR 1, 20; CA 1-4R;
SATA 13; DLB 8

Silverstein, Alvin 1933- .... CLC 17
See also CANR 2; CA 49-52; SATA 8

Silverstein, Virginia B(arbara Opshelor)
1937- .... CLC 17
See also CANR 2; CA 49-52; SATA 8

Simak, Clifford D(onald)
1904-1988 .... CLC 1, 55
See also CANR 1; CA 1-4R;
obituary CA 125; DLB 8

Simenon, Georges (Jacques Christian)
1903-1989 .... CLC 1, 2, 3, 8, 18, 47
See also CA 85-88; obituary CA 129;
DLB 72

Simenon, Paul 1956?-
See The Clash

Simic, Charles 1938-... CLC 6, 9, 22, 49, 68
See also CAAS 4; CANR 12, 33;
CA 29-32R; DLB 105

Simmons, Charles (Paul) 1924-..... CLC 57
See also CA 89-92

Simmons, Dan 1948-.............. CLC 44

Simmons, James (Stewart Alexander)
1933- .... CLC 43
See also CA 105; DLB 40

Simms, William Gilmore
1806-1870 .... NCLC 3
See also DLB 3, 30, 59, 73

Tellhard de Chardin, (Marie Joseph) Pierre
1881-1955 . . . . **TCLC 9**
See also CA 105

Tennant, Emma 1937- . . . . **CLC 13, 52**
See also CAAS 9; CANR 10; CA 65-68;
DLB 14

Tennyson, Alfred 1809-1892 . . . . . **NCLC 30**
See also DLB 32

Teran, Lisa St. Aubin de 19??- . . . . . **CLC 36**

Terkel, Louis 1912-
See Terkel, Studs
See also CANR 18; CA 57-60

Terkel, Studs 1912- . . . . **CLC 38**
See also Terkel, Louis

Terry, Megan 1932- . . . . **CLC 19**
See also CA 77-80; CABS 3; DLB 7

Tertz, Abram 1925-
See Sinyavsky, Andrei (Donatevich)

Tesich, Steve 1943?- . . . . **CLC 40**
See also CA 105; DLB-Y 83

Tesich, Stoyan 1943?-
See Tesich, Steve

Teternikov, Fyodor Kuzmich 1863-1927
See Sologub, Fyodor
See also CA 104

Tevis, Walter 1928-1984 . . . . **CLC 42**
See also CA 113

Tey, Josephine 1897-1952 . . . . **TCLC 14**
See also Mackintosh, Elizabeth

Thackeray, William Makepeace
1811-1863 . . . . **NCLC 5, 14, 22**
See also SATA 23; DLB 21, 55

Thakura, Ravindranatha 1861-1941
See Tagore, (Sir) Rabindranath
See also CA 104

Thelwell, Michael (Miles) 1939- . . . . **CLC 22**
See also CA 101

Theroux, Alexander (Louis)
1939- . . . . **CLC 2, 25**
See also CANR 20; CA 85-88

Theroux, Paul
1941- . . . . **CLC 5, 8, 11, 15, 28, 46**
See also CANR 20; CA 33-36R; SATA 44;
DLB 2

Thesen, Sharon 1946- . . . . **CLC 56**

Thibault, Jacques Anatole Francois
1844-1924
See France, Anatole
See also CA 106

Thiele, Colin (Milton) 1920- . . . . **CLC 17**
See also CANR 12; CA 29-32R; SAAS 2;
SATA 14

Thomas, Audrey (Grace)
1935- . . . . **CLC 7, 13, 37**
See also CA 21-24R; DLB 60

Thomas, D(onald) M(ichael)
1935- . . . . **CLC 13, 22, 31**
See also CANR 17; CA 61-64; DLB 40

Thomas, Dylan (Marlais)
1914-1953 . . . . . **TCLC 1, 8; PC 2; SSC 3**
See also CA 104, 120; SATA 60; DLB 13,
20

Thomas, Edward (Philip)
1878-1917 . . . . **TCLC 10**
See also CA 106; DLB 19

Thomas, John Peter 1928-
See Thomas, Piri

Thomas, Joyce Carol 1938- . . . . **CLC 35**
See also CLR 19; CA 113, 116; SAAS 7;
SATA 40; DLB 33

Thomas, Lewis 1913- . . . . **CLC 35**
See also CA 85-88

Thomas, Piri 1928- . . . . **CLC 17**
See also CA 73-76

Thomas, R(onald) S(tuart)
1913- . . . . **CLC 6, 13, 48**
See also CAAS 4; CA 89-92; DLB 27

Thomas, Ross (Elmore) 1926- . . . . . . **CLC 39**
See also CANR 22; CA 33-36R

Thompson, Ernest 1860-1946
See Seton, Ernest (Evan) Thompson

Thompson, Francis (Joseph)
1859-1907 . . . . **TCLC 4**
See also CA 104; DLB 19

Thompson, Hunter S(tockton)
1939- . . . . **CLC 9, 17, 40**
See also CANR 23; CA 17-20R

Thompson, Judith 1954- . . . . **CLC 39**

Thomson, James 1700-1748 . . . . **LC 16**
See also DLB 95

Thomson, James 1834-1882 . . . . . . **NCLC 18**
See also DLB 35

Thoreau, Henry David
1817-1862 . . . . **NCLC 7, 21**
See also DLB 1; CDALB 1640-1865

Thurber, James (Grover)
1894-1961 . . . . **CLC 5, 11, 25; SSC 1**
See also CANR 17; CA 73-76; SATA 13;
DLB 4, 11, 22

Thurman, Wallace 1902-1934 . . . . . . **TCLC 6**
See also CA 104, 124; DLB 51

Tieck, (Johann) Ludwig
1773-1853 . . . . **NCLC 5**
See also DLB 90

Tilghman, Christopher 1948?- . . . . . . **CLC 65**

Tillinghast, Richard 1940- . . . . **CLC 29**
See also CANR 26; CA 29-32R

Timrod, Henry 1828-1867 . . . . **NCLC 25**

Tindall, Gillian 1938- . . . . **CLC 7**
See also CANR 11; CA 21-24R

Tiptree, James, Jr. 1915-1987 . . . **CLC 48, 50**
See also Sheldon, Alice (Hastings) B(radley)
See also DLB 8

**Tocqueville, Alexis (Charles Henri Maurice
Clerel, Comte) de** 1805-1859 . . **NCLC 7**

Tolkien, J(ohn) R(onald) R(euel)
1892-1973 . . . . **CLC 1, 2, 3, 8, 12, 38**
See also CAP 2; CA 17-18;
obituary CA 45-48; SATA 2, 24, 32;
obituary SATA 24; DLB 15

Toller, Ernst 1893-1939 . . . . **TCLC 10**
See also CA 107

Tolson, Melvin B(eaunorus)
1900?-1966 . . . . **CLC 36**
See also CA 124; obituary CA 89-92;
DLB 48, 124

Tolstoy, (Count) Alexey Nikolayevich
1883-1945 . . . . **TCLC 18**
See also CA 107

Tolstoy, (Count) Leo (Lev Nikolaevich)
1828-1910 . . . . **TCLC 4, 11, 17, 28**
See also CA 104, 123; SATA 26

Tomlin, Lily 1939- . . . . **CLC 17**

Tomlin, Mary Jean 1939-
See Tomlin, Lily
See also CA 117

Tomlinson, (Alfred) Charles
1927- . . . . **CLC 2, 4, 6, 13, 45**
See also CA 5-8R; DLB 40

Toole, John Kennedy
1937-1969 . . . . **CLC 19, 64**
See also CA 104; DLB-Y 81

Toomer, Jean
1894-1967 . . . . . **CLC 1, 4, 13, 22; SSC 1**
See also CA 85-88; DLB 45, 51

Torrey, E. Fuller 19??- . . . . **CLC 34**
See also CA 119

Tosei 1644-1694
See Basho, Matsuo

Tournier, Michel 1924- . . . . . . **CLC 6, 23, 36**
See also CANR 3; CA 49-52; SATA 23;
DLB 83

Townsend, Sue 1946- . . . . **CLC 61**
See also CA 119, 127; SATA 48, 55

Townshend, Peter (Dennis Blandford)
1945- . . . . **CLC 17, 42**
See also CA 107

Tozzi, Federigo 1883-1920 . . . . **TCLC 31**

Traill, Catharine Parr
1802-1899 . . . . **NCLC 31**
See also DLB 99

Trakl, Georg 1887-1914 . . . . **TCLC 5**
See also CA 104

Transtromer, Tomas (Gosta)
1931- . . . . **CLC 52, 65**
See also CA 129; brief entry CA 117

Traven, B. 1890-1969 . . . . **CLC 8, 11**
See also CAP 2; CA 19-20;
obituary CA 25-28R; DLB 9, 56

Tremain, Rose 1943- . . . . **CLC 42**
See also CA 97-100; DLB 14

Tremblay, Michel 1942- . . . . **CLC 29**
See also CA 116; DLB 60

Trevanian 1925- . . . . **CLC 29**
See also CA 108

Trevor, William 1928- . . . . . **CLC 7, 9, 14, 25**
See also Cox, William Trevor
See also DLB 14

Trifonov, Yuri (Valentinovich)
1925-1981 . . . . **CLC 45**
See also obituary CA 103, 126

Trilling, Lionel 1905-1975 . . . . **CLC 9, 11, 24**
See also CANR 10; CA 9-12R;
obituary CA 61-64; DLB 28, 63

Trogdon, William 1939-
See Heat Moon, William Least
See also CA 115, 119

Trollope, Anthony 1815-1882 . . **NCLC 6, 33**
See also SATA 22; DLB 21, 57

Author Index

Webb, Charles (Richard) 1939- ...... CLC 7
See also CA 25-28R

Webb, James H(enry), Jr. 1946- .... CLC 22
See also CA 81-84

Webb, Mary (Gladys Meredith)
1881-1927 .... TCLC 24
See also CA 123; DLB 34

Webb, Phyllis 1927- .... CLC 18
See also CANR 23; CA 104; DLB 53

Webb, Sidney (James)
1859-1947 .... TCLC 22
See also CA 117

Webber, Andrew Lloyd 1948- ...... CLC 21

Weber, Lenora Mattingly
1895-1971 .... CLC 12
See also CAP 1; CA 19-20;
obituary CA 29-32R; SATA 2;
obituary SATA 26

Webster, Noah 1758-1843 .... NCLC 30
See also DLB 1, 37, 42, 43, 73

Wedekind, (Benjamin) Frank(lin)
1864-1918 .... TCLC 7
See also CA 104

Weidman, Jerome 1913- .... CLC 7
See also CANR 1; CA 1-4R; DLB 28

Weil, Simone 1909-1943 .... TCLC 23
See also CA 117

Weinstein, Nathan Wallenstein 1903?-1940
See West, Nathanael
See also CA 104

Weir, Peter 1944- .... CLC 20
See also CA 113, 123

Weiss, Peter (Ulrich)
1916-1982 .... CLC 3, 15, 51
See also CANR 3; CA 45-48;
obituary CA 106; DLB 69

Weiss, Theodore (Russell)
1916- .... CLC 3, 8, 14
See also CAAS 2; CA 9-12R; DLB 5

Welch, (Maurice) Denton
1915-1948 .... TCLC 22
See also CA 121

Welch, James 1940- .... CLC 6, 14, 52
See also CA 85-88

Weldon, Fay
1933- .... CLC 6, 9, 11, 19, 36, 59
See also CANR 16; CA 21-24R; DLB 14

Wellek, Rene 1903- .... CLC 28
See also CAAS 7; CANR 8; CA 5-8R;
DLB 63

Weller, Michael 1942- .... CLC 10, 53
See also CA 85-88

Weller, Paul 1958- .... CLC 26

Wellershoff, Dieter 1925- .... CLC 46
See also CANR 16; CA 89-92

Welles, (George) Orson
1915-1985 .... CLC 20
See also CA 93-96; obituary CA 117

Wellman, Mac 1945- .... CLC 65

Wellman, Manly Wade 1903-1986 .. CLC 49
See also CANR 6, 16; CA 1-4R;
obituary CA 118; SATA 6, 47

Wells, Carolyn 1862-1942 .... TCLC 35
See also CA 113; DLB 11

Wells, H(erbert) G(eorge)
1866-1946 ...... TCLC 6, 12, 19; SSC 6
See also CA 110, 121; SATA 20; DLB 34,
70

Wells, Rosemary 1943- .... CLC 12
See also CLR 16; CA 85-88; SAAS 1;
SATA 18

Welty, Eudora (Alice)
1909- .... CLC 1, 2, 5, 14, 22, 33; SSC 1
See also CA 9-12R; CABS 1; DLB 2;
DLB-Y 87; CDALB 1941-1968

Wen I-to 1899-1946 .... TCLC 28

Werfel, Franz (V.) 1890-1945 ...... TCLC 8
See also CA 104; DLB 81

Wergeland, Henrik Arnold
1808-1845 .... NCLC 5

Wersba, Barbara 1932- .... CLC 30
See also CLR 3; CANR 16; CA 29-32R;
SAAS 2; SATA 1, 58; DLB 52

Wertmuller, Lina 1928- .... CLC 16
See also CA 97-100

Wescott, Glenway 1901-1987 ...... CLC 13
See also CANR 23; CA 13-16R;
obituary CA 121; DLB 4, 9

Wesker, Arnold 1932- .... CLC 3, 5, 42
See also CAAS 7; CANR 1; CA 1-4R;
DLB 13

Wesley, Richard (Errol) 1945- ...... CLC 7
See also CA 57-60; DLB 38

Wessel, Johan Herman 1742-1785 .... LC 7

West, Anthony (Panther)
1914-1987 .... CLC 50
See also CANR 3, 19; CA 45-48; DLB 15

West, Jessamyn 1907-1984 ...... CLC 7, 17
See also CA 9-12R; obituary CA 112;
obituary SATA 37; DLB 6; DLB-Y 84

West, Morris L(anglo) 1916- ..... CLC 6, 33
See also CA 5-8R; obituary CA 124

West, Nathanael 1903?-1940 .... TCLC 1, 14
See also Weinstein, Nathan Wallenstein
See also CA 125, 140; DLB 4, 9, 28

West, Paul 1930- .... CLC 7, 14
See also CAAS 7; CANR 22; CA 13-16R;
DLB 14

West, Rebecca 1892-1983 .. CLC 7, 9, 31, 50
See also CANR 19; CA 5-8R;
obituary CA 109; DLB 36; DLB-Y 83

Westall, Robert (Atkinson) 1929- ... CLC 17
See also CLR 13; CANR 18; CA 69-72;
SAAS 2; SATA 23

Westlake, Donald E(dwin)
1933- .... CLC 7, 33
See also CANR 16; CA 17-20R

Westmacott, Mary 1890-1976
See Christie, (Dame) Agatha (Mary
Clarissa)

Whalen, Philip 1923- .... CLC 6, 29
See also CANR 5; CA 9-12R; DLB 16

Wharton, Edith (Newbold Jones)
1862-1937 .... TCLC 3, 9, 27; SSC 6
See also CA 104; DLB 4, 9, 12, 78;
CDALB 1865-1917

Wharton, William 1925- .... CLC 18, 37
See also CA 93-96; DLB-Y 80

Wheatley (Peters), Phillis
1753?-1784 .... LC 3; PC 3
See also DLB 31, 50; CDALB 1640-1865

Wheelock, John Hall 1886-1978 .... CLC 14
See also CANR 14; CA 13-16R;
obituary CA 77-80; DLB 45

Whelan, John 1900-
See O'Faolain, Sean

Whitaker, Rodney 1925-
See Trevanian

White, E(lwyn) B(rooks)
1899-1985 .... CLC 10, 34, 39
See also CLR 1; CANR 16; CA 13-16R;
obituary CA 116; SATA 2, 29, 44;
obituary SATA 44; DLB 11, 22

White, Edmund III 1940- .... CLC 27
See also CANR 3, 19; CA 45-48

White, Patrick (Victor Martindale)
1912-1990 ..... CLC 3, 4, 5, 7, 9, 18, 65
See also CA 81-84; obituary CA 132

White, T(erence) H(anbury)
1906-1964 .... CLC 30
See also CA 73-76; SATA 12

White, Terence de Vere 1912- ...... CLC 49
See also CANR 3; CA 49-52

White, Walter (Francis)
1893-1955 .... TCLC 15
See also CA 115, 124; DLB 51

White, William Hale 1831-1913
See Rutherford, Mark
See also CA 121

Whitehead, E(dward) A(nthony)
1933- .... CLC 5
See also CA 65-68

Whitemore, Hugh 1936- .... CLC 37

Whitman, Sarah Helen
1803-1878 .... NCLC 19
See also DLB 1

Whitman, Walt
1819-1892 .... NCLC 4, 31; PC 3
See also SATA 20; DLB 3, 64;
CDALB 1640-1865

Whitney, Phyllis A(yame) 1903- .... CLC 42
See also CANR 3, 25; CA 1-4R; SATA 1,
30

Whittemore, (Edward) Reed (Jr.)
1919- .... CLC 4
See also CAAS 8; CANR 4; CA 9-12R;
DLB 5

Whittier, John Greenleaf
1807-1892 .... NCLC 8
See also DLB 1; CDALB 1640-1865

Wicker, Thomas Grey 1926-
See Wicker, Tom
See also CANR 21; CA 65-68

Wicker, Tom 1926- .... CLC 7
See also Wicker, Thomas Grey

Wideman, John Edgar
1941- .... CLC 5, 34, 36, 67
See also CANR 14; CA 85-88; DLB 33

Wiebe, Rudy (H.) 1934- ...... CLC 6, 11, 14
See also CA 37-40R; DLB 60

Wieland, Christoph Martin
1733-1813 .... NCLC 17

Wieners, John 1934-.............. CLC 7
See also CA 13-16R; DLB 16

Wiesel, Elie(zer) 1928-..... CLC 3, 5, 11, 37
See also CAAS 4; CANR 8; CA 5-8R;
SATA 56; DLB 83; DLB-Y 87

Wiggins, Marianne 1948-......... CLC 57

Wight, James Alfred 1916-
See Herriot, James
See also CA 77-80; SATA 44

Wilbur, Richard (Purdy)
1921- .... CLC 3, 6, 9, 14, 53
See also CANR 2; CA 1-4R; CABS 2;
SATA 9; DLB 5

Wild, Peter 1940-................ CLC 14
See also CA 37-40R; DLB 5

Wilde, Oscar (Fingal O'Flahertie Wills)
1854-1900 .... TCLC 1, 8, 23, 41
See also CA 119; brief entry CA 104;
SATA 24; DLB 10, 19, 34, 57

Wilder, Billy 1906-............... CLC 20
See also Wilder, Samuel
See also DLB 26

Wilder, Samuel 1906-
See Wilder, Billy
See also CA 89-92

Wilder, Thornton (Niven)
1897-1975 ..... CLC 1, 5, 6, 10, 15, 35;
DC 1
See also CA 13-16R; obituary CA 61-64;
DLB 4, 7, 9

Wiley, Richard 1944-............. CLC 44
See also CA 121, 129

Wilhelm, Kate 1928-................ CLC 7
See also CAAS 5; CANR 17; CA 37-40R;
DLB 8

Willard, Nancy 1936-........... CLC 7, 37
See also CLR 5; CANR 10; CA 89-92;
SATA 30, 37; DLB 5, 52

Williams, C(harles) K(enneth)
1936- .... CLC 33, 56
See also CA 37-40R; DLB 5

Williams, Charles (Walter Stansby)
1886-1945 .... TCLC 1, 11
See also CA 104

Williams, Ella Gwendolen Rees 1890-1979
See Rhys, Jean

Williams, (George) Emlyn
1905-1987 .... CLC 15
See also CA 104, 123; DLB 10, 77

Williams, Hugo 1942-............. CLC 42
See also CA 17-20R; DLB 40

Williams, John A(lfred) 1925-.... CLC 5, 13
See also CAAS 3; CANR 6, 26; CA 53-56;
DLB 2, 33

Williams, Jonathan (Chamberlain)
1929- .... CLC 13
See also CANR 8; CA 9-12R; DLB 5

Williams, Joy 1944-.............. CLC 31
See also CANR 22; CA 41-44R

Williams, Norman 1952- .... CLC 39
See also CA 118

Williams, Paulette 1948-
See Shange, Ntozake

Williams, Tennessee
1911-1983 .... CLC 1, 2, 5, 7, 8, 11, 15,
19, 30, 39, 45
See also CA 5-8R; obituary CA 108; DLB 7;
DLB-Y 83; DLB-DS 4;
CDALB 1941-1968

Williams, Thomas (Alonzo) 1926-... CLC 14
See also CANR 2; CA 1-4R

Williams, Thomas Lanier 1911-1983
See Williams, Tennessee

Williams, William Carlos
1883-1963 ... CLC 1, 2, 5, 9, 13, 22, 42,
67
See also CA 89-92; DLB 4, 16, 54, 86;
CDALB 1917-1929

Williamson, David 1932-......... CLC 56

Williamson, Jack 1908-........... CLC 29
See also Williamson, John Stewart
See also DLB 8

Williamson, John Stewart 1908-
See Williamson, Jack
See also CANR 123; CA 17-20R

Willingham, Calder (Baynard, Jr.)
1922-..................... CLC 5, 51
See also CANR 3; CA 5-8R; DLB 2, 44

Wilson, A(ndrew) N(orman) 1950- .. CLC 33
See also CA 112, 122; DLB 14

Wilson, Andrew 1948-
See Wilson, Snoo

Wilson, Angus (Frank Johnstone)
1913- .... CLC 2, 3, 5, 25, 34
See also CANR 21; CA 5-8R; DLB 15

Wilson, August 1945-....... CLC 39, 50, 63
See also CA 115, 122

Wilson, Brian 1942-............. CLC 12

Wilson, Colin 1931- .... CLC 3, 14
See also CAAS 5; CANR 1, 122; CA 1-4R;
DLB 14

Wilson, Edmund
1895-1972 .... CLC 1, 2, 3, 8, 24
See also CANR 1; CA 1-4R;
obituary CA 37-40R; DLB 63

Wilson, Ethel Davis (Bryant)
1888-1980 .... CLC 13
See also CA 102; DLB 68

Wilson, John 1785-1854......... NCLC 5

Wilson, John (Anthony) Burgess 1917-
See Burgess, Anthony
See also CANR 2; CA 1-4R

Wilson, Lanford 1937-....... CLC 7, 14, 36
See also CA 17-20R; DLB 7

Wilson, Robert (M.) 1944-........ CLC 7, 9
See also CANR 2; CA 49-52

Wilson, Sloan 1920-............. CLC 32
See also CANR 1; CA 1-4R

Wilson, Snoo 1948-.............. CLC 33
See also CA 69-72

Wilson, William S(mith) 1932-..... CLC 49
See also CA 81-84

**Winchilsea, Anne (Kingsmill) Finch, Countess
of** 1661-1720.................. LC 3

Wingrove, David 1954-........... CLC 68
See also CA 133

Winters, Janet Lewis 1899-
See Lewis (Winters), Janet
See also CAP 1; CA 9-10

Winters, (Arthur) Yvor
1900-1968 .... CLC 4, 8, 32
See also CAP 1; CA 11-12;
obituary CA 25-28R; DLB 48

Winterson, Jeannette 1959-........ CLC 64

Wiseman, Frederick 1930-........ CLC 20

Wister, Owen 1860-1938 .... TCLC 21
See also CA 108; DLB 9, 78

Witkiewicz, Stanislaw Ignacy
1885-1939 .... TCLC 8
See also CA 105; DLB 83

Wittig, Monique 1935?-........... CLC 22
See also CA 116; DLB 83

Wittlin, Joseph 1896-1976........ CLC 25
See also Wittlin, Jozef

Wittlin, Jozef 1896-1976
See Wittlin, Joseph
See also CANR 3; CA 49-52;
obituary CA 65-68

Wodehouse, (Sir) P(elham) G(renville)
1881-1975 ... CLC 1, 2, 5, 10, 22; SSC 2
See also CANR 3; CA 45-48;
obituary CA 57-60; SATA 22; DLB 34

Woiwode, Larry (Alfred) 1941-... CLC 6, 10
See also CANR 16; CA 73-76; DLB 6

Wojciechowska, Maia (Teresa)
1927-...................... CLC 26
See also CLR 1; CANR 4; CA 9-12R;
SAAS 1; SATA 1, 28

Wolf, Christa 1929- ...... CLC 14, 29, 58
See also CA 85-88; DLB 75

Wolfe, Gene (Rodman) 1931-....... CLC 25
See also CAAS 9; CANR 6; CA 57-60;
DLB 8

Wolfe, George C. 1954-.......... CLC 49

Wolfe, Thomas (Clayton)
1900-1938 .... TCLC 4, 13, 29
See also CA 104; DLB 9; DLB-Y 85;
DLB-DS 2

Wolfe, Thomas Kennerly, Jr. 1931-
See Wolfe, Tom
See also CANR 9; CA 13-16R

Wolfe, Tom 1931-... CLC 1, 2, 9, 15, 35, 51
See also Wolfe, Thomas Kennerly, Jr.

Wolff, Geoffrey (Ansell) 1937- ..... CLC 41
See also CA 29-32R

Wolff, Tobias (Jonathan Ansell)
1945-...................... CLC 39, 64
See also CA 114, 117

Wolfram von Eschenbach
c. 1170-c. 1220 .... CMLC 5

Wolitzer, Hilma 1930-............ CLC 17
See also CANR 18; CA 65-68; SATA 31

Wollstonecraft Godwin, Mary
1759-1797 .... LC 5
See also DLB 39

Wonder, Stevie 1950-............. CLC 12
See also Morris, Steveland Judkins

Wong, Jade Snow 1922-........... CLC 17
See also CA 109

Literary Criticism Series
Cumulative Topic Index

This index lists all topic entries in the Gale Literary Criticism Series *Contemporary Literary Criticism, Literature Criticism from 1400 to 1800, Nineteenth-Century Literature Criticism,* and *Twentieth-Century Literary Criticism.*

Topic Index

TCLC Cumulative Nationality Index

Nationality Index

ISBN 0-8103-2425-3